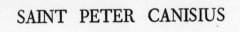

SAINT PETER CANISIUS

IHS

THEOLOGVS ✠ PETRVS CANISIVS

IESV · SOCIETATIS

Qui docti fuerint, fulgebunt quasi splendor.
firmamenti; et qui ad iustitiam erudiunt.
multos, quasi stellæ in perpetuas æ-
ternitates. Dan. 12.

Hunc habuit Petrum felix Germania · Patrem,
Quem stupuere olim Curia, Templa, Scholæ.
Nunc sculpta ære quidem fas est hæc ora tueri,
Illius at vita est suspicienda magis.

St. Peter Canisius in old age
A copperplate engraving by the Saint's contemporary, Dominikus Custos

SAINT PETER CANISIUS, S.J.
1521-1597

BY

J. BRODRICK, S.J.

THE CARROLL PRESS
BALTIMORE, MARYLAND
1950

DE LICENTIA SUPERIORUM ORDINIS:
J. BOLLAND, S.J.,
PRAEP. PROV. ANGLIAE

NIHIL OBSTAT: P. CAN. LONG
CENSOR DEPUTATUS
IMPRIMATUR: ✠ GULIELMUS EPISCOPUS CLIFTONIENSIS
DIE 4ᵃ JULII, 1935

First published 1935

Reprinted with permission of original publishers 1950

Manufactured by
Universal Lithographers, Inc.
Baltimore, Md.
U. S. A.

BONAE ATQUE ILLUSTRI MEMORIAE
OTTONIS BRAUNSBERGER, S.J.,
PRINCIPIS EDITORUM

CONTENTS

ILLUSTRATIONS

ix

PREFACE

A BOOK of this size, concerned with German life in the sixteenth century, necessarily involved a good many problems of style and method. For instance, some policy had to be adopted with regard to the Christian and place names that abound in it, and a consistent policy was by no means easy either to find or to pursue. Most of the characters in the book are priests having a claim to their title of 'Father' now and then, but that mild word would not consort too well with the explosive Jakobs, Heinrichs, and Albrechts of Germany's baptisms. It seemed the better course to give the English forms of the names in such circumstances while otherwise leaving them in their solid Germanity, especially when they belong to persons of greater dignity and consequence than Jesuits. Only in one case has this plan led to an apparent discrepancy, a saintly, unknown priest being referred to as Father Leonard Kessel, and a wily, well known chancellor of Bavaria as Leonhard von Eck. It would have been effrontery to deprive such a portentous person as Eck of his 'h'. Place names offered less difficulty than Christian names because the Royal Geographical Society has issued excellent lists to guide one in the prevailing confusion. These lists have been followed dutifully throughout.

As for the chronology and general architecture of the book, some attempt at artistic form was made by building according to a time sequence modified by regard for causal connexions and the necessity of grouping together events similar in character. Canisius, however, was such a peripatetic person that the result has turned out more like a Strawberry Hill than a sound, tidy house of modern design.

The book contains a very large number of passages translated from the Saint's letters and other writings, as this seemed the only right and honest way to present him to English-speaking readers. These letters, in their original Latin, German, and Italian, are far from being fine literature. Apart from the fact that he was not gifted imaginatively, Canisius had to write, as he says himself, *tumultuarie*, in a raging hurry, concerned only to tell his plain tale and have done. The idea of anybody writing a letter with a view to subsequent publication would have been utterly beyond his comprehension. He was certainly no literary man, and the problem of his queer prose is complicated by an excessive addiction to Scriptural quotations which frequently appear strained or irrelevant. Nevertheless, the letters, unpolished and arid though they might seem, have veins of purest gold, and suffice by themselves to authenticate their writer's spiritual greatness. Heinrich Denifle, the eminent Dominican scholar, used to read them in the evenings in order to sweeten and refresh his mind after laborious days spent in the study of heart-breaking anti-Catholic tomes required for the preparation of his great book, *Luther und Luthertum*. To read them, however, is one thing, and to translate them another. For the reasons given, they proved exceedingly recalcitrant to the process, nor was it possible at times to manage more than a free rendering which should reproduce the sense of the text exactly, without too much consideration for its syntactical nodosities. A precise reader, inclined to be shocked by such conduct, might see what he can make of the text himself before giving way to indignation.

Whether the book will be found interesting or not depends upon how the term is interpreted. Certainly it is not everybody's book, and Peter Canisius does not go out of his way to help things along. A wayfaring man all his life, he made journeys of thrilling interest and alludes to them as if they meant about as much as going by Underground from Baker Street to Waterloo. Even the great controversies in which he played an exciting though reluctant part have quite lost their colours, those once flaming purples and oranges and blues which used to act on men like intoxicants. As for the Saint himself, it would be too much to hope that his character has been caught even in such a huge web of words as is here spun around him. He was far too great for what little art this book contains to paint him truly, and its motto might well be the lines which Ghirlandaio wrote in sadness on the most perfect of his portraits:

Ars utinam mores animumque effingere posses
Pulchrior in terris nulla tabella foret.

Still, there is something of the real St. Peter in the following pages, adumbrations of him showing well enough that his life has as good a message and as fine an inspiration for Christian men in 1935 as it had promise of deliverance for Christian men in 1535, when, still a boy, he was about to leave his quiet Dutch home for the great unrevealed adventures of what, in after years, he liked to think of as his ' pilgrimage ' through the world.

The book would be much worse than it is but for the assistance of its author's friends, Mr. Edward Eyre, Father Henry Keane, S.J., Dr. Johannes Metzler of Munich, Mrs. George Blount, and Miss Susan Bliss. He thanks them with all his heart, as he does, too, his publishers and their printers, who shouldered a monstrous burden with the utmost good-temper, fortitude, and competence.

BIBLIOGRAPHICAL NOTE

THE two principal sources on which this book is based are:

1. Braunsberger, Otto, S.J.: *Beati Petri Canisii Societatis Jesu Epistulae et Acta.* Eight volumes large octavo, pp. 7,550, Herder, Freiburg im Breisgau, 1896–1923. It is difficult to speak of this superb work with restraint. By the consent of scholars of every nation it ranks among the greatest achievements of modern editing. Father Braunsberger spent more than thirty years on it, during which time he sifted upwards of 260 libraries and book-shops in England, Austria, Belgium, Denmark, France, Germany, Switzerland, Holland, Italy, Portugal, and Spain. Certainly no saint in the calendar of the Catholic Church has had his correspondence edited with more devotion and scrupulous accuracy than St. Peter Canisius.

2. *Monumenta Historica Societatis Jesu.* Sixty-two volumes octavo, Madrid-Rome, 1894–1933. This series, still in progress, is edited by a group of Spanish Jesuits and contains a reproduction, with critical apparatus, of all the letters of the principal early Jesuits, excluding Canisius. It is referred to in the following pages by the initials M.H., after which is given the specific title, e.g.: M.H., *Epistolae P. Hieronymi Nadal.*

The full titles of other books consulted, together with place and date of publication, are given in the foot-note references. These titles in their authors' spelling are repeated whenever occasion arises, even on the same page, in order to spare the reader a plethora of confusing *l.c.*'s.

SAINT PETER CANISIUS

CHAPTER I

THE START OF THE PILGRIMAGE

In the east of Holland, near the German border, there is an old Catholic town called Nymegen. One may spell it in about six different ways and be correct. It is not very famous, though a series of international treaties bears its name. The English wiseacre, Lady Mary Montagu, once took stock of the town and decreed that it was like Nottingham. " Never were two places more resembling," she said, and, true enough, each is built on a hill and has a river, like a few other towns in Europe. Nymegen's history goes back to Julius Cæsar who had a camp there that day he overcame the Nervii. But Charlemagne is a more substantial figure in the town's annals, because he liked it as a holiday resort and built himself a summer palace on its hill, of which there is a fragment still to be seen. For half an hour every evening curfew is still rung and still called by the people " Keizer Karels Klok " ; the finest square in the new quarter of the town is " Keizer Karels Plein " ; and the Catholic University is known as the " Universitas Carolina." Now, however, the Emperor of the West has a rival for popular affection in a man whom Nymegen bred within her own four walls. She may count for little in political history and for even less in the history of Dutch art, but her place in the history of the Catholic Church is secure as the native town of St. Peter Canisius. A colossal bronze statue of him stands in her central park, and under the high altar of a splendid church her children lovingly venerate an old pair of his boots and the stick with which he tramped more weary miles than ever did the legions of Cæsar or Charlemagne. Dutch Catholics are jealous of their claims to St. Peter for the good reason that the German Catholics are apt to appropriate their second great national apostle, just as they appropriated their first one, St. Boniface, and so assimilated him that it is difficult to believe he was born in the heart of Devonshire. Racially, at any rate, St. Peter was completely Dutch, and the fact that he wrote of himself as " either a German or a Belgian " is unimportant. Erasmus of Rotterdam wrote in the same way. Holland as now on the map existed during their lifetime only in the dreams of obscure patriots. Some of its provinces owned the suzerainty of France while others were included in the geographical jumble of the Holy Roman Empire. But Gelderland, St. Peter's native province, kept clear during his youth of both connexions, and Nymegen, its capital, went one better by repudiating any dependence even on Gelderland. Let who can, then, decide St. Peter's nationality, not that it makes the least difference one way or the other.

In the frequent feuds between Nymegen and the disreputable Dukes of Gelderland at the beginning of the sixteenth century a certain Meister Jakop Kanis so distinguished himself that his fellow-citizens elected him their Burgomaster nine successive times. By all accounts he was a fine type of man, brave and generous in the service of his town, so good at business that he had risen to be head of the powerful clothmasters' gild, and a scholar of such excellent attainment at the universities of Paris and Orléans that he had been engaged for five years as tutor to the sons of Duke Réné II at the Court of Lorraine.[1] His services there were requited with some title of nobility and an annual pension. The arrival of the pension in Nymegen each year by special envoy gave occasion for elaborate festivities.

Meister Jakop married in 1519 the daughter of a flourishing apothecary named van Houwenigen. In looks and style the pair must have resembled the portraits in the Rijks Museum, comfortable and competent people from their powdered heads to their silver-buckled shoes. Nowhere more convincingly than in Holland have men succeeded in making trade appear aristocratic. If the Dutch artists are to be believed, city fathers in conclave, all of them plain dealers in cloth and foodstuffs, might easily have been mistaken for a group of nobles discussing some high affair of state. Jakop was of that rich merchant class, a genial, sagacious man, with the usual Dutch gift for making the best of both worlds. His family name, Kanis, on which the Renaissance unfortunately laid its pretentious hand, provided him with an obvious charge for his shield when he became Burgomaster of Nymegen. The seals which he used are still preserved at the Stadhuis,

Canis is the latin for "dog"

[1] One of those boys was Claude, afterwards first Duke of Guise and father of the celebrated Cardinal of Lorraine. Claude's son and his tutor's son would afterwards be leaders of the two great opposing camps at the last sessions of the Council of Trent.

each showing in chief the figure of a rather dubious hound *courant*. It was a good name and a good symbol in sixteenth century Holland, because only sublime doggedness could have fashioned a home for a great nation out of what an envious English poet called "the undigested vomit of the sea." Incidentally, the name caused Protestant poets afterwards to indulge in atrocious puns at the expense of Meister Jakop's son.[1]

The home of Jakop and his wife was a big thatched house in the thoroughfare still known as "Broerstraat" or Street of the Brothers. There on May 8, 1521, Peter Kanis, or Canisius, came into the world, quite unconscious of the remarkable coincidences which biographers would afterwards triumphantly adduce in connexion with his birth.[2] The first coincidence, if such it should be called, is certainly impressive, for on the Edict of Worms, putting Martin Luther under the ban of the Holy Roman Empire and thus, as it were, officially marking the start of the Reformation, the date was also May 8, 1521. But there was more than that. The year of Peter's birth witnessed the momentous partition of the Habsburg dominions whereby Charles V made over Austria and its dependencies to his brother Ferdinand, keeping for himself Spain and the Burgundian inheritance. Thus was he freer to grapple with France, and in May, 1521, the great clash came. One of its first incidents was the wounding of Ignatius Loyola which, in a true sense, was the first incident in the history of the Society of Jesus. As Peter Canisius became the leading spirit of the Catholic Reformation in Germany and one of the greatest Jesuits of all time, it may not be fanciful to see in these facts an illustration of the way in which God balances accounts with rebellious monks and war-mongering princes.

Meantime Peter lay in his cradle at Nymegen blissfully indifferent to them. Nothing is known of his childhood except that his mother died during it and that his father, as Burgomaster, received a letter from Henry VIII exhorting Nymegen to hold out manfully against the perfidious Duke of Gelderland who had sided with France in the war. It was not a very happy time to grow up in. War and heresy between them distracted men's counsels and made ordered life almost impossible. The

[1] Some authorities have maintained that Jakop's family name was not Kanis at all but De Hondt, but neither Jakop himself nor any of his people were aware of the fact. They always signed themselves Kanis and others of their tribe were known indifferently as Canes, Kaniss, Kanigs, Kanisius, but never as De Hondt. A German worthy went further and maintained that Kanis has nothing whatever to do with dogs but derives from *Kahn*, meaning a skiff or style of boat used in old times on the Rhine. Pott, *Die Personennamen*, 1853, p. 567. Herr Pott made no disciples.

[2] The house was demolished some years ago and the site is now occupied by the Hotel Moderne.

trumpet blasts from Wittenberg had penetrated to the Netherlands and stirred so much discontented blood there that, according to the English agent, writing to Wolsey in 1527, two out of every three people "kept Luther's opinions." In Nymegen itself two women had been burned at the stake for heresy the previous year, so that the concern of good Vrouw Kanis on her death bed for the faith of her husband and her boy is readily intelligible. "As she lay dying," Peter afterwards recorded, "she warned her husband with wise devotion against the novelties in matters of belief which were then spreading among our countrymen, and adjured him to cling tooth and nail to the Catholic religion."[1]

Besides Peter, two junior sisters, Wendelina and Philippa, were left motherless by the death of Vrouw Kanis. Their father was so busy with administrative work and so often obliged to be away from home that he could not devote much time to his children, circumstances which made him decide, after a decent interval, that he ought to marry again. His second wife, Wendelina van den Bergh, came of good stock and must have been an excellent woman in her own fashion. Peter soon learned to love her, and wrote feelingly many years later, when he was a famous man, that nobody "could have been less of a step-mother to him than she." But there were limitations to her qualities, as will appear, due to the same mundane absorption which clipped the wings of the Dutch artists. She bore her husband so many children that Peter's early biographers seem to have lost count of them, some putting the number at nine or ten and others at nineteen. We are sure of at least eight, which must have been enough to keep Peter from boredom in his nursery. The mundane absorption of the Dutch artists is a help at this point because it enables anybody who so desires to see what the Kanis children were like, sedate little things who carried themselves in their acres of clothes with the dignity becoming the sons and daughters of the first citizen. Peter, the eldest, was the least sedate. By his own account he started life as a wilful, headstrong child, addicted to all sorts of mischief and a sore anxiety to his elders. Instead of saying his prayers while in church he used to play games of his own invention, or practise some antic on the stolid backs of the worshippers in front of him. He became conceited, too, he says, and used to swagger before other boys as the son and heir of the wealthy Burgomaster. At first for his education he was entrusted to the care of a pious governess who found him more than she could

[1] Braunsberger, *Beati Petri Canisii Epistulae et Acta*, vol. i (1896), p. 8. This work will be referred to as: Braunsberger, *Epistulae*.

manage. Soon he was transferred to the Latin school of the town, near the huge, battle-scarred Church of St. Stephen.[1] This school was a second-rate, poky establishment, even by the easy standards of those days. The buildings had fallen into disrepair, and the books used were mainly old and tattered Graduals and Antiphonaries which the choir of St. Stephen's had discarded. A rector and two masters constituted the entire staff. There is a story that Peter developed a special aptitude for writing Latin hexameters while under their care, and that is about all that is known of his early promise.[2]

When Peter was twelve a boarding school of some sort appears to have claimed him and his hexameters. At any rate he left home and found himself among boys who, in his own words, " thought it a grand thing to talk and brag about their wickedness." He goes on to explain that they did not stop short at dirty talk and that he was himself as bad as the rest of them. Still, amid all the murkiness of that passionate time there were gleams of the man he would be, small happenings to show that evil was not going to have a bloodless victory in his soul, and one direct premonition of his future allegiance. Thus it is known that, disgusted with himself for his backslidings, he would sometimes don a hair-shirt, however he came by that object. During these spells of repentance he used to spend hours at a time pouring out his sorrow and resolutions to God before the Blessed Sacrament in St. Stephen's, and there on one occasion he had a mystical experience that affected the rest of his life. Another time a curious incident happened while he was on a visit to some relatives in the pleasant, famous town of Arnheim. A certain lady of the town, revered by all who knew her for her holy life, called on the family and, seeing their small guest, announced that a new order of priests would soon arise in the Church to which in the providence of God Peter would afterwards affiliate himself. The precise date of that incident is not known but it must have been close enough to the August morning in 1534 when seven graduates of the University of Paris climbed to a little chapel on the slopes of Montmartre with no more elaborate ambition in their hearts than to vow a pilgrimage to Palestine where, if God willed, they would shed their blood for the love of Jesus Christ. They were the first Jesuits.

[1] This, the church of St. Peter's baptism, is said to have been consecrated by St. Albert the Great in 1273. It is now, through history's chances, a Protestant church, though Nymegen is almost entirely Catholic.
[2] For the details given the present chapter is indebted to a well-documented article, *De jeugd van Peter Kanis Noviomagus*, contributed by J. Tesser to the Dutch periodical, *Studiën*, vol. ciii. (1925), pp. 335-59.

About the year 1570 when Peter was at the height of his religious activities he committed to paper some reflections on the days of his youth. This manuscript has been called his *Confessions*, but it is not autobiographical in any strict sense of the word. It is addressed to God and intended for Him alone, as it were a combined *Te Deum* and *Miserere* for the mercies and sins of half a century. The following passages from it are very darkly coloured, but Peter the saint could hardly be expected to give much credit to Peter the unregenerate:

What shall I say about those first years of my wretched, senseless boyhood which I spent foolishly and without purpose, more asleep than awake . . . ? In truth many were the things shameful for a Christian child which in those days I thought and desired and planned and performed. Very often I deserved not only reproof but severe chastisement. Boyhood has its own graces, modesty, candour, innocence, but they were not mine to boast of, and it has also its special faults with which, O Lord, I even then began to stain the nuptial robe Thou gavest me. Woe is me, how many profitless hours, days, nights, weeks, months, years I have squandered! How empty, indigent and stupid I have been, living without Thy fear or Thy love as though I knew Thee not at all, the Giver, the Guide and the Preserver of my being. I used to waste much of my time in idleness or in play, wandering about absorbed in foolish trifles and all manner of childish pursuits. These were my delight even at sacred times and in sacred places. The diseases of my fallen nature clung close to me and, though opportunity for grave sin was lacking, an evil will daily made itself more evident. I grew wroth with the counsels of wisdom and gave my temper rein. I loved to annoy, and I was envious and full of pride. There was spite in my heart, too, and as far as I could at that tender age I carried out schemes of revenge. How often did I not then despise and offend my parents, my nurses, my playmates, and any who dared admonish me! Only tardily and reluctantly would I do what was required of me, led away as I was by vanity and I know not what foolish whims. . . .

But now I implore Thy grace, Lord Jesus, who when Thou wert a boy didst grow more than all other boys in wisdom and grace before God and men, a Child conceived and born and brought up without shadow of stain, in whom all other children are blessed. O Lord, who art glad when little ones come to Thee with their sins, remember not the transgressions of my youth and my ignorance. . . . Let Thy mercies speedily prevent me, wretched, miserable, ignorant, frail, empty, stupid man that I have ever been. I fear all my works, knowing that Thou dost not spare the offender. Thou art just, O Lord, and not only lovest justice but dost demand and judge it in every age and time. Grant this only unto me, O God of my youth, that as I have left my first charity and stained the white robe of my innocence I may recount unto Thee all my years in the bitterness of my soul, for what else can I offer Thee for those first slippery years with their countless falls but that by which Thou art gladly appeased, the sacrifice of a contrite and humble heart?

Once, while still a boy, I was praying in the Church of Nymegen devoted to St. Stephen, the first martyr, and prostrate adored Thy sacred Body, my Lord, near the high altar. Never can I forget the grace that Thou didst then bestow upon me. I was calling upon Thee anxiously and, I think, not without tears, I lay my heart open to Thee, for I saw in a manner I understood not the vanities and lying follies of the world, the many perils on every side, so that it seemed but few would escape. I therefore begged Thee to stand by me in danger and seemed to say to Thee: *Vias tuas, Domine, demonstra mihi et semitas tuas edoce me. Dirige me in veritate tua et doce me quoniam tu es Deus Salvator meus.* I firmly believe that Thou didst then give birth in my heart to the spirit of fear and holy solicitude, and afterwards didst preserve it so that my inconstant, frivolous youth, with fear for its master and keeper, might stray less in crooked ways. For Thou didst pierce my flesh with Thy fear and I began to be afraid of Thy judgments. Thereafter, as I think by the doing of Thy Angel, my guardian, I began to take delight in the pictures or carved representations of holy things and in the Church's ritual. I therefore gladly served the priests at Mass and myself used to assume the priestly rôle, imitating the way they sang and sacrificed and prayed. I would act the priest as best I knew how, which was childish foolishness, perhaps, but sometimes also foreshadows the future cast of a man's mind, and gives testimony to discerning eyes of the wonderful ways of Thy providence. The wise of this world little know in how many ways Thou, who art wisdom supreme, dost accommodate Thyself and Thy words to our childish capacity, and every day affords its own proof that Thou dost communicate the gifts of Thy bounty to little ones in a manner quite other than that of Thy dealings with adults and the aged.

Alas, if only my heart and all the ways of my young life had stood fast in that boyhood simplicity! But with increasing years my wickedness grew. A greater lust to sin possessed me and corruption of various kinds infected my heart. I used to sin, and it was accounted no sin but sometimes even a thing to be proud of, that wrecking of youthful innocence. I became more and more arrogant, thinking myself a knowing fellow and despising others in comparison. It used to be my desire also to express an opinion on the weightiest matters, and I would hold forth, as the saying is, like a blind man discoursing on colours. Nor would I give in easily if at any time advised or admonished, so swollen had I become and so much did impudence, self-love, folly and obstinacy possess my soul. And what am I to say about my contentiousness, my fits of anger, my jealousies, my secret hatreds? According to Thy mercy and not according to my perversity remember Thou me, for Thy goodness' sake, O Lord. Remember Thy bowels of compassion and Thy mercies that are from the beginning of the world. O Lord, rebuke me not in Thy indignation nor chastise me in Thy wrath, for my iniquities are gone over my head and as a heavy burden do they weigh me down.

When the time came for me to leave home for school the change only made my disease worse, for I fell in there with companions who taught me the licence of sin by both word and example. . . . I do not accuse them, O Lord, in order to excuse or cover my own iniquity. They sinned and I was a party to their sins. They merited chastisement and so did I. It shames me now to confess what I was not then ashamed to do. I beg for mercy because I fear Thy judgment, knowing that the greater the sin the greater the penalty and that lesser sins, too, will have their appointed retribution. Now, therefore, while there is yet time to be merciful, let Thy power conquer our weakness, Thy wisdom our ignorance, Thy goodness our iniquity, so that to none of us may be imputed the evil done secretly and openly against Thy law, by me, on account of those comrades, or by them, on account of me. Help us, O God our Saviour, and for the glory of Thy name, O Lord, deliver us and forgive us our sins. We sinned as children, we sinned as youths. Would that we had had some Tobias to teach us from infancy to fear Thee and abstain from all evil. Have mercy upon us, O Lord, and that others may have happier fortunes do Thou stir up in many hearts the spirit of Daniel and his companions to carry Thy yoke from youth. . . . Open, O Lord, the eyes of blind and foolish parents and masters that they may no longer lead blind and foolish children to perdition. Make them see the danger to themselves and to their charges that lies in their most criminal carelessness. Cause them to realize how prone youth naturally is to rush headlong into all manner of evil, and how, as a rule, it can hardly be turned to virtuous courses without strenuous effort. Let them reflect that the flower of virginity is the loveliest and most commendable of boyhood's graces but that it is also the frailest and most perishable of flowers. Once it falls it falls for ever, and the earliest regret is too late because it is irrecoverable.

Oh, if boys only knew the good things that they possess in their purity, with what care and diligence would they not hedge around and guard their golden treasure, what fierce battles would they not fight to defend it, and what cautious watch would they not keep on their domestic foe, the flesh, to suppress its rebellions. Never would they permit modesty to suffer damage or holy chastity to be violated by their own or another's action. Rather like alert and well-armed soldiers would they at once take the field against the enemy, burning with holy indignation, the moment he appeared with his allurements.

As for me, it is not my happy fortune to be able to say with a good conscience in the spirit of Thy true virgin, Sara: *Nunquam concupivi virum et mundam servavi animam meam ab omni concupiscentia. Nunquam cum ludentibus miscui me neque cum his qui in levitate ambulant participem me praebui.* But though I cannot so glory, I yet declare the grace Thou didst confer on me in delivering my body from fornication and never permitting me to soil myself with any woman. For this I thank Thee, the Author of all good, with my whole heart. . . . But meantime I know, O Lord, that I cannot and never could be continent except by Thy granting, who dost extinguish the burning flame of concupiscence in the torrent of Thy grace and renderest the vow and yoke of chastity not only tolerable but light and sweet. . . .[1]

Allowing for the profound humility and sorrow with which a saint must ever look back upon the least of his sins, there is still enough in these passages to show that Peter Canisius had plenty of red blood in his veins. What chiefly turned its ardours from their natural course and

[1] Braunsberger, *Epistulae*, vol. i, pp. 10–5.

canalized them for greater purposes appears to have been, under God, the voice of the mysterious lady of Arnheim. It was a voice that still echoed in his soul sixty years later when he wrote in Switzerland the " Nunc Dimittis " known as his *Testament*. " I remember," he tells us, " that once when I was on a visit to friends in Arnheim, a widowed lady of great holiness spoke in prophecy, under divine enlightenment, of a new order of priests about to come into existence, by whose means God would soon send reliable labourers into His vineyard, and she foretold that I also would be among them. At that time there was as yet no thought or mention, anywhere in Italy, France or Germany, of the men now called Jesuits."[1] Apart from the secret workings of grace that incident was the nearest approach to anything directly supernatural in Peter's early life.

His *natural* history, so to call it, does not properly begin until 1536 when he became due for a university. He was still some months from his fifteenth birthday, but since fifty counted for old age in those days it did not do to waste any time in making a start. Meister Jakop chose Cologne for his son as he had many business connexions with that city and even the right of nomination to a canon's stall in its famous Cathedral. On educational grounds it was a poor sort of choice, though, perhaps, no worse than any other open to him. Practically all the old universities of Europe had gone to sleep. For Cologne itself, on the other hand, the choice turned out providential and even fateful. One could go the whole way from Nymegen by water, as the Rhine links the two cities, or there was the alternative of the family coach over probably the worst roads in Europe. It was January, mid-winter, and—land or water—it did not matter very much which you risked because you were bound to suffer the worst in any case. The boats of the time were famous above all for their smells, and the coaches got " shipwrecked " so often in the slush that one exasperated traveller called for their inclusion in the Litany, alongside pestilence, famine, sudden death, earthquakes and other major human afflictions.

In Cologne Peter was placed under the care of a good priest named Andrew Herll who had a house close to the church of St. Gereon. That church is the most interesting of the many famous ones in the city and, perhaps, only rivalled by San Clemente in Rome as a place evocative of Christian and pagan memories. It was built by the mother of Constantine to the honour of St. Gereon and other reputed Theban legionaries

[1] Braunsberger, *Epistulae*, vol. i, pp. 37–8.

who, according to tradition, suffered martyrdom on its site. In the sixth century Gregory of Tours described it as the " Church of the Golden Martyrs " on account of its abundant and splendid mosaics, and the title has clung to it ever since. When Peter Canisius got into difficulties in after life it was his habit to write to Cologne for the gift of a Mass or prayer " ad aureos Martyres " or at the shrine of St. Ursula.[1] For a student of architecture St. Gereon's is very convenient as he can there contemplate pretty well every style evolved during the Christian centuries. Canisius, however, had no remarks to contribute on the fascinating subject. To him St. Gereon's was just a church like any other, except that it com- memorated a particular group of brave men whose stand for God fired his imagination.[2] By slow degrees, he too would learn to stand for God no less bravely, and his love for St. Gereon's came of the fact that it was there he learned the rudiments of Christian soldiership.

Considering what sorry specimens of their kind the German clergy were in the sixteenth century, Peter had amazing good fortune to be associated with Andrew Herll and his circle. They formed a tiny green oasis in a wilderness of indifference and corruption. Herll himself, friend of the famous humanist and battling theologian, Cochlaeus, combined true culture with the deep, instructed piety of Flemish mysticism, and his young protégé and lieutenant, Father Nicholas van Esche, had all the makings of a canonizable saint except the miracles. Father Nicholas, like Peter, came from Gelderland, a fact that helped to bring them together in the most momentous friendship of Peter's whole career. Peter was born a hero-worshipper and in van Esche he found his first, authentic hero. To Nicholas the expressive words of an English poet laureate have perfect application : " What men call nobility of soul does not consist of riches of imagination or intellect, but in harmony of mind which is most clearly perceived where a few fundamental essences attain simple co-ordination and easy stability—just as in music the true vocal intonation of the major triad, the common chord, is the sweetest of sounds, resolving

[1] The poet S. T. Coleridge, who detested Cologne, wrote the following doggerel lines, " On my joyful departure from the same City " :

As I am a rhymer,
And now, at least, a merry one,
Mr. Mum's Rudesheimer
And the church of St. Gereon
Are the two things alone
That deserve to be known
In the body and soul-stinking town of Cologne.

[2] Still, though he said nothing at the time, he must have been deeply impressed by the magnificence of the church because, nearly sixty years later, he referred to it in one of his books, as " precious, beautiful, artistic and wonderful."

all discords, and speaking of peace in its satisfied close." If we may believe one who knew him well, even as a child van Esche had striven towards that unity and integration. " While still a little boy," this man recorded, " he would often get up in the middle of the night to spend hours in prayer. Many times, too, he would steal away from home at the first rays of a wintry dawn, kneel down in the snow before the closed doors of the church, and there, with his arms extended in the form of a cross, keep vigil until the sexton arrived to let him in."[1] He used to put a stone under his pillow on the nights when he wanted to rise for prayer so that he might not sleep too soundly, but his mother discovered it and the tears which he saw her shed made him give up emulating Jacob. Afterwards he admitted that the practice was a foolish one. The adult years of his career did not belie such determined beginnings. While at school with the Brothers of the Common Life from whose ranks Thomas a Kempis had but recently gone to Heaven, and afterwards at the University of Louvain, Nicholas fascinated people by his purity and selflessness. He seemed, so to say, naturally supernatural, alive to God as the birds are to the air through which they move. His father, who was a prosperous merchant, tried hard to anchor him to earth. He made him dress well and kept expatiating to him on the dignity, the joys and the rewards of commerce. It was no good, for Nicholas had set his heart on commerce of another kind, that " traffic of Jacob's ladder " to which even as a child God had apprenticed him. One day father and son were driving through a Dutch city. " I want you to observe carefully, Nick," said the merchant, " what a thriving and beautiful city this is." " Certainly I will, Father," answered the boy, and gave himself up to contemplation of the Holy City, the Bride of the Lamb, whose twelve gates are twelve pearls. " Well, how did you like it ? " the father asked when their journey was done. " Immensely, sir," was the answer, " indeed I fell completely in love with it." And the merchant thought with satisfaction that his boy was getting sense at last.

With the exception of such brilliant freaks as Erasmus, who might have been born anywhere, Dutchmen at this period were very much of a piece, ponderous and unimaginative, extraordinarily good-natured and with a power of sticking to their aims that amounted to genius. Dying in the last ditch seems to have come natural to them. We think of Adrian

---

[1] These and the other details of van Esche's life given here are taken from a Latin biography, written soon after his death by one who had been closely associated with him. The biography was reprinted in de Ram's carefully edited work, *Venerabilis N. Eschii vita et opuscula ascetica* (Louvain, 1858).

of Utrecht, the brewer's son who assumed the government of the Universal Church shortly after Peter Canisius was born. Margaret, the widow of Charles the Bold, was a great lover of letters and made it her business to seek out poor, deserving students. While passing through Louvain very late one wintry night she noticed that a candle was burning in a window immediately under the roof of the *Collegium Portiorum*. Who on earth, she wondered, could be up at such an hour and on such a night? On enquiry she learned that it was a poor lad from Utrecht whom neither cold nor hunger could tear away from the few Greek and Latin books he had acquired at the cost of his stomach. Margaret was touched by the story and sent Adrian three hundred florins to buy books. That was the first step to the Throne of the Fisherman, but Adrian remained himself to the end, sublimely unromantic and with only one real hobby, to share his last crust with somebody as poor as himself. He was always poor because he gave everything away, and he had not an atom of poetry in him. To the horror of the cultured Cardinals round him, he said, when shown the Laocoön group, that it was only an old idol. And he died of a broken heart after a very brief reign because he had been unable to heal the gaping wounds of Christendom.

Mention of Adrian is not irrelevant in this place, for he was the brother in soul of Nicholas van Esche and Peter Canisius. They, too, were utterly pedestrian people and probably could not have told the difference between a marble by Michael Angelo and a bit of plaster-work by the local potter. They might easily have preferred the potter's effort. Though Canisius was in Rome while Michael Angelo was creating his masterpieces there, he never makes the slightest allusion to him or any other artist. All that side of life and, needless to say, the appeal of natural beauty too, apparently meant nothing to those matter-of-fact Dutchmen. But give them an item of human suffering to relieve or the chance to share with somebody their secret content, and then, how their hearts would sing! Perhaps, after all, we can find poetry in those prosaic lives, the lives of Adrian and Nicholas and Peter, and that Dutch Thomas who wrote: " Give me, O most sweet and loving Jesus, to repose in Thee above all things created, above all health and beauty, above all knowledge and subtlety, above all riches and arts, above all joy and gladness, above all gifts and boons that Thou canst give and infuse, above all the joy and jubilation that the mind can contain or experience, for Thou, O Lord my God, art the best above all things, Thou alone most beautiful and most loving, Thou alone most noble and most glorious, above all things, in whom all things are found together in all their perfection."

Besides van Esche there was another guest in Andrew Herll's house with whom Peter became intimate, a gifted boy from Protestant Lübeck named Laurence Surius. Though younger even than Peter he appears to have been already affected by the Lutheran opinions prevalent in his native city,[1] and might have gone over to them entirely had not Heaven intervened to save him to be the first systematic biographer of the Saints, through the influence of van Esche and Canisius.[2] The presence of a third guest in addition to Peter and Surius under Herll's hospitable roof is not certain, but there are some indications that Jörgen Skodborg, the exiled Archbishop of Lund, may have been of the company. No one better than he could have enlightened Peter on such hard facts of Reformation history as the ineptitude of much papal action and the brutal, selfish rapacity of kings and princes who used Lutheranism to further their villainies. He had been secretary to the bloodthirsty tyrant, Christian II, King of Denmark. In 1519 the primatial see of Lund was vacant through the death of Archbishop Berger, and Christian, desirous of acquiring some island property belonging to the see, thrust Skodborg on the unwilling chapter, who had already elected their dean. Very soon he discovered his mistake. Far from being the ready instrument he had supposed, the new Primate set his face like flint against any interference with the rights of the Church. Christian thereupon forced him to resign and compelled the chapter to elect a notorious rascal who was related to one of his mistresses. This person, Diederik Slaghök, formerly a Westphalian barber, had been responsible for the judicial murder of several Swedish bishops and noblemen. Opposition to his confirmation in the see was too strong for the king, and Slaghök, instead of being anointed, was burned to death in the public square of Copenhagen in 1522. Lund then remained without an archbishop until 1525. Meantime there had been a revolution, and Christian's brother, Frederick, as considerable a tyrant as himself, was on the throne. When his attention was called to the long vacancy of the see of Lund he decided to reinstate Skodborg, who had gone to Rome to lay his case before the Pope. By

---

[1] Lübeck, the chief city of the Hanseatic League, was the storm-centre of northern Europe at this time. Bartholomew Sastrow, who was a boy there with Surius, gives in his Memoirs a lurid account of the advent of the Reformation, which he embraced with great enthusiasm.

[2] Some writers deny that Surius was ever inclined to Lutheranism, but Peter Canisius is quite clear on the subject and he must have known : " Sub eo praeceptore [van Esche] vel potius doctore spirituali vixit mecum Laurentius ille Surius Lubecensis, ex haeretico Catholicus—me adjutore—Coloniae factus." Braunsberger, *Epistulae*, vol. i, p. 36.

this time, Clement VII had a candidate of his own, and, so ruinously did he mismanage the negotiations with the king, that Frederick, who was only looking for some excuse, broke off all dealings with the Holy See and set to work vigorously to Protestantize his dominions. Skodborg, the innocent cause of so much trouble, retired to Cologne where he was made a canon of St. Gereon's.

Herll's little family kept closely in touch with the Charterhouse of St. Barbara in Cologne, a venerable institution that did a world of good unostentatiously. St. Bruno, the founder of the Order, was himself a Cologne man, and his spirit of simplicity and self-effacement still lived on in the monks of St. Barbara. They were of the same type as their London brethren who, shortly before, had mounted the scaffold as serenely as they used to mount the steps to their choir. In Germany they were respected by Catholics and Protestants alike, and even Sebastian Brandt, who had so little good to say of priests and religious in general, devoted a chapter to their praise. Not they but their few detractors will be found on board his famous *Ship of Fools*. The evils of the age in which they lived did but inspire them to fresh generosity in the service of God and their neighbour. The lights of Heaven had gone out, so they would kindle whatever little lamps they could to guide men in the temporary darkness. Books of theology and devotion appeared at regular intervals from St. Barbara's private printing-press, bearing at the end as their only indication of authorship these few words : " *Ora pro Carthusia Coloniensi unde hic liber prodiit.*"

The prior of St. Barbara's[1] at this time was a man named Gerard Kalckbrenner, but he is better known as Hammontanus, from the Belgian village of Hamont where he was born. Prior Gerard had something in him of St. Anthony of Egypt. He was the gentlest and kindliest of people and a great lover of solitude, but the Church's need found him at once in the ranks of her defenders. His sub-prior from 1536 to 1539 was the famous ascetical writer, Johann Justus Landspergius, so called from the beautiful town of Landsberg, in Bavaria, where he was born, and from his family name, Gerecht, which is the German for just or righteous.[2]

---

[1] Immediately before and during the Reformation period the most popular saints in Germany and the Low Countries were St. Anne, St. Catherine of Alexandria, St. Barbara and St. Ursula, in that order. The artists did a good deal to help on St. Ursula's cause, as experimenters in grouping and design found her eleven thousand companions very useful for their purpose. Siebert, *Beiträge zur vorreformatorischen Heiligen— und Reliquienverehrung* (1907), p. 48.

[2] As will be seen throughout this book, people of the sixteenth century were afflicted with a mania for Latinizing or Graecizing themselves. For instance, the real name of the great Catholic humanist and apologist, Cochlaeus, was Dobeneck. That meant nothing whatever in Latin or Greek, but his native place gave the Doctor an idea. It was Wendelstein, *Anglice*, Windingstone,

Landspergius was a saint and mystic as well as a controversial theologian of considerable ability. One of his many devotional writings, the *Epistle of Jesus Christ to the Faithful Soul*, is familiar to Catholics in England through the translation made by Blessed Philip Howard during his long imprisonment in the Tower of London. A chief element in the spiritual teaching of the Carthusian is his insistence on devotion to the human heart of Jesus Christ as symbolic of the love which God bears to mankind. That devotion transfigured his own life and turned his constant suffering into joy. A hundred and fifty years before St. Margaret Mary had those revelations which stopped the creeping paralysis of Jansenism, Landspergius wrote the following counsels for his disciples:

> Take pains to stir up in your soul veneration for the most amiable Heart of Jesus, the Heart that so abounds in love and mercy. Resort to It in spirit. Through It ask for all you need and offer up all that you do. It is the treasure-house of every heavenly grace, the door by which we approach God and God comes down to us. Place, then, in some spot that you often pass a picture or image of Our Lord's Heart, or of the Five Wounds, or of Jesus covered with blood and bruises. It will be a constant reminder to you not to fail in your holy exercises but to go forward steadily in the love of God. Looking on it you will remember your exile and the sad captivity of your sins. So with sighs and a great longing you will lift up your heart to God, and mentally, without movement of lips or noise of words, cry to Him, desiring that He would make your heart clean and at one with the Heart of Christ, that is, that He would unite your will to His own adorable Will. You may, too, if your devotion inspires you, embrace the image of the Heart of Jesus, telling yourself that it is, in truth, no image but His very Heart on which your kisses fall. . . . Even should the hearts of all your friends and all the world cast you out or betray you, rest assured that this most faithful Heart will not deceive you nor abandon you for ever."[1]

---

suggesting a snail's spiral shell, in Latin, Cochlaea. One of the principal humanists who was part author of the *Epistolae obscurorum virorum* received from his father the honest but common name of Jäger, which in English is Hunter. This was soon changed to the Latin, Venator, but the gentleman considered it much too obvious and began signing himself Rubeanus, from his birthplace, Dornheim, which in English would be Brambleham. The Latin for brambly is *rubeus*. Finally he emerged in history as Crotus Rubeanus but where he got the Crotus from nobody has been able to discover. The modern Germany of Adolf Hitler is sternly opposed to all this kind of thing.

[1] *Pharetra divini amoris*, nova editio (Cologne, 1620), pp. 80-1. Landspergius was, of course, by no means the first to urge devotion to the Divine Heart of Our Lord. The roots of the devotion were always in Catholic theology, quite apart from the special revelations granted to St. Margaret Mary.

It was spiritual teaching of this kind, in which the stress is always on personal love of Our Lord, that moulded the most impressionable years of Peter Canisius. He and Surius were constantly at the Charterhouse, and van Esche even had a private cell there to which he used to retire now and then for his soul's refreshment. The course of Peter's story will show how strong were the ties that grew between him and the Carthusians of Cologne. It is pleasant to think of him and the others from St. Gereon's in quiet converse with their cloistered friends, and it is well to remember when studying the dismal records of Catholic life at the time of the Reformation that there must have been many like them, men of devout and peaceable mind whose prayers and tears did not find a chronicler. So dark are the pictures painted by contemporaries, including Peter Canisius himself, that it might appear as if the secular and regular clergy were entirely given over to the devil. A good proportion, if not the majority, certainly were, but their misdeeds are far from being the whole of the story. Wickedness is usually noisy and blatant and so attracts attention, whereas goodness, of its very nature, strives to remain unknown. Moreover, the average human being is sufficiently impregnated with ideals to expect goodness and take it for granted. His letters to friends will not, as a rule, contain reports on the daily routine of hospitals and orphanages, but should he have witnessed a good murder or have come in contact with thieves or blackmailers, then, at last, he has ' news.' In view of this familiar fact it is wise to bear in mind that no document nor mass of documents is likely to give a completely balanced account of such a hectic, many-sided age as the sixteenth century. And it is also well to remember Aristotle's dictum : " The function proper to any particular kind is the function of the good specimen of that kind. Thus the function of the musician is the function of the good musician."[1] It is men like van Esche and the Carthusians who are the true representatives of Catholicism, and it is their sober spiritual doctrine, and not any aberrations of popular piety, which bears the seal of the Church's approval.[2]

[1] *Nichomachean Ethics*, I, 1098a.

[2] It is commonly acknowledged now by those who have taken the trouble to study the matter at all adequately that the Church might have succeeded in reforming herself from within much sooner had not Luther's revolt supervened to complicate the whole issue. " Had the forces already at work within the Church been allowed to operate," writes a well-known biographer of Luther, " probably much of the moral reform desired by the best Catholics would have been accomplished quietly, without the violent rending of Christian unity that actually took place." P. Smith, *The Age of the Reformation* (1920), pp. 26–27. As for the contention that it was Luther who shamed the Church into respectability, it has to be remembered that such saints as Cajetan, Teresa, and Philip Neri were not primarily concerned with the Protestant Reformation at all. Even in the case of St. Ignatius Loyola, it only came as an afterthought. Had there been no Luther and no

Van Esche, taught by the Brothers of the Common Life and by the Carthusians, was, above everything, a mystic of the Passion and of the suffering Heart of Christ, as the various little ascetical treatises which he composed or edited testify. Their teaching is at once tender and bracing, for, while their author lays it down as axiomatic that the personal love and following of Christ is the sum and substance of true religion, he insists tirelessly that such love is not born of mere pious aspirations but only of strenuous activity with both intellect and will. "It is by the sacred humanity of Our Lord," he says, "that alone we are raised up to the very throne of God, Christ being the only door to salvation. He must be our all in all, the lodestar of our hearts, the Beloved whose embrace is sweet beyond the dreams of mortal lovers." But the divine love comes to a man down the same avenues of will and memory that true human love has always trodden ; the difficult, familiar ways of mind-fulness and sacrifice and self-devotion. Let him take up his cross daily and a man may find out something about love. He never will on any other terms. That was the essence of van Esche's doctrine, as old as the Gospels and as new as the dawn of to-day. How profoundly it influenced Peter Canisius may be understood from the following tribute to Father Nicholas in his *Confessions*.

Bless the Lord, O my soul, and forget not all that He hath done for thee in giving thee as master and daily counsellor in the ways of holiness one whose only care and love was thy salvation. With him for guide I gradually began to make small surrenders of my own good pleasure that I might the better please God whom as yet in the heyday of youth I knew but little and feared still less. His counsel, his practice, his example were like new light to my eyes. Aided by his firm discipline I learned to break or restrain the headlong impulses and vain ardours of my young blood. With him for a close friend I found it easy to forgo other companionship. No one in the world was as dear to me as he, or as much a part of my soul, and I gave him all the trust that a father could desire from his son. Nor was it only in Confession that I often laid my soul bare to him. Every night before going to bed I used to tell him, as we conversed intimately together, all the falls and follies and stains of the day's experience, that he might be their

---

Reformation his sons would have built their schools and carried on their mission just the same. Other orders and congregations that were destined to have enormous influence in reviving Catholic piety came into existence and functioned without any reference whatever to the cataclysm in Germany.

judge and sentence me to whatever penance he thought best. I
acknowledge and reverently praise Thy mercy, O God, faithful
guardian of men and protector of my life, who hast always and everywhere prospered my ways. In Cologne Thou didst in Thy sure providence destine this man to be for me another Ananias, who would instruct
me and bring me closer to Thyself. Every day his care for me increased.
He prayed for me, he wept over me, he took his pen in hand and
wrote for my instruction. My soul was indeed covered with his
blessings, his exhortations, his warnings. On one occasion I had to
leave him to go home. It was very pleasant there and I soon began
to fall into lax ways, but Thou didst send him to me when I had
been away too long, and by him didst rouse me, as a father his sleeping
son. Rebuking my negligence, Thou didst put me on my feet again,
and then, having won back Thy weak and lazy child, didst confirm
him in Thy ways through Thy servant's solicitous devotion. Ah,
how Thou didst make my heart to leap when I heard from his lips
and learned to repeat after him such maxims as these : To serve God
is to reign ; Know Christ well and it matters not if you know nothing
besides. He used to make me read each day a chapter of the Gospels
and choose from it some verse to be meditated and learned by heart.
In addition to this he provided me with books of piety and the lives
of holy men, by the frequent study of which Thou didst teach me
more and more of Thy love and fear. . . . May all Thy innocent and
holy ones thank Thee, my God, who didst lay Thy hand upon me
and care for me singularly during those years when the world's blandishments and the delights of the flesh lead so many far from Thee. I beg
Thee, O Lord, the faithful guardian and lover of mankind, to grant
to many other young people the same grace Thou didst accord to
unworthy me of good and holy directors for their souls. . . .[1]

Peter further records the 'sweet intercourse' which he and Surius
enjoyed with Landspergius and his Carthusian brethren, but he does not
give any details of their conversations. Certain it is, however, that he
derived from them and from van Esche's guidance a deep devotion to
the Sacred Humanity of Christ and he may also have learned in the same
environment to appreciate with especial enthusiasm the work of the
great medieval mystic, Tauler. The point depends on whether he was
the author of a certain book which has been confidently attributed to

[1] Braunsberger, *Epistulae*, vol. i, pp. 17–9.

him in recent years. As will be shown later on, there are grave reasons for doubting the attribution.

Having now placed Peter in his spiritual environment and indicated the forces that were moulding his will, our next step is to follow him as well as we can into that curious old scholastic world where he gathered his sheaves of learning. Scholasticism was still the queen of men's intellects, though her royalty had of late been very rudely questioned. In the course of time she had assumed every costume, " the old red robe of the cardinal, the cape of the bishop, the priest's soutane, the monk's frock, the judge's ermine, the professor's square cap, the warrior's coat of mail, and even the petticoat of the ladies." But the day of her monopoly was nearly over, and it was precisely at her favourite court of Cologne that she suffered the most deadly assault on her privileges. Cologne, the fourth of the German universities, was founded by the municipality in 1388. It was the first bourgeois establishment of the kind, as its predecessors, Prague, Vienna and Heidelberg, had owed their inception to the munificence of princes. Like them, it was constituted in general lines on the model of Paris, but the division of the students into " nations " and some other usages of the mother university were not adopted. Cologne had been from an early date the chief *Studium* or educational centre of the Dominicans in Northern Europe, a *Studium* made famous by the lectures of St. Albert the Great and St. Thomas Aquinas. There too, in the convent of the Franciscans, had taught and died the Dominicans' great philosophical and theological rival, Duns Scotus. It is only a few steps from the shrine of St. Albert to the grave of Scotus, but what memories of the wordy battles of long ago that little pilgrimage can evoke! With such an illustrious pedigree the university seemed destined for a splendid future, and during its first hundred years it lived well up to the high standards set for it. Then, as so often happens with both men and institutions, came a period of self-satisfaction and stagnation, out of which grew, like some giant fungus, one of the most embittered literary controversies that the world has ever known.

The unfortunate Jews were the cause of the trouble. One of them, a learned but intemperate person named Johann Pfefferkorn, became a Christian at Cologne in 1506. He then conceived that it was his mission to effect the wholesale conversion of his former co-religionists, and, as a preliminary to this large undertaking, asked and obtained from the Emperor a rescript commanding the Jews of Germany to deliver up all books hostile to the Christian faith. Armed with the document, he set to work in the most bigoted and blundering fashion possible, and, without any real authority, demanded that the Jews should surrender not only anti-Christian books but their own sacred writings, such as the Talmud and Cabbala. In this course he had the fullest backing from the theologians of the University of Cologne, who had, unfortunately, long ago forgotten the moderation and charity of St. Thomas Aquinas. Opposition in more enlightened Catholic circles soon made itself felt, however, whereupon Pfefferkorn suggested that Johann Reuchlin, the best Hebrew scholar in Europe, should be asked for a pronouncement. Reuchlin gave it, but not in the way that Pfefferkorn wanted, and so drew on his scholarly head the lightnings originally intended for the children of Israel. Next followed a sharp duel in print, with the usual weapons of abuse and slanderous insinuations. The outcome of this was a decision by the Cologne authorities that Reuchlin had fallen into heresy, but before proceeding against him judicially the theologians thought that they would see what they could themselves do in the arena. They did all sorts of unbecoming things, and so exasperated the old scholar that he allowed his temper to get the better of his judgment and vented on them a flood of scurrilous vituperation. Both his *Defence* on this occasion, and his previous answer to Pfefferkorn, were condemned by a number of universities, including Louvain and Paris, and he was summoned to appear before the Inquisitor General, a Cologne theologian, in September, 1513. He thereupon appealed to Pope Leo X who referred the unhappy controversy to the Bishops of Speyer and Worms. They declared entirely in Reuchlin's favour, and when the Inquisitor counter-appealed only one man of the twenty-two appointed to consider the matter in Rome upheld him.

That might appear to be the end of the story but it was really only the beginning, as the humanists and anti-clericals of Germany had meantime rallied to avenge outraged scholarship on the unwise doctors of Cologne, whose decadent theology and barren speculations afforded an easy target for the shafts of satirists. As a measure of self-defence Reuchlin published in 1514 a series of letters addressed to him by learned sympathisers—*Clarorum virorum epistolae*—his purpose being to show that serious students who knew what they were talking about did not consider him to have exceeded legitimate bounds in his criticism. The title of the volume suggested to Hutten and Crotus Rubeanus, two of the left wing humanists, the brilliant idea of publishing a similar one containing letters supposed to have been written by the Cologne theologians to their leader, Ortwin Gratius. Thus originated the *Epistolae obscurorum virorum*, a book with hardly a smile in it for a modern reader but which was then considered uproariously funny. The poor friars and theologians were made to talk the most preposterous nonsense in the most ridiculous Latin, it being the aim of the book to bring them into contempt, not as bad men, but as hopelessly stupid and uncultivated simpletons. The crude and heavy humour of the letters, their bitter personal tone, and nasty suggestiveness were exactly suited to immature minds and evoked whoops of delight from the student class in Germany. Cologne University became the great joke of the period. How seriously it suffered from the long struggle, which ended only with Reuchlin's death in 1552,[1] may be seen by a glance at the following figures. In 1516 the number of freshmen was three hundred and seventy. Ten years later it had dropped to seventy-two, and in 1534, just before the arrival of Peter Canisius, it was only fifty-four.[2] The authorities attributed the decline to the religious upheaval, but in sober truth the major part of the blame lay at their own doors. They had allowed their traditions to become fossilized, and refused blindly to recognize the claims of the New Learning which might have been turned to glorious account in the service of true religion.

As soon as he had settled down with Herll and van Esche at St. Gereon's, Peter Canisius took his matriculation, which merely meant in that easy age taking an oath to abide by the statutes and regulations of the university. Before the entry of his name in the *Matricula*, he would have been known, according to the custom of the time, as a *bejaunus* or *bajan*, derived from *bec jaune*, a yellow-beak or fledgling. Throughout history new boys have commonly been obliged to submit to some painful ritual before admission to the privileges of school life. At Cologne the *bajan* was regarded as a kind of wild beast that had to be tamed. This was accomplished at his " Depositio," or ceremonial laying down of rustic manners and ignorance, to which function he was conducted in garments suggestive of some animal or other. Stretched at full length on a bench he had then to endure a good deal of rough and painful

---

[1] Reuchlin died in full communion with the Church, though before his own death Pope Leo X had changed over to the side of his adversaries, frightened probably by the apparition of Luther in 1517. Reuchlin broke off all dealings with his grand-nephew, Melanchthon, whom he had at first dearly loved, on account of that man's defection to Lutheranism. It is a significant fact that Melanchthon alone of the great humanists—Ulrich von Hutten was not one of them—died outside the Church. Erasmus never left it and Pirkheimer, Crotus Rubeanus, Zasius, Amerbach, and others, who at first were enthusiastic for Luther, drew back when they perceived the evil consequences of his teaching. Their gradual disillusionment is traced in Döllinger's *Die Reformation*. The Reuchlin controversy as a whole is admirably described by Bishop Creighton in his *History of the Papacy*, vol. v, pp. 29–49.

[2] Janssen-Pastor *Geschichte des deutschen Volkes*, vol. vii, p. 164.

treatment with pincers, planes, saws, and other instruments that might be used to remove the tusks, horns, and claws of a dangerous beast. Though the university authorities endeavoured to keep this buffoonery within reasonable bounds, the *bajan* must have felt stiff and sore after it.[1] There followed his 'penance,' which invariably took the form of providing an elaborate feast for his tormentors. With this his "jocund advent" came to an end and he was hailed as an honourable member of the university. Peter Canisius says nothing about his own initiation but there can be no doubt whatever that he had to submit to the usual rites, as they were in full swing at Cologne in 1536.

Peter's first studies at the university were in the faculty of arts, which embraced the traditional *trivium* of grammar, rhetoric and logic. To this faculty four colleges or *Bursen*, as they were called, had become attached in the course of time. The oldest and most flourishing of them was the Montanerburse or Montanum, which received its name in honour of Gerard de Monte, an illustrious rector who died in 1480. It was at this college, largely a preserve for Dutch or Flemish students, that Peter entered himself, because, though he might board outside, he was obliged to belong to some recognized corporation of the university. One point in connexion with his choice is worthy of notice. In 1509 the chief bene-factor of the Montanum had made it a condition of his bequests that the students should be given St. Thomas Aquinas for their intellectual guide and master. On this account they were generally known in the City as the " Thomists," in contradistinction to undergraduates of other founda-tions who were called " Albertists," after Albert the Great, or " Scotists " after Duns Scotus.[2] The point is significant because in those days, before the great revival of scholastic theology initiated by the Dominicans of Salamanca, Peter the Lombard and not St. Thomas was the recognized authority in the schools. An old German book of moralizings entitled *Margarita philosophica*, which was published at Strasbourg, Alsace, in 1504, has a delightful woodcut representing the student's progress in learning. Wisdom in the guise of a lady stands at the entrance to a tower with superimposed terraces, something like a pagoda. A little boy approaches to whom she presents a horn-book, bearing the alphabet. On the ground floor of the tower the old grammarian Donatus, who tutored St. Jerome, is seen teaching, armed with a birch, while from the

---

[1] Wrede, *Geschichte der alten Kölner Universität* (Cologne, 1921), p. 27. Rait, *Life in the Mediaeval University* (Cambridge, 1912), p. 118. Rashdall in his *Universities of Europe in the Middle Ages* gives an interesting account of a " Depositio " in which Martin Luther was one of the executioners.
[2] Braunsberger, *Epistulae*, vol. i, p. 660.

windows of the upper tiers Aristotle, Cicero, Ptolemy, Euclid and other such representative worthies look down benignly on the reluctant scholar. At the top of the tower theology has a floor to itself, filled entirely by the ample bust of Peter the Lombard. Owing to his connexion with the Montanum the sympathies of Peter Canisius were soon fortunately diverted from that good anthologist but poor theologian to the true genius of Catholic thought, St. Thomas.

The first course at the university consisted mainly of Latin studies in continuation of what the undergraduate was already supposed to know about the language of Rome. All the lectures were delivered in that language and the students were expected to converse in it whenever engaged on their academic labours. This first course, which was merely preliminary, led up to the baccalaureate, a distinction corresponding to the French rather than to the English idea of a B.A. After less than a year's work on his authors, during which the spirit of genuine humanism began to steal over him, Peter Canisius took his degree. Certainly he acquired a very sound knowledge of the Latin classics, attested by his ability to quote them with point and ease. His letters are full of tags from Cicero, Horace, Livy, Vergil, and other worthies, but above all from the *Noctes Atticae* of Aulus Gellius, a second-rate piece of literature which appears to have been his special favourite. Though when the mood takes him his prose can toss its plumes in the lordliest manner of the Renaissance, his ordinary work-a-day Latin is by no means attractive. Only in his books do we find the measured dignity and lucid grace which prove his discipleship of the ancient masters. It must be said, however, as anybody reading him will soon and painfully discover, that humanism touched St. Peter only lightly and on the surface. A text from the Vulgate always meant more to him than the brightest eloquence of ancient poet or philosopher.

The next step in his course was to become a licentiate of arts, which involved a strict *tentamen* in private and then a public *examen* before the chancellor. An embittered student of the time said that these examinations were "like a trial for murder." They consisted, as did the subsequent tests leading to the Master's degree, of disputations and much questioning on the old *quadrivium* of music, arithmetic, geometry and astronomy, with which for good measure were thrown in the three philosophies, physical, moral, and metaphysical.[1] These philosophies embraced what

[1] All these branches of learning are symbolized in the arms of the University of Oxford, which consist of an open book with seven clasps, surrounded by three crowns. The clasps represent the seven liberal arts of the *trivium* and *quadrivium* and the crowns the three philosophies.

was then understood by natural science, derived almost exclusively from Aristotle, together with the same man's views on logic, psychology, metaphysics, ethics, political philosophy and astronomy. As a supplement or introduction to the works of " that damned heathen," if we may use Martin Luther's expressive terminology, Peter Canisius would have studied Porphyry's *Isagoge*, the *Summulae logicales* of Pope John XXI, Gerard of Cremona's *Theories of the Planets*, the inevitable *Material Sphere* of Joannes a Sacrobosco, whose mother knew him as John Holywood of Halifax, Yorkshire, a treatise on optics called *Perspectiva communis*, by the fiery English Franciscan, John Peckham, a sort of history book entitled *De calamitate temporum*, and various other treatises full of the quaint ideas and happy confidence of the Middle Ages.[1] It would not be true, perhaps, to say that Peter wasted his time over them but he would certainly have been better employed learning Hebrew and reading Plato. Of Aristotle there was more than enough, but he was not taught intelligently and the muddled, undiscerning professors tended to regard him with the awe due to a prophet of the Old Testament, verbally inspired. That attitude gave some colour to the tirades of the heretics and humanists. By barring its doors to the Renaissance, Cologne failed Peter Canisius, shutting out from his youth a whole world of wisdom and beauty. For the time being, however, he was contented enough with his poor Latin Aristotle and his Joannes a Sacrobosco, since there was always Vergil as a refuge from their aridities.

The universities of old times did not believe in making the way of wisdom too much of a primrose path. At Paris in the fifteenth century the students were obliged to sit on the floor during lectures, with a view to curbing the haughty ardours of youth—*ut occasio superbiae a juvenibus secludatur*. In a number of places, probably Cologne among them, the professors deliberately spoke very fast in order to prevent the making of notes which might be handed round or down and engender a spirit of independence in the scholars. This system had the advantage of encouraging private rumination but must have been a heavy tax on the scholars' memories and powers of attention. It was their duty after the lecture was over to discuss and repeat it among themselves, and at the end of the week they were expected to present their professors with a written résumé of the material expounded during it. Of course they took every chance of " getting a rise " out of their masters and indulged much more than their modern counterparts in booing, hissing, banging of desks, etc.,

[1] Braunsberger, *Epistulae*, vol. i, p. 663.

notwithstanding the earnest entreaties of vice-chancellors that they should behave *more virginum*—as young ladies are reputed to do.

Outside school hours the authorities found the control of their charges an exceedingly difficult problem, especially in large cities such as Cologne which had a cosmopolitan population. The Cologne students were notorious for their love of a fight, of beer and of gambling. Despite fines, floggings, imprisonment and the activity of the *lupi* or official spies deputed to keep an eye on their movements, they set upon the watch at night, played wild football in the streets, drank copiously, fiddled under ladies' windows and generally made themselves a nuisance to law-abiding citizens. These diversions were, however, peculiar to the German section of the community and not shared by the numerous Scotsmen in residence. For one thing the Scots were too poor to indulge in them, so invariably poor that in Cologne all poverty-stricken students came to be nicknamed Scots. Peter Canisius occasionally joined in the merry-makings at carnival time but used to let the wine and beer go by as a small act of reparation for the drunkenness with which the feasts nearly always ended.[1] There is no sign that he cared much for music or fine clothes, two things very dear to the hearts of the Cologne students long ago, probably, in the case of clothes at least, because it was forbidden to wear anything but clerical dress. Like the Oxford Clerk, Peter

> Was lever have at his beddes heed
> Twenty bokes clad in black or red
> Of Aristotle and his philosophye
> Than robes riche or fithele or gay sautrye.

He helped the poorer students as well as he could and from time to time denuded his little library of its treasured volumes that they might be sold for charity.[2] In a born book-lover that was not a bad form of self-sacrifice. There was characteristic Dutch deliberateness about his growth in sanctity, a steady, unostentatious advance such as might be expected in a man whose country's fortunes were made in silent, slow-moving barges. Nothing at all advertised him in those days as the destined engineer of God who would block with his sturdy dykes the advancing flood of the Reformation and reclaim a great deal of the lands over which it had already flowed so disastrously.

[1] Braunsberger, *Epistulae*, vol. i, p. 22.
[2] Braunsberger, *Epistulae*, vol. i, p. 22.

In 1539, after he had obtained his licentiate, Peter moved to Louvain, a daughter university of Cologne, in order to follow a brief course in canon law. Next to nothing is known of this journey to Belgium, but it was apparently undertaken to please his father, who hoped to see him become a brilliant jurist. Meister Jakop had grown suspicious of Peter's association with priests and monks in Cologne. He might commit the terrible mistake of drifting into a monastery, and so spoil the paternal ambitions for him. It was time, then, thought the Burgomaster, to put love's young dream into his head. An attractive girl would be the best remedy for too much religion and such a one accordingly was chosen and brought on the scene, but only to find her charms politely disregarded. Peter had got beyond that stage. The jaunty, care-free airs of his boyhood had gradually given place to an intense seriousness of purpose and strong feeling of vocation under the influence of van Esche and the Carthusians. Through his experiences as a student and from his intercourse with good and zealous men he came to realize more and more the terrible significance of the religious struggles going on around him. It was the day of doom and no time for marrying or giving in marriage. For his motto, just like a Dutchman, he took the word PERSEVERA, writing it thus in large capitals on his theme-book, the first of his millions of written words to be preserved. To encourage himself he would often repeat some dull Latin hexameters with the following sense:

> Live inwardly to God, revere His light within,
> Live utterly to God, the world without despise,
> Be all thy thought and anxious care to win,
> Contemning earth, approval from His eyes.[1]

There is not much poetry in those lines, but it was something other than poetry that Peter was seeking when he made them his own.

In May, 1540, at the age of nineteen, he became a Master of Arts of Cologne. This was a solemn affair beginning with a disputation known as the *Quodlibeticum*, or optional test, because the candidates had the privilege of choosing the subject. As a special mark of honour he was also allowed to indulge in "*jocosas questiones ad auditorii recreationem*" —humorous questions for the diversion of the audience. The ceremony of Inception followed in the Dom, Cologne's great cathedral, where he was given his *biretta* and other insignia, and then came the *Promotorialessen*, or elaborate banquet for the authorities, which Peter had to provide out

[1] Braunsberger, *Epistulae*, vol. i, p. 67.

of his own pocket. A few months before taking the degree he had countered his father's marriage manœuvres by vowing himself to perpetual chastity. Things were moving fast within him, though he did not yet know the precise direction in which his future lay. Meantime Meister Jakop tried other expedients to keep him in the pleasant ways of earthly salvation. Hopes of a fine marriage were gone and Peter seemed bent on being a priest, but he might still bring glory to the family if he could be persuaded to accept a rich benefice of which the Burgomaster had the bestowal. The rock that was Peter wrecked that project, too, whereupon his father, being a good man, abandoned further attempts to control the operations of Heaven. Peter confesses that his " love of quiet and contemplation attracted him to the religious life of the Carthusians," but the words of the mysterious lady of Arnheim who had assured him as a boy that God intended him to belong to a " new order of priests " kept ringing in his memory.

After obtaining the Master's degree a Cologne student was at liberty to specialize in one or more of the other three faculties, theology, law and medicine. In his state of mind Peter naturally chose theology, but how he worked at it during the years 1540–43 is not recorded. The university possessed a good library and doubtless he spent much of his time there. At the end of the fifteenth century an observant chronicler put down Paris as the best place for the study of the seven liberal arts, Bologna for law, Pavia for medicine, Cracow for astronomy and Cologne for Scripture.[1] Peter was aware of Cologne's speciality and so concentrated on the study of the Bible. To judge by the amazing ease and appositeness with which he quotes both Old and New Testaments on nearly every page of his voluminous writings he must almost have known the Bible by heart. Its text became the natural and usual vehicle of his thoughts, even in familiar correspondence, and is used to such an extent as at times to be positively wearisome or even comical. Thus, he not infrequently juxtaposes incongruous passages, without the slightest anxiety as to the resultant dreadful mixture of metaphors.

Surius and he grew so fond of each other during those student years that, like two small boys, they vowed one day never to separate. The terms of the pact were carefully inclusive, and laid down that, even should one choose to enter a religious order, the other must follow suit. In February, 1540, Surius joined the Cologne Carthusians, so bringing the pact into operation. That was an hour of severe testing for Peter

[1] Wrede, *Geschichte der alten Kölner Universität*, p. 39.

An old print of Nymegen, the birthplace of St. Peter Canisius

as both his promise and his predilections strongly inclined him to follow his friend. But still he held back, because above the voices of affection and inclination there sounded that other strangely insistent one reminding him of "the new order of priests," for which he must wait. Peter had no idea where to look for this order. It did not come into official existence until seven months after Surius had gone, and it was to remain unknown to him for three more perplexed and anxious years. Nevertheless, like St. Joan, he remained true to his voices and like her he was not deceived. Thirty years later when he was a scarred veteran of the battles with heresy he wrote to Surius, still in the peaceful seclusion of St. Barbara's, begging him for release from their boyhood compact. "Surius was smiling while he told me this story of Peter's scruple," says the good man who preserved it for us.[1]

The first letter from Peter's pen that has been preserved shows by its rather crude and violent conception of duty how earnestly he was striving to be found worthy of his vocation when God should reveal it to him. It was written to his sister Wendelina in January, 1541:

In your letter, my dear Sister, you beg me to pray that you may escape the snares of the world. Well, I would have you know that prayers are not going to bring about your complete reform unless you prepare your slow heart for the blessing you ask God to grant you. Neither will they help if you continue to be cold and negligent in God's service and to perform your duties so carelessly. This negligence will grow upon you more and more, and your soul will become progressively subject to more serious and dangerous contamination. Because you are so slack and lazy in your spiritual exercises your heart has lost the power to taste the sweetness and lovableness of God. You cannot know how pleasant are the further stages of that narrow way whose first part is sown with nettles and thistles and thorns. Through these the beloved must make her way on wounded feet to fall into the arms of that chosen Lover for whose sake all things else are to be abandoned, costly ornament, finery and fashion, and creature comforts and pleasures of every description. May God be merciful to you who seek Him and His Spirit in the midst of such things. I shall implore the Holy Spirit to enlighten the darkness in which you wander after folly and fleshly indulgence. You have my thanks for

[1] He was John Hasius, a German Jesuit of Dutch extraction. Braunsberger, *Epistulae*, vol. vi, p. 383. Hasius, who knew Surius in his old age intimately, says that he was "Societati nostrae addictissimus" and as keenly anxious for its welfare as for that of his own Order.

what you said to me, and I beg you to consider this letter as addressed to you alone. Learn to die, dear Sister, to the sinful inclinations and thoughts of your own heart. A very happy New Year to you. Your brother Peter.[1]

Poor Wendelina! She may have been somewhat worldly-minded but there is no reason to think that she needed such a stern homily. Larger experience would soften her brother's mood and give him a tenderer regard for the frailties of human nature, as, indeed, may be seen in his next extant letter, addressed to her at Eastertime, 1543, when she had been married a year and was expecting her first baby:

Sister dear, as Christ has risen again let us too rise to newness of life, leaving our old sins dead and buried in our Saviour's tomb. Remain strong in your Christian faith and so learn to despise the vanity of the world and the desires of the flesh. This wisdom, however, is only for those who stand firm in the fear of God. . . . Men permit themselves in their blindness to be led astray by a false confidence in the mercy of Our Lord, but you and I will consider rather the deep penitence of the Good Thief which caused him to cry out, " Lord, remember me ! " This spirit of penitence will not be given to us unless we listen carefully for the voice of God speaking in our consciences, and do or leave undone for His love that which it commands or prohibits. It behoves us, then, to examine whether we are employing our time piously and to the best purpose, carefully avoiding occasions of sin and useless worries. Be on your guard above all things against the pride of the world which manifests itself chiefly to-day in fashionable belongings, jewellery and the desire for pretty clothes. . . . You speak as if you were expecting a child and wanted to keep the matter secret. It is the way of mothers to go quite crazy about their first babies. Try to avoid that excess and remember that it is your duty, a duty grossly neglected in our time, to take the greatest care that your children keep their innocence and grow up in the fear and service of God. Thank you for the juniper berries. They agree with me very well and I hope to keep in good health with their aid. May God bless you all. Your brother Peter.[2]

[1] Braunsberger, *Epistulae,* vol. i, pp. 68–9.
[2] Braunsberger, *Epistulae,* vol. i, pp. 72–4. This letter ends with a postscript reflecting on the quality of the wine provided by Wendelina's husband when Peter last visited them. He advises them to purchase their liquor in Cologne when next they need some.

About the time when Peter wrote that letter something happened to divert him from his studies and other occupations. A young Spanish priest named Alvaro Alfonso came from Mainz to Cologne and attached himself to the Montanum. We are not told so in as many words, but subsequent events make it clear that Canisius and he must have become friends almost at once. Certainly the Spanish priest would have provoked Peter's interest by his appearance and behaviour, for though he seemed to be a religious of some kind he did not belong to any order with which the young Dutch student was acquainted. Mystery had come to school in the guise of this quiet stranger, and Peter must assuredly have wondered whether he might not be a herald of his long-desired "new order of priests." In point of fact he was, and we may legitimately suppose that from his lips Peter heard for the first time the inspiring story of St. Ignatius Loyola and his early companions. One companion, he would have learned, and the best loved of all, was another Peter whose child-hood in the mountains of Savoy resembled that of van Esche in its simple, unforced piety. Like St. Vincent de Paul at the end of the same sixteenth century, Peter Favre[1] spent the long day as a lad with his dog and his sheep, wandering from pasture to pasture and dreaming his young dreams. The dream that he cherished most was to be able to go to school. "*Flebam desiderio scholae*," he recorded of himself—I used to cry with longing to be at school—which he not only succeeded in satisfying, but even worked his way to the school of schools, the University of Paris. St. Barbara had her College there as well as her Charterhouse in Cologne, and on its lists Favre entered himself, sharing a room and his poverty with a young Spanish hidalgo named Francis Xavier, whose chief claim to glory so far had been the winning of the high jump in the university sports. In February of the year 1528 Ignatius Loyola arrived in Paris from Barcelona, having trudged five hundred miles alone through the snow-blocked defiles of the Pyrenees and over country made perilous by the contending armies of France and the Empire. Since the days of his convalescence after Pamplona, when, to pass the tedious, pain-haunted hours, he had idly turned the pages of the only two books available, some stories of the saints and the Life of Christ by a Rhineland Carthusian, God had taken complete possession of his soul. But he had not ceased to be a soldier at heart. The fires of Spanish chivalry would still and always burn in his veins, but burn now only to serve the King

---

[1] His name is spelt in various ways, Faber, Lefevre, Faure, etc., but Favre would seem to be the most correct form.

of Heaven. From his sick bed he had risen to win the world for Him, had kept a vigil of arms before the Mother of the King, and then, after a year of terrible penance and profound spiritual experience in the cave and little chapels of Manresa, had set out for Jerusalem to convert the Turks to Christianity. Only the intensity of his love for Christ, his King, could have kept him alive through the hardships and disappointments of that pilgrimage[1] just as, after his return to Spain, only the same love could have impelled the unbookish soldier of thirty-three to sit learning the elements of Latin with children, that he might study to be a priest. At Alcalá and again at Salamanca, to which places he had gone in hopes of acquiring a little philosophy and theology, he was thrown into prison on suspicion of being a heretic. When a compassionate lady asked him how he could endure it, he answered : " There are not so many chains and fetters in all Salamanca as I long to bear for the love of God." Then followed a year of slow starvation at Paris where he attended lectures at the Collège de Montaigu, lived in the poorhouse and continued to pursue with unquenchable ardour his one ambition of winning recruits for the service of his King.

In the late summer of 1529 Ignatius changed his lectures and joined the College of St. Barbara to prepare for a degree in arts. As a poor student he ' clubbed ' with Favre and Francis Xavier, sharing their room and whatever plain fare they had for a meal. Favre, who had graduated shortly before in arts and medicine, was appointed to help the newcomer with his studies and soon came under the spell of his holiness. While at Manresa Ignatius had worked out a system of prayer and meditation which he now applied to the troubled soul of his young tutor. Favre made these *Spiritual Exercises*, as they were called, and the *Spiritual Exercises* made Favre. Peace, which scruples and despondency had destroyed, came back to his heart and with it a profound love and veneration for the man to whom he owed his deliverance. In his own words " they became one in hope and will," two souls, like David and Jonathan, fused in a love passing the love of woman. He was the first steadfast disciple of Ignatius, the most loyal and the most lovable. One who knew him intimately bore this witness : " In his dealings with others there was a singularly charming sweetness and grace such as, to speak truly, I never found in anybody else. By some means or other he would win their friendship, gradually steal into their hearts, and with his amiable

[1] Bates, in his *Touring in 1600* (London, 1911), gives a blood-curdling account of what the pilgrim had to expect, even late in the sixteenth century.

manner and slow pleasant words kindle in them a mighty love of God."[1]

The ever fresh and delightful *Memoriale* which he composed as a record of God's mercies to him is the best window to Favre's soul. Through it one gets such glimpses as this : " On the feast of St. Elizabeth, Queen of Hungary, I felt great devotion and a desire to keep certain persons in mind that I might pray for them, regardless of their failings. These were the Pope, the Emperor, Francis I, Henry VIII, Luther, the Grand Turk, Bucer, and Philip Melanchthon. I felt in my soul that these men were being sternly judged in many quarters, and from this feeling there arose within me a certain devout compassion proceeding from the Good Spirit."[2] At another time he wrote : " While once pondering over the distaste and repugnance that is wont to arise in those who attend the sick, especially if they be poor people with contagious or evil-smelling diseases, I felt a conviction that it behoves everyone engaged in such or any other good works for the love of Christ alone to be ready to give his life very gladly in their exercise."[3] This was not only a conviction with him but his unfailing practice. Neither pestilence nor the perils of war had any power to hinder the movements of his charity. Wherever, in the cities he visited, human misery dragged out its course, there he would be found, no matter what the diseases or denominations of the sufferers. Catholic, Protestant, or Jew, it made no difference, for their troubles were the only necessary passport to his heart.

Common affection for Favre was the link between Ignatius and Francis Xavier, who at first had been inclined to laugh at the old soldier turned student with his extraordinary notions about loving God. After Xavier had been won, it was the turn of the intellectually brilliant James Laynez to succumb, and he was followed by his friend Salmeron. Then with the number made up to ten by the accession of five other masters of the university, Bobadilla, Rodriguez, Codure, Le Jay, and Broët, St. Ignatius laid the foundations of his Company. They took their vow at Montmartre, and six years later, September 27, 1540, after much heart-searching and heavy tribulation, obtained from Pope Paul III a bull establishing the Society of Jesus as a new religious order in the Church. It was only by slow degrees that the plan of the new order unfolded itself to Ignatius and his companions, and even at the time when the bull was granted they were still far from having determined the external scope and object

[1] M.H., *Epistolae PP. Paschasii Broeti*, Claudii Jaii, etc. (Madrid, 1903), p. 453.
[2] M.H., *Fabri Monumenta*, p. 502.
[3] M.H., *Fabri Monumenta*, p. 582.

of their corporation. Unlike so many of the tribe of Macaulay who would dabble in their history, they certainly had no idea that they were founded for the specific purpose of combating Lutheranism. It was for the Pope to decide what they should do and where they should go, "whether to the Turks or other unbelievers, or to the regions called India, or to the lands of heretics or schismatics, or to faithful Catholic populations." Should His Holiness not call upon them for special service beyond the seas or in heretical countries, then they would devote themselves "to preaching, hearing confessions, teaching children Christian doctrine, giving retreats and all other methods of advancing Catholic souls in the way of perfection."

After a period of strenuous activity in France Favre was sent by Ignatius in 1540 to a religious conference in Germany. His first experiences of that agitated land were sufficiently disheartening. "Would to God," he wrote to Ignatius from Worms in January, 1541, "that there were in this city even two or three priests not living in concubinage, nor involved in other public and notorious scandals!" Such was the story everywhere, for a year later he is writing from Speyer: "The marvel is that there are not many more Lutherans when one thinks of all the abuses."[1] From Speyer he journeyed to Regensburg, carrying his books in a bundle on his back. Then he was ordered to Spain, where he made a profound impression on the Viceroy of Catalonia, Don Francis Borgia, and gained two court chaplains as candidates for the Society of Jesus, one of them the Alvaro Alfonso, from whom Peter Canisius may be supposed to have learned the incidents here recorded. Not long afterwards Favre was back again in Germany, ending up at Mainz in November, 1542. On these various travels—travels that would render our degenerate limbs incapacitated for life—he met with dangers and hardships of every description, but he never worried where he slept nor how he fed or fared provided he could get men to turn their thoughts to God. When thrown into prison as a spy in France he immediately set about making good Christians of his gaolers. Bandits, gypsies, tavern-keepers, peasant lads, cardinals, grand ladies, hooligans of the back streets, all were dear and welcome to his limitless sympathies. His great weapon with the educated was a retreat according to the method that he had learned from Ignatius in Paris. After Ignatius he was the best exponent of the *Spiritual Exercises* among all the early fathers of the Order and while in Germany gave them to many of the most eminent ecclesiastics there, including Cochlaeus.

[1] M.H., *Fabri Monumenta*, pp. 59–160

With heretics he dealt according to the prescriptions that he had himself outlined for the guidance of his friend James Laynez : " In the first place it is necessary that anyone who desires to be serviceable to heretics of the present age should hold them in great affection and love them very truly, putting out of his heart all thoughts and feelings that tend to their discredit. The next thing he must do is to win their good-will and love by friendly intercourse and converse on matters about which there is no difference between us, taking care to avoid all controversial subjects that lead to bickering and mutual recrimination. The things that unite us ought to be the first ground of our approach, not the things that keep us apart."[1] Ordinary people, " Jedermann " and his wife, Favre wooed by such kindness and sympathy as exhales from this passage of the *Memoriale* : " On the Vigil of SS. Simon and Jude I happened to be saying my prayers in the silence of the night when I felt strongly inspired to use every effort to have the poor sick people who may be found up and down the streets of this City of Mainz gathered together and received into some hospital where they can be well tended and looked after. . . . I also felt myself inspired to pray to the Blessed in Heaven who had suffered from weakness and bad health in this life that they would deign to be the advocates of the poor sick people of this and other cities and that they would obtain for me fresh grace to help them." Such was " the great Peter Favre," as St. Francis de Sales called him, and of such a kind was the story to which Peter Canisius listened that spring morning in Cologne. No sooner had he heard it than he was sailing up the Rhine to find Favre and his destiny.[2]

It was a three days' journey then, full of discomforts and dangers due to the conditions on the ship, the numerous rocks and shoals in the river and the frequency of customs houses. Heine's poem had not been written to romanticize the adventure and the frowning crag of the Lorelei brought no vision of a lady combing her golden hair but only of a drowned sailor that might easily be the passenger himself.[3] At Mainz Peter was welcomed

---

[1] M.H., *Fabri Monumenta*, p. 400.

[2] A much vaunted but slipshod and most inaccurate book by a professor of history at the University of Brussels has another explanation of the interest shown by Peter Canisius : " Le jeune homme plein d'ambition et très intelligent, avait reconnu immédiatement quelle carrière cette Compagnie lui offrait pour jouer un rôle éminent, exercer une influence considérable, et arriver aux grandeurs." Philippson, *La Contre-Révolution Religieuse* (Brussels, 1884), p. 86. There is much more of the same astonishing insight into the motives of the Catholic reformers in this volume. It is distressing to find it listed as an ' authority ' in Dr. Kidd's recent history of the Counter-Reformation.

[3] Writing from Mainz in 1543 Favre speaks of Cologne " qu'est à trois journées loing d'ici." M.H., *Fabri Monumenta*, p. 202. In 1555 Sir Thomas Hoby sailing from Mainz to the Dutch frontier paid toll at twenty-one customs houses to fourteen different local authorities. E. S. Bates, *Touring in 1600*, p. 336.

with open arms and invited to share during his stay the modest comforts of the presbytery where Favre was lodging. Soon he was deep in the *Spiritual Exercises*, of which experience he wrote the following impressions to a Cologne friend :

I made a good voyage to Mainz and found to my great happiness the man of whom I was in quest, if indeed he is a man and not an angel of God. Never have I seen nor heard a more learned and profound theologian nor any man of such shining sanctity. His desire of desires is to labour in union with Christ for the salvation of souls. Though, whether he is writing or conversing familiarly or seated at table, all his words are full of God, he is never tedious or wearying to his listeners. He enjoys such great credit and reputation that many members of religious orders, many bishops and many learned doctors have taken him for their master and guide in the spiritual life. Among the number is Cochlaeus, who avows that he will never be able to repay the debt he owes him for instruction in the *Spiritual Exercises*. . . . For my own part, I can hardly find words to tell you how these *Spiritual Exercises* have changed my soul and senses, enlightened my mind with new rays of heavenly grace, and inspired me with fresh strength and fortitude. The abundance of the divine favours overflows even into my body, and I feel altogether invigorated and changed into a new man.[1]

St. Ignatius intended the *Exercises* to occupy about thirty days, and there is every indication that Peter Canisius devoted the full time to them.[2] All was not plain sailing for him during it. The *Exercises* when rightly and fully performed under experienced guidance turn a man inside out, and, however good he may have hitherto been, open up to him perspectives of sanctity such as only the rarest kind of courage can face without

---

[1] Braunsberger, *Epistulae*, vol. i, pp. 76–7. Similar testimony has been borne by thousands of other witnesses, some of whom, such as the distinguished French priest, Mgr. d'Hulst, were at first very shy of trusting their souls to the guidance of St. Ignatius. It is the witness of life as opposed to the criticism of mere intellect or literary fastidiousness, which objects to the formalism and 'mechanized' spirituality of the Exercises. Such criticism forgets that the Exercises were intended to be a practical guide-book for the master and not for the pupil. The master must adapt them to the needs of his pupil, put living flesh on their bones and show how their principles are to be applied in the acquisition of Christian holiness. As for the charge of being mechanical, there is nothing high or holy, not even poetry or love itself, which is independent of 'mechanisms.' Metre is a mechanism and so is habit, on which love and friendship are based. Though Newton's *Principia* is a dry book with very little obvious poetry in it, no one but a fool would deny its greatness. The book of St. Ignatius is a spiritual *Principia*, containing, if the critics like, the 'mechanics' of the spiritual life. To blame it for not being something that it was never intended to be is puerile. Only a superficial dilettantism could pretend for a moment that the spiritual life, seriously pursued, needs no prosaic foundation of habit, or that it is essentially lyrical and a matter of spontaneous raptures.

[2] Braunsberger, *Des ersten deutschen Jesuiten Berufsgeschichte*, in *Stimmen aus Maria-Laach*, vol. lxxxv, p. 51.

faltering. The sensation is somewhat like being flayed alive, for it means in essence the excoriation of that private will which wraps us about so comfortably, and the putting on instead of the holy will of God, strong as death and ruthless as the grave. A passage in Favre's *Memoriale* hints that Peter Canisius did not surrender without a struggle. Favre mentions him by name and says that after observing him at his prayers, he understood more clearly than ever before how shrewdly and softly the devil works to keep souls from venturing too much in the service of God.[1] But Peter had a generous heart and came through victoriously. In a letter to the Prior of the Cologne Carthusians written while the retreat was in progress, Favre speaks thus of his proselyte: " I am at present enjoying the company of Master Peter and I have no words to tell you how sweet I find it. May He be blessed who planted so promising a tree and may all those be blessed who helped in any way to bring it to perfection. I have no doubt at all that among the number is your Paternity who found so many means of assisting this young man to become what he is, and not like the rest of his generation. I have grown fonder than ever of our Cologne which knew how to cherish and guard such purity."[2]

Peter had found his " new order of priests," so there was only one thing to be done. On May 8, 1543, his birthday and the feast of St. Michael, he pronounced the following vows:

In the Name of Our Lord, Amen. I, Peter Canisius of Nymegen, now beginning my twenty-third year, do after mature deliberation vow simply to Almighty God, in the presence of the Blessed Virgin Mary, St. Michael, and all the Saints, that I shall henceforth transfer my obedience to the Society which bears the Name of Jesus Christ. In like manner I firmly promise and vow to the Lord God and His Saints that by the divine grace I am determined to take upon me actual poverty, except in so far and as long as the Superior of the said Society, or in his stead Master Peter Favre, who now deigns to receive me as a novice of his Society, shall prohibit me from doing so. I further vow to make a pilgrimage to the tombs of the Apostles in Rome, and this at the first opportunity unless Master Peter shall otherwise decide. If it should fall out that I am not received into the Society, I wish myself then to be under an obligation to enter any other approved order which the professed fathers of the same Society may advise. And all these things I promise and vow solely for the love and reverence of

[1] M.H., *Fabri Monumenta*, p. 638.   [2] M.H., *Fabri Monumenta*, pp. 198-9.

Jesus Christ Our Lord, and for the honour and service of the glorious Virgin Mary, of St. Michael, and of all the Saints, that I may save my soul. Amen.[1]

Peter looked upon that May morning as the date of his second birth and upon Favre as a second father who had begotten him in the Lord, the first German son of the Society of Jesus. On his return to Cologne after the retreat he visited his dear friend the Carthusian Prior to tell him about his experiences. A few days later this good man addressed the following letter to the Prior of the Carthusians in Trier:

> Venerable and very dear Father and Friend. Amidst the storms with which all Christendom is shaken in these deplorable times God has not entirely abandoned His Church but has raised up to help her some apostolic men, filled with His Spirit and adorned with virtue from on high. . . . There is one of their number with the Cardinal of Mainz, Master Peter Favre by name, a theologian of the University of Paris and a man of great sanctity. He puts men of good-will who come to him through certain wonderful exercises by means of which they obtain in a few days true knowledge of themselves and their sins, the grace of tears and a genuine and hearty conversion to God, together with progress in His service and a secret familiarity and loving union with Him. Would that some opportunity might present itself for travelling to Mainz! Assuredly it would be well worth a man's while to go even as far as the Indies in search of such a treasure. I trust that before I die God will grant me to see this man, His singular friend, in order that I may be guided by him to reformation of heart and union with my Creator.[2]

Having delivered himself of his good news to the Prior Peter returned to his books and his lectures with the zest of a man for whom the purposes of life have been transfigured. One very interesting and plausible surmise about his activities is that he put together and published at this time a German edition of the sermons of the great medieval mystic, Tauler. At any rate such an edition, the completest and most satisfactory up to that date, appeared at Cologne in June, 1543, with an introduction signed " Petrus Noviomagus "—Peter of Nymegen. It would be pleasant to be able to state definitely that Peter of Nymegen was Peter Canisius, if

---

[1] Braunsberger, *Epistulae*, vol. i, p. 75.   [2] M.H., *Fabri Monumenta*, pp. 447–8.

only for the reason that the first book ever written by a Jesuit, the well-spring of such a mighty torrent of print, would then have been issued in defence and honour of a great Dominican who had fallen into disrepute with Catholics because Luther professed to have received much help from his teaching in his struggle towards evangelical freedom. But our desire for it to be true must only make us the more cautious about admitting the identity of the two Peters. Father Braunsberger considered the matter as proved and he has been supported more recently by an impressive array of scholars from his own and other orders. Their arguments, briefly stated, are that no other Peter of Nymegen except Peter Canisius can be found for the rôle of editor, that Canisius and his Jesuit brethren in Cologne were closely in touch with Jörgen Skodborg, the exiled Arch-bishop of Lund to whom the work is dedicated, that Canisius, according to his own express statement, was at the time deeply interested in mystical theology, and that his known connexion with the Carthusians, who were devoted students of Tauler, would have afforded him the necessary stimulus and opportunities for the production of the work. These arguments are certainly very weighty and may very well be true, but, on the other hand, we have to ask why, if Canisius was the editor, not a single one of his brethren suspected it until, in 1890, 347 years after the event, Father Braunsberger came forward as a champion of the theory, following the lead of a Protestant scholar who had ventilated it in a history of medieval pantheism ? Never by a syllable does Canisius himself suggest anywhere in his voluminous writings that he had brought out an edition of Tauler. Moreover, though Peter frequently gives advice about spiritual reading in his letters, and though he possessed a copy of Tauler's sermons in Latin, he mentions the saintly Dominican only once and then to recom-mend, not his sermons, but certain meditations on the Passion which went under his name but are known now to be spurious. Surely this is a strange omission if, as is supposed, it was Canisius who wrote : " Among the other good books which convey God's word to us for the nourish-ment of our souls in this vale of tears, I have always found that the sermons of the Illuminated Doctor, John Tauler, suited me best."[1] St. Peter's early biographers, who faithfully mention his other works, are as silent as himself about any edition of Tauler.

But there is still another objection which the Dominican, Franciscan and Jesuit defenders of Peter's title must answer before they can consider

---

[1] Opening words of the introduction to the 1543 edition of Tauler's Sermons, signed "Peter of Nymegen."

themselves secure. As has been said, the Tauler edition of 1543, including the long introduction signed " Petrus Noviomagus," is in German. It was made to a large extent from manuscript sources, some of which, reports " Petrus Noviomagus," were " so old that the handwriting had become almost obliterated in places." Now it is quite certain that Peter Canisius did not know German very well in 1543, not, at any rate, well enough to be competent to deal with ancient and mutilated manuscripts in that language. Thus in 1550, seven years further on, Peter informed St. Ignatius that he was engaged in " learning the German language well at home," and twelve months later still he tells his friend, Leonard Kessel, that he is going on with his preaching, " having surmounted as best I could the difficulties of the German language."[1] Is it to be thought that a man who was still struggling with the intricacies of German syntax in 1551 had actually published a large book in excellent German prose eight years before? Perhaps some way will eventually be found of reconciling these conflicting data. One hopes that it may, but meantime St. Peter must do without this laurel that has been woven too hastily into his crown. It is the more easy to sacrifice it because, as will be seen, even without the Tauler edition he still retains the distinction of being the first Jesuit in any country to publish a book.

Peter's noviceship in Cologne was by no means a time of placid seclusion from the world. In the early days the Jesuit authorities had to provide for their novices as best they could, since money was lacking to build special houses for their accommodation. The plan followed was to gather them together in large university towns where they might both pray and study under official guidance. Such a community then existed at Paris and another was forming at Louvain. Peter Canisius, directed by Favre, started a third at Cologne in conjunction with two Spanish priests. In 1544 the number of recruits had grown to nine, but that increase did not bring with it any change in the external circumstances of Peter's life. He dwelt as before with Herll, near St. Gereon's, and went on with his theology at the university, while all the time progressing in the interior life under the inspiration of " his brother and particular friend," Favre. In the university annals he is mentioned as having preached a trial sermon before the Senate on the eve of All Saints. Then, in December, he was summoned to Nymegen, where his father lay dying. Not a word has Peter to say personally about the emotions

---

[1] Braunsberger, *Epistulae*, vol. i, pp. 340, 389.

of that hour, typical reticence in which some people might be tempted to discern the desiccating effects of Jesuit spirituality. But they would be wrong. Matthew Rader, the first man to write an account of Peter's life, says, on the authority of Peter's own half-brother, that after his father's death " he spent the whole night praying humbly to God with sighs and tears to grant his father pardon and peace. And God, the Father of mercies, heard his filial sighs and made known to Canisius that both his father and mother were in Heaven. Great joy and consolation possessed him then, and he thanked the Eternal God with all the thanks of which a mortal man is capable."[1]

Peter's step-mother would have liked him to stay at home, now that his father was gone. She was a good soul, but limited in her aspirations, and when Peter announced his intention of devoting his portion of the family inheritance to the service of the poor and the support of his struggling brethren in Cologne, she lost her composure rather badly. It was not that she herself and the others had received less than their due. They were very well off indeed, but the thrifty lady refused to admit it, and bitterly resented the intrusion of the evangelical counsels into her affairs. After returning to Cologne Peter received an angry letter from her denouncing Favre as a " vagabond foreigner " who had tricked him into parting with his property for the sole purpose of getting it into his own hands. The two Peters were very much astonished and dismayed by this outburst, and as women's tongues can work a great deal of mischief Favre decided to answer it himself:

Dear and respected Lady in Christ Our Lord,

You complain that Master Peter Canisius, hitherto a very loving son to you, has now completely changed his manner, and you consider that I alone am responsible for this. The very opposite is the truth, for I who know that this most excellent young man is united to me in the closest bonds of affection and aspiration, so that we might almost be said to have only one will between us, cannot but heartily desire and wish him every kind of good. Consequently, I feel myself indebted beyond expression to his relatives and friends, meaning by these not only men dear to him in the bond of Christian charity but also his friends and relatives by blood and family association. For this reason I pray much and often for the repose of his father's soul and for you and your children and relatives, that God may comfort

[1] Raderus, *De Vita Petri Canisii libri tres* (Munich, 1614), pp. 233-4.

you all. But why then, you will say, have you taken Master Peter away when you cannot but have known how much he helped and counselled and consoled us? My answer is, dear Lady, to ask you a question in turn. What would you do as a Christian if you saw on the one side Jesus Christ, yearning to take His delight in Peter's spiritual and intellectual progress, and on the other his natural relatives and friends wishing at all costs to enjoy his society in the midst of the unstable, transitory pleasures of the world? If you admit the legitimacy of this test, then I certainly could not but wish to help him in his resolution. Moreover, it was no interest of my own that I was seeking and I took good care not to benefit by a single penny of his money. The whole question as it seems to me is made one of worldly interests. Few have any care for the interests of Peter's soul, while many feel themselves aggrieved because he chooses to distribute outside their circle the property that is his by right of inheritance. We make a great fuss if one clod of our fields is separated from another, but remain quite unperturbed at the thought of our souls being torn and separated from God their Maker, in union with whom is their supreme felicity. For the rest, I most solemnly assure you that nothing of Peter's property has been applied to my advantage. God is faithful, and He has, I trust, kept me true to this extent that it would be impossible for me to give even a thought to worldly prospects. Why then, you may ask, did you not forbid him doing that to which, as you are aware, all his family most strongly object? As a matter of fact I do not know exactly how much property he has set aside, nor, to speak plainly, do I disapprove of his action. What you say has been alienated I know to have been applied to charitable uses, and that, from the standpoint of right reason, ought not to be considered alienation at all but rather restoration to God, the one real and rightful owner of everything upon earth. What is there wrong in this when the possessions he brought with him are his own to dispose of as he pleases? Our little Society aims at and covets advantages of a very different kind.

As for the reports spread around about myself, I think they are too trivial and contemptible to be believed, at all events by persons such as you who fear God and speak no evil of your neighbour. They say that I am an unknown foreigner. I admit that charge. Yes, I am a foreigner, a stranger upon earth, and so are all my companions, not only in this land but all the world over. And a stranger I shall remain until death, no matter where the goodness of God may direct my steps, for all I desire is to be made a servant in the house of God and a fellow-citizen of the saints.[1]

With the money that had come to him Peter Canisius assisted poor students at the university, among whom was a Bavarian youth named George Eder, afterwards famous as adviser to three successive emperors, and as rector eleven different times of the University of Vienna. In his letters and in one of his many learned books, this staunch defender of the Faith paid touching tribute to the friends who helped him when he was young and without resources. "Plurima accepi beneficia, praesertim a Patre Canisio," he says.[2] Many besides Eder were similarly assisted but Canisius never alludes to such charities. It is only when someone does *him* a good turn that he grows eloquent. Now that he had the means, he also rented a house in Cologne where he and other members of Favre's little group might live together and be a support to one another, but in this move he reckoned without Hermann von Wied, Archbishop of Cologne and Elector of the Empire, one of the strangest personalities produced by the mysterious upheavals of the Reformation.

[1] M.H., *Fabri Monumenta*, pp. 253–5.
[2] Aschbach, *Geschichte der Wiener Universität*, vol. iii (1888), pp. 169–70.

CHAPTER II

AN ARCHBISHOP BECOMES A HERETIC

WHEN Canisius arrived in Cologne in January, 1536, an important provincial synod was being held there, convened by Archbishop von Wied to remedy the abuses prevalent in his Electorate. Now, though well-meant, this synod was itself an abuse, as a general council of the Church had already been summoned by Pope Paul III, and local councils might not be held in the interim without infringement of canon law. Just then, however, canon law had lost its savour for the Archbishop. He was in a great sulk with the Pope over a decision recently given against him in the courts of Rome and in no mood to respect wishes emanating from that quarter. So his synod went its way, and doubtless Peter Canisius took a lively interest at least in the spectacular part of the proceedings. After the Archbishop himself the most important figure in them was the Chancellor, Dr. Johann Gropper. These two must certainly have attracted Peter's attention, and we may surmise that he asked questions about them and received a variety of answers. The Archbishop, he would have learned, was a most enigmatic person, described, on the one hand, by a member of his household as " a good, pious, peaceable master, very fond of hunting and not particularly well educated," and, on the other,. by Emperor Charles V, as neither a Protestant nor a Catholic but a proper heathen, with not enough Latin in him to get through the *Confiteor* at Mass.[1] Pursuing his enquiries, Peter would have learned to his further bewilderment that, though Archbishop Hermann patently loved the wild red deer much better than he loved the Pope, he nevertheless had shown himself not long before a most zealous and determined foe of Lutheranism, even to the extent of a few burnings and other muscular demonstrations of orthodoxy. But with the arguments of Catholic theology he was not so well at home. They bored him and made him sigh for his familiar

---

[1] *Das Buch Weinsberg*, ed. Höhlbaum (Leipzig, 1886), vol. i, p. 194 ; Druffel, *Briefe und Akten zur Geschichte des sechzehnten Jahrhunderts*, vol. iii (Munich, 1882), p. 8.

spear, or whatever it was that he used in the hunting field. Yet Catholic theologians respected him greatly. "To your eternal credit," wrote a doughty antagonist of the Lutherans in 1524, "there is hardly another man to be found who withstands these enemies of Christ more vigorously and vehemently."[1] On the whole, then, up to 1536, the balance, from a Catholic point of view, would seem to have been in the Archbishop's favour, though his lack of professional learning, his gullibility and his antipathy to Rome must have caused certain forebodings.

Then there was Gropper, of whom Peter would have heard nothing but good from his friends at St. Gereon's and St. Barbara's. Trained as a jurist, it was not until the Diet of Augsburg in 1530, when the Protestants presented their famous Confession, or profession of faith, to the Emperor, that he began to take a serious interest in theology. He studied it privately and without guidance, but nevertheless became so proficient in Scripture and patristic lore that the illustrious scholastic Pighius said he preferred him "to any supercilious product of the schools." Pighius, however, unwittingly did him a disservice by indoctrinating him with a theory of original sin and justification which afterwards made trouble at the Council of Trent. It was one of those 'mediating' theories, half Lutheran and half Catholic, and Gropper liked it because he was at heart a great mediator. In Cologne, all the honours went to him, except the doubtful ones which his master, the Archbishop, could claim, for having brought the synod together. He acted pilot to the synod, and, in 1538, brought out the lordly folio containing its acts and disciplinary decrees. As a private contribution to the good work, he included an *Enchiridion Christianae Institutionis* of his own composition, which would have been wholly admirable as a manual of instruction but for the appearance in it of the unfortunate Pighian theory of original sin. This book, of which another famous theologian, Ambrose Catharinus, said that he had "seen nothing in all his life more orthodox, learned, loyal, and worthy of complete acceptance," must speedily have come into the hands of Peter Canisius.

Peter, we have seen, lay somewhat *perdu* during his first student years in Cologne, as every good student should. But we can safely surmise his evolution, as we are now familiar with the men who moulded him. One and all, these devoted men were mainly preoccupied with the struggle against heresy. From them he would certainly have learned each new phase of the great fight and, in particular, how Cologne stood affected.

[1] Fabri, *Malleus in haeresim Lutheranam* (Cologne, 1524), Dedicatio.

It was a time of progressive disillusionment for sanguine Catholics, who, like Peter's future friends, Gropper and Bishop Julius Pflug, dreamed hopefully of reunion. Over against those "Expectantes," as they were called, stood the stalwart Johann Eck who had been in the front line from the beginning of the struggle and knew better than most men the temper of the Protestant leaders. Dr. Johann warned Gropper's party that they were pursuing a will o' the wisp and that anything but honest submission to the Pope by the Protestants was mere "wind and vapour, though one should go on disputing for a hundred years." Events proved him right, for the "Conversations" between the Catholic and Protestant leaders which took place at Hagenau, Regensburg and Worms during 1540-1541 resulted only in widening the breach that divided them.[1]

Meantime, the attitude of Archbishop von Wied to the Lutherans had softened considerably under the moderating influence of Gropper. Hermann became one of the "Expectantes," or hopeful people, himself, and, having no theology to speak of, began to wonder if after all the Protestants might not be right on a good number of points. He seems to have been perfectly sincere in his change of front and actuated by honest desire to better the conditions in his huge diocese. At his court in Bonn he employed two avowed Lutherans, the astronomer Bruckner, a former Augustinian monk and close friend of Zwingli, and the humanist Medmann, who had sat under Melanchthon at Wittenberg. These worthies persuaded the ingenuous Hermann that Melanchthon and Bucer might afford him much assistance with the disciplinary reforms on which he had set his heart. Why should his Highness be afraid of such people when they were great friends of the upright and orthodox Gropper? One strain in particular in the Archbishop's soul gave the pair a hold on him, his repugnance to the simplicities of Catholic devotion. People who ride to hounds are not usually the sort who light candles to St. Anthony, and Hermann, mighty hunter and theological ignoramus, began to think that religion in Cologne was altogether too complicated.

After Rome, Cologne is probably the greatest repository of saints in the world. In the eighteen marvellous churches, dating from the early Middle Ages or further back, are to be found such unexpected relics as those of the Maccabees and Magi, not to speak of St. Ursula and her eleven thousand companions. There, too, are the earthly remains of the most typical of medieval saints, Blessed Hermann Joseph, and a host of other

[1] They are described with interesting detail by Pastor, *Die kirchlichen Reunionsbestrebungen während der Regierung Karls V* (1879), pp. 184-217, 251 sqq.

holy bodies that once walked Cologne's cobbled streets and still make her name famous in the Martyrology. Luther scoffed at her claim to possess the skulls of the Magi, and men more wisely tolerant of popular traditions than Luther have been known to boggle at the eleven thousand Ursulines. Peter Canisius was the dead opposite of Archbishop von Wied in this respect. The more saints and relics for him the merrier, and a fig for the dryasdusts with their woeful tale of anachronisms, scribes' mistakes and archaeological impossibilities. Happily it is no business of ours to pronounce on these high matters, beyond saying that popular traditions have a way of avenging themselves on their learned traducers and that popular devotion, such as was poured forth at the shrines of Cologne, may be able to find its heavenly mark all right, without the antiquarian's fussy assistance.

In 1539, Archbishop Hermann, bent on purging Cologne of its saint-worship, decided to invite Melanchthon to Bonn. The great Philip could not come just then, but gave his old pupil Medmann, who had brought the invitation, some hints on the best way of managing his master and of fostering his reformatory inclinations. Like Cranmer, to whom the annalist Strype reverently compared him,[1] Hermann was not difficult to manage. He entered into correspondence with Melanchthon and with the Swiss reformer, Bullinger, who addressed him as " Brother in Christ " and pleasantly informed him that the Mass " was only a human invention, an empty ceremony, without any foundation in Scripture." For a great Catholic prelate to have permitted and even invited such liberties is proof that von Wied had already gone very far on the wrong road.

In September, 1541, he summoned a Landtag, or provincial Diet, that he might sound the deputies on the question of religious reformation in the Electorate. Finding them not nearly so enthusiastic about his plans as he had hoped, he turned for consolation to the much married ex-Dominican, Martin Bucer, whom a woman friend had described ecstatically as a " dear *politicus* and *fanaticus* of union."[2] Gropper still hoped that Bucer might live up to these titles and accordingly at first approved of the Archbishop's scheme to bring him to Bonn. By February, 1543, however, he had seen enough of the man to realize that he was about the most insidiously dangerous heretic of the age. With Luther one could at least be sure where one stood, but this Bucer was as slippery as an eel. Alive to the menace of his presence, good Chancellor Gropper, whose

[1] *Memorials of Archbishop Cranmer*, Oxford ed., vol. i, pp. 412–3.
[2] Owing to his connexion with England and his burial at Cambridge, Bucer is honoured with eleven columns in the *Dictionary of National Biography*.

only ambition throughout had been to serve the Church's interests, veered round and took his stand as leader of Cologne's opposition to the ominous policy of von Wied. "May God forgive him!" wrote Bucer piously to his friend, the famous schoolmaster, Sturm.

In due course Melanchthon himself arrived in Bonn to direct operations, and under his leadership various minor prophets of the new liberty were let loose on the ill-instructed people of the country surrounding Cologne. The city itself being as yet too dangerous for open propaganda, Bucer prudently kept the breadth of the Rhine between its cobbles and his heterodoxy. He concentrated on the village of Deutz, and thither curious and sensation-loving Catholics used to repair in boats to hear him preach, until the Senate banned their excursions. Other preachers took the local peasantry for their province, and their success is attested by the fact that many country districts quite near Cologne are to-day part of what German Catholics call the "Diaspora," or areas where their brethren form only small and scattered communities among a population predominantly Protestant. Thus hemmed in by heresy on all sides the faith of the Rhineland capital was in the very gravest peril, especially as the militant spirits of the Schmalkalden League had professed their eagerness to bring the gospel to the city on the tips of their lances. Melanchthon, writing to Luther from Bonn, expressed himself as hopeful about the prospects: "I think that scarcely anywhere else in Germany has there been or is there so much barbaric and utterly heathen superstition as in these parts. All the running to statues that goes on here is the proof of it. Now, however, I see great audiences listening to the sermons of Bucer and Pistorius, who both teach pure and correct doctrine. There are other preachers in some neighbouring towns and villages who also teach true doctrine and administer the sacraments in a godly manner. May the Almighty prosper these beginnings."[1]

In February, 1543, the clergy of Cologne published a detailed indictment of Bucer, and this was followed by a still more incisive charge, drawn up on behalf of the university by the Provincial of the Rhineland Carmelites, Eberhard Billick. Billick pointed an interesting contrast between the methods of evangelization employed by Luther and Bucer and declared his conviction that Luther's abuse, ridicule and blasphemies against the Church were less dangerous than the other man's honeyed poison, compounded subtly of Protestant error and Catholic truth.[2] This book

---

[1] *Corpus Reformatorum, Melanchthonii opera*, vol. v, p. 112.
[2] Postina, *Der Karmelit Eberhard Billick* (1901), pp. 46–8.

thoroughly angered Melanchthon, who described it as "the work of that well-fed Carmelite, priest of Bacchus and Venus."[1] A little later Philip the Mild wrote from Bonn to a friend: "Here I am, in contest with the Cologne sycophants. If only Europe had pious princes the furious onslaughts of these men would not be refuted with pen and ink but set right with cudgels."[2] The sycophants' sin was that they had unmasked Bucer's and Melanchthon's policy of penetration, so great a sin that a delegate of the Schmalkalden League was sent by Philip of Hesse to protest against it. Philip and the Elector of Saxony both guaranteed armed assistance in case of need, for which Hermann expressed warm gratitude.[3] Melanchthon's official reply to the Cologne clergy, *alias*, "the papal rabble, the bastard breed whose dirty, lascivious, infamous lives are before the eyes of the whole world," bore a preface by Luther describing the rabble, etc., as "not men but incarnate devils who deride God in His Heaven."[4]

Pope Paul III was aware of the battle in progress for the faith of Cologne and wrote several times exhorting the clergy and senate to hold out manfully against the machinations of their Archbishop. "In the Name of Our Lord Jesus Christ who dwells in you," he said, "we beg you to continue in your good purpose and to use every possible precaution that Bucer and the Lutheran preachers, now roaring around you and seeking whom they may devour, may not gain a footing in your city and seduce the people."[5]

On Easter Sunday, 1543, Archbishop von Wied said Mass in German at Bonn and afterwards distributed Holy Communion under both species. Thereupon the Pope addressed him a long letter expressing profound sorrow that he should be the first bishop to secede from the Church, and imploring him to remember his duty to God, his solemn oath of fealty to Rome, the constancy of his brother bishops, the unhappy fruits of blood and bitterness that the new doctrines had borne in Germany. It was all to no purpose, for Hermann's pope was now the versatile and plausible Bucer, "that great architect of subtleties," as Bossuet described him. That was the critical juncture at which the two Jesuit Peters, Favre and Canisius, came publicly into the story.

Shortly after Canisius had joined the Society of Jesus in Mainz, Bucer and Melanchthon started a fresh and more concentrated attack on the faith of Cologne. The younger Peter bethought him of the other, knowing,

[1] *Corpus Reformatorum*, vol. v, pp. 113-4.
[2] *Corpus Reformatorum*, vol. v, pp. 120-1.
[3] Varrentrapp, *Hermann von Wied und sein Reformationsversuch in Köln* (1878), pp. 139-40.
[4] Postina, *Der Karmelit Eberhard Billick*, p. 56
[5] Raynaldus [Rinaldi], *Annales ecclesiastici*, Paris ed., vol. xxxiii, p. 40.

from his own recent experience, Favre's gift for inspiring timid souls with enthusiasm. Accordingly, in conjunction with his friend, the Carthusian Prior, he wrote urgently begging Favre to come among them. The Cologne people had excellent and most zealous leaders in such men as Gropper and Billick, but something more was needed than good polemics if the city was to be saved. Hermann's secret agents were at work, distributing hand-bills and cautiously undermining the none too solidly grounded faith of students and other impressionable folk. Against such propaganda there was only one sure defence, a strengthening of the people's attachment to their religion through a revival of devotion and Catholic practice, and for such a task none was better qualified than the saintly man who had written his conviction, " que ces hérésies du temps présent ne sont aultre chose, sinon faulte de dévotion, faulte d'humilité, de patience, de chasteté et charité."[1] Favre's presence in Cologne proved such a stimulus to popular devotion that when the Cardinal of Mainz, to whom he had been lent by St. Ignatius, asked him to return, the Cologne leaders appealed to the Apostolic delegate, Poggio. " We beg you," they wrote, " and most earnestly implore you in the name of Jesus Christ to permit us, for the salvation and integrity of this holy City, to continue enjoying the greatly appreciated company of the Reverend Father Master Peter Favre of the Society of Jesus. . . . No sooner did he come amongst us than he won the admiration and singular love of good men. . . . By means of a certain divine discipline he has brought numbers into the way of holiness and continues increasingly each day to win very many souls for Christ. . . . It is of the gravest moment, in view of the thousand heretical snares with which Cologne is beset, that this man, who is prized by the highest in our midst, should remain here to help the sorely tried people with his incomparable wisdom. If necessary, we beg Your Lordship to petition the Holy Father, Pope Paul, on our behalf. . . ."[2] In all Favre's good work Peter Canisius was by his side, the recruiting sergeant for his retreats and instructions and the devoted companion of his hours of weariness.

In July, 1543, von Wied laid before his Landtag at Bonn the reformation scheme which had been drawn up by Bucer and Melanchthon. The secular estate, or lords temporal, gave their assent to the project, but the Cologne clergy refused even to consider it until Bucer and other innovating preachers had been expelled from the Electorate. Hermann thereupon tried to force his priests into acquiescence, but they appealed to the Emperor, who passed through Bonn in August on his way to war

---

[1] M.H., *Fabri Monumenta*, p. 202.   [2] M.H., *Fabri Monumenta*, pp. 451-2.

with the Duke of Cleves. Favre was chosen for the difficult and dangerous task of laying their case before His Majesty, as, not being a subject of the Electoral dominions, he ran less danger of being thrown into prison. At Bonn he had interviews with the Papal Nuncio and with the Emperor's Dominican confessor, after which these men related all that he had told them to the Imperial Chancellor, Granvelle. One event that impressed him very much was the High Mass *coram episcopo* which the Emperor attended. Hermann, he says, was most devout on this occasion and observed the ceremonies in such a careful, truly Catholic manner that numbers of people rejoiced, believing him to have had a change of heart. But it was all mere play-acting. After Mass, the Emperor, to whom Granvelle had communicated Favre's supplication, took the Archbishop aside and made him promise to expel the Lutheran preachers, to suppress his printed formula of reformation and to refrain from all innovations of doctrine and discipline until the royal wish in the matter was declared. Promises, however, are as easy to break as to make and no sooner was the Emperor's back turned than Hermann resumed his campaign. He did not know the sort of campaign on which Charles V was about to engage or he might have had a few misgivings.

Towards the end of 1543 the *Book of Reformation*, composed for His Highness by Bucer and Melanchthon, was given to the world. Each of the Protestant princes received a copy, and four years later an English version appeared, to provide, in the words of Strype, " a good pattern " for the divines of Edward VI.[1] The title of this volume, a faithful reproduction of the cumbersome original, was as follows :

A simple and religious consultation of us, Herman, by the grace of God Archbishop of Colone and Prince Electour, etc., by what means a Christian reformation, and founded in God's worde, of Doctrine, administration of the devine Sacraments, of Ceremonies, and the holy cure of soules and other ecclesiastical ministeries may be begon among men committed to our pastorall charge, until the Lord graunt a better to be appoynted, either by a free and Christian Counsayle, general or national, or elles by the States of the Empire of the nation of Germanie, gathered together in the holye Gost. Imprinted in the yere of the Lorde 1547 at London by John Daye dwelling in Sepulchres paryshe at the sygne of the Ressurection, a lytle above Houlbourne Conduyt.[2]

[1] Cranmer used a Latin copy, dated 1545, which is still preserved in the library of Chichester Cathedral.
[2] The book is a small, beautifully printed octavo in Gothic characters and runs to 260 pages.

On its appearance in Germany the book met with a mixed reception from the Protestants, because, owing to Bucer's Zwinglian proclivities, its section on the Holy Eucharist left the question of the Real Presence in the air. Luther, to whom the doctrine was sacred, became thoroughly angry and threatened to give Bucer and Melanchthon a piece of his mind in print. Melanchthon, knowing his master's powers of vituperation, hastened to explain that Bucer and not he was responsible for the offensive chapter, whereupon the one Martin hurled a few bombs of rhetoric at the other Martin, and only refrained from denouncing him as, " a devilish, damnable, superdiabolical blasphemer and liar," out of deference to the Elector of Saxony.[1] More to Luther's taste was the chapter entitled, " Of the unitie or concorde of the Churche," in which there is not a single syllable about the Pope. To Peter Canisius with his warm devotion to the " Golden Martyrs " and other saints of Cologne the following excerpt from the chapter, " Of abuse in Prayer," must have sounded peculiarly sinister :

> The second abuse in prayinge is when we aske any thinge of them of whom it ought not to be asked, as when men praye saintes, which nowe lyve wyth the Lord, that they will make intercession for them . . . as when they pray S. Sebastian to defende them agaynste arrowes and venimmes, S. Antonie agaynst the aposteme called commonly S. Antonie's fyer, S. Appollonie agaynst the touthache, etc. Item, when they call upon the Images and stockes of saintes, as the sayntes them selves, as they do which vowe pilgrimages to certayn stockes, which idolatrie hath welnigh overflowen the whole worlde, and that it maye be taken away the people must be diligently called backe from sayntes to God. . . .
>
> Seinge that no man can preferre the devises of men before the doctrine and exemples of the holy Goste wythout a most haynous dispite of God, and seinge that all the exemples of praiers delivered by the holy Goste teache to cal upon God only, neither is there any wherein sayntes be spoken unto, every man easily perceyveth how unworthie a thynge it is for Christen men . . . to use thys newe invention of callynge upon sayntes.[2]

Such mingled pietism and heterodoxy and such cleverly distorted pictures of Catholic teaching and practice were typical of the book as

---

[1] Janssen, *Geschichte des deutschen Volkes*, vol. iii (1888), p. 517.
[2] The pages of the book are not numbered in any way and the spelling throughout is as gaily inconsistent as in the passage quoted.

a whole. Besides the doctrinal sections the work contained the elements of a vernacular service to replace the Latin liturgy, some portion of which was taken over by Cranmer and embodied, after a little literary polishing, in the first Book of Common Prayer. These borrowings were retained with slight modifications in the Revised Prayer Book of 1552 and still form part of the services in the Church of England.[1] Cologne's great Dom might now be dedicated to similar services but for the sturdy resistance of such men as Gropper, Billick, Favre, and Canisius.

Gropper, Billick, and four others set to work immediately on a rejoinder to the *Simple Consultation*. Though a big book of a hundred and sixty folio pages crammed with miscellaneous learning, this rejoinder was ready in both a Latin and German form within three weeks. The zealous Cologne printer, Gennep, had his messengers waiting for each page as it was completed and the two editions were out and in circulation before Archbishop Hermann could recover his breath.[2] The book, entitled in Latin, *Antididagma, seu Christianae et Catholicae religionis propugnatio*, followed Hermann's work point by point and subjected its arguments to a raking fire of scriptural and patristic quotations. It was clear and business-like where Bucer was long-winded and vague, and it helped enormously to steady educated waverers in the Catholic ranks.

Meantime, Canisius and his companion, Alvaro Alfonso, devoted themselves with such enthusiasm to works of charity that Favre had to write from a sick bed in Louvain to restrain their ardour. Apparently they had put aside their studies in order to labour in hospitals or to wait on the poor people whom they had taken under their own roof.[3] It was the only contribution that their youth and inexperience could as yet make to the Catholic resistance, but von Wied was shrewd enough to reckon it quite as inimical to his cause as the good controversy of Billick or the diplomatic moves of the Cathedral clergy. At the urging of Peter and to please his friend Billick Favre returned to Cologne in January, 1544, bringing with him two young disciples, a Belgian named Lambert Duchateau, and Aemilian Loyola, a nephew of St. Ignatius. The five of them now went to live in a house situated "auf der Burgmaur," near an old tower in the city walls, Peter paying the rent out of what was left of his inheritance. This house soon became a busy centre of devotional

[1] The importance of Archbishop von Wied's *Simple Consultation* for the history of the English Prayer Book is described in detail by Jacobs, *The Lutheran Movement in England* (1892), pp. 224, 233–44, 253–80.
[2] Postina, *Der Karmelit Eberhard Billick*, pp. 151 sqq.
[3] Braunsberger, *Epistulae*, vol. i, pp. 99–100.

propaganda, and largely, we are given to understand, through the attraction of Peter's unostentatious goodness and charity new recruits began to muster round Favre's flag. In gathering his brethren under one roof, however, Peter had unknowingly broken one of the City's laws. Owing to the exemption from municipal taxes which the numerous convents and monasteries enjoyed, the Cologne Senate, in a natural desire to protect its revenues, had prohibited the foundation of new religious communities. Archbishop von Wied saw his chance and seized it. He called the Senate's attention to Favre's small family and demanded that it should be dispersed. But that was not enough. His agents in the city received instructions to spread defamatory rumours about the Jesuits. If they belonged to a proper religious order why did they not, like other religious, wear a distinctive habit and sing office together in choir? Their apparently free and easy manner of life could be made to look very suspicious and, as much mischief had been done in the Rhineland by pseudo-religious organizations in the past, soon even good and loyal Catholics began to wonder and ask questions. They had seen quite enough religious experiments in their country recently and were in no mood to tolerate one in their city. The mere fact that a thing was new made it suspect, even such a substantial thing as the Continent of America, which, twenty years after its discovery, was denied a place in his geography by the eminent Cochlaeus, as probably only a traveller's tale. The Society of Jesus was barely three years old, and, in Northern Europe at least, people knew hardly more about its sons than they did about the alleged Red Indians on the other side of the Atlantic.[1] Even Peter Canisius with all his ecclesiastical connexions had only come to hear of them by accident.

On June 27th the senators of Cologne decided to institute an enquiry, and a week later Favre was officially questioned. He explained exactly who they were, faithful adherents of the Catholic Church whom the Pope had authorized in a special bull to follow the rule of life according to which they were then living. The two " Stimmeister," or consuls, commissioned to see to the execution of the law and the preservation of public morals, were not entirely satisfied and returned to the charge on July 28th with a following of senators. Favre was no longer there to meet them, as he had been sent to the King of Portugal by St. Ignatius, so the difficult rôle of defendant fell to Peter Canisius. His account of the interview runs thus :

[1] By an extraordinary chance, two Red Indians appeared, of all places, in the woodcut border on the title-page of Leo X's first bull against Luther !

Finding Peter de Smedt and myself at home the same consul who was here before harangued us as follows in the name of the whole senatorial body : " We have reported to the Senate the explanations you recently gave us concerning your institute. We understand that your numbers which were then about eleven have since been increased." " No, no," I interjected at this point, " that is not correct, for we now number only nine." He took no notice of me, however, and thus continued his discourse : " The sentence and decree of our august Senate is that all of you living here together are to quit our City without delay. Your destination is your own affair, but we shall no longer tolerate you in our midst." As no reason whatever was given for our expulsion, I said to the consul : " If go we must we would beg our Lords the Senators for one sole favour, namely an honest testimonial to our good name and innocence by which we may prove in other places where people may be suspicious of us that we are not expelled for any crime." This request was refused as quite unreasonable. We had come without being asked, so without a character we should go. " Very good," said I ; " if your will, gentlemen, is to be your reason, I beg you to remember that you are ejecting innocent men who were pursuing their studies at no cost to anybody but themselves, and to reflect how you are going to account to God, the Supreme Judge, for the injury you are inflicting on them." At this they all shouted excitedly : " Is that a threat, sir ? " " Not in the least," I answered calmly ; " I merely point out that you will have to answer to God for this heavy sentence of yours." " Beware," thundered the Consul in conclusion, " of making us return here a second time. We grant you eight days in which to dispose of your effects and make preparations for your departure." As they passed out I said to them : " We shall pray for you all heartily wherever we may afterwards find ourselves."[1]

Peter was destined to be a pioneer Jesuit in many respects, and here we see him the first to be honoured with that decree of expulsion which would become a commonplace of his Society's history. He emphasized the fact that his visitors were honourable men and " the best Catholics in all Germany." Therein lay the virtue of the persecution, for it would not have been much of a trial, he says, to have been judged and proscribed by people of evil life or heretical belief. Moreover, owing to the skilful propaganda of von Wied's hirelings, practically the whole city considered

[1] Braunsberger, *Epistulae*, vol. i, pp. 672–3 ; 104–5.

the sentence to be just. "At every gathering and social festivity we are tried and condemned anew. Satires and songs turning us to ridicule are the vogue of the moment. At first we were accounted good men but now they say that we lead young people astray, enticing them into our company, and that we deceive women whom we know to be rich. So we pass through good report and evil report, found unworthy though we be to confess and glorify in our blood our crucified Lord and Master." According to the story of a good Cologne nun who died in 1650 at the age of a hundred and two, Peter and his company were given in derision the nickname of " The black chestnuts " by the common people. More usually, however, they were known as " Jesuits," an unfriendly label of Protestant invention which Peter resented, though not on account of its hostile origin. " The ill-will and malice of some people has fastened the name ' Jesuits ' on to us," he wrote. " Far be it from us who are but new volunteers in the service of the Cross to usurp to ourselves that sacred Name. . . . Well we know that the perils, hardships and opposition which we experience are the common lot of all devout souls, especially in this fretful age when all piety is derided as superstition."[1]

As the Prior of the Carthusians, Peter's " tantus amicus," was absent from Cologne at this time, he went for advice to two other good friends, his former host, Canon Herll, and Jörgen Skodborg, Archbishop of Lund. They counselled him not to obey the decree but to consult the Rector of the university. " The Rector kept me to supper," he reported, " and regaled me with all sorts of complaints, saying that in his opinion our institute could not last. Then he tried to persuade me that I should act wisely by abandoning it. I never thought that I should find so many men of different types lovingly anxious to withdraw me from my vocation. I have several times been urgently petitioned to become a professor at the university, and I have been offered a canon's stall in the two chief churches of Cologne, the Dom and St. Gereon's."[2]

It is interesting to notice how, even at that early date, Peter was regarded as a person of great promise. The critics of the Jesuits grieved to find him in such company. " Wherever there is talk about us," he wrote, " the chief lamentation is over me. ' He is a good fellow,' they say, ' and those others are trading on his innocence to promote the interests of their sect. They are taking him from us and leading him off into a far country.' " Such talk, however, only confirmed Peter in his love

[1] Braunsberger, Epistulae, vol. i, pp. 135, 670.
[2] Braunsberger, Epistulae, vol. i, pp. 105-6.

for the order he had chosen. He drew up a supplication to the Rector of the university, so eloquent and well argued that that good man capitulated and went himself to plead with the Senate. But the Senate remained obdurate, and the Rector, who dared not offend their Mightinesses, accordingly advised Peter to give in and disband his company. He and Lambert Duchateau thereupon returned to Canon Herll's friendly house with the words of the Psalmist on their lips, *Dominus dispersiones Israel congregabit*, while the others were given ready welcome by the Carthusians and Dominicans. The lovable Savoyard, Claude Lejay, who had attached himself to St. Ignatius long ago in Paris, was now working in the great Imperial City of Augsburg, and to him Peter sent a messenger for instructions, as Rome was too far away and the necessity too urgent for an appeal to the Founder of the Society of Jesus.[1] That Archbishop von Wied was the chief author of their misfortunes is made plain enough in Peter's report:

It is astonishing how heartily we are hated by our Archbishop, whose faith stinks so nastily in the nostrils of all Catholics. He has already several times admonished the Consuls of Cologne publicly and strictly that they are on no account to tolerate such pests and disciples of the devil as ourselves. He knows all about us, he alleges, and that we are nothing but spies, whom he is determined to thrust one and all out of his dominions. May God be blessed by whose will we are thus accounted more than a match for apostates, heresiarchs and renegade monks who are not expelled but rather bribed to come here and maintained in luxury. Some fear that owing to the Archbishop's determination the Senate will not allow us to remain until we receive Father Lejay's answer, even though we are living apart from one another. . . . Well, if this be God's good pleasure we shall not doubt the equity of His dealings, and the more we suffer the better we shall be assured of it. It is only the novitiate of the Cross, its mere show and shadow. Oh, would that some day we might be found worthy

---

[1] In a remarkable biographical essay published by the well-known Protestant *Verein für Reformationsgeschichte* under the title *Petrus Canisius, der erste deutsche Jesuit* (Halle, 1892), Paul Drews insinuated that at first Peter was a Jesuit only in name, as he had not the spirit of his order and acted without reference to its superiors. This mistake of a careful and scholarly writer was due to the fact that Drews did not possess Braunsberger's volumes which only began to appear in 1896. They prove conclusively that from the first Peter was scrupulously careful to consult Favre, Lejay or some other local representative of St. Ignatius. That he did not write direct to St. Ignatius on the present occasion was really due to geographical difficulties, and in no way to an imperfect spirit of obedience. An answer from Rome might take a month or, two months, or, as often happened, might get lost in the post and never come at all. The ordinary post was so unreliable that people used to send three or four copies of their letters by different routes in hopes of one of them getting to its destination. In referring to Lejay Peter was acting on the explicit instructions of Favre. Braunsberger, *Epistulae*, vol. i, p. 108.

to shoulder the stark reality so that our hunger and thirst and glory
and rest and peace and whole life might be in the Cross of Our Lord
Jesus Christ, the Father of all hope and consolation.[1]

Shortly after these brave lines had fallen from Peter's pen, instructions were issued to the police to arrest and cast him and his companions
into prison. One of them, a great friend of Peter's named Leonard Kessel,
told Favre how they felt about it : " We were all in high spirits, expecting
gaol or the whipping post. The whole of Cologne was talking about
us, imagining us to be members of some new sect."[2] " It had been
decided," wrote Peter himself, " that I, as the leader of my miscreant
brethren, must be the first to be thrown into prison," but from the chains
which he declared himself keen on wearing in such a cause he was saved
at the last moment through the intervention of the dean of the theological
faculty, a distinguished and noble-hearted Dominican named Stempel.
" I know not whether we ought to be glad or sad at missing such a
grace," he said.[3]

Meantime, dramatic changes were taking place in the big, unhappy
world of war and politics. Terrible disaster had befallen the Emperor
at the siege of Algiers in 1541, when only his magnificent personal courage
had saved his army from annihilation. Jubilant at the news, the French
King seized his chance to launch a vicious attack on the Habsburg Netherlands, in conjunction with the Protestant Duke of Cleves, who laid claim
to Gelderland. Naturally the German Protestants were in high spirits
over the embarrassment to their enemies caused by the new war, the
reported death of the Emperor, and the advance of the Turks along the
Danube. The stoutest champion of the old Faith in North Germany,
Henry of Brunswick, had been forcibly ousted from his dominions by
Philip of Hesse and John Frederick of Saxony, so that by the end of 1542
the Catholics could count on only two rulers of any military importance,
the Dukes of Austria and Bavaria. Then, just when the Church in Germany
seemed doomed, the whole scene underwent a sudden transformation.
Far from obligingly leaving his bones on the desert sands, Emperor Charles
appeared like an avenging ghost from Africa, turned on the recreant

---

[1] Braunsberger, *Epistulae*, vol. i, pp. 109–10. Writing in 1895, before Braunsberger's first volume
was published, a learned German Protestant historian, Joseph Hansen, dilated rather patronizingly
and pityingly on what he called the " fairy-tale complex " of Jesuit authors. He was quite sure
that the story of von Wied's persecution of Canisius and his brethren was part of that complex,
invented to make Peter look important. *Die erste Niederlassung der Jesuiten in Köln*, in *Beiträge
zur Geschichte vornehmlich Kölns und des Rheinlands*, p. 196.

[2] M.H., *Fabri Monumenta*, pp. 302–3.

[3] Braunsberger, *Epistulae*, vol. i, p. 111.

Duke of Cleves and, in a fortnight's campaign, sent his pretensions up in the smoke of burned towns and a ravaged countryside. At the Treaty of Venloo which followed, Jakop Kanis signed for Nymegen, making that town part of the Empire and his son, Peter, a German at least on paper. To balance the loss of his vanquished ally, Francis I sought the aid of the Turks, a move which so disgusted public opinion in Germany that the Protestant princes came round to the side of the Emperor. Francis had cut his own throat, and the last of the many wars between him and his Habsburg rival ended, much to Charles's advantage, with the Peace of Crépy, in September, 1544, just when the Elector of Cologne was endeavouring to secure the suppression of the Jesuits. A good authority has said that the fortnight's war between Charles and the Duke of Cleves " had probably momentous consequences for all time in the religious history of North Western Germany."[1] With the fate of Cleves, who had been compelled to undo all his evangelical achievements, staring him in the eyes, von Wied thought it safer to lie low for a while. During the lull, the people of Cologne were given the opportunity to revise their unkindly judgment of Peter and his brethren, whereupon the storm against them died down as suddenly as it had arisen. Many trials and privations still continued to be their portion but they scarcely noticed such minor rubs of fortune, striving as they were, in the words of one of them, " with all their might to love, reverence, imitate and hold in every hope, dream and aspiration their sole-sufficing Jesus."[2]

Only three companions now remained to Peter, as the others had been summoned to Italy by St. Ignatius. One of the three, Lambert Duchateau, was dying, and on Peter fell the responsibility of procuring for him whatever medical attention and sick-room comforts the state of their finances permitted. The love and sympathy that united them among themselves and to their brethren afar comes out in the following letter from Canisius to Favre, December 30, 1544:

Hard as it is for a son not to see his father nor to be able to greet him face to face, it becomes doubly hard when he gets no news of him. And so we are all very sad indeed, and greatly puzzled too, that, during this long time, we should not have had a single letter from your paternal hand. We have remained now many a month deprived of your company; Rome has sent us no word in the meantime; and

[1] Armstrong, *The Emperor Charles V* (1902), vol. ii, p. 15.
[2] Braunsberger, *Epistulae*, vol. i, p. 115.

nearly four months have gone by since last we had the pleasure of a letter from Father Lejay. . . . You can see, then, *Pater carissime*, that we might be described as forsaken sons. . . .

Owing to the hostile attitude of the Cologne people towards us, Father Lejay thought it advisable when last he wrote that we should all proceed to Rome. But in the interval it pleased God to let our dear brother, Master Lambert, become ill, which necessitated some of us remaining behind. . . . Yes, Father, he whom thou lovest has been sick and his sickness was unto death. Though it was a death precious in the sight of the Lord, we cannot but mourn it bitterly because it was also the death of one dearer to us than a brother and more esteemed than any friend. We left nothing undone that man could do to keep him with us. He was part of our souls, but if the Lord ordained to take him it was not for us to say nay, for whether we live or whether we die we are the Lord's. Lambert lived for God, lived master of himself and lived for his neighbour. . . . He might by the mere wishing have had great possessions, but he despised them all and kept nothing for himself, counting it a good bargain indeed to have Christ alone in exchange. Even his own flesh and blood he sacrificed, leaving his parents, though they were advanced in years, and flying from the pleasant studious leisure to which he was born. His learning had no trace of pride in it and he preferred to be a pupil rather than a master, to serve rather than to command. To ask him a favour was to do him a favour, and he looked upon opportunities for kindnesses to others as kindnesses shown to himself. Always ready and eager to help unasked, he would never raise difficulties, or question an order, or show the slightest sign of impatience or reluctance, it being his nature to find pleasure in what pleased others. . . .

In death as in life he was wholly Christ's, and remained up to the very end his cheerful, gay self, encouraging us and expressing his gratitude. . . . Then as the festive bells rang for the Vespers of the Holy Angels he went sweetly to sleep and so passed, happy soul, to join the Angels' festivities in Heaven. . . . He lies at rest among our great friends the Carthusians, a pledge of the love between us.[1]

The friendship between the Jesuits and the Carthusians mentioned here was cemented in a remarkable way this same year, 1544. At a general chapter of the Carthusian Order it was decided on the motion

[1] Braunsberger, *Epistulae*, vol. i, pp. 121–2.

of the Cologne Prior to admit the Society of Jesus to a share in all the merits of St. Bruno's family. " Having heard the fame of your holy lives and teaching," wrote the Prior General to St. Ignatius, " by which in the darkness of this age you lead men back to the narrow way of salvation, we rejoiced and gave thanks to God. . . . For our part, brothers, if there is anything we can do, by Masses, prayers, fasting, and other holy exercises we shall most gladly co-operate with your endeavours. And we make you and your successors in the Society shareholders with us, both in this life and the next, in all the merits of our good works, begging that you would in turn grant us a participation in yours."[1] St. Ignatius sealed the brotherly compact on June 15, 1544, and it still binds the two orders in closest friendship, a blessing they both owe in large measure to the Cologne Carthusians' admiration and love for Blessed Peter Favre and St. Peter Canisius.

By this time Canisius was also on intimate terms with Gropper, Billick, Stempel, and other eminent Catholic leaders, while within his own order he was gradually becoming the focus of affectionate correspondence with men of every standing and nationality. At that early stage the various Jesuit provinces were not as self-contained as now, and under the genial influence of a shared ideal national boundaries and prejudices dissolved like a mist in the sun. Peter Canisius became as much at home with Frenchmen, Spaniards, and Italians as with his own people and, indeed, found among them some of the chief loyalties that brightened his existence. Language was no barrier, as all Jesuits spoke Latin with nearly as much fluency as their mother tongues. It may be mentioned, too, that in the press of his multifarious occupations Peter never forgot his relatives in Nymegen. His step-mother, who had not shown herself particularly friendly after his entrance into the Society of Jesus, lost her youngest child in the first year of her widowhood. Peter's love for her and for his many brothers and sisters was of the good, durable kind that seeks above all the advantage of its objects, so when he wrote to console her towards the close of 1545 his letter took the following shape :

Dearest Mother,

I am sending you a picture of Our Lady as a pledge of affectionate remembrance. May it serve you as a mirror and bring you comfort when sorrow floods into your soul. All her life long holy Mother Mary

[1] Orlandinus, *Historia Societatis Jesu* (Cologne, 1615), lib. iv, n. 107. The letter is dated liturgically, " The Sunday after *Cantate* Sunday, 1544."

endured a thousand sorrows and anxieties on account of her dear Son, because even while He was still a child she saw clearly in the light of her heavenly meditations all the sufferings that awaited His tender limbs. Her tears used to fall on the little hands and feet that one day great nails would violently pierce, and she used to kiss the holy brow destined for its crown of thorns. So, dearest Mother, offer up all your affliction in union with the sorrows of the holy Mother of God. Place all your troubles and anxieties in the stricken heart of the Queen of Heaven, for she can protect you better than could all mankind put together. Do not take so much to heart what cannot now be changed. . . .

I beg you earnestly, in the name of God, to be more authoritative and strict in your dealings with the children and the servants. You are inclined to be too easy-going with them. Also, I am anxious that you should put away the many vain and unprofitable ideas by which the devil seeks to spoil the fervour of your prayers, and perhaps also to induce you to contract another marriage. In my opinion you would act wisely if you made up your mind not to marry again, at least during the next twelve months. Such a resolution would bring you great graces from God. I shall not forget you nor the crosses you bear. It is a cross that you should not merely tolerate, but desire and want and love, attaching to it all your hopes, even though every friend you possessed turned against you and neither from them nor from any other created thing could you obtain a particle of consolation. May God deign with His holy grace to strengthen and direct you.[1]

Just before Christmas, 1544, Peter was raised to the diaconate. He and Leonard Kessel, who was a priest, then took over and administered between them one of the many Cologne parishes which had been orphaned of their pastors. It was Peter's first experience of the pulpit and his first opportunity to engage in public argument on behalf of the Church's doctrines. Hardly ever again for the next half century would he cease to wield that sword of the spirit which is the Word of God, and it might be said with justice that his sermons as a deacon, of which no record has been preserved, were the beginning of the most indefatigable and fruitful pulpit career in the whole history of the Counter-Reformation. At the

---

[1] Braunsberger, *Epistulae*, vol. i, pp. 117–8. A month or two later Peter wrote to a certain Count Oswald, a friend of his father's, whose estates lay near Nymegen, to thank him for his offer of hospitality to the dispersed Jesuits of Cologne. The letter concluded with an appeal to the Count to be good to Peter's relatives, " memor quam sit salutaris orphanorum, pupillorum ac viduarum defensio."

University, where he still attended lectures, he had won such a name that, when he was down for a discourse on some sacred subject, all the professors of law and arts used to attend, as well as Gropper, some bishops, and all the students of theology who could squeeze themselves into the hall. He was appointed one of the *declamatores* in the ' Quodlibets ' or disputations about everything under the sun with which the dons liked to divert their academic souls at Christmas time, part of his duties being to lighten up the proceedings with a certain amount of facetiousness. Billick, Stempel and other prominent men urged him, young as he was, to take up professorial duties, but that would have meant tying himself to Cologne and sacrificing the mobility which St. Ignatius had made a cardinal principle of his order. He did lecture on the Gospel of St. Matthew, but only in a private capacity at the Montanum.[1]

In January, 1545, a mission of charity took him to Belgium in response to an appeal from his old friend and master, Nicholas van Esche. Like some other good men, that saintly soul was distressed by Peter's adhesion to the Society of Jesus, about which mysterious order he appears to have shared the usual suspicions. Master and disciple had, in consequence, drifted apart, to the disciple's genuine distress. When, then, Peter received an appeal from Father Nicholas on behalf of the woefully poor nuns in Diest to whom he was chaplain, he blessed God for the opportunity it afforded him to heal their misunderstanding. Going with his story to the Prior of the Carthusians, Peter came away with five hundred gold pieces for the nuns and another hundred for a priest named Cornelius Wischaven who had recently joined the Society of Jesus in Louvain. To the second sum Peter added a contribution from his own funds sufficient to wipe out the debts contracted by Wischaven before becoming a Jesuit. Diest is a good hundred miles from Cologne, and that particular January during which Peter covered them, probably on foot, has its place in history as one of the most terrible experienced in Europe since the ice age. For instance, if Peter wished to buy some wine on his journey to keep his blood from congealing, he had to do so by the pound and not by the pint, as all the vats in Germany had frozen solid. The reader will like to know that he does not say one single word about his journey, which must have been awful beyond belief. He hardly ever mentions such purely personal concerns, thereby rather draining the colour out of his story but leaving perhaps something that is even better, the physiognomy of a man drained of self as much as poor human nature

[1] Braunsberger, *Epistulae*, vol. i, pp. 112, 124–5, 664–5.

can ever hope to be. He did not take long to put things right with van
Esche. " Master Nicholas is entirely on our side now," he wrote to
Favre, " and blessed be God who has restored him to me as friendly and
kind as ever." They went to Louvain together to hunt up the debt-
burdened Wischaven, and while there van Esche used his considerable
influence with the Rector of the University and other prominent men
to procure their consent for the foundation of a Jesuit college in the
city. The complete success of these negotiations was Peter's first achievement in that delicate art of diplomacy for which his father had been
distinguished.[1] It is narrow-minded to think that the only great diplomatists
are the people who arrange wars and treaties of peace, because sometimes
to obtain a concession from a bishop or to avoid offending a parish priest
or a Mother Superior requires the dexterity of a Talleyrand.

At Louvain Peter developed an already existing friendship with his
saintly but very singular client, Cornelius Wischaven. Cornelius was
probably the oddest novice that the Society of Jesus took to her bosom
in those early days.[2] She speculated well, however, for under Favre's
discipline, which was stern enough at times, he became after many
tribulations one of her best-beloved and most hard-working sons.
Through him Canisius was introduced to a sinister aspect of sixteenth-
century life which had its bearing on his own development. Never was
there an age so full of gross superstition, of hearty belief in witches,
warlocks, were-wolves, vampires and such things. Educated and simple
alike dabbled in the occult; and Campeggio, the Papal Nuncio, even
felt obliged to include in his *Constitutio* of 1524 a clause whereby ecclesiastics
who took upon themselves the rôle of sorcerer, diviner or weaver of
spells were to be branded with infamy at the discretion of their superiors.
The illustrious scholar Reuchlin found comfort in the weird mysteries
of Cabbalism, and his highly cultured grand-nephew, Melanchthon, had
the most implicit faith in horoscopes and auguries. Comets, of course,
scared everybody out of their wits, but the worst affliction of the century
was its all-pervasive terror of the devil. It was the age of the original
Dr. Faustus, whose famous legend took shape and grew mightily in the
devil-haunted atmosphere. A healthy belief in the devil is an essential
and tonic part of religion without which Christianity would no longer
be the religion of Christ, but the belief of those days had turned to a
disease. Indeed, it was not so much a belief as a perpetual nightmare

[1] Braunsberger, *Epistulae*, vol. i, pp. 138–40.
[2] His vocation to the Society and subsequent training by Favre make a very good story, as given
in Favre's *Monumenta*.

that lay heavy on Catholic as well as Protestant imaginations. Fear of the devil pressed like an icy hand on Luther's heart and inspired a good deal of his theology, while on the Catholic side it created a whole body of literature on the problems of possession.[1] Often enough, ability to deal with cases of alleged possession was regarded as a touchstone of true religion, and in many places in Germany keen competition sprang up between ministers and priests to see which side could get a particular devil out first.[2]

In Belgium, Cornelius Wischaven had won renown as an exorcist, and his feats in that line certainly made a deep impression on Peter Canisius. The following extract from a letter addressed by Cornelius to Peter describes some interesting psychic phenomena, not unknown in more recent times:

On my way back to Bruges I fell into a river but escaped drowning by the mercy of God. I thought afterwards that this was a ruse of the devil to keep me out of that city where I might have done some good to souls. . . . The day before I left, a lady named Griffiers called on me and earnestly begged me to visit a young married woman who had been possessed by a devil for ten years. . . . This devil treated her so horribly that no priest had the courage to go near her. He mangled and roasted her in the most extraordinary way, very often throwing her naked into the fire and holding her in the flames for two or three hours at a time. Do what they would, the many witnesses present found it impossible to drag her out. She used to take the burning coals that were all about her body into her mouth and chew them. This I saw her do with my own eyes, and I also saw her swallow heaps of gold rings and more than two thousand pieces of stick which she afterwards cast up again. Other things that she swallowed in my presence were a huge iron nail, a complete glass siphon, a ploughshare with the nail attached, a pair of spurs, coins, projectiles, a quarter pound of lead and a knife ten inches long together with a dagger. All these and other things innumerable she had in her stomach and threw up again in my presence. I never saw the like. The devil used to hang her up by the neck, too, but he could not

---

[1] A typical treatise of the time is *Daemoniaci, hoc est de obsessis a spiritibus daemoniorum hominibus*, by Peter Thyraeus, a Jesuit professor of Würzburg. It argues elaborately such questions as whether heretics are all possessed by devils, whether devils enter human bodies by the mouth or pores or through some other channel, whether any who are not Catholics have power to eject them, etc. etc.

[2] Freytag's classic, *Bilder aus der deutscher Vergangenheit* (Leipzig ed., 1924–1925), vol. iii, part ii, gives a number of interesting cases in the section entitled, *Der deutsche Teufel*.

strangle her as he has no power against human life. When she threw
glass objects against the wall they did not break, and once after she
had buried her face in the fire there was not a mark on it nor were
her hair or clothes singed in any way. In her lucid moments she
received Holy Communion most devoutly and was a model of patience.
She made a general confession to me and felt better after it than ever
before, praise be to God.[1]

Peter did not show any unwillingness to credit his friend's experiences.
Indeed, he seems to have been a little proud of them and reported gaily
to Favre : " I pass over an infinite number of things I could tell you
about Father Cornelius, who is now all the more to be admired in proportion as he waxes more terrible to the demons themselves. In a short
time he put eight devils to flight that would not stir for the exorcisms
of other priests. It was a stupendous feat to witness, and had I not been
present I would have laughed at the story rather than believed it."[2]
Favre, however, refused to be impressed and answered sharply : " I would
have Master Cornelius know that I entirely disapprove of his exorcising
activities, as much fraud and deception lurks in that sphere. Let him
content himself with ejecting the devil from men's souls, which is the
proper office of a priest, and leave exorcists to do their own business."[3]
After his return to Cologne from Belgium in February, 1545, Peter
rented a house alongside his friends the Dominicans and there reassembled
his brethren when permission had been obtained from the civil authorities
through the good offices of the Carthusians. It was a pleasant house,
he told Favre, having five rooms or more, and a little garden at the back.
He paid ten gold pieces in rent for it out of his private resources, an
expenditure that gave him some anxiety. Though they were extremely
poor he would not allow his men to ask " even a farthing " in alms.
God would see to it that they did not starve, he said. The catalogue of
their library drawn up by Peter himself serves to illustrate the modesty
of their equipment. It contained eight volumes : Erasmus's *Paraphrase
of the New Testament*, *A Moralization on the Bible* by some unknown
author, *The Golden Legend* of Jacopone de Voragine, St. Bridget's
Revelations, *The Soliloquies* of St. Bonaventure, a work with the curious
title, *Opus trivium notabilium Praedicabilium*, an encyclopaedia called *The
Properties of Things* by an English Franciscan, and an *Annotated Book*

---

[1] M.H., *Fabri Monumenta*, pp. 471-2.   [2] Braunsberger, *Epistulae*, vol. i, p. 142.
[3] Braunsberger, *Epistulae*, vol. i, p. 156.

of notable Sayings.[1] There was not much help in that library, it will be agreed, for a young and eager student. Peter had to find his authorities where he could and to acquire learning under difficulties that would have driven anybody but a Dutchman to despair. He was anxious in an undecided way to sample the lectures and facilities of Paris or Louvain, as the German custom of moving about from university to university appealed to him, but the Cologne authorities became distressed at the mere possibility of his leaving them. In March, 1545, Billick and the other members of the faculty of theology addressed a petition to Father Bobadilla, one of St. Ignatius's first disciples who was at Brussels with the Nuncio, Verallo, urging that Peter should not be taken away for a few years more. His presence, they said, " would spell advantage to the city as well as to the university, for he was a most suitable young man to be a professor on account of his proved piety and learning."[2] Verallo, too, was asked to intercede, and Gropper, together with the Priors of the Carthusians and Dominicans, wrote independently to Father Stempel about the same business. That these eminent men should have been so anxious to retain him is some indication of Peter's growing importance at the age of twenty-four. When approached directly, he said that he believed his studies would profit by a change but that he had no personal inclination in the matter, since " he depended entirely on the judgment and authority of his superiors."[3]

Favre, who was then resident in Spain, expressed strong opposition to any change, not because he desired to see Peter the first of Jesuit university professors, but because he regarded him as the foundation-stone of the Society of Jesus in Northern Europe. Writing to Peter and Alvaro Alfonso from Valladolid, he said : " Though I knew well that you would make better progress in your studies elsewhere I preferred the good of many souls to your advancement in learning. My great love for Cologne induced me to expose you to risks and made me choose rather to see you unlearned there than wonderful doctors at some other university . . . I should prefer to hear, Master Peter and Master Alvaro, that you were both dead and lying beside Master Lambert in Cologne than that you were alive and flourishing away from that city, provided of course, obedience had not counselled or commanded your departure. For obedience is better than all sacrifice." Peter's answer was characteristic : " Let me say freely that if obedience does not call me away I am determined

---

[1] Braunsberger, *Epistulae*, vol. i, p. 671.   [2] Braunsberger, *Epistulae*, vol. i, p. 665.
[3] Braunsberger, *Epistulae*, vol. i, p. 144.

to devote myself body and soul, all my time and study and teaching and prayer, in a word, my whole self, living and dying, to the people of Holy Cologne."[1]

It was no mere sentimental attachment to towers dreaming of the enchanted past and exquisite shrines where the martyrs gleamed in gold that made these men write with such feeling. Peter certainly loved Cologne to some extent in a simple, human way, but he was too much of a realist to indulge in any emotion irrelevant to the great purpose that had won his allegiance. He knew that Cologne was the keystone of a mighty Rhenish arch of Catholicism. Within the jurisdiction of its powerful Archbishop in ecclesiastical matters came such distant places as Liége, Utrecht, Münster, Osnabrück, and Minden. " Should it fall," he wrote in December, 1545, " Gelderland, Jülich, Cleves, Brabant, and Holland must necessarily be involved in the disaster." But there was more even than that at stake. The succession to the crown of the Holy Roman Empire was not, in theory, hereditary, but depended on the votes of the seven Electors. One of these, the King of Bohemia, usually took no part in the proceedings ; two others, the Electors of Saxony and Branden-burg, had gone over to Lutheranism ; and a third, the Elector Palatine, had his face set in the same direction. If, then, Hermann von Wied, the Elector of Cologne, succeeded in maintaining his position, the Lutherans would have a majority in the Electoral College and the Crown of Charlemagne might easily become an apanage of Protestantism.

Hermann had by no means given up his determination to Lutheranize the Electorate of Cologne and its capital. No sooner was the Emperor in trouble again with one or other of his many enemies, including the gout, than he resumed the attack. The omens were again favourable to him by the spring of 1545, for when the Protestant princes were then asked at the Diet of Worms whether they would submit their religious proposals to the general council summoned by Paul III to meet at Trent in March, their answer was a scornful ' No.' " The Council at Trent or elsewhere indicted by the Bishop of Rome the Protestants do utterly refuse," reported the English agent at Worms to Henry VIII.[2] They could afford to be insolent just then as their League had 57,000 infantry and troopers to the Emperor's 28,000, but they overlooked the possibility that God might not always be on the side of the big battalions.

At Worms, during the Diet, the two Jesuits, Lejay and Bobadilla,

[1] Braunsberger, *Epistulae*, vol. i, pp. 155–6, 169.
[2] Gairdner and Brodie, *Letters and Papers of the Reign of Henry VIII*, vol. xx, part i, p. 453.

Cologne in the time of St. Peter Canisius
From an engraving made by Anton Woensam in 1531

were present as theological advisers to the Papal Nuncio and to Cardinal Otto Truchsess, Bishop of Augsburg. A few months earlier Lejay had written to Salmeron, another of the first fathers of the Society of Jesus : " We have in Cologne a young man named Master Canisius, the splendid promise of whose life and learning is to be seen in a letter of Dr. Cochlaeus. The Cardinal of Augsburg bears him great affection."[1] So it appears Peter's reputation had spread outside Cologne, though how or where he came in contact with the great Cochlaeus is not recorded. In May, Father Lejay summoned him to Worms and he went gladly, buoyed up with the hope of obtaining some assistance against von Wied from Cardinal Farnese, the Pope's nephew, who had put in an appearance at the Diet. Before he reached his destination, however, probably again by ship up the Rhine, Farnese had abruptly departed in disguise, as he believed himself to be in danger of being murdered by the Protestants. Peter remained a while to help his brethren with their preaching and ministrations to the sick. He loved his intercourse with the gentle Lejay, a man, he said, " who was ever full of piety and sweetness." But more significant for the future were his relations with Cardinal Truchsess, who esteemed him so highly that he contemplated sending him there and then to the Council of Trent. Before returning home, Peter witnessed the abortive efforts of the Emperor to attract the Lutherans to the Council, and acquired much sad insight into the bitter mind of their leaders who, he says, " were devoting all their attention to mobilizing troops and fortifying positions."

Day by day the clouds of civil war loomed more black and menacing over Germany but, in the midst of the gloom, Peter had the satisfaction of knowing that von Wied was becoming angry and anxious at the magnificent resistance put up by Gropper and his allies. Thus the English agents, Bucler and Mundt, reported to their master, Henry VIII, in July: " The Bishop of Cologne last week sent letters to the Emperor and the States of the Empire complaining of the clergy in the town of Colleyne who rail upon him as a heretic and thus diminish his fame and dignity of Electorship unworthily. He desires the Emperor and the States to prohibit this, and offers to purge himself before them if the clergy will lay aught against him for such mutations as he hath made in religion."[2] Plainly, Hermann had no great sense of humour !

[1] M.H., *Epistolae PP. Paschasii Broetii, Claudii Jaii*, etc., p. 290.
[2] Gairdner and Brodie, *Letters and Papers of the Reign of Henry VIII*, vol. xx, part i, p. 560. England, as well as other nations, maintained a high level of orthographical freedom in the sixteenth century. Cologne appears indifferently in the *Letters and Papers* as Colon, Colyne, Colloine, Collyne, and Colleyne, as above.

From this time onwards the defenders of Cologne's faith used Peter as their regular official envoy. From Nuncio Verallo at Worms he brought a letter to Billick, in answer to which that stout-hearted man detailed the latest manœuvres of von Wied. In order to dispirit the Cologne people rumours were spread that the Imperial Chancellor had become a Lutheran and that the Emperor himself had abandoned his hostility to Protestantism. Hermann's agents were constantly coming and going, holding secret meetings, and plotting in the dark. He intruded his heretical preachers everywhere and threatened the Catholics with dire penalties should they molest them. By dint of bribery and flattery he had now won over to his side the dean of the Cologne Chapter, and that person had weaned several others from their allegiance to the Church. Some even of the common people, seduced by his preachers, were beginning to say openly " *der Glaub ist frei* "—a man may believe what he likes—and all the time the thought of the 50,000 Protestant soldiers available, in the last resort, for a raid on their city made the general population restive.[1]

After his return to their midst, Peter Canisius was swept into a maelstrom of activity. "Never in my life," he wrote to Favre, "have I had fewer moments to call my own." It had already been brought home to him that what the Catholic Church in Germany needed in order to outface her foes was not an army of soldiers but an army of good and learned priests under the leadership of zealous and hard-working bishops. According to Lejay, who had had many opportunities for knowing, the study of Scripture was no longer pursued at the Catholic universities, and as for the study of theology, " *per tutto e sepolto*," he said—it was completely dead and buried.[2] Canisius now determined, as far as in him lay, to revive both, at least in Cologne, and so, though under age, he became a " Bachelor of the Bible " and started lectures on theology and Scripture for the benéfit of any students who cared to listen to him. On Sundays and feast-days he preached in German in St. Maria in Capitolio, or Zint Märjen, as it is called in the local dialect, one of the most interesting old churches on earth and one of the most important of Cologne's churches, while continuing, as before, his lectures on the Gospel of St. Matthew at the Montanum. In addition, he contrived to be the heart and soul of the weekly academic disputations because, though terribly burdensome, he believed that they served greatly to promote the study

[1] Postina, *Der Karmelit Eberhard Billick*, p. 158.
[2] M.H., *Epistolae PP. Paschasii Broetii, Claudii Jaii*, etc., pp. 286–7.

of theology. So now, at the age of twenty-five, he was launched on the chief work of his life, on those hidden, inglorious educational activities which are the true *seminarium* of both religion and civilization. The student class of mankind became now and for good his primary concern. "Any hard task seems sweet to me that I do for them," he confided to Favre. Behind the scenes he tried his best to crown their young lives with something more precious than learning, much as he prized that, with the self-renouncing, devoted, purposeful love which energized his own young life. The *Spiritual Exercises* of St. Ignatius were his great resource because his own experience of their tonic effects on both soul and body made him eager to share with others so potent a remedy for the slackness and apathy with which he was daily confronted. The life and joy had disappeared from many men's religion and what they most needed was the invigoration to be found in a spell of the disturbing, bracing drill which Ignatius, the convert swashbuckler, had wonderfully elaborated. Those *Exercises* had re-created the world for Peter himself, and he had the manifold witness of his brethren to confirm his belief that they were capable of working the same miracle for anybody who gave them a fair trial. Could he have looked into the future he would have seen, and exulted to see, his order driven by the spirit of the *Exercises* to a sort of specialism in martyrdom, so that there is hardly a land on earth not reddened at some time or other with Jesuit blood.

One whom Peter gained for God by them at this time had been an intimate of Luther and Bucer, a notable filibuster, proud of his many exploits in destroying and pillaging Catholic shrines. On these occasions it was his custom to grind up the relics of the saints and serve them, mixed with flour, to the stray dogs of the locality. What marvel of grace enabled Peter to persuade this fire-eater to make the *Exercises* is not told us, but we are earnestly assured that he came out of them the opposite of his old self, joined Peter's community and astounded them all with his great virtues, especially his passionate devotion to the saints.[1]

In August, 1545, the Emperor paid a visit to Cologne, whereupon the Catholic authorities delegated Peter to lay their case against von Wied before His Majesty. As the Archbishop was now the declared protégé of the powerful Protestant League, Charles could not for the moment promise Peter very much. He had to be content with an assurance that the Emperor would admonish and remonstrate with von Wied, which was poor comfort for people who knew their Hermann.

[1] Braunsberger, *Epistulae*, vol. i, p. 161 ; M.H., *Fabri Monumenta*, pp. 357–8.

No sooner was his liege-lord out of sight than that shifty prelate summoned the estates of his Electorate to discuss measures for the forcible over-throw of the Catholic party. Then, once again, Peter was dispatched in hot haste to explain the new development to the Emperor, who had gone on to Antwerp.[1] Though he was successful in the immediate purpose of his mission, he derived just as little satisfaction from his visit to Court this time as on the previous occasion. This he explains in a letter to Favre of December 22, 1545 :

> The Lord helping me I fulfilled my task and brought back what the clergy desired, namely an edict from the Emperor prohibiting the Archbishop and estates from arranging at their convention anything contrary to the faith. The Papal Legate gave me great comfort and held out good hopes of a happy ending to our troubles. But the Emperor's delay in pronouncing against the Archbishop is a source of intense grief and almost of despair to very many, as they feel that his heart is not in the business. If he does not soon adopt vigorous measures the Archbishop's efforts will bring the gravest disasters upon all Germany. Hitherto the menace of the Lutheran forces gathered for the destruction of the Duke of Brunswick served him as a reasonable excuse, and his present illness at Bois-le-Duc provides him with another. Meanwhile, the Archbishop pursues his evil policy with more vigour than ever, and only Cologne now remains to be captured for the new evangel. Who has the power to defend this poor city, surrounded by enemies on every side and with many of her own clergy and senators secretly in sympathy with the Archbishop ? To Heaven alone can we look for help, inspired with confidence by the presence in our midst of the bodies of so many holy martyrs and virgins.[2]

Had Peter but known what the seemingly apathetic Emperor was really thinking, as he sat resting his poor gouty foot on a stool, he would have danced the whole way back to Cologne. The vigorous measures for which he longed were to come sooner than he expected. Meantime, he returned to his studious ways and though, as he said, weighed down with so much work and so many cares that " leisure and quiet even to

---

[1] Possibly it was on this occasion that Peter wrote his long and very interesting *Agenda per me Petrum Kanisium*, now in the state archives, Naples. Braunsberger overlooked the document but Duhr published it in the *Historisches Jahrbuch*, 1897, pp. 827–9. Duhr opines that it belongs to the first months of 1546. If so, Peter must have been dispatched on yet another mission after his return from Antwerp.

[2] Braunsberger, *Epistulae*, vol. i, p. 165.

write a letter were almost impossible to find," produced in April and September, 1546, new editions of the works of St. Cyril of Alexandria and St. Leo the Great. The reason why he consecrated his young energies to these two holy patriarchs was his ever-deepening conviction that the Catholic Church must be, to a very large extent, what her bishops made her. In his dedication of the first volume of St. Cyril's works to the new Archbishop and Elector of Mainz, Sebastian von Heusenstamm, he held up the Patriarch of Alexandria as a model for the German bishops, inasmuch as the problems of his age were similar to the problems with which they were confronted. He had Nestorius, Eunomius, and Apollinaris to withstand, just as they had Luther and Calvin. Let them, then, give battle with the holy zeal and courage of Cyril in their hearts, for on them depended the salvation of Christendom. " Even the worst of men would not find it difficult to recognize apostolic authority in bishops if only they might first observe in them apostolic piety." The second volume of the work bore a dedication to Peter's " fellow-soldiers," the theological students of Cologne. In this he denounces in sufficiently elegant Latin the craze for elegant Latinity introduced by the humanists. " We turn up our noses, I am ashamed to say, at everything that lacks the seasoning and ornament of the rhetoricians. All our care is for style, and I fear that if St. Paul were with us to-day he would not have much of our esteem, being unskilled in oratory." St. Cyril should be the Cologne students' model and inspiration, for " his works breathe the pristine vigour of the Gospels. You will find no one to-day who treats sacred matters with sincerity such as his, or who avoids as carefully as he the least taint of erroneous doctrine. At all times and everywhere he bore himself as a true Christian bishop, full of fatherly compassion and combining perfect meekness with his authority as a pastor. Never in all his writings does he fail in moderation, and even when refuting the errors of heretics he is not forgetful of Christian forbearance. No bitter word escaped his pen, nor did he ever hunt about for striking phrases. These ancient theologians were so wrapt up in God that they had no desire to polish their periods or seek other elegance than that which a heart on fire with the love of Christ spontaneously suggested." This edition of St. Cyril made Canisius the pioneer author of the Society of Jesus, as no other Jesuit had yet found his way into print.

In June, 1546, Peter was raised to the priesthood by Johann Nopel, a coadjutor bishop of Cologne whom he numbered among his intimate friends. To this good man, whose zeal and eloquence had done much to baffle the machinations of Bucer and von Wied, he dedicated his edition of the works of St. Leo. It was the contempt shown for the Fathers of the Church by Luther, Calvin and other heretics that impelled him to engage on a task involving "Herculean labours," he told a friend.[1] Herculean the labours must certainly have been, for his editions of the two Fathers were the first ever published on critical and scholarly lines, though, of course, by modern standards, only moderately critical and scholarly. The volumes of St. Leo enjoyed great popularity. They were reissued twice in revised form at Cologne within the following two years. In 1553 and 1556 two further revisions appeared at Venice and Louvain, and again in the same places in 1566 and 1573. That was not too bad an achievement for a young man of twenty-five who showed himself also well versed in Tertullian, St. Cyprian, St. Vincent of Lerins, St. Augustine, St. Gregory, St. Jerome, St. Hilary, St. Epiphanius, St. Prosper, and St. Bernard. Lactantius he considered so much his private property that he wove the smooth periods of the Cicero of the Christians into his own text without the formality of any acknowledgment. Though these editions of the Fathers are now entirely superseded they have interest for us as showing that from the beginning Peter was an advocate of the new methods in theological study which humanism had introduced, namely intelligent investigation of Christian sources, and they prove too, as hinted above, that he was early possessed of his dominant conviction, heartily endorsed a little later by his brother Jesuit, St. Robert Bellarmine, on the all-importance of the episcopal office as the key to a genuine Catholic reformation.

At this time when anxiety for the fate of Cologne and grave domestic poverty might have weighed too heavily on Peter's heart, he was cheered by the receipt of a letter from St. Ignatius to himself and his two companions:

Jhesus

May the grace and the peace of Our Lord Jesus Christ be with you and with us all. Amen. This is my joy in Jesus when I see Him grow up and bear fruit in so many souls. I thank God for the ineffable mercy He shows us for the sake of His glorious Name. This is how I often feel when I hear of you and others who have been called to our Society in Christ Jesus. Study and explore in your hearts this vocation and grace which has been given to you in Christ. Exercise it, lean upon it, traffic with it and never permit it to lie idle or stand

[1] Braunsberger, *Epistulae*, vol. i, p. 205.

still. It is the Lord God who grants us both to will and to achieve. He will give you the spirit of Jesus in all things, and understanding and fortitude that by your means the Name of God may fructify and be glorified in many souls, with expectation of a better life in Christ Jesus. I write to you as one putting the spur to a galloping horse. You have made me all your own in Christ. I know your eager zeal in the vineyard of the Lord, and the splendid promise you give that in you Christ Jesus will be glorified to the end. . . .

If you have not heard from me as often as, I think, you would have liked, you must not be surprised. I have such an ever-increasing mountain of business to transact in Christ Jesus that I can scarcely escape it, even to write a letter about matters in which many people are concerned. Those whom I must answer or write to, form a veritable army, so many are the places in which the spirit of Christ is at work building up our Society for the glory of His Name. We have now a college at Padua to which a Venetian nobleman has assigned a revenue of a thousand ducats a year. There is question at present of founding a college at Bologna, and we have good hopes of soon seeing others at Trent and Paris where some of our Fathers are at work. The college at Valencia, in Spain, has already been opened, and enjoys a revenue of three hundred ducats. The Duke of Gandia is about to start yet another college in his domains with a revenue of seven hundred ducats. There are eighty of our men now in the college of Coimbra, in Portugal, and the King, who has assigned it a revenue of two thousand ducats, wishes the number of scholastics to be increased to a hundred. Besides these there are very many other places to which I have to write: to Barcelona, to the Spanish Court, to Louvain, to yourselves, to Trent, to India. About this last place I need only tell you that the King of Portugal is sending ten more of our Fathers there by the next vessel that sails. I pass over Alcalá, Toledo and Valladolid, where we either have scholastics or there are people who want letters.[1] So now if you do not hear from me frequently you will understand and take it in good part. . . . For the rest, let us beg and beseech God to grant us the knowledge of His holy will and the grace ever to do it.[2]

It was one of the proudest claims of the Protestant reformers (and is still a proud claim of their modern children) that they had reinstated Christ at the centre of religion and disengaged Him from His Mother's

[1] This letter was written in June, 1546, when the Society of Jesus was not yet six years old.
[2] Braunsberger, *Epistulae*, vol. i, pp. 189–92.

apron-strings and the mob of saints with which medieval superstition
had confounded His paramount rights. But from the letter just cited,
as indeed from almost any random letter of such thorough-paced
medievalists as Ignatius Loyola, Peter Favre, and Peter Canisius, it
appears rather plainly that the reformers must have been under a mis-
apprehension. Peter received too, at this time, copies of letters from
Francis Xavier in India, telling of ten thousand baptisms in a single month
and six hundred new Christians who had already laid down their lives
for their faith. What an answer that was to the squeamish Elector
in his arm-chair in Bonn ! And what a source of fresh enthusiasm
to Peter and his companions for the invincible cause which they
represented !

While Peter's reputation grew and spread, his elder brethren watched
solicitously from afar to see that no vanity of life should spoil his promise.
Thus Claude Lejay, while at the Council of Trent in June, 1546, took
Peter's ordination during that month as a good occasion on which to
whisper some fatherly advice. "I was deeply affected, my Peter, by
the news of your first Mass," he wrote. "Would that it had been possible
for me to assist at it and to fill my soul with the divine spirit that overflowed from yours. Who could possibly be without joy in the midst
of these Heavenly mysteries when God comes down at human invitation
to dispense His riches ? What a condescension it is on Christ's part to
come when you call and to give you the power to call Him that He may
come ! Show yourself worthy of this divine favour and think what a
shame it would be to stoop from the sublime heights on which God has
placed you to any mean ambition. I am led to advise you all the more
because I see you engaged in public work and the object of men's delusive
praises. Go down deep, then, into your own heart, my Peter, and school
yourself in profound humility. I do not think it wise for you to be
always hugging a book nor that you should immerse yourself unduly
in any other business. As the soul may be wrested from the body by
overmuch toil, so may the spirit or fire of God in your heart be gradually
damped down by the rush and hurry of external occupations, until at
last it is completely extinguished. Therefore I would most earnestly
wish you to cry a halt now and then, and cease not only from your sermons
to others but from the converse you hold with yourself, that you may
hear God speaking to you in the silence. It is not always the man who
is over his books from morning to night that makes the most progress.
The man of prayer often learns by not learning, as that great light of

the Church, Aquinas, did, whose best master was Christ on His cross."[1]
That Peter accepted those plain-spoken but affectionate counsels in the
right spirit is evident from a letter which he wrote shortly afterwards
to a Jesuit student of Louvain who had asked him for advice. This
letter has the additional interest of showing him a zealous promoter of
frequent Communion. We have called him a medievalist, and so he
was in his world-outlook, just like Luther, Melanchthon, Copernicus,
and other alleged heralds of modernity, but the true spirit of Christianity
is neither ancient nor medieval nor modern. It is out of time altogether,
and as authentic in this sixteenth-century letter as in the sixth chapter
of St. John, or the *Motu proprio* on Daily Communion of Pope Pius X:

> You have told me, dear Brother, your methods of study and how
> you pursue wisdom rather than knowledge. You do not neglect
> disputations, you diligently compare the text of the ancient theologians
> with the Scriptures, you instruct virgins and widows, you have much
> converse with learned men and you are on familiar terms with the
> graduates of the university. I do not condemn your programme, but
> neither do I approve it to the extent of adopting it myself. I, too,
> thanks be to God, have had my turn of public teaching, preaching,
> arguing, exhorting. But ah, what an ill twist those labours of mine
> took which I had begun in all sincerity. While toiling for others I
> began, like a candle, to be myself consumed. While counselling and
> prescribing for others I neglected the care of my own soul. My mind
> became habituated to vain concerns and my senses went astray in their
> obsession with trifles. The man who thought it a fine thing boldly
> to inspire all whom he met with the fear of the Lord himself grew
> proud and arrogant. But now that, by the singular mercy of God,
> opportunity to preach and lecture has been taken from me, I realize
> how much I have neglected myself while unseasonably bent on helping
> others. I feel how far I have strayed from the simplicity of the little
> ones of Christ, and how much need I have of steady purpose and purity
> and holiness before I can be accounted a true member of our Society,
> if only the least worthy member.
>
> While approving of your present occupations I think you should
> concentrate your efforts rather on gaining young men than on winning
> over theologians and other such important people. . . . Let your
> endeavour be to rouse in many students a happy shame and sorrow for

---

[1] Braunsberger, *Epistulae*, vol. i, pp. 206–7.

their sins, to get them to go to Confession weekly and to Communion often, to create in them a thirst for the Word of God, love of poverty, purity of purpose in their studies, contempt for the world and the flesh and a keen desire for the yoke and cross of Christ. Why should I say more, as if you did not know all this as well as I do? You tell me that you do not like the custom of more frequent Communion which has been introduced in many places. You point out the dangers that may arise, quoting what St. Basil says in his treatise on Baptism. But our concern is with young men serving their apprenticeship to learning. Surely they will not serve Christ the worse by more frequent Confessions and Communions? Where, I ask you in all earnestness, is to be found a more certain remedy for sickness of soul and a better spur to holy living than in Holy Communion.? Again, where do studies thrive best, where are the cold and apathetic set on fire most easily, where are men of the world taught with least effort obedience and the fear of God, where, finally, do married people learn best how to conquer and control the desires of the flesh? Is it not in those places where the practice of frequent Communion flourishes? You will object, however, that we cannot be sure if communicants are rightly disposed. My answer is, what harm can the perversity of those who abuse the Holy Sacrament do to It or to us? Be careful, I beg of you, not to require too much from your brother. He is to be led on gradually in the way of holiness by the reception of this divine food, and by assiduous, careful instruction. St. Augustine laid it down that it behoved all Christians to approach the Holy Table every Sunday, and that was the custom in the Church for many centuries. To be brief, for the worthy reception of this Sacrament it is enough that a man's will should be turned away from evil and resolved, in the strength of Christ, to pursue virtue. What would you answer if I were to ask you which is the better course, to abstain from Communion through humility or to approach It out of loving confidence in God? The man who partakes of the Body and Blood of Christ floods with new light the temple of his heart, strengthens his power of doing good, fortifies his soul against every evil, establishes himself in unfeigned love, and weakens and casts off the last relics of his sins. But my pen is running away with me. Forgive my volubility and put it down to my lack of sense. Good-bye and pray for me, a poor fellow with more words in him than wisdom. In great haste. *Tuus*, Peter Canisius.[1]

---

[1] Braunsberger, *Epistulae*, vol. i, pp. 207–9.

It will have been seen by now that Peter's letters are not exactly great literature. As he pointed out to a friend who was shy of writing to him on account of defective Latinity, he was himself no artist with his pen but just a plain, blunt man who spoke his mind in the first way that occurred to him. " Like you," he said, " I have never learnt to be elegant as a writer, but I cannot remain dumb on that account. I just pour out to my friends the first thoughts that come into my head."[1] By way of example, here is such an outpouring of himself to his step-mother in October, 1546, showing the special nature of Peter's " first thoughts " :

Dear Mother,

You must always try to carry your cross patiently. I received your letter but not the clothes you sent. Doubtless, they will arrive later on. It makes me glad to know that sufferings are your lot because they are proof that your faithful husband, my father, has not forgotten you, however much you may forget your own self. Patient suffering brings the sufferer to all tranquillity and peace. It prepares us to receive the highest graces, wipes out the stains on our hearts, opens blind and sin-sealed eyes, preserves us from all pride and vain-glory, delivers us from the terrible pains of Purgatory, and makes us careful and solicitous about our salvation. Indeed, for a widow to serve God truly it is necessary that she should tread the way of the Cross. Remember, dear Mother, that trials and sufferings are the genuine badge of the children of God. Many are the tribulations of the just but from all of them will the Lord be their deliverance. As to whether we have deserved our sufferings or not, what does it matter ? The great thing is to suffer well and patiently.

So therefore, dear Mother, gird yourself to fight bravely, not only providing for your children's temporal needs but taking care to leave them the example of a patient, loving mother who esteems their salvation of more account than all the riches in the world. Maintain a firm discipline over them. Each evening, see that they say their prayers, that they repeat the Ten Commandments, and recite four Hail Marys while recalling to mind the four Last Things. Sometimes, too, get them to say five Our Fathers, kneeling by their beds with their arms extended in the form of a cross.[2] Further, it is only right that in the morning, before breakfast, they should offer their thanks to God in prayer, and

---

[1] Braunsberger, *Epistulae*, vol. i, p. 227.
[2] This was an old form of devotion in honour of Our Lord's Five Wounds.

you will invite them, by means of some little reward, constantly to be learning new prayers, which they may become accustomed to say for the rest of their lives.

Let the dead bury their dead, Mother, and do not grieve over my father who is at peace in God, leaving you in a more perfect state than that in which he possessed you.[1] Good father and husband that he was, he formerly cherished and protected you. Now he has found for you an eternal and omnipotent Protector who is faithful above all the children of men. Dear Mother, look after yourself, and keep well and strong with the help of God, and always pray for me.[2]

Some people may not like that letter, but its forthrightness and emphasis on the less accommodating aspects of Christian truth meant nothing more terrible than a deep moral earnestness which by no means precluded all tender feeling. This became apparent when Favre died in Rome on August 1, 1546, worn out at the age of forty by his incessant labours for the Church. When he learned the news Peter wrote to St. Ignatius : " The death of my father, Master Favre, is not, indeed, in itself a matter for tears, but I have to confess that the news was a cruel blow to me. The sorrow in my soul is such that I cannot help expressing a little of it to your Reverence, and I beg of you to help my weakness with your prayers."[3] For the rest of Peter's life, Favre's name was to shine like a beckoning star in his memory, and fifty years later he would tell an inquirer such treasured details as the manner of his walk and how when saying Mass he used to weep abundant tears for the love and joy that filled him.[4]

All this time the struggle for the faith of Cologne was proceeding apace. The Archbishop's persistence had brought upon him sentence of excommunication and deposition in April, 1546, but he held to his post, confident in the might of the Schmalkalden army. It was probably this circumstance that finally determined the Emperor to throw down the gage to his domestic foes, though their forces were twice what he could muster, and their leader, the bigamous Philip of Hesse, had started negotiations with his foreign enemies. His patience was at an end. In the words of a dispassionate historian, " at every Diet he had endured

[1] " A woman is bound by the law as long as her husband liveth, but if her husband die she is at liberty. Let her marry to whom she will, only in the Lord, but more blessed shall she be, if she so remain, according to my counsel." I Cor. vii, 39–40.
[2] Braunsberger, *Epistulae*, vol. i, pp. 224–6.
[3] Braunsberger, *Epistulae*, vol. i, p. 223.
[4] Braunsberger, *Epistulae*, vol. viii, pp. 415–7.

vulgar insults to himself and his faith from the citizens of Imperial towns, from foul-mouthed preachers and from drunken princes. The Lutheran press had poured forth a muddy stream of pamphlets in which the pictures were as coarsely insolent as the text. . . . Every authority in the Empire had been set at nought; religion had become a cloak for shameless territorial greed."[1] But, more than any thing, it was the danger to the Habsburg succession from a fourth Protestant Elector in the person of von Wied that gave the Schmalkalden War to history.

If Charles could not rally as large a force as his enemies he had at least the satisfaction of commanding troops that knew all there was to be known about war as waged in those days. Also, he was a much cleverer diplomatist than anyone on the other side, as was shown by the way he managed Pope Paul III and Duke Moritz of Saxony. Paul provided subsidies on the understanding that the war was for the extermination of heresy, and Moritz, a capable soldier and heretic himself, became an ally on the understanding that it was no such thing. Charles gave both assurances without turning a hair, which was a perfectly normal thing to do in that age. The war was begun in the summer of 1546 by the Imperial cities of Ulm and Augsburg, both signatories to the League of Schmalkalden, but during the first few months nothing decisive came out of it. Notwithstanding the defection of the Saxon Duke, Archbishop von Wied continued to hope for the best and relaxed nothing of his efforts to Lutheranize Cologne. This pertinacity meant another long journey for Peter Canisius, as the clergy and university authorities decided to appeal to George of Austria, Prince-Bishop of Liége, who enjoyed the influence that comes of being the son of one emperor and the uncle of another. He became a bishop because emperors considered a mitre the most suitable decoration for their illegitimate male offspring. It was an uneasy time to stir abroad, but Peter, as usual, says nothing of his adventures. In Liége he devoted his leisure to preaching and lecturing, now that he had the authority of the priesthood to bear him out, and on Christmas Day was summoned without previous notice to regale the magnificent George and his Court with a sermon.[2] Afterwards, George regaled Peter with a banquet.

Then, in January, 1547, when the Emperor by brilliant strategy and magnificent courage had subdued nearly the whole of South Germany, Peter was directed to proceed to his camp at Geislingen in Württemberg.

[1] Armstrong, *The Emperor Charles V*, vol. ii, p. 136.
[2] Braunsberger, *Epistulae*, vol. i, pp. 233–4.

The distance from Liége to Geislingen is about three hundred miles by road, which, whether covered on foot or on horseback, must have been a sufficiently hazardous journey in the middle of war and winter. But Peter, in his two letters from Geislingen to Dr. Gropper, whom " he loved as a father " and revered as " the foremost and most fearless defender of religion," dismissed his adventures with a couple of Latin tags utterly unhelpful to an historian:

Geislingen, January 24, 1547.

JHESUS

The grace of Our Lord Jesus Christ be your protection, Reverend Sir, as it has been mine up to this hour. I arrived safely at the Emperor's camp, at least as far as my body is concerned. But while endeavouring to catch up with His Majesty I learned more than enough of the truth of those maxims, *Miseri qui castra sequuntur*, and, *Multa bellum habet inania*. Would to God that war was only a stupid thing and not a sink of all iniquity. The Emperor stayed two days at this place which is called Geislingen. It is only three miles from Ulm, whither the Legate, Verallo, had gone when I arrived here yesterday before dinner. I was, however, at once recognized and well received by Cardinal Truchsess, that most charming and illustrious man whose kindness I had first the happiness of experiencing at Worms. He wishes me now in token of his regard always to remain by him both in this town and in Ulm. I shall therefore be one of his household as long as your business keeps me in the Emperor's train. To come to news, Hermann von Wied has not sent any delegates to the Emperor. Personally I think it probable that they have gone to the Elector Palatine. As this Prince has recovered the Emperor's favour only with the greatest difficulty, he will not have had the heart for any plans against Cologne, especially as he has shown that he genuinely regrets his negotiations with Hermann.

When I had explained my mission to Granvelle, the Imperial Chancellor, he procured a writ summoning Manderscheid, Omphalius and other such abettors of the Archbishop to appear before the Emperor. As they show no signs of repentance for their temerity, you may now easily obtain justice at the Emperor's hands. . . . No priests in all Germany are more respected and honoured by His Majesty than the Cologne clergy, nor are there any more deserving of general public protection. As men of the highest rank and probity have given testimony to this effect, the clergy must henceforth put away all anxiety and confirm the brave people of Cologne in their holy resolution. It is not their cause alone that is in the balance but the cause of the whole Church. It is the cause of Jesus Christ, and from Him you will have your reward in proportion to what you expend in toil and money on His behalf. If to have obtained in your favour the sentence of the Supreme Pontiff and to have the support of all good and learned men be not enough, at least the Emperor's complete success in undertakings that seemed hopeless ought to inspire even despairing souls with the confidence of certain victory. The proud men of Frankfurt and the rebels of Ulm are now glad to be able to crawl as suppliants to the Emperor's feet. The powerful Duke of Württemberg is only too pleased to surrender, and haughty Augsburg exchanged its foolish dream of evangelical liberty for heavy servitude. Germany's strong and famous cities have now but one ambition, to be restored to the favour of the man whom they railed at as a tyrant and sought to destroy by their stubborn resistance and perfidious alliances. And shall one bishop, old in years but not in wisdom, who might well take for his crest a strutting peacock, stand out against you and against the true authority of his betters? Of what account are these feathered pretenders compared with the eagle that spreads his invincible wings on every wind of the world?[1] I am going on with the Emperor to Ulm and shall there explain everything to Mgr. Verallo. Further, with God's help I shall do my best to obtain a missive from His Majesty to Archbishop Hermann. . . . May God keep your Reverence and all the Cologne clergy.

Your servant,

P. Kanisius.[2]

Adolf von Schauenburg had recently been appointed to the See of Cologne in place of the deposed von Wied, and Peter explains in his second letter to Gropper the various negotiations with which he was busy on the new Archbishop's behalf. The long struggle was now practically over and Cologne had kept her faith. By a series of brilliant forced

---

[1] Peacocks formed part of the arms of the Dukes of Wied. A two-headed eagle displayed or with wings outspread was the device of the Habsburgs.

[2] Braunsberger, *Epistulae*, vol. i, pp. 234–7. Peter hated Ulm like poison, called it ' this Babylon' and wrote about it in the following terms to the Prior of the Cologne Carthusians : " Every vestige of piety seems to have completely disappeared. The churches, once famous for their ceremonies, are stripped of their statues, their altars, their relics, and there are no sacraments here any more. By I know not what just judgment of God, ecclesiastical property is given over to the most profane uses. The monasteries have no monks and now serve as places for sacrilegious love and incestuous intercourse. All this great city has not room for a single priest to expiate with the Holy Sacrifice the many terrible sins of the community."

marches Charles won the decisive victory of Mühlberg on April 24th, and made a prisoner of the brave Elector of Saxony. Thereupon Philip of Hesse surrendered, and before September 1, 1547, when the Diet of Augsburg opened, the Emperor was undisputed master of all Germany except the city of Magdeburg. That meant the total eclipse of poor, misguided Hermann, who, we may hope, had as little real malice in him as theology. Not during the whole course of the Reformation were more insidious and determined efforts made to capture any city for Protestantism than he made to capture Cologne, yet Cologne to-day, as always, is one of the most Catholic cities in the world. The story of her troubles, if not particularly exciting, at least enables us to study on a small and manageable scale the ideas and methods by which Protestantism was so successfully propagated elsewhere. Though Peter Canisius was far from being the principal hero of the resistance and played only a quiet and unobtrusive rôle, yet the city he loved was conscious of a bigger debt to him than might be considered owing from the few relevant documents now in existence. In these matters tradition and communal memory are safer guides than archives. At any rate, when he was canonized in 1925, Cologne honoured him as she had never honoured a citizen of hers before. Daily for a week the splendid ceremonies went on, in the Dom, St. Gereon's and sixteen other churches. Cardinal Schulte, successor to the office which, in his time, Hermann von Wied had betrayed, stood sponsor for the celebrations and with him were associated the Regierungspräsident, Siegmund Graf Adelmann, the Oberbürgermeister, Dr. Konrad Adenauer, and the then Chancellor of the German Reich, Dr. Marx. If the senators who had bullied Peter in 1544 could have come out of their graves for a few moments, how they would have stared !

CHAPTER III

ITALIAN INTERLUDE

DURING Peter's stay at Ulm in the spring of 1547 the question of his going to the Council of Trent came up again and this time the wishes of Cardinal Truchsess prevailed. Gropper was delighted with the news. " I am heartily pleased," he wrote to Peter, " that his Illustrious Lordship of Augsburg has persuaded you to go to Trent, as I am sure that you will be able to do our cause great service there. I beg you to send me the Acts of the Council when they appear. I am most anxious to see them, especially the Decree on Justification. . . . God keep and prosper you. *Tibi addictissimus*, Johann Gropper."[1] The part Peter played in this first phase of the Council of Trent was of small importance to anybody but himself. His time to help would not come till the last phase, sixteen years later. Nevertheless, his visit in 1547 deserves remembrance for the effect which it had on his outlook. Without reference to it, neither his hopes nor his subsequent achievements are properly understandable, for Trent polarized his thoughts as the Holy City where alone a divided Christendom might find its blessed vision of peace. There, too, he was brought into contact with great and good men of many nations, especially with the Spanish Jesuit, James Laynez, who had an enormous influence on his life. He learned at first hand the difficulties of a universal Church in a parochial world, and obtained a sobering insight into the queer mixture of motives with which much of the business of both Church and world is generally done. All this was very good for him, as well as the chance to investigate the most hopeful projects of disciplinary reform. In the course of time he would become the Council's greatest crusader in Northern Europe and so filled with its spirit that as somebody said, rhetorically but justly, if its decrees had been lost they might have

[1] Braunsberger, *Epistulae*, vol. i, pp. 244, 678. As pointed out in the preceding chapter, Gropper had private reasons for being interested in the Decree on Justification. It was promulgated on March 13, 1547, and included a condemnation of the theory of original sin and justification which he had put forward in his *Enchiridion*. He immediately submitted with all his heart. Hefele-Leclercq, *Histoire des Conciles*, vol. viii, pp. 1230–48.

been rediscovered engraved on his heart. Not a rhetorician but a well-known German Protestant historian recently wrote the following lines : " It may be that the decrees of Trent would have remained more or less a dead letter had not the Roman Curia found an auxiliary which made it its life's business to translate them into action—the Society of Jesus."[1] Now the Society of Jesus became established in Northern Germany through Peter Canisius, and for more than a score of years he was to be the great leader and inspirer of its activities. As the Council of Trent was the background of those activities, it is only right that we should endeavour to sketch it in here, particularly with reference to the part taken in it by the Jesuits.

When the number and size of the obstacles are considered, it must seem almost miraculous that the Council ever got beyond the stage of being a mere hope and proposal. Human imperfections and folly of every kind thwarted its progress at one time or another, the fears of the Pope and his Curia, the pride of the King of France, the Emperor's ambition, the prejudice of the Protestants, and the national rivalries of the conciliar Fathers themselves. Luther wanted it only so long as the Pope appeared reluctant, and the Protestants in general refused to co-operate except on their own impossible terms. At Rome the Curia was strongly opposed because, like all bureaucracies, it cherished the *status quo* in which alone vested interests are secure. Catholics generally were apathetic or sceptical, remembering the comparative futility of councils in the previous century, and the Popes, remembering another thing about them, wondered anxiously whether a new one would not revive the old disputes of Constance and Basle on the subject of their supremacy.

These, however, were minor difficulties. The real hindrance lay in the rooted, immitigable antagonism between the rulers of France and Germany, the same antagonism that cut short the Vatican Council in 1870. Before his death, in 1534, Pope Clement VII had made some half-hearted attempts to win the consent of King Francis, but Francis would not agree to anything which his detested rival, the Emperor, desired. Between Clement and Charles, likewise, no love was lost, so the strange, sad result of the negotiations was a Franco-Papal *entente* that led indirectly to the destruction of Catholicism in many parts of Germany. The next Pope, Paul III, promised better, but he, too, like his predecessor, had a powerful family, the Farnese, to hamper his good intentions and make bad blood between himself and the Emperor. Nevertheless, after fruitless

[1] Viktor Bibl, *Maximilian II, der rätselhafte Kaiser* (Hellerau bei Dresden, 1929), p. 112.

overtures to the Protestants, he issued a bull in 1536 summoning the Council to meet the following year at Mantua. Luther and his disciples replied with the " Schmalkalden Articles " in which that " sacrilegious Judas or Pope " was informed that they would accept this Council only if it recognized the doctrine of justification by faith alone, abolished the Mass, alienated to secular uses all foundations for private Masses and abrogated for ever the papal claims to supremacy.[1] As Luther was about to depart from the assembly of Schmalkalden in his carriage, he raised his hand in benediction over the theologians and princes, saying : " May the Lord fill you with His blessing and with hatred of the Pope."

With minds so disposed the Council could obviously do little to heal the wounds of Christendom, and accordingly the years passed without anything happening except frequent renewals of the papal bull of convocation. For one thing it was impossible to get the interested parties to agree on a locality. The Protestants would listen to no proposals that took the Council out of Germany, on which point the Emperor heartily agreed with them. Sincere Catholic though he was, Charles knew and cared next to nothing about theological questions. What he wanted was a Council that would restore discipline and bring the Protestants back to external communion with the Church, whatever they might privately continue to think about her doctrines. To ensure this programme he was determined to have the Council on German soil, and the Pope was naturally equally determined to have it off it, if possible. Nowhere in France would do, for, besides the opposition of the King of that country to a Council anywhere, the German bishops could never be got to congregate except under the protecting wings of the Habsburg eagle. Spain was out of the question for a variety of reasons, so there was only Italy left if the Pope was to keep the least measure of independence.

Eventually, after long and delicate negotiations, the Catholic parties, with the exclusion of the King of France, agreed upon Trent in Tirol, as it was technically a German city and yet predominantly Italian in population and sufficiently near the Italian border to ease the worst apprehensions of the Pope. To be a Pope with a conscience in those days was to be always on the rack. Show friendship to Francis and Charles became an enemy ; let Charles have his way and Francis would threaten schism. It was in conditions such as these, with Europe a perfect bedlam of hatreds

---

[1] *Articuli qui nostrae partis nomine exhibendi fuerant in Concilio Mantuae.* Published, Wittenberg, 1539. All the chief Lutherans subscribed their names without reservation, except Melanchthon, who added : " De papa autem sentio si evangelium permitteret pacis atque communis concordiae gratia, propter Christianos qui vel jam vel deinceps sub ipso futuri essent, ei superioritatem super episcopos quam alioqui habet, jure humano, etiam a nobis relinqui posse."

and intrigues, that Paul III reissued his bull in May, 1542: "Seeing with profound sorrow of soul the affairs of Christendom go daily from bad to worse, Hungary beleaguered by the Turks, Germany falling away, and all other nations cowering in fear and affliction, we have determined, independently of the consent of any monarch, to consult only the good of the Church and the will of the Most High." Then "one by one and at long intervals," a few bishops began to arrive in Trent, pathetically isolated and without power to achieve anything while the Emperor and the King of France kept the world in a state of panic. After a few months of waiting they were instructed to return home and three more years passed before another attempt could be made. On the eve of the new venture, in March, 1545, Luther issued his famous pastoral, *Against the Papacy of Rome founded by the Devil*, telling "the vicious scandalous knaves and cursed dregs of the devil at Rome, together with His Hellishness the Pope of Sodomites, to go to hell for ever," and expressing a desire "to curse them so that thunder and lightning would strike them, hell-fire burn them, the plague, syphilis, epilepsy, scurvy, leprosy, carbuncles and all manner of diseases attack them." This outburst was followed by the tract entitled, *Abbildung des Papstum*, consisting of verses by Luther to woodcuts by Cranach so gross in conception that German Protestants ever since have done their best to suppress them or hide them away for the sake of their master's reputation.[1]

At long last, on December 13, 1545, the host of difficulties had been sufficiently overcome to permit of the definitive opening of the Council. The Fathers present at the first sessions were four cardinals, four archbishops, and twenty-one bishops, a pathetic muster that the Papal Legate would not allow to describe itself as "*universalem Ecclesiam repraesentans*." These men, whose numbers, of course, increased very considerably as time went on, alone had votes and with them rested the responsibility for all doctrinal and disciplinary decisions. They were the Fathers of the Council proper, consisting, when everything was in due canonical shape, of bishops, abbots, and heads of religious orders. Before they registered their votes in solemn session on a particular point it had to be discussed, investigated and debated from every angle by a band of competent theologians and canonists. Each bishop brought his own experts with him and others were sent by the Pope, the Emperor, and

---

[1] There is a copy in the British Museum. Paquier in the introduction to his French translation of Denifle's monumental work on Luther gives an amusing account of the shifts to which he was put in his endeavours to gain access to the *Abbildung* in German libraries. As Luther has never been a saint in the English calendar, the British Museum let him have the book without demur.

various Catholic princes. From the outset the newly-founded Society of Jesus had some of its members at the Council in this capacity of spade-workers. Father Claude Lejay arrived in Trent a few days after the solemn opening as ' procurator ' of Cardinal Truchsess. For a long time he and another priest from Augsburg were the only German representatives in the assembly, as the bishops of that country could not or would not leave their dioceses for reasons good, bad and indifferent—chiefly bad and indifferent. The credentials of the pair were ample enough, for Truchsess had guaranteed " with his hand upon his heart to ratify and confirm what-ever should be said, done or brought about " by them at the Council.[1] During the early sessions Lejay enjoyed some peculiar privileges not accorded to any other priest then or afterwards. Thus he was permitted to state his views in precedence of the abbots and generals of religious orders, whereas other procurators might not speak at all except to present the excuses of their masters. For some time, too, he had the honour, though only a simple theologian, of debating on equal terms with the bishops. The Diary of the secretary of the Council, Angelo Massarelli, shows what good use he made of his privileges, to the satisfaction, it is said, of all who listened to him.

On May 16, 1546, Laynez and Salmeron, two of the first companions of St. Ignatius, arrived in Trent. They came as the special theologians of the Pope, selected by St. Ignatius, at the express wish of His Holiness, " after three days recourse to God by prayers and Masses."[2] Laynez at this time was thirty-four years old and Salmeron thirty-one. Their friend-ship dated from boyhood, when they were students together at Alcalá, and their names, as inseparably linked as those of David and Jonathan, are the best known of any theologians who figured in the debates of Trent. Before their departure for that city they had received the following instruc-tions from St. Ignatius, in which he writes, according to his custom, as though he were himself in the position of the persons addressed :

I should be slow to speak and should do so only after reflection and in a friendly spirit, particularly when a decision is to be given about matters before the Council or afterwards to be discussed by it. Rather should I profit by listening quietly in order to learn the frame

---

[1] Ehses, *Concilii Tridentini actorum pars prima* (1904), p. 441. The great collection of the documents of Trent to which this huge, magnificently edited volume belongs was begun in 1901 under the auspices of the Görres-Gesellschaft, a German academy of Catholic scholars. Several volumes have been published but the series is not yet complete. They render obsolete in a greater or less degree all the histories and appreciations of the Council that were written before their appearance.

[2] M.H., *Monumenta Ignatiana*, series prima, vol. i, pp. 359, 381.

of mind, the feelings and the intentions of the speakers, so that I might
be the better able to answer in my turn, or to keep silent. When speaking
about matters of controversy, it is advisable to enumerate the reasons
on both sides that you may not appear prejudiced, nor must you allow
yourself to give anybody cause for complaint. I should not mention
the names of authors in my discourse, especially if they be men of
consequence, unless I had first considered the matter thoroughly, and
should keep on friendly terms with all, without favouritism. If the
matters under discussion are so obviously right and just that one neither
could nor should remain silent, I should then give my opinion with
the greatest possible composure and humility, and conclude with
salvo meliori judicio. Finally, should I wish to speak in a discussion
on such a subject as acquired or infused qualities, it would be a great
help not to consider my own leisure, nor to hurry for lack of time,
that is to say, not to think of my personal convenience at all but rather
to adapt myself to the convenience and condition of the person with
whom I seek to deal that so I may influence him, to the greater glory
of God.

Our Fathers going to Trent will best promote the greater glory
of God among souls by preaching, hearing confessions, lecturing,
teaching children, setting a good example, visiting the poor in the
hospitals and exhorting the neighbour. In such works each should
strive according to his particular talent to encourage as much as possible
the spirit of prayer and devotion, in order that all may beg God Our
Lord mercifully to pour forth His Divine Spirit on those who are
engaged with the business of the Council. In preaching, I should not
touch upon matters that are in controversy between the Protestants
and the Catholics, but simply exhort the people to lead a good life and
practise the devotions of the Church. I should move them to acquire
a knowledge of their own hearts and a greater knowledge and love
of their Creator and Lord, appealing to the intellect. While hearing
confessions I should address my penitents in such words as might
afterwards be repeated publicly by them, and impose as their penance
some prayers for the Council. In giving the *Spiritual Exercises* and at
all other times I should speak as I would do before the world at large,
and I should not give more than the First Week of the *Exercises*, except
in the rare cases of people who were ready to order their lives according
to the rules for making an election.[1] Here also prayers for the Council

[1] These rules are to be found at the end of the second ' week ' of the *Spiritual Exercises*.

ought to be recommended. The teaching of children should be undertaken when opportunity offers, bearing in mind the preparedness and dispositions of both master and pupil. It will be well to start at the beginning and develop subjects in a greater or less degree according to the ability of the scholars, and at the end of the lesson or exhortation there should be prayers for the Council. The hospitals should be visited at such times of the day as are best for health, and you should hear the confessions of the poor people, comfort them, and also bring them little presents whenever you can, not forgetting prayers for the Council. . . .[1]

How that little phrase 'prayers for the Council' pulsates through the message of Ignatius! His sons were not slow to divine the longings and holy hopes that inspired it and set themselves with filial enthusiasm to bring them to fruition. On their arrival in Trent they were graciously received by the Papal Legates. Cardinal Cervini, who had then a little nephew aged four named Robert Bellarmine, offered them the hospitality of his palace, but they preferred to go and lodge with Lejay at the common guest-house of St. Elizabeth. From the first there was plenty for them to do, as the Council had attracted to Trent tramps, beggars, disbanded soldiery and unfortunates of every description. These poor wretches camped as best they could outside the city walls until some charitable cardinals found them a refuge. Touched with pity, the Jesuits promptly constituted themselves guardians of this institution and, having procured a list of all the prelates and important officials in the city, approached each in turn, beginning with the cardinals, to solicit alms for their charges. As a result of their begging campaign, Laynez was able to report to Ignatius in September, 1546, that they had "provided clothes for seventy-six poor people, giving each a shirt, a smock, leggings and boots." The clothes were a difficulty, as the Fathers soon found that the incorrigibles were using them for stakes in an improvised gambling den. They solved the problem by giving garments of such make that they could not be wagered away without leaving their former owners in a state of nature unsuited to the climate of the Tirolese Alps.[2] Each of the Fathers went weekly in turn to say Mass for the poor people, and afterwards cheered them up and taught them the truths of the Faith with great earnestness. The sick of the city were also constantly visited and consoled by the three, but with "other great matters," they wrote jointly to Ignatius,

[1] M.H., *Monumenta Ignatiana*, series prima, vol. i, pp. 386–9.
[2] M.H., *Lainii Monumenta*, vol. i, p. 49; *Salmeronis Epistolae*, vol. i, p. 23.

" we do not concern ourselves except in so far as we are bidden."[1] The many theologians of various religious orders present at Trent were prohibited by the Presidents of the Council from preaching in public, but an exception was made in favour of Laynez and Salmeron, as they were the Pope's special officers. Laynez accordingly occupied the pulpit of Sta. Maria Maggiore every Sunday and feast-day, his audience being composed largely of the Fathers and officials of the Council. On one occasion Salmeron preached so admirably before the same distinguished gathering that they required him to have his sermon printed and published, an honour that came the way of no other Tridentine orator who spoke outside the sessions.[2]

St. Ignatius was not ambitious for his sons to shine as great lights of the Council. Other things being equal, he preferred them to keep in the background and do good in unobtrusive ways. It was not long, however, before the Papal Legates and the bishops discovered from hearing them preach that they were no less learned and prudent than charitable. They were then called upon to take their place in the assembly of theologians to whom were submitted points of doctrine for preliminary discussion. At first there was very little order in the theologians' debates. They spoke as the spirit moved them and some of them had shocked the Legates by highly unorthodox pronouncements. To remedy this state of affairs Cardinal Cervini arranged that one of the two Jesuits should be given an opportunity to voice his opinion early in the discussions and that the other should always speak at the end in order to be able to refute whatever less estimable views had been given an airing. This and other matters are explained in a private letter from Salmeron to Ignatius, July 10, 1546 :

Our Lord has given us grace to speak in such a way before the Legates, bishops and theologians as to afford them all much satisfaction. Another way in which we were useful was this. The views expressed by some of the theologians were not sound, so at Cardinal Cervini's suggestion and with his approval one of us took to speaking among the first in the discussions, while the other kept himself in reserve till the end for the special purpose of refuting any dangerous opinions that might be ventilated. Moreover, we can honestly say that we have the love and esteem of all the prelates of the three nations, Italy, Spain, and France, and they are jealous if we do not visit them. The Spaniards,

[1] M.H., *Salmeronis Epistolae*, vol. i, p. 16.
[2] M.H., Polanco, *Chronicon*, vol. i, p. 181. Polanco was the secretary of St. Ignatius, and his *Chronicon* is a valuable annalistic history of the early Jesuits.

who were at first the most unfriendly towards us, are now the loudest
in our praises. They invite us to dine with them that we may give
them hints for their next speeches in the congregations. Many prelates
learned in theology explain their views to us before giving them out
in public in order to have our criticism, and others learned in various
faculties but not in theology require us to tell them word for word
what they shall say in the discussions. Cardinal Cervini who bears
on his shoulders the weight of these sacred labours shows the completest confidence in our judgment on matters of dogma and makes
use of our services in the drawing up of decrees. . . .[1]

The apparent boastfulness of this letter was really only an affectionate
effort of Salmeron's to encourage Ignatius, whom he knew to be anxious
about the continuance of his Society. The Jesuits were so little known
in those days that they were constantly being confused with other religious
orders. In the documents of the Council of Trent itself they are sometimes listed as secular priests. There was a very definite feeling among
the Fathers against the introduction of new orders, and legislation to
give it effect was part of the Council's programme. Knowing this, Ignatius
was naturally anxious that his men should make a good impression. How
good it was comes out in the reference which Salmeron makes to the
attitude of the Spanish bishops. They were at first plainly hostile, and
as "sensitive people"—gente cosquillósa—much resented the patched
and worn garments in which their two countrymen appeared before the
international assembly, thus lowering Spain in the eyes of the foreigners.
The unfortunate pair had nothing better to put on, but their minds were
so richly apparelled that when the bishops had heard them speak their
attitude changed forthwith to one of pride and satisfaction that not even
a shabby cassock could long conceal the glory of God's own Peninsula.[2]

Having now made the acquaintance of our three Jesuits, we may turn
to take a brief glance at the work of the Council. The first question we
might feel inclined to ask is why the Fathers devoted their attention to
such themes as justification, original sin, the Mass, indulgences, etc., for
had not all these matters been dealt with long before in other councils?
The answer would be, yes and no. Other councils had dealt with and
defined certain aspects of the doctrines, according as the need arose, but
not by any means did they clear up all the obscurity surrounding them.

[1] M.H., *Salmeronis Epistolae*, vol. i, pp. 26–7.
[2] M.H., *Salmeronis Epistolae*, vol. i, p. 19; Orlandinus, *Historia Societatis Jesu* (Cologne, 1615),
lib. vi, n. 23.

Catholic definitions were formulated usually, throughout the history of the Church, in answer to heretical challenges. Until the challenge comes, the Church, as a rule, is content to leave the issues open to her theologians, only interfering when some school or party goes counter to what might be described as the general instinct of her children. In the sixteenth century her traditional, though in many respects, undefined doctrines, and the practices that had arisen out of them, were challenged over a wide front by the Protestant Confession of Augsburg. As an exposition of belief that famous document contained much positive teaching on original sin, justification, Scripture, faith, the Church, the sacraments, good works, and the communion of saints, which did not square with the defined or long and generally accepted beliefs within the Catholic fold. On the negative side, the Confession denounced as abuses the denial of the chalice to the laity at Communion, clerical celibacy, private Masses, auricular confession, monastic vows, the obligation on priests of saying the Divine Office, indulgences, pilgrimages, fasting and abstinence, and various other practices alleged to be based on mere human unscriptural foundations.

This was the gage which the Council of Trent took up, the vast syllabus of doctrinal opinion which it had to put to the test of Scripture and Tradition. How thoroughly and conscientiously the Fathers went to work may be appreciated from the fact that they devoted no less than sixty-one general congregations and forty-four others, each occupying from three to six hours, to the single question of justification. Between July and October, 1546, three different drafts of the proposed decree on justification were drawn up, discussed word by word, and finally rejected. Far from being in any hurry to condemn a theory merely because it had Protestant patronage, the Fathers listened attentively while one of the most eminent among them, the holy and learned Girolamo Seripando, pleaded eloquently for the view that a double justice is necessary to salvation, the traditional inherent justice of Catholic theology *and* an imputed justice not unlike the kind championed with much force and ability by Martin Luther. This was the theory about whose fate Gropper had manifested his anxiety to Peter Canisius. It had much that was attractive in it, and many good men besides Gropper hoped that it might prove a *vinculum pacis*. But the only thing that mattered, after all, was its truth or falsity. To all the arguments urged in favour of it there sat and listened, utterly unconvinced, " a little pale-faced man, with big, bright eyes and a long aquiline nose." When his turn came to speak, on October 26th, this man, James Laynez, got up and delivered perhaps the most devastating speech heard during the whole course of the Council. The massed learning and sheer deadly logic of it rang the death-knell of the double justice theory, as far as Catholicism was concerned. So deeply impressed were the Legates and Fathers that they requested to have Laynez's speech in the form of a written treatise, and thus elaborated it was included word for word in the Acts of the Council, the one and only document from any Father's or theologian's pen to be so honoured.[1]

Parallel with the doctrinal discussions and decisions of the Council went others of scarcely less importance on questions of discipline and practical reform. In their very first proclamation to the Catholic world the Fathers had clearly stated their twofold aim: The extirpation of heresies and the reformation of morals. Monarchs and politicians more interested in the secular advancement of their realms than in purity of doctrine might wish and endeavour to prevent theological decisions, but the Church, conscious of her divine commission as the teacher of nations, held serenely on her way, reaffirming every article of belief that had been assailed and condemning fearlessly every contrary dogma of the assailants. She was not to be browbeaten by pressure from without into disavowing her immemorial dogmatic convictions, any more than she was to be cajoled by pressure from within into acceptance of disciplinary abuses. She would state her beliefs unequivocally once again but she would also mend the manners of her children. Thus during the fifth session, which began in May, 1546, the very necessary reform of the pulpit was the subject of lively debates, and a decree was published calling upon all ecclesiastical rulers and other prelates of the Church to preach the Gospel themselves, or, if hindered legitimately, to provide worthy substitutes. Parish priests were put under a strict obligation to explain the faith to their flocks on all Sundays and feast-days, and the regular clergy were forbidden the pulpit until they had obtained their bishop's sanction and a testimonial of good conduct from their superiors. To bear out all this sound legislation, provision was made for the expert instruction of priests in the Holy Scriptures. After the great Decree on Justification had been passed unanimously, another followed on such vital questions as the qualifications of nominees to bishoprics, the duty of bishops to reside in their dioceses and carry out canonical visitations, the maintenance and repair of churches, the conferring of Orders, the care of hospitals, and the evils of pluralism.

[1] Pallavicino, *Istoria del Concilio di Trento*, lib. xviii, cap. xv; Astrain, *Historia de la Compañía de Jesús*, vol. i, p. 534 and note. The disputation has been finely edited in modern times by Hartmann Grisar, *Jacobi Lainez Disputationes Tridentinae* (Innsbruck, 1886), vol. ii, pp. 153–92.

It was on the day of these auspicious events, March 3, 1547, that Peter Canisius walked weary and travel-stained through the gates of Trent, with a letter in his pocket from Cardinal Truchsess warmly commending him to Cardinal Cervini. He had had his first experience of what travellers of the time used to refer to with feeling as " the Purgatory of the Alps," but, as we have now learned to expect, he says nothing whatever about it in his correspondence. His route was from Ulm to Kempten in southern Bavaria, thence to Innsbruck, and from Innsbruck over the Brenner Pass to Brixen, after which he followed the valley of the Etsch or Adige to his destination. The Lutheran, Sastrow, made exactly the same journey the previous April and relates in his Memoirs that a mile from Kempten two huge, hungry-looking wolves were waiting for him, but he escaped them and reached the town trembling from the encounter. There he was warned " not to venture alone in those mountains where wild beasts and murderers prevailed." He did venture, however, and was rewarded for his courage with a splendid feast of music provided by the Tridentine Fathers, of all people. "At Easter," runs his account, "I heard most delicious singing in the Trent churches. I have heard the musicians of Duke Ulrich of Württemberg (and they were a source of pride with him), of the Elector of Saxony, of the King of the Romans, not to mention those of the Emperor, but what a difference ! Old men, with beards almost reaching to their waists, sang the upper notes with a purity and skill fit to compare with those of the most accomplished youngster."[1]

One could wish that St. Peter had treated his friends to such attractive details with which wide and varied experience must have richly stored his memory. But, as we know, he was not the type of person to comment on his private adventures, or on the strangeness and beauty of the scenes through which he passed. He was too much absorbed with invisible realities, and in his deepest heart he had come to care seriously about one thing alone, which was to revive the dormant but indestructible genius of Catholicism. With his introduction to Laynez and Salmeron he numbered five of the first companions of St. Ignatius among his intimate friends, high privilege for one so young, and a rare opportunity too, on the threshold of his career as a Jesuit. Favre was a saint pure and simple ; Lejay, a man of great holiness with an extremely attractive human

---

[1] *Social Germany in Luther's Time* (London, 1902), p. 143. This book is a translation of portions of Sastrow's Memoirs. News of Luther's death reached Rome while Sastrow was staying there in 1546. The people at the inn where he lodged spent the evening telling stories to Luther's discredit and otherwise reviling his memory, all except one, a procurator of the Rota, who kept murmuring to himself while the others talked, " O Jesu Fili Dei, miserere mei ! " Peter Canisius passed over the event in complete silence.

Alfonso Salmeron

Diego Laynez

personality; and Laynez, a profound thinker and scholar, somewhat dour and unsmiling, perhaps, but so straight, true, generous, and utterly lowly-minded that it was easy to forget the absence of more facile charms. Of him and Salmeron Peter wrote to the Roman Jesuits shortly after arriving in Trent: " I can sincerely and impartially testify that among the many men of profound and various learning who debate here . . . none are more esteemed or eagerly heard than Laynez and Salmeron."[1] Particulars of the work of the two, with which Peter himself was associated, are given in the following letter of Lejay to St. Ignatius :

At the present time two congregations are being held every day, one of prelates in the morning to deal with questions of ecclesiastical discipline, and another of theologians in the afternoon to discuss doctrine and examine false views concerning the Sacraments in general, Baptism and Confirmation. All have now said their say, and by the grace of Our Lord our companions Laynez and Salmeron have expressed their views in the most admirable manner. Certainly I do not think that there is anybody more trusted by Cardinal Cervini than those two, nor any to whom he shows greater marks of esteem. His latest commission to them was to extract from various works the errors of the heretics on all matters of faith. When they had finished their task the Cardinal Legate placed the results before a congregation, and then instructed them to make a similar catalogue of the decrees and passages of councils, Popes and Doctors of the Church wherein those errors are condemned. We have every reason to be grateful to Our Lord Jesus Christ for having deigned to use our Fathers' services in matters of such importance, to a greater extent, I believe, than those of any other theologians.

Father Laynez continues his preaching, but will stop during Lent, as it is the custom here to have only one preacher for all the Lenten discourses. Indeed the Father has sore need of rest from study and preaching for some days, as he looks to me quite exhausted and run down. But it is not easy to get him to stop work, however necessary the rest may be. Yesterday I begged him to put away his books for three or four days. As for Salmeron, it is just as difficult to lure him away from his labours.[2]

[1] M.H., Polanco, *Chronicon*, vol. i, p. 214.
[2] M.H., *Epistolae PP. Broetii, Jaii*, etc., pp. 332–3. Lejay at this time had a serious trouble of his own, as Ferdinand I, King of the Romans, was trying to coerce him into accepting the bishopric of Trieste.

It may be doubted whether the Spanish pair could have got through their laborious task of cataloguing Protestant doctrines from authoritative sources had their young German colleague not been at hand to assist them. Many outstanding treatises of the Reformation were published in German, of which language neither Laynez nor Salmeron knew a syllable. All that part of the programme must accordingly have fallen to Peter, and what a grind it was may easily be imagined. Are there any books ever printed quite so repellent to the touch and the eye and the mind as the Gothic-lettered theological lucubrations of the sixteenth century? The labours of the three men and the general work of the Council were carried on under increasingly great difficulties. Seven sessions had been completed, each involving an immense amount of study, debate and careful organization, when further progress was rendered impossible by renewed misunderstandings between the Pope and the Emperor. Spotted fever had broken out in Trent to complicate the situation, and there was peril, too, from the marauding soldiery of the Schmalkalden League. The Legates therefore decided to remove the Council to Bologna, in the Papal States, where Charles could not so easily employ his coercive tactics. On hearing the news, he described the Pope as " an obstinate old man working for the destruction of the Church," but the truth is that neither His Majesty nor His Holiness was now worrying so much about the interests of the Church as about the fortunes of their respective families. The victory of Mühlberg, won at this time, April, 1547, by his own brave right arm, raised Charles to the pinnacle of his power. It became plain at once that he had no intention of forcibly suppressing Protestantism, as he had promised to do, but the Pope unfortunately did not understand his very good reason, which was the utter impossibility of the task.

The crisis placed Lejay and Peter Canisius in a very awkward position because, as the delegates of a German prelate, they felt obliged to remain on in Trent with the Spanish bishops and other adherents of the Emperor. By dint of earnest pleading, however, they succeeded in obtaining permission to follow Laynez and Salmeron who had gone to Bologna. On his way to the new seat of the Council, Salmeron had fallen ill at Padua, and there Lejay and Canisius found him in a dying condition, but " resigned with full joy and content to the most holy will of God."[1] Owing to the munificence of a Venetian gentleman the Jesuits had been enabled to open a college at Padua, of which Canisius gave a very glowing account to his Cologne friends on April 12, 1547:

[1] M.H., *Salmeronis Epistolae*, vol. i, p. 38.

My dearest brothers, I am in so very little danger of forgetting you that I seize every pretext for sending you a few lines. This I do for fear my previous letters may not have reached you. I cannot tell you how much delight and edification I get every day from my observation of the men here. They strive one and all with common effort to obey and serve in everything, and no one is ever satisfied with his own deeds or desires. So wonderful and lovely to see is the order of this house that I doubt whether you would find better discipline in the best of monasteries. And yet there are none of the usual monastic sanctions of cells, hair shirts and long fasts, for all would rather do whatever task has to be done through the sweet compulsion of love and promptitude of obedience than through any fear of penalties or penances.[1]

The Paduan Fathers, for their part, were greatly pleased with Peter's visit. " He made a very learned speech one day this week," a member of the community wrote to Cologne. " On Easter Sunday he left for Bologna with our Father James Laynez. I know that you are all longing to have Master Peter back with you. . . . He has written to you several times." Their patient, Salmeron, was physically tough, and soon made a very good recovery to live to a hale old age. " I know in very truth," he told St. Ignatius, " the affection and paternal love with which your Reverence has us written on your heart, and I hold for certain that it was your prayers and those of my brothers that obtained for me from Our Lord what the doctors could not bring about with all their experiments and medicines."[2]

Owing to the Emperor's hostile attitude, the Presidents of the Council decided to postpone the promulgation of further decrees, and to concentrate at Bologna on the discussions concerning the Sacraments that had begun before they left Trent. Into this high argument Peter Canisius found himself drawn. He had learned enough Italian to speak publicly in that language at the meetings of the theologians, which, incidentally, was a very unusual accomplishment for a northerner in those days, and at home in his rooms he diligently sought out, in books that he had procured from Cologne, such testimonies of ancient faith as would help in the drafting of dogmatic decrees.[3] In both his *Diary* and *Acta* Massarelli, the secretary of the Council, mentions him and his religious brethren a number of times. The following are specimens of the highly compressed and sometimes highly confusing entries :

[1] Braunsberger, *Epistulae*, vol. i, pp. 246–7.   [2] M.H., *Salmeronis Epistolae*, vol. i, p. 38.
[3] Braunsberger, *Epistulae*, vol. i, pp. 250–2.

April 23. At the twentieth hour[1] a congregation of the minor
theologians was held to discuss the same fourteen articles about the
Sacrament of Penance. Five men spoke, namely Peter Canisius of
the Society of Jesus, a German; Brother John Anthony Delphinus,
Vicar General of the Conventual Franciscans; Brother Augustine of
Montecalcino, an Augustinian; Brother Barletanus of the Conventual
Franciscans, a Paduan; and Father James Laynez of the Society of
Jesus. As the congregation closed at half past six, Father Laynez had
not time to finish his oration and put off the rest of it to a future occasion.
The Most Reverend Cardinal Cervini presided and there were twenty-
six prelates in attendance, as well as many doctors and masters.

The first to speak was Don Peter Canisius, of the Society of Jesus:
He proved the doctrine of confession from various authorities and to
these he added the parable of the Prodigal Son who on his return to his
father said: "I have sinned against heaven and before thee." The fatted
calf that was killed for him might be taken as a symbol of Christ and His
Passion whose merits are applied to the penitent confessing his sins.

May 6. At the nineteenth hour there was a congregation of theolo-
gians on the same three sacraments. To-day five men spoke, namely
Brother Maurus of Ravenna, a Canon Regular; Father Claude Lejay,
Procurator of the Most Reverend Lord Otto, Cardinal of Augsburg;
Brother John Baptist Moncalvius, a Conventual; Brother Clement of
Florence, of the same Order; and Father Peter Canisius of the Society
of Jesus. The Congregation lasted four hours. Cardinal Cervini
presided and there were eighteen bishops present and many theologians.
Brother Maurus of Ravenna discoursed on the Sacrament of Order,
Claude Lejay on Matrimony, John Baptist Moncalvius on the same,
Brother Clement of Florence on Orders, and finally Father Peter
Canisius again on Matrimony. He judged that the articles now proposed
are all heretical in tendency because clandestine marriages cannot be
invalidated. A marriage of whatever kind, contracted by Christians
and consummated, cannot be rendered invalid by anybody, not even
by the Church herself, according to those words of Christ, "Whom
God hath joined together let no man put asunder." Wherefore St.
Paul said, "A woman is bound by the law as long as her husband
liveth, etc."

---

[1] The Italian 'day' in that era began with the Ave Maria bell at sunset. Consequently the
twentieth hour would be about three o'clock in the afternoon according to modern European
reckoning.

May 15. *Sunday.* After dinner I visited Fathers Claude, James and Alphonsus of the Society of Jesus, and showed them the censures on the canons with regard to the Eucharist. We discussed the censures for four hours, and I reported the results to Cardinal Cervini.

June 4. *Saturday.* The canons on the Sacrament of Penance were drafted for examination during the coming session. I showed them to Fathers Alphonsus, James, and Claude of the Society of Jesus, and to Brother Peter Paul Januarius of the Order of Preachers.[1]

A week after the last visit of Massarelli to the Jesuits, June 11, 1547, the Legates decided to prorogue the ninth session of the Council indefinitely, as there seemed to be little hope of overcoming the Emperor's opposition. Accordingly, with Cardinal Cervini's permission, Laynez and Canisius left Bologna for Florence on June 17th. A few days later Laynez was preaching in the Duomo to three thousand people and shortly afterwards expounding the Scriptures from the same famous pulpit to equally large congregations.[2] The Catholics of those days must have had cultivated tastes, for Scripture lectures were a regular feature in the ministry of most big churches. St. Paul's Epistle to the Romans formed the *pièce de résistance*, owing to its central importance in Reformation controversies. The number of discourses on this deep and difficult theme delivered by Jesuits to congregations of quite ordinary men and women would astonish modern lovers of twelve o'clock Mass who go to sleep under anything more intellectual than a simple homily. What Peter Canisius did with himself during that July and August, except, perhaps, perspire and improve acquaintance with the great Laynez, is not recorded. He hated the Italian heat, small blame to him, and begged his Cologne brethren to pray that he might either die at once or be recalled to Germany. Instead, he was summoned to Rome by St. Ignatius, while Laynez set off to preach, teach, and succour distress in Perugia, Siena, Padua, Venice, Bologna, Naples, Palermo, Monreale, and 'a camp in Africa.' The hundred and fifty miles to Rome with "those sunbeams like swords" drilling into one all the time must have been a hard purgatory for a man used to the reasonable summer ardours of Holland and Germany. But how well worth while it was

---

[1] Merkle, *Concilii Tridentini diariorum pars quarta*, pp. 644, 649, 652, 660 ; Braunsberger, *Epistulae*, vol. i, pp. 684–5. If Massarelli reported him accurately, Peter's views on clandestine marriages were mistaken. He may have obtained them from Laynez, who had gone astray on the same point. The Council of Trent did, in fact, invalidate clandestine marriages.

[2] M.H., *Litterae quadrimestres*, vol. i, pp. 45–6. These letters, containing accounts of Jesuit activities in various lands, were sent to Rome by local superiors every four months.

appears in a letter which Peter wrote from Rome some months later, November 20, 1547, to a Dutch friend, a canon of Zutphen, who had recently joined the Cologne Jesuits and was undecided whether he should stay with them:

JHESUS.

DEAREST BROTHER ANDREW,

May the grace of Our Lord Jesus Christ kindle and keep perfect in us all worthy desires, Amen. Separated as we are by such long distances, we must find our mutual consolation while apart in the one great, beautiful source, our rule of obedience. It is this that to our immense advantage keeps you in Germany, busy against your natural inclination with the study of law, and that severs me, who have but lately come to Italy, from your dear company, and from my country, unhappy restless Germany, though to be out of that upheaval is very good for one's soul. I wish I could explain to you with my tongue or pen the gladness which floods my soul, that you might understand, dear friend, how I am progressing before God, and also rejoice with me in spirit over this new good fortune of mine to be living here in such happy circumstances. You can imagine what a joy it is, after seeing at the Council so many great men, after the most intimate companionship with the chief fathers of our Order, after experiencing the wonders of many places and societies, to be now, as the crown of it all, one in heart and daily custom of life with the chosen company of our brothers here and with that best of men, our Father Ignatius. Others give all their days and dreams to the pursuit of gain or the acquisition of learning, and their toil, if not fruitless, is heavy, anxious and full of peril, while I live here in wisdom's home, apprenticed to humility and a pupil in the splendid school of obedience and every virtue. Here at work I would fain stay always, even if no tie of obedience bound me. . . .

Come then, brother mine, do you, too, take the road to Rome and share with us here, in the Lord, the exercises of holy humility and apostolic obedience. . . . You need have no fear that you will lose the opportunity to complete your studies. Our Reverend Father in Christ, Ignatius, will very gladly see to that in due course, for he is one who overlooks nothing that pertains to the greater glory of God and the spiritual welfare of his sons. Let it be your endeavour to bring with you a keen, submissive, simple heart, passing over all honour, security, reputation and private interest for the lowly service of obedience. Believe me, with the love of Christ crucified in your heart nothing in this life will seem to you hard or burdensome. Have you not experienced throughout life God's goodness and power always operative in your regard? He will not fail you now when you set forth on your travels in His Name, but will be the faithful guide and guardian of your steps. He never abandons His own, and even if the world despises them it is only for a little while; if they suffer in this brief life it is a blessed suffering. Hasten then, I beg you, and, as St. Jerome warns us, cut rather than untie the cable that binds your ship to the shore. . . . I am longing to see you again, and to have you share and become rich with the good things of Our Lord which we here enjoy so abundantly. I beg Him to increase in you the strength of His Holy Spirit, and to bring you here quickly, a free and happy man, for the loving welcome that awaits you. . . . [1]

When, after their vow at Montmartre in 1534, St. Ignatius and his companions found that they could not get to Palestine they decided to visit in couples some of the Italian university cities " to see whether the Lord wished to call some students to join them." The spirit that animated these " poor pilgrim priests," as they liked to be named, was shown when one of them was cast into prison at Padua on suspicion of heresy, for he " was so joyful that he did nothing but laugh the whole night through."[2] As long as they could they clung to their original project of going to Jerusalem, and only when it was seen to be quite impossible did they turn their steps towards Rome for the fulfilment of the second part of their vow, which was to put themselves entirely at the disposal of the Pope. This was not their first visit to the Eternal City, as they had gone there in batches on previous occasions, " walking barefooted through heavy rain and floods that sometimes reached up to their breasts, passing twenty-eight or thirty milestones a day, living on a little bread and water, *et hilares et psalmos cantantes.*"[3]

In the springtime of 1538 they were all reunited with Ignatius in Rome, preaching fervently in broken Italian and winning grace with the people by their untiring charity. The terrible winter of that year brought starvation into the Roman slums. At night the streets and squares were crowded with poor wretches half dead from cold and hunger. Numbers of these

---

[1] Braunsberger, *Epistulae*, vol. i, pp. 254–6.
[2] M.H., *Monumenta Ignatiana*, series quarta, vol. i, p. 118.
[3] M.H., Polanco, *Chronicon*, vol. i, p. 57.

were taken by Ignatius and his companions to the old, ramshackle building near the Torre del Melangolo in the Via dei Delfini which they called their home, and there tended with the utmost devotion. By dint of strenuous begging among the rich, beds were obtained for the sick, the others having straw couches prepared for them. The Jesuits fed them and looked after their bodily needs with their own hands, and then, when they were comfortable, gave them spiritual instructions. In all, more than three thousand men and women were thus succoured that winter.[1]

At this time, an old painting of the Blessed Virgin under the title of *Madonna della Strada* was venerated in a twelfth century church at the foot of the Capitol. St. Ignatius fell in love with the picture. His men were to be above all city workers, apostles of the market-place, and Our Lady of the Street would be a most appropriate patroness for them. Obsessed with this idea, Ignatius eventually went to the length of asking the parish priest outright to give him the picture. The good man, a Lombard named Peter Codacio, naturally refused, but he did not reckon with the power of his suppliant's prayers, and shortly afterwards gave not only the Madonna but the church and himself to the Society of Jesus. He was a great acquisition because, like a true Lombard, he had a splendid instinct for business. " Now," said the other Fathers happily, " we can leave all our financial worries to him and get on with the spiritual work."[2]

Through the good offices of Codacio, Ignatius acquired a little property in the parish of Sta. Maria della Strada and on it, in 1543, began the erection of a permanent residence for his sons. It was such a poor and unpretentious building that one observer did not hesitate to describe it as a hovel, but all the same, by the year 1545, there were more than thirty men living under its roof.[3] The four low and narrow rooms occupied by St. Ignatius and his lay brother assistant are all that now remains of it. When the flamboyantly grand *Gesù* was in process of building, the filial piety of the Jesuits had these rooms converted into chapels. The contrast between them and the baroque magnificence all around is one to stir the hearts of other people besides Jesuits. It was here that Ignatius wrote the constitutions of his Society and the letters that St. Francis Xavier, in far-off India, used to read on his knees; here St. Philip Neri came often for counsel; here St. Charles Borromeo said Mass and St. Francis de Sales many a time knelt in prayer; here St. Aloysius and St. Stanislaus gave themselves to the Society of Jesus; and here, hot and tired but assuredly

[1] M.H., Polanco, *Chronicon*, vol. i, pp. 65–6.   [2] M.H., Polanco, *Chronicon*, vol. i, pp. 66–7.
[3] Tacchi-Venturi, *La Casa di S. Ignazio in Roma* (1924), p. 25.

happy, St. Peter Canisius received the first embrace of the man whom Favre had taught him to revere and love years before.

As it was not until 1547, the year of Peter's arrival in Rome, that St. Ignatius began to draw up his constitutions, the institution known to Jesuits as the ' tertianship,' or third year of probation, was not yet organized in detail or clearly marked off from the ordinary first noviceship. It existed, however, in an experimental stage, and Peter fulfilled its main condition by going into retreat for about three weeks. He had his friend, the saintly eccentric Cornelius Wischaven, for company, and profited so much from the firm, affectionate direction of Ignatius that he declared himself tempted to " forget Germany and the rest of the world " altogether. But Peter was really incapable of forgetting Germany. " I will always carry you in my heart wherever I go," he assured his Cologne friends, and the dead, too, would go with him, " the shining memory of Master Favre and of that most dear brother Lambert," who lay at rest among the Carthusians. Outside times of prayer, St. Ignatius set him, for the good of his soul, to scrub pots and pans, wash the floor, help the cook and make himself generally useful as a domestic. These cannot have been very pleasant employments for one of his upbringing, to judge by the report of a fellow-worker who had also been nurtured in refinement. He was Benedict Palmio, afterwards a celebrated Jesuit, and he says that so dirty and unkempt were the lay servants with whom they had to consort that he could not look at them or their surroundings without getting sick.[1] St. Ignatius could not afford a better class of servant, and the dirt of the house must have tried him sorely, as he was famous for his love of cleanliness.

In the hospitals to which, in Advent, the ' Tertians ' were sent as helpers, Peter fared a good deal better than Cornelius Wischaven, as he was allowed time off to say Mass each day at " St. James's," whereas Cornelius at the rather inappropriately named " Our Lady of Consolation " found that the most he could manage was to hear Mass on Sundays. He was on his feet from morning till night " *huc illuc, sursum deorsum*," and besides attending to ninety beds, some occupied by two patients, he acted as official grave-digger and corpse-carrier to the institution. That was no sinecure as at least one patient died each day. Cornelius was so badly fed that he always felt " ravenously hungry " and " as if his stomach were going to pieces within him." The patients made game of him because he could not speak a word of their language and he had other troubles

---

[1] Tacchi-Venturi, *Storia della Compagnia di Gesù in Italia*, vol. i (1910), p. 609.

in abundance but, says the contemporary narrative, "in spite of everything he was invariably in the highest of spirits."[1]

It was by hard exercises such as these that St. Ignatius strove to foster in his sons the spirit of willing and prompt obedience, a virtue which he prized as necessary above all others for co-operative work in the service of God. He had been a good soldier and knew, as every good soldier knows, that efficient action by a body of men is impossible unless controlled by a single will. His military habit of mind was not put away with his captain's uniform but persisted to leave its mark on the order which he founded. The title of *Compañía*, by which he wished his order to be known and to which he clung, though the humblest of men, in face of all criticism and opposition, has itself a military ring, and *Regimini militantis Ecclesiae* are the first three words of its ecclesiastical charter. In an order so conceived, obedience necessarily emerged as the fundamental principle of activity. "The rule of obedience is simply the expression of that one among the military virtues upon which all the others depend . . . the corner-stone upon which rests the structure of coherent, unified action. . . . Where many wills have to act to one end . . . the many wills need to become one will; the many persons, in many quarters, simply the representatives, in the best sense, of the one person in whom the united action of the whole finds source and energy." Might not these words easily be mistaken for a pronouncement of St. Ignatius? They are in fact, the words of a dry, scientific authority on military and naval operations.[2] Ignatius, however, was a good deal more than an ex-soldier. He was a saint whose own deep spiritual experience had found in obedience not merely the guarantee of unified action but also the royal road to union with God. It merged for him into love so clear-eyed and swift of apprehension that it could discern Christ in the lowliest of His disguises and hear His voice where the natural ear, perhaps, caught only the growl of some hectoring authority. It was such obedience that he preached to his sons, a vital, creative virtue, giving dignity and coherence, not to a small area of a man's life, but to the whole of it, inasmuch as it puts all his willing into immediate relation with the will and the purposes of God. So well did he succeed with his son, Peter Canisius, that Peter became himself a great preacher and exemplar of obedience. The subject almost turned into an obsession with him. We shall find him harping on it constantly, whether himself a private or in command, and see him growing

[1] The document is printed in Tacchi-Venturi, *Storia della Compagnia di Gesù*, vol. i, pp. 619–23.
[2] Captain Mahan, *The Military Rule of Obedience*, in *Retrospect and Prospect* (London, 1902), pp. 255–83.

under its influence in the sober, unshowy heroism of action or endurance which characterized his work for the Church. The next episode in his career well illustrates the extent to which the Ignatian conception of obedience had already taken hold of him.

At the beginning of the year 1548, Juan de Vega, Viceroy of the King of Spain in Sicily, petitioned St. Ignatius to open a school for boys in Messina. During the preceding decade the Saint had received many similar petitions, but it was only by slow degrees that the idea of a college for external students, not destined to be Jesuits, gained ground with him and his advisers. It was the appeal from Messina that banished his remaining doubts and led to the momentous decision by which the culture of Catholic Europe was thereafter to be so profoundly influenced. Once having adopted the education of youth as part of the normal work of his Society, Ignatius, in his thorough way, flung himself into the Messina scheme with all his heart and soul. As the first independent boys' school to be opened by his Society it must necessarily provide the pattern for all others. He would therefore send of his best, and to discover them would submit to the Roman brethren a questionnaire of a kind unique in Jesuit history. For this purpose the whole household to the number of thirty-six was summoned together, even the cook, the historians note, being included[1]. Four questions were put to them by Ignatius:

(1) Was each one ready to go to Sicily and take whatever position and work might be assigned to him there by his superior?

(2) Were those who might be chosen for the mission prepared to do whatever manual and external work the superior should give them, supposing them to lack literary training, or if they possessed such would they be ready to teach any subject that obedience might enjoin, whether theology or Scripture or philosophy or letters?

(3) Would those who were not yet priests be willing to engage in scholastic work, according to the prescription of obedience?

(4) Would all judge that to be best which their superior might enjoin in matters not connected with teaching, and submit their wills and judgments to the dictates of holy obedience?[2]

Three days were given them to think over the questions proposed, after which time they were invited to hand in written answers to Ignatius. The following is an accurate translation of St. Peter's reply, delivered on February 5, 1548:

[1] Orlandinus, *Historia Societatis Jesu*, lib. viii, n. 8.
[2] M.H., Polanco, *Chronicon*, vol. 1, pp. 268–9 ; *Monumenta Ignatiana*, series prima, vol. ii, p. 50.

However much and long I consider the points briefly proposed by my Father in Christ and Superior, Master Ignatius, I feel myself, in the first place, by the help of the Lord, equally inclined in all things to both courses, either to remain at home here all my life should that be his will in my regard, or to go to Sicily, India or any other place whither he might choose to send me. If it is to Sicily I go, I declare simply that no matter what office or work I am enjoined to assume, I shall be perfectly content, whether it be that of cook or gardener or porter or student or professor of any subject, even one about which I know nothing. And I vow solemnly from this day forth, which is the Fifth of February, never again to act through human respect nor to trouble in the least about anything that may befall with regard to my abode, my work or other such matters of personal convenience, leaving concerns of that kind and every other anxiety to my Father in Christ and Reverend Superior. To him I humbly offer, completely submit, and confidently entrust, in Jesus Christ Our Lord, my intellect and body. 1548.

Written with my own hand, Peter Canisius of Nymegen.[1]

In the event, St. Ignatius chose four priests, among whom was Peter, and six men not yet ordained, to inaugurate the college at Messina. As the occasion was a very special one, he allowed the ten to settle by ballot who should be superior—another departure from custom that has rarely been repeated. All the votes except his own went to Father Jerome Nadal, a man from Palma in Majorca who had distinguished himself at the universities of Alcalá and Paris. Ignatius knew him while at Paris and, recognizing his quality, moved heaven and earth to win him, but all apparently in vain. Years later, when he was back in his pleasant island home, a letter from St. Francis Xavier in India came accidentally into his hands. After reading it, he immediately settled his affairs and went straight to Rome to offer himself to the Jesuits. So it was not only poor pagans at the ends of the earth that Francis could charm. Nadal, too, was his convert, a great man for whom was reserved the all-important mission of spreading the true spirit of St. Ignatius in nearly every European province of the Society of Jesus. Indeed, without exaggeration he might be called the second founder of the Society.

It is interesting to note the nationalities of the ten men chosen for Messina—French, Spanish, German, Italian, Belgian, Dutch, Tirolese,

[1] Braunsberger, *Epistulae*, vol. i, p. 263.

and Majorcans, almost the whole Continent in miniature. Their accomplishments were as varied as their countries, to judge by an account of them detailed in a letter of St. Ignatius. Nadal, besides being a doctor of theology and learned in Scripture, the Humanities, and Hebrew, possessed a Paris degree in mathematics. Andrew des Freux, *alias* Frusius, was good at those subjects, too, skilful in the use of scientific apparatus and endowed with what Ignatius calls " a special gift from God for making verses." Cornelius Wischaven was a Master of Arts and " knew a bit of everything." Benedict Palmio shone in Greek and had studied physics, and Hannibal du Coudrey was versed in the mysteries of medicine. To Peter Canisius the following tribute was paid : " He has been through a course of arts and a partial course of scholastic theology, but he is better equipped in Scripture, having lectured on that subject with much distinction at Cologne. He is a splendid Latin scholar, ready and elegant, and if he perfects his grasp of Italian he will preach well in it, for he has already given much satisfaction by his sermons in his own language."[1]

In letters to friends at this time Peter dwelt on the good work already being done by two Jesuits throughout Sicily, signalizing their great success in rooting out the favourite Italian vice of swearing and the custom then prevalent of using the churches as places for gossip and assignations. By their means, too, orphanages had been erected for little children, the *niños* who were irresistible to St. Ignatius ; and poor, fallen women and imprisoned debtors were the objects of other charities inspired from the same devoted source.[2] Peter, it is plain, would have loved to partner them in such activities but obedience had a more prosaic lot in store for him. He gives the key to his heart in a sentence of another letter written at this time : " *Uni animae prodesse et recte consulere posse totius mundi pretium superat in immensum* "—the power to benefit and promote the best interests of a single soul is immensely more precious than the value of the whole world. Whatever could be made to contribute to that end counted with Peter as part of religion, even the study of Aristotle and Cicero. They, too, had some bearing on the Kingdom of God, so he writes to his Cologne friends : " You will endeavour to fill the minds of the young men who visit you with zeal for souls and the desire of perfection, and you will spur them on to read Aristotle, even though they dislike the man. . . . Further, I think it would be well, and Father Ignatius quite agrees, if

---

[1] M.H., *Monumenta Ignatiana*, series prima, vol. ii, pp. 25–7.
[2] What St. Ignatius did for all these classes in Rome and how much he and his sons suffered on their behalf, is set forth in contemporary documents published by Tacchi-Venturi, *Storia della Compagnia di Gesù*, vol. i, pp. 624–76.

you devoted some time to the improvement of your style of writing, taking as your special model the letters of Cicero."[1]

The reader of the letters is never allowed to forget for long that they are the letters of a dedicated man. Peter·will discuss ordinary business, will talk of studies and tell a story or even a joke, but soon he is back to his dominant theme, the wonder of God's love for the world. On a single page of the letters the name of Christ will be found to occur ten or fifteen times. Love of Christ was the key-note that imparted tonal colouring to all Peter's major and minor scales, that knit the movements of his mind together and gave beautiful coherence to the diversity of his action. How the human tenderness of his heart was caught up and conserved in the great music is shown in the following passages from a letter to the Cologne Jesuits, written on the eve of his departure for Sicily:

Are souls which are very dear to one another sundered because obedience separates their mortal part for a little while—obedience, aye and the good of souls, and the providence of God to whom alone we owe all things for ever, not only these fleshly bonds of ours but the protection of the whole world? If I myself were ordered to India at any time, I neither could nor should feel the least anxiety, or trouble, knowing that God would be my guide on the journey. He would keep me safe and sound who for my sake built and upholds the universe. So, since our souls have come from God and are soon to be gathered to Him again in Heaven, let us despise, dearest brothers, the perishable globe of this earth, this dark prison that keeps from us the glorious eternal light and involves us, beaten and troubled, in the tangle of a thousand errors, snares, vanities, and concupiscences. One refuge and solace alone remains, which is that we who are bound to one another by charity's beautiful engagements should graft and establish our souls in Christ, serve Him with a freeman's service, drink of His spirit, win Him in our sufferings and our dying, and possess Him in everlasting beatitude.

I cannot omit a final petition that in the great, strong charity which Christ desires between us you will keep me ever in memory, and pray to God and His saints with loyal friendship for my salvation. Commend me to the prayers of all our friends, and remember me at the tombs of the holy Magi and St. Gereon and the Theban Martyrs and St. Maurice

---

[1] Braunsberger, *Epistulae*, vol. i, p. 267. Dislike of Aristotle did not die with the Reformation. In her essay, *Tradition and Experiment in present-day Literature*, Miss Edith Sitwell says : " Aristotle is one of the few people whom one can dislike with as fresh an intensity as if they were in the next room, though they died a couple of thousand years ago."

and all the virginal company of St. Ursula. If I dare ask so much, would you say a weekly Mass for me? I beg Father Prior of the Carthusians, my dearest friend, to get each priest to say one Mass for his Canisius, and to commend me, his unworthy but loving son, to the prayers of all the brethren. Reverend Father Ignatius and the whole Society of Jesus wish to be particularly remembered to him.

Now, though reluctantly, I must come to an end, my brothers, begging you again most earnestly for that weekly Mass. Certain I am that this rich alms will be my best viaticum as I set out indigent of soul on my travels. May the love of Jesus Christ bring us ever closer together, so that steadfast to the end in His grace we may become sharers of His eternal glory. Amen.[1]

On March 16, 1548, the ten Jesuits destined for Sicily went to pay parting homage to Pope Paul III and beg his blessing on their journey. Canisius acted as spokesman for the group and " made a graceful and pleasing Latin speech explaining the purpose of their expedition."[2] The Pope replied in affectionate terms, urging them particularly to combat Lutheran errors and inspire the people with confidence in the remedies to be provided by the Council of Trent. On Passion Sunday they rode out of the City in company with two couriers or postmen, " much pleased," says Polanco, " that they were the same number as the Apostles."

Some of them were not used to horses, and Cornelius Wischaven in particular nearly broke his neck by going over the edge of a precipice. " It was only the marvellous intervention of God that saved him", wrote Canisius. On this journey to Naples, where they were to take ship, " Father Nadal showed the greatest anxiety for the health and comfort of his brethren. He strove patiently and indefatigably with paternal care to help and relieve the troubles of those who were unaccustomed to riding, and took infinite pains to get them good lodging at the public inns. He was ever ready to look after all the horses, grooming them himself and providing for their refreshment. If anything was needed by his companions he would work night and day, begging and searching around until it was secured. Indeed, he left nothing undone that generous love and kindness could suggest."[3] Always on the look-out for a chance to do good, the travellers made a point of visiting the hospitals in the towns on their route. Thus they reported:

[1] Braunsberger, *Epistulae*, vol. i, pp. 266–9.
[2] M.H., *Monumenta Ignatiana*, series prima, vol. ii, p. 52.
[3] Aguilera, *Provinciae Siculae S.J. ortus et res gestae*, pars prima (Palermo, 1737), p. 12.

At Marino we had no time to do anything but go to the hospital. We found only one sick man there, so we heard his confession and left him much comforted in Our Lord. We arrived in the evening at Velletri, and as there were many people about because it was a feast-day one of us preached in the public square and some of the townsfolk made their confessions to us in the church and hospital, but not many as it was getting late. Nevertheless we were able to absolve the inn-keeper and his serving man. The courier was in such a hurry to be away that it was only with difficulty we could snatch a few hours of the night for a meal and repose. Still, we were always able to do a little good by the favour of God, and we especially remembered the work His Holiness had commended to us of fighting heresy. Thus we argued along the road with people we encountered in favour of vows and other matters of our religion. One night at an inn some gentlemen began to urge reasons against the use of images. We succeeded in refuting them, and a man who heard us, a person as far as we could judge of rank and authority, was so satisfied that he insisted the following morning on holding the stirrup while one of us mounted his horse. . . . Later three Moors joined our party, two of whom, we heard, were noblemen, and the third, actually a relative of the King of Tunis. This man knew a little Spanish, and first one of us who was not a priest began to talk with him about our faith, and then one of the priests. After a good deal of argument he was led to admit by the divine favour that the doctrine of the Holy Trinity was neither impossible nor against reason, and also that the whole history of Our Lord might well be true. It was shown to him that the ' Our Father ' was a suitable prayer to God, even according to his religion, and he was exhorted to say it and to beg for light. . . . If an opportunity offers we hope to be able to help those men to the best of our power.[1]

Naples was reached after a five days' ride, whereupon Peter found time to write to Leonard Kessel requesting him to send to Rome as soon as possible two skulls of St. Ursula's companions that had been presented to the Jesuits by some nuns in Cologne. From Rome, he said, these relics could easily be forwarded to Messina to be a protection and embellishment for the new college. His devotion to St. Ursula and the other Cologne saints was quite extraordinary, nor does he ever seem to have been visited by any misgivings as to the authenticity of the bones

[1] M.H., *Litterae quadrimestres*, vol. i, pp. 91–2.

he honoured or the legends he loved.[1] Despite his very considerable reading he possessed hardly any of the critical acumen that distinguished some other Jesuits of his own and of later ages. The saints for him were people to be worshipped and imitated, not people whose histories it was any business of his to scrutinize for anachronisms and other such treasure-trove of the scientific hagiographer. Passing from the saints to the sea, he said:

Father Cornelius and I most earnestly commend ourselves to your prayers, as according to report the voyage we are about to make usually proves perilous for those not accustomed to it. The thought of obedience keeps up my spirits, however, for whether alive or dead it makes us present and pleasing to Christ.... Long life or speedy death —is not either to be thought a glorious lot, provided we cling close to Him our Prince and Leader? Good-bye always in the tender love of Jesus crucified for us, and never forget the confident hopes and desires formed for his Cologne people by Father Peter Favre of sweet memory.[2]

As will be seen, Peter's premonition of an unpleasant crossing was more than fulfilled. Men in those days appreciated St. John's exclusion of the sea from Heaven. They dreaded it as an enemy whose moods were entirely incalculable and beyond control, and so hugged the coast for dear life on their voyages. The pirates, knowing the custom, also kept to the coast; but better, thought the sailormen, fall into their hands than be devoured by the horrible sea-serpents or other gruesome, nightmare monsters that waited for them in the wastes beyond sight of shore. What a merry trade the pirates plied in the Mediterranean may be guessed from the fact that there were twenty thousand Christian slaves in Algiers and that the two religious orders for the redemption of captives used to pay yearly sums equivalent to £70,000 in ransoms. A storm, as a rule, rendered the sailors quite helpless and panic-stricken. They were as superstitious as the shipmates of Jonah and knew as little about navigation. To determine their whereabouts they depended chiefly on

[1] The Protestants of the sixteenth century scorned the Catholics for their belief in the authenticity of saints' relics, but they were every bit as credulous themselves about unicorns' horns and such figments. The following words of a learned and impartial critic are to the point: " As for their belief in relics, it is only fair to point out what may not occur to every reader, that they had the same reason, neither more nor less, for believing so, as we for believing that the earth moves round the sun; it is common knowledge. ' Common knowledge '—is not all of it whether scientific or theological equally an act of faith? and is it more reasonable for us to quote Baedeker to ourselves than for pilgrim Nicholas to put his trust in Friar John? . . . Of two things we may be sure that the true history of a relic would probably be far stranger than its legend, and that whatever marvels the southerner saw or heard, he came across nothing more novel or more miraculous than the ebb and flow of the northern tides." E. S. Bates, *Touring in 1600*, p. 148.

[2] Braunsberger, *Epistulae*, vol. i, pp. 271-2.

landmarks, so if a mist came between them and the coast they were completely at sea in more senses than one.

The ordinary passenger ships of the period were dirty and evil-smelling, with about the same amount of comfort as a fishing-smack. One got sea-sick on them as a matter of course, and lay, like Pantagruel, " all of a heap on deck, utterly cast down and metagrobolized." Fynes Moryson, who did his travelling towards the end of the sixteenth century, has a few words of cheer for the destined victims :

> To speake something of preserving health by Sea : He that would not vomit at all, let him some dayes before he take Ship, and after at Sea, diminish his accustomed meat, and especially drinke, and let him take the following remedies against ill smelles and weakness of stomack. Some advise that he should drinke Sea water mingled with his wine, and some more sparing, that he drinke Sea water alone, which dries cold humours and shuts the Orifice of the belly and stomack. But I thinke they doe ill, who altogether restraine from vomiting, for no doubt that working of the Sea is very healthfull. Therefore I would rather advise him to use his accustomed diet till he have sailed one day or two into the Maine, or till he feel his body weake and thinkes it enough purged, then let him take meates agreeable to the Sea in small proportion, as powdred beefs, neates-tongues dried and like salt meates, and after eating, let him seale his Stomack with Marmalate. . . . To restrain the extremity of vomiting, till he be somewhat used to the Sea, let him forbeare to looke upon the waves of the Sea, or much to lift his head.
>
> To avoid the ill smelles of the ship, hee may in Summer carry red Roses, or the dried leaves thereof, Lemmons, Oranges and the like things of good odour, and in Winter he may carry the roote or leaves of Angelica, Cloves, Rosemary, and the aforesaid Lemmons, Oranges and Rose leaves.[1]

Moryson's prescriptions were intended to help on normal crossings, and his rosemary and marmalade would certainly not have been much use to the ten Jesuits, whose voyage, as related by Nadal to St. Ignatius, reads in places somewhat like an extract from Conrad's *Typhoon*. Since Peter Canisius was one of those blown about and battered by the murderous winds and waves, the letter may fitly be included in his biography :

> We went on board a frigate towards sunset on March 28th, and left Naples in the company of another vessel, commanded by Señor Juan Osorio, Captain of the Guard to the Viceroy of Sicily. When

[1] *Itinerary* (1617), part iii, book i, pp. 22-3.

we had sailed about ten or twelve miles Señor Juan was forced to turn back. As we were ahead we did not know what his trouble was, so our captain also swung round for Naples. We arrived at two o'clock in the morning and had the greatest difficulty in finding a shelter, which was very necessary as Master Benedict and myself were a good deal the worse for our short experience of the sea. Señor Juan who had reached port before we did was full of joy next morning to find us safe and sound. He told us that not knowing of our return his Excellency's majordomo and himself had been torn with anxiety on our account, fearing that we had met with some disaster.

As the weather was fairly good we set sail again that same day, in the late afternoon, and got on well until nightfall. Then the wind began to rise, and soon we were in the midst of a violent storm of thunder and rain, surrounded by mountainous seas, and in thick darkness that was broken only by flashes of lightning. We suffered a great deal, and lost sight of the other vessel, finding it again only on the following afternoon. At last we succeeded in bringing the ship to land at a place called La Scalea, in Calabria. I am not going to speak about the particular troubles of any one of us, because all that night Cornelius Wischaven was the only man who did not succumb. He never closed his eyes but kept watch and roused the sailors who were overcome by sleep. This he did on account of the great peril we were in of being engulfed by the sea, and also because there was danger from Moorish pirates who were reported to infest these parts and to have captured other frigates only a few days earlier. As for Master Benedict and myself, we felt and looked just as if we were half dead. However, once on dry land we were all, though battered, quite happy and satisfied, by the grace of Our Lord. We rendered thanks to God for our deliverance and especially for having brought us to shore in the nick of time, for immediately after our arrival such a dreadful storm began that we should almost certainly have been wrecked had we been caught in it. We searched for some place to lodge, but could not find rooms of any description, as the town is poor and without a common hostel. They told us, however, that the Franciscan Friars had a place some distance away, so we turned our steps thither to beg shelter for the love of God. The friars gave us a very small room and there the ten of us put up, together with a merchant from Messina. After we had recovered a little we thought that we should try to do some good in view of the approaching feast of Easter, so we began by exhorting the sailors to go to confession and communion. As they were busy then overhauling the frigate they put off coming until the night of Holy Saturday, when Father des Freux and I heard the confessions of ten of them.

Moved by the example of their mates the other sailors, though very tired, asked to be heard likewise, and all of them received Holy Communion from our Fathers on Easter Sunday. That was no small victory, as a number of them told us that they originally had no intention of going to the Sacraments. . . .

That same day we left the port and sailed with a fair wind for about four miles. Then once again a wild hurricane came down upon us and swept away our sailyards, to the imminent peril of our lives. But the sailors, with the help of God, took such swift measures in repairing the damage that we were saved, and rowed slowly and cautiously to a place on the mainland of Calabria named Paola. On that very day the feast of the St. Francis who is Paola's native patron was being celebrated there. We gave hearty thanks to Our Lord and so did the sailors who avowed that we had all had a marvellous escape. The most experienced amongst them said that in the ordinary course of events with such a wind the frigate must certainly have foundered or gone to pieces or been wrecked in some similar way. As it was, we had the greatest difficulty in landing, but by the mercy and providence of God we at last succeeded on Tuesday evening. . . . Next day we visited the monastery of St. Francis of Paola and were shown much kindness by the monks. . . . I, thinking to do some good in the city, sent one of our number, not yet a priest, to preach in the marketplace. A large crowd gathered to listen to him and so pleased were they that they begged me to appoint someone to preach in the principal church the following day. The governor of the city, the arch-priest and many nobles of the locality came to the sermon, and afterwards I was requested to arrange for a sermon each day while we remained in the town. This was accordingly done, the chief subject of our exhortations being always frequent Confession and Communion.

Amongst other good works that Our Lord brought about by means of our visit to the town, two deserve particular mention. The first was the foundation of a sodality of men devoted to frequent Communion, mental prayer and the practice of all kinds of works of charity, and the second, the inauguration of catechism classes for children. . . .

Late on the night of Friday, the day when those classes had been opened by one of us in the principal church with a great crowd of young people, the sailors came to inform us that the weather was then propitious for our voyage. We hurried away, but by the time we had reached the shore the sea had once more become angry. Still, as we were anxious to do what the sailors wanted and to be guided by their judgment, we proceeded to go on board, but after three of us had embarked the frigate broke its moorings and drifted away from the shore, and the waves were so huge that the sailors could not get it back to pick up the others. Instead, they had to put out into deeper waters to prevent the vessel being dashed to pieces. The sailors then tried to launch a boat, but as it was very small and did not look safe we were not particularly eager to trust ourselves to it. Not knowing what to do, the captain asked us to go along the shore on foot for about two miles, as we should there find a better place for embarkation. He then began to row back to the frigate with the intention of bringing it round to the place mentioned, but hardly had they left the shore when the boat upset, throwing its occupants into the water. By the goodness of God they all managed to scramble to land without much difficulty, and came after us on foot to the appointed spot. We had some trouble in crossing a swollen torrent on the way, as it was the middle of the night. I managed to get over after some acrobatics and I begged God to provide for the rest who were still on the other bank. Just then the sailors arrived to help them over, and at daybreak we reached our destination. This time by the grace of God, we climbed on board without difficulty and after a voyage of sixteen miles found Señor Juan with the other ship at a place called Maida. Señor Juan wished to have us with him during the next stage of the journey, but so heavy was the sea that we had to walk along the shore six miles before we could find a quiet haven. We went on board at Cape San Giuliano, but not entirely without risks as one of the sailors was thrown into the water. I tell you all this that you may more clearly see the working of God's mercy which delivered us so well from such great and frequent danger that we are now as though we had not experienced it at all. After embarking with Señor Juan we sailed that day for sixty miles and came in good style to Tropea, a town on the Calabrian coast. There we stayed over Saturday night, and a little before dawn on Sunday set off once more, passing the Faro, the most dangerous point on our route, quite safely and happily. By about nine o'clock in the morning we had covered the remaining sixty miles between Tropea and Messina.

On arriving in the harbour we found Father Jerome Domenech

with Doctor Inigo Lopez, a physician, waiting for us, whereupon we were so delighted that we quite forgot all the troubles we had been through. These were great enough in all conscience, especially in the case of Master Benedict and myself. Never during the whole of our time on the sea were the pair of us free from aches and pains of the stomach. The others did not suffer so heavily, but some of them say that the voyage made a very good noviceship. Now by the grace of God we are all well and happy in the service of Our Lord. May He mercifully grant us to know His holy will that we may carry it out completely and perfectly. From Messina, April 10, 1548.[1]

St. Peter had a few comments of his own to add to this long account. The rumour of pirates impressed him so much that it stirred in his memory twenty-two years later when writing his *Confessions*, but the chief mark left by the voyage on his soul was a deep sympathy for other victims of the sea's uncertainties. "Our experiences," he said, "though hard at the time, are good to recall, for they will make us think in future with pity on those wrecked or in danger at sea, and will spur us on to pray for them and do whatever lies in our power to help."[2] He goes on to tell of the fine reception they had on their arrival and of the pleasant ceremony that took place two days later in the principal church of Messina. With the viceroy, the civil magistrates and all the aristocracy of the city for audience, five of the Jesuits delivered Latin orations on various academic subjects, Peter's theme being the study of eloquence. It was a vapid and windy sort of subject but people liked it in those days when the agreeable delusion prevailed that orators could be made to order.

The citizens of Messina were very generous, and provided liberally for the needs of the new arrivals. Peter says, for instance, that they were able to spend the considerable sum of fifty golden crowns on books in a single fortnight. Meantime a college building was started, planned to accommodate fifty masters, and a regulation was made by the public authorities giving the newcomers an educational monopoly. That did not infringe any existent rights as there were no schools, properly so called, in Sicily before the Jesuits started their venture. Classes opened on April 24, 1548, when Des Freux, the laureate of the staff, celebrated the occasion with an appropriate ode.[3] The divisions and studies of the new school were arranged on the model of the University of Paris, which,

[1] M.H., *Litterae quadrimestres*, vol. i, pp. 94–9.
[2] Braunsberger, *Epistulae*, vol. i, p. 275.
[3] Peter reports that this gifted man was just then at work putting the *Imitation of Christ* into classical verse—a good indication of the peculiar taste of the period.

in old times, used to cater for students of all ages and degrees of ignorance. The Jesuits did the same, and, though the knowledge that they had to impart was limited, it was the best of its kind and quite possibly more effective in developing power of thought than the encyclopaedic curricula with which the brains of modern children are bewildered.

The lowest class in the college was composed of little boys who had not yet learned their alphabet. This they were taught by fellow-pupils of riper culture from more advanced classes. The boys of the second class learned to decline nouns and conjugate verbs out of a book entitled *De octo partibus orationis*, by the old grammarian Aelius Donatus, St. Jerome's tutor, whose name during the Middle Ages had become a synonym for all book-learning.[1] Next above them were superior persons who studied the *Commentarii grammatici* of a Dutchman named Jan van Pauteren or Despauterius. The master of this class had authority to reprehend or chastise his charges "according as it seemed good to him *in caritate Domini Nostri Jesu Christi.*" The fourth and highest class in this division of the school used for reference the grammar of a native Sicilian worthy, at the same time diligently repeating and polishing the information they had acquired during the earlier stages. The middle divisions of the school had two classes, in which works on syntax by Valla, Vives, and Erasmus were studied, with parts of Vergil, Terence, Cicero, Ovid, and Sallust as reading matter. Finally, there was the upper school, composed of older students qualified to deal with Homer, Aristophanes, Horace, Livy, Suetonius, Quintilian, and other Greek and Latin authors of heavier metal. From an early stage the boys were practised in the writing of Greek and Latin verses, not with any notion of discovering infant Horaces but in order to develop power of literary appreciation through personal experience of what it meant to try to express thought or feeling in terse and musical language. All the studies, high and low, were carried on in a lively, practical, healthily competitive manner, "*scribendo, componendo, declamendo, repetendo.*" Peter Canisius, who himself taught the principles of rhetoric, was in charge of this whole department of the Humanities. It was his duty to visit the various class-rooms frequently, to arrange syllabuses and generally to see that all was well with the boys in every stage of their evolution. Thus he was the first of the long line of important functionaries known in the Jesuit system of education as "Prefects of Studies."

---

[1] It is so used by Langland and Chaucer. Donatus kept his place on into the eighteenth century, in spite of his Grammar being so badly arranged that the Greek scholar Herder regarded it as a "book of martyrdom." Sandys, *A History of Classical Scholarship* (1908), vol. iii, p. 31.

Brought up as he had been in an atmosphere tense with momentous problems, Peter found the rhetoricians' bag of tricks a real burden, but even these "*studia insipida*," as he called them, were made tolerable by obedience and by the opportunities they afforded of influencing the boys' souls. All the pupils were expected to assist at Mass each morning, but further devotions were kept within wise limits and carefully adapted to the capacity of the various classes. The smallest boys had a custom that suited them down to the ground. Before being dismissed for the day, one of their number mounted a bench and gave out at the top of his voice the Our Father, Hail Mary, Salve Regina, Creed, and Ten Commandments, all the others repeating the words in lusty chorus after him.

In their solicitude for the welfare of youth the Jesuits did not forget the claims of maturer years. Father Nadal expounded the scholastic theologians, Durandus and Cajetan, whenever he could muster an audience, taught mathematics and Hebrew regularly, and lectured each Sunday on the Epistles of St. Paul from the pulpit of Messina's Cathedral. All that, however, was but a fraction of his usual programme, though his health was of the poorest. He had the souls of two hundred and thirty-eight students in his keeping and, being a pioneer, had to bear the anxiety of various unpredictable experiments. In such circumstances the Dutch phlegm and sturdy good sense of Peter Canisius were a great comfort.

Peter himself soon began to preach regularly in Italian on Sundays and feast-days, and in the intervals between his school duties used to sally forth "to dig and sweat in the garden," to comfort the sick and those in prison, to teach catechism and to do any other kind and good thing for which God might provide the occasion. One expedition of his at this time ended with a touch of comedy. The Dominicans were keeping a great festival of theology at their church and had invited the Jesuits to take part in the customary disputations. Four of them went, including Nadal and Peter. Now Peter's Latin, owing to his constant preoccupation with the figures and tropes of rhetoric, was apt to become somewhat unintelligible to people who had not Cicero and Quintilian on the tips of their tongues. On this occasion, according to Polanco, " he argued about the power of the Church in such elegant phraseology that the good friar who was to debate with him confessed frankly that he understood very little of what he had been saying. With that avowal he sat down *cum auditorii applausu*."[1]

National characteristics change very little in essentials with the passage of the centuries. Fynes Moryson noticed that Dutchmen and Germans

---

[1] M.H., Polanco, *Chronicon*, vol. ii, p. 370.

on travel invariably sought out and kept company with their own countrymen, just as they do to-day, whereas he " never observed any to live
lesse together in forraigne parts than the English." One German he met
" who, being reprehended that having been thirty years in Italy hee could
not speake the Language, did merrily answere : ' *Ach lieber was kan man
doch in dreissig Jahrer lehrnen ?* ' Alas, good Sir, what can a man learne
in thirty yeeres ? But the true cause of his not speaking the tongue was
his perpetuall conversing with his Countrey-men." The cause of the
perpetual conversing was German attachment to *Das Vaterland* which
impelled and still impels exiles to build up small Germanies in whatever
foreign places they might find themselves through misfortune or for
business reasons. In its way it is an amiable foible and Peter Canisius
certainly shared it to some extent, in spite of the fact that he got on so
well with men of other nations. With all his grit and practicality, those
fine Dutch qualities which carried a tiny people to empire in the teeth
of Spain and England, he had his soft side and was by no means exempt
from the *Heimweh* that so easily takes possession of the Teutonic soul.
We can imagine, without being too fanciful, that under the hot Sicilian
sun dreams would come to him of the changeful, misty skies beneath
which he was born, of the lordly Rhine on whose waters " new-mailed
in morning " he had gone to his first meeting with Favre, of Sancta
Colonia where the saints whispered their inspiration at every turn. However that may have been, Peter had to be admonished from Rome for
" brooding upon Germany."[1] Probably the severe illness that laid him
low in Messina had something to do with the homing tendency of his
thoughts. Still, though his mind would keep turning to Germany his
strong will remained completely loyal to immediate duty, as appeared
in a letter of encouragement addressed by him in May, 1548, to some
young Germans who were going through the Jesuit noviceship in Rome :

My Brothers in Christ, dear and desired, I have so much to tell
you, so many things glad and sad to say, that I scarcely know how
to begin my letter. It is a very sweet experience when a man folds
his friend to his heart and looks upon his face again, especially when
that friend has come from far away bringing with him the expectation
and ardent desires of many a month. So, too, men cannot help feeling
a certain corresponding sadness when they have reason to believe that
the long-sought means and opportunities to improve their friendships

[1] M.H., *Monumenta Ignatiana*, series prima, vol. ii, p. 131.

may be removed from them, not for a time only but for good. In this way I think it is possible that both you and I may find some small trouble taking possession of our souls, you at seeing your old friend Canisius, the one man you knew in Rome, spirited suddenly far away from you just as you arrived in the City, and I, because deprived of the chance to welcome my eagerly-awaited brothers, among the first of our Society's sons from Germany, after their long and arduous journey. . . . That journey, however, had a happy end, for it placed you in the centre of all that is mighty and magnificent in the world and gave you, as you now know, the best of fathers and the truest of brothers to delight your hearts. It seems to me that such an exchange might well make us all forget our unhappy Germany and give our undivided love to the City which has ever kept inviolate the faith of Christ and Peter, and which now bestows on us a new happiness, excelling immeasurably whatever delight there is in the pomp of the world or the gratification of sense. . . . In this new school you learn the abundant riches of poverty, the true freedom of obedience, the glory of humility and the supreme dignity and worth of the love of Jesus crucified. . . .

As for the solid development of our friendship, we must not measure that by our nearness to one another in the flesh, which is a mean and vulgar standard, for it consists rather in likeness of soul and harmony of will. Since, then, our endeavours to serve Christ are of one pattern and our ways of life very similar, how can we, with the breath of the Holy Spirit upon us, be anything but united wherever we are? How can the miles between us sunder our souls, or ever silence the converse of heart with heart? And then if we would think of the perfect union, may we not cherish the hope and desire, brothers, of going home together after this brief circle of years to the happy, happy country where death is dead and evil has no power to harm, where the Eternal Father waits to fill us with all delight, and where our beatitude will be crowned in the company of the brothers we loved so dearly? . . .[1]

Writing to another Jesuit friend at this time, Peter said: "As to your place of abode, convince yourself that we ought to settle down and be as completely at rest wherever Father Ignatius wishes us to dwell as if there was not the slightest chance of our ever moving again. Therefore, putting away every hope and fear and doubt about the future, let us not permit the least anxiety concerning a change of life to take

[1] Braunsberger, *Epistulae*, vol. i, pp. 278–80.

possession of our hearts, seeing that we cannot so much as promise ourselves to be alive to-morrow. Let us cling to obedience heartily and in all simplicity, not allowing even our minds to incline one way more than another." In the last sentence we find commended the blind obedience against which people who do not understand it are so fond of railing. It is blind only in the sense in which we talk of blind flying, or blind sailing. Instruments in the one case and the stars in the other supply all that is needed to keep direction. Maybe the blindly obedient man, too, has his stars, and shows more wisdom than the critics would guess in preferring them to his "little candle of experience." There can be no doubt about St. Peter's star, at any rate. "As we have once and for all surrendered everything that belonged to us to Christ," he wrote to a friend, "let us rest utterly in His most holy will, free from care and worry about finding our native land again, about our studies, about any change of time or place that may come upon us. . . . Our Captain and Leader is Christ . . . and no matter where in exile death meets us at last, it will not be able to sever us from Him."[1]

Peter thus stressed the duty of contentment because he had learned that certain good men in Germany, including the Prior of the Cologne Carthusians, were far from contented that he should remain in Sicily. Their efforts to bring about his return received no encouragement from him and remained unsuccessful until, towards the close of the year, a more powerful intercessor appeared in the person of William IV, Duke of Bavaria. This man and his chancellor, Leonhard von Eck, received high praise from Peter as good and zealous Catholics who deserved well of the Church, but the Catholic historian Janssen has nothing bad enough to say about them, and Riezler, the best general historian of Bavaria, describes Eck as "a master of Machiavellian and perfidious statecraft."[2] Eck's Catholicism does certainly seem to have sat lightly upon him, but there can be no doubt about the genuineness of the Duke's professions. He may have been ready to go to all lengths against the Habsburgs, but he remained true to Rome when he had everything to gain by throwing in his lot with her formidable enemies. Now, in 1548, he was deeply

---

[1] Braunsberger, *Epistulae*, vol. i, pp. 283, 291. With reference to blind obedience, we might mention that the superlatively great soldier, Stonewall Jackson, practised it on at least one occasion to a degree never required by St. Ignatius. In Allan Tate's biography we are told that he was summoned one bitterly cold night to the office of the Superintendent of the Military Academy of Lexington, where he was a professor. The superintendent was called away for a few moments and asked Jackson to take a chair until his return. Outside, he got into conversation with somebody and forgot all about the waiting professor. Entering his office next morning he found Jackson sitting bolt upright exactly as he had left him the night before.

[2] *Geschichte Baierns* (Gotha, 1899), vol. iv, p. 421.

concerned for the fate of Bavaria's sole centre of advanced studies, the University of Ingolstadt, which brand-new, Protestant Wittenberg threatened to put out of commission altogether.

The Duke knew of the Society of Jesus through Claude Lejay, who had worked in his dominions and for whom he had conceived the highest regard. Wondering whether those new priests might not be able to do something for Ingolstadt, he appealed to the Pope and to St. Ignatius to lend him some of them, specially asking for Lejay. As the reform of studies was a work of capital importance in those days and had been warmly commended and encouraged by the Council of Trent, the Duke's appeal fell on sympathetic ears. The universities played a tremendous part in the struggles of the Reformation, as from them were recruited the great champions of both causes, and in many countries the loyalty or defection of a university meant the preservation or disappearance of Catholicism over wide areas. Aware of this and of the consequent responsibility, St. Ignatius took counsel with Lejay, who knew best the type of man needed in Germany, and who would, of course, himself be going. Salmeron and Canisius were then chosen as his colleagues, the latter because in Lejay's opinion he was of " outstanding probity and learning." Nadal in Messina thought the same of him and showed such reluctance when ordered to deliver him up that Ignatius felt obliged to give the good Rector a penance for his dilatoriness.[1]

Peter was back in Rome by the end of June, 1549. On September 2nd he went once more to beg the blessing of Pope Paul III for himself and some other Jesuits who were about to travel. The audience took place appropriately at the Castle of St. Angelo, which is a monument to St. Michael, the patron Saint of the Holy Roman Empire of the German People. Peter always cherished a great devotion to him as his birthday, May 8th, coincided with the feast of St. Michael's Apparition. For this reason the ceremony at the Castle affected him profoundly. Writing about it in his *Testament* many years later, and about his visit to St. Peter's immediately afterwards, he said :

While the others went to pay their respects to the cardinals it pleased Thy immense goodness, O Holy Father and Eternal High Priest, that I should earnestly beg confirmation and happy issue of the Pope's blessing from Thy Apostles who are honoured in the Vatican. . . . There I felt Thy great consolation and present grace,

[1] M.H., Polanco, *Chronicon*, vol. i, p. 364, adnot. 1. There was trouble, too, in securing Lejay's release, as the Duke of Ferrara, for whom he was then working, refused to part with him until ordered by the Pope.

sweetly dispensed to me by those Thy intercessors. They gave me their blessing and strengthened me for my mission to Germany, and they seemed to guarantee their assistance to me as to an apostle of Germany. Thou knowest, O Lord, how much and how often Thou didst on that day commend Germany unto me. From that day forth Germany would occupy more and more of my anxious thoughts, and I would long, like Father Favre, to spend myself utterly in life and death for her salvation. Thus would I be a fellow-worker with St. Michael, the Angel of Germany. For a little while Thou didst hide from me the vast mountain of my unworthiness, showing me that in Thee and through Thee there was nothing too great to be achieved.[1]

On September 4th, Peter pronounced his last vows, including one of special obedience to the Pope, before St. Ignatius at the church of Santa Maria della Strada. A little earlier he had been again to the tombs of the Apostles, where, after commending to them his vows, he approached the altar of the Blessed Sacrament with St. Michael dominating his thoughts. The story of that visit and of the Mass of his ' profession ' that followed is thus recounted in the *Testament*:

My soul fell prostrate before Thee, my dull deformed soul, unclean and infected with many vices and passions. But Thou, my Saviour, didst open to me Thy Heart in such fashion that I seemed to see within it, and Thou didst invite me and bid me to drink the waters of salvation from that fountain. Great at that moment was my desire that streams of faith, hope and charity might flow from it into my soul. I thirsted after poverty, chastity and obedience, and I begged to be washed clean by Thee from top to toe and to be clothed and adorned by Thee. After I had thus dared to approach Thy Heart, all full of sweetness, and to slake my thirst therein, Thou didst promise me a robe woven of peace, love and perseverance with which to cover my naked soul. Having this garment of grace and gladness about me I grew confident again that I should lack for nothing and that all things would turn out to Thy glory.

At the beginning of Mass, which was said in the presence of the brethren by the Superior of our Society, Thy son Ignatius, Thou didst once more unveil to me my wretchedness and deformity, at sight of which I almost gave myself over to the dominion of black horror and despair. But about the time of the Elevation, Father of mercies, Thou didst console Thy unhappy servant, raising up my fallen hopes,

[1] Braunsberger, *Epistulae*, vol. i, pp. 53-4.

inspiring me with fresh courage, forgiving all my sins, promising me the best things of Thy bounty and sweetly inviting me to be thenceforward a new creature, with that hour as the date of my conversion. . . .[1]

As the chief duty of the three Jesuits destined for Ingolstadt would be to teach theology, St. Ignatius desired them on their way thither to stand for a doctor's degree in the subject at the University of Bologna. Bologna and Paris were the two great archetypal universities which provided all others in Europe with the main lines of their constitutions. Contrary to modern ideas, at Bologna the students, organized in gilds on geographical principles, ruled the University. This democratic system was followed in general by the universities of Italy, Spain, and Portugal, while the northern nations and England took Paris for their model. At Paris, the masters' or professors' gild was the governing body. The differences and comparative merits of the two systems had great interest for the early Jesuits, who were themselves to engage in many educational experiments, but at the moment Peter Canisius could think only of his examination. According to the diploma obtained by Salmeron from Cardinal del Monte, this was " *arduum, rigorosum ac tremendum,*" three adjectives fierce enough to scare any average candidate. The examiners were awe-inspiring, too, for among them was the celebrated Dominican, Ambrose Catharinus, one of the great lights of the Council of Trent. Peter confesses that he was " not a little frightened at the prospect " of facing such a giant because, " in his pride," he did not want to have his ignorance exposed. The examination was held on October 2nd, two days before the feast of St. Francis of Assisi and of Bologna's own patron, St. Petronius. To this saint's shrine and to the shrine of St. Dominic, who is buried in Bologna, Peter had recourse, earnestly beseeching Francis, Petronius and Dominic to help him and his two companions in the difficult hour before them. St. Dominic might put mercy into the heart of his son, Catharinus. Peter's mean opinion of his own powers was the most genuine thing in the world, yet it was combined with an extraordinary confidence, showing in a small matter the profound paradox of Christian humility in all matters. Looking at himself, he would, to his dying day, grow faint with apprehension; looking to God, he would be ready to endure anything and to withstand, serene and fearless, all the crowned and conquering iniquities of his generation.

On the appointed day the three Jesuits obtained their doctorate in

[1] Braunsberger, *Epistulae*, vol. i, pp. 55–6.

brilliant fashion, " comporting themselves during the examination," wrote the Secretary of the Council of Trent, " as everybody knew they would."[1] Then they were solemnly invested in their robes, " *cum potestate magistralem cathedram ascendendi, illamque regendi, legendi, glossandi, interpretandi, disputandi, ceterosque doctoreos et magistrales actus hic et ubique locorum exercendi.*"[2]

Shortly afterwards they set out for Bavaria. The stern winter of northern Italy had begun and their route lay through the Alps, but they had next to nothing to say about their journey. At Trent they found the Spanish bishops still in residence, pathetically intent on proving their loyalty to the Emperor. They were very good to the three travellers and showed much joy on hearing that their destination was Germany. The ride to Trent had taken them five days, but they were none the worse for it, and arrived, according to Salmeron, " safe and sound." They remained three days in the city " in order to rest the horses which were tired, and to visit the bishops."[3] The next stage of their journey took them to Dillingen, where they were welcomed with tears of joy by the good Cardinal Truchsess, who had conceived the plan of founding a new university under the direction of three men : Peter Soto, the learned and saintly Dominican confessor of the Emperor ; Martin Olave, a doctor of the Sorbonne who became a Jesuit shortly afterwards ; and Peter Canisius. For the present, however, Peter Canisius was not to be appropriated, but later he would make up royally for the disappointment he had to cause the Cardinal. At Munich the three Jesuits made their bow to the Duke of Bavaria and were received with every mark of kindness and affection by him and his powerful Chancellor. Next day, November 13th, they reached their journey's end. All the dons and doctors of Ingolstadt came to their lodging that evening to read them an address of welcome. Peter Canisius replied with an eloquent little extempore speech, offering their services very heartily to the University. Then there was a banquet at which they were the guests of honour. The following morning they were conducted to the principal college and assigned rooms that would have been quite comfortable but for the racket made by boisterous undergraduates. It was arranged, too, that they need not appear at high table but might dine and live in the private Italian fashion to which they were accustomed.[4] Such was the prosaic beginning of St. Peter's German apostolate.

[1] Braunsberger, *Epistulae*, vol. i, p. 685.
[2] M.H., *Salmeronis Epistolae*, vol. i, p. 86.
[3] Salmeron to St. Ignatius, October 15, 1549. Boero, *Vita del servo di Dio P. Alfonso Salmeron* (1880), pp. 33–4.
[4] M.H., Polanco, *Chronicon*, vol. i, pp. 413–4.

CHAPTER IV

THE BURDENS OF BAVARIA

THE Germany to which St. Peter returned was seething with unrest. Emperor Charles had beaten his high-placed enemies but, unhappy man, in the flush of victory made more dangerous ones by antagonizing the common people. His Spanish mercenaries got out of hand and by their insolent behaviour stirred all the placid Hänschens and Gretchens to the kind of slow anger that is the more terrible for being so forbearing. Spain and everything Spanish, including the Emperor, became objects of detestation, in spite of the fact that the first action of Charles on entering a town was to have a scaffold erected and a few Spanish heads duly chopped off, *pour encourager les autres*. The Emperor's treasury was empty, the Pope was estranged, and sleepless foreign foes, France on the one side and the Turk on the other, only waited for Charles to become embroiled in another domestic struggle in order to join in and destroy him. To judge from the great portrait by Titian, he was at this time a sick and disillusioned man, prematurely old. There seemed left to him but one alternative, to strive for such a pacification of his dominions as would reconcile the Protestant Princes and prevent them from selling their services to the eager buyers over the border, no matter how harshly the Pope might criticize his action. It was to this delicate task that he addressed himself at the Diet of Augsburg, convened shortly after the cessation of hostilities.

The Diet proved a sad disappointment to his hopes, as the Protestant Princes, whom he longed to see share his concern for Germany's welfare, did their best to turn the solemn affair into a carnival, in compensation for their recent asceticism under arms. Some of them, wrote the Protestant notary, Sastrow, who was present, so behaved " that verily the devil must have laughed " and, perhaps, the devil laughed, too, at the Emperor's efforts to solve the religious problem over the head of the Pope. For this purpose the Emperor appointed a private committee consisting of the conservative Lutheran, Johann Agricola, and some Catholics of conciliatory temper, among whom were two good friends of Peter Canisius, the Carmelite, Eberhard Billick, and Julius Pflug, Bishop of Naumburg. It was the business of these men to draft a scheme of religious accommodation which might serve as a provisional norm of belief and practice for the Protestant parts of the Empire until a general council more amenable to the Emperor's wishes than Trent should be convened. The formula which they produced was Catholic in tone, but it lacked theological precision and was worded with deliberate vagueness in the crucial sections on justification and the Mass. It also permitted marriage to the clergy, with certain reservations, and granted the chalice to the laity. Like the similar pacific measure of Regensburg some years earlier, the Augsburg formula became popularly known as the *Interim*, on account of its provisional character, but the Protestants, to whom alone it applied, chose to call it the *Interitum*, or measure of destruction.

This book is not a history of the Reformation, but a certain amount of digression into that field is necessary because it was there that Peter Canisius gathered his sheaves, and his work is not understandable without reference to the tares and cockle which made such a martyrdom of his harvesting. The *Interim* provided the soil for a fresh crop of every sort of doctrinal weed. Charles managed to pilot it through the Diet without too much difficulty by bribing the impecunious Elector of Brandenburg, who at this time was trying to ward off his creditors with promissory notes " powerful enough to poison a snake." But when the measure became law on June 30, 1548, it raised such a storm of protest as had not swept Germany for a generation. None were so easy-going as to do it reverence, not the Catholics who naturally regarded it as derogatory to the Pope, nor the Protestants who also quite naturally saw in it an insidious device for bringing back the Mass and other practices which they detested. " Nobody wants the *Interim*," a high court official reported sadly, while the French ambassador, de Marillac, described it sourly as " *la chose la plus mal considérée du monde.*"[1] De Marillac, who was an earnest-minded churchman and afterwards Archbishop of Vienne, did not object to the measure on religious grounds. The *Interim* was " *mal considérée* " because it might bring peace to Germany, which was the last thing that France wanted.

Moritz of Saxony, who had been requited for his valuable services in the recent war with the title and estates of his cousin the captive Elector,

---

[1] His amusingly hostile report is reproduced by Ranke, *Deutsche Geschichte im Zeitalter der Reformation* (Leipzig ed., 1925), vol. v, pp. 400–10.

liked the *Interim* as little as anybody. He wished to regain the respect of his fellow-Protestants which he had lost by siding with the Emperor, and the *Interim*, as it stood, was certainly not going to help him. Accordingly he determined to have it revised for his own dominions by Melanchthon, who was clever at such work. But this time Melanchthon failed because the conservative strain in his soul allowed far too many traces of old belief and practice—the so-called ' Adiaphora '—to stand in the Leipzig *Interim* for the taste of the more rigid Protestants. The captain of the opposition group was Melanchthon's former protégé, Flacius Illyricus, a man as exotic as his name, learned in strange ways, and the prize fanatic of the century. Up to the date of Luther's death in 1546 a certain amount of harmony had reigned in the Protestant ranks, as most of the leaders deferred to the authority of Wittenberg, but now, with the publication of the Leipzig *Interim*, " Whirl became king." Flacius broke off all dealings with Melanchthon, retired from Wittenberg and set up rival schools in Magdeburg and Jena. Within a short time, the Flacians and the Philippists, as Melanchthon's people were named, had begun a fierce theological war in which the stalwarts of both sides damned and anathematized one another far more heartily than did Rome the lot of them. Flacius, whom Melanchthon now regularly referred to as " the Viper of Illyria," was a man of incredible vehemence, and deafened the decent world ceaselessly with ringing blasts against Wittenberg and Rome. No weapon came amiss in the struggle, the foulest slanders, the vilest misrepresentation, the most scurrilous abuse, all darkened men's counsels and set the whole of Germany by the ears.[1] Later on, the " Variations " of these men would give Bossuet his splendid chance which he seized so effectively as to lure even that very queer fish, Edward Gibbon, for a time, into St. Peter's net ; and Döllinger, after him, filled three learned volumes with evidence proving that the direct result of their squabbles and clashing doctrines was an appalling decline of national morality. The most emphatic acknowledgment of the evil came from the belligerents themselves, especially from Melanchthon, who, in his *Commentary on St. Matthew*, expressed the conviction that it portended the end of the world.

It would be a great mistake, however, to think that the Protestants alone were responsible for Germany's misfortunes. The Catholic clergy and bishops must take their share of the blame. Some say it was the

---

[1] An informative study of Reformation verbal amenities was contributed by Dr. Friedrich Lipp to the series, *Quellen und Darstellungen aus der Geschichte des Reformation Jahrhunderts*, vol. viii (1908). It makes comforting reading as evidence of what God's great sacrament of time has done for men's tongues and pens.

larger share,[1] but, however that may be, it was sufficiently large to make Pope Adrian VI declare solemnly that the Reformation was "a punishment for the sins of men and especially for the sins of the priests and prelates of the Church."[2] Had they not been such faithless shepherds, had they done even the minimum that their calling demanded, it would have been impossible for the Reformation to stride with so much ease to its victories. How great those victories were may be estimated from the report of the Venetian Envoy, Badoero, writing in 1557, that nine-tenths of the German people were then Lutherans or other sectarians.[3]

In Bavaria, which we are accustomed to think of as a typically Catholic land, as Catholic as Italy or Ireland, Protestantism achieved complete, if only temporary, success over wide areas, and in the greater part of the country was pushing on to triumph under the patronage of half a hundred aristocratic families. That it failed in the long run was not due to any natural affinity of the Bavarian soul for Catholicism, as nearly all the great champions of the Church in the struggle were foreigners, while the chief Protestant aggressors were Bavarian born. The explanation of that curious reversal of rôles lay as usual in the failure of the native clergy and bishops to look after their flocks. Most of the bishops behaved purely and simply as German princes, wasting their time on what Chancellor Granvelle, who was no stickler for the proprieties, described as "la vénerie désordonée dudict Bavière." The few whose souls were above hunting the wild boar found other ways of shirking their primary duties, and even Cardinal Truchsess of Augsburg, whom Peter Canisius had learned to love, was so possessed by the traditional Kunstliebe of his people that he had no time for episcopal ministrations.[4] With the bishops in this state it is hardly surprising to find a good and faithful eye-witness deploring that the rural clergy spent most of their time in pot-houses, and that the clergy in general led "such lazy, gluttonous, drunken, dissolute, gambling lives as to be a scandal before God and the world."[5] Paumgartner, the

---

[1] For instance, the Catholic historian Knöpfler, in his Die Kelchbewegung in Bayern (1891), p. 42.

[2] Raynaldus, Annales Ecclesiastici, ad ann. 1522, lxv sq. "Scimus in hac sancta sede," continued the Pope, "aliquot jam annis multa abominanda fuisse, abusus in spiritualibus, excessus in mandatis, et omnia denique in perversum mutata. . . . Nec mirum si aegritudo a capite in membra, a Summis Pontificibus in alios inferiores praelatos descenderit. Omnes nos, id est praelati ecclesiastici, declinavimus unusquisque in vias suas nec fuit jam diu qui faceret bonum, non fuit usque ad unum. . . ."

[3] "Delle dieci parti della popolazione le sette sono de'luterani, due dell' altre opinioni, e una de' Cattolici." Albèri, Le Relazione degli Ambasciatori Veneti al Senato, first series, vol. iii (Florence, 1853), p. 182. This estimate cannot have been too far wide of the mark because it was borne out by other observers.

[4] Riezler, Geschichte Baierns, vol. iv, p. 104. Truchsess was 400,000 gulden in debt, owing to extravagance.

[5] Pfleger, Martin Eisengrein (1908), p. 17. Eisengrein was a great worker in the cause of true Catholic reformation. Further evidence from his pen will be given later on.

Bavarian ambassador at Trent in 1561, informed the Council that among the parochial priests of his country were to be found men professing the views of Zwingli, Luther, Flacius Illyricus, and other sectaries, and that at the visitation of 1558 more than 90 per cent of the clergy were discovered to be living in open or secret concubinage.[1]

Clerical education had suffered so terribly in the unrest and trouble of the times that numbers of priests could not stand the most elementary test in Christian doctrine.[2] As Lejay had said, Scripture and theology were dead and buried. For a long time these studies had been losing their lustre at the hands of verbose and uninspired professors who made a fashion of hair-splitting. When the Reformation came they afforded an easy target for the satire of humanists and Lutherans and soon were so discredited that nobody with anything better to do would listen to them. These were the days when to study the great Duns Scotus was to be a ' dunce,' and when a trivial person was one who followed the old scholastic system of the *Trivia*. Tradition wilted in that atmosphere of ridicule, and Bavaria's solitary university at Ingolstadt which championed it gradually sank into even worse decay than her sister institution at Cologne.

Like Cologne, Ingolstadt had once been a famous seat of learning. Founded in 1472 by a classically-minded Duke who conferred on his offspring all the rights and privileges of Plato's Academy in Athens, Ingolstadt's first fifty years were made illustrious by the teaching of Reuchlin and other equally great scholars. It was the university of which Melanchthon first thought when starting his career, and what might not have happened had he gone there to Johann Eck instead of to Martin Luther at Wittenberg ! The papal bull of foundation required that candidates at Ingolstadt should take an oath of allegiance to the Holy See, a provision in which one authority has seen " almost the first instance of anything in the nature of a test in university history."[3] This so-called test gave the new establishment a definitely Catholic stamp from the start, to which it lived up valiantly during the first decades of the Reformation. Eck, with his " solid square body and full German voice," stood at the head of the faculty of theology for thirty-two years and caused Luther the most serious embarrassment by battering away at him incessantly in language not much less violent than his own. He was easily the best match for Luther that the age provided, with the result that the name

[1] Riezler, *Geschichte Baierns*, vol. iv, p. 513.
[2] See below, Chapter xiv, p. 606 sq.
[3] Rashdall, *The Universities of Europe in the Middle Ages* (1895), vol. ii, part i, p. 272.

and fame of Ingolstadt spread all over the Continent. After his death in 1543,[1] the University began rapidly to decline because no scholar of equal ability could be found to replace him. Professors of the rival schools of philosophy known as Nominalism and Realism continued their traditional feud, regardless of the fact that Lutheran emissaries had begun to proselytize in their midst. Young people since the world began have been lovers of novelty, so the apostles from Wittenberg found ready listeners among the students, whose natural guardians were too intent on the fight over their metaphysical bone to protect them.

It was an hour of crisis for Bavaria and, indeed, for German Catholicism, to which Ingolstadt University stood in the same relation as Wittenberg to Protestantism. If Ingolstadt were captured by the Lutherans, as seemed dangerously probable, the supply of educated priests, such as it was, would forthwith cease, to the extinction of all hope of a Catholic restoration. Duke William IV realized the danger and, as already related, decided to appeal to the Pope and St. Ignatius for the help of the Jesuits. The Protestant scholar, Drews, notes November 13, 1549, the date of the Jesuits' entrance into Ingolstadt as "a day momentous in the history not only of that University but of Germany."[2]

In return for the services of his three men, Lejay, Salmeron and Canisius, whom he could ill spare, St. Ignatius had begged the Duke to grant them a home of their own at the University. He was well-informed on German affairs and felt that the members of his Order could work with real effectiveness only if they had a place where they might live according to their rule and train others to their ideals. Where was the good, he asked a little later, of providing professors if there was nobody to listen to them, and how better than by the establishment of a college could a contingent of sedulous, well-grounded students of theology be prepared for the University lecture-rooms?[3] The Saint had no wish to see his men secluded dons with their heads in the clouds. He

---

[1] He is buried in the Liebfrauenkirche of Ingolstadt. Many instances of his pawky sense of humour could be cited. Once a Bavarian blue-stocking of Lutheran sympathies challenged him and the whole theological faculty to a public debate, whereupon he procured a distaff and spinning-wheel and sent them round to the lady with his compliments. How much he was feared and detested by the Lutheran leaders may be guessed from the epitaph which Melanchthon wrote to his memory:

Πολλὰ φαγὼν καὶ πολλὰ πιὼν καὶ πολλὰ κακ' εἰπὼν
Τῷ δὲ τάφῳ Ἔκιος γαστέρ' ἔθηκε ἔην.

Having guzzled and fuddled up to the neck
Here lies the belly of foul-mouthed Eck !

Bretschneider, *Corpus Reformatorum*, vol. ix, p. 583. Some accentual and other misprints in the quotation as given by Bretschneider have been corrected.

[2] *Petrus Canisius, der erste deutsche Jesuit*, in *Schriften des Vereins für Reformationsgeschichte*, vol. x (1892), p. 26.

[3] *Cartas de San Ignacio de Loyola* (Madrid, 1875), vol. ii, p. 467.

was intensely practical and expressed a hope to the Duke that, given the college, the Jesuits would be able in due course to do much towards the restoration of Christian discipline in his dominions. Impressed by the argument, William promised faithfully to start the college without delay.

There was nothing dramatic in the beginnings of the three Jesuits at Ingolstadt, nothing more remarkable than the appearance of some new masters at a school. Peter Canisius delivered their inaugural lecture on November 26th, and had an audience that included most of the University staff. According to Lejay, who by temperament was not inclined to be unduly optimistic, the first efforts of his colleagues caused a mild sensation. Their lecture-rooms were crowded out and even the great and very busy Chancellor of Bavaria, Leonhard von Eck, did not disdain to sit under Canisius and Salmeron. Afterwards he professed himself highly delighted with the experience, but it was soon to appear that his and others' enthusiasm for the work of the newcomers meant little more than a gesture of politeness, based rather on curiosity than on any zeal for good theology. Theology, "*per tutto sepolto*," as Lejay had earlier reported, could not have had so swift a resurrection as all that. When the college question came to the fore von Eck showed his true colours. It was one thing to express admiration for the ability of the Jesuits, but quite another to spend money on them which Bavaria badly needed for her political war-chest. With his talent for procrastination and playing a double game, the Chancellor thought he would quietly shelve the issue and, by giving the Jesuits an occasional pat on the back, gradually reconcile them to the frustration of their hopes. Before he had been in Ingolstadt a month Lejay informed St. Ignatius that there seemed to be no prospect of obtaining the college and that the only thing giving him confidence and enabling him to work on "*in speranza contra speranza*" was the Saint's own assurance that the college would eventually be founded.

Pope Paul III, who died in November, 1549, had granted the Duke of Bavaria tithes on the clergy of his dominions for three years, as a contribution to the upkeep of Ingolstadt University. The first year, 1549, brought in more than 24,000 gold florins, which the Chancellor made a great show of employing scrupulously on the object intended by the Pope. He summoned the various professors, including the three Jesuits, to discuss with them the best way of investing the money in the interests of the University. There was a great deal of talk and sage advice, and that was the last that the University heard of its gulden. Lejay had hoped that some of them might go to the foundation of the promised college but forbore to suggest this to the Chancellor because, as he reported to St. Ignatius, a good friend of theirs, the Regent of the ecclesiastical Collegium Georgianum, "had warned Master Peter that if we tried to get a portion of the money set aside for the college we should have all the other doctors and professors up in arms against us."

After much prayer and consideration the three men at length decided to put their case before the Chancellor in explicit terms. Lejay thus tells the story:

Two days ago von Eck went to a lecture given by Master Salmeron and was so marvellously pleased with it that he came here after his dinner to consult Don Alfonso. We were all three together in my room at the time, so I seized the opportunity to embark on the explanation which we had agreed to lay before the Chancellor. The gist of it was that it would be to the honour of God and to the benefit of the University, of Bavaria and even of all Germany, if a college of our Society were established at Ingolstadt. To persuade him of this I said a good deal about our Institute and pointed out that if we had a college we could provide a continuous stream of students for the University and also give it a succession of good lecturers in theology and philosophy. Then I urged that we could not do otherwise than expect a college from a Duke who was genuinely Catholic, most liberal-hearted and keenly anxious to help the University. This point I enforced by speaking of the kings, dukes, signories and civic authorities who had given us colleges in other parts of the world. I concluded by saying that nobody was in a better position to promote such a project than the Chancellor himself, and I sang his praises a little, but modestly for fear we might seem to be flatterers.

He answered: "I have been thinking about this matter for two years and only a few days ago I spoke about it to the abbots here. Have no fear at all. Your wishes will be completely fulfilled, for I know the mind of my Prince." Then he said two or three times in Italian: "*Lassate fare a mi*—leave it to me. I like your Institute and way of life." Taking him up, I urged that the foundation of the college would be quite easy because there were vacant benefices and almost empty religious houses in the neighbourhood whose funds might be used for the purpose, with the sanction of the Pope. When I had finished, he said several times over: "Everything will be as you wish. Leave it to me." For this we rendered thanks to God and to his Highness.

Yesterday, at two in the afternoon, von Eck appeared with some gentlemen in Master Peter's lecture-room. He was mightily pleased with the lecture and sent us the enclosed document. We thereupon took him the letters of those cardinals who have shown singular friendship to the Society, namely Cardinals Farnese, Maffei, Cervini, Carpi, Borgos, and Verallo. Once again, to-day, the Chancellor came to Master Salmeron's lecture and appeared greatly satisfied with it. Afterwards he said that he had reserved ten thousand gold florins for the construction of a college building and that as soon as the new Pope had been elected he would expedite the matter by sending an envoy to Rome. The Duke would himself write to the cardinals whose letters we had presented. We asked the Chancellor how many scholars the new college would be able to support but to this we received only the vague answer, " a good number." Finally, we begged him, while expediting the matter, to be careful not to involve us in disedifying disputes over the question of applying the funds of vacant benefices. " Leave it to me," he said once again.[1]

The eagerness of the Jesuits to possess a college in Bavaria will be better understood before this chapter closes. In sober truth the situation in the country fell little short of being desperate. It was all very well for the Bavarian Duke to tell Cardinal Crescenzi that the three newcomers not only satisfied him but exceeded his highest expectations and made him confident that " their teaching and the example of their perfect lives would be most helpful in restoring true religion to those parts of Germany from which it had disappeared."[2] The Apostolic Nuncio, Lippomani, Bishop of Verona, had quite a different story to relate. A week after the Duke had penned his panegyric, March 5, 1550, Lippomani reported to Rome from personal observation on the spot that the Jesuits were " certainly wasting their time " in Ingolstadt, where they had only fourteen pupils between them, ten of whom were illiterate. " May God," he continued bitterly, " forgive those who were responsible for the removal of Don Alfonso Salmeron from Verona, where he was doing so much good."[3] That seems to have been more like the truth of the matter, though Lippomani was not entirely unprejudiced. The three doctors of Bologna, two of whom had distinguished themselves at the Council of Trent, could not find even a score of students interested in theology.

[1] M.H., *Epistolae PP. Broëtii, Jaii*, etc., pp. 345–9.
[2] Braunsberger, *Epistulae*, vol. i, p. 693.
[3] Braunsberger, *Epistulae*, vol. i, p. 694.

The brave fourteen came to their lectures probably because they had no other alternative, and they were to be the new pastors of Bavaria, the best she could produce from her population of half a million. Faced, then, as they were, with the spectacle of a depleted and ever dwindling native priesthood, sunk in ignorance and as lazy as sin, the Jesuits naturally concluded that the country could be saved only by a transfusion of new blood ; by the introduction of trained and zealous workers from Spain, the Netherlands and Italy. If they had their college they could import such men from their institutions abroad, a picked company who would attend the University courses and set the pace for the easy-going, comfortable Bavarians.

From the start, and despite the fact that his lectures, after the first deceptive fuss, found so little patronage, Peter Canisius seems to have made a deep impression on the notabilities of Ingolstadt. At any rate they did him the honour of accounting him a very present help in time of trouble. It was the custom in the University to hold a solemn service at the Liebfrauenkirche on Christmas Eve. This was attended by the whole academic body for the purpose of hearing a Latin discourse from some distinguished preacher. In 1549 the chosen orator fell ill or got stage fright at the last moment, thereby causing panic among the dignitaries responsible. They begged Peter to come to the rescue, and, " though he had not a moment to prepare," says the record, " he preached a sermon of the most satisfying eloquence."[1]

The Bavarians may have been slack and slow in other respects, but they certainly were not lie-abeds, to judge by the hours of the lectures at Ingolstadt. Peter's were timed for the fearsome hour of six o'clock in the morning. During them and in his private dealings with the students, he strove in whatever way he could to infuse a religious spirit into the life of the University. He began and ended his classes with prayers, a practice before unknown at Ingolstadt, and his intense, personal love of Our Lord shed its transfiguring glow even over the arid technicalities of his Lombard namesake whose *Book of Sentences* he was obliged by statute to use as the basis of his teaching. Some time in 1550 he started the compilation of a kind of theological dictionary. The first page of his manuscript contains fifty different titles of Our Lord, culled from Scripture and other sacred sources and all written in a pattern so carefully and neatly as to make evident the deep love that guided his pen. There is not much balance or style in the little anthology, but feeling, when intense,

[1] M.H., Polanco, *Chronicon*, vol. ii, p. 71.

transcends such planned expression; it is rhapsodical and repetitive, carving the loved one's name on trees or tracing it in the dust over and over again.[1]

Soon, through his kindness and devotion to their interests, Peter seems to have acquired considerable influence with the student body in general. They took to visiting him in his room and, rare mark of esteem, brought him before Christmas their private copies of Luther, Bucer, and Melanchthon, not, indeed, to keep or destroy but as a temporary surrender in consideration of the season, somewhat as a man might give up smoking during Lent. It was a disquieting sort of Christmas present for Peter, since no one was allowed to possess such books under pain of instant excommunication. When the Christmas festivities came to an end the young men reclaimed their unlawful property.[2] That people of their years should have been in possession of the books and so anxious to retain them is striking evidence of the efficiency of Lutheran propaganda, and also proof that discipline on the Catholic side had gone to pieces. The traffic in heretical books was one of Peter's most troublesome problems. Protestant printing-presses were many and prolific, and enterprising zealots abounded, eager to serve the cause and their own pockets by circulating what emanated from them in Bavaria. Though the Duke hated the subversive smuggling he was unable to do more than give it a spice of risk by employing detectives and ordering occasional police raids. As for the sentence of excommunication, it seems to have been about as much or little a deterrent as is nowadays Bernhard Tauchnitz's hopeful inscription, *Not to be introduced into the British Empire*, on the front of his volumes.

While very anxious to get the heretical books out of the students' hands, Peter greatly desired to get them lawfully into his own. Many worried people had begun to consult him on theological difficulties, and he needed to be well acquainted with the Protestant argument if he was to help such clients. But the Roman authorities, who plainly did not understand what was going on in Bavaria and apparently considered legislation suitable for the Papal States the right thing for Germany too, showed themselves exceedingly slow to grant his petition. Peter, on his side, was scrupulous to a fault and would not open an heretical book without explicit assurance that the bull, *In Coena Domini*, which contained the prohibitions, did not apply in his case. This assurance was denied him for a long time, to his very great inconvenience and uneasiness. As will

---

[1] A facsimile of this document is reproduced below, facing p. 822.
[2] M.H., Polanco, *Chronicon*, vol. ii, pp. 70-1.

Duke William IV and Duke Albert V of Bavaria

From the "Excubiae Tutelares LX Heroum" of Andreas Brunner (1655)

be seen, the *In Coena Domini*, together with the Index legislation that grew out of it afterwards, constituted one of the heaviest crosses of his pastoral career.

To the consternation of earnest Catholics Duke William and his great Chancellor both died in March, 1550. That catastrophe seemed to put a definite *finis* to the college project, because Albert V, who succeeded, had at first very little of his father's serious concern for the religious welfare of Bavaria. Music and art were his pieties, and to them he devoted all his resources and splendid ability. Munich's Medicean era now dawned with the inauguration of her world-famous collections, her magnificent Court Library and her festivals of song and dance. With schemes such as these absorbing his thoughts, and with a new chancellor to advise him who believed in conciliating the Protestants, Albert felt little inclina-tion to humour such people as the Jesuits, lost, as they seemed, to all sense of the value of art or, indeed, of any values short of the tiresome eternal ones.

. In the circumstances, Lejay and Salmeron began to despair of the promised college, but their younger brother's hopes were of tougher fibre and, instead of repining, Peter Canisius turned from his own troubles to comfort and encourage his fellow-labourers in other places. Thus on March 19, 1550, he addressed the following lines to the Jesuits of Cologne, enclosing copies of letters received from Jesuits at work in missionary countries :

JESUS

Dearest Brothers in Christ Our Lord, may the grace of the Holy Spirit, peace past all understanding and the immortal fruits of obedience be yours. Your letter reached me this very evening, good evidence not only of your diligence and progress in study but of your charity and courtesy to me, your brother. What could be pleasanter news for me and for all of us here than to learn of your undisguised contempt for worldly vanities, of your united ardour in bearing the yoke of Christ, of your strong determination to fulfil the precepts of obedience, and, finally, of the wonderful holy rivalry wherewith you pursue your studies and foster in your souls those desires which Christ suggests to His chosen ones ?

Though, I think, you have no need of my exhortations, I never-theless beg and implore you all, through Our Lord Jesus Christ, to prize obedience as the most beautiful and most holy of services and to bring into relation with it every detail of your studies and every movement of your hearts. For family love, learning, sermons, prayers, and all holy exercises ought to have their place and importance in our lives determined for us by their conformity with obedience. Anything that openly withdraws us from obedience, or causes us to be unfaithful to it in secret, profanes the temple of God, grieves His Holy Spirit, defeats His love and makes progress in all true religion impossible.

I would wish, then, that, as a rock-like foundation for your lives, you should daily consider with attentive hearts this your divine vocation, asking yourselves whether there is anything you ought to make good or improve in it, in order to be truly the companions of Jesus and to be justly so esteemed. . . . To this are you called, Brothers, for this are you ordained that you should in accordance with the simple rule of obedience surrender and resign yourselves to the guidance of another in all things, for the love of Christ. If you do this, as by divine and human sanction you should, then reckon yourselves novices, soldiers, brothers, disciples of the Society of Jesus; then judge that all is well with you, though there be few who approve the way you have chosen, nay, though everybody should neglect you utterly and visit you with their hate and scorn. . . .

I am sending you the records of what seem to me the most beautiful fruits of obedience which the Captain of our Army, Jesus, gathered from His soldiers only a few months ago. How true it is that the hand of the Lord is not shortened ! You will read in these letters about your brothers' most gallant struggles, about their burning zeal, their indefatigable labours, their apostolic faith, and their neighbourly charity, so great as hardly to be believed. And all this structure of God was built on the foundation of obedience. I shall be surprised indeed if you can read the story of such wonderful and perfect doings without profit to your souls. For myself, I was profoundly affected and felt myself quite a changed man, especially when I measured my meanness against the glorious example of my brethren.

We must pray to the Father of mercies that He may always keep us and our Society what it has so happily been from its beginning, namely, the good odour of Christ in almost every place, not only in Italy, Sicily, Spain, and Portugal, but in Arabia, India, and other regions where the holy name of Christ had hitherto been unknown. Of Germany I need not now say anything, though this land, too, has seen the Society's labours and will see them more and more as time goes on. Here in Ingolstadt many things promise well for us, even though the old Duke of Bavaria be dead. . . .

It was a great pleasure to receive from you the greetings of my Fathers of the Charterhouse. I am most anxious that you should remember me to them in turn. I shall not let pass any occasion of serving such excellent men, though, in truth, it is rather Canisius who needs the help of their prayers, Canisius whom they took so readily and kindlily to their hearts for many years that they deserve to be held dearer by him than all his dear ones. . . .

Good-bye, beloved Brothers, and continue to pray very much for us because of our great need.[1]

A marked trait in St. Peter's character was his keen appreciation of the efforts of other people. This is reflected in his correspondence thousands of times, as is also his sympathy with others in their setbacks and sorrows. It is a trait, by the goodness of God, not uncommon among men but it usually has very definite limitations. Kindly interest in the doings and sufferings of others is apt to wax or wane in inverse ratio to their distance from us in miles, those estranging miles that often make such sorry wraiths of our friends. It needs a big heart to bridge them with faithfulness, and a big heart Peter Canisius most assuredly possessed. He had the rare gift of stepping easily out of his busy hour to send a message of hope or comfort over frontiers or across seas. From his letters he appears to have been as keenly alive to the daily ups and downs of the Jesuit communities in Cologne, Louvain, Rome and Messina as if he actually belonged to them. But his brother Jesuits were far from being the only ones to experience his generosity as adviser, consoler, or bedesman. He was just as kind to people who had no obvious claim on him, to bishops, priests, nuns, men and women of the world, students, children, mendicants, and especially persons deservedly or undeservedly in prison. Most of the saints specialized in helping some particular form of human misery. For St. Ignatius it was fallen women; for St. Vincent de Paul, galley-slaves and orphan children; for St. Camillus de Lellis, the dying. St. Peter Canisius, all through life, took prisoners of every description as his favourite province.

It would be good indeed to know the secret steps by which he had climbed to his heights of selflessness at the age of twenty-nine. His

[1] Braunsberger, *Epistulae*, vol. i, pp. 301-5.

beginnings had shown small promise of such swift achievement, and later at Cologne Surius and he were for a time just

> Two lads that thought there was no more behind
> But such a day to-morrow as to-day,
> And to be boy eternal.

Alas, it is only the novelist who has the privilege of getting inside his hero's skin and listening to his most secret self-communings. The biographer must do what he can with a mass of dead documents which at the best are but poor, still-life pictures or photographic shots of a growing, evolving, uncapturable process.

Two features in the lives of the Jesuits at Ingolstadt won the special admiration of the Germans, their frugality, in contrast with the Germans themselves who, St. Peter says, had "no equals on earth as trenchermen and drinkers," and the fact that they gave their teaching free, unlike the other professors. From the scanty references here and there in his letters Peter appears to have been a man temperamentally akin to the old Caroline worthy who "loved littleness almost in all things, a little, cheerful house, a little company and a very little feast." The house in Ingolstadt was, perhaps, too cheerful because next door to the Jesuits lived some hearty Bavarian youths who had the miserable vice of bursting into song at all hours of the day and night.[1] As for the "very little feast" it meant in Peter's case more often than not a very big fast. All his life he was known for his abstemiousness, striving thus to "angelize" the body and also to make atonement for the excesses to which his beloved Germans were notoriously addicted. Far from hardening him, however, his austerities did but temper his soul to a greater serenity and establish in it that "central peace subsisting at the heart of endless agitation," which is the most beautiful triumph of conduct.

One of Peter's most frequent correspondents and dearest friends during many years was the Secretary-General of the Society of Jesus, Father John Polanco. Shortly after arriving in Ingolstadt he had written to this man at Rome: "It is impossible that I should ever forget your charity to me. You will remain always so fixed and engraved on my heart that, even though you write me never a word, though I may never be able to look upon my Polanco's face again, it is beyond my power not to love and cherish the very thought of you in your absence."[2] To Polanco, and later on to Father James Laynez, Peter was accustomed

---

[1] Braunsberger, *Epistulae*, vol. i, p. 376.   [2] Braunsberger, *Epistulae*, vol. i, p. 299.

to speak more freely than to others of his friends. " We have many well-wishers," he informed the first of the two in the letter just now cited, " and, what frankly astonishes me, we are not being tested by any misfortunes." If these were what he wanted he had only to wait a little. Two months later, March 24, 1550, he addressed Polanco again, this time in very different accents :

I shall tell you now in detail how we are faring and how this country is placed, for I am naturally given to speaking out, and even if I could slur things over it is not my way to do so, especially when writing to your Reverence. First of all, we have to be most careful in our lectures not to cite scholastic authorities often, nor to give allegorical interpretations of Scripture,[1] if we wish to retain our present audience of students. They are beginning to fall away already, though we try our best to please them by avoiding too much subtlety and neglecting no part of duty. Would that there were even four or five of them whom we might hope to benefit by our lectures! As for the majority, if our Reverend Father Ignatius had control of their education I certainly think no harm would be done by putting them back into the classes of grammar and rhetoric. In this university it is almost a convention that students need not trouble to study letters, least of all sacred letters.

To turn to another matter, as soon as I began to take a little interest in some of the students, to hear their confessions and give them Holy Communion at our house, the parish priest immediately flew to arms. He complained publicly that professors of theology were intruding into the province of pastors, thus, as he alleged, prejudicing the interests of his curates. We informed him that we had a papal privilege and that we had received a special commission from the Bishop of Eichstätt, who is both his and our Ordinary, to act as we did. But we did not think it advisable to show him our documents nor, indeed, to make much use of the privileges, at this beginning of our mission.

There is here a large concourse of students, especially students of law, from different parts of Germany, and, of course, various opinions and errors in matters of faith are prevalent among them. These opinions are not frowned on by the leading men of the University, either because they are unable or unwilling to stamp them out. The truth is, and

[1] It was and is the teaching of Catholic theology that the words of Scripture may bear other meanings than the literal. In her liturgy the Church constantly uses the sacred text in these derived senses, applying, for instance, the beautiful imagery of the Canticle of Canticles to the Blessed Virgin. The Protestant reformers, especially Calvin, denounced this practice and maintained that only the literal sense was legitimate.

they know it, that they have little share in the management of University affairs which for long have been controlled by the Duke and Chancellor von Eck. Eck was virtually master of all the faculties. May our most merciful Lord grant His peace to the souls of these two men.

Speaking generally, I may say that it is useless to look for practical interest in religion among present-day Germans. The divine worship of Catholics is reduced pretty well to the preaching of an uninspired sermon on feast-days. All that remains of the Lenten fast here is its name, for nobody fasts. And, oh, how rare it is for a man to visit a church, to go to Mass or to show by any outward sign that he still delights in the ancient faith. So much for the Catholics, or, rather, for those who keep the bare title of Catholic. At least one public Mass is said daily in our chapel which is quite near to the students' living quarters and in the centre of the town. Yet, though two bells are rung to invite them, I do not believe that even were we to bribe them with gold we could induce a couple of these men to come to the Holy Sacrifice. At the same time they are quite generous in their praise of what they judge to be our learning and piety.

One exceptionally good friend of ours here, who is provost of a college and a leading figure in the University, has lent us books and always shown us great kindness. Following the general custom, this man acquired possession of many Lutheran publications. At length we ventured to point out to him how dangerous this was, seeing that the retention of such books is strictly forbidden by the *In Coena Domini*. Also, for the sake of his soul we began to hold frequent devout conversations with him, but the only result of our exhortations was to throw him into such agitation that we are now wondering whether it would not have been better to have left him alone. And he is one of the best Catholics and finest theologians to be found here.

From this one case you can guess the difficulties and opposition with which we should be confronted were we to endeavour openly to get heretical books out of the hands of all who possess them. Even if we had a mandate from the Duke I doubt whether, being foreigners, we could strictly enforce it, especially as the people are so little in love with the Church of Rome. For this reason we do not greatly mind being without faculties for absolving from such sins, though we still desire to have them.[1] Before anybody here was in a fit state to receive

[1] By a bull of 1536 Pope Paul III decreed that those who kept or read heretical books could not be absolved from the sentence of excommunication, except *in articulo mortis*, by anybody but the Sovereign Pontiff.

absolution much preparatory work would have to be done. Reserved cases have never been promulgated in Germany and are so little regarded that, to our surprise, parish priests and monks absolve people in possession of heretical books. They plead that the *In Coena Domini* does not bind in Germany and that it cannot have been the Pope's intention to excommunicate learned Catholics who read heretical books for the good purpose of refuting them. Further, it is urged that up to the present time many learned men, good theologians and zealous defenders of the Church seem not to have worried whether they themselves or others incurred the censures.[1]

We would, therefore, ask your Reverence to write and tell us what you think about these and similar matters, and also how we are to change stones into men or, in other words, change Germans into people adapted to religious life in our Society. They have a positive horror of vows and of the evangelical counsels, and practically all the sincerity and simplicity of their faith have vanished. The situation is enough to numb the heart of one who gives it serious thought. Heresy is not being overcome either by force or by reform, and, with the best will in the world to restore the faith that has been lost, we are powerless owing to the fact that priests are too few or, indeed, entirely lacking.

My reasons for saying all this are, first, to convey to your Reverence some idea of the plight to which these and neighbouring parts of the country are reduced, and, next, to rouse your charity and compassion, that so you may be moved to pray to our Eternal Master for us and for the whole of Germany. Through you, to whom I have already made this petition, I shall not cease to urge it on all our dear fathers and brothers, that where sin abounds grace may one day the more abound. Blessed be the Father of mercies who consoles us in all these difficulties and gives us hopes for the speedy founding of a college whereby the remnants of Israel may be saved ; and this, too, notwithstanding the deaths of our noble patrons, on whose souls may the light of Heaven shine.

We do not think that the new Duke will abandon such a praiseworthy enterprise which was begun by his truly Catholic father and has the approval of princes of the Church. Moreover, we are strengthened and heartened by the faith and assiduous prayers of Reverend Father Ignatius, and the whole Society. It is well understood that by

[1] St. Peter's difficulty about the forbidden books is one of the stock problems of canon law. It would be answered easily enough at the present day, but in the troubled conditions of the sixteenth century the solution was far from obvious.

no other means than the college can the faculty of theology be kept alive. . . . Were it, however, to be founded easily and without opposition, it would not, I think, be in accordance with the history of those enterprises of our Society which have succeeded best. The Lord deigns to exercise us a little that He may bring us in due course to refreshment. . . .

The letters of our dear brothers in Cologne have given us great edification as we could see from them that Father Leonard and the other sons of the Society are continuing to bear fruit in the Lord through the vigorous exercise of obedience, humility and charity, each in his own office. When my Reverend Father, Peter Favre, who now most certainly lives in glory, first started his labours in Cologne, he and we had to contend with so many obstacles that I am in good hopes he is interceding for us and will secure for us the firm establishment and prosperity of the Society on that holy ground.

I beg your Reverence's forgiveness for this rambling and faulty letter. It is just my style. And I beg you, too, to advise your son Canisius from time to time how to deal with the people of this country. Finally, would you please supply me with a catechism suitable for the Germans? There I go with my exorbitant demands, I who have no claim to any consideration. We three most earnestly commend ourselves to the prayers and Holy Sacrifices of your Reverence and of all the fathers and brothers. May the Lord ever preserve and increase in us His holy grace.

Your son and servant Peter Canisius.[1]

There was at this time in Ingolstadt a famous physician and humanist named Johannes Agricola, who, like his namesake in Browning, used to indulge in meditations on what he saw going on around him. One of his meditations was on the three Jesuits. Thinking that they might not be happy and that Ingolstadt might lose them, he begged Heinrich Schweicker, secretary to Duke Albert, to persuade his master to write and " cheer them up a little." The Duke should try to ensure that they remained for three or four years at least. His father had long been endeavouring to procure learned professors from Paris, Louvain and other places, but it was not until the Pope sent those three men that his Highness's wishes were satisfied. What a pity, then, it would be if they were withdrawn. " Of a truth they are excellent men," continued Agricola, " and

[1] Braunsberger, *Epistulae*, vol., i, pp. 306–14. As it was Jubilee year, Peter added a postscript to his letter begging Polanco to get someone to visit the Seven Churches on his behalf.

lecture no whit less ably than did Doctor Johann Eck, most learned of theologians, some years ago."[1]

Agricola may have been correct in his surmise as to the despondency of Lejay and Salmeron. Not knowing German and apparently unable to learn it, those two were cut off from the social life of the University and much hampered in their pastoral work. But Peter Canisius laboured under no such disability. Though his Rhineland accent might sound a little strange to Bavarian ears, or occasional Dutch idioms obscure his syntax, he appears to have been understood quite well in Upper Germany. His first vernacular sermon was delivered on Laetare Sunday in the Lieb-frauenkirche. "Thanks be to God, all turned out happily," he informed Polanco, " for, contrary to general expectation, I was well understood and have been requested to occupy the pulpit regularly in the future." Owing to his knowledge of the language, an acquired knowledge because his native tongue was Dutch, the bulk of the pastoral work undertaken by the Jesuits in Ingolstadt necessarily fell to him, the preaching, visiting, retreat-giving, and confessional duties. He seems to have liked it well, judging by the quiet cheerfulness of his letter to St. Ignatius on May 28, 1550. Though Duke William was in his grave, he said, " a man for whom the whole Society of Jesus ought in gratitude to pray," they had not in the least given up hopes of obtaining their college. The Germans admired their method of life, and considered it a remarkable thing because so rare in Ingolstadt that nine or ten people should approach Holy Communion in one body at the church served by the Jesuits. Even the Rector of the University himself went to Holy Communion there on Whit Sunday. More important still, they had at last prevailed upon the Regent of the Georgianum to make a clean sweep of the Lutheran books in his library. There were other small successes, too, which Peter recorded the more readily because the credit could be given to his brethren. Father Lejay brought about the sincere repentance of an elderly priest who had taken a wife and gone over to Lutheranism ; two Spaniards walked fifteen miles to make their confessions to Father Salmeron ; a German soldier to whom Peter himself gave the *Spiritual Exercises*, though he omits to mention the fact, was so moved by them that he vowed to embrace the religious life ; and, finally, all three Fathers by their prayers and Masses laid a ghost which had been frightening the lives out of people. Of his own efforts in the pulpit Peter uses the word " *tentavi* "—" I have tried my hand at preaching in German and they desire and urge

---

[1] Braunsberger, *Epistulae*, vol. i, pp. 695–6.

me to continue this work. Now, also, because the Fathers think it advisable, I am giving Latin homilies to the students on feast-days. May Christ prosper these small efforts and render us useful in His vineyard. . . . We most earnestly beg you, of your goodness, Reverend Father, to pray to Christ for us, for this University, and for all Germany."[1]

That was the modest way in which the great work of the Jesuits in Germany began, with the saving of an unhappy soul here and there and the free tutoring of a handful of students in hopes of attracting them to the Sacraments. St. Peter's biggest preliminary feat was to bring about a remarkable change in the life of Erasmus Wolf, Regent of the Collegium Georgianum. With unerring instinct he had at once concentrated his attention on this man. The college which he ruled was a clerical seminary which still exists and flourishes in Munich. But it did not flourish under Wolf until St. Peter crossed his path. The Church's regulations with regard to fasting and abstinence had long been disregarded inside its walls, and the students, in other more serious ways, set a very bad example to their lay contemporaries. Wolf, urged on by St. Peter, agreed to make the *Spiritual Exercises* and prepare for ordination, for though head of a seminary he was not a priest. Like so many others, he came forth a new man and began to devote himself wholeheartedly to the restoration of discipline and piety among his students. " *Totus est noster,*" wrote St. Peter joyfully in December, 1550.[2]

Peter did not become downhearted at the lack of more spectacular successes, because he had invested his hopes in securities that he knew would not depreciate. Friends had offered him some relics of the Cologne martyrs, aware that nothing was more acceptable, but a papal ban on the removal of relics stood in the way of his obtaining the precious gift. Addressing himself to the Nuncio, Bishop Lippomani, for a dispensation, he said : " If, in your kindness, you can relax the law for us, we shall esteem it the greatest of favours and see to it, with the help of Christ, that the dispensation bears spiritual fruit. By beholding and touching relics pious souls are much helped to devotion and, not infrequently, others are moved to pray to God and the saints for Germany."[3]

When six months had passed without any further mention of the college, Lejay and Peter determined to appeal to the new Chancellor of Bavaria, George Stockhammer. After informing him about the negotiations with his predecessor and mentioning the explicit promises, confirmed in writing, which both von Eck and the late Duke had made, they continued :

---

[1] Braunsberger, *Epistulae*, vol. i, pp. 316–9.   [2] Braunsberger, *Epistulae*, vol. i, p. 346.
[3] Braunsberger, *Epistulae*, vol. i, pp. 320–1.

Now that Divine Providence has constituted you our patron and the protector of this University, what we hope for and look for from your Excellency is plain enough. You can scarcely have any misgivings about the great advantage that, with the help of Christ, would accrue to this whole Academy from the establishment of the college. You would, then, do us an immense favour by not denying us, this first time we appeal to you, your benevolent assistance in so sacred and worthy a business. As you enjoy authority with the illustrious Duke, we earnestly beg you to commend us and our cause to his favour. If we are heard and if the business succeeds, as very many in Italy hope and predict it will, then the first thing the Excellent Prince may be assured of, as far as we are concerned, is that a supply of truly Catholic and competent professors and doctors of theology will never fail in his University.

Secondly, besides the professors there will always be a stream of genuinely keen students to spur on the others by their assiduity.

Thirdly, in addition to the presence of professors and students of theology, the college can show the further advantage of possessing a number of thoroughly formed young men who by the example of their good lives and devout conversation may edify others in Christ, as appears to be the chief need of this age.

Fourthly, we consider it certain, and in the strength of Christ promise ourselves unhesitatingly that, in the process of time, many will go forth from this college on completion of their studies to engage worthily in public duties, seeking not their own advantage but the good of others and the things of Jesus Christ. They will lecture, teach, preach and devote themselves to other such offices of piety, in both public and private, doing all *gratis* and for love, as the spirit of this Society of Jesus demands.

As for a supply of students with a leaning towards our manner of life, there is no reason to suppose that the college will fail of it. By the grace of God we already have a number of young Germans in our Society, now pursuing their studies with repute of learning and piety at Paris, Louvain, and Cologne. There will be no difficulty in drawing on these men to start the Bavarian college. Besides, there are men even here in Ingolstadt at present, and always will be, we believe, ready to give themselves to our Society as soon as some signs of the college appear. Sincerity of life wedded to sacred learning is an attractive combination, and piety conjoined with discernible wisdom easily makes disciples. Truth rejoices to have its claims made good by word and example, and once thus vindicated it draws men, even against their will, to worship it, love it and follow its leading.

Further, we ask, what inconvenience could arise from mingling foreign students with young Germans, thus gracing one strong college with elements from different lands? Instead of obscuring the college this variety would render it illustrious. The Apostle's word stands for all time: In Christ Jesus there is neither Jew nor Greek, barbarian nor Scythian. Where we already have colleges, as in Messina, Palermo, Bologna, and Padua, not to mention those in Spain and Portugal, we support and reckon as of the family Germans and other foreigners, educating them in devout learning and instructed devotion. Spaniards and Sicilians, Germans and Italians dwell there together, all the more united in charity the farther their countries are apart. . . .

In truth, it may very well be considered a distinction for a university that it draws its professors from different nations. We three, invited here as theologians, are complete foreigners to one another by birth, unless you consider Spain, Savoy and Germany a single country. But faith and charity makes us one in Christ. His Precious Blood brings all peoples together, one's own and the rest of the world, and keeps them united in an indissoluble covenant. . . .[1]

For all their pleading and good arguments, which time would royally corroborate, the Fathers got nothing out of Stockhammer. He seems to have been one of those people who resent the mere suggestion that their country had anything to learn from other nations. Germans in general have their faults like the rest of mankind and undue exclusiveness would appear to be among them. At the present time, when America eagerly buys up the best intellects of Europe and when in the English universities professors of every nationality are welcomed, how rarely does one find a non-German teaching in a German academy! This has ever been the way, and the embargo on foreign brains proved a troublesome obstacle to the commerce in sanctities with which St. Peter Canisius was all his life engaged. That was the time " when the flowering strength of a new and almost irresistible nationalism was crushing oecumenical ideals, erecting subtle psychological barriers between the spiritual as well as the temporal lives of nations and seriously compromising the very existence of an international Church. In no other age was international

[1] Braunsberger, *Epistulae*, vol. i, pp. 323-7.

activity more necessary for Catholicism than in the sixteenth century: in no other age was it more difficult of achievement."[1] It must at least be granted to the Society of Jesus and to her great son, Peter Canisius, that they did their best to cope with the problem.

About the time now reached in Peter's history, Father Lejay, who had been lent to Ingolstadt only temporarily, received instructions from Rome to betake himself to Cardinal Truchsess at Augsburg. On hearing the news Duke Albert at once wrote to the Pope, saying that he " could not sufficiently praise the good work done in a short eight months by those three men of the highest learning and probity," and would His Holiness therefore forbid their removal from Ingolstadt, especially as he, Albert, was already " girding himself" to found them a college.[2] St. Peter's reaction to this panegyric was to exclaim: " Would that we had less favour and honour shown us and could count on a greater harvest of souls! " St. Ignatius, who had grown tired of mere talk, reacted by letting Lejay go in June, 1550, and Salmeron follow him in August.

Thus was St. Peter left alone to hold the fort. Nothing daunted, he continued to preach assiduously in both Latin and German and to lecture daily on the Sacraments. On September 12th he was joined by a fellow-Dutchman, Father Nicholas Floris, usually called Goudanus from his native town, Gouda, and by Father Peter Schorich, an Austrian of great ability and still greater independence. At this time Jesuits working at a distance from Rome were expected to send in reports every four months. These reports, known as *Litterae Quadrimestres*, are a valuable source of contemporary history. On September 29th one was due from St. Peter to St. Ignatius:

> To begin with mention of my revered and dearest Fathers Claude Lejay and Alfonso Salmeron, it is not easy to describe the regret with which this University saw them go. . . . Not only the ordinary people but the principal men of the town paid them openly the tribute of their tears and profound sorrow. While holding the Fathers in sweet memory these men are also moved by a certain indignation against the Cardinal of Augsburg and the Bishop of Verona, to whom their recall is attributed. On the day that Father Claude left for Augsburg, the principal men of the University here came to him to confess their sins and receive Holy Communion, that at least by this consolation

---

[1] Evennett, *The Cardinal of Lorraine and the Council of Trent* (Cambridge, 1930), p. 26.
[2] The letters are given in Druffel's *Briefe und Akten zur Geschichte des sechzehnten Jahrhunderts*, vol. i, pp. 441-5.

they might temper the sorrow which they felt over his departure. . . . Before Father Salmeron took the road to Verona, where I understand on good authority he is awaited most eagerly by all, the professors here made ready an exceptionally fine banquet for the two of us. This is the German way of cementing friendship and showing the dearest mark of trust and esteem. They promised also, if Father Alfonso would agree, to move heaven and earth to have his recall cancelled. If there were any means of avoiding it, they said, it was not to be borne that they should be robbed of such a distinguished ornament to the University, a man who was a second Dr. Eck and a greater than Eck. . . . They offered him his journey money, which he refused, and seven or eight of them, including the Rector and Vice-Chancellor of the University, accompanied him on horseback for several miles. . . ."

Six months later Peter once again expatiated to St. Ignatius on the merits of Lejay. After speaking of his unremitting toil in the confessional during the Diet of Augsburg, he continued:

He has a wonderful gift for getting on with all sorts of people, both high and low. His tact is such that there is no one he cannot handle and make a friend of, in Our Lord. Many have frequently expressed astonishment that this Father's modesty and simplicity should be found in one of such influence and public reputation. He has only to smile, it seems, to secure the fulfilment of his wishes; but whomsoever the Spirit of God once possesses, him He crowns with many graces, especially when the common good and the glory of Christ so require. It was not only the Catholics who found this Father a man after their hearts and an adviser competent to strengthen them in their faith. He gave satisfaction also to the foremost Lutheran members of the Diet who most willingly listened to him speaking on matters of religion. They asked him for his opinions on the chief points of controversy and put their own arguments before him, especially with regard to the doctrine of justification. . . . Like the wonderful artist he is in understanding and dealing with souls, he replied with the greatest modesty, solving difficulties, removing doubts and casting light on the truth in such a way that both Catholics and Protestants were filled with admiration.[1]

The foregoing passages are typical of St. Peter's correspondence which is packed with the praises of other men, generally to the exclusion

[1] Braunsberger, *Epistulae*, vol. i, pp. 331–3, 359.

of anything except dry odds and ends about himself. Lejay he had already canonized in his heart, just as he had Favre. He tells St. Ignatius that there are splendid hopes for the Society of Jesus in Germany because Father Claude is so much loved and respected on all hands. The King of the Romans had already promised him a college in Vienna, which, says the eager Peter, "presents us with an open door to Hungary and the Turks." But the Father's greatest success was with Cardinal Truchsess, the natural leader of the German Catholics. Only the previous year, this man, still worldly-minded and fond of display, had "vastly praised" the *Interim* in a sermon in Augsburg Cathedral, asserting that "all was right and good in it."[1] A prince of the Church who could thus speak of a formula doubtful in orthodoxy and promulgated in defiance of the Pope plainly needed a change of heart before he could be of much service to Catholicism. This radical change was brought about by Lejay, for St. Peter reports that, after he had guided the Cardinal through the *Spiritual Exercises*, his penitent became another man, "edifying great numbers by the simplicity of his dress, the frugality of his table and his progress in prayer."[2] Unfortunately Truchsess did not stand by his good resolutions and, though always a man of stainless life and lovable character, he failed through his prodigality to assume the leadership of renascent Catholicism for which he had seemed destined.

Though Peter and his two companions in Ingolstadt were very poor and, in fact, had nothing except their clothes and daily bread, they steadfastly refused to take a penny in fees, even on occasions when by statute the professors had a right to certain emoluments. They entirely disapproved of the heavy "tips" which students were obliged to furnish at graduation time and did their best to mitigate the hardships which the custom entailed. At home, a contest had arisen on the arrival of Peter's new companions. Each of the three wanted one of the others to have the main authority, a deadlock which Lejay, from Augsburg, endeavoured to remove with a text from St. Paul—"Let each esteem others better than himself." Eventually St. Ignatius was obliged to intervene and order St. Peter to accept the rôle of superior.[3] Peter now believed that the college "was certain to be founded at the conclusion of the Diet of Augsburg." On it he staked all his hopes for the regeneration of Bavaria, where the tares of heresy had so spread that there was "practically no

[1] *Die Chroniken der deutschen Städte* (Augsburg), vol. vii, p. 186.
[2] A few months later, March, 1557, the Cardinal retired with Lejay to a monastery, there to do a complete "long retreat" of four weeks. M.H., Polanco, *Chronicon*, vol. ii, p. 265.
[3] Braunsberger, *Epistulae*, vol. i, p. 330.

respect for authority left, no religion and no charity." The achievements of the three Jesuits, meantime, might seem paltry in the extreme, as when their leader, in his chronicle of small beer, informed St. Ignatius that they had settled a heated dispute among the professors and persuaded " a certain deacon " to go about more decently clothed. Peter was quite aware of it. " What our Portuguese, Spanish and Sicilian brethren judge to be a mere trifle," he wrote, " we here account a matter of great importance." To discover even ten thoroughly Catholic men in that City of the Plain would have been a joyful occasion, and, accordingly, he appeals " with all the earnestness of which he is capable " to St. Ignatius and to each and every Jesuit in the world, " by the Most Sacred Blood of Jesus Christ, by the common law and bond of fraternal charity and by the terrible danger to which so many shipwrecked souls are exposed, to succour us and our Germany with your daily prayers and Sacrifices."[1] Hardly a letter he writes but repeats this burning appeal, and it is, surely, coming from such a brave and sanguine heart, one of the most convincing indications of Germany's desolation.

The University of Ingolstadt, in common with all the universities of the Paris tradition, elected a new rector every six months. Elections took place on April 24th and October 18th, the procedure being as follows: All the doctors and professors of theology, law, and medicine, together with the dean and three masters of the faculty of arts, repaired to the Liebfrauenkirche to assist at the Mass of the Holy Ghost. They then registered their votes, and the man receiving a majority was bound to accept office or forfeit a fine of six gold pieces. No member of a religious order was eligible unless all the votes without exception went to him. To the acute distress of Peter Canisius this was his fate in October, 1550, nor had he a single gold piece, much less six, to buy himself out of his predicament. Shortly after he wrote about it to St. Ignatius :

In his last letter Father Nicholas informed your Reverence of my election, all unfitted as I am, to the Rectorship of this University. I have a few words to say about the matter. The government of the University is bringing me a great deal of trouble and mighty little in the way of obvious results. The Rector's principal duties are to register the names of new students, to compel debtors to pay their dues, to hear the complaints which citizens and women bring against the young men, to arrest, reprimand and imprison undergraduates who get drunk or roam about

[1] Braunsberger, *Epistulae*, vol. i, p. 334.

the town at night, and, finally, to preside at festive gatherings, academic meetings, and functions connected with the conferring of degrees.

To discharge these functions properly I ought to know German better than I do. As rectors are elected for a bare six months the custom is for them not to concern themselves with the reform of the curriculum or with the promotion of a religious spirit in the University. Seeing how badly such reforms were needed, I was totally averse to accepting the office until Father Claude, on your Reverence's instructions, wrote from Augsburg telling me plainly that I ought not to refuse, and adding that I must be careful to avoid any reforms or innovations for fear of creating prejudice against us at the start which might provide an excuse for not going on with the foundation of the college. My conscience is accordingly made up to act as directed unless your Reverence sends me instructions to a different effect.

There is a true saying that lawyers rule the roost in this place. The principal man among them told me yesterday that practically all the students of law are Lutherans. Even the four professors of the subject are not entirely free from suspicion of heresy. . . .

By the favour of Our Lord we are all well and comfortable enough. Father Nicholas has begun his schools and given general satisfaction. He made a great name for himself in a public disputation, showing that he was an adept in philosophy as well as theology. Would that he could learn German within a year, so as to be able to preach the Word of God and do good among the people here! . . . He and I have now agreed to study and learn German thoroughly at home; to help each other in our studies and to re-read the most important authors; to teach Christian doctrine once a week; and, apart from our lectures and Latin sermons, to work hard at Greek, as it is very necessary in this country. . . .

Our theological disputations, which, as we informed you, began well, have now so fallen off that we hope for practically nothing from the students here. Experience has taught us that only a few will attend our lectures, and they men unfitted for the schools, without appetite for study or desire of our assistance. . . .

The Lord grant us holy patience and true cheerfulness that we may be able to continue working in this desolate field. . . .[1]

In spite of all the apathy and obstacles referred to in Peter's letters, some progress had been made, and he could report two months later

[1] Braunsberger, *Epistulae*, vol. i, pp. 337–41.

that more students were approaching the Sacraments than for years past. Further, the college in Vienna was now a certainty and he had already begun negotiations for the establishment of another one in Trier. As Rector, the Saint did all in his power, within the narrow limits permitted him, to revive the spirit of study and stay the assaults of Protestantism. At the opening of the spring term in 1551 he posted a notice earnestly exhorting his six hundred and sixty students to give of their best, and promising that he would soon take measures to provide excellent facilities for the pursuit of every branch of learning. He addressed a secret memorial on university reform to the Bishop of Eichstätt, Ingolstadt's *ex officio* Chancellor, and endeavoured to procure an authoritative ruling against the sale or purchase of text-books by Protestant authors. These men were given in their zeal to introducing snippets of heretical doctrine in the most unexpected places, in Latin grammars, books on mathematics, manuals of law. Peter strongly objected to that irregular sort of campaigning and took measures to stop it by means of detectives who had authority to swoop down, not only on public book-shops, but on the private libraries of professors and students.

Other reforms claimed his attention, too. Most of the priests and deacons in Ingolstadt never said a word of the Divine Office on the plea that it was too long and difficult. For them he obtained a privilege to use the revised Roman Breviary of 1535, which was much simpler than the German versions, and armed with this he soon brought about a revival of liturgical prayer. In his anxiety for the welfare of the students he was not content to exhort and admonish them individually. He also wrote to their parents, if they lived at a distance, telling them of their hopefuls' faults and earnestly counselling them to take heed for their souls by checking their youthful follies and making sure that their home training was of a truly Christian kind.[1]

Perhaps Peter's greatest success as Rector was the speedy settlement of the long-standing dispute and enmity between the Nominalists and Realists. "Their immemorial hatreds and public quarrels are now at an end, thanks be to God, the Author of all peace," he wrote in December, 1550. Alas for his hopes, that same month of December witnessed the arrival of an entirely unmetaphysical pig on four legs to restart the mischief among the professors. One of them, eminent in the faculty of medicine, had cured a certain sick abbot of Ingolstadt, and the grateful patient sent his benefactor, Dr. A., a present of a live pig. As is the way of pigs the present went astray, and was in fact delivered to the address of Dr. B.,

[1] Braunsberger, *Epistulae*, pp. 346, 352-3, 364.

a notorious rival of Dr. A. Dr. B. refused to surrender what had come to him in so providential a manner, just in time for Christmas Day, so Dr. A. sued him in the University courts for restitution of the pig. St. Peter sat as judge, wearing his rectorial " *capitium*," or mantle with a flounce three fingers wide. On the plaintiff giving evidence of " fraudulent detention " the defendant retorted that he was " lying in his throat " and " a brawl ensued between them." After considering the whole affair and taking into account that the litigants were members of the Senate, the Court decreed " that such quarrelling must end and be abolished, for it was plain from the allegations of each party that they had not gone to law out of a spirit of hate and malevolence but only in a fit of anger and on account of the pig. Each had been attacked by the other, so they might consider, without prejudice to their reputation, that honour had been satisfied. Accordingly, they are sternly warned, under a penalty of twenty florins, to refrain from insulting or molesting each other in future." Sentence delivered, the two doctors placed their hands in those of St. Peter and swore to abide by it, " without, however," continues the old record, " coming to any agreement *super porco*."[1] What eventually happened to the pig is not known to history, but a month later the doctors were still squabbling over him or his memory.

The undergraduates, of course, provided the academic court with most of its cases. According to St. Peter, it was the opinion of the professors generally that " practically no university within or without the Empire was so full of licence or so lacking in discipline " as Ingolstadt.[2] By an old privilege the students were permitted to get married while still in residence. Perhaps that was the only way of stopping worse evils, but it led to much trouble for the authorities. Terrific celebrations used to take place on these occasions, in spite of proclamation after proclamation that there must not be more than thirty-two guests at any one wedding-feast, except when " by special grace of the Lord Rector and Senate, noble and excellent persons " might invite a larger number. St. Peter did not mind that form of indiscipline or, at any rate, did not attempt to interfere with it, knowing that to govern well one must not govern too much. The offences which he singled out for punishment were those affecting the general peace and security, as when he rusticated a pair of students for two years, " *tamquam grassatores et invasores hominum*." The exploits of these quarrelsome youths included the wounding of a clerical student at a dance, an unprovoked and armed attack on some nobles, and habitual

[1] Braunsberger, *Epistulae*, vol. i, p. 701.   [2] Braunsberger, *Epistulae*, vol. i, p. 376.

absence from lectures. At the intercession of Stockhammer, the Chancellor, who seems to have been related to them, they were allowed to return provided they engaged not to carry arms nor frequent taverns, to attend at least two lectures a day and to consider themselves 'gated' during winter at eight o'clock in the evening. They signed an agreement to this effect, but made hay of it before the end of a week, having in that short time broken the head of their landlord and nearly murdered another citizen. The Rector had no choice then but to commit them to the University prison, unless they could find somebody to stand their bail.[1]

One of the commonest charges preferred against the students was that of shooting off *bombardae* at night. These *bombardae* were a variety of musket that exploded with an ear-splitting bang, and by means of them the young bloods so murdered everybody's sleep that St. Peter was at last obliged to issue a proclamation denouncing the practice : " We are informed that certain students wander about the streets in gangs, barbarously and wickedly exploding *bombardae*, not only during the day but at night when Almighty God wishes every living thing on earth to be quiet. Others disturb the citizens by blowing trumpets and behaving like complete lunatics. By these presents we strictly prohibit such scandals, and recall to your memory the statute against *bombardae*, which we now declare valid and operative in perpetuity."[2]

In his administration of justice St. Peter showed much gentleness and appeared never so anxious to punish as to find excuses for the culprit. He considered the main functions of his court to be advisory and hortatory rather than punitive, but if he had to be severe he believed in making the punishment fit the crime. Thus a master of arts who disgraced himself by roaming about drunk at night was condemned to abstain from wine during the three days of Carnival. Peter locked students up only " when there appeared to be no better way of bringing them to their senses," and expelled them altogether only " if they seemed really desperate and incurable characters." It was with much reluctance, too, that he issued proclamations, in one of which he informed the students that the remedy against the appearance of such things was quite simple, for they had only to behave sensibly in order to see them stop. That the disciplinary duties of his office were not much to his taste is evident from the rueful little joke he made about them to St. Ignatius : " I cannot

---

[1] Braunsberger, *Epistulae*, vol. i, pp. 700, 704–6.
[2] Braunsberger, *Epistulae*, vol. i, pp. 354–5. In his *History of Universities in the Middle Ages* (vol. ii, p. 236) Rashdall says : " It was recognized that students in a medieval city required as much protection as Christians in modern Turkey or Jews in modern Russia." No wonder !

help admiring not only the variety but the contrariety of functions in our one Society. Thus while some of our fathers busy themselves liberating prisoners, behold me putting people into prison! . . . Our Lord Jesus grant us in His infinite kindness that like skilful physicians we may accommodate ourselves to each one's infirmities, becoming all things to all men that we may gain many."[1]

St. Peter's term of office expired towards the end of April, 1551. " By the grace of Christ I am through with the business," he wrote. " It involved a good deal of labour and anxiety, little conducive to spiritual progress, but still something was achieved for which I ought not to be ungrateful to the Author and Source of all blessings." This report to Rome, like so many others, is largely a panegyric of his companions with *their* achievements written out in full. Of himself he has the following tale to tell: " Before giving you an account of the last few months, I must say as a personal preface, Reverend Father General, that I have the best of reasons for being fearful and anxious with regard to the account which I shall have to render to God, my Judge, seeing that of these few months I am unable to give any answer except that they were badly employed." How much the troubles of Germany had bitten into Peter's soul is evident from the end of the letter: " No words of mine are strong enough to commend our thrice unhappy Germany to you, or to deplore its woes. The pass to which we have come is plain to the whole world. We are deserted by good men and oppressed by evil ones; we abound in scandals and are given over to sectarian strife; we are blinded by error and corrupted by the pursuit of all impiety. Therefore no work of mercy, of charity, of compassion, could appear more equitable than the succour of this one nation, of all nations the most afflicted, the most unhappy and the most depraved. May the God of all consolation stir up His perfect spirit in the hearts of our brothers that they may be ready and able to come and work for our Germany, aye, and to shed their blood time and again for the Church of Christ. Would your Paternity remember me in your prayers, but it is Germany rather than myself that I would throw upon your charity, though I know full well that I, of all in our Society, have most need of your holy intercession with God."[2]

---

[1] Braunsberger, *Epistulae*, vol. i, p. 364.

[2] Braunsberger, *Epistulae*, vol. i, p. 365. Valentine Rottmaier, who for nearly ten years was a lay professor of the Humanities and oratory at Ingolstadt, wrote a history of the University shortly before his death in 1574. Speaking of St. Peter as Rector, he said: " I know not what to write of this Rector Magnificus . . . for not I nor the most eloquent man alive could sing his praises adequately. . . . This only will I say then: *Lumen est nostro tempore inter Doctores Ecclesiae.* May he live for the Church and the Catholic Religion all the years of a Nestor," Braunsberger, *l.c.,* vol. vii, p. 823.

One result of Father Lejay's excellent work at the Diet of Augsburg had been an invitation to him from the ambassadors of the free-thinking Elector Moritz of Saxony to go thither and confer with Melanchthon and other Protestant leaders. Lejay showed willingness, and St. Peter, who believed him capable of converting the devil himself, grew thoroughly excited at the prospect of the faith returning to the original homeland of heresy. But the Pope did not approve of the prospect, and Lejay went instead to Vienna, taking with him St. Peter's helper, Father Schorich. As for Elector Moritz, however much his councillors may have been affected by Lejay, he had personally no great anxiety to be provided with a religion, and was already planning the rebellion which a year later would end the personal rule of Charles V in Germany.

Meantime Peter and Father Goudanus continued their humdrum round in Ingolstadt, lecturing, preaching, visiting the sick and imprisoned, and organizing disputations in hopes of reviving interest in theology. Peter's sermons now began to attract such large audiences that he had a number of times to transfer to a more spacious church than the one at which he was engaged, and his eloquence had the remarkable effect of making the people stay to the end of the service. That pleased him very much, for " here and elsewhere," he told St. Ignatius, " the custom is for the majority of the congregation to scamper off like so many dogs after the singing of the Gospel, or in the middle of the sermon, or immediately after the Consecration."

In their lecturing, both in public and unofficially at home, the two Jesuits strove hard to engage the affections of the students for St. Thomas Aquinas. With the same purpose in view, Peter addressed a very persuasive letter to a critical but learned Cologne doctor, pressing the claims of the *Summa* on his attention. This cantankerous " Dr. George " did not like Jesuits and had proved hostile to those in Cologne. Yet Peter writes to him in the following strain: " Would to God, my George, that we might often close our eyes to the world and look upon Him who offers us His cross for the best of golden books, who reveals Himself and His secrets to little ones, who both desires and is able to communicate Himself to us wholly that we may live safe and carefree, rich in poverty, happy in affliction, cheerful when despised, and in death more than conquerors."[1] What George, who had no great repute for orthodoxy or piety, thought of that letter may be left to the imagination.

St. Peter's capacity for friendship was remarkable. No man he had

---

[1] Braunsberger, *Epistulae*, vol. i, p. 367.

ever met on a friendly footing was afterwards forgotten and he always showed the greatest eagerness for news of these acquaintances. A letter from them constituted a festival in his heart's calendar, but there were only too many *feriae* in it owing to their neglect or preoccupation. Father Laynez, whom he had greatly reverenced ever since their short while together in Trent and Florence, was one of the sinners by omission. On his return early in 1551 from Africa, where he had been naval chaplain to an expedition against the Barbary pirates, Peter wrote to welcome him home and gently upbraid him for his silences :

I gather from a letter from Father Brouet that you are now in Florence to preach the Lenten Course. Would that I could be among your auditors! I could hope to derive more profit from your sermons than when I lived with you in Florence of old, for then I was a lazy person and unskilled in Italian. I have often regretted that I did not make better use of the chance then given me, and I therefore all the more earnestly beg your Reverence to commend me in your prayers to God whose graces I have not yet ceased to receive in vain, slow and unprofitable servant in our Society that I am. . . . We very rarely receive a letter from Italy. You in that land are probably too busy and we here of too little account to receive a few words of news in our exile. Well, if we may not have the comfort of your Reverence's letters in our loneliness, do, at least, help us, unhappy ones, with your prayers. I would like you to give my warmest greetings to Master John, the physician, and his wife.[1] . . . Please pray hard and obtain the prayers of our brethren for this deserted vineyard of Germany which goes to rack and ruin for want of labourers.[2]

In spite of the brave front which Peter and Goudanus opposed to circumstances, they were obviously beginning to be affected by the dreary conditions of their lives. Twice in March, 1551, and again in June, Polanco wrote to encourage them, promising that they should have more frequent letters from Rome. In July Peter thought that he was about to lose Goudanus, by now a bosom friend, and expressed his sorrow at the prospect : " He has brought me more help and consolation than I could ever have deserved. Still, the same grace of God assisting me by favour of which I have hitherto lived with so many dear fathers and brothers in Christ, I hope I shall keep a good and trustful heart, even though I

---

[1] Giovanni di Rossi, the Florentine doctor with whom Laynez and Peter had lodged in 1547.
[2] Braunsberger, *Epistulae*, vol. i, pp. 347-9.

be condemned to remain alone here in this sterile and thorny land. Holy obedience will turn into a paradise any place where your Reverend Paternity wishes me to live or die in the course of this short pilgrimage."[1]

The two friends were not to be separated, however, though St. Ignatius evidently contemplated removing them both to Vienna, where Father Lejay stood in sore need of their assistance. To help the General to a decision Peter submitted a perfectly balanced set of *pros* and *cons*, the chief reason against their removal being, he said, that Duke Albert, Stockhammer, the Bishop of Eichstätt, and the whole professorial body of Ingolstadt had begun to urge on him acceptance of the office of vice-chancellor which had fallen vacant. It might be difficult to refuse without giving offence to these eminent men, but, on the other hand, Peter pointed out, the office was for life and far more honorific than that of rector, carrying with it all sorts of dignities and emoluments quite unbecoming a religious vowed to poverty. "It annoys me," he concluded, "that these men should be so friendly to me personally and want to cover me with honours, while unwilling to look at our Society. . . . To make an end I can only say this : Master, send me where you will, not excepting the Indies."[2]

At last, owing to the insistence of Duke Albert with St. Ignatius, Peter received instructions to undertake the duties of vice-chancellor, though only for a few months and without the usual honours and stipends of the office.[3] In this way was frustrated the plan by which Albert evidently hoped to bind the Saint permanently to Ingolstadt. For all practical purposes the government of the University lay entirely in the hands of the vice-chancellor, as the Bishop of Eichstätt, the *ex-officio* Chancellor, was not in a position to help. Peter, accordingly, found himself burdened with a multitude of new and highly uncongenial demands upon his time and patience. It was his business to preside in state at all the more solemn academic functions, to pronounce sonorous Latin orations before the whole University, and to place on doctors' heads the cap which they had won, saying : "You may begin to teach, in the Name of the Father and of the Son and of the Holy Ghost." These doctors were obliged by statute to make a presentation to the vice-chancellor. Peter used to accept their gifts in public, but afterwards, calling the men aside privately, he would hand them back, saying that as one vowed to poverty he could not keep them.[4]

[1] Braunsberger, *Epistulae*, vol. i, pp. 371–2.   [3] *Cartas de San Ignacio*, vol. ii, pp. 469, 564–7.
[2] Braunsberger, *Epistulae*, vol. i, p. 377.   [4] M.H., Polanco, *Chronicon*, vol. ii, p. 563.

After a few months of the speechifying and promotions, the vice-chancellor informed St. Ignatius that he was " striving with all his might " to shuffle off the unwelcome honour, but that it clung to him like a burr, for anything he could do. It was all the more tiresome because at this time he had begun to cast longing eyes towards Saxony, whither he would willingly have gone to support his much-tried friend, Bishop Julius Pflug. " My heart is more in Saxony than anywhere," he wrote, " and I pray Christ that it may be given to me to help that land, the fountain-head of so many heresies." Another forsaken church had also cried to him for assistance, the church of the great, Imperial City of Strasbourg, where, owing to the energetic propaganda of Bucer, Hedio, and other prominent evangelicals, Catholicism was in the last stage of disintegration. After the Schmalkalden War Charles V had compelled the Lutherans to restore the Cathedral and some other churches to the Catholics, but he could not undo the mischief to men's faith, and so Strasbourg remained the chief bulwark of Protestantism in south-western Germany, famous the world over for the new system of education on Protestant lines started there by Johann Sturm. In September, 1551, the canons of the Cathedral, all of whom were princes, counts or barons, wrote begging Peter to come as their preacher, or, at least, to see at first hand the straits to which they were reduced. That appeal, too, won the sympathy of his apostolic heart, though, in his genuine distrust of himself, he had the greatest misgivings about his ability to be of much assistance. When such doubts came over him it was ever his way to think of Cologne and its array of saintly intercessors. He accordingly wrote to Father Kessel, saying:

If you love me you will offer three Masses to the Holy Trinity in the Golden Chapel of St. Ursula, and often commend this whole affair of Strasbourg to the Blessed Magi, Patrons and Kings of all Germany, to St. Gereon, and to my Bishop, St. Severinus.[1] I am in hopes that the great trust which I repose in you and in your sons and brothers will not be deceived, but that you will continue to help me in your goodness, unfitted as I am for the heavy burden awaiting my shoulders. I would say the same to dear Brother Arnold and to my Reverend Fathers in Christ, the Carthusians, whom I suppliantly beg to say Mass for me, at least now and then. Would you ask Father Prior on my behalf to do for me now in his goodness what he is wont

[1] St. Severinus, Bishop of Cologne, died at the beginning of the fifth century. Canisius calls him " my Bishop " because he himself was born, educated and ordained priest in the arch-diocese of Cologne.

to do whenever serious business impends, namely, to have recourse to the prayers of his special friends, either mentioning my name or not ? He could do me no greater service, for I feel nothing to be more necessary for me and for Strasbourg than that God should look benignly on my first efforts, enabling me so to win the hearts of the people that they may, at least, come to listen to me and give me a chance of influencing and helping them. You see how urgent and loquacious I am, but I do want to convey this one thing to you and to beg it of you with all my heart, that I may have the many prayers of many men for the sermons in Strasbourg. Your charity will not disappoint my hopes in the matter, but, God helping us, the seed I go to sow will have each day the water of your prayers, and you will also assist this poor husbandman in his labour and obtain for him and his work the intercession of the saints by every means in your power.[1]

Peter, however, was not destined to go to Strasbourg on this occasion for, before the time came, circumstances had arisen which led to a big change in the externals of his life. In the months between, Goudanus and he worked away more strenuously than ever, despite the irritating chains of office with which Peter continued to be shackled. Being the soul of kindness, he became greatly concerned for the health of his companion who suffered much from a melancholy temperament. This was due to incipient tuberculosis, but regardless of it, Peter relates, he went on with his lectures all through the long vacation and " even during the dog-days," for the benefit of the few students who remained in residence. Peter did the same himself, though he omits to mention the fact. In addition to his lectures on the Book of Sentences, the supposedly leisured and Olympian vice-chancellor was also engaged throughout the high summer expounding the Gospel of St. John and St. Paul's Epistle to the Romans. By this time his sermons had become the talk of the town, so much so that no church was large enough for the crowds who overflowed through the doors and gathered in knots round the open windows to hear him. Twenty years afterwards, a distinguished man, Samuel Quickeberg, Duke Albert's chief assistant in collecting the treasures of art and sculpture at Munich, recorded with pride that formerly at Ingolstadt he had " often listened to Peter Canisius preaching with the most superb eloquence in the Latin tongue."[2] But it was his German sermons that caused the biggest stir. At Christmas time, 1551, these

[1] Braunsberger, Epistulae, vol. i, p. 388.   [2] Braunsberger, Epistulae, vol. i, p. 361.

were being preached out on the confines of the town. The weather was *frigidissimum*—perishingly cold—and owing to the many duties awaiting the preacher afterwards the sermons had to be given, he says, " when dawn had as yet scarcely broken." Nevertheless, the people tramped through the dark and cold to hear him, which seems to show that he did not lack the peculiar fascination which in a later century would make such a magnet of the Curé d'Ars. He certainly possessed the Curé's essential qualities, simplicity and sincerity so radiant that even the coarsest consciences must feel their glow. Consciences in Ingolstadt were coarse enough to test the gifts of a hundred saints, and the sigh of Peter's heart is almost audible in the sentence that summed up the experience of his apostolate : " *Quam est operosum (heu me) Catholicos in religione veteri continere !* "——Woe is me, what a task it is to keep Catholics true to the ancient Faith ! And yet Ingolstadt was comparatively a strong centre of Catholicism. It looks to-day almost exactly the same as St. Peter saw it, with its ancient walls and towers commanding the broad reaches of the Danube. Baedeker called it " melancholy," but the adjective is a matter of taste and simply means that the fortress town bears the scars of the battles of long ago and lacks night-clubs, crystal palaces, and other famous modern amenities. It is strange that Protestantism, which was a new and forward-looking thing, should even temporarily have gained a footing in its beautiful old gabled houses whose very stones cry out allegiance to the past. Gables somehow do not fit on to Protestantism and one cannot help feeling that it is incongruous for old Heidelberg and Nuremberg to be Protestant strongholds. In all probability Ingolstadt would be one too, had there been no St. Peter Canisius.

Peter expended his charity on every section of the town's population. Owing to the scarcity of priests in Germany it had become the bad custom to ordain men with hardly any regard to fitness. Whoever wanted it could have ordination for the asking. Peter now started special courses of lectures and instructions for those about to be ordained and used his great weapon of the *Spiritual Exercises* to stir up their zeal. He gave the *Exercises*, also, to any priests whom he could persuade to listen, exhorting them and getting them to promise that they would foster frequent Confession and Holy Communion in their parishes. Hoping that, if financially assisted, some of the poorer students might turn their thoughts to theology he went about begging alms to start scholarships for them. But alas, he says, such was their state of mind that even then they would not give a little attention to " the most necessary of all studies at a time when every Tom, Dick and Harry argues and trifles about sacred things, out of the depths of his ignorance." As a frontal attack on their apathy did not bring much success, Peter tried other ways of winning them. He persuaded good numbers of them, whom he had helped with their ordinary studies, to come to his house on Sundays and feast-days. Each time, one was chosen by the others to deliver them an address in Latin or German. Doubtless, plenty of ragging and nonsense went on, but Peter did not mind that, provided he could teach his raw recruits how to speak effectively. Who knew but that some day they would turn into effective preachers? Rumour of the proceedings spread and then lordly M.A.s took to patronizing them. At the end of the address Peter recited public prayers, to which the students responded, for the success of the Council of Trent, for the peace of the Church, and for the extirpation of heresy. These prayers were followed by the Litany of the Saints. Owing to Peter's persuasive and persistent urging, other priests gradually adopted the practice of having public prayers in church for the Council, for the bishops, for the Emperor and all princes, and for the defeat of the Turks. In the course of time this custom of " *allgemeines Gebet* " spread throughout Catholic Germany and became immensely popular.

All during these years Peter naturally endeavoured to attract suitable young men to the Society of Jesus, and it speaks eloquently of conditions in Catholic Bavaria that the results of his unremitting efforts were two recruits, both Tirolese. However, he had the patience of a born angler and could at least pride himself on the quality if not the quantity of his catch, for they were fine fellows and afterwards did valiant service for the Counter-Reformation.

Such, then, was our Saint's apostolate in Ingolstadt, all as unromantic as a Monday morning, except, perhaps, the occasion when he emulated the sublime charity of St. Catherine of Siena in the service of a poor malefactor who had been condemned to death. " We trust," he wrote to St. Ignatius, " that he is now reigning with Christ and praying for us, as he promised me he would do, just before his execution."[1]

The year 1551 witnessed the opening of nine new Jesuit colleges in various parts of the world, including Vienna. King Ferdinand of Austria had kept his promises, unlike his son-in-law, the dilatory Duke of Bavaria, and St. Ignatius, who informed the latter that " the resources of the Society of Jesus were greatly exhausted," inclined to listen to the appeal of Ferdinand for the help of Canisius and Goudanus, provided

[1]Braunsberger, *Epistulae*, vol. i, p. 384.

they could be transferred to Vienna without antagonizing Duke Albert. To ensure this, Ferdinand was advised by Father Claude Lejay to write direct to the Pope, saying, without specifying any particular men, that he had urgent need of two accomplished theologians for the University of Vienna. On the Pope asking St. Ignatius to supply the men, he was informed that it could not be done because the most perfect pair for the purpose, and the only ones at all available, unfortunately belonged to the Duke of Bavaria. But, of course, if His Holiness were to order that they should be *lent* to Vienna until such time as Bavaria had a Jesuit college of its own, that would settle the difficulty. Duke Albert could not reasonably be annoyed because, after all, his men were only going on loan. Thus were wiles countered by wiles, and thus came their marching orders to the two Jesuits of Ingolstadt.[1]

They were given ten days in which to make their final dispositions. On February 24, 1552, St. Peter visited the Duke to thank him for his many kindnesses and obtain leave of departure, whereupon Albert " begged and prayed " him not to move, at least until he had time to make representations to his relative, King Ferdinand. But that would have necessitated going beyond the ten days allowed by the Pope, so the Duke on second thoughts decided instead to send his secretary to Rome with a petition for the return of Peter and Goudanus.[2] He was generous in defeat and presented the pair with a hundred florins to help them on their journey. Four days later, a Sunday, Peter preached his farewell sermon to the accompaniment of " much weeping and sobbing." Then followed a big round of good-byes, including a visit to the Bishop of Eichstätt, who gave the wayfarers his blessing, " *quamvis stomacharetur contra Patrem Claudium.*" The chief men of the town saw them on board their ship and some sailed with them, as a guard of honour, part of the way up the Danube. Soon the ship was out of sight of the men on the quayside, who turned home sadly, wondering, perhaps, who would now look after the students, comfort the poor fellows in gaol, teach little ones their Christian doctrine, and preach the Kingdom of Heaven with such unwearying love and devotion. " And that," says Polanco, " was the end, for the time being, of our Fathers' settlement in Ingolstadt,"[3]— only for the time being though, because the memory of St. Peter remained behind to work potently in his absence for the establishment of the college on which he had set his heart.

[1] *Cartas de San Ignacio*, vol. ii, pp. 468–9 ; M.H., Polanco, *Chronicon*, vol. ii, p. 564.
[2] Braunsberger, *Epistulae*, vol. i, p. 398.
[3] M.H., Polanco, *Chronicon*, vol. ii, pp. 564–6.

CHAPTER V

THE AUSTRIAN SCENE

PASSENGERS on slow-moving ships have plenty of time to think, and their thoughts naturally go back to what they are leaving behind and forward to what awaits them. In the sixteenth century there was little else to do on board a ship except think. The journey from Ingolstadt to Vienna took four days, and the ship, an open, evil-smelling tub, conspired in winter with the swollen Danube, which is blue about as often as the moon, to make things thoroughly unpleasant for everybody concerned. There was considerable danger, too, and the beauties of the passage through the Struden failed to impress people whose only anxiety was to get out of it alive. It is not difficult to guess the thoughts that occupied St. Peter's mind, as he gazed, hardly seeing them, at the castled hills and islands of romance by which his ship staggered uneasily to its destination. His had been a strange life so far. Only just turned thirty, he had seen more of the world and its troubles than do most men in a lifetime. Holland, Belgium, Germany, Italy, Sicily, all were known as only those know them who traverse them on foot. Difficult beginnings seemed to be his fate: Cologne, when all there was in turmoil; Trent in the first experimental days of the Council; Messina, while the college was finding its feet; Ingolstadt at the chilly, uncertain dawn of a new day; and now Vienna, Christendom's last bulwark against the insuperable might of the Turk. Each new field of labour that had opened to him seemed to be more barren and full of heartbreak than the last, and, for all his self-giving, he could as yet point to little in the way of secure achievement. Cologne, where he had worked so hard to establish his Order, was still suspicious and unfriendly, and Bavaria, the Promised Land of his dreams, now receded into the mist with all his holy hopes for it apparently shattered.

While Peter's ship ploughed its way by Regensburg on to Passau and Linz a manifesto was issued in the ultra-Protestant city of Marburg. *Henricus II, Francorum Rex, vindex libertatis Germanicae,* the heading

ran—Henry, King of the French, Champion of the liberties of Germany !
It was war once again, war in which Moritz, the victor of Mühlberg, was
to stand shoulder to shoulder with Germany's immemorial foe against
Germany's Emperor. Peter Canisius did not know all the tortuous intrigue
that led to this unprecedented treason, but he had seen and sorrowed
over the first moves of the miserable game. The Germany that his heart
burned to serve became again the pawn of detestable politics in which
the honour of God and the good of the plain and uncomplaining citizen
had about as much place as they are allowed in the masterpiece of
Machiavelli, the text-book of the recreant schemers.

Passau was reached, and Peter's thoughts must have been of that
City's princely bishop under whose jurisdiction much Austrian territory
lay. Now that he was on that territory, King Ferdinand, its ruler, would
naturally occupy the first place in his ruminations. He knew much about
him already and that he was a complete contrast to his brother, the
Emperor. Charles, though born and bred in the Netherlands, had never
been anything but a Spaniard ; Ferdinand, born and bred in Spain, became
a German to the tips of his fingers. He was jovial and gay, gracious and
unaffected, and so indifferent to ceremony that he would receive any
chance caller in his bedroom and talk to him in his night-cap while putting
on his boots—" *con poca dignità e reputatione sua,*" as a rather shocked
Ambassador Extraordinary from Italy reported. Unlike most of the
princes of his age, he was a faithful husband and, after her death, never
betrayed the memory of his adored Queen Anna who had given him
three sons and twelve daughters to tantalize the chancelleries of Europe—
girls and boys, all of whom would later enter into St. Peter's life, but
particularly the eldest son Maximilian, about whom he had already heard
disquieting rumours.

Though an excellent and devoted Catholic in most respects, King
Ferdinand had no great liking for the dogmatic and assertive side of his
religion. He believed in trying to please everybody and letting them,
as another Italian observer reported, " abound in their own sense while
pretending not to notice." For his sons' education at Innsbruck he
provided tutors about whose orthodoxy he did not trouble to enquire.
Afterwards, during the Schmalkalden War, he allowed the impressionable
Maximilian to consort freely with his brother's Protestant allies and to
contract friendships injurious to his faith. Indeed, from a Catholic point
of view, he brought the boy up thoroughly badly, addicted to wine and
women, lazy, and more given to strumming on his lute or playing with

his pet bear than to study or the transaction of business. Yet the genial and gifted Max learned to speak six languages fluently and became so popular that he was known as the " Joy of the World." But, owing to his father's carelessness, he very nearly brought doom on the House of Habsburg by going over to Protestantism.

King Ferdinand's easy and pacific temper proved a godsend to the enemies of Rome, who soon made a happy hunting-ground of Austria, Hungary, and Bohemia. Austria, as St. Peter knew, had been gravely affected by Lutheranism, the nobles as usual being the great champions of faith without good works. It was such a convenient doctrine for people who still believed heartily in the devil but found the old methods of keeping out of his clutches too irksome; and besides, with the downfall of the Mass, much valuable property must go begging for new owners. Ferdinand loved the Mass and hated heresy, but, even had he not been the too tolerant man that he was, he could do little to stay its ravages because the Protestant stalwarts had always a trump card up their sleeves, marked with a crescent moon. Since the terrible day of Mohacz, when he succeeded to the crown of Hungary, Ferdinand had been at ceaseless war with the Turks. It is a glorious story, that gallant defiance, over more than twenty years, of a ruthless foe who sought him under the very walls of Vienna. But Ferdinand needed Protestant money if he was to keep up the good fight, and the Protestants naturally required a bargain for their services. Hence arose the state of affairs described in Janssen's lurid chapter entitled, " Moral and Religious Anarchy in Austria." " Good God," wrote one worthy man of the age about his own part of the country, " the seven deadly sins have become as the daily bread of our clergy here," while another man, the distinguished convert from Protestantism, Frederick Staphylus, reported to King Ferdinand, after an official investigation, that the Austrian clergy everywhere were utterly perverted, that there were as many sects as there were parishes, and that hardly one priest in a hundred denied himself a wife or a concubine.

St. Peter Canisius may not have known the full extent of the moral and material troubles into which he was sailing, but he had plenty of information to worry him, particularly about the collapse of the famous and venerable University of Vienna. As at Ingolstadt, the University's faculty of theology, on which the supply of efficient priests for Austria depended, had gone steadily to rack and ruin. During the decade 1529–1539 it consisted of only two professors, with a mere handful of students, and after 1549 it disappeared altogether for a time. The result was a rapid decline in the numbers of the clergy, so rapid and steep that, according to the Bishop of Laibach, whom it most nearly concerned, in twenty years not a single priest had been ordained in Vienna.[1]

Had the decline gone much further Austria must inevitably have been lost to the Catholic Church, a prospect that at last so frightened King Ferdinand as to make him for a while indifferent to Protestant susceptibilities. The King knew that those men were getting a stranglehold on his University, and wrote in distress, asking St. Ignatius to help him. St. Ignatius, ever one to meet good-will more than halfway, agreed immediately, with the result that, at the end of May, 1551, Father Lejay and Schorich arrived in Vienna from Germany, to be joined a few days later by a splendid Belgian priest, Father Nicholas Delanoy, at the head of a band of young Jesuits from Rome. They had walked the whole way except the last stage from Innsbruck, which they covered in some sort of ship along the river Inn. As was nearly always the case with roaming groups of Jesuits in those days, this group was completely international in composition. On the arrival of Peter Canisius and Goudanus, the following nations had each a member or two among the Jesuits of Vienna : France, Flanders, Spain, Italy, Belgium, Germany, Austria, Holland, and Hungary.

From his outpost in Ingolstadt St. Peter had followed the fortunes of the new college with the liveliest interest, and was particularly pleased by the warmth of the reception which two bishops gave to his brethren, the Bishop of Vienna, Frederick Nausea, an old friend of Peter's own, and Urban Weber, Bishop of Laibach.[2] With Weber the men from Rome found Lejay, and remained, one and all, as the Bishop's guests until their college had been made ready for them. King Ferdinand had directed some of his advisers, including Bishop Weber, to look around for a suitable building to house the Jesuits and their scholars. After examining a number of places, they decided on a certain part of the monastery of St. Dominic which stood near the University and was then occupied by only a few friars. St. Dominic's was one of the most magnificent of Vienna's many monasteries, lofty, extensive, and fortified with towers. Sultan Suleiman and his hundred thousand Turks had burned it in 1529, but Ferdinand, after their repulse, repaired the damage. Owing to the sadly depleted numbers of the Dominicans in residence, a large part of the monastery had been let to workmen who were living there with their families. That

---

[1] Sacchinus, *Vita P. Petri Canisii* (1616), p. 96. Sacchinus was so careful of his facts that even the exacting Ranke expressed admiration for him as an historian.

[2] Weber, of course, called himself Textor. Nausea's real name was Grau. ' Grauen ' is the German for ' to shudder ' which suggested the Latin ' *Nausea*,' meaning more or less what it does in English.

was the part selected for the Jesuits, but taking possession was not so easy as has sometimes been imagined. Thus Braunsberger, the learned editor of St. Peter's letters, to whom the present biography of the Saint is so patently indebted, writes in another place : " Here it was that Canisius came to rest. Here, under the protecting hand of St. Dominic, the son of St. Ignatius prayed, preached and worked with his pen, and so the Order to which the world owes the *Summa* of St. Thomas was also, through its hospitality, to have a share in the merit of the *Summa* composed by Canisius."[1]　One could wish that that pleasant way of putting the matter tallied with the facts, but in reality, and quite naturally, too, perhaps, the Dominicans showed no enthusiasm whatever at the prospect of having the Jesuits for guests. Urged by King Ferdinand, however, they at length agreed to take them as paying guests but only temporarily, until another home had been found for them. The King himself guaranteed the Dominicans their rent.[2]

All at length being ready, owing to the good offices of Bishop Weber as a house-furnisher, the Jesuits entered their strange college and spent the first few days in a whirl of excitement, trying to protect their territory from the inroads of the workmen's wives and children whom curiosity made vexatiously aggressive. By the end of the year they numbered eighteen all told, five novices, eleven scholastics, and two priests. The priests started their public lectures at the University on June 22nd, Lejay taking the Epistle to the Romans as his text, and Delanoy, the fourth book of Peter the Lombard's *Sentences*, which deals with the Sacraments. Besides themselves there was one other professor left in the faculty of theology, and the number of students honouring all three with their attentions was, at the start, exactly ten, most of them semi-illiterate. To swell the microscopic audiences the young Jesuit scholastics came to the theology lectures but pursued their literary and philosophic studies at home, which annoyed the public professors of those subjects.[3]　The home life of these young men was strenuous in the extreme. From morning to night disputations, repetitions, declamations in both Latin and Greek went on merrily, while the non-Germans among the brethren made valiant assaults on the phonetics of the Fatherland. The phonetics proved too much for a few of them and they had to be returned to Italy, suffering

---

[1] *Entstehung und erste Entwicklung der Katechismen des Seligen Petrus Canisius* (1893), p. 17.
[2] M.H., Polanco, *Chronicon*, vol. ii, p. 267.
[3] Polanco assigns two reasons for his brethren's behaviour, first because many of the professors of literature had ceased to be Catholics, and, secondly—the young Jesuits not being paragons— " ne bona existimatio quam de nostris conceperant [Academiae professores], quod scilicet in linguis et philosophia eruditi essent, minueretur." *Chronicon*, vol. ii, p. 270.

from some unspecified trouble which may have been inflammation of the glottis. These vanquished ones had had their hour, however, among the neglected Italian children whose fathers, then as now famous engineers, were engaged in newly fortifying Vienna against the Turks. They achieved such wonders with the children, and Father Juan Vitoria, an energetic Jesuit Don Quixote from Spain, put such devotion into their elders by his fiery eloquence, that in a short time Vienna's Soho became the City's model quarter.

Meantime Lejay and Delanoy had been confronted with a problem that was to trouble the peace of the Viennese Jesuits for many a day. King Ferdinand, in his genuine zeal for the Catholic faith, wanted and was determined to see in print a new manual or compendium of Christian doctrine for the use of priests and people throughout his dominions. This manual had to fulfil a number of conditions which only one theological writer in a million could be expected to face with equanimity. It had to be complete and concise, deep but devoid of subtleties, controversial in detail and friendly in spirit, learned and easily comprehensible, in fine, a paragon of a book which professors more often dream about than produce. The King having commissioned the Senate of the University to find the ideal author, they answered with one accord, "Lejay!" Thereupon Lejay wrote in deep distress to St. Ignatius, October 9, 1551:

I told you in a previous letter that His Majesty the King had commissioned the Senate of the University to elect some theologian who, in the name of the faculty of theology, would write a compendium of Christian doctrine. The Senate has elected me, without consulting either myself or Master Nicholas, and the King now exhorts me to compose the work. So, too, does his Chancellor, Dr. Jonas. To escape from the task, which is beyond my strength, I mentioned, without saying anything of my incapacity, various compendiums recently composed by able men in Germany, namely Peter Soto's, Gropper's, printed last year at the behest of the Archbishop of Cologne, that of the Mainz Synod, and others. The Chancellor answered that His Majesty wanted a more comprehensive book, treating of Christian dogmas in direct opposition to modern errors. It is to be a methodical work and to embrace everything that a good Christian ought to know. His Majesty wishes it to be composed by his own theologians, printed in Vienna on his commission, and taught, by his express command, in the schools of all his provinces and kingdoms.

In consideration of His Majesty's good and sincere intention to help his unhappy dominions, and of the fruit that might result from such a compendium, I have not yet definitely refused the undertaking. . . . Master Nicholas and I are of opinion that, besides other inconveniences, we shall not be able to excuse ourselves before the King and the University without prejudice to the reputation of the Society. On the other hand, we are both convinced that to satisfy the demand is beyond our power, since, apart from everything else, we have neither the time nor the material, nor the ability to put the material in order. Master Nicholas is in charge of this college and has to lecture daily both at home and at the University. I, too, have to lecture every day, and we do not see when we are going to find the time for other work. If we were to give up our lectures in order to attend to the affair, people would not like it. Here in Germany they are given to producing a book overnight, and many of them think that we could easily perform a similar feat. Men say to us: " When are we going to have some books from you, Fathers ? "

We humbly ask your Paternity to make known your wishes to us and, if you desire this compendium to be written, we beg you, for the honour of God, to send us someone to attend to it. We shall help him in every way we can. . . .[1]

At the end of his letter Lejay mentioned Peter Canisius as a possible author of the compendium, but he did not wish him to be removed from Ingolstadt. It turned out that St. Ignatius could not help, and there was no alternative then but for Father Claude to shoulder his burden. Being a great and good man, he found time somehow without abandoning his numerous other activities, and gradually accumulated a huge mass of material on justification, predestination, the relation of faith to good works, and other subjects of Reformation controversy. But his goodwill outran his strength, and in a short time his health showed signs of giving way. The thought of the two brilliant men at Ingolstadt began to tantalize him in his weakness, and at last he succumbed to temptation and set going the machinery which put Canisius and Goudanus on the ship for Vienna.

The pair, having weathered the dangers of the Danube, went, accompanied by the two novices of whom they were touchingly proud,[2] to

---

[1] M.H., *Epistolae Paschasii Broetii, Claudii Jaii*, etc., pp. 372–4.

[2] Speaking of them to St. Ignatius, Peter said : " They testify that in their opinion it is as big a feat to get one German into the Society as to get twenty Italians or Spaniards." Braunsberger, *Epistulae*, vol. i, p. 380.

swell the Viennese Jesuit community to the imposing total of twenty-five. It was March 9, 1552, Lent, and the middle of term. St. Peter accordingly plunged straight into the activities which he loved: confessions, sermons, visits to the sick and prisoners, and work for the poor. But there was another activity much less to his taste. Lejay had at once placed the notes for the Compendium in his hands, urgently exhorting him to set to work on the book, as the King showed signs of impatience. He swallowed the pill without making a face, though he certainly did not think that it was going to be good for him. At the University he took over Delanoy's work because that good man's rather ponderous delivery had begun to bore the Austrians, but he did not take over Peter the Lombard. Instead, he based his daily lectures on the notes presented to him by Lejay, and so became the precursor of the long line of Jesuit controversial theologians whose chief glory is the great St. Robert Bellarmine. At home he assumed charge of the young Jesuits' studies, an office that was no sinecure as the men worked like Trojans and, being of different ages and attainments, their *omnium gatherum* of a syllabus needed much careful organization.

During that busy Lent, St. Peter alone of the Jesuit priests could speak a language comprehensible by the Austrians. The people had a modern taste in sermons and disliked the generally prevalent Italian style of preaching, which was too declamatory and pyrotechnical. Peter's quieter methods appealed to them, though some less intelligent listeners were at first puzzled by his unfamiliar turns of expression.[1] It was only by slow degrees, however, that the Saint acquired a standing with the charming but somewhat flippant and feather-headed Viennese. They were suspicious of him as a foreigner and rather inclined to laugh at his Rhineland "brogue." Moreover, he took little pains to veil the fact that he was after their souls and would have them return to the simple practices of piety which they had very largely discarded. So it happened that on more than one occasion only eight or ten people came to his sermon,[2] and even some clerical students of the city were heard to say: "Why should anybody want to listen to the sermons of Master Canisius? He's a Papist."[3] Curious clerical students they must have been and worthy of the disloyal unprincipled generation that bore them.

---

[1] M.H., Polanco, *Chronicon*, vol. ii, p. 567; *Litterae Quadrimestres*, vol. i, pp. 574–5. Delanoy, who was hopeless at German himself, criticized Peter's sermons for their lack of emoι on (M.H., *Epistolae Mixtae*, vol. v, p. 78). Emotion was greatly overdone in those days.
[2] Wiedemann, *Geschichte der Reformation und Gegenreformation im Lande unter der Enns* (Prague, 1879), vol. i, p. 103, note.
[3] M.H., Polanco, *Chronicon*, vol. ii, p. 580; *Litterae Quadrimestres*, vol. ii, p. 20.

Germany was in the throes of civil war, engineered against the Emperor by the treacherous Elector of Saxony and the drunken terrorist, Albrecht Alcibiades, whose pillaging exploits made the worst atrocities of the Peasants' Revolt seem tame by comparison. " Perhaps never," wrote St. Peter, witnessing the fury, " was there waged on German soil a more savage war than this." Leagued with the Lutherans and, incidentally with the Turks, was his Most Christian Majesty, Henri II, a combination that compelled the forsaken Emperor to fly for his life, and the Council of Trent, once again the victim of Habsburg-Valois rivalry, hastily to close its sessions. Albrecht, with his wild, white mane streaming in the wind like a banner of doom, swore to blot out Catholicism and reduce its great stronghold, Cologne, to smouldering ruin. Watchmen kept look-out day and night from the City's towers for the approach of the marauders, while the people prayed and prepared to sell their lives as dearly as they might.[1] St. Peter, ever mindful of friends in distress, wrote to encourage his Cologne brethren. His letter, penned, as he says, *tumultuarie*, is mainly a fervent exhortation to the closer following of Christ, according to the spirit of the Society of Jesus. That must be his brethren's answer to the challenge of evil all around them, evil so palpable as to seem the herald of the world's dissolution:

The several sorts of great misery incident to this life are before us. We have bitter experience of the difficulties of our generation and know the appalling changes of fortune to which practically everything is subjected, just as if the world was in its last delirium and about to collapse into nothingness. . . . In this place we hear with what terrible cruelty the Turk rages against our next neighbours of Hungary, often butchering many thousands of Christians in the most brutal way. And is there to be any measure or end to the multitude of stormy mutinies that have now begun ? We are borne down and disquieted from every side by a thousand treacheries and evil designs . . . and there is no place of rest and solid peace for us except in the wounds of our Crucified Lord. . . . In them is our home of refreshment, our harbour, our sanctuary. Let the world indulge its madness. Let it wear itself out, for it cannot endure and passes like a shadow. It is growing old and, I think, is in its last decrepit stage. But we, buried deep in the wounds of Christ, why should we be dismayed ?[2]

[1] M.H., Polanco, *Chronicon*, vol. ii, p. 585.
[2] Braunsberger, *Epistulae*, vol. i, p. 403.

To Peter's delight some novices from Cologne had arrived in Vienna, bringing with them a good number of books, which were the only presents he cared about. The books and their bearers abundantly consoled him, he said, as tokens of the love that united him and the Cologne men, though "sundered by so many miles." They had told him as a piece of great good news that his half-brother, Theodoric, seemed to be following in his footsteps, for he had joined Andrew Herll in the house near St. Gereon's. "Even at the cost of my blood," answered Peter, "I would wish him to live and to die in our Society, he whom I have so long desired, and coveted with many a sigh to see draw nearer to you and be one of you." Suffering is the great teacher of sympathy, and Peter could enter so generously into the troubles of his Cologne brethren because he had so many troubles of his own. He was now within immediate range of the Turks. "They are very near us," he told Polanco, "and daily make further progress in Hungary. We therefore beg your Reverence to obtain for us the help of the Fathers' Masses that we may always be ready and nothing loath either to die or to live in holy obedience. No words could express the gravity of the crisis that has come upon Germany and all the Empire. May we shed our blood for the sweet Name of Jesus."[1]

It was just at this time when the outlook for the Jesuits in Vienna seemed about as black as it could be that Lejay succumbed to his labours and died. The following day, August 6, 1552, Peter addressed himself to Polanco, telling how they had called in the best doctors and taken every other means in their power to save their beloved Father:

But in spite of every effort, because Our Lord in whose hands are all things wished to show His Providence and bounty our Reverend Father Claude rendered up his holy soul to its eternal and ever blessed Creator, in the presence of all the Fathers and Brothers. And so he departed from us his children to that other world, like St. Martin leaving in each one an intense longing to keep him, had it been the will of Almighty God. He showed us the straight way to Christ both in life and in death, a death for him all the happier, in view of the labours, dangers and calamities which now confront us.

It was the Feast of the Transfiguration when he was taken up out of this valley of sorrows and ascended the holy mountain to find the perfect vision of Christ and rejoice with St. Peter in the beauty of God....
I am not going to try to show in detail how admirably this blessed

[1] Braunsberger, *Epistulae*, vol. i, p. 413.

Father lived or what a grand example of virtue he set us. For you know, Father, that, up to now, no one of the Society had worked more strenuously among the German heretics than he, or had such a long experience of suffering. Always and in every place where he dwelt he left behind the sweetest memory, and so stirred up souls to piety that nearly all whom he met would fain have retained him. Though he was old,[1] he did not cease to teach assiduously, and that to the complete satisfaction of his audiences. There was a certain wonderful grace and sweetness in his teaching which made it almost impossible for anyone to take umbrage, no matter what he said. . . .

But, as I have already declared, it is not my intention to tell the life-story of this Father who was chosen by God to be among our first Fathers and afterwards appeared as a very apostle of Germany. To the German princes and bishops, who held him in the highest esteem, he was of great service at the Diets of the Empire. It is well known, too, how much his presence was appreciated at the Council, in both Trent and Bologna. When at that time the bishopric of Trieste was offered to him, indeed most urgently pressed upon him by the King of the Romans, he could not be induced to accept it or ever to accept any other ecclesiastical dignity. He was a great practiser of poverty and used to frequent the Court of the King in an old-fashioned thread-bare gown, notwithstanding the protests of the Court officials who offered to supply him with all that he needed.

His life was regulated according to a detailed plan. Each day, as he often told me, he used to meditate on some part of the Passion of Christ and he had many beautiful sermons on all the different phases of Christ's life. The method of prayer which we call the Rosary was a favourite devotion of his. He practised it with great piety, going over the Mysteries of the Incarnate Word in the way in which they are presented to us by the Church.

I feel sure that his death will cause widespread sorrow.[2] God grant that we his sons, now bereaved of so good a father, may inherit those shining gifts with which, by God's grace, his whole life was adorned and made resplendent. Everybody here is profoundly grieved by his death and calls him an angel of God and the father and protector of all Catholics. . . .[3]

---

[1] Fifty-two or less, as he was born between 1500 and 1504, the precise year not being certain. Fifty was considered the late evening of life in those days and, indeed, on into the nineteenth century.

[2] Cardinal Truchsess of Augsburg wept bitterly when told the news, and wrote begging the Jesuits in Vienna for Lejay's New Testament as a memento.

[3] Braunsberger, Epistulae, vol. i, pp. 406-9.

On the strong recommendation of St. Peter, Father Delanoy was now appointed Rector of the College by St. Ignatius, while Peter himself and Goudanus added the work formerly done by Lejay to their regular programme.[1] The Saint's worst trouble at this time, the great cloud overshadowing his life, was the Compendium, about which he poured out his heart to Polanco. " This task," he wrote, " has been such a burden to me hitherto, receiving as I do very little assistance from the other Fathers, that if I devoted all my time to it, it would scarcely be enough. Moreover, as I often represented to Father Claude, I would gladly devote my services to convents of nuns, to prisons and to hospitals, were I not prevented by this work. But the Father invariably answered that I should put everything else aside and give myself up entirely to the composition of the book. Yet after so many months I am still stuck fast at the beginning, nor do I see how I can make any progress in the near future. I am most anxious, then, to have your Reverence's advice, because, though I have worked so hard, I am neither satisfied nor easy in mind about the matter, fearing that the book may remain unfinished for years if I continue, as at present, both to teach and to write. May the Lord turn everything to his glory ! Oh, if only Laynez or Salmeron or Olave were here how much more easily would the work be done ! But I hope that your Reverence will give me trusty counsel in this and all other matters. May Our Lord Jesus teach us to do His will and discharge our duty of obedience."[2]

That the Compendium to which he devoted himself conscientiously did not entirely bar Peter's way to prisons and hospitals is evident from a letter addressed to the Cologne Jesuits within a month of his arrival in Vienna. " To-day," he said, " I found a way to get in touch with prisoners. I am going to supply the place of parish priest to them, if I may talk so grandly; to set souls free, with Christ's assistance, from the chains of sin and to feed those hungry ones, almost dead with long starvation, that they may recover their strength from the Word of God. There are many of them with no hope of being liberated but rather weighed down with fear of increased distress. May Christ who died for them console the poor fellows and, if not in this life, at least in the next, make them safe and truly free. I commend them to your prayers, Brothers, for does not the Apostle exhort us : ' Remember them that are in bonds as if you were bound with them ; and them that labour, as being yourselves also in the body ' ? "[3]

[1] Aschbach, *Geschichte der Wiener Universität*, vol. iii, p. 97.
[2] Braunsberger, *Epistulae*, vol. i, pp. 411–13.
[3] Braunsberger, *Epistulae*, vol. i, p. 403.

At first the gaol-birds made game of their self-constituted chaplain, laughing in his face or bursting into obscenities when he tried to address them. But he never minded, and continued patiently day after day at his thankless and apparently fruitless task. Not content with advice and encouragement, he used to bring the men small treats of food, drink, and clothes, bought with money that he had himself begged for the purpose, and would get his young brethren to come and alleviate their hours of loneliness by telling them the news or reading to them. What Polanco calls his "*magna solicitudo*" gradually began to have effect, and first one and then another would unburden his conscience to Peter and receive Holy Communion at his hands. After a few months the whole spirit of the prisons visited by him became transformed and, instead of the sour suspicion that was his first greeting, he met on his daily rounds with tokens of general love and reverence. Not only the prison communities but Vienna at large wondered to see him walk side by side with condemned men to the place of execution and there stand to bless and comfort while the last dreadful rites were done.[1]

But, though the prisoners had his special attention, poor and afflicted people in general were by no means forgotten. The Jesuits through persistent begging built up a fund to provide for their more pressing needs, and themselves went from slum to slum with parcels of food, clothes, shirts, and boots. In the autumn of 1552 the plague suddenly swept through Vienna, carrying off thousands of adults and children before the authorities could do anything to stay the havoc. All schools were at once closed, including the embryo college for external students started by the Jesuits, the University put up its shutters, and panic descended upon the City. It was for such an hour that Peter Canisius was born. Regardless of personal danger, he and his brother priests moved about among the stricken people from morning to night, hearing countless confessions, administering the Last Sacraments, comforting where comfort was possible, and supplying food and medicines. Three times a day the whole Jesuit community met for prayer together to avert the wrath of God from the people, their midday devotions being joined in by students and others from outside. Despite his tremendous exertions on behalf of the sick, Peter, during the plague, was to be seen in the pulpit more frequently than ever, so that the Viennese, says Polanco, "were lost in astonishment at the burning eagerness of Father Canisius for the salvation of souls."[2]

[1] M.H., Polanco, *Chronicon*, vol. i, pp. 577, 579; *Litterae Quadrimestres*, vol. i, p. 574, vol. ii, pp. 114, 117.
[2] M.H., Polanco, *Chronicon*, vol. ii, p. 574; *Litterae Quadrimestres*, vol. ii, p. 114.

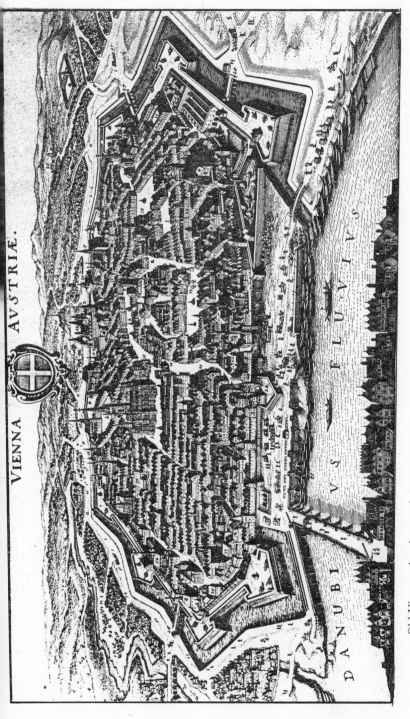

Old Vienna, showing on the extreme left, by the bridge, the Dominican Priory which first housed the Jesuits
The later Jesuit Church and College are marked No. 19, and the Royal Palace No. 29 at the top
From Merian's engraving (1643)

His fame as a comforter and helper in desperate cases began to spread throughout Vienna, owing to some remarkable successes which had attended his ministrations. One was with an unfortunate woman who appeared to have come under the power of the devil in a peculiarly distressing way. She believed that God had finally abandoned her, and terrified her neighbours by her shrieks for mercy. When not prostrate in bed she was constantly being thrown to the ground or dragged about with great violence by some invisible power. Priests had long since given her up, as their exorcisms did not seem to have the slightest effect. Then, in the last extremity, St. Peter arrived. By gentle management he persuaded her to make a confession of her whole life and, without any exorcism at all but only a simple prayer to God for her, bade her come to church, for she was cured. Next day, to the amazement of many witnesses, she appeared at Peter's Mass and received Holy Communion from him. After that she was always to be seen under the pulpit when he preached, and never again had she the slightest recurrence of her former affliction.[1] The result of this affair was that Peter became something of a hero with the women of Vienna, who pretty nearly elbowed the men away from his confessional altogether. The nuns, of course, were not to be outdone by these lay ladies, and what Polanco calls their " pious importunity " pursued the Saint relentlessly until he assumed the spiritual direction of two convents and agreed to oblige several others with exhortations in German at regular intervals.[2]

At this period scarcely one tenth of King Ferdinand's dominions could any longer be described as Catholic. In the country places religion of any sort was fast disappearing, while the wretched peasantry reverted to their ancestral pagan superstitions. The diocese of Passau alone, which adjoined that of Vienna, contained 254 parishes without a priest to attend to their needs, and in other districts, the bishops, driven almost desperate, had allowed men of doubtful orthodoxy to assume pastoral charge because they could find no others. Many of the incumbents were avowed heretics and made use of their position to destroy what remained of Catholic faith in the people.[3] St. Peter was given his first opportunity of going to the rescue of the forsaken parishes on Christmas Day, 1552. A small place in the neighbourhood of Vienna had sent a message begging for the services of a priest. That people should have wanted his help was

---

[1] *Litterae Quadrimestres*, vol. ii, pp. 115–6.
[2] M.H., Polanco, *Chronicon*, vol. iii, p. 243.
[3] M.H., Polanco, *Chronicon*, vol. ii, p. 579; *Litterae Quadrimestres*, vol. ii, p. 19, report of Father Delanoy to St. Ignatius.

the best of Christmas presents for a man like Peter. Having said Mass before dawn and distributed Holy Communion to large numbers at his usual church, he immediately afterwards mounted some sort of coach and drove over the frozen roads to the village. There he said Mass again and preached a Christmas sermon, the first Mass and sermon which the poor people had heard for ages. After Mass and a mouthful of breakfast Peter sallied forth to visit all the sick of the parish and bring them the consolation of the Sacraments. One old man of ninety wept his eyes out for very joy at the sight of a priest by his bed. Later in the day it was the children's turn, and Peter became so absorbed with their instruction that he forgot the passage of time and remained in the village much longer than he had intended. At his departure the people crowded round to bless and thank him. They all had little Christmas presents for him, and it was only with the greatest difficulty that he got away as empty-handed as he had come. Such pathetic gratitude for his ministrations indicates that Catholicism still remained a force in men's souls and might never have come to such a sad pass in Austria had the native clergy been worth the coats on their backs.[1]

At the beginning of the following year, 1553, the Jesuits received a special invitation from King Ferdinand, duly signed and sealed, to undertake similar missions in the country parts of his dominions. St. Peter alone could comply, as he was the only priest who knew German sufficiently well for the purpose, so, armed with full faculties from the Bishop of Passau, he set off into the wilderness during Lent. Abundant snow fell that winter, and it was piercingly cold in the mountain districts. Bands of robbers roamed about on the watch for lonely travellers, and armed heretics added another to the many perils of the road.[2] Through them all St. Peter moved undaunted from village to village, carrying out in each the same programme of Masses, Sacraments, sermons, catechisms and visits to the sick. How he found his way about in the snow is his own secret. Each turn of the track might bring him face to face with wolves or brigands, but the love in his heart had cast out fear. He had thoughts only for the deserted flocks, whose voices, like another St. Patrick, he heard calling and crying out to him. Typical of his whole life is the fact that though he visited scores of wild places on his mission and ran innumerable risks, he has himself hardly a word to say about them. Much snow, ice and frost, wild men and heretics, that is the whole of the story, except for the following few lines of a chance letter:

[1] M.H., *Litterae Quadrimestres*, vol. ii, p. 115.   [2] *Litterae Quadrimestres*, vol. ii, p. 250.

In order to do a little work in Our Lord's vineyard, I made a pilgrimage into our Austria during Lent. I visited parishes where conditions were piteous through neglect, and other parishes entirely bereft of pastors. Thanks to the grace of God, I was able to do something for these abandoned flocks by sermons, argument and exhortation. I had heard that there were more than three hundred parishes without shepherds and that many unfortunate people died in them unattended. It would be difficult for me to express in words how many and great sorrows, scandals, and dangers I everywhere encountered, troubles of such a kind as to render these most afflicted sheep of Christ deserving of the profoundest sympathy and compassion. I am in hopes that one day many of our Fathers will go forth and bring great assistance to the villages of Austria. There is a dreadful lack of priests here, but we are training in our college excellent young fellows with both the ability and the desire to devote themselves to the service of their native land. God grant that we may gradually have more and more of such labourers to train, not only for Austria but for all Germany as well.[1]

The Jesuit students mentioned here were to St. Peter as the apple of his eye. Nothing that he could do to inspire and help them was ever too much. His Compendium, his never-ending round of lectures and sermons, his women clients, his prisoners, all these might at times be a cross to him; the students were his unfailing comfort. Always planning to deepen their attachments to the Master whose service was his only ambition, to broaden their zeal beyond national limits, to make them intellectually efficient, and to increase their numbers, he became in the end, with the exception of St. Ignatius, probably the greatest single constructive influence in the history of the Society of Jesus. When the plague slowed down the wheels of education in Vienna, he seized the chance, busy as he otherwise was, to reorganize the studies of his young brethren, bringing them more into line with the methods of the University of Paris which St. Ignatius greatly admired. At the same time he set about providing for the accommodation of larger numbers of lay students, thus paving the way for the great college that would afterwards arise. The combined efforts of himself and Father Delanoy met, as usually happened, with plenty of opposition, due mainly to the fact that they gave their teaching free and welcomed everybody.

[1] Braunsberger, *Epistulae*, vol. i, pp. 421–2.

Opinions about the incipient lay college differed considerably. "This man thinks it a wonder," wrote Polanco, "and that man, a joke." One rumour going around was that the Fathers locked students into rooms with barred windows and then starved them for several weeks that thus "the Holy Ghost might descend upon them and give them a vocation to the Society of Jesus."[1] Tall stories such as that are more easily invented than exploded, so on the first Sunday of Lent, 1553, just before the reopening of schools, St. Peter decided on a daring step. After his usual sermon in the Church of St. Mary, the second largest and most beautiful in Vienna, he proceeded to give his listeners a short account of the Jesuit system of education.[2] His words appear to have had some effect with the ordinary people, those plain fathers and mothers of whom school-masters are supposed to stand in such wholesome dread, but with the University mandarins it was quite another matter. In human affairs the toughest of obstacles is a vested interest, and up against this St. Peter and his companions came full tilt.

The University resented the non-attendance of the young Jesuits at its schools of literature and was also, it would seem, nervous of the effect which a new academy, run on unfamiliar lines, might have on its own position.[3] So it adopted a dog-in-the-manger policy and, while itself unprepared to do its duty by the Church, would not permit others to try their hand. But Peter Canisius and his brethren, especially the large-hearted Father Delanoy, knew an argument to win popular sympathy which the cold logic of the professors could not refute. That argument was their charity, for the employment of which the circumstances of the time and the winds of heaven constantly provided scope. The heavens have many unpleasant winds, our own east one, the sirocco, the mistral, but perhaps none is quite so bad as Vienna's particular horror, the *Föhn*. It is a soft, warm wind blowing frequently from the Alps, and has such a devitalizing effect that dwellers in Vienna are apt to let everything slide and 'go to the devil' while under its influence. Whether or not it bore the name *Föhn* in St. Peter's day, it certainly blew then and made the kindly Viennese indifferent to the sufferings of the broken soldiers who arrived daily from the wars in Hungary. They straggled in half-naked, hungry, diseased, weak from their wounds, and many of them collapsed in the dirty, *Föhn*-swept streets, unable to reach whatever miserable shelter the authorities may be supposed to have provided for them. An eye-

---

[1] M.H., Polanco, *Chronicon*, vol. ii, p. 278.   [2] M.H., Polanco, *Chronicon*, vol. iii, p. 240.
[3] M.H., *Litterae Quadrimestres*, vol. ii, p. 249.

witness relates that it was the rarest thing to see a citizen take the slightest notice of them or so much as give them an armful of straw on which to rest. And so they died untended and unfriended, those poor Italian mercenaries who had done their bit

> " In the day when heaven was falling,
> The hour when earth's foundations fled."

They were herded together in a part of the city far removed from the Jesuits' quarters, but Father Delanoy at length came to hear of their condition and went in hot haste to alleviate it. Alms were begged by him and St. Peter from the Queen of Bohemia and other high ladies, and beds, food, clothing, medicines immediately procured. The younger Jesuits, for their part, scoured the city to bring in any soldiers who had fallen by the way. When their wounds and bodily needs had been attended to, the Fathers proceeded to give them the comfort of the Sacraments and to make arrangements for their future. To enable them to keep their independence they were provided with ready money and in other ways helped back to self-respect and good Christian living.[1]

The result of these and similar activities of the Jesuits among the other unfortunates of Vienna, for whom they were constantly providing shirts, clothes, boots, vegetables and all sorts of things, was, in time, a very definite turn of popular sympathy in their direction. The attentions even became embarrassing, as people took to bringing gifts to the house which it was difficult for the Jesuits to refuse without causing offence. St. Peter was the most embarrassed. One day a man led a calf up to the door and announced that it was for Father Canisius. Father Canisius declined the beast with many thanks, but, lo and behold, when next he looked out there was his calf tethered to the railings! He sent it back, however, as he always did the hens, pies, and what not which were constantly being presented.[2] More to his liking was the fact that people now began to show greater readiness to send their sons to the Jesuits' school. This, combined with the express sanction of King Ferdinand, enabled them to carry on in spite of the University, which for years to come would refuse the young Jesuits permission to stand for its degrees.[3]

The college had stout friends in the Papal Legate, Martinengo, and Bishop Weber of Laibach. The Bishop used sometimes to pay a surprise

---

[1] M.H., *Litterae Quadrimestres*, vol. ii, pp. 111–12 ; M.H., Polanco, *Chronicon*, vol. ii, pp. 575–6.
[2] M.H., Polanco, *Chronicon*, vol. ii, p. 578. " Alii gallinas, confectiones et hujusmodi afferentes, magna contentione ut reciperentur instabant."
[3] Braunsberger, *Epistulae*, vol. i, p. 415.

visit to the Fathers at their dinner hour, in order that the distinguished men whom he took care to bring with him might see for themselves how frugally St. Peter and his companions lived. One day King Ferdinand himself came to join the Fathers at dinner, having sent them beforehand liberal supplies of wine and *Delikatessen*. According to Polanco the good things were wasted because His Majesty and the courtiers forgot to eat, so engrossed did they become in the Greek disputation held by the young Jesuits for their entertainment.[1]

To build up a good library for his men was another of St. Peter's home concerns. He was a great bookman himself and used to say, " Better a college without a church of its own than a college without a library of its own." Lejay had been of the same mind, and shortly after coming to Vienna had started inquiries among the booksellers. Luck of a kind favoured him, for, owing to the disrepute into which scholastic studies had fallen, there were many volumes of St. Thomas, St. Bonaventure and other great theologians on the market. These for some inscrutable but certainly highly untheological reasons the apothecaries of Vienna wanted to possess. Lejay, however, anticipated them and paid cash down for the books out of the surplus of the journey money given him by the Duke of Bavaria. Other books were, in Polanco's words, " scraped together from all quarters," and thus, at its very start, the college possessed the nucleus of a satisfactory library.[2] St. Peter followed up Lejay's lead and considerably increased the stock, both by purchasing books and by begging them. This was a persistent hobby of his through life, and the libraries of the many houses in which he lived, including some that afterwards became very famous, owed to him either their inception or their first big developments. But he was not merely acquisitive in this matter of books. He was also a generous giver, both to people outside the Society of Jesus and to houses of the Society outside his own province.[3]

He was so keen about the provision of books because painful experience had taught him how little could be done without them. Every year his own commitments to various learned undertakings grew in number and importance. Father Lejay's Scripture lectures at the University had fallen to him, in addition to other courses, and he still laboured away

---

[1] M.H., Polanco, *Chronicon*, vol. ii, p. 273. A flippant person might suggest that a Latin disputation is bad enough, but that a Greek one must surely have been the destruction of anybody's appetite. Still, it was the century of the Renaissance, and educated men certainly took delight in these displays.

[2] M.H., Polanco, *Chronicon*, vol. ii, p. 275.

[3] Stonyhurst College Library possesses a copy of *Victor of St. Hugo*, purchased by St. Peter in Louvain, which afterwards travelled a good deal owing to his anxiety to make it as widely useful as possible. The title page contains notes in the Saint's hand, bearing on the matter.

at the Compendium, though unable to see any end to the business. His difficulty appears to have been that, to meet King Ferdinand's wishes, he must write a book suitable for two distinct classes of readers, different in aptitude and education. Only once in a hundred years does a book of that kind appear, some *Gulliver's Travels* or *Alice in Wonderland*, and the subject has never yet been theology. Great, then, was Peter's joy when he learned that Polanco had taken his suggestion and written to Father Laynez, proposing that he should compose an extensive treatise from which the Compendium might afterwards be extracted.[1] That news seems to have brought about a change in the Saint's own plans, for, though the matter is somewhat obscure, it looks as if, during these busy months of 1553, he had definitely abandoned the idea of producing a learned work for priests, and concentrated instead on the composition of a primer of Christian doctrine, adapted to the abilities of young students and children of ordinary intelligence. It was a happy chance that brought about the change, for it gave the Catholic world the greatest and most famous of its catechisms.

During 1553 Peter was not only the regular Sunday preacher at the Church of St. Mary by the river, but also preacher in ordinary to the King.[2] How he managed to fulfil all his obligations is a mystery, yet they never so absorbed him that he could not spare a thought for the worries of Cologne, Louvain, and Ingolstadt. To his old friend and host, Canon Herll, he addressed at this time a long and very beautiful letter, begging him to help his brother Jesuits in their hard struggle for existence at Cologne. They did not want a monastery or any such grand thing, he said, but only to be allowed to work unhindered, *pro Christo et Ecclesia*, either educating children or strengthening the devotional life of clergy and people :

> To this issue are we spurred on by the holy Magi Kings, by the Theban martyrs, the Maccabees, the Virgins of St. Ursula, and all that company so dear to God who by their choice rest in Cologne, making the city a magnet to the hearts of strangers. . . . But I have written more than I intended and would blush to send you this hasty scribble did I not know your kindness, and that I can deal with you as with a friend and most dear father. . . . I am anxious to know where your nephew is and what progress he has made in his theological studies. When I hear from you that he is doing well I shall return the greater

[1] Braunsberger, *Epistulae*, vol. i, p. 428.   [2] M.H., *Litterae Quadrimestres*, vol. ii, p. 376.

thanks to God for making him by your care a good and learned theologian. Would you greet the Reverend Doctor Gropper from me? I pray from my heart that he and Father Billick may never slacken in their zeal for the Church. . . . And would you also remember me to Father Prior of the Carthusians and Father Prior of the Dominicans, to both of whom I am heavily indebted? My remembrances and greetings to all my friends. In haste. April 27, 1553.[1]

A charity similar to that which inspired the letter to Herll was also shown the Louvain Jesuits, Peter and Delanoy having obtained for them recommendatory letters from King Ferdinand to Mary, Regent of the Netherlands.[2] As for Ingolstadt, the departure of Peter had given Duke Albert an unpleasant shock, and, the foundation of a Jesuit college seeming to be the only way to recover his man, the college at last received serious attention. The Duke's counsellor, Wiguleus Hundt, then at the head of Ingolstadt University, journeyed to Vienna to reopen negotiations. Peter and he got on famously together, and the college soon became a certainty, though the terms and details of its foundation remained to be settled later on. Only on one point did the two men disagree. Hundt wished the Jesuits to give an undertaking that they would provide professors of Latin and Greek for the University, but the sagacious Peter was entirely opposed, foreseeing how tongues would wag and spread a tale that the newcomers evidently wanted to deprive honest men of their jobs.[3]

A college that Peter found it more difficult to help directly was the German one in Rome, recently established by St. Ignatius for the education of priests to evangelize the northern nations. This great institution, whose red-gowned alumni still add colour to the streets of Rome, had at first a hard struggle to obtain students from beyond the Alps, and such students were the only ones fully suited to its purposes. St. Ignatius constituted Peter his recruiting sergeant and warmly urged him to his task. But it was a task beset with the most serious difficulties. The *Föhn* and overwork laid Peter on his back just as he was endeavouring to get to grips with it by addressing petitions to the King and various princes, bishops and nobles. " I have been ill," he told Polanco soon afterwards, " but thanks be to God I am beginning to feel better now and will get the letters done at once. Lest your Reverence should be surprised at our failure to supply the college with any Austrians, I must let you know this fact. It is exceedingly difficult to persuade the people of Austria to send their sons to Rome, as the conditions for entrance to the college are such as no northerners will tolerate, especially the one that requires students to bind themselves by oath to the service of the Pope."[1] Peter referred also to the rumour that the college had not so far proved a success, which caused St. Ignatius to answer sharply that it was doing very well, that the discipline was light, that the students had two days' holiday in the country each week, and that more progress in study was possible there in one year than anywhere else in two.[2] After that expostulation St. Peter co-operated most loyally with the General, though each man he sent to Rome was only secured by him after an amount of correspondence, explanation, and argument that would have been enough to make most people sick and tired of the business in a week. By April, 1554, he had dispatched twenty-three students, drawn from all parts of Austria and Germany.[3] It has to be remembered, too, as St. Ignatius himself readily acknowledged, that in sending these men to Rome, Peter was deliberately baulking his own immediate chances in Austria. The men would not be back for years, and meantime the northern lands must go without such help as they could have given. Austria, however, was far from being the limit of Peter's vision, and at this period he had entered on active negotiations with various princes and dignitaries for the establishment of the Society of Jesus in Holland, Bohemia, Tirol, Prussia, and Hungary. Somebody who had travelled in Turkestan spoke to him about conditions in that country, whereupon his Christian zeal immediately flamed out in a letter to St. Ignatius:

May Our Eternal Lord open a way for us to Tartary . . . for I hear that its people have never been Christians and that they are of a most cruel disposition, delighting in robbery and the spoliation of their Christian neighbours. The Polish Envoy tells me that their land, which is poorly cultivated, is larger than Spain, Italy and Germany put together. The natives, who live in tents and are always girded for fighting, feast on the flesh and blood of horses. In religion they are Mohammedans but worse than the Turks. May Almighty God who is helping barbarous India by our brethren also enlighten the darkness of Tartary that there may be one fold and one Shepherd.[4]

[1] Braunsberger, *Epistulae*, vol. i, p. 436.
[2] Braunsberger, *Epistulae*, vol. i, pp. 440–1.
[3] Braunsberger, *Epistulae*, vol. i, p. 457, note 3.
[4] Braunsberger, *Epistulae*, vol. i, p. 461.

St. Peter's Tartary, however, continued to be Vienna where, too, there was much darkness to enlighten. At the beginning of 1554 the Church in Austria seemed so near its end that the Saint wondered how the few remaining good Catholics escaped martyrdom. " May God in His great mercy send many workers to this country," he said, " for otherwise the people will become not merely heretics but like brute beasts, so much are they the slaves of malice and depravity." Vienna had now no bishop, for both Nausea and his immediate successor were dead. The problem of filling the vacant see exercised the wits of King and Council throughout the autumn of 1553 but no one suitable for the post could be found. Then suddenly a canon of the Cathedral chapter named Burchard van den Bergh directed attention to St. Peter himself, who happened to be related to him distantly.[1] He liked the Jesuits but did not really know very much about them or their constitutions. Probably he had no idea that the constitutions forbade the acceptance of ecclesiastical dignities, a wise provision of St. Ignatius for the safeguarding of the main purpose of his Order, and only thought that he was doing good men a service by strongly recommending Peter for the bishopric to the Nuncio, Martinengo, and other high officials of the Government. The news came like a bombshell to the Saint. He refused even to consider the matter, whereupon Martinengo and Canon Burchard begged him at least to dine with them and let them hear his reasons for refusing. They were in the following terms, as reported by the good historian Sacchinus :

First of all, since it is obvious that the originator of this scheme is Dr. Burchard, it must be equally obvious that the scheme in no way proceeds from the Holy Spirit but from the spirit of this world. I am not alone in thinking so, and it is what the ordinary people are certain to think. They will never be persuaded that I did not mount the episcopal throne by my own efforts and ambition, or, if not by my own, certainly by those of my stepmother's brother. But no one takes to himself an honour except him who is called by God ; and that I have not been thus called I am quite sure, not only from the fact that God never put such an idea into my superiors' heads, but still more clearly from the fact that God indubitably called me from the first to a different kind of life. Among other plain proofs of God's will in the matter there are the tranquillity of soul and supreme satisfaction which I have always experienced in this private life of poverty, as well as some

[1] The Canon's sister was St. Peter's step-mother.

successes in the affairs in which I have been engaged. Each of us is admonished by God to remain steadfast in his calling. That is God's will and ordinance, for He does not promiscuously desire all manner of service from everybody. Since He directs all things according to a wise and admirable plan He would not have called a person whom He wanted to serve Him by means of ecclesiastical dignities to a Society in which, by His own prompting, as I firmly believe, all doors to such dignities are shut fast. Then, again, I can urge the argument of public utility, for, supposing myself to possess any gifts, I shall be able to use them to best advantage if I am free to go where I am needed and if I am not tied to one place. . . . Finally, such is now the state of affairs in Vienna, so sunk are the people in error and so much at odds with their lawful pastors and with the Pope, that there would seem to be a far better chance of helping the country by ordinary works of mercy, sermons, and general friendly intercourse than by occupying a position of honour and authority.

On St. Peter coming to an end, Martinengo, according to Sacchinus, immediately jumped to his feet, " *magno ardore et clamore*," and held forth as follows :

I am astounded that a man of such wisdom and goodness should invent such excuses. You look for a divine call, as if a clearer voice than the cry of so many perishing men could be wanted by anybody. You say that it is not God's suggestion since it proceeded from Canon Burchard, as though the death of Christ by which He redeemed the world were not from God because Caiphas said : " It is expedient that one man should die for the people ! " You have experienced complete peace in your present way of life, but beware, Father, that it be not a treacherous peace and that under cover of humility you mask not the desire of leisure and liberty. . . . The throne to which you would be raised is no seat of honour and peace, as you seem to imagine. It is a throne of labour and martyrdom. . . . And as for your work being restricted, were you a very Apostle the effect of your efforts could not be more far-reaching since whatever you undertake as bishop of this Imperial City will redound to the service of the whole Empire. Come, then, and cheerfully bow your neck under this necessary yoke. Make a voluntary sacrifice to God and do not oblige us to use the full extent of our authority in the matter.[1]

[1] Sacchinus, *Vita P. Petri Canisii* (1616), pp. 76–9. The story is plainly somewhat dramatized by the author, but not to the distortion of the facts, about which Sacchinus always shows himself scrupulously careful.

The veiled threat contained in the Nuncio's last sentence scared Peter into writing immediately with a request that St. Ignatius would both beg the Pope to interfere and also send a dissuasive letter to King Ferdinand. Further, in case the Holy Father sided with his Nuncio and laid him under a command to accept the bishopric, he wished to know how he was to proceed. Ignatius advised that in such circumstances he should place the Brief upon his head in sign of obedience, but at the same time announce the necessity of writing two letters before anything else was done, a letter to the Pope confessing his defects and unsuitableness, and another to his Superior asking permission to accept the dignity. That, at any rate, would allow an interval for a renewed appeal to the Pope.[1] No second appeal was necessary, however, as King Ferdinand, in deference to the two Saints' wishes, bade his henchmen desist from their campaign until they received his further instructions. Peter immediately gave vent to his joy. "As for the bishopric," he wrote, "I thank the Divine Goodness with all my heart that Reverend Father General is protecting me with so much discreet care from this temptation and attack, which, if successful, would have brought a serious crisis upon us. Now I sail in harbour under the best and trustiest of steersmen." But the respite did not last long. By July, 1554, the King was again busily pulling strings, of which the man most concerned gleaned a hint from the new Nuncio, Delfino. " The Nuncio," he told Polanco, "has awakened in my mind the sad memory of the Viennese bishopric. I do indeed hope that I am wrong in the suspicion which his words compelled me to entertain. A little while ago I explained it to Reverend Father General. With the help of God, he will not allow unhappy me to be thrown into such a prison and labyrinth. *A dignitatibus liberet pauperes suos Dominus Jesus crucifixus*."[2] A month later the prospect had darkened, and Polanco was again made the confidant of Peter's trouble: " As for the wretched bishopric question I cannot help being anxious. I hear that letters are on the way from the King and the Papal Nuncio which will oblige me by the Pope's authority to submit to that yoke of all unhappiness. I have received no communication about the matter, but the person who wrote on the King's behalf to some cardinals has given the story away. They are now confident of success . . . so I promise your Reverence seven Masses in honour of the Holy Ghost the minute you give me news that their efforts have come to nothing. If it falls out otherwise I shall know for certain that God is angry with me for my sins, and all my life I shall have real cause to be

[1] Braunsberger, *Epistulae*, vol. i, p. 431.   [2] Braunsberger, *Epistulae*, vol. i, p. 478.

afraid."[1] Meantime the Pope was being besieged from opposite quarters. St. Ignatius used every ounce of influence he possessed to prevent what would have been a most dangerous precedent for his Order,[2] and King Ferdinand, through his representatives in Rome, worked just as heartily the other way. The King's men seem to have overdone their job. Their persistence annoyed the Pope, and that was St. Ignatius's chance to secure at least half a victory. The Pope refused to confirm St. Peter's appointment as bishop but agreed to his appointment as administrator of the diocese without titles or revenues, if St. Ignatius did not mind. As Ferdinand could secure no better bargain he accepted the arrangement with a show of thankfulness.[3]

Polanco was the most pleased man of anybody. " *Charissime Petre*," he wrote, " those seven Masses which you promised me in exchange for news that you were free from the bishopric of Vienna are owing to me, I believe, and I demand my rights from your charity. By the good offices of Father General, your Reverence will not be obliged to shoulder the burden." Peter said the Masses at once, but any joy he felt must have been tempered by the arrival of the following document shortly afterwards from Pope Julius III:

To Our Beloved Son, Peter Canisius, Priest of the Society of Jesus, Master of Theology.

Beloved Son, greeting. Desiring to set over the Church of Vienna, of the Province of Salzburg, which is at present bereft of the comfort of a pastor, a person useful and suitable according to Our heart, and to provide opportunity lest the same Church should meanwhile suffer spiritually and temporally, WE, observing that you of your piety to God, learning, providence in spiritual and circumspection in temporal affairs, and divers other gifts of virtue wherewith the liberality of the Most High has manifoldly adorned your person, would be able and willing usefully and happily to govern the aforesaid Church while the See is vacant, and that you would achieve much to its profit and advantage, DO hereby of Our own accord, of Our certain knowledge and with the fullness of Our Apostolic power, in consideration, moreover, of Our Beloved Son, Ferdinand, illustrious King of the Romans and of Hungary, Emperor Elect whom we understand to desire this very greatly, CONSTITUTE and depute you, of whom We have

[1] Braunsberger, *Epistulae*, vol. i, p. 487.   [2] St. Peter would have been the first Jesuit bishop.
[3] Braunsberger, *Epistulae*, vol. i, pp. 500-1.

the highest hopes in the Lord, by Our Apostolic authority, Administrator of that Church in spiritual and temporal matters for one year, within which time We shall provide for it a fitting and useful pastor; and We commit to you full and free charge of the administration of the said Church in the same matters spiritual and temporal during that year. . . .

Given at Rome, at St. Peter's, the Third Day of November MDLIV in the Fifth Year of Our Pontificate.

Only the first sentence of the Brief has been quoted. There are three others, making in all nearly a thousand words, with exactly four full stops to marshal them. They deal chiefly with practical details. St. Peter is to exercise jurisdiction either personally or through others appointed by him. In business for which episcopal orders are necessary he is to have the services of some neighbouring bishop, but in all other matters he must act as though he were himself the consecrated Ordinary of Vienna. The diocesan chapter, the minor clergy and the lay people are earnestly exhorted and commanded to obey and reverence him as their father and lawful superior, the Pope asseverating that he will reckon as his own and fully support any legislation, sentence or punishment decreed by St. Peter. In conclusion, King Ferdinand and the Archbishop of Salzburg are begged and exhorted to help him in every way.[1]

For any legislation, sentence or punishment that St. Peter decreed he might not have been in charge of the Church of Vienna at all. It was not in his character to play the commander-in-chief, and if he could not influence others by example or counsel he left them alone, except to pray for them. Besides, the conditions in Vienna were too bad and complicated for a simple priest to put them right by a wave of his hand. The secular power was guilty of constant intrusions into the ecclesiastical sphere. Ecclesiastical immunities and jurisdiction were openly violated, and the lay magistrates took it upon themselves as a matter of course to decide religious issues in the civil courts, and even to demand the appearance of bishops before their tribunal.[2] That was an external trouble of the Viennese Church. Internally, her plight was even worse. Divine service at the Cathedral had almost ceased from lack of priests, whose numbers had dropped in a short time from sixteen to six. Nor were the six much good. Too grand to hear confessions themselves, they neglected to provide

---

[1] Braunsberger, *Epistulae*, vol. i, pp. 506–9.
[2] Braunsberger, *Epistulae*, vol. i, p. 479; Bucholtz, *Geschichte der Regierung Ferdinands des Ersten*, vol. viii (Vienna, 1838), pp. 142–76.

substitutes at Easter-time until even the unsqueamish Government became disgusted and peremptorily ordered them to their duties.[1] For a long period the bishops of Vienna had had practically no control over their chapter. Even such good and zealous bishops as Fabri and Nausea could effect nothing in the way of reform owing to the passive resistance of their worldly-minded and partly profligate canons. " I am a man without any clergy and have no power whatever," wrote Fabri ; while Nausea, his successor, complained that he was equally impotent and had not the slightest influence over the schools and learned institutions of the diocese, in which the teachers " enjoyed perfect freedom to teach whatever they liked provided it was not in the spirit of the Catholic Church."

In all the confusion, St. Peter's sermons at the Cathedral alone sounded a clear and encouraging note. Though he in no way imposed himself, he became so obviously the leader of Vienna's forlorn hope that the more bitter enemies of the Catholic Church began to plot his destruction. At any rate, whenever he went to Court to preach, King Ferdinand thought it advisable to provide him with an armed guard.[2] Day by day the King grew to love and esteem him more and more. " Our King loves the Jesuits as brothers," wrote Staphylus to Hosius in February, 1555. " He has often said so before and recently repeated his sentiments to the Bishop-designate of Vienna, Peter Canisius."[3] Ferdinand in the goodness of his heart had set about transforming eight deserted monasteries into hospitals, a work that involved long and delicate negotiations with the Pope. All through, Peter stood by him and rendered the most valuable assistance. He knew even better than the King how badly the sick were neglected, and as a help for them planned and had printed in Vienna at this time a little manual of instructions and prayers entitled, *De consolandis aegrotis*. It was meant primarily for priests in charge of hospitals, but that the sick, too, might avail themselves of it, Peter had it printed in three languages, side by side, Latin, Italian and German.

His appointment as Administrator led to no change in his usual activities. Neither his lectures nor his sermons grew less. The sermons were his chief work, and it is characteristic of him that, even when preaching before the King, he harped incessantly on those particular Catholic doctrines and practices which were least popular at the time. Before his appointment to the charge of the Church of Vienna he had been commissioned

---

[1] Wiedemann, *Geschichte der Reformation*, etc., vol. ii, pp. 70–4.
[2] So Matthew Rader, Peter's earliest biographer, who learned the detail from eye-witnesses, *De Vita Petri Canisii libri tres* (Munich, 1614), pp. 48–9.
[3] *Stanislai Hosii Epistolae*, ed. Hipler and Zakrzewski, vol. ii (Cracow, 1886), p. 511.

from Rome to promulgate throughout Austria the Jubilee Indulgence granted by Pope Julius III at the accession of Mary Tudor. As the Indulgence was for the encouragement of prayer that England might return to Catholic unity, Peter had thrown himself whole-heartedly into his task. Martin Luther by his noisy and unbalanced tirades against indulgences had broken the unity of Christendom and engendered in the Teutonic soul a strong prejudice against the Church's doctrine of merit and good works. That doctrine had been abused, but it was in itself an essential corollary of the doctrine of grace and the supernatural life on which the whole theory of the sacraments is based, so Peter gladly seized the chance to rub into the muddled heads of the Austrians the seemliness, necessity and great spiritual value of indulgences. Prince Maximilian frowned on his efforts, and a babble of criticism enveloped him, but that was only a spur to his zeal. On receipt of the papal Briefs from the Queen of Bohemia, he translated them into German, had them printed and then affixed to the doors of the churches in the usual way. Priests in country towns and districts received from him with the Briefs a covering letter of instructions as to the method of publication and of warm exhortation to encourage their flocks not to miss so splendid an opportunity. At the Cathedral and at Court he devoted a whole series of sermons to the question of indulgences, explaining all so well and carefully that according to one who heard him " the people present could not restrain their tears for having been long defrauded through their ignorance of such manifold treasures and blessings."[1] He was a Court preacher of a very different kind from the Massillons and Bossuets, one who cared never a whit for the balance of his periods, and would as soon have spoken smooth flattery to a royal ear as John the Baptist himself. Ferdinand withal never ceased to love him, which says nearly as much for the King as it does for St. Peter.

The Saint was now being consulted from all sides about Church problems, education, good books and bad books, theology, heresy, administrative difficulties. He entered into close correspondence with the poet and scholar, Martin Cromer, private secretary to the King of Poland, hoping through his influence to find an opening for his brethren in ultra-Protestant Prussia, which was under Polish jurisdiction. On January 15, 1555, he told Cromer that he was ready to set out for Prussia that very day, on a sign from Rome.[2] With the letter went, as a New Year's gift, a little book about recent events in England, " which," says Peter, " unless

---

[1] M.H., *Litterae Quadrimestres*, vol. ii, p. 375.   [2] Braunsberger, *Epistulae*, vol. i, p. 515.

I am greatly mistaken, are going to be a source of immense joy to Catholic hearts." Queen Mary he calls "a new Judith" and sees in the recent reconciliation of England by Cardinal Pole a fair omen for unfortunate Germany. A few weeks earlier, in a Christmas letter, he had told the same friend that he had been "hunting about for a chance of labouring and suffering among the Poles, *pro Capite crucifixo, pro fratre misero, pro imperita pueritia.*"[1] Cromer, like nearly everybody else who came to know him intimately, fell a complete and willing victim to his *attrait.* He had a heart as big as the sorrows of the world. England, Poland, Tartary had each a secure place in it, but Germany and Austria naturally occupied the most room. Never to the end of his days did he cease literally pestering all the devout people whom he knew for an alms of prayer on behalf of those distracted nations. If ever a man believed heartily in the efficacy of prayer it was he. He had an insatiable hunger and thirst for it and by his persistent begging had already secured a splendid gift from St. Ignatius. Every Jesuit priest is now obliged by rule to say Mass once a month for the conversion of baptized non-Catholics of England and the northern nations, while those of the Society of Jesus who are not priests must say certain prayers for the same intention. This regulation is entirely due to St. Peter. On July 25, 1553, Polanco had written thus to him: "Your Reverence's petition to our Father that he would order priests to say Mass once a month and non-priests to offer prayers for the removal of the distress of Germany and other northern nations seemed to him very just when I proposed it. He has accordingly instructed me to write to all countries prescribing this, not for a certain time only but for all time, until the need shall have ceased. Which may God grant us soon to see. Amen."[2] The letter of St. Ignatius was as follows:

JESUS

Ignatius Loyola, General of the Society of Jesus, to his beloved brothers, both superiors and subjects in the Society, eternal happiness in Our Lord. As the law of charity, by which we are in duty bound to love the whole body of the Church in Christ Jesus, demands that assistance should be given above all to whatever part is affected by a grave and dangerous disease, it has seemed to me in my littleness that our Society ought to offer help and succour with particular love

[1] Braunsberger, *Epistulae*, vol. i, p. 514.   [2] Braunsberger, *Epistulae*, vol. i, p. 429.

and alacrity to Germany, England, and the northern nations, endangered by the most serious disease of heresy.

Now, though we may do our best to help in other ways also, and, though for many years several of the Society have been offering Masses and prayers for the needs of those nations, in order to increase the extent of this charity and to ensure its continuance I hereby enjoin that all our brothers, whether superiors or subjects, in my immediate jurisdiction and everywhere else, shall, if they are priests, say one Mass each month for the spiritual needs of Germany and England, and, if they are not priests, shall pray for the same intention, that the Lord may at length have mercy on those countries and on others infected by them, and may deign to bring them back to the purity of the Christian faith and religion.

It is my wish that this order continue in force as long as those nations remain in need of such assistance, nor is any province of our Society, even in the furthest Indies, to consider itself exempt from it. Rome, July 25, 1553.[1]

As time went on, the Jesuits in Vienna began to feel more and more cramped in their quarters at the Dominican monastery. Their work was developing and St. Peter cherished ambitions to start a boarding-school, especially for the sons of noble families, who might thus be prevented from falling under Protestant influence. Besides, the Jesuits' landlords had become restive and wanted them gone. King Ferdinand now suggested their migration to a Carmelite monastery, nearer the centre of the City, whose sole occupant at the time was the Father Prior. The Carmelites had been hit harder by the Reformation than most religious orders, and deserted monasteries like this one in Vienna were to be found in nearly every part of the Empire. For some years the King had been urging the superiors of the Order to send a fresh batch of friars to Vienna but they were unable to find the men, whereupon Ferdinand, rather unreasonably, lost patience and threatened to install the Jesuits. This high-handed way of finding a home for his new protégés did not at all commend itself to St. Peter, who spoke for once rather sharply about His Majesty in a letter to Rome: " He is treating the superiors of the Order in an imperious manner and writes saying that he desires to install us in place of their subjects, as though he possessed any authority to do so. It seems to me that by his action he is giving these religious a

---

[1] M.H., *Monumenta Ignatiana*, series prima, vol. v, pp. 220–1.

handle for complaint against our Society, since they may allege that they were shut out of their monastery by the King at our instigation."[1] There was another difficulty too, underlined by the Saint. The Carmelites, in their time, had sung the Divine Office publicly in the choir of their beautiful church, and had accustomed the people to expect a High Mass every day. Now the Jesuits by their constitutions were precluded from undertaking choir duties and High Masses. They were a completely new style of religious order, founded for a purpose with which such duties would have been incompatible. The King desired very much to see the old customs revived but did not insist, and so, at the beginning of 1554, when the Carmelites' full consent had been obtained, the Jesuits took possession of their new church and college. So difficult was the work of putting their topsy-turvy home in order that the whole twenty-two of them fell ill. The King granted them an endowment of 1,200 florins annually, which, owing to the cheapness of food and other things in Vienna, was wealth beyond their dreams. Two small houses adjoining the monastery were promptly opened as a boarding-school for boys of the upper classes, and a properly constituted novitiate, the first in German lands, was also set on foot.

To his great disappointment, St. Peter could not move in with his brethren, as the King had expressed a wish that he should reside in and preside over an institution of the University known as the Archducal College, which housed and supported twelve "Fellows," on the lines of All Souls' College, Oxford. From among them the professors of philosophy at the University were usually taken and it became St. Peter's delicate task to purge them of heretical opinions. He did not like it at all, and in Polanco's words "sighed all the time for a corner of our college where he would more gladly have served in the kitchen than occupy the post of superior in that college of professors."[2] He soon became so unwell separated from his brethren that the doctors ordered him home as the only way to save his life. "Infinite thanks to God," he wrote, "for bringing me out of the tempest to a haven . . ; from strangers to my very own fathers and brothers. Would that such comfort might long be mine, not for the sake of my health but for the good and peace of my soul. But I have been granted this respite only till I am well again, when I must return to my office of *Parens*, as they call it."[3]

[1] Braunsberger, *Epistulae*, vol. i, pp. 446–7. [2] M.H., Polanco, *Chronicon*, vol. iv, p. 239.
[3] Braunsberger, *Epistulae*, vol. i, p. 477.

At the college Peter was startled to discover his young brethren diligently at work under their Rector's baton, practising to sing office in choir! That kind of enterprise might easily have led to serious consequences for the Society of Jesus, so Peter felt in duty bound to protest to St. Ignatius. St. Ignatius ordered the poor Rector to do penance for a whole month, but it was quite a mild penance, merely " to accuse himself to God every day and to beg for the spirit of complete union and conformity with the Society throughout the world." Such unity and conformity was a great ideal of Peter's heart. To promote it he continued to write to the brethren in Cologne, recalling the holy memory of Favre and of Lambert Duchateau who had died in his arms ten years before. For the same end he would have given the world to obtain a visit from Laynez. " Would that he might be allowed to come here just once," he wrote to Polanco, " so that he might see for himself how we are placed, and tell us face to face what steps we ought to take for the general well-being. I could easily forgo the enormous private joy and consolation which I know well I should get from his company, but your Reverence will remember the common good and decide in your prudence what is most expedient for it."[1]

All men and women who helped his Order became shrined for ever in Peter's memory. It was he who obtained for King Ferdinand and his vice-chancellor, Dr. Jonas, a share in all the merits of the Society of Jesus, according to the beautiful old custom of the monastic orders from ancient times. Wiguleus Hundt, the good man with whom he was in relations about the college at Ingolstadt, commended a young protégé to him in March, 1555. To judge by Peter's anxiety for the lad's welfare he might have been some prince on whom the destinies of the Church depended. Recognizing in Hundt himself a kindred soul, he addressed him in the following terms : " Happy indeed may we count ourselves, though the common run of men despise us, if we devote ourselves whole-heartedly to the glory of Christ and the vindication of religion, in this time of storm which calls not only for patience but for all our faith and assiduity. How sweet it will be to remember one day, dear Friend, that, as enemies of the Church's enemies and friends of her friends, her true-born sons, solicitous for straying souls and consumed with zeal for the Household of God, we bore much and essayed great things, even though, perhaps, our achievement was small. So must we labour now as never before. Here is our chance, the field of battle and the hour of victory. With Christ is the

[1] Braunsberger, *Epistulae*, vol. i, pp. 472-3.

crown for those who stay the course in this most sacred contest, as did Dr. Eck of illustrious memory. Nor do I wish there to be any distinction here between priest and layman. It behoves each and all to do and dare with a great and noble rivalry for the same religion and the same spiritual home under one and the same leader, the Pope, just as a man would strive for the lives of those dear to him, for his country in danger or for his own deliverance."[1]

To achieve anything worth while in that age of black suspicion and covetousness became a labour of Sisyphus, as the following little history will show. Peter's step-mother, like the true Dutch *vrouw* she was, made him anxious by her continual absorption in worldly affairs. " Try to keep patient and sweet in your troubles, dearest mother," he wrote to her, " and remember Our Lord's words : ' Martha, Martha, thou art careful and troubled about many things, but only one thing is necessary.' The more sorrows and afflictions visit you, the more is Our Lord preparing your soul for Mary's part. . . . Why do you let your trade affairs and merchandise take up so much of your time when they must all be left behind and go back to the dust from which they came ? "[2] The relations between the Saint and his two half-brothers, Theodoric and Otto, were of the most affectionate kind, the elder, in particular, looking up to his distinguished relative with a charming mixture of reverence and familiarity. Young Otto, at St. Peter's special request, was sent to Vienna for his education, on which occasion Theodoric begged the Saint to make sure that the boy wrote often to his mother. Peter made sure, all right, and so affected his step-mother by his love and devotion, that she began to speak in high terms about the work of the Jesuits. The result was that her sister, a devout and wealthy lady, expressed a desire to bequeath to them her fine house in Nymegen. Peter, when he heard the news, advised St. Ignatius not to accept the intended gift. He knew his people too well, he said. They were a large and rapidly expanding clan who would very likely object in the strongest terms to any alienation of property.[3] They did ! In 1554 Leonard Kessel had gone from Cologne to conduct, by special invitation, a most fruitful mission in Nymegen. At the beginning of the following year he returned to assist at the death-bed of the lady who wished her house to become a Jesuit college. Then the storm broke and by a decree of the Senate, passed at the instigation of the clan, Father Kessel was ignominiously expelled from the town. Addressing a prominent

[1] Braunsberger, *Epistulae*, vol. i, pp. 518–9.
[2] Braunsberger, *Epistulae*, vol. i, p. 432.
[3] An astonishing proportion of the present Catholic nobility of Holland is descended from them.

Nymegen consul, as the good aldermen of the time liked to style themselves, St. Peter protested against the injustice. He could afford to talk
straight, as this Wichmann van den Bergh was married to his first cousin:

> Sad news has reached us here, my dear Wichmann, that some of
> our brethren are in bad odour among you and have received harsh
> treatment from your Senate. I believe that this is the work of the devil,
> whose delight it is to frustrate the efforts of good men, especially when
> they tend to the glory of Christ and the salvation of souls. . . . Now
> though I am confident that what has happened will redound more to
> our credit than to our shame, I am sorry for your sake, and for the
> sake of the Senate and my native town, that men should have been so
> ungently treated whom by rights the people of Nymegen ought not
> only to have tolerated but to have honoured. You must be aware
> that there are many of us from Nymegen now in our Society; and
> so, if regard for our common nationality, for the deserts of our relatives
> and friends among you, for our old acquaintance and the ties of blood
> that bind us, did not deter you, you might at least, in consideration
> of our common citizenship, have spared one man for the sake of many
> and shown not only a little indulgence, if that was necessary, but a
> little of your usual kindliness and helpfulness.
>
> It is easy enough to cast suspicion on good and upright action,
> and the world is ever prone to misinterpret, pull to pieces, and put an
> objectionable construction on whatever is said or done for the sake
> of religion. But I would ask you to believe me that we who have left
> all things for Christ are not covetous of your fortunes. We have put
> our riches safely away in the holy citadel of poverty and have no designs
> on the goods, houses, or possessions of other men. Far from wanting
> to be a burden to your town, our only desire is to ease, God helping us,
> the burdened consciences of our fellows. We are not anxious for your
> alms but rather to give you spiritual blessings, to serve our native land,
> to console its sorrowing and encourage its devoutly Catholic children;
> in a word, to enrich it with the true and eternal good things of God. . . .
>
> Let us have done then, wise Friend, with selfish counsels. Here
> there is no question of mine and thine, but of promoting the glory of
> Jesus Christ, of bringing refreshment to unhappy consciences, of sending
> trusty labourers into a much neglected harvest-field. . . . You can judge
> for yourself whether it is right to override the last wishes of a dying
> woman who was your friend, and make no account of her prayers and

entreaties. . . . . It was my duty to remonstrate and plead with you and
if what I have said in charity meets with your approval I shall owe
double thanks to God and to you. If not, well, I must run the risk
of your displeasure for the sake of the truth and of my native land.[1]

No man is a prophet in his own country, at least until he has been
some centuries dead, and Nymegen, now so rightly proud of Peter Canisius,
was one of the tardiest Catholic towns to admit Peter's brethren to her
civic privileges.

[1] Braunsberger, *Epistulae*, vol. i, pp. 541–3.

CHAPTER VI

FAILURE AND ACHIEVEMENT

WITH the flight of Charles V from Innsbruck in 1552, the political situation of the Empire underwent another of its kaleidoscopic changes. Elector Moritz became temporarily master, but afraid of his dispossessed cousin, John Frederick, " the big dog whom the Emperor held in leash," and also of King Ferdinand, he dared not go too far, and agreed to the patched up Peace of Passau which gave the captive Protestant princes their liberty and the Lutherans in general freedom to practise their religion. Ferdinand conducted the negotiations on behalf of his brother and showed once more his genius for compromise. The religious question in its wider aspects was postponed to a future Diet, and the Empire turned again to its daily affairs, interrupted only by a duodecimo war between the late allies, Moritz and the mad Albrecht, which came to an end in 1553 with the Elector's victory and death on the wild field of Sievershausen. The Protestants were now in a stronger position than ever before, especially as Ferdinand's son and heir, Maximilian, openly sympathized with them. Rejoicing in such protection they could afford to be bold even under Ferdinand's nose. But they forgot the proverbial warning not to be too bold, and at last in 1554 roused the King into ordering an examination of such professors at his University of Vienna as fell under suspicion of heresy.

Peter Canisius, in virtue of his position at the head of the faculty of theology, was obliged to take part in the inquisitorial proceedings, though, like Lejay before him, he felt a strong repugnance to such work.[1] It must not be thought that anything dreadful was contemplated. King Ferdinand was not a Tudor and desired only to remove from their posts men convicted of having broken the oath by which they had secured them. As their lives and goods were never in danger this policy cannot seem too oppressive to anybody acquainted with Elizabethan penal legislation, nor to anybody who remembers that Catholics could neither teach

[1] " Non libenter intererat P. Claudius examinationi professorum Universitatis in negotio fidei, et tamen Regi hoc officium, licet odiosum, quod eo praesente a ministris regiis exercebatur, negare non potuit." M.H., Polanco, *Chronicon*, vol. ii, p. 278.

nor learn at such centres of enlightenment as Oxford and Cambridge until the nineteenth century was well advanced.

The first man with whom Peter was called upon to deal in his new capacity was not a professor but the parish priest of a place near Krems, in Lower Austria. This person, a certain Andrew Cupicz, had so openly and defiantly preached Lutheranism that the local government felt obliged to arrest him and send him to prison in Vienna. The law of the land made such propaganda a criminal offence, and Andrew plainly got only what he had asked for. St. Peter visited him in prison and used all his powers of persuasion, *modeste ac sinceriter*, to convince him of the error of his ways. When that proved unavailing he submitted to the offender in writing answers to his various arguments, whereupon Andrew set about the composition of a large treatise to prove that the Pope was Antichrist and the Whore of Babylon. After that Peter confessed himself defeated.[1]

The next recorded case is a more interesting one, though the results were the same. Nicholas Bourgeois, a Belgian who had invented for himself the Greek name Polites, held a chair of philosophy at Vienna. Like Cupicz he made no secret of his Protestant sympathies and in consequence found himself one fine morning in the University prison. Peter, who knew him well and liked him, at once wrote him the following letter:

To the Eminent Master Nicholas Polites.

I hear, my Polites, that you are in trouble. Would to God that the trouble was not of your own making, for, as you know, the particular reason why we have inflicted on us the things which we suffer and endure, is of capital importance. You need not bother to sing me the old song, *Oportet magis obedire Deo quam hominibus*, etc., because, in the first place, you are but a man and under no obligation whatever to trust to your private judgment in matters of religion, nor to regard yourself as equally competent in the evaluation of things divine with men wiser and more learned than yourself, and more experienced in theology. If we follow the word and spirit of Christ we must necessarily defer even to bad men and unjust rulers. I should not mind your making an exception in the case of religion if you only rightly understood and were able to defend this preposterous kind of a new religion. Do you consider that our Emperor and King and

[1] Braunsberger, *Epistulae*, vol. i, p. 456. Cupicz remained in mild captivity for about ten months and then escaped to Hungary and oblivion.

the greatest princes on earth, with a few exceptions, know nothing at all, and that you and your new Christians are wiser than they? Do you embrace the errors of apostates and revolutionaries, condemned ages ago, and reject the common teaching of the holy Councils, of the Fathers of the Church and of theologians? It is the easiest thing to make profession of the Gospel and trumpet the Word of God with full blast, for there is nothing that the devil cannot turn to his own purposes, he who was not afraid to urge the Scriptures against Christ. But the Kingdom of God is neither in speech nor in the written letter, not on men's lips nor in their wrangling, though good men reverence the writings of Prophets and Apostles and receive them as infallible divine oracles. But Christ did not so bind us to them that He would have us neglect whatever else the Apostles taught, and they taught many things never put in writing: or, again, whatever has been decided and commonly practised by the pillar and ground of truth, the Bride of Christ, the holy and invulnerable Catholic Church. Why, then, do you so despise the beliefs and practices of the ancient Fathers and of the Saints, your ancestors, and appeal to the Scriptures alone, in the interpretation of which you shut us out, while admitting and approving the views of men condemned by Christendom? Why do you despise venerable authority, and, if you deny doing so, why, then, do you lean upon the Confession of Augsburg, that staff which is nothing but a reed?

I am not at all surprised that your proceedings should have given great displeasure to upright men, and I am the more grieved that you do not seem to mind. Leaving aside the question of scandal, that hurt to weak brethren of which a prudent man would be incapable and still less a charitable and devout Christian, I beg and counsel you, Brother, by the sacred wounds of Christ, to join, united in heart with me, in prayer and supplication to the Father of Light from whom is every gift, for the gift of sincere faith. Would to God that we might both be truly wise, cleanse our souls of stain, however contracted, and expiate it by true penance. . . . Let us ponder together what a serious sin disobedience is and how heavily God punishes rebels everywhere. Let us think, too, how unworthy of learned men are fickleness and insolent contempt for sacred things in which the majority of mankind and its wisest ones have always taken their delight. . . .

But why all this argument, you will say? Because I, too, am a man and your brother in Christ and I am sorry for what has happened to you, my Polites. I shall not cease to pray to Our Lord that this affliction may be for the good of your soul. No one has urged me to write to you, nor, I assure you, had I any idea that you were going to suffer imprisonment. The more truly I love you the more freely do I admonish you not to trust so much to your own judgment in matters of religion, which you do not understand and will never handle properly unless you submit yourself without reserve, not only to the letter of Scripture but also to the dogmas and doctrines of the Church. If that seems difficult to you, beg, with the Prophet, for light from Heaven : *Illumina oculos meos ne umquam obdormiam in morte.* . . . Become a little child and true wisdom will be given to you. In the Church the light awaits your eyes. Outside, search as you like, you will only increase your darkness, aye, even if you were a greater than Arrius himself in knowledge of the Scriptures. I write out of my love and anxiety for you, on the spur of the moment and, as you see, rather confusedly. You will, I hope, take all in good part, in the spirit in which it is written. I wrote thinking only of your salvation. Farewell, Brother in Jesus Christ, and render thanks to God for the divine visitation.

Peter Canisius, least of Theologians.[1]

Peter might have spared his pains for all the good his letter did the unfortunate Polites. Though he confessed in prison that he was no theologian and could not answer the arguments brought against his opinions, he remained obstinately wedded to them. The acts of his examination are extant and show how earnestly Peter strove to win him round. Courage is a fine thing even in a bad cause, and it is impossible not to admire this man who sacrificed his post and brought hardship on his wife and children rather than surrender convictions which he seems to have held sincerely, though unable to justify them. King Ferdinand's government gave him eight days in which to settle his affairs and depart from Austrian territory. It was a harsh sentence, but not quite as bad as the one which the victim's own friends had pronounced on Servetus in Geneva, less than a year before.[2]

That was a sad story, but St. Peter's short inquisitorial career did not lack comic episodes, too, as when he was asked to pronounce on

---

[1] Braunsberger, *Epistulae*, vol. i, pp. 462–5.
[2] The Acts and sentence are in Braunsberger, *Epistulae*, vol. i, pp. 733–9. Servetus was burned alive on October 23, 1553. Melanchthon called his execution " a signal act of piety " and became reconciled by it to Calvin, with whom he had not been on speaking terms for many years.

the extraordinary Croatian nobleman, Paul Skalich, who had invented a new kind of Euclidean theology and endeavoured to prove by means of squares, circles, and triangles that there must be three natures in Christ. He also published a treatise entitled, *The Dark Secrets of Hidden Things*, and wore a magic ring. When Peter remonstrated with him, he answered that he was " ready to argue about everything under the sun, and in opposite senses too, perhaps." That was no idle boast, because the previous year at Bologna he had, in his own words, publicly defended " divine, angelical, celestial, elemental, human, Christian, philosophical, metaphysical, physical, moral, rational, doctrinal, and infernal theses."[1] He was probably mad, but that did not prevent him being a great nuisance to Canisius for some years afterwards. His description of the *Spiritual Exercises* of St. Ignatius, given in a violent diatribe against the Holy See and Peter himself a few years later, is worth quoting : " In that Jesuit sect of yours this also is to be noted, that they give what they call Exercises to individual persons, but secretly and only to those of better education. To show that they are Christians, they begin the Exercises with the Lord's Prayer and the Hail Mary. Then during some days they demand a written confession of all sins, which they proceed to scrutinize for eight days. That done, they go through the life of Christ from His birth to His death, and propose for meditation day and night all the various classes of demons. Finally, they urge the exercitants, as they are called, to join the Society of the Jesuits. Should anybody refuse, he is immediately confronted with the document containing his sins and told that they will be revealed to the whole world. But few dare resist such a threat, especially if their sins have been serious, and those few are so unceasingly defamed and maligned that for very shame they have either to return and become Jesuits or else hide away from men's eyes altogether."[2]

Nearly as queer as Skalich was a famous mathematician and linguist named Postel, who had been for a time a Jesuit novice in Rome. He came to Vienna in 1554 in quest of a post as professor of Arabic, and importuned St. Peter to obtain it for him from the King, but Peter, who knew the fantastic speculations to which he was addicted, showed no enthusiasm. " I cannot see the use of his Arabic," he informed Polanco, " since there is no visible hope of finding men here who, armed with this language, would set out to convert the Turks."[3]

In the cases mentioned so far Peter had at least the satisfaction of

[1] Braunsberger, *Epistulae*, vol. i, p. 471.   [2] Braunsberger, *Epistulae*, vol. ii, p. 823.
[3] Braunsberger, *Epistulae*, vol. i, pp. 449–50.

seeing the proselytizer depart from Vienna, though he did not count that much of a victory. They merely changed their field of operations. One man, however, and the most dangerous of all, he was unable to stir an inch. Johann Sebastian Phauser, a priest born in Constance in 1520, had gained such a reputation as a preacher that King Ferdinand invited him to accept office at his Court. As he was living with a woman, herself the daughter of a priest, and had a family by her, Johann considered that Ferdinand's Court might prove an uncomfortable place of residence. He accordingly declined, but when Prince Maximilian, a little later, invited him as preacher to *his* Court he showed no hesitation. He was a shrewd man and knew that he would be safe under Max's wing. Max has been a puzzle to German historians. According to Ranke he was one of the most gifted, cultured, enlightened, and knightly princes of all time. Maurenbrecher, on the other hand, says drily of him: " No historian can become enthusiastic over Maximilian II. An advocate of his reign would at the most be able to plead mitigating circumstances at the bar of history, and those only in a very restricted measure." How and when precisely he came by his Protestantism is another problem that has exercised the experts. Holtzmann, in a long and most interesting study, contends that the Prince imbibed his Lutheran doctrines during his youth at Innsbruck,[1] but there are others, Hormayer, Stieve and Hopfen, who argue that he never imbibed such doctrines at all, that he never ceased to be a Catholic, only an enlightened one of the school of Erasmus, a " *Reformkatholik* " or a " *Kompromisskatholik*," who saw in the Jesuits and their allies the real enemies of the Church. The great Maurenbrecher has a thesis of his own for which there is much to be said, namely that Max, a waverer up to 1554, crossed the line owing almost entirely to the influence of Johann Phauser, who arrived at his Court in Vienna that year.[2] Whatever the rights and wrongs of these theories, St. Peter Canisius at once recognized in Johann Phauser his dearest foe.

Johann was a man of middle height, very fat in the face, clean-shaven, and bearing a resemblance to Luther. He had sharp wits and a fair amount of culture, but report had over-rated his eloquence. There was, however, a certain ardour and incisiveness in his sermons that attracted attention, and he had plenty to say which, coming from a priest, could not fail to stimulate curiosity. In fact he preached doctrines that were Lutheran in everything but name. This we know on the evidence of one of his friends,

[1] *Kaiser Maximilian II bis zu seiner Thronbesteigung* (Berlin, 1903), pp. 18 sq.
[2] *Historische Zeitschrift*, vol. xxxii (1874), pp. 221 sqq.

a person named Blahoslaw, who visited Vienna in March, 1555, on some mission or other from the sect of the Bohemian Brothers. His report was as follows :

I went early to the sermon on Sunday and found a large congregation waiting. People were hurrying in from all sides, carrying stools and other seats. This went on for over an hour until the church was packed. At last Maximilian arrived from the Castle, entering by the choir, and at the same time the preacher came. He gave out a short Lutheran hymn and then, having said some prayers, recited by heart the passage from the fifteenth chapter of St. Matthew which deals with the Canaanite woman. . . . . This preacher gave me throughout the impression of being an Evangelical, for he spoke altogether in the Lutheran style, but without mentioning Lutheranism, and explained the truth quite simply and supported it with passages from many writers. Still, he let it be plainly understood that by the Pharisees he meant the Pope and his regulations. . . . The people were there two or three hours in such a mass that a girl began to scream under the pressure. . . . After the sermon there were Lutheran prayers. Maximilian then departed, followed by the people, whose chairs had lost their legs in the crush. All classes were represented, Germans, plenty of Hungarians, Court officials, guardsmen, academic personages, plain citizens, and servants. There was not a whisper of blame for the preacher. Indeed, practically all the people, including the servants, praised him. They said that things must be changed and, though the preacher had mentioned no names, they all grumbled against the monks.[1]

That same Sunday, probably at the same hour, St. Peter, too, gave a sermon, but no chairs were broken by the massing of an audience in his church. The contrast shows as well as anything could how events were shaping in Austria. "This accursed plague of heresy ever increases here," he had told Polanco. "The professors and students are so terribly infected by it that our University seems a very monster, nursing impiety and destroying rather than saving the youth of our land. Those most addicted to the gospel of Luther are sought after diligently, and given fat stipends in more than one part of Austria. As for heretical books, I can assure you that the number of them is infinite both in the cities and in the little country towns. The Government and the common people

[1] Cited by Holtzmann, *Kaiser Maximilian II*, pp. 232–3.

openly bestow their favours on the innovators . . . and all the while there
is such a dreadful dearth of priests everywhere that the bishops, we fear,
may more and more prefer to tolerate married and apostate priests in
their parishes rather than see the people deprived of all services."[1]

On all sides men were clamouring for the concession of the chalice
to the laity, and even threatened King Ferdinand with riots and rebellion
if he refused. They still kept up a modicum of Catholic practice, but
it is significant that when they went to confession they refused to specify
their sins and received absolution after a mere recital of the Confiteor.
Such preachers as remained harped all the time on the merits of Christ
and the mercy of God, without ever a word about the Blessed Virgin,
the saints, indulgences, fasting and abstinence, or any other typically
Catholic devotion or obligation.[2] All the wholesome Catholic blood
had been drained from their religion, leaving an anaemic residue which
scarcely differed from Protestantism. Faced by such conditions, which
threatened the swift extinction in Austria of all that he held dearest, Peter
Canisius turned sorrowfully for advice to St. Ignatius. Ignatius answered
on August 18, 1554, with a letter that Protestants have never ceased to
execrate as a horrible Jesuit primer of persecution :

I gather that your Reverence in your letters of July 7th and 17th
asked with pious solicitude that I should write my views as to the best
methods of maintaining the Catholic Faith in the provinces of His
Royal Majesty, of restoring religion in them where it has fallen, and
of upholding it where it is in danger. . . . It will be the part of your
prudence to judge which of the proposals here made are to be put
before His Majesty for, though all of them seem to be most useful,
granted circumstances of persons, places and seasons favourable to
their employment, still, it may, perhaps, be necessary to rule out some,
owing to the contrary disposition of the men and countries concerned. . . .

As, in case of bodily illness, it is first necessary to remove what
causes the disease and then to apply restoratives which renew health
or establish it firmly, so in this plague of souls which various heresies
have made to rage in the King's dominions, the first thing to be done
is to see how the causes of it may be rooted out, and then, how the
vigour of healthy Catholic doctrine may be restored and confirmed. . . .

First of all, if His Royal Majesty were to profess himself not only
a Catholic, which he has ever done, but a determined and thorough

---

[1] Braunsberger, *Epistulae*, vol. i, p. 480.   [2] M.H., Polanco, *Chronicon*, vol. iv, p. 241.

adversary of heresy, and if he were to declare open and not merely secret war on all heretical errors, it would doubtless be the best and most effective of human remedies. From this would follow a consequence of the utmost importance, namely that he would suffer no heretic to have a place in his Council, and would still less give the appearance of highly esteeming such men, whose advice is believed to have for its ultimate aim the encouragement and promotion of the heretical wickedness with which they are themselves infected.

Again, it would be of the greatest help if he refused to allow anyone infected with heresy to occupy any official post or enjoy any dignity in the Government, especially in the supreme government of the various provinces. Finally, and would that this were known and witnessed by all, no person convicted or strongly suspected of heresy should be given any honours or riches but rather at once deprived of them. If, in order to show that the business of religion was being taken seriously, an occasional example were made by depriving a few offenders of life or by expropriating and banishing them, this remedy would be all the more efficacious.

All public professors of the University of Vienna and other universities,[1] as well as those who administer the government of the same, ought, it would seem, to be deprived of office if they fall into bad repute with regard to the Catholic religion. In my judgment this applies also to rectors of private colleges, to pedagogues and to lecturers, in order that those whose duty it is to train youth in piety may not instead corrupt them. Suspects ought therefore to be removed from their posts, and, much more, open heretics, lest they infect their youthful charges. Even students, it would seem, ought in similar case to be expelled, if they give no hopes of amendment. All schoolmasters and tutors ought to understand and know from experience that there is no place for them in the King's dominions unless they are Catholics and as such profess themselves.

It would be expedient either to burn or remove out of every part of the kingdom all heretical books which by diligent search were discovered in the possession of booksellers or private persons. Moreover, books by heretics on subjects such as grammar, rhetoric or logic, though not in themselves heretical, ought to be entirely banned, in testimony of hatred to the heresy of their authors. It is not expedient

[1] There were two others under King Ferdinand's jurisdiction, those of Prague and of Freiburg im Breisgau.

even to mention such books, lest young people, whom heretics would draw to themselves by such means, be influenced. Other and more erudite books can be found, free from this grave danger. It would help greatly, too, if booksellers were prohibited under heavy penalties from producing any heretical book, or commentaries by any heretic, bearing his name or containing a single example or word smacking of impious doctrine. One could wish, too, that it were forbidden under the same penalties to all merchants and others to bring such books, manufactured elsewhere, into the King's dominions.

No beneficed clergy or confessors in ill repute for heresy ought to be tolerated. On being convicted they should at once be deprived of all ecclesiastical revenues. Better a flock without a pastor than a flock with a wolf for pastor. Pastors who are Catholic in faith, indeed, but who subvert the people by their ignorance and the evil example of their public sins ought to be most severely punished, deprived of their incomes by their bishops and withdrawn altogether from the care of souls. It was their bad lives and ignorance that brought the pestilence of heresy upon Germany.

Preachers of heretical doctrine, heresiarchs and others convicted of spreading this plague ought, I think, to be subjected to heavy penalties. A notice should everywhere be publicly proclaimed that those ready to retract within one month from the date of publication would receive indulgent absolution in both the ecclesiastical and civil courts, but that those convicted of heresy after that time would lose their civil rights and be disqualified for the reception of any honour. It might also be determined, if thought advisable, that they could be punished by exile, imprisonment or sometimes even death. But I do not speak of the extreme penalty or of setting up the Inquisition, because such measures appear to be inappropriate for Germany in the present mood of the country.

Whoever shall style the heretics 'Evangelicals' might very well be mulcted in some fine, lest the devil should rejoice to see the enemies of the Gospel and of the Cross appropriate a name that is contrary to the facts of their profession. They ought to be called by their own name, which is 'heretics,' so that even in mentioning them we may express our horror of persons who conceal a deadly poison under the cloak of a salutary name.

The holding of episcopal synods and the proclamation of dogmas and decrees in Councils will, perhaps, by making the truth known to

them, effect the conversion of the more simple-minded clergy who
have been led astray by others. As for the people, it may be of
advantage if good preachers, pastors and confessors show openly
their keen hatred of heretical errors by denouncing them in incisive terms, provided that the people are professing Catholics and
believe what is necessary to salvation. With regard to other
matters which can be tolerated, perhaps a policy of non-interference
should be pursued.

That is the first half of St. Ignatius's famous, or if anybody prefers
to call it so, infamous, letter to St. Peter. Ever since in 1895 Professor
Gothein cited it in his massive, learned, and bigoted treatise, *Ignatius
Loyola und die Gegenreformation*, it has been used innumerable times to
damn the Jesuits, especially during the hot post-war controversy that
centred round the debates in the new Republican Reichstag on the abrogation of the law of 1872 by which Bismarck had made the Society of Jesus
an illegal corporation in Germany. In 1925, the year of St. Peter Canisius's
canonization, an enterprising Protestant review published the whole letter
in German, French and English, as though by such a broadcast it hoped
to neutralize the effect of Pope Pius XI's pronouncement. Yet what does
the letter amount to after all but such a commendation of coercive measures
in special circumstances as nine men out of ten in the sixteenth century
would have considered just and reasonable, provided, of course, that
they were for the protection of their own particular 'doxy'? From
numerous other passages in the correspondence of St. Ignatius it could
easily be proved that neither he nor any of his great sons such as Peter
Canisius set much store by police methods in the advancement of religion.
Their trust was rather in hard work, good example, and the power of
prayer, and when, as in the letter under discussion, police methods are
recommended, they are so only as purely defensive measures, to protect
a Catholic population from foreign assault, not at all in order to force
Catholicism on people who did not want it. The peaceable Protestant
who minded his own business and left Catholics to mind theirs was not
only never molested by Peter Canisius and his brethren but was often
enough the object of their regard and friendship. They sometimes even
had Lutheran doctors as their medical attendants, a little courtesy to
which one finds no parallel on the other side. Professors at the University
of Wittenberg had to take an oath subscribing to the Confession of
Augsburg. No Catholic was ever given a chance to occupy a chair there,

much less to propagate his religious views among the students, and why then should King Ferdinand, St. Ignatius, and St. Peter Canisius be accounted persecutors for urging or using, to protect the Catholicism of Austria, the same methods that the Protestants themselves followed rigorously in all their dominions? It is true that St. Ignatius appears to have approved of the death penalty for heterodox propaganda, though only as an example in flagrant cases, but in that too he had many of the other side to agree with him, without his reservations. In such a matter all depends on a man's sense of values. If he believes the souls of his fellows to be more important than their bodies, he will think murder of the bodily life less a crime than heresy which destroys the supernatural life of the soul. In the sixteenth century it was more natural, though erroneous, to jump to the practical corollary of such a view, than in the twentieth century when most men do not believe that they have souls at all.[1]

The second part of the letter deals with the measures to be taken to restore faith and piety as soon as the causes for their disappearance have been eliminated. These positive measures are, put shortly, the appointment of good Catholics, bound by oath to remain such, to all posts of authority; the careful selection of bishops, preachers, parish priests, and confessors; the diligent exposition of Catholic doctrine to the people; the proper payment of priests in charge of parishes so that intelligent and suitable men may not be deterred from accepting such work; careful inquiry before anybody is appointed to a teaching or administrative post in schools and academies, and the imposition of a Catholic test on all such candidates; rigorous censorship of books brought to the King's dominions from without or printed within; the provision of a uniform manual of Christian doctrine for children and the uneducated, of a more comprehensive text-book for curates and parish priests, and of a compendium of scholastic theology for advanced students; the introduction of good and learned priests from foreign countries to make up for the dearth of priests in Austria; the establishment of several seminaries in Austria from which a well-trained native clergy would in time come forth, and, finally, the setting up of colleges for the education of young

---

[1] The views of Ignatius and Canisius were almost identical with those of the gentle, peace-loving, magnanimous Saint Thomas More. "As touching heretics," he wrote in his *Apology* (chap. xlix), "I hate that vice of theirs and not their persons, and very fain would I that the one were destroyed and the other saved. . . . Howbeit, I will that all the world wit it on the other side, that who so be so deeply grounded in malice, to the harm of his own soul and other men's too, and so set upon the sowing of seditious heresies that no good means that men may use unto him can pull that malicious folly out of his poisoned, proud, obstinate heart, I would rather be content that he were gone in time, than overlong to tarry to the destruction of others."

noblemen, on whom, as things stood in those days, the interests of religion mainly depended.[1]

Such was the much-abused letter of St. Ignatius. Its suggestions coincided for the most part with those which St. Peter Canisius had long been urging, but in the way of their adoption stood always the inscrutable Prince Maximilian. Phauser, for all his corpulence and vanity, must have had some charm, because he certainly cast a strange spell over the Prince. Max gave him his complete sympathy and took the greatest delight in his sermons. St. Peter hardly knew what to do, up against such a combination. In the summer of 1554 he challenged Phauser to public debate and worked his hardest to convince the people that the man was a heretic. But that availed little because the people had no great objection to heresy provided its preacher continued to tickle their ears with exciting sermons. Phauser did not fail them in that respect. St. Peter declared him to be " *facundissimus*," and another witness informed Father Kessel that " so great was the concourse of ordinary people and noblemen at his sermons that many could not find standing room in the church and were obliged to listen at the doors. They run to him from all sides, as to an apostle sent by God, in coaches, on horseback, singly or in troops."[2]

Before the end of the year 1554, Prince Maximilian's Protestantism had become so objectionable to good Catholics that the Vice-Chancellor of the Kingdom, Jakob Jonas, was driven into reproaching him in the presence of his father for going about " with bad eggs "[3] and doing nothing but intercede for the " Lutheran rascals." Max retorted that his intercession was for an honest servant of the House of Austria, whereupon Jonas said that nevertheless the person was a Lutheran rascal. Max then lost his temper and called the Vice-Chancellor " a doddering old Papist."[4] Ferdinand left Vienna early in 1555 to preside at the fateful Diet of Augsburg on which the religious fortunes of the Empire were destined to be based for more than two generations. His departure gave Maximilian and Phauser a free hand, for the Prince was now the virtual ruler of Austria. Phauser seized the golden chance to pour out his pent-up Lutheranism, which made St. Peter so anxious that he wrote to Ferdinand at Augsburg imploring him to intervene. Ferdinand in answer to his appeal remonstrated with his son, but to no purpose, whereupon he sternly ordered the young Prince and his preacher to appear before him at Augsburg and exculpate themselves. Maximilian did not obey, but

---

[1] *Cartas de San Ignacio*, vol. iv, pp. 470–6.
[2] Braunsberger, *Epistulae*, vol. i, p. 527, n. 2.
[3] *Mit faulen Eiern*.
[4] Holtzmann, *Kaiser Maximilian II*, p. 234.

Facsimile of the concluding lines of a holograph letter written in Italian by St. Peter Canisius, Vienna
to St. Ignatius Loyola, Rome

TRANSCRIPTION

TUTTO questo sia per dar piena informatione alla Reverenda Vostra Paternità et prego che questo Principe[1] sia adgiutato appresso Iddio con le nostre orationi. Li sapienti dicono, et e molto probabile, che la conservatione della Religione non habbia altro humano subsidio qui et in Austria, se non per la vita del Re vecchio.[2] Certo li prelate vicini ecclesiastici sono tanto de pocho sive in doctrina, sive in disciplina, che non se potria dire. Onde li consiglieri pigliando una diffidenza impidiscono quello che il Re vecchio farebbe secondo le sue bone inclinationi. Item non se trovano li quali voliano far dal Catholico, non sentiscano piu missa in Austria, le prediche sono per stabilire le secte, et non per nutrire o defendere la fede, mangiano carne tutta via per Austria nella quaresima, dediti alla gula quanto se puo dire, et irrisori grandi delli Papiste, sicome chiamano tutti li Catholici.

Iddio ci conservi contra li Turchi, perche la malitia et perfidia commune pare che sia quasi matura a ricever li grandi flagelli. Non altro per adesso. Vostra Reverenda Paternità se raccordi de noi altri, accio possiamo servire fidelmente alla sua Maiesta eterna in medio nationis pravae et far frutto in patientia. 25 Martii 1555.

Prego per il Padre Erardo che habbia licentia et potesta d'absolvere nelli casi reservati.

della Reverenda Paternità Vostra

Indigno figliolo

PIEDRO CANISIO

[1] Maximilian.   [2] Ferdinand, King of the Romans.

nevertheless was sufficiently cowed by his father's wrath to advise Phauser " to go easy for a while and not launch out so intemperately until a better opportunity presented itself."[1]

Both the Prince and Phauser, who now openly inveighed against the Mass and the primacy of the Pope, had discovered that St. Peter was responsible for the stern letter from Augsburg. Phauser threatened to leave Vienna altogether unless Peter and his brethren were expelled, but Max had no power to expel them and must accordingly content himself with less obvious forms of petty persecution. The Bohemian sectary Blahoslaw reported that the Prince had become " *der offene Hauptfeind* " of the Jesuits, being so embittered against them that he would not see or speak with them on any account or permit them to approach his palace. In March, 1555, St. Peter told St. Ignatius that Max bore him personally a special grudge, as he considered him to be the chief opponent of his preacher, that he would not allow him to promulgate the indulgence recently granted by the Pope in thanksgiving for the reconciliation of England, that he interfered constantly in religious matters and kept about him Lutherans and others who made a mockery of the Lenten regulations and the Catholic faith generally. He would not see Peter himself but he summoned a non-Jesuit friend of his and rounded on him for associating with Phauser's wicked enemy. " I am now regarded," continued the Saint, " as the Lutherans' chief foe and traduced throughout Austria in defamatory writings. My friends fear for my safety, so much, for religion's sake, am I the object of heretical benevolence. *Sed si Deus pro nobis quis contra nos ?* "[2]

Thus the struggle proceeded till the summer, when news reached Maximilian that gave him pause. For many years, indeed almost since his coronation at Aachen in 1521, Charles V, a mystic in the guise of an Emperor, had been dreaming of retirement to some monastery in Spain. Now his dreams began to take definite shape, and Maximilian had joyous visions of himself as King of the Romans and heir to the Habsburg throne. Not even Phauser could be permitted to endanger such prospects, so in June he was politely told to take a month's holiday out of Vienna. In August, King Ferdinand added a codicil to his will which was addressed to his three sons and ran as follows :

> I look at the world and see how heresies and new sects are every-
> where spreading. . . . You are my chief anxiety, Maximilian, for I have
> seen and noticed many things to make me very apprehensive that you

[1] Holtzmann, *Kaiser Maximilian II*, p. 235.   [2] Braunsberger, *Epistulae*, vol. i, pp. 524-6.

wish to secede from our religion and go over to the new sect. God
grant that this may not happen, and that I do you an injustice by
suspecting it. God knows, no greater sorrow or affliction could befall
me on earth than that you, Maximilian, my eldest son and probable
successor, should fall away from true religion. That this should happen
to any of you, my Sons, would be a sorrow and grief to me so great
that I would far rather see you dead. Every day of my life I beg God
most earnestly to protect you from such a fate and to take you out
of this world while you are still, as I hope, good Christians rather
than let it befall you.[1]

From this time on St. Peter had to be away from Vienna for long
periods on the business of the Pope or of the King, but he never lost
sight of Phauser. He had written to Nadal and Laynez, who were at
Augsburg, asking their advice as to the best methods of silencing that
bumptious and wary evangelist. Pleading with him was no use, as Peter
had discovered, and to bring him before the courts, if that could be done,
would only raise a new storm. The best course, he thought, would be
for Ferdinand to send some trusty representative, not objectionable to
Prince Maximilian, who would tell him as a friend how much scandal
his patronage of Phauser was causing throughout the Empire and how,
by fomenting Lutheranism in Austria, he was playing into the hands
of his House's foes, the French and the Turks.[2]

Phauser was back in Vienna before very long, and a fortnight later,
October 20, 1555, King Ferdinand himself came to enquire personally
into the man's orthodoxy. This was again St. Peter's doing and doubtless
did not send him up in Maximilian's estimation. Father and son listened
to the preacher a few times. Ferdinand, at St. Peter's suggestion, bade
him let them have a sermon on good works for All Saints Day, but
Phauser in his over-confidence dilated instead on the sole sufficiency of
faith, which caused the King to inhibit him and introduce in his place
a suffragan bishop of Passau. This man, however, did not really supplant
Phauser, and twelve months afterwards the King and St. Peter were still
endeavouring in vain to get rid of him. Ferdinand, in conjunction with
Peter, put eleven questions before him in writing, with orders to submit
plain answers within eight days. Max himself took the answers to his
father. They appear to have been cleverly drawn up with a view to
confusing the King, who was no theologian. After brooding over them

[1] Holtzmann, *Kaiser Maximilian II*, p. 248.   [2] Braunsberger, *Epistulae*, vol. i, pp. 531–4.

for a whole week, even in the Council Chamber, he instructed his son to return them and inform Phauser that he desired no further disputation with him, as he was too learned for His Majesty.[1] It might have been different had St. Peter not been away in Regensburg and unable to advise. Max and Phauser then sent the articles with their answers to Melanchthon at Wittenberg for his opinion. He heartily endorsed their sentiments and wrote to Max, saying: " Pope, bishops, priests and monks are murderers, since they deliver up to death Christian men who oppose their false doctrines." From that time on, the pair avowed themselves Melanchthon's faithful disciples, while Melanchthon, in turn, regaled his friends with praise of Phauser's good work in Vienna. Maximilian also entered into friendly relations with the apostate, Vergerio, and invited the Unitarian, Sozino, to his Court. For three years he had not been to Holy Communion and he was doing all in his power to prevent his children being brought up as Catholics. His wife endeavoured in a friendly way to keep him within bounds, but she loved him too much to risk his displeasure by more strenuous opposition.

Everybody appears to have loved Max, even St. Peter, whose sole objection was to the Protestant leanings of the man whom he styled so appropriately " Germany's Absalom." There was very much of the big boy in the tall, slim, handsome Prince. He loved to make the Germans gape by taking round with him from place to place dromedaries, apes, peacocks, captive Turks, and, above all, an elephant. This beast made such an impression that when Max visited the Council at Trent in December, 1551, a huge wooden effigy of him was erected in the streets from which magnificent fireworks were let off in honour of the occasion. Incidentally, they nearly burned out the place, Fathers of the Council and all. The elephant's memory lives on in Tirol, where a *Gasthof* that once had the distinction of quartering him is still proud to be known as *Zum Elefanten*.

Max's menagerie helped the Protestant cause by distracting attention from his religious activities and rendering him personally very popular, whereas St. Peter had no gifts whatever as a showman. It is some indication how steadily the Saint kept up his opposition to Phauser that, according to a report of the time, Maximilian angrily summoned him to his presence in May, 1557, and thus addressed him: " Know that, God aiding me, a time will come when I shall make you remember and rue all your doings. I leave you alone just now for my Father's sake."[2] The following month

---

[1] Holtzmann, *Kaiser Maximilian II*, p. 263.
[2] Gindely, in *Fontes rerum austriacarum*, vol. xix, part ii (Vienna 1859), p. 176.

Vienna celebrated its great *Fronleichnam*, or Corpus Christi festival, and Max, as representative of the absent King, was asked to grace the proceedings with his presence. He replied that he could not do so as he had to attend a sermon. The ecclesiastical authorities then said that they would put off the start of the procession until Phauser had finished. All right, said the Prince, and instructed Phauser to hold his pulpit fort for three hours on end ! A week later there was a similar procession in Pressburg, where both Ferdinand and Maximilian had forgathered. The King asked his son to take part, but he feigned illness and then, on further urging, blurted out that it would be against his conscience, as there was no worship or honour of God in such ceremonies.[1]

In 1558 a new complication arose owing to the Prince's attitude, a complication destined to cause St. Peter Canisius many an anxious hour. Charles V resigned his crown that year and Ferdinand was elected Emperor, both formalities being carried out without any reference to the Pope, who, nevertheless, claimed that, according to the theory of the Holy Roman Empire, his sanction was necessary for their validity. By an unfortunate chance the Pope was Paul IV, and Paul had the best of reasons—defeat in war—for disliking everything that came out of Spain. But his blunt refusal to acknowledge either Charles's resignation or Ferdinand's accession was not due entirely to prejudice. Charles V, by his schemes for securing the reversion of the Empire to his son, Philip of Spain, had done much to throw Prince Maximilian into the arms of the Protestant Princes; and Ferdinand, too, in pursuit of his dynastic aims, had often shown himself careless about the religion of his children. He had given his daughter Mary in marriage to Duke William of Jülich-Cleves, a close friend of the Protestants, and seriously contemplated a further alliance between his daughter Leonore and the Lutheran King of Denmark. All this cannot but have made the youthful Max suspect that there was nothing very terrible in the creed of the new religion, many of whose professors had proved themselves to him genial and cultivated friends.[2]

In June, 1558, Pope Paul appointed a commission of cardinals to inquire whether Ferdinand by his careless upbringing of Maximilian had not disqualified himself for the semi-sacerdotal dignity of Holy Roman Emperor. They found unanimously that such was the case, and Paul accordingly refused to recognize him or to receive his ambassadors. That was a nice pass for Catholic Europe to have reached, and no way out

[1] Holtzmann, *Kaiser Maximilian II*, p. 316.
[2] Bibl, *Maximilian II, der rätselhafte Kaiser* (1929), pp. 70–71.

of it could be found during the remainder of the old Pope's life. Through the unremitting efforts of St. Peter and other good men a reconciliation was effected in 1559, with the advent of Pius IV. However, even the conciliatory Pius refused to crown Ferdinand unless he promised to disinherit Maximilian and let Philip II of Spain be elected King of the Romans. Max had recourse to the Protestant Princes in his danger, but received only cold comfort, their chief advice being to turn to God in prayer ! The crisis of his career had now come upon him, and under constant pressure from his father, who threatened not only to queer his election as King of the Romans but also to deprive him of the Crown of Bohemia, he bade a regretful, final farewell to Phauser. There it is necessary to leave him for the present, still anything but friendly to Catholicism or to the Jesuit who, in accordance with his name, had barked so persistently at the heels of his beloved preacher. Max, it is probably correct to say, was the one outstanding failure of St. Peter's apostolic life. He baffled him from the start, and seems to have been entirely impervious to the influence that worked so mightily on his great father and on Duke Albert of Bavaria. As to whether Peter was justified in campaigning so strenuously against Phauser, perhaps the judgment of the Protestant historian Holtzmann will suffice : " The Austrian Catholics and Jesuits cannot be blamed for agitating with every means at their disposal to bring about the removal of this man."[1]

Over against his failure with Maximilian Peter could set at least one great success during those busy and troubled years. It was a success at the other end of the scale, not with the high and mighty but with the simple. As has already been abundantly shown, the religious instruction and formation of youth were St. Peter's dearest ambition from the date of his return to Germany in 1549. On September 12, 1550, Lejay wrote as follows to St. Ignatius from Augsburg:

Canisius is anxious to teach Christian doctrine to the young students of the University [of Ingolstadt] in Latin, and to have a primer composed for public use. He has written asking my opinion on the matter and enclosing a copy of his first lecture which I am sending to you. I have told him that a catechism for children, containing the doctrines contrary to the errors now prevalent in this country, would not only be useful but that it is essential to possess it. The Lutherans exercise the greatest diligence in this matter and teach their catechisms

[1] *Kaiser Maximilian II*, p. 234.

in all their boys' and girls' schools. It seems to me that the composition of the Catholic catechism ought to be undertaken with great care by three or four of the most experienced and learned theologians in our Society and that, when it is ready, all who teach Christian doctrine, especially in Germany, should be obliged to use it as their text-book . . .[1]

Six months earlier St. Peter had written directly to Polanco begging for " a catechism suited to the needs of the Germans " ; so on the very threshold of his career the great preoccupation of his life already possessed him. To understand the genesis of his chief contribution to Catholic literature, and also to remove the misunderstandings created by a recent book with the extraordinary thesis that the catechetical method as understood in modern times is a Protestant invention, quite out of harmony with the tradition of the Catholic Church,[2] it is necessary at this point to interject a few words on the history of catechetics.

Luther's famous *Shorter Catechism* appeared first in 1528 in the old medieval form of *tabulae* or wall charts. He had been led to draw them up, and to devote his genius with great assiduity to the composition of the manual that grew out of them, by the revelation of appalling religious ignorance among the people in the Visitation of the Saxon Electorate in 1527. But it was far from his intention to break with the traditional methods of teaching Christian doctrine. Indeed, he declared in the plainest terms that he knew no better methods than " those in which such instruction had been given from the earliest days of Christianity and until now, viz., under the three heads : The Ten Commandments, the Creed, and the Our Father." Commenting on this statement, a recognized modern authority on Luther's work remarks : " Hence he himself was far from sharing the opinion of certain later Protestants, viz., that, in the selection and methodical treatment of these three points, he had struck out an entirely new line. He simply adapted the existing form of instruction to his new doctrines, which he cast into a shape suitable for popular consumption."[3] A cursory examination of both Larger and Smaller Catechisms shows how faithfully Luther adhered to the traditional division of subject-matter. Only on one point, as far as method goes, was he an innovator, in that he was the first to apply the name catechism to the booklet containing the instructions. Before his time *Catechismus* meant the subject-

---

[1] M.H., *Epistulae PP. Paschasii Broetii, Claudii Jaii*, etc. pp. 358–9.
[2] Tahon, *The First Instruction of Children and Beginners* (London, 1930), edited with an Introduction by F. H. Drinkwater.
[3] Grisar, *Luther*, Eng. tr., vol. v (1916), p. 489.

matter of the instructions which were given orally; so it is true to say, but hardly worth saying, that before Luther there were no catechisms in the modern sense of the word. Nor is the fact that he used the question and answer method in his Shorter Catechism of any greater importance. It had been used in medieval times, and dates back to the earliest days of Christianity. To sum up in the words of an expert Protestant writer on Luther's instruction books:

> The contents and form of his Catechism are not arbitrarily determined but borrowed from the venerable century-old practice of the Church. . . . Luther followed the usual custom of the Church in annexing for the composition of his Catechism the existing, generally accepted matter of instruction. This he bound into a whole and, under a name of venerable antiquity, dedicated it to the service of the Church. Not only did the chief articles, the Creed, the Our Father, the Sacraments, and the Decalogue retain their place in his work but the usual interrogatory form of the baptismal catechism and confession books was also preserved, while, in the answers to the questions, Luther took over a variety of material that is to be found almost word for word in the *Catechesis Theotisca* of the ninth century, in the exposition of the Our Father by Kero, and even already in the *Sacramentary* of Gelasius.[1]

The Catholics, on their side, had not been slow to produce instruction books for children and others, suited to the new conditions ushered in by the Reformation. The first Catholic catechism appeared at Augsburg in 1530. From that date onwards a whole series of similar manuals in German or Latin or both languages kept the printing-presses busy. Bishops, professors at universities, and members of religious orders all joined in the good work. St. Peter's friend, Johann Gropper, produced three catechisms on his own account, and six separate primers of the same kind saw the light in Cologne during the first half of the sixteenth century.[2] Indeed, by the middle of the century the trouble with the Catholics was not that they had too few catechisms but that they had far too many.

---

[1] Weidemann, in Schmid's *Encyklopädie des gesammten Erziehungs-und Unterrichtswesens*, vol. iii (Gotha, 1862), pp. 906–7. Probst, in his treatise, *Geschichte der Katechese*, pp. 89–94, gives a translation of the early medieval book, *Disputatio puerorum per interrogationes et responsiones*, and shows that its method of instruction by question and answer was a normal one from the ninth to the thirteenth century.

[2] Moufang, in his *Katholische Katechismen des Sechzehnten Jahrhunderts* (Mainz, 1881), reprints thirteen catechisms written in German during the sixteenth century, and they were by no means all. Of Latin catechisms there was no end.

As each of these manuals followed a scheme of its own the resulting confusion can be imagined. Moreover, large numbers of them were too long and learned for popular use, while others missed out the convenient interrogatory form. Worse still, they differed in the wording of essential formularies, as, for instance, the Ninth Article of the Creed which appeared in the five following versions: The Holy, Universal Church; A Holy, Universal Christian Church; The Holy, Christian Church; The Universal Church; The Universal, Holy Church. Similar discrepancies found their way into the statement of other articles and doctrines, and the result was that none of these early Catholic catechisms gained general approbation or wide diffusion. Meantime, as Father Lejay told St. Ignatius, Luther's book, a work of genius in its lucidity and conciseness, was penetrating into every corner of Germany. Matthesius, who was active on Luther's side, boasts that by 1568 at least a hundred thousand copies of his *Shorter Catechism* had gone into circulation.

In view of all this, of the ill-success attending the Catholic catechisms and of the triumphant progress of the great Lutheran one, it is not surprising that St. Peter Canisius should have been anxious to see the balance of popular favour redressed. As on other difficult occasions, his thoughts turned to Laynez, the most brilliant intellect of the early Society of Jesus. He, if anybody, might be the match for Luther, and Peter knew, too, what a zealous and successful catechist he had proved himself in Venice, Padua, Brescia, and Naples.[1] To Laynez he accordingly wrote on February 10, 1551:

Recently I have been in communication with Rome about a catechism for the youth of Germany. . . . Father Claude thinks as I do that the best and most advantageous thing of all would be if your Reverence deigned to put together a course of Christian doctrine by which the teaching of the Church, from which they have so much wandered, may be easily communicated to the children and simple people of Germany. I have often discussed the point with my brethren here and we are agreed that it would be the greatest help to ourselves and others if, using the gifts with which God has endowed your Reverence, you would write a more suitable manual for the proper instruction of children than most of the catechisms now in circulation. Often enough these only do harm to their youthful readers. I beg

[1] At Naples in 1548 Laynez had founded a special men's confraternity for the teaching of Christian doctrine.

you, then, most earnestly, for the public good of Germany, that should God inspire you with any ideas on the subject you would please let us have them, and send us here, if you at all approve, a manual of Christian doctrine. With the help of the Lord we shall see to it that your labour and kindness in consenting to the request of your sons do not go without fruit.[1]

The next stage in the story was reached when King Ferdinand imposed upon Father Lejay the duty of writing a compendium of theology. Lejay, as already related, found the task beyond his powers, and by his representations to the King brought about the transfer of St. Peter from Ingolstadt to Vienna for the express purpose of helping with the compendium. In the King's letter to St. Ignatius of December 4, 1551, he speaks of the work as a *Summa quaedam*—some sort of a compendium.[2] Nobody seems to have been quite clear as to the nature of the book wanted by Ferdinand, least of all himself, or as to the readers for whom it was intended. After Lejay's death in August, 1552, the whole responsibility for fulfilling the King's wishes, whatever they were, fell on St. Peter, and it has already been seen how little he relished it. This learned kind of book, meant for goodness knows whom, was not what he had set his heart on. He was thinking of students, children, and simple, unlettered folk who had souls to be saved just as much as priests or professors. As has been seen, he could not get on with it and, at last, on November 29, 1552, heard from his great friend in trouble, Polanco, the good news that Laynez was taking over his commission.[3]

Peter now appears to have changed his plans. Instead of the manual for theological students which had so far occupied and baffled him— if, indeed, that was the nature of the mysterious Compendium—he turned to the production of a manual of Christian instruction for *all* youth. In other words, he gave up the idea of writing a *Summa theologica* and devoted his attention to the composition of a *Summa doctrinae Christianae* or catechism, though, as far as the evidence goes, it is possible that he may have had both works in mind from the beginning. In many respects

[1] Braunsberger, *Epistulae*, vol. i, p. 348.

[2] *Cartas de San Ignacio*, vol. iii, p. 475.

[3] The idea was to produce a text-book of theology that would replace Peter the Lombard's *Liber Sententiarum*, which was no longer suited to the needs of students. Laynez planned a work on a large scale. It was to be in six sections, comprising extensive treatises on God, the Blessed Trinity, the Divine Word, the Procession of the Holy Ghost, Providence, the Incarnation, Scripture, and so on. By September, 1553, three books were completed, but after that Laynez became so involved in other business that he was unable to continue with his plan. His manuscripts, with the exception of two volumes of Tridentine dissertations, have never been published, chiefly owing to the illegibility of the eminent man's handwriting.

his catechism *is* a compendium of theology. Not very much is known about his methods of work or the material in which he quarried, but there are two codices still in existence to which he certainly had resort. One of these contains various theological opinions and tractates drawn from St. Thomas, Pico della Mirandola, Clichtovaeus, Eck, Gropper, Lindanus, Navarrus, and similar sources. It is written partly in Peter's own hand and partly by others. To it is appended a treatise, *De Justificatione*, in fifteen chapters, by Claude Lejay. The second codex is entirely by Lejay and consists of the notes he made when first commissioned to write the Compendium. It has 342 leaves, which St. Peter indexed and found of service in the composition of his catechism, though he went far beyond anything that it contained.[1] While he worked away at that congenial task the Saint showed the greatest avidity for the advice of his brother Jesuits and wrote often to Rome begging the favour of a criticism. By the beginning of 1554 he had so far advanced with his work that he was able to submit the manuscript of the first part to King Ferdinand. From the King, who was then at Pressburg, he received the following letter on March 16th:

Honourable, religious, devout and beloved Son,

We have seen and examined the first part of your Catechism which you sent to us for inspection. Our opinion and expectation of it is that on publication it will, with the help of God, greatly promote the salvation of our faithful subjects. Accordingly, We graciously beg you to finish the remainder of it without delay and so transmit to Us the whole and complete Catechism as soon as possible, for We have resolved and determined that this your Catechism be translated also into our German tongue, and, when printed in both languages, that it be expounded and taught publicly to youth in all the Latin and German schools of our five Lower Austrian provinces and of our County of Görz, to the exclusion of any other catechism under the severest penalty and the threat of our indignation. That this may the more conveniently be brought about, We return you herewith the first part, charging you before everything to note all through in the margin the books and chapters where are to be found the excerpts from Scripture, the Fathers and Doctors of the Church, and Canon Law, which are cited by you learnedly, appositely and devoutly in that Catechism. This is in order that even less learned schoolmasters and other men of less

---

[1] Braunsberger, *Epistulae*, vol. i, p. 416.

exact and profound knowledge may look up and see these excerpts, for We cherish not a little hope that in this way many who have lapsed through ignorance will be brought back to the bosom and saving embrace of our holy mother, the Catholic Church, and that far greater numbers than hitherto will render obedience to the meaning and admonition of these writings when they see the original sources from which you extracted them. As soon, therefore, as you have made these annotations or references, return that first part to Us immediately. While it is being translated into German you will be able, as is your duty, to finish the rest and send it to Us. In this matter We cannot refrain from courteously urging and admonishing you not to be troubled or reluctant in the prosecution of your pious labour. You will provide for many thousands of souls and receive from Almighty God a hundredfold reward. On our side, We, as a Christian King, sincerely and greatly desirous for the salvation and eternal life of our faithful subjects, shall see to it that you and your most religious Society are requited for this labour with all our Royal bounty. Given in our City of Pressburg, the XVI day of March, in the year of Our Lord MDLIIII.[1]

Before the receipt of St. Peter's manuscript, King Ferdinand had written to St. Ignatius, telling him of all the mischief that was being done in his dominions by Protestant catechisms and epitomes of theology, and urging on him the necessity of providing a manual that might serve for the instruction of theological students and others at universities and also for the consolation of country priests, who were in straits over their weekly sermon.[2] St. Ignatius replied suggesting that it would be better to divide the work into two distinct sections, one a manual for parish priests from which to instruct their flocks, and the other a separate textbook on which professors might base their lectures. Polanco, in communicating these details to St. Peter, gave him a strong hint that he ought so to refurbish the work on which he was engaged as to make it suitable not only as a catechism but as a manual for parish priests. This was too much for the Saint, who wrote back in the following terms, June 8, 1554:

I am astonished at the sudden change of decision as to the Compendium of Theology. We promised the King that there would be two manuals, one for parish priests and another for the theological students of this University, and his Majesty gave his approval to this

[1] Braunsberger, *Epistulae*, vol. i, pp. 454-5.   [2] *Cartas de San Ignacio*, vol. iv, pp. 501-2.

arrangement. I was at work on entirely different lines and his Majesty has likewise read and commended my poor effort. Now, if you will have me satisfy in one and the same book both the needs of children, for whom exclusively I have been writing, and of parish priests, the King will not be greatly pleased and I shall have to change everything for the fifth or sixth time. Moreover, the delay may bring me into serious disrepute without any countervailing advantage. The Chancellor is constantly exhorting and urging me to hurry with the work, on the ground that the printer, whom he has sent to me several times, is waiting, and that delay may be a source of grave danger to many souls who by publication of the Catechism would have pure doctrine on which to nourish their souls and so escape the poison now daily imbibed by them.

For this reason, though I should have been very glad indeed to send my Catechism to Rome for your inspection and correction before it saw the light, according to your wishes, I yet found it difficult to refuse the reasonable request of good men by deferring the issue some months more while the book went to you and returned here. Still, I did not want to trust my own judgment in the matter and so left everything open, to the disappointment, if I mistake not, of that excellent man, the Chancellor. By other means I then managed to secure the King's consent to postponement of the publishing until the work had had your censorship. It is only right, I think, that you who have in your hands the rest of the trilogy, the two Compendiums, I mean, should not be entirely ignorant of this third part which is offered as a kind of basis for elaboration in the other works. I am accordingly sending you a part of my Catechism for children and I desire with all my heart that everything in it may be changed or corrected at your hands, and then returned hither as soon as possible, in deference to the urgent wishes of the King. I beg you not to delay too long. Meantime, I shall have the remainder of the work transcribed and sent to you.[1]

At first sight it might appear that St. Peter's original intention to let his book be published without submitting it to the Roman authorities was not in accordance with the constitutions of the Society of Jesus, which require every Jesuit writer to place the fruits of his pen before censors approved by the General or the local superior. The answer is that the constitutions were not officially promulgated and made binding

---

[1] Braunsberger, *Epistulae*, vol. i, pp. 473–4.

in northern lands until a year later—to be precise, in May, 1555. In any case, Peter had the fullest permission and approval of his Rector, Father Delanoy. As related, however, he did send his work to Rome and, according to Sacchinus, the Roman censors heartily commended contents, arrangement, exposition and everything else in the Catechism.[1] Peter himself wanted the censors to be stern. Writing to Polanco, June 8, 1554, he said, referring to the very learned Rector of the Roman College: "I beg Father Olave also to join in the correction of my little work and not to have any mercy on its unskilled author, whether with regard to his style or his statements. From your Reverence I still more desire and look for this service. But, as I have said, please let there be as little delay as possible because the King's officials are in a great flutter."[2]

By August 16th, St. Peter had his manuscript back, a fact which, considering what the posts in those days were like, showed remarkable expedition on the part of Laynez, Des Freux, Olave, and Polanco, who acted as censors. They made a formidable combination, for Laynez and Olave were profound theologians, and Des Freux or Frusius had the reputation of being as good a Latinist as Cicero. Thanking Polanco for their services, Peter said:

Praise be to Christ who moved your charity to undertake in the midst of so much weighty business the censorship of that humble little effort and lucubration of mine. I would gladly send you the rest of it only that I am being pressed by the people here. They have been waiting a long time and it is not easy to find excuses for any further delay. Besides, the Reverend Fathers who promised me their services as censors and correctors are so overwhelmed with other work just now that it would not be right to bother them too often with the Catechism. I therefore trust that you will permit me to have the part of the work which I sent to you printed and also the later pages, as they are clamouring for them so urgently. I commit all the success of the book to your prayers and Holy Sacrifices to God. May our most merciful Lord grant it some success in these lands where religion is so much corrupted.

As to your suggestion that the name of the author might well be appended to the preface of the Catechism, I have thought the matter over carefully and consulted with the King's Chancellor. We came to the conclusion that, as the authority of one man would not carry much weight, especially with the people of this country, the suppression

[1] Sacchinus, *Vita P. Petri Canisii* (1616), p. 90.   [2] Braunsberger, *Epistulae*, vol. i, p. 476.

of his name might redound more to the glory of God and the common good. The more the book is taken for the work of several men, of better learning and wider influence than myself, the greater may be the credit given to it. So too, perhaps, will the honour of the King be better safeguarded, lest people should say that he was dependent on a single person. The Chancellor is therefore adding a new preface in the name of His Royal Majesty.

I thank Father Frusius and Father Olave for their kindness in undertaking the censorship. I heartily esteem them both and send them my respectful greetings. I am writing a separate letter to Father Laynez.[1]

The edict of King Ferdinand which forms the preface to St. Peter's Catechism is a long document but sufficiently interesting to justify reproduction in full. In its first form given below, it makes no mention of Peter at all and, without too much departure from the truth, cleverly conveys the impression that his single-handed achievement is a co-operative work. His name did not appear as author until four years after the publication of the *Summa*, when, quite unknown to him and against his will, a bold Venetian printer blazoned it on a new issue of the volume. The text of the King's edict is as follows :

Ferdinand, by the grace of God august King of the Romans, of Germany, Hungary, Bohemia, Dalmatia, Croatia, Sclavonia, etc., Infante of the Spains, Archduke of Austria, Duke of Burgundy, etc., Marquess of Moravia, etc., Count of Tirol. To all and sundry of Our faithful subjects, to ecclesiastical and lay dignitaries, counts, barons, lords, marshals, presidents of provinces, lieutenants, prefects, governors of towns, judges, burgomasters, consuls, soldiers, vassals and communities, and all others Our subjects and loyal people of Our provinces of Lower Austria and of Our County of Görz, of whatever grade, station, order or dignity, Our Royal Grace and all prosperity.

With great grief of soul We ponder and see by what serious agitations and perils the Christian world is shaken on all sides. But it is the wretched state of neglect and contempt into which Religion has everywhere fallen that is the chief and most frequent cause of distress to Us and to all devout souls. For Religion is the most sacred thing on earth and the most sure and excellent ornament and buttress of the State and, because it is so, Satan, the malign contriver of evil devices,

---

[1] Braunsberger, *Epistulae*, vol. i, pp. 482–3.

the fiercest foe of Holy Church and of all good men, well knowing how much the human race depended on true Religion for protection, has now for many years been attacking and disturbing the cause of Religion everywhere, in such a way that it would seem never before to have been attacked at one and the same time with greater vigour and resources, with more abundance of stratagems and deceits. Up to this moment he has not ceased to instruct his satellites and ministers who, by means of small published books, foster, disseminate and propagate all exercises of impiety, partly in order to confirm those who have abandoned the Church in the errors and sects to which they have seceded and partly to bring about the desertion from our Catholic religion, and affiliation to their own party, of such as still remain in the safe camp of the Church of God.

Among those little books, of which there is everywhere great abundance, the works called catechisms exercise much influence for the overthrow of Religion, inasmuch as, being often esteemed for their conciseness, elegance, and form, they singularly deceive and, to a grave extent, corrupt inexperienced and innocent youth, which is framed by nature for the sincerity of the truth. In the reading of those books, poison, alluring by reason of its sweetness, is held to the lips of the simple and unwary who, before they realize it, are corrupted in their souls with new and pestiferous opinions which are afterwards most difficult to eradicate. Hence it happens that, once permeated by this leaven of false doctrine, they have little regard for the Catholic Faith and the dogmas and venerable decrees of Holy Mother Church. They disdain them and sometimes, through contempt, even attack them.

In this matter We have not been wanting in our duty to do all that could be done by counsels, warnings, commands and public edicts befitting a Christian King to defeat these impious endeavours and uphold the rights of our sacred Catholic Religion. Nevertheless, this foul plague spreads more and more daily and new catechisms continue to appear, filled with new enticements. They are spread about and are read and expounded in schools, with greater danger than simple children, credulous and short-sighted youth, ignorant adults, or the majority of teachers can realize or appreciate. We have therefore decided that a good physician's practice in case of serious illness, or the action of trusty ship-masters in a storm, is not unsuited to Us, namely, that We should by some means either remove altogether or at least mitigate, so far as God assists Us, these present most serious dangers.

Wherefore, after mature deliberation, We judged that it would be most salutary for Our faithful subjects if, in such confusion of dogmas and sects, We were to have an orthodox book of catechetical instruction written, published and commended to Our people. We accordingly selected for the composition of this Catholic work men of sound faith and doctrine, whose knowledge of theology and also purity and integrity of life are well known, and submitted the book that they produced to the examination of censors. In this way We made more sure that nothing should appear by Our authority which was in any way opposed to the teaching of the Gospels and of the Holy Catholic Church.

When, then, by the grace of Almighty God, the aforesaid book had been written and had received the warm approval of Catholic theologians, We entrusted it to our faithful Michael Zimmermann for printing, expressly forbidding and, by Our Decree in this letter, prohibiting any other printer or bookseller in the Holy Roman Empire and in Our hereditary Kingdoms and Dominions from plagiarizing or printing this same book for a period of ten full years from the date of this first edition, or from daring to expose for sale copies of it printed elsewhere, no matter on what pretext, under penalty of Our severe displeasure, a fine of ten marks of pure gold and the confiscation of all the books. And We have decreed that half the said fine shall go to Our exchequer and half to the above-mentioned printer.

We therefore charge you herein addressed, particularly those who govern and administer justice as Our representatives in Our provinces of Lower Austria and County of Görz, to see to it most diligently that this Catechism alone and no other is propounded, explained and taught to school-children, whether publicly or privately, by schoolmasters, tutors and instructors, in so far as you and they desire to avoid Our severe anger and other penalties, reserved according to Our judgment for delinquents and contemners of this Our Edict. For this is Our express mind and will. Given in Our City of Vienna, the XIIII day of the month of August in the year of Our Lord MDLIIII.[1]

A diarist at the Council of Trent, whose identity has not been determined, reports some gossip to the effect that the Pope of the time was displeased with the Edict of King Ferdinand, as it showed His Majesty meddling with religious matters independently of papal or episcopal sanction.[2] However that may have been, no echo of the alleged displeasure

---

[1] Braunsberger, *Epistulae*, vol. i, pp. 752–4.
[2] Paolo Sarpi, as usual, improves the occasion in his *History of the Council* (London, 1619), book v, p. 377.

ever reached St. Peter, nor is it in the least true that Ferdinand's action went beyond legitimate bounds. Peter, who was very sensitive to lay interference, would have been the first to protest, whereas, instead, he threw himself with great energy into the business of helping Zimmermann to get the Catechism through the press. Zimmermann was a distinguished master of his craft and not only printed books in Latin, Greek, Syrian, and Hebrew characters, but was the first man in Germany to possess an Arabic fount. " I have delayed answering longer than I should have done," wrote Peter to Polanco on October 26, 1554, " chiefly because I have been very busy seeing the Catechism into print and helping the printer. I send you the first fruits of our co-operation, and I earnestly desire to have these things of mine not only revised but corrected and improved. God grant that they may find a better form, be successfully printed, and at length published to some purpose! There is still a vacant place at the end for corrections, if you deem any advisable. My sensations are like those of a woman in labour. I find it impossible not to be anxious while the child remains unborn that it may be such as can be offered and consecrated to God. Meantime, please promote its success by your prayers, that I may finish this debt to God and tribute to you under the same inspiration that began it. May Our Lord Jesus turn this trepidation of my mind to His glory! I have learned by experience how far I am behind those who have the skill to write with style and see their books through the press in an efficient, business-like way. I believe and hope that you will have less trouble with the composition of the other works.[1] The Court here and ourselves are looking forward eagerly to their appearance."[2]

Shortly after the date of that letter St. Peter was appointed administrator of the diocese of Vienna and became involved in the struggle with Phauser. Progress with the Catechism then stopped for a time, a delay for which Phauser gives the chief credit to his patron, Maximilian. There may be something in that story and in the preacher's boast that he had secured " at great risk " copies of the sheets already printed, but more probably the delay was caused by St. Peter's transmitting to Rome offprints of the second part of the Catechism as soon as he received them from Zimmermann. At any rate, old historians and bibliographers such as Orlandinus and Alegambe are emphatic that he submitted the *whole* work to St. Ignatius before it was published, either in manuscript or in proofs. Not until March 25, 1555, is there further definite news of it. On that date Peter addressed the following lines to St. Ignatius :

[1] The *Encheiridion Parochorum* and *Summa Theologica*.   [2] Braunsberger, *Epistulae*, vol. i, pp. 501–2.

As for the Catechism, praise be to the Lord by whose grace this work is now almost finished. I shall send you a complete copy by another post, and I entrust all correction and revision of the book to whatever Fathers your Reverend Paternity may appoint. I say this that the work, when it is reprinted, may issue thoroughly revised and well arranged, so as to satisfy even testy and critical readers. I confess that I am a poor hand at this kind of composition and not the proper person for it. But it was good for me as a penance for my sins. The Lord grant that the labour may not have been in vain. I humbly beg your Reverend Paternity to say a Mass for me and have all the other Fathers in the house do the same that the King's holy expectations from the publication of this little book may have happy fulfilment.[1]

A month later Peter sent a copy of the completed work to his friend Martin Cromer, which proves that the date of the first edition of the Catechism was the spring of the year 1555, a point on which many writers have gone astray.[2]

That first edition is not a very handsome little book to look at. It bears the marks of its laborious and painful birth, being a small octavo printed rather poorly on paper that would almost do at a pinch for polishing metal. Latin is the language throughout, the title being SUMMA DOCTRINAE CHRISTIANAE, *Per Quaestiones tradita et in usum Christianae pueritiae nunc primum edita*. After these words on the title-page comes an extract from the Edict of King Ferdinand, the complete text of that document following overleaf. The back of the title-page has a rough woodcut of Our Lord on the Cross with the Blessed Virgin and St. John beside Him, and a glimpse of Jerusalem behind. Above and below the picture run the words: *Jesus Christ Crucified, Author and Finisher of our Wisdom and Justice*. After the Edict of Ferdinand and immediately before the table of contents there is another smaller woodcut of Our Lord surrounded by children of different ages. His hands rest on two of them while an older pair stand by His side and seem to question Him. Above the group runs the Psalmist's verse: *Come, children, hearken to me; I will teach you the fear of the Lord*, and underneath, the invitation of the Prophet Isaias: *Come, let us go up to the mountain of the Lord and to the house of the God of Jacob and He will teach us His ways and we will walk*

[1] Braunsberger, *Epistulae*, vol. i, pp. 521-2.
[2] Braunsberger, *Epistulae*, vol. i, p. 537. Braunsberger states in another place that of the scores of Church historians, biographers and bibliographers whom he had consulted, only two gave the date correctly.

in His paths. The book contains 193 leaves, numbered on one side only and nine others unnumbered, eight at the beginning and one at the end. Nowhere is there mention of the place or year of printing, which explains why so many writers, relying on the date appended to Ferdinand's Edict, have confidently and erroneously assigned it to 1554. Even the all-but-perfect catalogues of the British Museum have been found wanting.

The plan of the work is extremely simple, perhaps even artificially simple. St. Peter starts from the text of Ecclesiasticus : *Son, if thou desirest wisdom, keep justice and God will give her to thee.* He divides Christian doctrine into doctrine of wisdom and doctrine of justice. Wisdom, as St. Augustine taught, has for its object the three theological virtues, faith, hope and charity. What we must believe is taught us by the Apostles' Creed and what we ought to hope and pray for, by the Our Father, while true charity, on God's own assurance, consists primarily in the observance of His Ten Commandments. Here it will be seen at once that St. Peter is completely loyal to the immemorial way of dividing religious instruction. The second part of the Catechism deals with that justice on the 'keeping' of which depends the bestowal of wisdom by Almighty God, namely the avoidance of evil and the doing of good. The two sections are linked together by a little treatise on the Sacraments, which are necessary both for the 'keeping' of justice and the acceptance of wisdom. The Catechism accordingly divides into five chapters or chief articles, (1) Faith, 22 questions, (2) Hope, embracing the Our Father and Hail Mary, 29 questions, (3) Charity, embracing the Decalogue and Commandments of the Church, 39 questions, (4) the Sacraments, 53 questions, and (5) Justice, embracing sin, good works, the cardinal virtues, the gifts of the Holy Ghost, the Beatitudes and the Evangelical Counsels, 86 questions. The questions are short and pointed, but the answers sometimes run to three or four pages, which shows that they cannot have been intended for mere parrot memorizing.

St. Peter had a definite class of readers in view when he composed the *Summa,* namely, undergraduates and the more advanced pupils of high schools who would all be familiar with Latin and capable of following an easy theological argument. In such circles Latin was then so far from being a dead language that it was considered an offence deserving of stripes for a boy to speak German during school hours.[1] But these more learned lads were not the only ones to engage Peter's solicitude. He was

[1] Braunsberger gives references to various church and school ordinances of the time which strictly enforced the custom of speaking Latin on both pupils and masters, *Entstehung und erste Entwicklung der Katechismen des seligen Petrus Canisius* (Freiburg im Breisgau, 1893), p. 30.

planning, too, as will be seen, for their younger brothers of about fourteen or fifteen and for the littlest ones who had barely learned to read their mother tongue. From the start it was his intention to have the *Summa* put into German and to issue in that language much abbreviated and simplified versions of it. Before a year was out he had achieved the first of those ambitions, for a German translation of the *Summa* appeared at Vienna in the middle of 1556, the Latin text having already been reprinted three times there and at Louvain. So much is plain sailing, but the historians, including such eminent men as Alzog, Hergenröther, Kraus, and Janssen, who have attempted to assign dates and places for Peter's smaller Catechisms, are all at sixes and sevens. Even Braunsberger loses his monumental calm while trying to steer through the confusion, and launches out at the 'sins' of librarians who mislaid or destroyed their early editions of the little books. "Where have we got to?" he asks truculently. "Are we concerned with works printed in the sixteenth century or peering back into the dim ages of hieroglyphs and cuneiform inscriptions?"[1] He peered to such purpose, however, that at last, after hunting through half Europe, he discovered in a Munich library a Latin grammar, containing, as an appendix, an abstract of St. Peter's *Summa* adapted to the capacity of little boys. The book was printed at Ingolstadt in 1556, under Peter's own supervision, and is certainly the long-lost first edition of his "Shortest Catechism." His idea in binding it up with an elementary Latin grammar was to take on at their own game such Protestants as Melanchthon, the "Praeceptor Germaniae," who made a practice of instilling their doctrines by means of school books. A German version of the little book appeared a few months later, probably also at Ingolstadt, and was reprinted in 1558 at Dillingen.[2] It is so tiny in format (a 32°) that the librarians can hardly be blamed for having let it slip through their fingers. The most significant thing within its covers is the series of prayers for all occasions which St. Peter provides: morning and evening prayers, prayers before and after meals, prayers to be said when the clock strikes or when anybody lights a candle, and a common, daily prayer for all the needs of Christendom. As related, Peter greatly prized this community prayer and desired children to be accustomed to it from their tenderest years. He himself in the pulpits of Ingolstadt and Vienna used regularly to fall on his knees at the end of his sermon and give out prayers which

---

[1] *Entstehung und erste Entwicklung der Katechismen des seligen Petrus Canisius*, p. 99.

[2] Braunsberger, *Entstehung*, pp. 98–106; *Epistulae*, vol. ii, pp. 884–8. Only three copies of the first editions of the " Smallest Catechism " are known to be extant, in the State and University Libraries, Munich, and the Alte Königliche Hofbibliothek, Berlin.

the people repeated after him, for the Pope, the Emperor, the bishops and other pastors of the Church, and all on whom the welfare of the Church depended. Prayer was the breath of his life, and in it lies the secret of the matchless courage that made him seem to carry in his frail flesh the invincible purpose of the angels.

St. Peter had now made provision for the two extremes of youth, small children and students on the threshold of manhood. There remained a third class to be considered, boys and girls attending middle schools. These formed in many ways the most important class of all, the most easily moulded for good or evil, and Peter accordingly devoted very special attention to his *Smaller Catechism* which was intended for their instruction. He began the work at Worms towards the end of 1557, continued it at Zabern in Alsace, and finished it at Ingolstadt during the first months of 1558. The different place names meant, as will be seen, that much other serious business had begun to demand his attention, but nevertheless the *Smaller Catechism for Catholics* appeared at Cologne about Christmas time, 1558, first of all in a Latin dress, like the others. It was reprinted at Vienna and Antwerp the following year, at Rome in 1560, and at Cracow in 1561. Three years later the Cologne printer, Maternus Cholinus, who was a personal friend of St. Peter, brought out a new edition, in which the Saint included an " Horarium of the Eternal Wisdom of God, Jesus Christ Our Lord, together with some exercises of Christian piety." The Horarium was based on the writings of the great Dominican mystic, Blessed Henry Suso, with whose spirit Peter had become familiar years before in Cologne. After it follow the exercises of piety, which consist in taking for consideration each day of the week some special virtue of Our Lord's life on earth. Thus Sunday is devoted to His humility, Monday to His meekness, Tuesday to His patience, and so on. In the introduction to the considerations, St. Peter writes : " Among all exercises of piety there is nothing more excellent, more pleasing to God or more serviceable and necessary to men for the leading of a good and holy life than diligent and constant meditation on the life and sufferings of Our Lord Jesus Christ."

This same year, 1564, appeared at Dillingen the third German edition of the *Smaller Catechism*. St. Peter had now made it into a combined " Catechism and Prayerbook," enriched with little pictures in the margins and 105 larger woodcuts, of which forty-three represent Our Lord and nine Our Lady. The rest are devoted to the Blessed Trinity, to the saints of the Old and New Testaments, and to various ceremonies of the Church.

In the section containing the prayers, St. Augustine, St. John Chrysostom, St. Bede the Venerable, St. John Damascene, St. Francis of Assisi, and St. Thomas Aquinas mingle their piety with the praise and tears of the Psalmist; and here, too, are devout instructions for the evening examination of conscience, for the proper observance of the saints' festivals, for the assistance of the souls in Purgatory. There is such an air of tenderness and love about many of these instructions that, as Braunsberger truly observes, " one might think one was reading Tauler, Suso, or St. Gertrude, and name the little book a late flowering of medieval mysticism."[1] In the prayers, St. Peter seems to have aimed particularly at impressing on children's minds the truth that Jesus Christ Our Lord is the Alpha and Omega, the foundation and the crown of all human holiness. The children are taught " how each by commending to God in the morning his day's deeds and omissions, may unite them with the service of Christ "; how, before going to sleep, he should recite the lovely old " Song of praise to Christ," beginning:

> Christus du ein Licht und Tag
> Die Finsterniss der Nacht verjag !

The whole life of Our Lord is brought to mind in fifty short prayers, and after that comes a sort of rosary of His Sacred Passion. In addition to the prayers, St. Peter provides a liturgical Calendar with many notes and hints on the observances of the Church. In order to associate the saints in the children's minds with the changes of the seasons, he cites verses from the charming old *Bauernregeln* or Shepherd's Calendar of Germany, such as:

> Sankt Clemens uns der Winter bringt,
> Sankt Peters Stuhl den Lentz herdringt,
> Den Sommer bringt uns Sankt Urban,
> Den Herpst aber Simphorian.[2]

Indeed, everything in this little book is attractive, and it deservedly became the most popular and famous of St. Peter's Catechisms. He knew,

---

[1] *Entstehung und erste Entwicklung der Katechismen des seligen Petrus Canisius*, p. 132.

[2] St. Clement's Feast doth Winter bring,
St. Peter's Chair will urge the Spring,
The Summer's here with St. Urban
And Autumn with Symphorian.

Another rhyme gives the approximate dates, " when the Sun begins to recede from or approach us ":

Auff Barnabä die Sonne weicht
Auff Luciä sie zu uns schleicht.

as must every great reformer, that children are the future, the Church and State of to-morrow. 'Win them and the world is won' became his motto, and for the rest of his life he never wearied, amid all his other duties, of revising and improving his gifts to them. One of his last actions on earth, as an old man of seventy-five, was to prepare an edition of the *Shortest Catechism* with the words divided up into syllables, "to enable my dear little children to learn it more easily."[1]

During the decade between the first edition of the *Summa* and the definitive edition of 1566 St. Peter had become a recognized leader of Catholicism in Germany. The two great Cardinals of the North, Truchsess and Hosius, were his intimate friends, while three Popes, Julius III, Paul IV, and Pius IV, had shown him marks of their trust and esteem. The Cathedrals of Vienna, Prague, Regensburg, Augsburg, Strasbourg, Worms, Cologne, and Osnabrück, had resounded with his eloquence, and the Protestant theologians had learned to see in him one of most the skilful and dangerous of their foes. In 1565 he received in Eisengrein's book, *Catalogus testium veritatis*, the extraordinary honour of a place with the great Saints and Doctors as a witness to the truth and, in the following year, the still more significant tribute of inclusion in a Protestant *Dictionary of the Heroes and Illustrious Men of all Germany*. Such recognition had been won by a life of almost incredible labour and hardship. He knew no rest and was here, there, and everywhere, preaching, teaching, writing, negotiating, planning for the Cause that spelt everything in time and eternity to him. As a prop to that Cause the *Summa*, in its first form, did not satisfy his zeal. It must bear more of the impress of the Council of Trent, which had meantime brought its sessions to a triumphant conclusion, and be better equipped to meet Protestant attack in any direction.

Peter had been promised the help of Salmeron, Nadal, and other learned men for the work of revision, as he was himself immersed in public affairs, but the help failed him and he had to grapple almost unaided with his task. The book appeared at Cologne in 1566 under the title, *Summa Doctrinae Christianae, per Quaestiones luculenter conscripta, nunc demum recognita et locupletata, authore D. Petro Canisio, Societatis Jesu Theologo*. Here for the first time Peter admits his authorship, and for compelling reasons. "I trust," he writes in the Preface, "that I shall be forgiven by all fair judges for having revealed my name in this edition. It has been revealed already, without my knowledge, in other editions, and the Emperor now mentions it openly in his Edict. Moreover, by

[1] Reiser, *B. Petrus Canisius als Katechet* (Mainz, 1882), pp. 73-4.

a law of the Church no book is permitted to appear without the name of the author.[1] For the rest, I will confess that in making this edition, or rather revision, I have done what other more learned men are wont to do, changing some matters and adding many others in order to bring out the sense better and help the reader. Kindly censors cannot take this proceeding amiss, knowing as they do by experience how truly it was said of old, ' Second thoughts are best '."

The principal addition to the book was an appendix of twenty sections on the Fall and Justification of Man, according to the teaching of the Council of Trent. But there are many other changes and enlargements besides, some of which afterwards brought upon Peter the charge of having shifted his ground. Thus, in the first edition he had room for only a few lines on the primacy of the Pope and gave references to his authorities, as usual, only very briefly in the margin. In the 1566 edition the primacy of the Pope stands out conspicuously, and the words in support of it written by St. Jerome, St. Optatus, St. Augustine, St. Cyprian, St. Ambrose, and St. Irenaeus are given their place in the text. But despite the complaints of the famous seventeenth-century Gallican, de Launoy, and the misunderstandings of the learned nineteenth-century Protestant biographer of St. Peter who admired him so much that he tried to portray him as out of sympathy with the papal claims, there is no fundamental difference between the two editions.[2] The primacy of the Pope is unmistakably in both, though more fully treated in the one under consideration. This editon had magnificent sponsoring, for, besides the Edict of Emperor Ferdinand, which now made its exclusive use compulsory in all the Catholic schools of the Empire, there was another ordering the same in every land subject to him from " Philip by the grace of God King of Castile, Leon, Aragon, England, France, Navarre, Naples, Sicily, the Majorcas, Sardinia, and also of the Islands of India and the Wide Ocean ; Archduke of Austria, Duke of Burgundy, Lorraine, Brabant, Limburg, Luxemburg, Gelders and Milan ; Count of Habsburg, Holland, Zealand and Zutphen ; Prince of Swabia ; Marquess of the Holy Empire; Lord of Friesland, Bourg-le-Sire and Bourg-le-Comte and the City of Mechlin ; Governor of Asia and Africa, etc."

A work such as the *Summa*, on which so much loving care had been expended, could hardly have failed of success. Before St. Peter died his Catechisms were circulating in fifteen different languages, including

---

[1] This regulation of the Council of Trent (Sess. IV) and of the Index of Pope Paul IV did not bind St. Peter, as it had never been promulgated in Germany, but he desired, all the same, to carry out the wishes of the Holy See.

[2] *Joannis Launoii Opera omnia*, vol. v, part ii (Geneva, 1731), pp. 684–96 ; Drews, *Petrus Canisius, der erste deutsche Jesuit* (1892), p. 46.

English and Lowland Scots, and had been re-edited or reprinted more than two hundred times. In 1615, only eighteen years after the Saint's death, his first biographer, Matthew Rader, wrote as follows : " Canisius is beginning to speak in the tongues of all peoples, in German, Slav, Italian, Spanish, Polish, Greek, Czech, English, Scots, Ethiopian, and, as I know from my own brethren on the spot, also in Hindustani and Japanese, so that nowadays he may fairly be accounted the teacher of practically every nation." Not only that but the *Summa*, for all its simplicity, was bringing some very remarkable converts into the Catholic fold, including the Lutheran Prince Wolfgang Wilhelm, Count Palatine of the Rhine, who testified in a book that " the principal cause of his conversion was the Catechism of Canisius."

The explanation of the book's success is not far to seek, but instead of proving its qualities by detailed analysis, it will be more appropriate here to cite two opinions out of hundreds on its merits. The first is that of Dr. Fr. Knecht, himself one of the most eminent modern Catholic authorities on the religious instruction of children, and runs as follows : " Anyone glancing at the work of Busaeus, who has assembled in four quarto volumes, making in the first edition 2,271 pages exclusive of indexes, the various passages of Scripture and the Fathers of the Church to which Canisius gives reference in the margins of his Catechism, cannot fail to be amazed by the abundance of erudition at the command of Canisius and to be struck with admiration for the skill with which he works on his rich stores of knowledge, reducing them to the compass of a little book that appears as if it had been cast from a mould and yet contains no sentence nor hardly even a word that is not from Scripture or the Doctors of the Church. It is not the genius of a particular man that speaks to us here : it is the spirit and the voice of the Church."[1] A year after Dr. Knecht's pronouncement, the Protestant Dr. Drews expressed the following opinion : " The Catechism of Canisius has taken his name through the world and down the centuries. Hardly any other book has had such a huge circulation as this, for 130 years after the date of its first appearance it had gone into nearly four hundred editions. . . . The whole plan and lay-out of it is skilful in the highest degree, and the execution a model of lucidity and exact statement, unequalled among Catholic books. All the moral doctrines and commandments of the medieval Church here come to life again, and the strong emphasis laid on them makes one feel that the age of the Counter-Reformation has dawned."[2]

[1] Wetzer und Welte's *Kirchenlexikon*, vol. vii (1891), coll. 303.
[2] Drews, *Petrus Canisius, der erste deutsche Jesuit* (1892), pp. 45–6.

Praises such as these greeted the Catechisms from the beginning, spoken by Popes, bishops, academic bodies, and learned men of many countries, but abuse and misrepresentation have also ever been their portion, Melanchthon being the leader of the attack. He had learned, probably from Phauser, that St. Peter was the author of the *Summa* and, within a few months of its first appearance in 1555, in the course of an address to the students of Wittenberg University, delivered himself as follows: " The Austrian Catechism is the latest to see the light. It sets up many false propositions, and, in particular, revives the mad doctrine of monkish vows. Sham poverty and certain other external practices are honoured with the name of Evangelical perfection by the impudent and odious author . . . of that Catechism, who, incidentally, derives his name from a dog."[1] Melanchthon was followed in 1556 by his Flacian enemy, Johann Wigand, the Lutheran superintendent of Magdeburg, who published a small octavo of 104 pages entitled *A Scriptural Refutation of the Catechism of the Jesuits.* St. Peter's concealment of his name on the title-page of the *Summa* did not bring him much advantage. Wigand, like Melanchthon, knew that he was the author, and refers to him throughout his book as " this dog of a monk," " a fearful blasphemer of God," " a gross blockhead," " an idolater," " a wolf," and " Papstesel," or the Pope's own ass. Now and then he addresses Peter directly, " You swindling trickster," and " Oh, you shameless and miserable devil " being two specimens of his courtesy. Wigand's master, Flacius Illyricus, also entered the lists against " the heathenish doctrines of the Jesuits as taken word for word from their Catechism," but it would be tiresome to reproduce his tirades, or those of the " Exile of Christ," Tillmann Hesshusius, who in 1564 published a book to prove that there is " no error, lie, or blasphemy in all the blind system of Papistry, no matter how terrible, which the shameless Canisius hesitates to cloak over and extenuate."[2] The poets, too, lent a hand, and an ode of the year 1566 has survived, *In Catechismum Canisii*, which begins:

> Forte canem genuit sub nigro Cerberus orco,
> Per tria partitos qui facit ora sonos.
> Forma cani similis rabido sed atrocior ille est.
> Namque malum in superos virus ab ore vomit.[3]

[1] Bretschneider, *Corpus Reformatorum*, vol. xii (1844), pp. 107–12. Melanchthon had nicknames for nearly everybody, many being highly abusive. St. Peter he used to refer to regularly as, " the Austrian Cynic," a poor sort of Graeco-Latin pun on the first two syllables of his name.
[2] Braunsberger, *Entstehung und erste Entwicklung der Katechismen des seligen Petrus Canisius* (1893), pp. 58–70.
[3] Three-headed Cerberus brought forth a whelp in Hell. Canisius in figure resembles a mad dog but outdoes such a beast in savagery, for he spews his foul poison forth against High Heaven itself. Braunsberger, *Epistulae*, vol. i, p. 755.

These attacks are all the more extraordinary in view of the fact that there is scarcely a single bitter or provocative word in the *Summa* or the other Catechisms. But perhaps it was their very restraint and serenity which annoyed persons unable themselves to write like gentlemen. St. Peter's only answer to the insults was to say: *Benedictus Deus !* [1]

To tell in detail the history of the Catechisms in the various countries where they circulated would require a separate volume,[2] and there is room here only for a short account of their fortunes in Great Britain. Their first appearance in an English dress dates from 1567, when the saintly Lancashire priest, Laurence Vaux, published an adaptation of them at Louvain under the title, *A Catechisme or a Christian Doctrine, necessarie for children and ignorant people, briefly compiled and set forth by Laurence Vaux, Bachelor of Divinitie.* John Fowler reissued the book from his press at Antwerp in 1574 and 1575, and it was reprinted again, probably at Liége, in 1583. In his preface the author says: " I have compiled this little booke for young scolers and the unlearned, and what I have set furth, the grounde and substance I have collected and translated out of the Scripture and generall Councells, out of the bookes of D. Petrus de Soto and D. Canisius, addinge here and there some sentences of the anncient Fathers. God send them eares to heare which shall learne it, and them that neede not learne it, because they knowe it, to take it quietly when they reade it, knowing that I have made it for the simple and ignorant and not for the fine felowes and learned." The two men here mentioned, Peter Soto and Peter Canisius, were very good friends, and the Jesuit would certainly have been pleased had he known that Vaux was combining his work with that of the holy Dominican confessor of Charles V to provide a catechism for the persecuted Catholics of England.[3] The Catechism became very popular, especially in the Manchester area, and often figured among the objects seized during raids on Catholic houses by the minions of Burleigh. As was only to be expected, Vaux himself spent many a weary year in London prisons and is given the title ' Martyr ' in some documents, which he undoubtedly merited in spirit if not in deed.[4]

---

[1] Braunsberger, *Epistulae*, vol. ii, p. 745.

[2] In Sommervogel's extensive *Bibliothèque de la Compagnie de Jésus*, St. Peter's Catechisms occupy forty-nine columns, vol. ii (Brussels, 1891), coll. 618–66.

[3] St. Peter's association with Soto began during his missions to the Court of the Emperor at the time of the struggle with Hermann von Wied. He describes Soto in one letter as " that confessor, who is truly a confessor of Christ " and says that he showed him and his brother Jesuits every mark of friendship. Soto used to send well-disposed men to Peter that he might guide them through the *Spiritual Exercises*. B. aunsberger, *Epistulae*, vol. i, pp. 237, 318.

[4] The Catechism was reprinted for the Chetham Society in their series, *Remains historical and literary connected with the Palatine Counties of Lancaster and Chester*, new series, vol. iv, 1885, with an admirable introductory memoir of the author by Thomas Graves Law.

Just about the time of Vaux's capture at Rochester in 1580, Blessed Edmund Campion issued an appeal to the Government of Queen Elizabeth to be allowed to return to his native land and hold public disputations with the Protestant ministers. In it he said :

> Moreover, I doubt not but you, her Honourable Counsaile, being of such wisdome and drift in cases most important, when you shall have heard these questions of religion opened faithfully, which many times by our adversaries are hudled up and confounded, will see upon what substantiall groundes our Catholike faith is buylded and how feeble that side is which by swaye of the time prevayleth against us, and so at the last, for your owne soules health and for many thousande soules that depend upon your government, will discountenance error when it is bewrayed and hearken to those which would spende the best blood in their bodies for your salvation. Many innocent hands are lifted up to heaven for you dayly and hourely, by those English students whose posteritie shall not die, which beyond sea gathering vertue and sufficient knowledge for that purpose, are determined never to give you over, but either to winne you to heaven or dye upon your pikes. And touching our Societie, be it knowne unto you that we have made a league of all the Jesuits in the world, whose succession and multitude must overreache all the practices of England, chearfully to carry the crosse that you shall laye upon us, and never to dispaire your recovery while we have a man left to enjoye your Tiborne, or to be racked with your torments or to be consumed with your prisons.

That famous declaration led to a short but very lively controversy, in the course of which the interesting fact emerged that St. Peter's *Summa*, in its original Latin, was easily accessible everywhere in England. The declaration or challenge, or call it what one may, was published in 1580 and taken up at once by a minister named William Charke in his *Answer to a seditious pamphlet lately caste abroade by a Jesuit, with a discovery of that blasphemous sect*. A few months later another minister, Meredith Hanmer, joined battle with his *Great Bragge and Challenge of M. Campion*. These tracts were immediately dealt with by the redoubtable Father Persons in his *Brief Censure*, printed at his own secret press in London early in 1581. Both Charke and Hanmer replied, and then Persons launched his *Defence of the Censure* which ends with the words, " Here the Authour was interrupted by a Writte *de removendo*." The pursuivants had been put on his track by the unchivalrous Mr. Charke, but the "half book" which he managed by something like a miracle to get into print was quite enough to settle accounts with that gentleman. Charke had meantime mercilessly bullied Campion in the Tower of London, and even at Tyburn, while the martyr swung dying in the air, continued to hurl insults at him. Now Persons loved "good Mr. Campion," and the Epistle to M. Charke with which his *Defence of the Censure* begins reminds one of nothing so much as of an entomologist putting a pin through a beetle and fixing the ugly specimen in its glass case for ever.

But Persons' terrible indictment is the concern of this book only in so far as it throws light on the history of St. Peter's *Summa* in England. Charke in his original answer to Campion had professed to draw on two sources for the doctrines of the Jesuits, which it was his purpose to show up in all their ungodliness. The first of these sources was a book called *Censura Coloniensis*, which had been written by three Jesuits and published in 1560 at the instigation of St. Peter Canisius in criticism of a Protestantizing work that had recently appeared, and the second source was St. Peter's own *Summa*. Now, as a matter of fact, Charke had not been to these sources at all, but had derived his alleged quotations out of them from a violently anti-Jesuit work entitled *Fides Jesu et Jesuitarum*, which a certain German Lutheran theologian had published in 1573, under the false name of Donatus Gotvisus. Canisius, "the foremost Rabbi of the Jesuits," occupies a prominent place in that book, being as atrociously misquoted and travestied as might have been expected to satisfy even an Elizabethan divine. But no. Charke must improve the shining hour and go one better than his German model, while at the same time, as he thought, carefully concealing his tracks. In all this, however, he did not reckon with Father Persons, who proceeded to blow his pretensions sky-high as early as page 7 of the *Defence*. He had already compelled Charke to admit that Gotvisus was his real authority and now went on : " Though upon necessitie he confesse the same, yet finding the things there reported in his conscience to be false, whereas his Author citeth always two Jesuites bookes for proofe of the same, that is, *Censura Coloniensis* (which is not to be had in England) and *Canisius his great Catechisme* (which every man may have and reade), M. Charke quoteth the page always in *Censura Coloniensis*, whiche he is sure cannot be seene, and concealeth the page cited likewise by his Author in Canisius, for that his reader, turning to Canisius his places, should find the falsehoode bothe of M. Charke and his Author. And sometimes also when Gotvisus did not belye the Jesuites

sufficiently M. Charke without blushing will falsifie his words to make
them more odious." Returning to the charge on page 98, Persons continues : " How then coulde M. Charke without shameless false meaning
lay down the very same reportes [of Gotvisus] againe without naming
his author or seeing the booke whence they were cited, especially having
(besides many others) Canisius, a Jesuit, before his eyes in England, which
teacheth the very contrary as shall afterwards be shewed ? Thirdly, his
Author, Gotvisus, in the most of these reportes, citeth not only the Censure
of Colen but also the large Catechisme of Canisius for his proofe, which
was common in England to be seene and whereby M. Charke must needs
know that Gotvisus slaundered the Jesuits most impudently. For covering
whereof M. Charke not only suppressed the quotation of Canisius and
cited only the Censure of Colen (which he knew was not to be had in
England) but also suppressed his chief Author, Gotvisus himselfe, to the
end the reader might not by him learne out the quotations of Canisius
and thereby discover the falsehoode." Persons refers to St. Peter's work
in several other passages of the *Defence*,[1] and his evidence, in brief, comes
to this, that the Latin *Summa* by the year 1582 was a book which in England
every man might " have and reade " for it was " common to be seen and
solde " in the country.[2] There is other good evidence, too, of its popularity with the Catholic recusants, for it often figures among the objects
seized by government officials. Thus in August, 1586, " a catechisme
in Latine made by Peter Canisius, a Jesuite " is included in some pur-
suivant's list of " Popish books found in the studies of George Browne
and his two sisters " and again, the same year, among " such books and
papers as were found in the wood-pipe hidden by John Lyon."[3] It was
also discovered in the library of Anthony Babington when that conspirator
was arrested.

The *Summa* was translated into English towards the close of the
century under the direction of the Gunpowder Plot martyr, Father Henry
Garnett. " Besides these," wrote Garnett to Persons, June 2, 1601, " I
caused Canisius' *Summa* to be translated and added some supplement
of pilgrimage, invocation of Saints and Indulgences largely."[4] The " Setter-
forth " of the book, who may have been Father Garnett himself, says

---

[1] *Defence of the Censure*, pp. 139–40, 155, 165.
  [2] Several Protestant catechisms in Latin were in use in England. Though the exclusive use of
Nowell's Catechisms, issued first in Latin, had been enjoined by the canons of 1571, the Catechisms
of Calvin and Bullinger were still obligatory at Oxford University in 1578.
  [3] British Museum, Lansdowne MSS., vol. i, pp. 76–7.
  [4] Stonyhurst MSS., *Collectanea*, p. ii, f. 553. This translation of the *Summa* was one of four English
books to which an official reply was prepared. Strype, *Annals of the Reformation* (Oxford, 1824),
vol. ii, part ii, p. 109.

that in his judgment two principal things are to be found in it, " first, the very naked and sincere truth very plainly and expressly set down, and second, the multitude of witnesses of her sincerity." As an example, the question on the Church may be cited from the St. Omer's reprint of 1622 :

I pray you then what is the Church?

The Church is the whole multitude of all those that professe the faith and doctrine of Christ, which Christ the Prince of Pastors committed both unto S. Peter the Apostle, and also to his successors to be fedde and governed.

And therefore all Heretickes and Schismatickes do not deserve the name of a Church but do falsely arrogate the same unto themselves : who although they seeme to professe the faith and doctrine of Christ yet they refuse to be the sheep of the high Pastour and Bishop which Christ hath made chiefe governour over the sheepfold of the Church in his own steed, and hath by perpetual succession in the Romaine Church continually preserved.

This Chaire of S. Peter, this primacy of the Church, whosoever doth deny and oppugne, first they do not understand the large promises of Christ made unto S. Peter and the mysticall keyes of the kingdome of heaven delivered to him only and many other things written of S. Peter, the Prince, the mouthe and head of the Apostles. Then they doe manifestly breake the peace and certaine order of the Church which without an highe Bishop and his supereminent auctoritie can neither be well governed nor kept long in unitie, nor holde that sounde strength that is necessarie to bear out the violence of hel gates. Lastly they do impudently dicredite the Fathers and their Councels and writings, consenting all together about this manifest note of the Church, yea and the consonant voice of all Christianitie.

This Church and Her dignitie acknowledges Saint Hierome whose words are these : He that is joined to Peter's chaire is mine. Optatus of Africke hath acknowledged Her, who witnesseth that among the true notes of the Church the Chaire of Saint Peter is the principall. S. Augustine hath acknowledged Her who writeth expressly that in the Church of Rome the Soveraigntie of the See Apostolicke hath always flourished. S. Cyprian hath acknowledged Her, who imputeth the cause of all Haeresies and Schismes that do growe to this alone, that men do not obey one highe Priest and Judge, in Christ his roome.

S. Ambrose hath acknowledged Her, in so much that he hath saide that in all things he did covet to followe the Romane Church.

And more auncient than all these and neere unto the Apostles time, that very Apostolicall man Ireneus giveth such a testimonial of commendation to the Church of Rome : To this Church, saith he, because of the chiefer principallitie, it is necessary that all the Church have recourse, that is to say, all the faithfull that are dispersed in all places : in which Church by those that are in all places of the world hath always been conserved the Apostolicall tradition.[1]

The detailed references given for almost every word of this single passage occupy nearly a page, thirteen of them being to the New Testament and fifty-eight to a great variety of Fathers, Councils, and ancient ecclesiastical writers. All told, there are well over three thousand of such references.[2]

The Lowlands of Scotland received their version of the *Summa* in 1588 from an Edinburgh man named Adam King who was professor of philosophy and mathematics at Paris. It was entitled *Ane Cathechisme or Schort Instruction of Christian Religion drawen out of the Scripturs and ancient Doctours, compyled be the Godlie and lerned Father Peter Canisius ; with ane Kallendar perpetuale containing baith the awld and new Kallendar.*[3] The first question and answer of the *Summa* run in King's translation as follows :

Quha aucht to be callit ane Christiane?

He quha professis the sound and helthfull doctrine of Jesus Christ verray God, and verray man, in his halie kirk. Quha saever heirfor is ane trew Christiane condemnis and detestis alluterlie al kynd of worshipping of God and all sectis quhilkis ar found in quhatsumevir place different frome the doctrine of Christis halie kirk : sic as praesentlie is the sectis of the Jewis, of Ethnicques, of Mahomeit, and all haeretiques.

---

[1] *A Summe of Christian Doctrine*, composed in Latin by the R. Father Petrus Canisius. At St. Omer's for John Heigham, Anno 1622, pp. 97–9.

[2] All the passages to which St. Peter referred are cited textually in the large folio entitled, *Opus Catechisticum*, which his fellow-townsman and brother Jesuit, Peter Buys or Busaeus, gave to the world in 1577. This huge volume contains each question and answer of the *Summa*, printed separately in large type, and underneath in double columns of smaller type all the passages of Scripture and the Fathers on which the answers are based. It embraces the substance of four octavo volumes published first at Cologne in 1569–1570. St. Peter himself was the heart and soul of the gigantic undertaking.

[3] King borrowed the scheme for his Calendar from another book of Peter Canisius, but ejected a great number of Peter's saints from it and installed Scottish ones instead. One man honoured in both Calendars on January 28th is " S. Charls the greit Emperour." In the Calendar of King, Noah and his Ark find a special place because the author was interested in maritime matters. Thus under February 7th there is the entry : " Noa sent from the Ark ane uther dow whilk returneit that nycht with ane branche of olive." The book contains also an elaborate " Table of full Sey at all the costes of Scotland."

СУММА

НАУ́КА ХРИСТЇАНСКО́ГА

СЛОЖЕНА УАСТНИМЬ НАУУН́
ТЕЛІ́ЕМЬ БО́ГОСЛОВЦЕМЬ ПЕТРОМЬ КА́
НИ́СЇЕМЬ, ТОУ́МАЧЕНА̀ И́ЗЬ ЛА́
ТИ́НСКО́ГА Ѩ́ЗИКА
ОУ̀ СЬЛОВИНСКЫ, И̇ ОУ́ТНЦЈЕНА̀ ПО́ЗА́
ПОКЕ̑ДЫ ПРЕ́СВЕТО́ГА
Ѿ ТЦА́ ПАПЀ
ГРЕГѠ́РЇА ТРИ́НАДЕСТО́ГА ❖

Ꙋ РИ́МОУ́ ПРН̀ ДОМИНИКУ́ БАЖН́, ЛѢТО ГОСПОДНЀ
‚А Ф П Г҃.

Title-page of St. Peter's *Summa Doctrinae Christianae* in Slovenian, printed
and published in Rome in 1583 by command of Pope Gregory XIII

The Catholics of Wales were the last to have the *Summa* done into their native tongue, though in 1579 Owen Lewis tried very hard to get a Welsh version printed in Milan. Money was the difficulty. Lewis wrote to Cardinal Sirleto saying that various heretical books had begun to appear in Welsh and that the Catholics had no antidote except a small work of Father Polanco. If he had 120 gold pieces he could get the *Summa* of Canisius and two other books printed in Welsh at Milan by Robert Grifid, " *vir linguae Britanicae peritissimus.*"[1] Alas, the gold pieces were not forthcoming, and the Welsh version of St. Peter had to be put off until 1611, when Dr. Rosier Smyth brought it out at Paris. Most people would not be much the wiser if a question and answer from it were reproduced here, so we may pass on with a salute to Dr. Smyth.

One of the most zealous promoters of the *Summa* and its daughter Catechisms during St. Peter's lifetime was the eminent Jesuit, Antonio Possevino, friend and confessor of St. Francis de Sales, prolific writer of learned works, wonderful missionary and perhaps the most distinguished, if not always the most discreet, papal diplomatic agent of the late sixteenth century. When preaching the Lent at Rouen in 1570 this zealous man sometimes had as many as fourteen thousand persons at his sermons. He relates himself that he devoted three afternoons each week to the instruction of children and those in prison. " It was necessary for me," he says, " to send to Paris six times that Lent for supplies of the Catechism of Canisius in French. It was reprinted six times and brought to Rouen, where the book-sellers' assistants paraded the streets crying : ' Here is the Catholic Catechism which the preacher teaches ! ' " In the Archives of the English College, Douay,[2] there is a memorial of Possevino on the subject of religious instruction in schools, written probably for Cardinal Altemps, Bishop of Constance, between 1573 and 1577.[3] In it the following words occur :

[I recommend] that the Smaller Catechism of Peter Canisius be taught in the Schools at least twice a week and that the pupils learn it by heart. In explaining its text masters can use the *Summa* of Peter Canisius, which has long been approved by the Apostolic See and is expounded in Rome and practically everywhere else in Europe. . . . Further, it would be better that this Catechism, which, with the exception of the Catechism of the Council of Trent, written for parish priests, is by far the most popular in all parts of Europe and the Indies, should

[1] Vatican Archives, Regina, 2020.   [2] Now part of the Westminster Cathedral Archives.
[3] So Braunsberger, *Epistulae*, vol. vii, p. 690.

be employed as a text-book rather than any pagan treatise on ethics, so that Christian faith may be safeguarded and the poison which the heretics are now spreading everywhere with their pestilential catechisms be checked in its flow. . . . Those Catechisms of Canisius, both large and small, may be purchased by anybody at Lyons quite cheaply. . . .[1]

Possevino's friend, St. Francis de Sales, states in one of his letters that during the five years of his famous mission in Chablais, which began in 1594, he had "preached without other books than those of the Bible and the great Bellarmine."[2] But that is not quite accurate, because he certainly had the Catechism of Bellarmine's brother-Jesuit, brother-Saint, and brother-Doctor, Peter Canisius, also. Writing to St. Peter from Thonon, near Geneva, July 21, 1595, St. Francis said: "Here I am in my ninth month among the heretics and from so great a harvest field I have been able to secure only eight ears of corn for the Lord's granary. . . . Among them was Peter Poncet, an erudite lawyer and, as concerning heresy, a much more learned man than the Calvinist minister here. In friendly talks with him I seemed to make some impression by urging the authority of ancient writers and usages. I then presented him with your *Opus Catechisticum*, wherein Busaeus has set forth the opinions of the Fathers in full, and by study of it he was gradually led back from his errors to the beaten path of the ancient Church and at last gave in his submission. For this we both owe you a great debt of gratitude."[3] Another Saint to owe the Catechisms a debt was Aloysius Gonzaga, for Cepari, his confessor and first biographer, related that the prayers and little meditations on the virtues of Our Lord which St. Peter had added to the 1564 edition of the *Shorter Catechism* profoundly affected the small Luigi when he first came across them, about 1580. Years afterwards he confessed that that Catechism was the first thing to give him leanings towards life in the Society of Jesus.[4]

To conclude the long story of the Catechisms, of which only the barest

---

[1] Knox, *The First and Second Diaries of the English College, Douay* (London, 1878), p. 256. At the Douay Seminary, according to Dr. Allen, the future cardinal, writing in 1580, the students, before going on to their higher studies, were instructed "*diligentissime in omnibus catechismi capitulis ex Canisio.*"

[2] *Oeuvres de St. François de Sales* (Annecy ed., 1892 sqq.), *Lettres*, vol. iv, p. 127. Incidentally the great Bellarmine composed a famous Catechism himself, but declared afterwards, when he had seen St. Peter's *Summa*, that had he known of it earlier, instead of writing his own work, he would have contented himself with translating St. Peter's into Italian.

[3] Braunsberger, *Epistulae*, vol. viii, pp. 403–4. A more complete version of this letter is given below in Chapter XVIII.

[4] Cepari, *Vita Beati Aloysii Gonzagae* (ed. 2a., Valencensis, 1609), p. 37: "Eo tempore in libellum incidit Petri Canisii de Societate Jesu Theologi, in quo certa quaedam ad commentandum capita, ordine quodam erant descripta. Ex eo non modo ad divinae consuetudinis amorem vehementius

outline has been possible in this place, one last name must be mentioned, that of Herenäus Haid. Herenäus was born in 1784, the son of a destitute Bavarian peasant who had not the means to allow him schooling of any description. The only two things which he learned as a boy were to say the Rosary and to recite the *Shorter Catechism* of St. Peter. By dint of great efforts and native ability, however, he succeeded in obtaining entrance to the seminary at Landshut, was ordained, and, in 1808, created doctor of divinity. Then began a career of extraordinary devotion and zeal which the opposition of anti-religious circles in Munich only served to quicken. His great work there and at St. Gall was the establishment of catechism courses to undo the evil effects of eighteenth-century rationalism, under the blight of which catechetics had withered and the *Summa* of St. Peter Canisius had suffered banishment from the schools. St. Peter was his guiding star through all the difficulties of his reform, and never had the Jesuit Saint a greater lover than this man who was not a Jesuit. In 1826 he published a new German biography of his hero, and in 1834 caused Rader's original Latin biography of him to be reprinted. During the years 1844–1851 he translated and published at Augsburg in five volumes St. Peter's exposition of the Gospels for Sundays and feast-days, having already brought out in four volumes a new edition of the *Opus Catechisticum* of Busaeus. The *Summa* itself he honoured with five separate reprints in Latin and four in German, and the *Shorter Catechism* of St. Peter also saw the light again four different times under his direction. At the start of his wonderful career as catechist and confessor he had published a book entitled, *Defence and Vindication of the Venerable Theologian and Doctor, Peter Canisius, and his immortal Work : Summa doctrinae christianae*. The *Summa*, as perhaps the chief *Feldzeichen* or field-badge of the Counter-Reformation,[1] had become an object of distaste to the liberals of Germany, and Haid in his book rounds on the " haughty inspectors of schools who turned its title into a sneering adage." Their attitude, he said, was one proof more of the wretchedness of an age " from which all true learning had departed."[2] Possibly that decline of learning

---

exarsit, verum etiam, quae tenenda meditandi ratio, quae tempora essent observanda, cognovit. . . . Narrare postea est solitus hunc eumdem, de quo memini, libellum, atque etiam epistolas Indicas plurimum animum suum Societati Jesu conciliavisse. Libellum quidem, quod se rerum in eo ordinem, ac multo magis spiritum, cujus impulsu scriptus esset, vehementer probasse, suique stomachi fuisse diceret."

[1] Gustav Kawerau, a distinguished authority on the writings of Luther, expressed his judgment in the *Theologische Literaturzeitung* (vol. xix, 1894, p. 84) that " the Catechisms of Canisius had certainly as much significance for the Counter-Reformation as the Catechisms of Luther for the Reformation."

[2] *Apologie und Schutzrede des ehrwürdigen Theologen und Lehrers Petrus Canisius, und seines unsterblichen Werkes : Summa doctrinae christianae* (Landshut, 1822), p. 68. Cited by Braunsberger, *Entstehung*, pp. 48–9. Haid lived on to 1874.

was in good part the reason for St. Peter's eclipse. His little book was too learned for the simple needs of our less stalwart centuries, when even a professor, let alone a schoolboy, might balk at being required to ask fifty-eight umpires for a decision on a single point of the game. And so it came about that the *Summa* passed into honourable retirement after generations of glorious service during which " Canisius " and " Catechism " were regarded as synonyms.[1] The catechisms used in most countries to-day have certainly some of its blood in their veins, and not a few of them can trace their lineage directly back to it through the illustrious Deharbe.[2]

[1] A German authority, writing in 1925, stated that " Even to-day in certain districts parents can be heard to ask their children : ' Have you yet learned your Canisius ? ' " Metzler, *Petrus Canisius : Ein Charakterbild* (München-Gladbach, 1925), p. 84.

[2] The most elaborate and sumptuous edition of St. Peter's three Catechisms ever published has been reserved for our own day. In 1933 and 1934 they appeared at Rome and Munich in two quarto volumes edited with consummate scholarship by Fr. Streicher, S.J.

CHAPTER VII

FOUNDATIONS

DURING the course of a remarkable speech at the Catholic Congress held in Aachen in September, 1879, Baron Felix von Loë made the following pronouncement: "If all else that Canisius achieved during his life by his eloquence, his writings, and his labours had not been achieved, if the sole fruit to be noted in his life was what he did for the instruction and education of youth, he would still deserve the name which the Church has conferred upon him, the name of an Apostle of Germany and a worthy successor of St. Boniface."[1] How little exaggerated that tribute was, may be seen from a bare list of the places where St. Peter either founded famous schools, or helped to found them, or prepared the way for their foundation—Cologne, Vienna, Prague, Ingolstadt, Strasbourg, Trier, Freiburg im Breisgau, Zabern, Dillingen, Munich, Würzburg, Hall in Tirol, Speyer, Innsbruck, Landshut, Landsberg, Molsheim in Alsace, and Fribourg in Switzerland. Anybody doubtful about the work involved in such undertakings has only to read the *Foundations* of St. Teresa. Indeed, it was not so much work that they involved as a minor form of martyrdom, the martyrdom of jealous tongues, of hopes deferred, of promises broken.

After much sobering experience of the uncertainty in human promises, St. Ignatius and his advisers had learned to divide prospective colleges into two classes, mathematical and real. Mathematics deals with abstractions, and a mathematical college was not one for teaching that science but a college in the clouds, desired, indeed, and hoped for by the Jesuits themselves or by other men without the means to set it on foot, but not seriously intended at the time by the dignitaries who proposed it. Father Nicholas Bobadilla, one of the most sanguine of the early Jesuits, was a great promoter of these airy nothings and wasted much ink and breath over them. Real colleges, on the other hand, were those projected on a basis of pounds, shillings, and pence, such as the establishment at Vienna.

[1] *Verhandlungen der XXVI Generalversammlung der Katholiken Deutschlands* (Aachen, 1879), p. 110.

253

The majority of the first Jesuit colleges went through both phases, starting like Ingolstadt and Breslau as mathematical and passing in the course of time into real. In spite of St. Peter's elaborate negotiations with Frederick Staphylus from 1554 onwards, a college was not opened in Breslau until nearly a hundred years later, but Ingolstadt had already come within measurable distance of realization and Prague had the unusual distinction of being a real college from the start.

Bohemia, land of the centre and melting-pot of many races, provided St. Peter with his first big chance to prove his mettle as an organizer, not by making things easy for him, but by putting every conceivable obstacle in his way, short of honouring him with martyrdom from a window.[1] The sixteenth-century traveller, Fynes Moryson, describes the situation of the country succinctly: " Bohemia hath a language proper to itself and hath two Provinces belonging to it, Moravia (having his proper language) and Silesia (using the Dutch tongue) and these three make a Kingdome, which is subject to the Emperour, and it is joyned by Geographers to the Provinces of Germany because the same compasseth it almost round about."[2] Germany's embrace led to much trouble, for, with the progress of time, the Germans, being keener and more enterprising students than the Czechs, gained complete ascendancy at the University of Prague, founded in 1347 on the model of Paris by the enlightened King Charles IV of Bohemia. From Paris Prague had adopted the system of national groupings of the students, a policy which the Czechs soon learned to regret. Of the four " nations " at the University the Germans predominated in three and so could always outvote the Czechs on questions of administration. That did not make for peace and, as so often happened, racial antagonism gradually swamped even the aloof plateau of metaphysics. Nominalism was the fancy of the Teutons, so the Czechs were Realists to a man. Oxford, where Wycliffe had propagated his own brand of Realism, became a resort of Czech students, owing to the connexion of England with Bohemia through the marriage of Richard II to the daughter of Charles IV, and these men introduced into Prague various writings of Wycliffe which made a profound impression on the mind of a gaunt, brave, hot-headed undergraduate from the Bohemian village of Husinec. He was nicknamed Hus for short, and in due course, with his rough eloquence and forceful character, became the leader and champion of Czech nationalism. Lollardry, which in the land of its origin

[1] That process, known as " defenestration," was the favourite Czech method for disposing of unwanted people. There are many famous " defenestrations " in Bohemian history.
[2] *Itinerary*, part iv, book 2, chap. 3.

had soon succumbed to the vigorous onslaughts of the State, found a new life in Bohemia under "the budding genius of modern revolutions."[1]

After the fiery exit of poor Hus a terrible time came for Catholicism in Bohemia. The wild, fanatical genius, Zizka, swept through the land with his hordes of gallant peasantry and revenged the death of their idol on the magnificent churches, monasteries, and educational institutions which had been the glory of the old order. Catholicism was practically wiped out. The archbishop of Prague apostatized, and the see, after his deposition by Pope Martin V, remained vacant for more than 130 years, during which time the great University came completely under Hussite control. With the Reformation new troubles began, for, bordering as the country is on Saxony, it could not have failed to be affected by Luther's rebellion. But, though a section of the Hussites went over to Protestantism, the majority of the people continued to base their religious position on the Council of Basle, and, except for the fact that they communicated under both species and ignored the Pope, were very little different from Catholics. Genuine Catholics who adhered to the Church's discipline with regard to Holy Communion and everything else numbered only about four per cent of the population, a fraction, however, that included the Court and the noblest families in the land. Maximilian enjoyed the title of King of Bohemia, but his father, aware of his Protestant tendencies, took the administration of the country out of his hands and gave it to his second son, Archduke Ferdinand, who was a devout and zealous supporter of the ancient Faith. The chaos into which the Hussite wars and the rise of various radical sects had thrown religious affairs, caused prominent Catholics to look about for some means of saving the remnant of their little flock. Catholic schools were the most pressing need, and that naturally led to thoughts of the Jesuits, whose work in Vienna had become known. They accordingly applied to King Ferdinand in 1552, but Elector Moritz's rebellion at the time rendered it impossible for His Majesty to do anything, greatly though he sympathized.[2]

In 1554 Ferdinand went to reside in Prague for a while, which gave his confessor, Bishop Weber of Laibach, an opportunity to revive the project of a Jesuit settlement in Bohemia. Possibly at the suggestion of the Bishop of Breslau, who wished to have the Jesuits in or as near to Silesia as might be, the King at first thought of starting the new college

---

[1] So Louis Blanc describes Hus in his *History of the French Revolution*, vol. i, p. 28.

[2] An historian of Prague University suggests that Ferdinand himself was the prime mover. Being at loggerheads with that institution, he is supposed to have decided on calling in the Jesuits and founding another independent university. W. Tomek, *Geschichte der Präger Universität* (1849), p. 159. Tomek gives no evidence worth considering for his opinion.

in an empty monastery out in the wilds on the Silesian border. The place is called Oybin and stands near the Saxon town of Zittau. Had the Jesuits settled there they would have been in touch with a number of heretical countries, Saxony, Silesia, Lausitz, and Moravia, but they were essentially an order for cities, and St. Peter Canisius did not relish the prospect of rural calm which the secluded monastery presented to his mind. Writing to St. Ignatius, October 14, 1554, he said:

On occasion of the King's visit to Bohemia, which country, since the trial and burning of Jerome of Prague as a heretic at the Council of Constance,[1] has strayed very far from true Catholic faith, it has pleased Divine Providence to prepare the way for the introduction of our Society among the Czechs. The first impulse to this holy project came from the Bishop of Laibach, who said, referring to some deserted monastery of Celestine monks, that as there was only one religious left it would be better to hand over the place with its revenues to our Society for the establishment of a college like the one in Vienna. The King not only received the advice very readily but showed a great desire for the suggested change. His Lordship the Bishop accordingly wrote to me from Bohemia, asking me to provide in good time for a staff and other things necessary to a college. He added that the monastery was situated on the borders of Bohemia, Oberlausitz, Meissen, and Silesia, which provinces are, indeed, large and important but, I think, only in a small degree Catholic. I replied that further particulars of the monastery were necessary, that it did not seem advisable for our Society to settle in retired and thinly populated places, such as some monastic lands are found to be, and that it would be more conducive to the glory of God and the edification of our neighbour if the college were established in the chief city of some province where a more abundant harvest of souls for the love of Jesus Christ Crucified might be anticipated. The letter, which went into greater detail than what I am writing now, was shown to the King, and His Majesty, in consequence, decided that the college should be set on foot in Prague, out of the revenues of the aforesaid lonely and unprotected monastery. To-day he spoke to me personally on the subject, saying that he would subsidize the college from his own privy purse, as he expects that no small benefit will accrue therefrom to his Kingdom of Bohemia. Indeed,

[1] It was Jerome of Prague who introduced John Hus to the writings of Wycliffe. Both men went to their dreadful deaths with marvellous courage.

we may hope for the greatest inspiration to goodness and an immense gain of souls if our Fathers find an entrance to the metropolis from which practically the first seeds and roots of heresy have spread into Germany.

I may inform your Paternity that we have friends in Prague so attached to us that, even before there was any mention of the monastery, they offered the King a fixed income to support men of our Order. At the moment they are about to write to Rome, petitioning for twelve of our brethren, who will be supplied with the necessary money for their journey. I hope that all our Germans now in Italy and Sicily will be appointed to this college. Two of them should be doctors of divinity, who will doubtless have opportunity for good work among the seduced and the seducers of Prague. The Senate, however, is for the most part Catholic, and so is the Administrator of the diocese. In the whole of Bohemia there is not a single bishop left, and the Kingdom has been now a hundred years in schism. May God have mercy on so many souls travelling to perdition, for in Bohemia there are partisans not only of modern but also of such earlier heresies as those of the Piccardites and Hussites, who are at one in their desire to communicate under both species.

It would seem, though, that, since they have had a taste of Lutheran liberty, they are falling away gradually from Hussitism and abandoning the rigid fasts and other practices characteristic of that sect, which in the beginning and for long afterwards they used to observe most conscientiously. May Our Lord give us grace to succour this noble part of the Empire, to reform the temples of God and to lead back the straying sheep to their true, first Shepherd, that so there may be one flock, one fold and one Shepherd. I have a desire that all who come to start this college may be well armed with holy patience, and with great zeal not so much for arguing as for long-suffering and for building up this country in God rather by deeds than by words. Thus having sown in tears they may reap with joy and bring home their sheaves.

Nothing remains now but that we should all commend ourselves to the holy prayers of the Reverend Fathers and Brothers, ever anxious as we are to have many intercessors and helpers for this most desolate vineyard, infested with beasts of prey which destroy more than the united efforts of others are able to restore. As His Majesty has now secured a very good and safe income for this College of Vienna, the first in German lands but not, I think, the last, he is plainly its real founder and patron. It would accordingly give me satisfaction if each priest of the Society said three Masses for him, as your Reverend Paternity will know best how to arrange. Besides his spiritual needs, His Majesty suffers much from the Turks in Hungary. They have made still another advance and may easily enough do us a great deal of damage. May God in His infinite goodness give us grace to help these northern countries.[1]

In reply to King Ferdinand's letter petitioning for twelve Jesuits to start the college in Prague, St. Ignatius said that, though fifty of his men were to leave Rome the following year for various employments, he would still somehow find a dozen others, including two doctors of theology, to satisfy the King's wishes.[2] The next thing to be done, then, was to choose a suitable home for the new college. This task fell to the Viceroy of Bohemia, Archduke Ferdinand, who deputed Henry Scribonius, the zealous Administrator of the long vacant See of Prague, Anton Brus, General of the Crutched Friars, and other eminent men to select a site, and meantime summoned St. Peter to the city. Arrived there, Peter took up his abode in a tiny room at the hospital of the Crutched Friars and began immediately, at the Archduke's invitation, to preach at the Cathedral of St. Vitus to the Court and such of the people as understood German. These sermons, according to the report presented to the King by the commissioners mentioned above, constituted the best foundation-stone of the new college, inasmuch as they had won the sympathy of intelligent observers for the project.[3] The building eventually chosen to house the pioneer Jesuits was the venerable but dilapidated Dominican Priory of St. Clement, situated close to the famous stone bridge of Prague from which, according to tradition, St. John Nepomucene was hurled to martyrdom in the river Moldau. The Dominicans, of whom only five remained out of a hundred, were very naturally in no great hurry to surrender a place dear to them through century-old associations, and

---

[1] Braunsberger, *Epistulae*, vol. i, pp. 495–9. The sentiments of that letter seem fairly genuine, by which is meant that St. Peter really had the glory of God in view, and not merely the glory of his Order, in urging the establishment of a college in Prague rather than in rural Oybin. But even moderate Protestants are slow to give him so much credit. Thus the Swiss savant, Aloys Gautier, wrote in 1905 : " Canisius sait fort bien, d'autre part, que l'Ordre a besoin de tous ses membres dans les villes ; une activité modeste et sans gloire au sein de la population rurale ne servirait en rien les intérêts de la Compagnie et ne favoriserait pas son extension en Allemagne." *Étude sur la Correspondance de Pierre Canisius* (Geneva, 1905), p. 55. Gautier wrote under the inspiration of Carl Mirbt, Professor of Ecclesiastical History at the University of Marburg and a delicately polite but thorough-going critic of everything pertaining to the Society of Jesus. Mirbt's well-known *Quellen z. Gesch. d. Papsttums u. d. röm. Katholizismus* (1911) is a masterpiece of the art of choosing documents to fit a preconceived theory.

[2] *Cartas de San Ignacio*, vol. iv, pp. 484–5.

[3] Braunsberger, *Epistulae*, vol. i, p. 763.

St. Peter, after his Viennese experiences, was determined that they should have no cause for complaint. Having been informed that the friars were ready to strike a bargain, he saddled his horse and set out on the long, lonely, nine days' ride to Augsburg to consult King Ferdinand. By the time of his return to Prague he had been on horseback or on board some dreadful river-boat of the Danube for at least thirty-nine days out of sixty. But his devotion was not without its reward, for he was able to offer to the Dominicans a fine, untenanted Poor Clare convent, situated in beautiful grounds on the outskirts of the city. This the friars were quite ready to accept in exchange for their old home, and the King accordingly petitioned the Pope in August, 1555, for licence to make the transfer. At the same time he wrote urging St. Ignatius to send his twelve sons to Prague before the winter set in.[1] The petition stated various reasons why the exchange seemed advisable, particularly the fact that the Dominicans, through fewness of numbers, were unable to serve the spiritual needs of the Catholics in their vicinity and, through poverty, unable to keep their ancient and collapsing house in repair :

With this opinion the Friars-preacher themselves also agree, desiring to cede their place and rights because they are in sure hope that such surrender will be of great advantage to the faith and religion of Prague and Bohemia. Lest, however, the Brothers of St. Dominic should suffer loss, the Convent of St. Agnes was offered to them, and seeing that it was a more extensive and beautiful property, with larger buildings in better condition, they willingly undertook to migrate thither. . . . In ceding their rights in favour of the Fathers of the Society of Jesus there is this condition that the goods and revenues of the monastery of St. Clement are to remain entirely as heretofore in the possession of the Dominicans.[2]

Fearful of something going amiss with his twelve pioneers, Ferdinand now wrote directly to the Pope, behind St. Ignatius's back, asking His Holiness to see that the Jesuits were dispatched to Prague immediately. Unaware of difficulties in Rome, St. Peter supported the King by emphasizing how dreadfully cold Prague could be in October and by suggesting in detail the best and quickest route for his brethren to take— Rome to Ancona, then by sea to Trieste if the winds were favourable, from Trieste to Vienna and from Vienna the sixty remaining miles to

[1] *Cartas de San Ignacio*, vol. v, pp. 583–5. [2] *Cartas de San Ignacio*, vol. v, pp. 587–8.

their destination.[1] On being summoned by the Pope St. Ignatius explained
that men were not to be conjured like rabbits out of a hat, that he had
to collect them from various places in Italy, and that one of the two
designated doctors of theology was in bed with fever. The Pope saw
his point, whereupon Ignatius wrote to Ferdinand saying that, though
most eager to comply at once with His Majesty's wishes, it seemed better
on every count, including the approach of winter, to defer the departure
of the twelve until the following spring : " But lest the people of Prague
be altogether deprived of the consolation and spiritual help which our
men might be expected to provide, the Holy Father considers it right
that, pending their arrival, Doctor Canisius should remain in the city,
where he will be able to occupy himself very usefully preaching and
making all necessary preparations for the reception of his brethren."[2]

St. Peter was well pleased with his first impressions of Bohemia.
" Neither in Austria nor in Bavaria," he informed St. Ignatius, " have
I seen circumstances as favourable as those here for the return of schismatics
to Catholic unity. In the first place, though the people communicate
under both species they are not opposed to other usages, practices, and
precepts of the Holy Roman Church but observe fasts and exterior
ceremonies more devoutly than any of the Germans. Secondly, though
the leaders of the clergy have no bishops to guide them in the whole
of Bohemia they are zealous and diligent workers for the revival of religion.
Then, finally, the Hussites are divided among themselves and have but
few learned men and priests. If there was available here a good supply
of native Catholic preachers it would be an enormous advantage, though
so many are the sects and so obstinate in error are the more cultured
classes that only three or four professedly Catholic towns are to be found.
All other places keep the day on which John Hus was burned at the
Council of Constance as a day of major solemnity."[3] Some years later
he paid the Czechs in general this fine tribute : " They are very simple
and urbane, and far more courteous to strangers than the Germans. They do
not travel much outside their own country, and so escape the vices of other
nations. . . . God grant that our Society may have many Czechs in its ranks
to bring back to the bosom of the Church those whom Hus has led astray."

Prague impressed him as being not unlike Rome in size, beauty, and
architectural grandeur, and he was highly satisfied, too, with the site

---

[1] Braunsberger, *Epistulae*, vol. i, p. 554.
[2] *Cartas de San Ignacio*, vol. v, pp. 414-5. The Pope himself wrote in the same sense : Raynaldus,
Annales Ecclesiastici, vol. xxi, 1555, n. 50.
[3] Braunsberger, *Epistulae*, vol. i, pp. 545-6.

for his new college, as it lay in the centre of the city and had possibilities in the way of a good garden and other amenities. Being practical and provident, Peter always showed nearly as much anxiety about his gardens as about his churches, for the staff of a college must have somewhere to take the air if health was to be maintained. They must, too, have a reliable source of income if their work was to endure, since their constitutions precluded the acceptance of fees from their pupils for the tuition they gave. The revenue for the support of the Fathers in Prague was to come from the monastery of Oybin, to the amount of a thousand thalers.[1] St. Peter considered it a princely sum and wrote exultantly to St. Ignatius :

Your Paternity may without hesitation send hither not merely ten but twenty or thirty men, if you so wish and can spare them. For the rest, the place gives me greater hopes than Vienna, in spite of the fact that the University of Prague is now almost non-existent. I am looking forward to seeing our men theologians and professors here, the first since the death of John Hus, as I shall explain more at length on another occasion. Certainly, it seems to me that the Divine Goodness desires soon to convert these hearts which already show some eagerness for virtue. So your Paternity need have no anxiety about sending men to this Bohemia which borders on Saxony. Neither favour nor persecution, consolation nor desolation will be lacking in this vineyard, where, I am told, there are thirty thousand towns and villages. I would ask that two of the men sent should be skilled in Greek, and several of the others, good teachers of grammar, for the most part Germans. Further, there ought, if possible, to be one German preacher. . . . As for the theologians, they should be men capable of coping with the various heresies which rise and spread here continually, through the malice of the Enemy of all Catholic truth. Thus there is no lack of Waldenses, Bohemian Brethren, Zwinglians, Osiandrians, and Schwenkfeldians, in addition to the ordinary schismatics.[2]

Bricks and mortar now became large subjects of St. Peter's meditations. The buildings of St. Clement's had either to be demolished and re-erected according to a new plan, or else to be much patched and repaired, and

---

[1] This coin, whose value in the sixteenth century is not easy to determine, was the ancestor of the Almighty Dollar, which, literally speaking, may be said to have had a lowly origin. The word ' dollar ' is derived from ' thaler ' and that from the German *tal* or *thal*, meaning a valley. The thaler originated about 1518 in a little Bohemian village named Joachimsthal, near Karlsbad in the Erzgebirge, where there were famous silver mines.

[2] Braunsberger, *Epistulae*, vol. i, pp. 549-51.

the whole responsibility for this work, as well as for the payment of the
Italian workmen, fell on his shoulders. The four class-rooms were to
be entirely new, and so spacious that three of them could easily accommodate two hundred pupils.[1] It has to be remembered that all this time
Peter was administrator of the Diocese of Vienna, preacher-in-ordinary
to the Viceroy of Bohemia, and agent-general for German and Austrian
affairs of the Roman Jesuits. In the midst of these many preoccupations,
he suddenly received a command from King Ferdinand to proceed to
Munich on business connected with the college about to be started at
Ingolstadt. This time his journey was made in the unusual comfort of
a private coach, put at his disposal by his Prague friends with a view
to getting him back to them as quickly as possible. He left the more
readily, because work on the buildings at St. Clement's had to be suspended
during the winter.

From some conversations he had had at Augsburg with Wiguleus
Hundt, the Curator of Ingolstadt University, Peter feared that the proposals
to be made to him at Munich would be unacceptable ; but to his surprise
and great relief, except in one respect, he found that this time Duke
Albert really meant business, his intention being to found a fully equipped
Jesuit college, with a small seminary attached for the education of at
least fifteen secular priests. At Ingolstadt, whither he betook himself
on October 26, 1555, he was to confer with the four chief ministers of
the Duke, to come to an arrangement about endowments and everything
else pertaining to the new foundation, and also to give his considered
opinion as to the best methods for the reform of the University.[2] " I
shall do nothing that might be prejudicial to the Society or to your
Paternity," he promised St. Ignatius the day he set out, " and I shall
report to you on everything that happens at the consultations. Afterwards I think I shall be going on to Vienna where the King is now
resident. . . . May God give us His holy grace to serve Him utterly and
to be useful to our neighbour in every place."

The negotiations opened on November 27th and continued until
December 8th. On the former date St. Peter put his views before the
ministers in a document which is worth reproducing for the light it
throws on its author's capacity as a business man. He would have the
scope of the new college clearly defined and leave no loophole for divergent
interpretations later on, especially with regard to the class of pupil for
whom the Jesuits would be expected to cater :

[1] M.H., *Litterae Quadrimestres*, vol. iv, p. 330.   [2] Braunsberger, *Epistulae*, vol. i, pp. 564–6.

As our illustrious Prince Albert has judged that your Excellencies should discuss and settle with me the holy project of a theological college, I felt obliged to submit to you this simple statement in explanation of my views and discharge of my conscience, at the same time humbly commending myself to your courtesy. As far as I can see, no other inducement moves me to the handling of this affair than a good hope of getting at the truth and of promoting the glory of God and the common good.

In the first place, then, I think that planning a college for the Fathers of my Order is not enough, and that we must look further afield if your views and mine are to reach happy agreement. As for our Fathers, I can certainly assure you that their only motive in coming hither is the general good of this University and country, which they are eager to maintain and advance by all care, attention and diligence, especially in matters pertaining to the sincere profession of our holy religion. They doubt, however, whether this end and the true fruit of their institute can be attained, if they must devote their labours to the education of the very few theological students of Ingolstadt, seeing that they are a doubtful quantity, unfitted for sacred studies, and so apathetic as auditors that teaching them is like singing to the deaf. Moreover, to concentrate attention on them would be an injustice to a better class of student, met with in other places, as it would mean depriving such men of good and acceptable professors. The professors of theology in our Order are few and we want to help as many as we can, so we must carefully avoid going against the precept of Wisdom: Where there is no hearing pour not out words. . . .

I have no other purpose in saying this but to convey to you the impossibility of our fulfilling our vows and answering to the needs of your University and country, unless the one thing discussed and decided be the foundation of a college which will give its services to a definite group of theological students, educating them under a definite system of discipline, so that they may hasten in due course as worthy labourers into the harvest-field of Bavaria. As an artist makes ready his material before setting to work, I should like to see discussed before everything else the question of our Fathers having under their roof young men whom, by the goodness of God, they can serve and educate in learning and piety. We have discovered by many years' experience that it is vain to look for progress if we are obliged to deal exclusively with the common run of students, whose lives are so un-restrained and whose pursuit of sacred learning is so little marked by enthusiasm. . . .

My desire, then, is that a college be founded, not only for young men of my Order but for others also, with a view to succouring Bavaria and the neighbouring dioceses in their great need of priests. If I am not mistaken the Sovereign Pontiff looks to this issue and awaits this consummation. It is also the desire of the bishops everywhere, who say openly and frequently that the tithes already collected are for that purpose. As far as I can judge, if we want to see religion in Bavaria safe, here is the best protection that can be afforded. But wise men know all this and have no need of my wordy reminders.

In the second place, I would ask that a church be not forgotten when the boundaries of the college are determined. It is not possible for us to do without one, as I recently explained in detail, for it would be intolerable if our Fathers had always to be sought out, approached and consulted at somebody else's church, especially when they were wanted for priestly duties. We hope in Our Lord that the people of Ingolstadt will come to us as physicians of their souls, and we shall strive with all our might that their advancement in the service of God may not be less with us than elsewhere. This, too, is part of our institute, to devote as much care to the people in church as to the students in school, since it is our conviction that what priests do for the edification of souls, not only by lecturing but by instructing the simple, by administering the Sacraments and by healing with the divine assistance every species of spiritual disease, is a most acceptable sacrifice in the eyes of God. Such services, however, are not conveniently rendered except in a church of one's own, which can afford great comfort to devout souls when easily accessible.

Finally, though I have the fullest confidence, relying on the gracious kindness of our Prince, that once the college is established our men will lack nothing necessary for their daily support, I think it would be well, for the greater glory of God and the lasting security of the foundation, if, like other colleges, it, too, has its regular income from an endowment. Our brethren in Vienna have an annual revenue of 1,200 crowns, with which thirty men are supported, and elsewhere other princes show us a similar munificence. In many places there is an arrangement, with the consent of the Pope, whereby ecclesiastical property is applied to our colleges or, to use the technical expression, incorporated with them. It is for your prudence to consider how much vicissitude and uncertainty hangs in these times over every rank of society. Not without good reason, then, is provision made against such a contingency as the succession of a prince of insufficiently Catholic sympathies, under whom professors of theology might be compelled through sheer need to become a burden to the University, or, as has happened, to migrate elsewhere and abandon the college. I can say for certain that not a penny of the funds will go to our Society, which has neither the power nor the desire to derive private advantage from colleges of this kind. Whatever is given goes only to provide for the needs of the students, and our Father General most loyally sees to it that they are educated free of charge. When their studies are completed the Prince can send them wherever he lists, that they may freely give what they have freely received.

I hope, Gentlemen, that you will take these suggestions in good part, even though written in haste and at greater length than I intended. . . . As for myself, I shall readily subscribe to any better proposals that may be made, and I pray Almighty God ever to advance your Excellencies in His grace, that through you He may restore sound learning and the cultivation of piety to this University.

Your Servant in Christ,

PETER CANISIUS,

Theologian of the Society of Jesus.[1]

This memorial of St. Peter was the signal for a fine spate of such documents. On the ministers answering very courteously that there was not money enough for the construction of an entirely new theological seminary just then, the Saint replied that he would be content either to have the students boarded at the already existing Collegium Georgianum, or else under the Jesuits' own roof. In the latter case he asked that his brethren might have the exclusive use of a garden, that the students might have their own manager for temporal affairs, and that nothing should be expected from the Jesuits in their capacity of guardians except what appertained to the training in piety, behaviour, and learning of their charges. He was not very enthusiastic about this plan, and held to his opinion that a completely new college was the only satisfactory solution. The commissioners, with an eye on the local clergy, also made difficulties about the grant of a church, to which he replied:

<hr />

[1] Braunsberger, *Epistulae*, vol. i, pp. 570-2.

In the first place I could wish that the spirit of our institute was better known, for then it would be seen at once that we are far from desiring to have the pastoral rights of parishes or monasteries. We never take upon ourselves the rôle of parish priests or monks, content as we are with the simplicity of the sacerdotal life according to the requirements of canon law. Much less reason is there for fearing that a church given to us may be prejudicial to the interests of others, since the greatest desire of our hearts is to preserve and increase divine worship in all churches. And I believe that, if a church is built for us, the sermons preached in it will encourage and incite the people to frequent other churches more diligently. When I spoke of administering the Sacraments I meant only two, Confession and Holy Communion, which right, however, we do not desire to have in contravention of the rights of parish priests, who wish the people on certain days to make their offerings, confess their sins, and hear Mass in their own churches. But what objection is there to such people seeking our church also at other times, if they feel so inclined, and, when they are not being taught elsewhere, learning the ways of God from us? Again, when certain priests prove either unable or disinclined to bring comfort to afflicted consciences, why should it not be obtained from our Fathers? But I do not want to argue the point here. Only I feel pity for such men and women as I foresee would acquire much spiritual treasure in our church, as happens in other places where we have colleges, men and women who certainly would not be as ready to go to other churches, especially when it comes to making their confession. We are not hunting after a magnificent temple. All we ask for is a place of spiritual consolation for ourselves and our students, a place where we can pray unmolested for our illustrious Patron, for your Excellencies, and for the whole country, and where both ailing men and hale men may say their Mass without inconvenience.[1]

Peter's next move was to draw up a form of agreement, with blank spaces throughout for the commissioners to complete as they thought best. The piece of ground chosen for the new college adjoined the town brewery. Part of it was to be laid out as a garden, and the Saint took good care in arranging this and other details that there should afterwards be no disputes as to the ownership of the property. Duke Albert contributed 14,000 florins towards the purchase and development of the land, which

[1] Braunsberger, *Epistulae*, vol. i, pp. 574–5.

sum Peter proposed should be entrusted to the architect, Jörgen Stern, to the Chamberlain of the University, and to a third person nominated by the commissioners. The three should set to work at once, so that by April of 1556 the foundations might be laid. A few sections of the document may here be subjoined to illustrate the minute care taken by its writer :

5. As to the form of the building, one entirely new house shall be erected, ... feet long, ... feet wide and .... feet high. In the lower part of this house there shall be a kitchen with .... windows, and a room for the *oeconomus*. There shall be at least .... stoves, one to serve the school, and another the refectory. The number of these stoves in the upper and lower parts of the house shall not be less than ....

6. To this building a church shall be attached, ... feet long, ... feet wide, and .... feet high.

7. Adjoining the college and near the church there shall be a garden, shut off from the neighbouring houses by its own wall.[1]

The insistence on the stoves and garden is typical, for however willing Peter might be to endure privation himself, he would always do his best to protect others from it. Stimulated by his example, the Duke's ministers now submitted a draft agreement in their turn. Peter, in the most courteous manner, at once put it under the microscope and suggested that parts might be more explicit and less open to a double interpretation. Thus, he would like some mention made of chairs, tables, beds, crockery, and other domestic necessaries. If the Jesuits had to provide such things out of their first year's income there would not be much left over for food and fuel. Books, too, were essential, for, though the former Chancellor of Bavaria, Leonhard von Eck, had bequeathed his fine library to him and his brethren, Peter apparently had small hopes of their ever getting possession of it. All these things he wanted put down in black and white, to save trouble later on. He wished, too, that the terms on which the college was endowed should be made more definite by the assignment of the money to specific persons, and that the right of the Society of Jesus to the college and its revenues should be made perfectly clear. Another point criticized was the apparent anxiety of the Duke and his advisers to have as many Jesuits as possible professors at the University. In

---

[1] Braunsberger, *Epistulae*, vol. i, pp. 577–8.

opposition to Polanco who favoured it, Peter had recently protested against this plan in his letters to Rome. Now he urged his point again, that it would be unfair to the professors already in possession and also that his brethren were coming to be taught as well as to teach.

The commissioners certainly seem to have been rather exacting in their demands, for they looked to their guests to run, not only their own house, church and college, but the Collegium Georgianum as well, and to supply preachers for pretty well the whole of Bavaria. St. Peter asked for detailed information as to what was expected, and gave a gentle hint that there were other places besides Bavaria which might like a sermon now and then. Finally, he urged that the architect, a thrifty person who worried him a good deal over sixpences, should hurry on the building operations and that provision should meantime be made for the temporary accommodation of his brethren at the Franciscan monastery, or elsewhere. That was the sum of what he could personally do or suggest, he added, the rest being a matter for settlement between the Duke and St. Ignatius.[1]

The final pact was signed by St. Peter and the commissioners on December 7, 1555. In it were embodied all the Saint's proposals. The Jesuits were to have a theological college with garden and church, and an annual endowment of eight hundred Rhenish florins, together with certain quantities of wheat, rye, and oats. In return for these favours they would provide two professors of theology for the University, open a school for the free education of boys, and also undertake the training of maturer pupils in good morals and knowledge of the Scriptures. As though to make sure that they had left out nothing, the commissioners concluded their contribution to the pact with the following words : " All those in the college will serve His Highness the Prince in matters of religion, wherever and in whatever way they can whenever he so requests them."[2]

The main business of the college finished, St. Peter gave his time and attention to the question of university reform, about which he was well qualified to speak. From old experience he advised that the undergraduates should be compelled to reside in hostels under the supervision of university officers, which would be no great hardship for them and an immense relief to the sorely tried townspeople. As for other disciplinary statutes, " they should not be issued without mature deliberation in order

[1] Braunsberger, *Epistulae*, vol. i, pp. 579–81.
[2] Pachtler, *Ratio Studiorum et Institutiones Scholasticae Societatis Jesu*, vol. i (Berlin, 1887), pp. 345–9.

to avoid prescribing what may not be easy to obtain, as, for instance, regulations about longer gowns, about dancing, public games, fencing, etc. . . . So, too, with regard to several other matters, I would counsel that the rigour of the law be moderated, in the hope of attracting students to us rather than repelling them." Other matters recommended were the inspection of the schools, "*singulis Angariis*,"[1] the restoration of Aristotle to a place of honour in the curriculum, the shortening of vacations, the supervision of the books printed and sold in Ingolstadt, the reduction of the expenses incurred by graduates at their promotion, and measures to secure that all professors were true, practising Catholics. All these suggestions were embodied in the *Reformatio* promulgated by Duke Albert in 1562. Lest it should be thought that they are of mere antiquarian interest as belonging to the history of an institution whose little lamp went out far away in the past, it may be well to say that Ingolstadt University played an even more brilliant part in the later stages of the Counter-Reformation than its fine performance in the early stages of the Reformation and that, far from having vanished in darkness, it still shines bright to-day among its peers under the new name of the University of Munich.

Two letters written by St. Peter while busy with the college negotiations in Ingolstadt give an inkling of his other toils. The first is to the Duke's secretary, Schweicker, resident at the Court in Munich, whom he tells about his pastoral work and his lectures on sacred subjects for the benefit of the students of the Georgianum. "I have a great desire," he says, "to do everything in my power for them during my stay." On Sundays and the frequent feast-days he preaches twice in the Liebfrauenkirche and is planning a series of Catholic books, including a Latin grammar, with prayers for children included, and a kind of simple missal, containing the Epistles and Gospels for Sundays and feasts and the principal collects, hymns, antiphons and other prayers of the Church's liturgy. There were many versions of the New Testament in circulation whose editors often showed more concern for style than for an exact rendering of the sacred writers' thought. Peter devoted a page of his preface to their castigation. "The Church," he says, "has always had her own special eloquence and manner of speech, not a gaudy but a manly one, venerable for its chaste simplicity and decent gravity." It is to this style that he would have the ears of children accustomed, as represented by the despised Vulgate which even in Catholic churches was often thrust aside for the more

---

[1] An interesting old name for what are now called Ember Days.

elegant phraseology of such people as Erasmus. And so he provides his handy edition of the Epistles and Gospels from the Vulgate, each preceded by a clear summary and explanation of the argument. The admirable little book was published at Ingolstadt in 1556 under the title, *Lectiones et precationes Ecclesiasticae in usum scholarum Catholicarum.* For the use of Catholic schools ! There in a phrase was the star of St. Peter's ambition. His letter to Secretary Schweicker bore the date, December 19, which accounts for the following Christmas wishes at its close : " May Almighty God grant us to give our whole hearts to the worthy celebration of Christ Our Lord's Birthday, so that we may share the joy of the angels, be at one with the shepherds in simplicity, with the Magi in faithfulness, and with Mary and Joseph in all purity of life. Happy he to whom Our Lord's Birthday is the occasion for a spiritual rebirth, as it is for glory to God and peace and good-will to His world ! We must be utterly born again, for our blessed Fatherland cannot tolerate the stains of our first nativity. Christ is born to be the Author of the world's rebirth."[1]

The second letter, dated January 17, 1556, has a sadder complexion. It is to Cardinal Truchsess in Rome, telling him of the latest religious troubles of Austria and Bavaria. These were largely the result of the Peace of Augsburg, concluded by King Ferdinand and the Protestant Princes the previous year. That famous pact gave Protestantism legal standing in the Empire, but also made the double-edged principle, *Cujus regio ejus religio*, the law of the land. A Catholic ruler could now invoke its authority to keep his Catholic subjects within the Church's fold or to repress his Protestant subjects, and a Protestant ruler could do the same to achieve the opposite result. According to St. Peter's report to Cardinal Truchsess, large sections of the Austrian and Bavarian nobility had already " begun to pester and plague their princes for the grant of general liberty to embrace the Confession, or rather, Confusion, of Augsburg." Peter had been with King Ferdinand in Augsburg during the time when the fateful Religious Peace was being negotiated, and there can be no doubt that he helped to stiffen the King in his resolve to maintain the famous " Ecclesiastical Reservation " by which bishops and beneficed clergy were required to surrender their titles and emoluments should they abandon the ancient Faith. That was the only clause in the Peace for which Catholics had cause to be thankful. Otherwise, it was merely a victory for territorialism, and an acknowledgment that

<hr />

[1] Braunsberger, *Epistulae*, vol. i, p. 589.

Protestantism had come to stay. The mischief of the Reformation received the sanction of law and was recognised for the first time, not as a passing affliction of the body politic, like a kind of religious cold in the head, but as a permanent condition, bordering, except for a miracle, on the incurable.[1] The Protestant Princes were strong enough to avail themselves of its advantages, but their Catholic peers stood on a different footing, as St. Peter, who naturally considered the Peace a misfortune, explains in the following section of his letter to Cardinal Truchsess:

> Though I have no doubt that the Princes themselves desire to be and to remain Catholics, and that the vexatious importunity of their subjects distresses them greatly, yet are they weakened by fear of damage to temporal possessions, by the injustices of the age, the growth and solid establishment of heresy, the fewness of priests and the small esteem in which they are held on account of the abuses in their lives, the quarrels of monarchs, the successes of their enemies, the apathy of prelates, the events and unhappy results of the last Diet, and the slow progress and long adjournment of the Council of Trent. These and other evils which I pass over increase the cares of the Princes and render them not only anxious but almost desperate in the midst of so much commotion. Meantime the devil joyfully adds fuel to the deplorable conflagrations, daily by the instrumentality of heretics withdrawing more and more sheep from the Fold of Christ, and by the instrumentality of officials who consider themselves Catholics weakening and oppressing ecclesiastical jurisdiction.

The best remedy for these evils of which Peter could think was a meeting of the German bishops to consult with a legate sent by the Pope as to some means of stopping the activities of heretics who held professional posts in nominally Catholic Bavaria and Austria,[2] of securing a supply of zealous priests, of purging schools and libraries of heretical books, of drawing up a plan of reform similar to that which Cardinal Campeggio had composed in 1524 by the Pope's instructions,[3] and, above all, of

[1] The Peace was not even, as it has often been acclaimed, a first step on the road to toleration for no *subject* obtained religious freedom. It was entirely in favour of the Protestant lay Princes, who acquired the right to worship and make their subjects worship according to the Confession of Augsburg. Calvinists and other Nonconformists were excluded from its benefits.

[2] Duke Albert of Bavaria had made the avowed Lutheran, Graf Pankraz von Freyberg, his 'Hof-marschall' in 1553. He acquired such influence with Albert that he was dubbed 'the Duke's other hand' and yet he was not only a Lutheran but an ardent apostle of Lutheranism. Preger, *Pankraz von Freyberg auf Hohenaschau* (Halle, 1893), pp. 14–5.

[3] A great and noble document, containing suggestions for reform to meet all the objections of the famous *Centum gravamina*. Had these suggestions come a few years earlier and been properly carried out there might have been no disruption of Christianity.

settling the thorny problems arising out of the relations between Church and State. All these worries of St. Peter make rather tedious reading, but they must, at least, be referred to, as they formed the permanent background of his life.

At the end of January, 1556, he went to Augsburg for a short time and then on to Vienna to see the King. From Vienna he worked his best to get everything shipshape for the arrival of his brethren in Ingolstadt, and had the satisfaction of seeing St. Ignatius approve his agreement with the Bavarian commissioners. He preached regularly before King Ferdinand and encouraged him to hold out against the anti-Catholic demands of the Austrian nobles. The King filled him with admiration. " I most humbly beg your Paternity," he wrote to St. Ignatius, " to order prayers throughout the Society and Masses to be said by all priests for this Excellent Prince, the founder of the College of Prague. His health and safety are of the utmost importance to religion in Germany." There are more tales of woe in this letter. The Turks had recently ravaged Hungary again, carrying off thousands of Christian captives, while in Austria and Bavaria heresy was making such strides that Peter thinks there will soon be a " *praeclara occasio* " of shedding his blood for the Faith. In Vienna, he says, " the name Jesuit is on everybody's lips and we are pointed at as though we were Hell's own demons come upon the stage."[1] To his friend, Martin Cromer, Secretary to the King of Poland, he writes concerning the deplorable state of affairs in that nominally Catholic country. He encourages Cromer to use his gifted pen in defence of the Church, instead of devoting it to poetry and courtly exercises, and puts heart into him in the following fashion : " In these great storms let us watch for a better wind. Christ sleeps, the ship is shaken and all is considered lost. But He shall neither slumber nor sleep that keepeth Israel. To Him, therefore, let us entrust with perfect confidence ourselves and all the Church's affairs. He hath a care of us. To Him be praise and glory for ever."[2]

On February 20, 1556, Peter returned to Prague to resume charge of the building operations at St. Clement's. What a joy that charge was may be understood from the following report to St. Ignatius, May 17, 1556 :

Two months have gone by since my last letter to your Paternity, at my departure from Vienna. As I did not afterwards write to you, though instructed to write at least once a month, I humbly beg your

---

[1] Braunsberger, *Epistulae*, vol. i, p. 604.   [2] Braunsberger, *Epistulae*, vol. i, p. 608.

Paternity to forgive this grave negligence. . . . Now, to tell you a little
. about the more important events since my return to Prague. I found
here a quantity of debts, contracted over the work of building, and,
despite these, it was very necessary to furnish the house with many
things for the use of the brethren. So far, my efforts have been greatly
obstructed because I find the mandate of King and Viceroy of little
use to me. Personally, they show me every mark of kindness, but
they are quite powerless to secure that we receive the money intended
for this college. Hitherto we have received nothing but fair promises,
not a penny in money for daily food and clothes or for other expenses
in connexion with the building and furnishing of the house. I am,
therefore, being driven to borrow money, to seeking it in various
places, to frequent appeals at Court and to begging from all sorts of people.
May the Lord grant me that patience in which Father Codacio excelled![1]

That, then, was the romance of college-founding in the sixteenth
century, going about with one's cap in one's hand to scrape together enough
for the payment of bricklayers' wages and for the purchase of a dozen
very plain beds, chairs, tables, and other such gear. St. Peter exhausted
himself over the task but, for all he could do, when his brethren arrived,
the furniture was still wanting, and the bricklayers, in the tradition of
their calling, had not nearly finished the house. During Lent, Peter preached
each Sunday before the Viceroy and would have done so more frequently,
he says, but for the many confessions he was called upon to hear. The
Hussites soon learned to dread his sermons, and, as they could not deny
his learning, they spread reports that at heart he was one of themselves
but lacked the courage to make open profession of his allegiance to Hus.[2]
One sermon in particular, preached on Ascension Day before King
Ferdinand who had come again to Prague, caused a mighty commotion.
At the time it seems that a custom had grown up of using the invocation,
"*Christe, ora pro nobis.*" Now, though that formula is capable, under
certain restrictions, of a perfectly orthodox interpretation, it might easily
be applied in a heterodox sense, and for this reason St. Thomas Aquinas
had explicitly rejected it. St. Peter, who was an ardent disciple of St.
Thomas, rejected it also and, according to a Hussite present at his sermon,
"inveighed vigorously against those who so invoke Christ, calling them

[1] Braunsberger, *Epistulae*, vol. i, pp. 612–3. Pedro Codacio was the first of Jesuit 'procurators,'
whose business it is to look after the finances of their Society. St. Peter had known him in Rome
in the early days when he proved, by his patience and acumen, a heaven-sent helper to St. Ignatius.
[2] Braunsberger, *Epistulae*, vol. i, pp. 613–4.

erring and impious people, inasmuch as they divide the two natures of Christ by invoking Him as a mere man, prostrate before His Father, while in fact He reigns equal in power with the Father." The preacher is then reported to have said that this error, condemned in the beginning by the Council of Nicaea, was being newly ventilated "for no other purpose but to discredit the invocation of the saints to whom it really belongs to intercede for us with the Father."[1]

News of the sermon soon reached Melanchthon at Wittenberg and disturbed him enough to show that he did not underrate St. Peter's importance. Writing to Johann Albrecht, Duke of Mecklenburg, June 18, 1556, he said: "I am sending your Highness some pages from which you will see that fresh attacks are being made on us concerning the invocation of the Mediator. The Cynic of Prague, whose name is Canisius, contends with much heat that the Son of God is not to be invoked as Mediator, whereas Cyprian cries: 'I beseech Thee, O Son of God, that Thou wouldst beseech the Father on my behalf.' With regard to this controversy I am about to publish, under the invocation of the Son of God, a refutation of the Cynic's folly."[2] Melanchthon's foe, Flacius Illyricus, applauded his action for once in a way, and himself joined in the merry game of slandering and vilifying St. Peter. Not for many a day would he be allowed to forget that sermon. What angered the other side was his clear perception and exposure of the artifice by which they thought to destroy the practice of invoking the saints, for they must have known perfectly well that neither St. Peter nor any Catholic ever dreamt of denying the mediatorial office of Our Lord.[3]

During Lent and again at the end of May Peter made the arduous, three days' journey to remote Oybin in order to inspect the monastery from which his new college was to derive its revenues. The place had been ravaged by Zizka in the Hussite wars and only one Celestine monk remained, by all accounts a rather testy old gentleman. It was an extensive block of buildings, half monastery and half fortress, beautifully situated on a mountain side in the midst of a forest. "No place better

---

[1] Braunsberger, *Epistulae*, vol. i, p. 768.

[2] *Melanchthonis Epistolae* (Halle, 1874), p. 393. The quotation from St. Cyprian is now known to be spurious.

[3] In a large treatise published later on St. Peter states: "Than Christ we recognize no other common Mediator and Intercessor for all mankind. He alone has merited, He alone could ever have merited, to bring about the complete reconciliation of men with God. It is through Him that all the gifts of God have come to us or rather, come to us continuously, and He intercedes, not by certain words or prayers as do human intercessors, but factually and by His very existence. Through Him all the gifts of the Eternal Father to the petitioning of both men and angels must be both sought and received. The saints, on the other hand, are, so to speak, constituted mediators by the Church with this same Mediator." *De Beata Maria Virgine incomparabili* (Ingolstadt, 1577), pp. 659–60.

suited for a life of solitude and expiation could well be desired," Peter
informed St. Ignatius, "especially in winter when the cold is extreme
and the whole locality terrifying and unapproachable." By the instructions
of King Ferdinand, he brought back with him from his first visit a variety
of articles for the church and house in Prague and also a quantity of books
to start a library. That was not plunder because the monastery in its
deserted state belonged, like other private property, to the King. On
his second visit he was accompanied by three royal commissioners who
directed him in making a survey of the monastic lands and an inventory
of all the farms, live-stock, ponds, woods, house-furniture, and other
possessions. As the place was too far from Prague for his brethren to
give it due attention, he came to an arrangement with the commissioners
by which the entire property was to be farmed out to the mayor and
corporation of the neighbouring town of Zittau, the lessees undertaking
to collect rents, till the land, see to repairs, and to pay to the Prague college
annually the sum of 1,400 thalers. Out of this money the Jesuits, on
their side, must find and support two or three secular priests to look after
the spiritual needs of the dependent villages, as well as a dozen or so
retainers for domestic work. This agreement was about the worst mistake
that St. Peter made in the course of his life. He took it too easily for
granted that his Zittau tenants, nearly all of them Lutherans, were honourable men. In reality they were a collection of thieves, and Oybin became
for Peter and his brethren their heaviest cross, or rather a millstone round
their necks. All the subsequent years are saddened and maddened by the
purgatory of a place in which nothing ever seemed to go right. The two
priests whom Peter found installed there had to be relieved of their charge,
as they had taken wives and were administering the Sacraments in the Lutheran fashion. Try as he might he could not get other more dependable ones
to replace them, and so was forced to the conclusion that one or two of
his brethren would have to be withdrawn from the college for the task.[1]

Before leaving Rome, the twelve Jesuits destined for Prague had
heard that there was a great dearth of books in Bohemia, especially of
Hebrew books, so they determined to carry a library on their backs. By
dint of begging from friends they secured a large assortment of books,
which they placed in sacks and carefully sewed up. As they were on the
point of setting off with the precious sacks over their shoulders, they
were informed that St. Ignatius, who was ill in bed, wished to say a final
word to them. Ignatius knew all that had been done about the books

[1] Braunsberger, *Epistulae*, vol. i, pp. 614–6, 625–30.

and, according to an old historian of the Bohemian Jesuit Province, he looked sadly at the sacks and turned to the leader of the twelve, Father Ursmar Goisson, with the following words : " Father Ursmar, what possessed you to accumulate such a *farrago* of books ? O thou of little faith, why hast thou doubted ? I do not like this excessive anxiety of yours, as though God was in Rome alone and not also in Prague to provide you with books. It is He who is sending you there and He will not see you in need of books or anything else. Plain common sense should have told you that it was not advisable to load yourselves with such burdens when setting out on so long a journey. If, when you reach Prague, you cannot obtain any particular books, order them in Vienna and they will be sent to you. I shall not fail to mention the matter to King Ferdinand. Come, then! There is no need for you to take a single book from here, except Gerson's *Imitation of Christ*, which, unlike those sacks of yours, will ease all the troubles of your journey."[1]

Goodness knows they needed comfort, for their journey, especially in its final stages through Moravia, was a terrible experience. None of them knew a word of Czech and, as they had unwisely gone clothed like Italian priests, the anti-Catholic population mocked and ill-treated them at every turn. The inns to which they were obliged to resort proved, as they afterwards reported, not places of rest and refreshment after their weary marching, but " *curricula patientiae*." Considering it a good joke, the Lutheran landlords used to put rich dishes in front of the famished men and pile their plates with meat, it being Lent, when meat was forbidden every day, including Sunday. Only with the greatest difficulty could they obtain anything else, and they were invariably outrageously overcharged.[2] Father Goisson, the leader of the expedition and a devout and simple soul, has much to say on the subject. But there is comedy as well as tragedy in the story. At Polna, a Catholic town, the twelve travellers—one Belgian, five Dutchmen, two Germans, two Italians, one Austrian, and one Swiss—found a kindly pastor, " also called a Rural Dean," who was good to them. When the priests of the company had said Mass, which they had not been allowed to do in other places, the whole congregation came to the inn where they were staying. " Men, women, and grave matrons saluted us, bowing with the greatest reverence," says Goisson. After the ceremony, which passed off in absolute silence, the rural dean stayed on to dinner with them at the inn. " While we

[1] Schmidl, *Historiae Societatis Jesu Provinciae Bohemiae pars prima* (Prague, 1747), lib. i, p. 87.
[2] Orlandinus, *Historia Societatis Jesu* (Cologne, 1615), lib. xvi, n. 19.

were at table," Goisson continues, " the trumpeter of the town suddenly arrived and played on his trumpet for a quarter of an hour outside our room. He had done the same thing as we first entered the town. I did not guess that it was for our benefit until it happened again in the next town on our route. Here singers welcomed us with what are called musical motets of Paschal time. Among other things they sang was that Alleluia which Master Peter Schorich used to sing sometimes for your Paternity. All these folk, however, communicate under both species and without previous confession. They observe very exactly many ceremonies of the Catholic Church, as they do also in Prague. But the singers and trumpeters were after nothing else but *Dringhelt*,[1] as we were told. When I had made certain of this and that we were the objects of those uninvited and unwanted attentions, I took care afterwards to warn our hosts not to admit such people. This the trumpeters and singers resented very much indeed and abused us roundly, saying that it was the custom of the country to act so when noblemen and others of account arrived, and that, in spite of our being Jesuits, they had held us for gentlemen and shown us reverence." Next, good Father Ursmar tells of their arrival at their destination. " As we entered Prague we screened the sides of the coach with our cloaks, so that we might not be too plainly recognized. But in passing through certain streets we were held up, once by an iron chain drawn across the road, and another time by baulks of timber, whereupon there ensued a rush for us, and men and boys, women and girls, came prying and searching to find out what was inside the coach, whether men or wild beasts, such as stags and boars. And so, unperturbed, we arrived joyfully at St. Clement's. May the Lord Jesus be blessed. Amen. We were welcomed with great joy by the charity of Rev. Father Canisius."[2]

King Ferdinand had given instructions that the Jesuits, before leaving Rome, were to be provided with ample funds for their journey. That was the theory, but the fact was that the travellers had to borrow 110 ducats from Roman friends and might not have been able to start at all if the Pope's vicar had not generously presented them with a pack-horse to carry some of their baggage. Ferdinand meant well, but his large family and the Turks at his door made havoc of his finances. The treasury officials, tearing their hair to make ends meet, could hardly have been expected to appreciate the importance of such things as schools, without which Austria and Bohemia had often before rubbed along well enough,

---

[1] Modern German, *Trinkgeld*, meaning literally a *pourboire*, or, inexpressively in English, a tip.
[2] M.H., *Litterae Quadrimestres*, vol. iv, pp. 328–9.

and so St. Peter and his college took a very secondary place in their considerations. He could not even get sufficient money to buy beds for his brethren, and relates that their clothes were in such tatters after their long journey that " for many days none of them could leave the house for lack of something to wear." They had ordered new suits when passing through Vienna, but Fr. Delanoy, himself poor as a church mouse, had commandeered them for his own ragged flock. It appears from Goisson's letter that the Dominicans had not yet left St. Clement's. " Up to the present," he says, " our cells have been in the dormitory with the friars and some laymen. So we have had to put up with being in a crowd all the time, dining in the same place as the rest and using the same kitchen, which was a very heavy bondage. We hope in the Lord that these troubles, too, will have an end, though we see little or no sign of the friars departing. I must not omit to say that we have received some alms from our friends —three vessels of beer, some wine, six hens, and a big piece of a salmon, from all of which it looks as if we were not despised by everybody." When they had acquired some clothes, the new arrivals repaired to Court to present King Ferdinand with the gift they had brought him all the way from Italy, a rosary. His Majesty, being a kind-hearted man, kept his face and received the trifle as gratefully and graciously as if each bead had been a ruby. Many an expedition to the North or South Pole has had less real, honest privation and discomfort to endure than these men had, and yet, writes St. Peter, " in spite of all our troubles we are full of joy in the Lord nothing doubting as to the providence and goodness of God."[1]

They had high hopes for their school, as a good number of parents had written to them, sometimes from very remote places, offering their sons. In his instructions for the College, which now being in existence deserves the honour of a capital initial, St. Ignatius said that they were to accept " all sorts " but that little boys might have to be excluded for the moment, as there were no masters with a knowledge of Czech to teach them. Both St. Peter and Fr. Goisson seem to have misinterpreted the instructions as though their General intended small boys to be excluded altogether. Now, small boys were the very ones that Peter, at least, was most anxious to provide for. They gave him, as he informed St. Ignatius, far better hopes for the future than older fellows, already set in their habits and full of miscellaneous ignorance. All was then soon cleared up to the satisfaction of both men.[2]

[1] M.H., *Litterae Quadrimestres*, vol. iv, pp. 330–1 ; Braunsberger, *Epistulae*, vol. i, p. 617.
[2] *Cartas de San Ignacio*, vol. vi, pp. 137–55 ; Braunsberger, *Epistulae*, vol. i, pp. 617–8.

Peter and his brethren had to walk very warily, as the Hussites looked at them askance, and the decrepit University, thinking it smelt a rival, was plainly keen on making trouble. The sort of thing they had to put up with is indicated in the following passage from Peter's pen: " I believe others will have told your Reverence that a week ago last Sunday while I was saying Mass at the High Altar a big stone came to greet me through the window." Another Father was assaulted while saying Mass on the Feast of the Ascension and might have suffered violence but for the timely intervention of a lay brother.[1] Despite such evidence of hostility and the general uncertainty of tempers which made even King Ferdinand doubt whether the new school could possibly succeed, Scribonius, the brave and zealous Administrator of the diocese, ordered all the Catholic preachers subject to him to announce the opening of the College from the pulpit in the following terms: " On Wednesday next, July 8th, the Fathers of the Society of Jesus, recently summoned hither from Italy to undertake the godly education of youth, . . . will open the school made ready for that purpose, and inaugurate their lectures publicly and solemnly. All persons, without respect to nationality, age, or condition, may freely attend the lectures of this College, or Royal and Catholic School, there to be educated and trained without charge, to participate in scholastic disputations and exercises and to be taught all the varieties of arts, letters and languages of the curriculum."[2]

As the new College was an institution such as neither Prague nor any other part of Bohemia had known since the days of Zizka, even the Hussites showed a certain readiness to give it a trial. The inauguration ceremony took place at the Cathedral, where a solemn High Mass was sung and three young Jesuits pronounced resounding Latin orations before a very distinguished company. The orators had been so carefully drilled by St. Peter that, instead of breaking down as he feared, they swept the people off their feet and ensured that whatever else the College might lack it would not be pupils. Before a month was out there were more than a hundred boys on the roll, ranging from " the youngest scholars just beginning their Donatus " to students almost of university age. All promised extremely well, then, except on the financial front, where things were as bleak as ever. At his departure for the Diet of Regensburg King Ferdinand earnestly exhorted St. Peter to exercise rigid economy in the use of money. That must have amused the Saint in private because he had no money whatever to use. " Our creditors are giving us no peace,"

[1] Braunsberger, *Epistulae*, vol. i, pp. 617-9.   [2] Pachtler, *Ratio Studiorum*, vol. i, p. 150.

he confided to St. Ignatius, and things became so bad for him shortly afterwards that his great champion, Scribonius, indignantly asked the royal treasurers: " Do you think that these Fathers were summoned hither by His Majesty to starve to death?"[1] Father Goisson reported to Ignatius that they owed a thousand thalers to the workmen engaged on their house, and so far had received a bare two hundred from the authorities for all purposes. " Where the thousand is to come from is a mystery. Still, we hope in the Lord, *quoniam ipse faciet.*"[2]

Meantime a new responsibility had fallen on St. Peter's shoulders. In view of the progress and expectations of the Society of Jesus in Austria, Bohemia, Bavaria, and Tirol, whose capital, Innsbruck, was soon to have a college of its own, St. Ignatius decided to constitute an " Upper German " province of the Order and, on June 7, 1556, made out a diploma appointing Peter the first Provincial Superior.[3] This document reached him in Prague about the middle of July and caused him such acute distress that he immediately wrote imploring the General to spare one by nature so proud, unbalanced, and wanting in judgment the perils of such a charge. He had no gifts for the government of others nor any experience of such delicate work, and, besides, there were men, whose names he mentioned, far better suited for the post. " Finally, Father," he said, " I thought that I should ask all my brethren here to put their opinions of me in writing and send them to you. Ah, if you only knew my hidden and open vices and how much this Germany has dulled and secularized me, you would rather pity me and be moved the more to help me with your prayers, which, though all unworthy, I most earnestly desire."[4]

A month before he had any idea of what was in store for him, Peter had made a similar confession to Ignatius in a very long letter mainly occupied with the difficulties of the property at Oybin: " I recollect that all the letters I sent to your Reverence this year have gone without an answer, except the one from Ingolstadt in January. My sins, I believe, are the obstacle to my enjoying your letters and counsels. In my dealings with the fearsome people here[5] I think I am guided too much by my own judgment, but my trust is in the merits, Masses, and prayers of your Reverence and the other brothers so dear to me. Great, indeed, is his need of such assistance who would enter into the presence of God and then go forth to deal with men such as the Germans and Czechs. I often

---

[1] Braunsberger, *Epistulae*, vol. i, p. 622.
[2] M.H., *Litterae Quadrimestres*, vol. iv, p. 331.
[3] Braunsberger, *Epistulae*, vol. i, pp. 622–3.
[4] Sacchinus, *Vita P. Petri Canisii*, pp. 109–10.
[5] *Terribilibus hisce hominibus.*

think that what I need is a censor like Anthony Rion.[1] If he were here, he would have many a chance to crush my pride and make me act more wisely than I usually do. May the Lord give me grace to reform inwardly and outwardly and to live in exact accordance with the spirit of the Society."[2]

The letters which Peter had begged the Prague Fathers to write to Rome in criticism of his shortcomings, were not much use. Here is one from a good man named Van den Bossche, who, excusably perhaps, preferred the more melodious title of Father Sylvius:

Prague, July 13, 1556.

Jhs + Maria

Blessed be God, the Father of Our Lord Jesus Christ, who hath blessed us with all spiritual blessings in Heavenly places, in Christ. Amen. Reverend Father Ignatius, Some time ago obedience imposed upon me the task of giving you a little information about our Father Peter Canisius, as to his general behaviour in all matters great and small, and I thought it would be wrong to neglect to do so. Well, the fact of the matter is, Reverend Father, that I could not describe or celebrate worthily enough the esteem in which he is held by all good and sincerely Catholic men in these parts, no, not if I used every word in my vocabulary nor if I had a hundred tongues and a hundred mouths. Not in Araby nor Egypt nor in any kingdom of the world could his match be found. He might well be called a John the Baptist who went before to prepare the way of the Lord among the Germans and Bohemians. As everybody knows, he is beautiful with all piety and happy in the possession of every form of virtue. He is the pride and ornament of all Germany. Day and night he sweats and toils unsparingly to propagate and promote true religion. What a dreaded hammer he is of Holy Church's wicked enemies is past all telling. So filled is this great man with the love of God that all people reverence, seek, and love him. In this City of Prague he blooms like a flower of the field, shining in beauty. It was he who founded, built, and inaugurated our College, giving it such credit and reputation that in quite an extraordinary way people know not what to say in sheer admiration. This, Reverend Father, is what I had to report about our Father Canisius, but far greater things might be said and certain particulars set down which for lack of time I must pass over.[3]

---

[1] Rion was a shrewd lay brother whom St. Ignatius used to employ as an admonitor. He must have been a highly objectionable person.
[2] Braunsberger, *Epistulae*, vol. i, pp. 632-3.
[3] MH., *Epistolae Mixtae*, vol. v (Madrid, 1901), pp. 371-3.

During St. Peter's first period in Rome he had taken a private vow
" never to express a wish to go from one place to another except at the
plain command of his superiors." This, to his extremely sensitive conscience, was an additional reason for shunning the office of Provincial,
but St. Ignatius set his mind at rest " bidding him, in reliance on the
goodness of God, to bow his neck to the yoke, as he was already in
practice Provincial and now merely acquired the title, which would bring
with it an increase of authority and special divine assistance."[1] The office
of provincial superior in a religious order is hardly an enviable one at
the best of times, for no man with a conscience could lightly assume the
responsibility of directing and governing his fellow-men in the profoundest relationships of their lives. But a provincial in an old established
order is, at any rate, the inheritor of a long tradition. He knows exactly
the lines on which to proceed and, as a rule, need not worry overmuch
as to how his men shall find their next day's dinner. With the Jesuits
of the sixteenth century and, more especially, the Jesuits of northern
Europe, the situation was very different.

In those days, [says the historian Sacchinus, who himself belonged
to them], the office of Provincial was not as cut and dried and happy
as inexperienced people might be inclined to imagine. For, though
the first love and enthusiasm of the Society of Jesus still burned brightly,
and though the Order had the patronage of princely benevolence, still,
as is the way in all beginnings, nothing was ready and complete, no
houses, churches, nor furnishings. All these things, and daily bread
itself, depended, not on secure sources of revenue but on the voluntary
gifts of princes, which, having to pass through the hands of many
administrators, were in the nature of day-to-day alms. But, indeed,
there were far worse difficulties than that one, arising out of the very
small and inadequate number of workers as compared with the many
employments and heavy business with which they were burdened.
Besides, most of these brethren were only beginners in the religious
life, for whom there existed practically no provision in the way of
noviceship. Nearly all were strangers to Germany and stood in sore
need, not only of consolation and direction, but also of a certain divine
charity and prudence on the part of their superior. They had still to
learn the ways of religious discipline, because the rules of the Society
were little known and had not yet been explained nor officially

---

[1] Sacchinus, *Vita P. Petri Canisii*, p. 111.

promulgated. Finally, the Society itself was hardly known at all, except to the heretics who hated it. Such was the state of the Province which Canisius had built up and which he was now called upon to govern.[1]

For a while after his appointment, St. Peter's chief concern continued to be the colleges in Prague and Ingolstadt. The Prague one, notwith-standing its excellent quiverful of the arguments that make a man strong against his enemy in the gate, had to battle its way through a long period of opposition and persecution. Some of the Fathers resided in temporary lodgings on the other side of the Moldau in Little Prague, while their quarters at St. Clement's were being made ready, and consequently had to cross the Karlsbrücke at least twice daily on their way to and from school. Soon after the opening of the College these men received warning from the Governor of the Castle that certain Lutherans were plotting to waylay them on the bridge and send them to Heaven by the same watery route as St. John Nepomucene had gone. " We live in expectation of martyrdom," wrote one of them, " and as we go down to the schools feel it likely that we shall never return home, but to our Heavenly home. *Ecce in Aquilone, India!* "[2] Even the Hussites, who were not inclined to violence and some of whose boys were at the College, often made life a weariness for the Fathers. They had to keep indoors and very quiet on July 6th, when the whole country celebrated the feast of " St. John Hus." This was not so much a religious celebration as a nationalist one, something like July 12th in Belfast. Hussitism had become, in fact, not so much a form of religion as a profession of nationalism, with Com-munion under both species as its rallying tenet. That the Jesuits were foreigners sufficed to make them anathema, but another disability, too, worked against their acceptance. The Czechs, who have always been great lovers of colour, ceremony, and song, scorned the sober black gowns of the newcomers, and said that they were " a disgrace to the priesthood and to the Christian religion " because they did not chant the Divine Office or celebrate High Masses.[3] For the amusement of people who understood Latin some wag of the City circulated a punning hexameter line on the names Hus, meaning in Czech, a gander, and Canisius, the allusion being to the famous old story of the Gauls' night attack on Rome when the dogs remained asleep but a flock of geese gave the alarm :

Hinc procul esto Canis : *pro nobis excubat* Anser.

[1] *Vita P. Petri Canisii* (Ingolstadt, 1616), pp. 111-2.
[2] M.H., *Litterae Quadrimestres*, vol. iv, p. 433.
[3] M.H., *Litterae Quadrimestres*, vol. iv, p. 410.

It is a sufficiently ridiculous line, but some old Jesuit writers took it seriously, one of them replying with a hexameter of his own:

At qui Canem odere haud oves sunt sed lupi.

Even Sacchinus went out of his way to show that the punster had played into the hands of the Catholics by failing to remember the distinction between a gander and a dog: "A gander is an unpleasant object by reason of its strident gaggling and its notorious dirtiness, whereas a dog has the merit of fidelity and vigilance."[1]

St. Peter himself took no notice of the incident and, indeed, it cannot have implied very much ill-feeling, to judge by another report of that worthy Father Sylvius who was quoted above. "It is marvellous," he informed St. Ignatius, "how much our Father Provincial Canisius is venerated in these northern regions. Not only the Catholics but also Hussites and other heretics and even the Jews are in love with him."[2] Similar was the testimony of the Rector of the College, Father Goisson, also given to St. Ignatius: "It is impossible to describe or even to estimate fully the pleasantness of Father Provincial's conversation and his gift for being all things to all men. His eloquence and learning joined with his prudence and charm of manner seem to me just the qualities for Germany. If there were many German preachers like him in the Society they would give the Lutherans something to think about. He is greatly beloved in Prague, especially by the Archduke and other illustrious gentlemen."[3] At this time the Archduke, true Christian and gallant soldier, set out for the wars in Hungary, wearing on his heart an *Agnus Dei* given him by St. Peter. At Peter's suggestion he had revived by decree throughout Bohemia the old custom of ringing the church bells at midday as a signal to the faithful to pray for the Christian army fighting the Turks. In addition, the Saint had secured official orders for processions and a Mass *de Sancta Cruce* to be sung in every Catholic Church of the land for a Christian victory.[4]

Meantime the College settled into its stride under Peter's inspiration. There were daily lectures on Scripture, Hebrew, and dialectics, while in the lower classes Latin and Greek were taught with great enthusiasm. Outside school hours the Jesuits went the round of the hospitals, and in their spare moments, after the midday meal, studied the excruciatingly difficult Czech language, which John Hus had further complicated by the invention of

---

[1] *Vita P. Petri Canisii*, pp. 107–8.
[2] M.H., *Litterae Quadrimestres*, vol. iv, p. 432.
[3] M.H., *Litterae Quadrimestres*, vol. iv, pp. 406–7.
[4] M.H., *Litterae Quadrimestres*, vol. iv, p. 431.

mischievous little wedges, circles, and strokes in order to simplify it.[1] How busy they all were may be guessed from the Rector's words to St. Ignatius: "It would be a good thing for me if each day had the length of two."

The very last of the thousands of letters which St. Ignatius wrote or dictated during the course of his life was addressed to St. Peter on July 22, 1556, in connexion with the College of Prague. The letter concluded with an ardent wish for news of the other incipient college at Ingolstadt, which institution came to be known among the Jesuits as their holy Founder's 'Benjamin,' the child of his old age, towards which his dying thoughts were turned. News of his death on July 31st reached St. Peter in Ingolstadt itself, whither he had repaired as soon as the Prague College was functioning normally. Writing to Laynez, the Vicar-General of the Society of Jesus until a successor to St. Ignatius had been elected, he said:

The account of the life and death of that blessed man, our Father Ignatius, sent by your Paternity was long in reaching us and yet reached us all too soon. This news has stricken many hearts and weighed them down with sorrow that they may no more look upon the face of such and so great a Father, from whom they had received the first fruits of the spirit. But I think we ought to be glad for his sake and that congratulations are his due on his happy, happy return to home and fatherland. He so lived that his death could not have been a sad thing, and so died that he has filled us all with longing for life in his company, instead of the daily dying we know. If, while on earth, he had the power and gift to govern and protect his sons, to adorn their souls, and spread them over the face of the earth, as he certainly had in a wonderful degree, we ought not to doubt but that he will have care of us and of our interests in Heaven, all the more surely for the greater love and other gifts and fruits of the Spirit with which he superabounds in that land of immortality. Would to God that I could be accounted a worthy son of such a Father, or that, by his intercession, I might win in Christ Our Lord were it only a shadow of his perfect spirit. . . .[2]

On July 10th five Jesuit priests and thirteen scholastics arrived in Ingolstadt from Rome, after being nearly a month on the road. Owing

[1] St. Peter, whom difficulties rarely defeated, resigned himself to ignorance of Czech. He could make neither head nor tail of it. A recent English traveller in Bohemia whose profession is the teaching of foreign languages, relates that, despairing of Czech, he and his companion were obliged to resort to such devices as ordering things regularly in fives because five in Czech [pet] is the only numeral that a non-Bohemian dare risk pronouncing without peril of strangulation. "Two each and toss for the odd" was the rule they made for themselves.

[2] Braunsberger, *Epistulae*, vol. ii, pp. 22–3.

to the usual mismanagement of lay officials they found everything in confusion and disarray at the house assigned to them for a home, no provision having been made even for cooking a dinner. They muddled along as best they could, however, until St. Peter was able to come to their rescue. Then, says a contemporary *Relatio*, "everything that at the beginning seemed difficult was rendered pleasant and easy, owing to his work and counsel and his ability in the management of affairs under the sweet guidance of God."[1] Though the long vacation had begun when they arrived, they started classes in Hebrew and other subjects for any students who cared to attend, and the priests gave themselves up to preaching and other ministerial functions in the town and its neighbourhood. St. Peter took infinite trouble, in the teeth of much opposition both Catholic and heretical, to put the College on a sure basis, not merely for the contentment of his brethren but for the general good of the University and Bavaria. His influence with the Curator of the University, Wiguleus Hundt, was very great, and he used it to the full, especially in the interests of sacerdotal education. Hundt empowered him to deal directly with the University Executive, in order to secure the complete restoration of the theological faculty, so long a byword for slovenly incompetence. The number of lectures was to be greatly increased and far more ground covered, now that competent professors were at last available. The Georgianum, whose neglected function it was to supply good priests for Bavaria, was placed immediately under the direction of the Jesuits in all matters of spiritual and disciplinary concern. That part of his work was completely successful, but St. Peter found it difficult to get his boys' school under way. The professors of classics and such subjects at the University strongly opposed him, fearing that the new institution might swallow up their scholars; and the parish priests also cried alarm, fearing for their parochial schools, though these were not schools at all in the ordinary sense but only rendezvous for choir practices. The Jesuits, they complained, would not teach their boys to sing, and then what was to become of the Divine Liturgy? Practical difficulties, too, stood in Peter's path, as no separate house had been set aside for a boys' school, and he feared that if the ' *abecedarii*,' or little fellows, and the more grown pupils under university age, who were known as " Bacchantes," were permitted to enter by the same door as the undergraduates, the latter would feel themselves insulted and probably boycott the Jesuits altogether. It was no easy matter arranging all these bits of the puzzle,

[1] Braunsberger, *Epistulae*, vol. i, pp. 721–4.

and Peter had besides to find such things as stoves and beds for his house, that duty having been neglected by those to whom it had been entrusted. Promised funds never materialized, and when the Saint ventured a reminder there followed what Agricola, the Bursar of the University, described as " much snorting."[1]

Duke Albert wrote a cheerful letter to St. Peter on August 20th, promising help and patronage and expressing great hopes for the new College. There the help and patronage largely ended, for that was the way of princes. In his acknowledgement to the Duke's Secretary, St. Peter said :

> You would be astonished were you present here to see how wretchedly we are treated and how little has been made ready for our accommodation. Up to now the new professors have not been able to procure the necessary clothes for them to appear in public. I shall not fail the hopes that the Prince and the Curator of the University have conceived of me. In fitting out the College there will be no extravagance, and the library project will be postponed for the present. Only please let us not lack clothes, beds, and other necessaries of daily life for ourselves and our many dependents. . . . The Bursar complains that he has not the wherewithal to pay us our promised revenue, but if he does not relieve our daily need I shall follow the advice of the Rector of the University and start borrowing.[2]

Apparently, the Franciscans, who had a large monastery in Ingolstadt, were obliged by the wretched Bursar to supply the Jesuits with bread and beer. St. Peter protested against that unfair toll and had it removed, but he was willing to accept some of the firewood with which the Friars' garden was plentifully stocked. Long after the boys' school had begun its operations, when the Jesuits were established preachers and professors in Ingolstadt, they continued in their state of dire poverty and dependence. After a whole year of planning and pleading, St. Peter again addressed the Duke's Secretary, the one man he trusted, in the following strain :

> I commend to your charity the poor of Christ, my brethren here, on whose behalf I wrote a short time ago to our patron, Dr. Hundt. But I have received no reply. The physicians are afraid, and the situation itself sufficiently indicates that our men, particularly the masters and professors, will not be able to carry on with so much study and work

[1] " *In re tam ardua tantum stertere.*" Braunsberger, *Epistulae*, vol. ii, pp. 4–8, 9, 12–3.
[2] Braunsberger, *Epistulae*, vol. ii. pp. 14–5, 17.

if, through poverty, they cannot taste wine even once a week. Should they afterwards become ill, as some of them are already, expenses will be doubled providing medicines, the students will lose their professors, and I know not what other inconveniences will follow. I leave it to your prudence, then, whether, as the Bursar[1] and others judge, it is not expedient to provide the Fathers with sufficient means to procure some wine for the refreshment of nature. Indeed, it seems not only a useful expense but a necessary one. Many of the Fathers who never before drank beer have now nothing else provided, while round about there are such multitudes who do not require it, drinking themselves to death on wine. I think it will be easy enough to come to some arrangement without making calls on the Prince's purse. All I ask is that my hint may be conveyed to our Patron, Dr. Hundt, without waiting for a complaint from the Fathers. They have known hitherto how to suffer poverty and to bear all privation gladly, rather than cause trouble to their Prince and Maecenas.[2]

It will be remembered that St. Peter had put a garden in the front of his plans for the new College. The authorities promised it with their usual readiness, but nearly two years passed, years of tireless urging and pleading on the Saint's part, before, through the good offices of the faithful Schweicker, he secured his prize. On April 23, 1558, Schweicker wrote to him from Munich : " The day before yesterday I forwarded six hundred gold crowns as the purchase price of the garden for your College. . . . There is nothing I more earnestly desire than to be, whenever possible, the instrument of divine grace in the full service of God's servants."

For many a year to come the colleges at Vienna, Prague, and Ingolstadt were to be the torment and joy of St. Peter's life. He watched with loving care over every step of their progress, and intervened at the least threat of internal friction or when outside causes affected the smooth working of the scholastic machinery. No detail was too trivial for his notice if it bore on the reasonable comfort of his men or the efficiency of the schools. And thus it was that institutions of such insignificant origin and of such troubled beginnings grew with the passage of the years into powerful forces for the regeneration of Catholic Germany. Ingolstadt soon regained its former fame as a great centre of intellectual

---

[1] Agricola was a famous professor of medicine.

[2] Braunsberger, *Epistulae*, vol. ii, pp. 120–1. The beer supplied to the Jesuits was of the kind known to the workmen on a certain Devonshire estate as " Just right." One of them, being asked to explain the title, said : " It's this way. If it were any better we wouldn't get it, and if it were any worse we couldn't drink it. So it's just right."

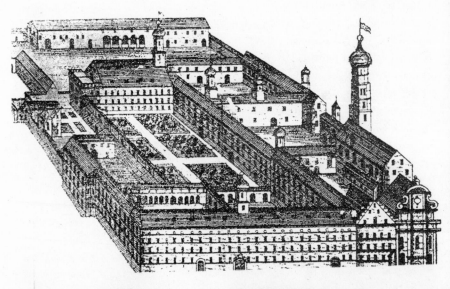

The old Jesuit College of Ingoldstadt established by St. Peter Canisius
and, below, the modern Canisius College, Nymegen

life, made illustrious by the teaching of such men as Gregory of Valencia and James Gretser. From the presses of the town, as in the brave old times of Eck, huge, learned tomes of polemics, history, and theology began to pour, including the best known books of that kind ever published anywhere, the *Controversies* of St. Robert Bellarmine.[1] Catholic theology, which Lejay had mourned as dead and buried, arose from the tomb in more comely robes than she had worn since St. Thomas finished the *Summa*, and a new race of priests and laymen, born of St. Peter's College, girded themselves for the regeneration of South Germany. The colleges in Vienna and Prague had equally glorious histories ahead and contributed in generous measure to the restoration and final stabilization of Catholicism in the lands to which they belonged. Details of the establishment of those three colleges have been given to show in some very small way the labour and long-suffering that such work demanded. Their success was a triumph of patience and holy hope, and the soul of it all was the gentle, humble, infinitely painstaking Peter Canisius.

It will not be necessary to describe so fully the beginnings of the other colleges which he set on foot. They were similar to those we know, matters of tedious negotiation, bargaining, eventual hard-won agreement and then, when the Jesuits arrived, the usual trouble to get the other party to stand by their promises. As soon as the colleges of Prague and Ingolstadt were more or less on their feet, St. Peter directed his attention to the needs of Bavaria's capital and seat of government, Munich. He loved the beauty of the city, and esteemed that his brethren's labours " would bring to Christ a rich return from that harvest-field " in which so many flowers of dream and illusion waved their heads.[2] Duke Albert's first idea was to obtain papal sanction for the transfer to the Jesuits of the Augustinian monastery of the City, in which only a few aged friars remained. This favourite plan of princes for an easy solution of the housing problem gave St. Peter acute anxiety, as it had done already in Vienna, Prague, and Ingolstadt. He appealed to Councillor Hundt to insist on the courtesies of the matter by making no move till, not only papal approval, but the full and free consent of the friars had been obtained. " We are very much afraid," he wrote, " lest we get a bad name with many people, and in Rome, too, as though we seemed to want to occupy a part or the whole of the monastery without the consent of the General of the Order. From the terms of its first foundation that monastery is the property

---

[1] The first edition of the *Controversies* appeared in Ingolstadt from the press of David Sartorius in 1586 (vol. i), 1588 (vol. ii), and 1593 (vol. iii), all during the lifetime of St. Peter Canisius.

[2] Braunsberger, *Epistulae*, vol. ii, p. 111.

of the Augustinians. . . . We are anxious, then, that when arrangements are being made for our place of residence you would leave no loophole for such hostile suspicions."[1]

In their casual and inconsiderate way the advisers of Albert suggested that if a few Jesuits, perhaps half a dozen, were billeted on the Augustinians a great deal of expense and trouble might be saved. Why should not the new arrivals club with the three remaining friars and make one happy family? To this St. Peter replied in the following terms:

If the foundations of this College are to be well and truly laid, not less than twelve or fourteen men should be sent in order to secure the best distribution of the necessary employments. There must be a rector, professors, domestic assistants, and priests for pastoral work so that, when necessary, they may render one another mutual service and, above all, help the sick. These numbers are further required in order that the men may live according to their rule. If only a few were in residence they might be too heavily burdened with teaching, and obliged to neglect domestic discipline, by which the healthy spiritual condition of a religious order is chiefly preserved. Many monasteries are now in a wretched state of collapse or daily deteriorate because the few persons left in them have neither the ability nor the wish to follow the practices of their order and institute.

Peter then goes on to express doubts about the wisdom of accommodating his brethren in the monastery under any circumstances. Its owners might easily find opportunities for complaint; there would almost certainly be disputes about the use of the monastery church; and any success that attended the Jesuits' ministrations might soon lead to invidious comparisons at the expense of the Augustinians. However, if the Government was determined to make the monastery serve, then the Jesuits must have a portion of it entirely separate from the Augustinians' quarters, and the latter must be asked to give an undertaking that they had received the Jesuits willingly and would permit them, whether in church or in school, to go quietly about their duties.[2] The undertaking was given in due course, but, as St. Peter's half-brother, Theodoric Canisius, opined, it was given not from love "but from fear of the Prince, and because the Father Prior of the monastery hoped that the Prince would show himself in turn more liberal towards the monastery in other matters."[3]

[1] Braunsberger, *Epistulae*, vol. ii, pp. 186–7.   [2] Braunsberger, *Epistulae*, vol. ii, pp. 217–9.
[3] Braunsberger, *Epistulae*, vol. ii, p. 873.

In his request to Laynez for men to staff the new College St. Peter signalized two worthies in particular after whom his heart pined, a good preacher and a good cook. By the end of November, 1559, four priests, four scholastics, and a lay brother had settled down in the infirmary wing of the monastery. What the lay brother was like as a cook we are not told, but there is evidence in plenty on the subject of the preacher, a clever hot-head named Martin Gewarts, who soon brought grievous trouble on his brethren by launching philippics at the secular clergy of Munich for their immorality and laziness.[1] The secular priests naturally retaliated, and in a short time Munich was buzzing with strange rumours about the Jesuits. As will be seen, St. Peter had many queer characters such as Gewarts to make a burden of his Provincialate. Even his own good and holy brother Theodoric caused him months of anxiety. Though he had been appointed Rector of the Munich College by Rome, the Cologne Jesuits captured him and only after a world of tedious argument and correspondence was St. Peter able to secure his return. In spite of all obstacles, however, the new College was solemnly inaugurated on March 3, 1560, with two hundred scholars on its roll. By 1576 the numbers had increased to six hundred, and in the last year of St. Peter's life his brethren had not only their magnificent, newly-built Church of St. Michael but one of the finest colleges in Europe, half of which, according to an observer of the time, would have afforded ample accommodation for a king and his court.[2]

Hardly was the Munich College out of its swaddling clothes before St. Peter was busily at work on the establishment of yet another great school. This time it was the turn of Innsbruck, beautiful capital of Tirol and favourite city of the Habsburgs. There in the Hofkirche, surrounded by the huge bronze statues of his ancestors and contemporaries, stout old Emperor Maximilian I lies at rest. Maximilian in his last will and testament had charged his heirs, Charles and Ferdinand, to build a church in Innsbruck where the Divine Services might be carried out with full solemnity. Ferdinand, on whom the pious duty devolved, determined to fulfil it thoroughly and to build not only a new church but a stately residence for the accommodation of a provost and twenty canons, as well

---

[1] Though St. Peter treated this man with the greatest kindness and consideration, he grew worse as the years passed and did the Society of Jesus considerable harm. In 1564 another Jesuit with whom Gewarts was on a preaching tour reported to Laynez that he was " facile a bever sicome e la consuetudine delli Germani di modo che quel che faceva in dece predice perdeva in uno pranso con il suo imodesto magnar et bere." Nor was that the worst to be said of him. Braunsberger, *Epistulae*, vol. iv, pp. 730–1.

[2] Cited by Duhr, *Geschichte der Jesuiten in den Ländern deutscher Zunge*, vol i (Freiburg im Breisgau, 1907), p. 185.

as other priests and students, numbering about forty all told. It was not a well-devised scheme nor had the King asked himself where, at a time when priests were so scarce, he was to obtain his provost and twenty canons. However, doubts did not assail him until the building had begun. Then they came in full force and, looking round for some way out of his difficulty, he bethought himself of St. Peter and his brethren, who had already more than once come to his rescue. He decided to turn the whole place over to them, regardless of the fact that the constitutions of their Order did not permit them to undertake such liturgical duties as old Maximilian had demanded. St. Peter had his first hint of the King's designs as far back as 1554. The following year he was definitely offered the new foundation with revenues sufficient to support forty men. Then, owing to Ferdinand's increasing financial troubles, another year passed without further developments.

On his return from Italy in December, 1556, Peter made a detour through Innsbruck to see how the building was progressing and, to his astonishment, found it a wilderness of scaffolding and half-finished walls. " It is hardly likely to be ready for bare habitation within two years," he informed Laynez, " and I therefore think it would be inopportune to hurry the King, especially as his treasury has been emptied by the wars." The two years passed and then, in April, 1559, while the Saint was busy with missionary work in Augsburg, Ferdinand, now Emperor, once more opened the negotiations. It was still his fixed intention to install the Jesuits, and, as he stipulated only for a daily sung Mass, without any reference to choir duties, St. Peter thought that the authorities in Rome might be able to stretch a point in his favour.[1] Rome apparently was not too happy about the liturgical part of the bargain, so Peter endeavoured to get the High Masses confined to feast-days and four annual commemorations of the dead. It was then Ferdinand's turn to feel a scruple, for the allaying of which he suggested that the Jesuits should co-opt six priests not of their Order who would carry out the liturgical functions. That plan presented obvious difficulties, but both St. Peter and his superiors in Rome professed their willingness to give it a trial. Ferdinand himself saved them the trouble. In conjunction with his Vice-Chancellor, Dr. Seld, and the Bishop of Fünfkirchen he evolved a new scheme, cancelling his gift of the recently constructed residence to the Jesuits and offering them instead, but only to the number of eight, an old Innsbruck property of the Habsburgs called the " Kreutterhauss."

[1] Braunsberger, *Epistulae*, vol. ii, p. 420.

Why he changed his mind is not clear, but it was probably owing to the depleted condition of his purse. In the new residence, which for St. Peter would have been such a grateful change from the dilapidated monasteries he usually had foisted on him, the Emperor proposed to install twelve canons instead of the original twenty. These men the Jesuits were asked to find, and also to accommodate in their own house a number of boarders, including twenty-four boys of noble families. The whole thing was rather exasperating and had involved Peter, burdened as he continued to be with much other business, in a whirl of vain negotiations and arduous journeys, but if he felt any disappointment he kept it carefully to himself. With never a complaint he set off once again for Innsbruck to discuss the new proposals. The "Kreutterhauss" he found to be a strange place for a religious community as it included a Habsburg prison, with torture-chamber and hangman's shed all complete. In fact, the place was quite impossible, and a few months after Peter's return to Augsburg he received a letter direct from Ferdinand asking him to come again to Innsbruck to inspect yet another building and discuss yet another scheme for the protean college.[1]

When Peter and Father Delanoy arrived in November, 1560,[2] they were taken over the house of the Dowager Duchess von Liechtenstein and asked what they thought about it for a college. They liked it very much and had only two objections, namely that it was too grand and that its windows looked on to the bridge over the river Inn, with possibilities of sights none too edifying for young Jesuits or their scholars.[3] The Dowager, however, wanted eight thousand florins for the property, which Ferdinand's Tirolese government declared to be "*nit ein kleine sondern grosse Kaufsumme.*" In any case, the Prime Minister himself, Count von Helfenstein, was living in the house and protested that he had nowhere else to go.

Dowager and Prime Minister between them made the Liechtenstein plan impossible, with the result that St. Peter was summoned once again to Innsbruck in June, 1561, to take stock of a residence called the "Hölz'-lische Behausung." It proved too small and narrow for the purposes of a college, as the officials expected it would, and they then took Peter to the Royal Hospital, where nineteen old men were cared for at the Emperor's expense. Peter did not at all like the idea of disturbing them, but was assured that, if he would accept the Hospital, the pensioners would not

---

[1] Braunsberger, *Epistulae*, vol. ii, pp. 661–4; 749–52.
[2] In the Innsbruck municipal archives there is a tavern bill for 10 florins 51 kreuzer, paid to Matthew Reychart, inn-keeper, for lodging St. Peter and Delanoy for four days.
[3] Braunsberger, *Epistulae*, vol. iii, p. 694.

be the losers by the transaction. He accordingly did so, and at long last the Jesuits had a home in Innsbruck. The only trouble was that Peter had no Jesuits to put into it. He sent his beloved Karl Grim there in hopes that his native Tirolese air might help his lungs, but poor Karl died within a few months. Peter mourned him deeply, and then, though he could spare no one to replace him, characteristically dispatched two of the best priests in his small Province to Genoa to embark for the Indies. All the alterations and furnishings of the Hospital were directed by Peter himself and he continued month after month to implore Rome to send him men. At last on June 25, 1562, he had his reward, as he said in the presence of Ferdinand's five daughters the first Mass of a solemn triduum arranged by the Emperor to celebrate the inauguration of the College.[1] The story of his work for it, if told in detail, would fill a volume, and the volume might fitly have for title, " The whole Art of Patience, illustrated by Examples." The magnificent University and Seminary with which Innsbruck is now equipped are the lineal descendants of St. Peter's College, which passed its early days in such poverty that the Fathers were able to balance their domestic budget only by cutting meat out of their dietary as far as possible.[2]

To conclude this chapter on St. Peter's first foundations, a few words may be said about the educational principles that guided him. They were simple and straightforward, like all the furniture of his mind, and had for basis no more recondite philosophy than the hard, unhappy fact of original sin. At the time of his canonization in 1925 Cardinal von Faulhaber of Munich said in a fine sermon that " the most Canisian thing about Canisius was his love for youth." His love, however, never blinded him to the fact that the golden lads and girls had not recovered in baptism, with the supernatural life, the true harmony and integrity of their nature. Reason in them is not born to the purple but has to fight for its throne, and it is the fundamental business of true education to guide and help reason to victory. Hence, for St. Peter, discipline wise and firm is the

[1] This Mass was the first to be offered in the new church, called the Church of the Holy Cross. To it the remains of Maxmilian I were transferred, and there his famous tomb is now to be seen.

[2] The chief documents are given by Braunsberger, *Epistulae*, vol. ii, pp. 879–82; vol. iii, pp. 694–717. There is an excellent chapter on Innsbruck in Kröss, *Der selige Petrus Canisius in Österreich*, Vienna, 1898. The Protestant critic, Gautier, has the following interesting remarks on the work of St. Peter and Delanoy in connexion with this College : " On ne peut pas se défendre d'une certaine admiration pour la prudence, la clairvoyance, la netteté de vues de Canisius et de son confrère. Mais il est trop évident qu'une adresse de ce genre, mise au service d'un confesseur en face de son pénitent constitue un terrible danger. La direction des affaires temporelles abandonnée aux mains expertes du prêtre, c'est l'abdication pure et simple de tout jugement personnel, de toute vie autonome. C'est la porte ouverte à tous les abus." *Étude sur la correspondance de Pierre Canisius* (Geneva, 1905), p. 63. That is an excellent example of giving with one hand and taking away with the other. It is also a well-known dodge when the prosecution when the defendant's case turns out to be too strong. Incidentally, St. Peter was *not* the confessor of Emperor Ferdinand.

first necessity; no mere easy, external dragooning, but the enlistment on the side of reason, by example, encouragement, and timely warning, of all that is best in a child's instinctive and emotional life. The home, he never tired of insisting in his sermons and books, is the first and most important factor in the making of souls, for, despite his great belief in colleges, he knew well that their proper function was not to supersede but to supplement the influence of home, and he would have subscribed heartily to George Herbert's dictum that " one good mother is worth a hundred schoolmasters." It was this conviction of the vital importance of home train-ing that caused St. Peter to lament in his *Confessions*, written in 1570, the in-difference of parents to their duties. Referring to his own boyhood he said :

From the sins which I and others then committed only too often, I now have learnt to grieve more and more for the hazards of boys of good family. In our time these boys are brought up in such a way that it would seem as if they had no worse enemies than parents, tutors, and others, bound to them by ties of blood or affection. Children at that generous age of boyhood are spoilt by those people in many deplorable ways, and are not only drawn aside from the path of virtue but infected with pride, love of ease, and impurity. If evil communica-tions corrupt good manners, what dreadful harm must come to children from the vicious habits of their parents and the scandalous behaviour of servants. Ah, what a reckoning there will be and what a terrible judgment for all who by word or deed scandalize Thy little ones, O Lord ; for all who hinder them or turn them back or laugh at them, when they would come to Thee to serve Thee !¹

As typical of many passages in St. Peter's sermons the following words to parents, spoken at Innsbruck in 1572, may be cited : " I beg and admonish all of you who are husbands and wives to reflect, for the sake of Our Lord and His bitter Passion, that God instituted marriage, not only that you might have children, but that you should with all care and discipline educate them for His glory and for the good of the Church. . . . Your children are the little ones whom Christ loves, whom He wishes to come unto Himself, of whom is the Kingdom of Heaven. Under pain of eternal malediction He will not have them scandalized. They are the best part of Christianity and the fairest hopes of the Church. God takes delight and joy in children. He hears the prayer and confirms

¹ Braunsberger, *Epistulae*, vol. i, p. 14.

the blessing that has them for its object. Think how weak, helpless, and pliant children are in their early years. They are like twigs that can easily be bent, or like blank tablets of wax on which anybody may write, and so, with little trouble, they can be moved and guided to every good habit. And again, think how the senses and hearts of men are prone to evil from their youth, how folly is bound up in the heart of every child, so that they need good discipline and cannot be healed unless kept in fear by both rod and tongue. Fear is the beginning of wisdom, and children ought, therefore, not only to be counselled and warned with earnest words, but to be punished with stripes when they deserve it. He that spareth the rod hateth his son, for if children are permitted to live according to their own sweet wills they become wanton and stubborn, not only learning evil habits but becoming so confirmed in them that it is afterwards impossible or most difficult to recall them to the right way and accustom them to virtue. For this reason such pagan writers as Aristotle, Cicero, Cato, Plutarch, and Quintilian issue urgent warnings about the education of youth.

" Next, consider the great evils, misfortunes and dangers which result from neglecting children in their youth, and not forcibly keeping them from bad companionship, bad example, and bad habits. Parents are often driven to anger and bitter sorrow, to complaint, anxiety, and torture of mind. Fear seizes them that their children will only become daily more wicked, disobedient, and ungrateful for every present or future kindness they would show them. They are robbed of all the joy which good parents have from their good and modest children, who are their treasure, their consolation, the staff of their old age, and the honour of their house and family. Often, they are disgraced in the eyes of the world by the follies of their sons, so that they could wish them absent, or dead, or at the devil. . . . And remember that you are responsible for all the evil which your sons may commit if badly trained, that whatever degradation they may descend to, with all its consequent scandals, is your handiwork. Oh, what an account you who scandalize children will have to render to God when He demands their blood at your hands. Oh, the undying worm that will torture you in the next world for this negligence, and, oh, the eternal, unspeakable sorrow which you will feel to hear your-selves cursed by your children in their own damnation, to hear them appeal to the justice of God against you because on earth you were so soft, careless, and compliant in your attitude to them, permitting them to do as they listed and never correcting their infidelities."[1]

[1] Braunsberger, *Epistulae*, vol. vii, pp. 629–31.

Some time during the years 1560–1561 a set of school regulations was drawn up for the Jesuit colleges of Prague and Ingolstadt. These regulations, if not the very first in the order of time, certainly belong to the very earliest attempts to draft a *Ratio Studiorum* and, according to the best authority on the subject, they were probably composed by St. Peter Canisius.[1] At any rate they bear all the marks of his composition, his attention to details of discipline, his care for cleanliness and health and, before everything, his solicitude for the spiritual welfare of the pupils. The document is in three parts, prefects of studies, masters, and pupils each having a long section devoted to them. The first part starts off in this fashion : " The prefect of the school will take great pains to see not only that the boys are diligently urged forward in the study of letters and piety, but also that everything pertaining to the external equipment, development, and cleanliness of the school is cared for. He will treat all the pupils of the school with paternal affection and speak to God about them continually in his prayers and Holy Sacrifices that they may the more easily make progress in both virtue and letters." All the other rules of the prefect of studies are in the same spirit. He is to see that the boys are given instructions about Confession and Holy Communion, that each class-room has a large and tasteful picture or statue representing some sacred subject, that poor boys in particular are provided with good lodgings, that no dust, dirt, or cobwebs are allowed to accumulate anywhere in the school, that the class-rooms are properly heated, that the edges of the doors are padded so as to prevent noise in closing them, that the boys have bats, balls, and other instruments necessary for their games, and so on. With regard to studies the prefect is to consider each pupil's ability and the subjects best suited to him, and in all other ways to promote the welfare of the individual. Stress is laid on the importance of the singing lesson at which all pupils, big and little, are obliged to be present each day. St. Peter and his brethren had the highest regard for the liturgical offices of the Church, and though, owing to the nature of the work for which their Order was founded, they might not themselves be able to carry out the liturgy in all its splendour, they spared no pains to prepare the children committed to them for such services.

The second section, dealing with the duties of the various form masters, opens as follows :

[1] Pachtler, *Ratio Studiorum et Institutiones Scholasticae Societatis Jesu*, vol. i (Berlin, 1887), pp. 154–5.

Each master will show paternal affection especially to the boys of his own class and continually recommend them to God in his prayers. He will shun no labour which he sees to be necessary for his pupils' good, not seeking his own advantage but that of his pupils and esteeming their progress both his business and his gain. In speaking with them he will take the greatest care never so much as by a syllable to try and attract them to the Society or to any other religious order, though he may and ought to foster their good desires generally, with caution, however, for fear of rousing suspicion. He is always at liberty to exhort them to virtue and to deter them from vice, without any reservations. . . .

In teaching in the schools, masters should always keep before their minds the image of the true and only perfect Master, Christ Our Lord, that they may imitate His forbearance and gentle courtesy with illiterate persons, fishermen, and people slow of mind, that they may teach with great diligence, stooping to the capacity of their listeners, admonishing them, solicitously and sedulously exercising them and gradually advancing them to higher things, and that they may wait patiently for the laggards, as did St. Paul. " We became little ones in the midst of you," he says, " as if a nurse should cherish her children."

With regard to corporal punishment, the general principle is laid down that the masters must endeavour to rule their charges by kindness and reproof, and that only when these methods have failed must they have recourse to the rod. In using it they are to observe " moderation, charity, and the prescribed number of strokes." Each offence has its particular tariff, the usual number of strokes being six, which, considering the ' toughness ' and insensitiveness of that age, was a remarkably low figure. When a boy violated the rules of discipline he was to be given a medal ' for demerit ' and obliged to wear it until his conduct showed improvement. Not to have got rid of the medal by the morning after its bestowal meant a penalty of two strokes. This custom, which St. Peter did not invent but borrowed from the medieval schools, bore hardly on the poor fellow who acquired the medal late in the day. It had, however, the advantage of making the boys more careful as the sun declined, which is the time when they are usually prone to riot. Here again emphasis is laid on cleanliness, each master being instructed to appoint two ' syndics ' from his class week by week who must watch the lavatories and corners of the corridors and report any boys " qui ista contaminant loca." After the disciplinary regulations, detailed instructions are given on the method of teaching the various subjects, of holding examinations, and of carrying out the elaborate programmes of exhibition days. As for the masters' ordinary dealings with the boys, "their conversation is to be such," says the document, "that the pupils may feel their gentleness and charity rather than fear their severity, but they must not be too familiar with their charges, rather keeping to a middle course, in order that their authority and influence may not suffer, especially in public."

Finally, it is the turn of the boys themselves to have their charter. Judging by the many misdemeanours against which they are warned, boy nature has not changed much in the intervening centuries. They carved their names on the desks then as they do now, they scribbled and drew faces on their books, they broke bounds and fought among themselves and hung about on the way to school and used swear-words and swam in forbidden waters. But there has been improvement in some respects, because boys do not now usually fight pitched battles with stones for missiles, though they may still hanker after the possession of " *arma bellica*." St. Peter had to lay down stringent rules against the carrying of weapons, the only knives he would allow being those which the boys required for cutting their quill pens. School, he said, " is not a military camp but a temple of the Muses." With an example of his directly spiritual counsels to the boys we may bring this chapter to a close : " Since, as the Wise Man says, wisdom will not enter into a malicious soul nor dwell in a body subject to sins, the study of all virtue and especially of true Catholic piety will be the first care of the students. Let them above all things fear, love, and worship God, and meditate assiduously on the life, Passion, and death of Christ Our Lord, printing them with devout affection on their inmost hearts. Accordingly, they will say with great care and diligence, not only their daily prayers in the church at time of Mass, but their morning and night prayers at home, that God may grant a happy beginning, a successful course, and a most blessed end to their lives and to their studies. They will listen to sermons reverently and attentively and take part in the divine services with the greatest modesty, devotion, and piety. All ought to be firmly convinced that their parents send them to school, and that their masters teach them, for no other purpose than that they may be the better able to seek and stoutly defend the glory of Almighty God and their own and their neighbours' salvation. Consequently, they will strive with all their might to extirpate self-love and the desire of empty honour from their hearts."[1]

[1] Pachtler, *Ratio Studiorum*, pp. 155–72.

CHAPTER VIII

TRISTIA

AT the Conference of Worms between the Protestants and Catholics in 1557, to which a chapter will be devoted later on, St. Peter Canisius learned the meaning and suffered the consequences of discord in what might be called the family next door. It was unpleasant enough, but not nearly so bad as what he suffered from discord in his own family, in the bosom of the Society of Jesus. To be traduced by Melanchthon had a certain glory attaching to it for a Catholic, but to be thwarted, criticized, and opposed by one's very brethren and fellow-soldiers in the battles of the Faith, there surely lay the most searching test of a man's capacity for endurance. We have now to see how St. Peter stood it, first in dealing with difficult characters who tended to make a ruin of schemes which he had set going with so much labour, and then as the victim of a great and good man's antipathy.

Peter had not long been superior of his Province before his domestic troubles began. In November, 1556, he felt obliged to tell Laynez that the new College at Ingolstadt was being disturbed by the strange behaviour of Father Couvillon, the eminent French Jesuit who had acted as theologian to the Duke of Bavaria at the second meeting of the Council of Trent. On their departure for Ingolstadt to start the College, St. Ignatius had given his men, including Couvillon, certain counsels as to their manner of conducting polemics with the Protestants. " Great care must be taken," he said, " to show forth orthodox truth in such a way that if any heretics happen to be present they may have an example of charity and Christian moderation. No hard words should be used nor ought any sort of contempt for their errors be shown. Let the Catholic dogmas be established and then the heretics will see that contrary doctrines are false. If the Duke considers that error should be publicly refuted in lectures and sermons, this must be done with modesty and a plain indication that love of the heretics' salvation is the motive."[1] That counsel was simple enough to

[1] Pachtler, *Ratio Studiorum*, vol. iii, pp. 470–1.

understand, but Father Couvillon's sharp tongue and ironic turn of mind flouted its wisdom. In lectures and sermons he let himself go to such an extent that he jeopardized the whole future of the College and awakened against his Order hostility which it could ill afford to face at that initial stage of its existence in Germany.

In addition to being rampageous, Couvillon was also a confirmed valetudinarian, and when not given whatever concessions he deemed due to his imaginary bad health, he broke out into abuse and criticism of his Rector. The truth is that, though a brilliant professor and a man of fine character generally, he was not quite right in the head. Restless and unbalanced, he belonged to the class of people whose chief itch in life is to be anywhere rather than where they are. No sooner had he been stationed in Ingolstadt than he began to pine for a change. As a theologian he possessed real ability and made a considerable success of his lectures at the University, but there again he showed his fickleness and importuned St. Peter to be relieved of the office. His *Wanderlust*, combined with his disedifying tantrums and discontent at his post, caused the Saint, who fully appreciated his value as a theologian, the gravest anxiety. He begged Laynez to write to him in friendly terms, pointing out that scarcity of professors made it impossible to relieve him at the moment, and urging him to go on with his lectures quietly and temperately until a substitute could be found.[1]

The Saint's gentle management of him had a good effect on the patient, but Peter put it down to something else. "Everybody thinks," he wrote, "that it is the beer which has set him up." To further the good work of the breweries he invited Couvillon to join him at Regensburg in January of the New Year for the sake of the change. There he used him as a sort of secretary to prove his confidence in him. Laynez, meantime, had written a stern letter to the culprit, but Peter held it back for a time until the cure had gone a little further. That precaution was of no avail, for when, in due course, Couvillon received the letter he merely counted it as yet another injustice. One cause of the trouble at Ingolstadt was that the Rector lacked authority to deal with such troublesome characters as this professor. In the early days of the Society of Jesus it was customary to limit a rector's jurisdiction by giving him an assistant or " *socius collateralis* " with independent authority. Place was also found for another official called a " superintendent " who enjoyed a good deal of autonomy in his own sphere. St. Ignatius had appointed Couvillon

[1] Braunsberger, *Epistulae*, vol. ii, p. 28.

to this post at Ingolstadt and he was not slow to take advantage of his immunities. St. Peter did not at all like this parcelling out of authority, and suggested to Laynez that it might be a good thing if the various rectors were relieved of these restrictions on their action. In particular, the Rector of Ingolstadt might with advantage to everybody have the millstone of Couvillon taken from his neck. " I beg your Reverence," wrote Peter, " to pay no attention when he petitions you to remove him from Ingolstadt and breaks out into his usual complaints. He is not *sui compos*, but, despite his unceasing lamentations, he does not seem as unwell as he imagines. I should like him to have no authority over the Rector, for the Rector has more than enough to put up with from him and might justly complain of his peevishness and asperity rather than suffer under his accusations."[1]

St. Peter's next report on the patient combines impartially strictures and admiration :

There seems to be no help for Father Couvillon, as scruples and hallucinations have taken such deep root in his soul. Sometimes they come upon him as strongly as if he were a lunatic or subject to the changes of the moon. . . . My attitude to him has been this. I considered that he was in no wise to be spared on account of his learning or because he is a professed Father, and so have put him under the authority of the Rector, at the same time reprehending and warning him in such a way that his love of comfort can no longer be disguised or defended on the ground of his profession, or on other grounds suggested by unregenerate human nature. Though he is timorous in disposition, he needs vigorous treatment on account of his excessive fastidiousness and inclination to pride, especially as he is so regardless of discipline and full of complaints. He does not pray much either, and indulges the flesh by taking far more sleep than is necessary, etc. He has a great loathing for study, a matter in which the devil scores his chief success by persuading him that he is not equal to his office, and troubling his soul with many scruples during lecture time. I believe that the devil is greatly annoyed at this Father's continued residence in Bavaria. For his influence increases every day and all students at the University esteem him so much that they neglect the other doctors. They love him and crowd to hear him for his wonderful gifts of disputation, lecturing, and exhorting. But, as I have said, all these exercises

[1] Braunsberger, *Epistulae*, vol. ii, pp. 48–9.

serve only to entangle him in evil. There is nothing he so much desires as to be freed from his scholastic pursuits, imagining that they are a greater hindrance to him than his self-love and self-will. With regard to your Reverence's letter, for several days he could not stomach that remedy. Utterly sick in soul, he put all the blame on his Rector, Father Thomas. I told him that, on the contrary, it was his pride which rendered your letter displeasing to him and which prevented him from seeing his errors, though they were perfectly obvious. He could not hide them even in his letters, which are full of the troubled motions of his soul. I accordingly sent him back to Ingolstadt, although he would have preferred to remain with me [in Regensburg], and I have given instructions that he is to be relieved of all domestic responsibilities and to apply himself solely to his office of lecturer and preacher. I have also written some counsels for his confessor, and I hope that he will be more at peace than in the past, now that he has received from you an admonition proportionate to his great faults. May the Lord grant him true moderation of soul and confirm him in the way of life to which he has been called against the winds of inconstancy and despair.[1]

Once again St. Peter's patience was successful in tranquillizing the poor professor for a while. It is significant that, though so critical of other superiors, Couvillon never uttered a word of complaint against his Provincial. Peter tried in all sorts of little ways to put heart into him and give him confidence. He consulted him often on business of the Province and urged him on to such honourable tasks as the translation into German of the inspiring letters which had come from the Jesuits in India. Probably he was in hopes that Couvillon might catch some of the infectious courage and resolution of his documents. As, according to the Saint, the Germans valued one writer more than ten professors, he also encouraged his patient to become an author. " This Father writes finely and pointedly," he told Laynez. But for all his efforts Couvillon was not cured and had frequent relapses into the abyss. Thus in February, 1558, more than a year after the events narrated, the Saint had to write in the following strain :

May God help Father Couvillon lest he be submerged in his fits of melancholia. Often they deprive him of all power of mind and body, so that he is unable to devote himself to his work or to be at

[1] Braunsberger, *Epistulae*, vol. ii, pp. 56–8.

peace in any place. His trouble seems to have become permanent and incurable. At certain times he is thrown to the ground by the attacks, and becomes burdensome and almost intolerable to himself and everybody else. . . . He is full of lamentations and always wants to be journeying about. In the summer I shall send him on travel, though his social manners are quite unsuited to Germany and he finds it impossible to live on peaceable terms with anyone. At his request, I obtained permission for him to deliver only three lectures in the week but no sooner had I obtained it than he changed his mind and wanted during this Lent to hold classes daily. So it is difficult to satisfy his wishes.

He is expecting some decision from your Reverence and hoping that by my offices somebody may be ordered to replace him in the schools. But I am sure that leisure would be more harmful to him than his work as a professor, though I could wish that he did the work with greater prudence. He says that he cannot go on with his schools until he has seen such and such books and authors—a great multitude of them. I have told the Rector to give him whatever he asks for in the way of food and dress, for in these matters also . . . he is very particular. I leave it to your Reverence to decide whether he is to remain in this College, of which he is a great pillar and a professor enjoying considerable authority with all men. He might be a splendid support to our brethren, if only he were or could become keener about his work.[1]

Two years later Couvillon was still in the depths of gloom, though absolved by St. Peter from all regular observance and " given everything he liked." He protested that he could not " abide the sight of anybody " and used to mope about the house or, at meal times, wander off goodness knows where. Three or four times a day he would order special food to be brought to his room and there, says St. Peter, in solitary state, " *ventris egit negotium*." Yet despite his physical and moral ailments he continued to do good work for the Church in Germany, work, it may fairly be said, that would never have been done but for the charity with which he was handled by his long-suffering Provincial. " I beg your Reverence to pray to God for him and to find some remedy for his unhappy state," is the Saint's last word to Laynez about him.

The case of the Ingolstadt professor was bad enough, but the palm for real blood-and-thunder insubordination belongs to a Prague professor

[1] Braunsberger, *Epistulae*, vol. ii, pp. 210-1.

named Tilianus or Linden, who, like St. Peter himself, hailed from Gelderland. He had been appointed by St. Ignatius in 1556 to teach scholastic theology at the new college in Bohemia, but owing to the disrepute into which his subject had fallen could not find any auditors. Father Goisson, the Rector, accordingly switched him over to philosophy and by that simple movement precipitated the storm. Though a man of great piety, Goisson lacked discernment and so made insufficient allowance for the weakness of his subjects. Now Father Linden's great weakness in another sense was his theology. He revelled in the subject and had attained to high proficiency in it. The change to philosophy gave him such annoyance that he forgot all his religious obligations in his efforts to have it cancelled. Goisson, as the author of the change, came in for the full fury of his highly disrespectful tongue. Linden plotted against his authority with fierce determination, formed a league in opposition to it and eventually came very near to destroying, not only community life, but the whole work of the Jesuits in Bohemia. He was an extraordinary person and, like Couvillon, claimed to be a sick man who needed all sorts of exemptions and indulgences. "I do not think," wrote St. Peter to Laynez, "that there is another man in the Society the like of Father Linden." He had the spirit of a wrecker and was both "rough and tough." Unhampered by the finer feelings that would have restrained a gentleman from exposing the troubles of his own family, he trailed his grievances in public and went to Scribonius, the Administrator of the archdiocese of Prague, with charges against his Rector and a request to transmit letters for him secretly to Rome. But he had come to the wrong address. "For the love of God," Scribonius answered, "I beg you to beware of letting the world know of your dissensions. Besides, those who have hitherto esteemed your Society would never believe your story."[1]

Linden then tried St. Peter's other good friend, Anton Brus, and was equally unsuccessful. Thereupon his temper became so violent that one night he invaded the room of another professor against whom he had some grievance and flung the astonished man right out of bed. The bad example was infectious, for when the minister of the house, whose authority came next after the rector's, imposed some small penance on a lay brother for a fault against discipline the culprit answered with his fists. And the minister himself was nothing wonderful. For one thing he had a monstrous appetite and used to disgust the others by the way he indulged it at table. Piqued now that Father Goisson should have

[1] Braunsberger, *Epistulae*, vol. ii, p. 58.

so easily freed the aggressive lay brother from the penalty of excommunication,[1] he left Prague without permission, betook himself to the Jesuits in Vienna, and shortly afterwards abandoned the Society altogether. After a few years he repented and was received back, but only to desert again. Then followed a stormy career out of which he at last emerged into peace and died holily, befriended by St. Peter.[2]

Meantime the Saint had transferred Linden to Ingolstadt, where he continued to agitate and be a nuisance until it suddenly came into his head to return to Prague. Writing of him to Scribonius and Brus, Peter said:

I thought it would be worth while to recall him from Bohemia and send him to some place where he might secretly unlearn certain vices and be the better formed to the rule of our obedience in Christ. But moved by I know not what unkindly thoughts of his superiors, and perhaps also by an unfounded fear for his own skin, he has elected to return to you and make fresh trouble rather than to go straight to Italy in order to serve holy obedience in simplicity of heart. Knowing this you ought not to allow any charges which he dares to utter against his Rector to disturb you. Let us put his offences down to perturbation of mind and imprudence of tongue. Do not, I pray you, suffer the accusations of one man to have as much weight as the innocent sincerity of a whole college. We, too, are men and not angels. As unfortunates, with the power to sin, do you who are spiritual reprove us in the spirit of meekness.

If you think that anything is necessary for the well-being of the College, Father Vitoria is with you in my name, as Superior unto edification of our brethren. Even the most holy college of Christ had its sinners and sorrows, and faults remained in it which only the coming of the Holy Ghost could completely eradicate. So it is less strange that among us, too, there should be blemishes, that faults should be committed and that not all attainments should be within the power of all. In conclusion, I would beg and implore you to give Father Vitoria every assistance, and to love and listen to him no otherwise than if he were your Canisius. . . .[3]

In the end Peter persuaded Father Linden to go to Rome and put his case before his superiors at headquarters. He gave him a letter of

[1] This was and is the penalty for " laying violent hands on a cleric or religious."
[2] Braunsberger, *Epistulae*, vol. ii, p. 61.
[3] Braunsberger, *Epistulae*, vol. ii, p. 109.

introduction to the Roman Jesuits, asking them to receive him with kindness, and made careful provision for the expenses of his journey. The Saint's feeling towards the turbulent man is expressed in a letter to Laynez announcing his departure : " Praise be to God, he set out to-day in sufficiently good spirits. We all desire that he should be his own accuser rather than that others should have to act the part. And we desire him also to be corrected in the school of obedience, so that from being a doctor he may become a disciple and from being a learned man, a little one in Christ, in all things wise unto sobriety. Most truly do I wish, as I have written, that he be received to penance and shown to those whom he has scandalized a reformed man. May Our Lord Jesus grant to him and to all of us the spirit of true simplicity that we may know, not only to subject ourselves utterly to our superiors, but also to give pleasure in every way to our brethren in the ranks."[1] That was the last of poor Linden. On his way to Rome he was struck down by a fatal illness at Loreto and died in the arms of Father Manare, the Rector, having publicly acknowledged his faults and bewailed them with tears of true penitence.[2]

Couvillon and Linden, though perhaps the most difficult cases, were far from being the only ones to add to the heavy burden of St. Peter's Provincialate. In 1559 he found seven men among the forty-four in the College of Vienna whose ideas of discipline would have been better suited to a students' club than to a religious order. Father Schorich, the erratic scholar whom he had been good to in the old days at Ingolstadt, had gone off to live with a bishop and pretty well defied Peter or anybody else to get him back to the common life, while another man, named Krieger, one of the pioneers of the Prague adventure, kicked over the traces altogether. Perhaps it was only natural that young Germans who had been brought up in an atmosphere of revolt against authority should have taken some time to learn the necessity and the nobility of obedience. At any rate a number of them gave St. Peter some of the saddest moments of his life.

His chief cross, however, did not come from the antics of raw recruits but from the vagaries and restless energy of a very fine man whom he counted as his second self, Father Juan Vitoria, so called from the Basque town of that name where he was born. The style of man Vitoria was is shown by this little cameo from the historian Orlandinus. It is carnival

[1] Braunsberger, *Epistulae*, vol. ii, pp. 121–3.
[2] Schmidl, *Historiae Societatis Jesu Provinciae Bohemiae pars prima* (Prague, 1747), p. 113.

time in Rome, 1549. Vitoria, not yet a Jesuit, has just been through the *Spiritual Exercises*. From his window he can see and hear the mob drinking, dancing, and singing its lascivious songs. In a storm of holy anger he strips naked, ties an old sack round his waist and rushes forth into the most fashionable streets, a heavy scourge in his hand. Along every street he goes where the crowds are noisiest, lashing himself so mercilessly that a trail of blood marks his progress.[1]

Vitoria's splendid work for the poor soldiery of Vienna and for his countrymen resident in that city has already been mentioned. There was no end to the good man's zeal. He flew like a bee from project to project in his longing to fill the Church with the sweetness of God's love, and it is scarcely surprising to know that, like the bee, he had a sting and could use it when made angry by other people's interference with his activities. His intentions were always noble but, like so many active people, he never seemed to know when it was time to stop. The long view was a thing nature had incapacitated him from taking. He must always " seize the instant by the foremost top " and spread himself on every side, irrespective of the dangers to which such scattered work is inevitably exposed. His crest might well have been a mushroom. Up they went, building after building, for this purpose and for that, without much thought where men and means would be found to keep them going. Such was Father Vitoria, an indisputably live wire whom to touch was to get a shock.

St. Peter, when appointed to the Conference of Worms, had petitioned Laynez for a substitute to represent him in the government of his Province. Vitoria was the man chosen, very probably at Peter's suggestion. His first duty in the new office was to visit the College of Prague, which had been overtaken by a succession of calamities. The revenues from the monastery of Oybin had ceased to come in, and nothing that the Rector could do by protest or representation availed to move the defaulting trustees. Frightened by his large and increasing debts, Father Goisson then started drastic economies. For some months the Jesuits did their hard day's work on a diet of bread and cheese with never a comforting glass to help it down, privations which, according to the Rector's diary, " were accepted by the brethren not only patiently but with gratitude, as making them like their Saviour."[2] A good indication of the poverty of the College is the fact that, when in 1558 four young

[1] *Historia Societatis Jesu* (Cologne, 1615), p. 262.
[2] Schmidl, *Historiae Societatis Jesu Provinciae Bohemiae pars prima*, p. 114.

Jesuits were to be sent from Prague to Vienna for their studies, the Rector
was unable to provide them with the few shillings necessary for their
journey and had to beg a thaler from the almoner of the Archduke. Father
Vitoria's visit eased the situation a little, to St. Peter's joy, for he was
good at getting money. The Saint watched his efforts with some anxiety,
as he had reason to fear imprudence, especially in his domestic reforms.
For all his piety Vitoria was a rather ruthless and inconsiderate superior.
He believed that everybody should be as vigorous and iron-willed as
himself, as ready to live on bread and water or to assume any conceivable
responsibility at a moment's notice. Already in 1557 Peter had informed
Laynez, after first warmly praising Vitoria's ability and zeal, that he did
not like the good man's idea of reducing the meagre amount of furniture
allowed to the Jesuits in Vienna nor his plans for the improvement of
their church. Such plans, he knew, would be carried out at the expense
of Vitoria's unfortunate subjects. They would have to pay the piper
while he called the tune. " I have written," said Peter, " counselling him
not to act precipitately. . . . The small improvements he desires ought
to be carried out gradually and without imposing fresh burdens on our
brethren. As your Reverence prudently observed, it is not expedient
for us to occupy a third professorial chair just now, nor for our Fathers
to preach in the morning at Vienna, against the custom of the country,
nor for us to have sermons during meals. I shall tell him about these
matters. Experience, the universal teacher, will give him more caution,
in the knowledge that not everything suits everybody and that certain
things may wisely and advantageously be winked at for a time."[1]

Complaints about Vitoria's high-handed methods of administration
soon began to flood in on St. Peter, particularly from Ingolstadt, which
College he had robbed of five men at one swoop to put them on to some
pet scheme of his own. After Peter's return to Worms from Cologne
in November, 1557, his first care was to give his lieutenant a detailed
account of the flourishing Jesuit colony in the Rhineland capital. " Let
us both write to Rome," he said, " and secure leave to seek and obtain
students from Cologne as props to our own colleges in time of need."
Vitoria is made the sharer of all his plans and hopes. On him the Saint
relied more than on anybody else for support in his great undertakings,
and perhaps also for a little human sympathy in his disappointments.
Alas, Vitoria himself would prove to be one of his saddest disappointments. By this time he was getting tired of Germany and yearning for

[1] Braunsberger, *Epistulae*, vol. ii, pp. 136-7.

pastures new, a symptom that caused Peter, who knew his worth, the deepest distress. Continuing his letter, he said :

I am fully conscious of your diligence and loyalty. The proof of both is seen in your continual journeying during these wintry months through Austria, Bohemia, and Bavaria, and in your great labours for the welfare of our colleges. . . . You now know, my dear Father, the human frailty of our brethren. You are experiencing the diversity of characters, some of them badly trained and some too, perhaps, ungrateful and disobedient. . . . For this reason I cannot refrain from congratulating our two selves. We have found our cross, and that we should bear it patiently, bravely, and joyfully for the Name of Jesus, is my heart-felt petition. For, as I have elsewhere stated, I should not like to interpret your reference to the possibility of our soon embracing in Rome,[1] as an indication that we are sick and tired of these worries, which must be our lot when going round on visitation. The best course of all, the one most befitting us and most pleasing to Christ, will be to lay aside the thought of Spain and Italy and to devote ourselves with all our hearts to Germany alone, not for a time only but for our whole lives, labouring for her might and main . . . and thirsting for nothing so much as the German harvest and the glorious success of its good workmen, particularly our own brethren. . . .

It grieves me to call to mind the complaints I have received from Ingolstadt on the score of the men whom you removed thence. The others fear that the College has been dangerously weakened by the big change. My point in mentioning such matters, Reverend Father, is that, as we have also been warned from Rome, we should avoid big changes as much as ever we can and not provide for one college at the expense of another. Rather should we consider carefully how to meet the present situation with the least offence all round. Meantime, I believe that you had good reasons for the many changes you made at Ingolstadt, but the people there are only human and need to be handled with a certain tact, so that as far as possible business may be transacted peacefully and inoffensively. . . .

One last point. Will you please instruct the rectors of colleges to say in future, when writing their quarterly report to the Provincial, whether they have put aside any money in savings which may afterwards be used for the common good, as necessity arises ? May Our

---

[1] At the general congregation, to which St. Peter but not Vitoria had been summoned.

Lord direct our efforts and those of the whole Society to His glory. . . .
I hope that you are feeling very well, Father, and taking good care
of yourself. Do not forget to tell me about your health always. . . .[1]

Father Vitoria was so keen about Italy that he used to send money
south which the poor colleges of his own province could very ill spare.
St. Peter remonstrated with him in the gentlest manner. " The Prague
house," he pointed out, " has not a penny to give anybody and the men
at Ingolstadt are saddled with the debts of Prague. If I am not mistaken,
the resources of the Viennese brethren are exhausted and they are
obliged to beg even for the building of the school." Vitoria himself was
a champion beggar, but his province did not benefit much from his
peculiar talent. Despite his Provincial's courteous hints he pushed on
with his pet schemes, wasting money and energy that could have been
much better employed. Good man though he was, he had only one
foot in Germany and began to hanker increasingly after the Italian sun.
The poet's words, adapted from Mary Tudor's cry when, at this time,
England lost Calais, would certainly have served as a motto for Father
Vitoria :

> Open my heart and you will see
> Graved inside of it, " Italy."

As he could not get there at the moment he determined as far as
possible to bring Italy to Austria. He would try to arrange everything,
even the cooking of an egg, on the Italian model, regardless of the
unfortunate northern stomachs that depended on him. His misdirected
efforts to secure a third chair at the University for a Jesuit professor,
preferably himself, were inspired by the hope of applying its emoluments
to the support of the Jesuits in Rome, a good object in itself, but hardly
fair to his half-starved brethren in Vienna and Prague.

St. Peter had already proved abundantly by his deeds that he was
second to none in his regard for Italian customs and for the needs of
the Roman College, but he possessed what Vitoria signally lacked, a
saving sense of proportion. With regard to the zealous Father's ambition
for a professorial post at the University, the Saint pointed out that to
accept fees for such work, as Vitoria desired to do, would be against the
spirit of their Order, and that it would be much better if, instead of
worrying about the Roman College, which was not his responsibility,
he were to concentrate on paying the debt owed by the College of Prague

[1] Braunsberger, *Epistulae*, vol. ii, pp. 144–8.

to certain booksellers in Ingolstadt. From Worms on November 18th he wrote again to give the complaints of the Ingolstadt Fathers in set terms : " They seem to have taken offence at your hint, conveyed, perhaps, too boastfully, that you have the King[1] in your pocket. They are astonished that you should make such a fuss about certain trifles. They say that you practically never consult the Fathers or call them together, and that, without a word to anybody, you make all sorts of regulations which you leave behind you in writing. These are small matters, Father, and such as I am sure you can justify, but we must constantly consider the claims of charity, the concessions which it is occasionally in our power to make, and the great importance of dealing gently rather than imperiously with the Germans. I know that your action in removing many of the Ingolstadt staff has not been welcome, and, indeed, a few days' inspection of the College could not have enabled you to judge adequately as to its needs. May Our Lord Jesus who alone is perfect order all things through us mightily and sweetly."[2]

As a help in the troubled state of his Province Peter begged Laynez to restore Father Delanoy to Vienna. Delanoy was a much kindlier and more level-headed man than Vitoria and might act as a brake on his Spanish impetuosity. " I am striving by letter," the Saint continued, " to moderate the good Father's zeal. Complaints from the brethren pour in, and I could wish that the business done by my locum tenens might be done with a minimum of offence. In small matters, I think that it is unnecessary to make a great display of authority, and at times a little indulgence ought to be shown to people. . . . I do not say this as though his zeal and piety were displeasing to me. Indeed, I know and testify that he has been of the greatest service to our German brethren, and I am in hopes that he will gradually become more and more useful to them. What I would emphasize is the great importance of settling affairs in a pleasant, amicable way, and of employing in the treatment of our northerners who are not seriously ill of soul gentle rather than drastic remedies."[3]

In subsequent letters Peter assures his General that, though Father Vitoria is too much given to making changes and innovations in domestic matters such as the hours of meals and the methods of cooking, under pretext of bringing everything into conformity with the usages of the Roman College, nevertheless he " is of great assistance in the government of the Province, gradually progresses towards the golden mean, and

---

[1] Maximilian, with whom, strange to say, Vitoria got on rather well.
[2] Braunsberger, *Epistulae*, vol. ii, p. 150.
[3] Braunsberger, *Epistulae*, vol. ii, p. 157.

the longer he remains with us will tend to become more mature and prudent in action." He accordingly begs the General on no account to recall him from Germany, even though that might be the Father's own desire.

To Peter's great contentment Father Delanoy was restored to Vienna in accordance with his request. He wrote at once to Vitoria begging him to take the new arrival as his ally, to consult him frequently, " to be gentle in his dealings with subjects, to moderate his sternness and not to consider changes of external discipline so important when no rule or custom of the Society called for them." Peter was the last person to think that he was himself a paragon of discretion. In all this sad story of two good men at loggerheads he constantly takes the blame for what is going wrong. Thus, writing to Laynez in February, 1558, he says : " I am greatly astonished that Father Vitoria has not approached the King in Prague during the last few months in order to obtain help for the College of that City which is being so abominably ill-used. *Deus semper laudetur*. With regard to that same Father, I thank your Reverence heartily for having prudently admonished me to treat him with tact and to encourage rather than dispirit him, so that you may be the better able to use his services in Germany. I hope that I shall be at one with him in all things and that I shall thus fulfil your Reverence's commands. For the love of God I beg you never to cease reprehending me about small matters as about great, and to point out my mistakes to me, above all such mistakes as I fall into in the discharge of this office of Provincial. Certain it is that I often fail and go wrong, acting as I do without that true understanding and discretion which are more necessary in this than in other Provinces."[1]

During the Lent of 1558 St. Peter went to Straubing to preach a course of sermons and thither Father Vitoria made his way from Prague to put all his cards on the table. He was in a humble and dejected mood at the time. His nerve had failed him a little and he needed encouragement. How the interviews passed off is explained by Peter :

I gave him, according to his wishes, full power to arrange matters as he considered best, but I also counselled him to consult the other Fathers and to seek the advice of superiors about affairs in the settlement of which antagonism to his plans was to be expected. With this I coupled advice to restrain his rather harsh disposition and to treat the brethren with greater gentleness, seeing that I had received letters of complaint from all three colleges. His Reverence remained three

[1] Braunsberger, *Epistulae*, vol. ii, pp. 205–6.

or four days with me and consulted me about everything, to my great consolation. He is full of excellent good-will and works very hard in the colleges of Prague and Vienna, which provide him with exercise in patience, owing to the frailties and contrariness of our brethren. I think that he is serving Our Lord in this way just as well as he could in a professor's chair. . . . His chief failing, it seems to me, is an itch and propensity for making regulations, and for chopping and changing when there is no real call for it. But there is hope that, with the help of Christ Our Lord, he will go forward from good to better."[1]

When Peter visited the College of Vienna in September, 1558, he was delighted with the excellent progress being made under Vitoria's management and wrote of him in terms of warm admiration to the General. Breaking into Italian he described him as " *un gran negotiatore* " and told of his fine sermons, his building operations, and the healthy state of discipline which he maintained in the house. But, alas, the old complaint had not disappeared. " I hear reprehended in Father Vitoria a certain importunity, and that he is too solemn, both outside and at home. He is not sufficiently affable, calm, and gentle. However, these are light and curable faults. I shall speak to him about them before I leave."

While Peter was on an unpleasant mission to Poland to be described later on, he received a most friendly letter from Vitoria, who avowed that he put forward the many suggestions it contained with the completest deference. That sounded very well, but when the Provincial ventured to criticize one or other proposal as being contrary to the wishes of Rome, Vitoria promptly wrote requesting to be relieved of his post. He was still wedded to his project of obtaining various chairs for the Jesuits, and primarily for himself, at the University of Vienna, in spite of the almost insuperable difficulties in the path of his ambition. Difficulties, however, were his daily bread. His appetite for them appeared to be Gargantuan, and he was not the sort of man to hesitate because it might fall to others to clean up the mess which his intemperate zeal showed every sign of making. St. Peter's opposition to his moves was certainly not prompted by mere faintheartedness or an unwillingness to adventure something for religion's sake. All his life was such an adventure, but he held strongly to the sound old principle that a little well done is better than much done slovenly. He tried in every way he could to procure good professors for the University of Vienna and, at the same time, maintained resolutely that no professor at all was preferable to an unsuitable one. But Vitoria could not see this, nor could he be brought to understand that he himself, with his strongly Spanish outlook and ignorance of the German character, was the least suited of any to hold a public academic post. Consequently he began to suspect his Provincial of deliberately thwarting him.

Another source of controversy between the two men was Vitoria's habit of piling up the burdens of his unfortunate subjects. Though St. Peter was heart and soul in all the good work being done at Prague and Vienna, he never lost sight of the human instruments. They came first and it was ever his first care to ensure that their health did not suffer from over-exertion. To prevent even the possibility of this happening he gave orders more than once that certain new departures in the colleges were not to be persisted in; and wherever work seemed to grow, as it were spontaneously, he would at once send any men he could possibly spare to relieve the pressure. Not so Father Vitoria. That fine old war-horse only cried Aha! at the sound of the trumpets, and could not for the life of him see why other men should be less ready than himself to have their backs broken. One little story of many illustrates his methods. On his journey to Prague in 1558 he had been fêted by the country people and conceived such a liking for them that he determined to send the young men of the College out as missionaries, *more Indico*, into the villages near the Bohemian capital. On Pentecost Sunday he started operations, setting off accompanied by two young men. None of them knew a word of Czech nor had they the least idea what sort of reception they would get from the Jews and Hussites among whom they were venturing. It proved so hostile that one of Father Vitoria's companions took to his heels. Vitoria pursued him and gave him such a rating for his cowardice that he faced about, preferring to brave the brick-bats and blasphemies of the peasants rather than the tongue of his irate Superior. Despite the strenuous endeavours of the three heroes, the whole expedition proved a fiasco. It could hardly have been anything else without a repetition of what happened on the first Pentecost Sunday, because the Jesuits could not speak any Czech nor the peasants any German.[1]

St. Peter was lost in admiration at his friend's enterprise on every front. Referring to the professorships project, he wrote to Laynez:

In this as in many other matters I do not so much disapprove as admire the stout-heartedness with which Father Vitoria embarks on

[1] Schmidl, *Historiae Societatis Jesu Provinciae Bohemiae pars prima*, pp. 117–8.

such large undertakings, nothing fearing those difficulties which would deter other men from attempts of the kind. And since I see that his daring and pious confidence in God lead to no evil results, I prefer to be a spectator rather than a disturber of his hopes. I therefore permit him, and shall go on permitting him, to abound in his own sense unless graver evils threaten, praying again and again this alone, that his pious solicitude may not lead him too far. For my part, I believe that we ought not at present to bother the Emperor about those professorships, first, lest we seem to promise more than we can perform, seeing that we are not sure of the number or quality of the men Rome may provide nor when they can come, and then again because the petition is invidious and may bring us, without any need or good result, into odium with other professors or masters who aspire to the posts. . . .

In brief, I think that as things are at present it ought to be enough for us to administer our own schools wisely and to form in them men who would, later on, with better opportunity, merit well of the faculty of arts in Vienna and elsewhere. . . .[1]

It is the quality expressed in these lines of seeing all round a subject that marks the true diplomatist. St. Peter was thinking ahead all the time, planning for a future which hasty counsels might so easily have compromised. And he wanted his men to be happy and at peace in their employments, not fussed into feverish activity by the slave-driving Vitoria. At the beginning of the year 1559, when he had started his magnificent apostolate in Augsburg, Vitoria still occupied his mind. " I am writing to him," he tells Laynez, " begging him to deal with people according to their characters and not to be sure that what he considers best should immediately be extorted. Patience, too, has its victories, and by going slow we go farther."[2]

About this time, Father Thomas Lentulus, the Rector of Ingolstadt, with whom Father Couvillon had had so many skirmishes, migrated from the Jesuits to the Carthusians, as he was perfectly entitled to do. But, like Couvillon, he was a restless soul and soon applied to St. Peter for re-admission to the Society, on the grounds that the Carthusians were not holy enough for him. The truth, of course, lay the other way round, as Peter knew very well. On the good man's return he found it extremely difficult to place him, as he refused to live under Vitoria, and the Ingolstadt Fathers showed no enthusiasm to have him back in their community. Only Prague remained, and there did not appear to be any

[1] Braunsberger, *Epistulae*, vol. ii, pp. 348-9.   [2] Braunsberger, *Epistulae*, vol. ii, p. 374.

suitable post for him there. Finally the Saint thought of sending him to Oybin to supersede the Father in charge of the few Jesuits there, who was "by nature too severe, and very particular in his government, thus, perhaps, proving burdensome to himself and to others." Before deciding anything about Oybin, Peter called Vitoria into consultation, as he had recently been to inspect that *damnosa haereditas*. They talked and talked, but could find no way of constraining the Protestants of Zittau, who farmed the monastery, to pay their just and reasonable dues to its owners, the Prague Jesuits. Vitoria was for having the agreement by which the property had been leased rescinded. But how was the rescinding to be brought about, and would the Jesuits themselves be able to run the place ? objected Peter. Would there not be endless trouble with the former lessees, who had already proved their determination and ability to balk any Catholic activities in their neighbourhood ? The anxiety caused by this and other misfortunes of his Province made Peter so ill that public prayers had to be ordered for him in Rome.[1]

All the time, as was his invariable custom, he kept his superiors informed about every detail of Province business, and wrote in the most childlike spirit for advice to such representative men as Nadal. Again and again he reports that Father Vitoria is a great help and consolation to him. "Just as he outmatches me in many qualities and virtues, so is he a more dexterous man of affairs and a better gatherer of alms." He was like that with everybody, no matter how much trouble they might have given. Father Lentulus, the former Rector of Ingolstadt, remains his "*carissimus Frater, Magister Thomas,*" to whom he sends warmest greetings, though he knew him to be on the point of abandoning the Society of Jesus a second time for a canon's stall at Nymegen. Similarly he many times begs the prayers of Laynez and the Roman Fathers for Schorich, Feyrabend, Lapidano, Krieger, and other priests and scholastics who, after giving all the trouble they could, had deserted the colours. "*Det illis Dominus spiritum compunctionis . . . ut ad suum ovile se recipiant, Domino miserante,*" was his prayer. In spite of the heroic forbearance and true charity which he had shown towards all the dissidents, he takes to himself the blame for the misfortunes which they brought upon his Province. Writing to Laynez in December, 1559, with reference to certain instructions on the observance of the recently promulgated constitutions, he said :

Would that in the members of the Society the same solicitude were found as is shown by its Head ! For my part, I am forced to confess

[1] Braunsberger, *Epistulae*, vol. ii, pp. 418–21.

that I do not at all live up to the obligations of a professed Father or Provincial, as set forth in the constitutions. My failure is due partly to indolence, as I have not hitherto given serious thought to this divine discipline, and partly to my ineptitude, imprudence, and singular blindness. I therefore suppliantly beg your Paternity's forgiveness and would ask you to impose some penance on me, so that corrected by your fatherly discipline I may begin with the new year, the Lord helping me, to show fresh diligence and complete obedience. I beg Him from my heart that by means of your Reverence He may some day deliver me from this heavy office, and provide me with better opportunities of exercising my soul freely in all humility and obedience, and of advancing in my vocation, to which I know I am not sufficiently faithful. Pray for me meantime, I beg you of your charity, and hold for certain that there is no Provincial in the Society who needs more help and better guidance than I do.[1]

The Saint need not have feared that he would lack opportunities of exercising humility while Father Vitoria was in the offing. That good soul had been puzzling for some time over the problem of helping the many poor scholars whom he had taken under his wing. Books were their great need and they had no money to buy them. Suddenly a brilliant light dawned on Father Juan. He would set up a printing-press of his own at the College and supply the students with their texts at a rate far below what any bookseller would charge. With Vitoria execution always followed close on the heels of conception, and very soon, by dint of begging, he was possessed of sufficient money to purchase type in Nuremberg. It was a hand press, of course, and the type could not have been called exquisite, but at any rate it was possible to read the impression it made. St. Peter hoped that in the course of time many good books would be the reward of Vitoria's labours. He doubted, however, whether the Jesuits themselves could manage the business unaided, and was confirmed in his doubt when Vitoria wrote asking for a compositor, a reader, a bookbinder, and other such experts. The Society of Jesus was not rich in that vein, as Peter discovered after some exploring. Reluctantly he had to tell the General that he considered the whole thing to be a luxury which would probably involve the Viennese Jesuits in a great deal of labour and bother, and that it might be much wiser to put the press in the hands of business-men, if any could be found to assume the responsibility. Vitoria quite agreed for once in a way, but the business-men were

[1] Braunsberger, *Epistulae*, vol. ii, p. 557.

shy when he approached them. Printing, after all, was a trade with traditions, and the good Father's amateur efforts failed signally to impress the hard heads of Vienna. He was left with his white elephant on his hands, which did not greatly improve his temper when Peter's forebodings of trouble began to come true.[1]

In spite of everything, at the beginning of 1560 the two men were still on the best of terms, Peter loving the eager heart of Vitoria, and Vitoria, on his side, doing his utmost in his own way to fall in with the wishes of his Provincial. The following letter which the Rector addressed to the Provincial in January, 1560, gives us many clues to the character of its writer and shows what a really fine and earnest man he was:

If I seem to address your Reverence sometimes in an excited manner, that, doubtless, is due to the fact that my old Adam is not yet transformed into the new. My difficulty is that I do not rightly see how I can satisfy everybody, so as to prevent them lodging quite fair complaints against me, who, more than others, ought to work without blame in the justifications and commandments of God. I regret that there are people who do not understand me properly, but your Reverence knows how difficult and troublesome it is to humble a proud heart. In your letter these words occur : ' Our titles may be different, I being called Provincial and Vitoria, Rector, but I beg that we may be and remain one in union of souls.' These are your words. I, for my part, make bold to affirm that by the goodness of God I in no way desire to keep my title and office, and that my one greatest desire has always been to know and completely fulfil the wishes of my superiors in thought, will, and deed. If I have not hitherto obtained this grace from God I feel sure that it is my sins which prevent it.

It saddens rather than frightens me that sometimes I do not know exactly what I am to do in order not to deviate a hair's breadth from the instructions and wishes of my superiors and my Father Provincial. I shall not comment, Reverend Father, on all the matters affecting me which appear on your last page, but there is one point I fail to understand, namely when you say that if I were in your shoes I should make less fuss at being entreated so often on behalf of the men in Prague, and would send the document promised with less delay. Well, I am entirely unconscious of having denied the Prague Fathers anything or of having made any promise. Your Reverence bade me send you the

[1] Braunsberger, *Epistulae*, vol. ii, pp. 528–9.

letters from the Prague College with my own opinion attached to them. I did so, and afterwards heard not a single word about the matter. . . .

At this point I shall quote your own very words. You say: 'I confess that I deal with other Fathers more freely than with your Reverence because you seem to be too afraid of me, and perhaps would take it hardly if I were to write to you more plainly and outspokenly.' Passing over all else that might be said with regard to this statement, I shall merely remark that I have more than once dealt with your Reverence in the manner you commend. I beg you, Father, to reflect carefully on everything according to your prudence and, if you discover for certain any occasion on which I have fallen short of your expectations, either by commission or omission, enjoin me, not a light, but a most severe penance. I have always been ready, praise be to Christ, and am absolutely ready now—speaking according to the interior man, for the flesh may burst if it likes provided the spirit retains its energy—not only for meals at the little table,[1] but also for stripes and every kind of mortification, if by your slightest nod you give me to understand that such are my deserts. . . .

This one thing I beg and implore, Father, *per viscera misericordiae Dei nostri*, that you will not allow anything in my letters, which I know I often write with little premeditation, nor any hints or words of others to deter you if you consider in Our Lord that a penance is expedient for me. The fear of you in which I stand is not servile, I think. Were my heart devoid of it and of those feelings of reverence which I owe to you and to God I would be much worse, Father, than you consider me. I do not therefore believe that I am more afraid than I ought rightly to be, and I am afraid not so much of anybody else as of myself, lest I fall short of my obligations to God and my vocation. By God's grace I desire to satisfy both to the full. . . .

You shall, then, Reverend Father, do with me what you will, and I, by the favour of Jesus Christ, shall so compose my soul that it may be as it were *materia prima*[2] ready to assume any form, provided I know from the judgment of the superiors whom it has pleased God to put over me that the forms are such as I may receive without offence to His Divine Majesty.[3]

---

[1] To eat one's meal, begged from the others in the refectory, kneeling at a little table apart from the rest of the community, is a form of monastic penance.

[2] An abstraction in Scholastic metaphysics. Think of a lump of soft putty and all the forms into which it might be shaped. But the lump itself is a form and the colour, size, smell, feel, and taste of it are other forms. Get rid of all these and of the atomic structure of the molecules of putty and you have *materia prima*.

[3] Braunsberger, *Epistulae*, vol. ii, pp. 574–6.

As St. Peter was overwhelmed with work at this time he asked his half-brother, Theodoric Canisius, to reply to the various points raised by Vitoria and, in particular, " to console him and bid him be of good heart." He continued to sing Vitoria's praises in his letters to Rome, making constant references to his wonderful diligence and sagacity. Peter was quite ready to let him have his own way in the conduct of affairs. Indeed, he had already given him *carte blanche*, only earnestly advising him to seek the counsel of other Fathers. The root of the difficulty between the two men was not in the sphere of external business at all, but in the sphere of internal government. Vitoria treated his subjects too harshly, and that Peter could not tolerate. In May, 1560, the Rector wished to have three of the Viennese Jesuits dismissed from the Society for indiscipline, and was annoyed when, instead, the Provincial transferred them to another college " to see whether for the love of God they might not be willing to turn over a new leaf." How little Peter was in danger of under-estimating Vitoria's worth was shown when the Roman authorities decided to send him to Poland. Peter argued might and main against the proposal, on the ground that Vitoria was indispensable to the welfare of the rapidly expanding College in Vienna. At this time the two were definitely drifting apart, though the Provincial had vowed to do all in his power to keep in the good graces of the Rector.[1] Now something happened to strain the relations more severely than ever.

In the summer of 1560 St. Peter received instructions that Father Vitoria and another Viennese Jesuit were to be professed of the four solemn vows the following February. According to the constitutions of their Order they had to submit to a number of tests beforehand, such as going on pilgrimage with nothing in their pockets, begging from door to door, waiting on the sick in hospitals, serving under the cook at home, and similar offices. Peter obtained for his two hard-worked men a remission of the more arduous of these exercises, but Vitoria, when the time came, made difficulties about being professed at all. He said that he was utterly unworthy and got as excited as if he had been elected Pope. Then suddenly, with a typical *volte-face*, he wrote to Peter, asking whether it would not be a good thing to carry out the ceremony with as much pomp and magnificence as possible, so as to show the scoffers of Austria and Germany that vows were not trifles to be despised. The Saint replied that he would prefer the ceremony to be quite simple, in accordance with Jesuit custom, but that he left the matter to Vitoria's discretion, merely expressing a

[1] Braunsberger, *Epistulae*, vol. ii, p. 740.

desire for a minimum of pomp.[1] Vitoria, however, was by now thoroughly
roused. His misgivings about his worthiness had changed into a crusading
pride. None but a cardinal to preside at the function would satisfy his
grand ideas, so he embarrassed Stanislaus Hosius, recently promoted to
the purple, with a request to fill the rôle. Hosius did not know what
to think and put his problem before St. Peter:

> Father Vitoria has asked me to receive his vows as representative
> of Reverend Father General. I have been advised that it would be
> highly improper for me to do so, as I represent the Pope and not Father
> General.[2] But Father Vitoria refused to be put off, as he wants the
> ceremony to be done with great pomp. This idea of his offends both
> the Emperor and King Maximilian. To speak the truth, I do not like
> it either, for, though he gives out that it will serve to edify many
> people, I foresee, on the contrary, that it will make a big scandal. I
> mentioned my own case to him as an example, saying that I had
> pronounced my oath of obedience to the Pope[3] without any show.
> But he is still wedded to his idea which pleases him better. I would
> willingly humour him, but I am compelled also to think of my position,
> which does not permit of my receiving his vows in place of Father
> General. I fear that I should become a subject of rumour if I did so.
> Still, if the affair could be carried through without pomp, I would
> not be so reluctant. At the moment I am trying to make up my mind
> as to the course to take.[4]

In the event Hosius refused to appear and showed Vitoria plainly
that he was disgusted with his proceedings. Nothing daunted, the Rector
then boldly invited the Emperor and King Maximilian to grace the occasion
with their presence. The confessor of the Emperor told St. Peter that
both monarchs had expressed to him their annoyance at the invitation,
but, not wanting to seem discourteous, each sent a bishop to represent
him at the function. The Emperor also gave seventy thalers towards the
expenses of decorating the Jesuit Church and lent beautiful hangings
from his private chapel for the same purpose. Vitoria, who did not suffer
from shyness, had probably asked him for them. On the great day, the
Bishop of Fünfkirchen, King Maximilian's representative, sang High Mass.
When the time came to pronounce the vows, a grand procession was
formed, at the head of which walked our hero carrying a crucifix and

---

[1] Braunsberger, *Epistulae*, vol. iii, p. 92.   [3] On being made a cardinal a few weeks earlier.
[2] He was Apostolic Nuncio in Vienna at this time.   [4] Braunsberger, *Epistulae*, vol. iii, p. 116.

Cardinal Hosius
From a print in the British Museum

lighted candle. Never before and never since in the Society of Jesus was there such a ceremony. When it had ended, seventy of the students decked out in gorgeous robes performed a play that lasted five hours.[1]

Such was Vitoria's triumph, a tragi-comedy that had at least the good effect of bringing an ordinance from Rome forbidding anything of the kind in the future. The General's letter, dispatched in his name to St. Peter by Polanco, May 24, 1561, was as follows:

> Our Reverend Father General understands that Dr. Vitoria, Rector of the College of Vienna, has made his profession with enough solemnity, or, indeed, more than enough, if we consider the simplicity which our constitutions require and of which our professed Fathers have hitherto given an example. In Dr. Vitoria's case we attribute the solemnity to a desire of giving edification, seeing that he arranged it at a time and in a country acquainted, apparently, with the collapse of solemn vows and the monastic life, his purpose being to restore them to honour in men's minds by the external pomp of the profession and the presence of illustrious persons. Nevertheless, so much festivity and splendour do not seem to our Father General sufficiently in accordance with the vows which we make, nor with the simplicity demanded by our constitutions. Wherefore he has deemed it proper to impose a penance on the Rector of the College for having in his pious zeal overstepped the limits of moderation, and he enjoins upon your Reverence to permit in the profession ceremonies of your Province only such solemnity as befits the humility and poverty demanded by our institute, in this imitating more closely the professions of our first Fathers.[2]

Troubles now began to fall thick on poor Vitoria's head. All his schemes went awry. He had rightly made a great point of cultivating friendship with King Maximilian, and to that end proposed dedicating to His Majesty a history book which he had caused to be compiled. St. Peter thought it an excellent idea—until he saw the history book. It was an uncritical and rather jejune piece of work, more likely to irritate than placate the highly cultured and fastidious Max. Vitoria had promised it to the King without previously consulting his superiors and, apparently, alive to its shortcomings, did his best to keep it from the eyes of his Provincial. Peter, however, secured a copy and put it before the Ingolstadt

---

[1] Braunsberger, *Epistulae*, vol. iii, p. 143.

[2] Braunsberger, *Epistulae*, vol. iii, p. 153. The penance was not a very heavy one, to say seven Hail Marys, "begging by the intercession of the Blessed Virgin the grace of complete discretion and true humility."

Fathers for censorship. Their verdict was entirely unfavourable, and, as the work had been written largely by a court official, the Jesuits could not themselves undertake to correct it. They, therefore, strongly advised against its publication, to Vitoria's great annoyance.[1]

Shortly after that contretemps, the Provincial and the Rector came into direct conflict. St. Peter cherished a scheme for specializing the work of the various colleges, it being his ambition to make Ingolstadt famous for the excellence of its theological studies, Prague for philosophy, and Vienna for classical learning. Plainly, it was a sound idea, but to bring it about it would have been necessary to transfer the course in dialectics from Vienna to Prague.[2] Now, that did not suit Vitoria's book at all, for he, too, hugged a scheme to his heart. He wished to transform his College in Vienna into a quasi-university. By dint of vigorous protests to Rome he succeeded in wrecking St. Peter's plan, but the only result of his bold ideas for the Viennese College was to make such bad blood between it and the University that the Emperor had to intervene and bid the Jesuits draw in their horns.

In the summer of 1561 three of Vitoria's subjects in Vienna, among them being Father David Eck, nephew of the illustrious Johann, decided that they could no longer endure the rigour of their Rector's law and must say good-bye to the Society of Jesus. At the time the Rector had made himself ill by his imprudent austerities. He used to take his sleep sitting in a hard chair, which certainly cannot have conduced to sweetness of temper the following morning. St. Peter appointed a special nurse to look after him, and then turned his attention to Eck, whose vocation he endeavoured in vain to save by every ruse of charity known to him. Vitoria was greatly distressed over the desertions and begged Peter to provide him with an assistant, or better still, to relieve him of his office altogether. The Saint would not hear of the latter course, and to help Vitoria obtained leave of absence from Augsburg for a fortnight. The days between June 22nd and July 7th, 1561, saw him at the College in Vienna, listening to the complaints of the community, comforting, advising, and encouraging everybody but most of all the Rector himself. To give an example of the spirit that ought to inform superiors he served the brethren at table and did menial work each day in the kitchen. The young

---

[1] Braunsberger, *Epistulae*, vol. iii, pp. 96, 107–8. The work was never published.

[2] Braunsberger, *Epistulae*, vol. iii, p. 52. Peter's reasons for his plan were not wholly scholastic. He desired to ease the burden of the Prague Fathers and to reduce the number of men in Vienna because the College there was " the most unhealthy in the Province owing to the insalubrity of the Viennese air." In other words, Peter wished to have as few of his men as possible exposed to the horrors of the *Föhn*.

Jesuits soon learned to love him, for he was always the same, genial and kindly, with a good word for every comer, even though it might sometimes have to be spiced with a reprimand. He proved, indeed, an almost perfect ruler of men, whose method is not to constrain by a parade of authority, but to guide the subject into willing obedience by making him feel the nobility of his surrender. If he did not succeed completely it was because poor Vitoria had become the prey of some mental disorder for which the salve of charity was of no avail.

Before leaving Vienna, Peter, at the Rector's own request, appointed Father Adam Höller, minister of the College. Shortly afterwards he received a plaintive note from this man, saying that nothing or next to nothing he did or could do found favour in the eyes of Vitoria.[1] The minister of a Jesuit college is also its " prefect of health," and in that capacity Father Höller had obtained from the Provincial a faculty to grant the young men under him permission for a drink outside meal times should their health require it. Presumably the drink in question meant something better than water. After the Minister had granted this leave on a few occasions, Vitoria delivered an exhortation to his community in which he sternly forbade any further quenching of thirst without special leave from himself. Should anybody in the house eat or drink without such leave he was to be accounted guilty of grave disobedience. Continuing his letter to the Provincial, Father Höller said :

These words of the Rector have made me most unhappy, for I would rather die a thousand deaths than act against obedience. And many of the brethren, too, have been disturbed by them. They have begun to say individually : ' I see that Father Minister is nothing but a servant in the College.' Would to God that I were! And they are also saying that before they would ask anything of the Rector they would rather die of starvation. I tell you all this, not because I think that the Rector who is such a prudent man, is unaware of what he is doing, but because I am now more in doubt than ever what I ought to do myself. Your Reverence desired me to make sure that the brethren lacked nothing, but the Rector will not allow me to carry out your instructions. Meantime the brethren are in a state of commotion and affliction which may easily lead them into temptation. I myself am the chief sufferer. Fresh temptations are ever assailing me, though, thanks be to God, not against my vocation. My whole difficulty is so to deal

[1] Braunsberger, *Epistulae*, vol. iii, p. 218.

with the brethren as not to offend God. If I act according to your Reverence's wishes I see clearly that I shall be opposing the will of the Rector. . . .

To open my heart completely to you, I think I have never been so greatly afflicted in my life, and I therefore beg you, as my first Father, to give me counsel. If I am to suffer for the most sweet Name of Jesus, I submit with all my heart. . . . During my time here I have never noticed such a change come over the Rector as has happened since his illness. Another thing he has done is to spoil the wine, for it is his wish that whatever wine is served be mixed half and half with water. Now these German wines, unlike the Italian ones, will not stand such treatment, and the Hungarian wine we have has already been ruined by it. I shall say nothing about the church, which, since the departure of your Reverence, has been so neglected. If anything is needed for it the Rector's usual reply is : ' Do whatever you like but the money I have I am going to use for building purposes.' . . . Things are going badly in the house, too, and it is I who am blamed. . . . He is constantly giving out that the rules for rectors require him to demand hard service from the brethren. I say all this, not because I want to accuse a Father who is so useful to this College and who manages business affairs so well, but in order to obtain a few words of advice from your Reverence as to the course that I ought to pursue.[1]

St. Peter was himself as much puzzled as Father Höller. He sent the letter to Rome with a covering note asking that Vitoria should be counselled to deal less hardly with his subjects, " and especially in the matter of food to treat them more generously and wisely." These are trivial things, but so was the shape of Cleopatra's nose, and it is just such small daily rubs and frictions that often enough spell the ruin of the finest enterprises. Another complaint against Vitoria was that he sent his men on journeys clothed in rags, to the disgust of everybody who met them and knew them to be Jesuits. " I do not dare to admonish him about these matters," wrote Peter, " for sad to say he is not at peace in his office. Rather is he doing all in his power to escape from it. I consulted with the Ingolstadt Fathers and, after praying for guidance, they each wrote to comfort him and confirm him in the post of Rector which he has hitherto held with great advantage. Perhaps he is placing on his shoulders more burdens than they can bear with his many big under-

[1] Braunsberger, *Epistulae*, vol. iii, pp. 218-20.

takings. . . ."[1] Father Delanoy, an independent witness, held the same opinion that the root of Vitoria's trouble was his incapacity to fold his arms for a minute. The grandiose edifices he had constructed, his printing-press and boarding schools for poor students and for the sons of the nobility, pulled him down because he had neither the funds nor the men to carry them on satisfactorily. " He does not seem the same man *qualis erat heri et nudiustertius*," wrote Delanoy in Scriptural phrase. " We have not failed to console the excellent Father. Father Provincial has done so himself by letter and by providing assistance, and he has instructed me and others to perform the same act of charity, as it were on our own independent account."

Certainly, it would be difficult to maintain that Vitoria was the victim of persecution. Whatever he asked for, within the resources of the Province, he received, and not only that but permission to follow his own will in the affairs of his College. Then, when in spite of urgent warning he had collapsed under the pressure of his intemperate zeal, his Provincial, without a word of recrimination, interrupted his own important work to comfort and encourage him. Even when it became necessary to point out some fault, the operation was performed with the most delicate tact. Thus Delanoy, writing in St. Peter's name, adverts to the old, old com-plaint of Vitoria's harshness in the following style : " We must try to remember, Reverend Father, that the Germans are rather susceptible and thin-skinned people. Hardly ever do they arrive at such a pitch of patience or become so proficient and perfect in virtue, as to be able to bear hard words or strong reprimands. It is the way they are made. But they atone for this failing by many good qualities which our Creator and Lord usually bestows on them. May your Reverence take this candid speaking of mine in good part and accept my words in the spirit in which they are uttered. Good-bye, dearest Father, and continue to love us as always."[2]

The Germans, as a matter of fact, are not half as touchy as Vitoria's own countrymen[3] but St. Peter and his allies were ready to pretend the opposite, in hopes that such an argument might soothe the Rector's feelings and manœuvre him into treating his subjects with greater forbearance. Peter had with him in Augsburg a Spanish Jesuit to whom he was devoted. This Father, Hurtado Perez, was his right hand man but, thinking that his nationality might render him acceptable to Vitoria, he parted with

---

[1] Braunsberger, *Epistulae*, vol. iii, p. 225.
[2] Braunsberger, *Epistulae*, vol. iii, p. 252.
[3] Still, generalizations about nations are very silly. William Shakespeare and Oliver Cromwell, Richard Cobden and Rupert Brooke, were all complete Englishmen.

him and sent him to Vienna, at the same time professing his readiness to let the Rector have any other particular helper he desired. In spite of all, however, Rector and Provincial became more and more estranged. A note of downright hostility crept into Vitoria's communications with his Superior. No longer did he object merely to Peter's government but to Peter's unfortunate self. "I dare answer him nothing," said the Saint, "nor give him any admonitions . . . for fear of making him angry. He owes four hundred florins to the Rector of the Prague College, but when I gently advised him to pay the debt, as had been requested, he took great offence and replied harshly that he suspected all sorts of things. I tell you this against my will, and only in order to secure the wise decision of my superiors. I beg them not to spare me at all in this matter but to reprehend me freely, so that the Rector of the College of Vienna may be helped and suffer no detriment through fault of mine."[1]

In the autumn of 1561 the trouble at Vienna became so serious that the authorities in Rome decided to appoint a new Rector, leaving to Vitoria only the administration of temporal affairs. Laynez was then absent on papal business in France, and the Society of Jesus was being governed by Father Salmeron as Vicar-General, with Pedro Ribadeneyra as his secretary. The General had written twice urging the removal of Vitoria, but his lieutenants in Rome, persuaded by the arguments of St. Peter, delayed until Laynez was put in possession of his letter. Laynez, however, held to his point, and Peter was accordingly informed by Ribadeneyra on October 18th that Father Hoffaeus, the Rector of Prague, must supersede Vitoria at Vienna, the latter remaining on as a sort of procurator of the Province but without any authority over the Jesuits of the three colleges whose revenues he administered. As this arrangement gave the good man's talents for business ample scope, St. Peter expressed warm approval.

Just before the news reached him from Rome, Peter had sent Father Delanoy to Vienna in the rôle of peacemaker. Vitoria saw in the move a new slight to his authority and wrote in sarcastic vein to Salmeron on the subject. Shortly afterwards his pent-up irritation boiled over completely in a Spanish letter addressed direct to Laynez at Paris. In this distressing document he invokes Father Delanoy as a witness without the slightest warrant, for that Father's own letters are extant to prove how little he sympathized with the tantrums of his Spanish colleague. After a preliminary gesture of humility in which he attributes some of the trouble in Vienna to his sins, Vitoria goes on:

[1] Braunsberger, *Epistulae*, vol. iii, p. 254.

Putting on one side that more secret reason, in the opinion of Father Delanoy a principal cause of the trouble is the fact that the Father Provincial has not the talent necessary for his office. Moreover, he undertakes other tasks which are not necessary but for which he feels a greater inclination and aptitude. There are, for instance, his sermons, which, according to Father Delanoy, he does not prepare properly. He neglects to think them out and merely dictates to somebody, in the intervals of his work as Provincial, such casual thoughts as come into his head. These he then delivers, often without any oral rehearsal. Again, he writes on many subjects, sometimes to no good purpose. He is in correspondence with various people on questions of ecclesiastical reform and what not, and converses with all sorts of people on such and other matters which are above my head. On one occasion, treating of an important question, he gave utterance to dangerous doctrine. In these ways he is a hindrance to the foundation of colleges of the Society, notwithstanding the good hopes there are that God Our Lord in His bounty and power will produce from them results tending to His glory. . . .

But leaving aside matters which may seem to be accusations and also the whole question of his behaviour in these and many other respects, especially in the realm of government, I have deemed it necessary for the discharge of my conscience to advise your Reverence that it is vitally important, and more so than I am now able to explain, that one of two things should be done. Either the burden of office ought to be taken from him and given to a more suitable man who is closer in spirit to the other superiors of the Society in the manner of government, or else—and this seems the more convenient and advantageous course—the Province should be divided and these colleges of the Emperor[1] put under another superior, more acceptable to King Maximilian. . . .

There are twenty-four or twenty-five plain reasons for this course, the principal being the Provincial's lack of aptitude for his post; his peculiar character which causes him to act out of tune with the customs of the Society; his occupations as a preacher, etc.; the fact that the Province is very much scattered; the great need in which the colleges stand of the Provincial's help and frequent inspection; the danger and inconvenience arising from the frequent summonses of rectors to consultations with him or with others in his name, which results

---

[1] Vienna, Prague, and Innsbruck.

in the abandonment of their colleges; the fact that he is not acceptable to King Maximilian, though he is so to the Emperor; . . . the further fact that he has no fixed place of residence except where the Court happens to be, and that he never makes one of the colleges his headquarters. He has lived hitherto under alien jurisdiction,[1] and in places remote from these parts which hold very nearly the last place in his consideration.[2]

Such was Vitoria's charge sheet, but not content with its wealth he added a final fling at St. Peter's life-long work for the promotion and sanctification of the Church's bishops. According to him, colleges were at that time much more important than bishoprics, which, to say the least of it, is not a very orthodox proposition. He was, of course, perfectly within his rights in complaining to Laynez, and some of his representations had sound common sense behind them. St. Peter assuredly *was* overburdened but that had come about because his superiors willed it so, and not through any Vitorian itch for new employments. Every single task he undertook had been given him by Rome, and if he was unable to live regularly in a Jesuit house that again was Rome's responsibility. Time after time he had expressed an ardent longing to be with his brethren, leading the good, common life in which he believed the best happiness outside Heaven was to be found, but not until the evening of his days did it become his portion. Maximilian's attitude to the Church neutralizes any sting there might be in Vitoria's grumble about Peter's disfavour in that quarter, and as for the sermons, the reader will see in a subsequent chapter whether or no the Saint scamped their preparation. The best of Vitoria's suggestions was that the Province should be divided, though in the natural evolution of events that must soon have happened in any case. As for his general criticisms, the Roman authorities answered them by leaving St. Peter in his post for eight years more, which, added to the time he had already served, was the longest term of office save one of any provincial superior of the German Jesuits down to the present day.

In his letter to Laynez Vitoria was within his rights. He said what he thought, however mistakenly, or what he thought Father Delanoy thought. But that is not the end of the story, for he carried on a sort of vendetta against his Provincial both inside and outside the Society. Father Pisanus, a distinguished member of the staff in Vienna, reported to the

[1] In Bavaria.   [2] Braunsberger, *Epistulae*, vol. iii, pp. 763–6.

General that " he did not treat his Provincial with due reverence privately, and in public spoke against him, taxing him with imprudence and inconstancy."[1] So complicated and unhappy did his opposition become that even the most judicious heads were puzzled as to the rights and wrongs of it. Father Pisanus, in his charity, assured the General that neither party was at fault, having said which he went straight on to mention several misdemeanours of Vitoria ! Polanco, on the other hand, surmised that both men must be guilty to some extent, the Provincial's crime being that he had not expressed his mind with sufficient clearness to the Rector. That was true, but Peter had more than once explained that he dared not express his mind for fear of causing an explosion. On the few occasions when he tried to do so the explosion came off as regular as the clock.

This distressing minor chapter of Jesuit history is now nearing its conclusion and, perhaps, it will be wondered why it was written at all. The answer is the following letter, to which all that has been related forms a necessary preface. The letter is from St. Peter to Alfonso Salmeron, Vicar-General of the Society of Jesus, and bears the subscription, ' Innsbruck, May 4, 1562 ':

The Peace of Christ be with us, Very Reverend Father. I wrote the day before yesterday, chiefly about the affairs of this College. Now, having received a letter from the Rector of Prague, I am compelled to tell you its contents that, knowing the disease, you may decide in good time about a remedy before worse evil befalls. I can solemnly testify that no word or deed of Reverend Father Vitoria on occasions when he appears to have been chagrined with me causes me to complain. Indeed, I earnestly beg your Reverence to put aside all consideration for me personally and, thinking only of the common good of this Province, to choose a more suitable Provincial, entirely free of those failings which Father Vitoria with good reason reprehends in me. I promise you that I shall not say a word to him respecting his accusations, and I beg you most urgently to forgive him if he has in any way acted less prudently, imputing to me rather than to him the blame for this raging storm, which could not have arisen but for my imperfections. I shall not feel it anything but a big blessing if I am given a heavy penance for my failure to treat that good Father with greater prudence and more tactful esteem. May the Lord be merciful to me and grant this Province an effective ruler, whether Father Vitoria

[1] Braunsberger, *Epistulae*, vol. iii, p. 769.

himself, or Father Delanoy, or some other man. To him I would gladly and unreservedly submit myself, by the grace of Jesus Christ, who for our sake humbled Himself, becoming obedient unto the most cruel death of the Cross.

The letter of the Rector of Prague is in the following terms : ' Father Vitoria, true to type, still goes on with his constant and sufficiently serious complaints against Reverend Father Provincial. He says that, though he loves and reverences him in virtue of his office and vocation, he is altogether unable to bear him out in matters of government, because it would be against his conscience and to the detriment of the colleges. Frequent assertions of his are that Father Provincial is not suited for his post but rather for the business of preaching and writing, that he himself is and always will remain the Provincial's opposite in every respect, and that Father Delanoy, too, cannot be entirely exculpated, as he is the Provincial's fellow-countryman.[1] It was for these reasons, he says, that he gave up the Rectorship of Vienna and is now striving by every means in his power to avoid meeting and speaking with the Provincial, as nothing more distasteful or terrible could happen to him than to have any further dealings with that man. Meanwhile, he laments grievously that, though he has several times written clearly enough to the Roman Fathers about these matters, they dissemble as if they did not want to understand the affair. Nevertheless, he is awaiting a letter from the Eternal City which will either relieve him altogether of his present office or give him freedom to deal with college business as he deems best.'

These and several other things which it is a greater pleasure to omit than to record are the burden of the letter from the Rector of Prague. He has advised me to be very careful in communicating them to your Paternity lest you should be scandalized, but by the grace of God I have no fear that a mere exhibition of human weakness will so affect you. I have therefore written freely in order to forestall future evils. The Rector concludes his letter as follows : ' In my opinion if this trouble goes on much longer there is reason to apprehend that Father Vitoria will gradually waste away and die under the stress of his thoughts. I have hitherto pretended not to notice, considering it better to lie low. On a few occasions I have spoken to him as gently as I possibly could, but now that all has been in vain I am in doubt whether it is advisable or even permissible to give him sacramental

[1] And so, presumably, should have understood his character and opposed his goings-on.

absolution unless he undertakes to speak and think more justly of his Superior in future. . . .'

Such are the Rector's own words to which I now add a few of mine. In the first place, I am extremely sorry that Father Vitoria is so sadly afflicted in body and soul, and even perhaps in danger, on account of my imperfections. Secondly, it is my very greatest desire and wish that I should be admonished and punished severely for all my previous negligence and blunders in the fulfilment of my duty, about which Father Vitoria might well be called as a witness. In the third place, I am sincerely convinced that Father Vitoria's prudence may be more safely trusted than mine. Fourthly, with regard to the absolution I am writing to tell the Rector that he should not deny the good Father this blessing, especially since, as I believe, he made known the aforesaid complaints to one person only and that in good faith, and meantime he is ready to do whatever his principal Superior, Father General, may command. Should the Rector think, however, that a secret and fraternal admonition was called for, he might proceed with it in order the better to extract the root of bitterness from Father Vitoria's soul. And he might also try to persuade him to refer everything which he disliked in the Provincial to Father General or to his Vicar in Rome, so that divine providence by the instrumentality of superiors may dispose all things more strongly and sweetly. . . .

Finally, I beg that Father Vitoria may be treated with kindness, lest on my account he continue to be so woefully afflicted, and that I may be made to pay the just penalty for my misdeeds, whether I remain in this post of Provincial, or whether, as I consider the more expedient course, I am left the sole function of a preacher. Pray to the Lord for me, Father, because I am in sore need of your Holy Sacrifices and prayers. . . .[1]

Sad to tell, Vitoria never seems to have made it up with St. Peter. He continued for a few years more to work and worry in the Emperor's dominions and was then recalled to the land of his heart's desire, Italy, where he served the Church with unflagging enthusiasm to the end of his days.

[1] Braunsberger, *Epistulae*, vol. iii, pp. 429–32.

CHAPTER IX

BETWEEN WHILES

THOUGH the establishment of new schools was St. Peter's principal work during this middle period of his life, it by no means absorbed all his attention. He had dozens of other irons in the fire and was involved in a whirl of disconnected activities which could not by any Procrustean trick of a biographer be made to come under a single heading. The only thing to be done, then, if we are to represent truthfully the complexities of a life which baffles our search for an external pattern, is to gather the fragments from time to time into as neat a pile as we can, with due respect to the exacting Titan, Cronus. To change the metaphor, the preceding chapter on St. Peter's work for schools has only a single theme or a theme with variations, but his life, like most men's lives, was ' contrapuntal,' or had many simultaneous tunes in its music. That must be the excuse for the omnium gatherum of the following pages.

In August, 1556, Peter, as provincial superior, was notified that the first general congregation of the Society of Jesus would be held in Rome in November. The main business of the congregation was to be the election of a new General in place of St. Ignatius, but the ratification of the constitutions of the Society also had a place in the programme. According to the constitutions, each province must send three representatives to Rome, including the provincial superior, and so it came about that St. Peter was on the long road to Padua in October, unaware of the storm that lowered upon the Eternal City. At Padua he heard of the postponement of the congregation to the following year, owing to the war which the Spaniard-hating Pope Paul IV had declared on King Philip II. It was a weary journey to have made all in vain, but Peter only said " *Deo gratias !* "[1] shouldered his pack and set off for Innsbruck to see how King Ferdinand's new building was progressing. Then he

[1] Like St. Patrick, he had the habit of saying *Deo gratias* on all occasions, sometimes with results that appear a little comic to the natural eye—" I have been in bed ill, thanks be to God " or, meaning a dear friend, " So and so has died, thanks be to God."

continued his wayfaring to Augsburg, and from Augsburg went to Dillingen to visit Cardinal Truchsess, who resided there. It is a mistake to imagine that Peter was constitutionally robust, and now an old gastric trouble laid him low, on the eve of the critical Diet of Regensburg, to which King Ferdinand had summoned him as his theological adviser. About these matters he wrote in his simple-hearted way to Laynez:

> The Cardinal treated me with the utmost kindness, not only when I was well but during some days when I was suffering a malady of the stomach. Wishing to greet the Duke of Bavaria at Ingolstadt before setting out for Regensburg, he desired to have me as his companion. Here [in Ingolstadt] I fell ill again, and, by the advice of the doctors, remained behind until I was well enough to follow the Cardinal to the Diet. He urged me to go with him in his own sedan-chair, and, as he departed, several times gave me orders that I was not to lodge elsewhere in Regensburg than with him. Though he knows well enough that, as I am now the King's man, he can no longer exercise over me the jurisdiction which he received from our Blessed Father Ignatius, he still greatly desires to have me, so to speak, at his elbow, and to confer with me frequently on the state of religion. At present, by the goodness of God, I feel sufficiently recovered soon to proceed to Regensburg for whatever business His Majesty wishes to use me. There will be many bishops there before long, and may God give me grace in their eyes that they may come to know the institute of our Society better than hitherto and also themselves to imitate it more closely.[1]

Regensburg was not an entirely new field for Peter as he had been there to preach in the Cathedral immediately before his fruitless journey to Padua. On that first occasion his sermons had so inspired the few Catholics of the rabidly Protestant city that the dean and whole Cathedral chapter afterwards wrote begging him to return for the feast of Our Lady's Nativity. The Protestants had thrown her statues out of the churches usurped by them, especially the image loved and venerated for generations under the title, " Schöne Maria "—Beautiful Mary. Peter, the canons suggested, must hurry back and publicly glorify the holy Mother of God in reparation. " It is impossible to describe," they said, " with what eagerness you are awaited here by all Catholics."[2]

[1] Braunsberger, *Epistulae*, vol. ii pp. 20–1.   [2] Braunsberger, *Epistulae*, vol. ii, p. 34.

At Dillingen, before the collapse of his health, Peter busied himself editing for the press " some old books admirably suited to the needs of the Diet." Arrived in Regensburg, he was lodged by the instructions of Cardinal Truchsess " in a handsome and most comfortable room close to his palace," and the Cardinal expressed a wish that he would come to dine and converse with him each day. He did not remain long in his handsome room, however, as he explains in the following lines to Laynez :

After a few days I begged to be excused, and proposed some reasons why it would not be fitting for me to remain in that room, the first being that the King, who had asked for me as his own theologian, might not like it if I saw too much of the Cardinal, and, also, that I might be the less bound to the Cardinal, better able to preserve a proper independence and to live in greater simplicity. Accordingly, with the help of the canons of the Cathedral, I discovered an empty house which had a stove in it and there myself and our Brother Stephen are now living. Our meals are sent in to us daily from the kitchen of the Bishop of Regensburg. The Cardinal continues to be as friendly as ever, and is present each morning while I say Mass at his residence.

I preach a sermon on Sundays and feast-days, and during Advent was in the pulpit three times a week. The bishops come to hear me and have shown themselves friendly, especially the Archbishop of Salzburg, who is the wealthiest of them all. Yesterday he spoke to me at great length about our colleges, and signified that he was ready to introduce the Society into his arch-diocese, which stretches far into the King's dominions. May our Blessed Lord give me grace to help those prelates according to the needs of the time, and may He enable me to go on preaching His holy Word in this desolate and ruined vine-yard.[1]

Besides the Archbishop of Salzburg, the Electors of Trier and Mainz, the Bishop of Strasbourg, the city fathers of Freiburg im Breisgau, and other authorities in Bavaria, Hungary, and Poland were all at this time urging St. Peter to come to the rescue of religion among them. It was physically impossible that he should personally satisfy all the earnest hopes and desires which his sanctity had created, but he at least prepared the ground and sowed the seed of the subsequent harvest. By the close of the century, when he had been dead only three years, his brethren had forty flourishing colleges or missions in northern lands, scarcely

[1] Braunsberger, *Epistulae*, vol. ii, pp. 39-40.

one of which but owed its existence, directly or indirectly, to his influence with secular princes or dignitaries of the Church. As already mentioned, his devotion to bishops and zeal for their true honour were so intense and obvious that certain Protestant writers have elected to paint him as a sort of ' episcopalian ' rather than as a genuine *Roman* Catholic. Therein they did less than justice to his equally intense, though, perhaps, less obvious loyalty to the Holy See which was so much a part of him that it did not stand out in relief.

At Regensburg he pursued the usual aims, and often the achievements, of his life, namely to make the bishops worthy of their sublime office, to provide an abundant supply of devout and zealous priests for the orphaned parishes of Germany, and to instil into the lay Catholics a practical and instructed pride in their religion that should arm them against all temptation. He drew up a memorial on the subject of ecclesiastical reformation, which, through Cardinal Truchsess, he submitted in all humility to the bishops present in the city. In February, 1557, he was able to tell Laynez that they seemed to be coming round to his point of view and had already begun to discuss the question of Church reform.[1]

During the four months, December, 1556—March, 1557, St. Peter was the regular official preacher of the Cathedral of Regensburg. Michael Helding, Bishop of Merseburg, an outstanding orator and Catholic leader of the sixteenth century, often went to listen to him, and on January 10th himself mounted the same pulpit to deliver a glowing panegyric of the Saint's sermons. The Protestants of Regensburg, not the even-tempered, courteous Protestants of modern times, but by all accounts as irascible and bigoted a collection of men as was to be found in the Empire, gave Peter such a dose of their hate that only the protection of King Ferdinand saved him from violence. All their pulpits rang with slanders and villainous charges against him, and at the Diet they agitated ceaselessly to discredit him and have him expelled.[2] No wonder that they " groaned " when they saw him invited to dine with the powerful Duke of Bavaria, or that they called down every curse in their language on his head when they witnessed his frequent closetings with the King. It was the chief aim of the Protestants at the Diet to secure the abrogation of the " Ecclesiastical Reservation " in the Religious Peace of 1555. That Reservation, which required any bishop or other dignitary who abjured Catholicism to resign his office, lands, and revenues, was one of the last bulwarks left to the ancient Faith. Ferdinand's temptation to give way on the point must

[1] Braunsberger, *Epistulae*, vol. ii, pp. 41, 68–9. [2] Braunsberger, *Epistulae*, vol. ii, p. 23.

have been sore indeed, as he was in terrible straits for money to fight the Turks, and this only the Protestants could provide. But he did not give way, and it is reasonable to suppose that the influence of his first and favourite theologian, St. Peter, had a good deal to do with the firm stand he made.[1]

Peter did not greatly relish the political business in which his office involved him. He had to witness too much of the bickering and bargaining that goes on behind the scenes, which explains the following distressful lines to Laynez: " As I know well the smallness of my ability and my great weakness and want of experience, I could wish to escape hence by any means, and rather beg my bread in India than be involved in dangerous trifling whereby the things of eternity are often treated with contempt and the rights of the Holy See violated. . . . But may the Lord speak to me through His servant, my superior . . . for in obedience is my hope and fortitude."[2] To console himself for the secular environment in which he found so little to his taste, the Saint devoted his spare moments to the re-editing and proof-reading of Bishop Hosius's large and very important *Confessio Fidei Catholicae*, which was published at Dillingen in 1557. At this time, too, he appears to have edited or helped to edit and publish some little tracts for priests, with instructions on the rubrics of the Mass and Holy Communion and the outline of a sermon to be preached to those approaching the altar.[3] His position brought him into contact with all sorts of interesting people, with a " poor Bishop of Ireland," whoever on earth that was, with a prominent, unnamed Jew whom he received into his house and prepared to be baptized by Cardinal Truchsess, with a high official of the Empire who has the distinction, under the aegis of Peter, of being the author of the very first published life of St. Ignatius and defence of the Order which he founded,[4] and, not to prolong the list, with the brilliant young fighting Catholic, William van der Lindt or Lindanus. In February, 1557, Lindanus sent St. Peter some controversial books he had written, chiefly on Scriptural subjects, asking for criticisms of them from the Saint and his friend Dr. Lucretius, who was a first-rate orientalist. Lindanus was impulsive, did things with a rush, and liked to make the sparks fly. St. Peter's answer was in the following terms:

[1] Braunsberger, *Epistulae*, vol. ii, pp. 51, 69.
[2] Braunsberger, *Epistulae*, vol. ii, pp. 51–2.
[3] Braunsberger, *Epistulae*, vol. ii, pp. 883–9.
[4] This was Dr. Johann Widmanstadt, who, dissatisfied with his unclassical name and unable to find a Latin or Greek equivalent, borrowed a title from his wife Lucretia and announced himself as " Dr. Lucretius." He was a religious-minded man and, under St. Peter's influence, decided after the death of his wife in 1556 to devote himself unreservedly to the Church in the priesthood. St. Peter helped him to provide for his three grown-up daughters. Braunsberger, *Epistulae*, vol. ii, pp. 19, 30–2.

May the Peace of Christ be with us always, Reverend Doctor. I have scarcely been able to find time for a reply to your three letters. They gave me some trouble to read, owing to the haste in which you wrote them. To begin with your manuscript address to bishops, Dr. Lucretius, whom we are felicitating on his ordination to the priesthood, complains that you have not left him enough marginal space for his comments, and he, like myself, wishes that your handwriting were more legible. For these reasons, and because he is extremely busy, he has read little or nothing of the document. There is not much chance of leisure for us in this place. I, however, have several times pleaded your cause with the learned men present at the Diet and I have also read to them portions of your manuscript. I shall give you my opinion on your writings presently. Would that I could bring to bear on the matter the competence with which you too generously credit me, and would that time and leisure were available for discussing the several points as they demand. I am late in answering, but you will forgive a busy man, and see in my comment on both works not a harsh censure but a fraternal admonition, candidly given.

Men of learning agree with me that much in your writings might be expressed with greater restraint, especially where you make unfair play with the names of Calvin, Melanchthon, and similar people. It is the mob-orator's privilege to riot in such blossoms, not the part of a theologian. With such medicine we do not heal the sick but render them the more incurable. The truth must be defended wisely, seasonably, and soberly, so that our modesty may be known to all men and we may obtain, if possible, a good report even from those who are without. I would not, then, have you give the Germans a handle for censuring in this and other works the juvenile exuberance of a new writer, rather than for commending and liking the sobriety and gentleness becoming in a devout theologian.

With regard to your proposed, 'Advice to Bishops,' there is this to be considered, that we temper zeal with Christian prudence, lest wishing to build up we, perhaps, through want of discretion, rather destroy, especially in these times when so little is left of the Church except ruins. But as I shall be reminding you of this elsewhere I forbear to speak further on the subject now.

Though Lindanus was such a whole-hearted and even pugnacious Catholic he appears to have held strong views on the faultiness of the

Church's official version of the Scriptures. These he expressed in the third book of his treatise, *De optimo genere interpretandi Scripturas*, which he had forwarded in manuscript to St. Peter, drawing from the Saint the following criticism :

My friends fear still greater danger from the doubts which you seem to raise about the Vulgate, for they think our opponents will make capital out of your remarks on its want of integrity. Of course the text needs emendation in places, but your offence is that you appear anxious to exaggerate the number of discrepancies and to make out that Catholics have long been under serious delusions about their Bible, as though the ancient codices had not been most carefully collated with our text. . . .

You were right to call attention to the faulty passage that you observed, but do not leave the reader with a scruple, as though the whole Bible abounded in all sorts of errors. This is not the way to defend the Council of Trent, but rather an attack on the Council, which has commended such a corrupt and mutilated version as you allege. The Protestant, Bibliander, wrote a book against the Council on those very lines. I should like you to read and ponder it. I know not what the Louvain and Paris theologians will say if they hear that the received version of the Bible is so full of mistakes that it cannot be corrected, even with the help of all the Latin codices, as you assert in the third chapter of the third book. However that may be, I thought it well to caution you, seeing that I am not alone in my opinion. Dr. Lucretius has a difficulty of his own about your references to the Hebrew, and thinks it would be advisable for you to send the whole treatise to Louvain for overhauling there by competent scholars.

To my mind the best thing you could do would be to leave aside the bishops' book and make a classified list of the inventions and lies of our opponents, issuing it with a straightforward commentary, as though you had proposed to yourself to refute the Confession of Augsburg or the *Loci Communes* of Philip.[1] Such a work would also be serviceable to the ill-instructed, and these are the people, I think, for whom we ought now chiefly to labour when we set about writing anything in Germany. Their ears are weary of old controversies, and good men and not so good alike abhor anything that savours of bitterness. Everybody looks for and approves modesty joined with gravity

[1] Melanchthon.

and soundness of argument. That, then, I think, is the right method to be pursued, but in such a way that the truth is nowise sacrificed. . . .

I shall again and again remind Dr. Lucretius that he must write to you. From the Most Reverend Archbishop of Salzburg I have obtained a promise that he will pay the printer for three hundred copies of your *Panoplia*[1] when they are ready. . . .

In case you do not know, I am leaving here for Italy within, perhaps, a fortnight on business of our Order. I am afraid we shall not be able to meet on the way, as my most direct route is by Salzburg and not by Augsburg. I urge and beg you, my very dear and distinguished friend in Christ Our Lord, to commend me much and often in your prayers and Holy Sacrifices. I am truly sorry that owing to the rush I am not doing enough for you, according to your desires and deserts. I am compelled to leave much undone that you may be expecting me to do and that I ought to do for you. . . . I advise you to get the *Panoplia* printed without delay, as I am anxious to see the preface before I leave. I beg you to tone down any harsh passages there may be in the book that we may admonish the erring in a spirit of meekness, rather than provoke them. . . .[2]

Among those to whom St. Peter sent greetings through Lindanus was Father Bartholomew Kleindienst, a Dominican professor at Dillingen who had once been a Lutheran professor at Leipzig on Melanchthon's appointment. Father Bartholomew appears to have assisted Lindanus in his Scriptural work, so, fearful lest he might be offended by the suggestion of sending the book to Louvain for revision, St. Peter added the following lines to his long letter : " Will you tell Father Bartholomew that I wrote from my heart and as I sincerely thought. . . . Perhaps I am timid, but so too are devout men of my acquaintance, lovers of the safer part, who go the King's highway, consenting to the humble and not seeking things too high for them. This does not mean, however, that others also may not abound in their own sense, as far as I am concerned."

That letter of Peter's, like most of his letters, is not a very exciting document as far as its style or contents go. Its charm is down deep and perhaps only discernible by people who have been very busy themselves but not too busy to be kind. Lindanus, was a young, rather bumptious, and wholly unimportant person at the time, however important he became later on.

---

[1] *Panoplia evangelica, sive de Verbo Dei evangelico libri quinque, contra omnes hujus saeculi haereses.* This is the soundest and most effective of Lindanus's many works.

[2] Braunsberger, *Epistulae*, vol. ii, pp. 72–7.

St. Peter treated him as though all Germany hung on his words. He treated with similar consideration everybody who showed the slightest desire to serve Almighty God, and by his generosity he very often developed in others qualities which at first they had possessed only in his charitable imagination.

The general congregation of the Society of Jesus in Rome was fixed to open on April 18, 1557. This time St. Peter had Father Goudanus for his travelling companion. They reached Padua on April 2nd, after more than a fortnight on the road, and the following evening Peter set off alone by ship to Venice to visit his brethren there, which done he returned to Padua, picked up Father Goudanus who had been ill, and departed for Florence. Another fortnight and the pair were in Rome. As the representatives of the various provinces had not yet all arrived, Peter busied himself while waiting "in firing the alumni of the German and Roman Colleges by public and private talks with enthusiasm for the northern mission-field." Then, when it only needed the presence of the Spanish and Portuguese Fathers, who were making hot foot for Rome, for the congregation to start, war broke out anew between the Pope and the King of Spain. As the King had issued an edict forbidding his subjects to enter papal territory, Laynez craved the Pope's permission to hold the congregation in Barcelona. This he was on the point of obtaining when the Society of Jesus suddenly found itself in the midst of one of the most terrible tempests of its very stormy history.

Father Nicholas Bobadilla was the cloud-gatherer, easily the most puzzling character among all the early Jesuits. He belonged to the original ten pioneers who had gathered round St. Ignatius, and he won the warm esteem of eminent men both inside and outside the Jesuit Order. During seven years he acted as theological adviser to a succession of nuncios in Germany. Peter Canisius saw a fair amount of him at the time and spoke of his "most pleasant company," particularly noting his "singular sharpness of wit, his powers of debate and decision, his simplicity of soul, his candour, and his charming affability."[1] The Saint also paid glowing tribute to the good work Bobadilla had done before he was expelled the country by order of Charles V for his imprudent denunciation of the *Interim*. That, however, is only one side of the picture, for, though the Father had many sterling virtues, it is equally certain that he was full of faults. The root of his trouble was that he had never really grown up. He carried on into mature years the boastful, headstrong, impulsive ways of a mettlesome boy. St. Francis Xavier used to twit him good-humouredly

[1] Braunsberger, *Epistulae*, vol. i, p. 159.

on his well-known weakness for the company of titled people, and Salmeron, Nadal, and others had much to say about him that was not complimentary. He was entirely without malice but imprudent and self-opinionated to the last degree. Once he conceived a thing to be right or wrong, wise or foolish, just or unjust, no power on earth seemed capable of stirring him. It was a case of Bobadilla *contra mundum*. At the time of which we write he had taken a violent dislike to Laynez, for reasons into which it is unnecessary to enter except to say that they were stupid, baseless reasons. Both orally and in writing he now began to assert that Laynez had not been legitimately elected Vicar-General of the Society, that he had usurped power, and that the Society, pending the election of a new General, ought to be governed by its " founders and first professed Fathers." In other words, Bobadilla ought to have a good share in its government. Soon he won a group of malcontents to his side, the chief of them being a very able French Father named Ponce Cogordan, who presented a memorial to two cardinals of his acquaintance, requesting them to show it to the Pope. In this he alleged that Laynez and his supporters were asking permission to hold the congregation in Spain for the sole purpose of electing a General according to their own tastes, and of drawing up constitutions for the Society independently of the Holy See. Paul IV, who had never been very friendly to the Jesuits, gave ear to the tall story and peremptorily ordered that the papal bulls, constitutions, rules, and everything else pertaining to the Society's discipline and government should be submitted to certain cardinals. At the same time he forbade any Jesuit then in Rome to leave the City.[1]

These untoward happenings put St. Peter Canisius in an awkward position, as he was required back in Germany by August to attend a new religious conference between the Protestants and Catholics at Worms. Eventually, through the influence of King Ferdinand's representative in Rome, he and Goudanus were permitted to leave, the congregation being once again postponed to the following year. By the good offices of some friendly cardinals, especially the Dominican, Michael Ghislieri, afterwards Pope St. Pius V, Pope Paul was made to see the injustice and utter falsity of the charges against Laynez, and Bobadilla himself, gradually coming to his senses, atoned by the zeal and holiness of his later years for all the trouble he had given.[2]

[1] The whole distressing story is well told by Astrain, *Historia de la Compañía de Jesús*, vol. ii, pp. 7–22.

[2] Cogordan, too, atoned by splendid work for his Order with the powerful Cardinal of Lorraine. Evennett, *The Cardinal of Lorraine and the Council of Trent* (Cambridge, 1930), pp. 61, 71, 87, 129, 131, 171–2, 341.

On his way home St. Peter addressed the following little note of sympathy to Laynez, posting it in Perugia:

I thought I must let your Reverence know that we arrived here to-day, *Domino adjuvante*, though only after a most difficult journey, owing to the ill-health of our companion, Brother Leonard. He is now feeling better. We found our dear brethren here quite well. To-morrow, with the help of God, we hope to set out for Florence, though I feel rather weak, either from dysentery or from the troubles of our journey. Father Goudanus's arm is better, and Father Vitoria and Alphonsus are both well, thanks ever be to Our Lord. We think that we shall not be able to reach Venice before the 10th or 12th of July. I hope that we shall be joined there by those whom your Reverence instructed to come from Loreto. I nearly forgot to mention our Brother Bartholomew, whom we helped with our horses to arrive here safely. For the rest, we put great trust in your Reverence's prayers. I shall commend you most earnestly to the brethren here that the Lord may turn all that you are now suffering to His greater glory and to the common salvation of us your sons. I shall write to you more in detail from Florence when it pleases the Divine Goodness. May He guide our steps and keep us always in His grace. . . . *Filius minimus*, Peter Canisius.

From Florence Peter wrote in conjunction with Goudanus, advising as to the best way of dealing with the Bobadilla difficulty. That document has not come to light, but there is a covering letter from which the following lines are taken: " If there is anything else you would like us to put down, we are entirely at the disposal of our Father and Superior. We take good care to recommend your Reverence to the prayers of the colleges on our route but we are saying nothing about the malcontents. God grant that they may some day behave better, and may Our Lord confirm us in His peace against these winds and waves. I am deliberately omitting to add the date and place of the document that our dual evidence may the better appear to have been given, not at Florence but in Rome, and so relieve me of any suspicion of having written according to private instructions. The doctor orders me to remain here a little longer, fearing I know not what from the dysentery. I earnestly commend the health of both my body and my soul to your Reverence's prayers. *Dominus Jesus nobiscum*."[1]

On the same day Peter wrote also to Father Nadal: " I have been

[1] Braunsberger, *Epistulae*, vol. ii, p. 88.

ill for some time with dysentery and fever, so Master John, our physician, insists that I stay in bed at his house to-morrow. May the Lord do what seems good in His eyes and make use of us, either sick or well, for His greater glory." Illness, however, had no power to prevent Peter from transacting business and planning great schemes for the help of Germany. Thus he submitted proposals to Nadal for the establishment on German soil of a seminary to replace the German College in Rome, which at this time owing to a variety of misfortunes seemed on the brink of dissolution. Peter had not a penny in the world on which he could call, as his letters to Polanco during the following weeks sufficiently prove. For instance, the expenses of the journey from Rome—the price of a horse, the fare for a boat, a night's lodging in some inn—had to be met in this fashion. On leaving Rome the travellers took just sufficient money to carry them to the next house of their Order. There they begged or borrowed the fare for the following stage, and so on until they reached home. Nothing was held in reserve against emergencies for the good reason that there was nothing to hold. "We did not take any money from our brethren in Florence," wrote Peter, "because we saw them to be very badly off at present, but Father Francis[1] has promised us ten scudi, though he is obliged to lend quite enough money. This will be sufficient for our needs. I think we have already spent twenty ducats on the journey. The rest the Lord will provide."[2] Father Francis, however, was not forthcoming with the ten scudi, so Peter borrowed thirty ducats from the Fathers in Venice and with them—a remarkable feat—repaid a debt to the Rector of the college at Loreto, bought some books, Venice being a great book-market, helped Father Vitoria and three companions back to Vienna, and covered the expenses of his own party of five on the way to Ingolstadt. Never were thirty ducats made to go farther.

Details such as these, of which there are hundreds in St. Peter's letters, show in what real poverty the early Jesuits lived. Yet when some costly scheme seemed necessary for the defence of the Faith Peter never hesitated. His trust in Providence knew no limits. To Nadal, then, he suggested from his sick bed that letters should be written in Rome which he might show to King Ferdinand and the Queen of Bohemia, the good Catholic wife of the Lutheranizing Maximilian. In these letters their Majesties might be urged to write personally to Spain, and to act through their representatives in that country with a view to obtaining financial

---

[1] Francis Palmio, Rector of the College of Bologna from which Peter is writing.
[2] Braunsberger, *Epistulae*, vol. ii, pp. 94-5.

support from wealthy Spanish noblemen for the establishment of a great new seminary to serve German ecclesiastical students. " I beg your Reverence for the love of God," Peter concluded, " to let me know quickly what you think of this scheme and to give me any suggestions that occur to you. . . ."[1]

Thus, whether sick or well, did he plot and plan all the time for the provision of good priests where they were most needed. And thus, too, did he carry his colleges in his heart wherever he went. No heavy business of writing books, preaching sermons, or working for the King could cloud his vision of the struggling colleges. During his stay in Rome and on the journey back he negotiated to obtain helpers from Spain and Italy, men who, " *praeter doctrinam aliquid elegantiae habeant.*" There is good reason for believing that Peter meant more than mere elegance of diction, that he meant external decorum. He was a thorough gentleman himself, and he liked, in the spirit of St. Ignatius, who was almost a fanatic on the subject, to see his men well-mannered and well-groomed. Throughout the negotiations his wisdom and charity shone with a beautiful radiance. Though he badly needed a particular man and had permission to take him, he would never do so at the expense of his studies. He was a great speculator in " futures," and would deprive no one of his educational chances, however awkwardly placed he might be to keep the colleges going. Always his vision went beyond the difficulty of the moment to the distant opportunity. The loveliest grace of his life was just this utter unselfishness which worked in terms that were not of time, and reckoned nothing of his personal convenience. Similarly, he was most careful of the health of his men. He would not take a certain young Jesuit named Peter from Bologna, though he had been assigned to Ingolstadt, because he had suffered from the quartan ague and was not in perfect condition for the journey at that hot time of the year ; and he urged that Father Everard Mercurian, Rector of the College in Perugia and a future General of the Society of Jesus, should be transferred to either Germany or Flanders, as his health was suffering from the Italian climate. It was the same consideration that made him so anxious to acquire good cooks for the German colleges. Writing from Bologna to Polanco he said : " I have not been able so far to find a cook in any of the three colleges of Perugia, Florence, or Bologna. I am pursuing my search anxiously, and I shall endeavour to secure one in some other college through which I pass. I shall report to your Reverence about the matter from Venice."

[1] Braunsberger, *Epistulae*, vol. ii, p. 90.

At Venice, however, Peter forgot about cooks and everything else in his concern for the few Fathers there who were struggling with dire poverty and overwork. " Owing to their poverty," he informed Polanco, " they are badly fed and they have so much to do that they cannot follow a common rule. The result is that nearly all of them are now so sick and weak as to be obliged to give up teaching and other good works, which might here be carried on with the greatest advantage if only there were plenty of labourers in this most promising harvest-field."[1]

Peter left Venice in the middle of July, and proceeding by way of Padua and Trent was back in Ingolstadt just a month after his departure from Rome. In Ingolstadt, too, poverty which was more like destitution confronted him. The original eight men there had been given so much to do that their backs would have broken under the burden had Peter not augmented their numbers. But when the time came for them to receive their meagre stipends the Government officials refused to pay for more than the number agreed to in the foundation deeds. To add to his troubles, the Saint had learned that the Prague College was still heavily in debt and without any prospect of clearing itself. He blamed nobody and left the issue to God. " These Princes," he said, referring to the Duke of Bavaria and King Ferdinand, " are in such financial straits that it is not in their power to help us. We must therefore as pioneers make allowances, sowing in patience and waiting on the grace of Our Lord by which all evil and every human difficulty is overcome."[2]

Though so lenient where debts to himself were concerned, Peter had a very tender conscience about paying what he personally owed. One of his first cares on returning to Germany was to reimburse the Italian Fathers for any expenses they had been put to on his account. He wrote to Polanco asking to be informed exactly how much the various colleges were out of pocket. The Pope had made a donation to the Society for travelling expenses and of this he begged a little to help settle his debts. " The rest," he said, " I shall scrape together as well as I can in the colleges here."[3] In his zeal for the propagation of good books Peter had guaranteed the *bona-fides* of a Prague bookseller who had obtained a quantity of literature on credit from an Ingolstadt publisher. The Prague person took a long time about paying, which so worried his guarantor that he wrote in the following strain to his friend, Anton Brus, who enjoyed great influence in the Bohemian capital :

[1] Braunsberger, *Epistulae*, vol. ii, p. 101. [2] Braunsberger, *Epistulae*, vol. ii, p. 66.
[3] Braunsberger, *Epistulae*, vol. ii, pp. 114–5, 118.

My chief reason for addressing you is that I want to be freed from a debt which I contracted here [in Ingolstadt] as surety for a Prague bookseller. Last year this man took to Prague from here many fine books, as my brethren are well aware, at the time promising faithfully to pay the price fixed by the Ingolstadt publisher shortly afterwards. I am ashamed at the delay, which the creditor neither can nor will endure any longer. I beg you, then, most earnestly to deal with the debtor at once, either through a Prague judge or a friend in whom you have confidence, so that my guarantee on this man's behalf may be honoured and the debt justly paid. . . . I would not trouble you with this shady business, so little in accordance with your position, did not necessity compel me. In my endeavours to furnish your City of Prague with good books, perhaps by trusting this man's big promises I proved myself too credulous. However that may be, would you please write soon to the brethren here telling them what immediate chance or future prospect there is of getting this debt paid. . . . May Our Lord Jesus snatch us away from the cares of the world to the study of true piety and the public good.[1]

Peter was constantly getting into trouble over books. While in Rome he had purchased a number for his colleges, leaving instructions that they were to be sent on after him by the primitive " parcels' post " of those times. They went astray, of course, and month after month their poor owner remained on tenterhooks as to their fate. All his many letters to Polanco at this time contain references to the unfortunate *sarcina libraria*, and when at long last they turned up in quite an unexpected quarter, Peter's joy was as great as if he had come into a fortune.

On his return to Germany he learned with disgust that uncharitable rumours were being aired in Catholic circles about Pope Paul IV. Paul's affection for St. Peter's Order could not be described as strong, but that fact in no way chilled the love and loyalty which the Saint bore to him as Pope. He was indignant that such things should be said, and expressed himself in strong terms to Scribonius and Brus :

I believe you must be well aware of the dreadful things that are being rumoured about the Supreme Pontiff. The people who say them are sons of Cham, taking delight in open jest and scurrilous action over their father's shame. It is not for me to pronounce on the cause

[1] Braunsberger, *Epistulae*, vol. ii, pp. 119–20.

of the great; they have God for their judge and vindicator. Only one thing I would say, that even if the Pope's case were more indefensible than the mob now asserts it to be, still the children of God and of the Church are in duty bound to speak and feel in a kindlier and friendlier way of the Head of the Church and the Vicar of Christ.[1] Wretched creatures that we are, we look at the human person and forget the divinely instituted office. We often let vulgar rumour affect us and, hasty in judgment, slow in wisdom, cold in prayer, the last thing we consider is a means to avert the wrath of God from ourselves, the clergy and the people, and to restore the peace for which we yearn, and general concord to the State. Perhaps, this outburst of mine is both too free and too long but I feel that your patience will not be much offended by my loquacity and that you may possibly even obtain some refreshment of spirit from it.[2]

As will be related further on, St. Peter left Ingolstadt for the religious conference at Worms on August 16, 1557. That business, which forms an important and self-contained chapter in his story, kept him occupied till the end of December when, in fulfilment of a long-standing promise to the Bishop of Strasbourg, he set out for that Protestant stronghold to study the situation and render what assistance he could to the afflicted Catholics. From Strasbourg he went on the same mission to Zabern in Lower Alsace, where the Bishop resided, and thence to Freiburg im Breisgau for the purpose of negotiating about the foundation of a Jesuit college in that beautiful old Catholic city. Among other places he visited and evangelized on this fatiguing, roundabout journey back to Ingolstadt were Breisach, Colmar, Schlettstadt, and Ruffach. He made Zabern his headquarters at the Bishop's desire, wrote part of his *Shorter Catechism* there, and diligently taught it to the pupils of the Latin school of the town.[3] In Strasbourg, where he found the Catholics "more cruelly oppressed and ill-treated than anywhere else" in his experience, he put new heart into them by stirring sermons from the pulpit in the grand old Cathedral which Geiler of Kayserberg had rendered illustrious in the past.

As a contrast to Strasbourg, dominated by the venomously anti-Catholic school of Johann Sturm, Peter delighted in the faith and beauty

[1] One of the rumours was that Pope Paul had invoked the aid of the Turks against King Philip. Unfortunately there was some ground for the rumour, though neither the Pope nor his appalling nephew ever sought a *direct* alliance with the Sultan. Pastor, *Geschichte der Päpste*, vol. vi (1913), p. 420.

[2] Braunsberger, *Epistulae*, vol. ii, p. 108.

[3] Braunsberger, *Epistulae*, vol. ii, p. 188.

of Freiburg, with its flourishing Catholic University. He liked the air
of the place, its architecture, its people and, indeed, everything about it,
as who would not that knows it at all ? It was the very place for a college,
he decided, the best place in all Germany, as he afterwards informed
Nadal. But the professors were much more anxious to talk about their
ancient University than about a new college, and Peter very readily discussed
with them ways and means of improving and extending it. On leaving,
after having had many dinners with the authorities, "*quae non minima
est Germanicae hospitalitatis tessera*," he took with him letters on the
subject of the University to King Ferdinand who, in that age, was over-
lord of the Breisgau.[1] In spite of his hopes and efforts, his brethren did
not secure a footing in Freiburg until 1620, when he was in his grave.
They opened houses in Schlettstadt and Ruffach in 1615 and in Colmar
in 1627, the towns he had laboured for during that winter mission of
1557–1558. And so the memory of him effected what his presence in
the body had been unable to achieve.

The mission brought him much consolation, so much that he found
it impossible " to explain in words," and told Laynez in his lowly way
that perhaps the reason of it all was because " as a child or weakling I
still need milk, the solid food of desolation and the Cross usually being
suited only for perfect men. I am not worthy to suffer big things for
the Name of Jesus nor to offer a perfect holocaust in the odour of sweetness." One special cause of his joy was a convent of Dominican nuns
in Strasbourg, gallant women to whom he gave conferences and who,
he said, " bore off the palm for constancy in the midst of Babylon,
declining neither to the right nor to the left from a stalwart Catholic
confession of faith."[2] The good Bishop of Strasbourg and his canons, all
of them noblemen in every sense of the word, were greatly pleased with the
results of Peter's efforts, and at his departure pressed on him a large sum
of money and other gifts. When he refused, they asked in wonderment
whether there was not some little memento he would like to have. There
was—a relic of some saint. Ushered into the sacristy, he was bidden to take
anything he wished and came away, feeling very rich and full of gratitude,
with small fragments of the sacred remains of St. Polycarp and St. Xystus.
His generous hosts gave him a royal send-off in a special coach and, without saying anything of their intentions, forwarded to Ingolstadt the money
he had refused. When he reached home he returned it to them.[3]

---

[1] It was known as " Vorderösterreich "—anterior Austria.
[2] Braunsberger, *Epistulae*, vol. ii, p. 191.
[3] Braunsberger, *Epistulae*, vol. ii, pp. 190–1.

In a letter to his lay friend, the good Catholic, Dr. Hundt, Peter, while still on his travels, laid bare the sources of his courage:

> The Lord sleeps, indeed, who guards Israel, but He sleeps only to test His chosen ones, letting the cruel tempest come upon them that when all hope seems over He may rise and with a gesture still the winds into peace. Meanwhile, however, He would have us admit our peril, our weakness, our nothingness; would have us pound on the door of grace with our prayers and tears so that He may open to us and crown our perseverance. Wherefore, let us not look for nor embrace human counsels of comfort, lest we seem to sin by our diffidence and too great fear against the eternal Truth and Goodness. Blessed are they who beg the Divine help with confidence and possess their souls in patience. He will come and will not tarry, the Father of Mercies, the Guardian and Helper of His Church for ever. He will come in His own good time, using the while between to put our faith and courage to the proof. Right well and truly was it said of old: *In Deo faciemus virtutem, et ipse ad nihilum deducet inimicos nostros.*[1]

On his way home to Ingolstadt the Saint called at Dillingen to confer with Cardinal Truchsess, who was in difficulties about the university which he had recently established in the town. His most eminent professors, such as the great Dominican, Peter Soto, were being removed by higher authority to even more important spheres of labour, and the Cardinal, finding it almost impossible to replace them, now proposed to Peter that the Jesuits should assume complete control of the university. Peter listened attentively, made notes, and offered suggestions, but declined to come to any agreement until he had put the whole case before his superiors in Rome. With Laynez he was always like a child to a well-loved father. He had the most implicit trust in him, and, though invested with wide discretionary powers, he would never take an important step until he had evidence that Laynez approved. " First of all," he said, reporting on the present affair to the Vicar-General, " I advised the Cardinal to offer some Masses for guidance and told him that I would get our Fathers to do the same. . . . But I shall promise nothing until I have your Reverence's decision on the whole matter." It took five years of planning and arranging to carry the project to success, and, as will be seen, Peter himself did most of the hard work which it involved. Cardinal Truchsess had such veneration for him that on this occasion he expressed an ardent desire to wash

[1] Braunsberger, *Epistulae*, vol. ii, pp. 184–5.

the Saint's feet. " Canisius," runs the record, "though out of respect not obstinate, was yet intensely reluctant, but at length gave way like his namesake, the Prince of the Apostles, lest he might hinder the work of the Lord."[1]

Back once more in Ingolstadt, Peter's first care was to beg Father Nadal's pardon for delaying an answer to one of his letters :

It is a long time now since I wrote to your Reverence, and I have no excuse to offer for so much negligence and ingratitude, shown constantly, not only to men, but much more to my Almighty and most faithful Creator and Redeemer who keeps me in this His holy Society, notwithstanding my utter unworthiness. . . . I was delighted to hear that His Excellency, John de Vega, wields the greatest influence in Spain.[2] Would that he and other noblemen might remember our poor, blind Germany. I beg you, Father, by the infinite charity of Christ and for the love you have always borne this province, to continue urging these men to explore every possible way and means of providing financial help for the Germans. . . . It has been a great comfort to us to know the holy desires for the salvation of Germany which Our Lord kindles in your Reverence's heart. You are our protector and father of fathers, to whom I most earnestly commend myself and the whole of this province.[3]

The Saint's next summons was to King Ferdinand, who rested, sad of soul, at Nuremberg. " He confided to me his most intimate secrets," Peter informed Laynez, " depositing in my breast the hidden things of his heart. I was moved to great pity, and consider that it is my bounden duty to help him, above all with the Sacrifices and prayers of your Reverence and the whole Society. For the love of God I implore you to have special Masses said by the Society for the King, that he may persevere manfully on his cross and be able to fulfil his Christian duty at this time, when he is in grave peril from his own flesh and blood,[4] from the Imperial Princes, from the Turks, and from his family Dominions, especially as he is so destitute of all human counsel and help in both religious and civil affairs."[5]

Cardinal Truchsess wished Peter to be present at the assembly of the Electoral Princes in Frankfurt on February 20, 1558. He would have

---

[1] Sacchinus, *Vita Petri Canisii*, p. 142. The Cardinal's servants are the authorities for the story.
[2] St. Peter had known de Vega in Sicily, where he acted as Viceroy of the King of Spain. Braunsberger, *Epistulae*, vol. i, p. 275.
[3] Braunsberger, *Epistulae*, vol. ii, pp. 197–200.
[4] From the intrigues of his son, the Lutheranizing Maximilian.
[5] Braunsberger, *Epistulae*, vol. ii, p. 205.

gone willingly had there been a prospect of helping the Catholic cause, but the matter to be discussed and decided lay altogether outside his sphere, no less than the transfer of the Imperial Crown from Charles V to Ferdinand. All that he had it in his power to do was to pray that Ferdinand would stand fast for the rights of the Church which the three Protestant Electors had determined to attack. And pray he did with all his might, seven hours of it a day being nothing unusual for him. Great, then, was his joy when, despite every effort for a revision of the immemorial oath, the Emperor-elect clung to the grand old formula of his ancestors, " to reverence, protect and valiantly defend Christendom, the See of Rome, the Pope's Holiness, and the Christian Church."

An additional reason for Peter's reluctance to go to Frankfurt was the commission given him at this time by Cardinal Truchsess to prepare for the press a new edition of Bishop Hosius's fine work against Brenz, *Verae, Christianae Catholicaeque doctrinae solida propugnatio.* In his epilogue to the book, which Maternus Cholinus published at Cologne this same year, 1558, Peter gives a brief account of his own labours on it, without revealing his identity. In its first form the work was not divided up in any way but ran on continuously page after page, to the utter bewilderment of those who desired to consult it. Peter provided, not only books and chapters, but paragraph headings and marginal summaries of the argument all the way through. The title, too, was his and he made an elaborate index for the convenience of students. None but a few friends knew till many years afterwards that he had undertaken this drudgery, at a time, moreover, when he was anxious above all things to be in Prague and Vienna, where his men were going through a period of acute distress.[1] Another literary project proposed to him, this time by the chancellor and theologians of the University of Louvain, was the composition of a text-book to supersede the *Sentences* of Peter the Lombard. He had had enough of that kind of work already but all the same did not refuse to try. It was his idea to epitomize the large, unpublished treatises of Laynez, and he might have written as good a manual for budding theologians as he had done for children if Laynez's dreadful handwriting and the press of much other business had not made it impossible.[2] He must go and write his zeal on the hearts of men rather than on paper, for Albert of Bavaria had appealed to him to save the Catholicism of Straubing.

[1] The Venetian reprint of Peter's edition of the book has 568 folio pages. Hosius wrote it in the first instance as a counter-attack on Brenz for a venomous onslaught which he had made on the Dominican, Peter Soto. Brenz at the time was the foremost Lutheran champion, and of more authority with the Protestants than even Melanchthon.

[2] Braunsberger, *Epistulae*, vol. ii, p. 213.

Straubing, which is situated on the Danube between Regensburg and Passau, was in those days one of the chief administrative centres of Bavaria, for which reason the Protestants had made special endeavours to win it to the Reformation. By the year 1558 they had very nearly succeeded, when suddenly St. Peter appeared on the scene. Before going he took care to arm himself with full civil and ecclesiastical authority, and then, having taken up lodgings with the Carmelites in the town, he started a whirlwind campaign of sermons, instructions, and appeals of every description. Three or four times a week he gave of his best in the old, lofty-steepled Church of St. James which is still a land-mark for voyagers on the Danube, and in the intervals busied himself to get the law put into operation against heretical activities. The town authorities had allowed Protestant schoolmasters and preachers complete immunity, which was a contravention of the Religious Peace of Augsburg. Peter did not like that Peace but he was determined that the Catholics should have the measure of protection it guaranteed them. Did they try to proselytize in Protestant territories the law was soon invoked, and Peter reasonably contended that what was sauce for the goose was sauce for the gander. Though gentle and kind by nature he could be adamant on this question, and let no opportunity slip to tell Catholic rulers their duty. The town authorities did their best to frustrate his efforts but he was more than a match for them, for all their gold chains. In a short time he so greatly stiffened the Catholic resistance that Straubing was out of danger.[1]

In all these efforts of his for the Faith there was sure to be an element of pain and frustration, caused, often enough, by those who should have been his best allies. King Ferdinand had been proclaimed and saluted Emperor at Frankfurt on March 14, 1558. In Rome Pope Paul IV absolutely refused to acknowledge his election. It was on a point of honour which might well have been waived in the circumstances, but Paul was not a man to make concessions. Charles V had not obtained his permission to abdicate, so Ferdinand might whistle for recognition, as far as he was concerned. He lived between two worlds, " one dead, the other powerless to be born," but he never realized it, and in consequence made a tragedy of his Pontificate. The tide had receded for ever from one particular creek where the first St. Peter's barque used proudly to ride, and Paul was stranded. For Peter Canisius his action brought about a conflict of loyalties of the most distressing kind. He found himself torn two ways, by his whole-hearted devotion to the Vicar of Christ and by his

---

[1] Braunsberger, *Epistulae*, vol. ii, pp. 221, 223–4, 807–11.

love for the Emperor with whose splendid, practical Catholicism he was intimately acquainted. The sad news of the *impasse* did not reach him for some time yet, however, and meanwhile, as he was working away in Straubing, his heart overflowed with joy at Ferdinand's election. He wrote to his friend Kessel at Cologne begging him to get each of the priests under his orders to say seven Masses that God might bestow the seven gifts of the Holy Ghost on the new Emperor and to ensure that the non-priests recited the litanies and the seven penitential psalms daily for a week for the same intention. In his own province priests and non-priests had, of course, been immediately given such instructions, and he appealed to Laynez to issue them to the whole Society of Jesus. The times were very evil, he said. The Lutheran ministers led better lives than the common run of Catholic priests, monasteries daily became emptier, and violent deeds, such as the recent murder of the Bishop of Würzburg, threatened to increase. The new Emperor was the Church's surest hope, and prayer for him was not only a true charity but a very wise investment.[1]

A letter of this time to Cardinal Truchsess illustrates not only Peter's concern for the Emperor's soul but his fearlessness in admonishing great people on the fulfilment of their duties. Though long, it is worth giving in full:

We ought to pray that the new Emperor may be given the qualities necessary for the successful management of the Empire, especially zeal for religion, which has now everywhere grown cold. Perhaps, by the just judgment of God, the reason why we lack rulers like Theodosius is that we have no bishops like Ambrose.[2] Meantime Judas prowls on the alert while Peter still sleeps, nothing recking of the account he shall render for so many perishing souls whose blood will soon be required at the hands of their pastors. Sara complains that Abraham

[1] Braunsberger, *Epistulae*, vol. ii, pp. 226–7, 263.

[2] The great Christian Emperor Theodosius was largely moulded by St. Ambrose. Chateaubriand's picture of the life of a Christian bishop in the fourth and fifth centuries, drawn for the most part from the history of St. Ambrose, was exactly the ideal cherished by St. Peter Canisius for bishops in the sixteenth century: " Rien de plus complet et de plus rempli que la vie des prélats du quatrième et du cinquième siècle. Un évêque baptisoit, confessoit, prêchoit, ordonnoit des pénitences privées ou publiques, lançoit des anathèmes ou levoit des excommunications, visitoit les malades, assistoit les mourants, enterroit les morts, rachetoit les captifs, nourrissoit les pauvres, les veuves, les orphelins, fondoit des hospices et des maladreries, administroit les biens de son clergé, prononçoit comme juge de paix dans des causes particulières, ou arbitroit des différends entre des villes : il publioit en même temps des traités de morale, de discipline et de théologie, écrivoit contre les hérésiarques et contre les philosophes, s'occupoit de science et d'histoire, dictoit des lettres pour les personnes qui le consultoient dans l'une et l'autre religion, correspondoit avec les Églises et les évêques, les moines et les ermites, siégoit à des conciles et à des synodes, était appelé aux conseils des Empereurs, chargé de négociations, envoyé à des usurpateurs ou à des princes barbares pour les désarmer ou les contenir : les trois pouvoirs religieux, politique et philosophique s'étoient concentrés dans l'évêque." *Oeuvres de Chateaubriand* (Paris, 1837), vol. xvi, pp. 12–13. Incidentally, this is almost a perfect picture of the life of St. Peter himself.

introduces handmaidens. She sorrows to find herself vilely used and neglected while her lord devotes himself to these strangers. But yet more hardly does she take it when besides the handmaidens there are strumpets on the scene who sway her husband's mind this way and that and permit him no leisure to be quiet at home, to care for his household or to preserve and increase his estate.

By Sara I mean the Church of Augsburg which is, as it were, the spouse of our Abraham[1] and might, according to her just deserts, be much better cared for if the handmaidens, that is the provostships, were excluded and the strumpets put aside, namely those new splendours on which money promised or contributed has been squandered. These gaudy shows distract the mind and keep the lover from his beloved.[2] Truth to tell, I am afraid lest the wiles of Satan should prevail by means of these entanglements and business worries, which he is at pains to cast about our feet. It ought not to be enough for us merely to have some honest purpose in view, such as the payment of debts, the foundation of a pious work, the service of our Catholic brethren. No ; such purposes can only have genuine and conscientious relation to our calling if for their sake more important things are not neglected, so that we may not appear to be serving Christ and the world at one and the same time or to be setting greater store by temporal rather than by spiritual things.

What shall I do, said simple-hearted Job, when the Lord shall come to judge ? What answer shall I make when He demands an account of my whole stewardship ? We have avoided, I think, most of the snares of the world and the flesh, but there yet remains to be conquered that spirit which deceitful cupidity and vain honour implant in the heart, so that we may learn to be content with little and to refuse such tasks and burdens as weigh down the conscience and hinder better and more necessary things. We are given only a short course in this life during which it behoves us to fight unencumbered, steadfastly, and like brave men. Let us not sit down on three chairs when one is enough. Let us put away rather than increase our burdens, seeing that the ones we bear are, alas, heavy enough on our shoulders. The

---

[1] " Our Abraham " was then Cardinal, protector of the German nation in Rome, Bishop of Augsburg, Prince of the Empire, Count consistorial of the Emperor, Provost of the Cathedral of Würzburg and of the collegiate church of Ellwangen, and Canon Cantor of the Cathedral of Speyer. As if that was not enough, he had set his heart on being Provost of the Cathedral of Freising also. For some reason, he received in addition to his many other stipends an annual pension of five thousand gold pieces from the Archdiocese of Toledo.

[2] As related earlier, Cardinal Truchsess was very fond of show and spent large sums on entertainment. Despite the remarkable influence of Lejay and St. Peter himself on him, he had obviously not yet thoroughly reformed.

way is narrow and does not easily admit travellers bent under so many packs, tied by so many chains, weighed down by so many cares. Let us, therefore, beg our holy father, St. Ulric,[1] that he would deign to counsel and help us in the proper discharge of this office which he himself once bore. . . . Let us go about our business in the Church of God as far as possible utterly strangers to the cares and concerns of the secular world, daily subtracting something from our vanities or pleasures or desires, so that we may ever more nearly approach to the ideal of the Perfect Pastor. . . . May Our Lord Jesus Christ grant us the plentiful fruit of His Passion and Cross, that in Him we may overcome the world and the devil and crucify our flesh with its vices and concupiscences. So shall we afterwards rise the more swiftly to newness of life and sing our well-earned Alleluia.[2]

With all its involved syntax and rather clumsy Scriptural metaphors, that letter is a winning document, but it did not completely win Cardinal Truchsess. Though he in no way resented St. Peter's hints and remained all through life his devoted client and friend, he never quite turned into a new St. Ambrose. He resigned some of his benefices, indeed, but, prodigal with money to the last, acquired others from later Popes to enable him to continue his patronage of the arts. All the same, he was a fine man and, in his limited fashion, a holy and zealous bishop to whom the Catholic Church in Germany is very greatly indebted.

The day after writing to him, St. Peter addressed another bishop, his friend Anton Brus of Prague, who had recently been appointed to the long vacant See of Vienna. " Blessed be God," he said, " for having given your Lordship this grand chance of helping Austria. . . . I would beg you not to be troubled by the first difficulties which you are fairly sure to encounter. It often happens that difficulties which it is rarely possible to evade at the moment are gradually overcome. Indeed, if you were to be too urgent, you might only make matters worse. The Emperor, whose reign may God Almighty prosper, will be at your call and, if I am not mistaken, he will prove himself all the more a Theodosius, the more plainly he sees that he is dealing with an Ambrose."[3] St. Peter was probably thinking chiefly of St. Ambrose's great success in securing by a firm attitude with the Emperor the restriction or repression of pagan propaganda in Italy and elsewhere. There was a clear parallel

---

[1] Bishop of Augsburg in the tenth century and the primary patron saint of the diocese.
[2] Braunsberger, *Epistulae*, vol. ii, pp. 228–30. The letter was written close to Passiontide and Easter, which accounts for the style of its concluding sentences.
[3] Braunsberger, *Epistulae*, vol. ii, pp. 231–2.

between the methods of that propaganda and the methods used by the Lutherans in Austria and Bavaria, just as there was a good deal in common between Theodosius and Ferdinand. What St. Peter longed to find was a modern Ambrose. Bishop Brus answered his letter in the following terms :

It is not a little part of happiness, *Suavissime Canisi*, to have a friend in trouble who, himself well acquainted with its sting, knows how to console the dispirited and be a true sympathizer. For this reason your letter and the booklets you enclosed were ever so welcome. It brought me the good news that you had not yet gone to Italy but that you were living and working fruitfully near at hand, and it consoled me in the most kindly way and gave me fresh courage, exposed as I am to every kind of annoyance and subject to the heaviest trials. Now I have practical experience of the labour and danger involved in conflict with the monstrous Goliath before his heretical head is crushed. I seem to have drawn on myself here in Vienna the hatred and malevolence reserved generally for the Jesuits, to use the nick-name of the enemy. Here the bishop alone is the stumbling-block. . . . I am described as a devotee of superstition, a papistical sycophant, and a seducer.

Blessed be God that I, a lowly and unprofitable servant, am counted worthy to suffer contumely for His Name and for His Church. May He, the Author of my vocation, look favourably on the work begun and grant His servant patience. . . . Believe me, I love and cherish the Fathers of your Society as none others,[1] for I have seen myself delivered from many troubles by their prayers. . . . Please try, my Canisius, to come back to us here sometime. I do not ask this for my own sake merely, greatly as I long to see you, but because I know that you have much influence in every quarter, beyond what other men have. Keep well, and pray for me as I do for you.[2]

Meantime, the hour approached when Peter must once again take the road to Rome, but his sermons in Straubing were doing so much good that Duke Albert petitioned his father-in-law, the Emperor, to forbid any interruption of his preaching before Pentecost. The Emperor complied, using the intimate pronoun " *Du* " in his letter,[3] to which Peter sent the following answer on April 4th :

---

[1] Brus was himself the General of a religious order, the Crutched Friars.

[2] Braunsberger, *Epistulae*, vol. ii, pp. 235–6.

[3] " Du mit deinem Predigen vil guets schaffen khundest, und ist unnser gnediger Beuelch an dich das du allso bissauf negstkhomennde Pfingsten daselbst zu Straubing verharrest, und mit deiner Predig furfarest." Braunsberger, *Epistulae*, vol. ii, p. 237.

Pax aeterni Regis suavissima nobiscum.

Personally, Sire, and on behalf of my brethren in Christ I return infinite thanks to Almighty God for giving us Your Sacred Majesty as our Sovereign and ever August Emperor, and I congratulate Your Majesty from my heart. We who live in this least Society of Jesus shall continue to fulfil our duty of offering prayers and Holy Sacrifices for you to Him who alone founded the Holy Roman Empire and, having founded it, rules it and renders it illustrious. May He deign to consecrate the fortunes of the new reign with the gifts of His supreme charity and to inform and grace Your Majesty with a fresh and ardent zeal for the cause of religion, which ought ever to be your first care. Amen.

I shall do as Your Majesty bids me that so I may wholly adjust my life to the wishes of the Excellent Prince Albert and to the needs of the country. With the help of God's grace I shall not desist from the task of preaching before Pentecost, but I would respectfully submit this information, that our Fathers in Italy are making every endeavour to secure the election of our new General and, if at all possible, to hold the ballot in Rome before Pentecost. I expect to hear definite news about the matter at any moment and I am instructed to be ready to start on the journey immediately it arrives, always, however, without prejudice to the authority of Your Imperial Majesty. I beg you earnestly, then, not to make it difficult for me to satisfy holy obedience if I am called to Italy, and to grant this favour to our Society, which, certainly, without a head, cannot flourish nor be rightly governed nor capable of helping others in Christ. . . . I would count it a great favour to have Your Majesty's decision on the matter, and if, as I hope, you grant our Society this little concession, I would be most obliged were you also graciously to inform Prince Albert, whose wishes in other respects it is both my duty and my pleasure to meet. May Our Lord Jesus plant in our souls the virtue of His Sacred Passion, that dead to sin we may live to justice and share blessedly in His Resurrection.[1]

Not content with that provision against misunderstanding, Peter wrote also to Duke Albert on receipt of the summons to Rome. He pointed out that the Jesuits were assembling for much other grave business besides the election of a new General, including particularly a discussion of ways and means of helping Germany, " that nation than which there is no other

[1] Braunsberger, *Epistulae*, vol. ii, pp. 238-9.

under the sun with better claims on our devotion." In view of this, he hopes that his departure will be excused and that Albert will himself write explaining matters to the Straubing authorities. Albert thanked him warmly for all the good he had done and, as a token of gratitude, sent him a ' cheque ' which on presentation to the Ducal almoner in Straubing would have procured him fifty crowns for the expenses of his journey to Rome.[1] Peter considered that the gift was more than a whole year of his sermons would have deserved but, grateful though he expressed himself, he returned the precious cheque to the Duke :

> I thank your Highness most heartily for your singular munificence, which I in no way merited. But, since it is not our custom to accept anything beyond what is necessary for daily life, and since we owe all of which, by God's grace, we are capable to your Highness and to Bavaria. . . . I beg you not to take it amiss if I return the letter you sent me for presentation to your almoner and decline to receive the money. It is not that I fail to appreciate the gracious liberality of so noble a Patron, for which I thank you again and again, and shall ever thank you, but because, in accordance with our rule of life, I am anxious to return honestly to God, my Creditor, what I have freely received, and to give it freely to my brethren in Christ. As your Highness knows, we are here to serve the Eternal Father as sons, and not as mercenaries, and our loyal desire is to please the best of Princes whenever and wherever we can. It will, then, be more than enough if, as I wrote last time, the Carmelite Prior in Straubing is compensated for the expense to which I put him for my keep. Jesus Our Lord, whose glory alone may we consider and untiringly promote in this troubled life, grant your Highness an increase of the sovereign and eternal good things."[2]

Before leaving for Rome Peter entrusted his much-prized Strasbourg relics to the care of a lady whom he used affectionately to address as his " mother." She was the wife of his friend Schweicker, Duke Albert's secretary. He had secured the services of some craftsmen to make a beautiful reliquary which nun friends undertook to line and ornament in the interior. Schweicker and his wife were given detailed instructions

---

[1] " Das wir Ewers vilfeltigen guethen geschefften nutz dise claine zeit, von andern guethertzigen, grundlich bericht seindt, haben wir ain sonders grose freudt gefallen und hoffnung entfangen, Der Allmechtig Ewig Gott werde sein gnad noch reichlich verleihen." Braunsberger, *Epistulae*, vol. ii, p. 248.

[2] Braunsberger, *Epistulae*, vol. ii, pp. 270–1. So determined was Peter that the Prior of the Carmelites, his " kindly host," should not be out of pocket on his account that he urged the matter in four other letters to the Duke or his advisers, and thus secured prompt payment.

as to measurements, together with drawings of suggested designs. The Saint asked them to pay any bills that came to hand in connexion with the work, but only as a temporary loan to himself which he would repay in full, " even if it was necessary to beg the wherewithal."

That off his mind, he proceeded to furnish the Duke of Bavaria with a variety of suggestions on the best way of preserving the Faith in Straubing and other cities. From Augsburg, where he made a short halt, he wrote again to Schweicker, who was in bad odour with the lay nobility of Bavaria on account of his stout resistance to their demands for religious liberty : "Your most charming letter has reached me, dearest friend, and I do not see what greater benefits I could expect from your kindness nor how you could possibly be more generous in your services to the undeserving. . . . Congratulate yourself, my Schweicker, that you are suffering something for the Name of Jesus and the defence of religion. Now is the time, if ever, to confess the Name of the Lord and not to blush for the Gospel which commands men to hear the Church, to obey its rulers, and to pass not beyond the bounds which their fathers have set. Would that zeal for the House of God might run away with us and inflame us against those madmen whose sport it is to trample on sacred things. . . ."[1]

In that letter and in one written the following day to Duke Albert, Peter urges, with all the earnestness of his zealous heart, that the Prince should show an unflinching front to the innovators. How much reason he had for anxiety was proved the following year (1559) by the general Church " Visitation " of Bavaria. Abundant evidence was forthcoming that the schoolmasters could nowhere be trusted, that they were usually ardent champions of innovation, that many of them caused the books of heretics to be read in their schools and even openly used Luther's Catechism as their manual of religious instruction. Against such perversion of the young, Peter Canisius would fight to his last breath. His letter to the Duke contained wise suggestions for the setting up of a new ecclesiastical commission, composed partly of laymen and partly of clerics, whose business it would be to investigate the Lutheran attack in all its forms and to discuss and propose the best methods for coping with it. This plan, of which Peter was the principal but not the only sponsor, was finally accepted and put into operation by the Bavarian Government in 1570. In urging it the Saint insisted on one vital point, the neglect of which only too often spoiled the chances of effective Catholic resistance. Addressing Albert, he said :

[1] Braunsberger, *Epistulae*, vol. ii, p. 267.

Concerning this matter, the Divine Bounty would be more favourable to our good desires and projects, were we to leave to the bishops
what is theirs by the ordinance of God, taking great care, as the saying
has it, not to put our scythe to another man's crop. I think that there
is no plague more hurtful to the Church, no more potent way of destroying all order, than the confusing of the ecclesiastical and civil juris-
dictions. The functions of both powers are entirely distinct and separate,
and it is a crime for lay people to intrude into the episcopal office,
whatever the bishops holding it may be like.[1] Your Highness is exceedingly well advised, then, to keep on the closest terms with the
bishops around you and to confer with them willingly on religious
affairs, on the heretical offensive, and on the best means of abolishing
scandals among the clergy. In my opinion it will help, too, if the
men I have referred to as spiritual counsellors apply for and receive the
approbation of their ordinaries or of a number of bishops that so their
suggestions may carry greater weight and have a more seemly basis. . . .

These things I say like the shoemaker going beyond his last, but I
say them out of love and special devotion to Bavaria, not as laying down
the law but to give wise men an occasion for deciding something better on
a matter of such grave importance. You are too gracious, gentle Prince,
not to take my counsels in good part for whatever they are worth, and
not to continue in your love and protection of the Fathers of our Society.[2]

St. Peter's route to Rome took him through the Bavarian Alps. At
Ettal, near Oberammergau, he was hospitably entertained at the well-
known Benedictine monastery, and given, when leaving, some relics of
the saints. Then he pursued his way to Loreto, where an incident befell
him of a rather comical description. On knocking at the door of the
Jesuit residence and announcing himself to be Father Canisius from
Germany, the lay brother, who had probably never heard of such a
person, demanded the identity papers, signed by their provincial superiors,
which travelling Jesuits were supposed to carry with them. Peter modestly
explained that he was himself a Provincial and consequently had no papers.
The brother, a cautious and suspicious person, thereupon slammed the
door in the Saint's face, saying, " You are not coming in here." Peter
turned away without a word, and, tired from his long journey, sat down

---

[1] The lay nobility of Bavaria, including sometimes Duke Albert himself, constantly challenged
the rights of bishops throughout the Reformation period, and violated those rights in almost every
way possible.
[2] Braunsberger, *Epistulae*, vol. ii, pp. 268–70.

on a bench near the door. There he remained for nearly an hour until one of the Fathers arrived back from the Basilica near by, who, recognizing him, asked in astonishment why he had not gone in. " Because the Brother wouldn't let me," answered Peter with a smile. When the Rector, Father Oliver Manare, and his community heard what had happened they ran to welcome their distinguished visitor and to offer him their profound apologies. These, St. Peter insisted, were entirely unnecessary, and, lest there might be reprisals on the unfortunate Brother, he took his part and warmly commended his vigilance.[1]

Peter arrived in Rome about the middle of May, 1558, and immediately set to work with some other prominent Fathers preparing the business to be transacted during the congregation. That work occupied more than a month. While engaged on it the Saint kept in close touch with his friends beyond the Alps and performed whatever services he could for them in Rome. The poor Bishop of Vienna was in sore trouble at the time. Owing to the exigencies of the situation, he had, on his appointment by the Emperor, immediately assumed office without waiting for the *placet* of the Pope. That was technically a breach of canon law, and Paul IV, being at loggerheads with Ferdinand, was not in the mood to overlook it. St. Peter might regret that the Pope's prestige as a maker of Emperors had come to an end, but he was too much of a realist to attach undue importance to its disappearance. He dreamt of a nobler presidency for the Vicar of Christ, a hegemony " whose crown is meekness and its life everlasting love unfeigned." To Bishop Brus he wrote, June 13, 1558 :

We have fallen, as you know, on most difficult times, which, in ways unexperienced before, test the mettle of the Church's good rulers and true bishops and pastors. There is little to be hoped from human counsels because, unless I am greatly mistaken, impiety and malice have prevailed over our natural ability and diligence. Let us fly, then, with tears to Christ, the Leader and Shepherd of the straying sheep. Let us rouse Him, as He sleeps in the boat, to succour the perishing, and let us beg Him to give us of His own power to steer our way. It would greatly help to this end if, as that light of bishops, St. Ambrose, did daily, your Lordship were frequently to offer the most efficacious Sacrifice of the Eucharist to God the Father, to devote much time and attention to prayer, the best weapon of a bishop, and steadfastly to transact the business of Christ and His Church in the midst of luke-

---

[1] Boero, *Vita del Beato Pietro Canisio* (Rome, 1864), pp. 185–6. Boero took the story from a manuscript of Father Borghese, who was in Loreto when the incident happened.

warm or wholly indifferent Catholics. . . . Though it is not my place to admonish a bishop, yet, relying on your singular benevolence to me, I exhort and most earnestly beg you to be ready for and manfully to despise the reproaches, hatred, and general malice of such people. We neither can nor ought to try to please two masters. Therefore, let us go on steadily, urging and executing the duties of our office without respect for persons, so that we may be seen to rely in our work on divine rather than human aid and authority. No doubt but that God, the Vindicator, will fight for us. Through Him we shall do mightily and He will bring our enemies to naught or assuredly turn their efforts to the salvation of His elect.

Peter next goes on to speak about the matter of Brus's confirmation in office by the Pope. He says that he has worked very hard to secure it but that there are serious difficulties in the way. If only the Pope and the Emperor would come to terms he might have some chance of success : " We are hoping that those Monarchs will soon be reconciled. Most people have little idea how difficult their quarrel makes things here. Believe me, all is being done here with foresight and prudence that religion may not suffer harm. Would to God that even the stone blind could not see, and that the present state of things did not make as clear as the day, how religion has been treated for many years by Catholics themselves. May Our Lord Jesus keep your Lordship safe, and with you, our Staphylus. If he is still on the scene I would like you to give him my greetings."[1]

The next letter from Rome is to the Duke of Bavaria and shows Peter in a guise that will not appeal to the modern imagination. He was a man of his age, as we are of ours, and everybody in the sixteenth century considered coercion of opinion as natural as we think it objectionable. Moreover, the ethics of religious persecution are hardly in question here, for Peter had no desire to see peaceable Protestant populations coerced. All he wanted was the repression of heresy when it became belligerent in a Catholic land. Incidentally, his letter to the Duke provides a lurid picture of the state of contemporary Europe. It begins with a reference to certain letters from the Jesuits at work in distant countries, generically described as the " Indies " :

The enclosure in my last letter to you, Illustrious Prince, gave some news of a new world. To tell you the rest of the story would take too long but perhaps I shall be able to another time. Even from the few reports I sent you the wonderful works and judgments of Almighty God can be understood, and they might well frighten us if we are indolent and ungrateful. The Father of the house lets nothing be lost. He searches on all sides that His house may be full, rejects those first called to His Supper for their thanklessness, and appoints strangers to their places. . . . Well, then, might our Germany be afraid which is rich in leaves but empty of Gospel fruit, which for so many years has been contending about faith and daily becomes more sterile in works, which has had such varied experience of the deceit and mischief of the new doctrine, and yet continues in ways so unquiet that there is hardly any constancy of belief or religion left, hardly any zeal, even among Catholics, hardly any of the spirit of penitence. What else, I ask you, do those evils portend but the destruction of the Empire and the devastation of Germany? Soon the Kingdom of God and its infinity of good things may be transferred from us, its unworthy possessors, to other nations, leaving, as it is written, our house deserted.

And, as though religious dissension were not causing enough trouble, behold the Turkish fleet off Naples, from which Calabria is bound to suffer an extremity of evil. There is good evidence that during the last few years forty thousand Christians have been dragged into miserable bondage by the Turks from the Kingdom of Naples alone. It is a terrible story of sorrow and anguish, that record of the raids on our brethren by a worse than barbarian foe. Good women and innocent maidens are violated, everything sacred is profaned, homes and temples are destroyed, men are led off as though they were beasts, free men are suddenly made slaves and rich men reduced to beggary, all family relationships are blotted out, husbands and wives are torn apart, treaties are scorned, and every right of justice and honesty is trampled on, while these barbarians and Mamelukes, as they are called, indulge in every licence and make everything serve their lust. What cannot be carried off as booty is given over to the flames so that the devastation is itself the monument of their abominable cruelty.

Such then, are the sufferings of our brothers and sisters, all bound to us in the closest union of Christ. So are these most unhappy ones endangered, and so do thousands of souls perish, while every year many splendid cities and provinces are torn from us and added to the Empire of the Turks. Meantime, our temper, and the Christian blood and spirit informing us amidst this greatest of public calamities, are sufficiently evinced by our dissensions and mutual strife which keep practically the whole world in agitation. Here, of a surety, is the reason why God in His anger sends or permits so many cruel wars, and such a plague of unending heresies that we can discover no measure nor term to our misfortunes.

In these terrible disturbances, I think that there are two services which by reason of your position your Highness might do for Christ and His Church. The first is that you might take great and frequent pains for the restoration of public peace and tranquillity, partly by earnest prayer to Christ, and partly by serious Christian exhortations in correspondence and conference with other monarchs. Secondly, your Highness might well imitate the example of the great Charles,[1] who should certainly be the model of German Princes, interested in the preservation of religion. . . . When this Catholic King heard a rumour that some Lutheran sectaries, including members of the nobility, had been arrested in the cities of Spain, he took up his pen in unendurable distress, conscious of the gravity of the matter and its dangers. Leisure, peace, prayer, and solitude were forgotten, and His Majesty, as though oblivious of his new way of life, urgently pressed the business, writing, issuing orders, laying commands on his daughter, the widow of the young King of Portugal, and proposing a strongly worded edict to the Cortes and to the Inquisition. The gist of his exhortations was that war must at once be declared on the sectaries, wherever they were found; that they must be routed, or, if captured, be made to pay the full penalty of their heresy as an example to others. He added that not even his own nephew should be spared if found guilty, though he held him dearer than anything on earth, for he would have no distinction made between one seceder from the Catholic religion and another. His aim in all this was to prevent by every possible means the entry into Spain of a plague which had so miserably ruined Germany and rendered her despicable in good men's opinion.

I gladly propose the example to your Highness because it is of very recent occurrence and well known to me, that it may be a comfort to your piety and a mirror of action, confirming your resolution against those who by their hesitation, connivance, silence, or consent, instead of restoring the Catholic religion let it be almost extinguished. Studying to appease lunatics rather than please sane men, these unskilful doctors only make the malady worse. Their first and last aphorism is: It

---

[1] Charles V, who after his abdication had retired to the monastery of Yuste, in the mountains of Estremadura. On the occasion arising, however, he once more took a part in public affairs by directing Spain's resistance to the onslaughts of heresy.

behoves us to obey men rather than God and His Church—for to such obedience their lives and policies are dedicated. In their eyes Christianity means merely politics. They would serve and satisfy both the world and God, and sometimes they even blush to profess themselves Catholics, lest they be considered adherents of the Pope.

I have run on longer than I intended and ask your Highness's pardon for my free speech. Being wise, you know that what I say is not imagination. . . . I thank you most heartily for providing the people of Straubing with a Catholic preacher and for removing the schismatical one, and I beg you, Christ assisting, to act boldly in the interests of religion, nowhere and at no time permitting wolves to rage either in the churches or the schools. So will be preserved the glory of your noble family, and future generations will know and publish the praises of the House of Bavaria, which almost alone in the Empire may lay just claim to the title of Catholic, having never failed in its faith though so many ways assaulted and surrounded on all sides by the sectaries.[1]

On June 19, 1558, after two years of anxiety and frustrated effort, the Society of Jesus opened its first general congregation. Immediately beforehand, the Fathers went to seek the blessing of the Pope, which was graciously accorded. The Holy Father wished, however, that they should submit the formula for the election of a General to the judgment of four cardinals. These men approved it but considered that the penalties to be visited on any Father guilty of " electioneering " and on his abettors were too severe. Nevertheless, the penalties remained, and, on June 28th, after a week spent in discussion of procedure, the electors began a solemn four days of penance and prayer to obtain the favour of Heaven on their work. During this time, the twenty electors, of whom St. Peter was one, discussed among themselves and endeavoured in every legitimate way to discover the relative fitness of various possible candidates. There were five of these, Paschase Broët, Francis Borgia, Nicholas Delanoy, Jerome Nadal, and James Laynez. Peter Canisius did not figure among the " possibles," either because not sufficiently well known to the majority of the electors of whom ten were Spaniards and three Portuguese, or else because those who might have voted for him knew that the Emperor would take it very ill indeed if he were to be permanently removed from Germany.[2]

[1] Braunsberger, *Epistulae*, vol. ii, pp. 281–4.

[2] The small number of the electors may cause surprise, considering that the Society of Jesus had over a thousand members at this time. The explanation is that St. Ignatius had been very sparing in granting the privilege of solemn profession and it was only the professed who had a right to take part in the election of a General. There were only thirty-five such men in the whole Society at the time of the Founder's death.

The day fixed for the voting was July 2nd. Preliminary to this a secret ballot was taken for the purpose of choosing the most suitable Father to deliver a Latin exhortation to the electors. St. Peter received all the votes. In the low and narrow room consecrated by the labours and holy death of St. Ignatius he addressed his brethren, gathered round Cardinal Pacheco as representative of the Pope. What he said we do not know, except that it met the solemn occasion perfectly.[1] When he had done Cardinal Pacheco retired to allow the electors an hour of private prayer, after which the voting at once began. Only one ballot was necessary as Laynez had a clear majority. Broët, Delanoy, and Francis Borgia each received one vote, Nadal four and Laynez the remaining thirteen. Broët, as the Father longest professed, thereupon declared Laynez General, in the name of the whole Society ; the electors proceeded to do him homage ; and, that finished, all with thankful hearts recited the *Te Deum.*

The days immediately following the election were given up to festivities, by which the Jesuits did not mean fireworks, banquets, and such things, but public disputations and lectures on theology, philosophy, and astronomy, with a play thrown in as a concession to human weakness. It was a religious play, of course, and, according to Nadal, delighted the College of Cardinals and the whole Roman aristocracy beyond measure. On July 6th the new General and his electors were received in audience by the Pope, who treated them with the most paternal kindness and, in a long address, warmly praised the good work the Society was doing. " We offer you all to God," the Holy Father continued, " and pray Him so to increase you in virtue, in number and in merit that you may carry His Name through the whole wide world."[2] That was a fine and noble *amende* from the man whose succession to the Papacy had so frightened St. Ignatius that " all his bones shook in his body."[3] But Paul IV could not cease in a day to be John Peter Caraffa, and the Jesuits, for all his kind words, were far from being at the end of their troubles with him. Returning full of gratitude from their audience they set to work on the second main business of the congregation, which was the careful editing and promulgating of the constitutions of St. Ignatius. By the end of August they were almost finished when, out of a blue sky, there broke on their heads

[1] Sacchinus, *Vita P. Petri Canisii*, p. 147.

[2] Braunsberger, *Epistulae*, vol. ii, pp. 286–91.

[3] So the Portuguese Father Gonçalvez in his *Memoriale* : " Todos os ossos se lhe reuoluérão on corpo." M.H., *Monumenta Ignatiana, Scripta de S. Ignatio*, vol. i, p. 198. Pope Paul, more than twenty years earlier, had been the co-founder with St. Cajetan of the Theatines. In 1545 he tried his best to have the Jesuits amalgamated with his own Order and on two other occasions had picked a quarrel with St. Ignatius.

another terrible storm, which came very near to washing away their constitutions altogether. As, luckily for his own peace of mind, St. Peter Canisius had left Rome at the time, the storm is no part of his story.[1]

Curiously enough, Peter's departure was due to a mission that had been confided to him by the Pope who was threatening the existence of his Order. The Saint had long been interested in the religious welfare of Poland and, while in Rome, corresponded on the subject with his friend Cromer, secretary to King Sigismund II. Cromer desired to see the Jesuits established in Cracow. " Go ahead," answered Peter. " Use your influence with the King for the promotion of this excellent scheme. We shall not be backward in providing Cracow with a colony of our men. . . . I shall devote myself completely to securing that you have no lack of learned, cultured, and devout men there. . . . I do not think that the Bishop of Ermland[2] will be aggrieved at our first offering this service to the King. From Cracow we can afterwards, God willing, pass over conveniently to Ermland."[3] By a happy chance Peter was given soon afterwards an opportunity for studying the Polish problem on the spot, a problem as serious as any with which his zeal had hitherto wrestled.

At a secret consistory, held in July, Pope Paul decided to send to the Emperor a legate who should expound the reasons why his election to the Imperial Crown could not be ratified by the Holy See, and who should afterwards proceed to Poland to be present at the forthcoming national Diet of Piotrków. A little later the Pope made a change in his arrangements and appointed Camillus Mentuati, Bishop of Satriano, as nuncio to Poland, postponing for the moment the dispatch of a cardinal legate. St. Peter and a professor of the Roman College named Father Theodoric of Amsterdam were instructed, " *praeter omnem expectationem*," to accompany the nuncio as theological advisers. The party left Rome about August 10th and, after a seven days' ride, reached Pesaro, all apparently well and cheerful. After a short rest there they took a coasting vessel to Rimini, from which town the gentle, lovable Father Theodoric wrote to tell his friends in Rome that Bishop Mentuati had fallen completely under the spell of St. Peter, and had adopted him for his spiritual as well

---

[1] For very sound reasons St. Ignatius had laid down in the constitutions that Generals of the Society were to hold office for life. Paul IV now forbade any General to rule for more than three years. After the death of the Pope the following year non-Jesuit canonists in Rome assured Laynez that Paul's regulation no longer bound him. Canisius and other leading Fathers of the Society pronounced in the same sense but Laynez would have resigned had not Pius IV expressly nullified his predecessor's injunction.

[2] Stanislaus Hosius, who had negotiated with St. Peter in 1554 for some Jesuit helpers in his huge diocese. Hosius was a Pole, and his real name was Hozyusz.

[3] Braunsberger, *Epistulae*, vol. ii, pp. 276-7.

as theological director.[1] From Rimini the party went by ship to Venice and thence made their way through Trent to Vienna, where they arrived on September 19th, all rather the worse for the wear. A rumour had gone ahead of them to the effect that St. Peter had been murdered in the mountains near Trent, and the Viennese Jesuits were in the lowest depths of sorrow and anxiety when their beloved Provincial appeared with nothing worse than the tertian ague affecting him.[2] The Bishop also had the tertian ague badly and Father Theodoric, who on arrival appeared to be in normal health, soon fell into a dangerous fever. What it was that had upset them *en route* they do not say, probably the terrible Italian sun which the two Dutchmen at least would have found more than their northern blood could bear. Poor Father Theodoric died on October 1st, after receiving the Last Sacraments from St. Peter. " He went without the slightest dread," the Saint told Laynez, " commending himself devoutly and unreservedly to Our Lord. His life was all innocence and sweet with piety. There was a rare charm in his manner and he possessed fine intellectual gifts. He could not have died in any way but well. . . . I arrived sick in Vienna and he sound, but, like Jacob, he has stolen away my blessing . . . and so I leave here bereft of my sweet companion and most dear brother, unworthy, I am afraid, of the spiritual and fraternal consolation he might have given me. . . . I desire with all my heart that his soul be commended to its Creator in the prayers of the brethren."[3]

Tertian ague notwithstanding, St. Peter made very good use of his enforced stay in Vienna. He obtained audience of Emperor Ferdinand three times and pleaded earnestly for his brethren at the College, who were faced with many grave difficulties. The University of Vienna continued to suffer from the activities of Protestantizing professors whose influence Peter now endeavoured to counter by securing that there should always be some Jesuits in the philosophical and theological faculties. This was easier suggested than brought about, however, because the University authorities would admit to its teaching staff none but men who could show a doctor's degree from some other recognized centre of learning. In 1552 Pope Julius III had granted the Society of Jesus the privilege of conferring its own degrees, after the General had submitted the candidate to a rigorous examination in which doctors and masters not of the Order had a right to participate. The Pope, moreover, decreed that such degrees were to be recognized by all Catholic universities, a stipula-

[1] Braunsberger, *Epistulae*, vol. ii, p. 826.
[2] Sacchinus, *Historia Societatis Jesu*, pars ii, lib. 2, nn. 113-14.
[3] Braunsberger, *Epistulae*, vol. ii, p. 309.

tion quite within his competence since the vast majority of those universities owed their existence to papal grace. But Vienna was very slow to honour the Jesuit diplomas. St. Peter himself had been allowed to profess theology in her schools because his doctorate was from Bologna, but others of his brethren, who had received theirs at the Roman College, found the way barred to them, though their qualifications were certainly as good as any lay university could have assured. Pure prejudice decided the issue and it was to overcome this that St. Peter approached the Emperor. He had complete success, for, when shortly afterwards Laynez submitted a list of his subjects whose doctorate he guaranteed, the Emperor " confirmed, approved, and corroborated it," and ordered all academic authorities in his dominions, both ecclesiastical and lay, to recognize the standing of the Jesuits, " under pain of his grave displeasure and other penalties." On Peter's further petition he granted, too, that Jesuits occupying academic positions were to be permitted to live according to their rule and not be precluded from such priestly ministrations as were compatible with their professorial duties. That victory marked a step forward in the work of the Counter-Reformation.[1] Peter was able to inform Laynez that the Emperor had received him more graciously than ever before, and that he had confided to him the secrets of his innermost conscience.

With his brethren at the College he did much good work, composing domestic troubles and putting fresh heart into despondent people. One young man named Volck, to whom he had already been very kind, was at this time a prey to melancholia and about to abandon the religious life altogether. His superiors had tried every method of helping him, but in vain, probably because they failed to put sufficient human sympathy into their efforts. Peter went about the business another way. In the words of Sacchinus: " He embraced his prodigal son and urged him to undertake some penance on his own account, and then on his knees with arms outstretched to beg his Heavenly Father to free him from the illusions of the devil. He did this, and on the following day returned to Canisius a completely different man, acknowledged his faults and, with many tears, made a general confession, after which he spontaneously begged for a public penance as an atonement to his brethren. Then he petitioned to be allowed to go through the Exercises of our Blessed Father Ignatius, which before he had obstinately refused, and did them with great ardour. To crown all he renewed his vows and entered with fresh enthusiasm upon the hearty

[1] Braunsberger, *Epistulae*, vol. ii, pp. 304, 316–17.

service of Almighty God."[1] The results of Peter's kindness and understanding in this case were far-reaching. He and Volck became the closest
friends, and the young man whom the Society of Jesus had so nearly lost
ended his days fifty years later as one of her most illustrious German sons.

From the Emperor Peter had obtained commendatory letters to the
King of Poland, and his Queen, Catherine, who was Ferdinand's daughter.[2]
The letter to Sigismund deserves to be reproduced as an illustration of
its writer's noble character :

The honourable and devout religious man, Our beloved son Peter
Canisius, Doctor of Theology of the Society of the sacred Name of
Jesus, has humbly made known to Us that, in company with the Nuncio
of Our Holy Father, he is about to proceed to the Diet which your
Serenity is assembling in a short time at Piotrków, there to help in
promoting all measures for the conservation, stabilization, and propagation of Our holy Catholic and orthodox religion in your Highness's
Kingdom. Wherefore he greatly desired that he and his Society should
be commended to your Highness by Us. Being thoroughly well
acquainted with the profound learning and piety, and extraordinary
zeal for religion of the same Dr. Canisius, and also knowing by experience with how much diligence and earnest endeavour that whole
Society of the Name of Jesus labours in the Lord's vineyard, We, for
Our part, could not suffer Dr. Canisius to come to your Highness
without a letter from Us, in paternal declaration of the regard and
affection in which We hold him and his religious Society. We commend him to your Highness and would have you receive him with
your royal favour and benignity, both in consideration of Us and on
account of his own outstanding services to holy religion.

As for the cause that impelled him to undertake the journey We
do not think that it needs much commending. Your Highness having
hitherto borne the merit and name of a devout Catholic King, We do
not doubt but that in the future also you will neglect or pass over
nothing which is considered to appertain to the praise and glory of
Almighty God, and to the conservation and promotion of the unity
of Our Catholic and orthodox religion. Thus will you join your will
and mind with Our paternal will and mind in this matter, setting at
naught and despising the endeavours of all who strive to obscure the

---

[1] *Historia Societatis Jesu*, pars ii, lib. 2, n. 115.
[2] Ferdinand was Sigismund's father-in-law twice over, as the Polish King's first wife had been
another daughter of the Emperor. Between the two Habsburg ladies he had married the beautiful
Barbara Radziwill. All three marriages were unhappy owing to the non-appearance of an heir.

glory of Christ and to stir up and foster schism and dissension in Christendom. This only would We say in Our paternal love for your Highness, that We consider it would be a great help to the preservation of the Catholic religion in the Kingdom of Poland if you were to establish a college of the Society of the Name of Jesus therein, especially at Cracow, thus enabling the brethren of that Society to produce abundant fruit by the soundness of their teaching and the example of their upright lives. We know from experience that Our own kingdoms and provinces have greatly benefited from such institutions. For the rest, we heartily wish your Highness all health and happiness *ad multos annos*.[1]

Now began a most trying and tedious period for St. Peter. The Nuncio's party entered Cracow on October 12th, having been nine days on the road from Vienna. By the good offices of Cromer, who enjoyed considerable influence, they were given an official welcome. But, though the Nuncio was treated with due respect, Peter and his new companion, Father Mengin, had very little done for them. They were obliged to fend for themselves—which their poverty made extremely difficult. The arduous journey had brought on a bad attack of Peter's old enemy, dysentery, and while thus suffering in a strange land, he had great trouble, he told Laynez, " to find a place to say Mass or a bed to lie down on." The Poles, at first, made a poor impression on him. With unusual asperity, he wrote : " They are rustic enough in all conscience, both as men and as hosts. Poland has not yet emerged from barbarism, and the German provinces, in comparison, appear completely civilized." Even the Nuncio, who was old and feeble, soon began to wish that he was back in Italy. The Roman authorities failed to replenish his scanty exchequer and at last he came to such straits that he knew not where to turn for the daily bread of his retainers. St. Peter, seeing how matters stood, went on his own account to plead for help with the Bishop of Cracow, who had plenty of money. Thus he managed to save the mission from immediate collapse, but he could do nothing to secure it the respect of the Polish authorities. His picture of conditions in the country is gloomy beyond what might have been thought possible. The nobility, who, like the Whig families of Hanoverian England, had filched most of the royal authority, were practically all on the side of the Protestant Reformation and used their wealth and influence to protect the multitude of Lutheran preachers that swarmed over the land. From Cracow alone, which was supposed to be

[1] Braunsberger, *Epistulae*, vol. ii, pp. 827–8.

a Catholic city, ten thousand people used to sally forth on feast-days in order to enjoy a Lutheran sermon from some hot-gospeller in a neighbouring village. Gibes and insults met St. Peter whenever he walked abroad, and he was given more and more evidence as each dreary day went by that the Polish priests and bishops belonged to the happy-go-lucky class of which he had had such sad experience in Germany.[1]

The Saint's stay in Cracow might truly be described as one long frustration and disappointment, but all the time he was much more concerned about the poor Nuncio's troubles than about his own. To help the old man, he greatly desired to speak with Queen Catherine, whom he knew to be a true Catholic despite her Utraquist leanings, but he was shy of asking for an interview until armed with her father's letter. Day after day he watched for the post expectantly and watched in vain, for the letter never arrived. Meantime, the Nuncio consulted him hardly at all on religious matters, possibly because the unfortunate man had given up hope of being able to do any good. The whole situation was topsy-turvy, as may be gathered from the following rather despondent lines of Peter to Laynez :

If you ask me what I am doing with the Nuncio, I announce that I have heard his confession once, at Pesaro. He uses my services for no other business whatever, except that of having dinner and supper with him each day. Sometimes he unfolds his plans to me and when he hears anything fresh of Polish affairs he lets me know, but not at all with a view to obtaining my help. On public occasions he wishes to be considered his own theologian. To sum the matter up, I am rather his consoler than his assistant. The result is that I am at liberty to write or read in private, and I do not think I can do much good with the old man or with his retainers. Whether I shall be able to do anything for him at the Diet, time will tell. At any rate, good will will not be lacking, though ability most decidedly is. It was for this reason that I warned you and begged you to let me have, if possible, a colleague who would prevent my incompetence from being injurious to the Church when it comes to more difficult negotiations about matters of faith. As I told you, Father Dominic, who is now my companion, is no theologian. But may the will of the Lord be done everywhere. What I am anxious about is to learn it from your Reverence and, having learned it, with God's help to follow it up to the very end. May God keep your Paternity and the Fathers and Brothers safe and sound for His glory. . . .

[1] Braunsberger, *Epistulae*, vol. ii, pp. 322–3.

The Most Reverend Nuncio has received no letters from Rome, to his grievous annoyance, nor has any notice been taken of his many pleas for a contribution to his expenses. Accordingly, he has asked me to beg your Paternity not to fail if by your authority you can do anything towards stirring up those whose duty it is to assist us on our mission. The Nuncio's officials have no clothes for the winter ; wine has been given up; and invitations to guests, customary and in accordance with the dignity of a nunciature, are no longer issued, not to speak of other inconveniences. Meantime, we are among people from whom it is scarcely permissible and certainly inexpedient to borrow anything, without the knowledge of the Pope.

There are so many things to trouble the good old man that some here fear for his life, and now, on top of everything else, comes the difficult journey to the King and then to the Diet at Piotrków, on which we must soon set out. I shall not say anything about the inhumanity of the Poles, Catholics included, and I pass over their anti-papal bias, their lack of faith and the negligible amount of zeal to be found in their leaders. In spite of all . . . the Nuncio leaves nothing undone to prove himself an indomitable and trustworthy leader of a most difficult expedition. I tell your Paternity this that you may deign to promote our cause both by your advice to the Roman Curia and by your prayers to Our Lord Jesus, lest the continued failure of temporal help may prejudice the religious negotiations.

Blessed be Our Lord who teaches us to be satisfied anywhere, neither gainers nor losers but content with Christ Crucified alone.[1]

It may be wondered what had become of King Sigismund all this time, especially as his wife lay ill in Cracow. The answer explains a good deal. He was away hunting wild boar, and much more interested in that beast than in either his poor Queen or in the representative sent to him by the Pope. A cunning, weak person, jeered at by the people as " King To-morrow," he treated Catherine shamefully for her failure to provide him with an heir, though his own effete blood was probably the cause. When the Queen's brother, Maximilian, who was a gentleman, protested against her ill-treatment, the King retorted that he could not be expected to live with an epileptic and that her malady—which he had invented for the occasion —must be the curse of God on him for marrying a deceased wife's sister. Though he had a clear papal dispensation for his marriage he made feeble

[1] Braunsberger, *Epistulae*, vol. ii, pp. 323, 325–6.

efforts to obtain a decree of nullity, being too afraid of the Emperor to attempt the solution adopted by Henry VIII. A few years later he died, and with him the line of the Jagellons passed unmourned out of history.

During his month in Cracow St. Peter was allowed to preach only a single sermon, which, however, his companion, Father Mengin, reports to have been a " phenomenal " success. His enforced leisure produced one interesting result in the shape of a long letter now to be cited, but first it is necessary to give some details about the man to whom it was addressed. When in the year 1529 the Turks had retreated from Austria, a baby boy was found among the corpses of the slain in the village of Pfaffstetten. The poor mite could only babble a few words to the effect that he was " Urban." From his way of saying the words his rescuers decided that he must be of Austrian parentage, and " Urban the Austrian " they proceeded to christen him without more ado. He turned out a clever lad, deserving of the patronage bestowed upon him by people interested in his romantic origin. In due course he rose to be Bishop of Gurk in Carinthia and was appointed Court preacher by Ferdinand as a make-weight to the unorthodox and irrepressible Phauser. Unfortunately, Urban was not himself wholly orthodox. Once, hoping to put Phauser's nose out of joint, Ferdinand praised Urban's sermons in presence of his rival but only drew the perfectly fair retort: " It is easy to preach the way he does. When he reaches some fundamental point he shies away and proceeds to make circles round the subject."[1] A few days later Phauser rallied him to his face on his shilly-shallying, and promised him his full support if he would speak out like a man against the Church of Rome. It was this position of affairs that drew from St. Peter Canisius the following characteristic letter:

Ever since I became acquainted with your Lordship two years ago, I have venerated your person and dignity, admired your erudite eloquence, and loved with all my heart your piety and zeal for the Church of God. Many eminent men share these sentiments with me, as does the most devout and prudent Emperor Ferdinand. All the greater, then, is my grief as often as I hear some men, not just of the common people but persons of standing and probity, speaking to your discredit. By pointing this out to you, for what it is worth, I judged that I should not be exceeding my duty, nor doing anything displeasing to your Lordship. Admonished thus in all friendliness, you can the more easily avoid in future what good men find objectionable in your conduct. . . .

[1] Holtzmann, *Kaiser Maximilian II*, p. 252.

In this affair it is not only your reputation that is at stake nor the benevolence of a handful of people towards you. Rather is it the salvation of many souls. On this account I ought not to be thought interfering by you or by anybody else. This is everybody's business. . . . But I must stop speaking in riddles and apologetic words, lest I seem to doubt your fairness. What, then, is the terrible charge I have against you? Well, in few words it is this. Some people say that your explanation of controverted doctrines is so ambiguous that the heretics claim you for themselves as much as do the Catholics, and assert that your sympathies are with them. The result is that the Catholics keep away from your sermons because you raise doubts in their minds about matters which they learned in the Church from their earliest youth. I am not the only one who has heard this report of you, and I have heard it more than once. . . .

But, you ask, did I personally notice this when I was at Court and followed your sermons regularly? I shall tell you truly and candidly before God and His holy angels. I noticed that on more than one occasion when the drift of your sermon led you, even against your will, to some controverted dogma, or when some text of the Gospel given out by you required a Catholic explanation owing to its distortion by the heretics, you dissembled and, like sailors avoiding a rock or travellers a snake, wasted time on questions less useful to the common people. Examples of your method were the occasions when the Gospel itself called upon you to say something about Holy Orders, the power of the keys, the remission and retention of sins, or again, when the season and the very tenor of your sermon demanded a few words on the invocation of saints and on prayer and Masses for the dead. In a recent sermon you omitted from your enumeration of the motives for holy living the most powerful one of all, not, indeed, to the Lutherans and Calvinists, but to holy David, to Christ Himself, our God and Saviour, to His blessed Apostles, and to the whole Church of God. I mean the recompense or reward. . . .[1]

But you will say that a man must preach seasonably and remember the ears he is addressing. If done for popularity, I do not agree, for popularity is not so precious that a single Christian soul should be placed

---

[1] St. Peter does not say that it is the *noblest* motive, at least to begin with, but only that it is the strongest, which it undoubtedly is. Only shallow thinking sneers at it as the 'sugar-plum theory.' The sneer would be justified if it were considered as something apart from and unrelated to the love of God, but that is not so. Its developed Catholic interpretation is that given in the hymn, *O Deus ego amo te*, beloved of St. Francis Xavier, or in the words of St. Catherine of Genoa: "I had given the keys of the house to Love . . . and I stood so occupied in contemplating this work of Love that if He had cast me, body and soul, into hell, hell itself would have appeared to me all love and consolation." In the sixteenth century, when the Protestants so strenuously denied that man could merit divine reward, i.e. more intimate union with God eternally, by his good works, the doctrine needed special emphasis from Catholic preachers.

in danger to gain it, but if the motive is to bring back gradually to the truth those who have been seduced by the heretics, I do not disapprove. Peter and Paul and other apostles and doctors have so acted, sometimes disguising matters lest their new auditors should shrink from their sermons. But they so acted only for a time, until they had won the people's confidence. Once the foundations of Christian doctrine were laid, they allowed nothing of the kind. Otherwise, what else would they have done by their inopportune silence except betray the truth? In your case you ought to exercise the greatest caution to prevent such a charge against you, especially when your auditors are not of the kind with whom you can afford to dissemble for long about many doctrines.

Many of your listeners are convinced from your methods that you think differently on several doctrines of the Christian religion from Her who is the pillar and ground of truth, the Catholic Church. And there are heretics who assert the same everywhere, twisting to their own sense words which, perhaps, were spoken by you with an entirely different intention. The result is that many souls are endangered for whom Christ died, and this rather by your silence than by the noisy asseverations of the heretics. Good and simple men beware of such people as they would of wolves, but if they think that you, a Catholic bishop and the Emperor's preacher, are of the same opinion as the heretics, they are easily led into error, trusting to your authority. I am not urging that you should undertake *ex professo* to refute the dogmas of heresy immediately. All I ask is that, whenever an occasion offers and the mention of some doctrine is natural, you should not pass it over, but devote a few words to explaining the Catholic position and giving an argument or two in its favour. . . . For myself, I am persuaded that you do not wish to dissent from the Catholic Church in any respect. Some of your actions prove this. But you seem as if you do not desire or dare to live up to your actions in your sermons. Now, owing to the infirmity of our human nature, the things we daily hear or read gradually become part of us, unless we are careful. So much is this the teaching of experience that it has passed into a proverb : Who lives with the lame will himself acquire a limp. And the Wise Man says : He that toucheth pitch shall be defiled therewith.[1]

---

[1] Urban had some strange friends for a Catholic bishop, e.g. the tempestuous rebel, Paul Skalich. Only the previous year, 1557, he had given the Lutheran, Mark Wagner, an introduction to all the Catholic dignitaries of Germany, testifying that the bearer had been commissioned by King Maximilian to explore archives for ancient documents. Wagner, all the time, was the paid employee of the Centuriators of Magdeburg, whose interest in ancient documents stopped short with whatever they could provide to the discredit of the Catholic Church !

You know now, my Lord, what it is that is expected from you, or rather from your sermons, and it has been told you by . . . your true lover, who writes secretly, and not to betray you but to put you on your guard. . . . It will be your part to take in a right and friendly spirit this warning offered to you in the same spirit. Your model can be St. Augustine, a man eminent in every kind of learning who . . . as a bishop advanced in years, willingly allowed himself to be admonished by a little child. . . .[1]

That letter is not without its point, even at the present day when dogma is so much discounted. St. Peter would not have addressed it to everybody. He knew his Urban and felt that just such a straight talk was what he needed to put him right. And he was completely justified, for not many months later an official of the Emperor's Court wrote of the man in question : " *Der ist in seinem predigen ganz römisch worden* "— He has become entirely Roman in his sermons.[2] Not only that, but he became a devoted friend of St. Peter's Order and did splendid service on the side of the Counter-Reformation.

From Cracow St. Peter went with the Nuncio to Lowicz, the seat of the Archbishop of Gnesen, Primate of Poland. With that aged Prelate the Saint obtained an interview to beg for his intercession with the King on the subject of Jesuit colleges in his dominions. But it was not only Poland's plight that Peter was thinking of. Writing to Laynez on November 27th, he said : " I should greatly like the Society to come to this country, as it offers such a wide and untilled field for the workers of Christ, and also because it affords an opening for the evangelization of neighbouring countries. The devil reigns over a great extent of Lithuania, Russia, Prussia, Muscovy, and in those vast territories of the Tartars which are said to range as far as China. Would that the light of the Gospel might dissipate the thick darkness of infidelity, and that the Society might achieve in these northern lands such results as it has already obtained in India. . . ."

Having concluded his business with the Archbishop of Gnesen, the Nuncio moved to Piotrków, where they found King Sigismund, two bishops, and a number of the nobility. The King had overdone his hunting and was ill, so the prospects for the Diet looked uncertain. Moreover, in spite of earnest entreaties the Nuncio could not rouse the Polish bishops from their apathy, even to the extent of appearing at the Diet, where the main question was supposed to be the religious one. " We are in

[1] Braunsberger, *Epistulae*, vol. ii, pp. 327–32. The last reference is to the pretty but probably apocryphal story of the child on the seashore who was trying to empty the sea into the small hole which he had dug in the sand.

[2] Hopfen, *Kaiser Maximilian II. und der Kompromisskatholizismus* (1895), p. 33.

trouble on all sides," wrote Peter to Laynez, his only consolation being that the weather was not as bad as might have been expected of Poland and that the Nuncio had begun to thrive remarkably on the Polish beer.[1]

To add to St. Peter's anxieties, he received orders from the Emperor to be in Augsburg by January 1, 1559, though there seemed little likelihood of the Diet at Piotrków introducing the religious question before that date. Suspecting that the Saint might not come, Ferdinand wrote asking Laynez to hunt him home, " *citra omnem moram ac tergiversationem.*" All his heart at the time was bent on helping Poland, for which country he said he longed to suffer, even to the extremity of laying down his life. Happily, the post was on his side. Ferdinand might summon him for New Year's Day but the Emperor's letter to Laynez, a much more serious affair, did not reach Rome until January 15th and then it took the General a further three weeks to get his orders to Piotrków. Meantime, St. Peter sat tight. He had been sent to Poland by his religious superiors, and Emperor or no Emperor there he would stay until his superiors recalled him. Duty and inclination chimed pleasantly in his conscience, but the inclination was also a renunciation. The Emperor's comfortable Court, where he was known and greatly esteemed, would have been much more agreeable to flesh and blood than the cold and dreary conditions under which he lived in Poland, an unconsidered nobody whose eagerness to bring the light and love of God to that gloomy backwater of Christendom only irritated the ridiculous self-satisfaction of its people. Who was this double Dutchman, to come advising the noblest nation on earth?

They were willing enough, however, to avail themselves of his charity in other ways, if we may trust the report sent by Father Mengin to Polanco on December 15th:

We are now at Piotrków among a host of the Church's enemies who try their best to nullify all our efforts. But Our Lord Jesus will help us, I hope. Father Provincial's concern at the moment is to assist both the poor and the nobles who commit to him affairs which they want transacted with the Nuncio. These people sometimes disturb and worry us a great deal by coming in crowds. Some of them beg to be recouped for damage they have suffered from the heretics; others seek the protection of the Church; and a third group petition to be freed from excommunications they have incurred. Often there is a multitude of such petitions, and Father Canisius never fails to do what he can for them all.

[1] Braunsberger, *Epistulae*, vol. ii, p. 335.

Mengin further reports that some of the people were very pious and came to the Jesuits' Masses, even though the hour was before dawn. Frequently they sought to force money on the pair while actually at the altar, and—characteristic touch—when the Fathers declined it, " rushed straight out of the church in disgust." Other details related are that the two Jesuits had entrusted to their care a boy somewhat like the dreadful Dauphin whom Fénelon's patience so utterly transformed. " Now," writes Mengin, " he gladly says his prayers on bended knees twice a day, serves our Masses, seems to love our company, and devotes himself to his studies at the times we have fixed for him. We found two beneficed clerics at the Court who formerly never opened a Breviary. These we have now persuaded to join us in reciting the Divine Office. Father Canisius has begun to offer thirteen Masses for the success of the Diet . . . and is striving to get other priests to do the same. After the Nuncio had said the first of his thirteen, he went to the King and found him extremely tractable and well-disposed to help the cause of religion. Finally, as the Bishop of Ermland's Dialogue on Communion *sub utraque* and on sacerdotal celibacy is out of print, Father Canisius has revised and carefully corrected the work with a view to a new edition."[1]

Only three Catholic bishops had appeared at the Diet, and of these one lay under suspicion of heresy in Rome. But the King thought highly of him and afterwards promoted him to the primatial see, in which office he showed indulgence to the innovators and strong hostility to the Pope. According to St. Peter, the Catholics had reason " to expect more danger from him than hope from all the other bishops put together! " No other ecclesiastics were expected in Piotrków. As emphasis on their apathy, the head of the Lithuanian Calvinists, Nicholas Radziwell, Chancellor of the Grand Duchy, did not fail to be present. This man, whom Hosius unhesitatingly called an heresiarch, enjoyed great influence with the King. "He arrived yesterday," wrote St. Peter, "and had a wonderful reception from the leading men and nobles. These people honour him, and the Catholics are very much afraid of him. In numbers as well as every other worldly advantage, our adversaries seem to have the upper hand, and I do not know whom the afflicted cause of the Church is going to find as its defenders. However, the King promised when I saw him three days ago that, as a Catholic ruler, he would not permit the affairs of religion to be mishandled."[2]

---

[1] Braunsberger, *Epistulae*, vol. ii, pp. 830–2.
[2] Braunsberger, *Epistulae*, vol. ii, p. 338. In another place the Saint adds that some even of Catholic bishops went out to meet and greet the ' heresiarch ', than whom there was " No one so bent on the destruction of the ancient religion."

St. Peter's next letter to Laynez sums up the whole situation and corrects any fancies we may entertain that Poland remained a Catholic country throughout the Reformation period:

It is now the fifth month since I left Rome in company with the Apostolic Nuncio, God, in His infinite goodness, having given me strength equal to these journeys. Meantime, though letters often come to this place from Rome, I have received nothing to inform me of your paternal wishes in my regard, or to tell me your opinion about the matters of which I have often written. . . . Certainly, whatever you might write could not fail to give me the greatest consolation, as I would at least feel that I was acknowledged by my Father, though I am in so many ways unworthy of the name of son. Many a time I am ashamed and vexed with myself when I think how useless a labourer I am and how I do nothing worthy of my profession or of your expectations.

As for work here, I do not see any chance of preaching. Of the few people who profess themselves Catholics there is not one with whom we are intimate, except that certain doctors come to see us occasionally. The Poles do not accommodate themselves to strangers. They are suspicious and distrustful, and keep all their love and courtesy for themselves.[1] The Nuncio is constantly complaining about their rudeness. He is astonished that they make so little of the Holy See, whose rights even the clergy neglect. As for the nobles, it scarcely enters their minds that such rights exist. . . .

To enlist your sympathy for the Poles in case you should be able to do something for them in Our Lord, I shall tell you what I think about the whole state of religion here. The defence and assertion of religion depend above all on the King and the bishops. The King has, indeed, made promises and offered his services to the Nuncio, but those who know him best hope for nothing and expect nothing worth while from such a poor-spirited person. They say that the burden of administering the realm has been thrown on the shoulders of others,

---

[1] Perhaps some reader will not have seen this up-to-date skit on alleged Polish self-centredness. The League of Nations is supposed to have commissioned four men—an Englishman, a Frenchman, a German, and a Pole—to write a disquisition on elephants. In a short time the Englishman submitted a brisk, objective, well-illustrated brochure entitled, *The Elephant: How I shot my first*. After him came the Frenchman with a yellow-back inscribed, *L'éléphant et ses amours*. The German took a long time and his work was in twelve volumes, *Der Elefant: was er ist und was er soll sein*. As for the Pole, he sent in a fiery tract, *L'éléphant et la Question Polonaise*. The following incident proves that the story is *ben trovato*. During the Verdun offensive in the Great War, a Polish nobleman who had fled to Moscow remarked seriously in the presence of the French military mission: "If Verdun is taken Paris, too, will fall. What a terrible thing that will be for the Polish Question!" Bruce Lockhart, *Memoirs of a British Agent* (1932), p. 148.

because the King, in his excessive hankering after leisure and peace, can hardly be got to listen with patience when it is a question of public affairs. Even by his own officials he is taxed with indolence. These officials, for their part, shy at the slightest reference to a strong policy against the sectaries. They will not tolerate men such as the Bishop of Verona, who endeavoured to persuade the King to remove the heretics from his Court and to show them less indulgence. And so in palace and council-chamber heretical influence is strong. The King treats them as friends, they are received at banquets by the bishops, and the canons of the Cathedral, mostly noblemen, are on extremely familiar terms with them.

The King blames the bishops for all the religious corruptions introduced during the last four years, and the bishops retaliate with loud complaints that the King does not use his authority to put in force measures demanded by the rights and liberties of the Church. . . . Would to God that their complaints had no foundation ! But, as far as I can see, the bishops themselves are physicians with no skill to treat the many and terrible diseases of this age, or like heedless and negligent mariners in the midst of a great storm. Their avarice very much diminishes any influence they possess and has made them hated by everybody. Moreover, they are practically all old and feeble men who spend their time nursing their health rather than ministering to their flocks. They seem to have given up everything for lost and to be concerned with making provision for themselves and their dependants, in case they have to fly the country. . . .

So much for the King and the bishops. I think the best way to put matters right would be to hold a provincial synod, under the presidency of some cardinal sent for the purpose of reforming the utterly depraved clergy and of making an apostolic visitation of every church in the land. . . . Would that the King and bishops might themselves petition for such a visitor and permit the correction of abuses. How much easier then should we find it to remove schism and heal the souls of the people, who, since the defection of the majority of the governing classes, cannot and will not be handled with firmness. . . .

Oh, that God in His goodness might grant His Church the remedy of a general council in these great troubles which are now driving the northern nations into destructive apostasy. If the council were held irreligion would not make such strides as to threaten Germany and Poland with the last and worst of all misfortunes. The Sovereign

Pontiff would acquire imperishable glory for himself and his Curia before both God and men, because the council is what all good men yearn and hope for and eagerly demand. . . .[1]

Just before the Diet opened, the Nuncio, who had lost all hope of being able to influence the course of events, signified to St. Peter that he might leave for Augsburg whenever he wished. Telling this to Laynez the Saint expressed his complete readiness for any course : " By the grace of Christ I sail in harbour. Let me be called or recalled to or from any place whatsoever, my mind is at perfect rest in the authority of my superiors. May what is pleasing to God, His perfect will, and that alone, be always done." The letter is one long cry for spiritual help for Poland. Laynez had asked the Fathers of the Society to say one Mass each for their General's intentions. St. Peter's answer was to say seven, that God might shower the Seven Gifts of the Holy Ghost on his superior and with them an eighth gift of anxious solicitude for Poland's tottering Catholicism.

In January, 1559, the old Primate died and was succeeded by John Przerembski, a man from whom the Church might at last expect more than the part of a helpless spectator. St. Peter was overjoyed and hurried at once, on the Archbishop's unexpected summons, to open his heart to him. The zeal that devoured him had not gone unnoticed by the new leader of Poland's religious hopes, and now his patient watch on the mount of desolation was to be rewarded with a glimpse of the promised land. The Archbishop informed him, he reported, that the first and firmest purpose of his episcopate was to introduce and solidly establish the Society of Jesus in Poland. With that news he could sing his *Nunc Dimittis*, content to wait on God for the great day when his brethren would play a foremost part in one of the most dramatic *contre-coups* of history, Poland's reconversion.

At last the weary Diet came to an end, without having decided anything on the religious question. Meantime, leave to proceed to Augsburg had come to Peter from the Sovereign Pontiff, whose authority, he said, he " put before that of any or of all princes in the world." On February 10th he set out on the sixty mile journey to Prague, his last words from Poland, addressed to the General of the Jesuits, being : *Quo sunt mundi quidem judicio res afflictiores, ac etiam desperatae, tanto magis nostrum erit desperatis rebus opem ferre quia sumus de JESU societate.*[2] That " quia " ought to stir a Jesuit's blood like the music of trumpets.

[1] Braunsberger, *Epistulae*, vol. ii, pp. 340–3.
[2] Braunsberger, *Epistulae*, vol. ii, p. 362. " The more afflicted and even desperate things are in the world's opinion, the more will it be our part to come to the rescue of forlorn hopes, because we belong to the Society of Jesus."

CHAPTER X

THE CONFERENCE AT WORMS

WE have now to consider an incident in St. Peter's life which brought him face to face with the leaders of Lutheranism in Germany, and is important as marking the final parting of the ways between Catholics and Protestants. No detailed account of the affair has ever been given in English, so there is the more need to set it forth, *sine ira et studio,* in as comprehensive a manner as the evidence of the disputants themselves will admit, without dependence on old sectarian histories or on such works as the *Annales* of Raynaldus in which Protestants are too often furnished with hoofs and a tail. The story has not lost its moral for our own age, when so much good-will is expended on efforts to heal the divisions of Christendom.

As mentioned in the previous chapter, St. Peter had been permitted by Paul IV to leave Rome in the summer of 1557, though his brethren there, gathered for the first general congregation of the Society of Jesus, were under a species of open arrest. The Pope let him go because he was wanted by King Ferdinand to attend a new religious conference between the Protestants and Catholics in the city of Worms. Now it is known that Paul IV was opposed to such attempts towards ' reunion,' so the question arises why he proved amenable. St. Peter's Protestant biographer, the learned Dr. Drews, has the answer pat. He was not only passively permitted to go but expressly sent by the Pope, in order, if possible, to wreck the conference.[1] How much truth there is in that contention will appear in due course. It is a fact, however, that, like the Pope, St. Peter cherished little hope of any good coming of such discussions. They had been tried already more than once, at Hagenau in 1540, and at Worms and Regensburg in 1545. In those earlier days, too, the chances had been much brighter because Protestant opinion had not yet

---

[1] *Petrus Canisius, der erste deutsche Jesuit,* pp. 68–9. Drews speaks of secret instructions, but no hint of such things is to be found in any extant record.

hardened on many points of doctrine. At Regensburg the two parties
even reached agreement on the crucial question of justification, which caused
Cardinal Pole to think joyfully that ' reunion ' was at last in sight. But
Luther rejected the agreement and so, on the Catholic side, did Cervini and
Caraffa, the latter of whom became Pope Paul IV. In spite of such warning,
Charles V and his brother Ferdinand abandoned nothing of their obstinate
belief in the efficacy of parleys between the Catholics and Protestants.

The Religious Peace of Augsburg had regulated the political standing
of both parties but left to a subsequent Diet the task of trying to find
some method of reconciling their confessional differences. It was to this
task that the Diet of Regensburg addressed itself in 1556. Peter Canisius
was present throughout as theologian to Ferdinand and had excellent
opportunities for observing the dispositions of both Catholic bishops and
Protestant princes. The debate turned on the alternative of a general
council or a conference similar to those held in the past, as a remedy for
the troubles that had come upon Germany. It will be interesting to listen
a little while to the orators. The Protestant Elector Palatine zealously
contended that a council would not serve, because his co-religionists
regarded the Pope as the author of all the mischief and would not attend
any meeting of which he was arbiter. Better rather to arrange a ' colloquy '
or conference wherein representatives of the two religions might submit
their differences to the judgment of Scripture, the four great Councils,
and the Fathers of the Church. Taking him up, his brother of Saxony
said that a free council after the pattern of the great four would be the
best solution but, as it did not seem possible to come to terms about the
presidency, the manner of voting and the matters to be decided, a colloquy
with Scripture as the criterion of doctrine would appear to be the only
practical substitute. The third Protestant Elector, Brandenburg, concurred.

Then it was the turn of the Catholic Electors. Mainz and Trier would
not allow that a general council was unattainable and Cologne supported
them by pouring a good deal of cold water on the idealism of those who
pinned their faith to friendly discussion. The Archbishop of Salzburg
would hear of nothing but a general council and, when the rulers of Austria
and Bavaria had in turn argued for a colloquy " by way of consultation,
not of disputation," Cardinal Truchsess of Augsburg rose to urge in
some detail the case against any such procedure. Colloquies had never
proved of much value, he said. They had been tried in Africa as long
ago as the time of St. Augustine, who put on record their futility. Subsequent attempts proved equally valueless, as history-books bore witness.

All the articles of the Augsburg Confession would have to be discussed in a thorough fashion, but even that would not be enough because several new doctrines, not included in it, must receive equal attention. And it was certain that neither party would be willing to give way. National councils had done good work in the past, but they were not adapted to a state of affairs such as that now confronting the rulers of Germany. The Cardinal accordingly voted for a general council and submitted reasons why the Pope should have the privilege of summoning it.

Brandenburg then said : " *Papa est ad quem omnia et a quo nihil ; ideo non debet habere indictionem* "—the Pope is one to whom everything goes and from whom nothing proceeds, for which reason he ought not to have the summoning. He was followed by Philip of Hesse and the Elector Palatine, who endeavoured to rebut the arguments advanced by Cardinal Truchsess. After them, the Saxon Elector made a fierce attack on the primacy of the Pope and dealt out quantities of theology against it. Cardinal Truchsess answered him, and then a vote was taken from which the colloquy plan emerged victorious. King Ferdinand signified his approval, but warned the Estates that the new colloquy must have a different spirit from past ones, whose only fruit was increased bitterness. It must be " a Christian and friendly consultation." Thereupon a long and rather heated discussion ensued as to the form of the conference. The Elector Palatine wanted a hundred or a hundred and fifty learned men to be chosen, over whom the King himself would preside or, failing him, his son Maximilian. Only the ancient Faith and the *Confessio Augustana* should be considered, " to the exclusion of all other sects." It is important to notice that this reservation, which carried the day, was a purely Protestant proposal. The unwieldy numbers suggested by Pfalz, and also his and Saxony's attempt to have their friend Maximilian appointed president were overruled, but in other respects their conception of the colloquy met with approval. The Catholic bishops merely stipulated that its findings must not be considered obligatory but in the nature of proposals for a future Diet to consider, and that it must not be allowed to encroach on the proper territory of a general council. Ferdinand succeeded in getting these amendments accepted and then the stage was set for as strange a comedy of humours as that or any other age has witnessed.[1]

Meantime, St. Peter Canisius had been watching developments with a critical eye. His first attitude to the conference question was one of undisguised hostility, which led him, greatly daring, even to write a

[1] Bucholtz, *Geschichte der Regierung Ferdinand des Ersten*, vol. vii (Vienna, 1836), pp. 361–8.

refutation of the decree by which King Ferdinand gave the colloquy legal
standing. "No good can be hoped from that conference," he warned
Laynez, "however it may be set up. Indeed, there is the gravest reason
to fear that it may have unhappy consequences for religion, if carried
through irrespective of the authority of the Holy See."[1] In addition to
his forebodings on general grounds, Peter had a private scruple about
converse with men whose aim was the destruction of the Catholic Church,
and begged Laynez to inform him whether it was legitimate to meet them
in daily life when there was no likelihood of such intercourse resulting
in their conversion. Though reassured on this point, his uneasiness did
not vanish, especially as King Ferdinand seemed determined to send
him to the conference as his own special delegate. "His Majesty," he
told Laynez in another letter, "has assembled for the business two bishops
and five theologians, among which latter men I am assigned the foremost
place. From that alone your Reverence can guess the learning and fitness
of the rest of the group! May God have mercy on us all. Everything
is being done for the King's sake, as he wishes before the conference
opens to hear from his theologians whether any conciliatory and moderate
approach to the chief dogmatic controversies can be found that will not
prejudice the rights of the Holy See. Do not doubt but that I, though
only a fool in these matters, am determined, God helping me, whose
cause is here in question, to decline neither to the right hand nor to the
left. The Cardinal of Augsburg is of opinion that I must obey the summons
of the King, if only to oppose excessive leniency towards the Protestants
on the part of the other theologians, who are all Germans. The Cardinal
has written to His Holiness on the matter. . . ."[2]

A little later the Saint informed his friend Lindanus that he was
"trying every avenue of escape from the whole affair." He even appealed
direct to the King to let him go free, on the ground that there were plenty
of better theologians and orators than himself available. "I am utterly
unsuited and useless for this business and also dislike the prospect of
it intensely," were his words to Laynez, whom he begged, if the worst
came to the worst, to see to it that nothing was decided about him which
might displease the Pope. Despite all the Saint's efforts, when the names
of the "collocutores" were published shortly afterwards he found himself
placed fifth among the principal Catholic delegates. It was a very
distinguished list, as was that of the Protestant party, and consisted of
the following men:

Braunsberger, *Epistulae*, vol. ii, pp. 40–1.   [2] Braunsberger, *Epistulae*, vol. ii, pp. 55–6.

Philip Melanchthon
From the etching by Dürer

Michael Helding, Bishop of Merseburg,
John Delphius, Suffragan Bishop of Strasbourg,
Jodocus Ravesteyn, Professor of the University of Louvain,
Martin Rithovius, Professor of the University of Louvain,
Peter Canisius,
Frederick Staphylus.

The Protestant representatives were :

Philip Melanchthon,
John Brenz,
John Pistorius,
George Karg,
James Runge,
Erhardt Schnepf.

Each side was given also six " *adjuncti* " or advisory theologians,
among the Catholic ones being Father Nicholas Goudanus. St. Peter
and other prominent men were most anxious to have Lindanus and Gropper,
the hero of the struggle with Hermann von Wied, present at the conference
in some capacity or other, but both refused. The blunt answer of Lindanus
to Peter's letter was that he " had no desire to be contaminated by an
affair of such ill-omen." Peter himself took some time to become
reconciled to his position. " I think it perfectly ridiculous," he wrote
to Laynez, " that I should be one of the delegates. The King has been
warned by the Cardinal of Augsburg that the consent of my superiors is
necessary. I cannot but fear that the Pope may disapprove of their choice
of me and consequently I am going to keep myself free from these chains
as much as by God's grace I am able. I shall watch for your Reverence's
decision about me. Nothing would I like better than the chance to free
myself from this entanglement and let others have the honour of negotiating
and disputing, which is a task that I know myself incompetent to perform
without very great difficulty." In April he wrote again in a more reconciled
frame of mind to explain to his General why exactly the conference had
been arranged and what it was intended to procure :

The delegates are desired to confer amicably together with a view
to discovering, if possible, some way of peace in the midst of such
great and long-enduring dissension of religion. The proceedings will
be taken down by notaries and submitted to the Estates of the Empire.
No final decisions or agreements are to be made. What the authorities

desire is a friendly attempt to find some plan for freeing Germany from so many sects. Meantime, the delegates are asked to promise that they will not reveal anything done at the conference and that they will deal with all matters before them according to the dictates of their piety and their consciences.[1]

When at length, after his visit to Rome, St. Peter perceived that his presence at the conference had the full approval of his superiors and, at least, the *nihil obstat* of the Pope, he began to take a more lively interest in the prospects and wrote to all his friends begging their prayers that peace and concord might be the result. Such behaviour is not very consistent with the wrecking policy that has been attributed to him. Truth to tell, any wrecking done was done by the other side. During the first months of 1557 the long-standing dispute between the two Protestant leaders, Melanchthon and Flacius Illyricus, came to a head, with results which a very temperate modern Protestant historian sums up in the words : " *Parteiung, Hass, und Krieg überall* "—faction, hatred and strife on every side.[2] Things became so bad that Johann Albrecht, Duke of Mecklenburg, felt constrained to intervene. Himself a rigid Lutheran of the Jena school, on February 25, 1557, he sent two envoys with letters and conditions of peace to Melanchthon at Wittenberg. Among these documents was a " *Formula Concordiae* " which the Duke hoped Melanchthon would accept. It embodied a profession of faith with regard to various disputed doctrines and also a series of anathemas against dissenters, among whom St. Peter Canisius was included on account of his Prague sermon in criticism of the invocation, *Christe, ora pro nobis*.[3] The relevant passage is in the section, *De Deo et Filio Dei Mediatore invocando*, and runs as follows :

> With consentient hearts and lips we confess, and, God helping us, will constantly defend the doctrine of the only true God . . . as it is set forth in Holy Writ, in the Nicene and Athanasian creeds, in the confession and writings of Luther and in the *Loci Communes* of Melanchthon. We, therefore, with all our hearts reject and detest the madness of Arius, Photinus, and Paul of Samosata, condemned 1,280 years ago and revived in our time by the books of Michael Servetus. . . .
>
> Moreover, we believe and confess that the *Logos* of St. John signifies a Person distinct from the Father and of the same nature as the Father. Wherefore, we further condemn the madness of the Jesuit, Peter Canisius,

---

[1] Braunsberger, *Epistulae*, vol. ii, p. 83.   [2] Holtzmann, *Kaiser Maximilian II*, p. 267.
[3] See above, p. 273 sq.

who, in order to establish the invocation of dead men,[1] asserts that the Son of God, Our Lord Jesus Christ, now sitting at the right hand of the Father, is Mediator only *ratione meriti*, but not *ratione intercessionis*, contrary to the express words of Hebrews vii. We therefore teach and confess that the Son of God is consubstantial with the Eternal Father, that He is true God and true Man, our Eternal Priest who now also intercedes and entreats for us. . . .[2]

The Formula of Concord failed to answer its zealous author's hopes. Finding himself gently taxed with ' adiaphorism ' in it, Melanchthon " flew into a great temper, and would not listen to the envoys who begged earnestly to be heard in the Prince's name. He came out with stinging invectives against Illyricus and others and, in the end, began to abuse the Prince himself and his messengers."[3] Meantime, ' the unquiet Flacius,' as the people of Magdeburg described their fantastic pontiff, was busy disseminating vile rumours and vitriolic tracts against his Lutheran brother of Wittenberg. Each had a prince to stand by him, Melanchthon, the Elector of Saxony, and Flacius, the Elector's dispossessed relative, pious, narrow-minded John Frederick. Between Elector and Duke, naturally enough, not much love was lost, a circumstance that gave an added zest to the theological animosities of their protégés. John Frederick was not able to secure the admittance of Flacius to the conference at Worms but Erhardt Schnepf satisfied him very well as an alternative. Schnepf proved a worthy disciple of Flacius and, as will appear, made things very hot indeed for Melanchthon at the Conference. On August 9, 1557, Flacius addressed a long, fervid exhortation to his crusaders about to depart for Worms. It began : *Salutem a Domino Jesu, unico omnium piorum Servatore, Amen*. Then came an introduction on the necessity of unity in the Church, after which the writer let himself go on the subject of his obsession, the *Interim*. " I feel with all my heart and soul," he said, " that your first duty is to work with the greatest possible ardour for the utter rejection from the Church of God and everlasting damnation of the impious *Interim*, with its allied corruptions of compromise, understandings, and bargainings with our adversaries." His hatred of the old measure of Charles V and of its Leipzig derivative from Melanchthon's adaptable pen was due to the fact that both retained elements of Catholicism and so bore the marks of the great beast and whore of Babylon. It would probably not be far wrong to say that Flacius was the most genuine, passionate, utterly devoted

---

[1] I.e. the saints.   [2] *Corpus Reformatorum*, vol. ix, col. 95.
[3] *Corpus Reformatorum*, vol. ix, col. 106.

hater the Catholic Church has ever known. At times his hatred burns so fiercely and intensely as to be almost sublime. In his exhortation he endeavoured, and not without success, to set his disciples on fire. They were to fight every slightest concession tooth and nail, and to work with all their energy for the public condemnation, aye, and even physical *Bestrafung*, of any Protestants who admitted as much as a petty ceremony practised by the Pope's carrion, or who deviated in the least from the straight path marked out by God's Anointed, Martin Luther. The Confession of Augsburg and the Schmalkalden Articles were to be their sword and shield. Before treating with the Catholics, all the Protestant delegates must be made to subscribe to them anew and to repudiate by name such people as Osiander, Major, Schwenckfeldt, and any who still defended the impious ceremonies of the *Interim*.[1] Such, then, was the frame of mind in which one section of the Protestants approached their " Christian and friendly consultation " with the Catholics. Was Melanchthon's party any better disposed ?

Melanchthon is a great puzzle. Despite his unimpressive appearance, his stammering tongue, and diffident manner, he had a fine brain and a character not only noble in many ways but full of charm. From an early date the Catholic humanists had made several attempts to win him back from Lutheranism, knowing as they did that he found his religious activities a weary burden and that what his soul longed for was a " *stilles Plätzchen*," a quiet little corner in which to pursue the study of his beloved classics in peace. Cardinal Campeggio made overtures to him through St. Peter's friend, Frederick Nausea. The gentle poet-bishop, Andreas Cricius, corresponded with him from Poland, each man using the intimate form of address, but it was Cardinal Sadoleto who showed the greatest eagerness for his return. Cochlaeus, himself a good humanist, thought that Sadoleto was going too far in his friendliness and wrote to Oleander, begging him to put the Cardinal on his guard. " In truth," he said, " I, too, would gladly have enjoyed Melanchthon's friendship and profited by his ability, if the Faith and the unity of the Church had not been dearer to me than anything in the world. He wrote to me once, suggesting that we should forget old animosities and become friends, devoted to mutual service. This proposal would have been advantageous and pleasant for me, and would have procured me the approbation and honourable recognition of Lutherans. But as soon as I noticed that he did not desist from his attacks on the doctrine of the Roman Church, I said good-bye to his

---

[1] *Corpus Reformatorum*, vol. ix, col. 199–213. John Frederick came out with an " Instructio " to the same effect as the Flacian exhortation.

friendship and am now an enemy, not, indeed, of his person or of his acute mind, but of his deeds and of his false teaching."[1]   The attitude of Cochlaeus was exactly that of St. Peter Canisius.   Both had noticed a gradual swing to the left in Melanchthon's opinions.   He was not a strong-minded man and, under the influence and flattery of such irreconcilables as Calvin, grew, not only more radical, but increasingly bitter towards the ancient Faith.   Somewhere in his soul there seemed to be chained a protesting Catholic whose voice so troubled his conscience that he cried his heresy the louder in hopes of drowning it.   Perhaps this is the explanation of his peculiar dislike for St. Peter's friend, Staphylus, who, like himself, had been an eminent Protestant professor.   For him he was " Staphylus the apostate."   Just before he was due to go to Worms the Lutheran King of Denmark invited him to his Court but, being a very superstitious man, he was afraid to accept, because at his birth his horoscope foretold shipwreck in the Baltic.   Writing to a friend on August 6, 1557, he said : " I would have preferred going to the godly colloquies of the wise and excellent King rather than to listen to the sophistries of Canisius, Staphylus, and similar sycophants."[2]   In other words, he had prejudged and condemned the Catholic delegates to the conference before hearing a syllable of their arguments.

The attitude of mingled hope and doubt which characterized Germany as a whole on the eve of the colloquy is well described by the excellent Protestant historian, Heppe :

> Days of great and fateful decision seemed to be approaching as the German princes, ecclesiastical and secular, prepared for the dispatch of their theologians to Worms.   Years ago, as it was believed, the Council of Trent had closed its sessions for ever, and so with all the livelier expectation did the whole of Germany look to the imminent Colloquy as to the crisis of its ecclesiastical future.   Even outside Germany men recognized that the Colloquy might prove of great significance for the whole Church, and Calvin, who had already come to an understanding with Melanchthon about it, bemoaned the fact that the Swiss Church could not take part in the proceedings owing to the opposition of Bullinger.[3]

Meantime, St. Peter Canisius watched in Ingolstadt for the post that would bring him his summons.   Before it arrived, he received the following letter from Cardinal Truchsess, then resting at Ellwangen in Württemberg :

[1] Kawerau, *Die Versuche Melanchthon zur katholischen Kirche zurückzuführen* (Halle, 1902), pp. 12, 17–8, 28, 40–1.   Even in the midst of an attack on Melanchthon, the honest Cochlaeus felt constrained to say : " For the rest I am privately very much in sympathy with this man."

[2] *Corpus Reformatorum*, vol. ix, col. 189, 196, 197.

[3] *Geschichte des deutschen Protestantismus*, vol. i (Marburg, 1852), p. 157.

My most beloved Brother in Christ, I congratulate Germany heartily on your return [from Rome] and I still more heartily desire to have converse with your Reverence about public business and my own private affairs. I beg you to let this be at your earliest convenience. From Ingolstadt you can proceed to Donauworth, thence to Nordlingen and afterwards safely hither. This is also the most direct and secure route to Worms. . . . I earnestly engage your Reverence in the Name of Jesus, and most urgently beg you to console me with a letter before setting out or, at least, by a visit in the course of your journey. And I likewise beg you to let me have without fail the memorandum you drew up in Regensburg at my suggestion, *De Officio et Reformatione Episcopi*. Believe me, I shall not read it without great fruit for my soul, and for the souls of others committed to my care. I shall prove by my deeds that I have read it, so do not deprive me of so great an advantage and, in your charity, satisfy my wishes. . . .

I am awaiting your Reverence's arrival here in Ellwangen with the greatest eagerness and burning hope. The place is only seven miles from Donauworth and the abbot of the Monastery of the Holy Cross will be pleased to provide you with a guide from among his servants, myself paying the expenses. . . .

Farewell, most beloved Brother in Jesus Christ. I beg you to commend me to the prayers of your brethren and I commend to you also my nephews and Kilian. Your most devoted Brother, Otto, Cardinal of Augsburg.[1]

At this time Peter was much saddened by the ill-health of his companion, Father Goudanus, who figured among the assistant theologians at the conference. " The doctor has scarcely a hope that he will be able to go," wrote the Saint to Polanco. " He seems so weak that we think he will never be fit for public lecturing again. If I take him to Worms perhaps it would be best to send him thence by ship to Cologne, from which place he could go on to Louvain, in hopes that the poor sufferer may obtain relief from his native air. The doctor is very much afraid of the autumn, which increases the danger for consumptives to an extraordinary degree. May Our Lord Jesus be present to him in his affliction and keep him safe for His own glory and our advantage. . . ."[2]

[1] Braunsberger, *Epistulae*, vol. ii, p. 116. Among the young nephews of the Cardinal then studying in Ingolstadt was the unhappy Gebhardt Truchsess, who afterwards as archbishop of Cologne followed the example of Hermann von Wied and seceded from the Church.
[2] Braunsberger, *Epistulae*, vol. ii, p. 117.

By August 16th, the day fixed for their journey, Goudanus was well enough to undertake it in Peter's sympathetic company. With them went a lay brother to do their cooking. As requested, they paid a visit *en route* to Cardinal Truchsess, who received them with the greatest kindness and provided them with a carriage for the remaining miles. That was a great convenience, because otherwise they would have had to provide for their horses in Worms or to find a purchaser for them.[1]

Worms lies in a fertile district known as the Wonnegau or " Region of Rapture." There was to be mighty little rapture associated with St. Peter's sojourn in that City of famous Protestant memories, but his first impressions of it were not too unfavourable. He and his companions were made welcome, after their week on the road, by one of his old pupils who held the post of chief preacher at the Cathedral. A chapel was put at their disposal by the friendly canons, and in other respects, too, they received every mark of considerate attention. St. Peter's first business, after he had settled down, was to write in hopes of inducing Dr. Gropper to come to the Conference. " At our own expense," he informed Laynez, " we sent a special messenger with letters to him, endeavouring by every means in our power to get this great defender of the Church to join us." But Gropper was beyond persuasion, as the following very pleasant answer to Peter shows :

Do not now for the first time think so badly of me as to entertain a suspicion that I am actuated by purely human motives in my obstinate refusal to take the place assigned to me at the Religious Conference. Believe me, that is not the case, most excellent Father Canisius. You know, I think, very well that I have not hitherto shirked any danger, however great, even danger to life itself, for the love of Jesus Christ and His dear Spouse, the Church, the Mother of us all. I hope always by the Divine Goodness to be of that same mind and never to refuse any task or undertaking by which I may be able to serve the cause of the Church, and not do it an injury. I do not think that anyone, and least of all my dearly loved Canisius, could be so unfair to me as to think, in the light of my past actions, that I ever considered men more than God when His Name, His doctrine, His faith, and His religion had to be publicly confessed.

It is not, then, as you think, the stubborn perversity of our opponents nor their overweening pride and inflated arrogance which deter me

---

[1] Braunsberger, *Epistulae*, vol. ii, p. 125. The usual practice in the sixteenth century was to buy a horse at the beginning of a journey and sell it, if one could, at the finish. A horse might have had a hundred different owners in the course of a year.

from assuming the office you adjure me so solemnly to bear. . . . Neither is it any distrust of the efforts of others, nor any consideration of the power and deceit of men, of the favour or inconstancy of princes and nobles, which the truly devout are wont to despise when there is question of great undertakings. No: my reasons are other and far graver ones than such human considerations, reasons of conscience which I have explained in detail in my letter to His Majesty the King. They prevent me by a sort of adamantine necessity from going to this new Colloquy or Disputation, now being held after the complete failure of at least five such efforts in the past. . . .

Could I have but one little hour's converse with you here, I am sure I should easily satisfy you, as I think I abundantly satisfied the Louvain theologians. They can testify for me at Worms, since I may not safely explain my reasons in a letter. Wherefore, Reverend Sir, for the sake of our old and, I hope, undying friendship, I earnestly beg and implore you to put away altogether any suspicion you may have recently conceived of indolence on my part in the business of Christ and His Church. . . . You can be certain that, just as your conscience moved you to invite me to the Colloquy, so mine does not permit me to accept. . . . Otherwise, be assured that I should never fail the Church and my country, even at the risk of life itself.

Go forward zealously with your work in Worms. We here shall diligently pray Almighty God so to bless you and prosper your holy meditations and efforts for the glory of His Name and the defence and the advancement of the Catholic faith and religion, that if our adversaries are not converted by your means they may at least be turned to confusion and hindered from further attacks on the Church. . . .[1]

Meantime, the Protestant delegates had begun to arrive in Worms, among the first being Schnepf and his little band of stout-hearted Flacians. They were disgusted at the respect shown to Melanchthon when he came, and did their small best to discredit him in the City. Flacius himself feverishly spurred them on with blazing exhortations from his stronghold in Saxony, bidding them stand fast by every jot and tittle of their creed and to beware of the kiss of Judas, that is, of Melanchthon, " with his pedagogue, the devil." They proved worthy disciples, Basil Monner in particular performing such miracles of backstairs intrigue that even some of Melanchthon's foremost supporters wavered in their allegiance.[2]

[1] Braunsberger, *Epistulae*, vol. ii, pp. 122–4.   [2] *Corpus Reformatorum*, vol. ix, col. 253.

Melanchthon, however, had his revenge not long after. As King Ferdinand could not preside over the Conference owing to pressure of state affairs, he had appointed the conciliatory and noble-minded Julius Pflug, Bishop of Naumburg, to represent him. One of the Bishop's first official actions was to ask the Protestants to try to reconcile their differences before the opening of the Conference. Flacians and Philippists met for this purpose at the Worms Rathaus on September 4th. Schnepf in a speech of great violence demanded that all present should subscribe to a solemn condemnation of Osiander, Major, the Zwinglians, and everybody who had bowed the knee to the *Interim*. Now Brenz, the second most important figure in the Protestant ranks at this time, was a confirmed Osiandrian, and Melanchthon was not only an unrepentant ' Interimist ' of the Leipzig brand but at the moment on close terms with the Zwinglians.[1] To demand the condemnation of two such men was merely to ask for trouble, and the Flacians, instead of triumphing, suddenly found themselves excluded from all further part in the private consultations of their co-religionists.

While waiting on these strange events, St. Peter Canisius did not remain idle. He preached in the Cathedral to an unusually large audience which included the two bishops, Julius Pflug and Michael Helding, and a good contingent of Protestants. One of these, a professor of Wittenberg named Paul Eber, wrote to give his friend Major an account of Peter's first sermon, not in very complimentary terms.[2] The three theologians from Louvain whom Philip II had sent to Worms very grudgingly, as he entirely disapproved of the Conference, were a great support to the Saint.

We have begun to join forces with them and with some others [he informed Laynez], so that we may have a victory in numbers and perhaps also in authority. Consequently, I do not see what danger or harm can come to religion and the Catholic cause from this Colloquy, if, indeed, God continues through your prayers to be propitious to us. Our able adversaries are now here, Melanchthon, Brenz, Schnepf, Pistorius, Sarcerius, each a very learned man of his kind and well equipped to deceive and impose upon people. They hold frequent meetings, we hear, and are armed with edicts and missives from their princes, charging them to bear loud testimonies against us. The fixed principle of their rulers now is to allow no agreement as to doctrines

[1] Melanchthon was ready enough to condemn the *Interim* of Charles V, but it was really his own Leipzig *Interim* that the Flacians wanted him to repudiate, on account of its toleration of some Catholic ceremonies.

[2] *Corpus Reformatorum*, vol. ix, col. 250.

of faith. They have determined to stand by the Confession of Augsburg tooth and nail, and, not trusting even their own delegates, they anxiously lay down rules for them and will not have them do anything of their private initiative. As is their wont, they employ cunning means and are always much more vigilant and keenly intent on propagating their views than the Catholics. The apathy of the German Catholics is a grief and shame to remember, nor are we stirred or roused from our deep and deadly sleep, to call it no worse name, though stimulated by such great and various evils. May Our Lord Jesus, the Prince of Pastors, give us at last pastors after His own heart who will have pity on the perishing multitude.

We are engaged now in thinking out and putting in writing sugges-tions for the more satisfactory arrangement of the Conference. The Louvain theologians are glad to use my services, and I think that throughout the Conference they will do nothing without letting us know and consulting us. We, in turn, willingly approach them about our affairs, and they have now delegated me to act as recorder of what we decide in common. . . . May God turn our efforts to His glory, and, through your prayers, may He prosper this Conference, especially as eminent and wise men forebode evil from it, and very few indeed encourage the hopes which, by the grace of God, we still entertain. I need not importune you with reminders to give thought in your piety to this business of such grave public importance. I believe and trust that you will spontaneously do what the magnitude of the danger demands. . . .

Some here think that the Conference will end almost as soon as it has begun, so much unfair treatment and invincible obstinacy do they expect from our opponents. . . . The Catholics are timid and afraid of an enemy that they have not yet seen. In matters of business they are unskilled and inexperienced, and so have frequent recourse to us, especially the Louvain men, whom to the best of our small ability we comfort and encourage. How much better it would be, though, for us and for them and for all Catholics concerned, if we had Father Nadal here as counsellor![1]

The Conference opened on September 11th at 7 a.m. All the secular and spiritual authorities of the Empire had sent deputies, and the assembly in Heppe's words, " was one of the most splendid and numerous that had been seen since the first appearance of Protestantism."[2] The inaugural discourse was delivered on the President's behalf by Vice-Chancellor

[1] Braunsberger, *Epistulae*, vol. ii, pp. 126–8.
[2] *Geschichte des deutschen Protestantismus*, vol. i, p. 173.

Seld and consisted mainly of an exhortation to keep to the paths of peace. The following is a typical passage :

It is no petty or common task with which we are concerned here. We are concerned with a matter of greater moment than any with which the history of the Empire of the Germans is acquainted, a matter which, in so many disputations and conferences, in so many dangerous agitations before unheard of, has now for forty years not only occupied the attention of the most learned men but has almost brought the whole social order to irreparable wreck and destruction. Towards you, then, as the few chosen and appointed to remedy this evil, the hopes of all are turned. Keep before your eyes not merely the present state of Germany but also those dangers which, though still in the distance, may yet fall upon us if we do not now restore harmony and end the utter discord by mutual reconciliation.[1] Our Saviour and Redeemer Himself is watching from Heaven your thoughts and wills. If you do His work with piety and sincerity, employing all the pains in your power, He will be present to this business which has been undertaken in His Name, and without any doubt will bring it to a happy conclusion. . . .

Far, then, from this assembly be all self-interest, ambition, and bigotry. . . . Nothing is more necessary now than good will and fairness and modest demeanour. If these be absent from the discussions, we can expect nothing of value to Church or State to result from them. . . .[2]

After some discussion as to procedure, which was eventually left to the discretion of the President and his assessors, Bishop Helding answered in the name of the Catholic Estates, saying that the Conference had great pleasure in greeting Bishop Pflug as President and that they would strive with united forces to second his efforts for the healing of the wounds of their Fatherland.[3] Melanchthon then rose and made the following very interesting speech :

We have heard with reverence the counsels and exhortation of the Right Reverend Lord President. Now, at the beginning, we earnestly

---

[1] The Thirty Years' War was the fulfilment of Seld's prophecy.

[2] Bucholtz, *Geschichte der Regierung Ferdinand des Ersten*, vol. vii, p. 370; Heppe, vol. i, appendix v.

[3] Heppe, *Geschichte des deutschen Protestantismus*, vol. i, p. 176. Helding, an extremely learned and courteous gentleman, was described by Flacius Illyricus a few years before as " a dirty, shameless sycophant," " an impudent rascal," " a desperate impostor," " a rogue whose mouth stank with lying," " a mongrel's excrement," etc. These flowers that bloomed in the Reformation spring have a good deal to do with the case. They show how much chance the Conference had of accomplishing its task.

pray the Son of God, Our Lord Jesus Christ, who assembles the Eternal Church by the voice of His Gospel, that He may guide us, and with His Holy Spirit gather unto Himself His Church amongst us. We offer to give a true and clear explanation of the doctrine of our Churches, doctrine which, for the glory of God and the salvation of souls, we desire to see shining like the sun and steadily propagated. But lest we be thought to fluctuate amid a welter of opinions, we testify that we embrace with godly and firm consent the prophetic and apostolic writings, understanding these to include also the Apostolic, Nicene, and Athanasian Creeds. We affirm that that doctrine is contained in the Confession of our Churches which was presented to Emperor Charles V at the Diet of Augsburg in the year 1530. We all testify that we hold this Confession with pious consent and that we have not departed from it nor ever shall.

Moreover, we reject all errors and sects at variance with that Confession, both ancient and modern, and, in particular, the impious decrees of the so-called Synod of Trent. We also repudiate the book called *Interim*, and all other policies repugnant to our Confession.

We believe with certainty that the Son of God assembles His Eternal Church by the voice of the Gospel and that the Church is not composed of a multitude which refuses the Apostolic writings and creeds, nor of any offscourings of Gentile, Mohammedan, or Jewish filth. Nor, again, is it composed of those who arrogate to themselves the title of Church and at the same time deliberately place themselves in opposition to the truth; who set up idols in contempt of God and help or encourage the murder of souls and bodies. The Church is rather that gathering which speaks the true accent of the Gospel, which, though it has its infirmities, yet stands fast on its foundations and does not wittingly defend idolatry. . . .

The second part of the Right Reverend President's oration in which he referred to the public calamities brought on by discord in the State has greatly increased my sorrow. . . . But we are not the authors of the discord. It is the criminal doing of those who strive to abolish the plain truth and to establish abominable idols. We are no deserters from the Church of God, nor do we wish to associate with those who dabble in the blood of godly men and defend idolatry.

The Reverend Lord President's request that we should expound our views peacefully, without prevarication or abuse, is entirely in keeping with the spirit of such a Conference as this, in which the simple truth is sought apart from all sophistry or bitterness, to the glory of

God and the salvation of souls. We therefore promise to set forth, with God's help, the true foundations of our doctrine from the prophetic writings, and to do so modestly and meetly, without juggling sophisms. Reciprocally, we beg that the authorities of the Conference may not permit our adversaries to employ sophistry, or to twist the prophetic and apostolic dicta to false meanings, or to string together excerpts from ecclesiastical writers in a distorted fashion. Our adversaries have now for many years been deluding the unlearned with such tricks.[1]

Not even his best friends claimed for Melanchthon a sense of humour and that speech shows plainly the reason why. It reminds one of the man in the story who mounted a horse and rode off furiously in all directions. One sentence approves Bishop Pflug's appeal for good feeling and courtesy, and the next trounces " the impious edicts of the so-called Synod of Trent," the shameless idolatry of the Catholics, and their open-eyed opposition to the known truth. The Flacian attack must have made poor Philip very sore indeed to distil so much concentrated bitterness. It is to be said for him that he suffered from the stone and that his wife was dying at this time, but his unfortunate victims in the opposite trenches were not aware of those tragic facts and still less, responsible for them. To judge, however, by a remark of his afterwards, it was not the Flacians nor the stone nor his dying wife that caused his outburst. The whole thing would appear to have been carefully premeditated. He uses the word ' certamen ' to describe the Conference, and says that " the beginning of the battle was a magnificent and jolly affair."[2] As the people of another country would put it, he seems to have been spoiling for a fight.

The second session, held on Monday, September 13th, was largely occupied with formalities of procedure and the taking of an oath of secrecy by the delegates. Here again Melanchthon made difficulties, though the oath had emanated as much from his own people as from the Catholics at the Diet of Regensburg. He was in a thoroughly contrary mood and had to be coaxed like a sulky child into good behaviour by the President. Bishop Helding opened the third session, the following day, with a renewed appeal for benevolence and peaceable counsels on both sides. He said that the Catholics took God to witness that they approached the Evangelicals with the sincerest good-will, for they saw in them, not enemies, but fellow-workers in the cause of brotherly peace. As for the Catholics themselves, if any hard words were uttered against them, let

them offer them up as a sacrifice to the sanctity of their common undertaking.[1] He then suggested that it might help if, in discussing particular
points of controversy, they were to start with the old doctrine as it was
generally held forty years earlier, and afterwards to seek for the causes
of division. Only those points ought to be discussed in which the Augsburg
Confession differed from the old teaching. That teaching might first be
expounded and then the other party could state in a friendly way what
displeased them in it and why. Afterwards, for the sake of clearness, each
party might commit its views to paper. To help the proceedings the
Bishop handed Melanchthon an " Index articulorum controversorum,"
drawn up by Peter Canisius in the same order as the articles of the
Augsburg Confession, and signed by four notaries. The mention of
Peter's name requires the statement that, though silent so far in the
Conference, he was, in his own words, busy in all sorts of ways " et
scribendo et loquendo et concionando et consulendo."

The chief event of the fourth session on September 15th was a long
reply to Bishop Helding by George Karg. His paper, which was largely
of Melanchthon's composition, consisted almost entirely of an abusive
attack on such Catholic practices and doctrines as Masses for the dead,
indulgences, confession, and the use of images. He began by saying that
the Protestants did not love strife but on the contrary were greatly grieved
by it. They brought with them neither hate nor ambition nor contentiousness. As for the other party, what sort of dispositions they brought,
what obvious errors they defended, even against their own convictions,
was as plain as the day. For argument he appealed to history and challenged
the Catholics to show their doctrines in the New Testament, a facile
argument still popular with people too dense to see the implications of
the parable of the mustard seed. The Catholics gave notice that they
would answer Karg's irrelevancies in the following session, and then
Bishop Helding rose once again to guide the debate back into its proper
channel by a discourse on the first article of controversy in the agreed
list, namely, original sin. As a preliminary to fruitful discussion he urged
that they must all admit and bow to the authority of some criterion, some
" judge of controversies " which should be the final court of appeal for
disputed questions. That was only common sense, and so was his further
contention, that the Scriptures by themselves would not suffice. They
must be ready to accept a uniform interpretation of them, and no interpretation had a better claim on their allegiance than that inherited from

[1] Heppe, Geschichte des deutschen Protestantismus, vol. i, pp. 181–2.

the Apostles and set forth in the works of the ancient Fathers and Doctors of the Church.[1]

The fifth session brought Peter Canisius into the limelight, as it fell to him to answer the charges of Karg. " The Catholics," he said, " are entirely opposed to bitterness and contentious language in the debates. Had our good friends of the opposite party wished in the same spirit to avoid such outbursts, they certainly need not have regaled us in the very first session of the Conference with lengthy and unseasonable reminders of ecclesiastical abuses. The Catholics also reprobate such abuses. But the Protestants reckon some matters as abuses which belong to the doctrine of the Faith, as, for example, the questions whether the saints are to be venerated, whether Christ is to be adored in the Eucharist, whether private Masses, as they are called, though in reality no Mass is private, are of recent introduction. The Catholics will deal with all these matters in due course and in the order in which they are set forth by the *Index Articulorum*. Turning to another point, since Melanchthon, its author, has made many and very important changes in the Confession of Augsburg, as, for instance, in the chapter on the Eucharist, and varied it from the first form which it possessed in 1530, we submit once again this petition, relative to the doctrine of the original Confession. In view of the fact that doctrines held by those who adhere to the Confession vary a great deal, and that at times they are in conflict with some of the Confession's most important articles, we ask those who stand by it to condemn openly and plainly, in common with ourselves, all teaching contrary to such Catholic truths as we defend and they do not repudiate."[2] That petition of St. Peter was made necessary by the split between Melanchthon and the Flacians, both of whom claimed to be the true inheritors of the Lutheran tradition. In the words of the Protestant historian, Heppe, " the Catholic party must rightly ask which of the two exactly represented Protestantism and with which were they to continue negotiations."[3]

As soon as Peter had finished speaking Melanchthon made a few remarks to the effect that " he could never help shuddering when he thought of the abominations that he had witnessed as a youth," and then Karg rose to answer what Bishop Helding had said in the fourth session concerning the acceptance of the patristic interpretation of Scripture. The gist of his speech was as follows:

[1] Bucholtz gives a long extract from the speech, *Geschichte der Regierung Ferdinand des Ersten*, vol. vii, pp. 373–5.

[2] Braunsberger, *Epistulae*, vol. ii, p. 796. The passage cited is, of course, merely a reporter's abbreviated version of a part of St. Peter's speech.

[3] *Geschichte des deutschen Protestantismus*, vol. i, p. 198.

The Word of God was not obscure, though the Fathers often disagreed as to its meaning. In the age of Pope Gregory barbarism brought in many superstitions with it, and there followed a time of great darkness during which the invocation of dead men, Masses for the dead, and the laws of celibacy were received, contrary to the law of God and ancient usage. Later still, under the prevalent sway of the Popes who made and defended impious laws, sacrificing monks came to the fore, bringing in new doctrines, as their books declared. And thus superstitions began to abound, for it is plain that the doctrines of penance, of justifying faith, and many others were corrupted at the hands of Thomas Aquinas, Scotus, and their kind. Consequently, the Protestant party refuse to accept the proposal that our controversies should be decided by appeal to the promiscuous sayings of ancient writers, to Pontifical decrees, or to the new-fangled labyrinths of monkish theology. Our desire is to have the controversies decided by the word of Prophets and Apostles.[1]

In the sixth session it was St. Peter's turn to reply to what Melanchthon had put forward by the mouth of Karg. Beginning with the all-important question of a fixed criterion, he said:

If, before all other agreements, some principle has not been found on this matter of a judge of controversies, or however we name it, the Colloquy cannot possibly proceed with any profit. Indeed, there is a real danger that it may break up prematurely, to the great prejudice of religion. How important it is for each party to a disputation or transaction on religious affairs to have sure and acknowledged principles, if any decisive result is to be obtained, may be seen from the universal proverb about the uselessness of arguing with a man who denies principles. This is the reason why we considered that, before all else, a sure norm or determinant should be proposed in the search for and confirmation of the truth; no deceptive or flexible norm, but a certain strong and unchangeable one, based on two foundations, the canon of Divine Scripture, and its true and genuine interpretation derived from the joint witness of the Fathers and the constant agreement of the Church. We urged this because it is not permissible for contending parties to introduce their private ideas and inclinations, nor to let their good pleasure be the interpreter of Holy Writ. . . . Men who do so

[1] Heppe, *Geschichte des deutschen Protestantismus*, vol. i, pp. 188–9.

make statements without evidence or demonstration, and give the appearance of benevolently providing laws for the Church instead of bowing to her legislation. They say that the Son of God, the Logos of the Eternal Father, who brought forth the Gospel from His Father's bosom, is a veracious Messenger, not to be considered as having carried down from Heaven ambiguities of language or Platonic figures of speech. But who is ignorant of that fact or ever called it in question? We, too, know and admit that not all the words of God are allegorical, but we contend that in the study of Scripture, meditation and careful thought are necessary to decide the subject of discourse, and that it helps to pay attention to the style, to the context, and to the circumstances under which the sacred document was written. . . .[1]

On one point we and the delegates of the other party are agreed, namely that we acknowledge the canonical Scriptures to be true, holy, internally consistent, and entirely divine, and of incomparable authority. Further, we hold that those Scriptures provide the best and soundest criterion for the adjustment of controversies in belief and religion. Whenever the Bible is clear and distinct in itself, we gladly submit to its testimony and ask for no other authority or evidence. But as soon as conflict arises about the meaning of an obscure passage and it is difficult to decide rival claims to the true meaning, then we appeal with perfect justice to the constant agreement of the Catholic Church, and go back to the unanimous interpretation of the Fathers. This is not in order that the Church may teach us without reference to the Scriptures but that the Church may show us the true and orthodox sense of the Scriptures; not that our faith may rest upon human authority without any regard to the Divine Word, but that we may learn from the explanations and instructions of holy men what the Divine Word really says. Where the sense of Scripture is clear and unambiguous we do not appeal to the Church, but, in doubtful places, we prefer the common agreement of the Church to the private exegesis of changeable men, who not seldom use diligent and pernicious endeavours to distort the sacred text.

It is not unreasonable for us to prefer the teaching of holy martyrs and learned confessors to that of individuals whose turn of mind is more open to suspicion—martyrs and pastors of the Church, distinguished by the holiness of their lives and their knowledge of the

---

[1] Karg had admitted that there might be difficulties in the sacred text due to style and idiom but held that they were not be cleared up by an appeal to the authority of ancient writers. It was the privilege of " the godly and learned " in any generation to pronounce on them.

Scriptures acquired by diligent comparison of the teaching of prophets and apostles from the earliest times. It is they who have bequeathed to us the symmetry of Catholic belief, with unanimous and harmonious accord.

Again, the contention that disputes arising out of the interpretation of obscure texts may be settled by comparing such texts with clearer ones, has against it the fact that the inherent difficulty of the matter is often too great, as St. Peter found in the Epistles of St. Paul, and as very learned and well versed men have frequently experienced in their study of the Bible. Then, too, the human understanding is so frail that it easily stumbles and goes astray in the profound obscurity which shrouds the sacred mysteries from its eyes. Even in matters within its competence, is it not always striving? Finally, a man's subjective mood and personal prejudices may very well hinder his understanding of things divine and baulk his search into the marvels of God's law. That is a task requiring a clean and upright heart and a mind ballasted with sincerity and devotion.

Now let me cite one or two examples to show more clearly that not all the doctrinal storms which shake the Church of God can be calmed by the sole means of appeal to the Scriptures. Well known is that passage containing the sacramental words of Our Lord at the Last Supper, *This is My Body*, and well-known, too, is the violent strife that has long raged about the interpretation of those words. By one school they are taken to mean the true and living Body of Christ which, with the rational soul and the Divinity, constitutes one Person. Others interpret them to mean only a symbol, though an efficacious symbol, of the Body of Christ, and with these men are allied the theologians who teach that the Body of Christ is present only in the eating and drinking of the bread and wine, but not otherwise. . . . Now, had the Scriptures themselves been sufficient to settle the controversy, the question would not have remained so long undecided among learned men. The same is to be said about the disputes relative to the number of the Sacraments, some putting it at two, others at three or four, as against the vast majority who hold fast to seven. The Scriptures provide different men with different views which they puzzle out in all sorts of ways and quarrel over among themselves. If all the mysteries of the Bible and all its evidences are so manifest why do men find contradictory meanings in it? Why does Osiander understand divine justification to be substantial justification while others make it out to be imputation, and a third party, imputation in this life and substantial justification in the next? Franz Stankar affirms that Christ justifies only by His human nature, and Osiander, on the contrary, that He justifies only by His divine nature. If there is nothing ambiguous or obscure in Scripture, whence have these men derived their various contradictory opinions? If there is nothing difficult or dark in the Epistles of St. Paul, why do Flacius and Gallus exclude good works as appertaining to Eternal Life, whereas Major and others include them in the sphere of salvation? How comes it that Gallus and Flacius derive the servitude of the human will from the same Epistles while others find there its freedom? that certain theologians who at one time were determinists and made God the author of evil as well as good now change their views and admit contingency in human action? They say that they think alike and harmoniously with regard to the fundamentals of doctrine but, verily, if the opposed points of view to which I have directed your attention are not concerned with fundamentals it is impossible to understand what is fundamental in Christianity at all.[1]

To sum up this question, there will be quarrelling in Germany about the sublimest objects of belief, a war of diametrically opposed views, so long as it is taught that each individual has a right to judge and decide for himself; so long as Scripture alone, interpreted privately, continues to be the final court of appeal; so long as some people arrogantly claim to be sons of God and despise others as mere human creatures. Tertullian says of such men: ' They appeal to the Scriptures, and thus emboldened endeavour to tire out the steadfast, to capture the weak, and to relieve waverers of their scruples. Therefore at the threshold of this matter we post a notice that we shall not admit them to any disputation on Holy Writ.'[2] According to St. Cyril all heretics derive their errors from the divinely inspired Scriptures by falsifying the true words of the Holy Ghost. ' You assail the law with the word of the law,' wrote St. Ambrose, ' in order to cloak the perversity of your minds with the law's authority.' When, therefore, any dispute that has arisen over the Scriptures is to be settled we ought to remember the warning of St. Clement of the apostolic age. The divine law, he said, must not be read or taught according to any man's private understanding of it, because in the Scriptures there is much that can be twisted to mean what some individual presumes to think it means. The sense

---

[1] The reference to determinism here is a dig at Melanchthon, who had completely changed his earlier views on the subject. It was he, too, who endeavoured to persuade the world that the Protestants were united in doctrine at the time of the Conference: " Videbatur inter nostros dulcis concordia esse." *Corpus Reformatorum*, vol. ix, col. 458.
[2] Karg had invoked the help of Tertullian for his own side.

of the text must be learned from those who have preserved it as it was truly delivered to them by their predecessors. . . .

Enough, and perhaps more than enough, of St. Peter's address, has now been given to illustrate his style of argumentation. He followed up his examination of the private judgment theory with a good defence of certain Fathers of the Church whom Melanchthon and Karg had accused of false doctrine, and then proceeded to show that such practices as the invocation of saints and prayers for the dead went back well beyond the time of St. Gregory the Great, from whose Pontificate Karg had dated their introduction. Karg's reiterated charge that the Catholics were in bad faith, and that many of their cherished doctrines were idolatrous or superstitious, caused Peter to remind him that they had been sent to Worms " *non certe ad calumniandum sed ad pie, docte et amice colloquendum.*" Let them as wise men, he continued, cease from berating the Church's magistracy, the ancient Fathers, and practically all orders of Catholics. It is only a bad cause that takes refuge in abuse. How much better to forestall one another with courtesy and to put their differences to the test of argument, supported by honest and rightly understood citations from relevant authorities. If the Catholics wished they could give tit for tat and say plenty to the discredit of the other side. But away with calumny, which is the nurse of dissension. " *Accedat autem per Jesum Christum oramus, qui pacis auctor et amator est, accedat, inquam, concilia-trix animorum evangelica charitas, quae non aemulatur, non agit perperam, non inflatur, non est ambitiosa.*"[1]

When St. Peter had finished, Bishop Helding, by the President's authority, asked the Protestants to state whether they regarded the Zwinglians, the Calvinists, and the followers of Osiander and Flacius Illyricus as true adherents of the Confession of Augsburg. The question was not otiose or put merely to annoy. It had been definitely laid down by the Diet of Regensburg that the Conference was to take place between Catholics and genuine Confessionists alone, as their religions were the only two recognized by law. The Catholics now wished to know where

---

[1] " We pray by Jesus Christ, the author and lover of peace, that evangelical charity, the reconciler of souls, may come instead, charity which envieth not, dealeth not perversely, is not puffed up nor ambitious." Braunsberger, *Epistulae*, vol. ii, p. 797. St. Peter's address as given above is taken from Bucholtz, *Geschichte der Regierung Ferdinand des Ersten*, vol. i, pp. 379-85, with a supplement from Riess, *Der selige Petrus Canisius* (Freiburg im Breisgau, 1865), pp. 221-2. Both authors had access to transcripts of the original documents in Augsburg and Vienna, but they supply no helpful details as to their character. St. Peter's address as given by them would appear to be more in the nature of a paraphrase than his actual words, though they enclose it in inverted commas. Braunsberger supplies only disconnected passages of the address.

they stood and with whom exactly they were dealing. The bargaining that went on between Melanchthon and Brenz[1] was no affair of theirs. Probably they knew nothing about it.[2] What they wanted was to be sure of the legal standing of the Colloquy, and the only guarantee for that was some such public statement as Helding requested. Instead of complying, however, Melanchthon flew into a temper and vented his annoyance, not on the Bishop, but on Peter Canisius. " You have been listening," he said, addressing the assembly, " to a sufficiently grandiloquent orator. If that is the way he wishes to contend with us we shall pay him out with interest. We looked for other methods of disputation. His is not the way either to investigate the truth or to bring about mutual reconciliation." Helding then endeavoured to soothe Philip's ruffled feelings but for his pains merely got the retort : " *Nos largiter vos remunerabimur, ne dubitetis* " —" Make no mistake, we shall settle accounts with you generously."[3] That was the end of the sixth session, held on September 20th, and, to all intents and purposes, of the whole Conference.

What St. Peter had surmised about it, that it might very easily come to an end almost as soon as it had begun, turned out to be less than the truth, for it never really began at all. A few days after the sixth session, Schnepf and his Flacians stole a march on " the holy Pharisees," as they styled Melanchthon's party, by handing to the President a written condemnation of Zwinglians, Majorists, and other dissenters from the Confession of Augsburg. Their action infuriated Philip, whose great aim and endeavour was to bluff the world into believing that Protestantism suffered from no divisions. The cat was out of the bag with a vengeance now, one powerful section of the Lutherans having publicly denounced other sections as heretical, and, unkindest cut of all, denounced them to none other than the common foe, the Catholics. Melanchthon took swift revenge. Using his influence with the legates of the Protestant princes present in Worms, he secured a majority for a mandate prohibiting the Flacians from further participation in the Colloquy, either inside or outside the chamber of deputies. Now, since the credentials of the Flacians had exactly the same legal validity as those of Melanchthon's people, the President and his assessors were faced with a serious problem. If they

---

[1] Melanchthon had undertaken not to condemn Osiander, whose views appealed to Brenz, on condition that Brenz did not condemn the Zwinglians with whom Melanchthon was on good terms.

[2] The Duke of Saxony, protector of the Flacians, did. Writing on the subject to Bishop Pflug, he said : " Thus did these two consuls sport together. And thus perish the truth and the Church of God. May God have mercy on us. Amen." Heppe, *Geschichte des deutschen Protestantismus*, vol. i, p. 201, n. 2.

[3] Heppe, *Geschichte*, vol. i, p. 191.

acquiesced in the exclusion of the Flacians, the Colloquy would cease to be representative, and degenerate into a mere private debate whose findings would have no claim on the attention of the Imperial Government. Melanchthon, on the other hand, could not be persuaded to budge from his position; so a deadlock resulted which not even the tact of Julius Pflug was able to modify in the least.

Contrasted with Melanchthon, the great leader of Protestantism and " Praeceptor Germaniae," Pflug, the Catholic bishop, might be said to have a few points in his favour. " The attitude adopted by Bishop Julius in this deplorable quarrel," writes the Protestant Heppe, " was as wise as it was dignified."[1] He refused to be drawn into the quarrel and held the balance of justice with perfect impartiality. On October 1st the Flacians came forward with another protestation and demanded that it should be read publicly at the next session of the Conference. Out of regard for Melanchthon the President negatived the proposal, whereupon Schnepf and his friends abruptly departed from Worms. Pflug then appealed for guidance to King Ferdinand.

Meantime the requital threatened by Melanchthon in the sixth session was duly paid on the heads of Peter Canisius and his allies. Peter was accused to his face of malice, blasphemy, idolatry, and other pleasant things, while rumour busied itself to breed hate against the cause which he represented. The Pope, it was whispered, had beheaded Cardinal Morone for Lutheranism, and had sent the most beautiful young courtesan he could find in Italy to the King of France, as an inducement to that monarch to persecute the Protestants. One of the meanest slanders spread about concerned St. Peter personally. Flacius Illyricus reports it as follows : " The chief author of the Jesuits, or certainly their restorer and propagator, is that Canisius about whose sanctity many excellent stories are told. Not the least of them is the one recounting what happened at Mainz in 1557 with an Abbess named Catella. Canisius was entertained by her in great style, and, when the two of them had reached the merry stage in their cups, they proceeded, as lovers with the common name of dog, to celebrate canine nuptials. That story was well-known to everybody at the Colloquy of Worms."[2]

Peter's letters are sadly uninformative on the inner history of the Conference because his oath of secrecy stood in the way. But he tells

---

[1] *Geschichte des deutschen Protestantismus*, vol. i, p. 202.

[2] *De Sectis, dissensionibus, contradictionibus. . . . Pontificiorum liber* (Basle, 1565), p. 77 ; Braunsberger, *Epistulae*, vol. ii, pp. 800–1. St. Peter never set foot in Mainz in 1557 and there was no abbess there of the name of Catella (=puppy). Decent Protestants resented the story as much as did the Catholics. St. Peter took no notice of it.

a good deal about his daily life and the worries and small joys of which it was composed. The lay brother, his cook, fell ill, and Peter, with his stout belief in the efficacy of "native air," sent him to Cologne for treatment. In the brother's place he asked for a strong man and received a poor invalid who died shortly afterwards. Meals must have been a problem under such circumstances and, to add to it, there was Father Goudanus's racking cough, which made the Saint, who loved him, terribly unhappy. But there were some joyful occasions as, for instance, the day when the box of books which he had purchased in Rome arrived at last after many adventures—"*sarcina nostra tamdiu desiderata*." It was Cardinal Truchsess who had rescued it and who added to Peter's content by hinting that there seemed to be a prospect of the Pope and King Ferdinand being reconciled. The Cardinal's letter had also the less happy effect of raising a serious scruple in its recipient's mind. He remembered how heartily he had backed up his Lordship's endeavours to procure Father Nadal for service in Germany, without too much consideration of the position of the Jesuits in Rome, and straightway wrote the following apology to Laynez:

I confess that I have sinned and I beg your forgiveness for not resisting our excellent friend, the Cardinal, when he petitioned for Father Nadal. Instead of that, I encouraged him with some hopes of success. In this my love of Germany led me astray, as I was rather confident that the country could be helped by Father Nadal better than by anybody else. That was my great desire. I dared to make some concession to the pious and ardent wishes of the Cardinal, who had urged me in so many ways to intercede for him that you might at last send somebody. I adopted the plan of giving him a promise that I would write to you in his name, suggesting that Father Nadal might possibly be able to quit Rome for a time during the present troubles,[1] and come here with counsels for the alleviation of Germany's manifold misfortunes. I thought that it would be easier for you to explain through the post than for me to give reasons which might prove unpalatable to our good Patron. But I do not wish to excuse myself. I beg forgiveness again that, contrary to the law once delivered, I entered into negotiations with the Cardinal before letting your Reverence know. I deserve whatever punishment you may enjoin and shall undergo it gladly. Though sinning and straying so frequently I get off scot free and suffer nothing for my many great trespasses.[2]

[1] Pope Paul's threat to change the constitutions of the Society of Jesus.
[2] Braunsberger, *Epistulae*, vol. ii, p. 136.

By this time the Saint had surrendered all hopes of the Conference coming to anything. If the Protestants would not agree on some fundamental determining principles, how was it possible to argue with them? His own spirit is revealed in a comment he made on the dispatch of some new Jesuit workers from Italy to Germany: "I do not look for any greater joy in this darkness and trouble than to see, sent by the Lord of the harvest, men, who offer themselves and their blood to God and His saints for so many perishing souls in Germany. We can, it seems, bear no fruit here except by labouring in patience and in hope against hope, making no account of anything if only we can help a few of the vast multitude in peril. Verily, the need here is for a great thirst to win souls to Christ, and for great patience in bearing with and comforting those who have begun to listen and are looking for the truth."[1]

In the seventh session of the Conference Melanchthon endeavoured to secure the ratification of his 'Pride's Purge' in regard to the Flacians, and the acceptance by the Catholics of some new delegates whom he had invited to Worms without any official authorization. The President was naturally obliged to refuse him both favours, as being contrary to his mandate from the Diet of Regensburg, whereupon Philip and all his henchmen rose and strode angrily out of the council-chamber. Writing to his friend Camerarius he said, speaking of the Catholics and Flacians: "They are making a mockery of us, like the Jews giving blows to Christ."[2] So, it would seem that, whatever other people thought, Philip was not vexed with too mean a conception of his own place in the scheme of things.

One more session was held which the Protestant party did not attend, and then some weeks passed without a further meeting, during which Bishop Pflug did everything in his power to save the Conference from complete collapse. St. Peter took advantage of the enforced leisure to pay a visit to his brethren in Cologne, where he remained from October 29th to November 6th. Just at this time he received news of his stepmother's death which affected him deeply. "It is the great longing of my heart that she may have the help of the Sacrifices and prayers of your Reverence and the other Fathers and Brothers," he confided to Laynez, while paying a filial tribute to her memory. The situation in Cologne interested him very much. A short while before, the Senators had transferred their Gymnasium of the "Three Crowns" to the care of the Jesuits, following upon the defection from the Church of its then regent. It was a great windfall for the Fathers, though the Senate drove a rather

---

[1] Braunsberger, *Epistulae*, vol. ii, p. 138.   [2] *Corpus Reformatorum*, vol. ix, p. 306.

hard bargain with them and attempted to interfere with their domestic concerns. Among them was a Father John Rethius, who belonged to one of the wealthiest and most aristocratic Cologne families. Being also an excellent religious he was very much astonished and distressed when the Senators suddenly appointed him governor of the Gymnasium, without so much as a 'by your leave' to any Jesuit authority. That would never have done, as Father Kessel was the legitimate superior, but it would not have done either to tell the Senators to mind their own business. Father Kessel and Father Rethius himself managed the stout gentlemen with such skill that St. Peter was lost in admiration for them both, as he was for the fine work carried on at their school. It already counted students from every part of Germany, and Rethius had started very clever negotiations to attract to it young Catholics who were attending or about to attend Protestant universities. St. Peter's conviction that those Cologne Jesuits were the best and most efficient of his brethren in northern lands spurred him to labour his hardest to alleviate the extreme poverty and difficult conditions of their lives. "They cannot live together apart from the students owing to lack of accommodation," he told Laynez, "and they have no garden, which makes it very difficult for them to provide for the sick." The Senate treated them shabbily, though fully alive to the value of the work they were doing, and, had it not been for the charity of Peter's own old friends, "the good Carthusian Fathers," they would have gone many a day without a square meal. "I marvel," continued the Saint, "how, deprived of the discipline of other colleges, which they consider it impossible to introduce here just now, they are yet all of one heart, and simple, charitable, diligent, and obedient in their mutual relations." Father Kessel, for his part, wrote to tell Laynez of the great comfort that Peter's visit had been to them all, and Father Rethius enthusiastically recorded his daily doings in a diary from which the following are extracts :

October 30th.—Father Canisius received and accepted an invitation to dine with Dr. Johann Gropper at St. Gereon's.

October 31st.—He visited the Chancellor of our Archbishop and secured for us licence to preach in the Church of St. Ursula. He also arranged that Father Rethius should have prompt access to the Archbishop whenever necessary. The same day he was invited to dine with Graf von Mansfeldt,[1] who promised that he would

[1] Von Mansfeldt became Archbishop of Cologne the following year.

deal with the Archbishop about entrusting to us the office of ordinary preachers at St. Ursula's. At the same time he asked Father Canisius to preach in the Dom on the Feast of All Saints. Father Peter excused himself, whereupon Graf von Mansfeldt dispatched two canons who urged him until he gave way.

November 1st.—Father Canisius said Mass and preached in the morning at the Convent of St. Ignatius of Antioch. At midday he preached in the Dom to some thousands of men. The Graf von Mansfeldt and many other nobles were present, as well as a great multitude of students, though at that hour very few usually came to a sermon. Such a well-attended, learned, and brilliant sermon had not been heard in Cologne for many years. When Father Peter was leaving the Dom people rushed to look at him, exactly as though he were some king or emperor.

November 2nd—The Senate dispatched an apparitor to him with gifts such as are usually reserved for the honouring of the ambassadors of princes and other illustrious people. The same day Father Canisius dined with the Carthusians, and preached such a fine sermon that the Prior gave him 400 thalers for our College, as well as a bond for another hundred the following day.

November 3rd—Father Canisius dined again with Dr. Gropper. At 4 o'clock in the evening he made an extempore Latin speech at our school on liberal studies, and, though we had told only our own scholars and a few others, so many men came from outside that the large hall could scarcely hold them. Before his departure, Father Canisius many times visited Herr Johann Hardenrath, and through him offered his services to Herr Constantine Lyskirchen,[1] in case that gentleman or the Senate should at any time wish him to approach the King of the Romans or other German princes on their behalf. His offer was gratefully accepted, and Herr Hardenrath is to write to him at Worms informing him about the Senate's petition.

November 6th—Father Canisius returned by ship to Worms.[2]

That simple record gives a fairly clear idea of St. Peter's influence and methods. He was still comparatively young, only thirty-six, and yet he seems to have been regarded by all classes of Catholics as among the best of their natural advocates and leaders. From Bonn, on his way back,

---

[1] One of the most influential of the Cologne senators.
[2] Braunsberger, *Epistulae*, vol. ii, pp. 804–6.

the Saint addressed a few pregnant lines to Father Kessel on the subject of courtesy at leave-takings. Perhaps he had observed a certain brusqueness in the way the Cologne Jesuits managed such things. The Germans, like the English, are apt to be casual over them, not because they have no feelings but because they hate to make a scene—and quite right, too. St. Peter, however, was all for southern methods. " I would like," he said, " all members of the Society to receive an embrace before setting out on a journey. It astonishes me that, whether through your fault or mine, the matter was so impolitely handled, and that more thought was not given to charity, which is fostered by and takes delight in these external offices. I think that our brothers of the Society should be treated in a more fraternal fashion. But I do not say this as though I had myself suffered any neglect at your hands. I merely want to urge that, on the arrival or departure of our brothers, Italian charity rather than German simplicity should be our practice. For the rest, and in my own case, I avow that you treated me while among you with far greater indulgence than I deserved."[1]

Back in Worms, Peter still had leisure to devote to preaching and catechizing while the ill-starred Conference went slowly to dissolution. King Ferdinand expressed a strong wish for its continuance, and suggested a compromise to which the Catholics readily agreed. But Melanchthon would not meet them half way. Instead, on December 1st, he and his confrères handed to Bishop Pflug three documents, in which they endeavoured to lay the whole blame for the adjournment on the Catholics. It would have been much better, they said, had good and learned men of their own churches gathered together for peaceful discussion of any matters requiring elucidation, instead of engaging in theatrical disputations with persons " *qui manifestas Idolomanias tueri solent.*" Yet, because the Diet of the Empire wanted such a conference, they had not refused. " We began the Colloquy modestly and without any shuffling, and we proposed absolutely nothing that could have held it up or been a hindrance to its progress."[2] To these contentions St. Peter drew up an answer in the name of all the Catholic delegates, which was laid before the President on December 6th. It is a lucid and trenchant piece of writing but far too long to cite in full. Beginning with a warm tribute to Bishop Pflug for his patience, tact, earnestness and impartiality as President—qualities which the Protestants also had duly acknowledged—it goes on to deal with the main charge of the opposition:

[1] Braunsberger, *Epistulae*, vol. ii, p. 142.   [2] *Corpus Reformatorum*, vol. ix, pp. 386–8.

We, the Catholic delegates and assistants, unhesitatingly appeal to the Acts of the Colloquy. There is nothing we desire more than that our case should be judged from our recent deeds, words, and writings, on condition that the judges are qualified by their standing, authority, and equity to decide. We are not much frightened by the words and opinions of those who wished to set themselves up as both plaintiffs and judges in this Colloquy. . . . We would like fairer and more disinterested judges, and ask only one favour, namely that the deeds, words, and writings of our party should honestly be compared with those of the other party, and then both, with the decisions and expressed wishes of the Estates and decrees of the Empire. . . .

In the first place, it is perfectly well known that the Estates pronounced for a courteous and orderly discussion of doctrine, but those who were present at the beginning of the Colloquy are only too well aware how bitter, cross-grained, and disorderly was the other party's opening. They began, straight away and quite irrelevantly, with most serious accusations, not blushing to charge us with cruelty and impiety. . . . As for the cruelty, let those whose business it is see to it. All who were present at the beginning of the Conference will testify that the other party brazenly and by name condemned as impious the declaration of his Imperial Majesty known as the *Interim* and also the decrees of the Council of Trent. Now even supposing these instruments to be impious, it was both unseasonable and unfair to rail at them so severely and to condemn them in that fashion, since it was with such matters that the Colloquy had to deal by means of argument and not by these bare condemnations. It is strange that our opponents should have been so forward and intrepid with this pronouncement and afterwards, at the right time, should have refused to join us in condemning the sects, though a decree of the Empire required their acquiescence. It was the same with regard to the Zwinglian doctrine of the Eucharist, which has always been plainly and constantly condemned, not only by every state of the Realm, but by Luther himself. These men would not allow it to be brought forward for discussion, but they were only too ready, without any discussion or reservation whatsoever, to brand with impiety the Emperor's book of the *Interim*, which contains so many articles and dogmas of faith and religion. They pretend meantime that they avoided condemnation of Zwinglianism and other sects, which are not less at variance with the Confession of Augsburg than with our Religion, because they feared that such action on their part might cause dissension and public disorder. But much more should they have anticipated and feared danger when they so lightly reprobated the book of the Emperor which is practically an epitome of Christian doctrine. And yet, after acting in this mischievous way, they would like to be considered models of orderly deportment at the Colloquy. . . .

With similar modesty and equity they make us out the authors of dissension and of many people's ruin, because we asked for the specific condemnation of the sects. In doing so we were merely obeying the decree of the Regensburg Diet, which His Majesty the King adheres to in his last communication about the Colloquy; and our petition was ratified as entirely consonant with the work of the Colloquy by the very colleagues and companions of our critics, colleagues whom the Estates of the Realm appointed as delegates but whom these men excluded from the debates. . . .

It is abundantly plain from the two Recesses of Augsburg and Regensburg that the princes of the Empire desired this Colloquy to be with those only who held by the true and genuine Confession of Augsburg, and also that they wished other sects to be condemned. Our friends, however, flatly refused to condemn the sects by name and so gave us reason to suspect, either that they were unwilling to obey the edicts of the Empire, or that, under cover of their Confession, they sheltered and encouraged several sects. That suspicion was confirmed by other plain tokens. It is matter of common knowledge that great strife goes on among those who adhere to the aforesaid Confession; strife, too, not about unimportant matters but about the chief articles of the Confession and the fundamentals of the Christian religion. Irreconcilable quarrels began among them some time ago concerning free will, justification, the theological virtues, good works, penance, the Sacraments, and, most of all, the Lord's Supper or the Eucharist. The Church, with her rites and jurisdiction, is also a bone of contention, as well as many other doctrinal questions of a similar kind. Everywhere in Germany various flocks of sectaries are to be seen, straying in the shadow of that same Confession, at war with one another and as much divided among themselves as they are from the Church which they hate. . . .

The chief cause of the Conference's suspension is, as we have said, the discord among these men which has led one set of them to exclude others with the same credentials from the Imperial Diet as themselves.

The discord has now gone so far that, if the princes and cities are counted which share the religious beliefs of Schnepf and the other excluded men, it will appear that the majority of those hitherto regarded as Confessionists are now cut off and debarred from having any part in this Colloquy and its attempts at reconciliation. . . .[1]

These excerpts are sufficient to show the style of the protestation. It was quite unanswerable, as may be seen by the verdicts of a few representative Protestant historians. Thus, referring to the uneasiness shown by the Duke of Württemberg and Prince Maximilian at the presence of Peter Canisius in Worms, Holtzmann says : " Christopher and Maximilian need not have worried very much about the representatives of Catholicism. The real enemy this time was in the Protestant ranks. It was their unhappy split into separate camps which not all the efforts of months were able to bring together."[2] Droysen is equally emphatic : " Owing to the sentiments which the adherents of the old and new faiths entertained for one another the Colloquy of Worms could scarcely have had much success. That it had no success at all was due to the split among the Evangelicals."[3] Finally, we may quote Ranke, alleged to be " the best equipped historian who ever lived " : " It is humiliating to be forced to record that the Conference was not broken up by disputes between the two great parties ; it never even got so far—the divisions among the Protestants themselves put an end to it altogether."[4]

Apart from everything else, St. Peter and his colleagues were quite ready—" *paratissimos nos offerimus*," they said—to continue the discussions with the truncated Protestant delegation if the President and his advisers so desired.[5] That the Saint personally had by no means decided to press for the closing down of the Conference after the expulsion of the Flacians is apparent from the letter which he caused Father Salmeron, then a visitor to Worms, to write to Laynez on November 21st. He gives all the pros and cons and begs for advice, which was not forthcoming.[6] Meantime, the President had decided that resumption at the moment was useless, and he accordingly prorogued the assembly *sine*

[1] Braunsberger, *Epistulae*, vol. ii, pp. 160–72.
[2] *Kaiser Maximilian II*, p. 318.
[3] *Geschichte der Gegenreformation* (Berlin, 1893), p. 52.
[4] *Ferdinand I and Maximilian II*, Eng. tr., p. 80. This judgment is repeated in Ranke's *History of Germany during the Reformation*, a work which he undertook, by his own confession, as a sort of makeweight to his *History of the Popes*. His co-religionists had complained that in the latter work he had been too favourable to Catholicism. It was a curious motive to inspire a great historian who prided himself on his icy impartiality.
[5] Heppe, *Geschichte des deutschen Protestantismus*, vol. i, p. 209, n. 1.
[6] Braunsberger, *Epistulae*, vol. ii, pp. 801–2.

die, in order to refer the whole question to the judgment of the Estates.

That was the last considerable attempt to bring the Catholics and the Protestants together until Leibniz made his great effort in the eighteenth century. The determination of the Protestants all along to wreck the Colloquy is evident from their conduct outside the debates. Schnepf and others are delightfully ingenuous as to their intentions, the one real business of all good men at Worms, say they, being " to smash the Papacy."[1] Protestant zealots, pensioners of the people who were supposed to be engaged in friendly discussion with the Catholics, thundered anathemas against Rome from many pulpits, and, not content with that, did their best to raise disturbances at Catholic services by open brawling.[2] One story current about Peter Canisius was that after his brush with Melanchthon he had suddenly gone dumb and fallen down dead in his tracks. To his amusement, some orators in Saxony used the tale to illustrate the wonderful judgments of God.[3]

Now that everything was over, St. Peter did not feel too dissatisfied with the results of the Colloquy. Most that he had expected from it had been achieved, as he explained in the following letter from Worms to King Ferdinand :

The Colloquy is at an end, Sire, and not, in the opinion of good judges, without having borne fruit. Blessed be Our Lord who confirms the unity of His Church by the division and confusion of the sectaries. May the experience teach us not to trust nor give in to the persecutors of the Church, who keep faith with neither God nor man, promising and pretending one thing but doing another. Would that we might not be fearful or faint-hearted. God would fight for us if only we stuck fast to Him and despised the wretched little bugbears of the world. May Christ give us the spirit of true and solid peace, which is not found

[1] Heppe, *Geschichte*, vol. i, supplement, p. 15.
[2] Braunsberger, *Epistulae*, vol. ii, pp. 170–1. As on other occasions, St. Peter was honoured with verse, the usual tedious stuff about dogs. Here are a few lines :

In cane sunt oris rictus foedusque latratus,
Errantes oculi, turpe voraxque caput.
Omnia conveniunt ; distorto lumine spectat
Canisius, similis rictus et oris adest.
Attribuit falso Sanctum sibi nomen Jesu,
Contra quem sparso saepius ore latrat ;
Atque canum rabies non raro infestat euntes :
Illius rabiem sic pia turba timet.

The poet then tells how this " dirtiest of dogs " disturbed the " pious Colloquy " with his mad yelping.
[3] Braunsberger, *Epistulae*, vol. ii, p. 178.

among the ungodly or in the camps of the rebellious. And may Our Lord, the King of Kings, grant us in all things understanding and zeal for His Name, now so many ways blasphemed. . . . I humbly offer myself and commend myself and all my brethren to Your Majesty, whom may Our Lord Jesus deign to comfort in these present troubles and to strengthen against all the tribulations of the world.[1]

The attacks on himself personally appear to have left Peter quite cold. He never replied to them nor did he at any time use vituperation as a weapon in public controversy. But in his private letters he gave his indignation rein, thinking of Melanchthon's insolent demeanour over against the Church of the centuries, of the fanatical determination of Flacius and his kind to keep every avenue of reconciliation closed, and of the unreasoning, almost maniacal hatred of the *Res Catholica* fostered so sedulously by the Protestant leaders. The dimensions of that hatred, its intensity and viciousness, are utterly out of proportion to any wrongs or abuses that may have originally engendered it. It is the most awful portent of the sixteenth century and worth study as a psychopathological disorder. St. Peter reacted to it as any decent, normal man might have been expected to do. " Blessed be Our Lord," he wrote to Laynez, " who has delivered us from the company of those absolutely hopeless people. We may well lament over them for many reasons, for their blindness, their hardness of heart, their malignity, their craft, their insolence, their sophistry, their obduracy, their pride, and their impiety. To satisfy them is beyond our power because they will not make the slightest concession. But Our Lord has not suffered this Conference, or rather conflict, to be altogether barren of result. In the first place, it showed forth the singular concord and constancy of the Catholics who were present . . . and the spirit of confusion which Our Lord sent among our adversaries. . . . A third advantage is that having had experience of the despicable opinions and small authority of those grumblers, we can the more easily strengthen others against such enemies of the Church, and fight it out with them in greater confidence. Fourthly, we hope that Catholics will be much strengthened in their faith by the revelation of serious discord among the sectaries ; that waverers will henceforth desert us in much smaller numbers ; and that those who have been fascinated by false doctrine will, in disgust and weariness with such dissensions, be the more ready to return to the fold of the true Church. Finally, the Estates of the Empire

[1] Braunsberger, *Epistulae*, vol. ii, pp. 173–4.

Des Ehrwürdigen Herrn Doctoris Martini Lutheri/ gottseligen/
TRIVMPH.

Und verantwortung/ Wider die gottlosen Schmehschrifft/der Newen Münch/der Jesuiter/ Welche sie unter
dem Titel/ ANATOMIA LVTHERI, ausgesprenget haben.

Luther's Triumph. A sixteenth-century cartoon against the Jesuits. It will be observed that the
legs of the Papal chair are supported on four books, the Works of Plato and Aristotle, Peter the
Lombard's *Liber Sententiarum*, the Commentaries of the Monks, and the Decretals. Staphylus is
called Judas because he abandoned Lutheranism for the Catholic Church. The first two figures in
the group on the right are Melanchthon and Flacius Illyricus.

will learn from the Acts of the Conference how spiteful, petulant, and brazen-faced these people showed themselves, and that there is no reason why we should try to establish sincere and full religious concord with men who deny first principles and cling might and main to opinions the most indefensible and the most alien from the piety of the ancient Church. Perhaps, too, the princes will conceive a dislike for such conferences in the future, and, taught by the event the futility of such remedies, be the more ready to embrace what seems the one and only means of restoring religion in Germany, namely a general council. . . ."

That passage is sufficiently strong to satisfy anybody who may have thought that St. Peter entirely lacked the fire of an Augustine or a Jerome. He concludes his letter with a few words about his own part in the Conference : " Among the Catholic theologians at the Colloquy none throughout laboured more strenuously with pen and voice than Father Goudanus and myself. Often enough we had not time even to say Mass, and I am astonished that we both kept so remarkably well in the midst of so much work. Our Lord was good to us, owing to your prayers. I believe we have increased the fear which our adversaries had beforehand conceived of us, so that it is not surprising if they wish the worst to the Jesuits, as they call us throughout Germany."[1] St. Peter's optimism as to the results of the frustrated Colloquy was justified. The Catholics had their problem clear-cut at last. Corporate reunion they saw to be a vain dream, and they accordingly transferred their hopes to a general council which would put their own house in order, irrespective of what their separated brethren might think or devise. On the other hand, the Colloquy, in the words of a distinguished historian, " marked the crisis of German Protestantism, for from it dated the ebb, the backward flow, and subsidence of the Protestant current in Germany."[2]

---

[1] Braunsberger, *Epistulae*, vol. ii, pp. 175–7.

[2] Maurenbrecher in Sybel's *Historische Zeitschrift*, vol. l (1883), p. 42. The break-up of the Conference was the signal for a pamphlet war of considerable violence. During it, early in 1558, St. Peter made a short but spirited reply to an apologia of Melanchthon and was himself answered by Melanchthon's henchman, Dathaenus. Only two copies of Peter's anonymous tract are known to exist, one being in the British Museum. The very abusive retort of Dathaenus is printed in Goldast's *Politica Imperialia* (Frankfurt, 1614), pp. 1261 sqq.

CHAPTER XI

THE CITY OF THE CONFESSION

As was recorded earlier in this book, Emperor Ferdinand showed great determination to secure the services of Peter Canisius for the Diet which opened at Augsburg on March 3, 1559. Peter came, and his coming marked a turning-point in his career. Augsburg for years afterwards remained his permanent home, the centre of his ministry and the city of his love. More than any other place in the Empire, more than Cologne or Ingolstadt or Munich or Vienna or Prague or Innsbruck, it claimed his devotion and grew under his care into something strangely different from what might have seemed its inevitable destiny. Why, at the height of his powers, did the Saint concentrate so much attention on Augsburg? Why did he anchor there so long and let the good winds from other quarters entice his sails in vain? The chief reason is that Peter was a fairly able strategist who recognized in the position and power of Augsburg a key to the future developments of religion in South Germany.

For hundreds of years Augsburg has continued to be one of the loveliest and liveliest cities in Europe. In the time of Canisius it owned allegiance to none but the Emperor, and was as free almost as the unique City in which the Pope now resides. Founded and named after himself by Augustus in the year 15 B.C., the town marked the northern terminus of the Roman road which formed the main artery of travel to and from Italy throughout the Middle Ages and long afterwards. It was not easy to get anywhere in South Germany without passing through Augsburg, and many who passed came back to stay. Among them in the fourteenth century was a weaver from Graben named Hans Fugger. Hans traded in linen and left a large fortune to his sons. The youngest of these, Jakob, was one of the greatest geniuses of commerce the world has known, and not many years passed before the Haus Fugger had its ships on every sea and its business agents in every important city of Europe. Such enterprise stimulated competition, and firms with world-wide ramifications, such as those of the Welsers and Baumgartens, vied with the Fuggers in making Augsburg the chief credit centre of Christendom.

When the Reformation came, the vast majority of Augsburgers sided enthusiastically with Luther. At first the civil authorities held out against the new teaching, but popular opinion gradually forced them to adapt their policy to the changing conditions. The City joined the Schmalkalden League at its formation and step by step began to restrict the liberty of its Catholic subjects. In 1537 the priests were expelled, and, until the Emperor broke the power of the League in the Schmalkalden War, Augsburg remained a purely Lutheran, or rather Zwinglian, city. It was the first of the cities to arm against the Emperor, a betrayal for which it paid dearly after the battle of Mühlberg. A colossal fine was imposed, and, as an additional burden, Charles V did the rebel burghers the equivocal honour of holding three Diets within their walls in the short space of nine years. The first and last of these are famous in history as the Diets of the *Interim* and of the Religious Peace respectively, while an earlier one, that of 1530, had made Augsburg sacred forever to Protestantism as the City of the Confession.

In the Reichstag of 1548 the Emperor forced the *Interim* on the reluctant people, compelled them to recall Bishop Truchsess, and restored to power the patrician party whose sympathies lay with the ancient Faith. Three years later the Protestant preachers were banished, a measure which so exasperated the dissident majority that in 1552, during Moritz's rebellion, they opened their gates to the Emperor's enemies and once again proscribed Catholicism. Within a month Charles swooped down on the City, but this time he was not sufficiently powerful to do more than secure toleration for the Catholics. How was it, we might ask, that he had power enough even for that, considering the enormous wealth and influence of the city? The Haus Fugger and the Haus Welser are the explanation, for they remained staunchly loyal to the Church through all the vicissitudes of the Reformation, and played, in both senses of the word, a capital part in the Catholic resistance by lavishly financing the Emperor. That is something a Catholic might remember when tempted by modern developments to deny even the ghost of a virtue to capitalism.

After the Religious Peace, Augsburg became a city of two faiths, functioning side by side in precarious amity. But amity is hardly the right word, for there was no love lost between them. They merely did not come to blows. The Catholics had succeeded in keeping control of some of the finest churches, even of the great cathedral itself, which to the Protestant majority must have seemed a palpable injustice. But the law had spoken and might was no longer right. How much the old blood-and-thunder methods of evangelization had changed is shown by the practice of the wealthy councillor and annalist of Augsburg, Mair, who records to his own glory that he used to offer eminent but impoverished Catholics a substantial sum down and a monthly pension if they would renounce the Pope.[1]

Such was the position of affairs when the Diet of 1559 assembled. The Protestants were still very sore over their discomfiture at the Conference of Worms but that only made them the more determined to secure the repeal of the Ecclesiastical Reservation which enabled the Catholics to retain possession of so much valuable ecclesiastical property. Their hopes centred on Emperor Ferdinand. He was such a contrast to his sullen brother who had bullied Augsburg in the past, breezy and accessible where the other could only scowl, and a thoroughly German Prince, despite his Spanish antecedents. The gracious and genial sovereign detested strife. Truly loving his people and longing to see them united and living friendlily together, he was willing to barter almost anything except the essentials of his devoutly held Catholicism to attain that happy result. Compromise had become a second nature to him in the pursuit of his noble aim, and from the Catholic point of view it was his great weakness just as from the Protestant one it was his principal virtue. He was understandably out of temper with the Pope, who refused to acknowledge his unquestionable title, and thoughtful, far-sighted men such as Peter Canisius wondered anxiously whether, in the circumstances, he might not be persuaded to make dangerous concessions—if only to spite His Holiness.

St. Peter trudged into Augsburg, then, with no elation in his heart. Though one of the Emperor's trusted and honoured advisers he passed almost unnoticed in the brilliant throng, a shabbily dressed, inconspicuous little priest, accompanied by a gawky clodhopper. He had discovered this person, a certain Wolfgang, at Prague, where he was trying his vocation and, incidentally, the patience of the community. A country lad with little aptitude for anything but giving trouble, he had so exasperated the Fathers that they appealed to Peter for relief. Peter's solution, as in many another case, was to take Wolfgang into his personal service, which was exactly what the young fellow desired. The Saint at once explained the situation to Laynez, and Wolfgang, from being a

[1] *Die Chroniken der deutschen Städte*, vol. xxxii, Augsburg, p. xxxiii.

malcontent, turned into a loyal and happy squire who had a thoroughly exciting time by his master's side at banquets and interviews.[1]

The splendour of the assembled Courts, the stately ceremonies and social functions in their setting of architectural perfection, made little impression on St. Peter's eyes. He saw beneath the glittering surface to the slimy, bitter depths that were seeping through and poisoning all the wells of goodness and gladness in his country. " Dear God," he wrote during the first days of the Diet, " how many men incline to schism ! As for the Catholics, with the exception of the bishops their thoughts and talk are all of taking up arms against the Pope. Sadly I say it, there is a dead set against the Holy See, as though the Turks and heretics did not provide a sufficiency of enemies. For the love of Our Lord I therefore beg all the Fathers and Brothers earnestly to implore the mercy of God on the Germans."[2]

Peter's heart at this time was dominated by two great desires, to see the German bishops initiate a campaign of local reform and to witness the reopening of the Council of Trent. During the Diet he worked and schemed indefatigably for both ends, only to discover that the second and more important was unattainable while the Pope continued to refuse recognition to the Emperor. But, through his friendship with Cardinal Truchsess and Bishop Julius Pflug, he had opportunities to do a great deal for the other cause and used them unsparingly. Truchsess was the acknowledged leader of the bishops, and to him Peter, who lodged only a few doors from his residence and at his expense, stood in the relation of adviser-in-chief. " He is so attached to me," wrote the Saint, " that he seems to forget his dignity altogether, wishing to abide by my opinion in everything."[3] The upshot was that a council of the bishops came into existence, with Julius Pflug as president, to discuss the main problems confronting the Church in Germany. Though nothing decisive could be done without the help of the Pope, it was something already achieved to have roused the episcopate, if only to that little extent, from its long torpor. Peter boldly presented himself to each bishop in turn, reckless of snubs provided he could get them to subsidize a student or two at the German College, Rome, or to give him an alms towards the purchase of a hostel for the poor scholars of Augsburg who were scattered in mean lodging-houses about the city, with no one to care for their morals or their faith. More often than not he came away empty-handed, for the

---

[1] Braunsberger, *Epistulae*, vol. ii, pp. 372–3.   [2] Braunsberger, *Epistulae*, vol. ii, p. 376.
[3] Braunsberger, *Epistulae*, vol. ii, pp. 372, 379.

prelates had no fire in them, no eager zeal to meet his own. To play the fine gentleman was their ambition, to have a good time, and to be left in peace.[1]

Cardinal Truchsess, however, made up for his brethren's indifference. He insisted on having Peter to live with him in his palace and soon broached the project of a permanent Jesuit foundation in Augsburg. To take advantage of the fine opportunity offered by the presence at the Diet of large numbers of Italians, Spaniards, and Frenchmen, the Saint had summoned Delanoy and Couvillon to assist him in the work of confessional and pulpit. Their coming made a tiny Jesuit community an accomplished fact, which, combined with the possibilities of Augsburg as a mission field and the fairly tolerant attitude of the Protestants, caused Peter warmly to espouse the project of his Cardinal friend. He pointed out to Laynez the convenience of Augsburg as a place of residence for a Provincial, situated, as one might say it was, " in the very marrow of Germany." Thence, as from a watch-tower, one might survey the whole country and send help where it was most needed, *co-operante Domino*. But he pointed out the difficulties, too, the chief being " the singular disfavour " with which the Jesuits were regarded, not only by Protestants but by many Catholics, on account of their undisguised devotion to the Holy See.

In Augsburg, during the Diet and afterwards, the Saint's work became so extensive and multifarious that no detailed record of it is possible. The Emperor and Cardinal Truchsess both seem to have regarded him as their proper man. He was always at their beck and call, ready to undertake journeys for them at a moment's notice, to advise or write or speak as they might consider that the interests of religion demanded. It might almost be said that he kept his finger on the Emperor's pulse, watchful for the slightest sign of weakness. If he thought he detected it he would at once begin to storm Heaven with his prayers and never rest until the real or imagined crisis had passed. At the Diet, business proceeded with exasperating slowness. Indeed, to judge by the report of Councillor Mair who was present, the chief business of princes and prelates appears to have been the consumption of strong drink. He says that the Emperor had " prayed and admonished the Electors and Estates in a gracious, paternal manner to put some limit to their everlasting and inordinate drunkenness."[2] To their Congress might have been applied the words

[1] Braunsberger, *Epistulae*, vol. ii, pp. 379–80.
[2] *Die Chroniken der deutschen Städte*, vol. xxxii, p. 350.

said of a more famous one: "*Il ne marche pas, mais il danse.*" What with banquets and social functions of every description, it was not until May that the members found leisure for State affairs. The Acts of the Colloquy of Worms, largely in St. Peter's handwriting, were then read publicly and caused much rejoicing in Catholic circles. But the Protestants soon had their revenge when the all-important question of the Council came up for discussion. Appealed to with great earnestness by Cardinal Truchsess, they replied that they would be delighted to patronize the Council on condition that it was held within the Empire; that the Pope first freed all Catholic bishops from their oath of allegiance to him; that all questions were decided solely by appeal to the Scriptures; that their theologians were allowed to vote on equal terms with the Catholic bishops; and that the former decrees of Trent were officially declared invalid. It was a hopeless *impasse*, but it had at least the wholesome effect of still further rousing Catholics from the vain dreams of ' reunion ' which had kept them from paying sufficient attention to the workable alternative of a reformation of the Church from within.

It was for such a reformation that St. Peter had long been pleading, and now he laboured might and main to stir up the enthusiasm of those best qualified to promote it. " If the Catholics were to show even a tenth part of the vigilance and diligence of their adversaries, I should not be so perplexed," he told Nadal. To obtain the help of Heaven he ordered the daily recitation of the Litany of the Saints in the colleges of Vienna, Prague, and Ingolstadt, a custom which was afterwards adopted permanently by the whole Society of Jesus.[1] On his urgent recommendation, the Fathers also had resort to corporal austerities. The most essential preliminary and, indeed, *sine qua non*, of the Council was to bring about a reconciliation between the Pope and the Emperor. Each letter of the many that Peter dispatched to Rome carried an appeal to Laynez to seize every least opening for a good word to His Holiness. Alas, Laynez no more than Ferdinand was in favour at the Vatican, but he did what he could through friends in the College of Cardinals, and a little later on, when the Pope lay ill in bed, he visited him and told him how generous the Emperor had been in all his dealings with the Jesuits, how true a Catholic he had proved himself and how anxious he was to promote the interests of the Church.[2]

To his deep disappointment St. Peter learned from Rome that

---

[1] St. Peter would seem to have imposed the Litanies on his colleges as something allied to fasting, disciplines and hair-shirts—in fact as a form of intercessory penance for a time of emergency.

[2] Braunsberger, *Epistulae*, vol. ii, p. 471.

Ferdinand was regarded in official circles there with the greatest disfavour, and even accounted a heretic. " Lovers and promoters of peace are not given a chance," he complained to Laynez. " We here see for ourselves that never before was the Emperor more conscientious in his duty to God or more solicitous for the approval of good men. Very soon, I hope, he will show his mettle clearly. May Our Lord Jesus by your Paternity's prayers confirm and increase what He has begun in the soul of this Prince. The chief obstacle to concord between him and the Pope is that neither man will trust the other."[1] The proof to which Peter referred followed almost at once. On May 15, 1559, the Protestant members of the Diet had presented a remonstrance to Ferdinand vehemently demanding that the Ecclesiastical Reservation of the Religious Peace should be abolished. It will be remembered that the Reservation was the only remaining legal guarantee of Church property which still remained unconfiscated in Protestant territories. The value of the measure to the Catholics was that, besides preserving their churches for a better day, it removed temptation from the path of their less saintly prelates. To go over to the Reformation, as it were in full pontificals, with all dear properties intact, was one thing, and to go over mitreless, prebendless, and landless was quite another. According to the Reservation, if a bishop or canon liked to secede from the Church it was his own affair, but he might not steal the diocese or the diocesan revenues from his flock.

At Regensburg two years earlier the Protestants had started their first campaign against the Reservation, but Ferdinand, counselled and encouraged by St. Peter among others, had held out against them. Now they tried again and with greater determination, demanding, according to the report of Queen Elizabeth's agent in Augsburg, " that it be free and frank for every man to accept and profess the Gospel, and that for this profession neither laymen nor clerks shall lose anything from their former livings : that if a priest or canon of the high colleges or cathedral churches give himself to this religion he shall not lose his prebend or benefice, for if they be deprived of their livings the just and right doctrine is defaced and condemned. Against this request the Papists do spurn and kick ; saying, if a clerk might have a wife and his benefice, then no clerks or few would be unmarried."[2]

Faced with these demands, Ferdinand was in a position of peculiar difficulty. The Protestants controlled much of the revenue of the Empire

[1] Braunsberger, *Epistulae*, vol. ii, p. 425.
[2] Stevenson, *Calendar of State Papers*, Foreign Series of the Reign of Elizabeth 1558–1559, p. 259.

and he was sorely in need of financial assistance. During May he almost went on his knees to the Estates for money to keep up his garrisons against the Turks along the 160 miles of frontier in Hungary and Istria. He had other costly commitments, too, which caused the English agent to write home that " the discovery of some gold-producing island would be necessary to bear such charges," so the temptation to make a bargain with the Protestants must have been terribly alluring. Yet the same English agent reported to Elizabeth that though " assuredly a most clement Prince, he was the keenest advocate on the side of the Papists." On June 13th he gave his answer to the Protestant remonstrance in the following terms : " No matter what sufferings and calamities the Emperor may be called upon to endure for the sake of the Catholic Faith, it is his firm purpose to persevere in the same unto death, nor will he ever consent to the withdrawal of the Reservation." With regard to the general council, Ferdinand was equally emphatic, avowing that he would not raise a little finger in support of the outrageous claims put forward by the Protestants. In his interviews with the Emperor Peter Canisius was bound by an oath of secrecy, so we shall never know exactly the extent of his contribution to this important victory of the Catholic Church.

One splendid result of the Emperor's stand was a change in the attitude of Pope Paul IV. Through his spies at Augsburg the English agent, Mundt,[1] discovered and reported to Queen Elizabeth, July 19, 1559, that the Pope had " recently written to the Emperor by the Cardinal of Augsburg, highly praising his constancy and piety in upholding the ancient religion and exhorting him to persevere in it ; promising that the approbation of himself and the cardinals for the Emperor's confirmation shall be speedily obtained."[2] Pope Paul died just a month later, before he could fulfil his promise, but it serves his memory as, perhaps, the best of epitaphs.

While history thus shaped itself in Germany, St. Peter's fortunes were being determined in Rome. Though by no means on good terms with their Bishop, nor themselves all exemplary ecclesiastics, the canons of Augsburg Cathedral had been impressed by Peter's character and ability. As Augsburg was the principal city of the Empire, its cathedral pulpit had come to be regarded as the chief platform of German Catholicism. The post of preacher there was no less important than that held by a *conférencier* of Notre-Dame in the modern world, for his was the representative voice of the German Church to which all parties lent attentive

---

[1] " Bribes for spies " formed an item in Mundt's bills to Cecil. Stevenson, *Calendar of State Papers, Foreign Series of the Reign of Elizabeth*, p. 414.
[2] Stevenson, l.c., p. 388.

and critical ears. It had been worthily held up to his death in 1558 by the eloquent and saintly Dominican, Johann Fabri, on whom St. Peter had conferred the doctorate at Ingolstadt in 1552. Until Peter's appearance in Augsburg the canons had been unable to find a successor to Fabri. Then they knew that God had sent them their man and, on May 9, 1559, jointly addressed the following petition to the General of the Jesuits:

REVEREND AND ESTEEMED FATHER IN CHRIST.

Dr. Johann Fabri, who for several years filled the office of preacher and writer at our Cathedral Church, died last year, to the profound sorrow of our people and of all good men. Seeing thereafter the remainder of the little Catholic flock in this most celebrated city of Germany as it were deprived of its pastor and scattered perilously in the midst of prowling wolves, we considered that nothing was more necessary than the immediate provision of a preacher who would fill the place of the dead man with equal distinction and success. But men of that kind are few in the present stormy age, when everything has been corrupted by the ferment of heresy, and, even if persons of suitable learning and doctrine are to be found, it is not safe to entrust them at once with the responsibility of teaching in public, since we have learned by experience how seriously at present we stand in danger from false brethren. Considering, then, the circumspection and care demanded of us by this difficult matter, which involves the Catholic religion and the salvation of souls, and wishing to be completely secure in the appointment of a preacher for the excellent people of Augsburg, a man who would nourish their souls by the example of his blameless life no less than by his orthodox teaching, we most urgently entreated and begged the profoundly learned Doctor Peter Canisius to undertake this task for the glory of God and the good of the Church. He at length consented, on condition that you, his Superior, sanctioned the arrangement.

As you understand, Reverend Father General, the great good that can be done for religion in this most famous City of all Germany, and as it is the chief purpose of your Order to help the Church wherever she requires assistance, we certainly think that you could scarcely do anything more pleasing to God and more serviceable to the Catholic Church than to grant us the services as our preacher of your noble brother, Peter Canisius, who is illustrious throughout all Germany for his learning and for the sanctity of a life beautiful with every virtue.

We now pray your kindness with all our hearts and beseech you earnestly to content us. By so doing you will earn the favour of God and make us permanently your and your Order's debtors.

> CHRISTOPHER FREYBERG, Dean, and the whole Chapter of the Church of Augsburg.[1]

Cardinal Truchsess added his entreaty to that of the canons, rendering it well-nigh impossible for Laynez to resist. But it was a strange position for a busy Jesuit Provincial to hold, and the General must have had serious misgivings. He warned Peter to be careful to keep his independence, as the visitation of his colleges and other Province concerns would necessitate frequent absences from Augsburg. It was not an easy matter to arrange to everybody's satisfaction. The canons provided the Saint with a small and rather dilapidated house which he accepted gratefully, but when they endeavoured to settle a regular pension on him he turned recalcitrant and obstinately refused to be drawn into such a contract. If they liked they might give him enough for the support of himself and his companion but it must be as a pure alms and not in payment for services. Reluctantly they agreed, and a tiny sum, barely sufficient to keep body and soul together, was put at his disposal. Thus it was that Peter became a householder, faced with the famous problem of finding a cook. He managed somehow, possibly, as one letter seems to suggest, by grappling with the mysteries of the kitchen himself. Having so much writing to do and so little time for it, he ventured to ask the General whether he knew of any unemployed young Jesuit who might help him as secretary : " If you possess such a one with a gift for literary composition, I would be very glad of his assistance, provided he is so good and mortified that he will not mind having me alone for company."[2] No Jesuit was available, but he had the luck to secure instead the services of a young layman named Andreas Stör, and, thus equipped, started his long campaign for the soul of Augsburg.

How vigorously it was pursued may be gathered from the fact that between June 24th, when he opened his course, and the end of the year he preached fifty long and eloquent sermons at the Cathedral. The pressure of this work varied a good deal, most of it being crowded into the sacred seasons of Advent and Lent. Up to October he had assistance from Bishop Dornvogel, a suffragan of Augsburg, but after that became sole master of the Cathedral pulpit and continued for several years to perform its heavy duties with only an occasional helping-hand from others.

---

[1] Braunsberger, *Epistulae*, vol. ii, pp. 835–6. [2] Braunsberger, *Epistulae*, vol. ii, p. 439.

When first entreated to shoulder the burden he had felt very diffident about his ability. "I have warned the canons," he told Laynez, "that I entirely lack the graces of speech and oratory which born Germans possess and which the leading preachers of this Cathedral have usually shown. This disability will prevent me from retaining the favour and the numbers of my auditors. Consequently I have often thought that I might do better if I devoted myself to writing, and were altogether employed in confirming the Catholics here with my pen against the leaven of the sectaries. I think I might thus hope to please our simple-hearted German brethren and also to do them some good in Our Lord. At any rate, I might make a fresh contribution by at least showing more charity and moderation than the majority of writers, who mix a sort of violence and human prejudice with the argument of their books. That harsh method of treatment and cure offends rather than heals the Germans. This is not to say that I believe in rushing hastily into print but only that my reflections on some matters of controversy might, perhaps, be worth submitting to our Fathers for correction with a view to their possible publication. I mention the matter, that as a son to his father I may lay bare to you the secrets of my heart and satisfy my conscience, which has thus often impelled me."[1]

Before he had been a year at his post Peter was the best loved and hated man in the great Imperial City. He had not been at work more than a couple of months when the Venetian Ambassador at Vienna reported home that his sermons were attracting larger congregations than had been seen for many a year and, six weeks later, Laynez was informed that, as a result of them, many Protestants had already abjured their heresy. In February, 1560, the Dean of the Augsburg Chapter had a similar tale for the Elector of Mainz: "Our Cathedral Preacher, Dr. Canisius, has in so short a time achieved magnificent and unhoped-for results with both the Government and the people of the City." The Dean spoke also of the daily converts being made, whom another man described as "fine, plump fishes." "The face of Augsburg has changed," he continued, "and who knows what it may not become in the future!"[2]

But the Protestant preachers, of whom there were many in the city, did not take Peter's assault with folded arms and silent tongues. They made their pulpits ring with denunciation of him and spread rumours reflecting on both his morals and his orthodoxy. Referring to these in a letter to Father Goudanus, he said:

<hr />

[1] Braunsberger, *Epistulae*, vol. ii, pp. 397-8.   [2] Braunsberger, *Epistulae*, vol. ii, pp. 856-7.

Your Reverence must congratulate me on being written down a heretic, and even a heresiarch, by the heretics. They are dubbing the Jesuits ' Canists ' and alleging that they deny Christ to be Mediator as well as Intercessor. Well, what would you ? Let us love those who persecute and calumniate us, and take it for praise to be thus treated and stigmatized for the Name of Jesus. Let us be glad and rejoice that we are accounted worthy to hear ourselves called *Jesuwider*, soul-murderer, hell-hound, ravening wolf, prince of hypocrites, etc. With these blossoms are we garlanded. Blessed be God who, perchance, intends them as the preliminaries to a harder battle and a violent death. . . .[1]

Another rumour spread abroad was that St. Peter would shortly abandon the Church of Rome, in which he did not really believe. Outside Augsburg, the apostate papal nuncio, Vergerio, carried on a savage campaign against him. He assured the Duke of Württemberg that the Jesuit leader was " a real heretic and a man of the most abandoned wickedness," quite capable of the infanticides to which, according to Lutheran belief, his brethren in Venice had recently had resort in order to cover up their infamies.

Peter shrugged his shoulders, as far as he was personally concerned, but he found it hard that the work of his Order should be hampered and prejudiced by such monstrous calumnies. Early in 1560, Stanislaus Hosius, Bishop of Ermland, was sent by the Pope to Vienna to treat with the Emperor about the reopening of the Council of Trent and other matters. His first request was that he might have St. Peter as his adviser at Court, and to it Cardinal Truchsess promptly demurred, whereupon Polanco, probably smiling to himself the while, informed Father Juan Vitoria that Peter could not go and that they must try to make the Legate content with his Reverence as a substitute. Hosius, however, knew his Vitoria too well, and continued to petition for Peter until the resistance of the Cardinal was overborne. Then the Augsburg canons started to lament, saying that in the Saint's absence there would be nobody to feed " *das hungerig Volcke mit solchen suessen unnd angenemen wordten unnd lere.*"[2] Their protests gave Cardinal Truchsess an opportunity to ventilate a subject dear to his and to St. Peter's heart. Replying to them, he said that he, too, had opposed the departure of their Preacher until convinced of its necessity for the good of the Church. Besides, the Preacher had stipulated for occasional leave of absence when originally accepting office.

[1] Braunsberger, *Epistulae*, vol. ii, p. 745. The nearest English equivalent of the epithet ' Jesuwider is Antichrist, but the paronomasia of the original, Jesuiter=Jesuwider, is lost in translation.
[2] Braunsberger, *Epistulae*, vol. ii, p. 859.—" With such sweet and pleasant words and instruction."

He was certain to be summoned to the Council of Trent when it reopened and his General also must be considered to have certain claims on his services. He, the Cardinal, had consequently come to the conclusion that the best way to provide for the pulpit of Augsburg during such necessary absences of its Preacher would be to establish a college of his brethren in Augsburg. Would the canons therefore kindly let him know what they were prepared to do in the matter? The canons answered that they were prepared to do nothing whatever, because the Protestants, who formed the majority of the population, heartily detested the Jesuits and might cause serious trouble if they were admitted.[1]

Peter remained away from Augsburg just two months, helping Hosius with his negotiations in Vienna and going the rounds of the widely separated colleges. Incidentally, as he had access to the Emperor on this occasion, he took much trouble to procure a whole series of privileges for the Catholic printers of Cologne, one indication among many of his life-long enthusiasm for the diffusion of good books. Back in Augsburg by the beginning of July, 1560, he resumed his ministerial work and had preached another fifty sermons before the year closed. That made ninety for the nine months of this year spent by him in the City, a remarkable total when it is remembered that they were all carefully prepared, often directly controversial, and full of patristic and theological learning. Every Catholic doctrine attacked by the Reformers was solidly defended in them, and every aspect of Catholic life and devotion explained and eloquently commended. One who knew him better than most, his half-brother Theodoric Canisius, Rector of Munich College, reported to Rome in the following terms after a visit to Augsburg: " Father Provincial seems to me to be weighed down continually by too heavy a burden. Besides the anxiety attaching to his office as ruler of this Province, he has several other responsibilities. I say nothing about the terribly laborious task of preaching, which, in such a place and at such a time, is ample work for the whole of a man's energies. I know that whenever he is to preach, which is very often indeed, he stays up preparing for it a good part of the night. Moreover, his life is one of unremitting abstinence."[2]

Within twelve months of his starting operations, the canons of Augsburg informed Cardinal Truchsess that Peter had already won back nine hundred people to the Church, men and women who, the previous Easter, had communicated according to the Lutheran rite.[3] A good number of these

[1] Braunsberger, *Epistulae*, vol. ii, pp. 860–62.   [2] Braunsberger, *Epistulae*, vol. iii, p. 600.
[3] Braunsberger, *Epistulae*, vol. ii, p. 653.

were probably lapsing or lapsed Catholics rather than formal Protestants, but of such people, too, his harvest was great. Thus, during the Lent and Easter of 1561, a hundred converts in the fullest sense are reported as the result of his sermons. "Not in living memory," said the narrator, "have so many people approached the Sacraments of Confession and Communion devoutly as this year. Some came who had never before been to Confession; and the *Spiritual Exercises* were given, not only to ordinary people, but to men and women of illustrious birth, such as Counts and Countesses, who all derived great profit from them. Great numbers have begun the practice of weekly Confession and Communion, with singular consolation and advantage to their souls. Meantime, the Lutheran preachers are making an uproar, furious to see their prey snatched from their very jaws. It is said here openly that if Dr. Canisius remains much longer in this City the heretical preachers will expel him by violent means."[1]

Among the distinguished people whom it was Peter's joy and privilege to restore to full Catholic communion, two great ladies figured prominently, Ursula, Baroness of Lichtenstein, and Sybil, Countess of Eberstein, the wives of George and Mark Fugger. The Lady Ursula does not seem to have been a professing Lutheran when she first heard Peter preach. Probably, like so many others, she was a very negligent Catholic who would have followed the example of her sisters-in-law and apostatized outright but for the restraining influence of her husband. In a letter to Cardinal Truchsess, September 20, 1560, Peter gives the following details about her:

At first the wife of George Fugger was hostile to the Catholics, but now, after a few heart-to-heart talks I have had with her, she loves us greatly, brings her whole household frequently to the Sacraments, and is most zealous in making converts, whom she nurses and strengthens in the faith. I might almost call her house a monastery, so frequently does she have family prayers. Forgetful of her high position and dignities, she devotes her time to almsgiving, to the preparation of ornaments for churches and altars, to the making with her own hands of vestments and other things required for the beauty of the House of God. She sees to it that her daughters do the same, and she and they also make clothes and shirts for the poor. Before this time, she hardly entered a church once in many weeks but now she spends many hours there almost every day, and, though she has a long way to come to the Cathedral, she never misses the sermon on a feast-day. . . . She shows

[1] Braunsberger, *Epistulae*, vol. iii, p. 591.

herself a generous patron and helper of poor Catholics whom we often commend to her kindness. But as regards ourselves, we have earnestly begged her not to send anything to our house, and have returned such gifts as arrived against our wishes. This is not because we think lightly of her good-will but rather to restrain her extravagant generosity in our regard, which we prefer to see exercised in the service of Christ and His poor. I hope that this hasty narrative will give your piety consolation, and excite you to thank Our Lord for the conversion and holy life of this noble lady.[1]

The other lady, Countess Sybil, was an ardent Protestant, so ardent that, to her honour, she had spurned a bribe of 80,000 gold florins, promised by her father-in-law, the famous Anton Fugger, if she would become a Catholic. It was not only the Protestants, we see, who used such inducements ! Sybil resisted all attempts to get her to speak with St. Peter, and, according to one man's evidence, would not allow his name to be mentioned in her presence. However, through curiosity or for some other natural reason she one day appeared in the Cathedral for his sermon. What affected her so much we do not know, but she at once sought an interview with the Saint, had several subsequent talks, and by January 19, 1561, when he wrote to tell the good news to Laynez, was making the *Spiritual Exercises* under his direction. On February 1st he wrote again : " Thanks be to God by whose grace I have now reconciled to the Church that Countess of whom I told you." Her conversion was the sensation of the day in Augsburg, so much so that Catholics felt it must have been miraculous. The story ran that the Saint had appeared to Sybil in a dream and that, troubled like Pilate's wife by her experience, she had sent for him next day, recognized him, and capitulated to his learning and sanctity.[2] As neither the Saint nor the lady herself have left a word of testimony to the truth of this story, we are justified in rejecting it. A good deal of the attraction and inspiration of Peter's life is due to the fact that he was emphatically a ' homely ' saint, and achieved his great results by means which God places at the disposal of everybody. He and his brother-Jesuit, St. Robert Bellarmine, were no thaumaturges, either during life or after death. Indeed, they are conspicuous among the saints for their economy in miracles ; and that is a singularity or distinction, or whatever one cares to call it, of which they should not lightly be deprived.

---

[1] Braunsberger, *Epistulae*, vol. iii, pp. 653–4. Peter procured for his convert from Cologne a copy of the admirable devotional work of his Carthusian friend, Landspergius, *Pharetra divini amoris*. He remained her spiritual director for many years.

[2] Braunsberger, *Epistulae*, vol. iii, pp. 658–60.

The conversion of the two ladies brought Peter into close touch with the Fugger family, a relationship that enabled him to assist many worthy causes. Even before the event, however, old Anton, the head of the House and for many years the greatest financial power in Europe, had been profoundly impressed by the Saint's activities in Augsburg. It was his intention to build a magnificent college for the Jesuits, a plan which he bequeathed to his heirs on his unexpected death in 1560, but which the opposition of the Cathedral Chapter frustrated. St. Peter and his companion, Father Elderen, who, like Father Perez afterwards, assisted him with his correspondence and in the confessional, now took spiritual charge of the *Fuggerei*, that famous, self-contained village of almshouses in the midst of Augsburg which still exists to delight the eye of a connoisseur in architecture. All through these years Peter worked tirelessly to help the deserving poor, people whose poverty was due to no fault of their own but to misfortune or illness, or because they had lost their jobs owing to their Catholicism. There were large numbers of them in Augsburg. Street begging was illegal in Germany then as it is to-day, and the old trouble of quarter-day, when rent fell due, was as familiar as in modern London.[1] Crowds of these unfortunate people used to come to St. Peter for assistance and, with the enthusiastic collaboration of Ursula and Sybil Fugger, he did marvels for them. He preached a great charity sermon during the bitter winter of 1559–1560 to procure clothes for the tattered and shivering students of the City who, with German grit, were martyrizing themselves for the sake of an education. Referring to the multiplication of the loaves in the sixth chapter of St. John, he said that he did not ask his hearers to feed several thousand people, as did Our Lord, nor to leave everything to the poor, as did St. Laurence and St. Cyprian, nor to give half of their goods, like Zacchaeus, nor if anybody had two coats, to part with one. " This alone I beg and urge that we should extend our generosity to poor students and contribute something to provide them with clothes, as was done last year. Truly it is a great work of mercy to clothe the naked and one that will have the blessing of God and an eternal reward." Then, piling text upon text, he showed how faith and justice, prudence and common gratitude, required the exercise of such charity. " Try," he said, a month later, " to do an alms-deed five times this week. And I hope you will not forget the poor students. If, besides, anybody is able to visit the poor, or to have some poor person to dinner with him for three days, it will certainly be an act pleasing to the eyes of God." How

---

[1] Braunsberger, *Epistulae*, vol. iii, p. 595.

little he spared the susceptibilities of the upper classes is plain from another sermon preached at this time :

If we consider those vested with civil authority, how pitiable it is that they have so little care for the common good, and that they impose all sorts of taxes, *steurgelt, tribut und schatzung,* instead of lightening the common burdens. If we consider the rich, what do we more frequently see than the abuse of property in the service of pride, luxury, and fleshly indulgence, with corresponding neglect of the poor ? And if we consider the plain, comfortable citizen, is it not too bad that he should be so wrapped up in his possessions as to neglect the poor and to show them neither justice, nor mercy, nor charity ? Alas, we do not stop at that, but even use harsh words and unfair judgments, saying that the poor man is undeserving of our pity or our alms, that he is unknown to us, and so on. And we prefer to let our goods perish rather than see them employed for our poor neighbour's advantage. Is it not a sin and a shame that rich people should spend as many florins on one banquet as would support ten or twenty or a hundred poor ? Is it not inexcusable that there should be so many people in rags while our clothes-chests are stuffed with abundance of garments ? And what defence can there be for women who are never done acquiring jewels and aids to beauty, who are always thinking of something new in hopes of out-shining rivals, who spend as much on clothes in one year as formerly would have sufficed for five or six years, who are never satisfied with the delicacy of the material, for whom no food is sufficiently dainty, no wine choice enough, no ornament good enough to comfort their stomachs and to deck out and exalt their bodies of clay ? Their ambition is to be of the nobility and to have *Junkers* for sons, and so they spend as much as counts and princes. What wonder, then, is it that God should have punished us with the present scarcity and famine ? We are so lacking in mercy, aye, and even so scandalously abuse the gifts of God, that it would have been better and more desirable had we all been born and remained mendicants. Better that, I say, than that our riches should lead us into sin and scandal, and perhaps even, in many a case, drag us down to certain damnation. Think, then, my brothers, of the example of Christ and take the poor to your hearts. Does not the very weather preach to us, this cold and bitter season when the poor have most need of our pity ? Who does not know the dearness of fire-wood and all other things which the poor must buy ?

We see every day the number of the poor increasing. Craftsmen cannot find anything to do nor unskilled workmen a job. They either have nothing to sell or get next to nothing for what they may have, and all the time they are faced with the problem of paying rent and of supporting wife and children.[1]

Besides the two ladies mentioned above, St. Peter brought many other persons of rank and distinction back to whole-hearted Catholicism. Lower down in the social scale his conquests were unending, among them being a genial Anabaptist named Hans Jakob, the head of his sect in Augsburg. The Anabaptists were regarded by normal men and women in those days as Bolsheviks are regarded to-day, and Hans had spent a long time in prison for his opinions. But he was a likeable man, despite his views, and both Protestants and Catholics strove earnestly to win him to *their* views and so to secure his release. When the ministers had failed, the civil authorities invited Father Canisius to come to the prison and see what he could do. Convincing Hans was a slow business, but Peter went on with it doggedly, until one happy morning he was able to produce him before the assembled Senate where he abjured his errors publicly.[2]

Had Cardinal Truchsess had his way St. Peter would have been not only Preacher but Administrator of his diocese. While in Rome for the conclave following on the death of Paul IV, he fell ill and was visited by the kindly Polanco. "Tell Father Canisius," he said, "that I shall not be able to write to him during the conclave but that I most earnestly commend my diocese to his care and beg him to consider himself, as it were, its bishop, and to advise me from his observations as to what measures he considers suitable or what provisions for the diocese he judges ought to be made."[3] That was a generous gesture of trust, but it did not afford Peter much consolation. He told Laynez that the diocese embraced " more than a thousand parishes in which an infinity of scandals abounded," that the clergy were ill-instructed and apathetic, that the Cathedral Chapter usurped the rights of the Cardinal, their bishop, that the Cardinal himself was " full of good desires but slow in carrying them out," that the Germans hated him because of his loyalty to the Pope, that hardly any priests of the diocese recited the Divine Office, either because unable to obtain the special Augsburg Breviary or because the

[1] Braunsberger, *Epistulae*, vol. iii, pp. 628–30.
[2] Braunsberger, *Epistulae*, vol. iii, p. 609; Sacchinus, *Vita P. Petri Canisii*, pp. 195–6.
[3] Braunsberger, *Epistulae*, vol. ii, p. 517.

Offices in it were too long.[1] It is typical of the Saint that he should have endeavoured to solve the Breviary problem on his own account. He was always a zealous promoter of liturgical prayer and had written books to help people to follow Mass more intelligently and profitably. In the same spirit he never missed a chance of impressing on priests the sacredness of their obligation to make the Divine Office the centre of their devotional lives, and all the greater, then, was his distress to find it so much neglected in Augsburg. That City, like Milan and a few other dioceses of the Western Church, enjoyed the privilege of a special liturgy which carried with it the use of a Breviary different in many respects from the one to which priests in general were bound. But the Augsburg Breviary had not been reprinted for some time and, like its Roman counterpart, stood in sore need of revision, a task from which, in both cases, responsible men shrank in terror. Local traditions and prejudices would have needed the most delicate and cautious handling and there were all sorts of other obstacles, economic and historical. Even to-day, after many revisions, the Roman Breviary is far from perfect because local minorities made such a pother when even the lightest of hands was laid on their traditions. St. Peter, however, in his eagerness to help the priests of Augsburg, brushed the difficulties aside. As nobody else showed the slightest inclination for the task he would revise the Augsburg Breviary himself, and for the purpose set apart two precious hours of each crowded day which he devoted to the rearrangement of the Scriptural lessons and the expurgation of the Second Nocturns. It was a gallant attempt but, in the nature of things, foredoomed to failure, except that it led to the formation of a commission which, after many years of hard work, produced a new *Breviarium Augustanum* in Rome in 1569.[2]

On December 26, 1559, the Catholic Church had been given her new Pope in the person of Gian Angelo Medici, a friendly, cheerful, and generous-hearted Milanese who assumed the title of Pius IV. Pius made a complete contrast to his haughty and imperious predecessor. Even before his election he had been known in Rome as the " Father of the Poor." But two things, in particular, promised well for the Church, the fact that the new Pope was an old friend of the Emperor, and that his best-loved nephew was Carlo Borromeo, the Saint who personified Catholic reform in the South just as Peter Canisius did in the North. Though Borromeo was only twenty-one years of age Pius immediately invited him to Rome and made him Cardinal and Secretary, nepotism, the old, disastrous weakness of Popes, being on this occasion completely justified.[1] It is not surprising, then, with all these friendly omens, that the hopes of German Catholics ran high—perhaps too high. The resumption of the Council of Trent seemed at last to have come within the range of practical propositions, an expectation that roused some of the German bishops to unusual bursts of activity. At the beginning of 1560, the Archbishop of Mainz, one of the great princes of the Empire, dispatched an envoy to Augsburg with an invitation to St. Peter to come and help him in the reformation of his Electorate. The other ecclesiastical Electors of Trier and Cologne followed suit, and so did the powerful Archbishop of Salzburg. Peter was very glad of these invitations because of what they indicated. " Never did Germany promise a finer harvest than I see to depend on these Prelates," he wrote to Laynez.[2] But the canons of the Augsburg Chapter had first claim on his services and refused, even when appealed to by the Emperor, to let him go to Mainz. He was far too valuable in their city, they explained, to be spared for work elsewhere, even temporarily. By September, 1560, he had come to be so greatly reverenced by his congregations that they remained on their knees all the time he was preaching, a fact which a Cologne visitor described as *summopere admirandum*, since in his own Catholic city to go on one knee for the Elevation at Mass passed for a remarkable effort of piety.[3]

Some of Peter's conversions, and particularly that of an eminent Lutheran preacher, so much interested the new Pope that he addressed a Brief of congratulation to the Saint in March, 1561 :

[1] Carlo was soon on intimate terms with the Jesuits, particularly with the good Spanish Father, John Baptist Ribera, who had a deep effect on his spiritual life. A few years later, however, when the Saint was Archbishop of Milan, his youthful ardour led him into extremes of mortification and self-renunciation, to the annoyance of his uncle, the Pope, who, giving ear to tittle-tattle, blamed the Jesuits for it. Ribera was then strictly forbidden to go near his friend and penitent and the whole Society of Jesus went under a cloud. But the Pope soon discovered the truth, that it was not Ribera nor any other Jesuit who was responsible, whereupon he made ample amends for his temporary harshness. All this is explained in a very interesting letter from Polanco to St. Peter, about May 20, 1564. Braunsberger, *Epistulae*, vol. iv, pp. 530–6.

[2] Braunsberger, *Epistulae*, vol. ii, p. 586. Peter had hopes, too, at this time, for the conversion of England, as Queen Elizabeth was toying with the project of an Austrian alliance. The idea was that she should accept Charles, the third son of the Emperor. She caused her agent in Augsburg to make elaborate inquiries about the young prince, and St. Peter received instructions from Rome to find a suitable confessor for him, in case he succeeded in his wooing. But Elizabeth was not serious. To the Emperor's private ear she whispered that though she was " not better affected to any house or family in Christendom than to the House of Austria, yet descending into the bottom of her heart she cannot find any inclination to leave this solitary life but rather a certain contenta-tion to continue still therein." When, not long afterwards, Peter became aware of the Queen's real sentiments towards the Church, he was sorely disappointed. " May the Lord be present to His Church in this darkness and storm," he wrote, " from which with all my heart I long to see England delivered." His own College of Prague would one day help in the deliverance, for out of it would come Edmund Campion. Stevenson, *Calendar of State Papers*, Foreign Series, 1558–1559, pp. 298–9, 395.

[3] Braunsberger, *Epistulae*, vol. ii, p. 863.

Pius PP. IIII.

Beloved Son, Health and Apostolic benediction.

It has come to Our ears through Our beloved son Otto, Cardinal of Augsburg, with what zeal, diligence and charity you labour in that City to bring back to the way of salvation the multitudes who have strayed therefrom, deceived by the frauds of the heretics, and how well you are succeeding, with the aid of divine grace. That news, for which We so much longed, has given Us great consolation. We thank Almighty God who in His mercy has already, We hear, recalled so many to the Catholic Church by means of your preaching. Press on, Son, as you have begun, and continue to strive that the greatest gain of souls may be yours. Be urgent with a business so holy and of God. Do not grow weary of the divine work. He whom you serve will requite your diligence with the reward which He has promised to good and faithful servants. If there is any favour you desire from Us which you think would help towards the salvation of souls, We shall gladly accede to your petition.

Given in Rome at St. Peter's, under the Seal of the Fisherman, March 5, 1561, in the second year of Our Pontificate.[1]

How Canisius answered to the appeal of the Holy Father may be understood from the following facts and figures. During the years 1561–1562 he was away from Augsburg six months on his Society's or the Pope's business. In the remaining eighteen months he preached at the Cathedral from 200 to 225 sermons.[2] In Lent and Advent four sermons a week was the almost invariable number, the Lenten sermons being supplemented by three discourses on Christian doctrine each week at the Cathedral or the Church of St. John the Baptist. Moreover, as in 1559 the Protestants had started catechism classes for all the children of Augsburg,[3] Peter persuaded the canons to build on to his cramped little house " *ain stublin für die knaben*," that is to say, a room in which he might gather the sons of the leading families in order to save them from the attentions of the Lutherans. There he and his companion, Father Elderen, taught the boys their religion once a week or so all the year round.[4]

---

[1] Braunsberger, *Epistulae*, vol. iii, pp. 64–5.
[2] Braunsberger, *Epistulae*, vol. iii, p. 623. It is certain that the number was over two hundred but some may have been preached in other churches.
[3] Mair, in *Die Chroniken der deutschen Städte*, vol. xxii, p. 363. Luther's *Shorter Catechism* was the text-book used.
[4] Braunsberger, *Epistulae*, vol. ii, p. 863 ; vol. iii, p. 596.

The same Father Elderen reports that "almost every day" the Saint left their house to guide somebody through the *Spiritual Exercises*. The campaign of the two men[1] worked up to a climax during the Advent of 1561, when it was Peter's privilege to publish the Indulgence granted for the reopening of the Council of Trent. There is a thrill in the reports of that time, as though the men writing them would say : Here is something unprecedented in the history of the Reformation, the spectacle of a great city that had turned Protestant slowly but surely facing about for Rome. Peter was in the pulpit every other day on this occasion, and, as for the confessional, "*integros dies et aliquam noctium partem dare debuimus*," wrote Father Elderen—we had sometimes to spend the whole day and a part of the night in it. A hint of the results is given in the following note of one of the canons to Cardinal Truchsess : " In a hundred years there has not been seen so much fervour and zeal for religion in Augsburg as during the publication of the Papal Indulgence. It was marvellous to observe the way people thronged to Confession and Communion, and to the processions. If the good Father Canisius remains here he will achieve incredible things. God be praised for it all."[2]

At this point we may be permitted to pause and cast a glance at the more domestic and intimate side of Peter's strenuous life. He was such a colossal worker, such a fighter, even, where the Church's interests were concerned, that it is possible to overlook the fundamental gentleness of his nature. And one might forget, too, owing to his preoccupation with the general business of the Church, how profound was his love for and loyalty to the Society of Jesus. That a man such as he, whose utter selflessness and noble integrity shine starlike through the murk of a terrible age, should have loved his Order and its least rules so dearly, must surely make an honest inquirer wonder whether all that has been rumoured about the ambition and mean chicanery of the Order can be the truth. Here, for instance, is a letter addressed by St. Peter from Augsburg to three young Viennese students who had offered themselves to the Society of Jesus :

My dearest Brothers in Our Lord. Your letters made me exceedingly glad, as they provided abundant testimony of the grace which Christ Our Lord has bestowed upon you and of your diligent efforts to co-operate with it. It is, indeed, a great grace to know the dark complexion of this world, and, knowing it, to detest it. Greater still is

---

[1] Father Elderen did not preach, but assisted St. Peter in instructing converts and hearing confessions.

[2] Braunsberger, *Epistulae*, vol. iii, p. 602.

the grace to offer one's entire self to the holy and lovely light of true piety which illumines the tabernacles of the just. But the greatest grace of all is to renounce the blandishments of the world and the fascinations of human life, in order to gain Christ alone, to follow Him in His poverty, to love His Cross, to despise oneself, and to have obedience for one's only law.

As you have now signed on under your Captain, Christ, so may you persevere in His high grace, never doubting but that the yoke of the Lord will daily become sweeter to you and His burden lighter. Now, having guides to direct you and masters to imitate, you hardly need any encouragement from me, but I most warmly commend your holy ambition, and with great joy inscribe your names on the roll of the brethren who have offered themselves for training in this new army of Our Lord Jesus. Your first care must be to declare war on yourselves and to achieve daily some little victory over the old Adam's concupiscences. And I beg you to become intimate with humility, the queen and mistress of God's servants, preferring nothing to your superior's will if ever you would become truly wise. May Our Lord Jesus keep and protect you for His glory, and may He give you that ardent charity which purifies, enlightens, and perfects our souls. Pray to Our Lord for me, dearest Brothers.[1]

During the summer months Peter's relatives in Nymegen hoped that he might take a holiday among them. Replying to his half-brother, Theodoric, who was at home, he said: " From my heart I pray that Christ may smile upon our kith and kin, especially on Wendelina and on all our brothers and sisters. I have no news except that it will ever be a source of intense joy to me if they remain loyal to their Catholic faith and bound together in true, mutual love, serving God rather than the world, the spirit rather than the flesh. As for seeing me, there is no reason why they should be anxious. Let us leave the question to God. To Him we live and die, the children of peace and love. And let us be assured that, in His goodness, Our Lord will do for us what is most pleasing in His eyes and best for our souls. Give to each and all my special

---

[1] Braunsberger, *Epistulae*, vol. ii, pp. 558–9. It would seem that young men in general turned almost instinctively to Peter for help and advice. There is extant by one such, " Verses to the most learned and honourable Doctor Peter Canisius, Preacher of the Cathedral of Augsburg," of which the following lines give the import:

Ad te confugio, tamquam miser exul, Asylum:
Da precibus nostris, magne Patrone, locum.
Nam mea spes in te solo inclinata recumbit,
Exhaustum nummis quaeso juvare velis.

greetings. I beg Our Lord to strengthen us all in His grace and to visit us, wheresoever we be, with His consolations."[1]

Now, reversing the procedure, we may give a letter, not written but received by St. Peter, its author a distinguished priest of Trier on whom he had conferred the doctorate when Vice-Chancellor of Ingolstadt University. It casts some light on Peter's character to know that, amid all the bustle of the subsequent years, he never lost touch with this man, though they did not again see one another :

Now at last, kindest of Fathers and most eminent doctor of the Church of God, I think it time to come to a decision about a matter on which I have long deliberated. Nothing now grieves me more, to speak the simple truth, than my failure to follow at once your Reverence's holy leading. It was at Ingolstadt that you first encouraged me in the ways of holiness, as a nobler ambition than any dignity, and ever after you failed not to exhort me along the road. The more I consider the reasons that then and afterwards deterred me from throwing in my lot with you completely, the better I understand my youthful immaturity and folly. The first of these reasons, if I remember rightly, was contained in the text, *Magister, ubi habitas ?* and the second in another text, *Unde ememus panes ?* I reflected, that is to say, that you had no colleges in Germany with secure revenues, that to beg was not a thing that could be done without loss of dignity and offence to the people of this age and country, and that I, personally, would be of no use to the Church or to your Order on account of my provincial manner of speech and my difficulty with Latin. But when our mutual, intimate converse, and still more the goodness and spiritual beauty of your life, had taken that scruple out of my heart, I became so affected by you, *per gratiam Dei,* that at the time of your departure from Ingolstadt I began to think seriously of your Order and to vow that I would one day join you in it.

On my return home, however, other snares awaited me, family trouble, love of my own diocese, and hopes of setting up a college therein. Though these things did not entirely destroy my resolution they revived my doubts. I yearned in my inexperience to be of the widest usefulness, and the result of my dreams was wasted time, broken health, and the frustration of nearly all my labours. . . . Consequently, I now think that my first concern is to see to the salvation of my own soul, and then, if it is in my power, to help the Church. . . . I will no

---

[1] Braunsberger, *Epistulae,* vol. ii, pp. 481–2.

longer hesitate and abuse the patience and goodness of God. Giving second place to the natural love I bear my parents, I fly for refuge in fullest confidence to you, the truest of Fathers, and beg you humbly, by the manifold mercies of God, of your goodness and sweet courtesy to receive me, your erring but trustful son, into your Society. . . .[1]

What his Society meant to St. Peter may best be understood from his efforts on its behalf during these years in Augsburg, when he was busier with direct apostolic work than he had ever been before. The Roman Jesuits in their unending struggle with poverty looked confidently to him for some assistance for their embarrassed colleges, so sure were they of the largeness of his heart. Appeals reached him constantly from Polanco and other representatives of the General, such words as these written in the summer of 1559 : " Praise be to God, we are terribly short of funds. But we have not lost heart or our confidence in. God." There were close on three hundred Jesuits teaching or studying in Rome at this time, and as many of these, together with large numbers of students for the secular priesthood whom the Fathers of the Society were educating gratuitously, would in due course take their place in the German mission field, Polanco could plead sound excuse for his petitions.[2] He mentioned the Fuggers as people who might be approached, but St. Peter, who had a poor opinion of his own ability as a suppliant, thought it best to leave such great ones in peace until he had found his feet in Augsburg. Instead, he composed a memorandum for Cardinal Truchsess, setting forth the reasons why the bishops and other rich German Catholics should do something for the colleges in Rome. This document was circulated and seems to have had a fair measure of success. By personal letters, too, the Saint endeavoured to help, or, if a chance offered, by begging on somebody's doorstep. Thus, he cultivated the magnificent Archbishop of Salzburg assiduously—" cui non parum laboravi," he says—and succeeded in getting a hundred ducats from him for Polanco. Writing about this exploit he said : " I am a rather cold sort of person and haven't St. Francis of Assisi's happy knack of extracting alms. If I manage to scrape together something besides the hundred ducats, I shall send it on, but not without

[1] Braunsberger, Epistulae, vol. ii, pp. 489–94.

[2] The Roman College of St. Peter's day still flourishes under the name of the Gregorian University and remains as true as ever to its ideals. Its original buildings were stolen by the Italian Government in 1870 but finer ones have recently replaced them, built out of funds collected over many years by the Jesuits themselves. Only a hundred of the Gregorian's 1,800 students are Jesuits. The total cost to the non-Jesuit men for a five years' course under the best professors that the Society can discover in any of its Provinces is about £2 in English money. Almost every nationality and a great variety of religious orders are represented among the alumni.

shame at my failure to provide more liberally for my needy Fathers and Brothers, to whom I owe all that I am." A little later he wrote again : " Would that I had it in my power to provide for the needs of the Roman colleges which I know to be in sore straits. It is indeed our duty to sympathize with the troubles of our Fathers and to do our little best to help by every possible means. I shall talk to the rectors of this Province on the subject and also to my brother, Theodoric, when he arrives, and to any of the Society who may be returning to their native places. I shall urge them not to forget our Fathers in Rome, to whom there is nothing that we do not owe, in Christ Our Lord."[1]

For years afterwards Peter continued this campaign, arranging credits with bankers for the Roman Fathers, securing donations from friends in Cologne and elsewhere, and eloquently urging their cause with bishops and others who had it in their power to help. " We thank your Reverence for showing us so much charity," wrote Polanco to him. It certainly was true charity because, on the one hand, Peter's own colleges, especially his first love, Prague, had a hard struggle to keep the wolf from the door, and, on the other, Rome did not treat him too considerately in the matter of men. Thus when the Prague College stood in sore need of a Father who could preach in Czech, Rome dispatched a certain young Wenceslaus Ssturem to assume the duty. Now Wenceslaus, though a Bohemian, had forgotten most of his native tongue during a long residence in Italy and also laboured under the more serious handicap of not being a priest. One sermon was enough for him. On the second occasion, a solemn one, he decided to be missing, which caused so much merriment among the Hussites and other critical people that the Fathers were reduced to adopting a very troublesome plan. They wrote out his sermon for Wenceslaus in Latin, made him put it into Czech as best he could with the help of a sympathetic townsman, learn it by heart, and declaim it twice over at supper-time to the meek, uncomprehending community. By persisting with this method he at last conquered the pulpit of Prague, but it was a victory built on the headaches of his brethren. He was only one of many recruits from Rome who complicated the existence of St. Peter Canisius, for, of course, the rectors concerned naturally laid the blame at Peter's door. He protested time and again to Rome but the authorities there, Polanco, Ribadeneyra, and other astute Spanish secretaries, were too clever for him. What, for instance, could one reply to such an argument as this from the genial Polanco : " Your Reverence must not be surprised

[1] Braunsberger, *Epistulae*, vol. ii, pp. 501, 543.

if the German Province is occasionally given a bit of bone with the meat.[1] A man who has to care for the common good of several provinces certainly takes a wider view and weighs everything more exactly when it comes to the distribution of subjects than a person who may have only one province or place to worry about."[2] That was excellently said but it did not help St. Peter very much to digest his " bones."

Not only was he constantly given men quite unfitted for the duties to which they had been assigned, but he had removed from his Province some of its most valuable workers, men on whom his hopes were staked for the future development of the colleges. Thus, he had to stand by helpless while Father Lambert Auer, his best preacher and professor, was whisked off to Prussia and Denmark in the train of Bishop Commendone. Though ready to make any sacrifice for the general good of the Church, he could not see how Father Lambert's peregrinations were going to help. Father Mercurian, Provincial of the neighbouring Lower German Province, appears to have been a little scandalized at his attitude, but in the end it was Peter who was justified. When his travels were over, Auer wrote earnestly begging him to warn superiors in Rome against allowing any other Jesuit to go running about with nuncios or legates. It was a mere waste of time, he said, for he had been able to do very little good and had suffered damage to both body and soul.[3] A heavier blow was to follow for poor Peter. Just when he had begun to congratulate himself on the return of the wanderer, Auer was appointed rector of the new college in Mainz, probably at the instigation of Father Mercurian, to whose Province it belonged. Meantime, a quintet of distinguished voices clamoured to have the elusive Father at Innsbruck, the voices of Magdalene, Margaret, Barbara, Helen, and Joanna, Emperor Ferdinand's five daughters who resided in the capital of Tirol.[4] The Emperor himself, too, joined in the chorus, saying that Auer as a preacher was worth more than all the Jesuit orators in Vienna rolled into one. How to placate these great personages St. Peter did not know, and if, hoping against hope, he continued to make representations to Rome, who shall blame him?

It was easy for Father Mercurian, with his fine army of workers,

[1] " Non è da maravillarsene nè anche di che tal volta avia un poco de osso con la carne la provincia de Germania."

[2] Braunsberger, *Epistulae*, vol. ii, p. 537.

[3] Nevertheless, Father Lambert was the " *dilectus Achates* " and mainstay of Commendone on his thankless mission to the Protestant Courts. Writing from Lübeck, July 24, 1561, to Cardinal Gonzaga, first President of the Council of Trent, Commendone said, speaking of the German Jesuits : " Certain it is, I have not found in the Church of Germany a stronger and greater bulwark of the Catholic religion than the colleges of these men, so may it please God to multiply them." *Miscellanea di Storia Italiana*, vol. vi (Turin, 1865), p. 202.

[4] Braunsberger, *Epistulae*, vol. iii, p. 309.

to profess a little mild disapprobation. Peter had already lent him two valuable men, Father Thyraeus, whom he badly needed at Ingolstadt, and Father Sylvius, one of the main props of Prague. *Nulla vestigia retrorsum !* Mercurian held on to them both. He must have felt uneasy in conscience about it, for Father Kessel reported that he wanted to write to Peter but was too ashamed. Peter, who all the time had been doing a great deal to help the Cologne Jesuits, expressed surprise to some friends at this queer return they were making him, whereupon he received a sharp note from Cologne inspired by Mercurian. " I don't know," said the writer, " whether the people to whom your Reverence complained were much edified by your letters." Such little rubs had no effect on the Saint's good temper. He wrote to the rector of Trier, whither Mercurian had transferred one of the stolen men, telling him that he might keep his ill-gotten recruit permanently, and shortly afterwards was again in friendliest correspondence with the Cologne Fathers. One piece of news he gave them was that, at his petition, the powerful Fugger people had obtained from the Archbishop of Malines a promise to help the Lower German Province by every means at his disposal. As for the new college of Mainz which had robbed him of Lambert Auer, no sooner had he said his " *Fiat voluntas Domini* " over that disappointment than he turned to render assistance. He wrote to the Archbishop of Mainz a number of times, spurring him on to do his duty by the college, and at Augsburg, though so hard pressed with other work, transacted a good deal of its business. The five men sent from Rome to start the college stayed with him a few days on their way through. One of them wrote from the spot to tell the Roman Fathers their impressions of the " *magnifica Città Dagosta,*" of Peter's marvellous work there all alone, of his need of a cook and a tailor : " *Ma di questo mi rimetto. Basta che ci ha fatto tutte le carreʒʒe possibile* " —he has shown us every possible mark of kindness.[1] Poor as he was, the Saint raised the money for the last stage of the young men's journey, with little prospect of ever recovering it from Father Mercurian ; and not only that, but he borrowed sixty ducats and sent them to the Roman Fathers when the Archbishop of Mainz failed to meet his obligations. He felt ashamed, he said, to keep the Fathers waiting any longer for their money.

Each year, though " *semper et nunc maxime occupatus,*" as his friend Perez wrote of him, Peter found an opportunity, or made it, to visit all his colleges in turn, Vienna, Prague, Ingolstadt, Munich, and Innsbruck.

---

[1] Braunsberger, *Epistulae*, vol. iii, pp. 600, 670. Another speaks of the " *gran charità* " with which St. Peter welcomed them.

That work of counselling and comforting his brethren face to face was the only thing in the nature of a holiday that he allowed himself. The canons, who grew suspicious if he spent a day out of Augsburg, used to create a great fuss over giving him leave of absence for the visitations. They were on tenter-hooks lest he should not return, and sometimes he had to bring pressure from Rome to bear before they would allow him out of their sight. During the visitation of 1561 he found that a number of the men in Prague were ill. Three of these he at once dispatched to Oybin for a holiday in the mountains, while two others were sent home to their native places in hopes that their health might benefit. It was similarly in the interests of health that he now began to plan for the foundation of a novitiate in Prague rather than Vienna. Prague, he explained to the Roman Fathers, was a quieter place and less subject to political disturbances, "to say nothing of the more bracing air, the Bohemian beer, and other advantages."[1] Whether the beer had anything to do with it is not apparent, but Peter, on this occasion, made strenuous attempts to secure the establishment of a college in Pilsen, the greatest brewery city in the world. Both there and at Ellwangen, whither he travelled in state in a carriage of Archduke Ferdinand, he delighted the good Catholic people with several inspiring sermons.

Then it was the turn of Munich, in which college great developments had been taking place. Joy must have possessed the Provincial's heart as he pronounced the ritual blessing on the fine new residence which Duke Albert had erected for his men. A whole stag came from the Prince's larder to celebrate the occasion, but Peter's happiness was clouded by a problem to which he could see no solution. He was in desperate straits for men to follow up the many promising beginnings which his own tireless zeal had created. All his letters echo with the cry for men. There were such glorious things to be done if only he had the right men to do them. Father Peltan, one of the greatest scholars of the early Society of Jesus, then resided in Munich. As his health was poor, St Peter sent him to Cologne for a change, begging him to do his best to secure a few helpers from the Cologne brethren, who had abundance of material. Munich alone urgently needed six new men, but all that Peter got for his entire Province from his close-fisted neighbours was two—a cook and an M.A. Referring to this visit, and to a previous stay of the Saint in Munich a few months earlier, the annals of the college record how "marvellously the brethren were comforted by the presence of Father Provincial," and

---

[1] Braunsberger, *Epistulae*, vol. iii, p. 190.

" in what a wonderful way his visitation confirmed the souls of all in the holy manner of life " to which they had dedicated themselves.[1]

From Munich Peter returned to Augsburg to preach on August 31st, September 7th, September 8th (twice), and September 14th. After the sermon on that last day he set out to make his visitation of the college in Ingolstadt. There he served the community at their meals, only sitting down when the brothers and everybody had finished. As at Munich he had the pleasure of blessing a new refectory and schools, erected for him by the Duke of Bavaria " on the ground where that big tree used to stand." Peter certainly was not easy to satisfy. Now that in both Munich and Ingolstadt he had colleges for day pupils whose parents were sufficiently well off to feed and clothe their children, he began to plan for the establishment of hostels where poorer scholars might have their board and lodging free. Under his direction and inspiration such houses had already been bought or built in Vienna and Prague,[2] and he was working hard at this time to acquire one for similar purposes in Augsburg.

Finally, there was Innsbruck. We have seen something of the difficulties that attended the beginning of the college there, difficulties that pursued and haunted Peter for years. When in 1562 he had made everything ready at last, he found it almost impossible to get the right men from Rome. A rector named Voyt was sent, who, Peter observed, badly needed a rector himself, so full was he of scruples and indecision. One of the appointed staff was a Bohemian who could not speak a word of German, and two others were so broken in health as to be incapable of work. To Peter's expostulations Rome replied with a certain amount of asperity. Thus on May 16, 1562, St. Francis Borgia wrote : " To speak plainly to your Reverence, I think you ought to be more content with the men sent to you in Germany, partly because they are suitable, and partly because no Province of the Society is being treated more liberally than yours." A fortnight later, he returned to the charge : " You are quite right to urge that we here in Rome should carefully test the men whom we destine for the German mission before sending them, but you ought not to be so persistent in asking us for a new man every hour of the

[1] Braunsberger, *Epistulae*, vol. iii, pp. 109, 692.

[2] Just before beginning his work in Augsburg Peter had been to Prague, where he circularized the clergy and had bills posted all over the city, explaining the project of the college for poor students and begging for help with its foundation. At the same time he composed a little treatise on the education of youth, setting forth the advantages that would accrue to both Church and State from the establishment of such an institution. This he sent to the zealous Scribonius, who had it printed out of his own pocket and circulated widely. These efforts were crowned with complete success, and before the year 1559 was out the new boarding-school had begun its beneficent activities, " a work," wrote a historian of the time, " than which the Society of Jesus achieved nothing more illustrious that year." Braunsberger, *Epistulae*, vol. ii, pp. 364-5.

day. We are not rich in well-tried masters and so are obliged to send you such as we have. I can tell your Reverence for a fact that we do more for your one Province than, perhaps, for all the other Provinces put together, so much so that we seem almost to have no other duty here except to prepare men for the service of Germany. Be content, then, Father, because we are doing more for you than really might have seemed possible." Undoubtedly the Roman Fathers were doing their best, but they did not understand the position as St. Peter did. At Innsbruck, the seat of the Lower Austrian government and favourite city of the Emperor, the reputation of the Society of Jesus was in Peter's keeping and he was not the sort of person to let it suffer without a fight. That explains his persistency. His apology was sincere at any rate : " I beg your forgiveness, Reverend Fathers, for being importunate in my petitions for men and too solicitous about the establishment of the Innsbruck College. Such a pest and nuisance deserved punishment, but your charity has triumphed over my crassness and conferred on me, instead, a very great favour."[1]

It was at the intensest points of his great spiritual crusade that Peter showed best what the Society of Jesus meant to him. About the beginning of Lent, 1560, printed copies of the Jesuit rules and constitutions reached Germany for the first time and were distributed by the Provincial to his various houses. He took the opportunity to address a letter to the rectors, one passage of which ran as follows :

Since the Eternal Goodness has endowed us with the infinite treasures contained in our constitutions and rules, and now, at last, has instructed us more fully than ever before about the holy and perfect form of our institute, so that there no longer remains any excuse for our neglect or ignorance, it behoves us all to bring a new solicitude to the devout execution of our duty, making it our first business to strive for the prize of our vocation. We must bend all our energies to this, that dead to self we may strengthen and confirm within us the true life of Christ, and labour to fit ourselves more and more for the work of raising others from spiritual death, and of spurring them on in the way of holiness. The grain of wheat that falls into the ground and dies will bring forth much fruit, such fruit as our thrice unhappy Germany expects and requires of us. God would seem to have sent us to her that our light might shine in the midst of a crooked and perverse generation, so depraved by vice and heresy that our hearts ought to

[1] Braunsberger, *Epistulae*, vol. iii, p. 459.

bleed with pity, and our wills leave nothing unattempted that may serve to bring the straying sheep back to their Shepherd and Fold. . . .[1]

In December, 1560, the Saint addressed his rectors again, charging them to see to it that all their young subjects were carefully instructed in the best methods of making their confessions, of receiving Holy Communion, of hearing and serving Mass, of examining their consciences, of meditating and praying, and of thinking according to the mind of the Church. Each of the men was to be given a copy of the *Imitation of Christ* and of the Society's Common Rules. From time to time they should receive a little coaching in controversy and the solution of moral problems. The rectors are urged to impress upon all their obligation of gratitude to pray hard for the whole Society and its head, Father General; for their own Province, so sadly beset by heresy and moral corruption; for the Emperor and the House of Austria; for the Duke of Bavaria; for Father Nadal, who represented the German Jesuits in Rome; "for the conversion of the famous City of Augsburg"; and, above all, for the general council soon to resume its sessions at Trent.[2]

A few months later, during the Lent of 1561, when Peter delivered a sermon or lecture every day, he once again drafted a letter to his rectors, writing in the third person:

Father Provincial thinks that, in accordance with the duties of his office and the demands of true charity and obedience, he ought to impress some matters on the rectors of this German Province. This he does in order that everything belonging to the institute of our Society may be the better carried out, especially during this Lent, to the glory of our Eternal Lord and with the desired fruit of souls. He begs the rectors, for the love of Jesus Christ Our Lord, to show themselves diligent in the observance of these matters, as far as by the grace of God they can.

1. Let them hold in high esteem the rules sent to them from Rome, in which the duties of rectors are clearly set forth and explained.

2. Besides these rules they should know and often call to mind the General Examen and the Common Rules; the ten sections of the constitutions and the *Officium Provincialis*, of which a copy will be sent to all in a short time; the rules to be observed when writing to the General; and finally, the concessions and privileges granted to the Society, which, owing to the circumstances of this age and country,

[1] Braunsberger, *Epistulae*, vol. ii, p. 602.   [2] Braunsberger, *Epistulae*, vol. ii, pp. 769–72.

we frequently need to use. Father Provincial would like all the rectors to devote at least half an hour daily during this present Lent to the study of these matters, taking care to imbibe and stir up in their souls by the reading the true spirit of our Society.[1]

3. Let each rector have a special book in which to preserve copies of the *Litterae Quadrimestres* sent by him to Rome, as well as the orders of superiors received by him, and all other suggestions or regulations which seem to him to bear on the maintenance, government, and progress of his college. In this way, not only Father Provincial on his visitation but future rectors in the execution of their duties will be able to acquire a better idea of the state of the college, whether regarding its spiritual or temporal condition.

4. Let the rectors show reverence to the consultors of Father Provincial and discuss with them freely . . . such matters as pertain to the progress of their colleges. . . . Afterwards, if necessary, the consultors, speaking for the rectors, will be the better able to admonish and stir up the Provincial, lest he neglect any part of his duty to the colleges.

5. It is to be specially and diligently observed that rectors write to the General once a year, informing him of any respects whatever in which they think the conduct of the Provincial can be corrected or improved. Similarly, let the consultors of each rector write concerning him to the Provincial, every fourth month or oftener. . . .

6. Care should be taken that the *Litterae Quadrimestres* are written correctly and punctually and that the prescribed number of copies is dispatched. When sending them to the Provincial there should be a covering letter describing in detail the whole state of the college, that so he may have better knowledge of it and be the better able to direct its affairs. Finally would the rectors kindly send to Augsburg in due course documents describing the course of studies mapped out for the next term in their colleges.[2]

How little the hard work of Augsburg was permitted to interrupt the Saint's communications with Rome may be seen from the fact that

---

[1] Among St. Peter's own New Year resolutions for 1562 were the following:
    "1. During January to read the constitutions either before or after supper.
    2. To do some spiritual reading each morning after Mass.
    3. To be slow to speak and to keep my heart up.
    4. To be content with a very modest repast."
Braunsberger, *Epistulae*, vol. iii, p. 807.

[2] Braunsberger, *Epistulae*, vol. iii, pp. 99–100. The idea of the *Litterae Quadrimestres* was to inform, not only the General, but the various Provinces of the Society, of the work being done in any particular place. They served both as a spur to zeal and as an incentive to prayer, emphasizing that the Society was one great family, all of whose members shared common interests and loyalties.

in a single year he addressed twenty-two very long letters to Laynez, giving him the latest news of the situation in Germany[1] and full details about the colleges. This, however, was only a fraction of his correspondence, which during the same period included letters to the Emperor, to the Duke of Bavaria and his Secretary, to various bishops and non-Jesuit writers and theologians, and to a host of his own brethren both inside and outside Germany. The spirit that breathes in so many of these documents may be illustrated by the following letters to Peter's friend, Goudanus, whom he had sent to Cologne on the chance that the Rhineland air might benefit his shattered health. He loved Goudanus and missed him sorely. "Our Lord has united us in spirit," he wrote, after the Father had gone, "even if in this life we must be separated in the body. May He bring us together again in our blessed Fatherland, where it will be plain to see how truly we are brothers." From Augsburg on October 15, 1560, he thus addressed his sick and despondent friend:

You are experiencing the unmistakable visitation of the Lord, and you do not cease, I hope, to thank the Father of Mercies for the singular love which has bestowed on you this broken health with its ever-present reminders of life's transitoriness. When we are well we forget it for the most part, or think of it in but a vague and listless way. Let my dear Father Goudanus be glad that he is being thus purified on earth, and let him joyfully offer and pour out the remainder of his human life to God, who is Lord of both life and death. What is more precious and pleasing to God than the good-will that no manner of death can diminish but only render perfect? The holy ones in whom it reigns have often sighed that the beginning of true life came so tardily and that they could not be wholly living and reigning with Christ. But let us pass on from good-will to the charity that casts out fear; let us not brood on the weakness of the flesh, which as sons of Adam we carry about us, but rather let us stir up our souls and put on fortitude of spirit, however God may choose to deal with us. Whether we live or die we are His, and to Him let us offer the sacrifice of a contrite and humble heart. . . .

Your Reverence must not allow exaggerated ideas, or rather temptations, about the expiation of sin, the pains of Purgatory, the severity of the Judge, to take possession of your mind. Exercise yourself in hope by contemplation of the divine mercy. Build yourself a nest

---

[1] The letters make frequent mention of portents in the sky, terrible assaults of the devil on men and women and other "erschreckliche Zeitungen" beloved of the sixteenth century. St. Peter tells the stories as they were reported. He seems to have given credit to the ones in which the devil figured.

in the wounds of Christ. Put your trust in the inexhaustible treasury of merits which the Body of Christ makes yours. Rely on the strength of the Sacraments, and offer daily to the Father, who is God of all consolation, whatever you do or suffer, in union with the merits of Christ and His saints. I say all this out of my love for you, or rather because of the long mutual friendship between us. Quit you manfully, my brother, and let your heart be strengthened in Our Lord. . . .[1]

Poor Goudanus, always a great worker, had grown discouraged at the prospect of having to pass the remaining days of his life in idleness. Naturally of a melancholy disposition, he tended, during his long illness, to look upon the gloomy side of things; so a few months later Peter wrote once again, endeavouring to put heart into him:

I see that God has been pleased to surround your Reverence with infirmity. But though you are not always able to pull the chariot of the body with the same vigour, you have at least the comfort in Our Lord of many companions to sustain and protect the slow and burdened vehicle. Your inability is the lot of many men, and to a Christian it can never seem strange; so why, I beg you, should we be chagrined? Have we not reached the stage where this life ought to have lost its edge of delight for us, and the passage to true life, its fears? Meantime, may your charity find its viaticum, by which you may be strengthened and set straight however much bodily powers fail and dread of death takes possession; the viaticum, I mean, of a lively feeling of the Passion of Our Lord. Let us bring before our eyes the blood and wounds of Christ, His sweat, His Cross, and His death. Let us with true and ardent faith rest in Christ crucified, drinking the waters of life from that fountain, glorying in His merits and rejoicing heartily that whether we live or die He is our life and resurrection, our Head and the propitiation for our sins. . . . But I must stop preaching. The Lord will give as He has given your Reverence understanding to meditate on these truths in season, and to derive from them the profit of consolation which they contain.[2]

It may be wondered at this point how St. Peter's own health stood the strain of his incessant activity. His contemporaries wondered, too.

---

[1] Braunsberger, *Epistulae*, vol. ii, pp. 742–3.

[2] Braunsberger, *Epistulae*, vol. iii, p. 15. Instead of dying, Father Goudanus got so much better that Pope Pius IV chose him for a perilous mission to Mary Queen of Scots. The arrangements were made through St. Peter, and it was at his house in Augsburg that Edmund Hay and William Creighton stayed when they passed through Germany in connexion with the mission. Both afterwards became Jesuits, the first-fruits of Scotland.

Augspurg.

Part of old Augsburg showing the Cathedral with its twin spires and, near by, marked No. 7, the Jesuit Church and College

The indefatigable Father Delanoy, whose personal exploits in the rôle of Martha used to astonish Peter, considered that his Provincial was making impossible demands on the resources of nature. "It will be very advantageous," he explained to the Roman authorities, "if he is provided with a capable assistant to help him in both temporal and spiritual affairs, someone vested with authority from your Reverence to moderate his studies and labours." Salmeron, who was then acting for Laynez, accordingly warned Peter against tiring himself out and endangering his health. Father Delanoy, he continued, had been instructed to find him a suitable lieutenant who should not only help him with his preaching and everything else but also act towards him as a sort of medical overseer, commissioned to ensure that he took sufficient food and sleep and rested at intervals from his labours. Peter replied :

I thank your Reverence with all my heart for your charity in warning me that I be careful to offer a ' reasonable service ' to God our Father. I confess that I have often exceeded the bounds of moderation, and have neglected many things that needed to be done both here at home and in the world around. The rectors and consultors of this Province would like to give me a helper in my weakness ; but I feel too sorry for the colleges, and would rather add to their depleted staffs than take a good worker away from them. Also, I fear that such a one might do himself more harm than me good, living the free and easy life of this place where, owing to our fewness, we are unable to observe the rules of the Society in every detail. Father Hurtado was indeed a comfort to me but I made a present of him to the hard-pressed brethren of Vienna and Prague, lest I might be serving my own convenience rather than the needs of other people. So now, like the paralytic at the Pool of Bethsaida, ' I have no man,' nobody I can summon here as a companion. But I will suggest to the consultors to look round for such a person.[1]

To help with the preaching, which was the principal burden, nobody could be found, so Peter continued at it alone. In Lent, 1562, he broke down for a time, " laid low by a fever," as he told Hosius, " which, perhaps, is the result of giving a sermon every day." He was soon up again, though, and at work as vigorously as ever. That work included much besides preaching and direct ministerial activity. There was, for instance, the hard, dull labour of the pen from which throughout his life the Saint

[1] Braunsberger, *Epistulae*, vol. iii, pp. 249, 271, 294.

so rarely rested. When in Rome in 1557 and 1558 he had worked in the Vatican Library collating Erasmus's very successful but very faulty edition of the works of St. Cyprian with the ancient codices. Though through pressure of other business he was unable to finish his task, he collected nearly a thousand emendations. At Augsburg in 1561 he resumed his labours but, hearing that greater and more leisured scholars than himself, such as Latinus Latinius, were also engaged on St. Cyprian, he retired from that field and turned his attention to the letters of St. Jerome which Desiderius Erasmus had previously edited with a good deal of anti-monastic bias. " Nobody," wrote Peter, " could fairly grudge Erasmus of Rotterdam the laurels which he won in the realm of polite letters. . . ."[1] Desiderius should have been content with that realm and either have left sacred studies entirely alone or else have shown himself less super-cilious in his judgments on the writings of the Fathers. As soon as he begins to play the theologian he becomes unduly self-confident and arrogant. Often more interested in words than in the facts they convey, he turns into a merciless critic and goes farther in his censure of theological writers than any Catholic, however learned and wise, has hitherto claimed or deemed to be permissible. . . . A monk, he inveighs against monks. Himself no very weighty philosopher, he barely refrains from treating the scholastic doctors with scurrility. Moved by I know not what spirit, he wished to apply a purely Pyrrhonic theology to the dogmas of the Church. But, while condemning and storming at others, he never ceases to excuse and exalt himself. He would give in to nobody and the authority of his name has suffered more from his own doing than from any attacks of his adversaries." That passage, showing St. Peter in a fighting mood, is from the dedication of his edition of St. Jerome to the rector, professors, and students of the University of Dillingen, which had taken St. Jerome for its patron. Explaining his reasons for bringing out the book he says : " I saw and was grieved to see that the immense, divine treasure of St. Jerome's letters lay hidden away in huge tomes which, owing to their high price, very few people could buy. . . . I thought it would be worth while, then, for the convenience of the private reader and of students generally, to make a selection of the letters from the various tomes in which they now lie scattered, to arrange them in better order, and to issue them in a single volume of moderate size and weight." The volume appeared at Dillingen towards the close of 1561, an octavo of 787 pages

---

[1] Peter showed practical appreciation of Erasmus as a literary man by very often quoting from his *Adagia* in his letters.

which afterwards ran into nearly forty editions.[1] According to his first biographer, it was this book that determined St. John Berchmans to embrace the religious life in the Society of Jesus, just as it was the *Shorter Catechism*, with the prayers and meditations added by its author during these Augsburg years, that helped St. Aloysius to a like decision.[2] With the third and best loved of the young Jesuit Saints, Stanislaus Kostka, Peter's influence worked, as will be seen, not through a book, but face to face.

He laboured a great deal at this time on the improvement of his Catechisms, of which new editions were constantly appearing, but the works of other men, too, had a large share of his attention. "Father Provincial," wrote Elderen in May, 1561, "is wont to devote himself to having new Catholic books printed, and old ones, after careful revision, reprinted. For this purpose he is in intimate relations with other learned men, such as Cromer and Staphylus, and also with Catholic typographers." Many of the works published by these men were read in manuscript, revised, and seen through the press by St. Peter. When, in 1561, the *Supplication* of the French Calvinists to Charles IX appeared at Nuremberg in a German dress, it was through Peter's efforts that the answer of the French Catholic nobility, similarly translated, came out to meet it at Dillingen almost immediately. As the saints were so much in the controversies of that period a zealous Catholic layman named Walasser determined to produce an enlarged German version of the Martyrology. So much did Peter help him with the work, by suggestions, by the revision and amplification of his manuscript, and by contributing a long, original, erudite introduction on the worship and invocation of the saints, that the grateful man put the Jesuit's name rather than his own on the title-page. When the book appeared at Dillingen in 1562, it bore the inscription: "MARTYROLOGIUM. Der Kirchen Kalender. . . . Durch Doctor Petrum Canisium, Thümpredigern zu Augspurg, in Truck verfertigt." In his preface Walasser says that he had set Dr. Canisius's name in the forefront of the book " *als des fürnemesten urhabers diser verteutschung* " —as the principal author of this German translation.[3]

In view of the imminent resumption of the Council of Trent, St. Peter showed the greatest interest in efforts that were being made to bring out more scholarly editions of the acts of earlier councils. Ephesus, the third of the General Councils, was particularly dear to Catholics of the

---

[1] Braunsberger, *Epistulae*, vol. iii, pp. 119, 274, 289–90, 782–4.

[2] Cepari, *Vita di Giovanni Berchmans* (Rome, 1627), part i, p. 13; Braunsberger, *Epistulae*, vol. viii, p. 876.

[3] For the Catechisms, the German version of the "Supplication," and the Martyrology, see Braunsberger, *Epistulae*, vol. iii, pp. 772–97.

Reformation age because of its definition that Our Lady, whom the Protestants dishonoured, was the Mother of God. St. Peter had an additional reason for being interested in it, as having himself, at the start of his career, edited the works of its leading personality, St. Cyril. Great, then, was his satisfaction when he learned in 1561 that a hitherto unknown Greek codex of the Council's acts had come into the hands of the Duke of Bavaria. Father Theodore Peltan, the Professor of Greek at the Jesuit College, Munich, was summoned to Court to report on the find. So sadly had the manuscript been ravaged by time that Albert himself, though a good scholar, could make nothing of it. " 'What on earth is it?' " he asked Peltan. "I read the inscription and replied that it was the acts of the Council of Ephesus. Then said he : ' Is not this one of the Councils which Pope Gregory the Great is reported to have ranked with the Four Gospels ? ' I nodded my head. ' Come, then,' continued the Prince, ' make me a synopsis of this whole work as soon as ever you can. I am anxious to know in summary form what is here taught by the Catholic Church.' To this request I could not well offer a refusal but all the same I was afraid that I should not be able to satisfy the Prince unless I studied the volume through and through, which even for a man of leisure would be likely to involve an enormous amount of work. Luck was with me, however, for just when I had girded myself for the labour, what should I find at the very beginning of the manuscript but an epitome of its whole contents. Within three or four days I had turned this into Latin and presented it to the Prince, thinking that he would be satisfied with it and let me go free. On the contrary, it merely whetted his appetite for more, so the following morning he bade me be informed that he most earnestly desired me to translate the entire codex into Latin."[1]

At first Peltan refused flatly to shoulder the huge burden, but when St. Peter pointed out to him that by continuing obdurate he might easily give deep offence to the Duke, who had been so generous to the Society, he surrendered. The Saint then wrote asking Laynez to send Peltan a few lines of encouragement and to obtain for him any help he might require in Rome. Cardinal Truchsess and Cardinal Hosius next received letters, begging them to do what they could for the gallant Father Theodore. A month later, November 22, 1561, Peter sent Salmeron a summary of what had been achieved so far, requesting him to have it collated with the Latin codex in the Vatican Library. "The copy in the Prince's possession," he continued, "is most troublesome to read on account

[1] Braunsberger, *Epistulae*, vol. iii, pp. 136–7.

of the abbreviations. Sometimes it is necessary to resort to guesswork. Father Theodore has slaved at his task with incredible diligence. His version is now being revised and polished up, as the Prince is pressing us to get it finished. If only we had the Vatican codex by us we should not find the work so burdensome. Father Theodore hopes and desires that, by your Reverence's good offices, he may have certain points elucidated for him from the Vatican manuscript. The places are those marked by a triple asterisk in the summary I enclose. I am sure that, of your goodness and singular charity in our regard, your Reverence will do us this service. Places in the summary marked by a double or single asterisk are not so important, but it would be useful, all the same, to have the version of the Vatican codex, unless indeed you would prefer us to put aside the work on which Father Theodore has toiled so industriously and to recommend the Vatican manuscript to the Prince in place of it." From this letter it seems fairly certain that Peter himself helped directly with the work. On receipt of Salmeron's answer, he wrote: "That your Reverence should deign to assist us with the Council of Ephesus has given us great consolation. Nothing at the moment could have afforded us more satisfaction or have been a better help to us in bringing the work to a happy conclusion. We shall eagerly await the annotations."

When, at last, after three months of incessant labour, the Latin translation was ready, Father Peltan, being, like most true scholars, an extremely modest man, begged that it should not be published, or, if it had to be, that both it and its original should first be collated in detail with the Vatican codex. This was because he had become suspicious of the competence of the Greek scribe to whose pen the Munich manuscript owed its existence. Tragedy was the result of his scholar's scruple. The precious Greek codex and its Latin daughter were taken to Rome by the Bavarian Ambassador in 1562. He handed them to Cardinal Truchsess, who passed them on to Cardinal Paleotto, who entrusted them to Cardinal Amulius, who left them with the savant, Onofrio Panvinio, who asked the other savant, Cardinal Sirleto, would he kindly see to them. Twelve years then went by without poor Father Peltan being able to get any news of what had happened to them. In 1573, while in Rome on other business, he hunted for them everywhere. Not a trace could he find. At last some knowing person advised him to seek out Cardinal Sirleto, who at the time was Prefect of the Vatican Library. "I told him my sad story," says Peltan, "and he was most kind to me. He racked his memory for a moment and then his face lit up with joy, for he had not known till that moment who was the translator of the Acts of Ephesus." The eminent and charming Cardinal had done as requested by the Duke of Bavaria twelve years before, but as for the Duke's codex, which contained the variant readings and annotations on interleaved slips, Heaven alone knew where he had sent it to. Try as he might he could not remember, so the unfortunate Peltan went home, as empty-handed as he had come. Two years more passed by, when, one day, some Jesuits, working in the Ducal Library at Munich, came unexpectedly upon an ancient Greek manuscript. Father Peltan, the expert on such matters, was called in. Rapidly turning over the pages, he discovered that it was the long-lost codex, with Sirleto's annotations all safely in their places. "How I danced for joy," says the good man, "not because I had found anything precious of my own but because His Serene Highness had not lost his priceless codex." The following year witnessed the publication at Ingolstadt of six quarto volumes containing all the Acts of Ephesus in Peltan's translation, a work which he would not have undertaken and certainly could not have carried through but for the encouragement and devoted assistance of Peter Canisius.[1] Encouragement and assistance of the same kind were a constant feature of Peter's literary life.[2] One other feature of it at this period is of sufficiently live interest to require inclusion here, namely the Saint's unceasing efforts to secure some mitigation of the Roman Index.

Two of the star words in Peter's first letters from Augsburg are "Index" and "Turks," the one causing him as much anxiety as the other. Learned Germans[3] have asserted in modern times that not a little of the rigour of the Roman Index was to be ascribed to Jesuit influence. Now, since there is no evidence that Jesuits used influence of any kind in the matter, except in the days of Canisius and Laynez, the question can be settled for good by finding out what *kind* of influence they exercised. All men with any sense are agreed that some sort of censorship is required for the stability of every society. The never-dying controversies on the subject are only about the extent and strictness of such necessary censorship. Obviously these must vary with varying circumstances. In time of war men cannot be permitted to air sentiments of treasonable colour that might be safely ignored in time of peace. Now the Catholic Church on earth is emphatically the Church militant. History has rarely seen her at peace from external aggression or from tumults

[1] Braunsberger, *Epistulae*, vol. iii, pp. 131, 136, 240, 296, 302–3, 340–4, 401–4.
[2] As illustrated, for instance, in Braunsberger, *Epistulae*, vol. iii, pp. 239, 273, 292, 320, 481–2, 516, 526, 538, 773, 797—8, etc., etc.
[3] Quotations from them are to be found in Hilgers, *Der Index der verbotenen Bücher* (1904), pp. 194–5.

raised by her own unruly children, and, as her mission is not primarily to make her children learned or to indulge their fancy for social or religious experiments but to save their immortal souls, she has more need and justification for censorship than any other society in the world. That does not mean that the authorities responsible for her measures of censorship have always been wise or tactful, since they have neither claimed to be nor ever been held to be by Catholics more infallible in this sphere than a Home Secretary or Lord Chamberlain.

During a long period of the Church's history there was no general legislation with regard to the reading of heretical or immoral books. The Lateran Council had issued a restricted ruling on the matter in 1515 and the works of Luther and some other individuals had been prohibited in special decrees. But that was all, and there was no Index such as we are familiar with to-day. Owing to this state of affairs the need for guidance was widely felt. Peter Canisius applied to St. Ignatius, who answered with the following rather stern suggestions in August, 1554. It would be expedient to burn or have removed beyond the boundaries of Bavaria and Austria all heretical works that diligent search had brought to light. Books produced by heretics, though not in themselves heretical, ought to be entirely excluded, out of detestation for the religious errors of their authors. Should such books be necessary in schools, the authors' names ought to be deleted and the authorities should take the necessary measures to prevent their charges becoming in any way keen or curious about the men who wrote them. Finally, printers and publishers ought to be prohibited under severe penalties from setting up or issuing heretical works and from adding to innocuous works any gloss or comment by a heretic that had the slightest taint of false doctrine.

Certainly some such measures as these were desirable at the time, since many nuns and other cloistered persons in Austria and Tirol had been found reading the works of Luther, Melanchthon, and Zwingli. People living apart from the world are apt to be innocent in their choice of literature, like the French nuns who devoutly arranged for Renan's *Vie de Jésus* to be read aloud to them in the refectory during Lent. But the problem in Bavaria and Austria turned out to be more complicated than St. Ignatius, or any other adviser or legislator who spent all his time in Rome, could have guessed. It was one thing to suggest measures in Italy and quite another to put them into practice in Germany. At the beginning of the year 1559 Pope Paul IV promulgated the first Roman Index of forbidden books, and about the same time withdrew all faculties for reading such books which had previously been granted, the only exceptions made being in favour of the Inquisitor-General and a few cardinals. All books by heretics were prohibited, even though they contained nothing whatever about religion; and works as innocent of anti-Catholic bias as Euclid's *Elements*, if printed by a typographer who had on any occasion devoted his presses to the service of Protestantism, might not be possessed or read without episcopal and inquisitorial sanction. The penalty for violation of this law was excommunication, from which no priest could free the delinquent without special faculties from the Pope.

That was certainly censorship in its sternest guise, and as such it was accounted by good Catholics, not only in Germany, but in Italy and in Rome itself. Far from having had anything to do with the elaboration of the Index, the Roman Jesuits were from the first very anxious about its possible ill-consequences. A manuscript in the Vatican Library contains the following reference to the matter under date, January 14, 1559, which must have been within a few days of the appearance of the decree: "It is reported concerning the forbidden books that, to prevent the necessity of burning them all, some milder ordinance is going to be published. A certain Father Natalis, of the Order of the Good Jesus, has been to the Inquisition with a view to securing a modification of the law by his representations. Doubtless he was not very graciously received by the President, but from the attitude of the others one may infer that he succeeded in obtaining some concession."[1] The Father Natalis, or Nadal, here mentioned was one of the greatest Jesuit educational authorities and, as we know, a very good friend of Peter Canisius. It was chiefly on educational grounds that both men regretted the harsh terms of the Index legislation. Canisius is quite explicit about the German attitude to it. Writing to Laynez from Augsburg in March, 1559, he said:

The Index of prohibited books has reached us here. People in all appearance excellent Catholics are not afraid to reject and condemn its severity, nor do I see how it will be possible to get from the Germans all that it demands. There will be the same difficulty with Bohemia and Poland, and it is rumoured that even in Italy all the book-sellers are crying out against it. I would like to know what line our Fathers are to take in the matter. The fate of the Index is similar to that of the bull *In Coena Domini*. It has not been officially promulgated in Germany and never will be, in my opinion.

[1] Hilgers, *Der Index*, pp. 197-8.

Less than a month later, March 25, 1559, Peter wrote again to the same man :

> The Catholics of Germany, Bohemia, and Poland consider the Index intolerably severe, nor do we see how its demands are to be met. The better sort of Catholics argue that as long as the law has not been promulgated in Germany it is not to be feared very much, so you might appropriately call it a rock of scandal. According to report, not even the Venetians are showing themselves submissive, which proves that obedience is sadly lacking in our age. Meantime, I am anxious to know what we are to do with people who, though excellent Catholics, cannot be induced to give their assent and approval to this papal law, or who refuse to get rid of forbidden books, when such people come to us for sacramental absolution. Are those to be held excommunicated and *vitandi* who openly refuse to submit ? . . .

Laynez answered through his secretary, Polanco, that he had spoken to the Inquisitor-General, Cardinal Ghislieri, O.P., and that permission had been given him, which he might pass on to others of the Society, to expurgate objectionable books and use them in schools when freed from error. Some weeks later Polanco informed Peter that after a certain amount of argument they had obtained from the Cardinal permission for the Jesuits to absolve for the space of three months all those who had not obeyed the Index decree, provided they were prepared to submit in future.[1] Peter was not entirely satisfied with these concessions, and wrote again to Laynez, May 27, 1559 :

> I am astonished that neither the Cardinal of Augsburg nor myself can obtain an answer as to the right attitude for us to adopt with regard to the Index. We are as it were stuck fast in the mud, and not a little afraid. In the colleges they are crying out for something to be settled. I am most eagerly awaiting a reply, and anxious to the last degree that concessions may be made to the German colleges, according to the needs of the masters and of this country. Then again, I do not know whether my own permission to read heretical books has been withdrawn. I hear that the legislation cannot be maintained even among yourselves, either in Venice or Milan, in spite of the efforts of the inquisitors. Much less chance is there of it having any force in Germany. May the Lord bestow upon us truly Christian prudence and simplicity, that we may avoid so much as the appearance of evil and hold fast sincerely to the good. . . .[2]

[1] Braunsberger, *Epistulae*, vol. ii, pp. 377, 380, 387, 422.
[2] Braunsberger, *Epistulae*, vol. ii, pp. 425-6.

In his next communication with Laynez Peter raises the question
of school text-books. What books are they using at the Roman College ?
he wants to know, and how are they in Germany to replace the very
useful *De Copia Verborum* of Erasmus, all of whose works had come
under the ban of Pope Paul ?

> May your Reverence forgive me for harping so much on the Index.
> The more we study and think about it the more puzzled we are to
> know what to do. In short, we do not see how we are to carry on
> our schools and classes if we must obey this severe decree to the letter.
> There is a great lack of books on the Humanities and other classical
> arts, and we cannot find any here that satisfy the requirements of the
> Index. I commit to your Reverence's wisdom to discover if possible
> some means of relieving our burdened consciences, and also of pre-
> serving our schools and their customary literary exercises. Meantime
> we shall provide for their needs as best we can, according to our practice
> in the past. Your Reverence can understand the difficulties in which
> confessors will be placed when their three months' faculty to absolve
> Index cases has expired. . . . If we get no further dispensation I am
> afraid that we may have to close our schools, or at least to send away
> many of the scholars who attend them. For the same reason, little fruit
> is derived from the confessions which we hear all the year round. May
> God grant us His divine light and direct us in His holy service.[1]

In answer to this letter Polanco gave renewed assurances that the
Roman Jesuits would do their very best to obtain some mitigation of
the law before the three months' grace had elapsed, but Peter was still
far from satisfied, even though he had his personal faculty to read forbidden books restored to him, and wrote as follows to Laynez in July :

> It would be most welcome if some further concession were made,
> allowing our pupils to retain at least the books dealing with classical
> literature which they now possess, even though they are prohibited on
> account of the notes and elucidations by Protestant scholars with which
> they are embellished. We should also esteem it a great favour if something
> were settled about the emendation of such necessary books in the future. It
> is most difficult to procure any that are not comprised in the Index, so much
> so that if we wish to obey to the letter we shall find it next to impossible
> to keep our schools open in this country from lack of necessary books.

[1] Braunsberger, *Epistulae*, vol. ii, pp. 441, 445–6.

In reply to this plea Polanco intimated that Cardinal Ghislieri had granted the German Jesuits permission to ' dissimulate ' with regard to the forbidden books in the possession of their pupils until new texts had been printed for their use at Vienna or elsewhere. Further, the Jesuits themselves might read and use any such books with a view to having them reprinted after objectionable glosses had been removed, or, better still, converted into glosses in favour of Catholicism. " For a year, then, you can breathe freely," was Polanco's parting consolation to Peter.[1]

The foregoing extracts show that the Saint was most scrupulous in his respect for the law. He did not approve of it but, while it remained in force and he was not dispensed, nothing would induce him to violate the least detail. Many distinguished canonists held that the law was not obligatory in Germany as it had not been promulgated there, but he was unwilling to take advantage of that sound opinion. Whenever there was question of obedience his conscience became fearful of liberal views. Only the central authority could satisfy him, so, in August, 1559, he again appealed to Laynez to obtain an extension of the faculty for absolving transgressors against the Index. The three months for which the faculty had been granted would soon be up, and then the German Jesuits would " detest hearing confessions." " Your Reverence may judge for yourself," he continued. " Here we are, trying to carry on in the midst of a crooked and perverse generation. Labourers in such circumstances need encouragement rather than the additional harshness and affliction which our good brothers of the Society are obliged to endure on account of the prohibitions of the Index. However, *diligentibus Deum in bonum omnia.* . . ."[2]

After the death of Pope Paul IV on August 18, 1559, Polanco expressed a hope that a more generous dispensation than any hitherto granted might soon be forthcoming. Meantime the Roman Jesuits continued to besiege Cardinal Ghislieri with appeals for the mitigation of the law, to Peter's growing satisfaction. He was not yet out of the wood, however, for in October he wrote as follows to Laynez :

Though I no longer feel myself obliged to observe the Index legislation in every detail, I yet hardly have the courage to examine the necessary books which Cardinal Truchsess left for my inspection, as I am still without greater light and licence from the Holy See. . . . New heretical books dealing with the dissensions within the sect have appeared, and it would be a great help if we were in a position to inform Catholics

[1] Braunsberger, *Epistulae*, vol. ii, pp. 467, 471.   [2] Braunsberger, *Epistulae*, vol. ii, pp. 500-1.

about them. Would your Reverence please deliver me from these
scruples that I may no longer be worried by the fear of excommunication? Meantime, I am keeping those books but do not dare to read
them. And would you also intercede with the new Pope on behalf
of our confessors, that they may not be prevented by the severity of
the Index from giving absolution to students who have forbidden
classical texts in their possession?[1]

Two months after the election of Pope Pius IV Polanco reported
to Canisius : " With regard to the Index, the Holy Father summoned
our Father General to him and explained that it was his intention to
mitigate the rigour of the legislation in some degree, in which work he
hoped to have his assistance. The Pope also said that no books except
heretical ones were prohibited and that confessors had faculties to absolve
those who had violated the law. At the same time, he wished it to be
observed in future. . . ." Owing to Peter's persistent representations and
the tireless efforts of his brethren in Rome, concession upon concession
flowed out to Germany, until by the end of 1560 there was little more left
for them to ask. The new year brought still better news, for Polanco was
able to report in January, 1561, that Laynez had spoken again to the Pope
about the Index question and that " His Holiness had formed a congregation
of many cardinals and some prelates and theologians to deal with it."
Laynez himself was one of those appointed, and spoke so well before the
cardinals that they requested to have his discourse in permanent form.[2]

On March 10th, Pope Pius, petitioned by Laynez, abrogated all the
more galling features of the Pauline Index, as far as the German Jesuits
and their penitents were concerned. The ban on classical texts and other
study books annotated or published by non-Catholics was permanently
raised and only books expressly heretical or immoral in intention were
excluded from the dispensation. That the influence of Peter Canisius
counted for much in this affair is plain from the words with which Laynez
began his address to the Pope : " Most Holy Father, as we may see from
information supplied by Doctor Canisius, and from experience, it would
greatly promote the service of God and the good of souls if Your Holiness

---

[1] Braunsberger, *Epistulae*, vol. ii, p. 533. Publishers tried all sorts of tricks to dodge the legislation. One of these was to bind a known orthodox writer with other more doubtful authors, using
only the orthodox man's name on the cover. A publisher of Alcalá did this, with the result that no
less a person than St. Francis Borgia found himself on the Spanish Index of 1559 ! Astrain, *Historia
de la Compañia de Jesus*, vol. ii, pp. 110–13.
[2] Braunsberger, *Epistulae*, vol. ii, pp. 604–5, 689–90 ; vol. iii, p. 27 ; M.H., *Epistolae Patris Nadal*,
vol. i, p. 388.

were to grant some of our Fathers the following faculties. . . ."[1] In addition to the faculties connected with the Index, Peter had earnestly petitioned for and been granted another important one, namely to dispense from the very fierce Lenten regulations of those days which forbade, not only meat, but butter, cheese, and eggs, every day of Lent including Sundays. As the faculties were not yet complete enough to meet the situation in Germany, and as Cardinal Ghislieri had imposed certain restrictions on those granted, Laynez instructed Peter to beg for fuller powers when answering the Pope's gracious Brief to him, cited above.[2] This the Saint did on May 10, 1561:

BEATISSIME PATER,

I owe and offer Your Holiness, whose dignity is the sublimest on earth, infinite thanks for deigning to write and comfort in so many ways your little, unworthy servant. Blessed be God and the Father of Our Lord Jesus Christ who operates in Your Holiness so powerfully and sweetly by His adorable Spirit that your solicitude extends, not only to the general administration of the Church, but in a special manner to the spiritual restoration of the German people and of the City of Augsburg. Would to God that we of the least Society of Jesus, who work in this devastated field, had it in us to satisfy worthily Your Holiness's noble desires and truly paternal counsels. Then, indeed, would this vineyard of Christ not only be delivered from the wild beasts and ravening wolves who have so long and ruinously made it their prey, but it would be immediately and completely restored to its supreme Shepherd, the only Vicar of Christ on earth, and to his Apostolic Fold. For that consummation we must assuredly promise all our labour and care. We must be ready to a man to pour out our lives and blood for it if we wish to live up to our profession and to do our duty by the Holy See.

We also owe and reverently offer Your Holiness our profoundest thanks for having, of your special grace and clemency, granted our Society, and especially that part of it settled in Germany, certain faculties, to the end that fortified with them we might the more easily secure here a rich harvest of souls for the glory of Almighty God. Only this I would add, that among the said faculties some are not included which, as I explained to our Reverend Father General, would help to remove every scruple and to make everything plainer for us. . . . We, therefore, with the greatest reverence, humbly pray Your Holiness that, of

[1] Braunsberger, *Epistulae*, vol. iii, pp. 69–71.   [2] p. 442.

your generous and most ready kindness in our regard, you would vouchsafe, as is your wont, to lend a willing ear to our Father General when he acts in this matter for us, and furnish us with the spiritual helps meet for the salvation of souls. Whatever favour is granted us we shall use sincerely and selflessly, as the institute of our Society demands, for the sole glory of the Most High and the spiritual advantage of our fellow-men. We pray and shall ever pray that Your Holiness, under the leading of divine grace, may duly feed the flock committed to your care, and, having finally put to flight the monsters of error, bring it with joy to the pastures of holy unity and eternal life.[1]

The letter was in Latin such as Cicero himself might have approved, but it did not at all satisfy its composer. Instead of addressing it direct to the Pope, Peter sent it to Laynez. "As it needs polishing," he said, "I most earnestly beg that it be corrected and, if necessary, rewritten, before being presented to His Holiness—should it, indeed, be thought advisable to present it to him at all. . . . I must confess that this style of writing is beyond my capacity."[2]

And now it is high time for this long Augsburg chapter to close, though St. Peter's intimate association with the City did not cease for many years beyond the point we have reached. Throughout the next exceedingly busy and important period it remained his headquarters, and he continued his sermons at the Cathedral with undiminished energy. Augsburg to-day is one of the chief industrial cities of Germany, and it has even been called by one of its enthusiastic sons, who knew not what he said, "the Manchester of the Fatherland." But in the midst of the machines the old Augsburg lives on, the Augsburg of famous Imperial memories, of Fugger greatness and of Peter Canisius. The Cathedral, dating from the eleventh century, stands tranquil in its garden close, unrestored, unmodernized, exactly as St. Peter knew it. Elias Holl, the Sir Christopher Wren of Augsburg, was too fine an artist to disturb its peace. Wandering there, one can hear in fancy the bustle of the dead generations, as the magistrates, the great families, and the hearty shop-keepers and gildsmen come in to Mass. Then there is a pause and an earnest voice speaks in pleasant old German, pleading with all preachers and teachers, Protestant and Catholic alike, to tell men of Christ as He was and not as shallow sentiment would have Him appear, of Christ, one and undivided, who lay a baby in the manger and will come in the

---

[1] Braunsberger, *Epistulae*, vol. iii, pp. 140–41.   [2] Braunsberger, *Epistulae*, vol. iii, p. 143.

clouds of heaven with great glory to judge the living and the dead:
" Heut findt man der Prediger viell die nur von der ersten Zukunfft
Christi durch das gantz Jar predigen und sagen gar liebliche susse
ding. . . . Wen sie aber demgleichen auch predigten von Christi urthel,
gerechtigkait, und der Ewigen straff, so wurde der gemein man nit
so grob und leichtferttig an alle forcht dahin lauffen, in alle sundt und
laster, sonder einen eingezogener wandel furen, und noch der beicht
und buess vleissiger trachten in disser kurtzen Zeit der genaden.
Demnach lass uns bitten dass sie und alle Prediger nit ein halben sonder
ein gantzen Christum predigen, wie uns die Christenlich Kirch gepredigt
und lang zuvor David gesungt hat, *Misericordiam et Judicium.*" —
To-day there are many preachers whose sermons all the year round are
on the first coming of Christ alone, and about it they have sweet and lovely
things to say. . . . But if they would preach, too, on Christ's Judgment,
on justice, and on eternal punishment, the common man would not so
easily and lightly lose his awe of God in the midst of sin and viciousness.
Rather would he turn aside and devote himself earnestly to confession and
expiation during this short time of grace. Let us pray, then, that such
preachers and all preachers may preach, not half a Christ, but Christ whole
and complete, Christ as the Christian Church has preached Him to us, Christ
as David sang of Him long before, the Christ of Mercy and Judgment.

In 1930 the Protestants of Augsburg celebrated the fourth centenary
of the *Confessio Augustana.* Once upon a time that compromise of
Melanchthon had been the creed of practically all the people, but the
sermons of St. Peter, preaching an uncompromising Christ, had started
a marvellous process of change. The Augsburg official directory for 1930
gave the City's population as 165,522. Of that total Jews numbered 1,203,
unbelievers 2,307, Protestants 32,693, and Catholics 129,319. In 1614, when
Peter had been seventeen years dead, the then Burgomaster of Augsburg,
Matthew Welser, who had won renown as an antiquary, wrote in the following terms to the Saint's first biographer : " The memory of Father Canisius
will always be, not only honoured, but held sacred by me. I learned to
venerate and revere him first when a boy or rather mere child at my father's
house and from that day to this I know the place which he has held in the
esteem of my parents and whole family, though his good offices were not
restricted to a few families but embraced the entire City with admirable
charity. With completest truth can we say of our Augsburg affairs : *Pater
Canisius plantavit, Pater Roseffius rigavit, incrementum autem Deus dedit.*"[1]

[1] Braunsberger, *Epistulae*, vol. viii, p. 377.

CHAPTER XII

THE LAST PHASE OF TRENT

THE difficulties and dangers which beset the third and final meeting of the Council of Trent from its opening on the frosty morning of January 18, 1562, to the December day in 1563 when Cardinal Morone pronounced the "*Andate in pace*," were so great that the final success is one of the strangest and most unaccountable events in history. Each of the three great Catholic powers, France, Spain, and the Empire, contributed its share of trouble, and that the Pope and his four Legates, defenceless in a material sense and mere children at diplomacy compared with some of their opponents, should have piloted the Church to safety through two terrible years of almost incessant darkness and storm argues something more than human skill or prudence behind the scenes. Naturally this book is concerned with the Council only in so far as it bore on the life of St. Peter Canisius, but it may help to elucidate his rôle in the story if a summary is given of the principal difficulties with which the Fathers of Trent were confronted from the beginning. These centred round three famous men, the Spaniard, Pedro Guerrero, Archbishop of Granada, the Frenchman, Charles de Guise, second Cardinal of Lorraine, and the Hungarian, George Drascovics, Bishop of Fünfkirchen. On the very day of the Council's opening, Guerrero, chief of its stormy petrels, demanded that it be officially declared a continuation of the previous meetings at Trent in 1545 and 1551. Though such a declaration would have immediately antagonized both France and the Empire, whose rulers desired the Council to be thought new and independent in hopes of conciliating their Calvinist and Lutheran subjects, Guerrero could not be made to keep quiet about it. At the other pole, the Emperor and the Cardinal of Lorraine, virtual ruler of France, were so determined to preclude even the semblance of a continuation that for long they blocked any attempt to resume the discussion of the Sacraments at the point where it had been left off in 1552. Neither man was much interested in dogma, and each insisted that measures of practical reform should be the main business of the Council.

Among the items on the Emperor's programme were the concession of the chalice to the laity in Holy Communion throughout his dominions of Germany, Bohemia, and Hungary; the permission for married persons to take Holy Orders and for men already in Orders to take wives; and, most sinister of the demands, the reform of the Pope and his Curia by action of the Council. With these startling proposals Lorraine and his French brethren were in close sympathy but, mindful of their place in Christendom, they had a point of their own to add, that the Council should solemnly affirm its superiority to the Pope. The Spaniards, on the other hand, headed by Guerrero and stimulated by frequent exhortations from King Philip II, declared war à outrance on the proposal of granting the chalice. That this attitude was not adopted out of any tenderness for the Pope and his Legates, who, as a matter of fact, were open-minded on the chalice question, quickly became apparent.

In order to appease the Emperor and the French authorities, the Legates, with the sanction of the Pope, restricted the first efforts of the Council to discussion of twelve articles of reform. The first of these ran: " By what means can patriarchs, archbishops, bishops, and all who have the cure of souls be compelled to keep residence ? " This question, innocent though it looks, was a veritable powder-magazine in those days, and Pedro Guerrero was the very man to put a match to it by asking in his blunt and injudicious way whether the duty of residence had its basis in divine or only ecclesiastical law. It was not Guerrero's intention merely to find a theological means of keeping migratory bishops tethered to their dioceses. Beneath the surface controversy aroused by his question lay one that " affected the innermost constitution of the Church, and involved in itself the old antithesis between the papal and episcopal systems."[1] It split the Council into two violently opposed camps, that of the Spaniards captained by Guerrero clamouring for a definition that bishops, not only in their power of Orders, about which there was no dispute, but in their power of jurisdiction, held their credentials directly from God. The Pope in conferring a bishopric was merely to be considered as designating the individual person on whose shoulders God Himself then placed the mantle of authority. As championed by the Spaniards the theory amounted to a denial of the Pope's universal jurisdiction, for it made each bishop a Pope in his own diocese. Guerrero

[1] Pastor, *History of the Popes*, Eng. tr., vol. xv, p. 272.

accordingly played straight into the hands of the Gallicans, headed by Lorraine, though on the question of the chalice the two parties remained violently opposed.

As the story proceeds, the Emperor, for all his loyal Catholicism, will be seen to have shared the French view on the power of the Pope, so it is not surprising that good men should have wondered anxiously whether the Church was not going to be faced again with the controversies of Constance and Basle. None of the parties concerned had the welfare of the Church as a whole for their aim. Ferdinand and Lorraine desired the chalice and the abrogation of clerical celibacy primarily as a sop to their discontented subjects, and Philip of Spain opposed such concessions for fear they might affect the peace of the Netherlands. In other words, it was fundamentally politics and not concern for true religion that governed the relations of the three great Catholic powers with the Council of Trent. How nearly they brought the Council to disaster may best be shown by anticipating at this point and citing a letter written from Trent more than a year after the Fathers had begun their activities. It was from Cardinal Hosius, one of the five Presidents of the Council, to St. Peter Canisius :

His Lordship, Bishop Commendone, has delivered to me the letter in which, according to your piety, you lament for the cause of the Church. And, indeed, it is a matter for the tears of all good men, as there is danger that, under pretence of reformation, some terrible deformation may come to pass. There are not wanting children of the Church who would lay under orders him through whom order and unity, aye, and the majesty of princes, have hitherto been maintained ; so that the Church might now very well make the plaint of the inspired writer her own : " The sons of my mother have fought against me. For if my enemy had reviled me I would verily have borne with it, and if he that hated me had spoken great things against me, I would perhaps have hidden myself from him. But *thou*, a man of one mind, my guide and my familiar. . . ! "

What we had looked to suffer from the Protestants we now see done by people who profess that they are children of Mother Church. The divine right of bishops is hotly maintained, but to me it seems any sort of right except divine, since God's command is that the servant of the Lord must not wrangle.[1] The matter is pressed with such violence that charity, whose divine right is beyond dispute, would seem to have

[1] 2 Tim. ii, 24.

died in the fray. . . . Those Fathers who contended that all of a bishop's powers are divine and that he holds his jurisdiction, not from the Pope, but directly from God . . . would immediately cry out that the liberty of the Council was being violated if the Legates ventured to admonish them that they should confine themselves to the Council's programme and leave alone questions on which there was no controversy between Catholics and Protestants. The liberty of the Council, they seem to think, consists in each Father saying boldly whatever comes into his head, even if it is calculated to throw the Church into confusion. Who is there among the Lutherans or the Zwinglians or the Anabaptists who does not boast that he has been chosen directly by God? But these men are heretics, because they would have themselves so divinely established that they deny their subjection to the Roman Pontiff. The champions of divine right in the Council will allow nothing or next to nothing to the Pope in the matter of episcopal jurisdiction. As among our Protestant opponents one hears only of God's word and the Gospel, so in the Council some people have Christ and the *jus divinum* in their mouths all the time. A dissentient from their view barely escapes the taunt of being an enemy of Christ. I was astounded when I realized what was going on, and filled with greater sorrow than I could ever express to you. I would sooner have expected such behaviour from the Saxon Lutherans than from the sons of our Mother, the Church. Clamouring their shibboleths of Christ and the divine right, their ears remained deaf to those who pointed out that it might also be part of the glory of Christ to recognize and pay due honour to His Vicar, since the master may be honoured in the honour given his servant and, contrariwise, reckon himself contemned when his servant is despised.

We endeavoured, as we thought our duty, to satisfy these contentious men, without prejudice to the authority of the Pope, by proposing, as a distinction between lesser pontiffs and him who is recognized as Supreme Pontiff, the statement that the Supreme Pontiff rules the Universal Church. Fresh clamour then ensued, the objectors saying that the words were intolerable as bearing the implication that the Pope was superior to the Council.[1] As we saw that a terrible storm was brewing we did not consider it permissible for us to proceed further

---

[1] Lorraine and the French Ambassador, de Lanzac, were the chief fomenters of trouble. De Lanzac and his colleagues said that they would be stoned on their return to France if they did not fight for the complete removal of the words asserting the Pope's universal jurisdiction, and Lorraine protested that he had received personal instructions from the King of France and 120 French bishops " *ne verbis hujusmodi . . . ullatenus assentiantur.*" So Gabriele Paleotto, who was present in an official capacity, in his *Acta Concilii Tridentini*, published for the first time in 1842 by the English Protestant

with the matter. I believe that they want to build a Babylon in this place. They would all like to play the part of Legates and have authority to put motions before the Council. If the Legates do not at once obey their orders they threaten to take over their office and carry it on themselves. So you see to what a pass we have come. At a time when it was the duty of all to work their hardest that the dignity and authority of that See by which the unity of the Church is maintained should be increased rather than diminished, all seem instead to have conspired against it. Should any difficulty arise, the last thing they will suffer is that it be referred to the Pope, though by the institution of Christ Himself that has always been the custom in the Church of God. Not one ambassador of a prince here but turns to his master if in doubt about some graver issue. But let the Legates turn to the Pope and they are at once accused of committing some terrible crime, as though they were sending to Rome for the Holy Ghost. . . . That is how we are placed, so you must pray more than ever that God, made angry by our sins, may convert us and cause these tempestuous winds to cease. There is nothing to which we are less opposed than true reformation, but now, as I have said, what we have greatly to fear is some dreadful deformation. . . .[1]

Now, having some general conception of the storms that assailed the Council, we are in a better position to appreciate the stand made by St. Peter Canisius on its behalf. It will not have been forgotten that he owed every college in his Province to the munificence of the Emperor or the Duke of Bavaria, and yet it was to the schemes of these men, for whom in many respects he had the deepest admiration, that he showed the most determined opposition. From the first Peter found himself unable to sympathize with their anxiety to conciliate the Lutherans or to share their sanguine hopes that if the Council followed their instructions the Lutherans would attend it and, perhaps, even return to the fold of the Church. The Colloquy of Worms had taught him his lesson. He knew

---

clergyman, Joseph Mendham (pp. 370–371). That Mendham's aims were not too strictly the service of pure scholarship is clear from his English preface to the Latin text: " Should the present publication, by the peculiarity of its character, contribute to evince the fact that a Christianity predominantly and pervasively vitiated, with all the aid of ecclesiastical and secular pomp and patronage, favoured, too, by every and the utmost efforts of abused learning, and the flattery of interested and capricious friends, is still unable for a moment to hold up her head in the presence of any form of Christianity in almost the slightest degree restored to its original purity,—should this happiest of all results be in any degree realized, the Editor will feel a joy and thankfulness far surpassing any which might reasonably arise from the conviction of having presented to fellow students in the same path of literature a new and interesting relic of human history " (pp. xxii–xxiii).

[1] Braunsberger, *Epistulae*, vol. iv, pp. 63–7. The agitation of Hosius is very obvious in the wild Latin of this letter, which in many places defies literal translation.

his Lutherans too well by now to be under the delusion that they would be satisfied with any concessions short of the one laid down by their founder in a letter to Melanchthon, August 26, 1530. " All this argument about concord in doctrine," he said, " is utterly repugnant to me, because such a thing is quite impossible unless the Pope is willing to abolish his Papacy." When, therefore, Father Lambert Auer, who was present, gave him a detailed account of the boorish welcome accorded the Papal Nuncios by the Convention of Lutheran Princes at Naumburg in 1561, Peter was sad but not surprised.[1] That they should have stood on their hind legs because the Pope addressed each one in traditional form as " Beloved Son," was just what he would have expected. They knew of no such Father, they said, and it was " a scandalous thing for a man to pose as arbiter of controversies and religious differences who is himself the fount and origin of all discord and dissension, or for a person to sit in judgment whose rightful place is with the criminals in the dock."[2]

Though St. Peter was convinced that no amount of persuasion or friendly advances would bring the Lutherans to Trent, in fact that nothing would bring them but the abdication by the Church of her immemorial traditions, yet, aware that with God all things are possible, he worked and prayed, and tirelessly exhorted others to work and pray, that there might be a miracle. Months before the Council's reassembly he caused special litanies to be sung by the students of his colleges for a Lutheran change of heart and other blessings contributory to the Council's success. His sermons in the Cathedral of Augsburg were always prefaced by a prayer for it and frequently devoted to explaining what it meant, or to refuting Protestant libels against it. For the success of his many undertakings in Germany he was largely dependent on the good-will of the secular power, yet he did not hesitate to assert emphatically from the pulpit that secular princes had no right whatever to interfere with the Council's decisions, and to cite as a warning the leprosy with which King Ozias was punished for his attempt to usurp the functions of the priesthood.[3]

It would not be too much to say that the Council obsessed Peter during these years. It was the biggest interest, the biggest hope and, at critical times, the biggest sorrow of his daily life. The delays of the German bishops in going to Trent astonished and troubled him greatly. *Mirum*

---

[1] Prince Maximilian, who was in close touch and sympathy with the Naumburg Protestants, described their reception of the Nuncios as " a detestable piece of bad manners." Holtzmann, *Kaiser Maximilian II*, p. 387.

[2] The whole story is well told by Raynaldus, *Annales*, sub. ann. 1561, nn. 25–29 ; also, Ehses, *Concilium Tridentinum*, vol. viii, pp. 149 sqq.

[3] Braunsberger, *Epistulae*, vol. iii, pp. 375, 392, 409, 457, 622, 726, 759.

et miserandum were his words for their procrastination. Some pleaded that they were too old, some favoured the Lutherans, and some were afraid of them. Peter would not allow their pleas. " We are afraid of everybody except God," he answered. Every shred of influence he possessed was used to the full in an unwearying effort to overcome their misgivings. He could even employ the weapon of scorn, as when pointing to the good example of other nations he exclaimed : " *Sola friget et dormit Germania* "—Germany alone remains in her frozen sleep. For some time he had been on terms of intimate friendship with Cardinal Stanislaus Hosius. In December, 1561, he suggested to this learned and zealous man " that the Council would appear far more distinguished if a letter or writing of some kind were printed either casually or of set purpose giving the names and qualities of its members and presidents. People are also of opinion that it would help if one or two of the Council's public orations were put in circulation. The world, which is exceedingly avid of such news, would then have the material for forming a more correct estimate, and the spirits of Catholics in distant lands would be increasingly strengthened." A little later in the same month he again appealed to Hosius : " I am on the look-out for an oration or anything else in print commending the Council. My hope is that the Council's authority may thus be increased, as I think strangers have not that high regard for it which is its due." Within a few weeks the same ardent wish is once more expressed : " I do so long to be in possession of some of the speeches pronounced at the Council."[1]

It was Peter's joy to assist from afar the Presidents of the Council by every means in his power. As always in his life, he remained the lowly servitor of God's servants, too greatly honoured to be able to ease their burden a little or to add a mite to their content. The Cardinal Legates' chief needs were the latest news and the latest books, both of which Peter supplied with unflagging diligence. For the books he sent an agent to the periodical fairs at Frankfurt, where the great printing firms used to display their wares. Every new Protestant work of any importance was there secured and dispatched to Trent, Peter himself doing the necessary packing. Scores of such books went off by courier, some of them being such ugly and ponderous tomes as the famous *Centuries of Magdeburg*.[2]

---

[1] Braunsberger, *Epistulae*, vol. iii, pp. 325, 346, 373, 383.
[2] Braunsberger, *Epistulae*, vol. iii, pp. 240, 322, 326, 363, 374, 393, 396, 409, 428, 485, 489, 530, 575. The " Sixth Century " of Flacius Illyricus and his band betrayed in its preface the hopeless state of confusion and internecine strife to which the German Protestants were reduced. In 1559 a Venetian envoy had counted fifty-five different sects among them, each antagonistic to all the rest. Only against Trent were they at one. Among the books sent to the Legates by St. Peter was a tract teaching that no Christian could appear at the Council without committing grievous sin.

The gentle reader might ask himself at this point how he would have liked the job, especially if he had been a busy man with five colleges and a few sermons a week on his mind. But what the reader may really want to ask is why, if Peter was such a great fellow, he did not receive a personal summons to Trent. To that point in his story we may now turn our attention.

In February, 1561, nearly a year before the Council opened, the Dean and Chapter of Augsburg Cathedral addressed the following letter to Cardinal Truchsess who was in Rome at the time:

It has come to our knowledge that Canisius will be sent to the Council which opens at Trent on the Feast of the Ascension. Should this happen, words cannot express the damage that our church will suffer through his absence. Since the day when Father Canisius was appointed by us, with your Lordship's approval and consent, to preach the word of God in the Cathedral Church of this City of Augsburg, or rather after he was sent to us by the apostolic commission of Christ Our Lord, all know well the great things that he has accomplished. Our church had hitherto been ravaged and devastated in many ways by impious men. The death of Father John Fabri, that eminent man and preacher, left it desolate and languishing. Then came the learned Father Canisius to comfort and refresh it anew with his salutary discourses, and, as concerns Catholic truth, to build it up once more from the foundations. . . . All the great fruits of his labours will endure only if he remains in Augsburg. As for the argument that the Council, being a public matter, ought to have preference to Augsburg affairs, which are private, there are many good reasons against it. So we most earnestly beg your Lordship to intercede with the Holy Father and with the authorities of the Society of Jesus that Canisius may not be summoned to the Council.[1]

Towards the end of 1561, when the danger of losing St. Peter again became acute, the Augsburg canons renewed their appeal:

Father Canisius has done wonders with his daily sermons and exhortations during this last Advent. We know for certain that the number of Catholics in our city is growing every day, and accordingly

[1] Braunsberger, *Epistulae*, vol. iii, pp. 589–90. The Feast of the Ascension mentioned in this letter as the date of the Council's reopening, was not the date fixed by the bull of convocation. That appointed Easter Sunday, 1561, but, owing to difficulties raised now by Spain, now by France or the Empire, the Council had to be postponed many times and did not actually start its sessions until January, 1562.

beg your Lordship to use every means in your power to prevent Father Canisius from being called to the Council. He could not possibly do greater good at Trent than he is doing here, where we seem to have nobody but him, whereas in Trent there are plenty of learned men. His absence might occasion the lapse of many new converts whom he has brought to the Church, and the Lutheran preachers would take heart of grace once more with him out of the way. While he is here they are all frightened and bewildered and know not what to do, as they see the people flocking to him in such numbers.[1]

Meantime, during the summer of 1561, St. Charles Borromeo, nephew and secretary of the Pope, had informed Cardinal Hosius at Vienna that the Holy Father desired four representative German scholars to be sent to the Council as papal theologians. Hosius could only think of Father Canisius as suitable for the post, and even to him there was the objection that the Emperor did not favour his presence at Trent. Ferdinand had appointed Archbishop Anton Brus of Prague, Graf Sigmund von Thun, and Bishop George Drascovics of Fünfkirchen his ambassadors to the Council, and for them drew up secret instructions which he submitted to the criticism of his privy-councillor, Dr. George Gienger. This man and the Vice-Chancellor of the Empire, Sigmund Seld, had great influence with Ferdinand, and both were decided "Gallicans," firmly convinced that a reform of the Church could only be brought about if the Council were recognized, at least in practice, as superior to the Pope. Gienger, in his answer to the Emperor, suggested that a few theologians might be attached to the ambassadors, "not, however, stubborn or supercilious ones, such as most of that class are." Ferdinand replied that he had given much thought to the matter and had discussed it with his advisers: "But the extreme scarcity of such men has proved an obstacle to Our good intentions. You are aware that We possess few theologians of international celebrity, or who are suited for the arduous business in hand. True enough, among the Jesuits there is Canisius and also Nicholas Delanoy, but both men seem to be somewhat reluctant about making concessions, and perhaps they would show less enthusiasm for the reform of the Roman Curia than the necessity of the case requires."[2]

Goodness knows St. Peter was no enemy to reform, of the Curia or anything else, but he wanted it done decently and in order, and not as part of a plot to lessen the authority of the Pope. How would the Emperor

---

[1] Braunsberger, *Epistulae*, vol. iii, p. 601.   [2] Braunsberger, *Epistulae*, vol. iii, pp. 723-4.

have liked it had the Council assumed the right to dictate to him about the composition of his cabinet, the number of his ministers, the extent of his taxation? And yet that was precisely what his advisers wished the Council to dictate to the Pope, believing, as they erroneously did, that it possessed the higher jurisdiction. St. Peter, on the other hand, having studied history and theology to some purpose, knew that in the design of God the Pope came first, and that it was for him and no other human authority to reform his Curia. Consequently, Peter was not the man for Ferdinand.

Meantime Cardinal Hosius had gone on to Trent where he conferred with his presidential colleagues, Cardinals Gonzaga, Seripando, and Simonetta, about the choice of the German theologians. On their behalf he wrote as follows to Cardinal Truchsess, December 17, 1561:

The Legates have now discussed several times the question whether Father Canisius is to be called. At first there was a variety of opinions, some considering that he ought not to be removed from a city where he was doing so much good, and others wishing most decidedly that he should be summoned on account of his learning and great experience of German affairs. So the pros and cons of the matter swung to and fro, but now finally all are agreed that he is to be summoned. Many men here think that he will prove more useful to the Council than Lindanus or anybody else. I may tell your Lordship that I have always desired his presence, but I do not think that he ought to come before next Easter, as it would not be wise to remove him from Augsburg during Lent. After that he will be able to come without inconvenience, as about Easter-tide he usually goes to Innsbruck or elsewhere on a visitation of the colleges of his Society. During those months that he annually spends away from Augsburg he can remain here without much damage to that City. I have heard that your Lordship desired his presence here as your personal representative and I explained this to the Legates, as we do not wish to arrange anything without reference to you. Would you please let me know your wishes. You may rest assured that we shall take no steps with regard to Father Canisius without your consent. . . .[1]

That neither the Jesuit authorities nor Peter himself were very anxious to accede to the demands of those who wished him at the Council is made abundantly plain in the following excerpts from their correspondence:

[1] Braunsberger, *Epistulae*, vol. iii, pp. 725–6.

Polanco to Canisius, March 29, 1561 : The Chapter of Augsburg Cathedral acted rightly in taking measures to keep your Reverence among them. It is better that you should remain unless there be great hopes of advantage to the Council from your appearance at it. We shall not fail to help you with our prayers.

Canisius to Salmeron, September 13, 1561 : The Lord Cardinal of Augsburg has written to me in such fashion that I suspect he wishes to use my services at Trent. If given the option of refusing I would gladly do so, as I am only too conscious that I would be of little or no use in that assembly of the learned. Moreover, if I have to go, there will be some difficulty in finding a man to take my place in the pulpit here, as the Cardinal wishes him to be one of our Society.

Canisius to Salmeron, October 12, 1561 : My heartiest thanks to your Reverence for having interceded with the Cardinal of Augsburg on my behalf and for procuring me permission to remain on here as a preacher, however poor and cold, instead of going to play the part of an incompetent theologian at Trent.

Canisius to Salmeron, December 27, 1561 : Cardinal Hosius has written again to say that they are still discussing at Trent the question of summoning me thither. The Cardinal of Augsburg has been informed and I am hoping that he will find some excuse for keeping me here during Lent, when there is a chance of gathering in the harvest of the Lord, if such be the ruling of holy obedience. . . . *Domini voluntas fiat.*

Canisius to Cardinal Hosius, December 29, 1561 : It astonishes me that great men should trouble their heads in the least about summoning me to Trent as I know right well that if I were to appear there I should be like a goose among swans. Your Lordship can judge whether it is expedient to withdraw this workman, mean as he is, from the Augsburg vineyard during Lent, the season when labour is most profitable in fruit. However, let the Cardinal of Augsburg decide what he thinks best. I am completely at the disposal of holy obedience, and I shall strive for the good of the Church wherever I be, with the help of the Lord. May He deign to increase His grace in our souls. . . .[1]

In order to encourage any Protestants who might feel inclined to put in an appearance, the Council issued a safe-conduct of the widest scope, and in the first of the resumed sessions postponed discussion of

[1] In another letter, addressed to Salmeron, March 14, 1562, St. Peter, quoting a favourite book the *Noctes Atticae* of Aulus Gellius, says : " For such a great matter as the Council your Canisius possesses about as much competence as an ass does to appreciate a melody on the lyre."

doctrine to give them time to get to Trent. It was a vain act of courtesy, and some there are who can see in it, not even courtesy, but an empty pretence.[1] It is a marvellous gift to be so certain of other people's motives. The activities of St. Peter and his Roman brethren had made the Index a live question, so with the Index the business of the Council began on January 30, 1562. The fractious Guerrero at once made difficulties, as he did on nearly every point of procedure, and it took several lengthy debates to crystallize the eventual decision that the task of forming a new Index and new legislation be entrusted to a committee of eighteen Fathers who might choose assistants from among the theologians. The Fathers, it may be repeated, were the bishops and other prelates and the generals of religious orders who held the franchise of the Council, while the theologians, to whom the adjective " minor " was attached, had the sole function of enlightening the Fathers by their discussion of doctrine and so enabling them to vote with wisdom.

At the second session of the resumed Council, or the eighteenth of Trent as a whole, held on February 26th, there were present the Legates, the Cardinal Archbishop of Trent, three patriarchs, sixteen archbishops, a hundred and five bishops, four abbots, five generals of orders, and fifty theologians. No French or German bishops had as yet appeared, but the Council was plagued with a swarm of clerical and lay emissaries from the rulers of both countries. Through his agents the Emperor requested that the Confession of Augsburg should be spared the indignity of inclusion in the new Index. Though the Lutherans professed the lordliest indifference to the activities of the " so-called synod of Trent," Ferdinand endeavoured to make the Legates' flesh creep by warning them that if they banned the Confession they might pay for it with their lives. He seems to have been in mortal terror of a Lutheran rebellion, just as the Cardinal of Lorraine was that the German Protestants might come to the assistance of his own mutinous Calvinists, and, however well or ill founded their apprehensions may have been, they explain and, to a certain extent, excuse the policy pursued by both men in their relations with the Council of Trent.

Certainly, things were going very badly for the Catholic Church in Germany. St. Peter, watching anxiously from his outpost at Augsburg, reported to the Presidents at the end of January the apostasy of the Archbishop of Magdeburg, and the forcible appropriation by the Saxon Elector of the vacant See of Merseburg. It was rumoured, he said, that the Archbishop and the Electors of Saxony and Brandenburg were going

[1] The writer in the *Cambridge Modern History*, for instance (vol. ii, p. 676).

to send agents to Trent for the express purpose of disturbing the Council. A story had been given wide currency by the Lutherans to the effect that the Pope and the Catholic monarchs were conspiring at Trent to form a league for the destruction by fire and sword of all who refused to accept the Council's decrees. So circumstantial was the preposterous calumny that people had the names of the princes and cardinals who were in the plot on their tongues and could reel off the precise sums contributed by each to the war-chest. In order to rouse the hatred of the populace against him the Pope was represented as the ringleader and chief organizer of the conspiracy. Continuing, Peter reported :

A friend of mine has told me about a French gentleman who has come to Germany on a mission to the Lutheran princes. He is an adherent of the King of Navarre, and according to rumour he will ask the princes what instructions and conditions they wish to have imposed on the bishops whom the French government are about to send to Trent, and also what measures they intend to take should the Catholics attempt to defend the decrees of the Council by force of arms, as was thought probable. He will endeavour to come to some agreement with them on this matter. There are men who consider that the object of the devil in these negotiations is to unite the Calvinists and Lutherans.

Perhaps I am following up these events more freely than my position warrants, but I do so not out of mere curiosity or any desire to be an investigator and censor of public affairs. I think it advisable that your Lordships should know what good men in this country suspect, and that you should sometimes ponder on these matters. May the Divine Goodness grant that our fears prove groundless with regard to the wiles and fraudulent dealings of those who leave nothing unattempted that they think will help to baffle and undermine the sacred Council. I am sending you herewith some widely circulated writings that have been many times reprinted with the object of winning the Lutherans over to Calvinism.[1]

During the months that followed, Peter pursued his labours for the Council and for the salvation of Germany with such self-forgetful zeal that his health gave way, but even on his bed he was an apostle. He circularized his brethren with never a pause, begging them, for the love

[1] Braunsberger, *Epistulae*, vol. iii, pp. 360–2.

of Him who died to make all men one, to pray and fast and offer daily penances for the welfare of the Council. To guide the faithful in general he composed special formulas of intercession, or selected such from the liturgy, and soon practically the whole Church in Germany was addressing to Heaven on the Council's behalf the ardent desires and petitions of his heart. He sent some copies of these prayers to Cardinal Hosius, who acknowledged them in the following letter from Trent, February 10, 1562:

Very welcome news must it be to all good men that the Council is at last open, for which you have waited with longing and devoutly prayed. I would urge you and your Society to continue praying, did I not know, as the adage says, that it is unnecessary to put the spur to a horse already in his stride. This I feel all the more since reading the selection of prayers which you made and edited. They have pleased me immensely. I have presented each of the Legates with a copy and they have given instructions for the insertion of some of the prayers in the solemn public litanies which are to be recited here during Lent. Our hope in God is that through the prayers of the faithful ' that which our sins do hinder may be hastened by the bounty of His propitiation.' Would that, according to the desires of all good men, it was given to us to see present here not only the German bishops but also the Protestant representatives. We should then have better hopes for the happy progress and success of the Council. However, God's goodness permits us to promise ourselves this boon, as it is easy for Him to put the desire of coming into their hearts.

It will be your part to persuade and encourage any bishops with whom you are acquainted, so that they may not be deterred by the difficulties of travel, or, if unable to come themselves, that they may send delegates. Your Society has houses in Mainz, Cologne, and other places. Urge your brethren who may have some influence with the bishops to leave no stone unturned in their efforts at persuasion. It was good to learn from your letter that the Electors of Saxony and Brandenburg and a third party whose name escapes me at the moment were going to send representatives. I pray God that they may come, no matter what their intention in coming may be. Saul who set out to persecute the Church was changed into Paul. . . . God is the same now as He was then, equally potent, equally kind, equally merciful. He can take away the stony heart and give a heart of flesh, and He can bring about that those who came to curse His people should change their hearts and utter a blessing. As He is the fount and source of all goodness, He not only can but wants to do this, provided we pray to Him in faith, nothing wavering. Even from the stones He will raise up children to Abraham. Oh, let them come, let them come, no matter what their purpose be. They will find here the welcome of paternal charity . . . and we shall vow in our hearts not to be overcome by evil but to overcome evil by good. This favour of the divine mercy we hope to obtain especially through your prayers, in which we have the greatest confidence.

Those rumours of which you gave us information are a mere pack of lies, and I know who their author is.[1] I beg you to keep me well posted about all the proceedings at the Convention of Ulm and about any other matters which you consider it would be advantageous for us to know. In doing this you will render not only myself but all the Legates a much appreciated service.[2]

Knowing that work had begun on the revision of the Index, Peter told Hosius that he was " waiting hungrily " for the results of the Fathers' labours. When the decree setting up the commission was published in March he expressed his joy and satisfaction with its moderate tone: " I pray God to confirm the Fathers in the spirit of apostolic meekness. It is such milk that Christ's little ones need, and it is by such a bait that wanderers will best be lured home." With April came the time for the visitation of the Jesuit colleges, a duty which Peter hoped might deliver him from the necessity of going to Trent. On receiving another urgent invitation from Cardinal Hosius he answered as follows from Innsbruck, May 4, 1562:

I am very grateful to your Lordship for the singular kindness which inspires you to desire my presence at the Council. Would that it was in my power to show you by every manner of service how deeply I appreciate your goodness, but unfortunately many grave reasons prevent me from being able to meet your wishes this time. It was only with the greatest difficulty that I secured permission from my Augsburg friends to make this small journey to our college here in Innsbruck. I had to promise them that I would be back in the Augsburg

[1] It was the viciously anti-Catholic Duke of Württemberg who concocted the story of the 'League of Trent' at the Convention of Ulm in January, 1562. Walter Goetz, Beiträge zur Geschichte Herzog Albrechts V, p. 235, note 3, in Briefe und Akten zur Geschichte des sechzehnten Jahrhunderts, vol. v.

[2] Braunsberger, Epistulae, vol. iii, pp. 375-9.

pulpit for Pentecost and for the daily sermons during the solemn celebration of the octave of Corpus Christi. . . . I shall say nothing about the responsibilities with which I am at present charged as visitor and provincial superior of our colleges; responsibilities which I cannot easily lay aside without grave injury to those institutions. Then again your Lordship knows that little is to be expected of me at Trent which other men more learned and better versed in German affairs could not supply. In a short time our Father General and Dr. Alphonsus Salmeron will be coming to the Council at the Sovereign Pontiff's behest, and I have no doubt at all that they will perform their duties well and satisfy the expectations which are held of them. For this additional reason I still more earnestly beg and implore your Lordship to take my excuses in good part, and to believe that I have only one end in view, which is the glory of the Divine Name. I feel that I shall be better able to help souls to their salvation by celebrating Pentecost in Augsburg rather than in Trent, should that be the will of God. . . .[1]

Hosius now played his last card by invoking the authority of the Pope. In his love for Peter he did not wish to convey the unpalatable news himself, so he employed the good offices of Father John Couvillon, already well known to us, who was at the Council as 'orator' or official spokesman of the Duke of Bavaria. On May 8th, Peter wrote in agitation to Salmeron:

This very day I was hoping to set out on my journey back to Augsburg, as I had finished quite satisfactorily all business here in connexion with the brethren, the house, the school, and the school buildings. To God be the praise and glory. But, lo and behold ! a letter is handed to me from Father John Couvillon at Trent, saying that the Lord Cardinal of Ermland has been expostulating with him about my conduct. I had been already several times summoned to Trent and the Cardinal of Augsburg had given his permission, yet I continued to put off the journey. Well, the Lord Cardinal wished me to understand on the authority of the Holy See that I must go now at this summons from Father Couvillon. He promised that I should be allowed to depart from Trent within a month.

On receipt of the letter and order I took counsel with my brethren and decided to put off the journey to Augsburg while I wrote to explain

[1] Braunsberger, *Epistulae*, vol. iii, p. 427.

to the Cardinal and Father Couvillon my grave reasons for thinking that it would be wrong for me to be absent from that City during Pentecost and the following days. If they admit my plea I shall go straight thither, God guiding me, but if they still insist, I shall obey, as Father General has told me to do so should I receive a further summons. May the Lord turn everything to His glory. I repeat what I have often written before, that I am but little inclined to go to Trent as I am not sure that those judge wisely who think I am the man to transact their business. . . . All the more, then, do I beg your Reverence to help me with your counsel, your prayers, and your Holy Sacrifices.[1]

Perhaps it might be thought that Peter's procrastination was rather inconsistent in one who judged the German bishops so sternly for their delays. But he was not a bishop with a deciding vote in the Council and, moreover, he had given a definite undertaking to the Augsburg Chapter, with the full sanction of his religious superiors, that he would not leave them in the lurch during the important seasons of Pentecost and Corpus Christi. Cardinal Truchsess was almost as reluctant in the matter as he, and permitted him to go only on condition that he was set free " *quam brevissime*," so the voice of obedience seemed to call him in two opposite directions. Cardinal Hosius mentioned an order from the Pope, but that might have meant anything, and certainly Peter was justified in his contention that there were plenty of theologians in Trent to do the business for which he felt personally that he had no special qualifications. At any rate, whether right or wrong, his attitude and that of his superiors would seem to evince a certain modesty in the aspirations of the Jesuits, surprisingly at variance with the opinion which many worthy people have held and hold of them. Had they wanted glory for their Society, Trent was undoubtedly the place to find it.

As Laynez was absent from Italy on papal business[2] and Salmeron had been instructed to resume his old position of leading 'minor' theologian to the Council, St. Francis Borgia had taken over the government of the Society of Jesus. To him Peter Canisius wrote from Trent on May 17th:

---

[1] Braunsberger, *Epistulae*, vol. iii, pp. 433–4.
[2] He had been sent with the Cardinal of Ferrara on a legation to France, where he had valiantly defended the faith and the rights of the Holy See at the famous Colloquy of Poissy, the village near Paris where St. Louis was born. Some of the Catholic authorities present—there were six cardinals, forty archbishops and bishops, and the whole royal family of France at the Colloquy, not to speak of such people as Beza and Peter Martyr—told Polanco that listening to Laynez saying out boldly what they had not the courage to say themselves was " as refreshing as a bath in rose-water." M.H., *Lainii Monumenta*, vol. vi, pp. 61–2. Other documents on Laynez's activities at the Colloquy and immediately afterwards are in vol. viii, pp. 759–68, 775–805. For an excellent English account, see Evennett, *The Cardinal of Lorraine and the Council of Trent* (Cambridge, 1930), pp. 283–393.

I arrived in Trent safe and sound three days ago, thanks be to God, whereupon Cardinal Hosius immediately gave orders that I was to be lodged in the quarters which he had made ready for me in his own house. Before my coming he had been ill in bed and seriously preparing for death. Now he is telling everybody as a wonderful thing that my arrival was the signal for his complete restoration to health. He treats me as a most intimate friend and consults me about much confidential business. In both will and deed he is assuredly a man who deserves well of the Council and we owe him the tribute of special prayers to Our Lord on his behalf. Many bishops here, especially among the Spaniards, are friendly to our Society. Father General is expected, and as there is a report that Father Salmeron has already left Rome he is likely to be here even sooner than his Paternity. Heaven grant that they may not be long, as I would like very much to see both of them, but hope, in accordance with the wishes of the Cardinal of Augsburg, not to be detained here more than a month. . . .

As to conciliar affairs, the number of bishops and theologians increases every day, but there will be no further public disputations for three weeks. Meantime, a serious and bitter dispute is going on among the Fathers as to whether a bishop's duty of residence has its origin in divine or ecclesiastical law. A pronouncement will be made on the matter in the next session on June 4th. Some here are scared by the tyrannical and seditious plots of the sectaries in France, and the position in Hungary looks serious to the last degree. If the Turks now in arms conquer again it will probably mean the end of everything, so I earnestly beg your Reverence to set our brethren praying for the Council, France, and Hungary. May God, who now vouchsafes to reform His Church, turn every chance to His own glory. . . .[1]

Having shepherded Peter to Trent, we must now consider as briefly as the matter allows how he occupied himself during the month of his sojourn. Apart from the angry and often disedifying debates and parleys about the question of residence, it was a rather slack and uninteresting period of the Council. This, however, was not the fault of the Fathers, who were only too anxious to get on with their work if the secular authorities of Germany, France, and Spain would permit them. Peter's impressions are best given in his own words, to which comment can be added when necessary :

[1] Braunsberger, *Epistulae*, vol. iii, pp. 442-4.

To a Roman Jesuit, May 25, 1562: It is astonishing that Father Salmeron, whom we have been expecting from hour to hour, has not yet put in an appearance. His arrival will not be very welcome to a number of people, especially the Spaniards, as they give out openly and often that he has been sent by the Pope to confute their opinion as to the divine origin of the obligation of episcopal residence. They consider that this opinion ought soon to be solemnly defined by the Council. Some say that Salmeron has written a book on the subject and others bring forward evidence from his letters. As I perceived that this sinister rumour might prejudice many people not only against Salmeron personally but against our Society, I endeavoured to remove the suspicion from the minds of certain influential men, for I do not believe that there is a word of truth in what is said.[1] The ardent souls of those who contend vigorously, perhaps even with excess of vehemence, that the divine right theory of episcopal residence should be declared an article of faith, are not entirely a mystery to me. Things have come to such a pass now that all feel how essential to the Fathers is the divine assistance, if tempers are to be moderated and the daily heated discussions brought to a happy conclusion. I therefore earnestly beg that there may be more diligent prayer than ever for the success of the Council, especially between now and the next session on June 4th. *Ab omni schismate liberet nos Dominus.* . . .

As for myself, I really cannot see that I am doing anything of importance here. The Fathers have appointed me to a congregation of bishops and certain theologians, whose business it is to decide about the reformation of the Index published by the Roman Inquisition. The new Archbishop of Prague also makes use of my services from time to time, but most of my day is given up to Cardinal Hosius, who is a close friend and treats me with the greatest kindness. There is not much to be gained, I think, by a prolongation of my stay here. The German field suits me better, and it would facilitate my return thither if the Cardinal of Augsburg were given a hint to write to Cardinal Hosius asking that I be set free. . . . Among the Spaniards our greatest friend and patron seems to be Archbishop Guerrero of Granada, with whom we went to dine yesterday. . . .[2]

[1] There was not, and no shred of evidence exists that the Pope had given Salmeron instructions of any kind. The evidence that does exist goes to show that Pius IV was singularly scrupulous just at this time in not interfering with the business of the Council, whatever he may have done later on.

[2] It is an interesting fact that the three men, Lorraine, Guerrero, and Drascovics, whose aims and views the Jesuits at Trent, and especially Laynez, opposed most determinedly, were three of the best friends their Society had. Without the generous patronage of the Cardinal of Lorraine it could not

Canisius to a Jesuit resident in Germany, Trent, June 4, 1562: I shall tell you something now about the Council. The world's most learned theologians are present here in greater numbers than I think it would be possible to find elsewhere on earth. In addition we have many experts on civil law who have been sent by princes and kings. Hither have come, and still come, men of all nations, and ambassadors invested with the authority of their governments, Germans, Hungarians, Spaniards, Portuguese, French, and Greeks, not to mention a vast number of Italians. In our time there has not been seen a more learned and distinguished gathering of the Church's prelates, which includes six cardinals, seventeen archbishops, and one hundred and sixty bishops all told. France promises to send forty more in the near future and as many are expected from Italy; not to mention the Englishmen who have signified their intention to come. Though at first the Council's affairs appeared desperate, by the wonderful power of God the Fathers have been brought together in such numbers, and secular princes have given such united support, that now thinking men confess in all sincerity *a Domino factum est istud et est mirabile in oculis nostris.* I myself have seen terrible difficulties that blocked the way happily removed and changed to bright auguries, by Christ, the Church's Defender. A woman cannot bring forth her child in joy without the antecedent moans and anguish of her labour.

To-day the Fathers celebrated a session, memorable as a truly worthy and dignified spectacle, whether we consider the devout and beautiful ceremonies, the solemn and deeply pondered orations, or the majesty and varying ranks of the ecclesiastical and lay persons who took part in it. After the ambassadors sent by France and the Catholic cantons of Switzerland had read their instructions and received the Council's courteous reply, the procedure to be followed by the theologians each day in their morning and afternoon discussions was arranged and promulgated. Then debates were set on foot about the use of the venerable Sacrament of the Eucharist and about the decisions to be taken with regard to Communion under both species. It is the duty of all devout men to render heartiest thanks to God for His goodness in thus starting the Council with greater strength and better hopes

---

have survived in France, while in Spain its most liberal supporter was Guerrero. Drascovics, for his part, was a close friend of St. Peter and, when he became Cardinal and Chancellor of Hungary, did a great deal for Peter's brethren. The story does credit to both parties; to the generous-hearted prelates who were incapable of petty revenge, and to the single-hearted Jesuits who did not hesitate to jeopardize their bread and butter when they considered that the interests of the Church were at stake.

than ever before, and to beseech Him with ardent desires for the success of this renowned and necessary instrument of the Church's life, that so the verities of true Faith may be established, the errors of the new sects extirpated, and the discipline of the Church restored to its pristine vigour. We must also pray to the Father of mercies for the heretics, that after having been so often called and earnestly invited and long expected, they may at last come to realize that they have no honourable excuse for staying away. Here is the Council for which they have so often petitioned at their own meetings, a free Council which they can approach with complete security to put forward their views before accredited and competent judges. Kindly and sympathetic will those judges undoubtedly be, ready with patient ears to listen to all that they have to say. Only let them come to the Great Supper, forgetting their first rude and graceless refusal. . . .[1]

Canisius to St. Francis Borgia, Trent, June 18, 1562: It is the opinion of everybody here that Father Salmeron is the best theologian at the Council. He has brought the Society great honour, and blessed be God who willed that its light should shine among men of such dignity and influence. I have no doubt that when Father General arrives he will still further strengthen the Council's friendly attitude towards us. I, too, have been ordered to speak my views, and some say that I was a success. The Lord was good to me through the prayers of the Society. To Him be all the glory. . . .

Canisius to a Jesuit resident in Germany, Trent, June 19, 1562: As you are anxious to know how the Council proceeds, here are a few details. The commotion caused by differences of opinion between some of the Legates has now died down.[2] Public disputations have begun and are being held in a very suitable roomy place before vast audiences. The first congregation begins at 10 o'clock in the morning, after solemn High Mass, and goes on for three hours. Three theologians speak, but on rare occasions there may be a fourth, and there are present cardinals, archbishops, bishops, and ambassadors of princes. In fact

---

[1] One of the chief Protestant leaders of those days, James Schmidelin, Chancellor of the University of Tübingen, bears out what Peter says about the learning of the Tridentine theologians. Schmidelin had written a book against the Council which was being printed at Frankfurt. On June 29, 1563, he wrote to a friend in that city: "I remember saying somewhere in my book that the Fathers of the Council were ignorant men. Please see that that remark is entirely deleted as I hear that men of immense learning have gone to Trent." Braunsberger, *Epistulae*, vol. iii, p. 458.

[2] Cardinal Gonzaga and Cardinal Simonetta had had a quarrel about the odious question of episcopal residence. Hosius and Simonetta, who was a great authority on canon law, saw in the Spanish theory of divine right a weapon against the primacy of the Pope and strongly opposed the attempts to have it defined. Gonzaga and Seripando did not share their forebodings. See Pastor, *History of the Popes*, Eng. tr., vol. xv, pp. 272–82.

nobody is excluded. After dinner a second congregation is held, when three or four other theologians speak for at least three hours. I understand that there are more than a hundred theologians at the Council, representing the public authority of different nations and provinces, or acting as assistants to the bishops and princes. At present they are dealing with the question of Communion under both species, which has been submitted to them in five articles that the discussions may be orderly and to the point. The articles are as follows :

(1) Are all and each of Christ's faithful obliged by a precept of God to receive the Most Holy Sacrament of the Eucharist under both kinds ?
(2) Are the reasons which led the Holy Catholic Church to administer Communion under the species of bread alone to lay people, and also to priests not saying Mass, still to be considered so binding that no condition would justify the administration of the chalice to the laity ?
(3) If for valid reasons of Christian charity it be thought good to concede the use of the chalice to any particular nation or kingdom, under what conditions is the concession to be made ?
(4) Does he who communicates under one species only receive less spiritual benefit than he who communicates under both ?
(5) Is it necessary in virtue of a divine ordinance to administer Holy Communion to children before they come to the use of reason ?

Forty theologians have now given their views on these articles. The first to speak was Father Salmeron, whom the distinguished assembly heard with the greatest satisfaction and no less admiration. How many times have I not wished that the Protestants were present . . . to see and hear theologians of such acumen, judgment, linguistic ability, and sincere charity. . . . You must not think that the speakers are hampered in the expression of their views. They are quite free. Those whose turn to speak comes later carefully criticize the words and reasoning of their predecessors and sometimes even openly reprehend them. This is done, however, with due modesty, in search of the truth rather than out of a spirit of emulation. Often enough learned men are beaten in argument by other learned men, and in the battle of wits new points of view on the matter under discussion are constantly brought to light. Great and singular indeed is the favour of God in assembling here picked and chosen experts from every nation to profess, illustrate, and vindicate the teaching of Christ with such united zeal. One thing alone I see to be lacking. Very many of those who were called to the Great Supper have chosen, with their futile objections, to appear in the light of ungrateful guests, rather than come and refresh themselves in the company of their brothers on the good things that the Lord has prepared for them. . . . Let us pray to the Lord to fill His house where all things are ready, compelling them to come in. Amen.

These interesting extracts show Trent as it was, its grandeur, its human imperfections, its freedom, and above all its friendliness. They show, too, that Peter Canisius had not much scope for the display of his theological gifts at the Council. No details have come down of his work on the congregation of the Index, but as he was an intimate friend of Archbishop Brus, in whose house and under whose presidency most of the meetings were held, and as the findings of the Fathers coincided eventually in almost every particular with the views that he had been ably championing for many years, it is reasonable to believe that he had a large share in the victory of moderate counsels. In October, 1562, he wrote to Hosius from Vienna : " I cannot but express my joy at the success of the recent session, though news of what was decreed at it has not yet reached us. There is great and widespread hope that the much desired mitigation of the Roman Index may have been brought about for the relief of certain good men's scruples. To speak according to general opinion in this part of the world, those will do a good work who help at the Council to make the Index more tolerable. . . ."[1]

A decree of the Council promulgated by Pius IV on March 4, 1564, swept away all the harsher provisions of the Pauline Index. Classical texts, dictionaries, concordances, and other works of science or scholarship edited or compiled by non-Catholics might be used freely by everybody, provided they contained nothing contrary to sound doctrine. Translations and editions of the Fathers of the Church by heretics or condemned writers such as Erasmus were also permitted on the same conditions, and bishops were given extensive powers for the revision and subsequent authorization of books that deviated into heresy only occasionally. While strictly prohibiting all deliberately obscene lucubrations the decree made an exception in favour of the ancient poets who sinned in this respect, " *propter sermonis elegantiam et proprietatem*," at the same time laying down that unsavoury passages were to be most carefully hidden from the

[1] Braunsberger, *Epistulae*, vol. iii, p. 490.

eyes of youth. The ' mancies,' on the other hand, were ruthlessly banned —geomancy, hydromancy, aeromancy, pyromancy, onomancy, cheiromancy, necromancy, and so were all other books of fortune-telling, magic, and astrology. It was a terribly superstitious age, but the superstitions certainly received no encouragement from the Council of Trent.[1]

The other negotiations in which St. Peter took a prominent part were those concerned with the question of Communion under both kinds. It was an old, old question and had troubled the Church since 1414, the year in which John Hus left Prague for the Council of Constance and eternity. Up to that time there had been no actual prohibition of Communion *sub utraque*. It was the common practice of the primitive Church, and continued, side by side with Communion *sub una*, right up to the thirteenth century, when, chiefly for reasons of health and reverence, it gradually fell into disuse in Western Christendom. The Church had always taught that Christ is whole and entire under each species, and that doctrine had not been impugned, except by isolated heretics such as Berengarius who rejected the Real Presence altogether, until in 1414 an obscure Prague professor known as James the Little began to proclaim that Communion under both species was a divine command and that those who received under the form of bread alone committed a sacrilege. Hus's numerous following rallied to the support of James, and the movement spread with such rapidity that the Council of Constance, knowing it to be based on a false doctrine of the Holy Eucharist, felt obliged to condemn it and to prohibit the use of the chalice to the laity in 1418. Then followed war and revolution, during which the chalice became the Czech national emblem. It replaced the crucifix in churches, was carved on the gates of towns and palaces, embroidered on the banners of the insurgents, and painted on their shields. In the interests of peace the Council of Basle decided to allow the laity of Bohemia and Moravia to receive Holy Communion *sub utraque*, on condition that they acknowledged Christ's integral presence under either species. The required guarantees were given by the secular and spiritual authorities of Bohemia in the " Compacts " of Prague, but they were soon broken, and in 1462 Pope Pius II denounced and abolished the concession, which had been tolerated but never ratified by his predecessors. That step led to immediate schism and the renewal of war. Ferdinand inherited the desperate problem when he succeeded to the throne of Bohemia in 1526, and, having his hands full with Turks and other troubles, felt obliged to tolerate the religious practices of his new kingdom.

[1] The full text of the decree is in Labbé-Hardouin, *Acta Conciliorum*, vol. x, col. 207–10.

Meantime Luther had appeared. It took him some years to be convinced of the necessity of the chalice for lay people, but the Confession of Augsburg taught it, and the Zwinglians and Calvinists, while denying the Real Presence, were urgent in the same direction. Soon Germany began to be flooded with books championing the practice, and great blocks of people still calling themselves Catholics suddenly found that they were being defrauded by the Pope of something necessary to their salvation. The tenderness of their consciences on this point is in curious contrast with their broadmindedness on matters of temperate living and sexual morality. The movement for the chalice spread like wildfire. Within a few years it had overrun Bavaria, disorganized the religious life of Austria, penetrated the Rhineland, and pushed over the border into France. Everywhere the Catholic laity threatened revolt and secession if they were not given the chalice. In answer to the persistent demands of Charles V, Pope Paul III sent three legates to Germany with power to grant the concession, but under conditions so severe that very little success attended their peregrinations.

As the labours of St. Peter Canisius were chiefly in Bavaria, Austria, and Bohemia, he had special opportunities to become well informed on the chalice controversy. In January, 1554, he told Polanco of the clamour that the Catholics of Austria and Hungary were making for the concession, and was informed by Hosius the following year that the Polish Catholics had taken the law into their own hands. In August, 1555, the Saint reported to the General of the Jesuits that " all the best Catholics in Prague were immovably obstinate in their determination to cling to Communion *sub utraque*," so it was not only the Hussites with whom the Church had to reckon. Shortly afterwards the Bavarian Catholic nobility compelled their Duke to issue a declaration that he would not bring legal pressure to bear on any of his subjects who administered or received the chalice. Writing to Father Vitoria from Worms in November, 1557, St. Peter revealed the fact that Holy Communion was being dispensed to the laity *sub utraque* in the Cathedral of St. Stephen, Vienna, quite openly and with the tolerance of the authorities. Significant too is the fact that when, in May, 1561, all was ready for his coronation at Pressburg as King of Hungary, Maximilian ruined the ceremonies and caused them to be abandoned by refusing to receive Holy Communion except *sub utraque*.[1] According to a statement of the same Prince, two-thirds of his father's dominions were at this time either using the chalice in lay Communion or on the verge of revolt because not allowed to use it.

---

[1] Holtzmann, *Kaiser Maximilian II*, p. 391.

The controversy brought the Bohemian Jesuits up against a practical difficulty, as they discovered that many of the Catholic youths coming to their school were in the habit of receiving the chalice. St. Ignatius instructed them not to refuse the boys sacramental absolution if they appeared to be in good faith, but never themselves to administer Communion under both species. In Ingolstadt the report spread that the Jesuits were surreptitious utraquists themselves, despite their avowed opposition to the movement, a mistake due apparently to their use of a dry chalice to contain the small hosts for want of a ciborium.

For some years St. Peter would seem to have been strongly against the concession of the chalice under any conditions. Hosius was the leader of the Catholic opposition, and with his attitude the Saint sympathized to the extent of revising and republishing his *Dialogue* on the subject in 1560. That remained his standpoint up to May, 1562, when he was called to Trent; for during a course of sermons at Augsburg in March of the same year he urged every possible argument from Scripture, the Church Fathers, councils, ecclesiastical history, and even the writings of Luther, Melanchthon, and Bucer, against the contention that the chalice was necessary or advisable for the laity.

At Trent, however, Peter certainly veered round a little to the side of concession, probably influenced by the arguments of his two friends, Brus and Drascovics, the Emperor's ambassadors to the Council. He seems gradually to have adopted a more sympathetic attitude in the controversy, and to have considered, though with much diffidence, that the concession might be worth while as a careful and guarded experiment in a limited area and under very strict conditions. Further than that he would not go; so, to say outright, as some have done, that he was in favour of granting the chalice is to exaggerate the extent of the change in his views. As for the parallel demand that the law of clerical celibacy be mitigated, he never for an instant gave it the least encouragement.

Intimately connected with the chalice controversy was another highly interesting one about the interpretation of the sixth chapter of St. John's Gospel. Many eminent theologians, especially among the Dominicans, held that throughout the whole of the chapter Our Lord was referring only to His Person and His mission of redemption, which He proposed to the multitude as objects of faith necessary for salvation. In other words, the eating of His flesh and the drinking of His blood were metaphors for faith in His Person and His preaching. The majority of exegetes, however, saw in the discourse a plain promise of the Blessed Eucharist. The eating and drinking were not metaphors but statements of marvellous future facts. At Trent the two opinions came face to face in the discussions about the chalice, because the utraquists based their principal argument for the necessity of Communion under both species on the text: " Amen, amen, I say unto you, except you eat the flesh of the Son of Man and drink His blood you shall not have life in you."

The debates on the five articles relative to the chalice question began on June 10th and continued without interruption, morning and after-noon, until June 23rd. They were held in the Church of Santa Maria Maggiore before the distinguished audience already described by Canisius. Sixty-one theologians gave their views, some briefly, some for two or three hours on end. The majority, including Salmeron and all the Spaniards, were strongly opposed to the concession of the chalice under any con-ditions. On the interpretation of St. John, twelve said nothing; nineteen, including Salmeron, Canisius, and two Dominicans, urged the Council to define that the chapter was about the Blessed Eucharist; nine, of whom five were Dominicans, argued vigorously that there was no reference to the Blessed Eucharist in it; and twenty-one, including the great Dominican, Peter Soto, put forward a theory of conciliation according to which both spiritual and literal interpretations ought to be declared equally orthodox. Salmeron was the most powerful advocate of the ' realist' opinion, but to judge by the text of his discourse in Raynaldus he was too fond of press-gang methods in his argumentation. Thus, after citing a few good patristic authorities to his purpose, he concluded with never a blush, *et alii omnes*.[1]

On June 15th Peter Canisius took up the argument for two hours or more. According to Massarelli's summary of his discourse he dealt first with the fifth article and showed by a wealth of quotations from early councils and Fathers that the Church had never considered it neces-sary to administer Holy Communion to children before they attained the use of reason. Then he turned to the first article, and, while main-taining stoutly the literal interpretation of the sixth chapter of St. John proved that the argument for Communion under both species drawn from it by Hussites and utraquists was altogether inconclusive. St. John, he said, makes no mention of the chalice or the fruit of the vine in that chapter, and at the end of it records Our Lord's explicit words, *Qui man-ducat hunc panem vivet*. The words of St. Matthew, St. Luke, and St.

[1] Raynaldus, *Annales*, sub. ann. 1562, n. 50. For an excellent discussion of the whole subject see an article by Ferdinand Cavallera, S.J., in the *Revue d'histoire ecclésiastique*, vol. x (Louvain, 1909), pp. 687–709.

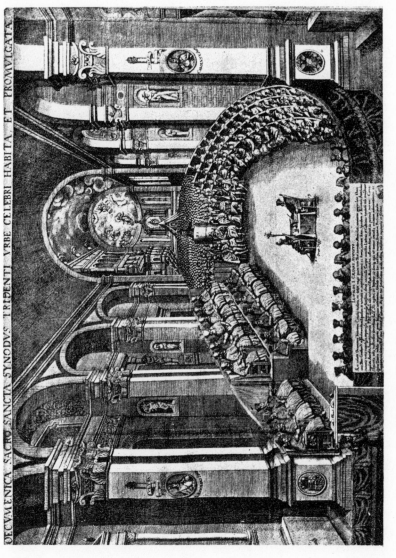

The Council of Trent in session during its last phase.

From a print of the seventeenth century based on engravings made at the time of the Council

Paul, *Bibite ex hoc omnes*, and *Hoc facite in meam commemorationem*, were addressed solely to the Apostles and could not have been intended as a law for the laity since they communicated the power of consecrating the sacred elements. As for the concession of the chalice to the laity, which came under the second and third articles, Peter held that the privilege ought never to be allowed to professed heretics, but that "it should not be denied to Catholics living in the midst of heretics if there was no other way of keeping them in the Church." This proposal he made with great diffidence and as a matter that ought to be most carefully weighed before any action was taken. The only people whose claims he thought worthy of consideration were the Bohemians. He then exhorted the Council to issue an authoritative decree on the Blessed Eucharist in which he devoutly hoped it might be declared that the literal interpretation of St. John's sixth chapter was the right and only tenable one. Chrysostom had put the matter beyond doubt, he thought, and as for the arguments of the opposing school he would show that they were by no means impregnable. In conclusion, he urged the Council to define that as much fruit and grace is derived from reception of the Holy Eucharist under one species as from reception under both.[1]

Peter's desire to have the equality of spiritual benefit from reception under one or both species made an article of faith arose from a well-grounded fear that many Catholics in Central Europe would object, if refused the chalice, that they were being defrauded of graces intended for them by God. Since medieval times there had been controversy among theologians on the subject and some at Trent urged that such great men as Alexander of Hales and Aquinas had not held the view to which Canisius was attached. How carefully and considerately the Council worked is well shown by its final ruling on this question and on the interpretation of St. John, to take but two examples. On July 16, 1562, it declared it to be Catholic faith that Holy Communion is not necessary for children before the age of reason; that the faithful are not under a divine obligation to receive the chalice; that the reasons which led the Catholic Church to change her early custom of administering Holy Communion under both species were just and valid; and that under the one

---

[1] Braunsberger, *Epistulae*, vol. iii, pp. 742–51; for the complete *Acta*, Ehses, *Concilium Tridentinum*, vol. vii (1919), pp. 537–61, 633–50, 691. That Peter's plea for the literal interpretation of St. John was more solidly founded than he knew, would appear to be the conclusion of modern scholarship: "The prevalent opinion among Continental critics now is that St. Paul and the writer of the Fourth Gospel did believe that Christ was really and substantially taken into the person of him who partook of the consecrated bread and wine, as Catholics have always maintained. Modern critical Protestants are free to admit this because they no longer feel bound to believe everything which St. Paul and St. John believed." Bevan, *Christianity* (London, 1932), p. 162.

species of bread Christ the author and source of all grace is wholly and entirely received, by which reception the faithful lose no spiritual benefit necessary for salvation. With regard to St. John, it was defined that his sixth chapter does not prove Communion under both species to be a divine precept, " no matter how, in accordance with the various interpretations of the holy Fathers and Doctors, the text is understood."[1] Accordingly, the theory that the reception of the chalice conveys a special and peculiar grace, and both theories on the sense of St. John, were left open questions and have remained so to this day. But history was to leave its mark on them. As time went on and the battle with Protestantism became more intense the purely metaphorical interpretation of St. John was abandoned by almost all Catholic writers. By a strange oversight many of them in our day appeal to the authority of Trent in support of their position.[2]

With all its reserves the speech of Peter Canisius gave great satisfaction to the ambassadors of the Empire and Bohemia. King Maximilian was informed on June 16th that Peter had spoken the previous day " in most learned fashion and made the Fathers more inclined to grant the use of the chalice." The same day Emperor Ferdinand was posted the following bulletin : " The theologians are now to be heard at their disputations daily. As nearly all of them are Spaniards with little knowledge of events and difficulties outside their own country, they argue as though everything were well with the world and there had been no religious upheavals or merely quite insignificant ones. Canisius alone spoke really to the point yesterday and prevailed somewhat with the Fathers to grant the concession."[3] But the real battle on that point was yet to be fought, as the Council in making its solemn definitions on Holy Communion left the disciplinary question of the chalice over for further investigation.

Meantime Peter had become involved in a minor tragedy of the Council, owing to the presence at it of his old friend and torment, Father Couvillon. Couvillon held a strange position for a Jesuit, that of Bavarian Ambassador. With him on the same footing was the high official of Albert's Court,

---

[1] Denzinger-Bannwart, *Enchiridion Symbolorum* (ed. 1928), nn. 934–7. Apparently when about to promulgate these canons the Fathers of the Council had overlooked, or intended to omit through lack of time, the doctrinal expositions with which the earlier meetings of Trent had prefaced its formal anathemas. From a letter of Truchsess to Hosius it seems to have been St. Peter who called attention to this oversight : " I agree with your Lordship in approving the argumentation of Canisius that teaching should come before anathematizing, nor should a few days' delay be allowed to hinder that arrangement. It is right and advantageous, and will help to reconcile the souls of many. Kindness and meekness ought to be given preference to severity, so that only when you have taught as fathers and educated as masters do you at length come to what necessity rather than your inclination demands." Braunsberger, *Epistulae*, vol. iii, p. 736.
[2] Knabenbauer, Fillion, Crampon, Calmes, etc. Calmes, for instance, says : " Theologians and exegetes have always been unanimous in recognizing Eucharistic teaching in the figures of John vi, 22–75."
[3] Sickel, *Zur Geschichte des Concils von Trient* (Vienna, 1870), pp. 330–1.

Dr. Augustine Paumgartner, whose instructions were to press by every means at his disposal for the grant of the chalice and the abrogation of the law of clerical celibacy in Bavaria. Couvillon felt very uneasy at having to be the promoter of such schemes and the worry brought on an attack of his old trouble, melancholia. St. Peter promptly came to the rescue by persuading him to write and beg release from his ambassadorial duties, a petition to which the Duke assented while requesting the Father to remain on at the Council as theologian to the Embassy. It was the saddest embassy that was ever seen, quartered in a wretched little house, desperately short of money and looked down on, not only by the haughty Florentines and Venetians, but even by the Swiss. Paumgartner grew more furious with every day that passed. That these people should rank themselves before his mighty Bavaria in the order of precedence was an indignity not to be endured; so he appealed to the Legates, who employed St. Peter as an intermediary between the contending parties.

Florence gave in, but the representatives of Venice and Switzerland held their ground, and the latter were eventually responsible for the departure of Paumgartner from the Council altogether.[1] The insight which St. Peter gained by such an experience into the all too human aspects of the Council made him yearn to be away helping his colleges or back with his flock in Augsburg. Cardinal Truchsess was the means of his rescue, secured by addressing some remarkable letters to Hosius, of which the following are extracts:

Truchsess (Rome) to Hosius (Trent), May 30, 1562. The priests of Augsburg are unable to endure their longing for Canisius, and much less can piety and religion put up with his absence. Since the day he left Augsburg, piety has tended to grow cold, and it is to be feared, if he remains away much longer, that the structure which he erected with so much labour and pains may fall to the ground, disturbing many souls. My ears have grown hot with the complaints of numbers who insist on his recall, and I would like him to return as soon as ever he has finished the business for which he was summoned. However great a help he may be to the work of the Council, the good he does by his presence at it cannot balance the evil caused by his absence from Augsburg.

[1] Paumgartner would not appear at any congregation if he knew that the Swiss were going to be present. This was very awkward for Drascovics and Thun, who badly needed his support in their campaign for the chalice, and they were reduced to begging the Swiss to make themselves scarce on at least one occasion, so that the Bavarians might have a chance of putting their country's position before the Council. Šusta, *Die römische Kurie und das Konzil von Trient unter Pius IV*, vol. ii, pp. 215, 237. The four volumes of this work, published as a sequel to Sickel's preliminary investigations (Vienna, 1904–1914), contain the complete correspondence of the Legates with Rome.

Truchsess to Hosius, June 6, 1562. The good men of Augsburg clamour and complain without ceasing. Their vehement cries and lamentations have become a torment to me, telling how they suffer from hunger and thirst for the divine word, and how they fear that their daily need and the absence of him who supplied it may give the purveyors of poisoned food a chance to intervene. . . . Why is Canisius, Augsburg's own man, detained by you at Trent? It cannot be your wish, or that of your colleagues who called him thither for the public good, that the adversary should scatter pestilent seed among the wholesome grain of his sowing. I think he has now fulfilled all that was required of him among you, or if there is any reason for still keeping him it cannot be so great as to justify the longer severance of the master from his disciples, and the father from the sons whom he has begotten and nurtured in the Lord. The loss to Augsburg is altogether greater than the gain to Trent, so that I regard it as an offence against religion not to return Canisius to the place whither he was sent by God, as the incredible results of his labours prove. I am besieged by the letters of my Augsburg flock and by the expostulations of his brethren here in Rome who all assert that Augsburg is suffering the gravest harm from his absence. Wherefore, I beg you to hasten his departure, or, rather, to let his own eager heart hasten it, for I know well how deeply the excellent man grieves to be separated from the people whose salvation is his continual thought and care. It will be the part of your singular piety and goodness to see that he leaves at the earliest moment, if he is not already on the road. Thus will you earn the greatest favour of God, do me an enormous service, bind his Jesuit brethren to you, and be the cause of salvation to many men in Augsburg.

Truchsess to Hosius, June 10, 1562. I think Canisius will already have left Trent. If not, I am very much surprised, nor can those who are delaying him be longer accounted without sin. . . . Though Laynez is said to be on his way to the Council I am unwilling on any account to sanction the delay of Canisius until his arrival. I am absolutely in torment from hour to hour, expecting the news of his departure.

St. Peter appears to have left Trent on June 20th, arriving in Innsbruck after a journey of four days. There he was bidden remain until Laynez came, which was not to be for another six weeks. During that time the new college gave him plenty to do. He presided over the solemn inaugural ceremonies, in which the five daughters of the Emporer took a prominent part, and busied himself building up a good library for his brethren in Tirol. His interest in books was insatiable. This time the Government of Lower Austria generously put 606 florins at his disposal for library purposes,[1] with which he purchased more than a hundred miscellaneous works from the sale catalogue of an old pupil of the great humanist and Hebrew scholar, Reuchlin. Among his acquisitions were several of Reuchlin's own books, including the *De arte caballistica ;* the poems of Sebastian Brandt, author of *The Ship of Fools ;* Averroes' *Destructio Destructionum ;* Summenhardt's *Commentary on the Physics of Albert the Great ;* the works of Duns Scotus ; treatises by Jamblicus-Proclus, Ficino, Bessarion, and other Platonists ; a commentary on the *Golden Ass* of Apuleius ; and several compositions of the humanists, Boccaccio, Pomponius Laetus, Lorenzo Valla, Filelfo, Erasmus, and Agricola. The list proves, at any rate, that Peter's taste in literature was sufficiently catholic, as does the larger one which he made out a little later of books to be purchased at the Frankfurt fairs. This included upwards of a hundred titles, some embracing several volumes. Owing to its length, the list has been relegated to the end of the present chapter, and is well worth a little study for the light which it throws on the methods and the sources employed by Jesuit educationalists in the sixteenth century.

Besides the care of his College, which opened with seventy-one pupils, St. Peter at this time became the preacher and spiritual director of the five royal ladies who resided in Innsbruck. A friendship quickly sprang up between him and them which developed with the years and had a profound effect on their spiritual lives. Already in September, 1562, Delanoy reported that they were overwhelming the Jesuits of Innsbruck with marks of kindness and had given them for their chapel magnificent vestments and altar linen embroidered by their own hands, as well as a beautiful silver tabernacle.

Meanwhile, Peter continued his good offices as the German correspondent of the Legates at Trent. In four days he wrote three times to Hosius, transmitting information received from his friend, the eminent statesman, Dr. Ulrich Zasius. It was reported, he said, that the dilatory Laynez had been seen not far from Augsburg :

I am waiting to hear his decision about my next movements. . . . There are various rumours concerning the Council, and I have been made somewhat anxious by the arrival here of missives from the

[1] Up to the summer of 1562, Ferdinand's treasurers had disbursed no less than 10,129 florins on the Innsbruck College, which must have been a considerable sum, as the annual amount assigned for the support of the whole staff was 1,500 florins. Braunsberger, *Epistulae*, vol. iii, p. 717.

Emperor's secretary, submitting to the Government proposals that seem calculated to undermine the Council's authority. I have also seen another document from Court in which the Pope and his supporters are very freely censured, as though they were bent on depriving the Council of its liberty. Now as the senators here have not all got clean records, and as documents of the same kind are also circulating at the Courts of various princes, your Lordship doubtless understands how much hurt and danger to the Church and the common cause of religion may be the result of them. As for myself, I think it my duty to stand on guard here that we may frustrate the arts and frauds of the devil, and, as far as lies in our power, prevent the business of Christ and the Church from being injured by the private prejudices and unfounded allegations of certain people. It might help somewhat if the Emperor's ambassadors at the Council were to issue prudent denials, and also if the Papal Nuncio at the Imperial Court were given a seasonable hint that the councillors and secretaries of His Majesty should be less free in their circulation of gossip, particularly when it is prejudicial to the authority of the Pope and the Conciliar Fathers. Your Lordship will forgive my seeming inquisitiveness and overlook the fact that I so freely offer my advice about a matter which, after all, may not be so urgent. It comes of my anxiety to serve the Church, which I cannot but grieve to see attacked by many enemies; helped and defended by few friends. I feel sure that the Emperor would be indignant, did he hear or read that the Council was being judged with such levity and contempt. . . . May Our Lord Jesus in His goodness preserve and defend it from the snares and devices of all who seek and love their own rather than the things of Christ.[1]

As the discussions on the Holy Sacrifice of the Mass had begun at Trent on July 21st, Hosius now asked St. Peter to draw up for him a memorandum *De abusibus Missae*. "Though it is going to be a difficult task for me," the Saint answered, "and though previously I had not thought it so necessary, I shall comply with the wishes of so good a friend to whom I owe far greater services." He had heard a rumour that the decree and canons on Holy Communion were to be altered in some respects. "Perhaps it is," he said, "because the Fathers wish to make the argument plainer, in order to meet the needs of this age, for whose diseases skilful physicians know how prudently to adapt their treatment.

[1] Braunsberger, *Epistulae*, vol. iii, pp. 469–71.

I am most anxious to learn what the Council may decide in the matter.
. . . But may the Lord keep in his place the Davus that is myself, and
fire with great zeal the hearts of those who, like your Lordship, are earnestly
devoted to the good of the Church."[1]

Within two days Peter had his memorandum on the Mass written
and dispatched to Trent. Then at long last Laynez arrived to give him
the signal for departure to Augsburg, where he immediately resumed
his preaching, catechizing, retreat-giving, and other ministerial labours.
Between August 15th and the close of the year, forty-one more sermons
went to swell his record in the pulpit. His eagerness for monastic reform
brought him during these months into relations with the Prioress of the
Dominican Convent of St. Catherine, a place inhabited by ladies of high
birth who made very little account of their rules. The Convent would
seem, in fact, to have become a sort of ladies' club, hospitably open to
lay friends and other persons, *dona ferentes*, without any regard for the
law of enclosure. Backed up by the Prioress, St. Peter appealed to Cardinal
Truchsess to get the General of the Dominicans to intervene, and also
secured an order from the Emperor for the appointment of two commissioners to visit and report on the abuses prevalent in the Convent.
Mair, the Protestant chronicler of Augsburg, took an interest in the Saint's
campaign and reported with a certain amount of satisfaction that it had
the effect of causing a flutter among the bright young things in the community, two of whom packed their cosmetics and left for home.[2] But nuns
were not Peter's chief concern. What he desired more than anything,
as he explained to Hosius, was that the Council should seriously undertake the reform of the "*filii Levi*," the priests both secular and regular
whose bad lives were the Church's greatest calamity.[3] His own efforts
in that direction never slackened, and the following year he invited plenty
of snubs and worse, by himself touring the monasteries in the old duchy
of Swabia to see whether he could effect any good by personal exhortation.[4]

Meantime the little Jesuit establishment in Augsburg had begun to
grow. Nadal came on ' visitation ' of the Province, and by his good offices
Peter and his companion, Father Elderen, were given a larger house,
and the comfort of three more of their brethren, one of them a priest.
It was arranged, too, that Father Delanoy should in future have the chief
responsibility for the three colleges of Prague, Vienna, and Tyrnau, Peter

[1] Braunsberger, *Epistulae*, vol. iii, pp. 472–3. Davus was the stock name for a servant or slave
in ancient Latin comedy, and came to stand both for a slow person and for a bumptious one.
[2] *Die Chroniken der deutschen Städte*, vol. xxxii, Augsburg, p. 394.
[3] Braunsberger, *Epistulae*, vol. iii, p. 485.
[4] Braunsberger, *Epistulae*, vol. iv, pp. 1036–8.

retaining merely a general sort of control. For this relief he expressed the deepest gratitude, as the seven houses of his Province, containing 163 men, were too widely scattered to be given adequate attention. And thus it was that the Austrian Province of the Society of Jesus came into existence. The difficulties these Jesuit pioneers had to surmount is some measure of the courage that they brought to their enterprise. In Cologne, according to Bishop Commendone, the Jesuits were nearly destitute. Ingolstadt had its own troubles, caused by the plain jealousy of the local clergy, who resented any intrusion into the preserves which they so grossly neglected; while in Munich, Prague, Vienna, and Tyrnau the plague raged for months with such violence that the colleges had to be dispersed. One of St. Peter's nephews, a young Jesuit at Tyrnau, was among its first victims. Nevertheless, despite their own penury, a glance at the state of affairs in 1562–1563 reveals Peter time and again trying to obtain a promised alms for the sorely embarrassed Fathers in Rome.

But far from being deterred by such misfortunes, Peter and his companions said welcome to each new responsibility that Providence sent them. Thus when, in 1562, the Bishop of Osnabrück asked for a college in his diocese, Peter spurred on his brother Jesuit, Father Denys, to the task and gave him all the help in his power. Denys occupied in Cologne Cathedral the same high post as Peter did in Augsburg, and the Saint wrote encouraging him to exploit his chances zealously for the faith. Using Augsburg as an enticement, he said: "It is grand to see how people now come to confession and Holy Communion who before never gave a thought to the Sacraments. I have to preach very often during this sacred time of Advent, so I beg you not to forget your Canisius in your prayers. . . . My greetings to Fathers Leonard and Francis, to Father Rethius, and to the whole community. How could it not be dear to me, placed in that holy and lovable City of Cologne which keeps my heart bound to it by many ties, and to whose saintly patrons I know myself so much indebted? A happy Christmas to you . . . dearest brothers, and be sure you pray for me."[1] A little later Peter wrote again to congratulate the Cologne Jesuits on their new foundations at Cambrai, Tournai, and Antwerp, mentioning in passing that his own Province was about to take over the management of the University of Dillingen.

Despite his many other commitments, the Saint's eyes were turned most frequently towards Trent. It gave him immense comfort to know that Laynez was now there, the man to whom he had looked up with

[1] Braunsberger, *Epistulae*, vol. iii, pp. 553–4.

such reverence and trust ever since their first meeting at the Council fifteen years before. And indeed his confidence was justified, for, by whatever standards we judge him, Laynez appears a great and noble character. It is admitted now by all but those who have some private axe to grind that he was the outstanding theologian of Trent. In each of its three assemblies, from 1545 to 1562, his able handling of the most subtle questions won the admiration of both friend and foe, and when, three centuries later, it was decided to place six statues of the chief figures of the Council in the church at Trent that had echoed to their voices, he was among the honoured, the others being the three Tridentine Popes, the Cardinal who acted as host to the Council, and St. Charles Borromeo.

The arrival of the Jesuit General at Trent in August, 1562, led to a rather unpleasant little dispute about precedence. This time he held the position of a Conciliar Father, and, as the head of an order of clerks regular or priests, which was the official designation of the Society of Jesus, the Master of Ceremonies assigned him a place in front of the Generals of the older orders of friars or brothers, who at once lodged a protest. Laynez said that he did not care where he was put, provided the status of his Society received no prejudice, and he even asked the Master of Ceremonies to let him take the last place. It was then the turn of the Legates to protest. Requesting the Father to refrain from appearing at public meetings for the moment, they discussed the matter among themselves and decided on a rather amusing compromise. Laynez was instructed to install himself on the opposite side of the church to the other Generals, immediately behind the bishops, from which position of honour his precedence to the gentlemen across the floor might be deduced. On the other hand, they were put down to speak before him, from which it would appear that *they* had the precedence; so anybody might think what he liked about the question.[1]

On September 6th Laynez unburdened his mind on the subject of the chalice, which had again come to the front in the Council. Before him no fewer than 166 Fathers had spoken, of whom 29 were unreservedly for the concession; 31 for it should the Pope be agreeable; 19 for it on the same terms but only in favour of Hungary and Bohemia; 38 unreservedly against it; 10 against it subject to the decision of the Pope; 24 for leaving the affair entirely to the Pope; 14 for putting off a decision until a later date; and one who could not make up his mind to support

[1] Astrain, *Historia de la Compañía de Jesús*, vol. ii, pp. 169–70; the Legates issued an official denial of the hostile rumour that Laynez had sought precedence of the other Generals. M.H., *Lainii Monumenta*, vol. viii, pp. 358–9, 469–71.

any of these conclusions.[1] All through the controversy the Pope himself displayed a very conciliatory temper, and, though convinced that the granting of the chalice would do little to heal the religious dissensions of the Empire, had instructed his Legates through St. Charles Borromeo to give the Emperor every satisfaction in their power. He also let it be known that he wished the matter to be settled in the Council rather than in Rome.[2]

Excitement reached fever pitch during the discussions, fiery Bishop Drascovics distinguishing himself by his terrific exertions on behalf of the concession. Significantly enough, the only German Father present, Leonard Haller, Bishop of Philadelphia *in partibus* and Vicar-General of Eichstätt, stood boldly with the opposition, though his liege-lord, the Duke of Bavaria, desired the chalice every bit as ardently as the Emperor.[3] As was to be expected, Haller's speech made a deep impression on the non-German Fathers, to the very great disgust of the Imperialists. But the most damaging criticism of their cause was reserved for the end when Laynez rose to wind up the long debate. His calm and moderation only enforced the power of arguments based on splendid theological learning and practical acquaintance with conditions in Germany.

Owing to the wide divisions of opinion, the Legates became convinced that a decisive majority for or against the concession would not be attainable in the Council and accordingly submitted a motion that the matter be left to the discretion of the Pope. The impetuous Drascovics and his colleagues, who thirsted for immediate results, thereupon raised such a clamour that the Legates, in the interests of peace, decided to redraft the motion in a form signifying the Council's approval of the concession, subject to whatever conditions the Pope might consider advisable. To this *via media* Laynez raised two highly pertinent objections. First, if, as alleged in the motion, the Council approved the grant of the chalice, then why on earth did the Fathers not make the grant themselves, seeing that that was what the Pope wished them to do? And, secondly, was it right to ask the Council to express antecedent approval of the terms on which the Pope might make it? In matters of faith the Pope's decision would be infallible and the Council could safely signify its *placet* in advance. But this was not a matter of faith. It was a matter of fact and of discipline,

---

[1] Ehses, *Concilium Tridentinum*, vol. viii, p. 906. This is Massarelli's list. Paleotto gives a slightly different one.

[2] Sŭsta, *Die römische Kurie*, vol. ii, pp. 278, 289–91.

[3] The other German Father, Bishop Rettinger, Procurator of the Archbishop of Salzburg, around whose head St. Peter had put a small halo for being the first of Germany's prelates to appear at the Council, prudently departed from Trent in order to avoid the necessity of recording his vote against the concession. His master, the Archbishop of Salzburg, was obstinately opposed to any change of the Church's discipline in the matter.

regarding which the Pope was liable to error. They did not know what the Pope was going to decide, and how then could they express approval, as though certain he would decide for the best?

As a result of these arguments the motion in its new form was defeated by ten votes, so the Legates abandoned it and submitted a simple proposal that the question of the chalice be left unreservedly to the judgment of the Holy See. Despite the heated protests of the Imperial, French, and Bavarian ambassadors, who looked, wrote Laynez, " as though they wanted to excommunicate the Council," this third formula carried the day by a majority of sixty. " God forgive them, for they knew not what they were doing," wrote the defeated Drascovics, referring to the " ayes." Laynez, as before, was among the " noes," because, as he shrewdly observed, the remission of the question unreservedly to the Holy See amounted to a tacit approval of the grant on the part of the Council, a point on which Drascovics was quick to seize in order to console the disappointed Emperor. How little taint there was of selfishness or mere human prejudice about Laynez's attitude all through may be understood from the words with which he closed his great discourse : " It is not because I am lacking in ready deference to the wishes of His Imperial Majesty, in all things unopposed to God and my conscience, that I have reached this conclusion. I know well that all of us who belong to this least Society of Jesus are bound to His Majesty's service by many ties. The Emperor was the first of Catholic princes to receive and foster our Society in his dominions. He has erected and founded colleges for us in various places, as those now in existence at Vienna, Prague, Tyrnau, and Innsbruck testify. Imitating the example of his father-in-law, the Duke of Bavaria has likewise given us colleges in Ingolstadt and Munich and is preparing to establish others. But the more indebted we are for favours and kindness, the greater has been my obligation to say out faithfully what I thought would best promote the glory of God and the salvation of such great Princes and their subjects."[1]

To the authority of Laynez, Drascovics and his allies now opposed that of Canisius. Writing to the Emperor, September 18, 1562, they said : " The arguments of Dr. Laynez were as weak as they could be, and he not only attacked us with pungent words but beforehand had striven to induce many bishops to do the same. He maintains his opinion in spite of the fact that Canisius of the same Society held the contrary

---

[1] For Laynez's part in the discussions, see Grisar, *Jacobi Lainez disputationes Tridentinae* (Innsbruck, 1886), vol. ii, pp. 13*–38*, 24–64 ; id., *Lainez und die Frage des Laienkelches*, in *Zeitschrift für Katholische Theologie*, vol. v (Innsbruck, 1881), pp. 672 sqq., vol. vi (1882), pp. 39 sqq.

view and testified to it in a public discourse."[1] The "pungent words" are a bit of the good bishop's imagination or irritation, nor in reality was there much material difference between the views of St. Peter and his General, as became apparent a month later. The Council by that time had turned over the whole affair of the chalice to the Holy See, which left the Emperor in a predicament as to his next move. He had no intention of sitting down to wait while the Pope made up his mind, nor could he reconcile himself to the fact that all hope was lost of obtaining the dispensation from the Council. His lay advisers, Seld, Gienger, and Zasius, of whose sincerity and loyal Catholicism there can be no doubt, held strongly to what they considered the teaching of Constance and Basle, namely the superior jurisdiction of Council to Pope. Staphylus, who, through the recommendation of his good friend St. Peter, had been appointed superintendent of the University of Ingolstadt, was another learned layman in whom Ferdinand trusted, and he, too, stood by the Gallican theory. As for ecclesiastics, there was the rather inscrutable "Urban the Austrian," Bishop of Gurk and Court preacher, whom St. Peter had taken to task some years before for the indefiniteness of his theology, and, ranged with him, the holy, headstrong Spanish Franciscan Cordoba, chaplain to Maximilian's wife. According to this latter worthy, the Pope was to be accounted a heretic if he refused to submit to the Council. Such were the men to whom Ferdinand most usually turned for light on his problems, all of them good men and true, but as after-events proved insufficiently alive to the dangers inherent in their policy of mediation.

As St. Peter's letters constantly testify, Ferdinand himself was a thoroughly upright Christian, bent on the Church's welfare. He considered, then, that the other side also must be allowed to proffer advice, and accordingly determined to submit his doubts, not only to some of the men mentioned above, but to Father Vitoria and Peter Canisius. In his instructions to Vitoria, of which separate drafts were forwarded to St. Peter, Staphylus, and Dr. Conrad Braun of Augsburg, the Emperor said that he "wished to consult the theologians of the Society of Jesus on the affair in consideration of their eminent learning, their piety, and their zeal to help the cause of religion." Vitoria was therefore requested to find out what his brethren of Prague and Vienna thought. His Majesty felt that the Pope, if applied to for the concession, might attach stringent conditions which would render it valueless. Would it not be sufficient if those wishing to communicate *sub utraque* gave an assurance to their

[1] Bucholtz, *Geschichte der Regierung Ferdinand des Ersten*, vol. ix (Vienna, 1838), p. 699.

confessors beforehand that in all else they were obedient children of the Catholic Church and believed exactly what the Church believed? Then follows a significant postscript : " His Imperial Majesty has been informed of the existence of a suspicion, by no means light or vain, that the relegation of the grant of the chalice to the Supreme Pontiff was brought about at His Holiness's own desire and by certain underhand practices. This was not done because he wished to deny the chalice, but chiefly in order that a kind of prejudice in favour of his authority and superiority over the Council might be established. In consequence thereof His Majesty has acquired a scruple, fearing lest he, too, by petitioning the chalice from His Holiness should seem to attribute to him this authority over the Council, and so to lessen and damage its credit and that of the whole Christian world. . . . His Majesty would prefer to leave this question severely alone. He therefore graciously requests Dr. Vitoria and the brethren of his Society to explain this difficulty also in the deliberations they are about to undertake."[1]

Vitoria, we know, was rather proud of the fact that he found favour with Maximilian, who desired the grant of the chalice even more ardently than did his father. It must have been somewhat of a shock to Dr. Juan in the circumstances, to discover that not one of his brethren had a good word to say for it. Having collected their views he rode post-haste to Trent—celeribus equis—in order to consult Laynez on the problem. Laynez, of course, heartily endorsed the conclusions reached, as probably did Vitoria himself, but he rightly wished to be sure there was no legitimate way of pleasing the Emperor and his son. He had, therefore, to be content with the addition of a few words to the effect that the chalice might safely be conceded " to certain great princes, should they desire it," personally, and not for their subjects. But " the chalice, absolute loquendo, is not expedient," nor should the matter be urged any further. In case, however, the Emperor determines to proceed, petition should be made to the Pope " with whom rests the supreme power of teaching and ruling," for it may no longer be even licit for him to treat with the Council, " lest by so doing he give the appearance of not recognizing the Pope as Supreme Head of the Church."[2]

St. Peter, for his part, wrote a personal letter to the Emperor on October 23rd, enclosing with it a long document setting forth his views on the problems submitted to him. The letter was in the following characteristic terms :

[1] Constant, Concession à l'Allemagne de la Communion sous les deux espèces (Paris, 1923), vol. ii, pp. 813-14. This monumental work, published under the auspices of the French Minister of Public Instruction, contains most of the documents relative to the controversy and its results, together with a profoundly learned commentary.
[2] Braunsberger, Epistulae, vol. iii, p. 514.

On the commands of Your Imperial Majesty being made known to us, Doctor Staphylus and I devoted many days to consideration of the documents regarding the question of Communion. Staphylus, I feel sure, being a prudent and erudite man, will send Your Majesty an admirable report on this grave matter. As for myself, though I can bring but slender competence and judgment to bear, I nevertheless think that I, too, ought to deliver my opinion in a plain and simple fashion. One thing only have I to say by way of preface and that is to beg Your Majesty with all the earnestness of which I am capable, by the most holy Body and Blood of Christ Our Lord, that you, glorious to this day as a Catholic Emperor, would deal with this matter religiously and prudently, according to its importance and Your Majesty's custom. For this is no mere profane or human business. It is altogether divine and of the gravest consequence, in that it concerns Christ Himself, God and Man, having to do with His most holy Body and Blood, both natural and mystical.

If the matter is dealt with unsuitably and unseasonably, and turns out unhappily, wise men forebode that it will spell dishonour to the Sacred Roman Empire, terrible disaster to the Church of Germany, and ruin to multitudes of souls. . . . Therefore, now, if ever, must we be diligent to transact the business of Christ and His Church with reverential fear and trembling, and careful to decide nothing in a matter of such importance without anxious and mature deliberation. So, under the guidance of Christ, will Your Majesty's honour in the eyes of all Catholics remain unimpaired. You will leave to posterity a public and undying memorial of proved faith and ancestral religion, and win immortal glory as a most Christian Prince, a truly Catholic Emperor, and a valiant advocate of the Church. Assuredly, there is nothing that we ought not to dare or do or leave undone, rather than ourselves violate the rights of Holy Church or, given the power, suffer them to be violated by others. This world raves in its old age and rushes headlong to all rebellion and impiety. We are therefore compelled to tolerate and suffer many abuses, owing to the evil of the times, but, as was well said of old, *ad aras usque*—only up to the altars. I shall continue to beg Almighty God that He may direct Your Majesty's efforts and desires to His glory and advance them for the good of the Church.[1]

---

[1] Braunsberger, *Epistulae*, vol. iii, pp. 499–501. The saying, "*sed ad aras usque*" is from Peter's favourite source, the *Noctes Atticae*. The story is that Pericles, on being asked by a friend to swear falsely on his behalf, answered : "It behoves me to help my friends, but only as far as the altars,' i.e., friendship's claims stop short where the claims of God begin.

As the document in which Peter expresses his views would fill twelve pages of the present volume, even in its compressed Latin, a résumé of it is all that is possible. He divides it into four sections, each headed by a question. The first runs : *Ought petition to be made for the use of the chalice in Holy Communion?* The answer is that the whole affair is best left to the judgment of the Pope, who knows German conditions thoroughly and truly loves the German people. No need, then, to hustle His Holiness. Should the Emperor, however, decide to go on urging the matter, *For what nations and persons ought the petition to be made?* Only for the Germans, Hungarians, and Bohemians, among which nations three classes of people are to be distinguished : non-Catholics, sound Catholics, weak Catholics. The first class, says Peter, are ruled out altogether by their own will and doing, for even the Hussites, who differed little from the Church in other respects, unfitted themselves for her favours by their rejection of her disciplinary authority. " Striving over external forms, they turned the symbol of unity into an emblem of schism." Loyal Catholics, on the other hand, neither needed nor asked for the concession ; and were it, so to speak, forced on them, it would lead only to confusion in the churches, to possible irreverence, and to certain trouble of conscience. In fact, all the inconveniences that had caused the Church in the past to give up Communion *sub utraque* would be sure to recur. As for the third class, the weak and vacillating Catholics who seemed to want the chalice purely from motives of devotion, but so insistently that they might fall away from the Church if not satisfied, to such the Supreme Pastor might certainly show some indulgence if no other way could be found to keep them in the fold. " Would to God," says Peter, who knew this class intimately, " that we could observe in them surer signs on which to rest our hopes of a reformation in character, if they are granted the chalice ! Large numbers of them prefer their private feelings of devotion to the common judgment of the Church, while others are to be met with on all sides whose devotion is a mere pretence and mixed up with serious error. They draw apart from the faith and unity of the Church, which has the perfect spirit of Christ, and, puffed up by their private feelings, wish it to be thought that they alone are persons of piety."

The third question is : *Whether the petition ought to be made, subject to certain conditions?* St. Peter replies emphatically that it ought, his urgency being due to the dreadful confusion of doctrine on the Blessed Eucharist that prevailed in Germany. By imposing conditions those who did not believe rightly about the Blessed Eucharist could be discovered and prevented from approaching the Altar until they had submitted to the Church's teaching, and it would become possible to tell at last who were and who were not genuine Catholics. Finally, *What should those conditions be, and how should they be expressed?* As seen above, the Emperor hoped that a mere general declaration of assent to the teaching of the Church would suffice but, on this point, St. Peter found it impossible to agree with him. Such a general declaration, he urged, might be made even by Anabaptists and Calvinists, who could use the word Church as meaning their own theory of the Church, and, moreover, it would afford learned and simple alike a chance of dissembling what they really believed. No ; something more explicit than the mere word " Church " was required. Peter cites the six conditions laid down by the Council of Basle when coming to terms with the Bohemians, and then gives in full the five revised ones that had been suggested and discussed recently in the Council of Trent. In them explicit submission to the Pope and to the decrees of the Council was required, which Peter realized would not easily be obtained in Germany. With consummate tact he proceeds first to show the Emperor the reasonableness and even necessity of the Tridentine demands and then goes on to see whether a formula more acceptable to His Majesty may not be, as it were, distilled from them. He considers that it may, and that by the addition of the adjective " Roman " in the simple profession of faith suggested by Ferdinand, all loop-holes for tergiversation would be adequately stopped up. Continuing, he said that he was well aware of the objections that would be raised to his proposal, owing to the way the very name of Rome was hated in Germany :

But in every difficult cause and, most of all, in the grave business of our holy faith and religion, we must be inspired rather by hope of good men than by fear of evil ones, nor should we so much dread the chances and uncertainties of the future as place all our trust in the wide providence and mercy of God Most High. . . . Assuredly, we are experiencing now the perilous times foretold by St. Paul when men would depart from the faith, giving heed to spirits of error ; when they would not endure sound doctrine but heap to themselves teachers, having itching ears. Is Catholic truth to be abandoned and betrayed or do we wish cravenly to conceal our profession because our adversaries demand surrender ? . . . True, the people shrink in horror from the name, the faith, the obedience of the Holy Roman Church, and even cover it with infamy. . . . But that is all the more reason why we should here and now, out of the charity which we owe our erring brethren, expressly profess and testify by our deeds that we are not ashamed of that Church and its Head which is the Mother and Teacher of all the Churches. . . . I fail to see any cause that would justify silence about the Roman Church and the Supreme Pontiff in the conditions, and I cannot understand the human timidity that makes us wish to dissimulate. Certainly, it is not by such methods that our sick and wavering brethren are going to be cured, whose unworthy neglect, if not actual contempt, of the Roman Church has become habitual. Many of them are intelligent and able men and as such have a strict obligation to profess their faith and render due obedience to the Roman authorities. As for the others, the simple and unlettered, who, perhaps, are not quite capable of understanding these matters, it will doubtless suffice if they have implicit faith. In dealing with them, I think we should strive by whatever means we can to lessen and gradually extinguish the hatred of the Roman Church which the heretics have kindled in their souls with their tales of clerical vices and abuses.

All the more earnestly, then, must loyal pastors and preachers work, instructing their prejudiced flocks with gentle kindness, exhorting them sweetly, praying devoutly for them, and leaving nothing undone to bring back the wandering sheep; for if they are not restored to the Roman Church there certainly can never be one fold and one Shepherd. . . .

It only remains for me now to admonish and, by the Body and Blood of Christ, to beseech all who may have a part in the transaction of this business that they ponder on it and never forget that there is more in it than meets the eye. . . . May the God of all mercy bring about that the decisions taken in this great matter be directed to His eternal glory, to the reverence of this Sacrament, to the good of the communicants, and to the edification of the whole Church. Amen.[1]

St. Peter's Augsburg friend and admirer, Dr. Conrad Braun, gave the Emperor eleven reasons against the concession of the chalice, some of them a little too strong for good theology, as when he declared his opinion that lay people who petitioned for it were downright heretics. Staphylus, on the other hand, took up the defence of such people. They were not heretics, he said, but only weak and troubled souls, groping for the truth. Mercy, then, should be shown them rather than severity.

[1] Braunsberger, *Epistulae*, vol. iii, pp. 499–513.

The conditions ought to be made as easy as possible, and, to prevent an outcry from those who opposed the concession in any form, the whole affair should be arranged privately between the Pope or the Council and the individual bishops concerned. But the report that pleased and influenced the Emperor most of all was that of Dr. Gienger. A learned man who knew how to argue effectively, Gienger esteemed that all conditions attaching to the concession ought to be swept away and replaced by a mere exhortation to right belief. That, however, was not the point that really interested him and roused his eloquence. It was the more delicate one, whether petition for the chalice was to be made to the Council or to the Pope. To go to the Pope, he said, would be to compromise the Council and to violate the decrees of Constance and Basle which established the superiority of the Council's jurisdiction. Since, however, the Council appeared unwilling to do anything in the matter, the only course left was to secure by some means that the Pope made the concession spontaneously and without any request from the Emperor. If this could not be done, Ferdinand, in conjunction with his bishops, might legitimately take the law into his own hands, either by promulgating a new *Interim* or by devising some other scheme at the forthcoming Diet. In conclusion Gienger insisted that the grant of the chalice would not be enough. With it must go permission for priests to marry, if the remnant of Catholicism in Germany was to be saved.[1]

The Emperor, having received and assimilated the reports, suddenly became inactive. He made Gienger's suggestions his own but for the moment refrained from putting them into operation. There was something more important on his mind, as the time had now come for the election of a new King of the Romans. Since that title designated the all but certain successor to the Imperial throne, Ferdinand greatly desired it for his eldest son, Maximilian, on condition that he remained a Catholic. In January, 1562, he had summoned the Prince to Prague and informed him that the Electors of Mainz and Trier would not vote for his election, nor would he, Ferdinand, support it, unless Max gave a solemn undertaking to be faithful to the Church. Max complied, and renewed his vows shortly afterwards. It was politics rather than conviction that determined him, but, once dissociated from the Protestant Princes, it might be hoped that he would in time arrive at something better than

[1] The full text of the reports of Braun, Staphylus, and Gienger is given in Constant, *Concession à l'Allemagne de la Communion sous les deux espèces*, vol. ii, pp. 817–34. "It is an undoubted fact," says Gienger, "that the Pope can both err and sin, whereas a Council cannot, especially in matters that immediately pertain to faith." Truly, as Peter Canisius said, there was more in this question of the chalice than meets the eye !

merely nominal Catholicism. Albert of Bavaria worked his best to help him along the difficult path. In September he was crowned King of Bohemia by Archbishop Brus, amidst great rejoicings, in which the Jesuits took a prominent part. Then, on October 29th, the Electors began their work at Frankfurt. Maximilian behaved with great dignity and considerable courage at this most critical juncture of his life, and was rewarded by success on November 24th. St. Andrew's Day witnessed his coronation at Frankfurt, to the great joy of both Protestants and Catholics.[1] Shortly afterwards Cardinal Truchsess wrote as follows to the Duke of Bavaria : " Rome and the whole of Italy is ringing with the praises of Maximilian. . . . That good man, Canisius, has written to tell me and others in what a spirited and truly Catholic manner His Majesty bore himself when pronouncing his Capitulation. He wavered on no point and said that it was his determination to follow in the footsteps of his ancestors and hold fast to the Catholic religion. This splendid testimony, coming from one so holy as Canisius, is rejoicing the hearts of good men everywhere."[2]

On December 24th the new King and Queen, accompanied by the Duke of Bavaria, paid a state visit to Augsburg. " The Catholics received the King and Queen with immense joy," reported Peter. " The clergy of the City went to meet them in solemn procession and led them to the Cathedral, where a public *Te Deum* was sung. The sectaries had spread a rumour that the King stood with them, but we rejoice to see that he in nowise fails to give the people an example of his Catholic profession. May Christ, the King of Kings, strengthen his faith." None, better than Peter himself, knew how much it needed strengthening. The Jesuits had long been praying and offering Masses for Maximilian, and Laynez now urged Peter to seek audience with His Majesty and lay the homage of their Society at his feet. But Peter was still beset with misgivings. Some instinct told him that Max would be anything but friendly, and that, before long, he would become a serious menace to both Pope and Council. Accordingly, he refrained from presenting himself at Court and resorted instead to audience with God in ardent prayer.

Meantime at Trent the twenty-second session of the whole Council, or sixth under Pius IV, had promulgated the decrees and canons on the Sacrifice of the Mass. That was on September 17th, and the next session was fixed for November 12th, but ten critical months instead of two were to pass before its realization. The Council now entered on its most

---

[1] By special dispensation from Rome, the King was allowed to receive Holy Communion *sub utraque* at the Coronation Mass.

[2] Braunsberger, *Epistulae*, vol. iii, p. 545.

perilous period. Archbishop Guerrero revived the dangerous controversy on episcopal jurisdiction, avowing that for his conviction of its immediately divine origin he "was ready to lay down his life." From the vehemence with which he and his Spanish brethren urged and argued the matter, their aspirations after martyrdom would seem to have been genuine. Nothing would content them but a solemn declaration making their theological hobby an article of faith, and so they brought the Council to a standstill and even threatened its complete disruption. What was really at stake in the controversy was not an obscure and debatable point in the theology of Holy Orders but the chief bond and guarantee of Catholic unity itself, the primacy of the Pope. Quick to see the drift of the apparently innocent arguments that bishops are under divine obligation to reside in their dioceses, Laynez at once stood out as the most determined and formidable opponent of his fellow-countrymen. According to Paolo Sarpi, who would not have minded seeing every Jesuit in Christendom skinned alive, the speech delivered by their General on October 20th against the Spanish theory was the greatest individual effort in the whole course of the Council.[1] Polanco reported to St. Peter that a Spanish bishop who heard it declared himself to have been completely "magnetized," and Paleotto, another listener, bore warm testimony to the profound learning and utter sincerity of Laynez.[2]

Almost every letter of the many received by St. Peter from Trent during the last months of 1562 contained some reference to what Polanco called "this blessed question of episcopal residence"—*tuttavia si tratta di questa benedetta residentia*. It had paralysed the proper activities of the Council, and that at a time when the Emperor was coming to life again, and when at the gates of Trent appeared the enigmatic figure of the Cardinal of Lorraine. St. Peter had long been observing the movements in France, and Charles de Guise did not inspire him with much confidence.[3] Like the Emperor's lay advisers, he was a good man, but like them, he, too, tended to regard religion as a department of politics. The great thing was to obtain or maintain political peace, and for that concessions of very generous scope seemed to him and to them the prime

---

[1] *Historiae Concilii Tridentini libri octo* (ed. 5a, 1658), pp. 553–6.

[2] Braunsberger, *Epistulae*, vol. iii, p. 497; Paleotto, *Acta Concilii Tridentini* (ed. Mendham), pp. 300–1. The discourse as expanded afterwards by Laynez himself occupies 370 pages of Grisar's *Disputationes Tridentinæ*. It is entitled, *De origine jurisdictionis Episcoporum et de Romani Pontificis Primatu*.

[3] The Cardinal's first speech in the Council was extremely reassuring and ended with a frank recognition of the Pope's supremacy. But nine months earlier he had just as frankly told the Duke of Württemberg that he had read the Confession of Augsburg, Luther, Melanchthon, and others, and entirely approved their doctrines. Evennett, *The Cardinal of Lorraine*, p. 434.

necessity. Their common programme included, not only the chalice for the laity and the abrogation of clerical celibacy, but the abolition of conclaves, the sanction of vernacular liturgies, and the removal of statues from churches. With Lorraine came thirteen French bishops, like himself good Gallicans to a man, and determined to secure practical recognition of their theory by insisting on the Council's right and duty to lay down the law to the Pope. Ferdinand, swayed by the advice of his lay mentors and by his love for Maximilian, now moved swiftly towards an alliance with the French for a combined assault on the Council's liberties. In order to be near the scene of events he determined to take up his residence in Innsbruck, and to convene there a bijou council of his own which would direct him in his dealings with Rome and Trent. On the last day of 1562 St. Peter received instructions from His Majesty to settle his affairs and make ready for departure to Innsbruck immediately he received the summons. It was the crisis at last.

APPENDIX TO CHAPTER XII

Catalogue of books to be bought for the College of Innsbruck as drawn up by St. Peter Canisius in July, 1562.

THEOLOGY

1. The Genoese Commentaries on the Bible.
2. A Dictionary of the Bible.
3. Many works of the Fathers, including St. Athanasius in the four-volume Basle edition of 1556.
4. A Catena of Greek authors on the New Testament.
5. The Opuscula of Perez († 1490) and his Commentaries on the Psalms.
6. Annotations to the New Testament by Jean Gagni, Chancellor of the University of Paris († 1549).
7. Francis Titelmann's Commentaries on the Psalms, St. Matthew, St. John, and the Epistle to the Romans, all directed against Erasmus.
8. Commentaries on the Epistles of St. Paul by Ambrose Catharinus, O.P. († 1553).
9. The Hebrew Lexicon of Santes Pagnino, O.P. († 1541).
10. The Hebrew Grammar of Elias the Levite († 1547).
11. The Opuscula of John Isaac, a converted Jew, professor at the University of Cologne.
12. The Commentaries of Durandus on the *Liber Sententiarum*.
13. The theological works of the Italian Dominican, Chrysostom Javelli, who taught Molinism before the Jesuit Molina was born.
14. The *Summa de Ecclesia* of John Torquemada, O.P. († 1468).

15. Books against the Wycliffites and Hussites by the English Carmelite, Thomas Netter, better known as Waldensis from his birthplace, Saffron Walden, Essex.
16. The dogmatic and polemical works of the Louvain theologians, Driedo, Latomus, and Tapper.

PHILOSOPHY

1. The Commentaries of St. Thomas Aquinas on Aristotle.
2. The Louvain Commentary on Aristotle's Logic.
3. The philosophical works of Chrysostom Javelli, O.P.
4. The works of Boethius.
5. Theophrastus.
6. The philosophical works of St. Albert the Great.
7. The Commentaries of the following writers on various treatises of Aristotle : Alexander Aphrodiseus (2nd century), Themistius (4th century), Simplicius (6th century), Ammonius (6th century), Avicenna (10th century), Averroes (12th century), Eustracius (12th century), Burleus (14th century), Apollinaris (15th century), Vimercatus (16th century), Donatus (16th century), Titelmann (16th century), Niphus (16th century), Mathisius (16th century).
8. *Catena aurea in Logicam Aristotelis.*

MATHEMATICS AND PHYSICS

1. The Works of Archimedes.
2. The Works of Ptolemy.
3. The *Tractatus de Sphaera* of John Holywood († 1256).
4. *Theoricae Planetarum*, or philosophical speculation on the planets, by Gerard of Cremona († 1184).
5. The Optics of the English Franciscan, John Peckham († 1294).
6. *Mappa Mundi cum arithmeticis.*
7. The Works of Johann Müller, known as Regiomontanus from his birthplace, the little Bavarian town of Königsberg.
8. The Astrolabe of Johann Stöffler († 1531).
9. The Works of Peter Bienewitz, Professor of Astronomy at Ingolstadt († 1552).

CLASSICS

1. Homer, with Commentaries in Greek.
2. The Fables of Æsop in Greek and Latin.
3. The Orations of Isocrates in Greek and Latin.
4. The Orations of Demosthenes in Greek and Latin.
5. The Works of Lucian, and separately, his Dialogues.
6. The Greek Homilies of St. John Chrysostom.
7. The Lexicon of Suidas.
8. The Greek Grammar of Bolsamius.

9. The Greek Grammar of the Swiss Zwinglian, Wiesendanger.
10. A Treatise on Greek Syntax by John Varennius.
11. The Works of Livy, edited by Heinrich Loritus († 1563).
12. The Commentaries of the French Calvinist, Ramus, on Vergil's *Bucolics*.
13. Commentaries on Sallust, Ovid and Horace.
14. The Philosophical Works of Cicero, with Commentaries.
15. The Commentaries and Annotations on Cicero of the Calvinist, Johann Sturm.
16. An Exposition of Cicero's *De Inventione* by Marius Victorinus, whose conversion to Christianity is described in St. Augustine's Confessions, and whose Exposition is much more difficult to understand than Cicero's naked text.
17. Bartholomew Latomus on Cicero.
18. *Thesaurus Ciceronis*.

RHETORIC AND GRAMMAR

1. Aristotle's Rhetoric, with the Commentaries of Ramus.
2. Observations on Aristotle and Quintilian by George Cassander († 1566).
3. The Rhetoric of Andomarus, together with the *Partitiones* of Arasius.
4. *Tabulae Rhetorices* by Cornelius Valerius († 1578).
5. The *Orationes* of Christopher Longolius († 1522).
6. The *Orationes* of Palearius, who was executed for heresy in Rome under Pius V.
7. The *Orationes et Carmina* of the Venetian, Andrew Navagerius.
8. *Orationes pro Lingua Latina* by Bernard Parthenius.
9. The *Orationes* of Carlo Sigonio of Modena († 1584).
10. The *Partitiones Oratoriae* of James Brocard.
11. *De Inventione et Amplificatione Oratorica*, by Gerard Buccolianus.
12. *De Schematibus*, by Antonio Mancinelli.
13. *De optimo genere Interpretandi*, by the Benedictine, Perionius.
14. The *Cornucopia* of Ambrose Calepinus.

HISTORY AND ARCHAEOLOGY

1. The Histories of Polybius, Diodorus Siculus, Dionysius Halicarnassus, Strabo, Eutropius, Procopius, Nicephorus and Berosus.
2. Fenestella's *Liber de Magistratibus et Sacerdotiis Romanorum*.
3. *Historia Romana*, by Flavius Blondus.
4. The *Fasti* and the *De Nominibus Romanorum* of Sigonius.
5. *Opera in Pandectas* by Budaeus.
6. The *Collectanea* of Caelius Rhodiginus.
7. The Chronicle of the medieval Benedictine, Sigebert de Gemblours.
8. *The Chronicle of the World* by Christian Masseus of Cambrai.
9. The *De Scriptoribus ecclesiasticis* of Trithemius, enlarged by Werlinus, Cologne, 1540.

CHAPTER XIII

EMPEROR VERSUS COUNCIL

To understand what happened at Trent and Innsbruck during the first months of 1563 it is necessary to go back for a moment to June 8th of the preceding year. On that day the Emperor's ambassadors in Trent put pressure on the Legates to have publicly read and discussed a long document known as the *Libellus Reformationis* which they had received from their Master. In one respect this famous and most interesting 'Plan of Reformation' reflects the greatest credit on the men responsible for its existence, among whom the chief appears to have been Staphylus.[1] While describing with grave eloquence the horrible abuses that had crept into almost every sphere of ecclesiastical administration they did not forget the respect due to the offices of the offenders. They spoke with great reverence of the Pope even as they detailed in forcible terms the misdeeds of his Curia, and from first to last, the sincerity of the moral tone that dignifies their remonstrance is beyond question. But sincerity and practical wisdom do not necessarily go hand in hand, and to have a good case is no justification for urging it under all circumstances. Everybody at Trent knew well that the Spanish bishops loathed the Papal Curia. From the first the Spaniards had been the most intractable party in the Council, grandees wrapped up in their own importance and ready to smell offence in the most innocent breeze that blew from the Seven Hills. To have thrown the Curia, the Pope's cabinet and executive, to their mercies would have been a gross insult to the Holy Father, yet that was the main demand of the *Libellus*. Before any further discussion of doctrine, the reform of the Pope and his cardinals must be undertaken by the Fathers of Trent and the number of the cardinals ought to be cut down to twenty-four. The Fathers ought further to place severe restrictions on papal

[1] It was first published by the Protestant scholar, Schelhorn, admittedly for reasons similar to those that led Mendham afterwards to print Paleotto's *Acta*. Certainly it would be difficult to find a more eloquent and impressive summary of the abuses that disfigured the life of the Church than the one given in the *Libellus*. The Catholic scholar, Le Plat, reproduced Schelhorn's text in the fifth volume of his Tridentine *Monumenta* (Louvain, 1785), pp. 232-59.

dispensations, exemptions, and ordinances, to grant the chalice to the laity of the Empire, to allow a married priesthood, to mitigate the fasting regulations, to permit partly vernacular services, to expurgate the Breviary and the liturgical offices, and to initiate other sweeping reforms.

But though a long and strong programme, it was not so much its matter as its manner that perturbed the Legates, the whole underlying suggestion that the Council was superior in authority to the Pope. The very first article gives the clue to the rest : " Our Most Holy Father, Pope Pius, should be exhorted and prayed graciously to suffer a reformation of such matters as he shall have perceived to need improvement, in con- nexion with the person, the office, and the Curia of His Holiness." *Ut reformari benigne patiatur*—there was the rub ! The Pope was not to be asked to reform himself but to submit to being reformed by the Council. Again, in the fourth article, it is demanded that exemptions from the common law granted by Popes be revoked *auctoritate Concilii*. In other words, the Council was to act on the old schismatical assumptions of the fifteenth century, never mind if all the ghosts of Constance and Basle began to walk again, with Heaven alone knew what consequences.

While urgently requesting the Emperor to withdraw the document, the Legates pointed out that many of its demands had already been discussed by the Fathers, and that the Pope was even then engaged on the reform of the Curia. Ferdinand had other matters to engage his atten- tion at the time, so, contenting himself with a very lengthy protest against the mild hint that it was not for secular princes to dictate to the Council, he retired temporarily from active intervention.[1] There the matter rested until at the end of the year His Majesty had seen Maximilian safely in possession of the Roman Crown. With that anxiety off his mind and stimulated by his Vice-Chancellor, he renewed his interest in the Council's doings. There came to him the idea of what Pastor calls a " bye-council," composed of the most distinguished theologians he could find to advise him in dealing with the slow-going Legates. Having instructed Peter Canisius and Staphylus to make ready for a journey to Innsbruck, he prepared to transfer his Court thither as soon as he should have had a sign from Heaven.

The sign came without delay, but whether from Heaven is not so certain. On January 2nd the French ambassadors at Trent, tired as they said, of waiting for something to be done about the Emperor's *Libellus*,

---

[1] Le Plat, *Monumentorum ad historiam Concilii Tridentini . . . spectantium . . . collection*, vol. v, pp. 328-9, 351-60.

submitted to the Legates in a new form the principal demands of that document and a few independent ones, in the name of Charles IX. There were thirty-four articles, nearly all, as Polanco informed St. Peter, " assai boni," but expressed by a remarkable feat without a single mention of the Pope or reference to his authority.[1] The Legates again patiently explained that many of the demands had already been satisfied or were in process of discussion, but the suspicious Frenchmen, strong in the support of Lorraine, refused to be placated and broke into loud complaint that the freedom of the Council was being strangled. Evil rumours had got about that the Pope intended to dismiss the Fathers if the Spaniards continued to agitate for a definition on the *jus divinum* of bishops, and this, coupled with the assurance that he now had the backing of the French, determined Ferdinand to assert himself vigorously. The end of January found him in Innsbruck where he was joined by Maximilian. Within about a fortnight he had set up his theological commission, with none other than Bishop Drascovics as its president.

St. Peter had received the Emperor's summons on February 3rd : " It is Our gracious command that you betake yourself hither immediately to Our Imperial Court and that you announce yourself to Us at once on arrival."[2] The Jesuit authorities had nothing whatever to do with Peter's appointment nor did he himself in the least desire it. Yet a well-known historian in a well-known historical series had the impudence to write : " The Jesuit, Canisius, knew how to insinuate himself into the Emperor's reform Commission in order to serve on it as the Curia's spy."[3] Peter arrived in Innsbruck on February 10th and found there his associate theologians, the layman Staphylus and the Spanish Franciscan Friar, Cordoba, chaplain to Maximilian's Queen. Cordoba was a peculiar person, so much so that Delfino spoke of him as " a fantastic old gentleman, very rigid in his opinions and too free with his tongue."[4] Two opinions in particular found favour with him, that the Council is superior to the Pope and that the Pope ought to be reformed by the Council. His official post at Maximilian's Court had not served to make him feel any kindlier towards Rome, or well-disposed to St. Peter. Peter invited him to dinner and tried to make friends with him, but it was no use. Staphylus,

[1] Le Plat, *Monumentorum*, etc., vol. v, pp. 631–43.
[2] Braunsberger, *Epistulae*, vol. iv, p. 45.
[3] Philippson, *Westeuropa im Zeitalter von Philip II, Elizabeth, und Heinrich IV* (Berlin, 1883), pp. 159–60. This is one of the reference books which one may use in the British Museum Reading Room without the formality of applying for it. We have already seen Philippson's egregious remarks on the meeting of St. Peter with Favre.
[4] Braunsberger, *Epistulae*, vol. iv, p. 952.

on the other hand, had long been regarded by Peter as amongst his "dearest and best of friends." Peter had warmly eulogized and defended him from the Augsburg pulpit and, on many another occasion, expressed high appreciation of his work for the Church. But he knew that the learned convert was a 'Gallican' and told Laynez that the "opinions of the Sorbonne were very much to be feared" from him. Delfino wrote him down a complete Gersonian and, worse still, a client of Drascovics, whom the Nuncio alleged to have held "*concetti terribili*" on the question of Pope and Council.[1]

Seeing Peter to be standing alone, the zealous Nuncio begged the Emperor that his own private theologian, the Dominican, Daniel Barboli, might be appointed to the Commission. In this he had his way, as Ferdinand admired Barboli and had recently appointed him to the bishopric of Pedena, but when he also endeavoured to secure the entrance of Father Nadal and so, as it were, to pack the jury, Ferdinand stood firm. St. Peter had already asked his General to send Nadal to Innsbruck, but only that he might consult with him about the business of his Province. Nadal came, and Delfino, who had boundless admiration for him, soon saw to it that, though not on the Commission, he played a foremost part in the negotiations.

Meantime, the Legates at Trent had dispatched Bishop Commendone on a mission of peace to Innsbruck. He was to explain to the Emperor why they had been unable to put the *Libellus* before the Council in its entirety, and to urge that the reform of the Curia should be left entirely to the Pope. Though Ferdinand esteemed him he was not exactly the right person for such delicate business, and the fact that he had to work with the rather fussy and interfering Delfino did not add to his chances of success. Leaving behind his secretary, Antonio Graziani, to report developments, he returned to Trent after a short stay at Court—"*dismissus non penitus e sententia sua,*" according to St. Peter. On the Legates' instructions he then wrote an account of his mission in the course of which he said : " It is great luck that among those theologians is Father Canisius, a man of the most perfect goodness and learning, and a great defender of the power of the Pope. But I fear that in this matter he will be alone, or almost alone."[2]

---

[1] Braunsberger, *Epistulae*, vol. iv, pp. 50, 952–3.

[2] Braunsberger, *Epistulae*, vol. iv, pp. 955–7. A little earlier, Commendone had committed to writing, at the Pope's request, his recommendations for the treatment of Germany, based on the experiences of his Nunciature there. In sum they were three : " Cioe la Compagnia de' Gesuiti in Germania, un' intiera et perfetta riforma, et una lega prima fra alcuni principi di Germania et poi con gl'altri re et principi Catholici.

Peter's position was, indeed, both difficult and unpleasant for the reason that his colleagues and the good Emperor had so much to justify their critical attitude towards the Holy See. To his principles they could oppose a number of brute facts, and to his idealism, a patch of very bleak reality. In Rome, the Pope, despite his gout, attended a congregation on reform almost daily but negatived the good impression thus created by raising to the purple, on January 6th, Federigo Gonzaga, nephew of the first President, and Ferdinando de Medici, son of the Duke of Florence, both of them mere boys, aged eighteen and thirteen respectively. On top of that deplorable blunder followed a rumour that the Sacred College was shortly to be augmented by ten or twelve new members. On January 23rd, Cardinal Truchsess wrote in dismay to St. Peter : " I cannot believe it and I shall not give my vote for it. Reform is more in words than in deeds. My ears are tingling with complaints from the provinces that the whole thing is a mere pretence." It is easy to imagine the distress of a man like St. Peter, especially when the Emperor summoned him and complained bitterly about the Pope's action and the stagnation at Trent. On February 29th, Delfino reported to the Legates : " His Imperial Majesty has again spoken with Canisius and with Barboli, saying much about the quality of the cardinals and that he could not get over what had been done in this matter in opposition to his wishes. Further, he styled the many papal dispensations ' dissipations,' and, almost in tears, declared that if a durable reform, safe from daily changes, was not carried out, he held the Christian Republic to be permanently incurable. At this point he mentioned that Paul IV, of holy memory, had made a great reform in the Court of Rome but that all of it is going up in smoke."[1] Polanco, however, had a good word to say to Peter for both Pope and Council. Things in Trent were not as peaceful as might be desired but neither were they as turbulent as people tried to make out. " The conclusion is that it will be a good thing for you to put your hopes in God." As for the Pope, he was a martyr to gout and physically incapable of doing all that he would have liked to do. " We here know that His Holiness is more inclined to the business of reform than many people imagine. The difficulty is to find the method."[2]

The method, indeed, was the thing, and it speaks volumes for the Emperor, that, knowing St. Peter to be opposed to *his* method, to be against the concessions he regarded as absolutely necessary, to be, in fact, from his

---

[1] Braunsberger, *Epistulae*, vol. iv, pp. 33, 961.
[2] Braunsberger, *Epistulae*, vol. iv, pp. 25, 37-8.

point of view, an unmitigated nuisance, he never showed the slightest sign of resentment. He need not have had Peter on his Commission at all. By a stroke of his pen he could have ruined all Peter's work in Germany, yet not once did he threaten or try to bargain. On the contrary, he gave almost daily some new token of his esteem for the men who opposed his reformation schemes so determinedly. At Peter's intercession he interested himself in so small a thing as the fate of the four hundred ducats with which he had endowed the Roman College and which some unscrupulous official had pocketed. Among the first things he did on arrival at Innsbruck was to pay a ceremonial visit to the Jesuit College, which one who was present described as follows:

He made the tour of all the rooms, both upstairs and downstairs. The friendly way he greeted us, giving us his right hand, and the extremely kind words he spoke, proved abundantly his gracious regard for us. Beside our College is a long extensive garden, fertile, and beautiful with flowers. On entering it he said it was just the place for the brethren to take recreation and that it ought to belong to us. Thereupon he made us a gift of it. When we petitioned for some things very necessary to us and the whole Society he willingly granted them, and, not only bade his officials see that we had what we needed, but gave instructions that we were at all times to be freely admitted to his presence. He said that he loved us as his sons, and that he would never cease to help and defend us. " Only go on," he concluded, " as you have begun, labouring strenuously in the Lord's vineyard."[1]

Shortly afterwards, the Emperor addressed himself to the Pope advising that the best way to help towards the restoration of true religion in Germany was to set up many Jesuit colleges there.[2] Indeed, so much friendliness did Ferdinand show St. Peter and his Innsbruck brethren that the English agent, Mundt, opined he must be planning, like his illustrious brother, to retire from the world—to the Jesuit College![3] As for Ferdinand's principal adviser, the most accomplished diplomat in the

[1] Braunsberger, *Epistulae*, vol. iv, p. 130.
[2] Braunsberger, *Epistulae*, vol. iv, pp. 118, 159. This view, already expressed by Bishop Commendone, was shared by Vice-Chancellor Seld and the Count di Luna, the Spanish Ambassador. When the Count visited Trent the Legates asked him what in his opinion, after his long experience at the Imperial Court, ought to be done to win back the Protestants and keep the Catholics loyal. He answered, they reported to St. Charles Borromeo, that " all he could tell us was the need in Germany of good preachers and of spreading as much as possible the Society of Jesuits." Pogiani Sunensis, *Epistolae et Orationes*, vol. iii (Rome, 1757), p. 286.
[3] So Mundt reported home to Cecil. *Calendar of State Papers*, Foreign series of the Reign of Elizabeth, 1563, p. 298.

Empire, Sigmund Seld, he not only admired the Jesuits but helped them to such an extent that St. Peter obtained for him in June, 1563, the rare privilege of participation in all the prayers and merits of the Society.[1]

Such were the men to whose policy St. Peter found himself the chief opponent. But he could at least honour their sincerity by matching it with his own and endeavouring by all legitimate means to save them from misunderstandings. He told Laynez that Ferdinand and Maximilian were having the very worst suspicions about the Council instilled into their minds; that the Cardinal of Lorraine was expected in Innsbruck shortly and would be certain to add fuel to their indignation; that the grim spectre of schism had begun to haunt his thoughts; and that he, therefore, begged his Paternity to have Masses and prayers said for the Fathers of the Council and the two Monarchs. Laynez instructed him to send information about the questions under discussion at Innsbruck, promising to keep the matter strictly secret. Though the Saint was under a bond to the Emperor, his General had a perfect right to know what he was doing and proposing, as the Society of Jesus would, of course, have to take the responsibility for his action. No Jesuit or any other man under religious vows has power to act independently of his religious superiors, and, besides, all theologians and clear thinkers on moral problems are agreed that even a *secretum commissum*, as was this, may be revealed in so far as necessary to ward off a grave public danger. The Seal of Confession comes under a special law of its own, but there is no other secret which can be considered sacrosanct under all circumstances and conditions. At Innsbruck the danger to the Catholic Church was indisputably grave, and to raise hands of horror to Heaven, as some have done, because St. Peter, in the most guarded way and by special messenger, sought advice from his General, is merely to trifle with the problem of conduct.

The Emperor was perfectly willing that Peter should take Father Nadal into his confidence, though he was not on the Commission. Indeed, Ferdinand himself had the Father to dine with him at Court in order to discuss the secret questions. It was only from Delfino that he wanted their exact nature carefully concealed, as he had no great liking for the Nuncio and feared that he might divulge everything in the wrong quarter. The Nuncio flattered himself that he could manage St. Peter. Writing to the Legates at Trent on February 20th, he said: "His Majesty had put the theologians under a promise of strictest secrecy, but, for all that,

---

[1] Braunsberger, *Epistulae*, vol. i, pp. 485, 503; vol. iv, pp. 275, 283.

Barboli and Canisius, who know very well their obligations to the Holy See, have taken counsel with me and will not say anything without the approval of Father Nadal and myself. I shall send Your Lordships a copy of their answers to the questions at the first opportunity. . . ."[1] St. Peter, however, steadfastly refused to let him see the answers and much resented his persistent endeavours to have them. Writing to Laynez towards the close of the Commission's work, he said: " The Most Reverend Lord Delfino is somewhat of a nuisance to me with his efforts to find out the matters treated of in our consultations. I have told him that as long as nothing happens which ought necessarily to be referred to him I do not think it right or reasonable to reveal secret matters, in violation of the promise given to the Emperor. . . . I am not sure to what extent I can trust him, as, in the opinion of many people, he seems to speak and to act on occasions rather imprudently. So I am going to go on refusing him, though he is most urgent to have the secrets out of me. . . ."[2] Despairing at last of Peter, with whom, however, he remained good friends and whose views he knew to be perfectly safe, the Nuncio turned his attention to the " fantastic old gentleman, Cordoba." From the beginning Cordoba had openly avowed his hostility to the Papal Curia, but at the end of May Delfino wrote in triumph to the first President of the Council : " I do not fail to practise exorcisms daily on the Franciscan, and I have so sweetened him that Canisius is amazed. . . . I am in the highest hopes that he will be completely ours. I have made him a present of a small *aspersorium*, with an *aspergillum* fashioned entirely of silver, a beautiful piece of work, worth twenty-five scudi, which has given him infinite pleasure. Then I kept him in humour with clocks, and I have promised him a beautiful one which, as I explained, I expect at any moment from Augsburg. . . ."[3]

The articles on which St. Peter and his colleagues had to pronounce originated as follows. Bishop Drascovics betook himself from Trent to Innsbruck in the mood of Saul on the road to Damascus, and, at the beginning of February, laid before the Emperor a document packed with grievances against the Pope and the Legates. The main allegation was,

---

[1] Braunsberger, *Epistulae*, vol. iv, p. 960.
[2] Braunsberger, *Epistulae*, vol. iv, p. 214.
[3] Braunsberger, *Epistulae*, vol. iv, p. 977. Delfino's clocks look uncommonly like bribery but the standards in that matter during the sixteenth century were different from and much lower than those recognized to-day. St. Charles Borromeo approved the Nuncio's action in general. Not many years afterwards Delfino changed his allegiance and went over altogether to the side of Maximilian. In 1565 the Spanish Ambassador spoke of him as " *el mayor adulador del Emperador del Mundo.*" To satisfy Maximilian, Pius IV created the Nuncio a Cardinal that year, though with great reluctance. In 1566 St. Pius V felt obliged to dismiss him from the papal service.

as usual, that the Council had been deprived of its liberty. To restore it, the Bishop urged Ferdinand and other princes to combine and insist on their right to a direct say in the Council's affairs independently of the Legates. Lest, as was to be feared, such action on their part should lead to an immediate break-up of the Council, the Emperor was advised to experiment with a few threats and warnings, as, for instance, that national synods must necessarily result from a dissolution at Trent. As the residence of bishops in their dioceses must be the basis of all genuine efforts at reform, the Emperor should see to it that a declaration on the subject was made without further delay. " Thereafter I consider," continued Drascovics, " that the chief and most necessary articles from the *Libellus* of Your Majesty and of the French Crown should be submitted to the Fathers by you, and not by the Legates." In conclusion, the Emperor was urged to come himself to Trent. Eight days later the other Imperial ambassadors, Brus and Thun, wrote to say that the time was now opportune for His Majesty to propose his articles to the Council " and to deliver it from the oppression of the Legates."[1] Moved by these representations the Emperor caused seventeen questions to be drawn up, four copies of which were delivered to Drascovics on April 15th, by the Vice-Chancellor, their principal author. Drascovics, as head of the theological Commission, retained one and distributed the others to Canisius, Barboli, and Cordoba.

The four men appear to have met for their discussions each day in the presence of Ferdinand, Seld, and other great personages. On April 16th a diversion was caused by the arrival of the Cardinal of Lorraine, accompanied by nine French bishops and some Sorbonne doctors. They were received in great state by Ferdinand and Maximilian, but St. Peter could have wished them at the other end of the map, as he feared " that there must be a little accord between Monsignor Delfino and the Lord Cardinal." How right he was may be seen from the report of Graziani to his master, Commendone, on February 19th :

The French gentlemen here have tried and continue to try every means of winning over Canisius. He has been visited by the theologians, the bishops, and the Cardinal himself, but his goodness is equal to his learning, as Your Lordship knows right well. Yesterday I said to him with a laugh : ' Beware of the Gauls, Father, as it is rumoured that they want to draw you over to their side.' He answered that, as a matter of fact, they had not broached such a question, but I heard

[1] Sickel, *Zur Geschichte des Concils von Trent*, pp. 427–30, 439.

from Signor Gasparo that it is being said in Court circles, and I also learned it from other people. Canisius tells me that the Cardinal related to him how Monsignor the Nuncio complained to his face that he and the other Frenchmen wanted to cause the Church's ruin by their demands for reform, aiming as they were at nothing else than the authority of the Apostolic See. . . . Canisius believes and fears that this misunderstanding between the two men must turn to the disadvantage of the Nuncio, as the Cardinal will join forces with the Emperor and leave him high and dry. . . . Yesterday the Nuncio gave dinner to some French bishops, but two of those invited, Metz and Orléans, would not go to it. . . . Canisius is afraid that the Council may be dissolved and says openly that, should such a thing happen, he does not see how Christianity can be saved from ruin. . . .[1]

Delfino had, at any rate, the courage of his convictions. He hovered round the little band of theologians like an inquisitive and hungry sparrow, ready to pounce on any crumb of information they might let fall. As the Dominican, Father Barboli, was his own theologian, he appears to have soon wheedled a copy of the questions out of him which he forthwith transmitted to the Legates at Trent. They contained nothing of which the Legates were not already only too sadly aware, and the answers rather than the questions formed the real subject of secrecy. These neither Barboli nor Canisius would divulge, though they felt justified in discussing the problems at large with Nadal, Delfino himself, and Graziani. By February 22nd they had their answers in the hands of the Vice-Chancellor. For the sake of clearness, St. Peter arranged some of them in groups as in Seld's *Indiculus*. Though the Saint's text is very long, a good portion of it must be reproduced here for the light it throws on his ecclesiastical standpoint :

Whether His Imperial Majesty should work for the continuation of the Council ; or should he bear with equanimity its dissolution or, at least, its suspension ?

I answer : Nothing would seem wiser and more advisable than that His Majesty should strive with all earnestness and diligence and with the full use of his authority to prevent the suspension and much more the break-up or dissolution of the Council. There could not be anything more worthy of so great a Prince than a serious endeavour to

[1] Döllinger, *Beiträge zur politischen, kirchlichen, und Cultur-Geschichte der sechs letzten Jahrhunderte,* vol. iii (Vienna, 1882), pp. 324–7.

secure the continuation and happy completion of the Council. By so doing he will prove himself to be in truth what he is styled and ought to be, the Church's Advocate. . . . He will serve the Church's public interest, which depends chiefly on the continuation of the Council, and will be enabled to avoid the grave inconveniences that the dissolution or suspension of the Council must indubitably bring with it. For who doubts but that the break-up or suspension of the Council would very seriously perturb all Catholics, as it would mean the frustration of their best and greatest hope? The task of many princes in conserving the faith and keeping out heresy would be made more difficult, and the ecclesiastical power, too, would everywhere suffer a great diminution of credit and respect, if the Fathers were to go home with their work unfinished. Moreover, the sectaries would be wonderfully strengthened by such a happening and find in it a splendid ground for launching everlastingly against the Catholics the taunt of shameful dissension in faith and religion.

Should threats be used to prevent the untimely dissolution of the Council, and if so, what kind of threats?

I answer: Threats ought not to be used until more gentle ways and means have been tried with both the Legates of the Council and the Pope. This is an extreme remedy which should be employed only with the greatest circumspection, if, indeed, it is hoped that by such a method the dissolution of the Council might possibly be prevented. Else would there be reason to fear lest other princes, abusing such an example of His Imperial Majesty, should more and more withdraw themselves from the unity and obedience of the Catholic Church and soon adopt the schismatical course of setting up and celebrating national synods, in defiance of the Pope. Nor do I think that any instance can be found of an upright prince using threats in such circumstances. Perhaps, indeed, an upright prince would deem such conduct unworthy. It is within the competence of princes to admonish, to petition, to rebuke, always with due regard to the law of charity. But that same law scarcely permits the chief pastors and rulers of the Church to be threatened and severely treated by secular princes.

His Majesty might instead explain the difficulty he would have in keeping his subjects to their duty and in defending the rights of the Church, were there to be a dissolution, and at the same time, protest that he gave, or would give, neither consent, nor assistance of any kind to such a thing, from which in all likelihood scandal and ruin would come upon the various provinces of the Catholic Church. Then, in place of threats, divers specific inconveniences that would arise from a dissolution might be mentioned: as, for instance, contempt and vilification of the Supreme Pontiff and the whole ecclesiastical hierarchy; prejudice, not only to the present Council, but to all future ones; opportunity for national synods, leading to deplorable disunion; and the impossibility of defending such a dissolution, which even good men would hardly interpret otherwise than as a manoeuvre for preventing a necessary reformation of corrupt ecclesiastics.

St. Peter next deals with three questions in one because, as he says, "they pertain to the same argument and spring from the same root," namely the fundamental question:

What and how great are the power and authority of legates sent to the Council by the Apostolic See; and what, that of other ambassadors sent by kings and great princes?

I answer: The power and authority of the legates is such and so much as the Supreme Pontiff wishes them to be. From ancient custom, observed in other councils and confirmed by constant and uniform tradition down to our own day, the Pope derives power to grant the Legates the right of initiative in the work of the Council, and of reference to himself about the matters treated. Assuredly there is no room for doubt that the *jus proponendi* belongs and ought to belong to the Legates. The matter was definitely settled in this very Council of Trent, namely that the Fathers should express their views on such subjects as the Legates proposed to them.[1] Should the princes now seek to change this procedure, there would be fresh and serious commotion, profitless to all concerned and detrimental to the Council. As in other affairs, so certainly in the Council it is necessary to observe a decent order, and this would be greatly disturbed if all the bishops present and, much more, the secular ambassadors, enjoyed the right of proposing and treating whatever they wished. Famous are the words of the Emperor Theodosius at the Council of Ephesus: *It is illicit for one not a bishop to intrude into the handling of ecclesiastical affairs.* And the Emperor Basilius gave expression to the same view when, at the eighth Oecumenical Council, he said publicly: *It is by no means permissible for us to move proposals on ecclesiastical affairs, nor to oppose the integrity*

---

[1] So it was, with only four dissentients, including, of course, Pedro Guerrero. Pastor, *History of the Popes*, Eng. tr., vol. xv, p. 265.

of the Council. Now, if even the greatest princes have no right to arrogate to themselves the functions of bishops, not to speak of legates, much less does it belong to their ambassadors either to demand or to exercise the ordinary right of proposal, against the constant custom and example of earlier Councils.

But to come close to the questions before us, the greater the power of the Legates (and it has always been supreme), the more diligently ought the Emperor to strive by the interposition of his authority that they make such proposals as may contribute in a serious degree to the salvation of Germany. If this cannot be obtained from them, then recourse should be had to the Supreme Pontiff that he may command the proposal of such measures. Furthermore, the inconveniences and grievances caused by having to await a reply from Rome on matters of little consequence, might be explained in the Emperor's name, as it means unwelcome and hurtful delay to business at Trent. Still, it is plain that in the ancient councils it was the received custom for the Legates to seek guidance on controversies or difficulties from the Supreme Pontiff, as from the one who alone had the power and right to summon, assemble, govern, and confirm æcumenical councils. . . .

In this connexion, however, it may be doubted whether the Legates have refused without rhyme or reason to accept, or to refer to the Fathers, proposals made to them in the name of His Imperial Majesty. . . . Perhaps some things are being urged which, if put to the Council according to the demands of the ambassadors, would raise disturbance and increase the present dissensions, rather than bring any advantage. As the times are so difficult there would seem to be need of caution in dealing with this matter.

The next question was about the Council's single Secretary, Angelo Massarelli, with whom many of the Fathers had become discontented. St. Peter answered briefly and sensibly that, in all such difficulties, petition should first be made to the Legates. If they failed to act, the Pope should be informed and asked for a remedy, in the name of one or several princes. It might also help, he suggested, if some members of the Council were given the rôle of censors, with a duty to report on any occurrences that might seem to lessen or prejudice the Council's liberty, as, for instance, malpractices such as bribery and subornation in the voting. As for the Secretary, if the Emperor pressed the matter he would doubtless easily obtain the appointment of two or three others to assist with the work which appeared to be too much for one man's energies. Then there followed the problem of how to get the stay-at-home German bishops to Trent. Peter suggested, as he had done before, a Papal Nuncio accompanied by an Imperial envoy, who would visit and stir up the ecclesiastical Electors. If the great three could be prevailed upon to come, the others might be expected to follow suit. As an additional persuasive, steps ought to be taken for the protection of their territories by means of alliances with neighbouring Catholic princes. If all failed and those men " for whom the Council had waited so long " refused to move, an effort should be made to get them to send procurators who might be allowed the right of voting in their masters' names.

The eighth question of St. Peter's numbering raised a momentous issue :

Ought the Emperor to betake himself to the Council?

I answer : It is a difficult point to decide, owing to the circumstances in which His Majesty, the Pope, and the Council are placed. Speaking generally, good men, anxious for the public interest, doubtless could not but approve the Christian mind and zeal of His Majesty were they to see or read of him, like another Constantine and faithful Advocate of the Church, in company with those Fathers who represent the whole Christian world. Who might not hope that from such a union singular light, peace, consolation, and advantage would flow to the Church, by the mercy of Christ ? But, on the other hand, if we scrutinize the present situation more closely, there will appear to be good arguments why His Majesty should not inconsiderately set out for Trent. If he treats there with the Legates it may easily happen that they will conclude nothing without first consulting the Pope, especially should he advance some proposal of great importance ; and if he treats separately with the Fathers, against the Legates' wishes, suspicion will at once arise of secret plots and conspiracies, making rather for division than for unity, and with possible offence to the Pope. Besides, there is danger of many people thinking and saying that the Emperor came in order to obtain certain concessions from the Fathers by the exercise of his authority, the implication being that the liberty of the Council is thus obscured, and any grant made, the result of cleverly applied constraint. Moreover, should the Legates or the Fathers refuse some request of His Majesty, the slight to his dignity would be the more serious for his presence in the Council.

Perhaps, too, there would not be wanting people to think and fear that the Emperor was minded to assume and use against the Pope and Roman Church that authority which some Emperors of old arrogated to themselves, without warrant of justice or legality. Thus would a handle be given to those who desire the break-up of the Council, which, if it happened, they would attribute to the Emperor's intervention. Furthermore, those who now take the Pope's side, or who in other respects are party-minded, would keep away from His Majesty and strive, we fear, the more diligently to ensure the success of their clique by new and factious methods. Besides all these dangers, it might easily come to pass that, on the failure of efforts devoutly and holily intended, His Majesty would be driven to speak or act somewhat sternly and thus, perhaps, become the cause of serious strife.

But, to say shortly what I feel, the Emperor might very laudably and advantageously seek to arrange a meeting with the Supreme Pontiff as soon as possible, either at Bologna, Mantua, or some other such neighbouring town. On that occasion, negotiations concerning the Council and the whole business of reform could, I think, be much more satisfactorily carried on than in Trent. Then would be the time to propose and urge whatever is desirable with regard to the reformation of the Pope and his Curia. It is hardly possible to imagine a better and safer plan than this for healing the wounds that now afflict us, and for the protection of the Council and all Christendom from graver perils to come. Spending himself utterly in that affair, no matter what the labour or danger involved, the Emperor would do for the Christian world and the peace of the Church the grandest and noblest service of which, with God's assistance, he is capable.

The next four questions are answered briefly. First, with regard to the controversy on episcopal residence, Peter distinguishes. The wordy warfare on the subject ought to be stopped, especially as most of the Fathers were against defining that residence was *de jure divino*. But, whatever the nature of the obligation, the actual residence of bishops in their dioceses was absolutely necessary and steps should be taken, by secular princes too, to compel them to it, unless they could prove to their superiors just and grave reasons for being absent. Secondly, to the question whether efforts ought to be continued to secure a division of the Fathers into two groups, one to deal with doctrine and the other with matters of reform, Peter replied that such a division would throw the whole voting system of the Council out of gear. The Fathers of one group would be unable to vote conscientiously on matters treated by the other group, as they would not have taken part in the preliminary discussions. Far better, then, to strive by every means possible that all the Fathers attended all the congregations on both doctrine and reformation. Thirdly, *Whether it be expedient to debate points of doctrine with so much subtlety, and would it not be better to give preference to the matter of reform?* Such close and detailed reasoning, answered Peter, could not always be avoided by the theologians, and it was ridiculous to wish it away in deference to the susceptibilities of people who spurned the Council in any case. But should there be ground for complaint on this score, the Legates might be asked to intervene and see that the disputants kept the needs of the time before their eyes. As for the business of reform, it ought to proceed *pari passu* with the discussion of dogma, so that the two greatest plagues of the Church, false doctrines and practical abuses, might be remedied simultaneously. The last question of this group brought up the matter of abuses and their reform. Should it still be urged and in what articles? Of course it should, Peter answered with all his heart. " Unchaste and evil-living priests of whatever order must be driven to judge and reform themselves before they are utterly ruined by the heretics." The Saint forbore to suggest specific articles of reformation, as such had already been drawn up many times. If the task were attempted again, he hinted that " a few items about the abuses prevalent among secular princes and noblemen " might well be included. Ecclesiastics, after all, were not the only sinners on earth.

The seventh of Seld's questions, St. Peter's thirteenth, is the most important of the whole series. It runs, with Peter's answers, as follows :

Ought those articles to be omitted which deal with the person of the Pope and with the Roman Curia? If it seems that they should most certainly be urged, what is to be done to avoid such offence to His Holiness and the Curia as might afford a pretext for breaking off the Council?

The articles touching the person of the Pope and the Roman Curia ought not to be omitted, but neither should they be urged upon the Fathers of the Council. The first dissuasive reason is lest it might seem that His Imperial Majesty who by divine law is, as it were, a sheep subject to the Supreme Shepherd, wished through the Council to give and prescribe laws for him to obey. Secondly, such action would strengthen the hands of those who now earnestly defend and wish defined the opinion that the Council's authority is greater than the Pope's. They would become less willing than ever to obey the Pope, and might withdraw themselves more and more from subjection to him. Thirdly, it is to be feared that some persons would seize on such action as an excuse to appeal from the government of the Pope to the Council, and, perhaps, when it so pleased them, they might the more easily claim exemption from the rule of the Roman Church. Fourthly, such a move, dangerous in these turbulent times, would bring the authority of the Supreme Pontiff, already in other ways opposed and generally despised, into even greater contempt. Finally, there are ancient and approved canons on the subject, and though many councils have been held under Popes from which similar but much greater reforms might have been demanded, we read of no such demand as this ever having been made. On the contrary, we find this ancient constitution: It is the will of God that the causes of other men be judged by men, but as for the Bishop of the Roman See, him God reserves without question for His own judgment.[1] . . . And that this was not merely constituted but also observed in ancient times we are taught by . . . that Roman Synod held under Pope Symmachus in which the Fathers declared with a loud voice : *Papae causam totam Dei judicio reservamus*.[2]

Since, however, it is of great importance that, if there is to be reformation at all, it should begin with the Head of the Church and the first of the Churches, all possible diligence should be used to procure that the Shepherd of Shepherds seriously applies his mind to this holy and necessary work of freeing the Roman Church from those abuses which offend the whole world, and are to-day a public scandal and a chief recommendation of the heretical cause to the multitude. His Majesty will therefore deserve well of the Church if he treats about this matter personally with the Pope, whose sentiments towards him are of the friendliest kind. And God grant that it may be soon, for their meeting would greatly help, not only to the reformation of ecclesiastical abuses, but also to the pacification of present disturbances. . . .

Should His Majesty be hindered by other affairs from soon meeting and talking with the Pope, the next best thing would be for him to

---

[1] This canon, from a work of the sixth century by Bishop Ennodius, was afterwards incorporated in the *Decretum Gratiani* (Migne, *Patrologia Latina*, vol. lxiii, p. 200). Peter gives reference to many other canons, including one now known to be spurious.

[2] Mansi, *Sacrorum Conciliorum nova et amplissima collectio*, vol. viii, p. 251.

choose some wise and God-fearing man to transact this most important business. The common good of the Church requires it and so does her necessity, especially in those regions where everything seems to threaten the speedy overthrow and basic ruin of religion unless succour is soon brought to a collapsing Catholicism. . . .

Having thus delivered himself on the explosive question of reform in *Capite et membris*, St. Peter turned his attention to the details of the programme. He is urgent for the strictest legislation on the subject of conclaves, but with regard to the limitation of the Sacred College says that it is neither permissible nor becoming so to restrict the Pope's authority in the matter " that he cannot choose, now many, now few, cardinals, according as the advantage of the Church, the merits of particular persons, and even the times themselves may seem to require." On the subject of dispensations he strikes a very different note : " Alas, great corruption has prevailed in this sphere by which good men have been given cause for serious offence, and evil men the opportunity for pernicious abuses. His Majesty would therefore do wisely and well to use all his authority and influence that dispensations might not be so frequently and lightly granted in Rome, without good cause shown and merely for some people's private gain. It is on account of such grants that ecclesiastical law is grievously violated, and so much relaxed on all sides as not to be merely neglected but openly despised and flouted. Nevertheless, the papal power of dispensation cannot be abolished because of such abuses, for it is not only useful but necessary to the Church of God. Indeed, there is no government that could function aright without some power to modify its own laws. . . ."

Peter mentions two classes of people from whom their privileges of exemption might well be withdrawn completely : Cathedral chapters, which should be rendered subject to the jurisdiction of their bishops, and priests belonging to religious orders, who ought to be compelled to revert to the strict discipline of their rule. As at the time there were many empty monasteries and many dioceses far too wealthy for their own good, the Saint urged that by arrangement with the Pope a certain redistribution of property should be carried out. The vacant monasteries might be turned into schools, and poor dioceses and poor scholars helped from the superfluity of the great bishoprics. One can imagine how pleased Pedro Guerrero and his hidalgos in the Council would have been with this suggestion ! Peter expressed strong sympathy with the Emperor's desire that excommunications should not be hurled about so freely; that the many abuses in the collation of benefices should be utterly abolished; that diocesan synods should be held regularly; that bishops should go on annual visitations of their dioceses; and that the Breviary, together with the liturgical and ritual books of the Church, should be carefully expurgated and revised, " in order to secure in the performance of the Divine Office and public services a reverent and seemly devotion." From all this it is sufficiently clear that the best-accredited defenders of the papal power in the sixteenth century were no enemies of reform. St. Peter's heart was consumed with longing for it, only it must be an orderly reform, carried out without prejudice to the hierarchal principle on which, by God's will, was based the whole structure of Catholicism.

The last lines of the Saint's document are headed with a question to which his answer is completely irrelevant. It was a vague question and he could not be bothered with it, so deeply did another matter preoccupy him:

What is to be said of those articles which are not all equally adapted to every kingdom and country?

I answer: It will be a right noble course for His Majesty, King of Kings that he is, to show all courtesy and benignity to the other Kings and Princes and their Ambassadors who come to the Council; to help them loyally with their articles and proposals; and, on every occasion, to strengthen them in their duty of reverence and esteem for the Supreme Pontiff and the Holy Council. Should they, perchance, produce and wish to propose to the Council articles specially concerned with the Pope and the Roman Church, then it will be the part of the Church's faithful Advocate to persuade and procure that they first negotiate amicably with the Legates on the matter; nor will he suffer articles to come before the Council, particularly at this period of conflict, which ought rather to be dealt with reverently and seriously in Rome. For partisan efforts ought to be shunned and put aside as they breed dissension rather than lead to Catholic unity and peace. . . . *Deo laus et pax Ecclesiae.*[1]

[1] Braunsberger, *Epistulae*, vol. iv, pp. 75–96. Graziani, who appears to have been somewhat of a scatter-brain, informed Commendone that he had caused St. Peter to modify a number of things in his *votum*. " Canisius," he said, " had the following sentence down: ' The Pope ought to be requested to permit himself to be reformed.' I objected that the words *ut patiatur reformari* were offensive and unfair, so he changed them to *ut reformet sese et Romanam Curiam.* . . . I tell you this that Your Lordship may judge what the *vota* of the others must be like when even Canisius, who may be called a saint, would say things offensive to Rome. In my opinion his whole *votum* is now very devout and full of learning, and it cannot but please the Emperor." Döllinger, *Beiträge*, vol. iii, p. 329. Graziani may be thanked for giving us unconscious evidence that St. Peter observed his pact of secrecy loyally. Each detail mentioned by the good Secretary is incorrect, proving that he cannot have seen the Saint's written answers at all.

Emperor Ferdinand I
From a print in the British Museum

Such was St. Peter's advice to the Emperor. Barboli shared his sentiments in the main but expressed them somewhat more rigidly, while Bishop Drascovics and Cordoba maintained their old standpoints. To the Bishop, who in many practical matters and in respect for the Pope was entirely with St. Peter, it seemed essential that the Fathers of the Council and the Ambassadors should have as much right as the Legates to propose motions for discussion; that the Emperor should go to Trent; that the chalice and marriage for priests should be sought from the Council; and that the age and quality of persons to be promoted to the cardinalate should be determined at Trent. Cordoba pinned his entire faith to the *Libellus*, and urged that every line of it, including those on the Pope, should be committed to the judgment and decision of the Council.[1] Ferdinand had, therefore, two opposite courses open to him, to follow Canisius and Barboli and make the Pope his confidant, or to go with Drascovics and Cordoba and stake everything on the Council. He knew well which way his son and his chief advisers would like him to turn his steps. Lorraine and all the power of France pointed him in the same direction and the solid phalanx of Guerrero would give him hearty welcome. Yet he hesitated, and on that scruple of his, engendered (can it be doubted?) at least in some measure by the voice of St. Peter, hung the fortunes of the Catholic Church and much of the future history of mankind. St. Peter himself, having done all he could, took the wintry, snow-bound road to Augsburg.[2]

Between March 7th and April 13th, thirty-seven days, there is record of his having preached thirty-three times. Besides such work, he was never without somebody for a retreat, visited the sick day and night, often spending a good part of the dark hours by their bedsides, heard numberless confessions, and persisted with his public and private efforts on behalf of the City's destitute population.[3] From Trent came a letter with sombre news. Polanco told him first of the visit of Laynez to Mantua, whither Cardinal Gonzaga, the first President and chief prop of the Council, had sent him to start a Jesuit College. The day after his return, February 21st, he had gone to dine with the Cardinal and had been shown every possible kindness. To the consternation of Laynez and of all who knew how much the Council depended on him, Gonzaga's temperature suddenly ran up to danger-point a few hours afterwards. For some days the sick

---

[1] Sickel, *Zur Geschichte des Concils von Trent*, pp. 428, 442–5.
[2] Nadal and others had lurid details to give of the weather that season, but Peter never mentions the subject.
[3] Braunsberger, *Epistulae*, vol. iv, pp. 802, 841.

man did not realize what had happened, that his physical reserves had been completely drained by the appalling strain of his labours for the Council. On March 1st, Laynez thought it right to warn him:

The good Cardinal replied that he was content and would be glad if our Father brought him Holy Communion. On his returning yesterday with the Blessed Sacrament, the Cardinal received and embraced him with much affection and willingly listened to his counsels. Then he made his confession to his ordinary confessor and with great devotion received Holy Communion from the hands of our Father. . . . Towards evening our Father returned and anointed him according to his desire. He asked spontaneously that the Passion of Our Lord should be read to him and that was done. Afterwards noticing that he was failing and at his last hour, our Father said the prayers for the dying, together with Father Salmeron and others. At the end of them the Cardinal rendered up his soul to Our Lord, it being three hours after nightfall. . . .

During this winter there was a great dearth in Mantua. As the poor began to suffer severely, the Cardinal issued instructions, which we, being at his house, saw carried out, that a thousand people whose need he had learned from his priests were to be provided with bread . . . until the next harvest. This and the daily alms that he ordered to be taken to poor families and poor monasteries cost him, it is said, fourteen or fifteen thousand scudi. He had advanced six thousand scudi for public works, and directed that they were not to be returned to him but paid into a *Monte di Pietà* for the benefit of the poor people. It would seem indeed that God had given him a special grace of mercy to the poor, which is a sure token that God will be merciful to him. Besides, he was always a zealous bishop, and governed his diocese so wisely that he was held to be one of the best prelates in Italy. Your Reverence will please order the usual Masses and prayers for the repose of his soul.[1]

The death of the first President brought such a gloom on the Council that one bishop likened the day to Good Friday. St. Peter, writing to Hosius, who was prostrated by the news, spoke of the Church as the widow of Naim mourning her son, at a time too when his wisdom and discretion were more than ever necessary to her. Then, rallying the

[1] Braunsberger, *Epistulae*, vol. iv, pp. 108–10.

despondent Cardinal he said: " I beg and implore you *per viscera miseri-cordiae Dei et Domini nostri Jesu Christi* to bear up under these difficulties, assaults, clamours, and sorrows, and to consider that nothing better beseems your wisdom and authority than the conquest of those hard and bitter trials by steadfastness of soul. . . . Place all your hope in Him who is and ever has been the unfailing Guardian, Guide, and Defender of His Church so that no power of Hell nor artifice of her enemies may ever prevail against the Rock on which she is established."

On March 14th Polanco reported to Peter a dreadful " *escaramuca* " between the retainers of the Spanish and Italian bishops. It was a sanguinary affair and only put down by the issue of an edict that anyone found in possession of arms would be summarily executed. Hard on that news followed the information that Cardinal Seripando was dead. The saintly General of the Order from which Martin Luther had sprung went to his longed-for peace on March 17th, leaving only Hosius and Simonetta to guide the distracted Council. Neither man was suited to the task, Hosius being too simple and straightforward a soul for its delicate require-ments, and Simonetta too hasty and hot-tempered. It was at this juncture, when the Council seemed irretrievably doomed, that Pope Pius IV suddenly rose to magnificent heights with a decision that puts him among the great seers and venturers of history.

On the death of Gonzaga the Pope was urged to appoint the Cardinal of Lorraine first President. The French and the Imperialists clamoured for his nomination, and, being an ambitious man, he eagerly desired it himself. But the Holy Father never even looked in his direction. With-out consulting a soul he decided one eventful night that Cardinal Giovanni Morone, the quondam prisoner of Paul IV, was the man. It was less than three years since he had emerged from the Castle of St. Angelo, after two ghastly years of confinement as a suspected heretic.[1] His com-plete rehabilitation followed, and now Pope Pius, who had long loved and admired him, made glorious amends for the injustice of his predecessor by honouring him with the heaviest and most sacred responsibility that could have fallen on any man's shoulders.

How splendid was the choice became evident from the expressions of delight which it evoked in every quarter. The Emperor applauded,

---

[1] Laynez had done all in his power to secure Morone's release. Writing to his General from Brussels, February 20, 1558, Salmeron said: " I had a long conversation the other day with the Archbishop of Toledo, and begged him to use his influence and authority on behalf of the Cardinal whom Father Polanco has so often recommended to us." M.H., *Epistolae P. Alphonsi Salmeronis*, vol. i, p. 235. Polanco also wrote in Laynez's name to Ribadeneyra several times, spurring him on to procure the intercession of the King of Spain.

the King of Spain heartily approved, Catherine de Médicis was pleased, and even Lorraine, magnanimous and noble gentleman, swallowed his private disappointment and sincerely congratulated his supplanter. A fortnight later St. Peter received the following Brief from the Pope:

Beloved Son, Health and Apostolic Benediction.

Our venerable brother, John, Bishop of Palestrina, called Cardinal Morone, has been constituted by Us, as We believe you will have heard, Our Legate *a latere* in the Council of Trent, after the death of the Cardinal Gonzaga, of happy memory. As he is to visit Our most dear Son in Christ, the Emperor, he will explain to you in Our name certain matters with which he is commissioned. You will rely confidently on what he says.

Given at Rome at St. Peter's, March 20, 1563, in the Fourth Year of Our Pontificate.[1]

The reason for Morone's mission to Innsbruck was that he might deal personally with the Emperor about two famous letters which His Majesty had addressed to the Pope on March 3rd. The second of these, an intimate and strictly private document, is the strangest mixture of respect and objurgation imaginable. The Pope is reminded of his advancing years and exhorted to remember the reckoning to come. In order not to be offensively personal, Ferdinand throws his fears into the future. The present Pope is a model, of course, but if young and inexperienced persons are made cardinals, who can guarantee the quality of the men they will afterwards elect? In the Council there is serious dispute about the nature of episcopal jurisdiction. The *bona fides* of those who oppose a definition of its immediately divine origin is open to grave suspicion. They are either aspirants to the purple or poor men dependent on the bounties of the Holy See. Only the champions of the opinion that residence was *de jure divino* could be safely trusted, the wealthy hidalgos whose bread and butter was safe, so would His Holiness kindly declare for them and bring pressure to bear that the matter be decided according to their sentiments? Next comes a ringing protest against papal interference with the decisions of the Council and against the Legates' monopoly of proposal. This point having been well rubbed in, Ferdinand exhorts the Pope " to seek and follow the advice and opinion of the two hundred Fathers of the Council rather than the suggestions of fifteen cardinals," with regard to conclave

[1] Braunsberger, *Epistulae*, vol. iv, p. 121.

legislation, the reform of the Curia, and the residence of bishops. The Council has the Holy Ghost to assist it but who dare affirm the same of the cardinals ? After much else the letter closes with an urgent homily to the Pope not to abuse his power, and to come to Trent in person : " I promise Your Holiness on the word of an Emperor, a King, and a good Christian, that you may come, remain, and depart in safety."[1]

The Pope replied in the most friendly and courteous terms, showing full appreciation of the Emperor's sincerity. He said that he deplored the long delays in the Council, " but these were caused by Your Majesty's Ambassadors, with their importunate demands and petitions on your behalf." As for the strange rumour mentioned by the Emperor that he wished to dissolve the Council, it was true that great princes had urged him to do so, "*sed id persuaderi nobis minime passi sumus nec vere umquam patiemur.*" He was quite willing to go to Trent if health permitted and any good result might be hoped from his visit. But the place was surrounded by Protestant and Zwinglian communities, and there would probably be riots in Rome if he ventured north, as the Turks were menacing that City.

Copies of the first and milder letter had been sent by Ferdinand himself to the Legates, the Cardinal of Lorraine, and others. The answer from the first party was pungent enough : " Your Majesty has the justest cause for grief that the affairs of this holy Council have been reduced to a state which gives great scandal and offence to the whole Christian world. But the responsibility is theirs alone who have arrogated to themselves without a tittle of justification the right of proposing here whatever matters they wish to have discussed." In other words, those very Spanish bishops for whom Ferdinand manifested such loving concern were the real cause of the Council's stagnation. It was they who started all the pother about the Council not being free, though, said the Legates, " were it being held in the middle of Saxony it could not have enjoyed greater liberty." And why should they not refer to the Pope for guidance ? They only did so when his authority was at stake, whereas the Emperor's own ambassadors and those of other princes wrote home about everything. As the Spanish bishops had so much to say about episcopal authority, was it not right that somebody should stand up for papal authority ?

When news reached Innsbruck that Morone was coming, Vice-Chancellor Seld remarked on the necessity of having an advisory body at Court to help the Emperor with the negotiations. It was therefore decided

[1] Le Plat, *Monumentorum*, etc., vol. v, pp. 690–703.

to reconstitute the theological Commission. Ferdinand put the Hungarian, Francis Forgách, Bishop of Grosswardein, in charge this time, and summoned Dr. Conrad Braun and Staphylus to join Cordoba and His Majesty's own confessor, the Dominican, Mathias van Esche,[1] on the board. After St. Peter's departure from Innsbruck in March, King Maximilian and the Cardinal of Lorraine appear to have done what they could to prevent his return,[2] but Ferdinand was too fine a man for the influences of mere prejudice. Early in April the Saint received his call, and, on arrival at Court by the middle of the month, was welcomed by His Majesty with great affection. Morone's short journey from Trent to Innsbruck took five days, owing to the weather and the dreadful state of the roads.[3] He arrived on April 21st and was shown all honour by the Emperor.

The negotiations began at once, Peter, as before, keeping in touch with Laynez. His instructions were as follows:

Father General considers that any private dealings you may have with the Emperor or the Legate ought to be kept secret. In matters pertaining to the service of the Pope and the Holy See, your Reverence will use the best offices in your power, according to your charity. Father General is further of opinion that you should give your answers in writing in order to ensure greater circumspection, though you may also confer orally, as you judge advisable. It is understood here that his Lordship has three matters for negotiation, the first and principal being about the phrase, *proponentibus Legatis*. According to report, the King of Spain has urged in Rome that others besides the Legates should have the right of proposal. . . . We have no doubt but that you will now again as formerly show good reason why the decree on this matter should not be changed. The second affair about which the Legate has gone to treat concerns the removal of the Council to Bologna, and the coronation of the Emperor there by the Pope. On this, too, your Reverence may be asked for an opinion. Father General judges that it would be more expedient for the Council to finish here in Trent where it has so often begun, on this ground among others that it will thus be considered to enjoy greater liberty than if held in Bologna. But he also thinks that, at the conclusion of the Council, it would be very fitting if His Majesty were to come to Bologna for

[1] Known also as Cythard or Sittard from the town of that name near Aachen in which he was born.
[2] Braunsberger, *Epistulae*, vol. iv, pp. 110–11.
[3] Constant, *La Légation du Cardinal Morone prés de l'Empereur et le Concile de Trente* (Paris, 1922), p. xxxix. This is a new collection of documents with a brief introduction.

his coronation, in order to bring the Empire and the Apostolic See closer together.[1] At a time of so much dissension and disaffection towards the Holy See, it appears the more necessary that a good Catholic Emperor, such as His Majesty, should give proof of his loyalty and set a fine example to his son and successor. . . . The third reason for the Legate's journey, we understand, is to persuade the Emperor to let the Council finish soon, after having first dealt with the necessary questions of dogma and reformation. If they should ask your opinion, know that Father General considers the proposal eminently reasonable and advantageous for the Church. The peoples are suffering a great deal from the absence of their pastors, and Christian souls are being kept anxious and in suspense until they see the Council determined on some good conclusion. . . .[2]

Meanwhile the bishops were leaving Trent in disgust at the delay caused by the allied Spanish, French, and Imperialist Fathers. In the opinion of Lorraine fifty others ought to have been driven from the Council as enemies of " salutary determinations," that is to say, Lorraine's determinations. The French could think of nothing but their domestic troubles with the Calvinists; the Imperialists of nothing but theirs with the Lutherans; and the Spaniards of nothing but " *questa benedetta residentia.*" Hosius and Simonetta were in despair. From the former Peter learned that the chalice question was again uppermost, not only in the Council, but in the local Diets of Bavaria and Austria, where it looked as if it might easily lead to revolution. What did his Reverence think about the matter? In a lengthy letter from Innsbruck on April 21st the Saint replied that the longer he lived in Germany and the more he heard, read, and observed concerning the subject, the stronger became his conviction that the grant of the chalice would involve far worse consequences than its refusal. He was persuaded that the general run of priests had neither the competence nor the zeal to instruct their flocks adequately in the new rite, and that error in Eucharistic belief would only increase and become more firmly rooted as a result of the concession. The whole attitude of the petitioners, the fact that most of them were hostile to the Pope and many of them scarcely distinguishable from Lutherans, made it plain how little was to be hoped from a policy of conciliation. Give such people an inch and they would take an ell, as indeed, they were already doing

[1] Bologna was in the Papal States, and Ferdinand was much too nervous of Protestant opinion to go there or to be crowned by the Pope.
[2] Braunsberger, *Epistulae*, vol. iv, pp. 147–9.

in Austria and Bavaria. Their triple slogan, *calex, caro, conjux*, the chalice for the laity, meat on Fridays for everybody, and wives for the clergy, would, if accepted, only lead to further and more radical demands, for "what good ever came or ever could come from giving way to the multitude in the sphere of religion? "[1]

This abandonment of the small scrap of sympathy which Peter originally entertained for the 'calixtines' led to some loss of temper in Innsbruck. Van Esche, the Court preacher, for whom when ill, not long before, the Saint had publicly prayed that he might "soon be well again for the evangelical office which he has discharged to this day with such great success and usefulness," now repaid the courtesy by saying to his face : "You worship the turpitude of the Papal Curia and its manifest vices. You are a bond-slave of the Pope."[2] It was given out, too, that Peter's change of front, microscopic as we know it to have been, belonged to the *quid pro quo* genus of actions. He hoped thereby, we are told, to wheedle some nice little unoccupied monastery out of the Pope.

Shortly after his arrival in Innsbruck Cardinal Morone was laid low with the gout, that subtle enemy of the Council of Trent. It did not, however, deflect him from his simple but masterly plan of campaign, which was to detach the Emperor and his people from the French and Spaniards. These he would deal with when he returned to the Council. The Emperor at first betrayed some restiveness, and certainly was not satisfied with Morone's preliminary explanations.[3] But the sick Cardinal was so sweetly reasonable, so ready to see His Majesty's point of view and even to sympathize with it, that there was no resisting him. Their bedside discussions centred at first round the answers to four questions which Ferdinand had submitted to Dr. Braun, Staphylus, Cordoba, and van Esche, just before the coming of St. Peter. The first was again on the tiresome old problem of proposal, to which the theologians had answered that, if the Pope or his Legates neglected to put forward such motions as seemed necessary for the defence of religion in Germany, then the Emperor would have a duty to supply the omission ; and not to him alone but to all Catholic kings, *imo et inferioris gradus Christi fidelibus*, it belonged of right to make necessary proposals. Morone let all this pass, except the clause including "the faithful of lesser rank," which, he said, needed some limitation. The second question concerned the Legates'

---

[1] Braunsberger, *Epistulae*, vol. iv, pp. 150–3.
[2] Braunsberger, *Epistulae*, vol. ii, p. 844 ; vol. iv, p. 982.
[3] Steinherz, *Nunciaturberichte aus Deutschland* 1560–1572 *nebst ergänzenden Actenstücken*, vol. iii (Vienna, 1903), p. 270.

habit of consulting the Pope, to which the theologians answered that recourse should be had to His Holiness, not before, but after the Council had made its decisions, in order to obtain the necessary confirmation. The cardinal found nothing objectionable in this advice either. The third question asked what was to be done should the Italian bishops " *quorum infinitus est numerus*," attempt to extort or decree anything " *in detrimentum Ultramontanorum.*"[1] The answer this time did not pass, and no wonder, for it was that either only a certain proportion of bishops from each nation should have consultative powers, or that the voting should be done by nations as at the Council of Constance. The fourth question raised the subject of papal supremacy directly, to which the answer was that the " *odiosa disputatio* " should be decided at Trent and in favour of the Pope. While agreeing that such was the correct decision, Morone altogether deprecated ventilation of the subject in the Council, as it was far too dangerous and would drag on interminably.[2]

Knowledge of the questions had reached Trent and been communicated to Laynez, who, like Morone, was in bed with the gout. On April 23rd the General wrote to warn St. Peter : " The theory of the Council being above the Pope is new," he said, " dating only from the days of Constance. It is held by comparatively few theologians, and undeserving that a serious-minded man should build upon it, or presuppose it as something certain. In truth, it appears to be the servant of seditious minds. All the more, then, will it be avoided by those who love peace and union in the Church, and who detest the spirit of schism which has such a hold on the men of our generation. . . . The secrecy which your Reverence counsels with regard to the matter in your letters is demanded by the very nature of the case, and I return your last letter without having shown it to anybody or having it copied."[3]

The result of the Emperor's consultations with Morone was yet another set of articles, fourteen in number, for the theological Commission. Ferdinand's faith in the efficacy of commissions seems to have been boundless and unshakable. The first seven articles reveal a surprisingly eirenic trend, due, obviously, to the diplomatic genius of the Legate, and, though the remaining ones are not of so peaceable a character, they are worded with remarkable moderation. They were not meant for Morone's eyes but he obtained a copy through some secret channel and proceeded to

---

[1] In the sixteenth century the label " ultramontanist " curiously enough bore the opposite meaning to its modern one. At that period an ultramontanist was a Gallican.

[2] Constant, *La Légation du Cardinal Morone*, pp. 68–70.

[3] Braunsberger, *Epistulae*, vol. iv, pp. 157–8.

annotate them for the guidance of Canisius and Dr. Braun, whose known loyalty to the Holy See was his chief comfort. His *avertimenti* coincided in almost every particular with the views often expressed by St. Peter, special stress being laid on the " true and common opinion that the Pope is above the Council." All the articles were discussed, defended, or pulled to pieces by the theologians, with the Emperor an interested listener to their oratory.

Some time after April 26th,[1] when the Imperial Chancery examined the Bull of Pius IV relative to conclaves, four fresh questions were added to the Commission's programme, three about the Bull, and the fourth in the following terms : " Why should it seem inadvisable for the Fathers of Trent to divide into national groups as was done at the Council of Constance ? " The next important event in the Commission's modest history was the receipt of a long letter addressed to the Emperor by the Cardinal of Lorraine. The letter consisted of an exposition and defence of the Gallican theory that the Pope is not " *Pastor Ecclesiae Universalis.*" Though the French Church, said Lorraine, had always held the Pope to be the Vicar of Christ, the Successor of St. Peter, and the first and highest Pastor in the Universal Church, they could not admit the titles which it was desired to grant him at Trent in the seventh canon on the Sacrament of Holy Orders, namely that his primacy was universal and that he possessed the plenitude of power as Ruler, Pastor, and Governor of the Universal Church. Taking the parts of the Church separately, the Church in France, the Church in Italy, the Church in Spain, etc., those prerogatives did indeed belong to him, but not so with regard to the Church taken as a whole. To allow that would be equivalent to admitting his superiority over the Council, which represented the Universal Church, and, therefore, a repudiation of the decrees of Constance and Basle. Having urged all that he could for his opinion, the Cardinal concluded with a detailed criticism of the thirty-three articles in proof of the Pope's universal primacy, which, at the Emperor's request, Delfino and Nadal had drawn up for presentation to the French and Spanish bishops in the Council.[2] The criticism is full of interest as showing how the mind of a Gallican worked in those days. Constance and Basle are the main props of the argument, nor is there any hint that the validity of their famous, unratified decrees, with which the Cardinal waves aside St. Thomas Aquinas and the Council of Florence, was ever contested or considered doubtful.[3]

---

[1] Braunsberger gives an earlier date but Constant argues convincingly for one after April 26th *La Légation du Cardinal Morone*, p. 72, n. 1.
[2] M.H., *Epistolae P. Hieronymi Nadal*, vol. ii, pp. 223–4.
[3] Text in Constant, *La Légation du Cardinal Morone*, pp. 48–64.

With matters such as these in its dossier the Commission could hardly have been expected to keep cool. No meeting could have kept cool with Cordoba in it. But Staphylus, too, was in arms, and with him, as far as can be gathered, stood van Esche. Against that coalition, of which Cordoba was the moving spirit, St. Peter and Dr. Braun could make no head. " The good Father Canisius is having a difficult time," wrote Polanco to Nadal, " as he finds his colleagues opposed to the authority of the Pope and the Apostolic See." The same letter referred to the heavy trouble that was then afoot between " *El Comendador* " and " *El Maestro*," discreet pseudonyms for Philip II and Pius IV. Polanco, being a most kindly man, wrote to Peter, too, to cheer him up : " We know the anxiety and affliction which your Reverence experiences in such company, but if God is with us let any man's hand fight against us. Continue to do all in your power by word or writing or any way that seems best to you to help the cause of the Church and the Holy Apostolic See, and as for the issue, let us commit it to the providence of God, praying Him without ceasing to look with eyes of mercy on His inheritance, won by the blood and life of His Son." That Peter did not fail in prayer is shown by his letter to the rectors of all his colleges, directing each priest to say Mass and the non-priests various prayers for Cardinal Morone.[1]

The theological Commission was meant to be a sort of jury, and consequently the Emperor expected it to return a joint and unanimous verdict on the articles. Soon, however, it became apparent that such harmony would be unattainable while St. Peter and Cordoba remained at cross-purposes. Peter argued and pleaded almost to tears but he could not budge the protégé of Maximilian. Rather did that vigorous man sweep the others, except Dr. Braun, with him to the composition of fourteen separate little booklets, each comprising an answer to one or other of the fourteen articles. On the backs of some of these, in the handwriting of Dr. Braun, who acted secretary, are the words, " read and approved," which meant that those particular answers had been endorsed by the entire Commission, including St. Peter. With the other answers Peter would have no truck. He thought at first of sending in a minority report, but, on consideration, decided that he might achieve more if he laid his protest before the Emperor in person. Though Ferdinand gave him little encouragement at the interview, he was undoubtedly impressed by the Saint's expostulation. In the first place, Seld, the Vice-Chancellor, received immediate instructions to revise and tone down the written

[1] Braunsberger, *Epistulae*, vol. iv, pp. 173-4, 188.

answers, after which pruning the booklets would again be submitted to the Commission. But that was not all. Seld, having explained the reasons for his many changes and omissions, handed the work to the Emperor's secretary, Singkmoser, for yet further abridgment. When finished, this second revision was only one quarter the length of the original text. Ferdinand himself then took a hand at the game and made all sorts of corrections and emendations in the margin. Finally, Seld went over the whole work once more, so that when it reached Cardinal Morone on May 7th, Cordoba would have been astonished at the suavity and conciseness substituted for his prolix criticisms.

Still, even thus sweetened and fenced about with almost excessive courtesy, the document contained a number of suggestions and ideas hardly calculated to expedite the cause of practical reform. Thus a definition of the question of episcopal residence was called for, the very matter that had spoked the wheels of the Council for so long, and the Emperor was urged to try his hardest to obtain the Pope's consent that the Council should have a say in the reform of His Holiness's person and Curia. By so doing, said the theologians, His Holiness " would win immense authority for the Council." A large section of the document is occupied with reasons excusing the Emperor from accepting the Pope's invitation to meet him, and with a perfectly gratuitous homily to the Holy Father not to transfer the Council to Bologna.[1]

On May 8th, the day following the presentation of the answers to Morone, St. Peter wrote as follows to Laynez :

Pax Christi.

Very Reverend Father,

I have received together your letters of May 1st, 2nd, and 4th, and I am now going to reply to them and to the one you sent me on April 27th. I thank your Reverence with all my heart for so carefully and so paternally instructing your son, and for supporting and strengthening him in his efforts for the common cause of the Church. The writings and replies which you sent were most welcome, though they arrived a little late and after the answers of the theologians had been committed to paper. Finding it impossible to obtain from my colleagues the only right and just verdict, as I see it, I changed my first plan of sending in a separate judgment and considered that I ought to visit the Emperor and freely explain my position and views to him. I,

---

[1] Constant, *La Légation du Cardinal Morone*, pp. 81–101.

therefore, went, and, after an apology, plunged into two narratives, first of the difficulties I felt with regard to the document drawn up by my colleagues, and then of the methods and procedure that His Majesty might more advantageously and auspiciously employ in the promotion of the Council and the work of reform. I pointed out that this document was not necessary or solidly argued; that it was composed in haste by a few persons ill-equipped for a task of such importance, owing to their inexperience of affairs and certain prejudices which hamper good judgment;[1] and that it little beseemed His Majesty to act harshly towards the Pope, who was devoted to him. The document might offend His Holiness and cool his ardour for the reforms already set on foot. Besides, instead of having his promises distrusted he ought rather to be congratulated and befriended for the efforts he was making.

Continuing, I said that the answers of my colleagues would come into the hands of the Fathers at Trent and give rise to fresh strife and agitation, thus hindering rather than helping the Council, which was already afflicted enough. Many men would consider that his Majesty was making common cause with those adversaries of the Church who never cease from vociferating against ecclesiastical abuses . . . while remaining wilfully blind to their own corruption. Again, I urged that this over-zealous effort would not merely prove useless as far as the Roman Curia was concerned. New grounds for irritation and annoyance would appear when the cardinals found the imperfections of their order so offensively and, indeed, unfairly set forth; when it was seen that the Pope was subjected to reformation by the Council; that the authority of the Legates was diminished; that a demand was made for national deputations; that the Secretary of the Council was held suspect; and that, finally, a weapon was being provided wherewith turbulent men might fill the Council with greater clamour and commotion than ever before. . . .

Having, in this manner, explained the difficulties from every angle, I proceeded to set forth what I judged to be the most helpful ideas on the other side. I urged that the opportunity afforded by the visit of so great a Cardinal ought not to be thrown away; that the Emperor, either personally or by representatives, ought to treat with him, not in writing but in intimate converse; and that he ought to hear him

---

[1] Cordoba was a Spaniard and had not been long in Germany at Maximilian's Court. Most of his company there consisted of his own countrymen.

out willingly on the best methods of avoiding and defeating the opposition with which both Church and Council were confronted. . . . Much, I continued, had already been excellently done in the Council which would promote the work of reformation in the highest degree, and negotiations might conveniently be started as to the confirmation and execution of the Fathers' decisions. Again, means ought to be sought of helping Germany's peculiar plight. . . . and this could be more easily effected through the Pope than through the Council. . . . I, for my part, would gladly do all in my power to assist with the devising of schemes for the re-establishment and advancement of religion, especially in the Emperor's dominions.

What more needed I to say? When I had finished speaking, freely, indeed, but as my conscience demanded, the Emperor answered very briefly. He gave me to understand that he would think about the whole matter. Learned men, he went on, were favourable to his plans and had voted for them. However, he wished well to the Pope and to the Council, and he would see that certain matters in the document were expressed less intemperately and offensively. To tell the truth, I was not satisfied by the Emperor on that occasion, nor afterwards in later consultations when he submitted the revised document to us again. I explained all this to Cardinal Morone and begged that no blame should be imputed to me or to our Society, if certain things in that long writing displeased him, as they undoubtedly will. He daily expects to receive the manuscript, and, though he has not yet set eyes on it, he bears it no friendly regard. He has commended me for the course I pursued and shows me the greatest kindness and favour. I think that when he receives the document he will make a list of its errors and inconveniences, perhaps remitting the rest to the closer scrutiny of the Council or the Pope. . . .

The result of it all is that I now feel myself freed from great anguish of mind. I have said my say to the Emperor, as conscience directed, so, whatever happens, I trust that I shall not be held accountable. I have made this quite plain to my colleagues. For the rest, I pray and would have others pray with me that Christ Our Lord may either completely suppress the Emperor's designs, especially as set forth in this document, or else turn them to the advantage of the Church. I shall not mention the name of the person who is rumoured to have whispered daily into the Emperor's ear those rigid counsels concerning the reformation of the Church in Head and members; the liberty of the Fathers at Trent; the right of proposal; the residence question; the abuses of the Roman Curia, etc.[1]

It is uncertain when we shall have the Emperor's permission to leave here because he awaits the Legates' answer, and wishes to confer with us about it. Personally, I would greatly like to get my dismissal from Court as soon as possible, so that I may look after my Augsburg flock rather than engage in distasteful and unavailing controversy with my colleagues of the Commission. And now your Reverence has a summary of the whole affair. I shall be glad to hear that you are considering it, and I greatly desire to have your further instructions as to what should be done in Our Lord.[2]

That Peter should have felt rather strongly about Cordoba's manœuvres is not surprising. He knew their sinister inspiration and it must have been exasperating to watch helplessly while an inexperienced blunderer fiddled with the delicate and complicated machinery of the Church. The Pope at the time was trying really hard to bring about necessary reforms in Rome, but Cordoba had not the vision to make any allowances for the difficulty of moving a bureaucracy. By being too hasty with the business in the past, another Pope had precipitated the Great Schism, a warning to which Cordoba and his kind remained completely insensitive. Indeed, the general trend of the document for which he and Staphylus were chiefly responsible would lead one to believe that neither knew anything about what was happening in the Council, or that they had been wilfully misled by the impatient Drascovics and Thun. These worthies came well within the scope of the gibe that ambassadors are persons who " lie abroad." They endeavoured to poison the Emperor's mind against Morone, and kept Cordoba and his clique supplied with biased tittle-tattle about doings at Trent. It suited the Franciscan's book well enough. Earnest and zealous he and his informants were no doubt, but they appear to have been incapable of seeing beyond their noses or of taking into consideration any views other than narrow national ones. To appease the Protestants, whose avowed aim was the complete destruction of the

[1] St. Peter must have meant either Cordoba or King Maximilian, two names standing for one policy.

[2] Braunsberger, *Epistulae*, vol. iv, pp. 174–7. The conclusion of the letter is about the affairs of Peter's Province which he continued to watch over assiduously in the midst of his Innsbruck anxieties. The Jesuits in Germany were being fiercely attacked by Martin Kemnitz and other Lutheran leaders. Some of the brethren wished to hit back but Laynez was opposed to all contention with heretics. While recognizing his point, St. Peter judged that some reply ought to be made, possibly by some friendly person, not a Jesuit, " non ut remordeamus sed ut veritatem doctrinae nostrae asseramus, ne, ut fit, multi putent vera esse quae nobis affingunt. Verum, quidquid Reverentiae Tuae placebit mihi displicere non potest."

Church, seemed the great objective, at whatever cost to the Catholic unity which rested and must ever rest on one only foundation, the authority of the Apostolic See.

Immediately after writing his letter, St. Peter learned of the final pruning to which the theologians' document had been subjected. " I now understand," he informed Laynez the same day in another communication, " that what I desired from His Majesty has been largely granted. . . . Blessed be God Who thus inspired and moved the good Emperor to change and modify his projects. To-day we were summoned again to consultation that we might give our opinions about the new canons on the Sacrament of Orders which a select committee had drawn up at Trent and submitted to the Fathers. The Emperor also put before us an expostulation from the Cardinal of Lorraine and the French bishops concerning one of the canons not yet promulgated. In this they seek to justify their denial of the primacy of the Pope, whom they refuse to acknowledge as Pastor of the Universal Church. . . . I should like to know what has hitherto been said or decided about this controversy, and the right reply to make to Frenchmen holding this theory of their Sorbonne doctors, in order that the authority of the Pope, already suffering more than enough opposition, may be preserved intact. . . ."[1]

To Peter's great satisfaction, all the theologians, including even Cordoba, apparently answered without hesitation that the Pope is superior to the Council, when the Emperor put them a straight question on the subject.[2] It gave him a momentary hope of soon being able to get back to Augsburg, but the hope had fled next time Cordoba opened his mouth. Cordoba might allow that the Pope was above the Council in theory, but in practice he believed the Council to be worth any number of Popes. Morone's friendly and moderate criticism of the theologians' answers so exasperated him that he wrote to the Emperor charging the Legate with rank hypocrisy as regards the matter of reform *in Capite et membris*. Owing to the Legate's magnificent diplomacy, that question and the two concerning the right of proposal and the transaction of business by groups of deputies from the various nations were the only outstanding ones towards the close of his sojourn in Innsbruck. To St. Peter he confided that the Emperor was " urging them tooth and nail," but again his diplomacy triumphed. " The rigorous suggestions of my colleagues have nothing availed," wrote the

[1] Braunsberger, *Epistulae*, vol. iv, pp. 182–3.
[2] Twenty-three years earlier Dr. Braun had written a treatise to prove that Councils derive their authority from the Roman Church ; that their decrees to be valid must have the Pope's ratification ; and that the Pope is infallible. N. Paulus, in *Historisches Jahrbuch der Görres-Gesellschaft*, vol. xiv (Munich, 1893), pp. 526–8.

Saint delightedly to Laynez. " Though their rejoinder to Cardinal Morone's criticism again gave the Emperor pause, it was rendered ineffectual, and the Legate has obtained all that he desired and even more than he hoped for. . . . He has persuaded the Emperor to desist from urging a new declaration on the words *Proponentibus Legatis ;* to leave the Bull about conclaves entirely to the discretion of the Pope, whether or no His Holiness chooses to submit it and other matters to the Council; and finally to relinquish the demand for national deputations. The result of this has been that the Cardinal, whom I left sad in bed after my visit to bid him good-bye, went away from here full of joy and consolation. . . ."[1]

The terms of Morone's compromise, by which he engaged to propose personally to the Council all the Emperor's reform projects except those relative to the Pope and the Curia, were substantially on the lines suggested by St. Peter in his February *votum*. Throughout the second period of the Commission he kept in close touch with the Cardinal and, by the Cardinal's own testimony, rendered him invaluable services. St. Charles Borromeo was so affected by Morone's references to Peter that he wrote : " It is incredible how careful and solicitous that good man [Canisius] is to protect and promote with all his might the worship and reverence due to Almighty God."[2] Peter on his side did not fail in appreciation of Morone. Writing to Laynez on May 12th, he said :

Yesterday the Lord Cardinal departed from here. He assured me that he held me in the closest bonds of friendship, and made me a present, as a seal on his extreme kindness to me. I have reminded the Fathers and Brothers of this Province to pray diligently for him, according to his own desire and your Paternity's wishes. He wants me to write often about the state of affairs here, sending the letters to your Reverence that you may confer with him about them. This is the best plan, I think, safer and more advisable than addressing them directly to him. . . . I cannot refrain from mentioning that, though many days confined to bed, the Cardinal achieved several splendid results. I believe that there is hardly another man alive who could have managed the Emperor so skilfully. . . . Thanks be to Christ Who sent him to us. It would have been difficult, I am sure, for anybody but him to secure so many concessions with regard to the Council, and to solve in good part the present problems of this Court. Doubtless, the Council

[1] Braunsberger, *Epistulae*, vol. iv, pp. 202–3.
[2] Braunsberger, *Epistulae*, vol. iv, pp. 235, 973–4, 975, 978.

will now progress more smoothly and peaceably, and the influence of certain of its sons who do not always envisage and plan the more honest course will be diminished. . . .[1]

Polanco, having learned from some Jesuit at the College in Innsbruck that St. Peter was quite worn out by his labours and anxieties, wrote suggesting that he should come to Trent for a change and rest. " I would like to go away for many reasons," he replied. " I do not possess enough judgment for negotiating with these gentlemen about matters of importance, and I find it extremely painful to see conclusions put in writing which tend, in my opinion, to lessen and obscure the authority of the Pope, Church, and Council. But God forbid that, if I can be of help, I should desert the cause of the Church in these unhappy times. . . ." Peter's renewed misgivings were due to that rock of offence, the *Libellus Reformationis*. On May 14th the Emperor had set his men the difficult task of extracting from it any ideas that might still be urged without violation of the pact with Morone. The theologians met every day and the very first thing to be brought up was the odious question of the chalice. All Peter's colleagues except Dr. Braun were in favour of again seeking the concession at Trent, though the Fathers had long ago shown their inability and unwillingness to deal with it.

Peter had other troubles, too, unconnected with his work on the Commission. The Rector of the College in Innsbruck gave him a world of worry, as, like Father Couvillon, the unfortunate man had become a prey to melancholia. The gentleness and generosity of Peter's action with regard to this human difficulty is in striking contrast to his inflexible determination where he considered that divine interests were at stake. He wheedled and humoured the invalid, rallied him in the kindest way, patiently listened to his interminable complaints, got others to write letters of cheer and comfort to him, and prayed and sought prayers tirelessly for him.[2] Eventually he sent the Rector off to Bavaria on holiday and took his place at the College himself. When the Archbishop of Prague was returning to Trent Peter said : " I would love to go with him in order to see my Reverend Fathers, who in their immense goodness and kindness towards me have offered me this singular consolation. But I must wait for a better occasion as I have had a hint that the Emperor might be annoyed,

---

[1] Braunsberger, *Epistulae*, vol. iv, pp. 192–3. If Peter in the last lines was thinking of the Cardinal of Lorraine, as seems likely, he did that great man an injustice. However wrong-headed much of his policy may have been, Lorraine's honesty and sincerity were beyond suspicion.
[2] Braunsberger, *Epistulae*, vol. iv, pp. 201–2, 222, 226, 248.

the Germans here offended, and the public good prejudiced by my going. *Fiat in nobis Domini voluntas ad suam gloriam.*" Finding it necessary to stay, Peter begged the Emperor to excuse him with the Augsburg canons who might resent his longer absence, and we may still read in the Acts of their Chapter under date May 28th: " *Die Römisch Kay. Maiestet excusirt D. Canisium.*"

Peter's great aim now was to keep the Emperor in a friendly mood. The pact with Morone had many enemies and he must be its defender. When Maximilian heard of it he was disgusted, and wrote from Vienna on May 24th reproaching his ageing father for his weakness: " From all that Your Majesty concluded with Cardinal Morone I am satisfied that we have very little or nothing at all to hope from the Council of Trent. . . . I, therefore, advise Your Majesty, with filial deference and out of my love for you, to remain no longer in that place, but to hasten hither at the first opportunity for the transaction of other important business. . . . As the Council is going to remain sterile, the farther you are from it the better. . . ."[1]

Meantime, Cordoba and his allies were busy with obnoxious rumours, calculated to spoil the good work of Morone. Ever since the visit of Lorraine to Innsbruck, St. Peter explained to Laynez, it was believed there that the Emperor had fallen under a cloud in Rome. The Roman people were reported to be afraid of that Cardinal and, in consequence, likely to resort to unfriendly practices against Ferdinand:

Thoughtful men would, therefore, like to see greater signs of genuine trust on the Pope's part and less place given to suspicion and those intrigues, of which, they say, the Italians are too fond. Another complaint is that practically no news can be sent to Rome without it immediately becoming public property. Secrecy is not properly observed, they allege, with the result that everybody knows at once about the Emperor's letters and plans. Again, it disturbs people very much to hear that in Rome things are done quite contrary to what has been decided in the Council, as when, according to rumour, quaestors were sent to the Kingdom of Naples, though the Council had prohibited such undertakings.[2] Finally it is alleged that due care is not taken, perhaps, indeed, scarcely any care, to put into execution the Bulls

[1] In Bucholtz, *Geschichte der Regierung Ferdinand des Ersten*, vol. ix (Vienna, 1838), pp. 689-93.
[2] The quaestors were officials appointed to promulgate indulgences and to collect money for building churches and other pious works. The Council had abolished the office altogether on July 16, 1562, but the decree had not yet become law. Still, the Roman authorities might well have refrained from taking advantage of the temporary respite.

recently promulgated in Rome, the suggestion being that the reform of the Curia is not receiving serious attention. I speak as a fool, but give you what I hear, partly that I may learn the right reply to such objections, and partly, that possible scandal and inconvenience may be warded off, by the grace of God. . . .[1]

Cardinal Hosius showed the keenest desire to have Peter with him in Trent for a time. " I thank your Lordship most heartily," answered the Saint. " Your wish for my presence is a good indication of your extremely kind and generous feelings towards me during these years, though I am all undeserving of them, and last year I gave you enough trouble when I was your guest. Just now the glory of God and the good of the Church seem to require that I should not leave the Court, how-ever much my personal leanings may call and invite me elsewhere. When there is no further use for Canisius here, then will I gladly seize the first chance of visiting my beloved Fathers and of placing myself entirely at the disposal of you, my excellent Patron."

Referring to the chalice question, always a great anxiety to Hosius, he said : " Let the princes think as they will. For my part I prefer to be mistaken with the bishops in this sacred business than to be wise with their Highnesses."

It was not only the chalice that had again come into the limelight. Despite the pact, Cordoba and his cabal continued to press for the reform of the Curia by the Council, even to the extent of making the Emperor waver. When St. Peter visited him on May 22nd His Majesty " spoke much on the subject of reform and censured the obstinacy of those who refused to allow the Council to undertake the reform of the Roman Curia. This is the old and popular song again and my colleagues appear to have increased rather than lessened its appeal. . . . I am most anxious to be counselled, and to be helped with the Holy Sacrifices and prayers of my Fathers and Brothers."[2]

Cardinal Morone expressed great satisfaction on learning that St. Peter was to remain at Court, and sent him an encouraging message " to persevere with a good heart in the way he had begun." By the Cardinal's express wish Peter was now commissioned to arrange an important negotia-tion with Albert of Bavaria, who seemed inclined to tolerate the use of the lay chalice in his dominions if refused the concession at Trent. The Council's Nuncio, Niccolo Ormanetto, journeyed to Innsbruck to receive the Saint's advice and instructions before setting out for Munich. Though

---

[1] Braunsberger, *Epistulae*, vol. iv, p. 203.   [2] Braunsberger, *Epistulae*, vol. iv, p. 213.

the mission was very successful, the Council had by no means heard the last of the chalice question, and in June St. Peter reported that Ferdinand and Albert were about to assemble a ' conciliabulum ' at Vienna for the purpose of deciding on their future policy with regard to it:

It is likely enough that I shall be summoned but much more certain that, if I am, I shall go with the greatest reluctance. . . . Am I to be always involved in these most difficult and grave affairs ? Must I have no respite from my single-handed opposition to a band of, so to speak, sworn allies, who if they were open enemies of the Church might be more easily circumvented and overthrown ? I confess that I find this cross very hard to bear, for experience teaches that great zeal and singular prudence and moderation are the principal needs of one who would engage in the religious negotiations of Germany. Perhaps you would use your influence to rescue me, a weak vessel, from these waves ? But if you think I should go to Vienna if summoned by the Emperor, then, in God's name, not my will but my Superior's be done. To come to more important matters. I would desire and urge that Cardinal Morone be got to write to the Emperor explaining why business in the Council proceeds so slowly. This is giving rise to fresh and harsh suspicions, as, for instance, that the tardiness is purposely planned in order to bring about the dissolution of the Council through sheer boredom with it. . . .[1]

The chief obstacle to progress at the moment was the sudden flaring up of a long-smouldering dispute between the French and Spanish ambassadors on the matter of precedence. King Philip had threatened to break off diplomatic relations with Rome if his man, the Count di Luna, was made to play second fiddle to the French ; and Philip being the only really ' safe ' monarch left, from the Catholic point of view, the Pope gave way to his demands on both the question of precedence and the other cherished one, that the Legates should no longer have the exclusive right of proposal in the Council. Morone, seeing his hard-won victory at Innsbruck thus thrown away, naturally became indignant, and even expressed a wish to resign his office of first President. That would have been the final disaster, but Pope Pius found a way out, and his great lieutenant remained to break, partly by means of this very dispute about

[1] Braunsberger, *Epistulae*, vol. iv, pp. 229–30. As a result of this letter, Morone asked Peter to explain to the Emperor on his behalf that the delay would not, perhaps, be accounted excessive, if the number of Fathers who desired to speak and the number of topics they wanted to discuss were ıaken into consideration.

precedence, the Franco-Spanish alliance of Fathers which had so long rendered progress impossible. How far the French envoys, backed up by Lorraine, were ready to go, may be seen in the protest which they drew up when the Pope gave precedence to the Spaniards: " We venerate, reverence, honour, and glorify to high heaven the Apostolic See, the Supreme Pontiff, and the Holy Roman Church, for the increase of whose dignity our fathers poured out their blood. But as for Pius IV, this successor but not imitator of St. Peter, we disown his authority and whatsoever he may decide or decree we reject and spurn with contempt." [1]

While these exciting things were happening at Trent, St. Peter went on doggedly with his efforts to keep the Emperor in the paths of peace to which Morone had so skilfully steered him. He persuaded Dr. Braun, the secretary of the theological Commission, to modify several things in its report on the Emperor's *Libellus* and to suppress a number of passages altogether. " These matters will come up for discussion to-morrow," he wrote on May 31st, " and I am afraid that the Spanish Friar may raise trouble and again force his drastic ideas on our attention. . . . Staphylus, a much more reasonable man, is ill, so, in consideration of the unhappy pass to which we theologians have come, would your Reverence please pray for us ? " Peter's surmise about Cordoba's attitude was more than fulfilled. He rejected the list of articles submitted by Dr. Braun and forced through one of his own, reiterating the demands for reform of the Pope and the Curia by the Council, and for a definition on the question of episcopal residence. When St. Peter protested that those matters had already been settled in the agreement between the Emperor and Cardinal Morone the old gentleman lost his temper and scribbled a hasty note to Ferdinand on June 6th, charging the Saint with having flagrantly violated his promise of secrecy and with being a persistent obstructionist and braggart. [2] Ferdinand, however, had grown tired of such tale-bearing. He had only to look at the two men to know which was the worthier of his trust, and he decided accordingly. To keep his Italian from rusting Peter wrote in that language to Laynez on June 12th: " As for these controverted matters, I observe that they make no great impression. In spite of the contrary views of my colleagues, His Majesty is content to pursue a peaceable course, according to the desire and counsel of Cardinal Morone." This assurance he had from the best possible authority, the Emperor himself. [3]

[1] Le Plat, *Monumentorum*, etc., vol. vi, pp. 116–20.
[2] Braunsberger, *Epistulae*, vol. iv, pp. 978–9.
[3] Braunsberger, *Epistulae*, vol. iv, pp. 246, 254.

Peter had won, and it was the Council's happy hour at last. Writing to Hosius six weeks later, he said: "I am full of gratitude to Our Lord for having crowned the recent session with such success.[1] The majority of men thought very differently about its prospects and anticipated anything but what has happened. Steep and dangerous indeed were the rocks among which we steered our way. May Christ prosper the rest of the voyage that the Fathers may soon reach harbour after so many terrible storms. . . ." Of his own contribution to the wonderful change, he spoke lightly. His praises were being sung in Rome, and the Pope had affectionately embraced him by proxy in the person of St. Francis Borgia. Hearing these things he said: " Would to God that I had done my duty and served the Church's need as faithfully as some people in Rome appear to give me credit for having done." That was all, and the reader, knowing his man by this time, will know, too, what to think of the trite old charge that the Jesuits stood by the Pope from motives of pure self-interest, hoping to get more out of him than they could from bishops or other authorities. St. Peter had worked so hard for the exaltation of episcopal authority that we have seen a good scholar, Dr. Drews, endeavouring to represent him as a sort of episcopalian, inimical to any extension of papal authority. This Innsbruck chapter corrects the exaggeration, and shows him and his brethren to have been nothing more or less than sincere men who believed honestly that God meant His Church to be monarchical and hierarchical. The world of their day was torn by dissension for which they felt convinced only one remedy would avail, the revival of loyalty and obedience to the central authority which Jesus Christ had constituted to make men one, even as He and the Father are one. Four years before the point of time now reached in this story, St. Peter had written to Nadal: "Another thing that Our Lord showed me on my recent travels was the immense importance of the special vow by which the Society of Jesus binds itself to the Apostolic See, completely and gratuitously, everywhere and at all times, without exception made or any thought of personal resources, trusting alone in the infinite goodness and power of Jesus Christ." That this fourth vow of the professed Fathers might, as it were, spread out and affect ever wider circles, St. Peter went on to urge with all his might the establishment in Rome of a college or colleges wherein young Bohemians, Poles, Germans, Danes, Norwegians, Englishmen, and others, might be trained in the various branches of learning, eloquence, and piety, and become, on completion of their course, what

[1] It was held on July 15th, ten months having passed since the last one.

he calls "Knights of the Holy See" in their own countries. Next, he recommended strongly that the Pope and cardinals in Rome should invite to their palaces boys of noble Bohemian, Polish, and German families with a view to bringing them up in true piety and devotion to the Holy See. Finally, he suggested the formation of congregations of specially selected prelates in Rome whose business it would be to keep in close touch with the much harassed bishops of the northern countries.[1] As time went by nearly all the schemes thus adumbrated came into existence in one form or another, to the permanent advantage of the Catholic Church. In their fallen nature men and women are provided, ready made, with all the centrifugal forces they require. Their profoundest need is a genuine *vinculum unitatis*, and it was St. Peter's realization of this that made him so sensitive and stalwart a guardian of the only adequate bond known to his world as to ours, the person of the Pope.

When all was over at Innsbruck the Saint invited his Franciscan foe, Cordoba, to lunch, and we may hope that the good friar accepted.[2] Perhaps he brought along his grand clock to show it to his host. Throughout the whole difficult period of the Commission's work, Peter was busy with various offices of kindness. Thus, he would write a number of times to cheer up a lonely Jesuit in Brixen; scrape together money to pay a debt somebody else had failed to pay; make arrangements for the convenience and pleasure of Father Couvillon; and plead earnestly with the Emperor on behalf of his struggling brethren in Rome and Prague. "All health to your Reverence," wrote the Rector of the college in the latter place, "and may you continue to love us, your Prague sons, and to help us on for the greater glory of Christ Our Lord. If we are unable to repay you, as is certainly the case, we shall, at any rate, never cease to pour out the humble prayers for your Reverence which this college owes you in perpetuity." That others should show gratitude for anything he had done used to cause Peter much astonishment. When Hosius occasionally sent him money for some of the many books which he had bought and dispatched to Trent, he said that such liberality covered him with confusion. Similarly, while making heroic efforts with the Emperor, Cardinal Morone, and others on behalf of the Roman College, he wondered why the Rector of that institution could be so good to him as to help an Augsburg youth in whom he was interested. "As soon as ever I get back to Augsburg I shall see about Hector's expenses," he wrote. But getting back to Augsburg was not going to be so easy, as the plague

---

[1] Braunsberger, *Epistulae*, vol. ii, pp. 366–71. [2] Braunsberger, *Epistulae*, vol. iv, p. 266.

was raging there with great violence. The frequent visitations of that terrible harvester in the sixteenth century presented the Jesuit authorities with a problem of peculiar unpleasantness. At first their men had been allowed and even encouraged to follow the bent of their hearts, which took them straight to the bedsides of the dying, but soon it became apparent that, if the Society's work was to continue, there must be some restrictions. Only the previous year, 1562, nearly all the Jesuits in Paris, including the Provincial, Father Paschase Broët, had died of the disease, contracted while visiting the sick. The Society could not afford to lose another Provincial in that fashion, so Laynez through Polanco, did his best to dissuade St. Peter from returning to Augsburg until the danger was over. Knowing his man, however, Polanco continued: "In case your Reverence should elect to return, Father General strictly orders you not to go to hear the confessions of persons infected with the plague." *Gl' ordina strettamente!* Nothing but that would have kept Peter from the sufferers' doors.

CHAPTER XIV

TROUBLES IN BATTALIONS

THE precise nature of the plague that ravaged many cities of Germany from the summer of 1563 onwards is not recorded. It does not seem to have had the horrible features that characterized, for instance, the Great Plague of London a hundred years later, but it made up by persistence what it lacked in virulence and probably accounted for more victims in the long run. In Augsburg, St. Peter records, forty or fifty people died of it every week. On July 18th he organized a public procession as an appeal to God to stay the havoc but, though all sections of the populace took part and prayed as only frightened people can, there was no lessening of the death roll for many months afterwards. Those who could afford to do so fled from the stricken city to the Bavarian highlands, among the first to go being the residential canons of the Augsburg chapter. St. Peter rallied the refugees on their faintheartedness, quoting the text, " O ye of little faith, why do ye fear ? " For himself, though the Roman Jesuits and such friends as Cardinals Hosius and Truchsess would have been greatly relieved to see him join the exodus, he not only remained at his post but by urgent entreaty succeeded in raising the embargo upon his personal ministration to the sick. At the same time the Jesuits of Vienna were allowed to revert to their old practices of charity, with the result that three of them died of the plague in rapid succession.[1]

Apart from the danger, for which St. Peter cared hardly at all, the plague involved him in grave anxiety for the well-being of his Province. His thirty subjects in Munich and eighteen in Ingolstadt lay open to its menace, and it hindered most seriously the easy commerce with Rome on which the smooth working of the colleges so largely depended. How, for instance, was he to get students over the Italian frontier, where a strict watch was kept to bar the progress of travellers from infected areas ? When he succeeded in smuggling through four young men, all British,[2]

[1] M.H., *Epistolae Patris Nadal*, vol. ii, pp. 426, 438, 460, 502.
[2] Robert Abercromby, James Tyrie, William Murdoch, and John Wick.

as far as Innsbruck, it was only to learn that they had been turned from the doors of the College there by the terrified Rector, Father Dyrsius. It is good to know that Laynez penanced the culprit, but he might have given him something more troublesome to say than the *Magnificat.* Dyrsius will shortly appear in a most peculiar rôle for a rector. At Ingolstadt, the trouble from the plague was complicated by private bickering between two of the best Jesuit professors, Fathers Peltan and Pisanus. Theodore Peltan was the fine scholar who edited the proceedings of the Council of Ephesus, and Pisanus was a theologian of eminence. But for some reason they could not stand one another, and for a long while taxed St. Peter's skill as a peacemaker. " Once again," he told Laynez at the beginning of 1564, " I have done my best to reconcile the pair and to make them shun all feelings of rancour and emulation. . . . Some allowance must be made for Father Theodore, as he has a difficult character."[1] Peter was a great hand at making allowances. More serious than that domestic fret was the possessive tendency shown by the Duke of Bavaria and his Cabinet with regard to the Ingolstadt Jesuits. They wanted to have the men completely under their thumbs, to turn them, in fact, into a species of civil servant, which would have stultified the primary purpose for which the Society of Jesus was founded. Easy mobility was one of the most treasured principles of the Ignatian plan, but local rulers who valued the services of his sons could hardly be expected to appreciate its necessity. Father Delanoy's removal from Ingolstadt to Vienna greatly annoyed Albert and his Court, though they were given in exchange a most capable, native-born German, Father Paul Hoffaeus. Subsequently, whenever St. Peter attempted the slightest shuffle of men for reasons of health or studies, Albert and his Chancellor would complain that such action was an infringement of the original contract by which the College was established. Much tact was needed to soothe the various ruffled spirits, and it speaks well for St. Peter's diplomacy that he kept both his independence and the close friendship of Albert and his Chancellor.

The anxieties of Ingolstadt, however, were a trifle compared with the torments of Dillingen, to which academic purgatory Peter was condemned in the autumn of 1563. Some months earlier, Cardinal Truchsess, who resided in Dillingen, had written in the following strain to King Sigismund of Poland : " It is plain and obvious to everybody that the brethren of the Society of Jesus are the most diligent and skilful of all labourers in the vineyard of the Lord. I am therefore consumed with longing past

---

[1] Braunsberger, *Epistulae*, vol. iv, p. 513.

belief to establish a college of that Society in Dillingen, in order thus to
protect the flock committed to me from the wolves around them. Poverty,
at present, is the chief obstacle to my hopes and the chief danger to my
people. I would, then, beg and beseech Your Majesty to favour with
your royal bounty an excellent design which will bring glory to God and
salvation to my flock."[1] Sigismund, however, did not consider the glory
of God so very important, and, as for the ' wolves ' of whom the Cardinal
spoke, he had plenty of them in Poland, and found them quite pleasant
creatures. The Cardinal, nothing daunted, went on with his plans, though
at this period his affairs had become so entangled through previous extravagance that he was obliged to spend most of his time in Rome, where
living was cheap and creditors ceased from troubling. Fine, likeable,
and devoted man though he was, nothing availed to teach him prudence
in the management of money. St. Peter, Laynez, and other Fathers
endeavoured by friendly counsel to put a check on his spendthrift ways,
but without any result. Whenever he came by some more money he spent
it as recklessly as ever, on the arts, of which he was a most generous patron,
or on lavish entertainment, of which, being a very generous man, he was
extremely fond. For many weeks he had been moving from place to place
in Northern Italy, awaiting the arrival of King Maximilian's two sons,
whom he was to escort to Barcelona, to their cousin, King Philip of
Spain. Almost by main force, he had attached to himself as chaplain the
Jesuit ex-soldier, Father Luys de Mendoza, a nephew of Laynez, and
through him pressed forward the scheme on which he had set his heart.
This was nothing less than the transfer to the Jesuits of his University
of Dillingen.

Many years before, the Cardinal, in the zeal of his heart, had founded
the College of St. Jerome as a seminary to provide good and learned
priests for the Augsburg diocese. In those days money was plentiful
and he stinted nothing to make his College a great success. So well did
it progress that in 1551 Pope Julius III raised it to the dignity of a university,
the first Catholic institution of the kind to be established during the
Reformation period. The privileges conferred upon it by the Pope were
ratified in due course by Charles V, and the formal inauguration took
place with great éclat on May 21, 1554. Lay students were then admitted,
as well as candidates for the priesthood, all being bound by an unusual
oath to earnest study and the diligent practice of their religion. It was
only a small university, of course, but for all that as genuine a member

[1] Braunsberger, *Epistulae*, vol, iv, p. 359.

of the great academic family as Oxford or Cambridge, or even proud Paris itself. For a time, under a band of gifted professors, the fortunes of Dillingen seemed assured, but the brilliant period soon faded into the light of common, impecunious day. The Cardinal could not meet his bills and the professors could not live on promises. The best of them drifted away to greener pastures, and the few who remained gradually lost both faith and interest in their baby University. The Cardinal, who had been a good father to it as long as he possessed the means, was profoundly grieved by its impending doom. What was needed to avert the fates was an assured supply of good professors, because, given them, the problem of students would solve itself. Now a corporation such as the Society of Jesus presented obvious advantages in this respect, and the Cardinal accordingly made up his mind to call the Jesuits to the rescue. He did not ask himself whether they would appreciate the dubious gift, or whether they had the men to spare for its management. He liked them and he knew that they liked him, so if he pleaded urgently enough they would not have the heart to refuse. He was right, but Laynez and St. Peter at once exchanged misgivings about the scheme. The Cardinal's large promises about revenues and other things did not impress Peter very much, as he had heard the same vain story before; and Laynez, for his part, did not know where the men for the new venture were to be found. He asserted more than once in letters to Peter that he accepted the very unwelcome and inopportune responsibility of Dillingen purely out of regard and friendship for the Cardinal. From the natural point of view it was certainly a very precarious investment, like buying, out of simple kindness, somebody's grand piano, without anywhere to store it or anybody to play on it. The town of Dillingen was barely on the map, a bit of a place that led nowhere and was famous for nothing. Moreover, the canons of Augsburg, who claimed rights over the University, had already shown that they were not enamoured of the Society of Jesus, however much they might once have appreciated the services of Peter Canisius.

In spite of the many inauspicious omens, Laynez directed Father Nadal, as 'commissary' for the German Jesuits, to go to Dillingen with Peter and spy out the land. There they soon found that the milk and honey of which their sanguine friend, the Cardinal, had spoken existed only in his imagination. The house intended for the Jesuits was a poor, incommodious place without so much as a square foot of garden or the most modest of chapels attached to it. But their good-will rose superior to circumstances and set about making the wilderness bloom. As usual,

Peter gives all the credit to Nadal. In his letters it is Nadal who is the supreme hero, the brain and spirit of every enterprise, without whom his Province must have gone to ruin. Still, as a matter of hard fact, it was not Nadal but Peter who bore the heat and toil of the day, who took the buffets of fortune and carried uncomplainingly for a decade of years the crushing burden of administration. Nadal planned and passed on ; Peter stayed to face the weary conspiracy of prejudices and enmities created by the plan, and all he has to say for himself, whether he won or lost in the encounter, is " unprofitable servant."

From Maguzzano, on September 16th, Cardinal Truchsess wrote to Peter : " Reverend Father in Christ and my honoured Brother. I have dispatched Cornelius Herlen, Rector of the University of Dillingen, with full mandate and instruction to transfer jurisdiction over the College of St. Jerome and the University to the Society of Jesus, according to the agreement made with Father General Laynèz. Nothing now remains but for your Reverence to overcome all difficulties and take possession of the house and revenues. . . . The Rector will supply part of the furniture, and you can obtain other necessaries with 208 florins to be paid to you by my quæstor. When my procurator, who is here with me at present, arrives, he will provide you with anything further that may be needed. And so I pray God that all may be to your liking."[1]

Nothing now remained, as the Cardinal said, but for Peter to overcome all difficulties, the chief of which was the Cardinal himself. Peter begged that his Lordship should obtain the written consent of the Augsburg canons for the new venture ; that he should engage in legal form to provide the Jesuit College with an annual income of a thousand florins ; and that he should make over to the College an unused library belonging to him in Ingolstadt, " lest otherwise the Jesuits seem to engage in battle like soldiers without arms." The Cardinal readily agreed to each of the suggestions but, in the event, carried through none of them. The Chapter of Augsburg refused to ratify his arrangement with the Jesuits, the thousand florins were not forthcoming, and the library remained in Ingolstadt. Next came the question of a staff. When asked from Rome what kind of men he required, Peter, made cautious by hard experience, said that masters with practised ability to teach were the need rather than " *doctores bullati*" who had not the art to communicate their excellent learning. Polanco showed caution of another kind by stipulating that the *viaticum*, or journey-money, of the men must be paid in advance, as he had lost faith in the C.O.D. method of transacting business. Nadal made a small contribution, and Peter begged the rest of a hundred crowns from friends in Augsburg, as the Cardinal's mythical quæstor could not be found. When transmitting the money to Rome, he said : " I ask you to accept the sum, such as it is, in good part . . . and, if there is a surplus, to give it to the poor. Also, I beg that many prayers be offered for us to God, as the pestilence is afflicting the people of Augsburg more than ever. May the will of God for us be always done. . . . Pray to the Lord for me, Father, and give my greetings to Father Francis, Father Ursmar, Father Emmanuel, Father Ledesma, and all the other dear Fathers and Brothers. In your great charity continue to help our Germans."[1]

In the course of four months, crowded with other business, Peter paid six visits to Dillingen, and his heart was there whenever the rest of him could not be. How hard put to it he and Father Nadal were to find a suitable staff may be gauged from the fact that they had to appoint the impossible Father Couvillon superior. He was the only person available, and available precisely because nobody wanted him elsewhere. The Jesuits at this time were in such demand that had they had twice their numbers they could not have contented all the petitioners. Therein lay a great dilemma for the authorities of the Order. Should they pursue the policy of training their raw recruits up to the last degree of efficiency before launching them on the world, meanwhile steeling their hearts to the appeals for help which reached them; or should they answer the appeals and hope for the best ? Their own convenience and reputation strongly suggested the first course but it was the second course that they pursued, thereby bringing much avoidable sorrow and anxiety on their heads. Certainly, the men who, in Peter's phrase, were " scraped together " for Dillingen could not be called model Jesuits. Many of them had only had a brief experience of the religious life, and the large freedom of social conditions in a new college, under such a man as Couvillon, proved too much for the little capital of virtue amassed by them in their noviceship. It only made things worse that they were clever men, as clever malcontents can do far more harm than stupid ones. St. Peter realized fully that the men were not entirely to blame, and made ceaseless efforts to provide them with a wise and firm superior. Try as he might, however, for twelve anxious months the superior could not be found. The problem became the bane of his life, and worked up Polanco to such an extent that he referred to it as " *questo benedetto Rectorato.*" To transfer a rector from

[1] Braunsberger, *Epistulae*, vol. iv, pp. 342-3.

Munich or Ingolstadt would have provoked the Duke of Bavaria, and it was no good taking Dyrsius from Innsbruck because, in Peter's dry words, "he needed a rector himself." Other men suitable for the post were already committed to employments from which they could not be removed without grave injury to some important interest, and so, for a whole year, Dillingen had to carry on under the unbalanced and melancholy Couvillon. "May the Lord," wrote St. Peter, "turn to His glory this College, which is built, it seems, on a fair hope rather than on a solid fact." The Cardinal's florins continued to remain a hope, as when Peter endeavoured to secure them one official played him off against another, so that he got practically nothing and was obliged to run into debt to provide for the needs of his men.[1]

The following letter to Laynez, written on Christmas Eve, 1563, gives some details about the unfortunate College:

It grieves me to be always sending you unpleasant news about Dillingen. Our Lord is humbling us, I think, over the beginnings of this College which got on so well while Father Nadal was there to guide the brethren. I told you in my last letter about Johann Albrecht, who, they say, has now abandoned the Society, though I do not know in what way or for what reason.[2] I fear he was a softer person than is suited to our institute. Father Torres writes to tell me that Father Nicholas Servatius, who was brought from Mainz to teach the Humanities, has issued a warning that we must look round for a successor to his post at once, as he is minded to leave us for another manner of life. . . . So now we are on the point of losing another professor from Dillingen, nor can we entertain any great hopes of Master Giovanni Facciardo, who finds his work of teaching rhetoric entirely against the grain. He will do no good, I think, as long as he remains out of sympathy with his backward pupils and treats them with no consideration. Your Reverence can see, then, that all is not well with the College of Dillingen. Love and enthusiasm for the instruction of youth is wanting in our men, and there is the further difficulty that Father Couvillon gives way to them too much. He permits heavy expenditure in hopes of assuaging their discontented souls, with the result that living at Dillingen is more luxurious than in any of the other colleges. . . . I have not recently been given a chance to visit

---

[1] Braunsberger, *Epistulae*, vol. iv, p. 411.
[2] Johann lectured on philosophy at Dillingen.

the good Brothers, whom, would to God, it was in my power to console and strengthen in their duty. Doubtless, the devil is envious of this College from which we may promise ourselves more than ordinary fruits, in Our Lord, as we see the number of students steadily increasing. All the more earnestly, then, do we expect and beg that many of our brethren may be sent to Dillingen, together with a good rector. . . . The first free week I can find will see me there, as they want me to come. I shall try to find some way of easing the situation. May God Our Lord bring the College to a better state. I shall only add that, in my opinion, it will be difficult to satisfy the desires of those who are so intent on recreation for the body while indifferent to true consolation of soul. Such people will never lack opportunity for complaint, no matter what the Cardinal promises and performs on their behalf. The prudence of a good rector would, however, do much to counterbalance these difficulties. . . . May Our Lord grant your Reverend Paternity, Father Nadal, Father Polanco, and all the community a happy New Year.[1]

As soon as the daily sermons of Advent and the Christmas octave were finished Peter travelled post-haste to Dillingen. Of his nine brethren there he found that five were ill through constant overwork and lack of physical exercise. And the men were ill not only in body, but in soul, discontented and unmortified people whom the other colleges of Germany had been glad to get rid of. After looking round, Peter exclaimed to Laynez : " Blessed be God who tests us in these first stages of the College. Only let us be helped by the sacrifices and prayers of your Reverence, that the trial may profit us all." The worst Jesuit in the house was the best professor, that Father Nicholas who had announced his intention of abandoning the Society. Another man, also a valued professor, had gone through a ceremony of betrothal some years before. Tiring of his fiancée, he became a Jesuit and pronounced his vows which, by canon law, dissolved the previous engagement. At Dillingen he became tired again, this time of his job, and gave out that he felt a divine impulse to return to his lady. No argument or persuasion of St. Peter had any effect on him. A third master, of Spanish origin, had begun, like Father Vitoria in the past, to sigh for the southern sun. He was a valuable man and much loved by his scholars, but as he was poor in health Peter gave way to his whim. Not satisfied with obtaining for him a Polish horse " of some renown " and providing him with ample funds, the Saint went to the trouble of finding him a group of friendly people for travelling companions, so that if he became ill on the way he would not lack attention. " I think he has the strength necessary for his journey," he explained to Laynez, " and I imagine that his longing to see Italy again will ease the toil of it for him. . . . He will tell you himself, I hope, about the sickness of his soul, which your Paternity will know how to cure. . . . *Deus adsit fratribus omnibus.*"[1]

Each day of his week's sojourn, Peter assembled the little community to address them on the true ideal of their vocation. " He urged and inflamed us all," reported Couvillon, " to a manly observance of our institute." To relieve overburdened professors he re-arranged the hours of lectures ; drew up regulations for the better management of studies ; strove to instil the principles of good government into Couvillon ; and did all in his power for the poor fellows whose health gave them trouble. " *Parva sunt haec quae curavimus*," was his comment on these efforts, but he felt that only Rome could solve the problem of Dillingen by sending masters of sturdier quality in both body and soul and, above all, that elusive rector of his dreams. In Nadal's instructions for the Jesuit superiors in Germany there was a counsel to treat their subjects " *spiritus suavitate* "—with sweetness of spirit. So scrupulously did St. Peter try to carry out the counsel that other superiors judged him excessive in tenderness and protested against the too great consideration which he showed to persons who, after causing much trouble, had finally seceded from the Society of Jesus.[2] His charity, however, did not save him from misrepresentation in Rome, whither querulous Jesuits carried their imaginary grievances. The result was an exhortation from Polanco that Peter should be more patient with his many valetudinarians, and not hesitate to run into debt for their comfort. His reply was as follows : " I deserve and willingly accept your reprehension in that, as one knowing to refuse evil and choose the good according to the letter rather than according to the spirit, I have not shown due patience, charity, and forbearance to my testy and ailing brethren. I humbly beg forgiveness for my neglect of charity and manifest impatience. In future I shall not complain so often but bear these burdens more patiently. Only let your Reverence pray for me. . . . May the will of the Lord be done with us all. . . ."[3] Peter's complaints were really mere statements of fact—that so and so had become

[1] Braunsberger, *Epistulae*, vol. iv, pp. 444–5.
[2] Braunsberger, *Epistulae*, vol. iv, pp. 711, 713, 796–7.
[3] Braunsberger, *Epistulae*, vol. iv, pp. 574, 591.

an epileptic or a consumptive, or that another man was in open rebellion. Nearly all the helpers who came to him from Rome had something wrong with them, the most usual trouble being tuberculosis. To start the first of Jesuit universities with such material must have been like trying to build a house with bricks that crumble at touch of the trowel. " *Dominus convertat in suam gloriam omnia quae possumus et non possumus,*" wrote Peter. One of the many things he could not do was to secure possession of a certain four hundred ducats, "*toties a Cardinale promissos.*" Polanco had airily invited him to incur debts on that slender security.

Meantime, Peter worked and campaigned for the Roman Jesuits, as though he had no anxieties of his own. In 1562 the German College was on the verge of bankruptcy owing to the shabby treatment accorded to it by those who should have been its most enthusiastic patrons. To save the situation, the Jesuits rented the Palazzo Vitelli and opened it as a boarding school for youths whose parents could afford a more or less expensive education. Within a short time two hundred boys had been enrolled, many of them, and these the best, through the direct agency of St. Peter. The Baroness Fugger's son, Octavian, was among those he sent, and figures as frequently in his letters as the most distinguished men of his Province. So keen was Peter's interest in the lad's physical and moral progress that Polanco felt it necessary to include a few lines about him in almost every letter from Rome. Laynez and his Secretary were not ungrateful for all that the Saint strove to achieve in their interest. In February, 1564, they determined to send him four excellent professors for Dillingen, among them the Oxford M.A., Jasper Heywood, nephew of Saint Thomas More and uncle of John Donne, Dean of St. Paul's. With the four came three lay brothers, including James Birura, who was deservedly regarded as one of the great Jesuits of that age. One has known such men, heroes of oven or broom, and felt dwarfed in their company.

The men from Rome arrived in Dillingen about April 12th, after being nearly six weeks on the road with only one horse between the seven of them. At long last, a rector, too, was appointed in the person of Peter's friend, Henry Denys, preacher of Cologne Cathedral. We have seen the type of person poor Couvillon was, a restless hypochondriac with a genius for finding trouble or making it. Now, on his supersession, Peter suggested that the good man should be joined, " *velut emeritus miles,*" to his own little community in Augsburg.[1] After heartily thanking Laynez for his generosity, he hastened to Dillingen to welcome the new arrivals. Other men were

---

[1] Braunsberger, *Epistulae*, vol. iv, p. 479.

sent to him, also, one pair on red and white mules, about which beasts the practical Polanco showed concern. He expected Cardinal Truchsess to buy the red one and to give a good price, "*perche la bestia è bona.*" The white one Peter must return to Rome somehow or other. Father Mendoza, the ex-condottiere, was yet another recruit to Dillingen, and to Polanco's keen satisfaction fell in love with the place. "We are delighted in Our Lord," wrote the Secretary, "that the air and life of Dillingen agrees with you so well, and that you have grown to like beer and even prefer it to wine." Part of Mendoza's contentment was probably due to the fact that the Cardinal, at Peter's prompting, had given the Jesuits the freedom of his own park, which Couvillon described as "a vast and most beautiful garden wherein, besides fish-ponds, there are summer-houses, trees of every variety, swans and game."

The reinforcements from Rome and the promise of another seven stalwarts in the near future enabled Peter to arrange with Cardinal Truchsess for the solemn change-over of administration at Dillingen on August 17th. As usual, he had obtained relics of the Ursuline martyrs for the occasion. When the canons of Augsburg learned what was contemplated, they promptly wrote warning the Cardinal against the Jesuits as fomenters of discord and ambitious intriguers who had no respect for any rights but their own. The Cardinal, who knew that dogs, horses and women interested the canons far more than the welfare of Dillingen, refused to be impressed and went on with his careful preparations for the ceremony of inauguration. On the day appointed, his coadjutor, Bishop Dornvogel, sang the Mass of the Holy Ghost in his presence, adding the collect of St. Jerome and, out of regard for the Jesuits, that of the Holy Name. When the sacred ministers had withdrawn, a low table covered with a cloth was placed in front of the Cardinal's throne. His secretary then read publicly the long proclamation handing over the University "to be taught, ruled, governed, regulated and promoted by the aforesaid professors of the Society of Jesus, now here present or afterwards to come, in the Name of the Father and of the Son and of the Holy Ghost. Amen." That done, the Cardinal intoned the *Veni Creator Spiritus*, which was followed by a panegyric of the retiring Rector, Cornelius Herlen. Having made his acknowledgments, Herlen proceeded to lay the insignia of office —silver sceptre, red silk cape, seal and keys—on the table before the Cardinal, who straightway invested him in the robes of a Protonotary Apostolic and Count Palatine. His Lordship then delivered a short address in confirmation of the deed of transfer, at the end of which St. Peter advanced and formally accepted jurisdiction over the University in his own name and that of the whole Society of Jesus. Immediately after, he and some designated Fathers repaired to the sacristy to carry out the formal ceremony of election. On Peter announcing to the assembled students that Denys had been chosen, the Cardinal bade him deck out the new Rector in his insignia and robes. When he was fully accoutred, Peter took him for the Cardinal's benediction, and then a procession was formed to escort him to his chair. A second proclamation was now read, constituting Cornelius Herlen " *gubernator* " of the University for all judicial and criminal proceedings, as by their constitutions the Jesuits were precluded from assuming such authority. Being a Prince-Bishop, Cardinal Truchsess was the civil as well as ecclesiastical ruler of his diocese, so Herlen's powers extended to all cases covered by the criminal law of the Empire. But he was made subject to the new Rector and could be removed from office by him.[1]

That was a great day for Peter, and, indeed for the Catholic Church, which, in due course, derived enormous benefit from the newly constituted Dillingen. The Rector, however, was not a success. His health gave way shortly after he assumed office, and Cardinal Truchsess, in Peter's words, " was by no means pleased with the good Father's manners." As he fell foul of his Gubernator also, Peter received instructions from Rome to visit him often and coach him in his duties, " *quia nemo nascitur artifex.*" In other words, to all intents and purposes Peter must himself govern Dillingen. Moreover, though the Cardinal continued to shelve the awkward question of revenues, he made such demands on the newcomers that Polanco protested a hundred men would be necessary to satisfy them all.[2] " It would be easier to have patience with him," wrote the Secretary, " if he could not afford to help financially, but the fact that he is able to indulge in other superfluous expenses which render endowment of the College impossible greatly damps our hope." Peter's only comment on this was : " *More suo facit* "—it's the way the man is made. To add to the joy of life for him, the plague suddenly revived and began to make havoc in Innsbruck, whose Rector, Father Dyrsius, was not a person for heroic occasions. Dyrsius promptly dispersed most of his staff, leaving it to the Provincial to find accommodation for them. Among the few who remained was Edmund Hay, the Scotsman whom St. Peter prized as one of the finest characters in his Province. Edmund's brother, Walter Hay, was just then toiling towards Dillingen by one route, while Father

[1] Braunsberger, *Epistulae*, vol. iv, pp. 917-27.   [2] Braunsberger, *Epistulae*, vol. iv, p. 650.

Thomas Darbyshire, quondam chancellor of the Bishop of London, approached the town by another. Each was accompanied by a little party, the two parties amounting to seven in all, of whom four were Britons, and they had been sent by different routes so as not to burden the colleges at which they had to break their journey. It shows how genuinely poor the colleges were that they must think twice about the few shillings involved in putting up seven men for a night or two. On hearing of the outbreak in Innsbruck, St. Peter wrote hastily to Rome in hopes that the seven might be recalled but, with the exception of William Stubbs, who had fallen ill at Padua, they were already over the German frontier and shortly afterwards he was nursing two of them in Augsburg. Andrew Avantianus remained on his hands for five months, " a great trouble to him," in the patient's own words, " and the recipient of his great charity and kindness."[1] As the Saint was by this time heavily in debt, the prospect of finding support and asylum for the men thrown on his exhausted exchequer appalled him, especially as Munich sternly barred its gates to strangers. " May Our Lord give me patience, through the Holy Sacrifices and prayers of your Paternity," he wrote to Laynez.

Father Dyrsius by himself would have been enough to test the patience of Job. The five ' Queens,'[2] daughters of the Emperor, who resided in Hall, near Innsbruck, had an irresistible attraction for the good man, far more so than the humdrum business of running a college. They were devout and generous women and, in spite of his melancholy humour, they certainly appreciated Father John as a spiritual director, though they had an official Jesuit chaplain of their own, Father Hermes Halbpaur. He returned the compliment with interest, to the disgust of Father Hermes. In January, 1564, Peter had written to Laynez : " The Rector of Innsbruck causes more fuss than almost all the other Rectors put together, and I fear it will be difficult to keep him there very long. He works hard and faithfully, both at home and in the school, and he is often unwell." A little later, Peter was in receipt of letters from Dyrsius and Halbpaur, each charging the other with poaching on his territory. " I have written," the harassed Provincial informed Laynez, " consoling the Rector, and cautioning him not to get into arguments with Father Hermes too easily, but rather to wink at many of his goings-on, as far as that can be done without scandal. Father Hermes wants to pay me a visit, and I dare not hinder him lest he become more obstreperous. Besides, it may be that

[1] Braunsberger, *Epistulae*, vol. iv, p. 817.
[2] These ladies were ' Queens ' only by a courtesy title. St. Peter regularly refers to them as such, and that is why they are thus named in the text.

he desires a rest and change, and not merely, as he says, to tell me his tale of woe."[1]

In April, 1564, when the first signs of the plague appeared in Innsbruck, the five royal ladies decided to migrate to Merano. Dyrsius immediately petitioned to be their chaplain, instead of Halbpaur. "I thought not," Peter told the General, "and have written to say that he should not desert the brethren or deny the Queens their usual chaplain." But the ' Queens,' bless their hearts, were quite keen on having both men and plagued Peter into consenting. "Tired out with their importunities, he gave in," reported Father Edmund Hay to Polanco. Shortly afterwards Dyrsius wrote to him saying that he was "ten times better in health" for the change, and for that reason Peter resigned himself to the Rector's absence. But he was determined that the ladies should not keep Father Halbpaur also for any length of time, and proceeded to take the necessary measures in Rome. In his fair way he added that both Fathers were "doing good work at the Queens' Court." When the ' Queens ' heard of his manœuvres, they countered with a direct appeal to Laynez, calling themselves the "spiritual daughters of his Reverence and of the whole Society of Jesus." Now the whole Society of Jesus was not supposed to have spiritual daughters, as St. Ignatius for good reasons very much objected to them. But Magdalene, Margaret, Barbara, Helen and Joanna were not to be put off. They needed the two Jesuits, they said, for confessions, sermons, and other work, and they could not replace them as, in Magdalene's words, the Tirolese clergy were "nearly all suspect in faith and patently ignorant, inexperienced and vicious." Would Laynez, then, kindly decide without reference to " *den frumben hern Canisii* "—the pious Mr. Canisius—and send them the only answer they could accept, an affirmative one? Having no option, the General did so, whereupon the five returned him their "eternal thanks." He had informed them that Canisius would pay them a visit soon. Secure of their two men, they expressed great pleasure at the news because of their unbounded admiration for him and of their knowledge that he had nothing but the kindliest feelings in their regard.[2]

The worst of it was that just at the time Dyrsius went away he had begun, under Peter's tactful management, to show real rectorial ability. Writing about him from Innsbruck in Italian which needs no translating, Peter said : " *Il Rettore si mostra un' buon Padre di famiglia, governando*

---

[1] Braunsberger, *Epistulae*, vol. iv, pp. 480–1.
[2] Braunsberger, *Epistulae*, vol. iv, pp. 948–50.

anche con buona quiete et ordine il Collegio et la schuola, Iddio sia lodato."
Another hard blow was the removal of Father Edmund Hay to be Rector
of the Jesuits in Paris. "As for Father Edmund," Peter continued, "I
do not want to hinder the common good, but this change will do considerable harm to Innsbruck College, of which he is, I might say, the
principal pillar. He is highly esteemed by the educated classes here and
listened to with great pleasure and applause. They will take it very ill
indeed if he goes, and it will be difficult to find another theologian capable
of giving them equal satisfaction with such eloquent and vivacious lectures.
It is true that he deserves to have greater scope and auditors of more distinguished ability, but your Reverence will know what is best, especially
considering the present danger to religion and the fact that Father Edmund
is so necessary, not only on account of his learning but also as an example
of true virtue to this College. There are not many like him here."[1]

Meantime, away in bleak, unfriendly East Prussia, that fastness of
Junkertum, dear old simple-hearted Hosius sighed for the presence of St.
Peter. Peter's letters were his great consolation and, if they failed, he
promptly made his disappointment known to Heaven. As always, the
Saint continued to send him whatever new books he thought of interest,
and to see the Cardinal's own books, or fresh editions of them, through
the press with unflagging devotion. After the old man's return from
Trent, a journey that nearly finished him, there appears to have been a
break in Peter's correspondence. Hosius was so upset by this that he
wrote to Rome almost angrily to know the reason. The reason was simple
enough—postal miscarriages or the Saint's inability to find leisure for
a letter. However, on August 8, 1564, just when he was most preoccupied
with the worries of Dillingen and Innsbruck, Peter addressed his friend:
"It could not but please me to learn of your Highness's desire for our
Society and that you wished some of its brethren, including your Canisius,
to come to you. I have written to Rome and commended the matter to
our Reverend Father General. As is only right, he will gladly fall in with
your wishes. For myself I would not find it hard to live in Prussia, under
the leading of obedience, and I promise you my services, dear Patron,
though perhaps they would not be worth much in your part of the world.
May the will of the Lord be done, and let Christ transfer me from Cardinal
to Cardinal, from Swabia to Prussia, if it be pleasing to His Holy Name
and advantageous for the Church. Farewell in Him, your Highness. I
reverently commend myself to you."[2]

---

[1] Braunsberger, *Epistulae*, vol. iv, pp. 580-1.   [2] Braunsberger, *Epistulae*, vol. iv, p. 609.

Once again, as at the start of Dillingen, *" per amor del buon Cardinale "* five Jesuits were collected with great difficulty from Cologne, Mainz, and other places, while three, including Robert Abercromby, came from Rome. As chief preacher of Ermland, Peter's old pupil and devoted lover, Father Fahe, was to go. Peter himself took charge of the whole affair, arranged routes and provided funds. When all was ready for his brethren's departure, he wrote thus to the Cardinal : " I wanted myself to take the road to you, my Lord, either before or with them, and made known my desire to the Cardinal of Augsburg. But the objections to my going away at present are too numerous in the opinion of judicious men, and I believe it to be the will of God that I should stay. May His will be ever done in us to whom alone we owe everything." This letter took four months to reach Hosius in Heilsberg, which shows what the posts were like. His Lordship answered :

Your brethren are with me now, and one thing only do both they and I equally desire, the presence of our Canisius. They consider that for the sole reason of his not having written to me during an entire year he should receive the penance of a journey to Prussia. Oh, if you were to come, I, for one, would derive greater joy from your visit than could be believed. . . . The illustrious Cardinal of Augsburg excuses you on the ground that, being Provincial, you have to visit the other houses of your Society. Well, what next ? So my men are to be considered outcasts from your Province ! They alone, forsooth, are to have never a Provincial and to be left in the lurch ! Is that what you think ? To me it seems that in excusing you the Cardinal has given me stronger reasons than ever for urging and being instant with you to visit us and see how things stand with your brethren here.[1]

In another letter Hosius repeated his little joke about the penance, adding that the expiatory visit to Prussia should be three months long. Peter, who would have been delighted to move into such friendly company, took him up and begged that his penance should be commuted into a stay in Augsburg where, for reasons soon to be seen, the heaviest trial of his life awaited him. The good Bishop of Würzburg, whose predecessor had been murdered by Protestant marauders in 1558, also desired his presence and could use the eloquence of misfortune to stir his sympathy. In October, 1563, the cruel and rapacious robber-knight, William of

[1] Braunsberger, *Epistulae*, vol. iv, p. 758.

Grumbach, had collected a troop of ruffians and seized and plundered Würzburg in the temporary absence of the Bishop, who lost more than 200,000 florins. All this was done with the connivance of the pious John Frederick of Saxony. The Bishop's chancellor told Peter while staying with him the following month about the horrible sacrileges that had been committed by the drunken soldiery, and in particular, how they had trampled on the Blessed Sacrament.[1] Having thus worked on his host's feelings, the Chancellor entreated him to help the stricken city by sending a band of Jesuits there as the beginning of a college. Peter showed the fullest sympathy and commended the prospect to Laynez, but he was then woefully short of masters, and so pressed for time that he could not even finish a letter which he had started to write in Dillingen. This letter is still to be seen, the first paragraph, a Latin panegyric on Nadal, scribbled in violent haste by Peter, and the rest done in Italian by another hand. Like the Bishop of Würzburg, he had been himself plundered at this time, as his cook in Augsburg, a novice of the Society of Jesus, absconded one morning with two hundred crowns which Ursula Fugger had given him for a charitable purpose. All Peter said about the fellow was, "May the Lord grant him a more wholesome heart," but Polanco, practical as usual, marvelled "*che tal quantita de denari sia stata tanto mal guardata.*" Next, the Bishop wrote personally to Peter, urging him to get something decided about the Würzburg college within a month. He wanted fourteen Jesuits and would give them the unoccupied monastery of St. Agnes, whose splendours he painted in attractive colours. But Peter noticed at once that he avoided the subject of an endowment, and, Würzburg being such a storm-centre and a notoriously ill-governed diocese, he wondered how his men, if he could raise them, would fare there.[2] A fresh rebellion of Grumbach at the beginning of 1564 made it impossible to do anything about the college until the summer. Then, at the end of August, Peter set off on the four days' journey to Würzburg, only to discover that the practical difficulties were far too serious to allow of an immediate solution. He would spend much of the following two years trying to straighten them out before the college became a reality. Würzburg itself would claim him for its apostle when ungrateful Augsburg rejected his ministry, and he would devote to its welfare the holy eloquence which breathed a more definite and exigent Christianity than the good canons of Augsburg had bargained for.

[1] There is a vivid account of Grumbach's rebellion in Janssen-Pastor, *Geschichte des deutschen Volkes*, vol. iv (1896), pp. 244–5.
[2] Braunsberger, *Epistulae*, vol. iv, pp. 411–2.

The canons had been dissatisfied with the tone of Peter's sermons for some time, though they could not deny the good he was doing and had themselves borne striking testimony to it not so long before. Now they complained to Cardinal Truchsess in a rambling angry letter that he had gone to Würzburg without their sanction and so left them preacherless when his services were more than usually necessary. The Cardinal would please inform him that if he did not show more zeal in his office he would be dismissed from it altogether. Coming from gentlemen who hardly did a stroke of pastoral work from one end of the year to the other, the letter moved Truchsess to indignation. He answered sternly that their charge was false in every particular, as, far from being guilty of the discourtesy attributed to him, Father Canisius had gone to great trouble to find the Dean and even journeyed to Dillingen in search of his plague-dodging Reverence.[1] He might have added that there was nothing to prevent a member of the Chapter from himself honouring Augsburg with a sermon once in a way. This outburst of the canons and their changed attitude to St. Peter were due to his Jesuit affiliation. The Jesuits had been remarkably successful, and success, in the present state of human nature, is apt to provoke reactions. Again, like every other religious order, but to no greater extent than they, the Society of Jesus enjoyed certain papal privileges and immunities, such as the right to absolve any who chose to come to them outside Paschal time, to administer Holy Communion, to preach, and to reconcile Protestants to the Church. In other words, they were given parochial powers to that extent, without being parish priests. Naturally, the parish priests did not much like it, though there is plenty of evidence that the Jesuits used their privileges with the utmost discretion. One could sympathize with the secular clergy of the period and see their point if they themselves had been willing or fitted to do the work from which they wished the Jesuits excluded. But with a few noble exceptions, they were neither the one thing nor the other. It was a parish priest himself, the illustrious Martin Eisengrein, who wrote the following instructive letter to Laynez from Ingolstadt, March 12, 1564:

Well may I confess myself most obliged to your Reverend Paternity, if only for this reason that over many years I have been the recipient of benefits and favours from the Society of which, by the grace of God, you are the supreme head. To say nothing of the steady support given

[1] Braunsberger, *Epistulae*, vol. iv, pp. 897, 900.

me by the Society recently. . . . I owe it, under God, to the same holy Society that I was snatched from the jaws of heresy and restored to God's Church. I am most profoundly grateful to you and there is hardly anything which gives me greater affliction than the lack of an opportunity hitherto to show my gratitude. You may be sure that when the chance offers I shall leave nothing undone to prove that I am one who desires with all his soul to see your holy Society spread far and wide throughout Germany and daily augmented in numbers. I think that no other remedy remains against the constant growth and power of heresy; no more efficacious antidote to it, than to station in the path of its progress men of character, erudition, and eminent goodness such as we see your Society produce in large numbers and with great distinction, to the untold benefit of the Church.

The rest of the clergy in Germany would seem to be fast asleep and as free of care as if nothing of the havoc which confronts us, nothing of the lamentable downfall of so many souls, could be laid to their charge. Your Reverend Paternity could not look without tears upon the wretched condition of some German dioceses, or upon so many of the clergy, rendered utterly hateful to Catholics and a mockery to heretics by the enormity of their wickedness. Up to this hour, they cling to their vices and neither the merited detestation of Catholics, the derision of heretics, nor the destruction of religion avails to make them amend their lives. Rather do they pile evil upon evil and daily more and more provoke the wrath of God. . . . Take for example, alas, the famous Cathedral of Regensburg. . . . You might say that the diocese of Regensburg is a sink of all iniquity. You can see there not only priests living in concubinage but adulterous and incestuous ones, and priests who have committed rape and homicide. And who is there to call attention to their crimes, by which very many are frightened away from the Catholic faith and all heretics are confirmed in their heresy?[1]

At the time of writing that terrible letter, Dr. Eisengrein, who had been converted from Lutheranism through the agency of St. Peter and the Viennese Jesuits, was pastor of the University Church in Ingolstadt and Rector of the University itself. His right to speak as he did came from his own holy and devoted life which ended in its prime as the result of his heroic labours for the Faith. Though he singled out the Regensburg

[1] Braunsberger, *Epistulae*, vol. iv, p. 493.

diocese as an appalling example of clerical corruption, it was not much worse than Würzburg or Augsburg or a dozen other places. The evidence on this unhappy subject is too abundant and clear for any question, and it was not only the minor clergy who sinned but the canons of the collegiate and cathedral chapters, and sometimes the bishops themselves. Indeed, St. Peter affirmed more than once that the canons were the very worst offenders, but as he was an interested party we may deny him the witness-box for the present. In 1542, when Morone, then Bishop of Modena, was acting as Nuncio in Germany, he came in contact with the Augsburg Cathedral Chapter at Dillingen. "I found it necessary," he informed Cardinal Farnese, "to admonish the Chapter individually and collectively with great earnestness about the concubines, the feasting and drunkenness, the gaming and hunting, the ignorance and lack of zeal, which led some of them into grave sin."[1] There is no suggestion of improvement during the next quarter of a century, but plenty of hints from Cardinal Truchsess and others that, with the exception of a few upright men such as Dr. Conrad Braun, the canons continued their irregular lives. Significantly, in 1567, they refused to accept the decrees of the Council of Trent relative to the reform of clerical, and especially, capitular abuses. Writing on the condition of the Church in Germany in 1585, Minutio Minucci said : " The chapters are for the most part composed of heretics or simoniacs or *concubinarii* or drunkards or men infected with some other vice."[2] Commendone, Staphylus, Ninguarda, Gropper, and others, bear the same deadly witness from their own observations, and there is not the slightest hint that the Augsburg canons were immune from the general degradation. In his terrible arraignment[3] Staphylus does not specify which chapter he had most in mind, but the Augsburg chapter was certainly the one he knew best. Dogs, horses and women, according to him and other earnest men, were the matters which chiefly interested the canons of the period and on which they expended the revenues of the Church. Few of them ever chanted the Divine Office or said Mass, and "excess and drunkenness were such common features of their lives that any who did not indulge therein were held for persons of mean quality and illiberal mind." In 1574 Cardinal Truchsess's successor in the see of Augsburg wrote as follows about his priests : "Most of the clergy having a cure of souls in this diocese lapse daily more and more, with unrestrained

---

[1] Laemmer, *Monumenta Vaticana* (Freiburg, 1861), p. 402.
[2] Cited by Constant, *Concession à l'Allemagne de la Communion sous les deux espèces* (Paris, 1923), vol. i, p. 602.
[3] Cited by Constant, *Concession*, etc., vol. i, pp. 600–1.

licence and wantonness, into every species of vice and scandal. They are given to almost continual drunkenness, surfeiting and lust, and, instead of being meek and gentle followers of Christ Our Lord, indulge in brawling and strife. Shameful as it is even to mention it, the abominable and damnable vice of concubinage has such a hold on them that, dead to all sense of decency, they advertise and openly acknowledge their condition."[1]

All this unblushing corruption ate into St. Peter's soul and so wrought on him that he could not forbear to voice his grief and indignation, even in the pulpit. Whether he was wise to do so is another matter, but he felt it necessary, he says, lest the laity whose vices he never failed to denounce, should consider him unfair and partial.[2] St. Ignatius in the *Spiritual Exercises* suggests that it rarely serves any useful purpose to criticize superiors, whether civil or ecclesiastical, in presence of their subjects, and, generally speaking, the advice is assuredly sound. There may be occasions, however, as Our Lord's own example shows, when plain words are in place. St. Peter considered that he was faced with such an occasion. We have seen already how he rounded on the easy-going preachers who were too fastidious and careful of their popularity to mention such unpleasant things as sin and Hell in their sermons, and how he adjured them to give the people " not half a Christ but Christ whole and complete, the Christ of mercy and judgment." In a sermon in Augsburg Cathedral, September 5, 1563, he said:

Where is charity now to be found ? Is it among priests and ecclesiastics, where, indeed, it should be seen ? Not so ; for these men perform the Divine Office and administer the sublime Sacraments without devotion. Often they honour God with their lips rather than with their hearts. Unlike David, they bring no love to their singing; unlike Jeremias, they have no zeal to bewail the sins of the people ; unlike Simeon, no ardour in God's House ; unlike Paul, no desire or practice of preaching; unlike Magdalene, no contemplation and devotion. Where is their care of the poor and of widows, such as the deacons showed ? We carry a fire in our breasts and remain cold. We put honey on our tongues and it has no savour. Ah, how many are the faithless pastors, the dumb dogs of Isaias, the teachers without sight in their eyes!

---

[1] Cited by Braunsberger (*Epistulae*, vol. iv, p. 546) from Steiner, *Acta selecta Ecclesiae Augustanae* (1785), pp. 87–8.

[2] Braunsberger, *Epistulae*, vol. iv, p. 856.

In festo Comem animarum Anno 1562.

In Matthæo legimus Christum aduersus Judæos inter alia prædicasse, quod similes essent pueris sedentibus in foro, qui clamantes coæqualibus suis dicát Cecinimus uobis et non saltastis, lamentauimus et non planxistis. Quibus uerbis indicat index incsabilem Judæorum duriciem et peruicaciam damnabilem, quod neque gratiosas et consolatorias prædicatiónes ac promißiónes acceptarunt, in quibus illis grá pax et óm bonum offerebatur. 2.° quod lapidea eórum corda emollíri non potuerunt seuerís terroribus legis, non prædicatiónibus pœnitentiæ, ita ut neque curarent Christi dulcem compellationem, neque austeram autem Ioannis, sed manentes qui fuerunt duri et in hartneckis sic cum cis semper spiritui sancto resistentes.

Illic ergo locum habet cantauimus uobis et ...

Quàm multi aut hodie inueniunt ur qui exemplo Judæorum nullis monitiónibus uel conciónibus à malo se auertere uel ad bonum impelli, ita ut neque amor Dei illos trahat neque timor excitet ad emendationem uitæ ut fideles idcirco prædicatóres etiam hodie conqueri poßint ac dicere cum plice. Cecinimus uobis ... quæ ad gaudium magnum prouocáret, si tantum considerare uellent cælestem Hierusalem, in qua ciues et habitatores, ab omnibus malis liberi et ... à quiescunt, cum Christo uiuunt, cum angelis regnant poßident summa æternaque bona, ut statis illórum et uitæ dican; y Beati qui habitat

Two pages from a codex of St. Peter's sermon notes, showing marginal and interlinear revisions of the dictated text in the Saint's hand
From the archives of the Society of Jesus.

That was straight enough, but Peter had still more incisive words to speak. On January 1, 1564, he began by wishing his congregation a happy New Year, and then went on:

I am minded to say that it is high time the ecclesiastical order had a good new year, for, alas, in the words of St. Paul, *propter vos blasphematur nomen Domini.* . . . Among the clergy many are to be found who, through ignorance or human respect, negligence or sloth, bury out of sight the Holy Name of God, instead of confessing it and making it known. They will not feed their poor neglected sheep with the Divine Word . . . and they sully their high calling with fleshly lusts and deeds, with worldly cares and affairs, so as to injure the Name of God in the eyes of both friends and enemies.

Speaking about the neglect of fasting and abstinence during the Lent of 1564, he said:

Scarcely one Catholic in a hundred now observes the fast, and it is small comfort to know, that, if the clergy were half as careful to keep the law as they are to indulge in surfeiting, the Lenten regulations would to-day be less despised and priestly chastity a less rare occurrence.[1]

In June the preacher was back to the charge, bewailing the contempt shown for the holy Sacrifice of the Mass:

As is the pastor, so are the people; as is the master, so is the disciple. But would to God that we could only be charged with ignorance and negligence. The same thing has happened to our priests as befell the ministers of the Church in the time of the prophet Malachy: *Who is there among you that will shut the doors and will kindle the fire on My altar gratis? I have no pleasure in you, saith the Lord of Hosts, and I will not receive a gift of your hand.* Indeed, we have defiled His altar with our unclean hands and lips, with our uncircumcized hearts, with our scandalous lives and grave abuses. Our avarice in dealing with this Sacrifice is notorious, and also our carelessness and neglect of decency in the divine services. What greater power could God give

---

[1] In the matter of abstinence, Heaven shortly afterwards had its revenge, as live-stock failed and the Senate of Augsburg was obliged to issue a decree prohibiting meat on all Wednesdays, Fridays, and Saturdays for the rest of that year. It was a Lutheran member of the Senate who sponsored the decree. Polanco was delighted, "though," as he wrote to Peter, "the gentleman's motive might bear improvement."

us than to be able with our lips to bring His Body and Blood to our altars, to touch Him with our hands, to distribute Him to others, and to offer Him in sacrifice for the Church Universal ? Such power and dignity are not given to princes or prophets or the very angels. . . . All the greater, then, is our sin when we abuse the dignity conferred on us, and, for God's sake or the Church's sake, or for the sake of our friends, or not to give a handle to our enemies, are unwilling to honour this Sacrifice and our calling as priests. So, on our account, is the Name of God blasphemed ; and, because we are not the salt of the earth, we are good for nothing but to be cast out and trodden on by all the world. So comes it that no men are to-day more despised than " Massing " priests. . . . How many are still to-day known publicly for their incontinence and drunkenness, who do not pray but blaspheme, who care only for temporal things, who are disgusted by the fact that they are priests, and are nowhere so bored as at the altar when saying Mass. . . . Such men, frequenters of taverns, do all their priestly work as a mere matter of routine. With them there is no honesty at home, no sobriety at table, no continence in bed, no study in books, no devotion in heart or soul. . . .[1]

About a month before St. Peter pronounced those last stern sentences he became aware that the parochial clergy of Augsburg were determined on revenge. Women who came to confession to himself and Father Elderen were taxed in the city with being " of the Jesuit sect," and mutterings were heard against the two men for administering Holy Communion at their Masses. " The criticisms sometimes upset Father William," Peter reported, " but I cheer him up and tell him to hope for better things." On June 3, 1564, the day following the last sermon quoted, the parochial clergy of the Cathedral delated Peter and Elderen to the Chapter as usurpers of their rights. Peter's one true friend in the Chapter, Dr. Conrad Braun, had died the previous year, bequeathing to the Jesuits his property in Dillingen. The rest of the canons, if not already hostile, were intensely suspicious and seized the chance now to give their grievances against the Jesuits an airing. Their charge-sheet, addressed to Cardinal Truchsess, contained such items as the following :

1. The Jesuits do not obey the Dean or anybody else.
2. They allow women to enter their house and yet wish to be considered above suspicion.

[1] Braunsberger, *Epistulae*, vol. iv, pp. 856–60, 864–6.

3. In their sermons and in the confessional they scandalously bring odium upon the clergy.

4. They would have it believed that they alone are virtuous men.

5. They keep themselves aloof from other people.

6. They comfort nobody but invariably drive people to despair.

These and similar charges are followed by a list of fifteen "*gravamina*," including such matters as that the Jesuits denied absolution to usurers, asked innocent young girls indelicate questions in confession, went into the pulpit late and preached too long, constrained people to attend their Masses, and indulged in invective against the ignorance and conduct of the clergy.[1] It will be observed that St. Peter's pulpit references to clerical corruption are set down in both documents, which seems to show that they were deeply resented. With regard to the indelicate questions, it is legitimate to wonder how the canons came to know that they were asked except through an inquisition of penitents, which suggests something in the nature of what is termed a 'frame-up.' However that may have been, it is an ascertained fact that very many, if not most, confessions made in Germany at this period were invalid owing to want of integrity. In 1565 Cardinal Truchsess found it necessary to issue a strongly worded denunciation of "the most evil custom" of confessing only in vague and general terms. In Augsburg, as previously in Vienna, St. Peter and his brethren found to their dismay that the people had no idea how to make their confessions. They would rush in and gabble: "I have sinned against God; I am sorry; give me absolution."[2] And they got it too, though as likely as not in a mutilated form. Here, as in many other matters, the tendency seems to have been to approach as nearly as possible to the Lutheran position, while still keeping the name of Catholic. In the circumstances, Peter and Father Elderen may well have asked questions, and if a young woman who had committed adultery or fornication thought it shocking that the priest, as in duty bound, should want to know which it was, one does not feel called upon to waste sympathy on her squeamishness.

In his detailed but modest and friendly reply to the criticisms, St. Peter pointed out that, according to the law of the Church then in force, it was permissible for Catholics to confess, except in Paschal time, to any priest they liked who had faculties from the local Ordinary, and to receive Holy Communion at his hands. Both Peter and Father Elderen

---

[1] Braunsberger, *Epistulae*, vol. iv, pp. 543–4.   [2] Braunsberger, *Epistulae*, vol. ii, p. 853.

possessed the fullest faculties from the Bishop of Augsburg and, over and above, a papal privilege, granted to all Jesuit priests by Paul III in 1549, whereby any Catholic was empowered to confess to them, *rectoris sui licentia minime requisita*. The same applied to the reception of Holy Communion otherwise than as Viaticum or within the Paschal season. Moreover, the Jesuits had been endowed by the Holy See with power to absolve certain reserved cases which fell outside the ordinary confessor's jurisdiction. Failure to exercise that power would have been a plain breach of charity, especially as they had been requested by the parish priest of the Cathedral area to help with the many confessions which were the direct result of Peter's sermons. As for their popularity with woman-kind which aggrieved the canons, Peter had the following observations to make :

Granted that in this matter the devotion of some of the weaker sex to these Fathers and, perhaps, over-zealous championship of them, may have 'aliquid humani' in its composition, cannot the foible be pardoned as merely the usual loquacity and fussiness of the daughters of Eve ? How are the Fathers to blame, seeing that they have no desire for such attentions and in no way encourage them ? Indeed, the difficulty is to cool them off. *Varium enim ac mutabile semper foemina.*

The Fathers withdraw no people from their parish priests or parishes nor do they canvass for people to receive the Sacraments at their hands. Rather are they heavily burdened by the numbers that come spontaneously, and often unable to satisfy all who desire their help. On the other hand, how are they to keep such clients at bay without harshness ? How deny their services to these petitioners or obstruct their good desires without breach of charity ? That people come in larger numbers to their Masses than to the Masses of other priests because, as some allege, they imagine the Masses of the Jesuits to be better and holier, is an utterly ridiculous invention.

Complaint is also made that the Fathers allow their penitents to approach Holy Communion too frequently, because some receive It every Sunday and feast-day. But what prudent man will venture to stand in judgment on another man's conscience and to condemn his good desires ? St. Augustine commends the reception of Holy Communion on Sundays to all the faithful . . . and what good man but would approve and promote a truly pious and Christian practice, whereby feast-days are wonderfully sanctified, and the consciences of many people immensely strengthened in the love of God and all devotion ?

Peter was also accused of dealing out 'hard sayings' to the people and of driving them to despair. To this charge he answered:

My auditors will readily testify that I often introduced the comfortable words of Scripture and, at the right time, spoke on the mercy of God. But if ever there was a time when men needed to be turned away from false consolation and stirred up to penitence and the fear of God, it is certainly now when the doctrine of salvation by faith alone, and the false persuasion that the mercy of God will do everything, have all but wrested and banished the fear and love of God from the souls of sinners. . . . There is no preacher but should be stimulated by this state of affairs to commending most earnestly to the people ardent prayer against evil habit, penitence for their sins, and the fear of God whom we have offended. In truth, thoughtful men will know that such a course does not breed despair, unless, perhaps, we would make out that Christ too drove the rich to despair with His terrible words: *It is easier for a camel to pass through the eye of a needle than for a rich man to enter into the Kingdom of Heaven.* . . . St. Paul was glad because he had made the Corinthians sorrowful, that their sorrow might work penance steadfast unto salvation; and would that Canisius might have the joy of seeing his Augsburg people made sorrowful according to God, that so they might work out their salvation in fear and trembling and bring forth fruits worthy of penance.

Peter's answer to the charge that he denied absolution to so-called usurers opens up an exceedingly wide and difficult question into which it is hardly the province of a book such as this to enter very deeply. Something, however, must be said, as the Jesuits of Germany became painfully entangled in the issue between nascent capitalism and the simpler systems which it ousted. Almost by instinct, we might say, Peter took the side of the underdog. Throughout life, he never failed to play the poor man's advocate and to urge their duty of neighbourly helpfulness on those better circumstanced. Thus, in a sermon preached in Augsburg Cathedral on July 7, 1560, he said, addressing his wealthy auditors:

You throw away a hundred ducats at the gaming tables and you make a pother about giving four or five florins to some poor man in need of bread. You serve a single guest of yours with thirty courses and neglect so many of the friends of Christ. . . . Ah, woe to merchants and to all who use false measure. Woe to usurers and deceivers and liars in buying and selling. Unless they restore, their sin will not be forgiven them.

On September 21st, the feast of St. Matthew, converted farmer of taxes, Peter again denounced the merchant and money-lending classes to which his best friends, the Fuggers, belonged:

Have we not many Matthews in Augsburg? They sit not only in the custom-house but in the council-chamber, invested in high office. The whole world is full of Matthews, full of publicans, usurers, and such as grind the faces of the poor by various newly-invented exactions. Everything is made a decoy for the poor; law-suits, ordinances of government, stamp-duties. Office-holders take advantage of their positions to feather their nests, even from the lightest of duties, so that everything both within and without the law has its price. Are not they Matthews who in every business relation think only of private gain, who mulct their neighbours in buying and selling, who lend money and take 6 per cent or 10 per cent on the loan, to the poor man's discomfiture? . . . The new preachers increase the licence, so that merchants sin without any conscience at all, while nobody makes restitution and whole families are ruined to provide others with ill-gotten gains and riches acquired through usury.[1]

Usury for St. Peter was not what we to-day mean by the term but something much more inclusive. It did not mean the exaction or acceptance of a very heavy rate of interest for a loan, but the exaction or acceptance of any interest at all, unless it could be shown that the security for the loan was not sufficiently sound, or that the lender could have used his money profitably had he kept it, or that he suffered loss by merely parting with it for a time. These extrinsic titles had gradually come to be recognized by theologians as justifying a claim to reasonable remuneration for a loan, but in their absence nothing might be exacted except the return of the capital. Underlying the teaching of the Church on the subject and the complicated argumentation of the schoolmen was the sound Christian principle that it is unjust and sinful to make profit out of another man's necessity. The Church was so stringent in her legislation because sad experience proved that there have never lacked

[1] Braunsberger, *Epistulae*, vol. iv, p. 855.

in this imperfect world human vultures ready to prey on the misfortunes of their fellows. The canon law, which was, of course, dodged to a large extent, even in medieval times when nobody questioned its rightness, raised no great moral difficulty until capitalism began to emerge. The crux of the whole complicated question came in the sixteenth century, and nowhere more acutely than in St. Peter's own City of Augsburg.

In the past, the problem had largely solved itself because money was, on the whole, unproductive. One kept it in a stocking or in the vaults of an obliging monastery, and withdrew from time to time whatever was needed to buy a cow or to pay a debt or, perhaps, to lend to a neighbour. But there was very little scope for investing it in the modern sense, because there was very little industry in search of capital. The doctrine that money *per se* was sterile had been taken over by the scholastics from Aristotle. It was put in the category of " fungible " goods, like bread or wine or fuel, whose use is in their consumption and for which an equivalent amount of similar goods is an equitable exchange. That theory of money rested on an economic fact, namely that labour and not capital was the source of social wealth, which shows us that Marx for all his modernity was a mere plagiarist. Unfortunately the fact was variable. Capitalism, of course, had always existed, but for long only the privileged few were in a position to take advantage of its possibilities. In the sixteenth century the few tended to become the many, under the stimulus provided by the influx of American gold, the discovery of new trade routes to the East, and the general ferment of the Reformation.

Naturally enough, Catholic moralists such as Laynez and Peter Canisius were considerably troubled by the new developments. When, in 1553–1554, Laynez found himself in Genoa, the city of Columbus, where bankers and company-promoters abounded, he felt it his duty to preach a course of sermons on the very pertinent subject of contracts and financial dealings. Such an impression did he make that the civil authorities published an edict ordering all merchants to submit their books and contracts for theological revision. Following on that success, Laynez composed a treatise, *De usura et variis contractibus mercatorum,* apparently for the use of confessors. This work affords a good idea of the difficulties with which Catholic theologians stood confronted at the period of economic transition. Money was yearly taking on more and more of the lineaments of productive capital, though not for nearly three centuries would it be completely transformed into the monster of fecundity that nearly throttled its Frankenstein in 1932. With these developments, the extrinsic titles to payment for a loan became the subject of general and sometimes extremely heated discussion. Merchants and financiers endeavoured by Procrustean methods to make the titles cover every sort of shady transaction, and the theologians, on their side, needed all their wits to solve the increasingly complicated problems of commercial justice. The following paragraph from Laynez gives some idea of the task:

As it is supremely necessary to avoid cheating one's neighbour in business or acting towards him unjustly, so is it extremely difficult to detect when such deception or injustice has taken place in commercial transactions. On the one hand, neither Scripture nor the ancient Fathers and philosophers deal with the matter in detail, and, on the other, the astuteness of the merchants, fostered by their lust for gain, has discovered so many tricks and dodges that it is hardly possible to see the plain facts, much less to pronounce judgment on them. This is the reason why modern writers, whether theologians or jurists, are so confused and at variance with one another. Finally, the matter, being a question of morals, only admits of a certain probability, because its nature is such that the least change of circumstances renders it necessary to revise one's judgment of the whole affair. Consequently, to decide such variable questions exactly one would need to be an Argus with a hundred eyes. As St. Basil says very well: To understand justice is, in truth, the part of a great intellect and of a very perfect mind.[1]

On the question of a price for loans Laynez held extremely strict views, and from him St. Peter derived the undoubted rigorism of his attitude. Peter had the plight of poor persons so much at heart that he tended to judge or prejudge the whole question of interest according to the broad principles of neighbourly charity rather than according to the exigencies of cold, dispassionate justice. When he blazed out against ' usury ' it was chiefly because he saw the suffering to which it led, poor men mortgaging their little properties for a loan and being distrained; or others, unfamiliar with the ways of high finance, buying misfortune as though it were a bargain. Capital, for Peter, had redeeming features only in so far as, like love, it was " *diffusivum sui.*" His truest friends in Augsburg were that City's principal capitalists, but such a consideration carried no weight at all, and he ended by seriously disturbing the tender conscience of Ursula Fugger, who became alarmed for the fate of her family in the next world. She communicated her *malaise* to her more stolid and less earnestly Catholic husband, George, and that was not a bad thing, because George's conscience needed a fillip. He hardly ever went to Mass, until, at this time, St. Peter got hold of him and wrought a big transformation.

The Haus Fugger derived much of its vast revenue from banking operations, but, being loyal Catholics, its members tried to keep within the letter of canon law, while using to the full every loop-hole afforded by theological speculation. It is said, though it has not been proved, that they financed the great Johann Eck on his expedition to the Italian universities in 1515 for the purpose of defending the popular species of partnership known as the "Triple Contract." The person in this contract on whom the theologians fastened suspicious eyes was a sort of sleeping partner or debenture holder who drew 5 per cent of the total profits, without sharing in the management of the business or risking the loss of his capital. It seemed like pure usury, that is to say drawing profit without labour, cost, or risk from the loan of a fungible commodity, and as such St. Peter Canisius held it in deep distrust. But, though Laynez declared it to be usurious, Peter would not condemn it outright, probably because he knew that many poor people, widows and small tradesmen were investing their savings in this way and deriving a modest subsistence in dividends. Peter also looked askance at the *Census* or rent-charges, which were another favourite device for eluding the usury laws, but on appealing to Laynez for guidance, he learned that this method might be tolerated.[1] He never for a moment, of course, questioned the extrinsic titles to interest but, like Laynez, he felt in his bones that the financiers did not greatly worry whether they possessed them in any particular case. "What is usury?" he asked in one of his sermons, and answered: "Everything a man takes over and above the bare sum he lent when this is done purely in consideration of the loan. For example, you lend your neighbour twenty florins on condition that the following year he returns you twenty-one florins. That extra florin is usury and you are bound to restore it." Then, referring to the excuses made for accepting interest, he went on: "A third person thinks that it is enough that this sin is not punished by civil law, which allows the giving and taking of 5 per cent interest. But brothels are also tolerated by the civil law, and a Christian who desires to act according to his conscience ought to make

[1] Braunsberger, *Epistulae*, vol. iii, pp. 543-4, 564.

more account of the canon law, natural and divine, which prohibits and condemns every species of usury."[1] Here Peter rather begs the question; but, at any rate, his motive, if not his argument, is above suspicion, and his stern attitude throughout the long dispute on the legitimacy of interest, of which more will be said later, may be understood and appreciated from his not unfounded conviction that merchants and money-lenders "oppressed the whole world and violated all charity and fair dealing."

The canons of Augsburg, who may very likely have been engaged in drawing comfortable incomes from the contracts about which St. Peter showed such annoying concern, decided at length to prohibit the two Jesuits from hearing confessions in the cathedral. But Cardinal Truchsess took up their defence so warmly that the Chapter relented to the extent of allowing Peter to go on administering the Sacraments "to persons of consideration and quality," on condition that he kept all others at arm's length and that Father Elderen abstained from pastoral work entirely. The restriction of Peter's ministry to " *ansehnliche und fürnemen Personen* " was a sarcastic stroke by which the canons would show their contempt for Ursula Fugger's hero-worshipping propensities. Let him have his Ursula! On his way to Würzburg in August, 1564, Peter wrote begging Cardinal Truchsess to get the invidious reservation removed, "lest in the administration of the Sacraments I be obliged to become an accepter of persons." Then continuing he said:

That my Lords, the canons of the Venerable Chapter, may know us for lovers of peace and tranquil counsels, who are profoundly distressed that the present scandal should have been stirred up and their minds embittered against us, I propose the following plan for Your Highness's consideration. It is that, with your good leave, we depart from the Cathedral so as not to be burdensome in the slightest degree to anybody. We can look around for another place of abode. According to the testimony of our opponents, we are responsible for the present storm; so, like Jonah, let us be thrown into the sea. . . . We only beg, through Christ Our Lord, to be allowed to carry on as priests of the Society of Jesus who may, in the spirit of their Order, promote the glory of God in Augsburg by their preaching and administration of the Sacraments. . . . Do not let us be forced against our consciences to give up our privileges which, no less than other men their privileges, we are in duty bound to maintain. . . .

[1] Braunsberger, *Epistulae*, vol. iii, p. 585.

I am writing these lines to your Lordship while on the road. They are not intended as a reflection on anybody but purely and simply as an explanation of the truth. I ask nothing else of your Lordship except in your wisdom to direct the whole affair to the glory of Almighty God. It will be our part to pray hard for their Reverences of the Chapter, to show them all respect and honour, and to love them steadfastly. And , we shall take good care not to let slip any least occasion of practising charity and patience. May the will of the Lord, the Searcher of hearts, be done, and may His glory and honour be our never-ending quest.[1]

Cardinal Truchsess had asked Peter for a copy of his Order's privileges but obtained only the item relative to the administration of the Sacraments. This his Lordship put before the canons, who retaliated by throwing at Peter's head the complete text of their own privileges and exemptions. He replied in September, saying that he was truly sorry to have to engage in such a style of correspondence and begging their Reverences to be patient with him. He had not, as they alleged, approached the Cardinal in the guise of an accuser but only as the accused, after sentence had been pronounced on him, that he might have the advice of the man who had first introduced him to the Augsburg mission-field. The privileges and statutes of the Cathedral Chapter had now become known to him for the first time, so if he had violated them in the past it was done in all innocence. As for his own Order's privileges, he had transcribed at the Cardinal's request only a tiny portion of them and made no petition that the dispute should be decided by reference to the extract given. As for the accusation that he had charged their Reverences with opposition to the Pope, he could not conceive how such a lie originated. They reprimanded him, too, for giving out that they obstructed the worship of God, but it never entered his mind to say any such thing. Augsburg was a hot-bed of gossip, even about the highest authorities, but he had given no handle to the busybodies. With regard to his alleged violation of parochial rights, he and Father Elderen had hoped to find favour with the Venerable Chapter as fellow-workers in the ministry of Augsburg, labouring side by side with them, denying their services to no soul in need but giving freely to all what they had freely received. " Heaven forbid that in a matter of such moment we should look to our private interest or be guided by human considerations rather than by concern for the glory of God and our neighbours' good."

[1] Braunsberger, *Epistulae*, vol. iv, pp. 644–5.

As for the decision whereby he was permitted to hear the confessions of noble or distinguished persons alone, Peter continued:

I do not understand why ordinary men and women, the poor and other simple folk, should be excluded from my ministrations, seeing that they often stand in no less need of consolation and spiritual help than the rich and noble. It is utterly unfitting that we should thus discriminate in connexion with the Sacraments and the common grace of God, which is offered to all men and ought, as a matter of justice, to be dispensed liberally to all who seek it. . . . As St. Paul says, Christ must be preached and souls saved *per omnem occasionem*. But we shall not invite anybody to confess to us if you will only allow free access to those who come spontaneously or for some good reason. . . . I plead guilty to the charge of having omitted some sermons, but, as many people know, I had a sound excuse and, in any case, it was arranged that Bishop Dornvogel should supply for me. Perhaps you will concede me a measure of forgiveness in consideration of the fact that I have preached extra sermons, to which I was not obliged, at such times as were most convenient for the people, especially during the holy season of Lent. I beg you then, my good Sirs, not to take it too hardly if I have now and then neglected a sermon, owing to being called away by princes on business touching the public interest. One other thing, in conclusion, I beg with all my heart through Christ Our Lord, namely that you would forgive anything hitherto done or left undone by me to your annoyance. Father Elderen and myself both promise all due reverence and respect to you, and we shall abide by whatever arrangements you make, only desiring that we be not compelled to anything against our vocation or repugnant to holy obedience and the wishes of our superiors. It would be the hardest trial in the world for us to remain in Augsburg, or to go on with our work at the Cathedral, against your wishes or with the least trace of offence to anybody. May Our Lord turn everything to His glory and be present to you, Sirs, with His Spirit. We reverently commend ourselves to you in Him.[1]

Meantime, Cardinal Truchsess had written to Laynez, assuring him that neither Peter nor Father Elderen were in the least responsible for the Augsburg storm. "It is entirely due," he said, "to the malice of

---

[1] Braunsberger, *Epistulae*, vol. iv, pp. 657–61.

some turbulent and ungrateful men among the depraved clergy who have striven out of hatred to damage the Jesuits in the eyes of the canons and others."[1] A little later, some of the foremost citizens of Augsburg, including George and Mark Fugger, addressed a long, warmly-worded expostulation to the Cardinal against the policy of the canons. After recording their distress at the persecution to which the two Jesuits were being subjected, they said : " We esteem Herr Canisius for a theologian and preacher of such profound learning and sanctity that he might in justice not only be treasured by the Venerable Chapter as a precious jewel, but even be named the outstanding glory of Germany and a pillar of the Universal Church."[2] Then, in four sections they detailed the evil consequences that must inevitably follow should St. Peter retire from Augsburg. In their opinion, the agitation against him was being engineered by a section of envious ecclesiastics who felt his presence to be a reproach to their scandalous lives. " Everybody knows in what high esteem the Jesuits are held, not only by His Holiness, the Pope, and His Imperial Majesty, but by all Catholic princes and nobles ; so much so, indeed, that their one complaint is the impossibility of getting enough of them."[3]

Shortly after this was written, a very different kind of document came to Peter from the hands of the canons, a lengthy, discourteous screed, full of new, petty allegations and sarcastic references. Then there followed a Brief from Pope Pius IV to the Dean and Chapter :

Beloved Sons, Health and Apostolic Benediction.

During these years there has come to us and to this Holy See the excellent and very gratifying report of the abundant profit which the City of Augsburg derived from the labours of Our beloved son, Peter Canisius, and other Fathers of the Society of Jesus. We have heard how many heretics have been restored to the Church by their learning and exhortations, and how great a solace their devoted labours have been to the Catholic citizens. As We were wont formerly to have joy in the hearing of such news, so a short time since did We grieve to learn that the Enemy of the human race had begun to obstruct such pious and salutary work, inasmuch as by his prompting, and through the base gossip of certain evil-minded persons, sympathies have been

[1] Braunsberger, *Epistulae*, vol. iv, pp. 898-9.
[2] Braunsberger, *Epistulae*, vol. iv, p. 901 : " . . . das er nit allein bei disem loblichenn Thumbstifft für ein costlich Edelgestain zuhalten, sunder unicum Germaniae decus et columna totius Ecclesiae billich genannt werden mag."
[3] Braunsberger, *Epistulae*, vol. iv, pp. 676-81.

alienated from the Society of Jesus. This turn of events is the more grievous to endure, not only because it hinders the work of God already begun, but because it must breed dissension and scandal between you and the lay Catholics and put new heart into the heretics. Therefore, in accordance with Our pastoral duty, and desiring to remedy this disorder and scandal, We exhort and admonish you that you cherish the same Canisius and others of his Society with your former charity and benevolence; that you diligently protect them, and not merely suffer them to engage in the ministry of the Divine Word and the Sacraments, permitted to them by the Apostolic See, but that you help them with your favour and co-operation therein, in obedience to the wishes of Our Venerable brother, the Cardinal of Augsburg, your Bishop. To him, as your Ordinary, you shall in future have recourse, if you desire to lay any charge against them.

Given at Rome, at St. Mark's, under the Ring of the Fisherman, September 30, 1564, the Fifth Year of Our Pontificate.[1]

Fortified by the Pope's Brief and the letter of the Augsburg patricians, Cardinal Truchsess now began to take the offensive. He informed the canons that their charges against the Jesuits had been investigated and found trumpery, except the one relative to Peter's occasional hasty departures from Augsburg, an offence which they might well have borne with " *ain bruederliche Geduld* "—a little brotherly tolerance—instead of making a mountain of it. He, their Bishop, had suffered much in his life and been twice in exile, but no previous sorrow wounded him so much as the dispute between the Chapter and the Society of Jesus. The canons might as well know that he would never suffer the Jesuits to be driven out of Augsburg, so the sooner they bowed to necessity and came to terms the better for everybody.[2]

The canons, however, were not yet beaten. They ignored the Papal Brief, scorned the letter of the patricians, and, in flat contradiction of their own previous and oft-repeated testimony, belittled Peter's record of holy activities. For instance, they said that his ministry to the plague-stricken was news to them, as well it might, seeing that they had all fled the City at the first sign of danger. But Cardinal Truchsess was not going to be bullied in his own house this time. He maintained pressure until the canons agreed to send representatives to Dillingen where, on

[1] Braunsberger, *Epistulae*, vol. iv, pp. 905–6.　　[2] Braunsberger, *Epistulae*, vol. iv, pp. 906–7.

October 20th, a pact was signed between them and St. Peter. This confirmed him in his office of preacher, while, for peace's sake, he resigned all claims as a confessor at the Cathedral. More than once, Peter had expressed a longing to be well away from the miserable squabbling, and there were plenty of other places that would have jumped at the chance of possessing him. But he could not abandon Cardinal Truchsess, especially as that good man guaranteed to find some other church where he might pursue his ministry in peace. The church chosen was that of St. Catherine, which belonged to the Dominican nuns with whose spiritual welfare Peter had been closely connected a little time before. "We have now begun to hear confessions in the Church of St. Catherine," he informed Laynez shortly after making it up with the canons. "Ursula Fugger is delighted because her residence is close to the convent, and she hopes that we, too, will soon find a house of our own in the vicinity. The Cathedral is a long way off so we have been obliged to take lodgings nearer St. Catherine's. God grant that this change, which annoys some people, may turn out for the best. The canons have begun to invite me to dinner, as a token of my restoration to grace after the Dillingen compact, but I am afraid they will not like it when they hear that we have been given a place where we can freely administer the Sacraments."

Unfortunately, St. Catherine's was too near the collegiate and parish church of St. Maurice for the fancy of its provost, Wolfgang Rhem, a canon of the Augsburg Chapter. He and his friends now started a new campaign against Peter, who wrote in distress to Laynez:

We had thought that we were over the cross of Augsburg . . . but a fresh commotion has been stirred up by another group of priests. They resent having us for neighbours and are working to prevent us from administering the Sacraments at St. Catherine's. It is difficult, too, just now to rent a new residence, so we are left suspended between hope and fear. Meantime, we have a chance to practise patience, as many people are gossiping about us and disparaging our efforts. . . . I think myself that the clergy of Augsburg will not easily tolerate our having a place for Confessions and Communions in any church of the city, so we have decided to refrain from giving Holy Communion during the next few months. It is indeed extraordinary that in this little flock of Catholics two priests, anxious to help quite gratis with the ministry of the Sacraments, should not be tolerated. Thus does

Our Lord put us to the test, and not by our Catholic brethren only but also by other foes who vociferate strenuously against the Jesuits as vagabonds incapable of settling down anywhere. . . .[1]

Simultaneously with the trouble in Augsburg which smouldered on for a long time, St. Peter's men in Ingolstadt were going through a very bad period, due largely to the same unhappy causes ; while in Rome such a vicious storm broke on the heads of the Jesuits, when Pius IV entrusted to their care the newly-established Seminario Romano, that Laynez had to order the prayers and penances of his subjects as for a major crisis. A certain Bishop Cesarini, whose pastoral misdemeanours the Jesuits had been called in to rectify, was the leader of the offensive and wrote a tract alleging that all Spanish members of the Society in Rome had Moorish or Jewish blood in their veins, while all its German members were stated to be concealed heretics, bent on undermining the faith of the students committed to them. This lucubration, which contained a whole string of other inventions, was posted to Germany, translated into that country's vernacular, and circulated widely at the Courts of the Catholic and Protestant princes.[2] St. Peter did an enormous amount with Cardinal Truchsess, Albert of Bavaria, Nuncio Visconti, and others, to counteract the damaging effect of the libels. In Italy, their author, who had already been relieved of his episcopal charge, would have found himself in a papal prison but for the intercession of Peter's brethren.

A greater misfortune in the Saint's eyes than any of these more personal troubles was the eventual concession of the chalice to the laity by Pope Pius IV. This victory of the Imperialists resulted from a bargain made in 1563, whereby the Emperor and his son, Maximilian, agreed not to hinder the winding-up of the Council of Trent, on which the Pope had set his heart, provided His Holiness promised the chalice. The Council came to a happy and successful close on December 4, 1563, having in its last session confirmed and approved the Society of Jesus as a new religious order. Then it was the turn of Ferdinand to demand his pound of flesh. At his request the Pope's Briefs, dated April 16, 1564, were addressed to the three Ecclesiastical Electors, to the Archbishops of Salzburg, Prague, Bremen, Magdeburg, and Gran, and to the Bishops of Naumburg and Gurk. These authorities were empowered to allow or forbid the chalice in their respective dioceses, as they judged best. On Sunday, June 18th, the Bishop of Gurk, our old friend " Urban the

---

[1] Braunsberger, *Epistulae*, vol. iv, pp. 712–3.   [2] Braunsberger, *Epistulae*, vol. iv, pp. 717–8.

Austrian," who had the administration of Vienna, promulgated the decree in the Cathedral of St. Stephen and constrained the Jesuits to read it in their church also. The Archbishop of Salzburg, whose jurisdiction extended over much of Bavaria, went more slowly and, ignoring the Emperor's mandate to put the concession in force without delay, convened a synod to talk the whole thing over. Salzburg and most of the great prelates of the North had all along been as much opposed to the concession as their Spanish brethren, and their hesitation may well have been based on a shrewder appreciation of the issues involved than the abounding confidence of Urban the Austrian, who was not celebrated for soundness of judgment.

The news of the grant came as a terrible shock to St. Peter. " Many souls have been perturbed by it," he wrote to Laynez, " nor do I see what more lamentable thing could have happened this summer. It means that a sword has been put in the hands of our raging enemies, so we soon expect to see the remnant of Israel turned into a Babylon. . . . May Christ grant us better times."[1] Since the Pope had not so much granted the concession as empowered the bishops to grant it, Peter and his brethren were at perfect liberty to continue in opposition till the bishops should have decided. And oppose they did with all their might. Abbé Constant, the best modern authority on the chalice question, talks a good deal about their " submission," but he is able to produce only one single person in the whole of Austria, Tirol, or Bavaria, to whom the Jesuits *may* have administered Holy Communion under both kinds.[2] They were actuated in their stand by two chief considerations : profound reverence for the Blessed Sacrament, which they felt must inevitably suffer indignities from the new rite, and a conviction that further concessions to weak-kneed Catholics, or further endeavours to conciliate Protestant opinion, must react injuriously on the life of the Church as a whole.

Cardinal Truchsess, who was as heartily opposed to the grant as St. Peter himself, dispatched a good and zealous canon of Freising named Pfister to report on what was happening at Salzburg. Pfister returned from the synod with news that the Archbishop was weakening; whereupon, at the request of Truchsess, St. Peter composed a long, secret instruction for the canon, copies of which were sent to the Archbishop of Salzburg and to the Bishops of Regensburg, Passau, and Chiemsee. In this the Saint set down very forcibly and cogently every possible dissuasive

---

[1] Braunsberger, *Epistulae*, vol. iv, pp. 590–1.
[2] *Concession à l'Allemagne de la Communion sous les deux espèces*, vol. i, pp. 662–5.

argument he could think of, drawing on both history and theology for the purpose. The chief claim of those who championed the concession was that it would promote peace, to which Peter replied, after stressing such practical inconveniences as the need of new chalices, new rubrics and ceremonies, new remedies and precautions of every kind : " Indeed the whole face of the Church will appear new, some worshippers desiring to communicate under one species and some under the two, in the same temple, around the same altar, at the same Mass. So will it come about that what Christ gave us as a symbol of unity will be turned into an emblem of division and disorder." That quotation must suffice, as the document, which was carefully anonymous, runs into nearly ten pages of print.[1] It did not succeed in its purpose, as the synod for which it was intended eventually gave a cautious sanction to the introduction of the lay chalice in some districts of Salzburg and Bavaria.

But there were compensations for Peter and for those who thought with him, owing to the changed attitude of Bavaria's Duke. At first Albert had been among the most enthusiastic supporters of the lay chalice, but, under Jesuit persuasion and as the result of a Protestant rebellion, he lost his keenness. His powerful vassal, the Graf von Ortenburg, had banded with other seditious nobles to introduce Lutheranism into their dominions. When refused the free exercise of the Confession of Augsburg by the Landtag of Ingolstadt early in 1563, Ortenburg issued a decree abolishing Catholicism in his territory. That act, insignificant in itself, was really a turning-point in the history of the Counter-Reformation. It roused Albert at last from his futile dreams of conciliation, and compelled him to embark on a policy of repression which, as St. Peter had been urging for years, could alone check the progress of Protestantism. As things stood, there was nothing whatever inhuman or unjust in the policy. It was merely an acceptance of realities and a belated imitation of what the Protestants had been doing all along. In December, 1563, the Duke seized the Schloss Ortenburg and shortly afterwards forcibly expelled the Lutheran ministers who had been introduced. Ortenburg then appealed to the Protestant princes and with their aid succeeded in re-establishing Lutheranism. In May, 1564, Albert replied by occupying the citadel of Mattigofen, where a collection of letters was found proving that Ortenburg and his associates had planned a large-scale insurrection for the purpose of destroying Catholicism throughout Bavaria. The Duke then indicted the ringleader for high treason and, on his flight,

---

[1] Braunsberger, *Epistulae*, vol. iv, pp. 623–32.

confiscated his possessions. Pankraz von Freyburg, who occupied a high official post, and other nobles of Lutheran sympathies were arrested and confronted with the damning evidence of their letters, but Albert, as always magnanimous, bade his judges be content with sentences of imprisonment.[1]

The whole affair made a profound and lasting impression on the Duke's mind. He began to ask himself whether the combative policy advocated by St. Peter had not been the right one from the beginning. And as for the chalice, were not the rebels, whom he had had such difficulty to repress, the loudest in their demand for it? All his patient efforts at conciliation had been repaid by the blackest treachery. The Protestants plainly did not want conciliation. They wanted the utter rout of Catholicism. Very good, then; their challenge would in future be accepted in the spirit in which they offered it. Under sway of such thoughts Albert began to attend more earnestly than ever before to the counsels of St. Peter and his brethren. Thus in January, 1564, he wrote to the Saint from Munich assuring him that he held the Fathers of the Society of Jesus in the very highest esteem and affection for all the good they had done in his dominions by their learning and example. Then, reminding Peter that many parishes of Bavaria had no pastors or only bad ones, he said that it would give him profound satisfaction if his Reverence would arrange for missions in such districts by some of his brethren capable of preaching in German. Though he knew that it was not the custom for Jesuits to live outside their colleges yet, in this matter, " die Christliche bruederliche Lieb " which comprehended all rules and vows must move his Reverence to consent. He would see to all expenses and he therefore asked " his singularly dear Dr. Peter Canisius " to come to Munich in order to arrange the whole affair with his councillors.[2]

Peter went gladly and did all in his power to meet the wishes of a prince who, as he informed Laynez, was now " seriously urging the cause of religion and opposing himself totally to the heretics." The difficulty was to find the men. Eventually, after much consulting and rearranging, during which he twice offered his personal services, the Saint appointed Father Couvillon, " as he needed a change," and Father George Schorich, the Court preacher in Munich. His own desire to go was frustrated by some of the Fuggers, who begged Albert to remember the desperate need of Augsburg. On May 5th, the two men set off into

[1] Riezler, *Geschichte Baierns*, vol. iv (1899), pp. 523–32 ; and for St. Peter's account of the conspiracy, Braunsberger, *Epistulae*, vol. iv, pp. 606–7.
[2] Braunsberger, *Epistulae*, vol. iv, pp. 438–40.

the wilds, armed with full instructions from their Provincial and ample credentials from their Duke. Their principal task was to undo the mischief wrought by ignorant, evil-living priests and Lutheran ministers in the territory of Graf von Ortenburg. To help them Peter dispatched a second pair of missionaries, Father Gewarts and Stotz, shortly afterwards, and himself took the liveliest interest in what was a new and exceedingly important departure for his men. It was not intended that they should be away very long, as Schorich, at least, held a position which Peter found that he could fill only by temporarily interchanging the rectors of Ingolstadt and Munich. So bad, however, were conditions in Lower Bavaria that he sent Schorich and Gewarts there a second time in August, having first drawn up a new set of suggestions regarding their work, for the guidance of Albert's zealous Chancellor. The eleventh of these runs : " It would help towards the restoration of monasteries if the monks were compelled to leave their concubines and return to their cells."[1] In September the missioners made a report on their discoveries. A large number of the clergy were practically illiterate ; most of them had concubines and children ; and others had gone through a form of marriage :

Some call Martin Luther, ' *Sanctum Doctorem Martinum et pretiosum Dei virum* '. They preach out of the books of Melanchthon and other Lutheran commentators. Only a very few—*perpauci*—use the correct form of the Sacraments, especially of absolution. Some absolve their penitents with these sole words, *Misereatur nostri Deus*. Others say, *Ego miserator Deus auctoritate et divinitatis Patris et Filii et Spiritus Sancti. Pax tecum.* Yet others omit everything except, *Ego absolvo te in nomine Patris*. . . . Despite all this they are held for Catholics and so wish to be held, with the result that nearly half the Bavarians in this district no longer care for either God or man.[2]

In November, 1564, St. Peter was summoned by Chancellor Eck to help reform the University of Ingolstadt, which, owing to the attitude of the professorial body, especially in the faculty of law, was again becoming a hot-bed of heresy. On this occasion he got Father Schorich to write a detailed report of his recent mission, of which some account must be given as illustrating the task and problem of the Counter-Reformation : " The Duke sent us with full authority to inspect the monasteries, schools and churches, and to put right anything in them

---

[1] Braunsberger, *Epistulae*, vol. iv, pp. 616–7.
[2] Braunsberger, *Epistulae*, vol. iv, pp. 672–3. The Latin is reproduced exactly as reported.

that needed improvement. He wrote to all his governors and officials so that we might everywhere be treated with the respect due to his own person. . . . Our peregrinations lasted six and a half months, during which time we examined and solved the difficulties of priests or rustics, the latter to the number of a hundred or two hundred daily. We gave each man a special exhortation and replied to his questions in a friendly fashion." The difficulties referred to by Schorich were generally against the Mass which the peasants did not want because, said they, it was unscriptural and detracted from the Passion of Christ. Against the saints they objected that honour given to them meant honour taken from Christ, while, as for invoking them, what was the good when they could not hear our prayers? Masses for the dead were of no use to anybody and were invented by the priests merely for the sake of the money they brought in. Images, holy water, processions, and other Catholic ceremonies they called "figments of the Papists" and contrivances to make an income. Against the priests they said that "they would not take the Sacraments from them unless they gave up their concubines, got married, and led a good life, like the holy Lutheran man sent to Ortenburg by the great Lutheran, the Duke of Zweibrücken." About the holy Lutheran man Schorich remarks that the peasants, who came two thousand at a time to hear him, "valued one word of his more than all St. Augustine or St. Jerome or the whole Council of Trent." The priests are reported to have been "mighty jesters and drinkers . . . always to be found in pot-houses or at weddings or other celebrations." The Jesuits ordered the arrest of such of them as did not know the formula of absolution or said Mass in German. "These and others," Schorich goes on, "we instructed, admonished, and finally set free from prison." The peasants who proved recalcitrant, after being admonished "with all charity, compassion and prudence," were put in prison for a day or two on bread and water to think things over. As for the churches, "God knows," says Schorich, "that each time I entered one I seemed rather to be entering a stable." It was strenuous work cleaning them and putting them in order, and hardly less fatiguing to collect and make bonfires of the large quantities of heretical literature in the houses of the priests and peasants. The missioners distributed good, simple Catholic books instead of the confiscated stuff, especially the shorter Catechisms of St. Peter.[1]

Meantime, the chalice question was the chief subject of controversy and agitation in other districts. Abbé Constant is inclined to disallow

[1] Braunsberger, *Epistulae*, vol. iv, pp. 724–31.

evidence showing that the concession was injurious, but how get over the fact that Bishop Drascovics publicly confessed his keen regret for having so urgently demanded it at the Council of Trent?[1] In July, 1565, Cardinal Truchsess informed St. Peter of the Archbishop of Salzburg's sad remark to him that " the concession had been the ruin of his people."[2] Peter himself continued his efforts to keep it restricted within the narrowest possible limits and suggested to St. Francis Borgia that new bishops ought to be made to take an oath not to extend it. His determined opposition and his influence with the Duke of Bavaria drove the ' calixtines ' to fury. " Is it possible," said one of them in Munich, " that the Duke allows himself to be hoodwinked by these accursed Jesuits, traitors and sons of the devil ? "[3] Even Maximilian, foremost ' calixtine ' though he was, had to admit that the concession did not give the results hoped for, but he attributed this to the refusal of marriage to priests, as, in his opinion, the two matters were intimately connected. St. Peter would have heartily agreed. The two matters *were* connected, not only to one another, but to a whole series of other coveted changes, such as vernacular liturgies, the abolition of the fasting laws, the removal of statues, and other diminutions of traditional Catholicism. Where the whittling process would stop if once it got a hold, Heaven alone knew. In St. Peter's opinion, the great need for the Catholic Church was, not to relax, but to stiffen her attitude; to have no further truck with heresy; to discipline her own children and to secure by stringent legislation that only avowed, practising Catholics held posts in centres of Catholic education. " Better," he wrote, " that only a few Catholics should be left, staunch and sincere in their religion, than that they should, remaining many, desire, as it were, to be in collusion with the Church's enemies and in conformity with the open foes of our faith."

The agitation against the Jesuits in Ingolstadt was due to their insistence on the University statutes which required graduates to swear allegiance to the Church. This rigour, as the lay professors styled it, annoyed the candidates and prevented them from coming forward. But Ingolstadt was not singular in its Lutheran trend. South of the Alps the same thing was going on, and with such unhappy results for Germany that St. Peter implored Laynez to seek a remedy from the Pope. He pointed out that many Lutherans and other heretics were taking degrees in law and medicine at Italian universities, from which they returned

[1] Hosius, *Opera*, vol. ii (Cologne, 1584), p. 241.
[2] Braunsberger, *Epistulae*, vol. v, p. 75.
[3] M.H., *Epistolae Patris Nadal*, vol. ii, p. 505.

well equipped to disseminate their false doctrines, while many German Catholics who attended the Italian universities suffered damage to both faith and morals in the process. The direct result of these representations was an article of Church legislation which is still in force and affects, not only all priests and professors, but all persons converted to Catholicism from Protestant denominations. Laynez laid St. Peter's petition before St. Charles Borromeo and Cardinal Simonetta. They took the matter to Pope Pius who, on November 13, 1564, issued a Bull enacting that in future no clerical or lay person was to teach theology, philosophy, law, medicine, grammar, or other liberal arts, nor to be created a master or doctor in the same, unless they had previously made public profession of the Catholic Faith according to the formula set forth in the Bull. That formula was the famous *Professio Fidei Tridentinae*, or *Creed of Pope Pius IV*, which appeared now for the first time.[1]

Reports reached Laynez at this period that Peter was killing himself with overwork. To the General's kindly remonstrance, he replied : " I could not but reverently take to heart your paternal admonition about moderating my labours. Would that I could keep discretion, the mother of virtues, in any department ! But I hope for better things through the holy prayers of the Fathers interceding for me with the Divine Majesty." He had the meanest opinion in the world of his work and ability. If things chanced to turn out well he would fix the credit on Father Nadal or some other man. If they went badly, it was always *mea culpa !* Towards the close of 1563 he had written to Laynez about the difficulties in connexion with the house in Augsburg and with some of the colleges : " I mention these matters," he said, " simply to provide a good opportunity for submitting the whole question to Father Nadal and for taking steps to help, not only this house, but our whole Province, by changing its head, the Provincial. On him the colleges chiefly depend, and I do not want them to be hindered and inconvenienced any longer by the prolonged absences or unworthiness of their Provincial. Perhaps, as I hope, your Reverence will be able to settle this question before you leave Trent so that we may begin the new year with a new government and happier administration of this Province, whatever may eventually be decided about Canisius. *Dominus in suam gloriam haec vertat omnia !* "[2]

The house in Augsburg referred to above was the cause of much anxiety because, utterly against Peter's wishes, his non-Jesuit friends

[1] Braunsberger, *Epistulae*, vol. iv, pp. 653-4 ;   *Bullarum Romanorum Pontificum amplissima collectio*, vol. iv, part ii (Rome, 1745), pp. 203-4.
[2] Braunsberger, *Epistulae*, vol. iv, p. 412.

had made plans to secure for him the Dominican monastery of the city. Writing to Laynez on December 16, 1564, he said: "Those who are urging the cause of a college for us here have drawn over the Duke of Bavaria to their view, and trust now that they will be able to obtain from the Pope that the monastery of the Dominicans may be ours. *Fiat voluntas Domini*. We are in terror about the whole thing and expect some persecution from it, especially as the friars have already got wind of the business. The Cardinal seems to be in a conspiracy with the Duke and the Fuggers to press the affair in Rome, no matter what the consequences afterwards."[1] That was how bad feeling was made between men than whom there should have been no better friends. Peter struggled with all his might to keep the peace, but what could he do with such wire-pulling going on in Rome? The Duke of Bavaria wrote telling the Pope that there were only four Dominicans left in the monastery and that they had not enough to live on or any hope of finding others to replace them when they became too old and feeble for work. He would provide for them liberally in another place where they would be able to carry on their mission with much greater comfort. So the plausible story ran, the only factor omitted being the fundamental one that men do not like to be ejected for the convenience of other people.

Meantime, the Catholic Church in general and the Society of Jesus in particular had suffered a terrible misfortune. On July 25, 1564, Emperor Ferdinand died, after a long and painful illness, during which he edified all about him by his deep piety and earnest concern for the Church. He asked his Dominican confessor to put away all ceremony and address him as "Brother Ferdinand," just as he would the simplest of the faithful. His last counsels and exhortation to Maximilian were that he should prove himself a loyal and obedient Catholic. Throughout his illness, St. Peter and the Jesuits everywhere had prayed unceasingly for the Emperor, and when he passed to God each priest of the Society offered twelve Masses for the repose of his soul. At the same time, Peter initiated a campaign of prayer that God would give Maximilian grace "to follow in his Father's footsteps."[2] But though the Pope and the King of Spain each appealed to the new Emperor to be merciful to the Jesuits he, at first, showed a distinct inclination towards revenge for such old scores as Peter's opposition to his beloved Phauser. The Viennese Jesuits expected to get their marching orders any minute. The courtiers, they said, were shouting,

[1] Braunsberger, *Epistulae*, vol. iv, pp. 763–5.
[2] Braunsberger, *Epistulae*, vol. iv, pp. 598, 607.

Crucifige! At the height of the crisis the good Duke of Bavaria expressed to Peter his readiness to give his brethren a refuge, should they be expelled, but Maximilian proved kindlier than the prognostications and not only let them stay in their college but gradually adopted a more friendly attitude towards them. Peter, however, continued to remain out of favour, but he did not mind that very much so long as Max kept friendly with the Pope. A thing that pleased the Saint immensely was that the Emperor retained the services of his father's confessor, Sittard, the man who had turned on him so roughly in Innsbruck a year before.[1]

Six months after Ferdinand's death Laynez followed him, worn to skin and bone at the age of fifty-three by his almost unbelievable labours for the Church.[2] Telling the sad news to Cardinal Hosius, St. Peter said : " Though we cannot but feel to the depths of our hearts the loss of so great and good a man, still we trust to be helped by his charitable intercession, so that the earthly warfare of our Society may be directed to successful achievement. May he live in Christ for ever, as he most certainly does." The General's death entailed a summons to Rome for Peter, where the congregation to elect a successor was appointed to take place on June 20, 1565. Before accompanying him thither we may round off the impressions of this chapter with a few illustrative odds and ends.

Though he showed such unflinching opposition to Protestant propaganda and such readiness to employ force in suppressing it, Peter by no means felt hostility to individual Protestants. He liked and praised the doctor who attended his brethren in Dillingen, for all that he was an avowed and practising Lutheran. Wolfgang, Duke of Zweibrücken, who was a convinced and even crusading one, he styled, " that good Prince," because sure of the man's sincerity. The Duke, on his side, appreciated Peter's goodness and expressed a desire to debate religion with him. The Saint would gladly have agreed, though, as usual, saying that somebody else would be a better choice, but the Pope frowned on the proposal and it never came to anything.[3] Similarly, though Peter might express the strongest condemnation of priests who neglected the laws of the Church, he was keenly alive to their difficulties and by no means blind to the frequent lapses of Rome. The Bull, *In Coena Domini*, which was so named because issued afresh each Holy Thursday, made him very sad when it reached him in April, 1564, as it contained nothing

---

[1] Braunsberger, *Epistulae*, vol. iv, p. 666.

[2] A very touching account of his saintly end from Polanco's pen will be found in Braunsberger, *Epistulae*, vol. iv, pp. 783–6.

[3] Braunsberger, *Epistulae*, vol. iv, pp. 682–3, 1046.

but threats and prohibitions. "Would to God," he wrote, "that we could find some means of helping both pastors and people in the present great corruption, especially as every mortal thing seems full of excommunications. Nobody cares to give a little aid and consolation to the unhappy pastors who still sweat and labour for the religion which is dear to them. . . . This is an old complaint, well known to Father Nadal, who promised to do something to secure a more kindly treatment for Germans in the matter of ecclesiastical censures, and to obtain greater consideration in Rome for parish priests who desire and are able to help the Catholic cause."[1]

Peter's letters are full of little stories that reveal his habitual kindness. He has a valued French subject in Munich, Père Henri Arduin, but the poor man is a martyr to insomnia. Perhaps, thinks Peter, it is the air of " la belle France " he needs, and home he goes, whatever the inconvenience to Germany. Another subject, a good and promising French novice, cannot get his tongue round the German gutturals. People laugh at him when he attempts to speak, so he is very unhappy until Father Provincial finds him a place among the Jesuits of his own country. Martin Florentius of Amsterdam is a very learned and useful master at Dillingen. But his health is poor and he sighs for Holland, though afraid to return to his family who have become estranged from him. St. Peter splits the difference, and supplies him with money and a horse to take him to Cologne, where he is well known and may be said to have one foot in Holland. "I shall write," he informed Laynez, "asking the Cologne Provincial to judge for himself by an interview with the good and learned man. He is in hopes of benefiting from food and air more like those of his own country, and offers himself for any sort of work, however lowly. He is a truly sincere and friendly man who deserves to have better health and to be kept in our Society."[2]

We have seen how Peter had to be warned from Rome more than once not to work too hard. Devoted man that he was, he never knew when he himself erred in this respect but quickly guessed when somebody else made the mistake. Thus, in a letter to Laynez, he says: " I must once again intrude into another's sphere and warn you about the Rector of Vienna. As if he had not already enough to do, he is now preaching Italian sermons and delivering a lecture daily in the schools. This burden makes it impossible for me not to feel deeply for him."

[1] Braunsberger, *Epistulae*, vol. iv, p. 509.
[2] Braunsberger, *Epistulae*, vol. iv, pp. 487, 498.

Finally, as a reflex of Peter's character, we may give a letter which he wrote to his sister, Wendelina, on April 13, 1564, when he was overwhelmed with work and worries:

May God's grace, love and peace be with us always.

Dear Sister Wendel, I have good hopes that you and all our brothers and sisters remain strong and steadfast in the holy Catholic Faith of our fathers. That is your greatest good, the most necessary and blessed thing for you in this world and the next. Woe, and woe again, to all disloyal, obstinate, and frivolous Christians who separate themselves in matters of faith from the unity and obedience of our beloved Mother, the Spouse of Christ, the Holy Roman Church.

Secondly, I earnestly beg and exhort you all to bring up your children in the fear of God, and, as upright and religious parents, to direct them by word and example in the way of quiet, Christian conduct, and not to give them too free a rein but to check them seriously should they be guilty of folly, or of sinful or knavish tricks. For you have to give an account before the Judgment Seat of Christ for these souls entrusted to your care.

Thirdly, I beg you all again and again often to pray God that He would give you grace to expiate your own sins with true confession and penance in this life before His justice overtakes and punishes in the other world what our sloth and negligence left unconfessed and unexpiated here below. . . .

Fourthly, I greatly desire to see among you love and unity, as true brothers and sisters and friends. Put away all ill-will, covetousness, hatred, and envy. Let each one counsel and help the others wherever and whenever there is need. Abide in love with all your neighbours. Be good to the dear poor . . . knowing that Christ will repay you abundantly for the kindness you show to His needy ones.

Finally, I know not what else to say than that I desire with all my heart to see you zealous in faith, devout in prayer, united in peace, God-fearing in conduct, and at last in our eternal Fatherland happy and blessed, through Jesus Christ Our Lord. . . .[1]

There is not much of Madame de Sévigné's grace and tenderness in that letter home, but St. Peter was no master of phrases and could only say the trite things which, meaning little to most of us, meant all the actuality of Heaven and Hell to him.

---

[1] Braunsberger, *Epistulae*, vol. iv, p. 495. Peter wrote in German, and the letter needs to be read in German for its full savour to be appreciated.

CHAPTER XV

WAYFARING YEARS

The financial difficulties of the Jesuits in Dillingen compelled their Provincial to take a strong line with Cardinal Truchsess. Being very fond of display, his Lordship maintained a fine choir and band of musicians at his court. St. Peter's personal feeling with regard to music is nowhere revealed, but he certainly held that there were a few other things in life more important than singing or playing on the virginals, and he told the Cardinal in equivalent terms that he must choose between his musicians and his Jesuits. Not for a moment did the lovable and magnanimous spendthrift become offended with his monitor. The most he did was to twit him gently for lack of confidence, and to suggest that he ought to display more of the optimistic spirit of his Apostolic namesake and less of St. Thomas's caution. All the same, he disbanded the showy choir to which St. Peter was hostile, and set himself in real earnest to the rehabilitation of his University. That the Saint loved him very dearly is proved by a hundred references, so the constant necessity of keeping him up to the mark must have been a thoroughly distasteful task. But Peter Canisius was never one to shrink from distasteful duties. How little the large-hearted Cardinal resented his interference became apparent when Peter received his summons to Rome. Writing to St. Francis Borgia, the interim ruler of the Society of Jesus, on February 16, 1565, the Cardinal said : " I know by personal experience and have learned from many other Princes with what ardour of Christian charity and erudition Canisius has employed his talents, especially at the Diets of the Empire. He is held in such great esteem by the Princes of Germany that he will be able to render inestimable services with his learning, his preaching and his saintly example. . . . It is incredible the amount of confidence these men repose in him." A new Diet, on which much depended, had been summoned at this time, and Truchsess dreaded the absence of St. Peter from it. To his relief, however, the meeting was postponed, whereupon he addressed himself once more to Borgia, urging the importance of sending Peter straight home as soon as a new Jesuit General had been elected. "Your Reverence and all others may tell yourselves for certain," he said, "that every time Germany is without Canisius she is deprived of assistance in matters of religion greater than you could credit. Such is the fruit of salvation to this country which comes of his incessant and most zealous labours that we may safely say his proper, divine vocation is in Germany."[1]

Peter left Augsburg on his long journey towards the end of April, 1565. He had with him two companions and at Munich was joined by a third, Father Paul Hoffaeus, a delegate to the general congregation. Hoffaeus cannot have been a very agreeable travelling companion because, though a most zealous and energetic Jesuit, he was an utter pessimist, especially about himself. The party halted at Innsbruck for St. Peter to give his sixteen brethren there a series of meditations preparatory to the renewal of their vows. The royal ladies also occupied his attention but, despite very earnest efforts, he failed to wean them from their excessive and highly embarrassing attachment to his Order. The next stage of the journey was the long one to Mantua, which city came in sight on May 8th. Four days later the wayfarers were in Bologna, among their brethren again. There they remained a little while, chiefly in order to rest Peter's horse, which had gone lame. From Bologna they proceeded to Forli, with two boys, the natural sons of Duke Ernest of Bavaria, added to the party. At this point St. Peter made a detour to Rimini and Pesaro that he might pay his respects to a good friend of the Jesuits who resided in the latter place. Resuming the journey, the party reached Loreto via Fano on May 19th, and three days later were off again for the last stage through the Roman Apennines, the Sabine mountains, and the desolate, fever-stricken Campagna.

It says something for St. Peter's reticence that even Loreto failed to drag a few picturesque lines from his pen. Like the Mother of God, to whom he had the tenderest devotion, he preferred to keep the deep things of his experience sealed in his heart. Luckily, however, reticence was not the strong point of Fynes Moryson, Esq., who made exactly the same journey through Italy twenty years after St. Peter, and so we are enabled to realize something of what it must have entailed. Travel in those days was certainly *travail*, to judge by Moryson's perpetual grumblings. Being a well-to-do English Protestant gentleman, Fynes

[1] Braunsberger, *Epistulae*, vol. v, pp. 728–9, 731.

made his way in comparative comfort, but that did not prevent him bemoaning the misery of the inns, the annoyance of the tipping system and the passport regulations, the bewildering variety of coinages, the dearness of food, hay, clothes, and the tricks by which landlords and guides fleeced the stranger. At Padua, where he remained for some months to improve his Italian, Moryson sold his horse for twenty silver crowns. Half a page of his famous *Itinerary* is devoted to lamentation over that bad bargain. How careful he was with his accounts may be seen from the following specimen out of his shopping-book in Padua : " I remember I bought a pound of butter for five sols and a halfe, a fat hen for two lires, six eggs eight sols, six oranges for one gaget, apples the pound two sols, a secchio of wine thirty-five sols, ten snailes foure sols, waxe candles the ounce two sols. I paid to my Taylor for making a cloake foure lires, and for my doublet and hose eight lires ; to my laundresse for making a shirt a lire, that is, twenty sols ; for washing it two sols ; and for washing foure handkerchers one sol. And this shall suffice for particular expenses." At the gates of Bologna customs officers were waiting for the travellers. " The souldiers demanded a curtesie of us," reported Moryson, " which we gladly gave them, perceiving they would not search our portmanteaus, which otherwise of their office they may do." Then there was trouble over a post-horse and the sad parting with two small coins before Fynes might cross a river at Bel' Aria. On reaching the March of Ancona he became nervous. " These inhabitants of Marca," he says, " are accounted a wicked generation, the greatest part of the cut-throtes and murtherers dispersed through Italy being borne in this Country. Our Hoste used us very ill, demaunding of each of us a *polo* for our bed and three *poli* for our supper ; and when we desired a reckoning demaunding for a little piece of an Ele one *polo* and a halfe, and for three little Soles tenne *bolinei*."

All the joyous bigotry of Cambridge comes out in Moryson's account of the Holy House of Loreto. He misinterpreted everything, and, gentleman though he boasted himself, allowed his hatred of Catholicism to get the better of his good manners. " Myselfe and two Dutch-men,[1] my consorts," he relates, " abhorring from this superstition, by leave entered the inner Chappell where we did see the Virgin's picture, adorned with pretious jewels, and the place (to increase religious horror) being darke, yet the jewels shined by the light of wax candles. When we were entered the Priest courteously left us, to give us space for our devotion :

[1] Germans.

but when we came forth it was necessarie for us to cast almes into an iron chest behind the Altar, covered with an iron grate. Therefore, my consorts of purpose to delight the Priest's eares with the sound of money, as with musicke, did cast into that chest many brasse quatrines, but of small value, and myselfe being last, when my turne was to give almes, did in stead thereof gather some tenne quatrines of theirs which lay scattered upon the grate, and got that clear gaine of that Idoll. God forbid I should bragge of any contempt to Religion ; but since it appears that such worship is unpleasing to God, and because Papists will have all their miracles believed, I will freely say by experience that having gotten these few quatrines in such sort as I said, yet after that God of his mercy preserved me in my long and dangerous travell, and from that time to this day by his grace I have enjoyed, though no abundant, yet a complete estate, and more plentifull than in former times."[1] That little story is a good example of the Protestant spirit with which St. Peter had usually to contend and it provides some justification for the very rare occasions when he used hard words about the Church's opponents. Nearly all Protestants in those days who wrote books or left other memorials of themselves, would seem to have forgotten common decency and humanity in their attitude to the Catholic Church. Montaigne saw one of them endeavour to snatch the Host out of the priest's hands at Mass in Rome. The same observant traveller was in Loreto shortly before Moryson and attests that, not only did the officials there refuse to accept gratuities, but that the ordinary craftsmen of the town declined any remuneration for making votive offerings commissioned by pilgrims, beyond the bare cost of the materials.[2]

As St. Peter rode by the sea to Ancona along the pilgrim's way he must have noticed the beacons dotted all down the coast for signalling the approach of a Turkish or corsair galley. Little did he dream that tragedy had befallen two young subjects of his own on those calm, blue waters only a few weeks earlier. He had sent them from Ingolstadt to Rome and, as one was a sick man, directed them to take ship at Venice for Ancona, so as to avoid the tiring journey by land. Not long afterwards the following letter reached him from one of the pair :

[1] *Itinerary* (London, 1617), part i, p. 100.

[2] With regard to Protestant fears when travelling in Italy or visiting Rome, Bates has the following remark : " It may safely be assumed that the danger was not quite so great as the fear, and that, where the former was incurred, the sufferer had only himself to blame." *Touring in 1600*, p. 112. In Churchill's *Voyages*, vol. vii, there is the story of an English Protestant sailor named Davis who fell ill in Rome in 1598. Though he made no secret of his religion he was civil about it, and relates that not only was he cared for in a hospital without charge but that he received food and money on his departure.

JESUS

May the peace of Our Lord be always with us. It has pleased the Divine Goodness, Reverend Fathers,[1] that on account of my sins I should be captured by the Turks on the way from Venice to Ancona. My companion, John of Trier, has been drowned, I am told. As the ship was not far from the shore he threw himself into the sea in hopes of saving himself from the Turks, but it was all in vain because he could not swim. Though profoundly grieved by his death, I could wish now, were it not a sin, that I had shared his fate. He has suffered only one death, but to me there remain as many deaths as the days I spend a slave in the galleys. My master has brought me to a place near Avlona[2] . . . and demands for my ransom a hundred and fifty *zecchini*. . . . Though I know, Reverend Fathers, that it is a heavy price and that I deserve nothing from the Society of Jesus for whose many benefits to me I have given only trouble in return, yet, seeing that I have been captured by the Turks on a journey ordered by the Society and that so much money is demanded because I belong to the Society, I beg you by the Wounds of Jesus Christ, if you cannot help me yourselves, as you did Brother Anselm, to recommend me in your sermons and to bring my case to the notice of bishops, cardinals, and other charitable gentlemen. . . . Oh, Reverend Fathers, Reverend Fathers, do not abandon me, but help me and let me not die in despair. I suffer more in this place than anyone could believe. Life at the oar is for me a continual death of blows and beatings. I see myself dying by inches, so I turn to you, Reverend Fathers, to free me from my chains. . . .[3]

The Jesuits were so miserably poor at this time that it took them five months to collect the necessary *zecchini*. St. Peter contributed a substantial part of the sum and promised more, but meantime the unhappy captive had been liberated through the good offices of some kind-hearted merchants in the East. He had been a very unsatisfactory Jesuit and a considerable worry to his Provincial, yet, knowing the style of man St. Peter was, he addressed him the following lines written on board ship in the Mediterranean, July 4, 1566: "Very Reverend Father in Christ.

[1] The letter was addressed to four others besides St. Peter.
[2] In Albania on the Strait of Otranto.
[3] Braunsberger, *Epistulae*, vol. v, pp. 58–61.

The heavy sorrow which the news of my captivity caused you makes me forget the danger from hostile craft, the stormy weather, and the discomforts of the vessel in order to send you the good news of my liberation, that from it your Reverence may derive joy even greater than was your sorrow over my servitude."

The fate of that young man illustrates one danger of travel in olden times but there were so many others that in German the two words, travel and danger, are apparently derived from a common root. An old English authority grimly advised a prospective traveller to make two things, his peace with God and his will; and another man, experienced on the road, comforted the stay-at-homes with the reflection that travel combined all the disadvantages of both death and Hell. Up and down the old guide-books are such hints as that you should not venture forth without food of some sort in your pocket, if only to throw to dogs which attacked you, and that you should not omit to look behind any large pictures there might be on the walls of your inn bedroom. Of travellers to Rome, in particular, it used to be said that they required " the back of an ass, the belly of a hog and a conscience as broad as the king's highway."[1]

For anything to the contrary in his letters St. Peter's journey Romewards might have been as easy as crossing the street. There is not a single word of complaint about the inns or the food or the weather or the roughness of the way, all things about which Fynes Moryson made such a doleful song. But then Peter was what one might call a specialist in hardship, with something to live for better than comfort or the satisfaction of curiosity. He rode in through the Porta del Popolo on May 28th, and at once set to work with the brethren already assembled to prepare for the forthcoming congregation.

The congregation opened on June 21st and ten days later St. Francis Borgia was elected third General of the Society of Jesus at the first scrutiny. As the other business of the assembly, in which St. Peter played a prominent rôle, was largely of a routine character, interesting only to Jesuits and not always to them, it is unnecessary to say anything about it. During the congregation the Saint received a letter from his half-brother, Theodoric, who was governing the Upper German Province in his absence. This letter mentioned the names of no fewer than nine men in the College of Dillingen who were either confirmed invalids or in other ways unsuited for their work. It is no joke to have half of one's staff out of commission, so Peter drew up a memorial for the Fathers in Rome about conditions

[1] Bates, *Touring in 1600*, pp. 58–9.

in Germany and the special qualifications required in those sent to labour there. Nadal once made a list of German 'vices' which events of our own day have curiously endorsed. He noted in particular a certain "*magnitudo animi*" which, being translated, means bumptiousness. It led, he wrote, to an almost complete disregard for people of other nations and to an especial aversion for Italians. The Germans tended to be bullies when in authority and abjectly servile when in a position of subjection. Their hankering after dignities, honours, and emoluments fairly matched that of the Spaniards, which was saying a great deal, but the Germans left the Spaniards nowhere when it came to demolishing quantities of meat or absorbing incredible oceans of strong drink. Unlike modern Germans, though, they deliberately set out to get drunk and were proud of it.[1] Better even than Nadal did St. Peter know the failings of his adopted countrymen, and he now urged that special care should be taken over the training of German novices. By attaching themselves to the Society of Jesus they did not relinquish their ancestry; and the wild, undisciplined conditions in which, often enough, their youth had been passed rendered a strict training imperative if they were to be of the least advantage to their native land. "Let it be held for a certain rule," wrote the Saint, "that those who cannot be cured of their faults in Rome will become worse on returning to Germany. Better, then, that they should be dismissed from the Society rather than sent back there. No Germans ought to be sent back but those whose constancy has been proved in Rome and whose virtue is known from the tests and experiments of our institute." After solid virtue the chief requirements were good health and commonsense. As life in the Upper German Province was more strenuous and arduous than perhaps anywhere else in the Society of Jesus, Peter begged his superiors not to dump invalids on him, and to be careful that Jesuit students in Rome did not contract tuberculosis. Then, speaking of other 'nationals' who might be sent north, he said: "In the training of the young men the Roman Fathers should remember to inculcate that there be nothing of hostility or superciliousness in their feelings towards the Germans but rather the most complete charity and benevolence. Let them not wax indignant with the heretics as men, or attack them by name, or in an embittered fashion, either publicly or privately. Let them believe that the Germans will be reconciled to our Society most of all by a certain courtesy and modesty in which its members ought to excel." In the pulpit of Augsburg the Saint had been led, half in sorrow and half in anger,

[1] M.H., *Epistolae Patris Nadal*, vol. iv, pp. 212–3.

to castigate the vices of the clergy, but he now recognized that this action was unwise. "Let superiors not suffer," he continued, "that anyone in the colleges or elsewhere should judge or spread rumours about even bad prelates, priests, or monks. Rather must they, as far as possible, carefully defend the authority of such people."[1]

Apart from the business of the congregation St. Peter found plenty to occupy his time in Rome. One matter that particularly engaged his attention was the fate of Germans who had fallen foul of the Inquisition. At this time, Rome, no more than Wittenberg or Geneva, made any pretence to be tolerant of heretics within her gates. If they kept quiet and made no parade of their Protestantism they might come and go as they pleased, but once their profession became public they were liable to arrest. Peter and Father Hoffaeus had some intimate talks on the subject with the Grand Inquisitor, Cardinal Ghislieri, soon to be Pope St. Pius V. As already shown, neither Peter nor any other Jesuit had the least desire to be mixed up in the affairs of the Inquisition. They certainly believed, in common with practically all the Protestants and Catholics of their day, that it was legitimate and right to use force in the repression of religious dissent but they considered it a last and desperate remedy with which priests as such should have no concern. Only with difficulty could they be persuaded even to visit prisoners and argue with them, so the remarks of St. Peter as reported by the worthy whose story follows must be taken with considerable reservations. He was a man aged twenty-eight, Philip, the son of the eminent Protestant scholar, Joachim Camerarius. After wandering through Italy quite freely for two months, Philip and his companion, Rieter, were arrested in Rome in June on a charge of being concerned in some brawl. When their identity became known they were transferred to the prison of the Inquisition where they found "several pious men confined in separate cubicles but without chains, on account of having confessed or being merely suspected of evangelical truth." Three days later Philip was brought before the Dominican Inquisitor, who, he says, put to him questions "full of devilish craft and delusion." Cardinal Ghislieri then asked St. Peter to see whether he could influence the young man, and this is how Philip reported the interview when he was safely back in Germany:

A few days later, Peter Canisius, head of the new sect who like to be called " Companions of Jesus," hearing of our detention from

[1] Braunsberger, *Epistulae*, vol. v, pp. 78–82.

some source unknown to us and, perhaps, also because of my name, obtained permission from the Cardinal of Ara Coeli and came to the House of the Inquisition, where is also the prison. On my being summoned to him in a private room he began a long-winded address in Latin. The fact that I was a German like himself, he said, had led him to visit me, that he might offer me all the assistance and service in his power in such great danger. He had obtained leave from the Cardinals of the Inquisition only after much labour and entreaty and he had put aside other weightier business in order to come. Many more were the honeyed words he uttered, for he had a fluent and garrulous tongue, but as his talk was then wearisome to hear I do not think that I need now report its idle futilities. At length, as though puzzled, he inquired how I had come to this calamitous pass; how I was being treated with regard to food; and was there anything I needed.

Though I had no difficulty in guessing from his dress the sect to which he belonged, I yet told him everything and begged him to carry out what he had spontaneously promised in words of extreme kindness. I said that I was now among strangers and destitute of all human assistance. Then I asked his name so that I might keep for ever the memory of his kindness. 'They call me Peter,' he answered smiling a little, and then turned the conversation into other channels with an exhortation that I should think seriously about my position. . . . Though I did not trust him (for I began to recollect having seen him several times at the Conference of Worms in 1557 and having heard him preach in the cathedral there), yet when he again offered his services in the most courteous terms I desired to test his good-will in a small matter. . . . I therefore asked him to have me sent the Psalms of David that I might seek comfort from them in my trouble. He promised to do so and anything else I liked, but said that I would be better advised to read carefully the book called *The Office of the Blessed Virgin*, commending the wonderful efficacy of the prayers contained therein. But when I persisted in my request for the Psalter, saying that I did not know what the other book contained, he went off simulating great friendliness.

Shortly after, I received from him Caesar's *Commentaries* in Italian and another book full of fables and idle stories, telling the exploits of a certain Amadis de Gaul.[1] Some days later I was brought by order

---

[1] This story-book was one of those in the library of Don Quixote. St. Ignatius revelled in it before his conversion and it was incidents in it that led him to keep his vigil of arms before the altar of Our Lady of Montserrat. That St. Peter should have sent Camerarius such light reading is surely proof of the genuineness of his human sympathy for the prisoner. Philip's disdain for the gifts does not make one love him the more. He was plainly a superior person.

of Canisius a book of the Polish bishop, Hosius, on Christian Doctrine. Among other things which this valiant champion of Papistry teaches are that it is unnecessary to be versed in the Law and the Scriptures, and that labour expended on the Scriptures is waste of time, seeing that they are a created thing and a beggarly element. When myself and my friend had read a few pages we easily perceived why Canisius had sent us this book. So we stopped forthwith and flung it aside in a corner of the cell amid the dust. . . .[1]

Philip and his companion did not have long to pine in prison. They were set free without any recantation after two months and given back all their belongings except one heretical book. When, in 1600, Philip was cited before the High Court of Germany on suspicion of having committed some crime during his visit to Rome, the Jesuits came forward to testify that religion alone was the cause of his imprisonment. He accordingly left without a stain on his character, but one may be allowed to think that hearty participation in a street fight, or even an adventure in burglary, is much less of a bad mark against a man than the conceit and ingratitude which misrepresent the honest efforts of somebody to do a good turn.

Far away in Poland, the good Hosius, whose book had been so rudely treated by Camerarius, was wondering what had become of his friends the Jesuits. "Should your Lordship happen to see Peter Canisius," he wrote to Cardinal Commendone, "give him my greetings and at the same time expostulate with him for having forgotten me altogether. Not only he but the whole Society has forgotten. I have not received a single letter from any of them throughout the summer. With the new General all things are become new." Peter, however, had by no means forgotten, and before his friend's complaint reached Rome the following letter was on its way to Ermland:

I have been here now nearly four months and those the summer ones, but I shall be returning to Germany shortly, with the help of the Lord. Meantime, I am thankful to the Divine Goodness for having given us an excellent Father and General, and for having graced our congregation with various blessings and saving counsels. Among those present was Father Salmeron, well known to your Highness. He desired me, before his return to Naples, to enclose a letter for you with my own.

[1] Braunsberger, *Epistulae*, vol. v, pp. 743–6. The remarks about Hosius are a complete misrepresentation.

As others often write to you about what goes on in the City, it would be pointless were I to repeat them, or give you news less well authenticated. I have had keen joy here from my intercourse with the most eminent among the cardinals, who are men completely devoted to the interests of the Church. May Christ preserve for us those strong, illustrious pillars of His Church, Cardinals Dolera, Amulio, Sirleto, and Ghislieri, to mention no others. As for Cardinal Borromeo, better be silent on the subject of his piety and goodness than say too little about them. But I beg and exhort your Highness not to cease stirring up these men by your letters to diligent care for the well-being of the Catholic Church. They need the spur, and frequent application of it, because, though they hear of and perfectly understand the diseases to which our German people are subject, yet, being far away from the sufferers and unable to look upon their sores and wounds, they are, perhaps, moved with less anxiety and zeal to cure them. Besides, it is difficult to estimate a situation to which we are not present with the same nicety as one under our eyes.

As for the Supreme Pontiff, I cannot but wonder at his benignity and tender regard for an ungrateful and largely rebellious Germany. He has expressed to me at great length the large benevolence, care, and solicitude wherewith he embraces our countrymen. He seeks remedies and tries various means of helping the illustrious nation, and sorrows that his efforts should be not only unavailing but even hurtful in the present perverse state of affairs. . . .[1]

St. Peter's delay in Rome weeks after the congregation had dispersed was due to another effort of the Pope to rescue the Church in Germany. No sooner was the Council of Trent at an end than His Holiness made earnest attempts to secure the enforcement of its decrees in the Catholic parts of that country. But the task was beset with difficulties, including the unexpected one of getting the decrees accurately on to paper. Eventually the Pope requested the great Venetian printer, Paolo Manuzio, to come to Rome for the purpose and then, when all was ready, he dispatched a secret envoy with copies of the newly-printed decrees to the Catholic bishops, princes, and universities of Germany. These, however, never reached their destination, as the envoy was waylaid and robbed of them *en route*. Once again, then, must Pius set to work, this time with more

---

[1] Braunsberger, *Epistulae*, vol. v, pp. 96–7. In the last sentence Peter is referring especially to the concession of the chalice.

PIVS · IIII · PONT · OPT · MAX ·

Pope Pius IV
From a copperplate engraving by Nicholas Beatrizet (c. 1515-1560)

elaborate precautions. The principle used in the choice of the new envoy was the one on which Father Brown carried out some of his criminal investigations, that there is nobody so invisible as the person one is most expecting to see. Peter Canisius fulfilled the conditions to perfection and had other qualifications to which neither the Pope nor the cardinals were blind. He was accordingly singled out for the mission, as explained in the following letter addressed by the Pope to Cardinal Truchsess on September 19th :

PIUS PAPA IIII

Venerable Brother, Health and Apostolic Benediction.

It has pleased Us to withdraw Our beloved son, Peter Canisius, for a time from the office which he is wont to fill in your diocese. For, owing both to his goodness and his great knowledge of German affairs, he seemed to Us a suitable person to be entrusted with the duty of visiting in Our name several parts of Germany and carrying to them instructions the nature of which you will learn from himself.

We beg you to take this arrangement in good part and to help towards the execution of Our wishes with your counsels and admonitions. Having saluted your Fraternity in Our words, he will disclose certain matters to you, concerning which We know that you will have confidence in his relation. We know, too, that it is unnecessary for Us to exhort you to persevere in your excellent labours for the Catholic religion. You have always done so with so much zeal that your example ought to have been a spur to other prelates of that nation. But while praising in the Lord your pious diligence with regard to other matters, We especially signify Our approval of your University of Dillingen and We desire it to be most lovingly and studiously cherished by you. From it as from a nursery We hope to see many devout and learned men come forth as defenders of the Catholic religion. You may be assured that Our help and favour will never fail you in its protection and in the advancement of your other pious designs.[1]

To avoid possible opposition in Germany the Pope decided not to constitute St. Peter a nuncio in the technical sense. As far as possible his mission was to be kept secret, so, to mask his real business, St. Francis Borgia appointed him official " Visitor " of the three German Provinces

[1] Braunsberger, *Epistulae*, vol. v, pp. 640-1.

of the Society of Jesus. This appointment was made widely known, but it is significant that the Brief containing it makes no mention of any power of jurisdiction. In fact, it was almost entirely a blind. A few days after the issue of the Brief, Peter received a letter of secret instructions from Polanco, directing him to keep in touch with Cardinal Amulio and another man disguised under the pseudonym of " Ausonio Gallo," who may have been the Pope himself or his nephew, St. Charles Borromeo, or his intimate adviser, Cardinal Tolomeo Galli. To ensure that there should be no tampering with these letters he was to employ a special seal and to transmit them to Rome through some trusted lay friend in Augsburg.

The purpose of the mission was not merely to present the bishops with authentic copies of the decrees of Trent. Peter must also confer with them and with the secular authorities on questions of ecclesiastical policy, and, in particular, use every effort to secure that they prepared for and acted in concert at the approaching Reichstag, about which there was cause, on the Catholic side, for serious foreboding. On the issue of this Diet would probably depend the future of the Church in Germany, as the Lutherans were more than ever determined to get rid of the restrictive clauses in the Peace of Augsburg.

Before leaving Rome, armed with the Tridentine decrees and a series of credential letters from the Pope, St. Peter made his way to the Roman College for the purpose of seeing a young student named Giulio Mancinelli who was rumoured to be something of a saint. Would Giulio in his kindness give the wayfarer " *alcune pie consideratione* " to sustain him on the long journey home ? The young man was greatly perturbed by the request but acceded when he saw how genuinely his distinguished visitor meant it. Afterwards Peter wrote from Augsburg to thank his young friend for all the spiritual consolation he had derived from his counsels.[1]

The journey home was made via Narni to Padua on horseback, from which city Peter went aside to Venice, probably by the regular service of river boats. When business was finished there he returned to Padua, and thence made his way through the Venetian Alps and along the broad valley of the Adige to Innsbruck. With regard to his luggage, it should be said that each copy of the Tridentine decrees was a portly tome containing two hundred and fifty pages. It was a matter of books, too, that had taken him to Venice, where he had purchased enough to fill three sacks and had dispatched them to Augsburg for his colleges by the Fugger agent.

---

[1] Braunsberger, *Epistulae*, vol. v, pp. 118–9. Mancinelli fulfilled his early promise and died, after many years of wonderful work, with a reputation for great sanctity.

The first thing Peter did when he reached Innsbruck on October 21st was to go to bed with a high temperature for eight days. Not even his sturdy frame was always equal to the intolerable burdens which his zeal imposed upon it. Despite his grave illness, he tried from his bed to put heart into the doleful Dyrsius who, however, refused to discuss college affairs with him and would scarcely acknowledge his authority. When a little later, it was decided to change this contumacious and exasperating Rector, Father Peltan, the man designated to succeed him, declared that he would rather leave the Society than accept the post, from which it may be seen that all Jesuits in those days were not Francis Xaviers. Indeed, Theodoric Canisius of Dillingen was so appalled at the prospect of having to govern them in St. Peter's absence that he wrote in the following pathetic strain to him:

I have had a letter from Rome bidding me in Father General's name to undertake the care of the Province without relinquishing the burden of my office as Rector. What I ought to think or do I know not, Father. I am perplexed, and greatly fear that God must be angry with me. I find myself weaker in spirit every day, while the burdens increase, and these the burdens of human souls. Scarcely do I breathe freely in obedience. Nevertheless, may the will of the Lord be done in everything, for it can never be other than good, even though these punishments mount up on account of my sins. I have written to Father General begging that he would have pity on my soul and not burden me above that which I am able to bear, lest I soon succumb and be rendered useless to God, myself, and my neighbour. Your Reverence well knows my weakness and the weight of the burden, so I commend my cause to you, *per Christi Jesu viscera*. I know that I am very different from what my superiors persuade themselves I am. They are deceived, in my opinion, by a certain exterior appearance of virtue, but within lie hidden the bones of the dead, rotten and foul.[1]

No sooner had the fever in his veins departed than Peter rode to Augsburg to pay a debt of a hundred and fifty ducats to George Fugger, and to give that friend and his saintly wife news of their two boys in Rome. Then, on All Souls' Day, he went to Dillingen for long conferences with Cardinal Truchsess. November 4th saw him again in the saddle, this time for the winter ride of more than a hundred miles to Würzburg.

[1] Braunsberger, *Epistulae*, vol. v, pp. 108–9, 770.

Those who knew their Germany were very anxious about him, but he got through safely and, at the strongly fortified citadel of Marienberg, placed in the Prince-Bishop's hands the decrees of Trent and a letter from the Pope which began as follows : " Venerable Brother, Health and Apostolic Benediction. We have directed this, Our beloved son, Peter Canisius, professed Father of the Society of Jesus, to visit and greet your Fraternity in Our name and to treat diligently with you about certain matters closely pertaining to your and Our office and to the service of God." The matters referred to were principally the promulgation and execution of the Tridentine decrees and the policy to be pursued at the impending Diet, but there was also much discussion of the college which Bishop von Wirsberg eagerly desired to see established in his dominions. Though St. Peter desired it, too, he was not blind to the difficulties ahead, apart altogether from the practical ones of obtaining the necessary men and money, as according to his report, Würzburg was one of the most disturbed and tragic dioceses in the Empire :

The City is gravely infected with heretical opinions, and the clergy, sunk in their vices, are more like soldiers than saints. From them and from the people our men may well expect as difficult and varied a species of opposition as they will find anywhere in Germany. Among the numerous Franconian nobility only a very few Catholics are to be found and these rarely send their sons here to be educated. Perhaps the Bishop will require a great deal of ministerial work from us, as a result of the many and heavy afflictions which his diocese has suffered. The parish priests apostatize in considerable numbers, to the great scandal of the whole people ; and, as the Principality is not yet at peace, there are multitudes of soldiers here, without whose protection the good old man, our Bishop, dares not go to the Cathedral or, indeed, venture out of his citadel at all. He has to fear the plots and ambuscades of his enemies more than any other bishop.[1]

In accordance with the usual procedure, the building offered to the Jesuits for their college was an old religious foundation, a Poor Clare Convent, still occupied by a few nuns. The chief idea of the Poor Clares when they put the place up was to segregate themselves as much as possible from the world. St. Peter found that they had achieved their purpose only too well and excluded not only the earth but the sun. Much

[1] Braunsberger, *Epistulae*, vol. v, pp. 128–9.

adaptation would be necessary to render the convent habitable as a college, and the Bishop had a reputation for parsimony. Moreover, the Roman Chancery demanded a "composition" of three thousand ducats for the Bull empowering his Lordship to transfer the convent, and that was a sum which his Lordship had no intention of surrendering. In the event, it required much diplomatic effort on the part of St. Peter and his Roman brethren to bring about an arrangement, because, though the Pope signified his complete willingness to grant the Bull without any tax, the curial officials, who received a commission on such transactions, would not give way. "Nothing is to be hoped from these gentlemen when money is in question," wrote the Imperial Ambassador in 1564. "So deaf are their ears to petitions that they seem rather marble statues than human beings."

From Würzburg St. Peter went on to Aschaffenburg, where Archbishop Brendel von Homburg, Elector of Mainz and Lord Chancellor of the Empire, had his palace. To this great Prince the Church in Germany owes an immense debt of gratitude. In his city, "Mainz the Golden," whither Peter repaired when the business of Trent was done, he had established a Jesuit college at which four hundred students attended in 1565. For some time the Archbishop had been striving to endow the college, and also a seminary for poor students under Jesuit supervision, out of the property of his see. The plan met with such determined opposition from the secular canons that Brendel felt obliged to appeal to the Pope over their heads. The Pope readily consented, but St. Peter judged that a mere verbal *fiat* was not a sufficiently safe provision for the future and so it came about that a Bull in set form was petitioned for and granted. To prevent the curial officials from exacting their customary dues the Pope had the document drawn up in secret and transmitted to Peter by Polanco, with the result that the college and seminary benefited to the extent of more than forty thousand Rhenish florins.[1]

Mainz must have awakened in the Saint's soul many a tender and holy memory. It was there, in the Presbytery of St. Christopher, that he had first met Favre and had been received by him as the first German son of the Society of Jesus. That was twenty-two years before; years during which the novice had outstripped the achievement of his wonderful master and done more than any man of the age to launch the tremendous redemptive forces of the Counter-Reformation. In Mainz, too, he met his old pupil and dear friend, Father Lambert Auer, who was

[1] Braunsberger, *Epistulae*, vol. v, pp. 123–4.

gallantly reviving the ancient glories of Rhenish Catholicism. From Father Vinck, the Rhineland Provincial, he tried earnestly to obtain help for the Bishop of Würzburg, but Vinck had not a soul to spare. It was everywhere the same story, mountains of work and dearth of men.

While at Mainz Peter heard rumours that his brethren in Ingolstadt were growing tired of answering the incessant attacks of the Lutherans. Schmidelin, the irrepressible, had just issued a new *Apologia* in which he contended with a wealth of vituperation that " the Koran of the Turks does not make less of Christ than these Zwinglian Jesuits." It was wearisome stuff to have to notice but, for the sake of weaker brethren and on account of Schmidelin's considerable repute, Peter felt an answer to be necessary and wrote urging his men once more into the breach. At this time, too, the old trouble of the Index revived, and we find the Saint busying himself as before to make the burdens of German priests lighter. For years he would continue striving to obtain some relaxation of the very stringent regulations governing the re-admission to the Church of convert Catholics who had relapsed into Lutheranism.[1]

From Mainz Peter travelled down the Rhine to Coblenz, where, in the massive citadel of Ehrenbreitstein which still commands the junction of the two majestic rivers, he renewed acquaintance with the Elector of Trier, Archbishop Johann von der Leyen. Eight years earlier the Saint had been in communication with this Prince about the foundation of a college in his metropolis, and at the Augsburg Diet of 1559 came to know him personally. He must have felt a little uneasy on the present occasion as, over and above his usual ambassadorial duties, he had to deal with a serious abuse in the conduct of his host. The Council of Trent, reaffirming ancient legislation, had decreed that a bishop must be consecrated within three months of his election or forfeit the revenues of his see during that period. Should he allow another three months to elapse without accepting consecration he *ipso facto* forfeited his bishopric. Now, though Elector Johann had been chosen Archbishop of Trier in April, 1556, at the time of St. Peter's visit nearly ten years later he was not yet even a priest. In his Brief to him, delivered by Peter, Pope Pius IV wrote : " The decrees of the Sacred Council of Trent are the chief and final remedy desired so long a time by all good men for healing the very grave and serious wounds of the Church. But this remedy will have been provided in vain by the continuous and great labour of so many illustrious Fathers unless the holy and beneficial decrees are faithfully and zealously made

[1] Braunsberger, *Epistulae*, vol. v, pp. 101, 129.

effective by all those whose office and duty it is to put them into execution."[1] The good and well-meaning Elector must have felt abashed as he read the words, but St. Peter was there to help him, commended by the Pope as one in whom he might repose as much confidence as in himself. The Saint now wrote urgently to Cardinal Amulio, begging him to secure the Pope's retrospective absolution for all that had been irregular in the Prince's conduct. He knew him to be a devout and generous man who, moreover, had this much excuse for his negligence, that at the time of his election the whole province of Trier was in a state of war and rebellion. Under Peter's persuasion he began to desire to put everything right but, for obvious reasons, did not want to be ordained and consecrated by his own suffragans or in his own archdiocese. For this, however, a dispensation had to be obtained, and it was Peter again who expedited the affair in Rome. Despite all his efforts, the Elector, owing to excessively long preparation for Holy Orders, died suddenly in February, 1567, still a layman.

One thing on this visit to Coblenz that must have given Peter immense comfort was the news of the Jesuit college in Trier. It had four hundred and fifty pupils, among them scions of the noblest families in the land. Not its escutcheons, however, but the magnificently Catholic spirit of the school delighted the Saint. Spontaneous devotion to the Mother of God flourished there, and such a detestation of heresy that the boys were in the habit of seizing and destroying all the Protestant books they could discover. Whatever the Electors of Trier may have been like (and the citizens never thought much of them), its ordinary men and women were great Catholics. Indeed, it was not possible to reside in the city on any other terms, as the Stadtrat had passed an ordinance in 1564 that each citizen must possess a voucher from his parish priest that he had been to his Easter duties. Studies, too, were in such excellent condition that a canon of the city could tell a Cologne friend: "Everybody here now philosophizes, and the whole town talks Latin." Through the good offices of St. Peter the work being done at the Jesuit college was put on a secure and permanent basis, for it was he who obtained from the Pope the sanction long desired by the Elector to endow it with the revenues of the derelict Sankt Barbarakloster. A Protestant historian, writing in 1591 of the colleges of Mainz and Trier as they were in 1565, made the following significant statement: "About this time the progress of the Holy Gospel was markedly hindered by the Jesuits, men whom the devil has hatched

Braunsberger, *Epistulae*, vol. v, p. 643.

out in these latter times as his final brood for the destruction of the Church of God."[1]

Peter's next stopping-place was Cologne, where, on November 21st, his dear friend and life-long correspondent, Father Leonard Kessel, received him with open arms. Kessel and the other brethren had been looking forward eagerly to his arrival, not only for the joy of seeing him again, but because they felt sure he must have in his baggage a certain papal dispensation, badly wanted by the University and Senate. Before Father Coster set out for the general congregation in Rome earlier in the year, the senators had impressed on him the necessity of bringing back the dispensation. Coster, however, had to return before he could procure it and, to lessen the shock of his failure, assured the senators that Peter Canisius would be certain to bring it along. Great, then, was the consternation when the Fathers, crowding round Peter, learned that the document was not among his effects. Peter made up his mind at once. Cologne was no place for him until the document arrived, so the following morning he stole quietly out of the city, accompanied by his nephew, Father Denys, and took the well-remembered road to Xanten, Cleves, and Nymegen.[2] Of his doings in the town of his birth on this occasion there are a number of contemporary accounts. It was twenty years since he had seen his family, decades during which they and all the citizens had learned to be proud of him. The magistrates accordingly decreed him an official welcome, and, as was the custom when receiving distinguished visitors, voted a quantity of wine to be drunk in his honour.[3]

The day of Peter's arrival in Nymegen was the feast of St. Catherine of Alexandria, patroness of students, so, barely had he dismounted from his horse when he was asked to address the scholars and staff of the Latin school of the town. The talk, which had necessarily to be extemporized, caused the Dean of St. Stephen's, who heard it, to let himself go as follows in a private letter to a friend: " We listened to him with great admiration at our school, and so beautifully did he speak that he drew tears from the eyes of many learned men. No one could sufficiently admire his eloquence. It was of the kind that baffles description, so intimately were fluent speech and learning united to modesty and humility. His voice flowed like a

---

[1] Cited by Braunsberger, *Epistulae*, vol. v, p. 182.
[2] There is a ridiculous story that, while passing through Marienbaum, the Saint saw a large collection of devils sitting on the roof of a Brigittine convent there; evidence, according to a seventeenth century chronicler, of the sanctity of the nuns. Perhaps it was the lack of visions and miracles in his life that drove pious writers to such concoctions.
[3] The minutes of the proceedings are still to be seen in the town archives: " Ons heren hebben geschenct D. Petro Canisio xxi kwart wijns in Novembri."

rushing river. In one word, the performance seemed to his listeners a very miracle. Who is there to tell adequately of this man's fame or to describe it in worthy terms? O happy age with such proof of faith in thee! O happy Church which has merited in this troubled time to possess such a defender!"[1] Such being his sentiments the Dean could not have failed to ask Peter to preach for him in the great church of his baptism. The canons hung tapestries from the pulpit to honour the occasion and thousands of auditors came, but the sermons were not comprehensible to everybody, as Peter, having forgotten his Dutch, delivered them in German. For the magistrates of the town he reserved a special address, which was given after his sister had put them in a good humour with an excellent banquet.

The other members of the family, envying Wendelina her privilege as Peter's hostess, insisted that he should at least come and dine with them severally. As they formed a numerous clan and each claimed to have a better right than the others, he settled the dispute in the following fashion. The various families were asked to bring all the dishes and wines they intended displaying at their homes to the hospice for the poor and there set them forth in splendid rivalry. Thus would they have a feast in common at which Peter would be present on condition that all the participants came to the hospice in the morning to receive Holy Communion from him. So it was done, and the poor of the town, being residuary legatees of the banquet, fed that day as never before in their lives.[2] But it was the sick ones among them who fared best, as Peter did for them what he would not do for his grand relatives, spending much of his scanty time by their bedsides.

One other little incident of this visit to Nymegen is worth recording. At Peter's suggestion Wendelina invited all their relatives and friends to dinner. On arrival the Saint drew each married pair aside separately into an inner room, where he earnestly exhorted them to constancy in their Catholic faith and asked them to promise with uplifted hand that they and theirs would ever remain true to the Church. They did so willingly and kept their word so well that half a century later, when a hundred and fifty direct descendants of St. Peter's father were alive, not a single one of them had ceased to practise St. Peter's religion, notwithstanding generations of disaster and persecution.

This was the Saint's last sight of his beloved birthplace. Again and again he had tried to secure a footing for his brethren in it, but it was

[1] Braunsberger, *Epistulae*, vol. v, p. 656.   [2] Braunsberger, *Epistulae*, vol. v, pp. 663-4.

not until he had been dead three centuries that the late-flowering seed he planted bloomed into the magnificent Canisiuskollegium, wherein, since 1900, the Jesuits of Nymegen have carried on an ever-developing apostolate of higher education.

Returning to Cologne on December 7th, St. Peter found that the dispensation, without which he dared not face the Senate, was still on its travels, so, the following morning, the feast of the Immaculate Conception, he set out for Düsseldorf to visit the Duke of Cleves. It proved a useless journey, as that semi-Lutheran Prince had gone off on some expedition. With a sigh for lost time the Saint then turned his horse's head towards Westphalia, little suspecting that at that very moment, December 9th, his credentials as a papal envoy had become valueless through the death of Pope Pius IV. Not for more than three weeks did a rumour of the event reach him. His first goal in Westphalia was its capital city, Münster, which, by road, is a good hundred miles from Düsseldorf. Again he found that his long ride had been to no purpose, as the Bishop of Münster was out of town. To save time, he transmitted the Papal Brief and the Tridentine decrees by a courier, and then busied himself with a report to Cardinal Amulio on the state of the diocese. It must have been a distressing task, as it drew from Pope Pius V on June 13, 1566, a letter to the Bishop of Münster and others which contained this strong sentence : " We learn that the chief cause of such gross heresy in Germany is the wicked, indecent, and disgraceful conduct of the clergy." Bishop von Raesfeld was then ordered to compel the priests to give up their concubines, but though, unlike his two predecessors, a fairly good and loyal man, he had not the strength of character for such a campaign and resigned.

Raesfeld's destined successor was the next prelate with whom Peter had to deal, Johann Graf von Hoya, Prince-Bishop of Osnabrück, who resided at Fürstenau in Hanover. The journey thither from Münster lay through seventy or eighty miles of Protestant territory but the Saint was not molested, possibly because he went in disguise. Both Protestants and Catholics vied in praises of his new host, Hoya, whose noble lineage, for he was nephew of Gustavus Vasa, declared itself by fine manners and a cultured mind. Devout of soul, too, he would have made an ideal bishop had he been a bishop, but, alas, he only bore the name and was not even a priest. His diocese was in a terrible state owing to the treachery of his predecessor, Francis von Waldeck, one of the Empire's champion drunkards. Only two churches in Osnabrück City remained to the Catholics, and such priests as survived had mighty little to commend them. In 1561 Hoya had made the acquaintance of the Cologne Jesuits, and at once conceived the idea of founding a college in Osnabrück. The negotiations, to which St. Peter was a party, proved abortive just then, but here he came now in person to start an Advent campaign of great intensity for the perplexed and eager Prince. As far as can be gathered he preached twelve sermons in the space of a fortnight, those following Christmas being rather in the nature of learned discourses on the chief controversies of the day. Between times, he spent long hours in converse with Hoya about the reformation of his diocese but, with all the good will in the world, neither man could do much to remedy its desperate troubles.

Advised by his host, Peter did not go in person to the holy old man of eighty-eight who was Bishop of Paderborn but sent him the Roman documents, with a covering letter, from Fürstenau. Very likely he used the same procedure with George, Duke of Braunschweig-Lüneburg, Bishop of Minden and Archbishop of Bremen, in which places there were so few Catholics that when the Duke died the following year the diocese died with him. Peter's heart bled for these unfortunate prelates. Writing a little later to St. Francis Borgia, he said :

Let it suffice for me to point out that there is hardly a class of men exposed to greater dangers, annoyances, and difficulties than the bishops of Westphalia in particular, and of Germany in general. Unless the Holy Father takes steps in good time, and this he could do in conjunction with the Emperor, I foresee that, on the decease of the bishops, the sectaries will at once rush in and possess themselves of their dioceses. At present they not only occupy but devour about eight sees, not to mention the Archbishop of Magdeburg, formerly Primate of Germany, who has now of his own initiative subjected himself and his church to the Confession of Augsburg. Perhaps it would help if bishops, in their lifetime, chose and associated with themselves coadjutors who would receive confirmation at once from both Pope and Emperor. In this way the sectaries would have less chance of thrusting themselves into the bishops' places and forcibly assuming their authority while the canons were still engaged on the election.

I think it is of great importance that, at the forthcoming Diet, the Emperor and the various rulers of States should be approached about this matter, in order to prevent future sacrilegious profanation, seizure, invasion, and pillage of churches, especially cathedral and metropolitan ones. For if the sectaries continue in their present course of seizing and laying claim to churches in their vicinity, the Catholic religion cannot long be preserved in Germany and the loss will be irreparable.[1]

From Fürstenau St. Peter retraced his steps to find the Duke of Cleves at Düsseldorf. He was a difficult man to handle as his sympathies appeared to be half way between Rome and Wittenberg. Among his chief advisers was the Erasmian Dr. George Cassander whose liberal, anti-Roman views Peter had tried to modify many years before. The Saint, then, had not much of a welcome to expect. Indeed, according to one historian, when the Duke heard of his coming he exclaimed : " What does this mischievous fellow want ? I should be glad if he, as the father of Jesuits, and all his progeny with him, were drowned in the depths of the Rhine." Peter reported on his experiences to St. Francis Borgia in the following terms :

On my arrival here from Westphalia at this Court of the Duke of Cleve-Jülich I heard for the first time of the death of the Pope. May he live with Christ. The news of his passing was sad and bitter for the Catholics everywhere in Germany for they have many reasons to revere the memory of Pius IV and to tell of the great things which he achieved. Notwithstanding the news, I made the Prince acquainted with the mind and wishes of the dead Pontiff and exhorted him to the fulfilment of his Catholic 'duty, especially that he should not give way to the innovations and profanations of the sectaries in the wide and illustrious territories under his rule. He promised that he would come to Augsburg and promote the cause of religion, in so far as it is agreeable to the Word of God, etc. May the Lord deliver him and his Court from the itch for novelty in religion.[2]

Peter's ' etcetera ' at the close of this letter represents a shrug of the shoulders, for the words of the Duke were the usual ones by which tepid Catholics excused their behaviour. It is not certain on historical grounds that the Saint's counsel had much to do with the fact, but from the time of his visit the Duke began to show much less favour to the Lutherans. He appeared in Augsburg for the Diet, according to his promise, and thereafter gradually abandoned his temporizing for a genuinely Catholic standpoint.

[1] Braunsberger, *Epistulae*, vol. v, pp. 169–70.　　[2] Braunsberger, *Epistulae*, vol. v, p. 170.

Back in Cologne for the great feast of the Magi on January 6th, Peter's first word to his brethren must certainly have been to ask whether the dispensation had come. It had not, and, perhaps, the brethren reminded him of the old jest that Bulls could not be expected to travel swiftly since they had feet of lead. This time they refused to let their visitor go into hiding, whatever the senators might say. Finding that Cologne knew nothing of the death of the Pope, he seems to have discounted what he had heard in Düsseldorf as an idle rumour. At any rate he did not relinquish his mission but only suspended it a little while in hopes that the wretched dispensation might arrive. The ecclesiastical situation, as he found it in Cologne, was full of anomalies. There were no suffragan or coadjutor bishops in the whole vast Electorate, and the Elector himself, Friedrich von Wied, nephew of the unhappy Hermann, was not a priest nor had his election as archbishop ever been confirmed by Rome. One can understand a little better now, perhaps, why the Reformation happened and went on happening. Of the four principal archbishops in Germany two were not priests and a third had gone over completely to Lutheranism.

The University of Cologne, too, had fallen on very evil days, so much so that the civil authorities were hard put to it to support the professorial body. In 1559 they had petitioned Pope Paul IV for a peculiar favour. By two concordats between the Holy See and Germany, signed in the fifteenth century, it was agreed that the right of appointment to benefices falling vacant during the odd months of the year, January, March, etc., should belong to the Pope. Paul IV was asked to confer such benefices as thus appertained to him in Cologne on the professors at the University for a period of three years. He graciously consented and his successor, Pius IV, extended the favour for another three years, so that it did not lapse until 1565. Then it was that the Senate laid upon Father Coster the sacred duty of procuring a further extension, not for three but for twelve years. Coster, on leaving Rome, bequeathed his responsibility to St. Peter and St. Francis Borgia. But by this time the curial officials had had enough of concessions and made such trouble that Peter, too, was obliged to depart empty-handed. St. Francis, however, was not the sort of person to surrender easily, and that knowledge kept Peter's hopes reasonably green.

Within four days of his arrival in Cologne he had twice addressed the students of the flourishing Jesuit Gymnasium. Then, on January 14th, he took his courage in his hands and faced the University and Senate. Presenting the Papal Brief which he had brought from Rome for them, he proceeded to comment on it and to make known clearly what the Holy See expected from their worships. In the first place, they must not allow anybody of whose faith they were not assured to preach or teach in the schools. Next, they must keep careful watch on printers to see that no immoral or religiously subversive books were issued by them. Thirdly, they must enforce the terms of the peace of Augsburg by excluding from their city such persons as refused to accept Catholic discipline, in the same way that Protestant cities excluded Catholics. Fourthly, they must be on their guard against admitting strangers who might be secret Protestant missionaries. Fifthly, they must not only pass but put into execution severe edicts against innovators and sectaries. Sixthly, the University must be reformed according to the decrees of the Council of Trent, of which an authentic copy was now in their hands, and, in particular, it must be seen to that nobody was admitted a professor in any of the four faculties who had not first made a profession of faith according to the form contained in the decrees. Finally, the benefices which the Pope would put at the University's disposal must be granted only to such persons as were ready and qualified to lecture and promote the studies of the University.[1]

City fathers and university dons are not as a class celebrated for humility, yet the Cologne men took Peter's dictation in the best possible spirit, which would seem to show that he conveyed it with considerable tact. They promptly voted him a large gift of wine as a mark of their esteem and, what was more to his liking, proceeded to inaugurate a veritable Catholic reformation of their city.[2] Peter's warm appreciation of their good-will came out at this time in the preface to the definitive edition of his *Summa* which he addressed to " The Senate and People of Cologne." After mentioning his personal reasons for gratitude and commemorating Cologne's secular greatness, he went on :

But the chief reason why I think you are to be congratulated, and God thanked most heartily, is that you have rendered yourselves worthy to have said of you what the Apostle of old said of the Romans, that your faith is spoken of in the whole world. To preserve intact and safe the religion of your ancestors, which is your holiest and dearest possession, you allow no place in your city for innovations and profanations but, no less prudently than firmly, cast out sectaries who oftentimes lay their plots against you. And thus you bring about

[1] Braunsberger, *Epistulae*, vol. v, pp. 681–2.   [2] Braunsberger, *Epistulae*, vol. v, p. 678.

with admirable zeal and piety that, while elsewhere confusion reigns in religion and utterly discordant sects flourish like poisonous things, among you there continues to be one heart and one soul, one sheepfold under one Shepherd. . . . I pray Almighty God most earnestly that He may make this grace and constancy of faith, whereby you are a shining light to Germany, continue with you for ever.

At Mainz, on his return there, Peter learned officially that his mission had come to an end and that he was to go to Augsburg to prepare for the Diet. Before doing so he wrote to Cardinal Truchsess, who was in Rome, setting forth the anxious thoughts that his experiences had awakened. He would have Truchsess plead with the new Pope, Pius V, whose election he considered a miracle of God's mercy, for the harassed German bishops, especially the three Electors. Their financial plight made it impossible for them to pay the fees demanded for necessary dispensations, and the Elector of Cologne, in particular, could not raise the large sum exacted by the Dataria for his long overdue confirmation as a bishop.[1] In the letter, Peter insisted once again that the bishops should be constrained to choose coadjutors, and that no bishop should in future be recognized by the Pope until he had been at least ordained priest. Finally, he dwelt on the grave importance of sending a legate to the Diet, authorized to treat with the German prelates about the promulgation of the decrees of Trent. Well he knew the difficulties likely to arise, especially from the privileges and customs of the cathedral churches. He had had sore personal experience in that quarter, but still he hoped for some measure of success. "If the whole Council cannot be promulgated," he said, " God grant that, by the common consent of the bishops, at least its principal chapters may be officially proclaimed and everywhere observed in Germany. I am afraid that, if wè neglect the opportunity offered by the Diet, there will not be another chance of commending the Council to these lands. I can see a struggle coming, prepared by the devil in order to weaken the authority of the Council at Augsburg, and I fear, and have good reason for fearing, that some so-called Catholic princes may put forward fresh proposals of conciliation between the Catholics and Protestants. I know that many men have it in mind to petition for the introduction of concessions. God grant that the Catholics may be

---

[1] To Peter's delight it soon became evident that Pope Pius was entirely opposed to the exactions of his officials, but when he promised Elector von Wied to send him his pallium without any payment if he would make the Tridentine profession of faith, that curious gentleman demurred and so rightly forfeited the sympathy of Catholics.

fortified to withstand the artifices of such men. . . ."[1] The letter ended with a cry in German from the depths of Peter's anxious heart : " *Gott helffe in disen grausammen Ungewidter* "—God help us in this violent storm.

Stormy the Diet certainly promised to be, and Peter was worn out after his travels. During that single year, 1565, he had visited twenty-nine different towns and ridden or walked well over five thousand English miles. With our high-powered cars we laugh at such a trifle nowadays but let somebody attempt it on horseback and see how he feels at the end! " I thank God who gave me strength to complete my journeyings during the four winter months," the Saint wrote to his General. " But for the last few days I have been feeling exhausted and without my usual vigour. May God's will be done in us and may He grant us to be sons of holy obedience in both life and death." About the vicissitudes of the way, all he had to say was this : " Troubles on the road and from the wintry weather were not wanting to us, but from greater perils God kept us safe. . . . And now I beg Him and your Paternity to forgive me for not having sought with greater diligence ways and means of carrying out my commission more satisfactorily, and for not having made better use of them when they offered. Being utterly inexperienced in this kind of mission, neither to myself nor to others was I as serviceable as I should have been, so I shall gladly welcome whatever penance your Reverend Paternity may choose to enjoin me."[2]

From Mainz Peter went to Speyer to comfort his well-loved friend, Lambert Auer, who again had taken up duties as preacher in the cathedral there. Merciless to himself, the Saint had ever the kindliest consideration for other men's powers of endurance and now affectionately urged Lambert to reduce his labours. The canons of Speyer were eager for a college and Peter would greatly have liked to satisfy them, as their city was the seat of the *Reichskammergericht* or Supreme Court of Justice. But it was also a fierce centre of Protestantism, and to settle Jesuits there seemed like asking for trouble. However, as will be seen, Speyer obtained its college in due course. From thence Peter returned to Dillingen to rest a little before the Diet, but Father Conrad Schwägerl, the most obstreperous Jesuit in the Province, wrecked his chances of a small holiday. He had already wasted a good deal of patience on Conrad, whose main object in life was now to abandon the Society of Jesus. Though from his subsequent activities one would hardly think it, the Father considered himself to be a martyr and wrote in the following strain to St. Francis Borgia :

[1] Braunsberger, *Epistulae*, vol. v, pp. 173–6.   [2] Braunsberger, *Epistulae*, vol. v, pp. 181–2.

The food of Upper Germany entirely disagrees with my health. Only once a week do we get a hot dish, generally salt meat or fish. Cold dripping is the stock condiment, and the doctors have frequently forbidden it as injurious to me. In this Province, Dillingen is the healthiest house. I have spoken to my superiors but they could find no more suitable place for me than here. I suffer from a violent sort of catarrh and for this the doctor in Augsburg, a most skilful man, judged that I should carefully follow the regime laid down for women at the time of childbirth, if I desire to get rid of a difficult and inveterate disease. I also suffer from horrible headaches, if, as is frequently necessary, I give myself up to study for a single hour. When the wind blows a little more keenly you would scarcely believe the trouble I have with my eyes. . . . At present I am affected almost daily with the most dreadful toothaches or pains in my head and sides. . . . During the night I try to sleep, in vain. If I succeed in getting off, the noise of the wind or a small sound in the house wakes me, and not for two or three hours am I able to close my eyes again. . . .[1]

Conrad was plainly what the gentle Theodoric Canisius thought him to be, a *malade imaginaire*. It would have been a thousand times more convenient for Peter to let him go, but, as he had taken his vows and was a priest, the Saint felt very reluctant to abandon him to his own devices. Eventually, in conjunction with Father Nadal, he made three proposals to the rebel: (1) that he should return to his native place for as long as he wished, while remaining subject to the Society of Jesus; (2) that he should go to Rome, if only to petition for a dispensation from his vows; (3) that, still remaining a Jesuit, he should enter the service of some bishop and live with him. It would be hard to imagine what more kindly offers could have been made, but Conrad rejected them all and went off, nobody knew where, full of wrath and accusations against St. Peter.

The next big event in Peter's life and in the history of Germany was the Diet of Augsburg. To his joy he learned from Polanco that he would have as companions at it Father Nadal and the saintly theologian of genius, Diego de Ledesma, who, like Peter himself, had been appointed by Pius V theologians to his Legate, Cardinal Commendone. On March 6th he welcomed his two brethren to Augsburg and, as they were tired out after their journey from Rome, went himself to present their respects to the Legate. The following day all three dined with his Lordship, and,

[1] Braunsberger, *Epistulae*, vol. v, pp. 611-4.

immediately after, successively with the Apostolic Nuncio, the Spanish Ambassador, and Herr George Fugger. Emperor Maximilian, however, did not at all appreciate their presence in the city and had even tried to prevent their coming by manœuvres in Rome. Nevertheless, Peter reported that " he set an example to everybody as a good, Catholic Prince, going to Church for Mass and attending sermons." With the exception of Max, the Catholic leaders showed much deference to Peter, for Nadal says that he had " great authority with the Legate and Nuncio " and that all the Catholic princes made their Easter confessions to him in the Cathedral.[1]

The relations of the Protestants with the Jesuits were of a mixed character. Opposite the Fathers' house in Augsburg Duke Christopher of Württemberg had taken up his quarters, with the ferocious enemy of Jesuits, Pastor Schmidelin, in his train. Some of the Duke's suite, Nadal reported, behaved courteously and saluted Peter and himself when they met in the street, but others, perhaps incited by Schmidelin, took to heaving bricks from their windows into the little patch of garden attached to the Jesuit house, when they observed any of the Fathers promenading there. The Fathers bore the bombardment without complaint, but not so the burly German lay brother who acted as their cook. One day, on the coming of the brick, he shot out of his kitchen in his apron, rushed into the Duke's kitchen and gave his opposite number there such a rating that the annoyance ceased forthwith. Duke Christopher, who was a gentleman, threatened with instant dismissal any of his retainers who dared to restart it.[2]

The canons of Augsburg also behaved better than might have been expected for, though they had previously declared that they would have nobody but the convivial Father Martin Gewarts, whom they described as " a jolly good fellow," for their preacher, they decided to invite Peter back to his old post during the Diet, when the Duke of Bavaria demanded the return of Father Martin to Munich. The preaching began at the Cathedral on Quinquagesima Sunday, February 24th. Between that date and Tuesday in Easter week the Saint had delivered thirty-three sermons, many of them learned, controversial discourses. On Holy Thursday he preached a Passion sermon lasting three hours, and followed, on Good Friday, with two more of the same kind which taken together lasted five hours. Even Nadal, who tells the story and was himself a fierce worker, began to wonder whether Peter's strength would hold out, for, besides the four sermons a week in the Cathedral or the Church of St.

[1] Braunsberger, *Epistulae*, vol. v, pp. 186, 577-8.   [2] Braunsberger, *Epistulae*, vol. v, pp. 580-1.

John, he used to give the ladies of Maximilian's Court a separate weekly address at the express wish of the Empress.[1]

Lutherans came to the sermons in good numbers, but not always to be edified. On one occasion they surreptitiously stirred a quantity of coal-dust into the holy water stoup so that the Catholics coming out from Mass might smudge their faces; and another time, during Lent, they brought cooked meats to the Cathedral doors and devoured them with great relish—"*como barbaros*," says Nadal—as the congregation passed in. The canons protested to Maximilian, who laid an injunction on the Protestant Princes to keep their retainers in order. The Duke of Saxony, to his credit, even threw a few of his lively family into prison.[2]

After Easter, the affairs of the Diet began to occupy so much of St. Peter's time that he could not continue his regular work in the pulpit. Nadal accordingly summoned Father Halbpaur from Innsbruck to replace him, and, a little later, in virtue of his position as 'visitor' of the Upper German Province, decided that Peter had better give up the Augsburg sermons for good. Thus ended seven continuous years of devoted ministry in the pulpit. Of the sermons preached this year two short excerpts may be given. The first is the exordium of a homily on penance:

If it were not Lent and if there were no Lenten regulations admonishing us to do penance, I would still have reason to treat of the subject on account of the state of the Empire. We can see how important it is that the Diet should begin well and have a happy ending, if we want true peace in both politics and religion. On the Diet's success must depend the preservation and defence of our country and the whole Empire, which years ago began to be weakened and troubled, as hardly ever in its previous history, by our dissensions and rivalries. Now comes in addition its most dreadful foe, than whom is none more powerful, cruel, or formidable. Far and wide he spreads himself, that undying enemy of the Christian name, ready with his mounted hordes to burst through Hungary into Germany, devastating and destroying us and our possessions with all the might of his sword.

The reference to the Turks, who had again become dangerously active, illustrates a common feature of Peter's sermons, their practical concern with events and movements of the day. Never was preaching less theoretical

---

[1] Braunsberger, *Epistulae*, vol. v, p. 561.

[2] M.H., *Epistolae Patris Nadal*, vol. iv, p. 733; Turba, *Venetianische Depeschen vom Kaiserhofe*, vol. iii (Vienna, 1895), p. 318.

or aloof from what might be called the newspaper side of life. The second excerpt, now to be given, illustrates another feature of it, its honesty and sincerity. The sermon was spoken in Holy Week and dealt with the subject of indulgences:

> Doubtless, many people do not wish to hear or think of indulgences. Indeed, they cannot abide even the name of them, considering them to be idle inventions, without warrant in the Word of God. The Papists, they say, and their head, the Pope, excogitated indulgences out of mere avarice and they are but fopperies and frauds to deceive the faithful. . . . The first and principal reason that moves our opponents to despise indulgences is nothing else than the fact of their having seen or heard them vastly abused in many places. To this our reply is that we Catholics in no wise deny but freely admit that in past years many and great churchmen have dealt evilly with indulgences, by granting them too readily. . . . Yea, in this matter they sought their own advantage and cultivated infamous avarice, gravely sinning against God whose gifts they put up for sale and rendered contemptible to the multitude.[1]

The Diet of Augsburg opened with great solemnity on March 23, 1566. There were two principal matters for consideration: the renewed activities of the Turks and the question of ratifying the Religious Peace indefinitely. That Peace had been concluded in 1555 as a provisional solution of Germany's confessional troubles until such time as a general council had spoken. Now Trent had spoken and the problem arose whether Catholics could conscientiously assent once more to the terms of the Peace as they had done in 1555, 1557 and 1559. It was a real crux, the first time in modern history when the issue of 'toleration' became urgent. In the inaugural address, which was read at a plenary session of the Diet by the Duke of Bavaria, Emperor Maximilian stated that, when elected King of the Romans, he had pledged himself to maintain the Religious Peace. That Peace, however, had legal force only between the Catholics and the adherents of the Confession of Augsburg. Besides these two parties various detestable sects, by which words the Emperor meant principally the Calvinists, had come to light in the Empire and it was of the first importance that they should be removed. He therefore requested the Estates to submit their opinions as to how this might best be effected.

[1] Braunsberger, *Epistulae*, vol. v, pp. 571–2.

Money was then voted for the Turkish war, after which act of grace the Protestant Princes demanded that the religious question as a whole should be brought into discussion. To this the Catholics were totally opposed, as they felt it would only lead to further strife and embitterment. Towards the end of March the Emperor decided that the two parties must carry on any religious discussions they desired independently of one another. If they had grievances or representations to put forward they could consign them to writing and submit them to His Majesty, who would then let each side see the document of the other, with a view to mutual reconciliation. It was a wise plan and might have done good if the men concerned had had the grace to appreciate it. Whatever the Catholics felt they said nothing, but the Lutherans made an unhappy show of their rabid animosity. At the instigation of the Dukes of Neuberg and Württemberg a memorial was put together and presented to the Emperor on April 25th. Somehow or other St. Peter obtained a copy, summarized it in Latin, and sent the result to Rome. It illustrates very well the temperament of the educated Lutheran at this period. They are obliged, they say, " by the command of God to flee the pagan abominations and idolatries of the Papacy," and they hope that, as a result of the Diet, many men will be " freed from Papistical tyranny." At the Council of Trent " such impious and horrible decisions were made that they think even Catholics must shudder at reading or hearing of them." In conclusion, they urge that, as " the Roman Church has stuck fast hitherto in blind and irrefutable idolatry, the Emperor should summon a national council in Germany as soon as possible and preside at it in person."[1]

In addition to that fulmination, the Elector Palatine, who was a leader among the Calvinists and savage about their exclusion from the Religious Peace, issued a separate tract to the Diet accusing the Jesuits of being responsible for all Germany's woes and demanding their suppression. St. Peter answered this preposterous outburst, but, in deference to the wishes of the Legate, persuaded Cardinal Truchsess, who wanted the work published, that it would be better to keep quiet. It was Peter, too, who put into German the long Catholic rejoinder to the Lutheran attack, which provoked another one, with himself in the middle of it. Endeavouring to show that there was serious confusion among Catholics on the subject of man's justification, the Protestant party made the following statement : " It is no secret in this city that, during the Reichstag,

[1] Braunsberger, *Epistulae*, vol. v, pp. 211-2.

Canisius preached on the text : *the seed of the woman shall crush the serpent's head*, and tried to make the promise apply, not to Christ, but to the Virgin Mary." True enough, there had been disagreement among commentators about the difficult text, Genesis iii, 15, but it was on a point of grammar rather than on a point of theology. The theological reasons for applying the promise in a secondary sense to Our Lady were set forth by none more clearly than by St. Peter himself in his great treatise on the Blessed Virgin, published in 1577 :

> Our opponents are deceived, or rather deceivers, when they would have us appear to the people ignorant and stupid enough to confine the whole promise to Our Lady because we read *ipsa* in the text, excluding that blessed seed in which all nations are blessed. Rather, indeed, are we certain sure and do for ever confess that Christ came into the world in order to crush the serpent's head. . . . Not otherwise has the Church ever taught or believed. To Christ alone has she attributed the honour that He by a certain absolute and excellent power should tread the serpent under foot and, at the same time, endow others and, above all, His Mother Mary with similar power. Nor do we thus make the Mother the equal of the Son, but rather proclaim His greater glory, in that, not only personally, but through His Mother and many others, He acts against the old serpent so powerfully that they, though by nature weak, triumph over so great a foe and reduce all his strength and cunning to nothingness.[1]

For the Catholics at the Diet, by far the most important task was to keep the Emperor in his friendly mood. The chief aim of the Lutherans was, as always, to have the Ecclesiastical Reservation abrogated ; and only Maximilian, whose father had been responsible for that safeguard of Catholic interests, could bring about what they wanted. St. Peter and Nadal, being well aware of this, wrote jointly to Rome urging their General to press on the Pope's attention the advisability of providing a subsidy for the Turkish war. For greater safety Nadal put the letter into the dialect of Catalonia and referred to the Pope cryptically as " the Friend of Rodriguez," because Pius had shown singular kindness to a Spanish Jesuit of that name. Maximilian's agents in Rome let him know that the Jesuits were secretly promoting his interests and that fact did not a little to keep him in a good humour, even though the Pope's decision

---

[1] *De Maria Virgine incomparabili* (Ingolstadt, 1577), lib. v, cap. ix.

to grant His Majesty a subsidy of fifty thousand scudi had been arrived at before St. Francis Borgia came on the scene. Certainly, His Majesty's three sisters in Innsbruck thought none too badly of St. Peter and his brethren, for when writing to congratulate Pius V on his election they declared that the Jesuits were " practically the only ones left who help the failing Church with their labours, vigils, and indefatigable zeal; who educate the young in order to win them for Christ; who guide doubting souls into the way of sure faith; who bring back those who have gone astray; and who, day and night, assist, raise up, console, and strengthen all whom they possibly can."[1]   A Jesuit can say with great pleasure that his brethren of those old times were by no means " practically the only ones left " to do all the good work mentioned.

Another most important way in which St. Peter, Nadal, and Ledesma helped to win over the Emperor and so ensure victory for the Catholic cause was by their attitude with regard to the final ratification of the Religious Peace. It was well known that the Pope did not at all favour the idea of ratification, and he had definitely instructed Commendone to make a public protest if anything derogatory to the Council of Trent came out in the proceedings. Now St. Peter knew well that such a protest would be just the thing to throw the Emperor into the arms of the Lutherans. He accordingly made it his chief aim at the Diet to prevent it, and slaved beside Nadal during May to such an extent that, in the latter man's words, on many days they had " no time for meals or sleep." Peter himself confessed that owing to the amount of writing, consulting, and running about they were obliged to do, the ordinary routine of life had to be abandoned altogether. Cardinal Commendone, too, said a word on the subject, which was that he and his henchmen had " scarcely time to breathe."[2]

Peter and his colleagues had this much in common with the Lutheran princes, that they were not enamoured of the Religious Peace. Neither party considered it anything better than an unsatisfactory compromise, required to prevent civil strife. Had they possessed the power, the Lutherans would immediately have cancelled its chief concession to the

[1] Braunsberger, *Epistulae*, vol. v, pp. 218-9, 223. Their high opinion of him did not prevent the good ladies from being a serious worry to St. Peter.   Magdalene, the eldest, would not make her confession to Father Halbpaur but only to Father Dyrsius, while, on the other hand, Margaret and Helen would not go to Father Dyrsius but only to Father Halbpaur. That meant the monopolization of two men by three women, which was altogether disproportionate, quite apart from the fact that Jesuits were precluded by their constitutions from being regular confessors to women under vows, as were the three. Peter's letters are full of this particular difficulty. All the help St. Francis Borgia could give him was to tell him to do the best he could, as they seem destined to carry that cross, however much they might struggle to be free of it.
[2] Braunsberger, *Epistulae*, vol. v, pp. 256, 590, 594.

Catholics; and the Catholics, on their side, would gladly have swept away the terms by which the Lutherans were legally recognized. But facts had to be faced. There was a stalemate in politics, and consequently the Jesuits judged that the Peace might legitimately be ratified "in order to avoid greater evils." At the same time they urged that, when the moment came for the Catholic Princes to signify their assent to ratification, they should make express mention of the Council of Trent and declare their adhesion to its dogmas. If they could not be brought to do so in a plenary session of the Diet they might, at least, be persuaded to make their profession of faith privately before the Legate. But, even should that small measure of deference to Trent prove impossible to obtain, Peter and his colleagues still urged with all their might that no public protest should be made. As, by a reasonable interpretation of the Pope's instructions, the protest might be waived if the Religious Peace contained nothing contrary to the dogmas and decrees of Trent, St. Peter drew up a long memorial in Italian to prove for the Legate that this was so, and that the Peace was a political rather than a religious instrument, which affected merely the discipline of the Church and not her dogmatic teaching.[1] Next, he and Nadal wrote to Rome praising Commendone to the skies, and begging Borgia to help him by making clear to "the Friend of Rodriguez" the difficulties of the situation, so that His Holiness might cease to press for the protest and leave everything to the discretion of his most judicious and trustworthy agent. Borgia took the matter up as though he had no other work in the world, and, by representations to influential cardinals and a personal interview with the Pope, to whom he submitted copies of the four statements drawn up by St. Peter and his colleagues for Commendone, succeeded in obtaining a free hand for the Legate.[2]

The Diet closed towards the end of May with the Catholics in the stronger position. From their point of view, practically everything depended on the maintenance of the Ecclesiastical Reservation and in that they had succeeded. Trent, too, had received a measure of recognition, though not to the extent that St. Peter desired. In the words of a good historian, Carl Maria von Aretin: "This was the first Reichstag at which the Reformation party quite incontestably lost ground. Hitherto the assailants, they now became the assailed and were obliged to look to their defences. The Papal Legate contributed in great measure to this result, as also,

---

[1] Braunsberger, *Epistulae*, vol. v, pp. 234–47.
[2] M.H., *Epistolae Patris Nadal*, vol. iii, pp. 130–2.

through his distinguished learning and piety, did the Jesuit, Peter Canisius."
St. Peter's best Protestant biographer is yet more emphatic. " That the
Diet ended as it did," he says, " was due before everything to the silent
work of the Jesuits."[1]

From Augsburg Peter travelled to Innsbruck on May 29th to arrange
the affairs of that distracted College, which, owing to the mismanagement
of Father Dyrsius, was declared by a person of authority to be an
"absolute Babylon." After Innsbruck it was Dillingen's turn, where
the Saint endeavoured to put the finances of the University on a sound
basis, a task made exceedingly difficult by the genial slipperiness of its
Cardinal founder. Having now to reassume his full duties as Provincial
he said to Borgia : " I beg you from the bottom of my heart by the
immeasurable charity of Christ to help me to drink this chalice and to
carry this heavy burden which is too great for my shoulders." The
bitterest part of the chalice continued to be the ill-health, inefficiency, or
faultiness of so many of his subjects. One master at Dillingen used to
go about arguing against the Immaculate Conception, and spent much
of his time making a sort of anthology of the more amorous passages of
the ancient poets with which he would afterwards endeavour to shock
the brethren. Of another subject Peter remarked with unusual vehemence :
" We may be compelled to dismiss him soon, as he is so troublesome,
silly, impudent and intolerable, that it seems impossible to fit him in
anywhere." But in many ways the worst offenders were Peter's three
most eminent preachers, Martin Gewarts, Hermes Halbpaur, and George
Schorich. They appear to have been somewhat spoilt by the attentions
they received in the Court circles of Innsbruck or Munich, and developed
peculiarities that rendered them unbearable in community life. When
appointed to the pulpit of Augsburg Halbpaur became so bumptious that
Peter was glad to lend him to the Provincial of the Rhineland. Reporting
the move to the General, he said : " May God deign to grant it to our
Germans to think more humbly of themselves and to continue in true
simplicity of heart when they discover that they are some good at
preaching."

His rectors were yet another source of anxiety to the Saint. At
Innsbruck, Father Delanoy, who succeeded Dyrsius, went in for such
Spartan discipline that charity was in serious danger of being forgotten ;
Father Leubenstain, at Ingolstadt, was obliged through lack of men to

---

[1] Aretin, *Geschichte des bayerischen Herzogs Maximilian des Ersten*, vol. i (Passau, 1842), p. 185 ;
Drews, *Petrus Canisius, der erste deutsche Jesuit*, p. 121.

assume himself the rôles of minister and cook; while in Dillingen the finest superior in the Province, Theodoric Canisius, appeared to be slowly dying of consumption. "Perhaps the only remedy left," wrote Peter to the General concerning Theodoric, " is one which necessity imposes on us against our will, namely that, however much we need his services, we bid him return to his native place so that the change and the air of his country may, by God's grace, restore his health. . . . When I go to Augsburg in a few days' time I shall consult the doctor there, and, if he agrees, I shall have no hesitation in at once sending this best of Fathers to Speyer, Mainz, Cologne, and perhaps also Nymegen, with a congenial companion."[1]

Another college whose successive rectors gave Peter much concern was that of Munich. The brusque and rough-mannered Father Paul Hoffaeus demanded so insistently to be released from his post that the Saint had to agree, but the change did not mend the situation, because, within a month of his appointment the new rector, Father Dominic Mengin, Peter's former companion in Poland, was " vehemently begging and praying to be allowed to lay down the burden." However, as there was nobody else he had to stay on until, in Peter's words, the Lord showed mercy on them all. About the troubles of his Province in general he wrote thus to Borgia : " We commend ourselves and this whole Province to the Divine Goodness through the sacrifices and prayers of your Paternity and the entire Society. We need them very much indeed, both on account of the various sick men in the colleges and because of the temptations and trials with which we are exercised at home and away from home. May Christ triumph and reign in our hearts that so we may perfectly fulfil our vocation and the will of our superiors."

Giulio Pavesi, the Dominican Archbishop of Sorrento, visited Dillingen at this time. Canisius and Nadal at once sought out this influential man, of whose compassion for afflicted Germany they were aware, to beg his help in Rome with regard to two matters dear to their hearts. Germany needed priests more than anything else. New vocations to the priesthood in their Society were numerous but, having no means to support many of the applicants, they were obliged to turn them away. If the Pope, in his goodness, would apply some of the revenues which he derived from Germany to the endowment of a Jesuit novitiate all these vocations might be saved. Secondly, the Catholic printers and publishers of Germany were few in number and straitened in circumstances, not having anything like the same patronage or resources which their Protestant confrères

[1] Braunsberger, *Epistulae*, vol. v, p. 451.

enjoyed. For instance, Sebaldus Mayer, in Dillingen, had been obliged through poverty to sell his plant and carry on as a mere employee. For such deserving and hardly-used men Peter made the following plea : " That books against the heretics, which are now a crying need of this country, may be the more easily printed, we beg that the Nuncio to Germany be given a faculty from the Holy Father to use an adequate sum each year in subsidizing the Catholic printers. It is a known fact that many works are suppressed or held up, owing to the poverty of the authors or printers, which on appearance would greatly strengthen the Catholics and restrain the activities of the heretics."

At Rome, Paolo Manuzio, son of the illustrious Aldus, had been granted a monopoly in the printing of standard theological works, which no other firm might infringe without incurring excommunication. It was he, for instance, who issued the *Catechism of the Council of Trent.* As excommunication held no terrors for the Lutherans they pirated the excellent patristic tomes and other productions of Manuzio, not seldom introducing glosses and comments of a controversial kind. If the Catholics wanted such books they had to buy the Protestant reprints of them because the Roman prices were too high for their lean purses. St. Peter and Nadal accordingly petitioned that a few chosen Catholic printers should be empowered to reproduce the editions of Manuzio in Germany. Finally, as a measure of relief, they begged that they might be entrusted with the loan of some books or manuscripts from the Vatican Library or the Library of Cardinal Sirleto with a view to having them printed and published for the advantage of German Catholics.[1]

The *Catechism of the Council of Trent,* mentioned above, appeared in September, 1566. It was composed principally by three Dominicans and put into Latin by the best stylist of the age, Giulio Poggiano, formerly secretary to Cardinal Truchsess. An eminent non-Catholic scholar recently described the work as a " classic both of theology and Latin."[2] For practical purposes the theology was much more important than Poggiano's elegant Latinity, so Pius V immediately instructed St. Francis Borgia to get the Catechism done into French and German. It was decided that Father Hoffaeus, who had a sound grasp of his native tongue, should undertake the German translation and that Peter Canisius should revise

---

[1] Braunsberger, *Epistulae*, vol. v, pp. 280–1. It should be said, in justice to the memory of Paolo Manuzio, that he did not use his monopoly to become rich. Ten years labour in Rome resulted in his having a very modest number of ducats saved, as a dowry for his daughter.
[2] B. J. Kidd, *The Counter-Reformation* (London, 1933), p. 166.

his work and see it through the press.[1] Peter devoted enormous care to his inglorious part of the programme and brought the Catechism out with great success in 1568. It is interesting to notice how much of his time was spent in this way, helping other men to achieve their purposes. Even during the Diet of Augsburg, when overwhelmed with other employments, he found time to assist the learned Father Torres in the preparation of his admirable *Confessio Augustiniana*, designed as a refutation from the works of St. Augustine of the Lutheran *Confessio Augustana*. The volume, partly written and wholly revised by St. Peter, though his name nowhere appeared in connexion with it, came out in Lent, 1567, and, in spite of its substantial size, was so well received that three thousand copies found purchasers within a few months. Through all these years Peter continued, too, to look after the printing of the many new editions of the works of Hosius, and there is evidence that he rendered valuable literary assistance to scholars such as Onofrio Panvinio who were devoting their talents to the service of the Church.

From September 9th to September 21st the Saint was at Wiesensteig in Württemberg, having been invited thither by the terrible hunter of witches, Graf Ulric von Helfenstein. Ulric and his brother Sebastian started to Lutheranize their territories in 1555. Both men went in terror of witchcraft, which made them so cruel that in 1563 they had tortured and burned no fewer than sixty-three unhappy women. Under torture, one of these poor creatures confessed that only holy water, as used by the Catholics, could nullify their magical arts. This piece of information led Ulric to write to his sister, who was a Catholic, begging that she would find some devout and learned man to teach him the Catholic Faith. So it was that St. Peter came to Wiesensteig. What he did there is not recorded, beyond the fact of his having reconciled two of the alleged witches who had abjured the Church; but shortly after his visit Graf Ulric publicly renounced Lutheranism and developed into one of the most ardently Catholic rulers in Germany. Though the family became extinct as long ago as 1627, they had impressed their new-found faith so thoroughly on the people that, to this day, the territory of Wiesensteig remains a little Catholic island in the midst of a sea of Protestantism.[2]

[1] Hoffaeus was a splendid Christian. In his character, however, there appeared a curious contradiction or disharmony, for, while having the meanest opinion of himself as a man, he considered his opinions and decisions utterly beyond criticism or reproach. In the matter of the Catechism he requested St. Francis Borgia to obtain him, not a plenary, but a *plenariissimam indulgentiam*, " for his agony " over the translation, and also " participation in the good works of all those who should read the German version, or in any way whatever hear about the same." St. Peter asked nothing for his own share in the labour.

[2] Braunsberger, *Epistulae*, vol. v, pp. 317–8, 780–90.

Peter's attitude to the ordinary Protestant or lapsed Catholic was one of deep compassion. Only against those who led them astray did he feel or express that righteous anger which is the glow of strong and sincere convictions. The harsh requirements of Rome before the lapsed could be reconciled puzzled and saddened him greatly, for he felt that German conditions were not understood there nor the frailty of human nature sufficiently taken into account. "Daily life is passed in the midst of heretics," he explained to Borgia, "and many cannot avoid converse, argument, and business dealings with them. Sometimes it happens that they are moved by the reasons and arguments of the heretics, and the passage to heresy is easy for them because they imbibed it in the past and took it in, as it were, with their mother's milk. But when admonished they come to themselves and ask absolution from us. I beg, for Our Lord's sake, that we here be not compelled to quench the smoking flax, nor to render our ministry odious to many, through seeming to want to introduce the rigour of a new inquisition. . . . Not thus shall we build up but rather destroy, I fear. . . . While, then, we praise the ardent zeal of the Holy Father, we also suppliantly beg that our hands may not be tied against helping the Germans in their peril, especially since all their ways are so beset with heresies and excommunications as to deceive, if possible, even the elect. . . ."[1]

During that winter of 1566, Peter and Nadal reopened negotiations with the Bishop of Würzburg[2] about the foundation of a college in his city. After much discussion a draft agreement was drawn up, with which the Bishop expressed himself satisfied. Nadal had then to go away on other business and Peter was left to settle details with the Bishop's chancellor. According to the Jesuit constitutions, a college, before being accepted by the Society, had to be endowed to support, not only masters and professors, but a good number of young Jesuit students also. The reasons for this stipulation are understandable enough, for only by some such arrangement could the continuance of the various colleges be secured ; but in a country like Germany, where the pressing need of the moment was all that bishops could be expected to consider, it was exceedingly difficult to get the conditions satisfied. The Bishop of Würzburg had his heart set upon obtaining a large number of masters for his college. That would have been right enough had he not also insisted on the provision of a preacher and two professors of theology and philosophy. Peter and Nadal tried as hard as they could to dissuade the Bishop from

---

[1] Braunsberger, *Epistulae*, vol. v, p. 361.　　　　　　[2] Friedrich von Wirsberg.

demanding the professors, knowing how scarce were those precious persons; and they did their best to escape promising a regular preacher because it would have been directly contrary to their constitutions for such a man to act as a salaried official, which was what the Bishop intended. However, they could not stir his Lordship's resolution and so put their hands to the agreement as the best attainable under the circumstances.

Towards the end of February, 1567, Peter repaired to Würzburg to be the first Jesuit occupant of the pulpit there. His Lenten course consisted of set sermons on three days each week of the season, together with catechetical homilies on two of the remaining days. Saturday was mostly spent in the confessional. In all he had preached twenty-nine times by April 1st. Religious conditions in the city were so bad, he reported to Borgia, that scarcely a confessor could be found who knew the words of absolution. All the interests of the priests seemed to be absorbed by women, or by the military exercises which were everywhere being practised. "This Franconian mission," the Saint warned his General, "requires workers of proved virtue and ability, ready for a life of unremitting charity and patience."

To help the situation, if he could, he now composed two memoranda for the Bishop, the first being a series of general fundamental theses from consideration of which those concerned might be led to thought for the reformation of the German dioceses. It is a sad document indeed, for it shows that the Church in Germany was slowly dying, and dying through the negligence or timidity of her official guardians:

Even the more wise and judicious bishops and prelates are to-day afraid lest if they demand a slight reformation they may suffer repulse at the hands of their canons. They are frightened by the misery of the age and always in terror of new commotions. One man waits for another to break the ice, and if they attempt anything their efforts are deprecated by lay counsellors and politicians. So it is that visitation of dioceses has been neglected for many years; that synods are not held; that the Council of Trent is neither received nor promulgated; that candidates for ordination are not properly examined; and that clerical vice of the most horrible kind can go on with impunity. While Peter sleeps Judas is vigilant, and everything deteriorates to such an extent that now we are left with scarcely a shadow of the ancient Church.[1]

[1] Braunsberger, *Epistulae*, vol. v, pp. 410–2.

At any rate there was one Peter who was not asleep. His second memorandum signalizes with true Christian compassion four classes of " sick men " for whose cure the bishops ought to strive might and main. The first consisted of the lapsed or relapsed Catholics for whose condition he felt so sorry because it was due, in his judgment, less to their own fault than to the ignorance and neglect of their priests. Then there were the priests themselves, some apostates, others married or living in concubinage, and nearly all ignorant, inefficient, and without the slightest regard for the prescriptions of canon law. The third category contained the worst offenders, the canons and beneficed clergy who so often obtained their advancement by the most unblushing simony and, once installed, utterly neglected the duties which they were paid to fulfil. Most of them dressed in lay clothes, and numbers hardly ever said Office or even Mass, openly flouted the laws of fasting and abstinence, and spent the Church's money at the card-table or on banquets and mistresses. That Peter was not painting the picture too black is sadly proved by the episcopal registers of the time.[1] The fourth class of his sick men were the religious in monasteries who " appeared utterly oblivious of their promised poverty, chastity, and obedience." For each class he suggested appropriate remedies, characterized by the broad charity and understanding which were typical of him. It was easy for Rome to fulminate excommunications and lay down strict laws. In a Catholic country such disciplinary measures might prove salutary, but in Germany they only served to make good and loyal men unhappy. The others simply laughed at them. That is why the Saint never relaxed his efforts to secure whatever mitigation he could of the laws regulating the absolution of persons who read heretical books or in other ways fell under the ban of the Church. No man of his time worked harder to make Rome understand that Germany was not Spain, and that measures which might be a medicine for the one country could easily prove to be a poison for the other. It is a very sad thing that there was nobody to perform a similar service with St. Pius V for England.[2]

In the midst of his labours at Würzburg Peter fell seriously ill. " Delivering sermons in that vast church has been a sufficient tax on my weak body," he told Borgia. It did not help to cure him when, towards

---

[1] Pluralism was rife, of course, and, curiously enough, we find Canisius and Nadal on one occasion in the surprising rôle of its defenders. The Council of Trent had enacted that no ecclesiastical person might have more than one benefice, but if the law had been carried out to the letter in Germany the Lutherans would certainly have taken possession of many of the benefices vacated. For that reason Peter and his friend urged caution on the Roman authorities. Braunsberger, *Epistulae*, vol. v, pp. 201-2; M.H., *Epistolae Patris Nadal*, vol. iii, pp. 193, 343.

[2] Braunsberger, *Epistulae* .vol. v, pp. 413-7.

the end of Lent, he received news from Rome that St. Francis felt unable to ratify the terms of his agreement with Bishop von Wirsberg. Indeed, he was thrown into consternation by the news, especially as Borgia required him to do all the necessary explaining and apologizing to the Bishop, who was a man of rather violent temper. Meantime the Saint had returned to Dillingen, where he collapsed and made the doctors anxious for his life. On April 17th, when he had recovered a little, he wrote from his bed explaining to Borgia in the most child-like way the reasons that had induced Nadal and himself to concede what the Bishop of Würzburg so urgently wanted. Continuing, he said:

But I am not so much convinced by all these reasons as to think that I may deflect from the opinion of your Paternity, whose business and duty it is to put right authoritatively whatsoever is done by your sons imprudently. The liberties of our institute have to be vindicated, the prescribed rules observed, and such dangers and inconveniences as this agreement might entail forestalled. . . . I have therefore written to Father Nadal asking for instructions as to how I should reply to the Bishop, that he may receive the unexpected news with less offence. . . . I was thinking that it might be a good thing if your Paternity answered the Bishop directly, at least to the extent of saying that, for good reasons, you could send only a few professors this year who, however, would be able during it to test the capacity of their students and find out what sum was needed to support our Fathers at the college. Meantime, you might return to His Lordship the document containing his offers and promises so that he, too, may, if he desires, declare himself free from all obligation. Father Ignatius, of holy memory, did something of the kind on one occasion. . . .

In all this I feel pity for the German mission-field, for I foresee great difficulty in setting up colleges there and in securing approval for our Society if we insist on talking about its freedom and making so many requests for ourselves. I remember that this was said in the last general congregation. Nevertheless, God is powerful to do more than we think or understand, especially if the Holy Sacrifices and prayers of many men plead with Him. . . .[1]

[1] Braunsberger, *Epistulae*, vol. v, pp. 431–2. Spanish influence was very strong at this time in the government of the Society, and affairs were apt to be arranged according as they suited conditions in Spain. The question of the Society's private prayer came up in the second general congregation. St. Ignatius had left the matter absolutely open in the constitutions, and in his letters expressed the view that it was better to endeavour to find God everywhere and in everything than to devote much time to set prayer. The Spanish Provinces, however, under the influence of St. Francis Borgia, had adopted the custom of an hour's mental prayer in the morning, and when Borgia became General

No sooner had Peter's fever subsided than he was off on his travels again, to hear the confessions and receive the renewed vows of the brethren in Innsbruck, Munich, and Ingolstadt. As usual, his activities in those places were by no means confined to the affairs of his Order, and at Innsbruck, for instance, we find him in conference with the Archduke Ferdinand about the foundation of a seminary and other measures necessary to preserve the faith in Tirol. The visitation over, he hurried back to Dillingen for the diocesan synod which Cardinal Truchsess and he had been planning for some time. One who was present in the town during it says that the Saint stood by the Cardinal's side as his right-hand man throughout, and the Cardinal himself wrote as follows to Borgia on June 26th : " I have held my Synod and, by the grace of God, it has passed off with all the peace and good results which I could have desired, for the salvation and excellent order of the affairs of my diocese. I render everlasting thanks to the Divine Majesty, and also give infinite praise to Fr. Canisius and Dr. Pisanus for the great solicitude and prudence which they showed. I can truly say that it was their help and virtue which enabled me to overcome every difficulty standing in the way of the Synod's success."[1]

This Synod is noteworthy as marking the first definite triumph of the Council of Trent in Germany. It was attended by representatives of the Augsburg Chapter and by abbots, other prelates, and heads of religious orders from the whole diocese, to whom were read a series of decrees drawn almost entirely from the acts of the Council. All parish priests of the diocese were strictly charged by the Cardinal, not only to possess and ponder, but to promulgate annually to their flocks the terms of the Bull, *In Coena Domini*, and they must further each acquire and study Father Polanco's excellent *Directory for Confessors*. Schoolmasters were obliged to make the Tridentine profession of faith, and were prohibited, under the severest penalties, from going themselves or sending others to Protestant universities. The Cardinal with his own lips pronounced a fierce denunciation of concubinage and other clerical vices, while, to stamp out drunkenness " in abbots, prelates, and parish priests," he forbade entirely the favourite German social custom of " treating," even going to the length of saying that anyone who stood a round of drinks would be guilty of a mortal sin of disobedience. That was the kind of talk that the clergy of Germany needed to put them on

this local custom was changed into a law for the whole Society. The whole story of the change is admirably told by Dr. Karrer in his *Der heilige Franz von Borja* (Freiburg im Breisgau, 1921), pp. 249–74.
[1] Braunsberger, *Epistulae*, vol. v, p. 638.

their feet. Even if the decrees of the Synod did not bring about an immediate reform they, at least, set a standard and a splendid example for the other bishops. The hoary old subterfuge that priests might read what they liked and act as they listed, because the legislation of Rome and Trent 'had not been promulgated in Germany, now fell to the ground in one important diocese, and at least one prop of the general moral insouciance was removed for good.[1]

At the end of the Synod Father Jasper Heywood, who was something of an eccentric, delivered the official sermons. In connexion with his appointment he wrote the following comical and (shall we say?) slightly cynical letter to Polanco :

I am now going to tell you a merry tale. The Reverend Fathers, our Provincial and Rector, have often counselled me during the preceding months, in Father Nadal's name, to prepare a solemn disputation with a view to acquiring the doctorate in theology in the near future. I put the matter off. Again and again they urged me to it, so at last out of obedience I did what I was told. There was a public disputation, and my Act was looked for and prepared for. Nothing happened, however, except dead silence. After a little while the Fathers renewed their plan, ordering that the solemn theses should once more be got ready and posted up in a public place for me to defend on an appointed day, so as to acquire the degree. This was done, and, on the instructions of the Rector, I myself issued invitations to professors of theology. But shortly before the day of the disputation dawned Father Provincial called me in and said to me, laughing merrily : ' Master Jasper, you would acquire greater praise and glory if the disputation were put off until we could get the theses printed, in order thus to make your promotion more distinguished and to secure that you have a finer audience.' But I replied : ' Father, if obedience allows I beg that the disputation may be held before the University alone, without any influx of outsiders, as a great deal of labour has already been expended in collecting theses, writing them out, rewriting them, and making them public. For myself I desire to be at once freed from this burden, lest it further hinder my lectures and studies.' When I had said this Father Provincial's smiles vanished altogether and he sent me back to Father Rector, who was absolutely of opinion that the affair should come off without any more delay. And so it did come off. I again gave a

[1] Braunsberger, *Epistulae*, vol. v, pp. 492, 497, 635-8.

public disputation before the University, and Father Rector appointed me a day in the middle of last Lent for my promotion. The house filled up with people and the whole town was talking about the coming event. Who but myself should be the Messer Magnifico? *Parturiunt montes, exit ridiculus mus; sicut erat in principio et nunc et semper.*

After Easter Father Provincial returned to us from Würzburg. In the sweetest and most affectionate way he smiled on me and said : ' I would like you to proceed with the business of your doctorate. Why do you not want to receive the degree when it is necessary to you for the greater glory of God?' At the same time he asked me to be good enough to deliver a discourse during the Synod which is to be held here shortly, and he praised me to my face, saying that there was nobody else to whom he would entrust the sermon except myself. ' For,' he continued, ' you have splendid natural gifts of both speech and action.' At that I immediately burst out laughing in such a way that I must have guffawed had I not remembered that I was dealing with my Superior.

I write this to your Reverence that you may join in my merriment. Every time I think of the affair I laugh heartily again. But enough of that. *Spectatum admissi, risum teneatis, amici.*[1] This is just a merry tale. Your Reverence will pardon me if I have interrupted your graver occupations. I write to cheer you up. As I am good for nothing else I can now at least heartily rejoice that I am able to make my superiors merry by providing them with material for laughter. I would not, however, be aggrieved if Father Provincial got it into his head that I have not so much as dreamt of acquiring an honorific title, nor do I willingly forgo my public lectures in order to prepare for disputations of this sort, except purely out of obedience. As just now he is on to me again about the matter, your Reverence, in my opinion, will not sin if you write from Rome to prevent me being given a degree which I neither deserve nor want, and to put a stop to such public Acts in future, as far as I am concerned. When I was a child I spoke as a child, I understood as a child, I thought as a child. But when I became a man I put away the things of a child. *Tempora mutantur nos et mutamur in illis.*[2]

---

[1] Horace, *Ars poetica*, line 5. " Could you, my friends, refrain from laughter, were you admitted to such a sight ? "

[2] Braunsberger, *Epistulae*, vol. v, pp. 633–4. The famous dictum with which the letter ends originated in the sixteenth century, but who deserves the credit for it is not certain. In this letter may be detected a shadow of the mental aberration which came upon poor Father Jasper afterwards. St. Peter always had the highest regard for him. He got his doctorate at last but events proved that he would have been better without it.

After the Dillingen Synod had closed Peter repaired to Würzburg to face the Bishop, who was impatient to hear about his college. There he was joined by Father Anton Vinck, Provincial of the Rhineland Jesuits, but himself did most of the talking. According to Vinck's report, he explained that it was not at all the wish of the Society of Jesus to avoid sending preachers and theologians, but only that, in the endowment of the college, the services of such men should not be contracted for, as such an arrangement would be contrary to the Jesuit constitutions. On hearing this the Bishop jumped up and angrily demanded why he had not been told so before. He then left the room to recover his equanimity. When he returned, Vinck says, Peter pointed out " *con la sua eloquentia* " that by its very institute the Society of Jesus was bound to the avocations in question, only they must be pursued gratuitously and not as part of a contracted bargain. If His Lordship would but trust the Jesuits he would find that they did not fail him.

At last the worthy old man gave in and consented to the alteration of the agreement in the sense required by the authorities in Rome.[1] St. Francis wrote to thank him heartily and to say that he most gladly accepted the responsibility of the new college. On receipt of the news the Bishop, for his part, " lifted his hands to Heaven " like another Simeon, in his joy and satisfaction. Could he have seen into the future he would have been still better pleased, for, in less than ten years, the modest Würzburg College which opened its six classes with one hundred and sixty boys in October, 1567, had been raised to the rank of a university by the Pope and Emperor. On the other hand, could the Jesuits have seen into the future they must have shrunk in dismay from the task they were undertaking, seeing their brethren, under Bishop Friedrich's successor, wretchedly housed, half starved, and provided, in the bitter words of Hoffaeus, with only " sour wine in small quantities and very bad beer." Still, by the turn of the century they had nearly a thousand students on their roll, and the University was playing a valiant part in the later battles of the Counter-Reformation.[2]

Meantime from Rome came a letter imposing yet another burden on St. Peter. The Bishop of Strasbourg was an old and infirm man. After his death, which could not be far distant, it was feared that the Chapter, which apparently had badly deteriorated in the preceding decade, might easily elect a successor quite unfitted to preserve the remnant of Catholicism

[1] Braunsberger, *Epistulae*, vol. v, pp. 709–11.
[2] Duhr, *Geschichte der Jesuiten in den Ländern deutscher Zunge im XVI Jahrhundert*, vol. i, pp., 123–7.

still left in the great Imperial City. The only way to prevent that happening was to secure the immediate choice of a suitable coadjutor with right of succession, and to Peter fell the delicate task of persuading the apathetic and disheartened Bishop to adopt such a course. After a final sermon in Würzburg Cathedral he set off in company with Father Vinck on June 30th. One reason for their keeping together was that bands of the peculiarly bloodthirsty type of Calvinist nicknamed the *Gueux*, who had been banished from the Low Countries, were prowling about the Rhineland and Palatinate. They met with no adventures, however, and after spending a little while on business in Frankfurt and Mainz, arrived at Speyer, where a few months earlier a school had been opened under the leadership of Father Hermes Halbpaur. Father Hermes may have lost his head in the pulpit, but up against the bellicose Protestantism of Speyer he found it again, and was carrying on valiantly in the face of appalling obstruction. In an effort to kill the school the civil authorities had issued an edict forbidding the citizens to give lodgings to Catholic schoolboys but, for all that, Hermes soon managed to collect 152 of them. Here, as in Würzburg, the real difficulty was the determination of the ecclesiastical authorities to bind the Jesuits by a contract to provide them with preachers and theological professors. St. Peter and Father Vinck did their best to straighten out the situation, but many a month was to pass before they succeeded in obtaining for the nascent college a charter guaranteeing its continued existence.

Then, accompanied by a representative of the Archbishop of Mainz, Peter set off on the long journey to Zabern in Alsace, where the Bishop of Strasbourg resided. That good man had just returned from a cure, quite ill and worn out as a result of the doctor's remedial measures. He received Peter well, as they had already been on friendly terms with one another, but, owing to bad health and natural timidity, showed little inclination to stand up to his haughty canons. Reporting the interview, Peter said:

I tried to show him how important it was to obviate with the greatest prudence the dangers of the election after his death, by the timely provision of a coadjutor to whom afterwards the administration of the diocese could be safely entrusted. I urged, too, that he should himself designate a Catholic man as his successor and not leave so grave a concern to the discretion of his canons, who were mostly, perhaps, suspect and wavering in their faith. I told him that he would have the support and favour of eminent men in Rome who heartily desired that his diocese should fare better than the majority of the Saxon ones, now, as we know, in the control of the heretics. He should then, I warned him, embrace the safer course and not expose his diocese and its Catholic flock to serious peril. Rather ought he to think of the neighbouring princes who were merely waiting for his death to make the diocese their prey; and he should remember the unsound faith of the electors, whom, if he was not prepared himself to suggest a suitable Catholic successor for election and confirmation, he might at least constrain to provide a coadjutor by an election held in a true and Catholic manner. . . .

I also used other arguments which I thought relevant, but with what success I do not know. All I could do was to plead with him. He has not yet decided on his course, as he is somewhat remiss and inexperienced in the transaction of business and appears not to have his heart in the present affair. We must pray to Our Lord that this illustrious diocese may not be wrested from the Catholics and subjected to the power of the sectaries. . . .[1]

The second part of Peter's very lengthy letter is taken up with some sharp criticism of the Strasbourg higher clergy, who lived "like gentlemen, enjoying the fruits of their benefices, instead of attending to the service of God and the ceremonies of the Church." Then he continues with a number of suggestions "for the preservation and advancement of the German dioceses at the present time." These were: (1) that the Pope should take counsel with the Emperor about the appointment of coadjutors with right of succession; (2) that, if the Emperor refused to help, the Pope might well adopt strict precautions to prevent the advancement of anyone to a canonry who had not first made the Tridentine profession of faith; (3) that each canon capitular, meaning one with a voice in the election of bishops, should be compelled to make the Tridentine profession a second time before recording his vote; (4) that the newly elected bishop should be obliged to promise under oath that he would not start innovations, or tolerate them from others, or permit married priests to officiate, or allow Communion under both species; (5) that, if any of these provisions failed to be carried out, the election should be declared void and confirmation refused in Rome.

Trent had already legislated for the canons in the sense described by St. Peter, but he replied that they ignored the law completely and would

[1] Braunsberger, *Epistulae*, vol. v, pp. 514-5.

not be likely to improve until the Pope used his personal intervention. It is interesting to observe how much the canons occupied his thoughts. The fact that they were drawn almost exclusively from aristocratic circles seemed to him a grave disadvantage, because such people could not easily be taught to toe the line. " They compel new bishops," he writes, " to swear respect for their privileges and exemptions, nor will they receive the Council of Trent in so far as it clashes with their ancient statutes. It cannot be denied that the vices of the cathedral clergy are both public and most abominable. By them they scandalize all parties and bring the whole ecclesiastical order into dishonour and opprobrium."

Having finished with the canons the Saint turns to the case of the monks and other religious. The Archbishop of Mainz had said to him more than once that the monasteries of his Electorate could scarcely survive beyond another decade, so few were the religious remaining and so irreligiously did the few demean themselves. " Indeed, words fail to tell," Peter continued, " how wretched and contaminated are the surviving monasteries of any order in Germany. Their superiors would seem to devote themselves to entertaining and keeping up a sort of public pot-house rather than to the good government of their communities. That is why Germany is full of apostates and vagabond monks who roam about without their order's habit and disgrace the parish churches in which they are nearly always to be found." His suggested remedy for this state of affairs is that the Pope should compel the superiors-general of religious orders to send trustworthy visitors to Germany with a commission to close down monasteries where there were only a handful of monks left and to amalgamate the various small groups into larger communities. The vacant monasteries might then be turned into seminaries, if there appeared to be no hope of their revival.

At the very end of the long document Peter comes back to the bishops again—" venerandos mihi semper Episcopos nostros." The root of their trouble is that " they lack confidence and strength of mind, thinking that the affairs of the Church in Germany are almost beyond redemption." He pleads their cause, makes excuses for them, and begs that they be given comfort and encouragement. And so we reach the close of this wonderful letter which almost by itself would have been enough to justify Peter's canonization. Its last words are a humble apology for the liberty he has taken.[1]

---

[1] Braunsberger, *Epistulae*, vol. v, pp. 515–9.

CHAPTER XVI

THE CENTURIES OF MAGDEBURG

St. Peter's long period as Provincial of the Jesuits in Upper Germany was now drawing to a close, but before it ended he had to endure a few more of fortune's frowns. For one thing, the royal ladies at Innsbruck became daily more exacting, their latest desire being that the Jesuits should undertake the spiritual direction of the house for pious women which they had established at Hall. Such a charge, as a regular ministry, is precluded by the Jesuit constitutions, but St. Peter had to make many weary journeys to Innsbruck before he could persuade their devout but intensely obstinate Highnesses to have some regard for other people's scruples. The two ladies still monopolized the services of two Jesuits as confessors and preachers, which might have been tolerable if they did not so enervate and spoil them. Thus, they used to send in special dishes each day to the Jesuit College, recently established in Hall, for the comfort of those privileged Fathers; and in other ways made onslaughts on the common life which belongs to the essence of a religious order. The two sisters who had married, Barbara and Joanna, had already carried off a Jesuit apiece from St. Peter's Province to act as chaplains at the ducal Courts of Ferrara and Florence. Apart from the sore need of them which he had at home, Peter intensely disliked the association of his men with the nobility, as he had learned by hard experience that Court life was the worst thing in the world for their souls. It had made his best preacher, Gewarts, an impossible person to manage, and turned Schorich, who was capable of better things, into a sulky grumbler who resented the mildest comment on his correspondence and gossip with the great ones of this world, both male and female. When these men and others like them fell foul of their rectors, as very often happened, it became St. Peter's responsibility to soothe the ruffled feelings on both sides. In some respects this was the most exhausting part of his labours as Provincial. The Province was still raw and without fixed traditions. Most of the men in it were overworked, for the good reason that their numbers did not at all answer to the amount which bishops and princes called upon them to do. The consequence was a certain fraying of nerves which, in the circumstances, must be counted an honourable infirmity. Page after wearisome page of Braunsberger's small print is occupied with these domestic upheavals, and, if one thing more than another proves the heroic sanctity of Peter Canisius, it is that his temper never lost its even sweetness under so much provocation. Not once is it possible to detect a note of personal grievance in his correspondence. As far as that evidence goes, and goodness knows there is plenty of it, he had no thought for self at all. The welfare of the Church, of his Order, of his individual subjects, these were what absorbed him. His men were not all heroes by any means, and the life of secular Courts damaged whatever ideals their Order had succeeded in putting into them. " *Mallem ego nihil cum Aula nostris esse commune*," he wrote to Borgia in October, 1567—I would prefer that our Fathers should have nothing in common with the Court. And as before that date, so for many years after it, he continued with the patient gentleness which was his great strength to withstand the encroachments of Bavarian Dukes and Austrian Princesses on the liberties of his Order.

On one of Peter's visits to Innsbruck for the purpose of placating the royal ladies there, an adventure befell him which was afterwards related in detail by his genial, simple-hearted companion, Father Rocca. Rocca, an Italian who had made his studies at Dillingen, has a claim to remembrance as the confessor and spiritual director for more than twenty years of St. Robert Bellarmine. The following is an account of what happened in December, 1567, when St. Peter Canisius and he were traversing the Bavarian Alps, on the outskirts of Oberammergau :

We two left Augsburg and made towards the Alps. As the rain which had been falling some time still continued to pour down, our ride through those high mountains was not without danger and hardship, due especially to the fact that the countryside was flooded. Nevertheless, by the grace of God we reached a certain monastery of the Black Monks of St. Benedict.[1] Shortly before coming to it, we had to cross the river Ammer, usually a small stream, but then so swollen by the rains that it covered the bridge, barely leaving visible the two wooden rails at the side. On both sides of the bridge there was so much water that it had the appearance of a lake. When we came to

---

[1] Ettal, well known to all visitors to the Passion Play at Oberammergau.

the spot, Father Canisius said to me: "Do you see those two wooden rails in the water, Father? We must cross over between them." I, who had never made the journey before, replied: "Father, where would we go? We run a terrible risk." But he, having more trust in God, was resolved, and answered me: "Do not hesitate, Father. I have been over this bridge on other occasions and there is no danger. So don't doubt but go ahead." With that I remained silent, and, making the Sign of the Cross, told myself: This is my Provincial; he bids me proceed, and, trusting in obedience, proceed I will. So I rode into the flood towards the bridge, which was a wooden structure, and found that the water reached up to my horse's girth. Father Canisius followed. As it was a Sunday the whole village stood watching us in amazement. Half way across, my horse put his foot on a large stone, which caused him to rear on his hind legs to the great consternation of his rider. Had he fallen, it would have been all up with the companion of Father Canisius. I then saw to it that the Father avoided the stone, and so we came over the water and into the village where all the rustics were standing about. With one voice they reproved us for rash men, saying we had done the one thing in the world that none of them would dare to do.

Shortly afterwards we came to the monastery, at which Father Canisius was received with great charity by the Abbot and the monks. After resting a little while, the Father desired to move on, but the Abbot would not hear of his going that day, because the valley below, two German miles in width, was impassable owing to being flooded to a great depth. Not long before, a peasant on a good horse had tried to cross but was obliged to return to the monastery. As the weather was fine that day and a strong north wind had begun to blow, the Abbot expected that the floods would subside during the night and enable us to travel more safely the following day, with the afore-mentioned peasant as our guide. We therefore remained that night at the monastery, and Father Canisius, at their request, gave the good monks an exhortation in the evening, to the satisfaction of all.

Having said Mass the following morning and thanked the Abbot and the monks for their great kindness to us, we started our journey towards the valley, preceded by the peasant who knew the lie of the land. We came down the mountain-side briskly, as the day was calm and fine, but when we reached the valley there was nothing to be seen but water, with high mountains on both sides from which torrents roared down. Though the river which runs through the valley is a large one[1] it was impossible to trace its course. Everything was a sea ; and on the ordinary paths the water reached up to our horses' girths. I wanted Father Canisius to be in the middle, between myself and our rustic guide, but he would have me take that position, saying that his horse was a good and safe one. I gave way against my will, for I was afraid that something might happen to Father Canisius, as indeed, afterwards fell out. We rode three or four Italian miles through the water prosperously enough, by the grace of God, during which time I often looked around to see how Father Canisius was faring. Once on turning I saw that he was almost completely submerged. He had one foot on the ground, but the other was in the stirrup, from which he could not disengage it. Thus, clinging to the reins and saddle, he was held fast and beyond helping himself or being helped by us. The guide told me not to stir from my horse, as I should be swamped before I could reach Father Canisius, and, indeed, I think he spoke truly, for the deep and rushing waters would have borne me and my horse away.

In that predicament, and unable to find any human remedy, I commended Father Canisius to God with tears. Then, looking round, what should I see but a giant of a man moving ahead of us on foot. I cried out and made signs to him to come. He went to Father Canisius, drew his foot out of the stirrup, and guided him and the horse to some dry ground. When I reached the same spot, I dismounted and embraced Father Canisius, saying : " Father, I was filled with pity for you, and, not knowing any way to help you, commended you to God." He replied that he had never been so content as then, turning over and over in his mind the words : *Cupio dissolvi et esse cum Christo.* Speaking to the man by whose good offices he had been drawn from the water, he said : " To-day we shall dine together at the inn, and I shall give you your honorarium." The man, who was smiling, answered something which I could not catch, as though pleased with the Father's words. Then, having helped him to remount, we all entered the water once more, and the man, who appeared to be a peasant, was seen by us for some time walking ahead. But when we had nearly crossed the flood and were near the inn, he was not to be seen any more, and I have always thought that he was an angel from Heaven, sent to deliver that holy Father in order that he might labour for some years more in the vineyard of the Lord and propagate the Catholic faith in Germany. . . .

[1] The Loisach.

The reasons which led me to believe that it was not a man but an angel were these : (1) he was not seen until the danger arose ; (2) he disappeared as soon as it was over ; (3) if he had been a man he would not have relinquished the dinner and honorarium promised to him, for, though the people of these parts are good and kindly and readily offer their services, yet they also readily accept a gratuity and a glass of wine, etc. And so concludes the story of what happened on that journey.[1]

On arrival in Innsbruck, Peter discovered that he had more than women's troubles to settle, as his Rector, Father Delanoy, was acting very strangely. He had developed a passion for gardening, and spent most of his time with a spade in his hands. Judging by their complaints, he appears to have devoted what remained over to harrying his subjects. Canisius endeavoured repeatedly with great tact to render him more genial and considerate towards them, but he had become a stern martinet, and the Saint's efforts were of no avail. All through, nevertheless, he speaks of Delanoy in an appreciative, sympathetic way as a " good and holy old man " and a " miles emeritus " who well deserved the rest for which he craved. Eventually, on his way back from Rome in January, 1569, Peter felt obliged to remove the Rector from his office and substitute Father Hoffaeus. He, too, was a martinet, but of a more tolerable kind, and he possessed the advantage of being in the good graces of the ' Queens,' who regarded him, he says, as their " albae gallinae filius " or white-headed boy. On this occasion St. Peter assisted at the death-bed of the former Rector, poor, well-meaning, melancholy Father Dyrsius, of whom the ' Queens ' were so fond. " It was marvellous," he wrote, " to see the care which Queen Magdalene had for the sick man, and how diligent she was in preparing his food for him daily and providing him with the most costly medicines. . . . After receiving the Sacraments of the Church and giving his brethren a shining example of piety, he to-day rendered up his soul to God who made him. May he live in blessedness with Christ through the sacrifices and prayers of the whole Society."[2]

At Ingolstadt trouble of a different kind, partly self-made, had come upon the Jesuits. Two of their professors in the faculty of arts were warring with secular colleagues to such an extent that the Chancellor of Bavaria

---

[1] Braunsberger, Epistulae, vol. vi, pp. 724–30. Rocca's account of the pleasant people of Oberammergau is very shrewd. They are extremely friendly and good-natured, and they do not resent a gratuity. Their children are surely the most likeable in all Europe, utterly unspoilt and with a courtesy and quaint little dignity in their bearing which makes them seem to be the children of princes.
[2] Braunsberger, Epistulae, vol. vi, pp. 245–6.

begged for St. Peter's intervention. Promptly answering the appeal, he found that the quarrel, like most quarrels, was about money. The two Jesuits insisted on returning to the candidates whatever fees they received at examination time, while the other professors claimed that the money thus renounced should come to themselves. Then again, the Jesuits were great sticklers for the observance of the University's statutes, any violation of which they denounced to the Senate. Though they might have had the letter of the law on their side, St. Peter considered that they had acted too pugnaciously, and without the humility and modesty that became them as religious. "Both sides, however, admitted me as judge and mediator," he informed Borgia. "I took Dr. Eisengrein as my partner so as to have greater authority in settling the dispute. . . . With the help of the Lord we succeeded in soothing the ruffled tempers and in bringing about a sincere mutual reconciliation. I have spoken with many of our Fathers regarding other points of the controversy, and shown them that the best way to preserve peace in future is for them to put argument aside and freely and willingly renounce the right by which they considered themselves the equals of other professors in the faculty, leaving all administrative cares to their colleagues and contenting themselves with the sole office of teaching. This way seemed both simple and secure, and by means of it the seeds of discord were removed. Our men have now been recalled to the modesty and simplicity proper to their profession. . . . God grant that, made wise by these troubles, we may in future beware of all appearance of evil and sincerely pursue and promote what is solidly good, in both the letter and the spirit."[1]

So far, the reader must admit, this biography of St. Peter Canisius has not been over-reticent concerning the internal disorders of the Society of Jesus in Germany, but perhaps the most terrible threat to its credit still remains to be mentioned. That was the infiltration of heretical opinions. Dillingen University which had already caused St. Peter so much disquietude, was now the centre of this totally unexpected and ominous visitation. About the year 1564, a young Englishman named Edward Thorn arrived in Louvain, where he hoped to improve his education. According to a declaration made by him later on, he was not a Catholic and had no intention of joining the Church. But he wanted to join the Society of Jesus, as he apparently considered that step the best way to arrive at *otium cum dignitate*. He accordingly feigned Catholicism and played the part so well that neither the Jesuits of Louvain nor those of

---

[1] Braunsberger, *Epistulae*, vol. vi, pp. 40–2, 560–2.

Munich, where he made a year's novitiate, had the slightest doubt of his genuineness. They even allowed him to pronounce what are called " vows of devotion," and then, in 1566, sent him to Dillingen for his literary studies, his age being twenty-four. What happened the following year is told in a letter from the Rector of Dillingen to St. Francis Borgia. Owing to the frequent changes in his staff, the Rector thought that it might be a good thing if all the professors and some of the Jesuit students were to make the Tridentine profession of faith. The community accordingly assembled in the chapel on the feast of the Assumption, where, the formula having been read to them, first the professors and then the lower masters testified on oath that they accepted it. The sequel may be given in the Rector's own words :

It came to the turn of Edward, the Englishman, who about two years ago was received into the Society in this Province and did a year of noviceship at Munich most satisfactorily. The rest of the time he has been studying rhetoric, first at Ingolstadt and then here, so peacefully and with such an air of humility and obedience that he was considered to be among the more perfect of the brethren. Well, when this Edward was admonished to make his profession of faith with the others, he openly protested that he could not do so conscientiously. Asked for his reason, he said that he would explain in another place. I therefore called him to my room shortly afterwards, where were present some other theologians, and requested him to let us hear what he had to say. He replied that he could not swear to belief in the legitimacy of venerating images, nor to obey the Pope, etc. We then dealt with him gently, using many arguments but, finding him stubborn, I bade him go to his room and had him provided with Catholic books. Practically every theologian here has dealt with him in private for several hours each day, both in conversation and by note. But he only became the more obstinate and would admit none of their arguments. His one reply was that his own mind testified otherwise to him, and that he would suffer every species of torment rather than recede from his opinions. His language was exactly like that used by the heretics of our time. When asked how he had learned to speak thus, he answered that he had always so believed, and that he was certain of its truth, whatever a Pope or Council or other congregation of men might define. . . . At last, when we saw that there was no moving him, we sent him to Father Provincial, then in Munich, but he went off instead to an heretical town near here called Lauingen, where, according to rumour, he has had a good reception from the ministers. . . . And thus ends this Englishman, who, if always a Protestant, as he says, has certainly proved himself a wonderful hypocrite. We commend him to the prayers of your Paternity and of the other Fathers and Brothers, if perchance some day God may have mercy on him.[1]

The well-known Lutheran, Tillman Heshusius, brought out a book at Basle to celebrate the acquisition of Thorn. It was not so much his abandonment of the Catholic Church as his defection from the Jesuits which rejoiced the hearts of the Protestants. Perhaps the black Company of "Esauites" would be crippled by a blow so public and unexpected. Their hopes ran high when, shortly afterwards, another young Jesuit of Dillingen fled to them, and, in conjunction with Thorn, endeavoured by letter to attract other malcontents of the University to the Protestant ranks. Much of the disquiet at the University was caused, strange to say, by the ideas of the twelfth-century Arab philosopher, Averroes, whose pantheistic doctrines had somehow laid a spell on certain Jesuits. Among them was another young Englishman named John Wick, who, in his philosophy lectures, took Averroes as master, belittled St. Thomas, and severely criticized Pope Pius V for putting that prince of theologians among the Doctors of the Church. Wick must have been an able man, in spite of his vagaries, because, when deposed from office and assigned the less risky task of expounding the principles of rhetoric, he gained such an ascendancy over his new students that they threatened to quit the University *en masse* if superiors interfered with him. For a long time, he and another insubordinate Averroist defied both their Rector and their Provincial. To relieve Dillingen of Wick's presence, St. Peter offered himself as a victim to his sarcastic tongue by taking him to live with him in Augsburg.

Among the remedies which the Saint proposed to his General against future misfortunes of the dreadful kind that had come upon them were the following:

Let the wretched tares of Averroes be utterly extirpated. It is thought that the philosophy of Averroes has made, not so much heretics, as atheists, of some of our men. . . . Those who came to us from Rome this year have shown the unhappy fruits which Averroes bears in many

[1] Braunsberger, *Epistulae*, vol. vi, pp. 29–30.

souls. They wish to rely solely on their own reasons, and have reverence for the authority of scarcely any man or any theologian. May God prevent our men from deriving this profit of their philosophical studies, as it is impossible to think of anything that makes it more easy for them to become heretics. Would that it might never on any account be permitted to one of ours to hold and defend, either publicly or privately, his own or another's opinion as against the common teaching of the schools. Some of our people have now the temerity to call the Arab " the divine Averroes," and by his authority, as I have said, they are confirmed in the spirit of contradiction and in their contempt for scholastic theology. Moreover, they defame by I know not what titles others who hold and defend the received doctrine of the schools. I thought that a public injunction should be issued, severely prohibiting and eradicating this seed of doctrine which appears to have taken root in the field of our Society. . . . I do not put forward these proposals as wishing to lay down the law, but only because I would lay before the best of Fathers such thoughts as occurred to me. I beg that, on account of these apostasies, due measures may be taken to safeguard the integrity of our Society, which depends most of all on soundness of faith. . . . Would your Paternity please pray for us, and see, I beg you, how important it is to send to this Province men strong in their faith and vocation. . . .[1]

How necessary it was for Rome to take the steps indicated by St. Peter became apparent a little while later when Father Klessel, the Court preacher at Innsbruck, publicly embraced Lutheranism. The Lady Magdalene was so indignant that she protested she would gladly light the faggots at his stake with her own hands when he was captured ! St. Peter's reaction took another form. " May our most merciful God forgive him and us," he wrote to the General. The affair prostrated him with grief, and he urged that no German should be received into the Society of Jesus in future until he had first made a public profession of faith according to the Creed of Pope Pius IV.

At the time when the Saint was worrying over the danger from Averroes to his own men and expiating their defection with his prayers and tears,

[1] Braunsberger, *Epistulae*, vol. vi, pp. 67–8. In the fifth general congregation of the Society of Jesus, held in 1593–4, it was decreed that Jesuit professors must, as far as possible, strive to lessen the credit of Averroes. If they found it necessary to mention some good argument of his, they should do so without lauding his philosophy as a whole, and show, when the chance offered, that his good things had been borrowed from other sources. That was a fair enough suggestion, as the Arabs had originally derived their Aristotelian and other lore from Christians in the East.

he was also brooding anxiously on the intolerable difficulties which confronted the German bishops. Between August and December, 1567, he drew up, at the request of the Bishop of Würzburg, yet another series of counsels for that much-afflicted Prelate. His Lordship should set aside regular hours for reading the canons of the sacred Councils, above all those of the Council of Trent. He should study, too, the Acts of the Provincial Council of Mainz, held in 1549, as Würzburg appertained to that Province, and the Plan of Reform promulgated on the authority of the Pope by Cardinal Campeggio at the Diet of Regensburg in 1524. Besides these, he should constantly peruse the Catechism of the Council of Trent and other books which set forth the proper methods of holding divine services, of administering the Sacraments, and of maintaining ecclesiastical discipline. The Bishop ought to have by his side a trustworthy confessor, and also an adviser skilled especially in canon law who would admonish him as to his duties. It is of great importance that he should acquire and study the decrees issued by the Pope, in particular such ones as the Bull, *In Coena Domini*, which pertained to the cure of souls and the office of bishops. He would do well to hold a weekly council of the best priests in his diocese, discussing with them how discipline might be rehabilitated and prelates and pastors helped in their work. " The diseases of many people would be cured gradually, with no great trouble, if the Bishop were known to be really vigilant; if he often sent round men to inspect and report; and if he combined fatherly meekness with the just severity of a judge." Parish priests and confessors should be instructed in the methods which they ought to employ in hearing confessions, and a selection should be made from the decrees of the Council of Trent for communication to the people, especially with reference to the Sacrament of Matrimony.[1] If the Bishop found it impossible to hold a solemn synod annually, as the Council prescribed, or to get the other provisions of the Council accepted by his clergy, he should inform the Pope in detail about his difficulties.

Such was the gist of St. Peter's " Consilium Theologicum," which he set forth with his usual modesty " and deference always to the judgment of better minds."[2] Just three hundred years after he wrote it, a learned canon of Würzburg described the document as " a precious relic . . . enshrining many solemn truths that deserve to be deeply pondered at all times, not excluding our own." From this time forth the Saint became

---

[1] St. Peter always had the problem of clandestine marriages very much at heart.
[2] Braunsberger, *Epistulae*, vol. vi, pp. 75–9.

as much the trusted adviser and counsellor of the Bishop of Würzburg as he was of Cardinal Truchsess and Cardinal Hosius.

To offset the domestic sorrows of this period, Peter was granted a passing glimpse of sanctity at home. Attending the Jesuit College in Vienna was a young Pole of noble birth named Stanislaus Kostka. Stanislaus had set his heart on being a Jesuit, and for two years endeavoured to secure his desire from the Austrian Provincial, Father Maggio. But the relatives of the boy offered strong opposition to his project, and, as they were a powerful influence in Poland, Maggio naturally feared to compromise his brethren in that country by going against their wishes. At last, in 1567, on the advice of the Emperor's confessor, Father Francis Antonio, Stanislaus determined to seek his fortunes outside Austria. He was only seventeen and had been delicately nurtured, but the seal of God on his heart made him resolute beyond his years. Rising very early on August 10, 1567, he slipped unobserved out of the Lutheran house where his elder brother and he had been lodging, because the Jesuits were not permitted to have a boarding-school. Then, after Mass and Holy Communion at a near-by church, he left Vienna and sought the shelter of a wood, where he changed his fine clothes for those of a peasant lad. Evidently he had studied his map carefully beforehand, as, in the rather confused narrative that has come down to us, there is no sign of hesitation about the route. Augsburg and Father Canisius were his objectives, and they lay, as the crow flies, 253 miles away. By the winding roads and paths which he must have taken he probably covered nearly twice that distance. A comparison of dates shows that he was a little over a fortnight on the road, which means that he cannot have covered much less than thirty miles a day. How he lived during that time nobody ever knew, but we hear, and may well believe, that angels attended him, as they did Elias, bringing him the Bread of Heaven in whose strength he walked steadfastly to his Mountain of Expectation.

Not finding Father Canisius at Augsburg, Stanislaus went straight on to Dillingen, apparently without having broken his fast. One could wish for a few details about the meeting between the old Saint and the young, but nothing has come down except a bald paragraph in a letter from Canisius to Borgia, addressed from Munich, September 25, 1567:

Very Reverend Father, *Pax Christi*.
Those who bring you this letter under the guidance of Christ are sent from our Province. The first is James of Genoa, well known in

Rome, whom your Paternity bade me return, in accordance with his own wishes, that he might have better opportunities for study. He lived among us in two colleges as a good, obedient brother, but perhaps his health will be better in the air of Italy. The second is Master Fabricius of Liége who has taught rhetoric for many years with credit in the College of Munich. He is a peaceable man, constant in his vocation, whom others can easily get on with and love for the singular candour and sincerity of his character. Of only one thing am I afraid, that his health may suffer if he stays overlong in the climate of Rome.

The third person sent is Stanislaus, a young Pole of noble birth, virtuous and devoted to study. Our Fathers at Vienna did not dare to receive him, for fear of provoking his family. He came to me desiring to fulfil a long-cherished project; for, some years ago, he engaged himself entirely to our Society before being admitted into it. In Dillingen, he was tested for a while at the boarding-school[1] and showed himself ever faithful to his duties and constant in his vocation. Meantime, he conceived a desire to be sent to Rome that he might be further removed from his relatives, of whose persecution he was afraid, and that he might make greater progress in piety. He has never lived among our novices, but might be aggregated to them in Rome. We hope for great things from him. . . .[2]

It has sometimes been thought that Father Canisius dealt rather inconsiderately with Stanislaus. In a penetrating and most admirable sketch of the young Saint[3] it is stated that he was placed as " an ordinary servant " in the College of St. Jerome and that " the work was heavy." But we know nothing of the work except that it consisted in waiting on the students while they dined, and such service can hardly be reckoned either humiliating or excessively laborious. As for the journey to Rome, St. Peter's letter shows that it was undertaken at the desire of Stanislaus himself and made in the company of two excellent and congenial fellow travellers. " Nos de illo praeclara speramus," wrote the Provincial, having no hint that the boy's constitution was already undermined by the intensity of his inner life and that he would " die in his glory and never be old." When in Rome the following summer on the business of his Order, St. Peter was asked to address the Jesuit novices at Sant'Andrea. He spoke on August 1st and had Stanislaus, still apparently quite strong and well,

---

[1] The College of St. Jerome.   [2] Braunsberger, *Epistulae*, vol. vi, pp. 63–4
[3] By Father C. C. Martindale.

among his listeners. The way, he said, to be sure of passing a month advantageously and happily was to persuade oneself by a form of make-believe that it would be one's last month on earth. This simple suggestion set Stanislaus on fire. One can hardly describe him except in terms of fire. He did not so much live as burn away before God with sheer longing for the eternal union, and so the words of St. Peter rang for him like the bells of Heaven. Exactly a fortnight later, the Feast of Our Lady's Assumption, Stanislaus was inexplicably taken ill and died.[1] He was beatified by Clement VIII in 1602 and canonized by Benedict XIII in 1726, the youngest confessor ever raised to the altars of the Church.

And now from Stanislaus, the happy Slav, we must turn to another man of that extraordinary race, the gloomy Croat, Flacius Illyricus. Rarely in human history has there been, outside asylums, a man whose life was so governed by a dark and crazy conviction. Introduced to the writings of Luther at the age of nineteen by his faithless cousin, the Provincial of the Franciscans in that indefinite region called Illyricum,[2] Flacius first spent some time in the circle of the Basle Protestants, brooding on his sins and contemplating suicide as the only way of escape from conscience. Next he wandered to Tübingen in search of peace and, not finding it, sought refuge with Melanchthon at Wittenberg. Melanchthon befriended him and taught him Luther's doctrine of justification by faith, which ' comfortable word ' made him for good the most enthusiastic of Luther's disciples. But he discovered on his own account the chief dogma of his creed and the one that supplies the key to his whole life. " It is now my absolute conviction," he wrote at the time, " that the Pope is, in very truth, the Antichrist."[3] What a useful recruit to the Lutheran cause he became may be gauged from the fact that only Luther himself surpassed him in literary productivity. Luther gave the world about four hundred different writings, and Flacius, close on three hundred. These writings of the Croat nearly all emanated from a blazing hatred of Catholicism in every shape and form. Hatred can be as great a motive power as love, and there is no denying that it turned Flacius into a worker of heroic quality.

In the long and bitter strife with the Catholics, the Lutherans gradually came to see that the weakest link in their own armour was history. During the last years of his life the same fact dawned on and distressed even the

[1] Sacchinus, *Vita Stanislai Kostkae Poloni* (Lyons, 1616), pp. 56–9.
[2] It corresponded roughly to modern Yugoslavia.
[3] Preger, *Matthias Flacius Illyricus und seine Zeit*, part i (Erlangen, 1859), p. 23. Preger is a panegyrist.

utterly unhistorical mind of Luther. In a Prefatory Epistle to the book of an Englishman against the Papacy, he wrote as follows:

All those who possess the spirit of Christ are doubtless well aware that by reading, speaking, and writing as much as they can against the bloodthirsty, shameless, blasphemous Whore of the Devil, they are accomplishing the highest and most excellent sacrifice of praise. I, who at the first was not experienced in historical study, assailed the Papacy *a priori*, as we say, with a frontal attack out of Holy Scripture. Now, to my huge delight, others are doing the same from the rear, that is out of historical documents. It seems to me an extremely good plan and makes me very happy, since I see so clearly that history and Scripture are in agreement. What I have learned and taught from St. Paul and Daniel, namely that the Pope is an offence to both God and humanity, is now plainly revealed by the historians.[1]

Spurred on by the wishes of his beloved master, Flacius conceived the ambition to provide Lutheranism with an ancestry. As a first sketch of a family tree, he brought out in 1556 a book entitled, *Catalogus Testium Veritatis*, wherein were listed the names of several hundred men and women who, throughout the Christian centuries and even at the height of the papal power, had not " bowed the knee to Baal." Among these fore-runners of Protestantism we find St. Bernard, St. Catherine of Siena, and St. Thomas Aquinas, which shows, at any rate, that Flacius was broad-minded in his principles of selection. Although ludicrously uncritical, the book gave the Protestant communities great satisfaction, and its success encouraged Flacius to go ahead with his ambitious scheme for a complete history of the Christian Church. He was a capable organizer and set to work, like a general preparing for war, to collect money, munitions, and troops. The money came in in such good quantities that the rivals of Flacius in Wittenberg, probably a little jealous, dubbed his History " the Golden Book." Munitions in the shape of manuscripts and old sources were sought diligently in all quarters by Flacius himself and his two henchmen, Marcus Wagner and Caspar von Nidbruck, the latter of whom, owing to the favour and recommendation of King Maximilian, was enabled to obtain entrance to Catholic archives and collections. Flacius obtained entrance by putting on a monk's habit with roomy sleeves. The

[1] Preface to *Vitae Romanorum Pontificum quos Papas vocamus*, by Robert Barnes, Chaplain to Henry VIII. The book was published at Wittenberg, in 1536. It is extremely rare, but there is a copy in the London Library.

Wittenbergers gave out that these sleeves used to come out of the libraries with something more than the arms of Flacius inside them. That they spoke more truly than, perhaps, they guessed is, according to Salig, the Lutheran historian of the Confession of Augsburg, easily seen by examination of the manuscript remains of Flacius in the Wolfenbüttel Library. When Flacius undertook the project of the *Centuries*, writes this authority, " he travelled about widely, oftentimes in disguise, and inspected the libraries in the monasteries. If he found something to his purpose, he was dishonourable enough to cut or tear out whole pages, or take away whole manuscripts with him. That is why the ' Flacian Knife ' and the ' Flacian Hand ' are still proverbial." But it was not only Catholic libraries which Flacius plundered. Salig found among his relics at Wolfenbüttel several holograph writings of Melanchthon which, as the Wittenberg doctors had alleged long ago, he must have procured by some burglarious practice.[1]

As for the troops, Flacius had the good fortune to enlist Johann Wigand and Matthew Judex, two stalwarts of uncompromising Lutheranism who hated the Catholic Church almost as heartily as he did himself. Wigand's style may be gathered from his references to Father Canisius in print as " a dog of a monk," " the Pope's own donkey," and " an impudent and miserable devil " ; while Judex wrote calling upon temporal rulers to exterminate the Papacy with the sword. Others, too, rallied to the colours, and soon a board of fifteen men had been set up to carry the vast project through. Five of these were constituted a sort of executive to seek for collaborators, share out the work, and pay fees—this last an important part of the programme. Seven others devoted their attention to the collecting of documents and the search for material in printed sources. Their finds were set in order by a pair of ' censors,' so as to enable the whole ' Collegium ' to pass judgment on them, and then all was ready for the actual composition. That is the account of the proceedings given in the preface to the first volume of the completed work.

One may laugh at Flacius or be horrified at him, but there is no getting away from the fact that he was a great man in his own most peculiar fashion. So cross-grained and cantankerous was he that no town, however fervently Lutheran, could stand him very long. Magdeburg drove him out in 1557 but that calamity made no difference to his plans. Owing to his association with the city and to his division of the History into centuries the work became known popularly as the " Centuries of

---

[1] Salig, *Vollständige Historie der Augspurgischen Confession*, vol. iii, p. 279. Melanchthon certainly did not make Flacius a present of the manuscripts, for his detestation of the man was notorious.

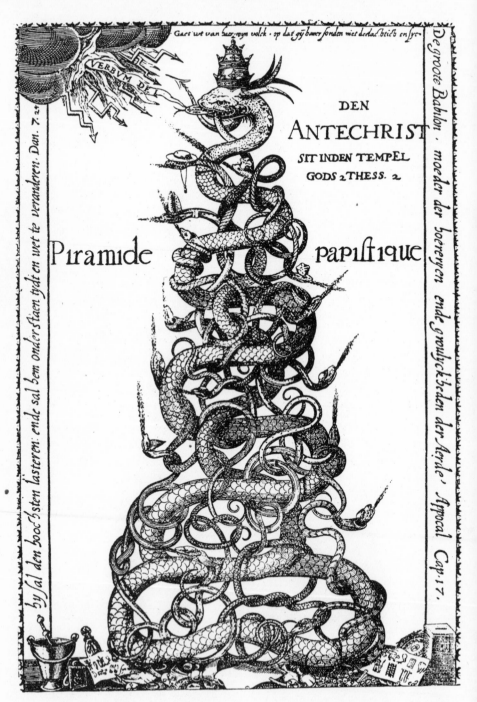

The fundamental idea of the Magdeburg Centuries: The Hierarchical Church
as Antichrist and enemy of the Word of God
A Dutch cartoon of the sixteenth century

Magdeburg." Some such handy name was a necessity, as the real title runs thus : *An Ecclesiastical History, giving in clear order a complete idea of the Church of Christ century by century ; planned and executed with singular diligence and honesty on the basis of the most ancient and reputable historians, the Fathers, and other writers, by some studious and pious men in the City of Magdeburg*. The first volume, dealing with the first three centuries, appeared at Basle in 1559 ; the fourth century in 1560 ; the fifth and sixth centuries in 1562 ; the seventh and eighth in 1564 ; the ninth in 1565 ; the tenth and eleventh in 1567 ; the twelfth in 1569 ; and the thirteenth, and last, in 1574. The seven massive tomes are repulsively printed and an exasperation to handle, but they met a crying need of Lutheranism and so received a magnificent welcome. From the time of their appearance the zealous preachers of the New Evangel had no lack of material with which to educate their flocks in devout horror of Rome, and that though they might know no Latin, as Flacius considerately issued a German translation of the first four volumes.

What is to be said about the value of the work as history ? Just this, that by modern standards it has no value at all. Ranke, indeed, found it in him to speak of its authors' " earnest endeavours to shatter the gross ecclesiastical fictions which had grown up in the course of time," and to declare that, " by dispersing the fogs with which the hierarchical power had veiled its real origin, they did general historical science a great service." There can be no doubt about the " earnest endeavours," but the " great service " is mere nonsense. What they did was to create new myths for old and to give general currency to such fables as the story of Pope Joan. The following judgment passed on their work by a scholarly modern biographer and admirer of Luther is much nearer the mark than Ranke's pontifical utterance : " Save for the accumulation of much material it deserves no praise. Its critical principles are worse than none, for its only criterion of sources is as they are pro- or anti- papal. The latter are taken and the former left. Miracles are not doubted as such, but are divided into two classes, those tending to prove an accepted doctrine, which are true, and those which support some papal institution, which are branded as ' first-class lies '. . . . The psychology of the authors is as bad as their criticism. All opposition to the Pope, especially that of the German Emperors, is represented as caused by religion."[1]

A little study of the scheme of the work is sufficient to prove its historical worthlessness. Each " Century " is divided into sixteen chapters

[1] Dr. P. Smith, *The Age of the Reformation* (New York, 1920), pp. 584-5.

dealing with the spread of Christianity, the rise of heresies, the introduction of liturgical usages, and so on. The principal purpose of the work is to reveal the gradual corruption of the primitive Apostolic ideal and the intrusion of antichrist into the Temple of God. Everything is made to point towards antichrist. Already in the first " Century " the reader can observe Flacius laying his lines. According to him, the history of the antichrist falls into three periods, during the first of which the Man of Sin disseminates his influence secretly. It was necessary to say this because the opening centuries of Christianity show no very definite trace of him in their records. But with Pope Boniface III in the seventh century, the Centuriators consider that they have found their deliverer from silences a little awkward for their thesis. Thenceforth they are in their element, as the period of the declared and identifiable antichrist has begun. In the judgment of Flacius, he is not merely a person but a whole system of government, the government, namely, set up by the devil in the City of Rome, for the destruction of all men's souls. The reign of the antichrist reached its climax with Pope St. Gregory VII, " the most monstrous of all monsters which this earth has brought forth." The third period of the antichrist's history is that of his showing up, which God in His mercy brought about by His servant, Martin Luther. Luther it was who finally unmasked the Beast, tearing away his century-old disguises and revealing him in his true colours as the very Abomination of Desolation sitting in the Holy Places.

Besides being a history of the hidden and open reign of antichrist, the *Centuries* were also intended to prove that the religion of the Gospels and the Primitive Church was good, sound Lutheranism, which, however, the antichrist succeeded in so obscuring and disfiguring as time went on that God had to send Martin Luther to rediscover it. Luther's central doctrine of justification by faith is put into the mouths of St. Paul and the Evangelists, and their seemingly Catholic deliverances are shown to be a misunderstanding. Needless to say, all this is done in the vituperative style without which the Flacian pen was incapable of moving many lines. He had an inexhaustible vocabulary of abuse.

The appearance of the huge volumes in fairly rapid succession aroused mixed feelings in Catholic breasts. Some were of opinion that the work might safely be ignored as too palpably biased to do any harm, but other and better-informed men took a different view. From the outset, Peter Canisius pleaded earnestly with Cardinals Truchsess and Hosius to secure, by their influence in Rome, the services of some leisured scholars who would reply to the Centuriators. Thus, on December 7, 1560, he wrote as follows to Truchsess who was in Rome: "It is a great shame and crime that ecclesiastical history should be distorted in so many ways by the sectaries. In Rome there are plenty of learned men skilled in historical investigation, and it would be a great blessing if one of them were chosen to write the lives of the Popes. At present, the sectaries invent whatever they like, while we snore away to a man."[1] Again during the Council of Trent in 1562, Peter expressed to Hosius his ardent wish that some learned bishop or theologian, of whom there were so many present, would undertake to refute "that most pestilent work of the Magdeburgers." As the heavy tomes appeared, he regularly transmitted copies of them to Hosius, Truchsess, Foscarario, and other eminent men, hoping all the time that they would get something done. When in Rome in 1565, he renewed his personal efforts and had the satisfaction of seeing Fathers Salmeron and Ledesma deputed to answer Flacius. But they made little progress owing to preoccupation with other tasks, and not Rome but Dillingen was to have the credit of providing that same year the first Catholic refutation of the Protestant History.

Shortly before his death in 1563, St. Peter's close friend, Dr. Conrad Braun of Augsburg, had written it, at the request of Cardinal Truchsess, and none other than Peter himself now revised the manuscript and saw it through the press, furnished with a short introductory sketch of its author's life and labours. The following year, William Eisengrein, a young cousin of the eminent Dr. Martin Eisengrein, came out with a small volume at Ingolstadt, dealing with the misrepresentations of the Flacian first "Century." Next in the field were two Englishmen, Alan Cope, a canon of St. Peter's, Rome, and Nicholas Harpsfield, once archdeacon of Canterbury, but, under Elizabeth, a prisoner in the Tower of London. Harpsfield composed "Six Dialogues" against the Centuriators, which Cope secured by some daring means and had printed at Antwerp. These few books were of very modest dimensions, but in Rome, according to report, the best Catholic historian of the time, the Augustinian, Onofrio Panvinio, had begun an extensively planned refutation of the *Centuries*. This report was not quite accurate, though, in the event, Panvinio did produce something. Finally, on May 31, 1567, St. Francis Borgia informed Father Canisius that the Pope desired the German Jesuits to bring out as quickly as possible a book designed, not so much to refute, as to discredit the Centuriators, by giving specimens of their contradictions, false

[1] Braunsberger, *Epistulae*, vol. iii, pp. 30–1.

allegations, and mutilation of documents. Peter was to circularize the various colleges and obtain from their professors such contributions as they could offer, which he would then set in order himself, and see through the press. Thus did his cherished project come home to roost, greatly to his embarrassment.[1] The reply which he sent to St. Francis was in the following terms:

> With regard to the short refutation of the Centuriators which the Holy Father desires from me and others of our theologians, I see clearly, after having discussed the whole matter with them, that it is going to be very difficult indeed. . . . The time has now come for me to make the usual visitation of the colleges that I may receive the confessions of all and see to the forthcoming renovation of studies. Besides, our theologians already have plenty to do with their ordinary teaching and preaching. Hardly a man among us is even moderately versed in ecclesiastical history. We also lack the necessary books, and they could be procured only at a high price, and with greater trouble in Germany than in Italy. My own unfitness, too, is to be considered, for, being sorely distracted by the external cares of the Province, I feel a distinct repugnance to these graver studies. In addition, I am by nature an extremely slow and plodding person when it comes to serious writing, and I have to work at the revision of the Roman Catechism, which Father Paul is turning into German but has not yet completed, in order that, when corrected, it may be published here in Dillingen. Many people are looking forward to its appearance with great eagerness.
>
> As for the *Centuries*, Father Onofrio[2] has practically carried through the very thing we want, having written against them a volume in three parts which displays clear and authentic knowledge of nearly all matters pertaining to Church history from the time of Our Lord to Pope Gregory, especially with regard to the office and power of the Roman Pontiffs. This work, which is completed but not yet in print, runs to 150 folio pages. I should not have known about it but for information recently given to our Cardinal by the author, who is the only man absolutely competent to carry out the task successfully. He might well be encouraged in every way, as he has hardly an equal nowadays in knowledge of history, which is a science, I may say, requiring the whole of a man's powers and attention if he is to expound it properly to others, especially in opposition to learned and contentious people.

---

[1] Braunsberger, *Epistulae*, vol. v, pp. 480–1.   [2] Panvinio, the Augustinian scholar.

These and other difficulties which occur to me will loom up if I am obliged to undertake the task. But, all the same, I do not decline any labour which I know to be the due of holy obedience. Only I beg your Paternity again and again to consider and tell me what you judge most expedient, lest we attempt something which we may afterwards have to regret as a failure. And, if I cannot escape the burden, would you also instruct me as to how I may obtain more assistance with it?[1]

Plainly, Peter Canisius had no great opinion of himself as an ecclesiastical historian or desire to see himself in that rôle. It was not false modesty but sensible self-knowledge which made him speak of his natural slowness with the pen. He *was* slow, and he could no more help it than he could the colour of his eyes. On the other hand, he was hypersensitive to the calls of obedience, taking for sacred duty the accomplishment of the Holy Father's least desire. These two things, his natural slowness and supernatural sensitiveness, were to be the cause of no little commotion when emphasized by the task of refuting the *Centuries*. But, whatever he might think of himself, his appreciation of other men's qualities and achievements lacked nothing in generosity. The young scholar, Onofrio Panvinio, who died in his thirties and was panegyrized by the Protestant classical genius, Scaliger, as the "Father of all History," found in Peter the warmest and most devoted of his admirers. Some paragraphs of a very long Italian letter which the Saint addressed to him from Dillingen, September 29, 1567, will help to illustrate this point:

Very Reverend and most learned Father Onofrio.

You must know that Monsignor the Cardinal of Augsburg has conferred with me about your works, which, for their erudition and accuracy, are so much praised throughout Christendom and so useful to the Holy Catholic Church that we may well thank Almighty God, the Author of all good, and express our gratitude to your Paternity. Now, as to the principal business, I regret that, chiefly owing to the poverty of the printer, you are unable to have these eminent works produced here in Dillingen, as they indeed deserve to be. For this reason, Monsignor the Cardinal, who loves you dearly and is a great admirer of your books, has negotiated with another famous Catholic printer, Calenius of Cologne. This learned and energetic craftsman,

[1] Braunsberger, *Epistulae*, vol. v, pp. 522-3.

who recently printed the new volumes of the General Councils, is very glad to deal with books on ecclesiastical affairs. I sent him a list of your works, with an indication of what you desire and an expression of your gratitude. Monsignor the Cardinal has now an answer to the effect that he will be pleased to accept your Ecclesiastical Chronicle, the three books against the Magdeburg History, the Universal Chronicle, and the fifteen ritual books. The other works, he thinks, would not be so useful a proposition either for himself or for readers. . . .

Maternus Cholinus of Cologne, who also is a good Catholic publisher and a friend of your Paternity, will print your new edition of Platina's *Lives of the Popes* and the Ecclesiastical Chronicle. . . . I think it would be much better if you had one publisher in Cologne rather than two, chiefly in order to preclude that spirit of emulation which is easily aroused between such men, and which has already, in a degree, started. I know both publishers and regard them as good Catholics. Calenius, I think, is the better equipped and more careful of the two. But let your Reverence do as you think best in the matter. . . .

Two new *Centuries* of the Magdeburg people, the tenth and eleventh, have just been issued. Copies will be sent to you immediately by the Cardinal, according to your wishes. God grant that your Reverence and other learned men may withstand these petulant and fraudulent enemies of Catholic truth and piety. Their leader appears to be Matthias Illyricus, who never ceases to obscure and pervert the truth of ecclesiastical history with his calumnies, and is always issuing new tracts . . . and other pestilential lucubrations to the great prejudice of the Holy Apostolic See. I think that there is no other heretic so persistent in attacking the dignity and truth of the Roman Church. For the love of God let your Reverence not neglect any chance of showing up the lies of this man and the false principles which he is given to laying down in his books with such wonderful deceit and colour that sometimes even learned readers may be led into error.

I pray God, Our Lord, to favour and prosper the holy zeal of your Reverence in defence of the Church and of the authority of St. Peter and his successors. May He be with you in your endeavours to elucidate matters of great consequence in ecclesiastical history. I shall gladly strive in conjunction with my brethren to serve and satisfy your Reverence, whether by revising some of your books or in any other way that you may desire of me. . . .[1]

[1] Braunsberger, *Epistulae*, vol. vi, pp. 69-73.

Panvinio was but one of many scholarly and zealous men whom St. Peter thus encouraged and helped. So much had he the cause of the Church at heart that he even took advantage of people's affection for him and his for them as an argument with laggards of the pen. " I cherish the hope," he told Martin Cromer, whose writings he desired to see published in an ' omnibus' volume, " that you will grant something of this kind to the love which I bear you, for the good of many men and the glory of Our Lord." Thus, too, did he plead with Cardinal Hosius, whose literary activities had come to a stop, and he was always urging his Jesuit brethren to fresh exploits of learned composition. Now the time had come for him to practise what he so often preached, as, in the middle of November, 1567, St. Francis Borgia let him know definitely that the Pope required him to answer the Centuriators. That he might be freer for the task, and also enabled " to take some rest," he was to be relieved of the burden of government for six months, during which period Father Paul Hoffaeus would act in his stead as Vice-Provincial. On receipt of this news he wrote as follows to Borgia :

As the Supreme Pontiff and your Paternity, to whom I owe all reverence and obedience, judge that I should henceforth devote my energies to the difficult matter of the *Centuries*, I humbly beg, before all things, the blessing and special grace of the Holy Father on the commencement and progress of my labours. Fortified with it, I shall be the happier in my approach to a task so hard and beyond my powers, and able to satisfy the good desires of His Holiness. Then, I covet and earnestly beg the prayers of your Paternity to Our Lord for the same intention. Would you also please give me leave to purchase with Province money such books, and they are neither few nor common, as shall be necessary for the work ?

Meantime, I shall carefully carry out your Paternity's wishes that I should not allow the business of the Province to weigh on my mind but retain merely the name of Provincial. . . . In order to arrange this matter promptly I am hastening to see Father Hoffaeus. I shall gladly confirm your Paternity's decision to him, and, at the first opportunity, transfer to that good and wise Father the office which I have filled so many years, quite unworthily and with trouble to my superiors. I shall write soon and tell you the result of our meeting. Only one thing must I add at present, namely that he has not yet turned the fourth book of the Roman Catechism into German, nor will he be able to complete the work before Christmas or the Epiphany, on account of the frequent sermons which he has to deliver, being the ordinary preacher of Munich.[1]

The Ordinary Preacher of Munich did not at all relish the prospect of being Vice-Provincial, and conceived the beginnings of a grudge against St. Peter on account of it. Unhappily the grudge took on substance with the passage of time and led to sad misunderstandings. Both men were terrible ascetics in their private lives but a difference showed itself in the visible results of their austerity. Of Peter's practice we have the following report from the Rector of Dillingen to Borgia at this time : " With regard to Father Provincial, I have this in particular to say that he is rather negligent about his health. He is immoderate in vigils and fastings. Practically every day is a fast day with him, and there are frequent extraordinary fasts. To this must be added the continual occupation of his mind, so that he can scarcely take his food in peace, much less have recreation after it. These practices proceed from private devotion, but he weakens himself greatly by them, especially his voice which, after fasts and vigils becomes strained and very feeble."[2] But though his vocal chords might suffer, no one complained that Peter's temper did. With Hoffaeus it was different. He had not the other's wonderful control and was apt to revenge on the innocent brethren around him the pangs of a cheated stomach. Brusque and abrupt, the sentences of his letters come like shots out of a gun. Even so they have a certain frosty attraction, a masculine and ironic tang that evince an able but rather intolerant mind. For the present, however, he and Father Canisius are going to get on passably well together. Between them they completed the German version of the Roman Catechism of the Council of Trent, early in the new year, and then Peter retired to Dillingen for the work against the Centuriators.

Hardly had he settled down to it properly when he was whisked away to Ellwangen by Cardinal Truchsess, there to preach the Lent and help with reforms which his Lordship had projected. He hesitated about going until the Dillingen Fathers assured him that by so doing he would not contravene the wishes of the Pope. In less than a month he preached more than a dozen long sermons, nearly all on the Sacraments, and made

[1] Braunsberger, *Epistulae*, vol. vi, p. 138. Peter's request for his General's prayers did not fall on deaf ears. There is extant a note-book in which St. Francis used to enter each day the various intentions for which he purposed to pray and had prayed. Under the date, February 5, 1568, there is the following item in Spanish : " Prayers said for that matter of Canisius." He also reminds himself that the prayers are to continue till Easter or the Ember Days following it.
[2] Braunsberger, *Epistulae*, vol. vi, p. 722.

by them twenty-eight converts from Lutheranism. As a specimen of his concrete and homely style, the following passages from a sermon on the multiplication of the loaves and fishes may be given. He is exhorting the people not to be deterred from approaching the Sacraments by the lack of personal virtue in those who administer them:

The ministers of the Church are the dispensers of the mysteries of God, but it is not necessary that such ministers should be as holy as the Apostles. It is the same Bread and the same Sacrament, whether dispensed by Judas or Peter. The Apostles themselves were very imperfect at the time when Christ desired to feed the multitude. They set more store by money than by His power and, indeed, had no proper belief that He possessed the desire or power to perform the miracle. None the less, Christ wished them to distribute the bread and feed the people.

If the minister of the Sacraments leads an evil life, think of him as an old basket in which good bread is carried. Permit that the bread be given you and leave the basket alone. Good pears and apples taste well, even if taken from a dirty wooden dish. And is not he a fool who despises a gold piece or a gem because he found it in the mud? Think, then, that it is God's will we should honour, even in bad ministers, the power which comes from Him alone, and do not pass judgment on the servant of Another.[1]

It is a pleasant picture that the good historian Sacchinus paints of the doings of St. Peter and his Cardinal friend that Lent. We see them going about the town searching for cases of poverty or sickness, bringing food and medicines with their own hands to such as needed them, cheering with friendly words and encouragement the poor patients in the hospital. But in Peter's life things never remained very long on that level of serenity. News now arrived that the Lutherans were spreading a rumour of his apostasy throughout Franconia. In those days people had credulity enough to believe anything, so the Bishop of Würzburg begged the Saint to come and kill the preposterous story. He did so in three sermons at the Cathedral, declaring himself to be for ever "the child, the disciple, and the defender of the Holy Roman Catholic Church," which assuredly must be in a strong position if her enemies had no better support for their cause than barefaced calumnies and impostures.[2]

[1] Braunsberger, Epistulae, vol. vi, p. 553.
[2] Sacchinus, Historia Societatis Jesu, pars tertia (Roma, 1649), lib. 4, n. 193

A rumour of an opposite kind to the one mentioned reached the Emperor at this time from his ambassador in Rome. It was that Pope Pius V intended to create Father Canisius a cardinal at the next promotion. Peter himself appears either not to have heard the story or to have ignored it, but it must have had some basis in fact, because, after the Pope's death, a document came to light containing the names of men to be honoured with the purple, and Peter's was among them. How much the Pope trusted him was shown by the commission which he received through Borgia to act as adviser to the Holy See on German affairs. Part of the new duty was to inform the Pope about persons in Germany who could safely be employed on the Church's business; a difficult task, Peter explained in a letter from Ellwangen, " seeing that one can scarcely find a man in this country who willingly declares or desires others to believe that he is in any special grace with the Pope." Conditions were still very bad, though perhaps Peter's account of them is made a little darker than the reality by such a depressing experience as that of meeting a parish priest who had not been to confession for seventeen years.[1] He would have cheered up if he could have seen a little distance into the future, for already the seed which he had scattered on the stony ground was beginning to sprout and give promise of a rich harvest.

At the end of his letter to Borgia he begged forgiveness for having stolen a month from work on the *Centuries*, as though he had gone to Ellwangen for a holiday. But even after that Lenten break he could not get back to his task, as he was elected by the German Fathers to represent them in the approaching triennial congregation of ' procurators ' in Rome. Though he at once demurred, "*pro sua modestia*," as Hoffaeus put it, objecting that the *Centuries* had first claim on his time, he was overruled and told that he could carry on his writing even more conveniently in Rome than in Germany. He wondered very much, and asked the eight Fathers to give him a testimonial for the sake of his conscience. They preferred instead to refer the case to the General, who answered, to their confusion, that Provincials, such as still was Father Canisius, could not be elected procurators. The answer came too late because, in the meantime, Cardinal Truchsess, who was going to Rome, had pleaded so urgently with Hoffaeus and his consultors for Peter's company that they gave way to him. "*Fece grandissima instantia*," wrote Hoffaeus afterwards in his own defence. "If we have erred in this matter," he continued, "the

[1] Braunsberger, *Epistulae*, vol. vi, pp. 179–84.

greater part of the blame will be mine and I therefore ask pardon, etc."
That "etc." is very characteristic of Father Paul.

The two friends made their journey Romewards in a leisurely fashion.
Not till June did they reach Ancona, where, quite unexpectedly, as such
things are wont to happen, St. Peter was visited by an experience that
moved him deeply. In his *Confessions*, written shortly afterwards, he
speaks of it as follows:

I thank Thee from the bottom of my heart, O my God most pitiful,
my Creator, my Saviour, my Protector, my Life, my Refuge, my
Salvation, every day and moment that I sail at random on this stormy
sea of human life, and am so strangely impelled in various ways to good
and evil that I often know not what wind it is which frets me, whither
my ship is borne, where I stand, or how I ought to set my course.
That also was my experience at Ancona when I came thither in June
of the year 1568 with the Cardinal of Augsburg. For, while I was
examining my conscience in the cathedral, Thou didst open the eyes
of my mind, O Light Eternal, and mercifully illumine him who lay in
darkness, so that he should know himself, abase his mind in the truth,
and learn in a new way to be submissive to Thee and serve Thee, O
holy Lord God, the complete and only good of every creature.

This light which Thou didst pour into my soul was of such sort
that I might learn, both then and ever after, to put all my intentions
and actions on a true and solid foundation. I understood from Thee
that the foundation is knowledge of self and of one's own vileness and
nothingness, so that looking upon myself I should see how, in the
realm of goodness, I am nothing, know nothing, wish nothing, do
nothing, possess nothing, for in Thee alone is the beginning, middle,
and end of all good, and in Thee alone ought every rational creature
to place his good always. Thou didst teach me, O perfect Master, the
foulness of much that is in me, for I had neglected and little considered
the foundation of my own nothingness and nakedness in the eyes of
Thy Majesty. I looked upon and appraised myself and my deeds with
human eyes, and cried not with St. John, *Non sum, non sum*.[1] Oh
would that Thou mightst increase in me Thy grace to walk with the
Magi in this new light, and to regard myself in all my ways as I truly
am and not as I seem to be; so that I may be able to say from my

---

[1] A reference to the answers of St. John the Baptist when interrogated by the priests and Levites.
John i, 20–23.

heart, *Abyssus abyssum invocat*, the abyss I mean, of my nothingness . . . ever calling to the abyss of Thy infinite majesty, power and perfection. I confess my sin, O most loving Father, in that I referred not to Thee the gifts which I received from Thee, but oftentimes took credit to myself for them or gladly allowed others to praise me on their account, neither saying nor doing in the spirit of him who cried : *Non nobis, Domine, non nobis, sed nomini tuo da gloriam*. But now I am resolved with Thy help . . . to look upon myself with new eyes and to walk, as I ought, in humility and simplicity of heart.[1]

When St. Peter reached Rome it was decided that he might as well act as procurator for his German brethren, despite his technical disqualification. This time he made a long stay in the Eternal City and during most of it was ill. Nevertheless, he managed to achieve a great deal, not only for his Province in the congregation, but for the Church at large by his influence and advice. He had interviews with the Pope, and was largely instrumental in bringing about the formation of two new commissions of cardinals to deal with the affairs of the Church in heretical or pagan lands. The cardinals of the first commission decided that sternness must be their cue in relation to Germany, but, as the Emperor was informed by his ambassador in Rome, Father Canisius intervened and persuaded them to proceed rather " *con lenità et piacevolezza.*"[2]

Sometimes a man's influence can be gauged more truly from small indications than from big advertisements, because it is not always the people whose names are in electric signs that really make the world go round. Shortly before St. Peter's arrival in Rome, Emperor Maximilian had granted the nobility of Lower Austria freedom to embrace Lutheranism, whereupon the Pope dispatched Cardinal Commendone to remonstrate with His Majesty. It was a mission beset with the greatest danger and difficulty, and Commendone needed all the comfort he could obtain. He was familiar with everybody who mattered in Rome, from the Pope downwards, but to none of them did he turn for advice and consolation. He turned to Father Canisius.[3]

One of Peter's principal endeavours while in Rome was to help the sadly neglected German College. Its funds at this time had become so depleted that they sufficed for the support of no more than thirty ecclesiastical students. According to a contemporary document, Peter

[1] Braunsberger, *Epistulae*, vol. i, pp. 29–31.   [2] Braunsberger, *Epistulae*, vol. vi, pp. 582–3.   [3] Braunsberger, *Epistulae*, vol. vi, pp. 223–6.

" cherished the poor remains of the college *tamquam sua viscera.*" That was the simple truth, and, but for his efforts, it might have collapsed altogether before it found a splendid saviour in Pope Gregory XIII. The Jesuits had five houses in Rome and at each the Saint was in eager demand for exhortations. " The Roman brethren," we are told, " derived immense joy of heart from the sight of so great a man and the rare example of his virtues."[1]

Among those with whom he now became intimately acquainted were St. Philip Neri and his illustrious son, Baronius. Baronius, still young and raw but infinitely devoted, had already been set by St. Philip the task of preaching and writing on Church history, with direct reference to the *Centuries of Magdeburg.* Though the first volume of his famous *Annals* did not appear until 1588, Baronius was at work on his sources from 1559 onwards, and there can be little doubt that St. Peter and he discussed their common burden together. Neither man was in love with it, but the Oratorian had two great advantages denied the Jesuit—youth and leisure. Also, he had the encouragement, whole-hearted, even if sometimes uncomfortably expressed, of his immediate superior, whereas Canisius got for his pains only the sulks or ill-concealed sarcasm of Paul Hoffaeus. " Reverend Father," wrote that good man to him in Rome, " the times seem to require that our Society should press upon the heretics more frequently than has been our wont. Goodness knows, they do not keep their mouths shut but, astute men, allow us to go on with our ' Latinizing,' while themselves ' Germanizing ' to the poor people, with great success.[2] Why do we not write more in German, Father ? Are there not more than enough Latin books already for the needs of learned people . . . and who, anyway, understands the mysteries of Scholasticism ? "[3]

During the months that Peter was in Rome he got very little opportunity to work at his book, nor was he more fortunate when he returned to Germany, for he was obliged to resume his full duties as Provincial and also to replace Father Hoffaeus in the pulpit at Augsburg. He began his Lenten course there on February 20, 1569, and between that date and April 12th, preached twenty-five times, always in the Church of St. Maurice, as his brother Jesuit, Father Rosephius, occupied the Cathedral pulpit. How effective the two men proved was shown by the reactions of the fifteen Protestant preachers in the City, whose anger led them to

---

[1] Braunsberger, *Epistulae*, vol. vi, p. 578 ; Sacchinus, *Vita P. Petri Canisii*, p. 260.
[2] *Latinizare . . . germanizant.* The point is that the Catholics usually wrote their polemical books in Latin whereas the Lutherans used the vernacular.
[3] Braunsberger, *Epistulae*, vol. vi, p. 218.

indulge in such feats of obstruction and vituperation that the magistrates had to restrain them for fear of a riot.

At the beginning of April, St. Francis Borgia decided to set Peter completely free from his office of Provincial so that he might devote all his attention to the *Centuries*. Up to that date, he had been able to devote very little time to the work. When notifying Hoffaeus of the change and of his own succession, the General said : " Father Peter Canisius has carried this troublesome burden so many years that it is only fair to relieve him of it, at least for a time. Nevertheless, according to his charity and from the experience which he has accumulated of persons and affairs in Germany he will help your Reverence with advice in matters of importance, and you will treat him with the respect, consideration, and love which are his due as the Father of all the Society's sons in Upper Germany and the neighbouring Provinces." To this letter Hoffaeus replied in the following engaging way : " I humbly beg your Paternity for the love of Jesus Christ and the salvation of the Province to change your mind and not force on me a burden which is likely to be the ruin of my soul and a terrible grievance to many who have discovered what an annoying and bitter thing it is to sweat under my ' Pharaohnical ' rule. Relying on this hope, I do not see how I can undertake the business of the Province. I have told Father Canisius so, and asked him not to withdraw until I have your further reply."[1]

Plainly ambition was not among the faults of which Father Paul could be accused. He was a truly humble man, and might have made a wonderful superior had he also been a little more meek. In accordance with his wishes, St. Peter continued to administer the affairs of the Province for the moment, and, meantime, addressed the following lines to the General :

The eternal peace of Christ be with us, Very Reverend Father. I thank the Divine Goodness and your Paternity with all my heart for releasing me from this burden which I have borne nearly fourteen years, and for providing me with a successor whom I know by experience to be a better, wiser, and more suitable man. . . . There is one petition which I cannot now refrain from making to your Paternity, that you would enjoin me in my freedom a good penance for the very many offences of commission and omission against the duties of my office of which I have been guilty. Then, I beg you more than ever

[1] Braunsberger, *Epistulae*, vol. vi, pp. 294, 321.

to obtain for me from God a new mind, that I may know and rightly esteem the grace now granted to me, by which I can pull myself together and make up to some extent for all that I have hitherto wretchedly neglected. I have no doubt but that this change of Provincials will be, not only a comfort to me personally, but a pleasure and advantage to others in Christ Our Lord. To Him be honour, praise, and glory.[1]

The news of Peter's retirement " disturbed us all exceedingly," wrote one of the Jesuits at Ingolstadt, while St. Francis Borgia, who was not an emotional person, spoke with feeling about the manner in which he laid down a burden " borne for fourteen years so patiently in the continual stress of government and with so much good zeal, integrity, and prudence." When the letter confirming the appointment of Hoffaeus arrived, Peter retired once more to Dillingen, hopeful that now at last he might be able to pursue his task without interruption. " The intention of the Pope," Borgia told him, " is not that you should write against the Centuries in their entirety, as that would involve too much time and labour, but that you should select some absurdities of the Magdeburg History and make of them a book calculated to destroy its credit." That is exactly what the Saint did, but in a far more thorough fashion than Borgia contemplated. Peter was constitutionally incapable of scamping any work to which he had set his hand. He must lavish all his care on it, dream of it night and day, and drive himself and others half way to distraction in his efforts to get it perfect. But even while thus absorbed he could never resist an appeal from others for help in their difficulties, and so we find him at Dillingen editing various lucubrations that had nothing to do with the Centuries, and collaborating with Father Torres in the production of that scholar's learned treatises. The General sent him as assistant Father John Rastell, a Marian priest, educated at Winchester and Oxford, who had joined the Society of Jesus the previous year. " I am now going ahead with the work," Peter wrote on June 28th, " but it scarcely admits of great haste, both on account of the natural slowness of my mind and of the difficulty inherent in the questions to be debated with such adversaries. I thank your Paternity for giving me as colleague Father John, the Englishman. In my company he is having scope enough to exercise himself in patience. I shall not let him be too heavily burdened with work but, Our Lord guiding me, shall take care that we observe moderation in our studies. All the same, I find that no little strain of mind is necessary

[1] Braunsberger, *Epistulae*, vol. vi, pp. 309–10.

to collect, digest, and put into shape such a large amount of material. May God in His goodness help us, through the Sacrifices and prayers of your Paternity, so that I may be able to satisfy holy obedience and finish the work within a year."[1]

Poor Peter ! He little dreamed that eight years would go by before he was through, and that even then only half of his plan would have been completed. Father John, the Englishman, soon proved less heroic than the occasion required. Perhaps the elegant amenities of Winchester and Oxford were not the best preparation for the bleak austerity of Dillingen. At any rate, he began to complain of overwork, probably with some justice, and after a short time made way for a man of tougher fibre. How St. Peter demeaned himself at Dillingen is told by one who was with him in the house. " It was wonderful to see," wrote this observer, " with what deference, charity, and intimate friendliness he lived and worked among us. Nothing was so agreeable and pleasant to him as to devote all the time which he could steal from necessary studies to the public and private instruction of children and illiterate persons, and to relieving cheerfully our domestic burdens, particularly by hearing the confessions of Germans. A short time ago, when he learned that the house in Augsburg suffered from a dearth of confessors and desired his help for a while, he betook himself thither at once, ungrudgingly relinquishing the conveniences for his work which he possessed here. He is there now, to the great advantage of many souls."[2] Another item mentioned by the same writer is that Peter made a three days' journey from Dillingen to bring peace to a household disturbed by quarrels over property. If ever a man deserved to inherit the beatitude kept for peacemakers it was he. All his story is full of homage to the spirit of peace. Only shortly before, he had gone to Ingolstadt to restore concord between the Franciscans and Jesuits, broken by the intemperate language of that hot-head, Gewarts ; and he moved heaven and earth to end the long territorial dispute between Archduke Ferdinand and the Bishop of Trent.[3]

Augsburg demanded Peter's services a third time that year in October, when he had recovered from an illness brought on by his immoderate exertions to get the work against the Centuriators finished. Earlier in this book there was occasion to speak of a peculiarly dark and forbidding feature of social life in the sixteenth century, its superstition and terror of the preternatural. It was this that now obliged Father Canisius to

[1] Braunsberger, *Epistulae*, vol. vi, p. 334.   [2] Braunsberger, *Epistulae*, vol. vi, p. 539.
[3] Braunsberger, *Epistulae*, vol. vi, pp. 245, 310-1.

abandon his studies and spend some months in Augsburg, where his friends, Ursula and Sybil Fugger, and their brother-in-law, Johann, lay in thrall to a very dangerous kind of spiritism. The trouble had been developing for a considerable time. In the letter which Hoffaeus addressed to Peter in Rome the previous year these words occur : " The demons are wonderfully exercising our patience, and would to God that we might be delivered without loss of honour. Susanna is devouring glass." This last cryptic utterance refers to a maid in the service of Ursula Fugger who had contracted a great appetite for glass objects which she ate with appreciation and apparently without injury. Susanna was not the only one to manifest such strange phenomena. So queer was the behaviour of Anna von Bernhausen, a maid-of-honour to Baroness Sybil Fugger, that the family believed her to have become possessed by a whole legion of devils. The two mistresses were naturally very frightened and turned to Father Hoffaeus for help. " They implored me with tears," he informed Borgia, " to allow Father Völck to take charge of the afflicted women." In consideration of all that the family had done and continued to do for the Church and the Society of Jesus, Hoffaeus could not well refuse, but he insisted that Völck, who was confessor to the Fuggers, must never be asked to attend the patients at night-time, or to perform exorcisms on them in public or oftener than once a week.

The next chapter in this queer story tells of the plan suddenly conceived by Johann and Ursula Fugger to take their unhappy charge, Susanna, on pilgrimage to Loreto and Rome. Of course they would want their confessor with them, and let Hoffaeus beware of trying to stop him going ! " According to rumour," wrote Father Paul to Borgia, " Johann and Ursula have had a revelation from the devil that whoever tries to prevent Father Völck from accompanying them will be severely punished. I, for one, am not afraid."

When Father Canisius first became involved in the affair, he showed a certain readiness to believe and sympathize, owing largely to his profound admiration for the piety of Ursula Fugger. He had seen strange things happen with his own eyes, and, besides, he was not such an advanced Christian as to feel superior to the evidence for demoniacal possession in the New Testament. Preaching once on the subject, he assigned seven reasons why God might permit men to be so afflicted, deducing them from the two general ones given by St. Cyprian, namely as a punishment of men when they are evil, or as a probation and opportunity for merit when they are good. In his practical way he then emphasized that it was a worse misfortune to commit a mortal sin and thus have the powers of Hell besieging one's soul "than to be possessed and tormented by a thousand demons in one's body alone."[1]

As in many cases of modern spiritism, the alleged demons of Augsburg at first gave utterance to unexceptionable counsel through the mouths of their victims, but gradually the style changed and with it the simplicity and humility of Ursula and Johann Fugger's obedience. It was the news that Johann had taken to astrology and necromancy which caused St. Peter to pull up and become suspicious. When in Augsburg in June, he warned the two against the dangers to which they were exposing themselves. The tone of his letter to Borgia on this occasion has completely changed. He is now in opposition and alarmed at the persistence of his friends in their credulity, all the more because he suspects them of believing that, not only souls from Purgatory, but the souls of the damned, may seize on human bodies and secure their salvation through exorcisms. In July he wrote again, more anxiously than ever. It was impossible, he said, to wean the pair from their superstitions or to persuade them to abandon the project of their pilgrimage. The whole affair was made doubly unpleasant by the fact that the Roman Jesuits were at this time endeavouring to collect funds for the purchase of the site of their new church, the Gesù, and the Fuggers had been very generous to them. St. Francis Borgia did not know what to do. He was very much opposed to his men acting as exorcists, and it did not ease his worry to learn from St. Peter that Ursula and Johann were going to Rome for the express purpose of telling his Paternity all about their visions and wonders. "I see," Peter continued, "that whatever we may say or feel, we shall not prevail much with those people. We are driven to fear that they lack, to some extent, due humility and prudence and require a more judicious confessor." Hoffaeus was more explicit: "They put more trust in their own judgments and revelations than in all the Doctors of the Church."

In spite of anything that Hoffaeus or Peter could do, Ursula and her necromantic brother-in-law set off in October with Father Völck, Susanna, and such quantities of baggage that twelve mules were required for its transport. The whole city of Augsburg gaped, and the Protestants were not slow to make capital out of the grotesque occurrence in their war with the Jesuits. Among the stories circulated one told of a Father who was alleged to have dressed up in the guise of a horrible-looking demon and prowled about Ursula's house at night until a courageous footman

[1] Braunsberger, *Epistulae*, vol. vi, pp. 530–1.

ran him through with a sword ! And there were cartoons in plenty, including a drawing of a sow with a tiara on its head bringing forth a litter of Jesuits. St. Peter was now obliged to leave his academic calm for that atmosphere of intrigue and bitter hostility, as somebody must take the place of Father Völck whom the pilgrims, wrote Hoffaeus disgustedly, " were dragging about wherever they listed." Peter arrived in October and was unable to get back to Dillingen until the following April. His principal duty in Augsburg was to advise and help Mark Fugger who, in the absence of his sister-in-law, had assumed responsibility for Anna von Bernhausen. Anna's case was peculiarly sad as she was only seventeen years old and belonged to a distinguished family. She had been afflicted since she was a little girl, and found no relief until St. Peter pronounced the Church's ritual prayers over her. But he did not succeed at his first attempt, and repeated the exorcisms later in the Oratory of Our Lady at Altötting, a popular place of pilgrimage in Upper Bavaria. The illustrious Dr. Martin Eisengrein was provost of this church, and wrote a long account of what happened at the exorcisms, to which fifteen masters of arts, canons, and public officials put their names as eye-witnesses. By some invisible power the afflicted girl was raised into the air and flung back to the ground in a fainting condition several times. Those who were present testified that she must have been " torn into a thousand pieces " had not God and His Blessed Mother protected her. It was a terrible scene and made them all weep with compassion, but, on the third day, St. Peter's prayers and tears prevailed. He constrained the demon who had used Anna's innocent lips for blasphemies against the Mother of God to repeat the Hail Mary in atonement before departing out of her, and then there came a great peace. As a conclusion, say the witnesses, Peter preached them " a fine Christian exhortation to penance and amendment of life." Mark Fugger and his wife then presented the Oratory in thanksgiving with a beautiful chalice which is still preserved there and known as the " Chalice of Canisius."[1]

In Rome, meantime, the unfortunate woman Susanna had also found her deliverance under very dramatic circumstances. That meant the return of the pilgrim party and freedom for St. Peter to resume his labours against the Centuriators. This time he had the unwonted experience of remaining attached to one place for a year continuously, except for a few excursions, as when he attended the dying Duchess Renée of Bavaria at Friedberg, or was sent by Hoffaeus to placate the disgruntled preacher, Schorich, in

---

[1] Braunsberger, *Epistulae*, vol. vi, pp. 641–51.

Munich. Hoffaeus himself was disgruntled in a different fashion, to judge by the following letter which he addressed to Borgia on May 27, 1570:

Considered from every angle, it seems not only expedient but necessary to set Reverend Father Canisius free from the work on the *Centuries*. He is too much entangled in it and unable to extricate himself. Never satisfied with what he has done, he gets worn out and despondent, and now desires to be allowed to put together some sort of book from his previous labours and publish it at once. Practically the whole of Germany knows what he is engaged on and expects a huge work, after all the time the Father has been occupied with it. Our Fathers at Dillingen say that the work will by no means respond to these expectations, and all the less the longer it is put off.

I pass over the fact that he does not refute even the first of the *Centuries* in full, but deals only with four persons, omitting matters of controversy. In order, then, to save the despondent and over-burdened Father, whose health is often bad, and also lest we keep the Germans on tenter-hooks too long, only in the end to disappoint their great hopes, it seems necessary that your Paternity should admonish Father Canisius to finish off his book or make an excerpt from it and publish it at once, afterwards leaving the *Centuries* alone and employing his time in writing smaller books, according as he feels inclined. If that is done Father Canisius can reassume the office of Provincial and I, the post of preacher somewhere, as, for instance, at Innsbruck, where I think I should not be unwelcome to the people and the Government.[1]

There was much superficial truth in that report, but the underlying impression which it conveys of an obstinate old man clinging to his ideas is completely erroneous. St. Peter was indulging no private inclination. He had more than once made known his repugnance to the work and declared his unfitness for it, but the Pope's wishes stood in the way of any surrender. In this smaller matter as in other more important ones, he took the words and decrees of the Pope with scrupulous literalness and refused to admit an interpretation favourable to his own convenience. Thus it had been over the *Index* legislation; over the Bull, *In Coena Domini;* over the question of usury. He was made that way, as direct and uncasuistical as a child. The Pope had told him to answer the Centuriators, and answer them he would, did he die in the attempt. It was an attempt both

[1] Braunsberger, *Epistulae*, vol. vi, pp. 699–700.

heroic and tragic, and, reading about it, one has a sense of frustration as when watching a fine actor cast for a part unsuited to his powers. Peter realized himself, even better than Hoffaeus, or the Rector of Dillingen who shared that Father's views, that he was a misfit in the rôle of learned controversialist, and he desired nothing more eagerly than to be free of it. Writing to Borgia on December 8, 1570, he said:

Very Reverend Father in Christ, the peace of Jesus and a Happy New Year to you. I have received the letter of your Paternity in which you exhort me, your unworthy son, to conclude my book, so that having done with the labour of writing I may turn my attention to other work more in accordance with our institute. Indeed, I wish that the work was finished. It has grown under my hands and involves heavier toil and anxiety than, perhaps, many people imagine. May the good God and your Paternity forgive me for being so tardy in showing obedience over the book, and for affording satisfaction neither to myself nor to my superiors, while unhappily turning this great stone. I am such a wretched and utterly incompetent writer that I certainly need the prayers of many intercessors.

With regard to publication, the work will go to press next month, but the printing may not be finished before Easter Sunday. I earnestly beg your Paternity and the Roman Fathers to commend the whole affair to God in your Masses and prayers, so that publication may have a happy issue. I have launched a big campaign in the book, not only against the Centuriators, but also against other innovators, in order, as was necessary, to make the refutation of heresy more complete. I hope that, by the goodness of God and your Paternity's approval, the whole book will be completed next summer, or, in other words, that I shall have finished what I have now in hand on the subject of three holy persons in the New Testament, St. John the Baptist, Mary, and St. Peter. I am anxious to expend more than ordinary pains in glorifying them and defending them against the heretics. . . .

I confess that I have often sinned by allowing too much anxiety to creep into my studies. Perhaps I torment myself more than the matter warrants, as do finicky and scrupulous characters who are not easily satisfied with themselves and often change their views. May the Lord be merciful to me through the intercession of your Paternity, from whom I humbly beg pardon and penance for these faults and all others of the year.

With regard to the government of the Province, I have only to say that it is very well with us to whom your Paternity has given a most admirable and prudent Provincial in the person of Father Paul. I hope that he will gradually make up by his diligence for what was omitted or badly done through my negligence, over so many years. . . .

I feel now, dear Father, how much more desirable a thing it is to obey rather than to rule. Would that I might be more grateful to God and my superiors who have set me free from a burden which was too much for me. . . .[1]

The concluding portion of this letter is taken up with a plea for the formation of schools of writers in his Order, which he had very much at heart. " I beg Our Lord Jesus," he said, " to initiate this most important project through your Paternity and to grant it successful progress. There is hardly any work, I think, which our Fathers could start and develop of more direct significance for the general good of the Church, especially in France, Germany, and Poland. In these countries new books dealing with religion are eagerly welcomed and bring to the much-afflicted Catholics a world of consolation at a period when heretical books are circulating everywhere and cannot be suppressed." Peter was so keen on the idea that he infected other men, including Hoffaeus for a time, with his enthusiasm. A decade earlier he had expressed the view that " one writer was more valuable in Germany than ten professors," and now his learned friend, Father Pisanus, went further and declared that one book was worth more than a thousand sermons! But it would not do to let such statements go by without remarking that, of course, it all depended on the professor, the writer, and the preacher.

As a contribution to the cause, St. Peter turned aside from his own work, which he was so anxious to get finished, in order to revise and see through the press a German edition of the Spanish Franciscan De Vega's great treatise on justification.[2] He also brought out at Dillingen a little book of prayers and instructions for Confession and Holy Communion, and a second small illustrated volume containing the Epistles and Gospels for the Sundays and Feasts of the Church's year, both of his own compilation. At this time, too, when in the throes of his work against the

---

[1] Braunsberger, *Epistulae*, vol. vi, pp. 418–9.

[2] This book, to which he added a huge preface in refutation of the Centuriators for the benefit of Prince Ernest of Bavaria, was cited as evidence more than a hundred years later to prove that Peter held the Thomist theory of efficacious grace. It is not clear, however, that De Vega himself held it, and, even if he did, St. Peter's general approval of his work is hardly a sufficient reason for claiming him as a forerunner of Thomism—not by any means that that would be a discredit to his memory.

Centuriators, he prepared and published a specially revised and amplified edition of his Catechism for the schools of Bavaria, as in 1569 Duke Albert had made the teaching of it obligatory throughout his dominions. This edition he dedicated to Albert's heir, the devout Prince William who a little later would crown and justify all Peter's hopes and labours by his great work for the restoration of Catholicism in Germany. Peter too it was who caused to be printed at Dillingen a Latin version of the inspiring letters which had come from Jesuits at work in the East, so that they might be available for the Society everywhere. Indeed, there was no end to the activities of his pen or to the encouragement with which he spurred on other writers. When in Frankfurt for a day or two in 1567 he paid a friendly visit to a sick canon there, and before he left had fired the invalid with keenness to produce a compendium of St. Augustine's Confessions. This appeared at Cologne in 1569 with a preface by the author devoted almost entirely to Peter's praises. Similarly, Father Torres in the preface to his important treatise on Holy Orders, published at Dillingen the same year, made open avowal of his debt to Peter, without whose continuous help the work could never have appeared. These were little circumstances that escaped the notice of Father Paul Hoffaeus.

Hoffaeus, however, plainly had cause for justifiable annoyance with Peter's hesitations and delays over the work against the Centuriators. As the Saint had explained to Borgia, it was his plan to produce three or four volumes against them, each pivoting round a central figure of the New Testament. They would show how the Centuriators had perverted the sense of Scripture in their treatment of the persons in question and so help to discredit the Magdeburg History, as the Pope desired. But, in the zeal of his heart, he went far beyond the minimum required of him. Believing the Centuriators to be by far the most dangerous foes of the Church then alive, he tended, when once on their track, to forget such considerations as his own health and the health of his assistants, the very busy life of the Dillingen professors, and the limitations to a printer's patience. At any rate, as the following extracts show, not only Hoffaeus but his own half-brother, Theodoric Canisius, the Rector of Dillingen, could have wished him otherwise occupied :

Theodoric Canisius to Borgia, February 1, 1571 :
        The first volume of Dr. Canisius is now printed and will be forwarded to your Paternity, that you may decide whether and how other volumes shall be prepared. Some people' here are doubtful about the

solid learning of the book, thinking it to be furnished with style rather than with good arguments. They think, too, that the Father's mental disposition is not suited for this kind of writing, which requires scholastic acumen rather than fluency of the pen. The good Father torments himself over the work, and harasses beyond endurance, not only himself, but several others, in order that the book may answer the expectations of obedience and the high hopes of the Catholics. Perhaps it would be better not to proceed to the publication of the second volume until the judgment of the public is known about the first.

Theodoric Canisius to Borgia, May 11, 1571 :

The labour involved in bringing out the first volume of Father Canisius has been immense, and the author and his assistants came very near to succumbing under it. God grant that he may gird himself for the publication of the second volume in a happier fashion. If only the method and present memory of Scholastic doctrine would serve him, after so many years devoted to other employments, his health would not frequently be in such grave danger. Now, even after an eighth, or sometimes, a tenth revision or correction, the good Father is not satisfied and often changes everything. It would seem, then, very necessary, if we wish to preserve his health, that he should be freed from this labour or adopt some other method of carrying it on. . . .

Paul Hoffaeus to Borgia, June 8, 1571 :

I could wish that your Paternity would suspend the work of Father Canisius against the Centuriators, at least for the remainder of the year. Though what he writes is good, it is expedient neither for himself nor for others that he should be solely responsible for the reply. We know what the Fathers of Dillingen have been through; and, besides, he has nearly killed himself over it. If your Paternity desires the good Father to remain with us long, he must not be thus occupied, writing on deep matters all by himself. He can never satisfy himself with what he has done ; the censors are without a basis for their judgment because he so constantly changes what he has written; and he has caused the printer quite enough worry. Your Paternity has but to ask the opinion of the Dillingen Fathers. For myself, I would urge that, if he *must* go on writing against the Centuriators, your Paternity should allow him only three days each week for the purpose. . . . If such be his wish, let him devote the remaining days to the composition of easy books in German.

Paul Hoffaeus to Nadal, July 9, 1571:

Care should be taken that the Pope does not impose on Father Canisius a fresh injunction to go on with the other two volumes of his work. . . . Otherwise, he will torment himself with scruples on account of the Pope's orders. . . . I could wish that, in this and other matters, I might have a free hand to dispose of my subjects, and that Father Canisius should know it. His health now needs attention more than ever. He should not be allowed to kill himself, as he does, with his writings. . . . If these suggestions are not approved, I entreat and demand that he be exempted altogether from obedience to me.

Like other men of intense purpose and high courage, St. Peter " saw the end so brightly that he could not see the way." That would seem to be a fair deduction from the passages given. In the following ones, the first of which was written when forwarding an advance copy of his book to Rome, he tells us himself what he thought about the whole affair :

Peter Canisius to Francis Borgia, April 20, 1571:

The eternal peace of Christ be with us, Very Reverend Father. Here are the first fruits of my work, which God grant that I may be able to publish soon now, slow as I have been about it. But I think that no pains are ever too great when writing at the present time on such a subject and against such adversaries.

To begin with, I humbly beg your Paternity's forgiveness for having, perhaps, gone beyond the intention of those who assigned me my task. . . . I did not think it enough to contend with the Centuriators alone but drew into the discussion others of the leading sectaries of the age, so that the work might be rightly entitled, *Falsifications of the Word of God.* The matter itself required that I should not pass over those others, whose opinions, errors, and very words the Centuriators have copied. . . . But, perhaps, I have been too diffuse in giving all this space to the single person of St. John the Baptist. If I have indulged myself unduly here, grasping out in every direction for whatever had an affinity with the argument or was supplied by the vanity of the heretics, I have also, I hope, illustrated the history of St. John . . . in such a way as to show the heretics that we do not lack means to defend and celebrate the persons of the Gospels, in company with Holy Church. I have an equally large amount of material ready wherewith to vindicate and glorify the history of Mary, the Mother of God. Though the abundance of proofs may displease some readers, I hope that others will be found to approve of labour expended for the glory of God's saints, especially when the heretics attack them and endeavour to weaken devotion to them.

There will also, I am afraid, be people in Rome to say that I have cited too many passages and opinions of the heretics . . . but Cardinal Hosius will understand my reasons and other prudent men of these parts will grant that such textual citations are adapted to the ills under which our Germany labours. . . . However, I have not been asked to defend myself or my book! I beg God of His infinite goodness and kindness to rectify whatever in the making of it I have omitted or admitted, wrongly and unwisely. In case it should be brought to the notice of the Holy Father, there is nothing I desire more than to be granted a plenary indulgence for my sins and negligences. On the other hand, I shall not doubt at all but that I well deserve whatever penance your Paternity may officially enjoin on me.

Now to indicate in a few words what I chiefly desire to be noticed with regard to the first part of the work, so that, if I am to go on with it, I may do so better prepared to finish the task quickly, to the greater glory of God. In the first place, I earnestly beg that there be appointed as reader and censor of the whole work some good theologian who will carefully note . . . the places in which the text of the book is deemed to require alteration. I shall be glad if, according to the judgment of the Fathers, marginal corrections are added in Rome before the book is communicated to persons not of the Society. Should it be thought necessary to suppress many passages or to remove whole pages, I would like to receive notice without delay. . . . I look and long for an admonitor who will speak his mind freely, for I am ready to accept whatever criticisms are passed on my book, not only with patience, but with alacrity and gratitude.

If from this present specimen of the future work it is judged not to be worth while that I should continue with it—and before God and your Paternity I declare that I am in many ways unworthy and unfitted to sustain the burden, especially in comparison with other more learned theologians—please let nobody imagine that I shall be aggrieved. Rather shall I think it an excellent decision . . . and shall pass on the lamp to others who are competent and prepared to carry through in worthy fashion a business of such importance. I know that there is other work, more in accordance with my vocation, to which, when holy obedience so permits, I could devote the time now given to these most troublesome studies, and devote it with, perhaps, better results and more satisfaction of heart. . . . I shall not go on with the task until your Paternity so decides and sends me fresh instructions, either because of the Pope's wishes or because it is thought that there may be some advantage in having the second and third volumes on the Blessed Virgin and St. Peter published. . . .

Peter Canisius to Everard Mercurian, May 5, 1571 :

As for my book, Father, I cannot but be in trepidation about the Roman censure, which I know will be no ordinary one, but exact and searching. Still, why should I dread the condemnation of my labours, seeing that I should be only too glad to break them off and throw the responsibility on somebody better versed in this wide and difficult field ? You have now in Rome a specimen of either my stupidity or my ignorance. Give but a hint that I should leave off and you will find me absolutely amenable, for it is not without distaste and aversion that I oppose myself to those outrageous enemies of Christ and His Church. But if I must go forward, I beg of your Reverence to admonish me freely as to what I should avoid or amend in my work. . . .[1]

Though, to demand stout volumes from critics of stout volumes before heeding their objections would be dangerously like supposing that he who drives fat oxen must himself be fat, still, a little productivity on their part is a help to greater confidence in their judgments. Now, of the two critics, and the only two, of St. Peter's book, Theodoric Canisius has not a single printed line to his credit, apart from some correspondence, and Paul Hoffaeus is remembered in bibliographies merely for his translation of the Roman Catechism. On the other hand, those who praised the book warmly were men such as Hosius, Sirleto, and Nadal, themselves experienced writers and one a scholar of the highest attainment. On July 11, 1571, St. Peter received the following characteristic letter from Hosius, then staying with the Benedictines at Subiaco :

Nicholas Delanoy used to be a man for whom I had very great esteem on account of the fine gifts which he possessed from God. But now I have a complaint to make about his Reverence. Since he

---

[1] Braunsberger, *Epistulae*, vol. vi, pp. 436–9, 441. The Latinity of the letter to St. Francis Borgia is so involved and awkward that St. Peter must have been either very tired or very worried when he wrote it. One does one's best with the translation of such documents, cherishing a hope that the reader may be neither tired nor worried but in an amiable, generous mood when he comes to see it.

came to Rome[1] he has paid me only one visit, and never again have I rested eyes on him. There is another of his Society not unknown to you who used to be a still more intimate friend of mine, and this person has written me scarcely a single letter during three whole years. Another man might have been vexed at such negligence, but I bore it with equanimity, especially when I had read a certain book on St. John the Baptist, written by this person. I realized then the thoughts which absorbed him, to the apparent exclusion of any concern about me.

The more this person is dissatisfied with himself, the more does his book give satisfaction to the devout and learned men who have read it, and to me also. God forbid that a work so pious and signally beneficial to its readers should be suppressed. Rather must you continue as you have begun and add Mary and Peter to John. These works cannot be read without great profit, whether by the Catholics or by the heretics themselves, since we discover in them true teaching, rare devotion, and a great lucidity, which I judge to be the principal virtue of style, all conjoined with no mean power of argument. Blessed indeed was the obedience which impelled you to undertake this labour. You say that you will not refuse a penance. For myself, I do not see what other penance can be enjoined on you for your deserts than that of completing your admirable work by adding Mary and Peter to John, but so that John is first given the light. This, then, is the penance which I would enjoin, had I any authority over you. However, I have advised those who possess such authority to enjoin it, and I think that they have done so. Good-bye, and accept your penance with a cheerful heart.[2]

The old Cardinal who had done the Church in many lands royal service by his own books of controversy was so strongly impressed by St. Peter's book that he wrote to the Pope commending it. It had been studied, he said, by the immensely learned Prefect of the Vatican Library, Cardinal Sirleto; by the distinguished theologian, Fontidonius; by the Oxford scholar, Alan Cope; and by many prominent Jesuit theologians. " Omnes uno ore probarunt vehementer "—with one voice they all approved of it thoroughly. "I hear now," the letter goes on, " that Your Holiness wishes, nevertheless, to have the judgment of the Master of the Sacred

---

[1] He had been appointed Penitentiary at St. Peter's.
[2] Braunsberger, *Epistulae*, vol. vi, pp. 445–6.

Palace on it. That is a design at which nobody could cavil, but if carried
out, it would be necessary to put off publication of the book for a long
time because the Master's eyesight is giving him much trouble. As it is
certainly a book to bring its readers the greatest profit, I entreat Your
Holiness to study the verdicts of those who have read it and to be satisfied
with them. There is danger of the printer suffering heavy loss if publication is long delayed . . . and he might also be deterred from setting
up the future writings of Father Canisius. Would to God that we had
many of his kind to devote themselves with equally happy results to
the task of refuting the Centuriators!"[1]

In conversation with Polanco the good Cardinal avowed that the
devout tone of St. Peter's book made him think of the ancient Doctors
of the Church. He loved its modesty and considered that no other work
of its author showed a finer style, but the pages that delighted him and
Polanco most were the concluding three which contained Peter's personal
confession of faith.[2] It had been added, for two reasons, because of the
recurrent rumour spread by the Protestants that Peter had joined their
ranks and because a number of Protestant writers were fond of declaring
him a hypocrite who did not believe the doctrines which he defended.
It was in the following terms:

I confess to Thee, Father, Lord of Heaven and earth, my Creator
and Redeemer, my strength and salvation, who hast not ceased from
my childhood to feed me with the sacred bread of Thy Word, and
to strengthen my heart. Lest I should wander with the straying sheep
who have no shepherd Thou didst gather me into the house and home
of Thy Church and there bring me up and conserve me, with those
for masters and pastors in whom Thou hast commanded all Thy children
to recognize Thyself. . . .

Luther I know not; Calvin I reject utterly; to all heretics I say
anathema. I desire that there should be nothing in common between
me and those who do not speak and feel and hold the same rule of
faith with the One, Holy, Catholic, Apostolic, and Roman Church.
. . . Of that Roman Church which others despise with blasphemy and
persecute, execrating it as the work of antichrist, I profess myself the
child, nor by a hair's breadth do I depart from its authority. I would
not refuse to pour out my blood and life in witness to the Church of

[1] Braunsberger, *Epistulae*, vol. vi, pp. 710–1.
[2] Hosius had only one small criticism to offer, that his friend might have been more brief on the
subject of St. John's locusts, and indeed he might, for he gives them over twenty pages.

Rome, and certain sure I am that nowhere else but in unity with her are there for me and all men the saving merits of Christ Our Lord and the gifts of the Holy Ghost.

With St. Jerome I freely profess that whosoever is joined to the Chair of Peter is mine; with St. Ambrose I desire to follow the Roman Church in all things; with St. Cyprian I reverently acknowledge her to be the root and matrix of the whole Church Catholic. I rest in the faith and doctrine which I learned as a child, confirmed with my growing years, taught as a man, and hitherto have defended to the best of my small ability. It is for no temporal advantage nor any man's favour nor in despite of my conscience (as I desire Thee, my God, ever to be merciful to me) that I have hitherto borne or shall afterwards sustain the part of a Catholic theologian. Nothing else demands and draws this confession from me but the honour of Thy Name, my God, and the power of the known truth. . . . I beg of Thee this grace, that living and dying I may never fall away from Thy charity as a partaker with all who fear Thee and keep Thy commandments in the Holy Roman Church, to whose judgment I submit myself and all my writings with no less gladness than reverence. . . .

When Pope Pius V, advised by Hosius, had read this confession, he immediately changed his mind with regard to further censorship of St. Peter's book and intimated that it might be published at once.[1] Nadal, who loved Peter, was delighted, because, as he explained to him, if the censors of the Holy Office had captured his work he " would probably not have got it back for at least a year." Peter was not very much excited by the warm welcome which greeted his book. " I have enough to be sad about," he told Nadal, " when I think how unworthy and unequal I am for such labour, and how many miseries and imperfections I import into it. The praises of some cardinals stir me very little. Would that I had it in me to give satisfaction to God and my superiors! "

In Innsbruck, meantime, the zealous but contentious and easily ruffled Archduke Ferdinand required a preacher. He does not appear to have liked Father Canisius very much, possibly because of his sturdy independence in face of the world's great ones, and Peter, on his side, certainly had no desire for a post at Court. But St. Francis Borgia wished him to take it, and to continue at Innsbruck his work against the Centuriators. He doubted very much his ability to bear the double burden of writer

[1] Braunsberger, *Epistulae*, vol. vi, p. 711.

and preacher, especially as the latter office carried with it responsibility for the souls of the Archduke's sisters at Hall. " Nevertheless, I shall gladly try," he told his General. He did, and promptly broke down in health as a consequence. Shortly afterwards, the Archduke departed for Vienna to be present at his brother's wedding, which gave Peter an opportunity of visiting Dillingen to see to the final revision and publication of his book. It appeared before the end of September, a bulky quarto volume of 796 pages, printed in fine, clear type on good paper. All the way through there are marginal headings and references, and the work is furnished with two excellent indexes. Its motto is a sentence from St. Gregory Nazianzen : " *Principium tibi sit, tibi finiat omnia Christus* "—Christ be thy beginning, thy finisher of all things, Christ.

Perhaps it may be wondered how Peter was able to stretch out the few passages on St. John in the Gospels to such a prodigious length. The answer is that, far from being a mere heavily-padded " life " of the Baptist, the book is a profound treatise on various aspects of Catholic doctrine and practice which the Reformers had attacked. Its author never forgot the precise terms of his commission from the Pope. He was to discredit the Centuriators by revealing their contradictions and absurdities. Already in his long preface he sets to work, showing how by the misuse of Scripture the Protestants had fallen into utter doctrinal confusion. The wide range of his reading is clearly evident from the start. Luther, Calvin, Melanchthon, Peter Martyr, Bucer, Stephanus, Carlstadt, Servetus, Major, Beza, Schwenckfeldt, Brenz, Stancar, Chemnitz, Bullinger, he has studied them all and cites their writings textually. The Greek Fathers in their original tongue come to him as readily as do the Latin ones. He quotes from St. John Chrysostom and St. Augustine with the ease and appositeness born of long familiarity with their teeming pages. The historians, Josephus, Eusebius, Nicephorus, Rufinus, Bede, and others, are drawn on in such a way as to make it evident that he had consulted them at first hand. Indeed, the learning of the book, which includes, of course, an intimate knowledge of the Catholic theologians, both medieval and contemporary, is, if anything, too great. One is rather swamped with references and allusions and, for our own bright age at least, the compliment of supposing the reader himself to be enormously erudite, is pushed to extremes.

Needless to say, a good deal of the argumentation has now lost the point which it once possessed, but there remain some interesting affinities between the naturalistic tendencies of much modern Biblical criticism and the crude methods of the Centuriators. Only the motive is different, that of Flacius and his allies being the removal, not of all supernaturalism, but of all "Romanism" from the Gospels. They desired, for obvious reasons, to make away with whatever in the story of the Baptist had a savour of monasticism. John's garment of camel's hair becomes an ordinary peasant's dress, and the locusts turn out to have been a sort of crab or other succulent shell-fish, supplied to him by the fishermen of the Jordan. Thus is the Baptist's life shorn of its unique features and reduced to terms of ordinary experience. Having disposed of the Catholic ideas of fasting and mortification, the Centuriators then proceed to show that the Precursor of the Messiah was also the Precursor of Martin Luther. St. Peter answers with forty-four closely reasoned pages, wherein he calls more than a score of ancient saints and sages to witness to the traditional practice of the Church in the matter of penance. Towards the end of the section, he forgets for a few pages his rôle of detached and critical scholar in order, like St. John, to become a preacher of penance himself. "The reader will forgive me, I hope, for this digression which is longer than I intended," he says in apology. "After all, it is not entirely irrelevant, for I was led into it by the love and zeal which constrain me to vindicate the cause of our John and of the Ancient Church against the impudent calumnies and base designs of those men."[1] The practice of celibacy in the Church and the whole doctrine of good works are defended in the same way with great and glowing erudition that has in it the throb of Peter's apostolic heart.

In connexion with the baptism of St. John, the Centuriators had introduced their chosen theories of faith and justification, which gives Peter occasion for another lengthy excursus on Protestant "variations." He supplies a wealth of commentary from Scripture and Christian tradition to show that faith and good works, faith and the Sacrifice of the Mass, faith and penance, are sanctities which God has joined together and which no man can put asunder. Another matter ably vindicated in connexion with St. John's stand against the Pharisees and Sadducees, is the teaching and disciplinary authority of the Church, while the Baptist's martyrdom and posthumous worship provide opportunity for much pertinent and highly effective criticism of the Protestant attitude to the Catholic practice of invoking the saints and venerating relics.

It is plain to see, then, that the book embraced a good portion of the whole Reformation debate. The style of it throughout is Ciceronian

[1] *Commentariorum de Verbi Dei Corruptelis liber primus*, editio princeps, cap. iv, fol. 93 verso.

to a degree unusual in books of theology. At times it rises to a fervent eloquence of pleading or expostulation, and at times, too, let us confess, the strident note so common in the polemics of the sixteenth century makes a discord in its harmonies. But, though St. Peter not infrequently refers to his opponents as " impudent," " audacious," " impious," and even " blasphemous," the epithets are aimed at the doctrine and not at the man holding it. He is never directly abusive or personal in the way favoured at the time by the majority of religious disputants, whether Protestant or Catholic, and it need hardly be said that the scurrilities with which the other side so frequently bespattered his own good name have no place in his pages.[1] The last word on the book, the truest estimate of its qualities, was given by the great theologian and scholar, Salmeron, when he said : " It breathes of nothing else to me but my Peter Canisius, by which I mean that it reveals piety rare and wonderful, deep learning, careful reading of the Fathers, grand controversy, and the genuine, orthodox interpretation of God's Word, all set out in a style so limpid and finely wrought that the reader is arrested, stirred, and marvellously charmed."[2] The fact that a reader in 1935 might not experience those pleasant sensations is no objection whatever to the truth of Salmeron's testimony.

[1] Flacius Illyricus not only wrote scandalous tracts against the Jesuits, singling out Canisius for his worst tirades, but earnestly incited his friends to traduce them. " What are you doing against the Jesuits and Schwenckfeldists ? " he asked a Frankfurt disciple in January 1569. Three weeks later the same man is again addressed : " Dear Brother, I await an answer to my recent letter as to what you are doing against the Jesuits." Again in July he inquires, " What are you writing or preaching against the Jesuits ? " His friend and colleague, Wigand, who helped him more than any other man with the Magdeburg History, published a lucubration somewhat earlier in which Canisius was traduced and insulted in the most abominable fashion.

[2] M.H., *Epistolae P. Alphons Salmeronis*, vol. ii (Madrid, 1907), pp. 311–2.

CHAPTER XVII

FATHER PETER AND FATHER PAUL

St. John off his mind, Father Canisius turned again towards " the Alps," by which term he liked to signify mountain-girt Innsbruck. Being a true Dutchman, he had no love for high altitudes and surmised that they might be the death of him. According to the standards of the period he was now an old man, for he had passed his half-century. And what a half-century it had been, the hyphen between medieval and modern history! Nearly all its strange happenings had cut deeply into Peter's life, so, perhaps, by the standards of any period he was old, if age be a matter not of years but of intense experience. Nevertheless, his vitality showed no signs of waning, despite the ill-informed statements of Protestant commentators who have imagined that with the end of his Provincialate he was out of the race. On the contrary, it would be more true to say that this was the time of his greatest influence, when he had so many and such various contacts with the changing world beyond his mountain home that it is impossible to find room for mention of them all.

Thus, he soon won over the Archduke Ferdinand, to whom he had dedicated his work on St. John, and became a power in the government of Lower Austria so far as its religious policy was concerned. Cologne, which had been gravely afflicted by the rebellion in the Low Countries, found in him, as always, a most sympathetic and devoted counsellor. The Cardinal of Trent sought his intervention to terminate the long-standing differences between himself and the Archduke. The coadjutor Bishop of Brixen, in Tirol, regarded him as a sort of patron saint of the diocese and wrote to him early in 1572 : " It gave me the keenest pleasure to receive your letter, in which I recognized that your continual, watchful care for the preservation of the bishopric of Brixen waxes ever greater and greater." Cardinal Hosius had such faith in his power to sway men that he pressed Albert of Bavaria to send him to the Elector of Saxony, who seemed favourably disposed to Catholicism, but Albert replied that he would not be admitted to the country for fear lest his fame as a theologian might cause too much excitement. And so it would be possible to continue for page after page, giving indications of the exceptional authority which had come to be attached to the name of Peter Canisius.

As mentioned, his duties in Innsbruck were of two kinds, to be the ordinary, official preacher of the City and to finish his work against the Centuriators. During the nine years which he was now to spend more or less continuously in Tirol he delivered close on three hundred sermons. These were all sermons in the grand manner, not such facile little things as a man might excogitate going up the pulpit steps. It was ever Peter's habit to write out each sermon, then carefully to revise the first draft, and finally to add marginal directions and catchwords. Sometimes he used to write two or three different versions of a sermon, or put down alternative openings and conclusions. The infinite pains which he took are very evident in the vast collection of manuscript notes still extant. But the notes were only to get the matter clear in his own mind and not for use in the pulpit. They are on all sorts of topics from ghosts to earthquakes, and usually, as the times demanded, have a 'heart of controversy' in them. One complete set of the sermons was devoted to an exposition of the Book of Job. Through all Peter's preaching there runs a vein of profound compassion for the poor. The poor, indeed, he had always with him and that made him the more severe on merchants and officials whom he suspected of exploiting them. There is no trace of self-conscious rhetoric in the sermons. They are entirely colloquial, a speech of heart to heart in the unstudied terms of every-day life. Penance and sorrow for sin are their great themes, introduced even on the most festive occasions; but that Peter was no kill-joy may easily be seen from the following passage of a sermon preached on Quinquagesima Sunday, 1572, immediately before the *Fastnacht,* or Shrove Tuesday carnival:

How may and ought a Christian man to celebrate his *Fastnacht* merrily and honourably with God ? I have heard it said that the devil does more harm to the Church and men's souls during these three days than all the preachers are afterwards able to undo throughout the whole of Lent. I have no wish to prevent or condemn the *Fastnacht.* Indeed, I think that not Peter and Paul themselves nor Emperor and King could stop it. But I would like to persuade and beseech you all to spend this time providently and discreetly. In the first place, then, I exhort the nobles and rich and all who have it in their power, to keep the *Fastnacht*, not only for themselves, but also for others less well off who need recreation and refreshment in their great poverty, infirmity, and trouble. Listen to how Christ teaches us to celebrate the *Fastnacht : When thou makest a feast call the poor, the maimed, the lame, and the blind, and thou shalt be blessed because they have not wherewith to make thee recompense ; for recompense shall be made thee at the resurrection of the just.* Perhaps you have no desire to be so liberal and compassionate in inviting and treating the poor ? Well then, I beg of you to give them at least of your superfluity, according to the words of Christ : *Gather up the fragments lest they be lost.* . . .

I urge one and all to celebrate the *Fastnacht* who have a quarrel or cause of dispute with their neighbour or keep any rancour, envy, or enmity in their hearts. It is a thing pleasing to God and in accordance with Christian charity to be merry at this time with people who are not in our good books, to make it up with them and become friends again before the season of penance. This is what Christ Himself teaches us : *Go first to be reconciled to thy brother and then coming thou shalt offer thy gift.* That is the order, first to make peace with our neighbour and then afterwards with God by offering to Him the sacrifice of a contrite heart. As a sign of this peace I exhort you all to act friendlily with those who have offended you and whom you regard as enemies. Be merry at your feasts, as I believe our forefathers used to be for this same purpose of making it up with people, and show an honest joy in your exterior. . . .[1]

Among the most interesting of the Innsbruck sermons was the one which St. Peter preached at the beginning of his course, on November 12, 1571. The previous day, which was a Sunday, he had announced that the Archduke desired the whole population to be present the following morning at 7 o'clock in or about the Church of St. Martin, in order to hear a " joyful *Te Deum laudamus*." Then they would walk in procession to the Premonstratensian Abbey of Wilten, outside the City, to assist at a High Mass " celebrated with great pomp and magnificence " in presence of their Sovereign ; all of which would be " to praise and thank God Almighty, the Heavenly Father, for the tremendous, amazing, and unparalleled victory which our Christian and Catholic Armada gained recently on the sea." Peter must have had inside information about the Battle of Lepanto, probably obtained from dispatches sent to the Archduke by

[1] Braunsberger, *Epistulae*, vol. vii, pp. 631-2.

his cousin, Don John of Austria, Captain General of the combined Spanish, Venetian, and papal fleets. At any rate, the sermon which he preached during the High Mass at Wilten had itself the style of a dispatch. " On Sunday, October 7th," he began, " God was pleased to bring low the pride of our foes. They came on merrily with a great shout, all their sails and oars in action, absolutely certain of victory. Our men, having first reconciled themselves to God by confession and penance, vowed, according to the pious exhortation of their Captain General, to fight only for the Name and honour of Christ,. putting their trust in the Living God.[1] No sooner did our Armada approach the Turks than the wind veered and the sea became calm. A stiff sirocco wind then began to blow and caused the smoke of the battle to drift towards the enemy's ships, which was an advantage for our ships because the Turks could not see them or in consequence easily resist their attack. Though they were superior to us in numbers, resources, power, and equipment,[2] their ships were, with few exceptions, at length either captured, burned, sent to the bottom, or otherwise put out of action. It was the work of God that of so many Turks not half or a quarter got away alive. Even their pashas and chief captains were either wounded or killed, only Aluch Ali managing to escape.[3] A hundred and eighty galleys were captured or destroyed, not to speak of the thousands of Turks killed or taken prisoners.[4] It was the work of God that fourteen galleys which had escaped were afterwards captured ; that great treasure of gold, silver, and jewels was taken, together with vast quantities of firelocks, cannon, military weapons, powder, armour, and provisions ; that the Christian captives were inspired to turn

[1] " At a certain signal a crucifix was raised aloft in every ship in the fleet. Don John of Austria, sheathed in complete armour, and standing in a conspicuous place on the prow of his ship, now knelt down to adore the sacred emblem and to implore the blessing of God on the great enterprise which he was about to commence. Every man in the fleet followed his example and fell upon his knees. The soldier, poising his firelock, knelt at his post by the bulwarks ; the gunner knelt with his lighted match beside his gun. The decks gleamed with prostrate men in mail. In each galley, erect and conspicuous amongst the martial throng, stood a Franciscan or a Dominican friar, a Theatine or a Jesuit, in his brown or black robe, holding a crucifix in one hand and sprinkling holy water with the other, while he pronounced a general absolution, and promised indulgence in this life or pardon in the next to the steadfast warriors who should quit them like men and fight the good fight of faith against the infidel." Stirling-Maxwell, *Don John of Austria* (London, 1883), p. 408.

[2] Hardly in equipment, as the guns of the Christians were more powerful and much more skilfully used.

[3] This pasha's name has been spelt in scores of different ways by the historians of Lepanto. St. Peter wrote it " Ucialj " but the true sound of it was probably something like " Ouloudj-Ali." The spelling in the text is that adopted by most Spanish writers. It was a disaster that Aluch escaped, as he lived to reorganize the Turkish fleet and become its high admiral. The Catholics took great interest in him because he was really an Italian who had renounced Christianity and risen to be the Sultan's viceroy in Algiers. He was known for his savage hatred of the religion which he had abjured.

[4] According to a " News-Letter " sent to the House of Fugger in Augsburg from the Christian Armada the day after the battle, " Almost all the Turkish nobles and nearly 18,000 men were killed, 10,000 taken prisoners, and 15,000 Christians who had been slaves on the Turkish galleys were set free." The letter ended : " Praise and glory be to God Almighty and His Blessed Mother in all eternity. Amen."

their arms against the Turks and so help our soldiers to victory. . . . It was the work of God that the Catholics should have gained such a triumph in the space of four hours, greater than anything that was hoped for or expected and without its like in all written history. A most powerful foe, made proud and insolent by countless triumphs, is routed in confusion by one Christian army under an Austrian Captain General who publicly professed his faith, and, crucifix in hand, exhorted his men to fight bravely for the honour of Jesus crucified."[1]

The main impression which one receives from St. Peter's sermon on Lepanto is of the astonishment and almost awe with which the Catholics regarded this victory. Never since Charles Martel's great achievement in the eighth century had such a thing happened. Turkish invincibility had been so often proved that Christian Europe inclined to take it for granted. The most that might be hoped for seemed to be a measure of successful resistance, and now in four short hours the whole naval power of the infidel was in ruins. No wonder that the Catholics regarded the result of the battle as a miracle, wrought by the " man sent from God whose name was John,"[2] through the prayers of Mary's clients everywhere in Europe on that October Sunday which is now consecrated in gratitude to the Feast of her Rosary.[3] Alas, owing to hateful national jealousies the great victory was not followed up, but, all the same, it brought a new spirit of confidence into Catholic life and so is a notable milestone in the progress of the Counter-Reformation.

Not Lepanto, however, or any other preacher's topic was the main preoccupation of St. Peter's thoughts at this time. The Centuriators still enjoyed that honour. Escape from their toils he could not, for, in spite of his unconcealed antipathy to the work, he still felt himself pledged, all the more since it was not now John the Baptist but Mary, the Mother of God, who claimed the chivalry of his pen. *Si vieillesse pouvait!* He was so ready, being her devoted lover, to spend himself in Our Lady's cause, but what could all the will in the world do when memory, too much overladen, tended to sink under its burdens, and words, those treacherous servants, came so tardily to his summoning? For such sad reasons he gently suggested to his superiors in Rome that perhaps he had

---

[1] Braunsberger, *Epistulae*, vol. vi, pp. 637–8.

[2] These words were applied to Don John of Austria by the Pope himself. Under God, it was undoubtedly his genius as a strategist that had won the day.

[3] The Jesuits did their part in the intercession for, on July 21, 1571, St. Francis Borgia had ordered all the priests of the Society in Europe to offer Mass each week for a Christian victory. Borgia had himself gone to Spain with the papal legate to help organize the league planned by Pius V. The legate sent to the Emperor for the same purpose was accompanied by Father Francis Toledo, a distinguished professor of the Roman College, afterwards cardinal.

better retire. But, influenced very likely by the great success of his first volume, they would not consent. When Pope Pius V, from whom he held his commission, died on May 1, 1572, he wrote again to enquire whether he might not now be considered free, though half of his book was written. "I leave it to my Fathers to judge," he said, "if it would not be better for me to give up this work and turn to other things more in accordance with my vocation." It was Hoffaeus who had infected him with that vocational scruple, but Nadal, the Vicar-General of the Society of Jesus at this time in the absence of St. Francis Borgia on papal business, let him know very definitely that his work was by no means alien to the proper engagements of his Order.

It was work of excessive difficulty on many counts, pioneer work in one of the most obscure departments of theology which no writer before him had explored with any great thoroughness. Our Lady walked in a garden enclosed. The texts about her were few and sometimes strange, so all the theology of her (and how grandiose and out-of-place the word seems when she is in question!) had to be a deduction from the theology of her Son. It went and will ever go, not so much upon texts, as upon the truest, surest, noblest instincts of the human heart. The high humanity of the Church is nowhere more apparent than in her appreciation of Our Lady. She fills up all the gaps in the evidence with an unanswerable *decet*. Thus and thus must Our Lady have been and be, for so it was becoming that God should deal with the Mother of His Son. It is an argument which no number of texts could make stronger but to urge it against men like the Centuriators, whose gentler feelings had been blasted and withered by heresy, would not have helped at all.

Somehow or other, then, Peter must find every available text. He had at first intended to refute only the Centuriators, but his love for Our Lady gradually led him to examine and criticize whatever arguments had at any time in the Church's history been used against her prerogatives. Still, it is the heretics of his own day who principally engage his attention, as may be seen from the fact that Luther appears in his work more than 140 times, Calvin upwards of a 100 times, Brenz about 110 times, Melanchthon 70 times, not to mention the galaxy of minor Thersites whose cavils are reproduced and confuted. For his positive arguments Peter went through the Fathers and great theologians, it might almost be said with a fine comb. But the results of his patient, laborious research in printed books were very disappointing, and he thought longingly of the many precious Greek manuscripts hidden away in the cupboards of Roman libraries which might contain the very evidence he required. He accordingly begged Cardinal Truchsess, who was in Rome, to intercede on his behalf with Cardinal Sirleto, the Prefect of the Vatican Library, and a well-known private collector of manuscripts. The following passage of a letter of thanks to Truchsess, written at the beginning of 1572, shows how truly scholarly and painstaking were Peter's researches:

> I am, indeed, greatly indebted to his Lordship, Cardinal Sirleto, for his promise to supply me, who have no claim on him, with ancient texts that may serve to defend the Mother of God against the heretics. Whatever so eminent a man may send me will be most acceptable. I am at present using only the ordinary editions of the Fathers which have been printed, as it is not easy to find Greek codices. I know that there are many manuscripts in Rome of such writers as the two Saints Cyril, St. Proclus, St. Amphilochius, Procopius, Flavian, Caesarius, and Miletus, which have never been translated into Latin. . . . So far, I have certainly found little in the more ancient sources which is concerned with the praise of the Mother of God. Indeed, some of the writers, such as St. John Chrysostom, Origen, and Theophylact, appear to find fault with the Blessed Virgin.[1] I have come upon nothing more beautiful than what is to be found in St. Athanasius, but the authenticity of that sermon is questioned by some scholars, as is also the authenticity of the Masses and Liturgies of St. Chrysostom, St. Basil, and St. James.
>
> To be brief, I can find no other authors to support me beyond those mentioned in my Catechism in connexion with the Angelical Salutation . . . and I therefore beg your Lordship most earnestly to confirm me in the good graces of Cardinal Sirleto and to secure from him whatever he may consider helpful in establishing the innocence and singular sanctity of the Virgin Mother, or relevant to the history of her life and death or to her peculiar prerogatives here below and in Heaven. There has scarcely been a passage ever written about Our Lady which the sectaries do not pull to pieces. . . . It is hard work answering the calumnies of all these men, but I shall strive to set forth under the guidance of Christ whatever thoughts suggest themselves for the vindication of His Mother. . . . I beg of your piety to support my effort by collecting

---

[1] St. John Chrysostom, following Theophylact, appears to have thought that there was a taint of vainglorious self-assertion in Our Lady's action at the Marriage Feast of Cana, which is surely a most unwarranted deduction from the Gospel text. As far as Catholics are concerned, that question has, of course, been settled long ago. Not even the faintest breath of sin ever touched Our Lady's soul. Origen and some others thought that her virginity was to some degree affected in the birth of Our Lord but it is a truth of Catholic faith that they were wrong.

whatever testimonies of the Fathers may be found in the libraries of learned men in Rome. I would gladly offer myself to the sectaries to be butchered for Mary's sake.[1]

The first batch of Sirleto's transcripts came to St. Peter by three different routes, a precaution necessary in those days when the post was liable to be waylaid and robbed at any stage of its journey. In his letter of hearty thanks to the two Cardinals he begged Sirleto for " some more of this generous wine to slake a thirst which the first draught provided had only increased." Further encouragement came in an enormous letter from Naples, dictated by the kind heart of the Jesuit Provincial there, Alfonso Salmeron, a man for whom Peter always showed the profoundest veneration. Having first congratulated him very warmly on the volume devoted to St. John the Baptist, Salmeron continued : " You are now engaged on a higher endeavour, fighting bravely and nobly with your pen for the glory of the Blessed Mother of God. Bravo, and all prosperity to your enterprise ! Meantime, I exult in high hopes that, having outstripped all others with your previous book, you will now with this one easily surpass yourself. For if it was given to you to fight so successfully on behalf of one who was but the servant of Christ, though a great servant, what may we not hope and promise ourselves from your pen when it is engaged in defence of Christ's most holy and spotless Mother who by her salutation sanctified John in the womb and caused him to leap for joy ? " There is a great deal more in this strain which reveals Salmeron's own tender devotion to Our Lady. Next comes a charming passage in which Father Alfonso rallies Peter for the too great modesty of his letters. " There was no reason," he said, " why you should so abase yourself when addressing me, calling yourself a coarse, dull, ignorant German fellow. The facts tell a very different tale, namely that you are a man of subtle, active, and ready mind, gifted with deep insight into the Heavenly mysteries. Well I know that you were not merely using the tricks of self-depreciatory language familiar to orators[2] but speaking out of the profound humility and Christian modesty of your soul, wherein there is no pretence or craft or dissimulation. And I recognize you for a true *Germanus*, whether

---

[1] Braunsberger, *Epistulae*, vol. vii, pp. 2–3. Peter's eager hunt for evidence in ancient, unprinted sources is very interesting in view of the following recent comment on his work in a learned English journal : " A reply was needed to the Magdeburg Centuriators, and by Papal orders Canisius undertook the task which Baronius was to fulfil. He was grotesquely incompetent . . . satisfied with unverified references and citations at second hand." E. W. Watson, D.D., in *The English Historical Review*, January, 1934, p. 127.

[2] " Nec tamen per Tapinosis figuram Rhetoribus notam te loqui quam per summam animi tui submissionem . . ." Ταπείνωσις=an abasing of oneself.

that word be taken in its Latin meaning of close kinship, or according to the derivation of *Germania* suggested by Tacitus.[1] Indeed, might I not ask what else is a *Germanus* but a complete and integral man; one endowed, I mean, with the unimpaired strength and resolution of human nature, in whom there is nothing weak or childish or effeminate? So you see, the more you try to disparage yourself the more you cause everybody to esteem and appreciate you!—you who think so little of yourself and speak in such modest tones. Blessed be God who of His incomparable goodness first rendered you the imitator of the Virgin Mother and the great Precursor of Our Lord in their rare and admirable humility before electing you to be their defender by the spoken and written word."

Having thus turned the tables on Peter, Father Alfonso passed to another matter which had come up between them. As it is an interesting point and shows well the persistence of Peter's zeal, we may be forgiven for letting Salmeron continue to speak:

In the last part of your letter you urge me to stir up those of our brethren who possess a good style or abundant learning that they may arm for the defence of God's Church, suffering so dreadfully in France and Germany, and with busy pens fight against the many raging plagues of heresy. Sure I am that it was zeal for the glory of Christ and the vindication of His truth which inspired your appeal to me, but you know, my wisest Father, what a big distance there is between us and the peoples of France and Germany,[2] so big as to make it almost impossible for us to learn what is going on in their midst, or, should news come, to render it too late for the purposes of controversy. As for the principal heresies that are abroad, the prevalent views of the sectaries, and the books circulated to seduce the people, nobody knows anything about them. Such being the case, I leave it to you to judge whether anything solid or distinguished could be written. You cannot be unaware of the strict laws under which we have lived during the past few years; of the obstacles put in the way of heretics who desire to visit Italy; of the ban on the importation of new books; and of the great difficulty experienced by those seeking permission to read heretical books, even when they might do so to the glory of Christ

[1] There is an elaborate play on the word at this point. The strict Latin for a German is " Germanicus." " Germanus " was an appellation of brothers and sisters who have the same parents or at least the same father. It also meant genuine, real, true.

[2] It will be remembered that Salmeron was writing from Naples.

and with profit to the Church. . . .[1] These are the reasons why Italy has produced few champions against heresy.[2] As it is the part of a brave soldier when on the field of battle to engage the enemy hand to hand and deal him smashing blows, so is it his fortune when out of the ranks to lead a tranquil life and meditate only thoughts of peace. You in Germany are on the battlefield. . . . It is therefore your part to fight valiantly, to engage daily in fresh battles, to strike down and slay with his own sword—the Word of God, produced for the support of his false doctrines—each fierce and insolent heretic who challenges you to combat like another Goliath. But for us who live in peace a different duty is reserved, namely to keep Catholics in their ancestral faith and to pray for all the blessings and favour of Heaven on you who face the foe. . . .

Once again, Father Alfonso has turned the tables on his correspondent. Peter had begged him to prepare his own many exegetical and other works for publication but they were in such a chaotic state, Salmeron said, that, like the bear-cubs mentioned by Pliny, they would need a great deal of licking to get any recognizable shape into them.[3] " But I will not refuse any labour that may give pleasure to you who ask me so urgently, exact of me so anxiously, and stimulate me so lovingly. Indeed, I give way to nobody in my love and reverence for you. . . . Good-bye, dearest Father, and, if it is not too much trouble, would you let me know whether you have finished half of your work in defence of the Blessed Virgin and when you think it will be published ? Take care in future not to suffer that I be deprived so long a time of the fruit which I obtain from the reading of your books! As soon as they come out send one or two copies to Rome at my expense, as they can easily be forwarded to me from there, wherever I happen to find myself."[4]

St. Peter's feelings of veneration and humility when in correspondence with Salmeron were due, in some measure, to respect for the good scholar and great theologian, but far more to remembrance of the fact that Father Alfonso was of the fast diminishing little company who had been with St. Ignatius from the beginning. Among the virtues of Peter's heart not the least was *pietas*, that lovely, tender regard for the ties by

---

[1] Salmeron himself, though so eminent a theologian, had not been able to obtain permission while Pope Pius V lived.

[2] But a few years later she was to produce the greatest of all champions, St. Robert Bellarmine.

[3] Braunsberger gravely informs his readers that though bears do lick their cubs, this is not to shape them, as Pliny imagined, but to cleanse and purge them!

[4] Braunsberger, *Epistulae*, vol. vii, pp. 40–5.

which God particularizes our human relationships. The memory of Ignatius and those first Fathers of the Society of Jesus counted for much in his life, as appeared at this time when Father Pedro Ribadeneyra wrote to him for comments on a biography of their holy Founder which he had prepared. The occurrence of Ribadeneyra's name is a serious temptation to digress, but we must resist beyond mentioning that, as a boy of fourteen, he had been the delight and bane of St. Ignatius's existence.[1]

Father Canisius did not approve of everything in the biography of his hero which Ribadeneyra now sent him for criticism. Thus, he deprecated the use of the term " illustrations " as applied to the spiritual experiences of St. Ignatius at Manresa, and desired it to be said rather that the Saint had received much remarkable knowledge of divine things. " For I would not," he continues, " thus give substance to the calumnies of people who suspect us of illuminism, and it might be a good thing to add a passage showing the difference between true and false illuminations, so as to preclude all opportunity for cavil and suspicion." Peter also disagreed with Ribadeneyra's rendering of Our Lord's words to Ignatius, Io saro con voi, as " I shall be favourable to you." He thought them to have a much deeper meaning, though he could not allow that they were the sole or even chief reason why St. Ignatius clung to the title, " Society of Jesus," for his Order. Peter was greatly interested in this question and asked for further light on it in Ribadeneyra's book, as well as for a statement that the Fathers of the Society had never arrogated to themselves the name of " Jesuits." That was perfectly true, but whether the name first came to be applied to them in compliment or in contempt has never been determined.

Criticisms such as those reported are of small account, but some others, concerning Ribadeneyra's omissions, have a bearing on the character of the man who wrote them. In a previous chapter there was occasion to speak of the intrigues which Father Nicholas Bobadilla had carried on to prevent Laynez from being elected General of the Society of Jesus. Bobadilla had become in consequence something of a disgraced man in the Society and was passed over by Ribadeneyra with a bare mention

---

[1] The way he came to know Ignatius was typical of his mischievous, impulsive boyhood. While a page at the Court of Cardinal Alessandro Farnese in Rome, he one day played truant from his duties and wandered off on a private sightseeing expedition. A Spanish friend had shown him a poor, dilapidated house in Rome and told him to knock on its door if ever he found himself in trouble. He was in trouble at the end of that day's truancy, fearful of what would happen to him when he got back to Court, so he knocked on the door of the tumble-down place which had been pointed out to him. It was opened by Ignatius, who treated Pedro with such irresistible kindness that the boy forthwith determined to abandon the service of Cardinal Farnese for this new master. Luckily, Ignatius and Farnese were very good friends, so the matter was easily arranged.

of his work in Germany. Now St. Peter had been personally acquainted with him and knew the leal and zealous heart that beat under the surface contrariness of his character. How true and generous he was deep down may be seen from the following delightful *suffragium* which he sent to Laynez on May 5, 1561, with regard to the question whether the term of the General's office should be for life, as in the Jesuit constitutions, or only for three years, as Pope Paul IV had desired:

> Very Reverend and most esteemed Father in Christ.
> *Gratia et pax Christi Domini sit semper nobiscum. Amen.* As regards the office of General, my vote is that it be always for life, according to the constitutions, and that, in the case of your Reverence, it may be so firmly established as to last for a hundred years. Should you die and be immediately raised from the dead, my vote is that you be confirmed in office until the day of General Judgment, and I beseech you to · accept the burden for the love of Jesus Christ. . . . I write all this from my heart in full sincerity, *ad perpetuam rei memoriam.* God keep your Reverence. . . . Your son in Christ, Bobadilla.[1]

It grieved St. Peter that Ribadeneyra should have nothing to say of this good man's work in the Empire except the bald remark, " *in Germaniam, Pont. Max. jussu, missus est,*" so he suggested the following amplification:
" He was sent to Germany and there through peace and war sustained for many years very heavy labours and grave dangers, fighting stoutly for the Catholic religion, especially in the Diets of the Empire." So too, with regard to Favre and Lejay, his one-time beloved companions, Peter wanted far more given than Ribadeneyra had found room for, and him-self supplied the material in the shape of two beautiful little panegyrics. Lest it might be thought that, in his eagerness to pay tribute to the great men whom he loved, he forgot to be fair to Ribadeneyra, we may give his final remark about the biography: " It seems to me that this work could not be too highly praised. . . . *Deo sit omnis gloria.*"[2]

St. Francis Borgia died on October 1, 1572, worn out by his exertions in Spain on behalf of the Catholic League against the Turks. Pope Pius V had preceded him to the grave in May, and his successor, Gregory XIII, was moving heaven and earth to keep the League in being in order to follow up the victory of Lepanto. His great hope was that Greece might be freed from the Turkish yoke and return to Catholic obedience, but

[1] M.H., *Bobadillae Monumenta* (Madrid, 1913), pp. 377–8.
[2] Braunsberger, *Epistulae*, vol. vii, pp. 252–70.

neither Maximilian, the Emperor, nor Charles IX of France who supported the Turks for his own dark purposes, would join the League, and Venice resigned her membership at the beginning of 1573. Observing the Pope's great sorrow, Cardinal Truchsess pointed out to him that there were places nearer home which needed his help as much as did Greece; Germany, for instance, with its wounded soul crying for the hand of a physician. When the Pope, impressed by his arguments, asked to whom he should turn for information and advice on German affairs, Truchsess at once answered, " Father Peter Canisius."[1] The immediate consequence of this interview was the following letter of the Pope :

To Our beloved son Peter Canisius, priest of the Order of Jesuits, Gregory P. P. XIII. Beloved son, health and Apostolic benediction. Among the cares by which We are extraordinarily troubled in this pastoral office assigned to Us by God, that has always been regarded by Us as the first and heaviest which We know to belong to this office in the highest degree and to be the object of God's chief solicitude, namely whatever appertains to the salvation of souls by the employment of all zeal and resources. We think that there is no difficulty, however great, which ought to free Us from this concern, for We trust that God Himself will stand by His cause, it being easy for Him to remove the stony hearts and replace them with hearts of flesh.

We have no doubt but that, of your charity, you too most willingly devote yourself to this concern. When, therefore, We learned that you were coming hither to the general chapter of your Order, We desired to have you as a helper in the promotion of Our wishes, and that you should consult with Archduke Ferdinand of Austria, the Duke of Bavaria, and the Archbishop of Salzburg, about certain affairs which Our beloved son, the Cardinal of Como, will declare to you fully by letter. Having explored and ascertained their views and intentions, you will explain all to Us on your arrival in Rome. Those princes are to be visited as soon as possible and you will attend to this business with the greatest diligence, coming to Us that We may know what plans We ought to make and be enabled to put them into execution. Pray to God, the Author of all rectitude in Our will and action, that We may have strength for the purpose.

Given at Rome, at St. Peter's under the Ring of the Fisherman, the twenty-third day of January, 1573.[2]

---

[1] Braunsberger, *Epistulae*, vol. vii, pp. 664–5.   [2] Braunsberger, *Epistulae*, vol. vii, pp. 106–7.

The Cardinal of Como's letter of instructions to Canisius has perished, but we possess the Saint's reply after his visits to the Princes and may guess from it the nature of his mission. A comparison of dates seems to show that he entered on it within a few hours of receiving the instructions. Archduke Ferdinand told him that the best way for the Pope to help Germany was to reorganize and strengthen the Catholic League against the Turks by every means in his power. At the same time he should endeavour to win the good-will of the Protestants by dealing with them in a friendly manner and showing that he loved them; but as for Catholics of bad life, and especially the canons of cathedral churches, these he should punish without mercy, " *adhibito etiam si velit Pontifex brachio seculari.*" Albert of Bavaria was of the same opinion. Bad priests, he said, did more than any other cause to prevent the return of Germany to the Church. The Pope should therefore concentrate on the establishment of seminaries and continue to promote the German College in Rome with all his power. Both Princes desired the Holy Father to keep on the best terms possible with the Emperor and to favour the election of his eldest son, Archduke Rudolph, as King of the Romans. The Archbishop of Salzburg agreed heartily with regard to the last affair. It was a piece of far-seeing statesmanship for, afterwards as Emperor, Rudolph reversed the temporizing policy of his two immediate predecessors and dedicated all his power and influence to the service of Catholicism. Not less wise was the recommendation of the three Princes that the Pope should send more nuncios to Germany and have a legate at every future Diet of the Empire, for these officials were to play a principal part in the drama of the Catholic revival.

Having fulfilled his mission to the Princes, St. Peter visited Augsburg to purchase a large supply of Protestant books which the Pope desired to have examined in Rome. He was given no money either for his mission or for the books, so he was obliged, as often happened in his life, to go into debt. Then, towards the middle of March, he joined Fathers Hoffaeus, Peltan, and Pisanus, who had been chosen delegates of the Province for the election of a successor to St. Francis Borgia, and set out for the fifth time on the long walk and ride to Rome. Trains and motor cars have unfortunately ruined our capacity for appreciating what those journeys must have meant in terms of fatigue and hardship.

St. Peter's report from the German Princes, backed by his personal pleadings, had considerable weight in turning Gregory XIII into " the Pope of the Seminaries." Through his liberal patronage the Roman

College became the magnificent Gregorian University, the English College was founded, and the German College rose from its moribund condition to a life of enduring usefulness. But that was not all, for, under Gregory's impulsion, the seminary movement, which was the soul of the Counter-Reformation, spread into Germany, Austria, France, Spain, Portugal, and even to India and Japan.

As Canisius had not been delegated officially to the third general congregation of the Society of Jesus he took no part in the election of the new superior but was chosen with three others to "enclose" the electors, as cardinals are enclosed in a conclave, and to see to it that none of them emerged or had anything to eat except bread and water until they should have made their choice. When the Fathers were on the point of casting their votes on April 22nd the Cardinal of Como made a dramatic appearance in their midst. Having taken a seat, he informed the congregation that, as all the Generals of the Society had hitherto been Spaniards, the Pope now, not only desired, but ordered them to elect a man of some other nationality, because he was certain that the change would be for the common good of the Church and of the Society itself. On the Cardinal's departure, the Fathers, who were naturally concerned for the freedom of the congregation, drew up a memorandum to the Pope explaining their difficulties. Five men, including Peter Canisius, took it to His Holiness at Frascati the same day, and returned before nightfall with Gregory's answer, which was to the effect that he entirely revoked his injunction, as he did not wish to prejudice the Jesuit constitutions in the slightest degree, but nevertheless he would be very pleased if a non-Spaniard were elected. Next morning he had his pleasure, as the Belgian, Father Everard Mercurian, was declared General after the first scrutiny. On April 26th, St. Peter himself became the subject of a vote and it was decreed, "ex quadam aequitate," that he should be admitted a member of the congregation, though without a voice in the election of the General's assistants. An exception of this kind is very rare indeed in Jesuit history and it testifies with some force to the regard in which Peter was held. His principal work in the congregation was to investigate in conjunction with Salmeron, Nadal, Edmund Hay, and three others those sections of the Jesuit constitutions which appeared to be out of harmony with the new decrees of the Council of Trent.[1]

Peter's visit to Rome was saddened by the deaths there of Father Lambert Auer, his first novice, who was so loved in Mainz that the whole

---

[1] Braunsberger, *Epistulae*, vol. vii, pp. 667-70.

Everard Mercurian
From an old print by Arnold van Westherhout

City went into mourning for him, and of Cardinal Truchsess, a man so humble and generous-hearted that even his faults are sweet in remembrance. After his return to Innsbruck in July, Peter asked Hosius, then resident in Rome, to fill the place of his dead friend in obtaining for him transcripts of old manuscripts from Cardinal Sirleto. He was now able to devote more attention to his work against the Centuriators, as a Franciscan named Johann Nas had taken over the office of preacher to the Archduke. But however much he might try to be the concentrated scholar, Peter was far too kind to keep the world at bay, and we find him supplying Surius with material for his *Lives of the Saints*; helping the zealous Nuncio, Portia, in his good work on behalf of the seminaries; writing to the Archduke a letter of 4500 words to urge the revival of Eucharistic devotion at a local sanctuary; spurring on the Cologne Fathers to bring out Latin versions of the ancient Greek theologians; begging the new General to provide for a refutation of Martin Chemnitz's very dangerous *Examen Concilii Tridentini*; acting as the spiritual director of the dioceses of Brixen and Würzburg; and, of course, fostering with filial devotion the growing strength of his Order in Germany. The following letter which he addressed on May 7, 1574, to the newly-elected Prince-Bishop of Würzburg, Julius Echter, is typical of his spirit:

Most Reverend Lord and Illustrious Prince, the eternal grace of Jesus Christ be with you. The sweeter to me is and ever will be the memory of the noble Church of Würzburg which took me to its heart with uttermost kindness in the past, the greater now is my delight at knowing for certain that Your Lordship has not succeeded to the administration of this Church and of the whole land of Franconia but by the singular providence of God. Blessed be that Father of mercies who has given such a pastor to His flock as all good men desired. I shall not be so arrogant as to offer instructions or advice to a great Prelate and dearly loved Prince, but with all my heart I pray the Lord Almighty to preserve and increase in you His manifold graces, especially that you may be enabled to put the new administration on a solid basis. Well I know that difficulties many and great will not be lacking to baulk your Highness's endeavours on every side. Both clergy and people are easily roused to opposition, for it is their fancy to make laws rather than to bow to them, but there are no deceits and powers of envious devil or treacherous world too great for the fear of God, the love of our Catholic faith, and the zeal of true piety to rout and scatter them.

Ever available are the divine promises by which all Christian rulers very rightly take courage and confidence, even in the midst of the greatest sorrow and peril. Antiquity is full of examples of how powerfully God has come to the assistance of bishops and princes while they were engaged in reforming their clergy and endeavouring to recall their subjects to a Christian mode of life. I feel sure, then, that the infinite goodness of God and your Lordship's devout fidelity are the guarantee of such happy results for Franconia as are consonant to the times and to your high function, and eagerly awaited by men of good will.

As for our college in Würzburg, which has been a concern of mine from the beginning, I greatly desire and reverently petition that it may always continue an object of your Highness's benevolent regard. The more of our men are supported there, the greater will be the supply of priests to help the clergy and people of Würzburg and all Franconia, *Domino cooperante*. May He mercifully continue as He has begun to crown and prosper you with His divine blessings that the clergy may undergo a thorough reform, the lapsed be restored to genuine faith and all the Franconian people kept to their Catholic duties.

A short time ago your Reverend Dean and Secretary passed through here on their way to Rome. I offered both men my services and gave them some hints for the journey. Would to God that I had the power and chance of doing something for your Highness and the diocese of Würzburg ! Certainly I should not fail to show you my esteem and gratitude on every occasion.[1]

Peter wrote to the Pope also at this time, just such a typical letter as the one cited, for it was to promote the cause of the seminaries and to obtain favours for the nuncios in Germany. The old hampering regulations about the absolution of persons who had fallen into heresy still prevailed, and he tried once again, as on other occasions, to have them removed for the benefit of both priests and people. To Andreas Fabricius, the Bavarian ambassador in Rome, he addressed a charming letter begging help for the good Cologne publisher, Gervinus Calenius. Calenius was bringing out a new and fuller edition of the Councils. " He has implored me for assistance in this holy work," wrote the Saint, " and I thought I should turn to you who have influence with the most learned and eminent people in Rome. I therefore beg you most earnestly to collect whatever

[1] Braunsberger, *Epistulae*, vol. vii, pp. 209–10.

may be useful for this new edition, especially documents relative to the first and second Councils of Nicaea, the first Council of Constantinople, the Council of Lyons, and other similar texts which so far are lacking to us or circulate in a defective form. . . . I would add further persuasion if I was not sure of your good will and ability to help, kindest Friend. . . . Lucky man to be in the Holy City now and able to gain the Jubilee ! Belgium needs our prayers at present for I hear that the Catholics there are in sore straits. May Our Lord come to the aid of the afflicted everywhere. Good-bye, dearest Sir, and keep your Canisius ever in remembrance."[1]

In the midst of his literary toil Peter did not forget his sister in Nymegen or his old friends in Cologne. When sending greetings to his relatives through Wendelina, he said : " With all my heart do I desire that they may be constant in their Catholic faith and ever charitable to the poor and afflicted in these unhappy times " ; while of Leonard Kessel, the Rector of the Cologne Jesuits, he begged that, should he go to Heaven before him, he would not forget his brother in exile but commend him to God and to the dead brethren whom he had known and loved. Shortly afterwards, to Peter's intense sorrow, both Kessel and his other good friend, Rethius, were stabbed to death by a lunatic.

Distress of a different sort was caused him by the strange behaviour of Johann Nas, his Franciscan successor as preacher to Archduke Ferdinand. By all accounts this man had a terrible tongue. For reasons not apparent he disliked the Jesuits heartily and used his public position to malign and discredit them. He must have been a clever and plausible person, as he certainly turned the Archduke against the Fathers and rendered their position in Innsbruck extremely uncomfortable. After bearing with the insults patiently for a time, Hoffaeus, whose temper was not of the best, wrote as follows to the General : " I see that our brethren are full of grief, and I hear and know for a fact that the people, including many devout friends of ours, have been alienated. . . . The Prince himself is a complete Nasian. . . . If we may risk His Highness's indignation and danger to the colleges, I myself shall take the pulpit . . . for the people are not edified by our continued silence. . . . I ask you, Father, may we not dare something for the greater glory of God either to the Prince's face or before the people ? It will not be anything new or matter much if we have to suffer for a time, or even to migrate from Innsbruck *propter zelum domus Dei*. . . . It is my firm belief that Germany's troubles cannot be

[1] Braunsberger, *Epistulae*, vol. vii, pp. 243-4.

completely healed without the blood of martyrs." Whatever Hoffaeus may have lacked it was not courage, but Father Mercurian deprecated any resort to pugnacious tactics. "Besides prayer," he answered, "and the holy Sacrifice of the Mass, with which we shall assist you . . . the following course seems advisable. First, let our Fathers bear with the same patience as they have hitherto shown any future injuries inflicted on them by that man, casting all their care upon the Lord Jesus. . . . I do not see that a public reply to Nas would, have any other effect than that of further antagonizing the Prince. Then, I think that your Reverence and the other Fathers should notify the Papal Nuncio and ask for some remedy from His Holiness whereby Nas's blustering conduct may be controlled and the Prince made to understand that the interests, not only of the Society of Jesus, but of Germany and the Holy See are at stake."[1]

Among other peculiarities of Nas's preaching there was a definite hostility to the practice of frequent Communion, by which men in those days meant Communion once a week. St. Peter took him up on that question, but in such a deft and courteous way as to make resentment impossible. He warned his listeners against criticism of preachers. " I would have you be quite sure in your own minds," he said, " that we Catholic preachers are all at one in the Catholic faith." No one had any right to judge his neighbour even if he went to Communion only once a year, but, on the other hand, it was just as bad to frown on people who were more diligent than oneself in the reception of the Sacraments. As for the abuses connected with the Sacraments, whether on the part of the priest or people, " no thoughtful person defends such things, which have been and are and will be in the Church until the end of the world," but it is against charity to attribute them to anyone in particular and against all reason to give up a good practice on account of them. " Rather should we be the more diligent about the right use, so that we may hold fast to it and promote it among all men, to the edification of our neighbour."[2]

Friar John's attacks on the Jesuits were all the more painful for the men concerned because he possessed many sterling qualities and proved himself a valiant and redoubtable champion of the Church in Germany. It was St. Peter's ill-fortune to incur the dislike of more than one such man. The excellent Father Vitoria had made his life miserable with criticism and suspicion in the past, and now the even more admirable Father Paul Hoffaeus was to repeat the sad story. Apart from some disapproval of his rigidity and secretive methods in government, Peter had

[1] Braunsberger, *Epistulae*, vol. vii, pp. 177–8.   [2] Braunsberger, *Epistulae*, vol. vii, pp. 711–2.

nothing but feelings of profound esteem for Father Paul. In virtue of his position as a consultor of the Province he was obliged to report to Rome periodically on the behaviour of the Provincial. This is what he said on July 29, 1572 : " In the visitation of this College he gave us a grand example of the many virtues which shine brightly in his character. . . . Perhaps the good Father would effect more in his visitations if he admonished in private those whom he is considered to reprehend and denounce too severely in public exhortations. Sometimes he uses written exhortations which do not lack a sting, and I wonder whether such things are not more hurtful than helpful. . . . In some matters he appears to be a scrupulous and rigid exactor of discipline, which, perhaps, is not the best way to win the affection of the brethren. . . . I think that he should take greater care of his health, as he is not very well and finds himself much exercised by the various anxieties and troubles of the Province. It might, there-fore, be a good thing for him to have an admonitor, *ex parte corporis*, in whatever house he is staying at."[1]

When Father Paul's constitutional term of office drew to an end in 1572 he made it plain that he was going to oppose the renewal of it. There-upon nine Fathers of the Province, headed by St. Peter, addressed a letter to the General in which they wrote as follows : " Though it is true that our constitutions prescribe a change of Provincials every three years, yet we think they allow of some dispensation for the common good of the Province. . . . We therefore most earnestly beg and entreat that we may keep our Father Provincial for some time longer and that your Paternity would turn a deaf ear to his reasons for declining the office . . . which he holds to the great satisfaction and advantage of us all." Father Paul's confirmation in office as a result of this appeal seems to have had the effect of heightening his natural imperiousness. At any rate St. Peter, though his official adviser, had to explain ruefully to the General more than once that he could not make a report as he knew nothing of the Provincial's plans or doings. He kept everything to himself and treated the consultors with complete indifference. As he was an excellent man of affairs, that might not have mattered so much had he only mellowed a little in temper. Instead, he became more brusque and angular with every year that passed, and so full of his own ideas that not even the General could get him to see another point of view. One big idea he had was that writing books amounts to much the same thing as wasting time. Probably many people would agree with him. When St. Peter wrote to Mercurian in September, 1574, warmly commending the project of a " *collegium scriptorum*," Father Paul had a word of his own to add : " The whole world is already full of books," he said. " What we need are examples. Let us concentrate on these. Many of our men evade more necessary labours through a pretext and itch of writing. If your Paternity agrees with me, I shall somewhat cool the fervour of those especially who take criticism in ill part and write nothing of such distinction as to be very worthy of our Society. In my opinion non-Jesuit writers are more diligent, accurate, and careful in their work than our people. I do not approve of large sums of money being spent in Rome to the account of this Province on a fuller edition of the Acts of Nicaea, as I know Father Pisanus is urging. We are now poorer than, to my knowledge, we have ever been before."[1]

That Father Paul had Father Peter principally in mind when he thus expressed himself is clear enough from the sequel. It is strange that he should have been so obtuse as not to see the example for which he called transcendently exhibited in Father Peter's daily life, but then prejudice does make people obtuse. For all his good qualities, Hoffaeus was deficient in true nobility of character. He resented very much the deference paid to St. Peter's views in Rome, and complained because the General was in the habit of communicating with him directly about the affairs of the Province. Human nature can be very inconsistent. It is not altogether uncommon to find men genuinely convinced of their unfitness to rule others and determined as far as in them lies to avoid any such responsibility. But once force the reins into their hands, and heaven help the horses ! They shed their misgivings overnight and become as jealous of their brief authority as a child of his part in a pantomime.

St. Peter's solicitude for the well-being of the German Provinces led him to speak plainly and frequently about the behaviour of rectors and other important people. Indeed, as a consultor of the Provincial and of his own Rector in Innsbruck it was his duty to do so, but Father Hoffaeus strongly objected to his candour all the same. Thus in July, 1575, he let himself go to the General in the following style : " It seems expedient in the Lord that, though Father Peter Canisius is consultor to myself and to his Rector, your Paternity should prohibit him from writing anything in future to Rome, to me, or to others, about the state of the Province or College, or concerning the faults of individuals. . . . It will be enough if he gives his views when asked for them." Father Paul,

[1] Braunsberger, *Epistulae*, vol. vii, p. 238.

however, was quick enough to avail himself of Father Peter's experience when in a tight corner, and he got into many tight corners owing to his tactlessness and rusticity. For a long time he was at loggerheads simultaneously with the Duke of Bavaria, Archduke Ferdinand, and the ecclesiastical authorities of Augsburg. It was typical of him that he should have wanted to risk the whole position in Innsbruck by an open attack on Nas. He had very little diplomacy in him, and, but for the good advice and good offices of St. Peter, his disrespectful attitude to secular authorities might have had serious consequences for the Province.

In November, 1574, Peter reverted, at the order of Hoffaeus, to his office of preacher, this time in the parish church of St. Martin, as Nas continued to be the preference of the Archduke at Court. During the year that followed he delivered close on a hundred sermons, but the following extract from a letter to Father Mercurian shows that he found the double burden of writing and preaching a terrible strain on his resources :

Your Paternity has repeatedly exhorted me to get the *Opus Marianum* into print, and many others are expostulating with me by letter for holding up the expected volume so long. I shall tell you once for all how the matter stands, and afterwards not say another word but leave everything to the judgment of my superiors. When I first engaged on this work at the behest of my superiors I was relieved of the administration of the Province and given as companion in my studies Father John, the Englishman. I also enjoyed the quiet of Dillingen and intercourse with the professors of theology there, and so I carried through and published the defence of St. John. But afterwards I was obliged to take over the pulpit in Innsbruck and lost the companion of my labours. Now I have been changed from Court preacher to parish preacher and am held up by so many distractions at the College that I make little progress with my book.

I think that Father Provincial does not regard my writing activities with a very favourable eye. He promised to obtain me a helper from your Paternity but so far he has not appeared. I become the more willing to devote myself to the book the more sure I am that not many people enjoy my sermons, especially here in Innsbruck. They spell more labour for me than success, perhaps because advancing age has deprived me of vigour and the power to please. I am very much dissatisfied with myself in this post and would gladly have this chalice, which I drink out of obedience, removed from me. Meantime, Father

Provincial has written to say that I must carry on here alone as preacher for six months, that is, until Easter. I am doing so now, though very much at the expense of my studies. If, after Easter, I might have a breathing space and could spend at least the summer months in Dillingen I would devote myself to the completion of the *Opus Marianum*. I want to wipe out the annoyance which I cause to so many people by my delays over it.

But when I consider my own weakness and think what an unskilful writer I am, I cannot but agree with Father Provincial's judgment. I have not the courage to go on asking for an assistant, who perhaps could not be given to me without inconvenience to Dillingen or to the Province as a whole. The talent I received is small, yet it is possible that, with the favour of God, I might achieve more as a writer than in any other ministry proper to the Society of Jesus. But at the same time I often feel and see clearly in the presence of God that I am very useless for any form of good work, and so a longing grows in me to make an end of both my life and my sins. Forgive me, your Paternity, that I should make such a fuss about a matter of so little consequence, pouring out these petty woes of mine on your fatherly bosom. . . . Pray for me, your unworthy son, and obtain for me the grace to struggle on, whatever the burden I may be called upon to bear. *Filius exiguus*, Petrus Canisius.[1]

Father Mercurian paid no attention to the complaints of the Provincial and the Rector of Innsbruck against St. Peter, but continued as before to repose absolute trust in him. The letters of Mercurian and his Secretary, the brilliant Father Antonio Possevino, to Peter, breathe an affection unusual in official correspondence. They are more like the letters of friends to friend, full of solicitude for Peter's health and of encouragement for his labours. Provincial and Rector between them had completely antagonized Archduke Ferdinand, and to Peter was now assigned the delicate task of undoing the mischief. It took time, but two years later he was able to tell Mercurian : " The Prince is now entirely reconciled to us here in Innsbruck." The reader may be interested to learn that the cause of His Highness's indignation was the refusal of Hoffaeus to give him a Jesuit tutor for his son. Jesuits of all people should surely have jumped at such a chance ; but surprisingly they didn't, and St. Peter was just as much opposed as Hoffaeus, though he heartily disapproved of

[1] Braunsberger, *Epistulae*, vol. vii, pp. 274-5.

that good Father's rather churlish way of rebuffing the petition. His churlishness with regard to the *Opus Marianum* made Peter wonder very much whether he should not abandon such labours, as appears in the following letter to Possevino of April 26, 1576:

Your Reverence spurs me on to the completion of the *Opus Marianum* of which I have now sent two parts to the printer. But some people think that all the parts should be finished before any of the work is published. The question is not yet decided, though personally I remain of opinion that the three parts which I have more or less ready should be printed as soon as possible to form a separate volume. If this volume has a poor reception I shall willingly abandon the rest of the work and descend to some less lofty theme. . . . Would you, therefore, please tell me your opinion or the mind of Father General, so that I may enter on safer paths and overcome certain scruples which trouble me? There are people who think I would do better to give up this learned style of work . . . and write instead small, pious books more to the taste of ordinary men and women, and also, perhaps more suited to my slender abilities. But as the Pope and Father General imposed on me my present task of confuting the heretics . . . I shall not abandon it until I have their permission. So nothing will give me more comfort than to learn from your Reverence what you think I ought to do in order to come nearer to the wishes of my superiors and obtain greater fruit of holy obedience. I know too well how busy and preoccupied Father General is to bother him with such a trifle. It will be enough for me to have secured by this letter the protection and faithful intercession of my dear Father Possevino.[1]

At this point it is necessary to say a few words about another cause of friction between Hoffaeus and Canisius. St. Peter, as we have seen, took up a very rigid attitude with regard to the lending of money at interest. He tended to regard all such transactions as usurious and denounced them with hardly less vigour than the Protestant Englishman, Dr. Thomas Wilson, who wrote as follows on the subject in 1572: " I say and maintayne it constantlye that all lendying in respects of tyme for any gaine, be it never so little, is usurie, and so wickedness before God and man, and a damnable deede in it selfe. We do all feare the plague marveyously . . . and yet what a blesse were it to thys whole realme if in one yere there

[1] Braunsberger, *Epistulae*, vol. vii, pp. 338–40.

were an universall murren of all usurers in England ! "[1] Their hatred of injustice rendered both the Jesuit and the Protestant somewhat blind to the fact that social conditions were changing rapidly and widening the area in which the traditional titles to interest admitted by Catholic theology could be legitimately invoked. Money had become capital to an extent never known before, a productive commodity which to lend meant to deprive oneself of a source of gain. For such deprivation it had long been considered lawful by practically all jurists and theologians to receive a reasonable indemnity in the form of interest, but during the sixteenth century opinions were sharply divided as to whether the title of *lucrum cessans* applied when money was the object lent. The minds of many good men still ran in the old grooves and continued to be governed by medieval conceptions of money as a sterile thing, for the loan of which nothing might be exacted. St. Peter Canisius was certainly of that way of thinking and let the merchants and bankers know it in the plainest terms. On the other hand, he can with equal certainty claim the indulgence which an excellent authority on the subject allows to the old preachers and theologians : " Their precepts on the contracts of business and the disposition of property may seem an unpracticable pedantry, but rashness is a more agreeable failing than cowardice, and, when to speak is unpopular, it is less pardonable to be silent than to say too much."[2]

Two forms of investment in particular exercised the wits and consciences of sixteenth-century theologians, a financial transaction so common in Germany that it came to be known throughout Europe as the *Contractus Germanicus*, and another favourite German device for acquiring an income called the *Census*, or rent-charge, whereby a man parted with goods or money and secured an annuity in exchange. The *Contractus Germanicus* was an investment at five per cent. It had been justified by influential theologians, including the great Johann Eck, long before St. Peter's time, on the ground that it really involved three contracts, each of which was recognized to be beyond reproach if made with different persons. The problem was, could they all be made between the same two persons and remain innocent ? In 1562, long before the point we have now reached in his story, St. Peter denounced the Contract as plain usury, " no matter what certain jurists oppose, who, arguing according to the prudence of the world, think that many things of this kind are to be winked at, against the common and received doctrine of both ancient and modern theologians

---

[1] *A Discourse upon Usury* (1572). Tawney's edition, 1925, p. 230.
[2] Tawney, *Religion and the Rise of Capitalism* (London, 1926), p. 287.

and canonists."[1] Peter plainly was no casuist, but that, despite his brave words, he had misgivings about the wickedness of the Contract is evident from his many appeals to Rome for a decision on the subject. On being asked by St. Francis Borgia, Pope Pius V declared as a private theologian that he thought five per cent derived from the combined contracts of partnership and insurance, of which, its defenders maintained, the *Contractus Germanicus* was composed, might lawfully be taken, at least in the case of minors and other such persons who could not themselves traffic with their money. This unofficial ruling, vague as it was, gave St. Peter much comfort and encouraged him to send more questions to Rome. But an official Bull denouncing certain developments in the theory of rents which appeared not long afterwards made the situation more obscure and difficult than ever. That was in 1569, the year when Father Paul Hoffaeus succeeded St. Peter as Provincial.

Father Paul was very much more 'modern-minded' than Father Peter in his appreciation of the theological problems raised by the expansion of credit. He had come to the conclusion that the *Contractus Germanicus* was lawful,[2] and now as Provincial used his authority to propagate that view. A commission of Jesuit theologians met in Rome in 1573 to discuss the ethics of interest. Both Hoffaeus and Canisius were in the City at the time, but for some reason St. Peter took no part in the deliberations. It is strange, considering his position, that he did not, and Braunsberger may very well be correct in attributing his exclusion to a manœuvre of Hoffaeus. If so, Father Paul wasted his pains, for the other men of the commission proved quite as conservative as Peter himself, and their report left the question of the *Contractus Germanicus* very much where it had been before.

Though, in default of a definite judgment by the Holy See, St. Peter continued to regard the Contract as usurious, there was nothing bellicose or propagandist in his attitude. He was simply puzzled and expectant. But his friend, Father Jasper Heywood, who lectured on theology at Dillingen, took a different stand. The Contract was to him so much anathema that he stuck at nothing to get it abolished. He even argued the new Bishop of Augsburg, who liked him, into issuing a decree in March, 1575, prohibiting the priests of his diocese, under pain of suspension, from absolving those who put their money out to interest at five per cent. At the same time the Bishop declared that anybody who defended

---

[1] Braunsberger, *Epistulae*, vol. iv, p. 563.

[2] In the circumstances, this was probably the right conclusion. These circumstances have changed in our times and the whole question of interest and usury is again in the melting-pot.

the Contract would incur excommunication reserved to himself. Father Hoffaeus was naturally very indignant with Heywood for his part in the proceedings, but the difficulties which he had raised soon solved themselves, as the Bishop died a few months later and his successor promptly quashed the decree. This man, Marquard von Berg, constituted himself a vigorous champion of the Contract and made things very unpleasant for Heywood and his brethren at Dillingen. The following letter addressed by the Rector of the University to the General on February 12, 1576, tells of their troubles:

We daily find our Patron [Bishop Marquard] more difficult to deal with. He has already withdrawn six hundred florins of the University's annual revenue. . . . Just recently, some priests of this diocese, formerly our pupils in theology, showed themselves unwilling to absolve those who desired to use in future that *Contractus Germanicus* by which five per cent is received, with power to recover the capital. Their chief reason for refusing was the very serious ordinance which the previous Bishop had published and which had been approved by leading theologians and jurists, forbidding the absolution of such persons. . . . So incensed was our patron with these priests that he gave orders for their imprisonment, and said that, if they remained wedded to their opinion, he would deprive them of their pastoral office. The same was to apply to all who should in future deny absolution in such circumstances. He also suspended Father Jasper Heywood from his office of lecturer, because he had enlarged on the question in class when dealing with the subject of usury, and threatened the rest of us with prison if we should dissuade priests subject to him from giving absolution in such cases.

On one occasion when I was present, our Patron denied that the *Contractus Germanicus* was against the divine law, for if it had been, he said, he would not permit confessors to absolve those who employed it. But those people themselves recognize and confess that it is a mere contract of loan, nor can learned theologians and jurists, who are often asked about the matter, find in it another legitimate contract. At last we have brought about that Father Jasper should not be stopped from lecturing at present. I have been informed by various learned men that they had more than once heard recently from our Patron's own lips that he was not such an ignoramus and tyro (he is a doctor of law) as not to know that the common *Contractus Germanicus* was usurious, but that he wished it to be tolerated by confessors, just as it is tolerated by civil magistrates (though it has never been approved by the Estates of the Empire but often condemned). . . . This affair has caused much scandal, especially as priests throughout the whole diocese are ordered to absolve from this usury until it is condemned again by the Pope and the Imperial Courts *et in specie et in Germania*. . . .[1] The Bishop, who is learned in the law, is unwilling to be advised by others, and least of all by those of our Society, with regard to the matter. The Fuggers are backing him up and so too are some of the principal officials of this diocese. . . .[2]

As I was writing these lines I received a summons to the Bishop. . . . In presence of his chief officials he admonished me seriously and with great weight of words that I must not henceforth suffer anything to be taught in our schools against the *Contractus Germanicus*, or allow his parish priests to be frightened by our men from granting absolution to those who use it. He added that to condemn the Contract publicly is a heresy more pernicious than all other heresies now in Germany. . . . He also threw in some serious threats as to what he would do if he found we were not fully obedient. I replied that we should take pains to ensure his having no just cause of complaint against us, and with that we parted.[3]

Appeals from Canisius and Hoffaeus now caused Father Mercurian to consult the new Pope, Gregory XIII, about the attitude which the German Jesuits should adopt in the Augsburg crisis. Gregory advised that they should not absolve persons who used the *Contractus Germanicus*, but neither should they, on the other hand, publicly denounce that method of finance. Being a loyal and obedient man, Hoffaeus immediately instructed his subjects to refuse to hear the confessions of any who declined to renounce the Contract, while at the same time warning the General that further action on the Pope's part would only cause trouble without changing anything whatever. Nevertheless, Gregory sent his Nuncio to Bishop Marquard with a serious admonition about his behaviour.

Meantime Cardinal Morone had been appointed Papal Legate to the forthcoming Diet of Regensburg and, at the express wish of the Pope, communicated by his Secretary, the Cardinal of Como, St. Peter was

---

[1] This is a reference to the Bull of Pope Pius V, which did not condemn the Contract *in specie*. The Bull was not promulgated in Germany.

[2] The Augsburg canons, who strongly objected to the strict views of St. Peter Canisius on the subject of usury.

[3] Braunsberger, *Epistulae*, vol. vii, pp. 341–2.

to act as the Legate's theological adviser.[1] Knowing this, Mercurian instructed the Saint to explain the difficulties about the *Contractus Germanicus* to the Cardinal, whereupon his Lordship addressed another admonition to Bishop Marquard. Like Hoffaeus, the Bishop was prompt to obey externally but, also like Hoffaeus, he remained internally convinced that the Contract should be permitted. Within the Jesuit ranks the question gradually developed into a kind of duel between Hoffaeus and Heywood, with Canisius as a very anxious spectator. Hoffaeus accused Peter of seconding Heywood but the documents are there to show that that was merely his imagination. Indeed, though he disapproved of the Contract, Peter's sympathies were entirely with Hoffaeus in the struggle. " I grieve for Father Provincial," he wrote to Rome, " as he is suffering a good deal of affliction and annoyance from this Englishman." He also spoke in glowing terms of the Provincial's " strenuous and successful labours " for the Church and thanked God heartily that the Society of Jesus in Bavaria had such a capable director.

Cardinal Morone stopped a short time at Innsbruck in May, 1576, before going on to the Diet of Regensburg, and chose St. Peter, already his consultor, for his confessor also. A little memorandum is extant in which Peter set down the points that he desired to urge on the Cardinal's attention. They deal entirely with Archduke Ferdinand, and start off under the heading, " *Laudandus videtur Princeps*," which is followed by a warm eulogy of His Highness's zeal and Catholic piety. Then the heading changes to the words, " *Indiget autem admonitione*." The subjects about which Peter deemed him to need a reminder are indicative of Peter's own wonderful concern for the welfare of the Church. Alsace and Baden might be far away on the map but their religion was near to his heart, and, as they then appertained to Austria, the Austrian Archduke was the one to help them. He should be exhorted to do all in his power for the Catholic nobility of those lands, as on their faith depended to a great extent the faith of the people ; to found a seminary whereby the deplorable dearth of priests on all sides might gradually be remedied ; and to restore and rehabilitate the once flourishing theological faculty of Freiburg University which had fallen on evil days. Nearer home, the Prince had other obligations which he ought to be encouraged to fulfil, especially that of making peace with the Cardinal Bishop of Trent, whose jurisdiction he had invaded. While about it, Peter begged, too, that His Highness should be asked to back up with his authority the reforming activities

[1] Braunsberger, *Epistulae*, vol. vii, p. 337.

of several other bishops whose territories adjoined his own. An extant letter of Morone shows that he adopted Peter's counsel in every particular with happy consequences for the many good causes in question.[1]

During the Diet of Regensburg, to which he came at the beginning of July, 1576, St. Peter preached about seventeen times in various churches of the City, and, for the rest, was kept busy by the Legate's affairs. To stimulate that great Churchman's zeal he drew up a memorandum on " some means by which Germany may be helped at the present time." The chief means of all, he urged, was the foundation of seminaries on German soil. If the bishops could not be induced to undertake this important work themselves, they should at least be persuaded to support eight or ten students at one or other of the existing Pontifical seminaries. As the bishops were the key to the whole situation, St. Peter showed the deepest concern for their work, welfare, and independence, above all desiring that the Pope should encourage them to make regular visitations of their dioceses; to ordain none but those who had pronounced the Tridentine profession of faith; to tolerate no married or heretical priests; and to exercise special care in the granting of faculties to confessors. Once again, the Saint urged the great importance of sending good nuncios to Germany, " *viri docti in controversiis, prudentes, mites, zelosi, vitae inculpatae, et ab omni avaritiae specie abstinentes.*" There is much else in the memorandum, especially about the reform of the religious orders, but enough has been reproduced to illustrate the persistence of Peter's ideas, for what he urges here is what he had been urging ever since he came to work in Germany and would urge to the day of his death.[2] It was exactly by such means as he suggested that the Catholic Church in the Empire eventually found her salvation.

Peter's horror of Court life, which was almost an obsession with him, is evident in his letters to the General from Regensburg. To avoid it as much as possible, he and the two Austrian Jesuits who had come to the Diet hid themselves away in a private house, rigged up a bell, and carried out their rule to its sound just as they might have done in a college of the strictest observance.[3] But Peter's thoughts did not run as calmly as the domestic horarium. He had a great many things to worry him: a book written by the Provincial of the Rhineland Jesuits which caused an outcry by its denunciation of the bad custom of choosing bishops and chapters exclusively from the nobility; difficulties in connexion with

---

[1] Braunsberger, *Epistulae*, vol. vii, pp. 344–6.　[2] Braunsberger, *Epistulae*, vol. vii, pp. 358–66.
[3] Braunsberger, *Epistulae*, vol. vii, p. 351.

the projected colleges in Augsburg and Regensburg; and the tragic fate of his Society's good friend, the Benedictine Abbot of Fulda. With regard to the colleges a curious situation had arisen, for the Fugger family were working might and main in Rome to have the Monastery of the Holy Cross, Augsburg, transferred to the Jesuits, while the Jesuits were striving equally hard in secret to prevent any such thing happening. They had suffered enough on the score of those monasteries. At Regensburg during the Diet, Cardinal Morone was instructed by the Roman Congregation which had charge of German affairs to see to the foundation of a Jesuit college in the City. Straightway the "Monastery of the Scots" was proposed for the purpose, whereupon Mercurian wrote to St. Peter cautioning him against acceptance. But Peter stood in no need of cautioning. He was utterly opposed to taking the property of other Orders, no matter how useless it might be to them or how generously they might be compensated by his own Order's friends. Of those friends and their efforts Mercurian said to him : " It is no new thing that our Society should have to make expiation for the excessive zeal and benevolence of others in its regard."[1] But that such zeal and benevolence could sometimes be as dangerous for those who showed the kindly qualities as for those who benefited by them was proved by the case of the Prince-Abbot of Fulda who, because he loved and fostered the Jesuits in his dominions, had been driven into exile and deprived of his dignity and possessions. St. Peter wrote to comfort the persecuted man and, in conjunction with Mercurian, used every means in his power to bring about his restoration.

Towards the close of the Diet, at which the Catholics had maintained and consolidated their position, Peter obtained leave from Hoffaeus and Cardinal Morone to retire to Ingolstadt in order to see his *Opus Marianum* through the press. There he passed a laborious winter of discontent; discontent, as he told Hosius afterwards, with his " babblings on so sublime and difficult a theme." Three of the five parts into which the work was divided had already been printed, but Peter absolutely murdered the proofs sent him by the unfortunate David Sartorius. This we learn from his first assistant, the Englishman Father John Rastell, now Vice-Rector of the fifty Jesuits in Ingolstadt. " I have only one thing to report," wrote Rastell to Mercurian on January 5, 1577, " and it is a thing for which Father Provincial can find no remedy. Reverend Father Canisius has been here four months and more for the purpose, as he requested originally, of watching over the printing of his book. But he did not

[1] Braunsberger, *Epistulae*, vol. vii, p. 374.

ask to come that he might make a new book out of the one already censored and approved. Excessive care in the matter not only holds up his Reverence but disturbs the peace of other people. Father Provincial bears with him and neither wishes nor is able to deny him the assistance of our Fathers and Brothers, which is quite right as it is only natural to show mercy to those in trouble. Father Canisius either says or insinuates that such assistance is very necessary to him, but all the same he was not given permission to come here in order to have the help of men who are committed to other employments. No wonder he needs it, seeing that, when he might be tranquilly engaged in composing the fifth part of his work, he spends all his time adding to and polishing the first three parts which had already been finished very satisfactorily. He over-exerts himself, and others too, in seeking for new material, writing, making changes, sighing for the unattainable, so that now there can be no remedy for the situation except patience." Father Mercurian's comment on this protest was sufficiently laconic and inscrutable : " We shall make use of what you tell us about the diligence and labours of Father Canisius at the proper moment." Six months passed and Peter was still in the toils, to the unconcealed disgust of Hoffaeus. " Perhaps with great trouble and inconvenience to many of our Fathers and Brothers he will finish his book in time for the Frankfurt Fair in September," wrote he to the General. " Your Paternity should not permit him to employ his pen in future on anything except small books of devotion in German. He can be useful to me in other affairs of the Province." Finally, Peter's half-brother, Theodoric, had a word to say on the subject, writing from Ingolstadt on July 18th : " Father Canisius has been here now for nearly a year working on his *Opus Marianum*. It is incredible how much the good Father fatigues and torments himself and many others with this business. We and all who know his studies consider it almost a miracle that he has not been overwhelmed and killed some time ago by the immensity of his labours. . . ."[1]

The impression conveyed by these extracts, that St. Peter had nothing else to do during his ten months in Ingolstadt except attend to his book, is erroneous. For one thing, the excellent Apostolic Nuncio, Portia, was residing there and monopolized a good deal of his time. During practically the whole of April he was employed first at Landshut as preacher to Prince William of Bavaria, and then in Augsburg on business entrusted to him by the Pope. When he was with Prince William, soon to be Duke and a great champion of Catholicism, a pleasant thing befell. One day Peter's lay brother companion, who used to do a certain amount of dictated writing for him, had to be absent for an hour on some errand. Peter remained in his room, sitting with eyes closed while he thought out the next paragraphs of his work. The door opened and in came Prince William, whom Peter, still lost in his thoughts, imagined to be the brother returning. "You were certainly quick about your business, Brother," he said. "Good man! Now sit down and write." The Prince sat down "as silent as a fish," says the reporter, and for more than an hour wrote to Peter's dictation. While thus engaged the lay brother walked in on the two of them and, amazed by what he saw, exclaimed: "Good heavens, Father Peter, open your eyes and see who deigns to be your scribe!" Father Peter did so and, covered with confusion, threw himself at the Prince's feet, begging forgiveness for his blunder. "It was no blunder," replied the Prince, "for I wanted very much to be your scribe, especially in this most devout work. Indeed, I congratulate myself on having had a part in it."[1]

Peter dedicated the work to Prince William's father, Duke Albert, in a very long preface which concluded as follows:

> Another reason that moves me to put Your Highness's name on my book is the desire I cherish of leaving some sort of public testimony of my respect and gratitude. It is now twenty-seven years since I first came from Rome to Bavaria and began to teach theology at Ingolstadt. During all that time my brethren of the Society of Jesus have again and again experienced your kindness and liberality, especially in Munich and Ingolstadt. Speaking for them and for myself I would like to testify publicly that our Society is indebted to Your Highness in a measure for which no thanks of ours could ever be an adequate return. . . . But we shall beseech Jesus Christ, the Son of God and of the Virgin Mary, to reward your kindness abundantly and to compensate you for your goodness to us with those blessings which truly enrich and beatify the immortal souls of men.[2]

Having at last finished his book, Peter felt a great weariness of controversial writing come over him. He was too old for the task, he said, and there were others who could do it far better, but if he must go on, obedience settled the matter. "Otherwise, I think it would be easier for

[1] Braunsberger, *Epistulae*, vol. vii, p. 772. [2] Braunsberger, *Epistulae*, vol. vii, pp. 386–7.

me, more useful to the people, and a satisfaction to some of my brethren, if I confined myself to the writing of small books in German. For that purpose Dillingen or Ingolstadt would suit me better than Innsbruck. *Verum ex voluntate superiorum totus pendeo . . . quomodocumque de me tandem statuant.*[1] Father Mercurian, whose sympathetic and lovable character is evident in all his letters to St. Peter, wrote now to Father Hoffaeus about him. " Father Peter Canisius tells me," he said, " that owing to his years he is unable to go on with his usual work of refuting the heretics and might be better employed on the composition of German books. . . . I should therefore like your Reverence to consult at the first opportunity with Father Peltan, Father Theodoric Canisius, and others, as to how and where the good Father may continue his labours, not only with greater advantage to souls, but with greater convenience to himself. When you have decided on the most suitable course you will so commend it to him, and so deal with him in every particular, as careful regard for his health and age demands."

In spite of Hoffaeus's gloomy forebodings the *Opus Marianum* was out by the middle of July, 1577, a volume of 780 pages with the title: *De Maria Virgine incomparabili et Dei Genitrice sacrosancta libri quir.que.* How complete was St. Peter's treatment of his subject may be seen from the titles of the five sections in the work ; (1) On the birth, childhood, character, and perfect life of Mary. (2) On Mary's admirable and perfect virginity. (3) On her Divine Motherhood. (4) On the various texts of the Gospels which have been wrested in this age to Mary's dishonour. (5) On Mary's Assumption into Heaven and her worship by the Church. In the first section he devotes four chapters to the strenuous defence of the doctrine of the Immaculate Conception, about which at that period Catholic theologians were still divided. He also champions the belief, not yet of faith but in our own day more and more discussed and advocated, that the Blessed Virgin is the Mediatrix of all God's graces to mankind. The fourth section in which he examines such famous Protestant *loci communes* as Our Lord's words to Our Lady in the Temple and at the Marriage Feast of Cana could hardly be improved as an example of victorious controversy. He brings all his batteries into action : great learning, deep piety, shrewd common sense, and a vigour of language that reminds one of St. Jerome in his encounters with Jovinian. Peter, as we have seen, was a sedulous student of Jerome and there are echoes of Jerome's rather savage polemic up and down his book. The hardest

[1] Braunsberger, *Epistulae*, vol. vii, p. 392.

knock to a heretic in it is where Luther is referred to as a " *subantem porcum* "—a hog in heat ! Now, doubtless that was a very shocking thing for Peter to say, even though Luther may have asked for it by his own shocking diatribes against the celibate and continent life, but it will seem less strange that he should have said it when we find the uncommon and unpleasant verb *subare* applied in exactly the same way by St. Jerome to Jovinian : " *Nunc restat ut Epicurum nostrum subantem in hortulis suis inter adulescentulos et mulierculas alloquamur. . . .*"[1] Apart from that one outburst where he let his indignation be the master of his manners, Peter's controversy is relatively urbane, and for the sixteenth century even a model of decorum.[2]

The learning of the book may be gauged to some extent from a few figures. Of Holy Scripture, its chief authority, no fewer than four thousand different texts are cited. Among the Fathers, St. Augustine heads the list with 670 appearances, while St. Jerome is quoted 280 times, St. Ambrose 235 times, St. Bernard upwards of 200 times, St. John Chrysostom 170 times, Tertullian 100 times, and many others, including the principal scholastic theologians, often enough and variously enough to show that St. Peter and they were familiar acquaintances. Altogether there are more than ten thousand marginal references to patristic and scholastic authorities in the revised edition of 1583. Deep piety and filial devotion quicken these dry bones of learning with a human warmth, as, for instance, to give but one example of hundreds, when the Saint comes to speak of Our Lady's Purification :

If to see and hold the Christ Child for one little hour kindled in the heart of a spent old man such transports of bliss that, aflame with heavenly love and weary of human concerns, he wished to die, and sang his swan-song in farewell to the world, what tides of love must have surged through the heart of the Child's Blessed Mother ! For not only did she have the high satisfaction of gazing constantly upon her Little One so beautiful, but with a Mother's right she handled and dandled Him, carried Him about in her arms, caressed Him, and covered Him with her kisses. He was the intimate, overflowing delight

---

[1] The passage is a terrible one and hogs figure prominently in it. *Adversus Jovinianum*, ii, xxxvl (Migne, P.L., xxiii, 333–4).

[2] One Protestant writer, the parson Wolfgang Platz, who found himself sharply handled by Peter, thought that it might be a good idea to shame the Saint with a very magnanimous reply. He had been compared to Goliath and described as living up to the first half of his Christian name by his attacks on the Catholic fold. " While you thus execrate, revile, and persecute me," he says to Peter, " I shall bless you, and pray from my heart for you and all who stick in the darkness of false doctrine that the merciful God may enlighten you and bring you to the knowledge of His divine Word." But the good man could not keep it up and in the next paragraph rails at Peter in the approved style of the age. Braunsberger, *Epistulae*, vol. vii, pp. 529–30.

of her heart through the years, and she cherished and bore upon her breast so precious and prized a treasure with not less faith and love than joy and consolation. The maternal instincts and affections which nature had put powerfully into her heart had received new strength from her faith and by her charity had been made complete.

On the last page of the book Peter threw aside his reserve and, forgetting the Centuriators and all other superior persons, addressed the Mother of God in the following terms:

Most august Queen and most true and faithful Mother Mary whom none implores in vain, I beg of thee reverently from my heart that thou, to whom all mankind are bound in everlasting gratitude, wouldst deign to accept and approve this poor testimony of my love of thee, graciously measuring its littleness by the good will that went to its making. . . . I shall care nothing what men think if only my labour is by thy kind judgment, I will not say commended, but at least excused. . . . I am no Ephraem who could make bold to say: *Dignare me laudare te, Virgo sacrata.* . . . For me it will be reward enough if thou dost suffer my name to be added to the roll, not of thy sons or lovers maybe, but at least of thy little clients and servants. . . .

Though St. Peter's reading was extraordinarily wide, it cannot be said that his book is scholarly in the deeper sense of the word. He possessed very little critical acumen, and rather tended to make piety a test of historicity in his judgment of old legends and traditions. But he allowed that there were " probable and improbable, true and doubtful or questionable stories " connected with the cult of the Blessed Virgin. " The Church," he continues very soundly, " does not require that we should believe indiscriminately whatever has been said or written on the subject. She leaves devout and prudent men free to judge for themselves, to prefer some authors to others and to pin their faith to this version of a story rather than to that. On the other hand, Christ in the Gospel requires that we should not rashly judge or condemn other men or by a single word cause scandal to the least of our brethren."

Peter experienced very great difficulty in having copies of the *Opus Marianum* transmitted to Rome, partly because it was so big that couriers fought shy of it, and partly because Venice, through which the post usually passed, was in the grip of the plague. Away in Naples Salmeron chafed at the delay, and wrote for information to Mercurian. Mercurian replied

on April 11, 1578 : " We have received only two copies of the book,
one for the Pope according to the wishes of Father Canisius, and one
for myself. I shall willingly surrender my copy in your Reverence's
favour, as you so greatly desire to have it. I am very sure that you will
derive much consolation from it, as have done all the Fathers here who
have read it. Perhaps Father Canisius will send you a copy for yourself.
Meantime enjoy my copy."[1] Subsequent to this letter another copy
must have reached Rome, for on May 9th Mercurian informed St. Peter
himself that it was worn out owing to the constant thumbing by the
community—" *volumen quod habemus horum patrum omnium deinceps
manibus jam attritum est.*" When Hosius eventually acquired his copy
and had it read aloud to him as his eyes were failing, he declared that
he could not imagine in what particular it would be possible to better
Peter's achievement. That was the general opinion at the time and it
has been endorsed by excellent authorities down to our own day.[2] In
1866, Migne, the portentously industrious editor and publisher of the
Greek and Latin Fathers, printed at his *Ateliers Catholiques* a collection
in thirteen volumes of the finest extant treatises on Marian theology,
which had been selected and arranged by Canon Jean-Jacques Bourassé.
In this well-planned and very valuable work, which bears the title, *Summa
Aurea de Laudibus Beatissimae Virginis Mariae*, St. Peter's treatise, " known
to all Mary's lovers and never to be known too well," as the editor describes
it, is honoured with reproduction in full, though it takes up 1245 columns.

The success that had attended his efforts against the Centuriators so
far and the entreaties of persons whose judgment he respected made
Peter desire to complete his original scheme by adding a volume on the
Prince of the Apostles. Entirely approving of the idea, Father Mercurian
authorized him to reside at any house in the Province which he might
deem most convenient, but in this his Paternity reckoned without Father
Paul Hoffaeus, who on receiving notification from Rome replied in the
following excited terms, January 20, 1578 :

Your Paternity wrote one thing about the studies of Father Canisius
on September 1st and another thing, quite different from what I had
very reasonably petitioned, on December 28th. I judged in common

---

[1] Braunsberger, *Epistulae*, vol. vii, p. 437.

[2] To give two modern opinions, Scheeben in his well-known *Manual of Dogma* (Freiburg, 1882,
vol. iii, p. 478) described it as " a classical vindication of the whole body of Catholic doctrine on
the Blessed Virgin," and Bishop Janssens, long rector of the Benedictine College of St. Anselm, Rome,
said that " it is now to be ranked among the most important books which devotion to the Blessed
Virgin has ever inspired." *Tractatus de Deo-Homine* (Freiburg, 1902), p. 146, n. 1.

Title-page and quaint wood-cut representing the Tree of Jesse, from the 1583 edition of St. Peter's work against the Centuriators, two volumes in one, numbering 1,193 folio pages

The copy from which the photographs were taken, now in the British Museum, was bound for the Royal Family of Bavaria

with others of this Province that the good Father should not be employed in writing theological books in Latin. Your Paternity now desires him to go on with this very work and to choose whatever college of the Province he likes for his residence. To these proposals I answer that it is absolutely inexpedient to have Father Canisius at Ingolstadt and that, if he is to be further occupied writing Latin treatises, I desire him transferred to another Province. The men here have learned by hard experience whether I was right in my first advice to you, but though I may have diminished greatly in your esteem I shall continue to love you always and to show regard for holy obedience as dutifully as I am able. Were I to be freed from this office of Provincial (which God grant!) I would desire no greater charity to be shown to me by a future Provincial than I have hitherto shown to Father Canisius, to whom you in Rome may, perhaps, consider me harsh because he applies to you for what he wants rather than to me, as though apprehensive that I might not deal with him fairly.[1] I am sorry that I should have to trouble your Paternity from time to time with such unhappy tales, but you must know that I, too, have very little comfort in this office of mine, to say nothing more. Anyhow, I reverently submit myself to your Paternity, knowing that there must always be people who, though sincerely trying their best, never seem able to do right in the eyes of others.

No sooner had Father Paul sent off that letter than he developed a scruple which caused him to follow it up with a second and longer one four days later :

A few days ago I wrote to your Paternity rather intemperately about the literary work of Father Canisius. I cry *mea culpa*, Father, and beg pardon and penance. My confessor has admonished me to write to you again setting forth with greater restraint the reasons why I think Father Canisius should not be permitted to treat of theological questions. Therefore, laying aside all prejudice, I shall give you my candid opinion and speak the more fully because it is others' battles I am fighting rather than my own. Father, that *Opus Marianum* of Father Canisius was a most grievous burden to this Province for eight or nine years on end. Good assistants were given him, the first being Father John Rastell, the Englishman, *piae memoriae*, who though a

---

[1] Right of appeal to the General over the heads of local superiors is one of the fundamental liberties of the Jesuit constitutions.

learned and holy man could not endure the irksomeness of working with Father Canisius. Then Father Anthony Guisanus, a man deeply versed in patristics, was appointed, but he too, found it impossible to tolerate for long the Father's occupations. He had other writers and collectors also from among our brethren who similarly groaned under his yoke and at last deserted him. Then he had recourse to extern assistants but neither could they help him in the way he wanted, and the result was that he nearly killed himself with overwork.

In addition to this, he has been a great trial and trouble to the censors, as he would always change the same passage ten times over after judgment had been pronounced on it. Never being able to satisfy himself, he had eventually to dispense with censorship and trust to his own devices in the completion of many passages. The good Father is not a theologian, and others more learned than he are consequently obliged to bear most of the burden of his books. . . . He amasses large quantities of heretical opinions but often assails them in a very feeble fashion, merely concealing the weakness of his replies under a certain grace of language. Even with his style, though, he is no longer satisfied and so submits all his writings to our professors of rhetoric, who find the imposition a nuisance. Finally, he is never able to get done with the matter under his hands and, in consequence, distresses the printers, who have to look on while their work is altered throughout.

If your Paternity can discover even one rector in this Province who is ready to put up with such annoyances from Father Canisius at his college, I shall not oppose in any way but rather help to promote the arrangement. Certainly, no theologian or consultor will give approval to these efforts of Father Canisius. It is true that we all owe obedience, but we have now obeyed so many years in the matter of this confounded writing[1] that your Paternity should guard our good Fathers and Brothers from being burdened afresh, especially as it is not enough for Father Canisius to have one assistant but he must engage the services of entire colleges. . . .

In his *Opus Marianum* there is much useful material, but his book on St. John is little read, nor do people in these parts care about such works, restricted to some one saint. If he now wants to deal with St. Peter also, what, I should like to know, can he bring forward which has not already been adduced by countless writers? A work on St. Peter must involve questions of the gravest importance, and these, Father Canisius, not being a learned man, will be unable to treat satisfactorily

---

[1] " *Obedivimus jam in ista benedicta scriptione tot annis. . .* "

without causing the brethren a great deal of trouble and annoyance. He would not get the work done in ten years, and if the brethren were free they would prefer to publish something in their own names rather than give their ideas to the world under another man's name.

It did not edify me that the good Father should have dispensed with the ordinary procedure of obedience and dealt, not through your Paternity, but directly, with the Pope about his writing activities.[1] Though he says that he petitioned to be released from the obligation of writing, he must surely have urged his point half-heartedly or rather, seeing how bent he is on the business, have procured a mandate to go on with it. Moreover, he ought not, perhaps, to have found, through your Paternity, a place in which to do his writing without consulting me, as he had no knowledge of the situation in either Ingolstadt or Dillingen. I was forced to explain it to him two days ago. Whatever be the case with regard to Dillingen, he cannot reside at Ingolstadt without that College, which is now peaceful and well-governed, being thrown into confusion. . . . The fact is that the Rector of Ingolstadt cannot endure the presence of this Father or his brother in his house, as both of them have often judged and spoken depreciatively of him, even in the presence of wavering brethren. . . .[2] Should Father Canisius now return to Ingolstadt, everything will be upset and the whole mischief will come back on my head eventually. . . . All in this Province know that the Father is most virulent in his writings and remarks about people. . . .[3] This is one of many troubles which beset my government. I shall bear them as long as your Paternity wishes, even if my reward is seemingly to be the loss of your confidence.

Should your Paternity expressly desire Father Canisius to continue writing on theology, I beg *per Christum* that he may do so in another Province. . . . In other respects he is useful and very dear to me, but I will not have the Province burdened for his sake as heretofore. These are the matters which I desired to put before your Paternity without any bias. I shall resign myself to your determination, even if ill-effects follow from it. Pray for me, Reverend Father.[4]

---

[1] This charge was entirely false.

[2] The Rector was Father Wendelin Völck, of whose conduct when confessor to the Fuggers some years before Hoffaeus himself had been fully as critical as St. Peter. Peter had a duty as consultor of the Province to report to the General on the conduct and administration of local superiors. Unfortunately one letter containing some criticisms of Völck came, through an accident, to the knowledge of that Father and stirred him to deep resentment.

[3] " *Mordacissimum in scribendo et syndicando.*" *Syndicare* = *examinare ; in alicujus mores vel acta inquirere, notare, acri censura carpere* (Du Cange).

[4] Braunsberger, *Epistulae*, vol. vii, pp. 785–6.

While Father Paul in his room at Augsburg was writing that letter whose Latin is as turgid and undisciplined as its emotions, Father Peter, in another room of the same house, was also addressing himself to the General. Both letters bear the same date, so the General probably received them together. In Peter's this is what we read:

I received with reverence the letter which your Paternity sent me towards the end of December and thank you immensely, my most indulgent Father, for replying in such a kindly way about the literary plans and desires of which I have spoken to you more than once, but not always in the same sense. I shall, therefore, now open my heart to you, as you wish, and confidently refer everything to your judgment. When it had been decided by Popes Pius V and Gregory XIII that I should write a public refutation of the heretics, Father Borgia of happy memory, our General, relieved me of all other responsibilities and gave me an associate in order that I might devote myself entirely to my task. This I did successively at Augsburg, Innsbruck, and Ingolstadt, and by God's grace, under the leading of obedience, completed the vindication of the Precursor and the Mother of God Our Lord against the heretics. In the course of my labours, Christ augmented in me the inclination and desire to fight these many beasts,[1] for I saw that their detestable errors were directed against the most illustrious persons of the Gospels . . . and that it behoved us very pressingly to lay bare and refute opinions which warred with the very light of Revelation. As for the contribution made to this argument by my feeble little forces let others decide who have read my books or will read them. At any rate, the adversaries whom I assailed have shown plainly enough by their silence that they have nothing to reply. Thinking, then, that my continuance with this work for which as yet I feel no particular aversion would be in accordance with the Pope's wishes and pleasing to your Paternity, I wrote to you about living at Ingolstadt as more suited to the matter in hand, and you kindly signified your willingness in letters to Father Provincial and myself.

Now I shall lay before you the considerations which draw me in the opposite direction and cause me to feel a repugnance to this literary undertaking. The fact is, Father Provincial makes no secret of his displeasure at my having written to Rome about the affair, and he

---

[1] This is but an echo of St. Paul (1 Cor. xv, 32) and of St. Ignatius of Antioch whose dictum: "From Syria to Rome I fight with beasts," meaning his brutal guards, was a commonplace in sixteenth century controversial literature.

not only disapproves of my going to Ingolstadt or Dillingen but judges that the whole idea of a new treatise might well be abandoned. He says that several Fathers of the Province are of the same opinion, and that St. Peter the Apostle, about whom I intended to write, has been the subject of many works which I am not likely to surpass. These objections have led me to argue with myself in the following fashion : You ought to regard and accept the will and judgment of your superior as your law, which granted, your duty is clear to cast off all solicitude about writing and compose yourself for some other work more in accordance with your vocation. Probably it will be easy to settle the matter with the Pope and obtain permission for me to desist at my time of life, especially since, in addition to Father Torres, who labours manfully against the heretics, several other writers of far greater learning than I possess can be found without any difficulty. I own my feebleness and incapacity and I know that the literary vocation is beset with various anxieties, faults, and temptations. Having experienced them many a time, I shall be very glad to acquiesce in the judgment of Father Provincial and pass the rest of my days in the peace of religious simplicity and obedience, whatever place of abode or work or burden my superiors may destine for me. In their judgment rather than in my own desires or inclinations will my heart repose its trust.

That, then, is my fixed determination. I do not wish to resume my writing, and, perhaps, I have a duty in conscience not to resume it as long as I remain in this Province and Father Provincial does not show more approval of the work. As for being transferred to another Province on some plea or other, I have never asked for such a change and shall never ask, because I would not have the perfect order of obedience injured on any account nor do I want to be troublesome to my superiors in the matter. Perhaps the Lord sees fit to warn me that, now fifty-six years old, I should, as the saying is, collect my baggage and put my house in order . . . preparatory to quitting this earthly lodging altogether. At all events, whatever your Paternity may decide about the whole affair will be to me an oracle. . . .[1]

The Pope readily set Peter free from further obligations because, as Mercurian wrote, " he did not want to fatigue your Reverence any longer with such a burden, now that you are advancing in years and rather worn out with past labours." And so the Saint's decade of concern with the

[1] Braunsberger, *Epistulae*, vol. vii, pp. 430–1.

Centuriators came to an end without his being able to say his say on the first Pope and the Papacy. Some modern Protestant scholars have indulged in an amusing surmise of their own about the matter, esteeming that Peter was stopped because he was too much of an ' episcopalian ' whose " past record afforded no security that he would treat the doctrine of the Papacy with all the decisiveness which, in Jesuit opinion, the times demanded."[1]

Though Peter had collected a good deal of material for his third volume and naturally would have liked to work on it, he expressed not a syllable of grievance or resentment against the man who made the venture impossible. " I shall now willingly lay aside all desire to write," he told the General, " and devote my energies to what I hope will be better labours, at the discretion of Father Provincial. God grant that I may rightly appreciate the grace which has been conferred on me in my unworthiness and derive from it the fruit most profitable for myself and my neighbour, whatever work or charge may now be committed to me. Probably this year, as last, I shall be Father Provincial's ' socius ' in the visitation of the colleges. As for any change of my status, I hope that I shall never again breathe a single word about such a thing."[2] The General, however, had some idea of changing his status, for he loved him and plainly wanted to deliver him from the hard yoke of Hoffaeus. Going round the country with Father Paul must have been something like going round with an imperfectly tamed bear. Mercurian, therefore, thought of transferring Peter to the college in Mainz, because it appertained to the Rhineland Province of which he had recently appointed superior the Saint's old friend, Father Francis Coster. After the tragic death of Rethius in 1574, Coster had been recalled from Douai at Peter's suggestion and made headmaster of the flourishing Tricoronatum College in Cologne. There he introduced the newly founded " Sodality of the Blessed Virgin " among the students with such success that it numbered four hundred members in 1577. On the appearance of St. Peter's *Opus Marianum* the Sodality, prompted by Coster, made a public act of thanksgiving to God for the book. Peter, who had been himself instrumental in setting up the Sodality at Ingolstadt, was deeply touched by the gesture of his Cologne friends and wrote to congratulate and encourage them. The revival of devotion to Mary, he said, was the surest ground of hope for the restoration of Catholicism. " By the same never-to-be-sufficiently-honoured Virgin Mother, I most earnestly beg and entreat all who have

[1] So Drews, *Petrus Canisius der erste deutsche Jesuit* (Halle, 1892), p. 133. Others have expressed a similar view.
[2] Braunsberger, *Epistulae*, vol. vii, p. 447.

embraced this sacred Sodality to be resolute and generous in their under-taking, assuring themselves that God's wonderful graces and protection will be with Mary's clients not only at the beginning of their course but much more abundantly as they go on in her service. . . . Let the heretics jeer if they like or rebuke the little ones of Christ as they chant their Ave Maria. . . . Blessed are they and worthy of a special crown."

At this date Father Hoffaeus received a letter from the General for Father Canisius which he was directed to pass on or suppress as he judged best. The gentle, peace-loving Mercurian must have smiled as he dispatched it, for it contained his offer to Canisius of transfer to Coster's jurisdiction at Mainz and so, in a manner, called the bluff of the good Hoffaeus. Addressing Hoffaeus personally the General said : " Your Reverence signified when writing to me that you suspected I had begun to think less well of you over this affair of Father Canisius, and at the same time you dilated on the favours which you had shown that Father. . . . It was absolutely unnecessary for you to make any such excuses or defence. I never had any doubt of your charity nor has Father Canisius ever by the slightest hint called it in question. On the contrary, I assure you that as often as he has had occasion to mention you in his letters he has invariably said such things as you could not read without blushing, so honourably has he always thought and spoken of you."[1] Mercurian here told the literal truth. Again and again Peter had given him most flattering reports of Father Paul, while his only substantial complaint against the Provincial was that he practised too much austerity on himself and on his subjects. There is plenty of evidence to show that this was the case and that Father Paul had much in common with the saintly tenth-century Abbot Maiolus of whom the old record says that he was unto his subordinates an example and a terror—*exemplo fuerit et terrori*.[2] The General had protested to him several times about his indiscretions in the matter of health and, effecting no change, at last appointed Canisius to be a sort of infirmarian to his Reverence, greatly to his Reverence's indignation. " There was no reason whatever," he wrote, " why your Paternity should have subjected me to the discretion of another man, charged with the care of my health. By the grace of God I am as well as I have been these many years, nor can anyone point to a single particular in which I have offended against the laws of health. So let your Paternity free me from this regulation. I promise you before the Lord never deliberately to do anything which

---

[1] Braunsberger, *Epistulae*, vol. vii, p. 439.
[2] *Vita Sancti Maioli*, Migne, P.L., vol. cxxxvii, p. 752.

I consider injurious to my health. If you do not set me free, my guardians may prescribe me something pleasant to flesh and blood but scandalous to my brethren." To this Mercurian replied: "I change nothing, but rather exhort you to prefer another's judgment to your own in your own cause and therefore to carry out cheerfully and exactly whatever is prescribed."

Father Paul had now found yet another grievance against Father Peter, but the remedy was in his hands, since all he had to do was to give Father Peter the letter addressed to him by Mercurian. Despite his previous protestations, however, he kept the letter back and wrote in the following strain to Rome: " For the love of God I beseech your Paternity not to take Father Canisius away from us. Our poverty is great and he is extremely necessary to us. I shall act towards him with the uttermost sweetness, as I have always done."[1] Once again Mercurian must have smiled and thought to himself what a curious person was Father Paul Hoffaeus. One minute he has hardly a good word for Father Canisius and the next chooses him to be his companion and adviser during months of travel. Not only that but when in spring, 1578, he had to go to Lucerne, where a new Jesuit College had been started, he appointed Father Canisius to rule the Province in his absence.

While acting as Vice-Provincial Peter was chosen by the Pope for a delicate mission to the Duke of Cleves, who received official assurance that he might trust His Holiness's envoy as a man " known to everybody on account of his learning, piety, integrity, and religion."[2] Owing to some hitch in the negotiations the Saint was not required to carry out that mission. Instead, at the request of the Prince William of Bavaria, he went to preach a Lenten course of seventeen sermons at Landshut, the capital of Lower Bavaria, with such effect that His Highness's Court took on for a time the semblance of a Carthusian monastery.[3] William belonged to the new race of princes who had been educated by the Jesuits to make the defence and restoration of the Church the central aim of their politics. Of him, the heir to the Bavarian throne, Peter wrote with enthusiasm to Mercurian: " Nowhere in all Germany have I found so much virtue and true piety as in this Prince. . . . Often, with but a tiny retinue, he visits the churches, the hospitals, and the sick in their own homes, exhorting and consoling them if confined to bed or dying. He admonishes the clergy of their duties, tolerates no heretics at his Court, is devoted to

[1] Braunsberger, *Epistulae*, vol. vii, p. 442.
[2] Braunsberger, *Epistulae*, vol. vii, p. 791.
[3] On this occasion St. Peter had the rare satisfaction of converting and baptizing a Turk.

his prayers, and has none of the vices common in princes. . . . How could I but serve so rare and fair a Prince? With all my heart do I beg your Paternity to have him remembered before Our Lord in the Society's prayers." That tribute was very well deserved but, as must now be told, the piety of noble persons can sometimes have awkward consequences for their admirers.

The confessor of Prince William and his Lorraine wife during many years was Father Dominic Mengin, the Lorraine Jesuit who had accompanied Canisius to Poland in 1558. The Saint then reported of him that he was a good but simple soul. Seven years later he succeeded to the rectorship of the Jesuit house in Munich, a post which out of deference to his princely penitents he was allowed to retain for fourteen years, though by no means an ideal superior. In 1578 Prince William petitioned for a Jesuit adviser who could be more closely and continuously attached to his Court than was possible for a rector, and Hoffaeus, thinking this to be a good pretext for deposing the unsatisfactory Mengin, appointed him to the new office. Owing to his long association with the Court, Mengin appears to have lost the spirit of his vocation. At any rate, he bitterly resented his removal from the rectorship, and made himself out such a martyr that his noble penitents, but especially the Princess, were full of sympathy for him. "They worship him like an idol and will not have him saddened," wrote Hoffaeus to the General. To add to the difficulty, Prince William's mother, a daughter and sister of emperors, rallied to Mengin's support. It was a powerful combination and, for all his simplicity, Mengin knew how to make skilful use of it. "If he goes on, he will appear to be leading the life of a swine rather than that of a religious," declared Hoffaeus in a temper, exaggerating everything as usual. Nevertheless, he had good cause for annoyance seeing that Mengin was deliberately egging on the Prince to demand either his reinstatement as rector, or his appointment as regent of the new Jesuit boarding-school in Munich. At last things came to such a pass that the Provincial, who apparently had some misgivings about his own personal qualities as a peacemaker, sent Canisius to Munich with full authority to settle the dispute. Peter was empowered to let Mengin reside at Court, or to make him regent of the Munich boarding-school, or to exempt him from obedience to all local Jesuit authorities if he would agree to live at the boarding-school in a private capacity. In other words, the Provincial's idea of a settlement was complete surrender. Not so Peter's idea, and he worked on Prince William to such good purpose that he finally waived his demand for the reinstatement of Mengin in a position of authority. Mengin was very tearful over this result, but by using great tact Peter managed to soothe him for the moment, without, however, conceding a single one of the privileges which he claimed.

Meantime at Hall, in Tirol, Father Hoffaeus had been engaged in a battle-royal with the Lady Magdalene on the subject of *her* confessor. She spoiled her man in exactly the same way as her nephew, Prince William, spoiled Mengin, causing him to live in a style absolutely incompatible with his Jesuit profession. On the surface it might seem too petty a matter for all the fuss which Canisius and Hoffaeus made about it, but, as Mercurian emphasized, it really involved and put in jeopardy the whole principle of government by which the Society of Jesus was held together. The Society could not abdicate its rights over its subjects or its responsibilities for the salvation of their souls, even to oblige such admirable people as William and Magdalene. An easy solution for the Jesuits would have been to release the two confessors from their vows, but when St. Peter made this proposal Magdalene was horrified. Her director must be a Jesuit even though she must render it impossible for him to keep his Order's rules. Finding that he could do nothing with her, Hoffaeus turned the negotiations over to Peter on his return from Munich, but for him, too, the autocratic lady was more than a match. Indeed she bullied him unmercifully, and we are given in his correspondence an amusing glimpse of the poor man seated at a table writing under her dictation a long letter of complaint to Father Mercurian!

Towards the close of the year 1578 Hoffaeus dispatched Peter once more to Munich, where he spent three unpleasant weeks endeavouring to come to some arrangement about Mengin which would not entirely override the Jesuit constitutions. Mercurian had summoned Mengin to Rome and sent another Lorraine Father to replace him as confessor, but Peter soon found that the problem was not to be solved on those easy lines. The following is his report to the General of the interviews which he had had with Prince William:

> At first the Prince was kind to me and spoke with moderation, but after a conference with his wife and mother about the affair he gave me the following answer in their joint names : They were greatly astonished and unable to approve that their good and satisfactory confessor should be so suddenly summoned to Rome. By this move the Father would be rendered suspect of having performed his duties

badly, though undeserving of such an unfair censure. If he had committed some serious fault they desired to know what it was, and, unless told, they would consider that Father General's harsh treatment of an innocent man was due to the enmity and ill-will of his brethren.

Upon this I delivered myself at considerable length in defence of your Paternity's action and in exculpation of our brethren from the shocking suspicions conceived against them. I showed, too, not only in conversation with the Prince but in a written document, how very important it is that your Paternity should possess full authority to send your subjects from place to place; an authority which belongs to our constitutions and has hitherto been very widely exercised, irrespective of any fault on the part of the persons changed.

But the excessive tender-heartedness of the Prince's wife and mother vanquished my reasons, and I seemed to be talking to deaf ears. They clung might and main to their point, protesting that, though anxious not to prejudice or do violence to your Paternity's government and the Society's constitutions, they yet had many grave reasons for retaining their present confessor, nor would they have him changed even for a more learned and suitable man. They had good hopes, they said, that superiors in their benevolence would not deny them this favour. They intended writing to the General about the matter, and also, if necessary, to the Pope. Meantime, while awaiting an answer from Rome, they requested that I should permit the Confessor to remain at his post.

Thereupon, I abandoned myself to reflections on the fastidiousness and obstinacy of these good ladies. Further resistance on our part . . . is not likely to change their attitude, as there seems to exist between them and the Confessor a very close compact and bond which, owing to their long, their far too long friendship, it is vain for us to hope to destroy. Then, too, considering that the Confessor, who is weak in both body and soul, shows himself so averse to the Roman journey, I thought that the best course might be for your Paternity to cease urging it on him. . . . I would therefore beg you earnestly to write to Prince William as soon as possible, saying that you have learned from me the reasons which make His Highness think it necessary to retain Father Mengin for the present, including the Father's unfitness for travel. . . . If a letter in some such friendly terms is addressed to the Prince, I have good hopes that it will render him more tractable, even if now, owing to his immoderate fondness for his Confessor, he is not ready to embrace the more salutary counsels which I desired to urge upon him. . . . May Our Lord Jesus deliver us from these miseries and preserve in holy discipline all of us who ought to be dead to the world and the life of palaces.[1]

In 1579, as in 1578, Prince William invited Father Canisius to be his Lenten preacher at Landshut. Peter delivered twenty sermons in a single month, and, exhorted by Mercurian, preached privately to the Prince on the theme of his confessor. But there was no stirring him from his determination to keep Mengin in his service. Indeed, that Father had gained such an extraordinary hold on him that he even wrote a threatening letter to Mercurian as a deterrent from action. The day that Mengin was removed, he hinted, would be a black one for the Jesuits of Bavaria. At this juncture, which was critical enough, goodness knows, Hoffaeus proceeded to execute a remarkable somersault. Though St. Peter had scrupulously referred every new development in the affair to him and never took a step without his approval, he began to complain that he was being ignored and that the General placed too much trust in the judgment of Canisius. Suddenly he finds himself " feeling sorry " for Father Mengin, about whom only a short time before he had written fierce, denunciatory letters to Rome. He grumbles that the case had not been left in his hands. He knows Mengin better than Canisius does. Canisius is being too severe with the man and has muddled things so badly that the situation is desperate, etc. etc. This extraordinary change of front was too much for the patience of Mercurian, who replied in the following terms on June 5, 1579 :

You say that you are sorry for Father Mengin because he has been driven into this labyrinth by the imprudent counsel and officiousness of other people. By these words your Reverence apparently wishes to shift the responsibility for this affair on to others, as though you had not been the prime mover in it yourself. Who but your Reverence first advised that I should leave the Prince his confessor ? It was by your orders, after you had gone to Lucerne, that Father Canisius and the other consultors wrote to me setting forth many reasons why I should not refuse the Prince's request. On the other hand, with regard to recalling Father Mengin, who wrote more sharply and vehemently than your Reverence in demand of this ? You often complained

[1] Braunsberger, *Epistulæ*, vol. vii, pp. 475–9.

of his conduct, but especially in your letter of August 9th when you said that as soon as he ceased to be rector he began to grow so idle, so disgusted with everything in the house, and so corpulent that if he went on he would seem to be leading the life of a pig rather than of a religious. I pass over several other statements of yours which were sufficient to make me wish to remove him as far from the Court as lay in my power. When you now assert that this was somebody else's advice you seem to forget your own letters to me, and I am therefore obliged to tell you that you must observe our *Formula scribendi* which requires the keeping of copies or summaries of all letters sent to the General. . . .

Finally, I cannot quite understand whom your Reverence had in mind when you requested that I should not make use of so many Provincials in the government of the Province, but I suspect that your hint applied to Father Canisius, whose services it was sometimes necessary for me to employ in this affair. What else was I to do seeing that you yourself had chosen him to deal with the Prince concerning it? . . . Recollect what you wrote to me on September 21st, signifying that you had sent Father Canisius with instructions to the Prince at Munich the previous day, and remember how on October 10th and December 6th you explained to me what he had achieved with your consent and approval. So far, then, from introducing a new Provincial, I did but use the services of one whom your Reverence had expressly delegated, and to him wrote practically nothing at any time which I did not also communicate to you. I even sent you a copy of the letter which I had addressed to the Prince.

Such, then, were the circumstances, but no matter what they had been or what the business in which I chose to use the help of Father Canisius, you had no call to censure the judgment of your superior. It ill became you as a prudent and obedient man. I have put up with the same thing many a time from your Reverence and overlooked this brusque and unseemly manner of writing to superiors, but I am now obliged to give you a serious warning and exhortation that you must learn to conduct yourself more moderately, decently, and considerately towards your superiors in future.[1]

In a letter addressed at this time to Father Theodoric Canisius, who had written praising Hoffaeus, Father Mercurian said: " All these years

[1] Braunsberger, *Epistulae*, vol. vii, pp. 500–1.

he has never ceased sending me letters full of complaints and stinging remarks, such as should not be written by a subject to a superior. I at first put this down to a certain simplicity and candour, and now and then gave him a light reproof or rather admonition about it. But this year his acerbity has been intolerable. What your Reverence mentioned about his prudence, diligence, and integrity was not unknown to me, but I cannot allow that meekness and true submissiveness should be wanting to his other virtues."[1]

Father Paul's way of accepting the General's reprimand is a good indication of his type. " I am astonished," he replied, " that your Paternity should try to make me the author of the trouble which Father Canisius has stirred up for us in the case of Mengin. You must forgive me if I deny this outright, and I can prove my point . . . without taking back a word of what I wrote to you about Mengin. His conduct neither pleased nor pleases me, but just as little am I pleased with the method of curing him which, unknown to me, Father Canisius adopted, and adopted in vain. In this miserable affair your Paternity left nothing to my disposition and discretion until the trouble had been made irremediable. I am compelled to say this, not in order to complain about the past, but by way of humble reminder that when in future you wish to transact any invidious or dangerous business with princes you should leave the Provincial room to intervene sweetly in its direction. For I, too, love the Society and, by the grace of Christ, shall be its faithful son as long as I live, whatever most of you in Rome may think about me."

Poor Father Paul! It piqued him that the General should deem Father Peter's conduct of the negotiations to have been *optime acta*— excellently managed—and he accordingly set out for Munich, where Prince William now reigned as Duke of Bavaria,[2] to show those Roman Fathers how a real diplomat gets to work. " I am here," he informed Mercurian in January, 1580, " cleaning up the mess made by Father Canisius."[3] His method was to give Mengin everything he wanted, including a more liberal supply of wine at meals than the other Fathers enjoyed. Alas for his hopes, a few months later he had to write to the General in the following terms : " Father Mengin seems to be getting worse, and other malcontents are joining forces with him. Unless something is done they will be the death of the excellent Rector, but nothing can be done without upsetting the Duke." Before the year was out Mengin had begun to

---

[1] Braunsberger, l.c., p. 577.   [2] Duke Albert V had died on October 24, 1579.
[3] " Ego hic nunc exedo quod ipse intrivit."

complain as loudly about Father Paul as previously about Father Peter, and who will say that it did not serve Father Paul quite right? " The Lord deliver us from such confessors !" he groaned, thinking also of the contrary gentleman at Hall, to whom, he said, he would gladly pay a pension of a hundred florins a year if he would oblige the Society of Jesus by leaving it.[1]

All this time, through every misunderstanding and difference of opinion, Father Peter continued to be the ' socius ' and right-hand man of Father Paul. In homely phrase, Father Paul knew far too well which side his bread was buttered to cashier Father Peter. Peter was his most loyal and devoted servant, ready at a moment's notice to fill any gap or assume any rôle. In 1580 he once more took over the government of the Province at the request of Hoffaeus, who had to be absent for a period. On appealing to the General for advice Hoffaeus had been instructed to appoint " somebody whom he considered suitable," whereupon he immediately put the helm in Peter's hands. Nevertheless, in spite of such tokens of confidence, that same year witnessed another outburst of the Provincial against his unfortunate lieutenant. The usury controversy had again revived owing to the action of Father Heywood in egging on the new Duke of Bavaria to condemn the Contractus Germanicus in his dominions. Hoffaeus, it will be remembered, regarded the Contract as legitimate, and, knowing that Father Canisius shared the Englishman's speculative objections to it, he now jumped to the utterly false conclusion that St. Peter must be backing up Heywood's manœuvres at Duke William's Court. He even told Mercurian that Peter had threatened to refer the whole question to the Pope, above the heads of the General, Provincial, and everybody else. How much truth there was in that reckless charge became evident when Heywood issued the threat, for Peter then moved heaven and earth to dissuade him from carrying it out. " Would to God that Father Heywood might spare himself and us," he wrote to the Superior of his Order in Rome on November 20, 1580. " In his zeal he has set on foot a strange new kind of appeal, desiring to defend himself against his superiors by a judicial process and by those offensive demurrers which he has already sent to the Pope. In my opinion his action was contrary to all decency and religious prudence, and will certainly, with good reason, give displeasure to everybody in the Society. . . . At Father Provincial's request I have written my views on the subject. I think that, though

---

[1] One of the Hall confessor's grievances may be of interest to Jesuit readers : " Recitantur litaniae non est regula; et tamen fui coactus meo damno interesse."

Father Heywood lodged his appeal without any good cause and is far too distrustful of his superiors, he should, nevertheless, not be punished or cast off. That might only give him a grievance and seriously alienate the Duke of Bavaria from the Society. . . . I recommended, therefore, that he should be allowed to have his way and to go to Rome to put his case before the Pope, for if he remains with the Duke, who is already beginning to look askance at our brethren, I am afraid that the Fathers in Munich and Ingolstadt may suffer."[1]

So much, then, for Father Paul's charge against Father Peter. Utterly groundless though it was, he wrote to Rome demanding that Peter should be removed from his Province. " I regret that I prevented this on a former occasion," he said. " He is a good man, but does many things with a good intention which are dangerous to us and have hitherto greatly obstructed my government. I therefore cannot any longer tolerate his way of going on." Two days later the irate Provincial repeated his demand for the removal of Peter and then, meeting the Saint at Dillingen, repri-manded him severely for conduct of which he was entirely innocent. It was not in Peter's nature to protest or defend himself when his superior accused. Instead, he asked forgiveness and promised amendment in such a child-like, self-effacing way that even Hoffaeus was touched, though, when reporting the incident to Rome, he could not refrain from giving his imaginary grievances another airing : " Father Canisius has asked my pardon very thoroughly," he said. " I love the good Father, and as long as I have been in this office I have most willingly let him go his own way. But he has certainly abused his Provincial's benevolence and indul-gence to some considerable extent. He is and has been liberal with promises but easily slips back into his old ways, not so much through a defect of will as through the weakness of old age. Indeed, for thirteen years he has exercised my patience in an uncommon degree, but I am still prepared to put up with him, provided he keeps to himself and God, without any interference in the counsels or government of the Province or any comment thereon in his letters. . . . Lo and behold, he has again most urgently begged my for-giveness and made promises, etc. Well, well, I'll be patient with the good Father."[2] Father Paul was not required to strain himself too long in the prac-tice of forbearance because six weeks later Providence put all the mountains of Switzerland between Father Peter and his long-suffering Reverence.

---

[1] Braunsberger, *Epistulae*, vol. vii, pp. 588–9. Heywood was not the only Englishman whose conduct grieved St. Peter at this time. He also mentions a certain " Father Christopher " as being very troublesome, the same unfortunate man who afterwards as Sir Christopher Perkins played the spy for Queen Elizabeth and sent numbers of English Catholics to prison or the gallows.

[2] Braunsberger, *Epistulae*, vol. vii, p. 577.

Before closing this chapter of imperfect sympathies it is only fair to add a remark made by Duke Albert of Bavaria about the two men concerned. According to writers who had contemporary evidence to draw on, he used often to say of them : *Petrus Apostolus et Paulus doctor gentium ipsi nos docuerunt legem tuam, Domine.* This association of names and epithets was shrewdly conceived, for to Peter Canisius truly belonged the spontaneous love and measureless devotion of Peter the Fisherman, together with no small amount of the great Apostle's obstinacy and undue conservatism, while Paul Hoffaeus had much of the fiery zeal and unappeasable energy of Paul of Tarsus, together with double his proclivity to wield the flail of apostolic indignation. Canisius was Dutch and Hoffaeus, in spite of his Latin-looking name, was pure German. If blame must be apportioned for the disagreement between them, a thoughtful man will remember that difference. Blood will tell, we say, but it sometimes tells other than beautiful stories, without its owner being entirely responsible. Whatever the rights and wrongs of the case, Hoffaeus stands among the greatest of sixteenth-century ecclesiastics, a fine, forthright character of whom neither his country nor his Order has any reason to be ashamed.

CHAPTER XVIII

PILGRIM'S REST

BEFORE relating how Canisius came to leave Germany behind him for good, it may be of interest to glance at a few facts and figures about the Jesuit provinces which he helped to establish and the colleges which owed to him either their existence or a good measure of their prosperity. The list opens with Cologne, his city of predilection, where he had begun a Jesuit settlement in 1544. Fifty years later, despite the unkind fates which dogged its every step, the college there numbered more than a thousand scholars, including groups from France, Belgium, Switzerland, Hungary, and Scotland. A large proportion of these boys afterwards became priests and played a prominent part in the revival of Catholicism. The college of Vienna, founded in 1552, had likewise a thousand students before the century closed. Prague's college, which followed, seemed at first to be the most forlorn of Jesuit enterprises, but under the Emperor Ferdinand II its influence developed in the most amazing fashion, until it leavened the whole of Bohemia and turned that age-old refuge of heresies into a Catholic land. Like Prague, Ingolstadt owed its college almost entirely to St. Peter's exertions. Though it had not the numbers and fame of many of its sister institutions it was there that, towards the century's close, Jesuit masters educated the future Emperor Ferdinand and Bavaria's first Elector, Maximilian, who in alliance secured for the Counter-Reformation some of its most resounding victories. The Munich college was opened by St. Peter in 1559, and by 1597 had nine hundred pupils on its roll. Mainz obtained its Jesuit school in 1561, principally through the efforts of Canisius and his great friend Rethius. By 1590 it numbered eight hundred students, of whom forty were preparing for ordination. Innsbruck and Hall, those colleges of many tribulations, remained small and undistinguished during St. Peter's lifetime, but afterwards repaid all his care for them by developing into a famous university. Dillingen was a university from the time when the Saint accepted its direction in 1563. The three hundred students of

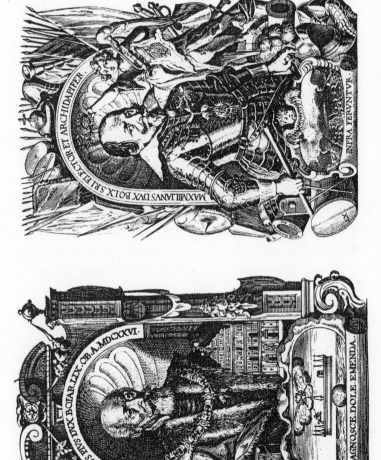

Duke William V and Maximilian, first Elector of Bavaria. The Church which Duke William is holding is that of St. Michael, Munich, which he built for the Jesuits, and named after the Archangel in deference to the wishes of St. Peter Canisius. The Church became the traditional burying place of the Bavarian Royal Family

From the " Excubiae Tutelares LX Heroum " of Andreas Brunner (1655)

that period had become nine hundred forty years later, a very large number of whom were destined for the priesthood. Würzburg college when accepted by St. Peter in 1567 had only 160 scholars. In 1601 it had grown to the same impressive numbers as Dillingen. With the foundation of the college in Speyer the Saint was intimately connected, and it was he who, by arrangement with Cardinal Hosius in 1565, set on foot the Braunsberg mission in East Prussia from which the powerful Polish Province of the Society of Jesus derived its existence. Peter was himself the first Jesuit to enter Poland. By the year 1600 no fewer than 466 of his brethren were at work there and the mighty spectacle of a nation's reconversion had begun to startle and thrill all observers. "A short time since," wrote an awed papal nuncio in 1598, " it might have been feared that heresy would entirely supersede Catholicism; now Catholicism is bearing heresy to its grave." In Regensburg St. Peter prepared the way by his courses of sermons and other services to the bishop and diocese for the foundation of a Jesuit church and school in 1589; while at Augsburg his long devotion and sufferings bore their fruit in 1582, when, " as by a miracle," he said, his friends the Fuggers and especially his old protégé, Octavian Fugger, succeeded against all opposition in building a fine church and college for the Jesuits. The numerous other Jesuit colleges and missions which sprang up in Germany, Austria, and Hungary during the sixteenth century were nearly all indebted to Canisius for help of various kinds. When he came to Germany in 1550 it was with two companions, Lejay and Salmeron. When he left it for ever thirty years later there were one thousand one hundred and eleven of his brethren at work within the Empire.

Some Protestant writers who admired St. Peter himself but detested his Order have imagined that his relegation to Switzerland was a form of banishment inflicted on him for being insufficiently Jesuitical and papistical for the liking of his superiors. The true explanation of his departure from Germany is much less sinister. He went to Switzerland simply because he was needed there. A glance at a map of that country will show that the relatively small Catholic canton of Fribourg is completely isolated from the other Catholic cantons by the huge bulk of Protestant Bern. To the west, Fribourg is surrounded by the Protestant canton of Vaux and, except for a tiny corridor to the Lake of Neuchatel, Vaux and Bern have had her in their tight embrace since 1536. For forty years after that critical date the pressure on Fribourg never ceased. Apart from the threat of absorption by force which always hung over her, she was necessarily the victim of a kind of spiritual osmosis, equally dangerous to her religion. Being small and poor, she had no system of higher education, and her younger sons were consequently tempted to seek opportunity for their talents at the excellent Protestant institutions in Basle, Bern, Lausanne, or Geneva. The civil authorities of Fribourg were well aware that the key to their country's future lay in the school. If they were to survive as a Catholic state they must provide for the intellectual needs of their Catholic people. How to do it with their limited resources was the great problem. Ever since 1540 they had pressed their claim on the deputies of the other Catholic cantons in the Swiss National Assembly. All were agreed that an institution for higher studies must be founded, but each esteemed that his canton had as good a right as Fribourg to possess the institution, and the result, as usual in such human equations, was no institution anywhere. Fribourg then endeavoured to meet her responsibilities by the appointment of a sort of board of education and the establishment of a small Latin school. In these moves the chief agent was Peter Schneuwly, Provost of Fribourg's venerable old collegiate Church of St. Nicholas, and later Vicar-General to the dispossessed Bishop of Lausanne. Schneuwly was one of the heroes of the Catholic revival in Switzerland. Impressed by the growing fame of the Jesuits as educators, he cherished the project of bringing them to Fribourg, especially after Lucerne had obtained their services in 1577. Two years later his chance came with a visit from the newly-appointed papal nuncio, Giovanni Bonomio, Bishop of Vercelli. Bonomio was a man of very strong character, " un saint parfois terrible,"[1] who knew exactly what he wanted and took good care that he got it. He enjoyed the exceptional advantages of being intimate with such great persons as Pope Gregory XIII and St. Charles Borromeo. On being named nuncio to Switzerland, he swept through the country like a whirlwind, everywhere infusing new life and hope into the despondent Catholics. On some occasions he rode from dawn to dark without once setting foot on the ground. Like so many strong and masterful characters, he was deficient in tact, and left much bad feeling in his wake among both Protestants and Catholics. Being strongly partial to Jesuits, he claimed one of the Lucerne Fathers as his interpreter on tour and got the unfortunate man into serious trouble. Away in Dillingen Peter Canisius heard of it and expressed hearty disapproval of the Bishop's behaviour. But his Lordship never minded. People could say what they liked about him provided they did what he desired them to do.

[1] Berthier, *Lettres de Jean-François Bonomio à Pierre Schneuwly*, etc. (Fribourg, 1894), p. 167.

At Fribourg Bonomio immediately decided, without reference to the Jesuit authorities, that the town must have a Jesuit college. To endow it, he looked round in his ruthless way for some monastery to suppress and found his perfect victim in an old Premonstratensian Abbey, situated at Marsens near Fribourg, in the world-famous ' County ' of Gruyère. This twelfth-century foundation had fallen on very evil days. Only six monks were left there and these led lives utterly unbecoming to their profession. Having decided on their doom, the Nuncio rapidly extorted consent from the local civil and ecclesiastical authorities and then, in February, 1580, obtained a Bull from his friend Pope Gregory by which the monastery was suppressed and its revenues transferred to the proposed new college.

All this time not a word had been said to the Jesuit superiors about the part that they were expected to play. The Upper German Province had its hands full trying to man the new college in Lucerne and to start the new college in Augsburg which had at last been secured by the energy and generosity of the Haus Fugger. It was therefore with no great enthusiasm that the Jesuit General, Father Mercurian, received orders from the Pope, inspired directly by Bonomio, to accept the Fribourg responsibility. "I strove to avoid this new burden," wrote the General to Hoffaeus, "but His Holiness absolutely insisted on our taking it, and even forced it on us." Hoffaeus was accordingly instructed to visit the Nuncio in Switzerland and endeavour with all his might to dissuade him from his purpose, at any rate for some time to come. In May, 1580, while the Provincial waited on the Nuncio's good pleasure at the Lucerne college, he received an intimation from the authorities in Fribourg that they had changed their minds and no longer wanted the Jesuits, as they did not consider that the revenues of the suppressed monastery would be sufficient for the support of a college. "I am delighted," wrote Hoffaeus to Mercurian, "that this affair has collapsed for the present, without any fault of mine." Father Canisius showed equal satisfaction, not because he was opposed to the college in itself but because he knew that his brethren had more than enough to do already, and because he hated the idea of their living on the revenues of a suppressed monastery.[1]

At this point there began a three-cornered contest between Hoffaeus, the Fribourgeois, and Bonomio. Hoffaeus smouldered and protested, the Fribourgeois played for the safety of their pockets, and Bonomio sailed smilingly on to his goal. The hesitation of the careful Fribourg

[1] Braunsberger, *Epistulae*, vol. vii, p. 543.

authorities was overcome by a solemn deed of assurance, with the Nuncio's seal attached, that they would never have to provide a single sou for the Jesuits out of their own treasury. How should they have to, wrote His Lordship, when the revenues of Marsens would suffice, not for ten Jesuits, as stipulated, but for twenty of them? And this he said knowing next to nothing about the revenues of Marsens. His irresponsible insistence on the adequacy of a thousand ducats a year for all purposes made Hoffaeus angry. "Impossible!" he cried, writing to Mercurian, "for where are we to get our church, our schools, our garden, our books, our furniture, and a thousand other things? . . . Also, we have not now the men to staff a new college. Indeed, all our old colleges are very badly provided for, and the Augsburg college is not yet begun. *Chi abbracchia molto stringe puogho.*" Hoffaeus was quite right, but his protests made no difference whatever to Bonomio. In vigorous letters from His Lordship to the Pope, the Pope's Secretary of State, and St. Charles Borromeo, they were brushed aside as trivial or irrelevant. "We want this college," he said, "and this college we shall have, in spite of the Jesuit Provincial." A peremptory command from the Pope at length settled the matter. Hoffaeus knew when he was beaten and wrote as follows to Rome on September 23, 1580: "Now that I have put up enough resistance fruitlessly, it gives me great consolation to feel sure that God designs us to have a college in Fribourg. I give in, therefore, lest I seem to oppose the will of God and of the Holy See, and I shall now begin to entertain good hopes for the success of this college, especially as your Paternity promises me an adequate supply of men."

A fresh complication arose towards the end of the year, as Hoffaeus was summoned to Rome for the election of a successor to Father Mercurian, who had died on August 2nd. Bonomio, fearing that the Provincial might now once again try to wriggle out of his engagement, as, indeed, he did try, came all the way to Ingolstadt for the sole purpose of urging him to visit Fribourg. Father Paul was completely won this time by the good Bishop's zeal and enthusiasm, but when the day arrived for his promised journey to Fribourg he lay in bed seriously ill. "My advisers are of opinion," he wrote to Rome on November 14th, "that it would be most foolish of me to undertake so long a journey, and therefore, in accordance with their counsel and command, I shall send somebody else to Fribourg in my place. His Lordship of Vércelli will take this very badly and complain about me in Rome, but the facts are as I have told you." As his deputy, Hoffaeus first thought of sending Father Martin

Leubenstein, the excellent superior at Lucerne, but he, too, was due in Rome for the general congregation. The only other person available was Father Jasper Heywood. That Hoffaeus should have asked him to go, after what had passed between them, is a good indication of the straits to which he was reduced. Heywood at once refused on the ground that he must await in Munich the answer of the Pope to his appeal in connexion with the *Contractus Germanicus*. Then, as though by a mere afterthought, Father Hoffaeus remembered Father Canisius, to whom he and the authorities in Rome had recently and very willingly granted a period of leisure at Dillingen for the revision of his works against the Centuriators. There was to be a second edition, and the Saint longed intensely to make it as correct and persuasive as lay in his power. His books had cost him dearly in anxiety and weariness. They were bone of his bone and flesh of his flesh, so, being human, he cherished ambitions for them, not because of any glory that they might bring him but for the good that they might do. Scarcely, however, had he settled down to his difficult task, which he diversified with much work for the Duke of Bavaria and with loving exhortations to his three half-brothers in Nymegen,[1] when there came a note from Hoffaeus instructing him to go to Fribourg and prepare the way for the new college. " I set out to-morrow, *favente Christo*," he informed Father Manare, the Jesuit Vicar-General, on November 20th, " and greatly desire to be granted your Paternity's blessing for this important mission. One of our Fathers has been appointed to spend the winter with me in Fribourg. God grant that our stay there may be to His glory." This letter, the last which he was to write on German soil, is full, as usual, of concern for the interests of the Church and of his Order. He begged that grave and erudite Spanish Fathers should be sent to help in Germany ; that Father Torres should be encouraged to revise and reissue his learned books and also to answer a certain " doctum et eloquentem " Protestant antagonist ; that the German Fathers going to the congregation in Rome should not return without a " Visitator Provinciae " ; and that they should also bring with them a clear and definite ruling on the *Contractus Germanicus*, " which so perplexes our men and so greatly endangers people's consciences." Of his own frustrated literary work he merely says : " I am obliged to abandon it for a mission of greater importance." And the postscript to this last of his thousands of letters from Germany is also typical : " Would you give Father Salmeron and Father Bobadilla a very special greeting

[1] Braunsberger, *Epistulae*, vol. vii, pp. 563–8.

from me. I owe them so much. Father Bobadilla has sent me a sweet letter with a copy of a book by the Patriarch Gennadius."

St. Peter's journey from Dillingen took him, by direction of Hoffaeus, along the Danube valley through Württemberg to a convent of Augustinian nuns near Sigmaringen. He knew that these good women were very poor and very much neglected, so, though he had travelled nearly a hundred miles, apparently on foot, he heard their confessions on his arrival and "rejoiced them with a comforting exhortation." He then resumed his journey through Constance to the canton of Thurgau, in order to perform a similar charity for the Poor Clare nuns of a convent bearing the name of "Paradise." The notes of the German exhortation which he gave on this occasion have survived in a mutilated form and are worth quoting in part, despite their rather mixed metaphors and faulty imagery :

I am very glad that Our Lord should have made me worthy to come here and see this house of God, excellent and well-ordered, which but a short time ago lay in the power of the Church's enemies, deserted and profaned. . . . All Catholics ought to thank God, who alone does wonderful things, for this change and ought also to rejoice with you on the recovery of your Paradise. Now that we are met together *in nomine Domini*, I shall tell you in a few words how we can preserve and increase our Paradise, so that it may bloom and bear much fruit to rejoice the eyes of the angels. . . .

God planted a Paradise and therein placed Adam and Eve, giving them a precept whereby they might practise obedience to His Divine Majesty. We see, then, that Paradise was a home of obedience. . . . There man owned his allegiance to God lovingly, and was blessed by Him and given many revelations. . . . No *meum* and *tuum* had place there. Man lived without desire of gold or silver . . . content with little and unsolicitous about food or drink, raiment or display. But when he was in honour he understood not and lost his robe of innocence. God, however, provides another Paradise for such as would live in this place, desiring to serve Him perfectly. He has given them the rule of St. Francis whereby to exercise themselves in their vowed poverty, chastity, and obedience, and He desires them to establish a spiritual Paradise, a garden beautiful and pleasant to Him and His angels, where many sweet fruits are ever to be found growing.

Now, that our Paradise may also become for us a spiritual Paradise we need a good and trusty gardener, a stout wall, and fruit-bearing trees. First, we need a good gardener, namely the Heavenly Husband-man who planted a garden from the beginning. He, we know, could not tolerate disobedient persons in His Paradise but at once expelled and excluded them for ever, so great and jealous a lover is He of obedience. . . . Woe, then, to those who fail in obedience to God and their superiors, as did Adam and Eve. Who knows but that it was on account of this sin that your predecessors here were cast forth ? . . .

Then, secondly, we need a strong wall, by which I mean perfect enclosure, to defend us from enemies and wild animals. This wall must be threefold, separating our bodies from those of secular persons outside ; keeping our tongues from too much talk and injurious or idle words ; and, finally, guarding our souls and all our senses. Such walls had the Mother of God around her at home when the Angel came. . . . It is not enough to have a good exterior enclosure . . . unless our tongues are kept in restraint. That gate and door to the house of our souls must be kept well shut if we wish to have interior peace.

In our Paradise all must keep united in the bonds of love and concord, yielding nothing to anger, contention, or bitterness, for the place of Christ is in peace. And we must grow in spirit and become fruitful trees in our Paradise, for which increase we need the good root of humility, born of a profound knowledge of ourselves and our sins ; the daily knife of mortification to prune our trees lest they bring forth bad fruit ; and good nourishment to strengthen us, namely the daily sustenance of meditation on the Passion of Christ and our last end. . . .[1]

Canisius reached Lucerne on December 2nd and remained a week at the college there, waiting for Bishop Bonomio, before setting out on the last stage of his journey. At Lucerne in those days an English Jesuit, Father Robert Ardren of Chichester, belonged by some turn of Providence to the community. He was the man chosen to keep St. Peter company in Fribourg but, unfortunately, though a breezy, likeable character, he had faults which rendered him unsuitable for the part. Bonomio having arrived, the three men rode out on December 10th along the rocky road to Bern. They were accompanied by a guide in the uniform of the Lucerne militia, as a hint to the Zwinglians *en route* that it might be wiser to leave them alone. By a piece of ill-luck, however, they arrived in Bern

[1] Braunsberger, *Epistulae*, vol. vii, pp. 849–51.

at exactly the wrong moment, when the whole populace was in the streets in boisterous mood to see a criminal executed. Unable to get through, Bonomio and his companions took refuge in an inn, but not before His Lordship had been recognized. Almost immediately the police arrived and informed the Bishop that he was under arrest, or as Father Ardren put it in his amusing English-Latin, " illos enim ipsum arrestare." Then the mob invaded the inn, shouting that the Bishop and priests should be taken to the gallows. There might have been violence but for the timely intervention of the two chief magistrates, or *avoyers*, as they are called in Switzerland. They came attended by six councillors and proceeded to arraign the Nuncio, who kept his head admirably and extended his hand to them as though sure that they desired by their presence to honour a distinguished foreign visitor. He was all smiles and courtesy, while they were all stiffness and formality. For a moment they refused the hand which he offered but, abashed by his fine manners, shook it and removed their hats. Then, sitting down, the Bishop motioned the 'Dominos Bernenses' to do likewise, "which they couldn't," says Ardren, " because there was such a crush." Quickly recovering from their embarrassment, the magistrates accused Bonomio of having called them heretics and of having plotted in divers manners against their cantonal majesty, for which offences he was to consider himself banished from the soil of Bern. At this " His Lordship flamed up and warned them to have a care since such a sentence violated the law of nations." They replied that they would write to him within three days about the question, whereupon there was more handshaking and a last word from the Nuncio that they should not be so ready in future to listen to tittle-tattle against him. Unfortunately, it was not all tittle-tattle, and the Bernese authorities must be said to have acted, on the whole, with forbearance. But the populace in general was not so complacent. When, after dinner at the inn, the three strangers remounted for the short ride to Fribourg, they were set upon by a howling mob and treated with the greatest indignity. " Some emitted sounds as of an ass braying," says Ardren's report, " while others put their hands to their swords in a most threatening manner, calling us knaves and rascals, and wishing for us death on the neighbouring gallows." As they rode out the forlorn three were bespattered with mud and pelted with snowballs and rotten turnips. The identity of the hated 'Jesuit, Canisius, was not known or there might have been more serious consequences. All that Peter had to say about the snowballs was that he hoped " God would turn them into a good foundation for the college of Fribourg." At the time, Bonomio showed equal fortitude but afterwards, when safe, almost precipitated a war between the Catholic cantons and Bern by his complaints and objurgations.[1]

Though it was evening and pitch dark when the travellers reached their destination they received a welcome which atoned for the inhospitality of the Bernese. All the school children of Fribourg were drawn up in festal array to greet them, while a small boy reeled off a speech in elegant Latin, telling them how delighted everybody was to see them. Unknown to St. Peter, except for a few minor excursions this was the end of his journeying, the very sea-mark of his utmost sail. Holland, Belgium, Germany, Italy, Sicily, Austria, Poland, all the lands for which he had laboured so devotedly during forty years were behind him for ever.

After resting and being entertained on the following day, which was a Sunday, Bonomio and Canisius appeared before the "Little Council" of Fribourg. The Nuncio, greeting Messeigneurs, said that though, to his disappointment, he had not been able to bring them many members of the Society of Jesus, he had at least, brought them its most distinguished member. The good man, who had already begun to address St. Peter as his "dearest brother in Our Lord," was certainly not sparing of compliments for, shortly afterwards, writing to the Vicar-General of the diocese, he exhorted that dignitary " to preserve and cherish the venerable old man, Reverend Father Canisius, with the utmost care as though by having him wrapped up in cotton wool."[2] St. Peter, on his side, was fully appreciative of the Nuncio's good intentions, but distrusted his judgment and regretted his tendency to ignore the rights of other people.

The transfer of the Abbey of Humilimont, at Marsens, to the Jesuits took place on December 21st, Pope Gregory's Bull having reached Bonomio the previous day. The ceremony began with solemn Mass of the Holy Ghost, sung by the monks, presumably under pressure from the Nuncio. Canisius then advanced to the Bishop's throne and, in presence of Provost Schneuwly, three Fribourg councillors, and a notary, read aloud the Pope's very decisive words. There followed the usual rites for such rather melancholy occasions, during which the Abbey bells were rung a full peal to proclaim the tidings to the countryside. One cannot help feeling sorry for the monks, whatever their faults. After all, the Abbey had been theirs for more than four centuries. The bells must have sounded in their ears like a funeral knell, nor can their music have

<hr />

[1] Braunsberger, *Epistulae*, vol. vii, pp. 853-8.   [2] Braunsberger, *Epistulae*, vol. vii, p. 861.

been any more welcome to the country people, signifying, as it did, the end of free meals and other such privileges.

No sooner was the monastery in Jesuit hands than St. Peter found it to be, like other monasteries forced on his Society, a truly "damnable inheritance." A large part of it had been destroyed by fire two years before and what remained was encumbered with debts and other obligations. Peter also discovered, when the deed was done, that the entire property, with the exception of the vines, had been farmed out by the Nuncio to some local tenants who engaged to pay the Jesuits an annual rent of nine hundred crowns. Many years before, when establishing the college in Prague, the Saint had had bitter experience of those leased properties. He was not conversant with the legal mysteries of amortisation and emphyteusis, nor, had he been, would his knowledge have helped him much at Marsens, because the deed was drawn up in French, a language which he could not understand. When he begged for a Latin or German version of the document, the Nuncio pooh-poohed his suspicions and bade him not look such a magnificent gift horse in the mouth. Twelve months later, Peter was seven hundred crowns in debt.

But there were worse troubles than debts. Three of the former monks had been allowed by the Nuncio to remain on at the Abbey as pensioners of the Jesuits. Not long afterwards the same Nuncio was fulminating against them and desiring their expulsion from Switzerland because, among other misdemeanours, they used to console themselves for their dispossession, poor fellows, by getting drunk almost every day. And then there was the question of the "Burgundian salt." By an ancient deed of gift the monks of Marsens had a claim to an annual supply of salt from the Counts of Burgundy, which claim, though long neglected, passed with the Abbey property to the projected college of Fribourg. Now salt in the Europe of that age was a commodity as precious as it is to-day in India, so Father Canisius valued the privilege that had come to him very highly. But, alas for his hopes, the salt did not come, even when the Pope and the King of Spain, to whom Bonomio had appealed, conjured it. For a whole decade the negotiations went on and then, in April, 1590, St. Peter wrote sadly to a Belgian friend : "We would seem now to have lost all hope of obtaining the salt." On the other hand, a right which he by no means desired fell to him all too readily. The monastery enjoyed temporal jurisdiction over two villages in the neighbourhood, and Peter found to his dismay that the Jesuits would henceforth be responsible for law and order in them, which entailed the provision of policemen, judges, and even an executioner. Father Ardren wanted to retain this jurisdiction for the sake of certain property involved, but the Saint was utterly opposed and later on secured its renunciation.

Apart from the annoyances connected with the management of Marsens, Peter liked his new surroundings very well indeed. As everybody knows, Fribourg is a beautiful town and as full of exciting holes and corners as one of its own admirable Gruyère cheeses. Did not Ruskin declare it to be " the most picturesque town in Switzerland " ? But our practical-minded Dutchman was not much affected by such aspects of the place. It was the Catholicism of Fribourg which appealed to him, and also, its good husbandry. The very stones of this " petite Rome, silencieuse et cachée, pleine de vieilleries naïves," exhale an aroma of the Faith. It stands over against Geneva and has so stood since Calvin's day, as the Catholic capital of Switzerland, and vies with Geneva too, in modern times, as a " clearing-house " of international activities. Here is what St. Peter, himself so good an ' internationalist,' wrote about it in a letter to Hoffaeus :

The clergy and people are matchlessly kind to us, and I am absolutely convinced that in Catholic Switzerland there is no healthier air nor land better cultivated and productive of wine and all other necessaries than the soil of Fribourg. The City is the rival of Bern, but for native courtesy and affability its people have no equals in this part of the world. They have preserved their Catholic piety in the very midst of violent and raging heretics, which is something that may be accounted a miracle. With one accord clergy and people defend the rights of religion, and I certainly think that this Republic is most deserving of all the favour shown it by the Holy See, and of our Society's earnest work and care on its behalf.

With regard to the college, there is no reason why your Reverence should fear to prescribe conditions concerning the number of men to be supported and the maintenance of our privileges. But be merciful to them at the start, I beg you, and do not ask too much, lest we seem to be crying out against the Bishop, or should give a handle to persons here and in Lucerne who talk invidiously about what they call the greediness of the Jesuits. The Fribourgeois will be satisfied if we begin with one or two classes when some sort of place has been made ready for the college. Afterwards it will not be difficult to support half a college out of the monastery property. People think that if we sold the property, which we are entitled to do at any time, we would realize a sum large enough for the support of an entire college. . . .

One most earnest request which I have to make is that your Reverence would come here after Easter, so as to be on the spot when the Lord Nuncio returns. In this way His Lordship will be enabled to transact more satisfactorily and freely whatever business he has with the Government, *Christo duce*.

The confines of Bern are only two miles from here and Lausanne is only six or seven miles away,[1] while one can get to Geneva in a three days' journey. From their slanderous lampoons against us, it can be seen how much the people of these places fear the Jesuits. They strive, in consequence, to advance their schools, and engage learned professors in them, as an offset to whom it will be worth our while to have uncommonly good masters at the college here. Certainly both the clergy, who are wonderfully friendly to us, and the magistrates who have faced and surmounted many difficulties for our sake, expect great things from us.[2]

St. Peter's first sermon in Fribourg was preached in the Church of St. Nicholas a week after his arrival. According to Bonomio it was a great success and won for the Saint universal applause, including that of the cantonal Government. He began by describing himself as an unknown, foreign theologian and begged their Lordships and his " dear brothers and sisters of Fribourg " charitably to put up with his weak voice and other defects of body and mind. Then he asked them to pray that he might be enabled to preach wisely and they to receive his words profitably. " Should it happen that any of my auditors fail to understand me or desire to criticize something I say, or are offended by it, I would beg them in friendship not to judge and condemn me too hastily, as Christ forbids, but rather to admonish me in Christian charity, either themselves personally or through others. Let them come and see me, knowing that I

---

[1] Peter was a poor judge of distances, unless he understood ' *milliarium* ' to mean five. English miles. Bern at the nearest point is seven miles from Fribourg, and Lausanne, the capital of Protestant Vaux, is almost exactly thirty miles away.

[2] Braunsberger, *Epistulae*, vol. vii, pp. 600–1. A pamphlet issued by the Protestants in 1575, *Contra impias Scholas Jesuitarum*, addressed the Jesuits in the following terms : " The Pope of Rome, Christ's principal adversary, was your father ; impiety was your mother ; madness your midwife ; and the tutor of your manners and doctrine, the devil. . . . There have been men who denied the existence of God, men who impiously doubted whether He existed, men who contended that there were many gods, men who worshipped as gods bulls, serpents, crocodiles, and various other kinds of animals, men who numbered among the gods Aesculapius, Mars, Mercury, Bacchus, impure beings and obscene prostitutes, and others notorious for every manner of vice. But of all the numberless impious classes of men the Jesuit swine are easily first in audacity, crime, folly, rage, and cruelty." Braunsberger, l.c., p. 745.

am ready to explain myself with all meekness." So much was enough by way of preamble, he continued, lest in the cold weather he should detain them too long.[1]

That sermon was the first of a feast-day series which lasted without intermission for eight years. Feast-days were holidays of obligation apart from Sundays, and Fribourg observed no fewer than thirty-four of them in the year, not counting all feasts of Our Lord, Our Lady, and the Apostles.[2] Peter preached a total of more than 320 sermons in Fribourg, but these were not distributed evenly throughout the eight years, as he had become so feeble from constant prayer and austerities towards the end of the period that he could scarcely speak in more than a whisper. Thus he preached fifty-four times in 1583, but only eight times in 1588. As always in his life, each sermon was carefully prepared, its main points written out in a mixture of Latin and German, and directions for the delivery inserted in the margin of the manuscript. Taking the eight years of preaching at Fribourg with the seven consecutive years at Augsburg and five at Innsbruck, and adding to them the long spells in Vienna and Ingolstadt, the many Lenten and Advent courses in Cologne, Prague, Würzburg, Regensburg, and Landshut, the very numerous occasional sermons, and the scores of exhortations delivered to his brethren of the Society of Jesus, it would not be too much to claim for St. Peter that, while by no means the most eloquent preacher of his age, he was at least its most indefatigable preacher. The extant notes of his sermons alone cover more than twelve thousand large sheets of paper. Assuredly, too, never preacher lived whose motives were less open to challenge. The very form of his sermons bespeaks their utter sincerity. It is the rarest thing to find a coloured phrase in them or anything but the simple, unconscious rhetoric of earnestness. Whenever he could, Peter renounced his private vocabulary to clothe his thoughts in the language of Revelation, or perhaps it would be more accurate to say that his thoughts ran naturally into Scriptural form owing to his ceaseless meditations on the books of the Old and New Testaments. At any rate, the number of texts which he quotes is astounding, and justifies a surmise that he must almost have known the Bible by heart.

Peter had a characteristic way of beginning and ending his sermons. He used to open with the words : " The love of God the Father, the grace

[1] Braunsberger, *Epistulae*, vol. vii, pp. 863–4.
[2] Thus, the feasts of St. George and St. Thomas of Canterbury were holidays of obligation in Fribourg, entailing not only attendance at Mass but at a sermon morning and evening and at Vespers and Compline.

and mercy of Our Lord Jesus Christ, the indwelling and comfort of God the Holy Ghost, be with us all now and for ever." Then he asked all who desired such a fulfilment to say with him a fervent "Amen," and continued: "We shall beg God's blessing and say together an Our Father and Hail Mary that I may deal with the Word of God rightly and that you may hear it fruitfully." At the end of the sermon he said: "I commend your souls and bodies, honour and possessions, to the protection of God the Father, Son, and Holy Ghost, Amen."[1] Between him and his audience there was much more intimacy than is common in the modern pulpit. He did not so much preach as talk to the people, taking them into his confidence and telling them the Church's troubles or wishing them a Happy New Year, as though they were all at some family gathering. But he could be very stern, too, at times, and even on such joyful feasts as that of St. Nicholas, the patron of Fribourg, he never hesitated to emphasize unpalatable truths. Thus on the Saint's feast in 1581 he said:

If St. Nicholas were here to-day, for what would he praise his people of Fribourg? He would praise them for not giving way to the reformers and changing their religion; for being readier to visit the Sepulchre of Our Lord and the Holy Places than all others of their countrymen; for abstaining, as some do, on Wednesdays and Fridays, in imitation of the practice of their Patron and, indeed, of the ancient Church. Next, for what would he reprove them? First, because neither in youth nor in the prime of life are they ready to undertake a little abstinence, but by gluttony and drunkenness hinder all that is good in their characters, dissipate their property, ruin their health, and destroy themselves body and soul. Secondly, he would have a serious rebuke for the heartlessness, meanness, and injustice of Fribourg's people towards the poor, arising out of usury and the new business practices of worldlings. Thirdly, he would blame us for our politics, inasmuch as we allow many good laws and customs of our fathers to fall into oblivion and even contempt, with resultant licence and levity among the people, many of whom are Catholic only in name and sin with impunity owing to the too great indulgence of the Government. . . . Indeed, it is a strange thing that we should praise St. Nicholas so grandly in his church and should show such pride in him, while at home we forget entirely the lessons of his life. We show our devotion to him

[1] Braunsberger, *Epistulae*, vol. vii, p. 574.

by stuffing ourselves and getting drunk, he who was such a pattern of Christian abstinence and moderation. We have forsaken our ancient Patron and adopted Bacchus. As long as he reigns here Saint Nicholas will not worry much about us . . . no matter what we may sing or hold about him.[1]

As in his courses of sermons at Augsburg and other places, St. Peter's preaching at Fribourg nearly always had some bearing on the urgent controversial topics of the day. The Catholic practices which he most commended were those which the Reformers decried, such as devotion to the Blessed Virgin, pilgrimages, jubilees, processions, the veneration of the saints, frequent Confession and Communion. Penitence, especially as manifested in fasting and abstinence, was one of his constant subjects, for the good reason that his flock relished it so little. " Among all good works," he said at the beginning of his first Lenten course in Fribourg, " there is not one which both Catholics and Protestants love less, and find so heavy, hard, and bitter, as fasting. Fasting is a guest that never gets an invitation, but is shunned by practically everybody and put off, if possible, to Holy Week. Rich people make excuses and the poor are unable to entertain this guest. Nobody is at home to him."

But though Peter's words were often hard, in condemnation of slackness and superstition, there runs through the majority of his sermons an explicit note of tenderness and sympathy. Whenever the needs of the poor or afflicted engaged his attention, as they so often did, he made no scruple about wearing his heart on his sleeve or laying himself open to the censure of more cautiously charitable persons. The winter of 1586 was a time of great scarcity in Fribourg. Preaching on November 23rd that year, the Saint took upon himself to outline a scheme of relief for the consideration of the Government :

It is a difficult matter that I am going to discuss, and I fear some people may be annoyed by my temerity in giving my views on such a grave subject. But I have this much comfort—that my words may, as I desire them, give wise men an occasion to think more diligently about the common misery and need which presses upon so many, and well-nigh compels all who have it in their power to come forward and help to avert the general danger, to preserve the State, and to comfort the poor.

[1] Braunsberger, *Epistulae*, vol. viii, pp. 518–9.

Having asserted what he considered to be the principal assurance against such visitations, namely prayer and penance, he proceeded to detail some special remedies :

The first is for the magistrates to follow the example of Christ who, though Himself wisdom supreme, yet desired to consult with His disciples as to how the poor should be supported in their need. Thus also did the Apostles when they saw that poor widows were being neglected, constituting seven deacons to look after them. . . . It is, therefore, not only fitting and praiseworthy but necessary that the magistrates should be vigilant, and, either personally or through their four tribunes or other officials, undertake serious measures of relief. . . . Among other things, they might consider whether it would not be advisable to find out how people are living in the four quarters of this town. . . . There should be at least a weekly inspection and the names of persons more gravely afflicted by poverty should be discovered and written down. . . .

It would help, too, if men appointed by the Senate were to prohibit and suppress the extravagance which goes on at weddings and festive gatherings. There is no need for such display, and it is greatly prejudicial to the poor, of whom a large number could be supported with the money spent on grand banquets and feastings. The gilds, in particular, might well be ordered to restrain their spending, especially at Christmas time, but most of all on Epiphany Day when practically to a man the members get drunk and behave with great levity, under pretext of honouring the three Kings.

Another remedy would be to find or provide money, food, houses, or shelter for the poor. This could be done by begging alms from noble and rich men, who may thus make unto themselves friends of the mammon of iniquity. . . . Secondly, there might be collections on Sundays for the poor. Thirdly it would help if the rich acted mercifully towards their debtors and exacted less from them than they might in other circumstances. Fourthly, the rich should care for their necessitous neighbours, acquaintances, and friends, lest otherwise they be like Dives who forgot poor Lazarus at his feast. Oh, blessed are they that now feed, refresh, clothe, and visit Christ in His members . . . who are as dear to Him as we are and often dearer. Whosoever receives them not, receives not Christ, nor is worthy of that kingdom which Christ has promised to the poor.[1]

[1] Braunsberger, *Epistulae*, vol. viii, pp. 730–3.

Of Peter's lighter style in the pulpit many examples could be given. One whole sermon at Fribourg, and a long one too, was on the life of the bee as a model of industry and the community spirit, but it has to be said that the preacher did not derive his bee-lore from personal observation of a hive. He derived it entirely from Pliny's highly imaginative *Natural History*, which was a way they had in those pre-scientific times. On Christmas Day, 1584, he gave his sermon in the form of a dialogue between the congregation and the Angel Gabriel, " the first preacher of the Feast," and often, on other occasions, varied his discourses in some such innocently dramatic way. In general it can be said that the chief characteristic of his preaching was its simple piety. The truths of which he spoke were not mere cold abstractions, but burning, vital realities to him, and so there is an unction in his unadorned sentences worth many measures of more academic eloquence. Even in the sadly truncated notes of his sermons given by Braunsberger it is possible to discern a vestige of their ancient flame. The common people, with their very unromantic sins and sorrows, liked them exceedingly well and did them the high compliment of moulding their lives by them, nor were the others, the people of taste and discrimination, less appreciative, to judge by the testimony of one of them who confessed that he " shed abundant tears " every time he heard Father Canisius preach.[1]

Besides the sermons in Fribourg town, St. Peter did a good deal of mission work in country districts where German was spoken. "I have known him," wrote a Fribourg worthy, "traverse the country places of this Republic in winter, when he was already broken with age. And he made his difficult journeys through the snow not only without reluctance but gladly, in order to preach the Gospel and the truths of the Roman Faith. . . . On being urged by his friends to spare himself these and similar labours in his old age, he used to reply that he had not yet satisfied his desire of struggling against the enemies of the Christian faith, for he was ready to spend his blood and his life in that employment."[2] Of one such excursion the Saint was particularly fond, to a little shrine of the Blessed Virgin still happily in existence at a place near Fribourg called Bourguillon. It is not easy of access for it stands on a rugged eminence more than two thousand feet high, but Peter loved to make his slow way to the top, thinking the while of Mary's journey through the mountains to visit Elizabeth, and of her Son's climb up Calvary.

The domestic life of the two Jesuits at Fribourg in those early days must have been full of discomfort. They lodged with the Precentor of

[1] Braunsberger, *Epistulae*, vol. viii, p. 797. [2] Braunsberger, *Epistulae*, vol. viii, pp. 558–9.

St. Nicholas's and paid him for the privilege, but they had to go out for their meals to another house, than which no seaside landlady ever invented a more detestable arrangement. Being a shy and austere man, St. Peter suffered agonies from it. The abundant fare and liberal drinking at his host's table seemed to him out of accord with the professions of people vowed to poverty, and Father Ardren's hearty English appetite and thirst served to emphasize the disproportion. To redress the balance, Peter ate hardly anything. "I think he is letting himself die of hunger," wrote one who noticed his manœuvres, in August, 1581. Hunger is not conducive to large-mindedness, and the same observer had to report that the Saint was sometimes rather difficult to deal with, being extremely scrupulous and, perhaps, too exacting for flesh and blood less finely controlled than his own. The result was that Ardren and he did not see eye to eye. Peter was critical of Ardren's business methods, and Ardren retaliated by criticizing Peter's theology. On each side it was very mild criticism, but two men living together cannot afford to indulge even in that if they want to be happy. The situation made Peter sigh for his favourite remedy in difficulties, an official ' visitor ' from Rome. In June, 1581, the remedy came, no less a person than the wise Frenchman, Oliver Manare, who had been ruling the Society of Jesus as Vicar-General since the death of Mercurian.

Manare reported soon afterwards to the new Jesuit General, Father Claude Aquaviva, that he found his two brethren " con sanità et molto grande riputatione appresso del popolo." Father Canisius, he said, apart from his sermons, was leading a very secluded life, while Father Ardren had immersed himself completely in the affairs of the monastery at Marsens. Twice a week this active Briton found time to give Catechism classes, but, says the Visitor, " he does the work in such a muddled fashion that he is not understood and I don't know whether he understands himself. He gets through a great deal, but he wants to be too universal and learned. However, the goodness of both men and the great esteem in which Father Canisius is held for his learning and virtue make up for all our short-comings."[1] Among the records of Manare's visit is a long list of doubts and difficulties submitted to him by Canisius. Trivial though some of these may appear, they illustrate very well the delicacy of St. Peter's sense of obedience and show how loyally determined he was not to involve his Order in any obligations inconsistent with its rule. Thus he wanted to know whether if one of them was invited to dinner he could go without

[1] Braunsberger, *Epistulae*, vol. viii, p. 538.

the other; whether when the two of them had meals at their lodging they should have reading throughout; whether they might keep their French-speaking servant and if so how often he should go to confession; whether it was lawful for them to take anything in alms; whether if people contributed to the expenses of the new college on condition that they acquired right of sepulchre in its church he should accept such conditions.[1]

Mention of the college brings us to the next point in the story. More than a year had now passed since Peter's arrival in Fribourg and there was still no sign of it. Meantime, he had been putting together all the crowns he could find, but his little hoard would hardly have sufficed to build a barn. However, he could choose the site for his college and did so, in conjunction with Manare, as confidently as though he had a fortune to spend. Like Rome, but in a very much more painfully literal fashion for its visitors, Fribourg town is built on hills, of which the highest was called in old times Belsex, or the Beautiful Rock. The town has long since flowed over and round it, but in St. Peter's day it was still a green pleasance of meadows and orchards; undeveloped, as we say, except for a sort of citadel at the top. Up there would he pitch his college and dedicate it to St. Michael, the Saint of high places, on whose feast he was born sixty years before. The first thing to be done was to obtain a licence from the cantonal Government to purchase land. For this, three different sets of authorities had to be approached, involving many tiresome visits of Canisius and Manare to the Rathaus. One of the chambers there bears the quaint name of *La Salle des Pas perdus*. To Manare, at least, it must have seemed a highly appropriate name, as objections of every description, partly instigated by the Calvinists of Bern and Geneva, were raised against his petition. Eventually, however, the influence and personal popularity of Father Canisius prevailed, and he was then free to purchase his hill as soon as he could find the money. Its chief owners, moved also by regard for his character, agreed to let him have it at so moderate a price that by the summer of 1582 he had been able to sign the conveyances and take possession of the citadel with its orchard and garden. Then he acquired a house and some fields adjoining, together with the use of a reservoir on the hill as a water-supply and fishery.

These are trivial facts and would hardly be worth recording except as evidence of the great esteem in which Peter was held. Certainly he had no special gifts as a man of affairs, and he won his victories in business simply because he was such a genuine man of God. In their agreement with Bonomio the Fribourg councillors had emphatically stipulated that the Jesuits were to expect no assistance from public resources, yet the same men now voted quite spontaneously the large sum of twelve thousand florins for the purchase of two houses in the Rue de Lausanne to serve as temporary class-rooms and chapel while the college was being built. They did so because they judged Father Canisius to be well worth twelve thousand florins. As for the Saint's actual management of affairs we have Manare's report that he was no good at such work, but " totus abstractus " and quite unable any longer to apply his mind to it, despite the most earnest endeavours. The Visitor accordingly relieved him of further responsibility for temporalities, and a little later, in August, 1582, Peter himself begged Father Aquaviva to let him resign his office of superior also. The General, who reverenced him deeply, agreed at once "in order that he might devote all his energies to promoting the salvation of souls." A young Silesian Jesuit, just half St. Peter's age, arrived in Fribourg on September 11th to take control, and was followed ten days later by four of his brethren, including the Englishman, Father John Howlett, destined to be the first prefect of studies of the new college.

A month afterwards, October 18, 1582,[1] the college opened its doors and won such favour that within a single term the Jesuits had been crowded out of their rooms by invading boyhood and compelled to purchase a third house in the Rue de Lausanne. The congestion made everybody sigh for the college on the hill which the Fathers could not find the money to build. " We are burdened with a debt of two thousand crowns," wrote St. Peter to Bonomio in January, 1583, "and only trust in the help of Heaven keeps up our spirits in this penury." A year later the help of Heaven came in the shape of a Government decision to build the college at the expense of the cantonal treasury. Work began on it in March, 1585, but owing to the difficulty of getting materials up the hill, to threats of war, to civil dissensions, to the plague, and to other calamities, a whole decade went by before the new buildings were ready for habitation. Even then there was no sign of the church for which the Jesuits had been endeavouring to collect the necessary crowns.

Though St. Peter Canisius took no part except that of an adviser in the management of the college, he was yet regarded as the good angel of its fortunes. Others may have done the work, but he it was who by

---

[1] New Style, as the Gregorian Calendar had been promulgated to take effect from October 4th, 1582. The day following was to be called October 15th, but it required a long time to persuade Protestant countries, and particularly England, to adopt the reform. They preferred to be wrong with Julius Caesar rather than right with the Pope.

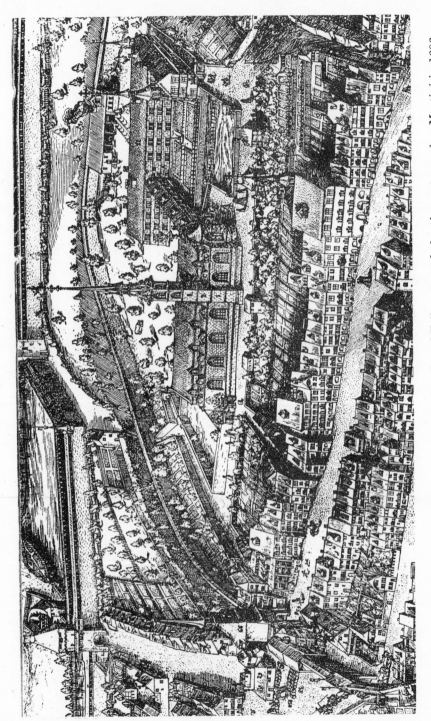

The Church and College of St. Michael, as shown in the plan of Fribourg made by the cartographer Martini in 1606

the influence of his holiness made the work a possibility and gave to it its fine edge of idealism. That highest of high tributes which George III paid to the dying Chatham, "your name has been enough to enable my Administration to proceed," was paid to St. Peter in his day by the best priest in Switzerland. "Even were he to do nothing at all, being now broken in health," wrote Provost Schneuwly to St. Charles Borromeo in July, 1583, "yet would he, saying not a word, keep all the rest to their duties."[1] The college, then, was truly his and remains his to this day, for, though the Jesuits have long since ceased to be its guardians,[2] his spirit still guides its beneficent activities from that room, now a chapel, where he gave his great soul to God. St. Michael's plays and has always played a prominent part in the Catholic life, not only of Fribourg, but of all Switzerland. It is primarily due to the work and influence of the College that Fribourg has become in modern times the chief European centre after Rome of Catholic international activities and the home of a university in which the teaching of St. Thomas Aquinas is given the full honour that is its due. Both the *Pax Romana* and the *Catholic Council for International Relations* were founded and have their centres in Fribourg. Speaking of them and of the University in 1928, M. Guillaume de Weck declared that St. Peter Canisius "a été le symbole et l'inspirateur de toute la politique d'intellectualisme catholique de Fribourg."[3]

Turning now to St. Peter's activities apart from the College, we may signalize first his foundation of sodalities. It was then the hey-day of the sodality movement, and none showed himself more enthusiastic for its spread than Peter, who in his own person was the living embodiment of its twofold ideal, devotion to the Mother of God and to the service of one's neighbour. Having first obtained permission from higher superiors, he started in Fribourg on September 8, 1581, a men's sodality which was joined in good numbers by senators, priests, and other persons of standing. The original sodality in Rome to which this was affiliated in due course made no provision for women, but in Fribourg St. Peter found a means of satisfying their good desires by adapting the men's organization and rules for their benefit. Then came the turn of young people, for whom the Saint established a students' sodality on November 1, 1581, nearly a year before the College of St. Michael was opened. Though intended primarily for the sanctification of their members, the sodalities

[1] Braunsberger, *Epistulae*, vol. viii, p. 115.
[2] They were expelled from Switzerland by the Federal Government after the brief civil war of the Sonderbund in 1846 and have not since been permitted to return.
[3] *Fribourg : l'Action catholique et universitaire*, p. 51.

had a marked social bearing and embraced many of the functions now more commonly associated with the Society of St. Vincent de Paul. Thus at Fribourg it became the sodalists' duty and privilege to collect alms for the poor; to visit the poor in their homes or refuges; to wait on and watch with the sick, which they often did the whole night through; to make peace between enemies; to teach Catechism to unlettered persons; to help prisoners; and in general to be Good Samaritans to all in misfortune. How wide and generous was the spirit which St. Peter fostered in his sodalists may be seen from the prayers which they used to say in common at their meetings, prayers for the whole Church and for those parts of it such as France and Germany which were more specially afflicted, prayers for all poor and unhappy people, for confessors, for priests in general, for the Bishop of Lausanne, for help against the Turk, for the other needs of Christendom. And the members, young and old, did not confine themselves to prayers but fasted on bread and water and practised other stern forms of mortification to win the mercy of God for their country and the world.[1] That they were not unmindful of their debt to St. Peter Canisius is shown by the number of rosaries, litanies, and other prayers which they offered regularly for him during his last years on earth.

Though Peter's body was almost worn out at this time, his mind, or rather his spirit, retained all its old keenness. No sooner had he arrived in Fribourg than he began to agitate for the establishment of a printing-press in the town. Books for him had something sacramental about them, and now that he could no longer preach as much as of old he felt an overwhelming urge to send out many of these silent ambassadors of his devotion. In June, 1591, Peter's Provincial told Aquaviva that without writing he simply could not exist—*sine scriptione vitam nequit agere*. The one talent left to him by infirmity and old age he must traffic with up to the very end, even though, as the Provincial reported, the labour sometimes nearly killed him.[2] His campaign for the printing-press met with all sorts of checks and disappointments, but he never thought of giving up and in 1585 had the reward of his perseverance. Applying that year to Pope Sixtus V for the usual papal privilege, the Fribourg senators said: " At the persuasion of Reverend Father Peter Canisius, who greatly adorns this our city by dwelling therein, we have purchased a printing-press at considerable expense and hired the services of a printer."[3] This printer, Abraham Gemperlin, became a dear friend of Peter's—" *Abrahamus noster,*

[1] Braunsberger, *Epistulae*, vol. viii, pp. 824, 840–1.
[2] Braunsberger, *Epistulae*, vol. viii, pp. 820–1.
[3] Braunsberger, *Epistulae*, vol. viii, pp. 214–5.

mihi amicissimus "—which, considering all the trouble that Peter caused him by maltreating his proofs, speaks eloquently for the characters of both men. The first of the Saint's books to be issued after his arrival in Fribourg was a revision of his two volumes against the Centuriators which were published in one at Ingolstadt in 1583. On this work he had been engaged for more than two years, endeavouring with scrupulous care to strengthen his arguments and meet whatever criticisms had been urged against his theology. He had once more appealed to Cardinal Sirleto for texts from Roman manuscripts, and sought also the help of Father Torres and other scholars among his brethren. Far from being satisfied, however, with this very thorough revision, which appeared at Lyons and Paris as well as Ingolstadt, he at once set to work on a third overhaul of his material. There still exists a copy of the 1583 volume containing more than two thousand further additions and emendations, written in ink between the lines or in the margins. The most interesting of the changes here is Peter's renunciation of the opinion, borrowed from St. Albert the Great, that the Blessed Virgin had received all the Sacraments except Holy Orders. His eminent brother in religion, Francis Suarez, very rightly challenged the statement as it appeared in the first edition, whereupon Father Alber, the then German Provincial, protested to Aquaviva against such domestic censuring, but we are happy to report that the General took no notice of his objurgations. That was in 1594, and very likely it was the perfectly fair and courteous animadversion of Suarez which led Peter to part company with St. Albert. Of the revision order too, the most tiresome of all literary drudgery, was Peter's work on the many new editions of his Latin and German Catechisms which appeared during his years at Fribourg. As there were more than forty of them and their publishers naturally desired to have a fresh word or two from the author, it can be guessed that his pen ran little danger of rusting.

Peter's first entirely new book during this period was printed and published at Fribourg by his friend Gemperlin in 1586. It contained 288 pages and bore the following long title: *Ninety-two Considerations and Prayers of the devout Brother Claus of Unterwalden, together with his Precepts, Maxims, and Prophecies, now printed for the first time.* Brother Claus was Blessed Nicholas of Flüe, a fifteenth-century Swiss hermit who, after a strangely varied life as farmer, magistrate, judge, and soldier, ended his days as a solitary with such repute for holiness that he was beatified by Pope Clement IX in 1669. St. Peter's book began with a life of Brother Claus and short sketches of St. Beatus and St. Meinrad, all based on traditions with which the Bollandists have since dealt very mercilessly. Nevertheless, those learned men did Peter the honour of reprinting part of his preface in the *Acta Sanctorum*. It was the prayers and meditations that had attracted him, and, though with our superior modern knowledge we can point out that they were not, as Peter thought, composed by Blessed Nicholas, but merely adapted by him from much older sources, his book did not help souls to sanctity any the less because of its poor scholarship. To get people to pray was his aim, not to contribute to the advance of learning. For the same purpose he reissued the following year, 1587, his *Manuale Catholicorum*, a stout little prayer-book of 480 pages with many naïve woodcuts to help simple imaginations. It bore a charming dedication to the eleven-year-old Prince Philip of Bavaria, encouraging him to be a good boy in the most affectionate terms.

During the last decade of his life St. Peter was very active as a hagiographer on devotional lines. In 1590, at the request of some Benedictine monks, he wrote and published with Gemperlin the life of a saintly married lady named Ida who was much venerated in Switzerland. This book, which ran to 137 octavo pages, was intended primarily for husbands and wives. " As gold," says the author, " excels all other fine metals, so is the love of husband and wife to be esteemed and held above all other human love." The same year witnessed the appearance of a large volume devoted to the biographies of St. Beatus and St. Fridolin. Fridolin was a genuine Irish missionary saint, though his legend is almost worthless historically; but whether a Swiss Beatus ever existed is more than doubtful. If he did, he certainly was not a disciple of the first St. Peter nor sent by him to evangelize Switzerland, as the old documents alleged. Our St. Peter reported the story as he found it, not having in him the modern sensitiveness to historical atmosphere. With an advance copy of his book, dispatched to a friend in Soleure, he enclosed the following note:

The eternal peace of Jesus Christ be with us, your Excellency. My Beatus comes to you now, though not as neatly and finely garbed as was his due. Of your kindness you will receive the poor guest courteously and not grow wroth with his tailor, who failed to prepare better clothes for the excellent man. The style of the book and the prolixity of the story will displease people . . . but I came to the task of writing it an old man and foreigner. Should it, however, give you any satisfaction I shall think that I have done very well indeed. Only please don't despise the poor little thing. . . .[1]

[1] Braunsberger, *Epistulae*, vol. viii, p. 295.

Ever since his Cologne days Peter had been devoted to the soldier saints, Maurice, Ursus, Gereon, and their companions, associated by tradition with the famous Theban Legion. In 1594 he produced yet another quarto of 195 pages devoted to the lives of these men. The book and especially the part devoted to St. Ursus, whose relics were supposed to be in the Swiss town of Soleure, cost him a great deal of trouble. A dear friend in Soleure, the patrician, Johann von Staal, supplied him with documents. "I could wish, indeed," wrote Peter when thanking him, " that I had more strength and ability to deal with the collection which you sent me, so as to make something of it answering to your expectations and acceptable to the people of Soleure. I foresee, though, that to put this chaotic and undigested material into shape and to accommodate it to the needs of modern soldiers is going to be a very laborious business. I therefore turn to God for help and put my trust rather in the prayers of the saints than in my own efforts. May the good people of Soleure help me too, and commend me earnestly and frequently to God while I sweat with my pen."[1] Peter's young friend, James Keller, who was a master at the College at this time, composed a " Carmen heroicum " to be prefixed to the book. It pleased the Saint, but the Rector was a more exacting critic and stopped its publication, whereupon Peter spoke such sweet comfort to the disappointed poet that he declared himself lucky to have failed—" *nam si meliora lusissem meliora non audissem.*" The Government of Canton Soleure were so delighted with the book that they presented to " the devout, incomparably learned, and most profound theologian, Reverend Father and Doctor Peter Canisius of the Society of Jesus," a handsome edition of St. Jerome in nine folio volumes which had come from Plantin's famous press in Antwerp in 1579, and an equally beautiful edition of St. Ambrose in four volumes. Two years later Peter re-edited the life of St. Maurice under the title, *A Mirror for Soldiers*. The Swiss were a soldiering race, and the civil wars in France at this period lured large numbers of them to arms, either on the side of the League or under the flag of Henry of Navarre. It was not glory that they sought but pay, and St. Peter, knowing the temptations to which mercenaries were peculiarly open, desired in the goodness of his heart to give the Catholics among them a message of hope and encouragement, since other services lay out of his power.

At this point we may put the question, what is to be thought in our own day of those hagiographical lucubrations? When the writer of this

[1] Braunsberger, *Epistulae*, vol. viii, pp. 304-5.

book asked his opinion of a famous Belgian scholar, himself a Jesuit and the greatest living authority on the subject, he received for answer the one expressive word, "*épouvantables*"! Judged by modern critical standards they are doubtless very dreadful. So long as Peter had a document of some antiquity he does not seem to have worried about its value as evidence. That good men of the past might have invented stories or confused one saint with another or skipped through the centuries, blithely indifferent to anachronisms, seems not to have occurred to him. But it has to be said in his favour that he was one of a large company and no worse, for instance, than the Protestant Archbishop Ussher whose *Antiquities of the British Churches* abounds in similar historical naïvetés. Unlike Ussher, Canisius made no pretence to scholarship in these books. He wrote, as he says quite openly, partly for edification and partly with the controversial purpose of defending the cult of the saints from heretical attack. For this reason he introduces many Scriptural quotations and excerpts from the Fathers into the books, it being his aim to strengthen the faith and deepen the piety of the simple readers whom he had in view.[1] He therefore used his sources, such as Gregory of Tours' *De Gloria Martyrum*, without any attempt to estimate their historical worth, and treated the incidents provided as so many pegs on which to hang his own thoughts about time and eternity. Thus the lives of St. Maurice and his companions are made the occasion for an excursus on the duties of soldiers and the legitimacy of waging war on the part of the Christians, wherein Peter uses as a text Horace's famous line, *Dulce et decorum est pro patria mori*. That does not mean that he had any romantic illusions about war, for his letters show that he hated the thing as the foulest and beastliest horror with which mankind can be afflicted, and detested equally heartily the petty, brazen-voiced nationalism which is so often its cause.

Whatever may be said about the worthlessness of such works as contributions to scholarship, there can be no doubt about the tremendous pains that went to their making. A letter which the Saint addressed to a Benedictine monk of Einsiedeln in June, 1588, shows that he was conscious enough of the inadequacy of his sources and eager for more enlightenment. "I regret," he said, "that trustworthy memorials of ancient saints, containing the light of history which we desire, are not available. Perhaps our forefathers, in harmony with the simplicity of their times, touched only lightly and sparingly on what concerned the lives, teaching, and deaths of the saints. . . . Would that we had an ecclesiastical authority

[1] Braunsberger, *Epistulae*, vol. viii, pp. 284–90.

with zeal in his heart to search through various monasteries for whatever documents may exist concerning the sayings, writings, and deeds of the saints and patrons of Switzerland. . . ." On another occasion, writing to a layman of Soleure who was collecting documents for him, he said : " I quite approve of your decision to take your time over the collection of the various monuments of antiquity. It is not a hardship to me but a downright pleasure, because I am very keen to have sought out every scrap of evidence from old sources which bears on the matter in question."[1] Peter's laborious essays in biography are all now superseded and forgotten. As lives of the saints with whom they dealt they never had much value, but as avenues to the heart of the Saint who wrote them they will always be precious. For is not the learning which they lacked a poor and perishable thing compared with the love which was their inspiration ?

In 1591 St. Peter had a severe illness from which he emerged so bent and broken that he required the support of a stick to enable him to totter about. But he was far from being vanquished in spirit, and the following year produced an admirable little spiritual work in Latin for the twenty-year-old Ferdinand, eldest son of Charles, Archduke of Austria. This youth, who later became the great Catholic Emperor, Ferdinand II, was then a student under the Jesuits at Ingolstadt. Peter called his manuscript, which in the German version now in the Palatine Library, Vienna, is a codex of 180 pages, *A Manual of Piety, containing Instructions on Prayer for a Christian Prince*. The work is preceded by an interesting epistle dedicatory in which the Saint explains why he, an old man and stranger to the Prince, has written this book for him. It is because he has heard such golden report of his Highness that even far away in Switzerland he has learned to love and honour him. The letter continues as a little homily on the necessity and value of prayer.[2] After it come instructions on how to pray well, and then a series of prayers and meditations for each day of the week ; prayers for spiritual and temporal rulers ; a prayer to be said for the Prince himself ; prayers for relatives, friends, enemies, heretics, and persons hostile to the Church ; prayers in time of war, famine, and other calamities ; prayers for the afflicted and sorrowful, for all classes of Christians, and, finally, for the Prince's dead father. The work concludes with the life of the good Emperor, Theodosius the Younger, as related by the historian Socrates, followed by " Some Golden Christian Rules " of St. Louis IX of France. It pleased Prince Ferdinand's mother

---

[1] Braunsberger, *Epistulae*, vol. viii, pp. 263–4 ; 301.
[2] Braunsberger, *Epistulae*, vol. viii, pp. 336–40.

so much that she felt she must present a copy to the King of Spain. " My Ferdinand," she wrote to her son in January, 1599, " get your scriptor to copy for me the Prayer Book of Father Canisius, and send it to me at the first opportunity, wherever I may be. I desire to send it to the King. Also get me a fine binding of shagreen, but do not have the book bound, as I shall see to that myself. Take care that the work is done in the most exact and beautiful fashion."[1]

Another work of the prayer-book class which St. Peter produced at this period was a devotional commentary on the *Miserere*. He had planned but did not achieve a " Little Book of Consolation for Forlorn Catholics," and also began a German translation of the well-known medieval book of devotions, the *Paradisus Animae*. Braunsberger prints the two versions of an introduction which the Saint had prepared for the work. Though very short, only about a page and a half in length, they contain over eighty emendations and revisions, evidence of the scrupulous care and pains that Peter took with all his compositions.[2]

Finally, in the matter of books, there were the two remarkable volumes of *Notes on the Gospels* which came from Gemperlin's press in 1591 and 1593. The first, devoted to the Sunday Gospels, is a substantial quarto of 1,172 pages with good indexes, and the other, devoted to the Gospels read at Mass on saints' days, runs to 864 pages. The volume on the Sunday Gospels was dedicated to Peter Schneuwly and the other priests of Fribourg, in testimony of the writer's deep regard for them. " I cannot," he said, " but thank the Author of all good and rejoice in my heart that I was led here by obedience to be your colleague and fellow-worker in the common cause. If I have done a little for it, it was due to the incentive of your example, for well I know the great battle you have fought for the true faith over these many years." The dedication of the second volume to the Senators of Fribourg is a huge affair concerned chiefly with the defence of the Church's attitude towards her saints. In thanks for it the Senators presented to Peter a fine edition of St. Augustine in ten volumes which they had purchased at Lyons for 152 *livres*. Peter's extraordinary knowledge and love of Holy Scripture comes out well in this great work, for he cites upwards of twelve thousand texts in the margins. " No manna," he says, " will be to me more sweet, no token more dear, no study more lovely and delightful than to exercise myself night and day in the Word of God." God was such a glorious and absorbing reality to him that the Scriptures became less a printed book than the living

[1] Braunsberger, *Epistulae*, vol. viii, p. 828. [2] Braunsberger, *Epistulae*, vol. viii, pp. 870–2.

voice of his greatest Friend. The idea that inspired him to devote his old age to such an incredibly laborious task as the writing of this huge commentary is revealed in some lines of a letter addressed to a Roman Jesuit on August 25, 1591. " I have been now a whole decade in Switzerland," he said, " and must struggle ever increasingly with the infirmities of old age, so that I may well prepare for my end. Since it is impossible for me to preach to others, I am writing something, so far as age and health permit, that may be of help to a few preachers for the glory of God."[1] In his dedication of the book to the Fribourg clergy he said that he did not intend it to be a learned commentary. Such commentaries already existed, so he would put aside for the most part minute discussion of the text and content himself with giving the chief heads of doctrine in a form suitable for meditation and prayer, " in order to help, if not learned persons, at least good and simple readers, according to my small ability." Love of the Church's liturgy which inspired so many of St. Peter's smaller books was also the inspiration of this big one. " I know not why it is," he says, " but not many people to-day apply their minds earnestly to the Church's feasts and ceremonies, putting on like true sons the spiritual thoughts and affections of their most holy Mother." His desire, then, is to recall people to the liturgy by explaining the spirit of the Church's offices as reflected in their respective Gospels.

When the volumes appeared the Bishop of Lausanne considered them so helpful that he ordered all the deans, parish priests, and preachers of his diocese, whether seculars or regulars, to buy copies without delay and study them sedulously. They certainly deserved the honour, and even to-day a preacher or person seeking material for mental prayer, might do worse than turn to those old pages distilled from the heart of a saint. The very way they were written would have made them precious, apart from their intrinsic excellence. After Peter's death, his friend, James Keller, testified that, though at the time he was only a young man in his twenties and not a priest, the Saint used to climb two flights of stairs to his room, leaning on a stick, to get his opinion of the " Notes." Keller protested that it would be easier and more becoming for him to go down to Father Canisius, to which Peter replied : " A useless old fellow like me has plenty of leisure, but you are very busy."[2] It was typical of him that no sooner had the two volumes appeared than he immediately set to work revising and improving their contents. He spent a year at this task but unfortunately the three volumes which resulted have never been published.

[1] Braunsberger, *Epistulae*, vol. viii, p. 334.　　[2] Braunsberger, *Epistulae*, vol. viii, p. 844.

To conclude, we may give two short extracts from the "*Notes*," taken quite at random, as an indication of their quality. The first is on the Holy Eucharist, from the commentary on the Gospel assigned for Corpus Christi :

It was not enough that Christ should for our sake be made obedient unto death, even the death of the cross. He desired further to be, in a manner of speaking, consumed utterly by us and blended intimately with us in all our infirmities. As St. Chrysostom says, it did not suffice Him to become a man and be beaten with scourges, but He must form, so to say, one kneaded mass with us, and that not by faith only but by truly making us His body. . . . Thinking of this, I will reproach myself for the strange thoughtlessness that makes so little of this profoundest and sweetest miracle and but rarely embraces it with due devotion. I will argue myself a person cold of heart who in the presence of so sublime a mystery of love in perfection is not more touched and moved to a warmth and even melting fervour of heavenly love. . . .

Would that the spirit of the Psalmist might flower again in my heart, so that I, too, might sing with joy when I approach this sacred Table : *Quam dilecta tabernacula tua, Domine virtutum !* Till then I may well be displeasing to myself and charge myself with ingratitude, seeing that I make so poor a return to the Lord who loves me so bountifully, and am not wholly concerned to give Him love for love, as the nature of love demands. . . . Therefore, when in future approaching the Holy Sacrament, I will try my best not only to have the house of my conscience clean and in order—*Domum enim Dei decet sanctitudo* —but also to foster diligently in my heart that fire of divine love which Christ came on earth to spread and desires to be kindled chiefly by Holy Communion. I will put out all fires of alien love and keep at bay the stormy gusts of passion.

But from what source is the flame of true love to spring up in my heart ? It will do so, partly from devout consideration of the wounds and afflictions of Christ crucified, and partly from the thought of His incredible generosity and charity in coming and operating in this Sacrament. He loves me with a greater love than that which I bear myself and is more glad to confer His gifts on me than I am anxious to receive them. . . . What kinder host could be imagined than He who invites all suffering souls without distinction or exception, and cries to us ceaselessly : Come unto Me all ye who labour and are heavy laden ?

What more could He have promised than His present Self, the blessed life of the soul and the body's glorious resurrection. . . ?

For the rest, among the other benefits and blessings of this Sacrament when worthily received there is a certain wonderful communication and even incorporation, not only with the Angels, but with the Angels' King. As it happens to a coal to be changed and totally converted into fire, so by a worthy reception of the Eucharist we bring about that we become changed in a wonderful manner into Christ, are rendered sharers of His divine nature, and, as Cyril of Jerusalem says, grow somehow to be the very blood brothers of Him our Head. For so great is the power of this divine food that whoever eats of it worthily is not only joined to Christ by a spiritual relationship but even made one with Him by a certain natural and most intimate incorporation. . . . What the Holy Sacrament does is to put us in Christ and Christ in us, not only refashioning our souls, but preparing our flesh for life and immortality.[1]

The second extract is from the commentary on the Gospel for the ninth Sunday after Pentecost, and deals with the subject of charity to the poor, which was always one of St. Peter's favourite themes. Here, he is meditating on the text, " Make to yourselves friends of the mammon of iniquity " :

I shall sorrow from my heart that there are to be found so many niggardly and extravagant persons of standing, nobles and rich men, who rarely give a thought to the question of helping the poor, and never take it on themselves to care for the poor seriously. Hardly one rich man in a multitude could say honestly with Job : I was an eye to the blind and a foot to the lame ; I was the father of the poor ; I broke the jaws of the wicked man and out of his teeth I took away the prey. . . . How difficult it is to persuade rich people to have full faith in these words of Christ : Give and it will be given to you ; give to the poor and you shall have treasure in Heaven. For my part, I shall feel all the greater pity for the poor and treat them with the greater humanity and kindness the more sure I am that they are often without any human comfort and assistance . . . for what says God in the Old Testament on this subject ? He says : There will not be wanting poor in the land of thy habitation ; therefore I command thee to open thy

[1] *Notae in Evangelicas Lectiones quae per totum annum Dominicis diebus in Ecclesia Catholica recitantur* (Fribourg, 1591), pp. 753–7

hand to thy needy and poor brother that liveth in the land. . . . But now how rarely do we find a Paul and Barnabas who labour for the relief of the poor, making collections and distributing the gifts with their own hands. . . . If I am poor myself and unable to give money, food, drink, and clothing to those who need them, I shall at least gladly bestow the gift of my sympathy and compassion. It is a beautiful thing, pleasant to the angels and beseeming a Christian man to be able to say with Job : I wept for him that was afflicted and my soul had compassion on the poor. . . .

In what more persuasive way could Christ have stirred us up to be merciful than by saying that whatever we gave to a poor person He counted as given to Himself? Remember the words of the Angel Raphael : Prayer is good with fasting and alms more than to lay up treasures of gold ; for alms delivereth from death, and the same is that which purgeth away sins and maketh to find mercy and life everlasting. On this St. Cyprian comments that without alms our prayers and fastings have little power with God. Many works of piety have been commended in the faithful, but no persons have been singled out by Christ so conspicuously or will be praised by Him at the Last Day so openly as those who have shown themselves kind and helpful to the poor. They are His chosen ones and He will invite them as His most intimate friends to their place on His right hand and assign to them the kingdom of His Father, prepared for their possession from all eternity. . . .[1]

St. Peter concludes each of the commentaries, of which there are seventy-three in the first volume, with three practical applications. Thus, to the section containing the second extract given above he has appended the following words : " I must petition God on behalf of eminent and wealthy men, that they may serve Him with fear, and remember that they are not the lords but the stewards and dispensers of their possessions, from whom an account will be exacted, all the stricter in proportion to the wealth conferred on them. Moreover, I will pray for rich men that it may be given to them to put away all prodigality and avarice and to help the poor and afflicted with charity unfeigned, for it is written : Give alms out of thy substance and turn not away thy face from any poor person ; so it shall come to pass that the face of the Lord will not be turned from thee. Finally, I will beg God's grace for myself that I may pass

[1] *Op. cit.*, pp. 894–9.

this time of penitence wisely and end it happily, being enabled to give God, my Judge, a good account of my vocation, and to enter by the help of the saints into their blessed company for ever." The hundreds of such subjects and suggestions for prayer which Peter thus adds to his commentaries have a special interest as showing how all-embracing was the charity that possessed him. He had indeed come unto a wide heart for there is hardly a verse in the whole breviary of human sorrows which escapes his compassion.

St. Peter's belief in books as bulwarks of the faith remained strong to the end. At some unspecified date during the last period of his life he addressed an urgent letter to the General of the Jesuits, begging that a number of competent Fathers might be appointed to write a new manual of theology in accordance with the needs of the new age. Peter the Lombard's *Book of Sentences* was out of date, he said, and needed badly to be refashioned with the Protestant controversialists in view. In October, 1583, he again appealed to the General :

As God in His goodness has supplied our Society with many fine and solidly learned theologians from various nations who could be of great use against modern heretics, I most earnestly beg and entreat your Paternity, though but your unworthy son, to have at least a few of our non-German theologians set aside for the purpose of confuting these pestilential enemies of the Catholic Church. The honour of Christ, the common good of the Church, the special position of our Society, which has never been more viciously attacked, and finally the weakness of so many people who are somewhat scandalized by our silence, would seem to demand that a chosen group of our Fathers should undertake the public championship of Catholic truth, not only with their voices, but with their pens, prudently adapting to the needs of this age the fruit of their able researches. . . . I am sure that this excellent project is in the highest degree conformable to our institute and will not be less effective as an office of charity and obedience than that which our Fathers exercise in the conversion of the heathen in India. May Our Lord Jesus direct all things to the glory of His Name.[1]

But Peter was not content merely to exhort superiors. When he considered that somebody had a talent for writing, he ran after him and begged and cajoled until a promise of a book had been obtained. It was thus

[1] Braunsberger, *Epistulae*, vol. viii, pp. 56, 176–7.

that he prevailed upon the eminent Roman theologian, Emmanuel Sa, to publish his Scriptural and other works, as in the past he had prevailed upon Salmeron and Torres. Bellarmine's *Controversies*, which were coming out at this time, gave him the profoundest satisfaction, and we find him sending affectionate greetings and congratulations to their author, whom he was not privileged to know personally. Jesuits, however, were far from being the only persons whom Peter endeavoured to enlist in the writer's brigade. " I remember hearing on one occasion when I was in Rome," he told Cardinal Sirleto, the Vatican Librarian, in March, 1584, " that your Lordship contemplated publishing certain studies you had made on many parts of the Bible. . . . If I may do so without presumption I would most earnestly beg and entreat your Lordship to urge on and complete this admirable and holy project. Christ will reward you abundantly for your labours, and you will have the deep gratitude of the Church and the rare satisfaction of knowing that you have kept your promises to Almighty God. I pray from my heart that Christ, the fount and source of all wisdom, may render us fitting and faithful workers while we live; for the night cometh when no man can work. . . ."[1] Of the same order as that letter was another which Peter addressed in September, 1586, to Melchior Zanger, Provost of the collegiate church of Ehingen on the Neckar. " The thought of you, dear Provost," he said " could not but be pleasant to me, knowing well, as I do, how valiantly you have been fighting the battles of the Church, not with your lips only but with your books against the heretics. Blessed be God who maintains and prospers such wise and brave theologians as yourself in the German mission-field. . . . I mentioned to you on one occasion that you would do a good service to German Catholics if you were to collate the various German versions of the Bible, or, at any rate, of the New Testament, and publish the results with an illustrative commentary. The attention of the reader might usefully be called to such passages as make against the heretics. This is what René Benoit of Paris has done with his annotations, so providing Catholics with arms against the heretics. I pray God Almighty to prosper your holy labours for the Church and to have you long safe and sound in His keeping."[2] The layman, Mark Welser of Augsburg, was similarly encouraged to bring out a life of St. Ulric, that City's patron. " I am very keen that you should go ahead with the work," wrote Peter, at the same time expressing his joy to hear that the Jesuits of Antwerp were planning to produce lives of the Belgian saints. It was

[1] Braunsberger, *Epistulae*, vol. viii, pp. 187–8. [2] Braunsberger, *Epistulae*, vol. viii, p. 251.

when Hussites, Lutherans, and other sectaries were raging fiercely in Bohemia. . . . I therefore beg you earnestly, Brothers, always to keep green in your hearts the memory of your patrons and friends, irrespective of whether I am alive or dead, and I cannot live much longer now in this decrepitude of old age. You will think with gratitude especially of those by whose patronage, favour, and care your illustrious college was begun and has been to this hour defended against the designs of envious enemies. Of such the chief was the House and Royal Family of Austria, than which Europe to-day knows hardly another more glorious. You and your successors must hold that Family in deep esteem as the agency by which Almighty God mercifully introduced our little Society into Austria and Bohemia, and supported it there with all kindness. May they live forever in Christ, those men who by their counsel and assistance vouchsafed to institute, promote, and fortify your college, and also those who graciously help you to-day. But you owe no less a debt of gratitude to your patrons and friends among the saints, for I am certain sure that it is their faithful intercession which has enabled you to stand hitherto and will enable you to go on. Therefore let devotion flourish among you to St. Adalbert, the first Apostle of the Bohemians, to St. Wenceslas, their King and Martyr, to St. Clement, your Patron, to St. Sigismund, and other saints whose names and merits have been celebrated for so many centuries in the Church of Prague. Believe me, many gifts of divine grace which you experience in your lives and work are the result of their intercession.

Finally, I beg of you again and again to be mindful of your vocation and to esteem greatly the Bohemian field entrusted to your care, labouring indefatigably at its cultivation with the assistance of Christ. Let your lives be irreproachable, and shining examples of holy poverty, perpetual chastity, and religious obedience. Make it your particular care that, in the matter of patience and charity, not only Catholics but enemies of the Catholic name and false brethren may learn by actual experience how the Name of Jesus is more and more glorified by you. For you ought never to forget that you were called to Bohemia, not merely to teach and preach but to bear the cross and be of service to everybody. May that fervent zeal for souls which our Father Ignatius chiefly demands wax strong in your hearts, so that endowed with it you may bend your whole minds to the task of restoring the strayed sheep of Bohemia to their fold and true Shepherd, Amen, Amen. . . .[1]

[1] Braunsberger, *Epistulae*, vol. viii, pp. 388–90.

Those letters get us so close to the heart of St. Peter's mystery that, perhaps, the reader will have patience for a third and final one, addressed to the college in Munich, probably on February 1, 1595. That college and the magnificent Jesuit church, which is the Westminster Abbey of Bavaria, had been dedicated to St. Michael at Peter's petition:

With each recurring Feast of Our Lady's Presentation, Brothers, I cannot refrain from thinking of your college because it was on that day that it began a happy existence, by the grace of God. The thought of the occasion is very pleasant to me, as I took part in the inauguration with your first Rector, Father Nicholas Delanoy, whose dear and gracious memory ought to be treasured by you. I call to mind, too, with joy, the favour and concern shown for the college by the then reigning Duke of Bavaria, Albert, and his illustrious Chancellor, Dr. Simon Eck. It was they who petitioned Rome for the first Fathers to start the college and they who laid the first foundations. I thank God with all my heart and you will join me in thanking Him for inspiring Prince Albert to show his paternal care for your college by the large sums of money and other benefits which he bestowed upon it. Once and again he built new schools with ample accommodation for the many students whom you were to instruct in letters and piety, and, in addition, found places for our Fathers as preachers and ministers of the Sacraments at the Church of St. Augustine, in order that the functions of our Society might become familiar to the people of Munich. You owe much to his father, the senior Duke William who first summoned three of our theologians to Ingolstadt and gave them good welcome; you owe still more to Albert himself as the founder of our colleges at both Ingolstadt and Munich; but you owe most of all to Albert's son and the heir of his piety and liberality, our unparalleled Maecenas, the junior Duke William, who during many years has attempted and achieved so much for the prosperity of your affairs that numbers of men have been not only astonished but in some measure scandalized by his munificence. . . .[1]

---

[1] That the Jesuits themselves did not want elaborate and grandiose structures is apparent from a decree passed at the first general congregation of the Society in the year 1558. It runs as follows: "In so far as it rests with us, let there be a limit put to our residential and college buildings. They should be convenient, healthy, and solidly constructed as residences and places wherein to carry on our work, but in all these respects we are to show ourselves mindful of poverty, and therefore buildings must be neither sumptuous nor affected." The Munich Jesuits had tried to restrain the generous impulses of Duke William but without avail. In Fribourg St. Peter was similarly perturbed about the college there. "Many people say," he wrote to Father Hoffaeus in 1596, "that in the whole of France there are no college buildings to equal ours in magnificence. We seem, therefore, to have

But let us not talk of this matter. Our business, dearest Brothers, will be to recall often the rare benefits, spiritual and temporal, which we have received from those excellent Princes, to proclaim the goodness of God as shown forth in them and in their families, and to turn our desires and efforts with strenuous will to the task of satisfying their holy expectations, especially by doing all in our power for the Church in Bavaria. We who know the kindness and generosity of those great men must surely stint nothing and set no limit to our exertions for the religious welfare of their country. . . . Blessed be the Author of all good who has given me, the oldest among you now, not only to see but in a manner to taste the sweet fruits which you gather every year in the garden of Munich. You have shown yourselves true instruments of salvation to multitudes of men. May Christ, the prince of benefactors, confirm what He has begun in you and increase in your hearts the genuine spirit of our Society, so that you may continue to promote, not your own advantage, but the common good of souls in Bavaria, especially the souls of the priests and people of Munich. . . . You have the golden law of charity which Christ commended dearly and St. Paul often inculcated. So practise it in Munich and the rest of Bavaria that you may win an ever increasing number of souls for the living God. . . .[1]

About a year after the date of those letters, when he was so feeble that he could scarcely walk, St. Peter took up his pen to address similar affectionate farewells to the colleges of Innsbruck and Fribourg. He begged the Innsbruck men never to forget their obligations to Emperor Ferdinand and his daughters, for whom it was their duty of gratitude to be diligent intercessors before God. " You have a grand field for your labours in Tirol," he concluded. " Give it your love gladly, working for the advancement of its people and inspiring them with desire for the better gifts by your word and example. . . . Good-bye in Christ, dearest Fathers and Brothers, and keep always before you the ideal of your great vocation so that you may be poor men as you profess, simple in obedience, fervent in spirit, and aflame with zeal to win and nurture for Christ a multitude of souls."

declined somewhat in this matter from the humble and holy poverty which we vowed." He objected in particular to windows with armorial bearings which various noble families were having put up. " It seems to me that we shall thus lose something of our freedom and be reduced to a sort of servitude towards the donors, whose children and heirs will want to come and inspect their escutcheons at the college of the Jesuits." Braunsberger, *Epistulae*, vol. viii, pp. 428–9. Peter's ideas of magnificence were rather restricted if he considered that the Fribourg College displayed it. It is, in fact, a very plain, unpretentious building, but constructed as solidly as a fortress.

[1] Braunsberger *Epistulae*, vol. viii, pp. 385–7.

To the Fribourg Fathers Peter offered a touching apology for his seclusion in their midst. It was not his will but his need that had made him withdraw " to pack up his baggage for the end of the pilgrimage." As for his work in Fribourg, he would " lovingly admonish and entreat them to make up by their holy labours for what he had neglected to do, accommodating themselves to all men by a vigilant charity." They must ever remember their debt to Bishop Bonomio, hold the clergy and Senate of Fribourg in deep esteem, and show by deeds rather than words that they are conscious of their obligations to their benefactors. " If I die a member of your community," he concluded, " I beg you, after the burial of my perishable body, to remember me faithfully before God, that of His mercy I may be rendered spotless for the fellowship of His chosen priests and be able to pray for you, your college, and town in the land of the living. *Fiat, fiat.*"[1]

In January, 1583, as on many other occasions in the past, St. Peter, at his General's request, composed a long memorandum dealing with the duties of Jesuits. One section of this document entitled, " Our duty of helping heretics, especially the heretics of Germany," runs to more than six hundred words ; and another, dealing with the education of students at the German College, Rome, occupies nearly seven full pages of Braunsberger. Peter had that College, which was the chief hope for the future of the faith in Germany, always in mind and wrote often to encourage its staff and alumni. How they, in turn, regarded him is well shown by the following letter which the Rector addressed to him on May 21, 1594 :

Having received your Reverence's letter, full of love and charity for our college, I made it my first business to hand it to one of the students that he might read it aloud to the others. It made the profoundest impression on all to hear of your fraternal charity towards them, of the misfortunes of Germany, of the present dangers that threaten to destroy that country unless God in His mercy intervenes, and, finally, of your Reverence's devout and efficacious suggestions as to the manner of placating God's anger and imploring His divine assistance. For myself, I must confess that nothing would please me more than to be honoured more frequently with such fruits of your charity. As a matter of fact, this our college, which with entire justice reverences you as its second founder, values your salutary exhortations and counsels with the regard due to the best of fathers, whose authority,

[1] Braunsberger, *Epistulae*, vol. viii, pp. 412-4, 442-3.

made venerable by grey hairs, is the highest we know. It would indeed be a great thing for these young men of Germany if they could look upon your face and hear the very tones of your voice. . . . Your Reverence can understand my desire for this from what I told you when thanking you for your former services to us, though I know well that it is not so much thanks as some tangible results of your counsels which you eagerly await. . . . It will be my care, and I shall certainly do my very best, to see that these results are forthcoming. . . . May God Almighty, the Lord of the world, mercifully hear our prayers and, appeased by them, establish a Christendóm wherein all may acknowledge Him for their King. . . .[1]

Father Aquaviva, who was one of the greatest and wisest men that the Society of Jesus has produced, loved and venerated St. Peter to the extent of being eager to do anything for him. " If ever your Reverence should judge anything to be necessary for your consolation," he wrote immediately after becoming General, " you will confer a favour on me by letting me know about it with all confidence and freedom. It will always give me pleasure to gratify you and I shall esteem it as but your just due for the labours which you have sustained in the service of Christ and of our Society." The correspondence between the two men was very frequent and marked on both sides by a note of deep affection which is extremely rare in such official documents. The General's eagerness for the prayers of " that most dear and good old man, Father Canisius," is touching in its insistence, while Peter's absolute trust in his superior, his reference to him of every difficulty that arose, and the confiding way in which he laid before him all the cherished hopes and ambitions of his heart for the Church and the Society of Jesus are radiant with the white simplicity of childhood.

Another great correspondent with the Saint was Bishop Bonomio, who loved him with all his heart. When appointed nuncio to the Emperor Rudolph II in 1581 the Bishop made the journey to Court through Lucerne, which was entirely out of his way, partly on the chance that he might see Peter there. " Oh if I could only get a glimpse of you," he wrote, " I should consider myself almost in Heaven and believe the happiness and success of my journey and mission secure. . . . *Vale mi Pater humanissime ac deliciae meae in Domino.*" He liked to regale Peter with whatever items of news came to his knowledge, such as that the Lutherans of Tübingen

---

[1] Braunsberger, *Epistulae*, vol. viii, pp. 366–7.

had endeavoured in quite the modern fashion to win the benediction of the orthodox Patriarch of Constantinople for the *Confessio Augustana*, only to receive from his Beatitude a letter and vituperative treatise, damning the Confession in the heartiest terms. Peter in turn reported that an earthquake had destroyed two villages in Vaud, killing 122 people and inspiring the Calvinists of Geneva with such terror that they kept a black fast even on Easter Sunday. The Prince-Bishop of Basle was another of Peter's devotees. "If you will pay me a visit here," he wrote from his castle at Porrentruy in March, 1582, "I shall be delighted to send you horses and all else that may be required for the comfort of your journey." When in 1582 Pope Gregory XIII appointed St. Charles Borromeo his Visitor and Delegate to Switzerland, that great reformer wrote to Peter at once for information and advice about Swiss ecclesiastical affairs. The long answer was typical in its modesty and prudence, its praise of Bonomio, Schneuwly, and other good men, and its urgent pleas for the much-harassed Bishops of Lausanne and Sitten whose cause Peter had made his own. It was like him to put in a plea also for persons who desired to be reconciled to the Church, that their return might be made easy, for he was aware that Borromeo tended to be a very stern and exacting judge in these matters. St. Charles then wrote requesting Peter to join him at Bellinzona or Roveredo, but the Jesuit Provincial intervened, saying that such a journey in the depths of winter would be too dangerous for an old, infirm man like Father Canisius. "The people of Fribourg hold him dear," he added, "and would take grievous offence if his health were to be imperilled." Peter himself was glad to escape going. "I prefer to be out of Cardinal Borromeo's company rather than in it," he told Aquaviva, "because I consider him too rigorous a physician for the spiritually weak and delicate Swiss."[1]

Another great contemporary Saint besides Charles Borromeo who held Peter in veneration was Francis de Sales. Once, while on his famous mission in Chablais, Francis had an argument about free will with a Calvinist and quoted in its favour the words of God to Cain as given in the Vulgate version of the Book of Genesis: "If thou do well, shalt thou not receive? but if ill, shall not sin forthwith be present at the door? But the lust thereof shall be under thee and thou shalt have dominion over it." The Calvinist retorted that this text was no good as an argument because the Hebrew pronouns corresponding to "thereof" and "it" are masculine and so could not refer to the word "sin" which in Hebrew

[1] Braunsberger, *Epistulae*, vol. viii, pp. 170–5, 177, 201.

is feminine. Worsted for the moment, St. Francis looked up the treatise on free will in St. Robert Bellarmine's *Controversies* for a solution of the difficulty but found that, though the text was there, St. Robert, cautious man, had left the puzzle of the pronouns severely alone.[1] This non-committal attitude had the interesting consequence of making one Doctor of the Church appeal to a second Doctor of the Church to supply the deficiency of a third Doctor of the Church, as may be seen from the following letter of St. Francis to St. Peter Canisius :

Thonon, July 21, 1595.

Most Esteemed Father,

As you know so well, the splendour of virtue is a thing that no distance can dim and that renders those clothed in its brightness conspicuous and lovely to all who honour so much as its name. That is why I, an insignificant and obscure nonentity, think that I need not plead excuses for venturing to write to you. For you are not unknown and obscure ; you, if I may humbly say so, who have found your way to the hearts of all Christ's faithful on account of so many deeds and words and writings on Christ's behalf. It is no wonder that you who have written so often to Christians of every condition should receive letters from many people on the sole score of their Christian profession. Since, then, I am not far away from you, separated, I understand, only by the Lake of Geneva, I thought I should do something not unpleasing to you and of immense future utility to myself if I were to approach you through the post, as I cannot do so in the flesh, for the purpose of putting questions to you from time to time about theological matters and difficulties and of receiving an occasional letter of instruction from you, according to your neighbourly charity. . . .

Here I am now in my ninth month among the heretics, having been able in that time to gather only eight ears of corn for the Lord's granary, out of such a huge crop. . . . Among them is Peter Poncet, an erudite lawyer who on the subject of heresy is far more learned even than the Calvinist minister of the place. When I observed in our talks that this man was somewhat influenced by the authority of the ancient writers I handed him your Catechism, with the opinions of the Fathers given in full in it by Busaeus. The perusal of this work led him from his error into the well-worn highway of the Ancient

[1] The text is a famous one for its difficulty and has been interpreted in a variety of conflicting ways. Both the Latin Vulgate rendering and that of the Protestant Revised Version are faulty. The text in its original Hebrew would seem to have no bearing at all on the problem of free will.

Church and at last he made his submission. For this favour, too, both he and I owe you our deepest gratitude.

A short time ago, when I was urging as an argument for free will that text of Genesis iv., 'The lust thereof shall be under thee and thou shalt have dominion over it,' Poncet objected out of Calvin that the pronouns referred to Abel and not to the word 'sin,' making the sense be 'thou shalt have dominion over thy brother,' not over sin. The reason he gave, also on Calvin's authority, was that the pronouns are masculine in the Hebrew text, whereas the word sin is feminine. I was not able to answer this difficulty, not even with the assistance of Bellarmine's illustrious *Controversies,* for when I looked them up I found that he did not touch at all on the enigma of masculine relatives going with a feminine noun. . . .

As a mere unlearned and inexperienced tyro in these matters I beg for an interpretation of the Hebrew phrase from a most skilled and kindly master, basing my hopes on your readiness to help all your neighbours. For the rest, may God Almighty long preserve your venerable old age for His Church, and do you, I pray, hold me for your most devoted humble servant and son in Christ, as I became some while ago to Father Antonio Possevino, of your Society,

Your servant in all humility,

FRANCIS DE SALES.

Among men of lesser eminence who loved St. Peter none showed their affection more plainly than the good people of Fribourg. In 1581 their youthful parish priest, Sebastian Werro, determined to make a pilgrimage to Jerusalem. With a letter from Peter as his passport, he went first to Rome whence he wrote to tell the Saint that he had seen the Pope one summer evening at Frascati and how, on his beginning to supplicate for a reform of the Calendar, His Holiness cut him short with the deadly question: "Pray, sir, are you a mathematician?" When he embarked at Venice he carried with him a little book of meditations recommended by St. Peter to cheer him up "should the hurricanes and tempests last too long." It was this very likeable young man who wrote as follows to Bishop Bonomio in June, 1584, on hearing that Peter had been summoned to a meeting of the Jesuits in Augsburg: "That excellent, saintly man, the venerable priest of Christ, Father Canisius, is to go to the congregation of his Society at Augsburg. Both his Rector and Provincial have guaranteed that he will return, but, nevertheless, I am afraid lest he may be called away from us altogether. If this man of God does not come back, it is all over with us. I, therefore, have recourse to your Lordship and implore you with every prayer of my heart that, in addition to your former services, you would secure the return of Canisius to us by dint of your letters."[1] Bonomio thereupon addressed himself to the papal Secretary of State and further promised Provost Schneuwly, who also was anxious, that he would "work with all his might" for the restoration of Father Canisius to Fribourg.

In Augsburg the Saint was welcomed with enthusiasm by his old friends, particularly by Sybil Fugger, who received him, according to a witness of the scene, "*incredibili gaudio et veneratione.*" To a father at the Congregation Bishop Bonomio wrote from the Emperor's Court : "If I too could be at your meeting, especially in order to embrace my most beloved companion, Father Peter Canisius, how much I should rejoice and be heartily refreshed in the Lord!"[2] But perhaps the most convincing mark of esteem was shown by the Fribourg Senators, for they paid all the expenses of Peter's journey.

Early in 1585 Father Aquaviva decided, owing to the ruinous state of St. Peter's health, that he should leave Fribourg for some college in Germany where he might enjoy greater comfort and peace. To this the German Provincial, Father Bader, replied that a change of scene would not be of much avail, because Peter's real trouble was an inability to stop working, and he would probably find more temptations that way in Germany than in Switzerland. Besides, the Fribourg people would intensely resent his removal. Still unconvinced, Aquaviva answered that, whatever the obstacles, he "considered some peace and a more comfortable place of abode entirely due to the good old man." As for the Fribourgeois, if the state of Peter's health were explained to them they would not oppose his departure. Bader thereupon did his best to arrange matters, with the results detailed in the following letter to the General :

Concerning the recall of Father Canisius, I have spoken to himself, to the other Fathers at Fribourg, and also in veiled terms to some externs. Our men deprecated his recall much more vehemently than he entreated for it, and the others not of the Society used their prayers almost like weapons in their intense opposition to it. The common argument was that the Senate, people, and clergy of Fribourg would be most seriously offended, seeing that all of them hold him to be

[1] Braunsberger, *Epistulae*, vol. viii, p. 642.   [2] Braunsberger, *Epistulae*, vol. viii, p. 647.

the stoutest bulwark and finest ornament of their republic, on account of his repute for holiness and his general celebrity *secundum Deum*. Indeed, they openly boast of his presence among them before both Catholics and heretics. Finally, all are of opinion that his removal would mean great detriment to the college, as far as its new fabric is concerned.

It was not possible to get the Father to plead his own cause with externs. He desired that I should allege some not quite solid nor valid reasons, as, for instance, that he had been asked for by the Duke of Bavaria, or that he had some writing to do and required access to books. Now, everybody knows very well that nothing is so detrimental to his health as unremitting study, and from that he will be all the less able to abstain if he has plenty of good books.

As a last resource he thought that I might secure his release without difficulty if I were to promise his reappearance after a year, but this course also seemed rather unsafe. Eventually, he gave up. I have left instructions that great care is to be taken of him, but the good Father is too hard on himself and does not easily acquiesce in measures for his comfort, because of some scruples or other. However, I hope he will do something in the matter.[1]

In 1587 Peter once again received the call to a provincial congregation of his brethren in Augsburg and answered it faithfully, though, in his Rector's words " quite worn out with age and hard work." A Fribourg nobleman gave him a horse for the journey, but he was able to achieve only half of it, as far as the Swiss Baden, when increasing weakness obliged him to turn back. " It became plain to me," he said with a smile, " that St. Nicholas would not let me leave the town of his patronage, and I shall end my days in Fribourg." Still, ruined health did not prevent him from preaching an eloquent panegyric of Bishop Bonomio, who had died in Belgium earlier in the year, nor did it stop the flow of his converts, who sometimes came to him from very distant places. Among them in 1587 was the junior Johann Pistorius, distinguished son of a famous father, who held the post of privy councillor to the Margrave of Baden and afterwards brought that nobleman into the Church, with results to be seen in the Catholicity of Baden at the present day.[2] Two years later an eminent Calvinist arrived from Heidelberg, " attracted," as the record puts it, " by the wide fame of Reverend Father Canisius." So grateful

[1] Braunsberger, *Epistulae*, vol. viii, pp. 677–8.
[2] Braunsberger, *Epistulae*, vol. viii, pp. 299, 764–6.

was this man for his conversion that he undertook a pilgrimage to Compostella on Peter's behalf.[1] Before his death the good old man was being invoked as a saint by people who were ill or in danger. A story is told, for instance, of a poor, possessed woman who wrote to him from Straubing, imploring him to deliver her. When he had read the letter he wept and said with a deep sigh : " Unhappy me, who do they think I am ? " Then, telling the lay brother who looked after him that he wanted no dinner until he had settled this affair, " he took up his pen and for about two hours continued to put in writing whatever suggestions he thought might help the good woman."[2]

As the Saint's long earthly pilgrimage drew to a close his concern for the interests of the Church seemed ever to widen and deepen. " It can truly be said of him," wrote a non-Jesuit who knew him well, " that he was never less at leisure than when at leisure, never less alone than when alone, and never less free from care than when entirely unencumbered, for it was then that thought for the Church's welfare absorbed him." His last letters are full of anxious references to the religious wars in France, to the Cologne upheaval, engineered, alas, by the recreant nephew of his old friend, Cardinal Truchsess, to the agony of the Netherlands under Calvinist oppression. As late as 1595, just two years before Peter's death, we find Hoffaeus reporting to Aquaviva that " Father Canisius does not cease to plan various works of usefulness for the Church in Germany with a devotion greater than his physical strength will support." That was Peter all over, the Peter whose chief failing consisted in an inability to rest. Though first cousin to a dozen virtues this hunger for activity was still a fault because it gave other good men concern, and the finer attitude is that indicated by the simple lines of resignation :

I am not eager, bold,
Or strong—all that is past.
I am ready *not* to do,
At last, at last!

It took many hard blows of disease and pain to render Peter Canisius ready not to do, but eventually that grace also was given him, though he tried to stave off the hour of acquiescence by means of a broom with which he used to make assaults on the dust of the College corridors. Provost Werro, who related this detail, goes on to tell of seeing the old Saint in the scullery, helping " *trementibus manibus*," with the washing-up.

[1] Braunsberger, *Epistulae*, vol. viii, pp. 800, 814.
[2] Braunsberger, *Epistulae*, vol. viii, pp. 469, 853.

Very likely he was more of a hindrance than a help, but quite certainly he went to the work for no motive of ostentation or even edification. He merely could not see why he should be different from the other Fathers who were expected to do a certain amount of house work each week.[1]

An interesting glimpse of him at this final stage is afforded by an outside witness, the French poet and historian, Pierre Matthieu, who enjoyed some renown under Henri IV. In his posthumously published *Histoire de France* this man wrote of St. Peter :

Je le vis en l'an 1594 à Fribourg en Suisse, où je passois allant à une diète pour les affaires qui entreront en leur temps dans cette Histoire. Il estoit lors aagé de plus de quatre-vings ans[2] et neantmoins je le trouvé sur les livres, et le vis dans les actions communes aux plus jeunes Religieux, admiré le grand respect qu'il portoit à un jeune homme qui estoit Recteur du College, et m'estonnois comme un homme de cet aage, qui avoit tant de pouvoir aupres de l'Empereur Ferdinand, s'abbaissoit si fort.

The new buildings of the Fribourg college became ready for habitation in 1596, and the Jesuits staged joyous ceremonies which were attended by all the important people of the town to celebrate their inauguration. After High Mass, " symphonica hilaritate rite confecto," St. Peter tottered on to the sanctuary of the provisional church with the aid of his stick. There was hardly anything of him left, a bare wisp of the man that he had been, and his voice rose scarcely above a whisper as he explained what Jesuits were made for, " to teach the young, to preach to the people, to absolve sinners in the confessional, to help the sick, to comfort the sorrowful, to strengthen the dying, to bring those lost in heresy back to the way of truth." It was a summer's day and a feast of Our Lady when thus he spoke in public for the last time on earth. Of his many good-byes we need give in this place only the one addressed to Aquaviva in the shaky hand of old age :

The eternal peace of Jesus Christ be with us, Very Reverend Father. Among the consolations which support a broken old man such as I am, the greatest is that I should feel at perfect peace with the superiors whom God has placed over me as His substitutes in this Society. Therefore I who long ago in 1549 made my profession at Rome to our Father

---

[1] Braunsberger, *Epistulae*, vol. viii, p. 883.
[2] Matthieu should have said that he *looked* over eighty. He was in fact only seventy-three.

Ignatius of holy memory would like now in my seventy-fifth year, when I am useless for any good work, to set down in this letter such points as seem calculated to render me truly and solidly at peace with your Paternity, the high priest of our institute. First then, on my knees in spirit and in very deed I humbly beg to be forgiven all my secret and open offences, not only against Almighty God but against you, the fifth Vicar of Christ our Redeemer in the government of this Society, to which sublime vocation I was called in my unworthiness. And I offended, alas, very often and very much, doing badly the duties given me years ago, especially when among our professed Fathers I was a provincial, preacher, and writer deserving of blame on many counts.

I also confess my fault that I have lived in colleges like a non-professed father,[1] receiving, through the indulgence of superiors, many comforts that ill became a religious man vowed to poverty. When at length set free from duties proper to our Society, I took to having my meals in my room and to saying Mass in a private chapel, and now I render no brotherly assistance to anybody in the house or outside it. And so I am become for all to see a useless, fruitless sluggard, undeserving of the bread which I eat and the kindness which my brethren show me. I know that these favours have been conferred upon a sick old man in order to lighten the burden of his years, but still I have reason to grieve and to beg forgiveness, Reverend Father, seeing that I have not used such privileges more carefully and gratefully for the glory of God and the salvation of my soul. . . . I therefore beg your Paternity with all my heart sometimes to commend me, your worthless, unprofitable son, to God in your Mass, to make me a sharer of the privileges and spiritual graces which you have received from the Holy See for the consolation of your sons, and finally to enjoin on me a penance that I may obtain in fuller measure the grace of your fatherly benediction.

Inutilis filius, Petrus Canisius.[2]

At last, in 1597, there came a time when St. Peter had to keep to his room altogether. The lay brother who looked after him during the nine months before he died, a man of good education named Sebastian Strang, recorded that " there was hardly anything left of him except skin and bone, and he could not remain long in any position, lying or sitting, without

---

[1] Colleges might be endowed and have fixed revenues, but by the Jesuit constitutions professed Fathers were required to live in unendowed houses on the charity of the faithful.
[2] Braunsberger, *Epistulae*, vol. viii, pp. 431–2.

torture." To his other ailments the dreadful one of dropsy was added towards the end and caused him intolerable suffering. But he only made a joke of it, and when his Rector asked him one day how he felt the answer was, "Very fat, Father, thanks be to God!" Hardly a word would he utter but there must be a *Deo Gratias* attached to it, for thankfulness had become a second nature to him. As has been abundantly shown in the preceding pages, he never forgot any service, however small, done to himself or to his order, and continually impressed upon his brethren their duty to pray earnestly for all benefactors. The first chapter of a long instruction which he wrote for some nuns in Hall, near Innsbruck, is devoted entirely to the subject of *Danksagung*—the returning of thanks—and he begs the good ladies in his quaint, attractive old German to walk always " auf den schenen rightigen weg der danckbarkhait"—along the beautiful straight highway of gratitude.

The right use of illness was a thing much insisted on by St. Ignatius Loyola, " seeing," as he said, " that it is no less a gift of God than health." But it is the hardest thing in the world to use rightly, and for that reason the last months of martyrdom in St. Peter's life have a particular nobility. " He was always contented," wrote his nurse, " no matter what was done with him . . . nor would he ask for anything to relieve his pain, being perfectly satisfied with whatever was given him." Indeed, contentment was his habitual attitude, whether sick or well. When, after his death, Father James Keller was required to report on what he had observed in him during the period 1590–1594, the worthy man wrote : " I can say nothing about his patience in time of trouble because he never seemed to have any troubles, so well did he accommodate himself to all persons and circumstances." Brother Strang was so conscious of having a saint in his charge that he used even to try experiments to see how the old man would react. One very cold day his patient asked him to light the stove near his room. " I pretended to carry out his wishes," the Brother recorded, " and made a good deal of noise so that he might hear me and think I was doing as he wanted, but I did not light the wood which I had put into the stove. The Father waited a while for the heat to come through to him. When it failed he did not show the least trace of annoyance, but crept quietly back to bed, blessing God and thanking me for my services." On another occasion Strang refused point blank to do some little thing that his patient wanted, with the same misguided idea of seeing what would happen. " So sweetly and patiently did he answer me," says the experimentalist, " that I was pierced to the heart and had to leave the room, all shaken with contrition." Strang records, too, that during the whole of his long illness St. Peter never once gave him an order, but always used a kind of prayer to him when he needed to have something done. Summing up the conduct of his patient throughout, he says that " he allowed himself to be treated after the way of a little child "—*se instar infantis tractari permittebat.*

During the afternoon of December 20, 1597, the Brother found Father Canisius kneeling on the floor by his bed, absorbed in prayer. When he rose he was seized with a violent fit of trembling which so alarmed Strang that he rushed off to summon the Rector and various members of the community. But the paroxysm passed away, and Peter would not allow his good nurse to watch with him during the night. By the grace of God, he said, he would live it through. At midnight the anxious Brother visited him again, only to be entreated to return and take his rest. Strang noticed the same considerateness in all his patient's dealings with himself and other men, recording, for instance, that the Saint would hardly ever " permit anything special in the way of food to be brought to him, for fear of being troublesome to the cook."

At daybreak of December 21st, the Rector brought the dying man Holy Communion, which he received with the utmost devotion, repeating over and over again, *Benedictus Deus, Deus, Deus.* The mere sound of God's name seemed to give him rapture. Then for an hour he read slowly a series of prayers and aspirations which he had copied into a notebook long before. He could do this though the writing was blurred and worn by much thumbing because his eyes retained their keenness and lustre up to the end. It is also recorded that his abundant dark hair had hardly a streak of grey in it at the time of his death. About three o'clock in the afternoon of the same day, December 21st, the Rector anointed him. The little room was full of Jesuits and other visitors, but save for the voice of the Church helping her great helper in his agony, an extraordinary stillness pervaded it. " In one hand," reported the Rector, " he clasped his crucifix, and in the other the blessed candle which I assisted him to support. We could not tell the exact moment of his death, but we think it was when the words of the Litany, *Ut nobis indulgeas, Te rogamus audi nos,* were being pronounced. There was no sign of death nor motion of any kind."[1]

The quietude of St. Peter's end which was so perfectly in keeping with his simple, undemonstrative character disinclines one to embark

---

[1] Strang's evidence and the other references for the account given here of St. Peter's last illness are supplied in full by Braunsberger, *Epistulae,* vol. viii, pp. 892–943.

on any long account of his posthumous glory or of the wonders attributed to his intercession. In any case he was no thaumaturge, either during life or after death, and he had to wait 267 years before he was even beatified. However, as Louis Veuillot observed on his visit to Fribourg in 1838, the good people there and multitudes elsewhere had anticipated the judgment of Rome from the day that Peter died. Against the wishes of his brethren, whose tradition in these matters is one of the utmost simplicity, he was given a public funeral and laid to rest before the high altar of the grand old Church of St. Nicholas. Only with the greatest difficulty did the Jesuits succeed in recovering his relics for their own Church of St. Michael when it was completed a quarter of a century later. On May 21, 1925, Pope Pius XI canonized him and declared him a Doctor of the Catholic Church—328 years after his death. A believer in God knows that these delays are not fortuitous. He glorifies His Saints *in tempore opportuno*. "All peoples," said the Pope addressing the German pilgrims in Rome for St. Peter's canonization, "all peoples who to-day live impoverished and unhappy lives can perceive the holy love and true peace of this genuinely international Saint. . . . He looks down on them all to-day and calls them into a fellowship of peace." Peter's shrine is very near Geneva. If only the League of Nations desired to have a patron in Heaven what a perfect one he would make!

EPILOGUE

It is to be feared that the mass of details given in the foregoing pages may have sadly blurred the image of the man whom the book was intended to portray. Let us see, then, if we cannot get him a little better into focus, briefly and without repetition. First of all it is safe to say that Peter Canisius was not a natural genius as that word is commonly understood. He seems to have possessed only moderate powers as a thinker, and certainly he could not for a moment be matched with such giants of intellect as St. Augustine and St. Thomas Aquinas. True, he wrote one book which fell little, if at all, short of being a masterpiece, but it was a masterpiece for its age, and not for all ages like the *De Civitate Dei* and the *Summa contra Gentiles*. It would probably be no exaggeration to say that St. Peter never wrote a truly memorable sentence in his life, that he was entirely incapable of those winged words which so often fell from Augustine's magical pen. Peter read very widely in many fields. It is recorded that he used to re-read Cicero's entire works every year. But he never became either a genuine stylist or an authentic scholar because he lacked by nature the intuitive flair and vision that are required for the making of such people. Even in the practical sphere where he certainly achieved marvels he was not an expert and owed his successes to something other than a genius for negotiation. Yet in spite of all these limitations, in spite of the fact that whatever cross-section of him we take we come upon nothing but what might be called sublime mediocrity, he was unquestionably a very great man. It was the integrity of his character that made him such, marshalling his average powers and giving them a glow and forcefulness utterly beyond their inherent worth. In this he resembled another bourgeois saint of average endowment, Teresa of the Child Jesus, who died almost exactly three centuries later than he, and attained canonization three days before him.

Though so far apart in time and so completely dissimilar in their careers, Peter and Teresa were kindred souls who reached the heights by the same paradoxical road of simplicity. Both became great because they remained obstinately small and kept in their dealings with God the stark sincerity and realism of childhood. When one reflects on the life and work of St. Peter, the picture of a child at play in the greatest of modern ballads comes easily to mind :

Through the long infant hours like days
He built one tower in vain—
Piled up small stones to make a town,
And evermore the stones fell down,
And he piled them up again.

A whole book could be written about St. Peter's vain efforts to make a town, that Heavenly Jerusalem which he tried so hard to build on Germany's waste-land. In one sense his life was full of frustration, yet losing so many causes which he cherished he never lost heart, and worked away for them to the end with almost ferocious resolution. It was the child's heart in him that made such stability possible, a heart too dependent on God to be affected by the raiding moods of dejection which often assailed him. Towards the end of his life, in a long memorial to Aquaviva of which mention has already been made, he suggested some principles for the guidance of Jesuits destined to work among non-Catholic populations. They were as follows :

Let this be the beginning of all attempts at healing the evil of heresy, whether in Germany or elsewhere, that our men beware of the spirit of fear and diffidence which insinuates that their work for heretics must be fruitless and as vain as trying to make a white man of an Ethiopian. For the Apostle tells us that he that plougheth should plough in hope, and he that thresheth, in hope to receive fruit, and we must therefore not be broken by any labour which the love of Christ, the good of our neighbour, and our vow of obedience prompt us to undertake. As for the secrets of God's wrath and judgments, whether with regard to individual men or to whole nations, let those scrutinize them who will. . . . We shall rather imitate the prudent and skilful physician who, called to attend his friend in serious illness, carefully applies all the remedies of his science, and day and night watches over the patient; but for the outcome, leaves it to God, whose help he implores while diligently co-operating with Him. . . . Then again, in order that we may stand on firm ground in our dealings with heretics we must not only put away all feelings of pusillanimity and discouragement but conceive a tremendous confidence in the immense goodness of God, who even from the stones raiseth up children to Abraham. . . . especially when with Abraham, against hope we believe in hope and magnanimously depend upon the Author of all grace. Supported, then, by this hope and trust, let us commit the issue to God, and not make so much account of the arguments of human reasoning as ever to abandon our efforts and diligence by prayer, exhortation and persuasion. Should our success be small and obstacles plentiful, we can think that for us, too, was it said : Be patient, brethren ; behold the husbandman waiteth for the precious fruit of the earth, patiently bearing till he receive the early and the latter rain. . . .[1]

The courage evident in those unpretentious lines came from St. Peter's habit of prayer. Brother Strang testified that during his last illness he used to spend seven hours each day in prayer, " pleading with God not only for himself but for every class and condition of mankind." Those seven hours, four in the morning and three at night, were not merely a practice of old age but the custom of his whole life. It was possible because he used to rise daily at four o'clock. People loved to be present at his Mass, even though he took an hour to say it in his devotion and scrupulous care for the smallest rubrics. One witness testifies that " he pronounced the words almost with an actor's precision," and another tells how he was so affected by the tones of Peter's voice while saying Mass that " he exulted for six whole weeks " after once hearing him.

His prayer, like everything else in him, was characterized by the utmost simplicity. He never in his life went into an ecstasy and the documents are silent about any profound mystical experiences. But they do tell us that he loved such humble devotions as the Rosary and the Little Hours of the Blessed Virgin. After the martyrdom of Blessed Edmund Campion at Tyburn in 1581, a friend in Rome procured his beads for St. Peter and on them he probably said his Rosary during his last years on earth. He used to ' go the round ' of his beads several times a day. Though simple in the sense that it bore no discernible marks of higher contemplation, Peter's conception of prayer was exceedingly wide. Indeed, everything with him turned naturally to prayer, even such a common act as taking a mouthful of food. Brother Strang noticed that he had some little whispered liturgy of praise and gratitude, not only for his whole meal but for each time that he raised his fork, which, incidentally, was not very often as " he never ate more than a quarter of an ordinary man's share."[2]

[1] Braunsberger, *Epistulae*, vol. viii, pp. 128–9.   [2] Braunsberger, *Epistulae*, vol. viii, p. 920.

Peter's overwhelming personal love for Christ Our Lord needs no further proving. It was the mainspring of all his activities, and as evidence of it his letters can stand comparison with those of St. Paul. A man could not talk with him for five minutes without Christ coming into the conversation. He looked out on the world through the eyes of Christ and assessed the worth of everything by Christ's standards. If we adapted a famous expression and wrote, " Cor Christi, cor Petri," we should be doing no violence to the truth. " Would that thou alone, good Jesus, sweet Master, mightest possess my heart," he used to pray. " O Thou, my rest, my life, and my salvation, would that I might seek Thee only, and know no influence but Thine, and cling to Thee indissolubly. For what need I besides Thee, and what good is anything to me without Thee ? When shall I see Thee, my Eternal Light and Enlightenment ? When shall I be with Thee, my Peace and my Refreshment ? When will this world be silent for me and its changefulness end, O my Refuge and Joy and Desire ? "[1]

All the actions of Peter's day were directly linked up with the labours and sufferings of Christ. Thus " at the sound of the clock striking and at the beginning of any work," he used to say this prayer : " I praise and glorify Thee, sweetest and kindest Heart of Jesus, in and for all the good things which Thy most glorious Divinity and most blessed Humanity have wrought in us through the noblest instrument of Thy Heart, and will continue to bring about in us for ever and ever." So, too, each ' Hour ' of his office was put into relation with some aspect of Christ's sufferings, as, for instance, None, " in honour of Christ dying for thee on the Cross, that His loving death may become so sweet in thy heart as to render all else displeasing and of no account " ; or Vespers, " in memory and praise of Christ taken down from the Cross, when with joy it will be recalled by thee how after death and the toils of this life thou wilt rest happily in sinu Domini."

In the manuscript prayer-book which the Saint had put together for his private use and clasped as he lay dying, the following Morning Prayer of Salutation to the Heart of Christ is to be found :

I praise, bless, glorify, and salute the most sweet and bountiful Heart of Jesus Christ, my ever faithful Lover. I thank Thee for the constant care wherewith Thou didst protect me last night and didst offer to God the Father on my behalf praise, gratitude, and all duties

---

[1] This prayer, of which only a part has been reproduced, is from the Expositio Virtutum in the documents relative to Peter's beatification.

IESVS CHRISTVS α et ω, principium et finis, I
filius Dei et hominis, Salvator mundi, Rex coeli et terrae, pri=
mogenitus omnium creaturarum, Dominus dominantium, Rex Regum,
Deus deorum, Princeps pacis, Mediator Dei et hominum, caput Ecclesiae,
Corona Sanctorum omnium, Agnus Dei, Pastor bonus, Propitiatio pro peccatis
Summus Pontifex, Fons sapientiae. Propheta magnus ac potens in opere et serm[one]
Mors mortis. Domitor inferni, Victor Sathanae, Antiquator Iudaismi, des:
tructor Ethnicismi, Interfector Antichristi, Iudex victorum & mortu:
orum, Speciosus forma prae filiis hominum, in cuius vultu desi:
derant angeli prospicere, Via veritas et vita, Iustitia, Re:
demptio, Resurrectio, Consolatio, gaudium et voluptas
nostra, Legifer noster, doctor noster, Refrigerium
animarum nostrarum, Sanctus Sanctorum. Divus
Divorum, Doctor Doctorum. Secundus Adam, La:
pis angularis, Supremus apex surri
ædificii, Cardo virtutum, pulchritudo rerum,
Reparator salutis æternæ, Monarcha visibilium et
invisibilium, quem adorant angeli, tremunt Diaboli,
prædicant sancti, horrent impii, Lex confitetur, Prophetæ
nuntiant, Apostoli demonstrant, Euangelia describunt, mi:
racula comprobant, Martyres clamant, Virgines docent, Philosophi
profitentur, Reges agnoscunt, Mundus veneratur, Coelum ac terra
testatur. Qui seipsum quidem redimendis omnibus impendit, vult qs sol.:
nos non in universum fieri: sed qui etiam in revelatione iusti iuditii
sui reddet unicuiq[ue] secundum opera eius: iis quidem qui secundu[m]
patientiam boni operis, gloriam et honorem et incorruptionem
quærunt, vitam æternam: iis autem qui sunt ex contentione, et qui non acquiescunt veritati, credunt
autem iniquitati, ira et indignatio. Rom. 2.
Ei autem qui potens est nos conservare
sine peccato, et restituere ante ror:

Iesus Hebraicè, spectrum gloriæ suæ immaculatus   Orig. Hom. 27
& ΣωΤΗΡ Græce, in exultatione. SOLI DEO   Sicut auro ... in psal
Seruator Latinè. SALVATORI NOSTRO   ... ... dogma
Abunt. Graeco in   ... ...
Deo Jesu meo, qualiter   gloria et magnifi-   ... ... Babylonis
tio magis Augustino   tia, imperium et
placet: si quod illi nihil   potestas et nu[n]c
in secundione meo. Lib.   et in omnia
18 de Civit. Dei. c. 32,   sæcula
sunt habent LXX.   AMEN.
                             N.

Vidi ... librum fol. 114   IS . 50.
Spernere mundum, Spernere nullum, spernere sese,
Spernere se sperni, tibi ... hæc bona ... Hieronis.

                    I   Ludovici (Cradini)

Handwriting of St. Peter Canisius, being the titles and praises of Our Lord
which he selected from the Old and New Testaments as a prologue to an
unfinished dictionary of theology
From the archives of the Society of Jesus.

which I owed Him. And now, O my Lover of Lovers, I offer Thee my heart to be as it were a rose in bloom attracting Thy eyes all day with its beauty and delighting Thy Divine Heart with its fragrance. I offer it to Thee, too, as a chalice from which Thou mayest drink Thy own sweetness, with all that Thou wilt this day deign to operate in my soul. More, I offer my heart to Thee as a fruit for Thy banquet of most exquisite savour, which eating Thou mayest so take to Thyself that it will feel blissfully conscious of being within Thee. And I pray that every thought, every word, every deed, every stir of my will this day, may be directed according to the good pleasure of Thy most beneficent Will.

Equally eloquent of the love which he bore to Christ was Peter's last exercise of the day, " when in bed and about to fall asleep." It began with this little prayer : " Let my eyes take their sleep, but may my heart watch always unto Thee. May Thy right hand bless Thy servants who love Thee." Then, drawing a deep breath or sigh, " as of divine love," five successive times, he made five aspirations " in union with the praise which flows from Thee, Lord Jesus, to all Thy saints ; in union with the gratitude drawn from Thy Heart, good Jesus, which causes Thy saints to thank Thee ; in union with that Passion, good Jesus, whereby Thou didst take away the guilt of all mankind ; in union with the divine longing which Thou, good Jesus, didst have on earth for the salvation of mankind ; in union with every prayer which welled from Thy divine heart, good Jesus, and flowed into the hearts of Thy saints."[1]

Finally, as examples of Peter's prayers we may be pardoned for reproducing two which he composed and used to say on behalf of the Society of Jesus. He was the most loyal of men, and that Society to which he had given his bond in youth remained to the end a chief object of his love and solicitude. Even as late as 1595, only two years before he died, he was to be found devoting a whole hour every other day to the study of the Jesuit rules and constitutions.[2] The two prayers are in the following terms :

O Lord Jesus Christ who dost frequently send new workers to labour in the vineyard of Thy Church, I thank Thee with all my heart for Thy immeasurable goodness in wonderfully constituting this Society bearing Thy Name through Thy chosen servant, Saint Ignatius ; in

---

[1] These and the other prayers mentioned above are reproduced in full in Schlosser's book, *Beati Petri Canisii Exhortationes domesticae* (Roermond, 1876), pp. 452–5.

[2] Braunsberger, *Epistulae*, vol. viii, p. 862.

propagating it widely throughout the world; and in choosing to make me, unworthy as I am, one of its sons. Increase in me the genuine spirit of its Founder, and grant that all of us who belong to it may, in accordance with his teaching, die to self-love, and, established in perfect obedience, show ourselves fruitful branches of Thy vine, turning all things with sincere hearts to the greater glory of Thy Name. May we be assisted by the merits of our holy Father Ignatius and by the virtue of the divine Sacrifice of Thy Body and Blood to be undeviatingly true to the standard of evangelical poverty, to serve Thee and Thy laws faithfully as Ignatius showed us how, and to practise, as he everywhere demanded of his sons, the solid virtues of a good religious until death. Amen.

•   •   •   •   •

I commend to Thee, Lord Jesus, this whole body of our Society that in its superiors and subjects, its sound men and sick, its sons who progress or fall away, and all its business spiritual and temporal, it may be rightly governed to the glory of Thy Name and the advantage of the whole Church. Through Thee may we everywhere increase in numbers and merits, and may we know our vocation thoroughly and knowing it love it, so that all grades of our Society may serve Thy Majesty worthily and faithfully; cling fast to the evangelical precepts and counsels; and, united in the bonds of fraternal love, feel Thy efficacious blessing on their provinces, colleges, missions, and ministries. May they be sober, simple, prudent, peaceable, and studious of solid virtues, so as to make their lives accord with the Name they bear and their deeds answer to their professions. Confirm, Lord Jesus, what Thou hast begun in this Thy congregation, that with Thy help we may practise until death the religious obedience, poverty, and chastity which with Thy help we vowed. To Thy mercy I commend not only the living members of this Society but all its dead brethren and bene-factors.[1]

The reader may have noticed that Ignatius Loyola is honoured with the title of 'Saint' in the first of those prayers, though at the time when Peter Canisius wrote it he was not yet even beatified. That pardonable attribution, which being in a purely private prayer in no way contravened canon law, bespeaks St. Peter's profound love and veneration for his great Father in God. Up to the end he continued to manifest the liveliest

[1] Braunsberger, *Epistulae*, vol. viii, pp. 691–2.

interest in the efforts of the Jesuit authorities to produce a satisfactory biography of Ignatius. Indeed, he might have been writing the biography himself, so keen was he about it. In an exhortation given to his brethren of Fribourg on July 31, 1587, the anniversary of Ignatius's death, he described him as " the mirror and exemplar of all perfection," stressing particularly his personal love of Christ and his spirit of prayer, the two things in which Peter himself most resembled him. " Nothing is more true," he wrote in his memorial to Aquaviva, " than that which Christ Himself affirmed : *Qui manet in me et ego in eo, hic fert fructum multum.* It will greatly help us to this if we try to see God present in all things, and not only raise up our minds to Him in prayer but refer everything and every deed we do to Him, feeling no less a spirit of devotion in our work than in meditation itself, as our Father Ignatius wonderfully did and taught us to do." To see God present in all things—that was Peter's secret as much as it was Ignatius's. He had no shred of poetry in him and no feeling whatever for natural beauty as a mere source of aesthetic delight. But as the creations of God and evidences of His power, will and wisdom, he derived other satisfactions from flower and tree and fountain playing. They can be divined very easily in the following simple and delightful exhortation which he delivered to his brethren at Fribourg in May, 1583 :

Having to say something to you to-day by way of the usual exhortation, I long remained in doubt as to what it should be. At last I decided to speak about our garden in this lovely, pleasant month of May, and I hope that no one will object to the idea. In common with other religious we have a garden attached to our house, and the monks of ancient times were careful that each monastery should be similarly provided. Now, why was this? It was because they knew that the bow cannot always remain bent; that religious men cannot always be praying, chanting, studying, meditating, or engaged on other spiritual exercises, but need recreation of the body. They were aware, too, of the many advantages which religious men may derive from a right use of their garden. It reminds them, for instance, that they are the sons of their first father, Adam, for whose sake God planted a garden in the beginning . . . and brings home to them how, through disobedience to God, he was driven from it into unhappy exile. But a garden speaks, too, of the second Adam, who chose to begin His Passion therein and expiate by His obedience the sin of the first Adam. . . . Where was

Christ accustomed to pray at night but on Mount Olivet, where there was a garden, a fact known to Judas, who sought Him there with the cohort? Where did He elect to be buried? Where did He appear to Magdalene? And when He appeared, He, the sower who went forth to sow his seed, it was in the guise of a gardener. . . .

Let us see now what is the true and praiseworthy way to use our garden. When we are about to enter it and have reached the fountain, we ought to purify our intention, as indeed, we ought to do about every particular act on which we engage. . . . It needs a climb to reach our garden and each of us might, therefore, call to mind such texts as, *Ecce ascendimus Hierosolymam*, or, *Petrus et Johannes ascendebant ad Templum ad horam orationis nonam*, or again, *Petrus ascendit in superiora ut oraret circa horam sextam*. . . . Anyone who goes into the garden, not expressly in order to pray, ought to think of it as an open book offered to him in which he may learn to know God and himself. The leaves of that book are the leaves of the trees and the flowers and all green growing things, if we would read and understand them, for there is nothing that God has made, however lowly, which does not declare to the wise the wisdom, power, and goodness of its Creator, or fails to remind them to praise and love Him, since all things were created on their account in measure and number and weight, some for man's use, some for his pleasure and some to give beauty to his world. But our garden has another lesson for us, too, inasmuch as its flowers and trees teach us obedience in our vocation, and gratitude, subjection and reverence to God, while at the same time convincing us of the folly and faithlessness of our ways in thinking, desiring, speaking, and doing so many things against God's laws and ordinances. I can say of the garden, ' Winter is now past, the rain is over and gone, the flowers have appeared in our land '; but I still have mid-winter in my soul and my tree has no bloom to show. Woe to me should the Gardener return to seek fruit and flowers in His garden.

Another subject for consideration is afforded by the sight of the earth, embellished at this season with so many varieties of flowers, grasses, plants, and trees in their finery, which feed the eyes and delight us with their fragrance. No artificer, even if he had Solomon's cunning, could devise such variety or produce such beauty. What, then, will this world be like after the last resurrection . . . when the sun will shine with a ten times more glorious ray? . . .[1]

[1] Braunsberger, *Epistulae*, vol. viii, pp. 603–6.

In another exhortation the Saint represents the soul as " a host watching at the window of the senses if anywhere she might behold the Beloved whom she would run to meet. Should she see a lovely flower or tree or bird she at once thinks within herself : Oh, how beautiful and lovable and good must He be who made them! Or should she hear the birds in song or bells sweetly sounding or the strains of music, she reflects in her heart : Oh, how sweet is the voice of the Beloved from whom proceeds all sweetness when He calls souls to His embrace! " All this is no doubt jejunely expressed, for Peter had only a poor command of language. But it is the feeling behind the lame analogies that matters, and about its genuineness and profundity there can be no doubt whatever. Peter's soul was so attuned to God that all his longings and desires had truly become " whispered dialogues of the daily hours with eternity."[1]

A man who so truly loved God, to whom God was so real and personal, could not but have sincerely loved his fellow-men. For St. Peter, who was an entirely masculine character, love meant, not a facile emotion but a practical and steadfast attitude of the will. Loving spelt doing, striving, self-giving, working might and main for the true perfection and durable happiness of the one loved. In that sense Peter's love knew no limits and included the heretics of his day just as much as the Catholics. He would have done anything in the world to save them, in spite of the fact that he occasionally used hard words against their leaders and for heresy itself had a hatred as deep as was his devotion to Catholic truth. In the first volume of his *Notes on the Gospels* he described the thing as " a disease more pernicious than any leprosy, a plague more deadly than all other plagues, a crime more detestable than all thievery or other wickedness." But for the ordinary heretic, the common man and woman who had been born or drifted into Lutheranism, he felt nothing but the most genuine compassion. It was wrong, he held, to judge all heretics alike and " make no distinction between masters and disciples, seducers and seduced." He even goes out of his way to defend the general run of German heretics from harsh criticism. " Certainly an infinite number of them adhere to the new sectaries and err in religious belief," he explained to Aquaviva, " but they do so in such a way as proves that their errors proceed from ignorance rather than malice. They err, I repeat, but without

---

[1] From a verse of the deeply contemplative Austrian poet, Rilke, which, Christianly interpreted, might have been written to sum up the spiritual trend of St. Peter's soul :

Das ist die Sehnsucht : wohnen im Gewoge
Und keine Heimat haben in der Zeit.
Und das sind die Wünsche : leise Dialoge
Täglicher Stunden mit der Ewigkeit.

contention, without wilfulness, without obstinacy. Most Germans are by nature simple, homely folk. Born and bred in Lutheranism, they receive with docility what they are taught in schools, churches, and heretical books. And that is why they go astray."[1]

Even for Lutherans of a more pronounced and belligerent type the Saint has a charter of indulgence. He strongly deprecated any discourtesy towards them and, to prevent it as far as Jesuits might be concerned, submitted to his General a list of " ill-advised approaches " which they should be cautioned to avoid :

> First, it is assuredly wrong to meet non-Catholics in a temper of asperity or to treat them with discourtesy, for this is nothing else than the reverse of Christ's example inasmuch as it is to break the bruised reed and quench the smoking flax. Those whom heresy has made bitter and suspicious, estranging them from orthodox Catholics and especially from our Fathers, ought always to be instructed in a spirit of meekness, to the end that by whole-hearted charity and good will we may win them over to us *in Domino*. Again, it is a mistaken policy to behave in a contentious fashion and to start disputes about matters of belief with argumentative people who are disposed by their very natures to wrangling. Indeed, the fact of their being so constituted is a reason the more why such men should be attracted and won to the simplicity of the Faith as much by example as by argument. . . .
>
> Another mistake is to bring up in conversation subjects to which the Protestants have an antipathy . . . such as confession, satisfaction, Purgatory, indulgences, monastic vows, and pilgrimages; the reason being that, like fever patients, they have infected palates and so are incapable of judging aright about such foods. Their need, as that of children, is for milk, and they should be led gently and gradually to those dogmas about which there is dispute. . . .[2]

It is not intended by these citations to suggest that St. Peter was a tolerationist in any modern sense. The sixteenth century knew nothing of toleration, which only came into being much later as the unwanted offspring of indecisive wars. Peter was a man of his age and believed, as did everybody else, whether Protestant or Catholic, that force might legitimately be used to repress religious propaganda of a colour different from one's own. But it can be claimed for him that, while stern in his

[1] Braunsberger, *Epistulae*, vol. viii, p. 131.   [2] Braunsberger, *Epistulae*, vol. viii, p. 130.

attitude towards Protestant leaders and proselytizers, he knew how to be friendly and sympathetic towards the vast majority whom he styled their unwitting dupes. But even the leaders were not entirely outside his compassion. " I shall sorrow for the lot of the sectaries," he wrote in one place, " seeing that, though so much at cross-purposes among themselves, they yet conspire . . . to bring in the reign of the pestilent Antichrist and labour indefatigably towards an indescribable sort of atheism. For my part, I shall not fail to show both seducers and seduced the charity which is owing even to our enemies, and I shall strive by every means in my power to deserve well of them." That Peter practised what he preached is shown, to take one instance of many, by his letter to Aquaviva begging that prayers might be said throughout the whole Society of Jesus for the pugnacious Calvinist, Chandieu, whose attacks on Jesuits and Catholics in general were notorious for their savagery.[1] With all reserves made, then, as in other matters so in this of chivalry to his foe Peter stands high among his contemporaries. Certainly, no eminent Protestant of the time matched him in moderation of language or in willingness to believe well of those who differed from him.

Otherwise than as a controversialist Peter's bounty was absolute. Up and down the present volume much evidence has gone to prove that, despite a certain natural ruggedness of character, he was a very human saint and such a one as most men, whatever their religious affiliations, could hardly help regarding with both respect and affection. When told of somebody's mismanagements or misdemeanours his comment would usually take this form : " *Dominus Jesus et nostri et miserorum omnium misereri dignetur* "—may the Lord Jesus deign to have pity on us and on all unfortunate people. Again, it is characteristic of him that when referring to the victims of economic misfortune, as he so constantly does in his books and sermons, he seems to have been almost incapable of omitting the adjective, *lieb*. To him they were always " the dear, the beloved poor." Were he alive in the world to-day he would assuredly never weary of denouncing the social injustices that are carrying our civilization headlong to destruction.

Though a great stickler for discipline in the young, as must anybody be whose care for them is more than a mere form of self-indulgence, Peter by no means frowned on high spirits or required that boys should be sages. In a sermon on the Book of Job delivered at Innsbruck in 1574, he said :

[1] The whole question of St. Peter's attitude to the Protestants of his time is most carefully and impartially studied by Dr. Johannes Metzler in his brochure, *Der hl. Petrus Canisius und die Neuerer seiner Zeit* (Münster in Westfalen, 1927).

"Job was not a rigid and austere father to his sons, but easy and kind, allowing them honest recreation. He did not prevent young people meeting and having a good time together at table, for he knew that it is natural in youth to love and seek some diversion and external form of enjoyment. Indeed, young people need such that they may afterwards the better obey and serve God in spiritual things. It is right and advantageous that they should relax and have their fun in smaller things so as to be the more ready and keen for such important things as study, prayer, virtue, and mortification. Let cruel and indiscreet fathers take note of this."[1] Peter saw to it that they took notice when he was given the opportunity, as the following small example shows. A lad named Küng had been placed at the Jesuit college in Fribourg by the magistrates of Soleure. They expected him apparently to repay their kindness by behaving with sena-torial gravity and studying his head off to do them credit. St. Peter warmly commended their interest in the boy but emphasized that they should not demand too much from him. "We must," he said, "make some allowance for the vacillating moods of youth. Maybe your protégé will rise above himself, conquer his dullness, and advance in his studies better than some people think him capable of doing. At any rate I admire him for his keen anxiety to meet the expectations of his Soleure patrons by being daily more diligent over his work. . . . Let us be patient, I beg you, in this matter, because the usual result of pushing boys on too rapidly, in excess of the right measure of discipline, is to break their spirits rather than correct them. . . ."[2]

Though St. Peter was not always discreet in his personal asceticism and pushed his fasting, for instance, to dangerous lengths, he was ever a great counsellor of moderation to other men. To keep a good middle course—*bonum servare medium*—was one of his chief principles and watchwords, not only with regard to penance but in the entire manage-ment of the spiritual and natural life. In a sermon which he preached at Augsburg in 1562 he touched on the question of dancing as a form of recreation on Sundays. Beginning with St. Paul's text, "Let your speech be always in grace seasoned with salt," he said: "This is ever a good and useful rule, even in worldly business, but it has a special importance in the affairs of conscience. Concerning them, there is need to speak discreetly and to keep a good middle course, so that there may be no exaggeration or straining of precepts. . . . I say this not only with regard to dancing but with regard to all pastimes on holidays of obligation, such

[1] Braunsberger, *Epistulae*, vol. vii, p. 767.   [2] Braunsberger, *Epistulae*, vol. viii, p. 473.

as the playing of games, shooting, sports, rambling, and other forms of recreation. I would not approve but rather consider it an impertinence were anyone to judge, condemn and despise his neighbour because he indulged in such recreations, even though they be accompanied by many sins. For it is difficult to prove that men, by virtue of the Sunday precept, are obliged to concern themselves exclusively with the service of God, without allowing any room for diversion."[1]

In Peter's life the good social virtue of *pietas* was peculiarly prominent. He was deeply attached to his family, and some of the longest letters which he wrote had love of his relatives for their inspiration. Owing to the disturbances in the Netherlands and the victories of Calvinism, he felt the profoundest anxiety for the faith of his half-brothers, Gerhard, Otto and Gisbert, who had been driven from their homes in Nymegen by the rebel bands of William the Silent. His letters to them, huge documents in Dutch or German, read like speeches to soldiers before battle. He comforts them, praises them, exhorts them, holds up to them the example of their ancestors, strengthens their faith, and by every manner of argument and persuasion seeks to create in them a detestation for heresy and an unalterable attachment to the Church of the centuries. Beyond such conventional expressions as " My dear—or dearest—Brothers," there is little show of affection, but how deeply it ran is apparent in almost every burning line of the letters. He knew their faith to be the most precious thing that his brothers and their children possessed, and his love went straight to the point without any sentimental divagations. To a nephew who had become a Jesuit and been recently ordained, the Saint addressed himself in this fashion in March, 1596, when he was almost incapable of holding a pen :

The eternal peace of Christ be with us, dearest Nephew. Joyfully do I thank Christ Our Lord for the news which I have received from Father Hoffaeus that you continue steadfast in your vocation and, as a priest and engaged in the other functions proper to our institute, you comport yourself in a way beseeming a child of holy obedience. Blessed be the Father of mercies under whose leading you increase and make lovely the grace given to you, and, having truly died to the world, so join yourself to the spirit of Christ that His holy and perfect will has you completely in bondage. Indeed you have chosen the better part, whatever the world—that *mundus vere immundus*—may think of

[1] Braunsberger, *Epistulae*, vol. iii, pp. 648–9.

you. Go on, I beg you, as you have begun, contemning all else and denying your own self in your zeal for the greater and better gifts. Love with all your heart our Crucified Lord who gave Himself gladly and utterly for our redemption. The Divine Goodness which has supported your efforts hitherto in class-room and church will not fail you in the future either, so that you may reap no ordinary fruit from the functions which superiors assign you. . . . You know, I am sure, that to one who loves God and walks in the royal road of obedience nothing is difficult, for all things give way to us felicitously when we co-operate with divine grace. . . . See that you do not forget old Canisius, who is now a sick man, incapable of helping other people. . . . You would do me a great favour if you were to commend the remainder of my life to the Blessed Trinity in three Masses. . . . I most heartily wish you and all the community a holy and happy Easter.[1]

Another nephew of Peter was a boy of thirteen at school in Fulda. To him the old Saint wrote as follows in January, 1597, when on the verge of his last illness :

The eternal peace of Christ be with us, dearest Nephew. It was a pleasure to receive towards the end of last year your very first letter to me. I had been on the look-out for it a long time, and am truly delighted to learn that you are well and living among Catholics. . . . You must earnestly and frequently implore Almighty God to strengthen in your soul and in the souls of your friends the light of Catholic faith, esteeming no wickedness more dreadful than to tarnish the purity of true religion or to depart even by a hair's breadth from the doctrine of our Holy Mother the Church.

Go on, Beloved Nephew, being a devout member of Mary's Sodality and a studious member of your third class in school, so as to give daily a bright example of modesty, uprightness and diligence. You are named James after my father in order that you may resolve to follow in his footsteps, knowing what an exceptionally good man he was. It is left for you, then, to brush aside trifles and gird yourself for the attainment of those things which befit your birth and abilities, remembering in all times and places to show yourself constant in the Catholic religion, the only religion of which no man need be ashamed. . . .

[1] Braunsberger, Epistulae, vol. viii, pp. 422-3.

You would please me very much by writing often and by sending me a specimen of your work. Give your masters an affectionate greeting from me. Good-bye in Christ, my James, and pray to God persistently that your studies may be directed to His particular glory and the advantage of your neighbour.[1]

It is in keeping with this family aspect of Peter's life that the last of all his many letters should have been one of affectionate farewell to his half-brother, Theodoric, written laboriously with his own hand the day before he died.

A most attractive feature in the characters of some great saints was their capacity for friendship. We think of Augustine during the idyllic time at Cassicium and, indeed, in all times and places, " longing for the absent with impatience, welcoming the coming with joy " ; or of Augustine's friend, the lovable Paulinus, with his tiny garden near Nola which, he said, was " hardly big enough to grow a cabbage in " but where, nevertheless, he was so eager to have all his friends about him. Madame de Sévigné's " bise de Grignan " is celebrated, but how many people are aware that Paulinus anticipated the sentiment of her exquisite line by more than a thousand years ? " I speak truly and feign nothing," he wrote to a friend whose wife had died, " when I tell you that every time I think of your sorrow I feel my own bowels shaken with your sighs." Now, Peter Canisius was a man of the Paulinus type and, though he did not possess the old Saint's lucid and lovely gift of words, could yet thus express himself on the subject of friendship : " Without friends there is no living, and to take friendship away is nothing else than to take the sun out of the sky."[2] Among his own intimate friends were persons of many nations and of every rank from lay brothers to cardinals. Once to be his friend was to be his friend for ever. He seemed incapable of forgetting those whom he had known in the past, no matter how many sundering years and miles might have cut them off from him. " I can-not but write you a few lines," he would say, when the chance offered, " to confirm the memory of our old friendship "—*ut veteris amicitiae nostrae confirmetur memoria*.

In the Augsburg Jesuit community there was a Belgian lay brother named Godfrey Hannartz. He had been with Peter in the pioneering days and when, twenty years later, Peter heard that he was ill he at once

[1] Braunsberger, *Epistulae*, vol. viii, pp. 449–50.
[2] *Notae in Evangelicas Lectiones quae . . . Dominicis diebus . . . recitantur* (ed. princeps, 1591), p. 1114.

wrote to offer his sympathy. "If report speaks truly," he said, "illness has come upon my Godfrey with whom I lived on intimate terms so many years and whom from my heart I would like to help in any way I can. I am therefore writing you a few lines so that you may know I have not forgotten you and am devoted to you, even if a long distance separates us. How fine it is that you should have borne so many labours and burdens in our Society and in the starting of the Augsburg college! If Christ now calls you to a better life, acknowledge the favour and do not be afraid, for we have a good Master. Without dying it is impossible for us to be happy. . . . You certainly owe God great thankfulness for giving you the resolution to live and die in your holy vocation. Let others worry about their wives and children and families; all that need concern you is to have a good conscience and Christ for your intimate friend. Pray to the Lord for me, dearest Godfrey, and have no doubt but that I shall always be faithful to you in my prayers, which it is a joy to offer for such friends and brothers as yourself. May our Lord Jesus have you both body and soul in His keeping, for the glory of His Name. . . ."

St. Peter's next letter to the same good Brother who had recovered from his illness contains an amusing little touch of superstition. "I am grateful to you, dear Godfrey," he says, "for writing to me now and then, and for the true-hearted friendship which you display towards old Canisius. You would do me a great favour if you were to procure me in Augsburg and Dillingen a gift of Masses and prayers. They say, you see, that the new year is coming in with I know not what doleful portents and will prove fatal to many. As a result, old people are frightened and anxious. . . . For myself, I do not worry about the health of my body but I think I could not be too solicitous as to the good estate of my soul, and that is why I seek and beg for many intercessors with God." The remainder of this letter is about other people, including a new rector to whom the kind Saint had already written a letter of congratulation, a sick man for whom he asks Godfrey to pray, a certain Augsburg bookseller with whose faith or morals or business methods there must have been something amiss, as Peter says of him: "I am sorry for Willer, whom after so many years we have not been able to bring to a better mind. Please give him my affectionate greetings." The letter ends with encouragement for Godfrey: "*In Christo vive et vale, Frater,* and continue as is your wont to merit well of your brethren out of charity unfeigned. Our liberal Master will pay you an immense reward for the labour which you have borne so many years. I shall pray for you always and you in turn will not cease,

I beg, to pray for me and to commend me at the shrines of St. Ulric and St. Afra."[1]

Among other special friends whom Peter delighted to write to were a lay brother tailor named Höffner, a young Jesuit student named Eberlin, and a Bavarian priest of the Society named Salbius, of whom it is recorded that he spent most of his time "visiting the homes of the poor or the resorts of lepers, and was never happier than when he had to suffer something for their sake." In Peter's last letter of many to this lovable man the first person mentioned for remembrance was the community cook —" Will you please greet the cook from me and Philip and the other Brothers; then the Rector, Father Julius and all the Fathers." It is not uncommon to find the names of five or seven men thus set down for greetings in Peter's letters. He had a particular affection for the lay brothers. Once, during his last illness, his infirmarian, Brother Strang, conceived a regret that he had not studied for the priesthood. Though he had given no sign of what was passing in his mind, he records that his patient suddenly said to him : " My Brother, put away those thoughts and let us stand fast in humility. Had it been possible for me to obtain the leave of superiors I would have embraced your grade of lay brother with both my arms."[2]

Among the friends very dear to St. Peter was Father Francis Rocca, the Italian Jesuit with whom he had waded through the floods near Oberammergau in 1557. Rocca had gone to Rome, there to become the confessor of St. Robert Bellarmine. Fourteen years after their adventure together he received from Peter a letter which opened in this fashion : " I cannot but write to my ever dearest Father Francis[3] and remind him of our old friendship. I am perfectly sure that he does not forget his Canisius, especially in Mass, and when he visits the holy places in Rome. You would do me a favour by writing to me sometimes here at Fribourg." Peter's other extant letters to Rocca teem with the names of old friends to whom he would be remembered. Among them are those of two lay brothers, " carissimi fratres," who, it delighted him to learn, were praying for him. And the dead are not forgotten, Delanoy, Nadal, Polanco, and so many others whom he had worked with and loved. In the last year of his life he inquires whether " good Father Polanco " had left any literary remains which he might get published for the advantage of his Province

---

[1] Braunsberger, *Epistulae*, vol. viii, pp. 246–7 ; 260–1. The saints mentioned at the end of the second letter are the two patrons of Augsburg City and diocese.

[2] Braunsberger, *Epistulae*, vol. viii, p. 896.

[3] "Patrem Franciscum mihi semper dilectissimum."

and "of a devout posterity." Hearing of the death of Father John Couvillon who had been such a worry to him when he was Provincial, he refers to him as "good Father John" and says to Rocca: "God grant that you and I may work out our vocation as happily as he did, and that, when the time comes, like him we may truly die in Our Lord." Similar was his reference to the death of that other torment, Father Dominic Mengin: "May good Father Dominic live eternally in Christ, having deserved so well of the novices, of the Munich College, and of the Ducal Court." The truth is that in each of these positions good Father Dominic had been an intolerable nuisance.

Of quite a different type from Mengin was another master of novices, Father Bonaventure Paradinas, who died at Landsberg towards the end of 1595. "I hear that venerable Father Bonaventure has been laid to rest among you," wrote Peter to the community shortly afterwards. "Oblivion now will never be able to steal so great a Father from present and future novices. Rather will the sweet, immortal memory of him be always green. Blessed be God who prospered the sowing of His servant so many years at Landsberg and gave his splendid efforts completion with such a happy end that dying as living he afforded an example of rare holiness." Peter, who had so genuinely contemptible an opinion of his own worth and work, used to be lost in admiration for the characters and deeds of other men. When his dearly loved friend, Father Martin Leubenstein, Rector of the college in Lucerne, died a victim of his devotion to the plague-stricken in 1596, he addressed a glowing panegyric of him to the bereaved community: "In the midst of the turmoil of his life he remained ever himself, hard and strict where his private comfort was concerned, but to others all kindness and affability; never seeking his own ends but striving all the time after whatever might make for the greatest glory of Christ and the salvation of souls. I would call you fortunate men, Brothers, if, as becomes you, you prove yourselves enduringly the heirs and sons of so great a Father. He had schooled himself to live frugally and to be content with little, rejoicing to do penance in secret, but to give full and open expression to his burning love for the poor and the sick. . . . Therefore let us not mourn him, but rather thank God joyfully who chose this His faithful and prudent servant to govern His new family in Lucerne . . . ; a blameless man, true and sincere in his service of God, indefatigable in the service of the Church. . . . Why should we sorrow as though such a Father had been snatched from us, when he has but gone to the true immortal life to join the grand company of our

Fathers who now reign with Christ their King? . . . As long as your school and church remain, the memory of this illustrious man will remain to admonish you, his brothers, heirs, and sons, that you must hold nothing dearer than fraternal love. What was it but such love, burning like a flame, that kept him so often till all hours in his confessional, when he had so much to do besides in the house? It was his joy to help both sick and sound . . . but the thing that touches me most of all is the way he staked his very life without a qualm for the victims of the plague, thus in his love of Christ so loving his fellow-men that he preferred death to failing them in their need. . . . What was this but the perfection of charity, loving not in word nor in tongue but in deed and in truth? However, as wise men like yourselves have no need of my sermonizing let me put an end to it with some words of the great Apostle: Comfort ye one another, and edify one another; always rejoice; pray without ceasing; in all things give thanks, for this is the will of God in Christ Jesus concerning you all. Pray to the Lord for me, dearest Brothers."[1]

Among Peter's extant letters are several addressed to new rectors, congratulating and encouraging them, and counselling them *not* to act like new brooms. Thus, when in 1597 another old friend, Father Itaeus, succeeded Father Leubenstein at Lucerne and was much frightened by the prospect of responsibility, the Saint wrote at once to put heart into him, though at the time his hand could just barely control a pen. " I am praying," he said, " that your Reverence may be given special fortitude and courage against all pusillanimity and that anxious care which so torments some people in their office of rector that they are hardly ever at peace. It would be wise for you at the start to overlook any blemishes there may be in the conduct of the brethren, so that they may love rather than fear their superior. . . . *Sapienti pauca!* May the Lord increase in us the grace of holy discretion, in order that of our very need we may create strength proportionate to our burden." *Facilitas* and *suavitas* were the qualities which Peter chiefly commended in superiors—approachableness and gentleness. Given these, he held, superiors could reform to their hearts' content without hurting anybody. In the year of his death, 1597, an Austrian Jesuit wrote to the General of the Society protesting against the severe methods of his Provincial. As a contrast, he mentioned the names of five eminent men who had ruled by kindness rather than by severity. Four of these, including Father Everard Mercurian, were dead, and the living one was old Father Canisius.[2]

[1] Braunsberger, *Epistulae*, vol. viii, pp. 453–6.   [2] Braunsberger, *Epistulae*, vol. viii, pp. 891–2.

One does not like to parade such delicate words as love and affection, but what else can it have been that made Peter write in the style with which the reader is now acquainted? Even in his little flicks at dilatory correspondents there is evidence of deep feeling, as when he says to Rocca: " Give Father Augustine my greetings and tell him from me that if he loved his brother Jesuits he would cheer them up no less than he does his outside friends with one of his letters." Even when himself desperately ill, Peter was a great hand at cheering people up. To one sick and despondent man he wrote in the following strain only five months before his own death: " I felt that I must send you a few lines, Father, when I heard recently that you had been laid low with a fever, for I was anxious lest while in that state some traces of your old despondency might reappear. Let us rather play the man and find our comfort in the Lord who is our strength ; and let us also rejoice that we should be thus visited in fatherly love by Him whose way it is to chastise the sons dear to Him and to purge and prove them as gold in a furnace, in order to make them ready for a blessed immortality." Father Paul Hetzcovaeus, who, as chaplain to Archduchess Magdalene, had caused Peter the gravest anxiety, received a similar letter while he lay full of melancholy in his last illness at Hall :

My Brother Paul, I beg of you with all my heart by our common Lord who bore so many and such terrible pains for our sakes to strengthen us on our cross and in the hour of death, that in these sufferings which are, as it were, the precursors and forerunners of death, you would rouse yourself and cry out courageously : " Where art Thou, Lord Jesus? Look mercifully upon the son of Thy hand-maiden, yea of Thy Spouse, the Church, which bore me to Thee. I am Thy servant, redeemed with the great price of Thy Blood, and it has pleased Thee to make me a member of Thy Body, and not only Thy brother but Thy co-heir in the Church militant and triumphant. I know that only pains and stripes are my due as Thy unprofitable servant. Here burn and here cut, that Thou mayest spare me in eternity. Thy rod and Thy staff are my comfort. If Thou didst not love me Thou wouldst not chastise me. It is good for me that Thou hast brought me low, so that, forgetting the world, the flesh and my very self, I may learn Thy justifications and depend on Thee alone who art become our way and truth and life."

These considerations are suggested, Brother mine, that you may acknowledge the hand of the Lord upon you as one of clemency and paternal love. . . . Have a brave heart then and fear not, keeping Christ Crucified before your eyes. . . . I beg and shall gladly continue to beg that He may increase in you holy patience, which is the medicine you now most urgently need. . . . Fight in Christ; and through Christ conquer and triumph, dearest Brother. I shall look forward with desire to seeing you in our Heavenly Fatherland, where we shall embrace one another affectionately. *Frater ex animo tuus, Petrus Canisius.*[1]

But it was not only in illness that people received comfort and encouragement from St. Peter. Any sort of trouble used to awaken his compassion. Thus, when Father Heidelberger of the Munich college became afflicted with grave temptations against faith, and miserable in consequence, the Saint wrote to him from his sick-bed in 1597, suggesting remedies and begging the sufferer to let him know whenever the temptations returned. " It is not for your destruction," he continued, " but for your salvation that God permits you to be thus assailed. You will derive inestimable benefit from the trial, if only you hold out and keep trust with Him who taught us to say : ' I have hoped in the Lord ; I shall not be put to confusion for ever.' "

Peter's successor in the pulpit at Augsburg was a holy and zealous man named Gregory Rosephius. He appears to have been subject to fits of dejection, brought on by his interminable labours. Peter had the profoundest admiration for him, and in April, 1597, addressed him, " *tremente jam dextra,*" in the following terms :

See how well, Father, this rough paper and my feeble old hand are matched! I beg you in your charity to pardon my awkward and uncouth way of addressing you. You have now, I trust, successfully concluded your Lenten labours and come in excellent health to the pleasant peace of Easter. As for me, I find that my legs will not do their duty, so sometimes it is difficult to say Mass. Blessed be God, the fountain of all good, who increases in us old men lassitude, distaste for food, loss of memory and the power of attention, troublesomeness, and other such miseries, which admonish us that we dwell in frail tabernacles and are on the way to a better life. But come, Father. Let us join in thanking Him who has our lots in His hand and by Whose providence you and I have been so many years connected with flourishing Augsburg. We have known the Truchsess

[1] Braunsberger, *Epistulae*, vol. viii, pp. 193–5.

family, and the Fuggers, the Rellingers, the Welsers, and other excellent patrons and friends, to whose generosity we owe so much. Let us follow the fine example they have set of service to their city, for the succour of which we were so strangely chosen. You are now so well housed and have such friendly congregations and pupils to listen to you with joy, while all the time the number of devout persons increases to praise the Name of the Lord in the true spirit of the Church, that we may well proclaim the singular favour which God has shown us. . . . May all the Fathers and Brothers of your college, men whom I hold dear in memory, enjoy the best of health and prosperity, together with all our patrons and friends. Take good care of your own health so as to allow no room for dejection or faint-heartedness, and do not, I beg you, forget me in your prayers.[1]

One more letter and this point of St. Peter's long memory for friends will have been sufficiently treated. It was addressed to the rector of the Jesuit college in Augsburg just twelve weeks before its writer died :

The eternal peace of Christ be with us, Reverend Father. I have received a large number of letters, from Father Hoffaeus, Father Haller, Father Rosephius, Father Valentia, Herr Mark Welser, Father Julius, and several other friends. Will you please make excuses to them for my silence ? Blessed be the Father of mercies who is visiting His old man these months with a new and heavy weariness, so that I may truly pray : *Bonum mihi quia humiliasti me.* There has come on me, too, a troublesome attack of dropsy which prevents me from saying or assisting at Mass, leaving my room, or doing anything to help other people. You see, then, what a useless sort of pack-animal I continue to be in God's splendid house which so many of my great brethren are diligently adorning. It was with pleasure that I read of your achievements in Augsburg this year, and I thanked God, the source of all good, with my whole heart, who by your labours improves this vineyard increasingly. . . . It makes me the more sorry, though, to think that I should be so far from imitating you, living as I do a life of useless dependence in this old age, which, perhaps, will soon deliver me to the dreadful and inescapable tribunal of Christ. You can gather from this how greatly I stand in need of your Masses and prayers and those of the Sodality.

[1] Braunsberger, *Epistulae*, vol. viii, pp. 474-5.

I loved and continue to love the people of Augsburg on whom God has conferred many and signal benefits. Anything I may have done for them was done very gladly, and, though it is not to be compared with what others of my brethren who succeeded me have done, you will not, despite his unworthiness, forget your first brother and preacher but commend him to the mercy of God in both his living and his dying. . . . I would like you to give my affectionate wishes to all in the community, whether I know them personally or not. May God restore our Procurator safely to us when he has finished in Italy the business of the Province and of the whole Society. Will you also please give my respectful greetings to my old friends and patrons, especially the members of the Fugger and Welser families, to whom we are so much indebted? As for the revision of the writings left by Mark Welser of holy memory, I suppose I need not worry too much while this sickness of old age barely leaves me alive and makes me disinclined for study. Farewell in Christ, dearest Fathers and Brothers, and go on praying, not only for me, but for our Swiss people who are troubled with the plague in many places.[1]

That letter reflects very well an aspect of St. Peter's spiritual life about which a few words may be said before concluding. Throughout the book the reader must have noticed how insatiable was his thirst for the prayers of his friends. He felt it because he genuinely thought himself in danger of being cast off by Almighty God if better men failed to inter-cede for him. His conviction of personal unworthiness and his utter self-abasement are two of the most obvious things in his story. Those who loved and venerated him were aware of them and strove with " *Xenia spiritualia*," or spiritual alms, to comfort his anxieties. If they chanced to forget he was quick with a reminder. Each year he used to write regularly to the Jesuit novices in Landsberg that he might wish them all blessings and make sure of receiving his spiritual present. The last item in one of these lists of gifts which a good Father in Munich had obtained for him from his scholars is thirty-two Paters and Aves, said by " those whose age did not permit of a larger offering because they are little fellows "—*parvuli enim sunt*. The offerings were sent by the boys, according to the same Father, " as a token of their gratitude, for they know the perfect way your Reverence has served their country."

[1] Braunsberger, *Epistulae*, vol. viii, pp. 482–3.

On the matter of self-abasement in the lives of the saints a thoughtful writer has made some observations which apply with peculiar force to the life of Peter Canisius: " Consider the saint's *humility*—the real fear for his salvation which seems to us so superfluous, the consuming remorse for sins which scarcely seem sins to us, the life-long tears over this and that mistake that seems to us so natural and not worth worrying about, the profound conviction of personal unworthiness, even when the rest of the world is already on its knees in reverence. Such humility seems to us mistaken, something intrinsically impossible, forced, unjust. . . . But who does not know the passionate, inarticulate confession of the heart bowed to the dust, abashed and trembling, because it is so utterly unworthy of the love given to it, unworthy of choosing, and being chosen by, the friend? Doesn't an undeserved love show up our defects and faults in a light incomparably more glaring than all the reproofs and scorn of our enemies? . . . What, then, when a man apprehends as a living reality with the whole of his startled soul the tremendous fact that God wishes to be his friend . . . that God has called him from eternity to this, to be His own, and not only that he should be God's, but, far more difficult to understand, and infinitely more difficult to believe, that God will be his . . .? Do you think that that man will study moral theology to reassure himself of all the sins he has *not* committed? Can he do otherwise than remain tremblingly aware of his infinite and unalterable unworthiness, in silent adoration of a choice which he can never, never understand, but by whose reality, notwithstanding, he lives every hour of his life? That is why the humility of the saints is so immeasurably deep, so passionate, so alert, so unforgetful, inexorable and implacable."[1]

The spiritual uneasiness of the saints, so well analysed in that passage, turned Peter Canisius into the most persistent of mendicants. Besides his ceaseless petitions for an alms of prayer from his living friends, he was ever on his knees to the holy ones at whose shrines he had been privileged to worship. Thus, to give but one example of scores, he wrote in the following strain to a friend in Cologne within six months of his death: " In this old age of mine I feel my poor body gradually dissolving . . . but I comfort myself with the sweet memory of the Theban and Ursuline martyrs whom I used gladly to worship in Cologne, and whom, though now distant from their shrines, I never cease to invoke. I have a great desire that one Mass should be said for me at the shrine of St. Gereon, because there I often experienced the grace of God, as I did, too, at the

[1] Ida Coudenhove, *The Nature of Sanctity* (London, Sheed and Ward, 1932), pp. 62–4.

House of the Carthusians." And so in Peter's end was also his beginning. Gereon who had inspired him as a boy to be a good soldier of Christ comforted him as a worn-out veteran, timorous through perfect humility at the prospect of meeting the Captain whom he had served so well.

The last extant letter of the Saint was sent during Advent, 1597, to his great friend and constant correspondent, the soldier-senator of Soleure, Johann von Staal. Like so many of his letters, it was one of consolation and reassurance, but the near approach of the Ember Days of Advent caused him to digress for a moment in order that he might sing the praises of fasting and penance " as a worthy and genuine rather than mere commonplace preparation for the Feast of the Nativity." There we have a last fleeting glimpse of Peter the inextinguishable ascetic, but quickly the other Peter reappears, the tender, patient, sweet-souled man whose austerity itself was but the good root of personal discipline from which his beautiful sympathies grew. " Good-bye in Jesus Christ, my dearest sir," he concluded, " and do you and all your family embrace joyfully with both arms the Child who is born unto us. As for myself, I jog along in the usual way, the sick old man you know. But if we have received good things at the hands of God, why should we not also bear the evil?" Exactly a week later he died.

INDEX

al. = allusion to. *C.* = Canisius. *quo.* = quoted as authority or otherwise.
ref. = given as a reference.

A

Aachen, Charles V crowned at, 217; Catholic Congress, 253
Abercromby, Robert, S.J., 566 n., 581
Adelbert, St., of Bohemia, 803
Adelmann, Graf Siegmund, 84
Adenauer, Dr. Konrad, 84
'Adiaphora', Melanchthon and the, 130
Adrian VI, Pope (Adrian of Utrecht), 12 f., 131
Afra, St., 835
Africa, Laynez in, 101, 161
Agricola, Johann, 128, 146 f., 287 f., 503
Aguilera, ref., 111 n.
Alacoque, St. Margaret Mary, 16
Alber, Ferdinand, S.J., 789
Albèri, quo., 131 n.
Albert, Duke of Bavaria, and *Acts of Ephesus*, 460 ff.; Augsburg, 644; and C., 337, 353, 358 ff., 364 f., 560 f., 602, 608, 701, 712, 724 f., 744, 765; death of, 762; and Jesuits, 139, 146, 151, 162, 166 f., 188, 221, 262 f., 266, 269, 271 n., 287, 289 f., 450, 509, 567, 572, 610, 804; and Lutherans, 604 ff.; and Maximilian, 517, 611; *Reformatio*, 269; and Trent, 476
Albert, St., the Great, on BVM, 789; study of, 20, 23, 503, 520
Albrecht Alcibiades, 176, 204
Albrecht, Johann, S.J., 572
Alcalá, Jesuits, 32, 75, 89, 108; Index question, 468 n.
Alegambe, 233
Alexander of Hales, 499
Alfonso, Alvaro, S.J., 31, 34, 53, 67
Algiers, slaves, 113; siege of, 58
Allen, Dr., Catechism, 250
Aloysius, St., *see* Gonzaga
Alsace, C. on, 740
Altemps, Cardinal, and Possevino, 249
Altötting, shrine of, 697
Aluch Ali, Pasha, 715
Alzog, al., 236
Amadis de Gaul, 622 n.
Ambrose, St., of Milan, 240, 248, 363, 708, 746, 791; C. on, 357, 407; Chateaubriand on, 355
Amerbach, Bonifacius, 22 n.
America, Cochlaeus on, 54
Amphilochius, St., 718
Amulio, Cardinal, 461, 624; and C., 626, 631, 634
Ancona, travellers by, 616 f., 689

Andomarus, al., 521
Anna, Queen of Austria, 169
Anne, St., 15 n.
Anne of Bohemia, 254
Anthony, St., of Egypt, al., 15
Antididagma, 53
Antonio, Fr. Francis, and Kostka, 674
Antwerp, C. at 72; Jesuits, 506, 800; printers, 237, 243, 681, 791
Apollinaris, heretic, al., 73
Apuleius, al., 503
Aquaviva, Claude, S.J., 784, 813; and C., 789, 799, 806 ff., 811 ff., 814 f., 820f., 827 ff.
Arabia, Jesuits in, 140; Arabic, 208, 233
Arasius, al., 521
Ardren, Robert, S.J., 773 f., 777, 784
Arduin, Henri, S.J., 612
Aretin, Carl Maria von, quo, 648
Aristotle, study of, 17, 24 f., 109 f., 269, 296, 520 f.
Armstrong, ref., 59 n., 81 n.
Arnheim, C. at, 5, 10, 28
Ars, Curé of, 165
Aschaffenburg, C. at, 629
Aschbach, ref., 43 n., 179 n.
Astrain, ref., 95 n., 343 n., 468 n., 507
Athanasius, St., 519; on BVM, 718
Auer, Lambert, S.J., 448 f., 477, 629 f., 640; death, 726 f.
Augsburg, Breviary, 439 f.; C. at, 239, 259, 262, 292, 316, 327, 335, 384 f., 422–471, 477, 479 f., 482, 487 f., 498, 501 f., 505, 541, 568 ff., 576, 582 ff., 587 ff., 596 ff., 620 f., 657, 691, 694 f., 733, 779, 810 ff., 830, 839 ff.; Catechism, 223, 251; St. Catherine's, 505, 601; Confession of, 94, 206, 211, 214, 392, 398, 400, 402 f., 408 f., 416 f., 423, 471, 483, 496, 518 n., 589 f., 604, 606, 635, 644, 678, 808; Diet of, 45, 84, 128, 216, 424 f., 630, 636, 639, 641 ff.; Jesuits at, 57, 151 f., 160, 426, 609 f., 742, 767, 769, 833 f.; Maximilian, 517; Peace of, 129, 270, 354, 386 f., 423, 626, 638, 644, 647 f.; plague, 564 ff.; population, 471; Schmalkalden War, 81 ff.; usury question, 737 f., 739
Augustine, St., al., 74, 235, 237, 240, 247, 379, 521, 652, 701, 709, 746, 794, 819; quo., 78, 386; at Cassicium, 833
Augustine of Montecalcino, Brother, 100
Augustinians, Munich, 289 f; nuns, 772
Augustus, al., 422
Aulus Gellius, 24, 482 n.
"Ausonio Gallo," 626

845